Lecture Notes in Computer Science

Commenced Publication in 1973
Founding and Former Series Editors:
Gerhard Goos, Juris Hartmanis, and Jan van Leeuwen

Moti Yung   Yevgeniy Dodis
Aggelos Kiayias   Tal Malkin (Eds.)

Public Key Cryptography – PKC 2006

9th International Conference
on Theory and Practice of Public-Key Cryptography
New York, NY, USA, April 24-26, 2006
Proceedings

 Springer

Volume Editors

Moti Yung
RSA Laboratories
and
Columbia University
Computer Science Department
1214 Amsterdam Avenue, New York, NY 10027, USA
E-mail: moti@cs.columbia.edu

Yevgeniy Dodis
New York University
Department of Computer Science
251 Mercer Street, New York, NY 10012, USA
E-mail: dodis@cs.nyu.edu

Aggelos Kiayias
University of Connecticut
Department of Computer Science and Engineering Storrs
CT 06269-2155, USA
E-mail: aggelos@cse.uconn.edu

Tal Malkin
Columbia University
Department of Computer Science
1214 Amsterdam Avenue, New York, NY 10027, USA
E-mail: tal@cs.columbia.edu

Library of Congress Control Number: 2006924182

CR Subject Classification (1998): E.3, F.2.1-2, C.2.0, K.4.4, K.6.5

LNCS Sublibrary: SL 4 – Security and Cryptology

ISSN   0302-9743
ISBN-10   3-540-33851-9 Springer Berlin Heidelberg New York
ISBN-13   978-3-540-33851-2 Springer Berlin Heidelberg New York

Springer is a part of Springer Science+Business Media

springer.com

© Springer-Verlag Berlin Heidelberg 2006
Printed in Germany

Typesetting: Camera-ready by author, data conversion by Scientific Publishing Services, Chennai, India
Printed on acid-free paper   SPIN: 11745853   06/3142   5 4 3 2 1 0

Preface

The 9th International Conference on Theory and Practice of Public-Key Cryptography (PKC 2006) took place in New York City. PKC is the premier international conference dedicated to cryptology focusing on all aspects of public-key cryptography. The event is sponsored by the International Association of Cryptologic Research (IACR), and this year it was also sponsored by the Columbia University Computer Science Department as well as a number of sponsors from industry, among them: EADS and Morgan Stanley, which were golden sponsors, as well as Gemplus, NTT DoCoMo, Google, Microsoft and RSA Security, which were silver sponsors. We acknowledge the generous support of our industrial sponsors; their support was a major contributing factor to the success of this year's PKC.

PKC 2006 followed a series of very successful conferences that started in 1998 in Yokohama, Japan. Further meetings were held successively in Kamakura (Japan), Melbourne (Australia), Jeju Island (Korea), Paris (France), Miami (USA), Singapore and Les Diablerets (Switzerland). The conference became an IACR sponsored event (officially designated as an IACR workshop) in 2003 and has been sponsored by IACR continuously since then. The year 2006 found us all in New York City where the undertone of the conference was hummed in the relentless rhythm of the city that never sleeps.

This year's conference was the result of a collaborative effort by four of us: Moti Yung served as the conference and program chair. Moti orchestrated the whole project and led the Program Committee's efforts in the careful selection of the 34 papers that you will find in this volume. Yevgeniy Dodis served as the general and sponsorship chair, coordinating the sponsorship efforts. Aggelos Kiayias served as the publicity and publication chair, tending to the conference's publicity aspects, Web-site, submission and reviewing site as well as the editorial preparation of the present volume. Tal Malkin served as the general and local arrangements chair and was responsible for the very critical job of hosting PKC 2006 at Columbia University.

The selection of papers for this year's program was a delicate and laborious task. PKC 2006 had received a total of 124 submissions by the day of the submission deadline, November 15, 2005. Each paper was refereed by at least four committee members who were frequently assisted by external reviewers. The online discussions together with the reviews that were posted on the online reviewing site, if printed, would require more than 450 pages of densely printed text. The present proceedings volume contains the revised versions of the accepted extended abstracts as submitted by the authors after an alloted three week revision period based on the Program Committee's comments. The PKC 2006 Program Committee had the pleasure of according this year's *PKC Best Paper Award* to Daniel Bleichenbacher and Alexander May for their advancement of RSA cryptanalysis in their paper entitled "New Attacks on RSA with Small Secret CRT-Exponents."

We would like to thank the Program Committee members as well as the external reviewers for their volunteered hard work invested in selecting the program. We thank the PKC Steering Committee for their support. We also wish to thank the following individuals: Shai Halevi for providing his Web-review and submission system to be used for the conference and for providing technical support; the submission and reviewing-site administrator David Walluck as well as the other students of the CryptoDRM Lab at the University of Connecticut for providing technical support; and Michael Locasto for Web-site administration support at Columbia University. Finally big thanks are due to all authors of submitted papers whose quality contributions make this research area a pleasure to work in, and made this conference a possibility.

March 2006

Moti Yung
Yevgeniy Dodos
Aggelos Kiayias
Tal Malkin

Organization

PKC Steering Committee

Ronald Cramer	CWI and Leiden University, The Netherlands
Yvo Desmedt	University College London, UK
Hideki Imai (Chair)	University of Tokyo, Japan
Kwangjo Kim	Information and Communications University, Korea
David Naccache	École Normale Supérieure, France
Tatsuaki Okamoto	NTT Labs, Japan
Jacques Stern	École Normale Supérieure, France
Moti Yung	RSA Laboratories and Columbia University, USA
Yuliang Zheng (Secretary)	University of North Carolina at Charlotte, USA

Organizing Committee

Conference and Program Chair	Moti Yung
General and Sponsorship Chair	Yevgeniy Dodis
Publicity and Publication Chair	Aggelos Kiayias
General and Local Arrangements Chair	Tal Malkin

Industrial Sponsors

EADS
Morgan Stanley
Gemplus
NTT DoCoMo
Google
Microsoft
RSA Security

Program Committee

Masayuki Abe	NTT Japan
Feng Bao	I2R, Singapore
Paulo S.L.M. Barreto	University of São Paulo, Brazil
Amos Beimel	Ben Gurion University, Israel
Xavier Boyen	Voltage Technology, USA
Serge Fehr	CWI, The Netherlands
Pierre-Alain Fouque	ENS Paris, France
Juan Garay	Bell Labs, USA
Rosario Gennaro	IBM Research, USA
Nick Howgrave-Graham	NTRU Cryptosystems, USA
Dong Hoon Lee	Korea University, Korea
Wenbo Mao	HP Labs, China
Alexander May	Paderborn University, Germany
David Naccache	ENS, France
Rafail Ostrovsky	UCLA, USA
Kenny Paterson	Royal Holloway, U. of London, UK
Giuseppe Persiano	University of Salerno, Italy
Benny Pinkas	Haifa University, Israel
Leonid Reyzin	Boston University, USA
Kazue Sako	NEC Japan
Jean-Sébastien Coron	University of Luxembourg
Alice Silverberg	U. C. Irvine, USA
Jessica Staddon	PARC, USA
Ron Steinfeld	Macquarie University, Australia
Edlyn Teske	University of Waterloo, Canada
Wen-Guey Tzeng	NCTU, Taiwan
Susanne Wetzel	Stevens Institute, USA
Yiqun Lisa Yin	Independent Consultant, USA
Adam Young	MITRE, USA
Moti Yung	RSA Labs and Columbia U., USA

External Reviewers

Michel Abdalla	Melissa Chase	Paolo D'Arco
Ben Adida	Lily Chen	Michael De Mare
Luis von Ahn	Liqun Chen	Breno de Medeiros
Giuseppe Ateniese	Benoît Chevallier-Mames	Nenad Dedić
Joonsang Baek	Chen-Kang Chu	Alex Dent
Paulo Barreto	Mathieu Ciet	Glenn Durfee
Daniel Brown	Scott Contini	Pooya Farshim
Jan Camenisch	Yang Cui	Marc Fischlin
Ran Canetti	Martin Döring	Jun Furukawa

Table of Contents

Number Theory Algorithms

Pairing-Based Cryptography

Cryptosystems Design and Analysis

Signature and Identification

Authentication and Key Establishment

Multi-party Computation

PKI Techniques

New Attacks on RSA with
Small Secret CRT-Exponents

Daniel Bleichenbacher[1] and Alexander May[2]

[1] daniel_bleichenbacher@yahoo.com
[2] Department of Computer Science,
TU Darmstadt,
64289 Darmstadt, Germany
may@informatik.tu-darmstadt.de

Abstract. It is well-known that there is an efficient method for decrypting/signing with RSA when the secret exponent d is small modulo $p-1$ and $q-1$. We call such an exponent d a small CRT-exponent. It is one of the major open problems in attacking RSA whether there exists a polynomial time attack for small CRT-exponents, i.e. a result that can be considered as an equivalent to the Wiener and Boneh-Durfee bound for small d. At Crypto 2002, May presented a partial solution in the case of an RSA modulus $N = pq$ with unbalanced prime factors p and q. Based on Coppersmith's method, he showed that there is a polynomial time attack provided that $q < N^{0.382}$. We will improve this bound to $q < N^{0.468}$. Thus, our result comes close to the desired normal RSA case with balanced prime factors. We also present a second result for balanced RSA primes in the case that the public exponent e is significantly smaller than N. More precisely, we show that there is a polynomial time attack if $d_p, d_q \leq \min\{(N/e)^{\frac{2}{5}}, N^{\frac{1}{4}}\}$. The method can be used to attack two fast RSA variants recently proposed by Galbraith, Heneghan, McKee, and by Sun, Wu.

Keywords: RSA, small exponents, lattices, Coppersmith's method.

1 Introduction

Let $N = pq$ be an RSA modulus. The public exponent e and the secret exponent d satisfy the equation $ed = 1 \bmod \phi(N)$, where $\phi(N) = (p-1)(q-1)$ is Euler's totient function. The main drawback of RSA is its efficiency. A normal RSA decryption/signature generation requires time $\Theta(\log d \log^2 N)$.

Therefore, one might be tempted to use small secret exponents to speed up the decryption/signing process. Unfortunately, Wiener[14] showed in 1991 that if $d < N^{\frac{1}{4}}$ then the factorization of N can be found in polynomial time using only the public information (N, e). In 1999, Boneh and Durfee[1] improved the bound to $d < N^{0.292}$. One can view these bounds as a benchmark for attacking RSA (see also the comments in the STORK-roadmap [11]). Thus, improving these bounds is a major research issue in public key cryptanalysis.

M. Yung et al. (Eds.): PKC 2006, LNCS 3958, pp. 1–13, 2006.

It remains an important open problem whether there is an analogue of these attacks in the case of small secret CRT-exponents d, i.e. exponents d such that $d_p = d \bmod p - 1$ and $d_q = d \bmod q - 1$ both are small. For the construction of such small CRT-exponents with a given bit-size, we refer to Boneh, Shacham [2]. Notice that small CRT-exponents enable to efficiently raise to the dth power modulo p and modulo q, respectively. The results are then combined using the Chinese Remainder Theorem (CRT), yielding a solution modulo N. For the normal RSA case with balanced prime factors p, q and full-size e, the best algorithm that is currently known has time and space complexity $\mathcal{O}(\sqrt{\min\{d_p, d_q\}})$.

At Crypto 2002, May[9] presented two polynomial time attacks for the case of imbalanced prime factors p and q. His attacks are based on Coppersmith's method for finding small roots of modular equations. His first attack is rigorous and solves a polynomial equation modulo p. This attack works whenever $q < N^{0.382}$. May's second attack is a heuristic method that is based on a resultant heuristic for Coppersmith's method in the multivariate modular case. This attack works whenever $q < N^{\frac{3}{8}}$.

Let us have a look at the size of d_p that can be attacked by May's approaches as a function of the size of q. In Fig. 1 we present both of these sizes as a fraction of the bits of N.

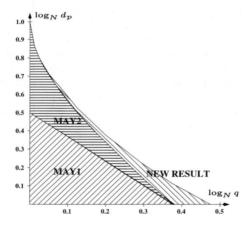

Fig. 1. The attacks of [9] in comparison with the new approach

A close look at the functions presented in Fig. 1 reveals that there is a tiny region where May's first method is better than his second one. Hence, it is a natural question to ask whether there is a unifying method that covers both regions of the key space.

In this work, we present a new attack that solves this question. In Fig. 1, we give the improved sizes of d_p that can be attacked by our new approach as a function of q. One can see that the new attack works up to $q < N^{0.468}$ and covers the key spaces of the previously known attacks. Thus, we are able to improve the benchmark for attacking CRT-RSA up to almost balanced prime factors.

Interestingly, we get the improvement by making just a small twist to May's second method. He solved a polynomial equation $f(x, y) = x(N - y) + N$ with a small root (x_0, q) modulo e. In this work, we make additional use of the fact that the desired small solution contains the prime factor q. Namely, we introduce a new variable z for the prime factor p and further use the equation $yz = N$.

Our new approach immediately raises an interesting open problem: The polynomial $f(x, y) = x(N - y) + N$ used here is very similar to the polynomial $g(x, y) = x(N + 1 - y) + 1$ that is used in the Boneh-Durfee approach to show the currently best bound of $d < N^{0.292}$ for attacking small secret exponent RSA. Notice that both polynomials $f(x, y)$ and $g(x, y)$ have the same set of monomials, i.e. the same Newton polytope. In contrast to $f(x, y)$, the polynomial $g(x, y)$ has a small root $(x_0', p + q)$. It is a natural question to ask whether one can improve the Boneh-Durfee bound by using the fact that this root contains the sum of the prime factors p and q.

We should point out that our new attack works for small d_p and arbitrary sizes of d_q. It is an open problem how to make use of a small parameter d_q in this attack. Maybe a clever use of d_q could already help to push the bound from $q < N^{0.468}$ to the desired normal RSA-case of balanced prime factors.

As a second result, we are able to give a different lattice-based attack on RSA with small CRT-exponents that works in the case of balanced prime factors, but with the restriction that the parameter e is significantly smaller than N. This second attack makes use of small d_p and small d_q. The result is achieved by multiplying the equations $ed_p = 1 \bmod p - 1$ and $ed_q = 1 \bmod q - 1$ and then using a linearization technique. Our attack works whenever $d_p, d_q < \min\{\frac{1}{4}(N/e)^{\frac{2}{5}}, \frac{1}{3}N^{\frac{1}{4}}\}$, i.e., up to roughly half of the bit-size of p, q for sufficiently small e. The attack requires to find a shortest vector in a 3-dimensional lattice and is extremely fast. As an application of our second result, we show that recently proposed RSA variants by Galbraith, Heneghan and McKee [5] and Sun, Wu [12] are vulnerable to the new attack.

We would like to point out that both new attacks are heuristic methods. We implemented both methods and provide several experiments that show that the heuristics work well in practice.

The organization of the paper is as follows. In Section 2, we state some lattice basis theory and in Section 3 we review May's result. In Section 4, we show how to achieve the improved bound of $q < N^{0.468}$. In Section 5, we present our second attack for $d_p, d_q < \min\{\frac{1}{4}(N/e)^{\frac{2}{5}}, \frac{1}{3}N^{\frac{1}{4}}\}$ and show how this attack breaks recently proposed fast RSA variants. We conclude our work by providing some experimental results for our attacks in Section 6.

2   Lattice Theory and Definitions

Let $b_1, \ldots, b_n \in \mathbb{Z}_n$ be linearly independent. Then these vectors span a lattice of dimension n defined by

$$L := \left\{ x \in \mathbb{Z}_n \mid x = \sum_{i=1}^{n} a_i b_i, \text{ where } a_i \in \mathbb{Z} \right\}.$$

We call the set $B = \{b_1, \ldots, b_n\}$ a basis of L. There are infinitely many bases. A basis can be transformed into another basis by a unimodular transformation, i.e. a multiplication by a matrix with determinant ± 1. Therefore, the absolute value of the determinant of a basis matrix is an invariant of the lattice L. We call this invariant the determinant of L, which is denoted by $\det(L) = |\det(B)|$.

A famous theorem of Minkowski gives an upper bound for the length of a shortest vector v in a lattice in terms of a function of the determinant and the dimension n:

$$\|v\| \leq \sqrt{n} \dim(L)^n.$$

In lattices with fixed dimension, a shortest vector can be found in polynomial time. In arbitrary dimension, approximations of a shortest vector can be obtained in polynomial time by applying the well-known L^3 basis reduction algorithm of Lenstra, Lenstra and Lovász [8].

Theorem 1 (Lenstra, Lenstra, Lovász). *Let $B = \{b_1, \ldots, b_n\}$ be a basis. On input B, the L^3-algorithm outputs another basis $\{v_1, \ldots, v_n\}$ with*

$$\|v_1\| \leq \|v_2\| \leq 2^{\frac{n}{4}} \det(L)^{\frac{1}{n-1}},$$

in time polynomial in n and in the bit-size of the entries in B.

Let $f(x, y) = \sum_{i,j} a_{i,j} x^i y^j \in \mathbb{Z}[x, y]$. We define the norm of f by the Euclidean norm of its coefficient vector: $\|f\|^2 = \sum_{i,j} a_{i,j}^2$.

Based on the L^3-algorithm, Coppersmith [4] presented in 1996 a method that finds small solutions to modular polynomial equations. The idea behind Coppersmith's method is to construct a polynomial which has the desired small root over the integers. Howgrave-Graham [7] in turn formulated a useful condition how to find such a polynomial in terms of the norm of a polynomial.

Theorem 2 (Howgrave-Graham). *Let $f(x_1, \ldots, x_k)$ be a polynomial in k variables with n monomials. Furthermore, let m be a positive integer. Suppose that*

(1) $f(r_1, \ldots, r_k) = 0 \bmod b^m$ where $|r_i| \leq X_i$, $i = 1, \ldots, k$ and
(2) $\|f(x_1 X_1, \ldots, x_k X_k)\| < \frac{b^m}{\sqrt{n}}.$

Then $f(r_1, \ldots, r_k) = 0$ holds over the integers.

3   Revisiting May's Attack on Small CRT-Exponents

Throughout this paper, we assume that $e < \phi(N)$. Furthermore, we assume that $q \leq N^\beta$ for some $\beta \leq \frac{1}{2}$. We start by writing the RSA equation $ed_p = 1 \bmod (p - 1)$ in the form

$$ed_p = 1 + k(p - 1),$$

for some unknown $k \in \mathbb{N}$. Rewriting terms yields

$$ed_p = (k - 1)(p - 1) + p. \tag{1}$$

A multiplication with q leaves us with the equation

$$ed_p q = (k-1)(N-q) + N.$$

We assign the variables x and y to the unknown parameters on the right-hand side and obtain a bivariate polynomial

$$f(x,y) = x(N-y) + N, \tag{2}$$

with the root $(x_0, y_0) = (k-1, q)$ modulo e. In order to bound the term $k-1$, we observe that by Eq. (1)

$$k-1 = \frac{ed_p - p}{p-1} < \frac{e}{p-1} \, d_p < (q-1)X < N^\beta X.$$

Let us fix a parameter m. We define the following collection of polynomials that all have the root (x_0, y_0) modulo e^m:

$$g_{i,j}(x,y) = e^{m-i} x^j f^i(x,y) \quad \text{for } i = 0, \ldots, m; \; j = 0, \ldots, m-i \quad \text{and}$$
$$h_{i,j}(x,y) = e^{m-i} y^j f^i(x,y) \quad \text{for } i = 0, \ldots, m; \; j = 1, \ldots, t. \tag{3}$$

The parameter t has to be optimized as a function of m.

Since each polynomial of the collection has the small root (x_0, y_0) modulo e, every linear combination of these polynomials also has the same root modulo e.

A lower triangular lattice basis can be build from the coefficient vectors of $g_{i,j}(xX, yY)$ and $h_{i,j}(xX, yY)$. According to Howgrave-Graham's theorem (Theorem 2), linear combinations of the vectors with sufficiently small norm give raise to bivariate polynomials that have the root (x_0, y_0) not only modulo e but over the integers. Having two polynomials $f_1(x,y)$ and $f_2(x,y)$ with this root over the integers, one can take resultants in order to extract the desired root. However, the last step is a heuristic, since the resultant computation may fail due to a non-trivial gcd of f_1 and f_2.

In [9], it was shown that with the optimal choice of parameters one obtains an attack that works up to $q < N^{\frac{3}{8}}$, see also Fig. 1 in Section 1.

4   An Approach That Works for $q < N^{0.468}$

Our improvement of the algorithm presented in Section 3 is based on the observation that in Eq. (2) the polynomial $f(x,y)$ contains in its small root $(x_0, y_0) = (d_p, q)$ modulo e the prime factor q. We will use the fact that we do not deal with just an arbitrary small root but that q is already determined by N.

Let us introduce a new variable z for p. We multiply the polynomial $f(x,y)$ by a power z^s for some s that has to be optimized. Additionally, we can replace every occurence of the monomial yz by N. Let us look at the following new collection of trivariate polynomials that we obtain by multiplying the former collection from (3) with z^s:

$$g'_{i,j}(x,y,z) = e^{m-i} x^j z^s f^i(x,y) \quad \text{for } i = 0, \ldots, m; \; j = 0, \ldots, m-i \quad \text{and}$$
$$h'_{i,j}(x,y,z) = e^{m-i} y^j z^s f^i(x,y) \quad \text{for } i = 0, \ldots, m; \; j = 1, \ldots, t.$$

What is the impact of a multiplication with z^s, i.e. the changes from the collection g, h to the collection g', h'? Every monomial $x^i y^j$, $j \geq s$ with coefficient $a_{i,j}$ in the former collection is transformed into a monomial $x^i y^{j-s}$ with coefficient $a_{i,j} N^s$ in the new collection. In case of a monomial $x^i y^j$ with $j < s$, we obtain a new monomial $x^i z^{s-j}$ with new coefficient $a_{i,j} N^j$.

The obvious advantage is that the coefficient vectors of $g'(xX, yY, zZ)$ and $h'(xX, yY, zZ)$ contain less powers of Y, which decreases the determinant of the lattice spanned by these vectors. On the other hand, the coefficient vectors contain powers of Z, which in turn increases the determinant. Hence, there is a trade-off and one has to optimize the parameter s subject to a minimization of the lattice determinant.

As in Section 3, the resulting lattice basis built from the coefficient vectors of $g'(xX, yY, zZ)$ and $h'(xX, yY, zZ)$ is lower triangular. Therefore, every polynomial from our new collection contributes with just one coefficient to the diagonal. If the coefficient of this diagonal entry has a factor of N^j, we eliminate this factor by multiplying the polynomial with the inverse of N^j modulo e. I.e., we eliminate powers of N in the diagonal entries in order to keep the lattice determinant as small as possible.

Let B be the lattice basis defined by the coefficient vectors $g'(xX, yY, zZ)$ and $h'(xX, yY, zZ)$, where we eliminated powers of N on the diagonal as explained above. Moreover, let L be the lattice spanned by these vectors with dimension $\dim(L)$ and determinant $\det(L)$.

We have to find two vectors in L that are shorter than the bound $e^m / \sqrt{\dim(L)}$ given in Howgrave Graham's theorem (Theorem 2). These vectors are the coefficient vectors of two trivariate polynomial $f_1(xX, yY, zZ)$ and $f_2(xX, yY, zZ)$. By Howgrave-Graham's theorem, $f_1(x, y, z)$ and $f_2(x, y, z)$ have the root (x_0, q, p) over the integers. We will later show that the desired short vectors can be obtained by applying the L^3-algorithm to our lattice basis B.

Suppose for now that we have computed two such trivariate polynomials f_1 and f_2 with the previous property. Then we can eliminate z from the polynomials by setting $z = N/y$. Since the resulting bivariate polynomials are rational we multiply them by a suitable power of y in order to obtain polynomials $\bar{f}_1, \bar{f}_2$ in $\mathbb{Z}[x, y]$. Afterwards, we take the resultant of these integral polynomials $\bar{f}_1, \bar{f}_2$ with respect to the variable x. We obtain a univariate polynomial $g(y)$ with root q. If $\bar{f}_1$ and $\bar{f}_2$ do not share a non-trivial gcd, $g(y)$ is not the zero-polynomial and we can easily extract q with standard root finding algorithms. This completes the description of the attack. The only heuristic assumption that we make in our approach is that $g(y) \neq 0$.

Assumption 3. *The construction described above yields a non-zero polynomial $g(y)$.*

We are able to confirm Assumption 3 by various experiments in Section 6. This shows that our attack works very well in practice.

It remains to give a condition under which we can efficiently find two sufficiently short vectors in the lattice L spanned by the basis B. The following lemma gives an explicit condition, under which the L^3-algorithm finds two such vectors.

Lemma 4. *Let $\epsilon > 0$, $t = \tau m$ and $s = \sigma m$. Let N and m be sufficiently large and*

$$X^{2+3\tau}Y^{1+3(\tau-\sigma)(1+\tau-\sigma)}Z^{3\sigma^2} \le e^{1+3\tau-\epsilon}.$$

Then on input B, the L^3-algorithm will output two vectors that are shorter than $\frac{e^m}{\sqrt{\dim(L)}}$.

Proof: Let $n = \dim(L)$. By the L^3 theorem (Theorem 1), the second shortest vector of an L^3-reduced basis satifies

$$\|v_2\| \le 2^{\frac{n}{4}} \det(L)^{\frac{1}{n-1}}.$$

Suppose that we can upperbound the right-hand side term by $\frac{e^m}{\sqrt{n}}$, then the claim follows. That leaves us with the condition

$$\det(L) < ce^{m(n-1)}, \tag{4}$$

where $c = (2^{-\frac{n}{4}}/\sqrt{n})^{n-1}$. Since c does not depend on N, we let c contribute to the error term ϵ and omit it in the further calculations. Now we have to find an expression for the determinant of L.

It is not hard to see that the contribution of the coefficient vectors in $g'_{i,j}$ to the determinant contains powers of X, Y and Z that correspond to the monomials that appear in $z^s f^m(x,y)$. The coefficient vectors in h' contribute to $\det(L)$ with powers of X, Y and Z from the additional monomials that appear in $z^s y^i f^m(x,y)$, for $i = 1, \ldots, t$. A straight-forward but tedious computation (details are provided in Appendix A) yields that

$$\det(L) = \left((eX)^{2+3\tau}Y^{1+3(\tau-\sigma)(1+\tau-\sigma)}Z^{3\sigma^2}\right)^{\frac{1}{6}m^3(1+o(1))}.$$

Now, we have an expression for the left-hand side of our condition in (4). In order to find an expression for the right-hand side, we observe that $n = \dim(L) = (3+6\tau)\frac{1}{6}m^2(1+o(1))$ (for details of the calculation, see Appendix A). Neglecting low-order terms, we obtain the desired new condition

$$X^{2+3\tau}Y^{1+3(\tau-\sigma)(1+\tau-\sigma)}Z^{3\sigma^2} \le e^{1+3\tau}. \qquad \square$$

We are now able to state our main theorem for our first attack.

Theorem 5. *Let $\epsilon > 0$. Under Assumption 3, the following holds for sufficiently large N: Let $N = pq$ be an RSA-modulus with $q \le N^\beta$ and $p \le 2N^{1-\beta}$. Moreover, let $e = N^\alpha$ be an RSA-public exponent satisfying $ed_p = 1 \bmod p - 1$ for some $d_p = N^\delta$ with*

$$\delta \le \frac{1}{3}\left(3 - 2\beta - \beta^2 - \sqrt{12\alpha\beta - 12\alpha\beta^2 + 4\beta^2 - 5\beta^3 + \beta^4}\right) - \epsilon.$$

Then N can be factored in polynomial time.

Proof: We can define the upper bounds $Y = N^\beta$ and $Z = 2N^{1-\beta}$ for q and p, respectively. Notice that the parameter β must not necessarily be known in advance. If β is unknown, we can brute-force search in polynomial time over the bit-size of q and obtain a suitable parameter β that satisfies our preconditions.

From Section 3, we know that the polynomial $f(x, y) = x(N - y) + N$ has the small root $(x_0, y_0) = (k - 1, q)$ modulo e. Using Eq. (1), we obtain

$$x_0 = k - 1 \leq \frac{ed_p}{p - 1} \leq \frac{N^{\alpha+\delta}}{N^{1-\beta} - 1} \leq 2N^{\alpha+\beta+\delta-1}.$$

Let us define $X = 2N^{\alpha+\beta+\delta-1}$. Now we take the condition from Lemma 4 and plug in our bounds X, Y and Z. Neglecting low-order terms and the error term ϵ, we obtain the new condition

$$(\alpha+\beta+\delta-1)(2+3\tau)+\beta(1+3(\tau-\sigma)(1+\tau-\sigma))+(1-\beta)(3\sigma^2)-\alpha(1+3\tau) < 0.$$

Our goal is to minimize the expression on the left-hand side. Therefore, we differentiate the term with respect to τ and σ. After some calculations, we observe that the expression is minimized for the parameter choices

$$\tau = \frac{(1-\beta)^2 - \delta}{2\beta(1-\beta)} \quad \text{and} \quad \sigma = \frac{1-\beta-\delta}{2(1-\beta)}.$$

Plugging in these values, we obtain the desired condition

$$\delta \leq \frac{1}{3}\left(3 - 2\beta - \beta^2 - \sqrt{12\alpha\beta - 12\alpha\beta^2 + 4\beta^2 - 5\beta^3 + \beta^4}\right). \qquad \square$$

In Fig. 1 (see Section 1), we presented the function from Theorem 5 for the special case $\alpha = 1$, i.e. for the important case where the magnitude of e is of the order of the size of N. In this case, our attack works up to $\beta = \frac{1}{6}(\sqrt{61} - 5) \approx 0.468$.

In [5] and [12], the authors suggested to combine medium size e with small CRT-exponents. In the balanced RSA-case, i.e. for $\beta = \frac{1}{2}$, our bound from Theorem 5 yields a polynomial time attack whenever $\alpha \leq \frac{7}{8}$. However, in the subsequent section we present a polynomial time attack on RSA with balanced prime factors whenever $\alpha < 1$.

5   An Attack for $d_p, d_q < \min\left\{\frac{1}{4}\left(\frac{N}{e}\right)^{\frac{2}{5}}, \frac{1}{3}N^{\frac{1}{4}}\right\}$

In this section we assume both that $d_p < \min\{\frac{1}{4}(N/e)^{2/5}, \frac{1}{3}N^{1/4}\}$ and $d_q < \min\{\frac{1}{4}(N/e)^{2/5}, \frac{1}{3}N^{1/4}\}$. We want to point out that we did not optimize the constant terms $\frac{1}{4}$, $\frac{1}{3}$ in the bounds for d_p, d_q in order to keep the calculations simple. We further assume that $e < \phi(N)$ and $1/2 < p/q < 2$, i.e. that p and

q have about the same size. We show *heuristically* that the modulus N can be factored under these assumptions.

We start with the RSA equations $ed_p = 1 \bmod p - 1$ and $ed_q = 1 \bmod q - 1$. We rewrite these equations as

$$ed_p = 1 + k(p - 1) \quad \text{and}$$
$$ed_q = 1 + \ell(q - 1), \tag{5}$$

where k and ℓ are positive integers. Hence we get

$$ed_p + k - 1 = kp \quad \text{and}$$
$$ed_q + \ell - 1 = \ell q.$$

Multiplying these two equations gives

$$(ed_p + k - 1)(ed_q + \ell - 1) = k\ell N.$$

Next we linearize this equation as

$$ex + y(1 - N) + e^2 w = z,$$

with the unknowns

$$w = d_p d_q,$$
$$x = d_p(\ell - 1) + d_q(k - 1),$$
$$y = k\ell,$$
$$z = k + \ell - 1.$$

In the following, we show that the unknowns can be obtained heuristically by lattice reduction techniques. Using our bound $d_p, d_q \leq \frac{1}{4} e^{-\frac{2}{5}} N^{\frac{2}{5}}$, we can upper-bound

$$k = \frac{ed_p - 1}{p - 1} \leq 2ed_p N^{-\frac{1}{2}} \leq \frac{1}{2} e^{\frac{3}{5}} N^{-\frac{1}{10}}.$$

The same bound holds for ℓ. This enables us to give the following upper bounds for x, y and z:

$$x \leq \frac{1}{4} e^{\frac{1}{5}} N^{\frac{3}{10}},$$
$$y \leq \frac{1}{4} e^{\frac{6}{5}} N^{-\frac{1}{5}},$$
$$z \leq e^{\frac{3}{5}} N^{-\frac{1}{10}}.$$

Let us look at the lattice L_1 that is spanned by the row vectors of the following lattice basis

$$B_1 = \begin{pmatrix} 1 & 0 & e \\ 0 & 1 & 1 - N \\ 0 & 0 & e^2 \end{pmatrix}.$$

Notice that L_1 contains the target vector $v_1 = (x, y, w) \cdot B_1 = (x, y, z)$. We want to balance the target vector, i.e. to make every entry in v_1 approximately of the same size. Therefore, we multiply the columns of B_1 with suitable factors, such that the size of each entry of the resulting target vector is bounded by $e^{\frac{6}{5}} N^{\frac{3}{10}}$. This gives us the lattice L_2 defined by the span of the row vectors in the basis

$$
B_2 = \begin{pmatrix} 4e & 0 & e^{\frac{8}{5}} N^{\frac{2}{5}} \\ 0 & 4N^{\frac{1}{2}} & e^{\frac{3}{5}} N^{\frac{2}{5}}(1-N) \\ 0 & 0 & e^{\frac{13}{5}} N^{\frac{2}{5}} \end{pmatrix}.
$$

The new target vector $v_2 = (x, y, w) \cdot B_2$ has norm at most $\|v_2\| \leq \sqrt{3} e^{\frac{6}{5}} N^{\frac{3}{10}}$. We want to argue that v_2 is among the shortest vectors in L_2. By Minkowski's theorem, L_2 contains a vector with norm smaller than

$$
\sqrt{3} \det(L_2)^{\frac{1}{3}} = \sqrt{3} \left(4^2 e^{\frac{18}{5}} N^{\frac{9}{10}} \right)^{\frac{1}{3}} = 4^{\frac{2}{3}} \cdot \sqrt{3} e^{\frac{6}{5}} N^{\frac{3}{10}}.
$$

We use the heuristic assumption that the vector v_2 is the shortest vector in L_2, i.e. v_2 is the only vector with norm below the Minkowski bound. Notice that L_2 also contains the vectors $(x - \lambda e, y, w + \lambda) \cdot B_2 = (x - \lambda e, y, z)$ with $\lambda \in \mathbb{Z}$. Thus $v_2 = (x, y, z)$ clearly is not the shortest vector in L_2 if $x > e/2$. However, this is not a problem because the condition $d_p, d_q < \frac{1}{3} N^{1/4}$ implies

$$
x = d_p(\ell - 1) + d_q(k - 1) < \frac{1}{3} N^{\frac{1}{4}} (\ell + k) \leq \frac{1}{3} N^{\frac{1}{4}} \cdot \frac{4}{3} e N^{-\frac{1}{4}} < \frac{e}{2}.
$$

Under the heuristic assumption that there are no vectors shorter than v_2, we can recover v_2 by a shortest vector computation in L_2. We confirm our heuristic by experiments in Section 6.

Notice that v_2 gives us the unknowns w, x, y and z. From y and z, we can recover the unknowns k and ℓ. This enables us to recover from w and x the unknown parameters d_p and d_q. Finally, we obtain p and q by solving Eq (5). This completes the description of our second attack.

5.1   Applications

As applications of our attack, we present the cryptanalysis of two fast RSA-variants that were recently proposed by Galbraith, Heneghan, McKee [5] and Sun, Wu [12]. In [5], the following parameter choice is suggested: 1024-bit N, 508-bit e and 200-bit d. Similarly in [12], the suggested parameters are: 1024-bit N, 512-bit e and 199-bit d.

Both schemes are vulnerable to our new attack, i.e. the factorization of N can be obtained from the public parameters (N, e) in a fraction of a second. However, the construction in [5] allows to arbitrarily tune the RSA parameters within some constraints. Thus, the parameters can easily be adapted in such a way that our attack becomes infeasible. Indeed, after learning from our attack Galbraith, Heneghan and McKee [6] as well as Hinek, Sun and Wu [13] revised their constructions in such a way that the present attack does not work. On the other hand, we want to warn that a lack of an attack for a certain part of the RSA key space is not a guarantee of security!

6   Experiments

We implemented the attack described in Section 4 using Shoup's NTL [10]. We ran our experiments on a 2.4Ghz-Pentium under Linux. In each test, we used an 1000-bit RSA-modulus N with varying bit-size of q. The sizes of d_p and the lattice parameters are given in Fig. 2. We would like to point out that we could not find one example, where Assumption 3 failed. Thus, the resultant heuristic seems to work perfectly in practice.

q	d_p	Lattice parameters	L^3-time
405 bit	10 bit	$m = 3$, $t = s = 2$, $\dim(L) = 18$	5 sec
370 bit	50 bit	$m = 3$, $t = s = 2$, $\dim(L) = 18$	5 sec
330 bit	100 bit	$m = 3$, $t = s = 2$, $\dim(L) = 18$	5 sec
280 bit	160 bit	$m = 3$, $t = s = 2$, $\dim(L) = 18$	5 sec
420 bit	10 bit	$m = 4$, $t = s = 3$, $\dim(L) = 30$	50 sec
385 bit	50 bit	$m = 4$, $t = s = 3$, $\dim(L) = 30$	50 sec
340 bit	100 bit	$m = 4$, $t = s = 3$, $\dim(L) = 30$	50 sec
290 bit	160 bit	$m = 4$, $t = s = 3$, $\dim(L) = 30$	50 sec
430 bit	10 bit	$m = 5$, $t = s = 4$, $\dim(L) = 45$	6 min
395 bit	50 bit	$m = 5$, $t = s = 4$, $\dim(L) = 45$	6 min
345 bit	100 bit	$m = 5$, $t = s = 4$, $\dim(L) = 45$	7 min
300 bit	160 bit	$m = 5$, $t = s = 4$, $\dim(L) = 45$	9 min
440 bit	10 bit	$m = 6$, $t = s = 5$, $\dim(L) = 63$	35 min
405 bit	50 bit	$m = 6$, $t = s = 5$, $\dim(L) = 63$	35 min
355 bit	100 bit	$m = 6$, $t = s = 5$, $\dim(L) = 63$	44 min
305 bit	160 bit	$m = 6$, $t = s = 5$, $\dim(L) = 63$	53 min

Fig. 2. Experimental results for the attack from Section 4

An implementation of the attack in Section 5 using PARI/GP [3] needs approximately 15 ms on an 3Ghz-Pentium to find the factors of an 1024-bit RSA modulus. In a test we generated 1000 RSA moduli with 512-bit e, and $d_p, d_q < 2^{200}$. Our implementation was in all cases successful. The success rate however fell to about 90% when we generated the moduli such that $d_p, d_q < 2^{204}$.

Acknowledgements. We thank the anonymous reviewers of PKC 2006 for their very helpful comments.

References

1. D. Boneh, G. Durfee, "Cryptanalysis of RSA with private key d less than $N^{0.292}$", IEEE Trans. on Information Theory, Vol. 46(4), pp. 1339–1349, 2000
2. D. Boneh, H. Shacham, "Fast Variants of RSA", CryptoBytes Vol. 5, No. 1, pp. 1–9, 2002
3. H. Cohen et al. "PARI/GP", http://www.pari.math.u-bordeaux.fr

4. D. Coppersmith, "Small solutions to polynomial equations and low exponent vulnerabilities", Journal of Cryptology, Vol. 10(4), pp. 223–260, 1997.
5. S. D. Galbraith, C. Heneghan, and J. F. McKee, "Tunable Balancing of RSA", Proceedings of ACISP 2005, Lecture Notes in Computer Science Vol. 3574, pp. 280–292, 2005
6. S. D. Galbraith, C. Heneghan, and J. F. McKee, "Tunable Balancing of RSA", full version of [5], online available at http://www.isg.rhul.ac.uk/~sdg/full-tunable -rsa.pdf
7. N. Howgrave-Graham, "Finding small roots of univariate modular equations revisited", Proceedings of Cryptography and Coding, Lecture Notes in Computer Science Vol. 1355, Springer-Verlag, pp. 131–142, 1997
8. A. K. Lenstra, H. W. Lenstra, and L. Lovász, "Factoring polynomials with rational coefficients," Mathematische Annalen, Vol. 261, pp. 513–534, 1982
9. A. May, "Cryptanalysis of Unbalanced RSA with Small CRT-Exponent", Advances in Cryptology – Crypto 2002, Lecture Notes in Computer Science Vol. 2442, Springer-Verlag, pp. 242–256, 2002
10. V. Shoup, NTL: A Library for doing Number Theory, online available at http://www.shoup.net/ntl/index.html
11. STORK, Strategic Roadmap for Crypto, http://www.stork.eu.org/index.html
12. H.-M. Sun, M.-E. Wu, "An Approach Towards Rebalanced RSA-CRT with Short Public Exponent", Cryptology ePrint Archive: Report 2005/053, online available at http://eprint.iacr.org/2005/053
13. H.-M. Sun, M. J. Hinek, and M.-E. Wu, "An Approach Towards Rebalanced RSA-CRT with Short Public Exponent", revised version of [12], online available at http://www.cacr.math.uwaterloo.ca/techreports/2005/cacr2005-35.pdf
14. M. Wiener, "Cryptanalysis of short RSA secret exponents", IEEE Transactions on Information Theory, Vol. 36, pp. 553–558, 1990

A   Details of the Calculations in Lemma 4

It remains to give the dimension and determinant calculation from the proof of Lemma 4. Therefore, we recall our collection of polynomials from Section 4:

$$g'_{i,j}(x,y,z) = e^{m-i}x^j z^s f^i(x,y) \quad \text{for} \ \ i = 0, \ldots, m; \ j = 0, \ldots, m-i \ \ \text{and}$$
$$h'_{i,j}(x,y,z) = e^{m-i}y^j z^s f^i(x,y) \quad \text{for} \ \ i = 0, \ldots, m; \ j = 1, \ldots, t. \quad (6)$$

The dimension of L is the number of polynomials in this collection:

$$\dim(L) = \sum_{i=0}^{m} \sum_{j=0}^{m-i} 1 = (3 + 6\tau) \cdot \frac{1}{6}m^3(1 + o(1)).$$

We order the monomials in our collection such that the coefficient of the monomial which appears on the lattice basis diagonal corresponds to the monomial $x^i y^i$ in $f^i(x,y)$. I.e., the coefficient of the monomial from $g'_{i,j}(xX, yY, zZ)$ which contributes to the lattice determinant is the coefficient of $x^j z^s (xy)^i$, where we cancel out all terms yz using the relation $yz = N$. As explained in Section 4, we also eliminate all powers of N from the coefficient. Analogously, we proceed with the coefficient vectors of $h'_{i,j}(xX, yY, zZ)$.

Let us first calcute the contribution of the coefficient vectors of $g_{i,j}(xX, yY, zZ)$ to the determinant. We denote by e_g, X_g, Y_g and Z_g the contribution of all of the coefficient vectors of $g_{i,j}(xX, yY, zZ)$ to the exponents of e, X, Y, Z in the determinant of L, respectively.

From the description of our collection in (6), we derive

$$e_g = \sum_{i=0}^{m} \sum_{j=0}^{m-i} m - i = 2 \cdot \frac{1}{6} m^3 (1 + o(1)),$$

$$X_g = \sum_{i=0}^{m} \sum_{j=0}^{m-i} i + j = 2 \cdot \frac{1}{6} m^3 (1 + o(1)),$$

$$Y_g = \sum_{i=s}^{m} \sum_{j=0}^{m-i} i - s = (1 - \sigma)^3 \cdot \frac{1}{6} m^3 (1 + o(1)),$$

$$Z_g = \sum_{i=0}^{s} \sum_{j=0}^{m-i} s - i = (3\sigma^2 - \sigma^3) \cdot \frac{1}{6} m^3 (1 + o(1)).$$

Similarly, we derive the contribution of the coefficient vectors of $h_{i,j}(xX, yY, zZ)$ to the determinant of L:

$$e_h = \sum_{i=0}^{m} \sum_{j=1}^{t} m - i = 3\tau \cdot \frac{1}{6} m^3 (1 + o(1)),$$

$$X_h = \sum_{i=0}^{m} \sum_{j=1}^{t} i = 3\tau \cdot \frac{1}{6} m^3 (1 + o(1)),$$

$$Y_h = \sum_{i=0}^{m} \sum_{j=\max\{1, s-i\}}^{t} j + i - s = (\sigma^3 + 3(\tau + \tau^2) - 6\sigma\tau) \cdot \frac{1}{6} m^3 (1 + o(1)),$$

$$Z_h = \sum_{i=0}^{s} \sum_{j=1}^{s-i} s - i - j = \sigma^3 \cdot \frac{1}{6} m^3 (1 + o(1)).$$

Summarizing we obtain the determinant

$$\det(L) = e^{e_g + e_h} X^{X_g + X_h} Y^{Y_g + Y_h} Z^{Z_g + Z_h}$$

$$= \left((eX)^{2 + 3\tau} Y^{1 + 3(\tau - \sigma)(1 + \tau - \sigma)} Z^{3\sigma^2} \right)^{\frac{1}{6} m^3 (1 + o(1))}.$$

An Attack on a Modified Niederreiter Encryption Scheme

Christian Wieschebrink

Federal Office for Information Security (BSI),
Godesberger Allee 185-189, 53175 Bonn, Germany
christian.wieschebrink@bsi.bund.de

Abstract. In [1] a Niederreiter-type public-key cryptosystem based on
subcodes of generalized Reed-Solomon codes is presented. In this paper
an algorithm is proposed which is able to recover the private key of the
aforementioned system from the public key and which is considerably
faster than a brute force attack. It is shown that the example parameters proposed in [1] are insecure.

Keywords: Public key cryptography, McEliece encryption, Niederreiter encryption, error-correcting codes, generalized Reed-Solomon codes,
Sidelnikov-Shestakov attack.

1   Introduction

The McEliece [2] and Niederreiter [3] encryption scheme are the most well-known
code-based public key cryptosystems. Their security rests on two intractability
assumptions: on the one hand it is difficult to decode an arbitrary linear code,
on the other hand it is difficult to recover the structure of the underlying code
from an arbitrary generator matrix which forms the public key in these systems. Indeed, the general syndrome decoding problem was shown in [4] to be
NP-complete. Moreover there is practical evidence, that it is hard for random
instances, too. Several quite sophisticated algorithms to attack the decoding
problem were published (for example [5, 6]), but their running times remain
exponential.

The hardness of the structural problem crucially depends on the kind of codes
being used. The original Niederreiter scheme made use of generalized Reed-
Solomon (GRS) codes. A polynomial time algorithm reconstrucing the code parameters from an arbitrary generator matrix was found afterwards by Sidelnikov
and Shestakov [7]. Therefore the original Niederreiter scheme is completely broken. On the other hand McEliece proposed Goppa codes for his scheme. Up to
now no efficient way is known to compute the parameters of these codes from
the public key.

In [1] Berger and Loidreau propose a variant of the Niederreiter scheme which
is intended to resist the Sidelnikov-Shestakov attack. The idea is to work with
a subcode of a GRS code instead of a complete GRS code in order to hide its
structure. In this paper we develop an attack on the modified system which is

M. Yung et al. (Eds.): PKC 2006, LNCS 3958, pp. 14–26, 2006.

feasible if the subcode is chosen too large. It can be considered as a generalization of the Sidelnikov-Shestakov algorithm.

The rest of the article is structured as follows: after having presented the Berger-Loidreau variant in detail in Sect. 2 we describe the basic attack in Sect. 3. In Sect. 4 we show how to speed up this attack considerably and in Sect. 5 we give some results of a test implementation.

2   The Modified Scheme

First of all let's recall some basic facts about generalized Reed-Solomon codes. In the following let F be a finite field.

Definition 1. Let $m, k, n \in \mathbb{N}$, $k \leq n$, $\alpha = (\alpha_1, \ldots, \alpha_n) \in F^n$, $x = (x_1, \ldots, x_n) \in (F \setminus \{0\})^n$, where the α_i are pairwise distinct. The generalized Reed-Solomon code (or GRS code) $GRS_{n,k}(\alpha, x)$ is a linear code over F given by the generator matrix

$$G_{\alpha,x} = \begin{pmatrix} x_1 & x_2 & \cdots & x_n \\ x_1\alpha_1 & x_2\alpha_2 & \cdots & x_n\alpha_n \\ \vdots & & \ddots & \\ x_1\alpha_1^{k-1} & x_2\alpha_2^{k-1} & \cdots & x_n\alpha_n^{k-1} \end{pmatrix}.$$

Consequently $GRS_{n,k}(\alpha, x)$ consists exactly of those words c in F^n which can be written $c = (x_1 f(\alpha_1), \ldots, x_n f(\alpha_n))$ for a polynomial $f(x) \in F[x]$ with $\deg f < k$. GRS codes allow efficient error correction. Given x and α one can apply the Berlekamp-Massey algorithm which can correct up to $\lfloor \frac{n-k}{2} \rfloor$ errors in polynomial time. (For details see [8, 9].) In context of cryptography it is always assumed that $GRS_{n,k}(\alpha, x)$ has full length, i.e. $n = \#F$ and char $F = 2$. For a fixed GRS code $GRS_{n,k}(\alpha, x)$ the parameters α and x are not uniquely determined:

Proposition 1. Let α, x be defined as above. Then

$$GRS_{n,k}(\alpha, x) = GRS_{n,k}((a\alpha_1 + b, \ldots, a\alpha_n + b), (cx_1, \ldots, cx_n))$$

for all $a, b, c \in F$, $a, c \neq 0$.

Proof. See [9].   □

It follows for example that two of the α_i can be chosen arbitrarily. Each of the different parameters for a given GRS code is equally suited for the above mentioned decoding algorithm.

Proposition 2. Let α, x be defined as above and $u := (u_1, \ldots u_n)$ where $u_i := x_i^{-1} \prod_{j \neq i} (\alpha_i - \alpha_j)^{-1}$. Then the dual code of $GRS_{n,k}(\alpha, x)$ is given by

$$GRS_{n,k}(\alpha, x)^{\perp} = GRS_{n,n-k}(\alpha, u) .$$

Proof. See [9].   □

Proposition 2 will be helpful later for reconstructing x if α is known.

The Berger-Loidreau modification of the Niederreiter public-key scheme works as follows (we present the dual version of the scheme given in [1], which has the same security, see [10]):

Key creation: Let $n = \#F$, $k \in \mathbb{N}^{\leq n}$ and a small $l \in \mathbb{N}^{\leq k}$ be given. Alice chooses a random GRS code $GRS_{n,k}(\alpha, x)$ with generator matrix $G_{\alpha,x}$ and a random $(k - l) \times k-$matrix A over F of rank $k - l$. Then her public key is given by $T := A \cdot G_{\alpha,x}$. The secret key is (α, x). (*A* must be kept secret, too.)

Encryption: To encrypt a message $m \in F^{k-l}$ Bob chooses a (secret) vector $e \in F^n$ of Hamming weight $\leq \lfloor \frac{n-k}{2} \rfloor$ and computes the cipertext $c := mT + e$.

Decryption: Using (α, x) Alice applies the decoding algorithm to c getting mT. By multiplying this with a right-side inverse of T she gets m.

3   The Attack

We fix some additional notation. For a $(k \times n)-$matrix $T = (t_{i,j})$ let $E(T)$ be the echelon form of T and $<T>$ the code generated by T. The $i-$th row of T is denoted by t_i. Given a permutation $\pi : \{1, \ldots, n\} \rightarrow \{1, \ldots, n\}$ let T_π denote the matrix $(t_{i,\pi(j)})$, i.e. the columns of T are permuted according to π. Analogically for $v = (v_1, \ldots v_n) \in F^n$ we define $v_\pi := (v_{\pi(1)}, \ldots v_{\pi(n)})$. If T is a generator matrix of $GRS_{n,k}(\alpha, x)$ then obviously T_π is a generator matrix of $GRS_{n,k}(\alpha_\pi, x_\pi)$.

Now let T be the public key of the aforementioned encryption scheme. Clearly T is a generator matrix of a $(k - l)-$dimensional subcode of $GRS_{n,k}(\alpha, x)$. Our aim is to find the parameters α and x (or equivalent parameters, see Proposition 1) where only T is given. The attack consists of two steps. In the first step (which is the more expensive one) the permutation of the field elements α is calculated. In the second step x is recovered.

Let $c \in <T>$. Recall that c can be written in the form

$$c = (x_1 f(\alpha_1), \ldots, x_n f(\alpha_n)) , \tag{1}$$

where $f \in F[x]$ with deg $f \leq k - 1$. Now let $d \in <T>$ be another codeword, $d = (x_1 g(\alpha_1), \ldots, x_n g(\alpha_n))$. For all $i = 1, \ldots, n$ we then have

$$\frac{c_i}{d_i} = \frac{x_i f(\alpha_i)}{x_i g(\alpha_i)} = \frac{f}{g}(\alpha_i) ,$$

unless $d_i = 0$. The main idea of the attack is based on the following

Proposition 3. *Let T be the generator matrix of a $(k - l)$-dimensional subcode of $GRS_{n,k}(\alpha, x)$ and $E(T) := (t_{i,j}) = [1_{k-l}|A]$ the echelon form of T. Then for each pair $(i, b) \in \{1, \ldots, k - l\}^2$ there are polynomials $P_i(x), P_b(x) \in F[x]$ of degree $\leq l$ such that*

$$\frac{t_{i,j}}{t_{b,j}} = \frac{(\alpha_j - \alpha_b)P_i(\alpha_j)}{(\alpha_j - \alpha_i)P_b(\alpha_j)} \tag{2}$$

for all $j = 1, \ldots n$ with $t_{b,j} \neq 0$.

Proof. For given i, b let t_i, t_b the respective rows of $E(T)$. Since $E(T)$ is in echelon form both rows contain (at least) $k - l - 1$ zeros, and there are (at least) $k - l - 2$ positions where t_i, t_b have common zeros. Let $a_1, \ldots, a_{k-l-2} \in \{1, \ldots, k-l\}$ be these positions. According to the properties of a GRS code there are polynomials $f_i(x), f_b(x) \in F[x]$ of degree $\leq k - 1$, s.t.

$$(t_{c,1}, \ldots, t_{c,n}) = (x_1 f_c(\alpha_1), \ldots, x_n f_c(\alpha_n))$$

for $c = i, b$ and they must have the form

$$f_i(x) = (x - \alpha_b) \cdot P_i(x) \cdot \prod_{r=1}^{k-l-2} (x - \alpha_{a_r}) \,,$$

$$f_b(x) = (x - \alpha_i) \cdot P_b(x) \cdot \prod_{r=1}^{k-l-2} (x - \alpha_{a_r})$$

with P_i and P_b having degree l at most. So for all $j = 1, \ldots, n$ with $t_{b,j} \neq 0$ we have

$$\frac{t_{i,j}}{t_{b,j}} = \frac{f_i(\alpha_j)}{f_b(\alpha_j)} = \frac{(\alpha_j - \alpha_b) P_i(\alpha_j)}{(\alpha_j - \alpha_i) P_b(\alpha_j)} \,. \qquad \square$$

Note that P_i, P_b in the above proposition may have common factors, so these polynomials are not unique in general. Since P_i and P_b have low degree we can now try to reconstruct the coefficients of both polynomials. If we do so for different rows t_i of $E(T)$ it is possible to recover the α_i as we will see below.

First of all we need a simple

Lemma 1. *Let $f(x) = \frac{P(x)}{Q(x)}$ be a rational function over F with $\deg P, Q \leq i \in \mathbb{N}$, P, Q relatively prime and Q monic. Let $x_1, \ldots, x_{2i+1} \in F$ be pairwise distinct values, for which f is defined. Then the coefficients of P and Q are uniquely determined by the pairs $(x_j, f(x_j)), j = 1, \ldots, 2i + 1$ and can be computed in polynomial time.*

Proof. Let $\bar{P}, \bar{Q}$ be another pair of relatively prime polynomials over F with $f(x) = \frac{\bar{P}(x)}{\bar{Q}(x)}$, $\deg \bar{P}, \bar{Q} \leq i$ and $\bar{Q}$ monic. Then we have $P(x_j)\bar{Q}(x_j) = \bar{P}(x_j)Q(x_j)$ for $j = 1, \ldots, 2i + 1$. Since $P\bar{Q}$ and $\bar{P}Q$ are polynomials of degree $\leq 2i$ it follows $P\bar{Q} = \bar{P}Q$. According to our assumptions P and Q have no common divisiors, so we have $Q|\bar{Q}$ and analogically $\bar{Q}|Q$. $\bar{Q}$ and Q are monic, so $\bar{Q} = Q$. It follows $\bar{P} = P$ immediately. This shows the uniqueness of P and Q.

Now let $P(x) = p_i x^i + \cdots + p_1 x + p_0$, $Q(x) = q_i x^i + \cdots + q_1 x + q_0$. As the $f(x_j)$ are defined, we get

$$f(x_j)q_i x_j^i + \cdots + f(x_j)q_1 x_j + f(x_j)q_0 - p_i x_j^i - \cdots - p_1 x_j - p_0 = 0$$

for $j = 1, \ldots, 2i+1$. This yields a (inhomogenous) linear system in the unknowns $q_i, \ldots q_0, p_i, \ldots, p_0$, which can be solved with $O(i^3)$ operations in F. The solution space may have dimension $d > 1$. In this case the unique solution polynomials P, Q in the above sense have both degree less than i. To find them one has to compute the element of the solution space with $q_i = q_{i-1} = \cdots = q_{i-(d-2)} = 0$, $q_{i-(d-1)} = 1$. Obviously this can be done in polynomial time, too.   □

Now consider (2) again. We're fixing an arbitrary b, for example $b = k - l =: r$, and put

$$\tilde{P}_i(x) := (x - \alpha_r)P_i(x), \tilde{Q}_i(x) := (x - \alpha_i)P_r(x) \tag{3}$$

and $g_i(x) := \frac{\tilde{P}_i(x)}{\tilde{Q}_i(x)}$ for $i = 1, \ldots, r - 1$. The first step is to reconstruct the coefficients of $\tilde{P}_i$ and $\tilde{Q}_i$. These polynomials have degree $\leq l + 1$ so according to the lemma above we need to know $2l + 3$ pairs $(\alpha_j, g_i(\alpha_j))$ to do so. The $g_i(\alpha_j) = \frac{t_{i,j}}{t_{r,j}}$ are given, but the α_j are unknown. The strategy is now to guess the values $\alpha_{r+1}, \ldots, \alpha_{r+2l+3}$ (for example) and sieve out the wrong guesses. W.l.o.g. we assume that $t_{r,r+1}, \ldots, t_{r,r+2l+3}$ all are nonzero (otherwise we can choose a different set of $2l + 3$ indices $i_1, \ldots, i_{2l+3} \in \{r + 1, \ldots, n\}$ with $t_{i_1}, \ldots, t_{i_{2l+3}} \neq 0$ and guess the values $\alpha_{i_1}, \ldots, \alpha_{i_{2l+3}}$) and that $\alpha_{r+1} = 0, \alpha_{r+2} = 1$ (by Proposition 1), s.t. in fact only $\alpha_{r+3}, \ldots, \alpha_{r+2l+3}$ have to be guessed. Given the pairs $(\alpha_j, \frac{t_{i,j}}{t_{r,j}})$ we calculate relatively prime P_i^*, Q_i^* of degree $\leq l + 1$ with $\frac{P_i^*}{Q_i^*} = g_i$ for $i = 1, \ldots, r - 1$ by solving the appropriate linear systems, see Lemma 1. Note that $\tilde{P}_i$ and $\tilde{Q}_i$ may have a nontrivial common factor, so in general $\tilde{P}_i \neq P_i^*$ and $\tilde{Q}_i \neq Q_i^*$. However, if the guess was correct then the following conditions hold:

C1. The $P_i^*(x)$ have a common linear factor (namely $(x - \alpha_r)$).
C2. There is a sequence $\alpha_1, \ldots, \alpha_{r-1}$ of pairwise distinct elements of F different from the $\alpha_{r+1}, \ldots, \alpha_{r+2l+3}$, such that $(x - \alpha_i)$ divides $Q_i^*(x)$, and the least common multiple of the $\frac{Q_i^*(x)}{(x-\alpha_i)}$ has degree $\leq l$ (the least common multiple divides $P_r(x)$).

If there are two distinct polynomials P_i^*, P_j^* with degree $l + 1$ then $Q_i^* = \tilde{Q}_i$ and $Q_j^* = \tilde{Q}_j$ (assuming that these polynomials are monic), and condition C2 can be replaced by

C3. Let $Q := gcd(Q_i^*, Q_j^*)$. Then $\frac{Q_w^*(x)}{gcd(Q_w^*(x),Q(x))} = (x - \alpha_w), w = 1, \ldots, r - 1$ for pairwise distinct $\alpha_1, \ldots, \alpha_{r-1}$ different from $\alpha_{r+1}, \ldots, \alpha_{r+2l+3}$ (it is $Q = P_r$).

The advantage of C3 is that it is straightforward to check from an algorithmic point of view, while C2 is more complicated (but also can be checked in polynomial time). So we always assume first that there is such a pair P_i^*, P_j^*, which is the case with high probability. Condition C1 can be verified easily, too, by the Euclidian algorithm. If the guess was right we can reconstruct the parameter $\alpha = (\alpha_1, \ldots, \alpha_n)$ of the GRS code from the P_i^*, Q_i^*: α_r can be reconstructed from condition C1 and the values $\alpha_1, \ldots, \alpha_{r-1}$ can be derived from condition C3. $\alpha_{r+1}, \ldots, \alpha_{r+2l+3}$ are given so it remains to find the $\alpha_{r+2l+4}, \ldots, \alpha_n$.

Suppose $\alpha_{i_1}, \ldots, \alpha_{i_{r-1}}$ belong to the unknown values. Choose a permutation $\pi : \{1, \ldots, n\} \to \{1, \ldots, n\}$ with $\pi(j) = i_j$ and $\pi(i_j) = j$ for $j = 1, \ldots, r - 1$ and

$\pi(b) = b$ for $b = r + 1, \ldots, r + 2l + 3$. Let $\beta := (\beta_1, \ldots, \beta_n) := (\alpha_{\pi(1)}, \ldots, \alpha_{\pi(n)})$. The matrix T_π is a generator matrix of a subcode of $GRS_{n,k}(\beta, x_\pi)$. Since the $\beta_i = \alpha_i$, $i = r + 1, \ldots r + 2l + 3$ are given, the $\beta_1, \ldots \beta_{r-1}$ – and thereby the $\alpha_{i_1}, \ldots, \alpha_{i_{r-1}}$– can be determined exactly the same way as described above when working with $E(T_\pi)$ instead of $E(T)$. This process can be repeated for different suitable permutations until all α_i are found.

We summarize the complete procedure in Algorithm 1. It makes use of the function $getAlpha$ which is defined in Algorithm 2.

Algorithm 1. Reconstruction of α

Input: Generator matrix T of a subcode of $GRS_{n,k}(\alpha, x)$ of dimension $r = k - l$
Output: Set B of candidates for α

1:   $B \leftarrow \emptyset$
2:   $\beta_1 \leftarrow 0$
3:   $\beta_2 \leftarrow 1$
4:   **for all** $(\beta_3, \ldots, \beta_{2l+3}) \in (F \backslash \{0, 1\})^{2l+1}$ with β_i pairwise distinct **do**
5:      $I \leftarrow \{1, \ldots, r - 1, r, r + 2l + 4, \ldots, n\}$
6:      **repeat**
7:          $b \leftarrow \min(r - 1, \#I)$
8:          **for** $j \leftarrow 1, \ldots, b$ **do**
9:              $i_j \leftarrow$ least element of I
10:         $I \leftarrow I \backslash \{i_j\}$
11:         **end for**
12:         **for** $j \leftarrow 1, \ldots, b$ **do**
13:             $\pi(j) \leftarrow i_j$
14:             $\pi(i_j) \leftarrow j$
15:         **end for**
16:         **for** $j \leftarrow b + 1, \ldots, n$ **do**
17:             **if** $j \neq i_1, \ldots, i_b$ **then**
18:                $\pi(j) \leftarrow j$
19:             **end if**
20:         **end for**
21:         calculate T_π
22:         $\gamma := (\gamma_1, \ldots, \gamma_{r-1}) \leftarrow getAlpha(\beta_1, \ldots, \beta_{2l+3}, T_\pi)$
23:         **if** $\gamma \neq NULL$ **then**
24:             **for** $j \leftarrow 1, \ldots, b$ **do**
25:                $\alpha_{i_j} \leftarrow \gamma_j$
26:             **end for**
27:         **end if**
28:      **until** $I = \emptyset$ or $\gamma = NULL$
29:      **if** $\gamma \neq NULL$ and $\alpha_1, \ldots, \alpha_n$ pairwise distinct **then**
30:         $B \leftarrow B \cup \{(\alpha_1, \ldots, \alpha_n)\}$
31:      **end if**
32: **end for**
33: **return** B

Algorithm 2. $getAlpha(\beta_1, \ldots, \beta_{2l+3}, T)$

Input: $(r \times n)$-matrix T over F, $\beta_1, \ldots, \beta_{2l+3} \in F$ pairwise distinct
Output: $(\alpha_1, \ldots, \alpha_{r-1}) \in F^{r-1}$

1: $(t_{i,j}) \leftarrow$ echelon form of T
2: **for** $i \leftarrow 1, \ldots, r-1$ **do**
3:    calculate relatively prime $P_i^*(x), Q_i^*(x) \in F[x]$ with degree $\leq l+1$ and Q_i^* monic and
$$\frac{P_i^*(\beta_j)}{Q_i^*(\beta_j)} = \frac{t_{i,r+j}}{t_{r,r+j}}$$
   for all $j = 1, \ldots, 2l+3$
4: **end for**
5: **if** the $P_i^*(x), Q_i^*(x)$ satisfy conditions C1 and C3 **then**
6:    $Q \leftarrow gcd(Q_i^*, Q_j^*)$ with i, j such that $i \neq j$ and $\deg P_i^* = \deg P_j^* = l+1$
7:    **for** $i \leftarrow 1, \ldots, r-1$ **do**
8:       $\alpha_i \leftarrow root(\frac{Q_i^*}{gcd(Q_i^*, Q)})$
9:    **end for**
10:    **return** $(\alpha_1, \ldots, \alpha_{r-1})$
11: **else**
12:    **return** $NULL$
13: **end if**

Once the set of candidates B is given is remains to check for each $\alpha' \in B$ if there is a $x = (x_1, \ldots x_n)$, s.t. $<T> \subset GRS_{n,k}(\alpha', x)$. (We know that there is at least one such α'.) This can be done using Algorithm 3.

According to Proposition 2 the dual code of $GRS_{n,k}(\alpha, x)$ is also a GRS code $G = GRS_{n,n-k}(\alpha, x')$. Let g be a row of the canonical generator matrix of G. Since each row vector t of T is an element of $GRS_{n,k}(\alpha, x)$ the inner product $t \cdot g$ is equal to zero. That's why $x' = (x_1', \ldots, x_n')$ has to be a solution of the linear system

$$t_{i,1}\alpha_1^j x_1' + \ldots + t_{i,n}\alpha_n^j x_n' = 0, \quad i = 1, \ldots, r, \quad j = 0, \ldots, n-k-1 .$$

If such a x' is found, the vector x can be calculated with help of Proposition 2.

Let's analyze the running time of the above algorithms in the worst case. First consider the function $getAlpha$. It is dominated by the computation of the echelon form in line 1, which takes $O(r^2 n)$ operations in F, and the for-loop in lines 3–4. In each step of the loop a linear system with $O(l)$ equations and unknowns has to be solved, which can be done with $O(l^3)$ operations. Verification of C1 and C3 and computation of the α_i takes $O(rl^2)$ operations at most. This yields a total running time of $O(r^2 n + rl^3)$ for Algorithm 2.

The main loop in lines 4–32 of Algorithm 1 is run $\frac{(n-2)!}{(n-2l-3)!} \in O(n^{2l+1})$ times. (We assumed $n = \#F$). The inner loop in lines 6–28 is called $\left\lceil \frac{n-2l-3}{r-1} \right\rceil$ times. Since in practice $\frac{n}{3} \leq r \leq \frac{2n}{3}$ we can assume that this value is bounded by a constant. With the above result we get a total running time of $O(n^{2l+1}(r^2 n + rl^3))$ operations in F. Note that the procedure can be optimized by computing the

---

Algorithm 3. Reconstruction of x

Input: $T = (v_{i,j})$, B as in Algorithm 1
Output: (α, x') s.t. $<T> \subset GRS_{n,k}(\alpha, x')$

1: **while** $B \neq \emptyset$ **do**
2:     $(\alpha_1, \ldots, \alpha_n) \leftarrow$ arbitrary element of B
3:     $X \leftarrow$ solution space of the linear system in $x_1, \ldots, x_n$ given by

$$v_{m,1}\alpha_1 x_1^j + v_{m,2}\alpha_2 x_2^j + \cdots + v_{m,n}\alpha_n x_n^j = 0$$

for $j = 0, \ldots, k-1$ and $m = 1, \ldots, r$
4:     **if** $dim(X) > 0$ **then**
5:         $(x_1, \ldots, x_n) \leftarrow$ arbitrary nonzero element of X
6:         **for** $i \leftarrow 1, \ldots, n$ **do**
7:             $x_i' \leftarrow (x_i \prod_{j \neq i}(\alpha_i - \alpha_j))^{-1}$
8:         **end for**
9:         $B \leftarrow \emptyset$
10:    **else**
11:        $B \leftarrow B \setminus \{(\alpha_1, \ldots, \alpha_n)\}$
12:    **end if**
13: **end while**
14: **return** $((\alpha_1, \ldots, \alpha_n), (x_1', \ldots, x_n'))$

---

echelon forms $E(T_\pi)$ for a fixed set of suitable permutations π in advance instead of computing them in each call of $getAlpha$. In this case we get an upper bound $O(r^2n + n^{2l+1}rl^3)$.

In Algorithm 3 the main loop is run $\#B$ times, and the dominant step in each loop is the linear system. It has n unknowns and $(k-1)r$ equations so it takes at most $O(n^2kr)$ operations to find a nontrivial solution. We get a worst case complexity of $O(\#B \cdot n^2kr)$ operations. In general $\#B$ is expected to be quite small so that Algorithm 3 is feasible.

In [1] an attack on the cryptosystem is given, which uses the original Sidelnikov-Shestakov attack as a black box algorithm. Its average running time is lower bounded by $\Omega(n^{kl})$ operations, so for practical choices of n, k, l the attack given here is much faster.

4 Refinement of the Attack

The above algorithm can be improved if there are two rows in the echelon form $E(T) = (t_{i,j})$ which have more than $k - l - 2$ zeros in common. Suppose the i-th and the b-th row, $i \neq b$, have $k - l - 2 + s$ zeros in common positions. It is $0 \leq s \leq l$. With the same argument as in proof of Proposition 3 there are two polynomials $P^*(x), Q^*(x) \in F[x]$ of degree $\leq l - s + 1$ (instead of $l + 1$) s.t.

$$\frac{t_{i,j}}{t_{b,j}} = \frac{P^*(\alpha_j)}{Q^*(\alpha_j)}$$

for all $j = 1, \ldots, n$ with $t_{b,j} \neq 0$. So to find these polynomials only $2(l-s+2)-1 = 2(l-s)+3$ of the α_j have to be known according to Lemma 1, and the number of guesses which have to be made is reduced by a factor $O(n^{2s})$. To check whether the guess is correct we make use of the following

Definition 2. *Let S be a (finite) set, $n, k \in \mathbb{N}, n \geq k$ and $v = (v_1, \ldots, v_n) \in S^n, w = (w_1, \ldots, w_k) \in S^k$. We say that v dominates w, if*

$$\#\{i | v_i = s\} \geq \#\{j | w_j = s\}$$

for all $s \in S$.

Obviously for given $v \in S^n, w \in S^k$ it can be checked with $O(n)$ operations if v dominates w.

Let $J \subset \{1, \ldots, n\}$ be the set of those j, where $t_{i,j} \neq 0$ or $t_{b,j} \neq 0$. For $\gamma \in F$ with $\gamma \neq 0$ we define $\frac{\gamma}{0} =: \infty$. Suppose the elements of F are ordered in some way. If the guess of the α_j is correct then the vector $\left(\frac{P^*(\gamma)}{Q^*(\gamma)}\right)_{\gamma \in F}$ has to dominate the vector $\left(\frac{t_{i,j}}{t_{b,j}}\right)_{j \in J}$. In this case it may be possible to reconstruct some of the (not yet assigned) α_j : suppose the function $f(x) := \frac{P^*(x)}{Q^*(x)}$ takes the value $\delta \in F \cup \{\infty\}$ for exactly one $\gamma \in F$, $f(\gamma) = \delta$, and there is a $j \in J$ with $\frac{t_{i,j}}{t_{b,j}} = \delta$. Then $\alpha_j = \gamma$. If we can find at least $2s$ additional α_j with $t_{b,j} \neq 0$ this way we can try to compute relatively prime polynomials $P^*_{i'}(x), Q^*_{i'}(x) \in F[x]$ of degree $\leq l+1$ for $i' \in \{1, \ldots k-l\} \backslash \{i, b\}$ with

$$\frac{t_{i',j}}{t_{b,j}} = \frac{P^*_{i'}(\alpha_j)}{Q^*_{i'}(\alpha_j)} \tag{4}$$

for all $j = 1, \ldots, n$ with $t_{b,j} \neq 0$. Of course the right polynomials have to comply with conditions C1 and C2 / C3. This allows us to reconstruct the remaining α_j as seen above.

If there are not enough δ s.t. $f(\gamma) = \delta$ can be solved uniquely, then at least we can extract a list of candidates for each α_j, $j \in J$, which consists of all γ with $f(\gamma) = \frac{t_{i,j}}{t_{b,j}}$. We can then choose a sufficient number of short candidate lists and try to solve (4) with the different possible assignments for the α_j.

What can we do now, if a pair of rows in $E(T)$ with more than $k-l-2$ common zeros does not exist? In this case we can try to find such a pair in the echelon form of an equivalent code of $<T> \subset GRS_{n,k}(\alpha, x)$. Let $\pi : \{1, \ldots, n\} \to \{1, \ldots, n\}$ be a permutation. Remember that due to the definition of GRS codes the matrix T_π is a generator matrix of a subcode of $GRS_{n,k}(\alpha_\pi, x_\pi)$. So we can replace T by T_π for distinct permutations π and look for rows in the echelon form $E(T_\pi)$ which have more than $k-l-2$ common zeros. When such a pair is found we apply the above method which eventually finds a set of candidates for α_π, which can easily be transformed to a set of candidates for α. When choosing the permutations we can restrict ourselves to those π which satisfy $\pi(i) > k-l$ for at least one $i \in \{1, \ldots, k-l\}$, since otherwise $E(T_\pi)$ differs from $E(T)$ only by the order of rows.

Note however that such a pair of rows does not necessarily exist in any equivalent code. For example the subcode C can itself be a GRS code of dimension $k - l$. As such it is a MDS code and any pair of rows in the echelon form can have $k - l - 2$ common zeros at most. But for random instances there should be a good chance of finding a pair at least for small s.

The improved approach is summarized in Algorithms 4 and 5.

We try to give a rough estimate for the running time of Algorithm 5. The main loop in lines 12–30 is run $O(n^{2(l-s)+1})$ times. Solving the linear system in line 13 takes $O((l-s)^3)$ operations. If the condition in line 15 is passed (verification takes $O(n(l-s))$ operations) the for-loop in lines 21–28 is called $O(\max_j\{B_j\}^{2s})$ times at most. Each loop takes $O(r^2 n + rl^3)$ operations. Since $\max_j\{B_j\} \le l - s + 1$ we get an upper bound $O(t_1 + n^{2(l-s)+1}((l-s)^3 + n(l-s) + (l-s+1)^{2s}(r^2 n + rl^3)))$ for the complete algorithm, where t_1 is the (undetermined) running time of Algorithm 4. Here we assumed that the condition in line 15 is always passed, which won't be the case in practice. The average running time should be well below the given bound.

Note that there are still several possibilities to improve the presented algorithms but for the sake of clarity we didn't include them here.

5   Experimental Results

Algorithms 4 and 5 were implemented in JAVA (with some minor modifications) and executed for different instances of the encryption scheme. We always chose s such that $l - s = 1$. Table 1 shows some example running times on a 2.6 GHz Pentium 4, 512 MB system. In particular we see that $findPemutation$ performs well for small s.

Algorithm 4. $findPermutation(T, s)$

Input: $(r \times n)$-matrix T as in Algorithm 1; $s \in \mathbb{N}^{\le l}$
Output: (π, i, b) s.t. i-th and b-th row of $E(T_\pi)$ have $r + s - 2$ common zeros

```
1:  S ← set of all permutations π ∈ S_n with π(i) > r for some i ∈ ℕ^≤r
2:  repeat
3:      π ← random element of S
4:      S ← S\{π}
5:      calculate E(T_π)
6:      for all (i, b) ∈ {1, ..., r}² with i < b do
7:          if rows i and b of E(T_π) have r + s - 2 common zeros then
8:              return (π, i, b)
9:          end if
10:     end for
11: until S = ∅
12: return NULL
```

Algorithm 5. Reconstruction of α, improved version

Input: Generator matrix T of a subcode of $GRS_{n,k}(\alpha, x)$ of dimension $r = k - l$, $s \in \mathbb{N}^{\leq l}$

Output: Set B of candidates for α

1: $(\pi, i, b) \leftarrow findPermutation(T, s)$
2: **if** $(\pi, i, b) = NULL$ **then**
3:     **return** $NULL$
4: **end if**
5: compute $(t_{i,j}) := E(T_\pi)$
6: $(a_1, \ldots, a_n) \leftarrow i-$th row of $E(T_\pi)$
7: $(b_1, \ldots, b_n) \leftarrow b-$th row of $E(T_\pi)$
8: $B \leftarrow \emptyset$
9: $\beta_1 \leftarrow 0$
10: $\beta_2 \leftarrow 1$
11: find pairwise distinct $i_1, \ldots, i_{2(l-s)+3}$ s.t. $b_{i_j} \neq 0$ for all j
12: **for all** $(\beta_3, \ldots, \beta_{2(l-s)+3}) \in (F\backslash\{0, 1\})^2$ with β_i pairwise distinct **do**
13:     compute relatively prime $P^*(x), Q^*(x) \in F[x]$ with deg $P^*(x), Q^*(x) \leq l-s+1$
    s.t.

$$\frac{P^*(\beta_j)}{Q^*(\beta_j)} = \frac{a_{i_j}}{b_{i_j}}$$

    for all $j = 1, \ldots, 2(l-s)+3$
14:     $c \leftarrow (\frac{a_i}{b_i})_{i \in \{1,\ldots,n\}, a_i \neq 0 \text{ or } b_i \neq 0}$
15:     **if** $(\frac{P^*(\gamma)}{Q^*(\gamma)})_{\gamma \in F}$ dominates c **then**
16:         $I \leftarrow \{r+1, \ldots, n\}\backslash\{i_1, \ldots, i_{2(l-s)+1}\}$
17:         find pairwise distinct $i_{2(l-s)+4}, \ldots, i_{2l+3} \in I$ with $b_{i_j} \neq 0$
18:         **for** $j \leftarrow 2(l-s)+4, \ldots, 2l+3$ **do**
19:             $B_j \leftarrow$ set of all $\gamma \in F\backslash\{\beta_1, \ldots, \beta_{2(l-s)+3}\}$ with $\frac{P^*(\gamma)}{Q^*(\gamma)} = \frac{a_{i_j}}{b_{i_j}}$
20:         **end for**
21:         **for all** $(\beta_{2(l-s)+4}, \ldots, \beta_{2l+3})$ with pairw. distinct $\beta_j \in B_j$ **do**
22:             **for all** $a \in \{1, \ldots, r-1\}\backslash\{b\}$ **do**
23:                 compute relatively prime $P_i^*(x), Q_i^*(x) \in F[x]$ with degree $\leq l+1$
    s.t.

$$\frac{P_i^*(x)}{Q_i^*(x)} = \frac{t_{a,i_j}}{b_{i_j}}$$

    for all $j = 1, \ldots, 2l+3$
24:             **end for**
25:             **if** the P_i^*, Q_i^* suffice conditions C1 and C2/C3 and α_π can be computed
    as in Algorithms 1,2 **then**
26:                 $B \leftarrow B \cup \{\alpha\}$
27:             **end if**
28:         **end for**
29:     **end if**
30: **end for**
31: **return** B

Table 1. Perfomance for different key parameters

				running time	
n	k	l	s	*findPermutation*	total
32	16	3	2	3 sec	<1 min
64	32	3	2	2 sec	16 min
64	40	3	2	2 sec	16 min
64	32	4	3	2 min	18 min
128	64	4	3	20 min	5 h 44 min

6 Conclusion

In [1] the values $n = 256$, $k = 133$, $l = 4$ are given as secure example parameters for the modified Niederreiter encryption scheme. It is claimed that $\approx 2^{2000}$ executions of the Sidelnikov-Shestakov algorithm for a structural break are needed in a brute force approach. However the above results suggest that these choices for the modified Niederreiter encryption scheme are highly insecure. Extrapolating the data above we estimate that an optimized implementation of the above attack can break such a system in a few days or even hours on a PC.

The encryption scheme is not completely broken though. To thwart the attack n and l should be chosen sufficiently large. However this has other drawbacks. A large n leads to large public keys and a large l causes bigger message expansion. It is unclear if the parameters can be chosen in such a way that it has higher efficiency and security than the McEliece cryptosystem.

References

1. Berger, T., Loidreau, P.: How to mask the structure of codes for a cryptographic use. Designs, Codes and Cryptography **35**(1) (2005) 63–79
2. McEliece, R.: A public-key cryptosystem based on algebraic coding theory. DSN Progress Report, Jet Prop. Lab., California Inst. Tech. **42-44** (1978) 114–116
3. Niederreiter, N.: Knapsack-type cryptosystems and algebraic coding theory. Problems of Control and Information Theory **15** (1986) 159–166
4. Berlekamp, E., McEliece, R., van Tilborg, H.: On the inherent intractability of certain coding problems. IEEE Transactions on Information Theory **24**(3) (1978) 384–386
5. Brickell, E., Lee, J.: An observation on the security of McEliece's public-key cryptosystem. In: EUROCRYPT '88. Number 330 in Lecture Notes in Computer Science, Springer-Verlag (1988) 275–280
6. Canteaut, A., Chabaud, F.: A new algorithm for finding minimum-weight words in a linear code: application to McEliece's cryptosystem and to narrow-sense BCH codes of length 511. IEEE Transactions on Information Theory **44**(1) (1988) 367–378
7. Sidelnikov, V., Shestakov, S.: On insecurity of cryptosystems based on generalized Reed-Solomon codes. Discrete Math. Appl. **2**(4) (1992) 439–444
8. Gabidulin, E.: Public-key cryptosystems based on linear codes (1995) http://citeseer.ist.psu.edu/gabidulin95publickey.html.

26   C. Wieschebrink

9. MacWilliams, F., Sloane, N.: The Theory of Error-Correcting Codes. North Holland (1997)
10. Deng, R., Li, Y., Wang, X.: On the equivalence of McEliece's and Niederreiter's public-key cryptosystems. IEEE Transactions on Information Theory **40**(1) (1994) 271–273
11. Garey, M., Johnson, D.: Computers and Intractability. A Guide to the Theory of NP-Completeness. W.H. Freeman and Company (1979)
12. Overbeck, R.: A new structural attack for GPT and variants. In: Mycrypt 2005. Number 3715 in Lecture Notes in Computer Science, Springer-Verlag (2005)

Cryptanalysis of an Efficient Proof of Knowledge of Discrete Logarithm

Sébastien Kunz-Jacques[1,2], Gwenaëlle Martinet[1],
Guillaume Poupard[1], and Jacques Stern[2]

[1] DCSSI Crypto Lab, 51 boulevard de La Tour-Maubourg,
F-75700 Paris 07 SP, France
{Sebastien.Kunz-Jacques, Gwenaelle.Martinet,
Guillaume.Poupard}@sgdn.pm.gouv.fr
[2] École normale supérieure, Département d'informatique,
45 rue d'Ulm, F-75230 Paris Cedex 05, France
Jacques.Stern@ens.fr

Abstract. At PKC 2005, Bangerter, Camenisch and Maurer proposed an efficient protocol to prove knowledge of discrete logarithms in groups of unknown order. We describe an attack that enables the verifier to recover the full secret with essentially no computing power beyond what is required to run the protocol and after only a few iterations of it. We also describe variants of the attack that apply when some additional simple checks are performed by the prover.

Keywords: Public key cryptanalysis, discrete logarithm, proof of knowledge.

1 Introduction

Since the seminal paper of Diffie and Hellman [10], the discrete logarithm problem has been considered a fundamental stone of public key cryptography. In order to define this problem in a general setting, we consider a multiplicative group $\mathcal{G}$ and an element $g \in \mathcal{G}$. We note ω the multiplicative order of g in $\mathcal{G}$ i.e. the smallest non-zero positive integer ω such that $g^\omega = 1$. The set $\langle g \rangle = \{g^i\}_{i \in \mathbb{Z}}$ of powers of g is a subgroup of $\mathcal{G}$ with ω elements. For any member $y \in \langle g \rangle$, there exists a unique integer $x \in \{0, ...\omega - 1\}$ such that $y = g^x$; by definition x is the discrete logarithm of y in base g. The computation of such discrete logarithms is considered to be intractable in many groups of cryptographic interest such as modular groups or elliptic curves.

An interesting question is how to prove knowledge of a discrete logarithm of a public data without revealing any other information about this value. Such a problem is closely related to the concept of zero-knowledge introduced in 1985 by Goldwasser, Micali and Rackoff [13]. A well-known and very nice solution was proposed by Schnorr [17] in 1989. In this two party-protocol, a prover who knows the discrete logarithm x of a public value y interacts with a verifier; if the prover is able to correctly answer the verifier's challenges, he proves knowledge of x. Two

M. Yung et al. (Eds.): PKC 2006, LNCS 3958, pp. 27–43, 2006.

complementary security aspects can be analyzed; firstly, the soundness property shows that if a prover is able to correctly answer the challenges then he must know the secret x. This proof is based on the notion of knowledge extractor that can extract the secret from the prover using rewinding techniques. Secondly, the zero-knowledge property shows that the execution of the protocol does not leak any information about the secret x, even if the verifier tries to bias its challenges. The proof is based on the notion of simulation of the communications.

In the Schnorr scheme, the soundness property can be easily proved since the secret is immediately derived from two correct and distinct answers corresponding to the same "commitment" sent by the prover as its first message. Deciding if the protocol is zero-knowledge is still an open problem when large challenges are used and if they are not randomly chosen by the verifier. It is significant to note that the proof of soundness strongly relies on the knowledge of the order ω of the basis g. Surprisingly, if this order is not known, for example is the context or RSA groups, the basic extraction strategy no longer applies. It is still possible to prove the security of the scheme used as an identification scheme [12, 16] but, in groups of unknown order, Schnorr based proofs cannot be considered as proofs of knowledge. This interesting open problem has attracted the interest of several research papers [11, 9] and, at PKC 2005, Bangerter, Camenisch and Maurer [1] proposed an efficient protocol, the so-called Σ^+-Protocol to prove knowledge of discrete logarithms in groups of unknown order. This scheme is derived from the Σ-Protocol whose paternity is unclear. The name was first proposed in 1997 by Cramer [7] in his PhD thesis and used by Cramer and Damgård [8] but original ideas can be found in the Schnorr scheme [17] and even previously in [5, 4, 2]. However, Girault [12] was the first to observe, in 1991, that the knowledge of the underlying group order was not necessary to carry Schnorr's like proofs.

In this paper, we show that the proposal in [1] is not secure since a dishonest verifier can obtain the secret of the prover. The main flaw in [1] is that the authors assume that some parameters needed for a protocol run are honestly chosen by the verifier; in the Σ^+ protocol, the prover never checks, and is not able to check, that these parameters actually have the correct form. Our attack takes advantage of this mistake. Thus, even if the protocol if proved in [1] to be a zero-knowledge proof of knowledge, the assumptions made in the proof cannot be verified with the described protocol. To fulfil the proof's assumptions, some additional and non obvious checks are needed which may drastically reduce the protocol efficiency. Some other solutions may be considered but they require to revise the protocol's proof.

Notations and Organization of the Paper. Throughout this paper, we use the following notation: for any integer n,

- $\mathbb{Z}_n$ is the set of integers modulo n,
- $\mathbb{Z}_n^*$ is the multiplicative group of invertible elements of $\mathbb{Z}_n$,
- $\varphi(n)$ is the Euler totient function, i.e. the cardinality of $\mathbb{Z}_n^*$,
- $\mathrm{ord}(g)$ is the order of an element $g \in \mathbb{Z}_n^*$,
- $\lambda(n)$ is the Carmichael's lambda function defined as the largest order of the elements of $\mathbb{Z}_n^*$.

It is well known that if the prime factorization of an odd integer n is $\prod_{i=1}^{\eta} q_i^{f_i}$ then $\varphi(n) = \prod_{i=1}^{\eta} q_i^{f_i-1}(q_i - 1)$ and $\lambda(n) = \mathrm{lcm}_{i=1...\eta}\left(q_i^{f_i-1}(q_i - 1)\right)$.

The paper is organized as follows: section 2 recalls the Σ^+-protocol [1]. Then, in section 3, we make some security related observations which lead to a practical cheating strategy. We also observe in this section and in section 4 that several simple and natural countermeasures do not succeed into defeating our strategy. Finally, annex A gives a detailed analysis of the attack complexity and annex B describes a detailed algorithm of independent interest, strongly inspired of the Pohlig-Hellman algorithm [14], to compute discrete logarithms in our setting.

2   The Σ^+-Protocol

Let us now briefly recall the Σ^+-protocol using the notations of [1]. Let H be an arbitrary group whose order needs not to be known. For example, H can be the set $\mathbb{Z}_n^*$ for a composite RSA modulus n. Let h be an element of H such that the computation of discrete logarithms in base h is intractable.

The Σ^+-protocol is a proof of knowledge of discrete logarithms of elements in H, in base h. Roughly speaking, this means that, for a given $y \in H$, a prover can convince a verifier that he knows an integer x such that $y = h^x$. As we will see in the rest of this paper, this protocol is not a zero-knowledge proof of knowledge of discrete logarithm since the prover reveals some information about his secret x when interacting with a dishonest verifier.

The proof requires a generator $\mathcal{D}_{\mathcal{S}}(k)$ that outputs a pair (n, g) s.t. n is an RSA modulus, $g \in \mathbb{Z}_n^*$ and it is hard to compute $u \in \mathbb{Z}_n^*$ and an integer $e > 1$ fulfilling $u^e = g \bmod n$. It is stated in [1] that "[the authors] *assume that* $n = (2p + 1)(2q + 1)$ *with* p, q, $(2p + 1)$ *and* $(2q + 1)$ *being primes, and that* $g \in QR_n$, *where* QR_n *is the subgroup of quadratic residues of* $\mathbb{Z}_n^*$". However even if this assumption appears to be used in the security analysis, at least in a side remark to prove the statistical zero-knowledge property of the protocol, it is not guaranteed by the protocol itself.

We still need a few additional notations coming from [1]:

- k is a security parameter,
- $a \in_U A$ means that the element a is randomly chosen in the set A using a uniform distribution,
- the equality symbol $\doteq$ is used to denote definitions,
- the secret exponent x is in the range $[-\Delta x, \Delta x]$ and the related public element of H is $y = h^x$,
- l_z is an integer parameter related to the security parameter k,
- c^+ is another parameter that determines the set $\{0, \ldots, c^+\}$ in which the verifier picks its challenges c,
- $\mathrm{commit}(\gamma, r)$ is a computationally binding and statistically hiding commitment scheme that commits γ using the random value r; to open the commitment one reveals γ and r.

The typographic convention of [1] is to use sans serif font for elements related to computations in $\mathbb{Z}_n^*$ and standard italic font when dealing with elements of H.

Prover	Verifier
Private input : x in $[-\Delta x, \Delta x]$	
Common input : h and $y = h^x$ both in H	
	$(n, g) \leftarrow \mathcal{D}_\mathcal{S}(k)$
	$\rho \in_U [0, 2^k \lfloor n/4 \rfloor]$
	$g_1 \doteq g^\rho \bmod n$
$\xleftarrow{\quad (g_1, g, n) \quad}$	
$\mathsf{x} \in_U [0, \lfloor n/4 \rfloor]$	
$\mathsf{y} \doteq g_1^x g^{\mathsf{x}} \bmod n$	
$r \in_U [-2^{l_z} c^+ \Delta x, 2^{l_z} c^+ \Delta x]$	
$t \doteq h^r$	
$\mathsf{r} \in_U [-2^{l_z} c^+ \lfloor n/4 \rfloor, 2^{l_z} c^+ \lfloor n/4 \rfloor]$	
$\mathsf{t} \doteq g_1^r g^{\mathsf{r}}$	
Choose r_y; $\overline{\mathsf{y}} \doteq \mathrm{commit}(\mathsf{y}, r_\mathsf{y})$	
Choose r_t; $\overline{\mathsf{t}} \doteq \mathrm{commit}(\mathsf{t}, r_\mathsf{t})$	
$\xrightarrow{\quad (\overline{\mathsf{y}}, \overline{\mathsf{t}}, t) \quad}$	
	$c \in_U \{0, \ldots, c^+\}$
$\xleftarrow{\quad c \quad}$	
$s \doteq r + cx$	
$\mathsf{s} \doteq \mathsf{r} + c\mathsf{x}$	
$\xrightarrow{\quad (s, \mathsf{s}) \quad}$	
$\xleftarrow{\quad \rho \quad}$	
If $g_1 \neq g^\rho \bmod n$, then halt.	
$\xrightarrow{\quad ((\mathsf{t}, r_\mathsf{t}), (\mathsf{y}, r_\mathsf{y})) \quad}$	
	If the equalities
	$\overline{\mathsf{y}} = \mathrm{commit}(\mathsf{y}, r_\mathsf{y})$
	$\overline{\mathsf{t}} = \mathrm{commit}(\mathsf{t}, r_\mathsf{t})$
	$h^s = ty^c$
	$g_1^s g^\mathsf{s} = \mathsf{t}\mathsf{y}^c \bmod n$
	hold, then output 1
	else output 0

Fig. 1. The Σ^+-Protocol from [1]

The Σ^+-protocol described in figure 1 performs a kind of parallel proof of knowledge of discrete logarithms in two mathematical structures, H and $\mathbb{Z}_n{}^*$, in a way similar to proofs of equality of discrete logarithms. However, the main original part is that the second structure is not a parameter of the system but is chosen by the verifier and changes from one proof to another.

3   Some Security Related Observations

3.1   A Preliminary Observation

A first simple security related observation is that some basic checks should be added to the scheme, exactly as for the original Σ-Protocol. This may be considered implicit but it is probably better to make checks explicit in order to avoid dramatic consequences in practical implementations.

More precisely, a remark made by D. Bleichenbacher about the GPS identification scheme during the NESSIE selection process [6] is relevant to the present context; consider a cheating verifier that does not choose the challenge c uniformly in the range $[0, c^+]$ but sends a value much larger than c^+. If the prover does not check that $c \in [0, c^+]$, he reveals $s = r + cx$ with $r \in [-2^{l_z} c^+ \Delta x, 2^{l_z} c^+ \Delta x]$. Then, $s/c = x + r/c$ and, if $c > 2^{l_z+1} c^+ \Delta x$, the verifier obtains $s/c - 1/2 < x < s/c + 1/2$ and consequently the secret $x = \lfloor s/c + 1/2 \rfloor$.

As a consequence, a check on the range of c must be performed by the prover. In the same vein, even if the consequences are not so important, the verifier should also check that the answers s and s lie in consistent ranges; this may be important to perform a full security proof.

This preliminary observation is not used in the sequel and we consider that the order of magnitude of any transmitted data is always checked.

3.2   First Observation: n Can Be Chosen in Such a Way That Discrete Logarithms in $\mathbb{Z}_n^*$ Can Be Efficiently Computed

The first immediate idea to attack the Σ^+-Protocol is to make the verifier choose a group $\mathbb{Z}_n^*$ in which he can efficiently compute discrete logarithms. For example, such a computation can be made if the Pohlig-Hellman algorithm [14] can be applied efficiently, *i.e.* if the multiplicative order of g is the product of only small prime integers. This situation occurs if n is computed as the product of two primes p and q s.t. $p-1$ and $q-1$ are "smooth", *i.e.* are equal to the product of only small prime factors.

Note that this kind of attack was somewhat considered by the authors of [1] since, as we already mentioned, they explicitly restricted themselves to the opposite situation where p and q are strong primes *i.e.* $(p-1)/2$ and $(q-1)/2$ are also primes. But, even if such a choice seems to be specified for a honest verifier in order to protect him against dishonest provers, a dishonest verifier can choose different kind of parameters to try to attack a honest prover. Such a cheating strategy does not seem to be taken into account since the prover does not try to detect it. The situation is even worse since the prover does not have enough information to check the correctness of n as a product of two unknown strong primes. In [3], Camenisch and Michels have shown how to prove that a modulus is the product of two safe primes. Adding such a proof in Σ^+ would drastically reduce the claimed efficiency of the protocol and render it totally unpractical.

The consequence of this first observation is that a cheating verifier can choose the modulus n s.t. he can further compute easily the following information:

1. $x\rho + \mathsf{x} \bmod \mathrm{ord}(g)$ $(= \log_g(\mathsf{y}))$
2. $r\rho + \mathsf{r} \bmod \mathrm{ord}(g)$ $(= \log_g(\mathsf{t}))$

Furthermore, he obtains from the regular execution of the protocol the answers s and s:

3. $s = xc + r$
4. $\mathsf{s} = \mathsf{x}c + \mathsf{r}$

However, even if we obtain four equations with four unknowns (x, x, r and r), this system cannot be solved to recover the secret x since the equations are not independent. Some more work is therefore needed.

3.3   Second Observation: Some Information May Be Revealed by a Honest Prover

If a dishonest verifier chooses the prime numbers p and q s.t. $(p-1)/2$ and $(q-1)/2$ are relatively prime, we know that the maximal order of an element in $\mathbb{Z}_n{}^*$ is given by the Carmichael lambda function $\lambda(n) = \mathrm{lcm}(p-1, q-1) = (p-1)(q-1)/2$. The verifier can choose an element g with such a maximal order which is close to $n/2$. In this case, g is not a quadratic residue in $\mathbb{Z}_n{}^*$.

Then, an idea is to choose $\rho = 1$ in combination with a group $\mathbb{Z}_n{}^*$ where the verifier can compute discrete logarithms. The consequence is that the attacker learns $\log_g(\mathsf{y}) = (x + \mathsf{x}) \bmod \mathrm{ord}(g)$ which can be seen as the secret $x \bmod \mathrm{ord}(g)$ masked with x randomly chosen in the range $[0, \lfloor n/4 \rfloor]$. Since $\mathrm{ord}(g) \approx n/2$, the mask x does not fully hide the value of $x \bmod \mathrm{ord}(g)$ and, from an information theoretic point of view, one bit of information is revealed if x is uniformly distributed modulo $\mathrm{ord}(g)$.

It is quite plausible that by repeating this approach one can deduce the exact value of the secret x from this partial information. However, we propose an additional trick to make the attack straightforward and effective.

3.4   Third Observation: Parameter ρ Can Be Chosen in Such a Way That the Multiplicative Order of g_1 Is Small

Using both previously exposed ideas, let us consider that the verifier chooses n and g s.t.

- p and q are prime integers,
- $(p-1)/2$ and $(q-1)/2$ are relatively prime,
- $p-1$ and $q-1$ are smooth,
- g is an element of $\mathbb{Z}_n{}^*$ of maximal order $\lambda(n) = (p-1)(q-1)/2$.

Let us now choose $\rho = \lambda(n)/2$. As a consequence, $g_1 = g^\rho = g^{\lambda(n)/2} \bmod n$ has multiplicative order 2.

As explained previously, a cheating verifier is able to compute discrete logarithms and thus obtains from a regular proof

$$\log_g(\mathsf{y}) = x\rho + \mathsf{x} \bmod \mathrm{ord}(g)$$
$$= \left(x \times \frac{\lambda(n)}{2} \right) + \mathsf{x} \bmod \lambda(n)$$
$$= (x \bmod 2) \times \frac{\lambda(n)}{2} + \mathsf{x} \bmod \lambda(n)$$

As a consequence, since the mask x is chosen in a range of size approximately $\lambda(n)/2$, the observation of the most significant bit of $\log_g(\mathsf{y})$ reveals the least significant bit of x, *i.e.* the value $x \bmod 2$.

Indeed, if $x \bmod 2 = 0$, then $\log_g(\mathsf{y}) = \mathsf{x}$ is uniformly distributed in the range $[0, \lfloor \frac{n}{4} \rfloor]$. If $x \bmod 2 = 1$, then $\log_g(\mathsf{y}) = \mathsf{x} + \frac{\lambda(n)}{2}$ is now uniformly distributed in $[\frac{\lambda(n)}{2}, \frac{\lambda(n)}{2} + \lfloor \frac{n}{4} \rfloor]$. These intervals are not disjoint but their intersection contains approximately only $\frac{p+q}{4}$ points. Thus, with overwhelming probability, the least significant bit of x leaks from a single execution of the protocol with such a cheating verifier.

In short, we have seen that a dishonest verifier can choose special parameters n, g and ρ in such a way that he can learn the secret x modulo two. Note that this is not detected by a prover who follows the protocol.

Then, the next bits of x can also be obtained by extending this attack. Suppose the verifier knows the k least significant bits $x_0, \ldots, x_{k-1}$ of x, where $x = \sum_{i=0}^{\ell} x_i 2^i$. He then tries to infer the bit x_k. To this end, he chooses the parameters n and g as before with the extra condition that 2^{k+1} divides $\lambda(n)$ and $\rho = \lambda(n)/2^{k+1}$. From the prover's answers during the protocol, he computes $\log_g(\mathsf{y}) = \mathsf{x} + x \times \lambda(n)/2^{k+1} \bmod \lambda(n)$ and considers the value

$$\log_g(\mathsf{y}) - \sum_{i=0}^{k-1} x_i 2^i \times \frac{\lambda(n)}{2^{k+1}} = \mathsf{x} + \sum_{i=k}^{\ell} x_i 2^i \times \frac{\lambda(n)}{2^{k+1}}$$

$$= \mathsf{x} + x_k \times \frac{\lambda(n)}{2} + \sum_{i=k+1}^{\ell} x_i 2^{i-(k+1)} \times \lambda(n)$$

$$= \mathsf{x} + x_k \times \frac{\lambda(n)}{2} \bmod \lambda(n)$$

which is either in the range $[0, \lfloor \frac{n}{4} \rfloor]$ or in the range $[\frac{\lambda(n)}{2}, \frac{\lambda(n)}{2} + \lfloor \frac{n}{4} \rfloor]$ according to the value of the bit x_k. As before, the verifier can deduce x_k with very high probability from a single execution of the protocol. The precise algorithm is given in figure 2. In this description, for clarity, the commitment of the values y, t and t are not described. This does not change anything in the attack.

A strategy for breaking the protocol is thus to choose a special value for n, *i.e.* a modulus computed as the product of two primes p and q with smooth values $p-1$ and $q-1$, and a generator g which is of maximal order and thus not a quadratic residue in $\mathbb{Z}_n^*$.

The total number of protocol executions to recover a ℓ-bit secret x is finally $\ell \times (1 + 1/\sqrt{n})$, since each bit requires at least one protocol execution, and the intersection of the intervals contains approximately $\sqrt{n}$ points.

The attack is no longer possible if the prover checks the correctness of n or g. However, as we will see in the next subsection, if only the quadratic residuosity is checked, a variant of the attack can be applied.

In annex B, we review some technical details related to the computation of discrete logarithms in groups of smooth order in order to provide a complete

---

- Inputs: the bits $x_0, x_1, \ldots, x_{k-1}$ of x
- Output: the bit x_k of x

1. Generate $n = p \times q$, with p and q prime, $(p-1)/2$ and $(q-1)/2$ relatively primes, $p-1$ and $q-1$ smooth and $p-1$ is divisible by 2^{k+1};
2. Generate $g \in \mathbb{Z}_n^*$ of order $\lambda(n) = (p-1)(q-1)/2$;
3. Set $\rho = \lambda(n)/2^{k+1}$ and compute $g_1 = g^\rho \bmod n$;
4. Execute a protocol with the prover:
   (a) Send (n, g, g_1) to the prover;
   (b) Receive $\mathsf{y} = g_1^x g^{\mathsf{x}} \bmod n$, $\mathsf{t} = g_1^r g^{\mathsf{r}} \bmod n$ and $t = h^r$;
   (c) Finish correctly the protocol with the prover;
5. Compute the discrete logarithm of y in base g using the Pohlig-Hellman algorithm (see annex B):

$$\log_g(\mathsf{y}) = \rho \times x + \mathsf{x} \bmod \mathrm{ord}(g)$$

6. If $\log_g(\mathsf{y}) - \sum_{i=0}^{k-1} x_i 2^i \times \rho \in [0, \lfloor \frac{\lambda(n)}{2} \rfloor[$ then set $x_k = 0$;

7. Else, if $\log_g(\mathsf{y}) - \sum_{i=0}^{k-1} x_i 2^i \times \rho \in]\lfloor n/4 \rfloor, \frac{\lambda(n)}{2} + \lfloor n/4 \rfloor]$, then set $x_k = 1$;

8. Else, go to step 4;
9. Return: x_k

Fig. 2. The attacker strategy to recover x_k from $x_0, x_1, \ldots, x_{k-1}$

description of the attack. We also provide in section 5 practical complexity estimates for realistic parameter sizes.

3.5   Final Observation: The Modulus n Can Be Prime

Let us assume that the protocol is slightly modified so that the prover checks the quadratic residuosity of g. This can be easily implemented: the verifier sends g_0 of maximal order $\lambda(n)$ and the prover sets $g = g_0^2 \bmod n$. We still assume that the prover does not make any verification on the modulus n so that it can be chosen by the cheating verifier without any restriction.

The verifier can then choose n as a **prime** number such that $n-1$ is smooth and divisible by 2^ℓ. In this case, he can still compute discrete logarithms. The generator g is a quadratic residue of maximal order $\lambda(n)/2 = (n-1)/2$. The attack we have described previously takes advantage of the short size of the mask x so it can be applied here. Indeed, by iteratively choosing the value ρ equal to $\lambda(n)/2^{i+1}$ for all the values i less than ℓ (the bit length of the secret x), the verifier is able to recover x bit by bit with approximately ℓ executions of the protocol.

In the next section, we describe an extension of the attack when the prover checks that n is not a prime number. This extension works for any unbalanced modulus, but its complexity grows exponentially with the length of the smallest factor of n.

4   Extension of the Attack for an Unbalanced Modulus

In this section we consider the special case where the prover checks that g is chosen in the subgroup of quadratic residues of $\mathbb{Z}_n{}^*$. This can simply be done by sending g and g_0 such that $g = g_0^2 \bmod n$. We also assume that g is a quadratic residue of maximal order $\lambda(n)/2$. However we still consider that the sole check that the prover performs on n is that n is not prime. In that case, the attack of section 3.5 applies. Thus, n can be chosen by the verifier so that :

- n is unbalanced: its prime factor p is much smaller than q. With such a choice for n, the approximation of $\mathrm{ord}(g)$ by $n/4$ might not be tight, and the bias could be exploited by a dishonest verifier;
- p is small enough, and $q - 1$ is smooth and divisible by a large enough power of 2, so that it is possible for the verifier to compute discrete logarithms in $\mathbb{Z}_n{}^*$.

- Inputs: the bits $x_0, x_1, \ldots, x_{k-1}$ of x and a bound $\tilde{k}$ depending on the allowed error probability
- Output: the bit x_k of x

1. Generate $n = p \times q$, with p and q prime, $(p-1)/2$ and $(q-1)/2$ relatively primes, $p < 2^{20}$, $q - 1$ smooth, and 2^{k+1} divides $q - 1$;
2. Generate $g_0 \in \mathbb{Z}_n{}^*$ of order $\lambda(n) = (p-1)(q-1)/2$;
3. Compute $g = g_0^2 \bmod n$;
4. Set $\rho = \lambda(n)/2^{k+1}$ and compute $g_1 = g^\rho \bmod n$;
5. Set $j = 0$ and $S = 0$;
6. While $j < \tilde{k}$, do:
   (a) Execute a protocol with the prover:
       i. Send (n, g, g_1) to the prover;
       ii. Receive $\mathsf{y} = g_1^x g^{\mathsf{x}} \bmod n$, $\mathsf{t} = g_1^r g^{\mathsf{r}} \bmod n$ and $t = h^r$;
       iii. Finish correctly the protocol with the prover;
   (b) Compute the discrete logarithm of y in base g using the Pohlig-Hellman algorithm of annex B:

   $$\log_g(\mathsf{y}) = (x \times \rho + \mathsf{x}) \bmod \mathrm{ord}(g)$$

   (c) If $\log_g(\mathsf{y}) - \sum_{i=0}^{k-1} x_i 2^i \times \rho \in [0, \mu]$ then $j = j + 1$;
   (d) If $\log_g(\mathsf{y}) - \sum_{i=0}^{k-1} x_i 2^i \times \rho \in [\dfrac{\mathrm{ord}(g)}{2}, \dfrac{\mathrm{ord}(g)}{2} + \mu]$, then $S = S + 1$ and $j = j + 1$;
7. End while;
8. If $S < \tilde{k}/2$, set $x_k = 0$,
9. Else $x_k = 1$;
10. Return: x_k

Fig. 3. The attacker strategy to recover x_k from $x_0, x_1, \ldots, x_{k-1}$ in the unbalanced case

From the value $y = g_1^x g^x = g^{\rho x + x}$, the verifier can recover $X = \rho x + x \bmod \mathrm{ord}(g)$, where x is uniformly distributed in $[0, \lfloor \frac{n}{4} \rfloor]$.

Let $\rho = \mathrm{ord}(g)/2$. Then X is either $x \bmod \mathrm{ord}(g)$ or $x + \mathrm{ord}(g)/2 \bmod \mathrm{ord}(g)$, depending on the least significant bit of x. The distribution of the X values is thus dependent on this bit. Since g is a quadratic residue of maximal order in $\mathbb{Z}_n{}^*$, we have:

$$\mathrm{ord}(g) = \frac{\lambda(n)}{2} = \frac{n}{4} - \frac{p + q - 1}{4}$$

We set $\mu = (p + q - 1)/4$. Thus, $n/4 = \mathrm{ord}(g) + \mu$.

The cheating verifier's strategy is detailed in figure 3. The attack consists in computing the discrete logarithm of y for each execution of the protocol, with a suitably chosen value ρ. The distribution of this value, translated according to previously computed bits, allows to infer one additional bit of the secret x.

The complexity is larger than in the previous attacks since many protocol executions are required to obtain a single bit of x. This complexity and the attack analysis are both given in annex A. With error probability $1/B$, an average of $8p \ln(B)/9$ executions of the protocol are needed for a cheating verifier to recover each bit of x from the distribution of $\log_g(y)$.

Figure 3 describes the attacker strategy to infer a bit of x knowing all the previous ones.

5   Practical Application of the Attack

The attack has been implemented using NTL. Using RSA moduli with very small prime factors in $\lambda(n)$, a log can be computed in less than 1 second for a 2GHz PC with a 1024-bit RSA modulus. The optimum seems to be reached when using prime factors of about 5 bits.

In the cases where g is a non quadratic residue or n is prime, only one protocol run is required per secret bit, and the attack is therefore very practical: for a 160-bit secret, it requires 160 protocol runs and a few minutes of computations.

In the unbalanced case, several protocol interactions and log computations per secret bit are needed. Typically, 200 runs per bit ensures an overall success probability above 90% for a 1024-bit modulus and a 160-bit secret: only several hours of computations are required, but the secret must be extracted from the data of $160 \times 200 = 32000$ protocol runs, which might prove difficult to acquire with a real prover device.

6   Conclusion

We have described a cheating strategy for an attacker acting as a verifier in the Σ^+ proof of knowledge of discrete logarithm described in [1]. It enables to recover the full secret with essentially no computational power beyond what is required to run the protocol and after only a few iterations of it since each iteration reveals one bit of secret. We have also described variants of the attack that apply when some additional simple checks are performed by the prover, namely verifying that the modulus chosen by the verifier is indeed a composite integer and that the basis is a quadratic residue.

The correction of the Σ^+-protocol is out of the scope of this paper but it clearly appears that additional checks would probably be a sound idea. Some solutions, such as adding a proof that the RSA modulus provided by the verifier is the product of two safe primes, would drastically reduce the claimed efficiency of the protocol. Another direction would be to choose the parameter x in a large enough interval so that there is no usable bias in x mod ord(g), even if the parameters n and g are chosen by a dishonest verifier. While this option only adds negligible complexity to the Σ^+ protocol and thwarts all our attacks, it does not address the question of the soundness of the protocol proof.

References

1. E. Bangerter, J. Camenisch, and U. Maurer. Efficient Proofs of Knowledge of Discrete Logarithms and Representations in Groups with Hidden Order. In *PKC 2005*, LNCS 3386, pages 154–171. Springer-Verlag, 2005.
2. T. Beth. Efficient Zero-Knowledge Identification Scheme for Smart Cards. In *Eurocrypt '88*, LNCS 330, pages 77–86. Springer-Verlag, 1988.
3. J. Camenisch and M. Michels. Proving in Zero-Knowledge That a Number Is the Product of Two Safe Primes. In *Eurocrypt '99*, LNCS 1592, pages 107–122. Springer-Verlag, 1999.
4. D. Chaum, J. Evertse, and J. van de Graaf. An Improved Protocol for Demonstrating Possession of Discrete Logarithms and some Generalizations. In *Eurocrypt '87*, LNCS 304, pages 127–141. Springer-Verlag, 1988.
5. D. Chaum, J. Evertse, J. van de Graaf, and R. Peralta. Demonstrating Possession of a Discrete Logarithm without Revealing it. In *Crypto '86*, LNCS 263, pages 200–212. Springer-Verlag, 1987.
6. NESSIE consortium. *Portfolio of recommanded cryptographic primitives*, 2003. Available from `http://www.cryptonessie.org`.
7. R. Cramer. Modular Design of Secure yet Practical Cryptographic Protocol, 1997. PhD thesis, University of Amsterdam.
8. R. Cramer and I. Damgård. Zero-Knowledge Proofs for Finite Field Arithmetic or: Can Zero-Knowledge Be for Free. In *Crypto '98*, LNCS 1462, pages 424–441. Springer-Verlag, 1998.
9. I. Damgård and E. Fujisaki. A Statistically-Hiding Integer Commitment Scheme Based on Groups with Hidden Order. In *Asiacrypt 2002*, LNCS 2501, pages 125–142. Springer-Verlag, 2002.
10. W. Diffie and M. E. Hellman. New Directions in Cryptography. In *IEEE Transactions on Information Theory*, volume IT–22, no. 6, pages 644–654, november 1976.

11. E. Fujisaki and T. Okamoto. Statistical Zero Knowledge Protocols to Prove Modular Polynomial Relations. In *Crypto '97*, LNCS 1403, pages 16–30. Springer-Verlag, 1997.
12. M. Girault. Self-Certified Public Keys. In *Eurocrypt '91*, LNCS 547, pages 490–497. Springer-Verlag, 1992.
13. S. Goldwasser, S. Micali, and C. Rackoff. The Knowledge Complexity of Interactive Proof Systems. *SIAM journal of computing*, 18(1):186–208, february 1989.
14. S. C. Pohlig and M. E. Hellman. An Improved Algorithm for Computing Logarithms over GF(p) and its Cryptographic Significance. *IEEE Transactions on Information Theory*, IT–24(1):106–110, january 1978.
15. J. M. Pollard. Monte Carlo Methods for Index Computation (mod p). *Mathematics of Computation*, 32(143):918–924, July 1978.
16. G. Poupard and J. Stern. Security Analysis of a Practical "on the fly" Authentication and Signature Generation. In *Eurocrypt '98*, LNCS 1403, pages 422–436. Springer-Verlag, 1998.
17. C. P. Schnorr. Efficient Identification and Signatures for Smart Cards. In *Crypto '89*, LNCS 435, pages 235–251. Springer-Verlag, 1990.
18. P. C. van Oorschot and M. J. Wiener. On Diffie-Hellman Key Agreement with Short Exponents. In *Eurocrypt '96*, LNCS 1070, pages 332–343. Springer-Verlag, 1996.

A   Analysis of the Unbalanced Modulus Case

In the following we show that the attack, described in section 4 in the case of prime modulus, can also applied if the modulus is unbalanced. In that case, we will show that its complexity grows exponentially with the length of the smallest factor.

We recall that the modulus n is unbalanced and that g is a quadratic residue of maximal order. In the following, we analyze the attack in detail. We briefly recall some notations already given in section 4. Let x_0 denote the least significant bit of x, *i.e.* $x_0 = x \mod 2$, X^0 the value of X for $x_0 = 0$ and X^1 the value of X for $x_0 = 1$. Since g is a quadratic residue of maximal order in $\mathbb{Z}_n^*$, we have:

$$\mathrm{ord}(g) = \frac{\lambda(n)}{2} = \frac{n}{4} - \frac{p+q-1}{4}$$

We set $\mu = (p+q-1)/4$. Thus, $n/4 = \mathrm{ord}(g) + \mu$.

For $x_0 = 0$, $X^0 = \mathsf{x}$ is uniformly distributed in the interval $[0, \lfloor \frac{n}{4} \rfloor] = [0, \mathrm{ord}(g) + \lfloor \mu \rfloor]$. Taking the values modulo $\mathrm{ord}(g)$, we have :

$$\Pr(X^0 \in [0, \lfloor \mu \rfloor]) = \Pr(\mathsf{x} \in [0, \lfloor \mu \rfloor] \cup [\mathrm{ord}(g), \mathrm{ord}(g) + \lfloor \mu \rfloor])$$
$$= \frac{2\lfloor \mu \rfloor}{\mathrm{ord}(g) + \lfloor \mu \rfloor} \approx \frac{8\mu}{n}$$

$$\Pr(X^0 \in [\lceil \mu \rceil, \mathrm{ord}(g)]) \approx 1 - \frac{8\mu}{n}$$

We can easily infer the distribution for $x_0 = 1$ with a circular shift of width $\mathrm{ord}(g)/2$. Since $X^1 = \mathrm{x} + \mathrm{ord}(g)/2$ is uniformly distributed in the interval $[\frac{\mathrm{ord}(g)}{2}, \frac{3\,\mathrm{ord}(g)}{2} + \lfloor \mu \rfloor]$, we thus obtain

$$\Pr(X^1 \in [0, \mathrm{ord}(g)/2] \cup [\mathrm{ord}(g)/2 + \lceil \mu \rceil, \mathrm{ord}(g)]) = \Pr(\mathrm{x} \in [\mathrm{ord}(g)/2 + \lceil \mu \rceil, 3\,\mathrm{ord}(g)/2])$$

$$= \frac{\mathrm{ord}(g) - \lceil \mu \rceil}{\mathrm{ord}(g) + \lfloor \mu \rfloor} \approx 1 - \frac{8\mu}{n}$$

$$\Pr(X^1 \in [\mathrm{ord}(g)/2, \mathrm{ord}(g)/2 + \lfloor \mu \rfloor]) \approx \frac{8\mu}{n}$$

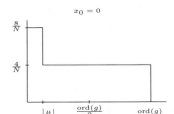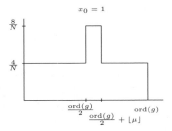

Fig. 4. The distribution of X^0 and X^1

The verifier should run the protocol several times to distinguish these two distributions. Each time the value X obtained is not in the intervals $[0, \lfloor \mu \rfloor]$ or $[\mathrm{ord}(g)/2, \mathrm{ord}(g)/2 + \lfloor \mu \rfloor]$ the verifier gains no information. Accordingly we consider only the values X in these intervals and try to distinguish $x_0 = 0$ from $x_0 = 1$. We set $\tilde{X} = 0$ if $X \in [0, \lfloor \mu \rfloor]$ and $\tilde{X} = 1$ if $X \in [\mathrm{ord}(g)/2, \mathrm{ord}(g)/2 + \lfloor \mu \rfloor]$. We ignore the other cases so that we keep in average only 3μ values amongst $\mathrm{ord}(g) + \mu$. Depending on the bit x_0, $\tilde{X}$ has the following distribution:

$$\text{if } x_0 = 0, \ \Pr(\tilde{x} = 0) = \frac{2}{3} \quad \text{and} \quad \Pr(\tilde{x} = 1) = \frac{1}{3}$$

$$\text{if } x_0 = 1, \ \Pr(\tilde{x} = 0) = \frac{1}{3} \quad \text{and} \quad \Pr(\tilde{x} = 1) = \frac{2}{3}$$

Let $\tilde{k}$ be the number of values collected by the verifier lying in the suitable ranges. Let $S_{\tilde{k}}^b$ the sum of the $\tilde{x}$ depending on the value b of the bit x_0. The Chernoff bound shows that, for every $\varepsilon > 0$,

$$\Pr\left(\frac{S_{\tilde{k}}^0}{\tilde{k}} - \frac{1}{3} \geq \varepsilon\right) \leq e^{-\tilde{k}\varepsilon^2 \times \frac{3}{4}}$$

and

$$\Pr\left(\frac{S_{\tilde{k}}^1}{\tilde{k}} - \frac{2}{3} \leq \varepsilon\right) \leq e^{-\tilde{k}\varepsilon^2 \times \frac{1}{6}}$$

If ε is the sample mean of the two distributions, *i.e.* $\varepsilon = 1/2$, this allows us to have a bound on the number of values needed so that the error value is not too large. For an error probability less than $1/B$, then the number $\tilde{k}$ of collected $\tilde{x}$ values should be such that $\tilde{k} \geq 16\ln(B)/3$.

Taking into account the number of unused values X, we obtain that the total number of verifications to learn 1 bit of information with probability $1/B$ is:

$$k \geq 16\frac{\ln(B)}{3} \times \frac{\text{ord}(g) + \mu}{3\mu}$$
$$\geq \frac{16\ln(B)}{3} \times \frac{n}{3(p+q-1)}$$
$$\geq \frac{16p\ln(B)}{9(1 + \frac{p-1}{q})}$$
$$> \frac{8p\ln(B)}{9}$$

Practical Results. Such a bound on the number of runs needed to learn one bit of information allows us to estimate the complexity of the attack depending on p and q. If p is really small, for example if $p = 3$, we obtain $k \geq 26$ for an error probability per bit equal to $1/1000$.

When p is larger, the number of runs explodes. Indeed, the number of queries strongly depends on the length of p and becomes too large as soon as p is larger than say 2^{30}. For such a value, and for a 256 bits secret x, the total complexity of the attack can be approximated by 2^{40}, for an error probability for each bit of x which is $1/B = 1/1000$.

Using Additional Information in X. To improve the overall success probability of the attack, we can analyze what happens when a bit was guessed incorrectly. In that case, when treating the next bit, one gets the distributions of figure 4, with a circular shift of $\text{ord}(g)/4$. Irrespectively of the correctness of the previous guess, the two candidate distributions for X are equal up to a shift by $\text{ord}(g)/2$. As a consequence, the distribution of $2X \mod \text{ord}(g)$ can take two values: a distribution D_1 when the previous bit was guessed correctly, and a distribution D_2 otherwise. D_1 and D_2 have the same shape as the distributions of figure 4, with $\mu = 2^{\frac{p+q-1}{4}} = \frac{p+q-1}{2}$. Because of the multiplication by 2, the peak is only $3/2$ as high as the rest of the distribution.

These remarks can be used to add new experiments regarding bit x_i when performing the experiments on bit x_{i+1}. D_1 and D_2 are harder to distinguish than the distributions of X^0 and X^1; therefore, the new experiences are less conclusive, and "weight" less than the first series; the weight ratio is $\ln(3/2)/\ln(2)$. This is partly compensated by the higher probability to land in the peaks of distributions D_1 and D_2, which are twice as wide as for the distributions of X^0 or X^1. Overall, with the same success probability per bit, these additional experiences save up to 54% of the log computations, depending on μ. The most attractive case is when the two μ-wide peaks of distributions D_1 and D_2 do not overlap, in which case the saving ratio is $\frac{2\ln(3/2)}{2\ln(3/2)+\ln(2)} \approx 0.54$.

The algorithm finally obtained is described figure 5.

- Inputs: a bound $\tilde{k}$ depending on the allowed error probability
- Output: the secret x

1. Generate $n = p \times q$, with p and q prime, $p = 3 \mod 4$, p small, $p-1$ and $q-1$ smooth, $(p-1, q-1) = 2$ and 2^{k+1} divides $q-1$;
2. Generate $g_0 \in \mathbb{Z}_n^*$ of order $\lambda(n) = (p-1)(q-1)/2$;
3. Compute $g = g_0^2 \mod n$;
4. $S[i] = 0$, $i = 0, \ldots, k-1$
5. $X[j] = 0$, $j = 0, \ldots, \tilde{k}$
6. $z = 0$, $\eta = \mathrm{ord}(g)/2$
7. For $i = 0, \ldots, k-1$, do
    (a) Set $\rho = \lambda(n)/2^{i+2} = \mathrm{ord}(g)/2^{i+1}$ and $g_1 = g^\rho \mod n$;
    (b) While $j < \lfloor \tilde{k} \times \mathrm{ord}(g)/(2\mu) \rfloor$, do:
        i. Execute a protocol run and extract

$$\log_g(y) = (x \times \rho + x) \mod \mathrm{ord}(g)$$

        ii. $X[j] = \log_g(y) - z \times \rho$
        iii. If $i > 0$, do
            A. If $2X[j] \in [\max(0, 2\mu - \eta), \min(2\mu, \eta)]$ then $S[i-1]- = \ln(3/2)$;
            B. If $2X[j] \in [\max(\eta, 2\mu), \min(\mathrm{ord}(g), \eta + 2\mu))]$, then $S[i-1]+ = \ln(3/2)$;
    (c) End while;
    (d) If $i > 0$, do
        i. If $S[i-1] < 0$, set $x_{i-1} = 0$;
        ii. Else $x_{i-1} = 1$;
        iii. $z = z + x_{i-1}2^{i-1}$
    (e) While $j < \lfloor \tilde{k} \times \mathrm{ord}(g)/(2\mu) \rfloor$, do:
        i. If $X[j] \in [0, \mu]$ then $S[i]- = \ln(2)$;
        ii. If $X[j] \in [\eta, \eta + \mu]$, then $S[i]+ = \ln(2)$;
    (f) End while;
8. End For;
9. If $S[k-1] < 0$, set $x_{k-1} = 0$;
10. Else $x_{k-1} = 1$;
11. Return: $x = \sum_{i=0}^{k-1} x_i 2^i$

Fig. 5. The attacker improved strategy to recover x in the unbalanced case

B   Practical Computation of Discrete Logarithms in Groups of Smooth Order

In the following we show how to compute discrete logarithms when the order's factorization of the group element is unknown, but only small factors are known.

Let $\mathcal{G}$ be a multiplicative group. We do not assume any specific property of this group in this section. Let g be an element of multiplicative order ω.

Generic algorithms to compute discrete logarithms, such as Baby step-Giant step or Pollard rho and lambda methods [15, 18] have complexity $O(\sqrt{\omega})$.

---

1. input: $y \in \langle g \rangle$
2. initialization: $Y = y$, $G = g$, $\Omega = \omega$, $P = 1$, $X = 0$
3. for i from 1 to ℓ do
   (a) for j from 1 to e_i do
       i. $\Omega = \Omega / p_i$
       ii. $z = \log_{G^\Omega}\left(Y^\Omega\right)$
       iii. $Y = Y/G^z$
       iv. $G = G^{p_i}$
       v. $X = X + P \times z$
       vi. $P = P \times p_i$
4. return: X

Fig. 6. A variant of the Pohlig-Hellman algorithm to compute discrete logarithms

However, in some cases, more efficient techniques apply. The well-known Pohlig-Hellman algorithm [14] takes advantage of the factorization of the order ω when it is applicable. If we choose the group parameters such that this order is smooth, this algorithm enables to compute discrete logarithms efficiently.

We now describe a variant strongly inspired from the original Pohlig-Hellman algorithm. We note

$$\omega = \prod_{i=1}^{k} p_i^{e_i} \quad \text{with} \quad \begin{cases} \forall i \in [1,k] \;\; p_i \text{ is a prime integer} \\ \forall i \in [1,k] \;\; e_i \in \mathbb{N}^* \\ 1 \le i < j \le k \Rightarrow p_i < p_j \end{cases}$$

and we consider the algorithm of figure 6.

Note that if we use this algorithm with $\ell = k$, it just computes discrete logarithms using the Pohlig-Hellman idea, performing the Chinese remainder computation whenever it is possible. We can also use it with $\ell < k$; in this case we can compute some partial information about the discrete logarithms. This may have important consequences when some optimizations such as so-called short exponents, *i.e.* exponents much smaller than the order ω but larger than 160 bits are used for efficiency reasons. In such a situation, the complete factorization of the order of g may be unknown but enough small factors p_i may still enable to recover some secrets.

Theorem 1. *On input $y \in \langle g \rangle$ and $\ell \in [1,k]$, the algorithm of figure 6 computes $X = \log_g(y) \bmod \prod_{i=1}^{\ell} p_i^{e_i}$. The time complexity is $O\left(\sum_{i=1}^{\ell} e_i \times \sqrt{p_i}\right)$.*

Proof. The justification of the result is done recursively. For any value of indexes i and j, we have, just before line "i." the following relations:

- $P = \prod_{\alpha=1}^{i-1} p_\alpha^{e_\alpha} \times p_i^{j-1}$
- $G = g^P$
- $\Omega = \omega/P$
- $X = x \bmod P$
- $Y = g^{(x \ \mathrm{div} \ P) \times P} = y/g^X$

After execution of line "i.", the new value of Ω is $\Omega = \omega/(P \times p_i)$. Then, in line "ii.", we have

$$G^\Omega = g^{P \times \frac{\omega}{P \times p_i}} = g^{\omega/p_i}$$

and
$$Y^\Omega = g^{(x \text{ div } P) \times P \times \frac{\omega}{P \times p_i}} = g^{(x \text{ div } P) \times \frac{\omega}{p_i}}$$

so the computation of $z = \log_{G^\Omega}\left(Y^\Omega\right)$ leads to

$$z = \log_{g^{\omega/p_i}}\left(\left(g^{\omega/p_i}\right)^{x \text{ div } P}\right) = (x \text{ div } P) \bmod p_i$$

An important fact for the complexity of the algorithm is that z is an integer in the range $[0, p_i - 1]$ because g^{ω/p_i} has multiplicative order p_i. Consequently, if p_i is small, we can use generic discrete logarithm algorithms with running time $O(\sqrt{p_i})$ to efficiently compute z.

Then, after computation "iii.", we have

$$Y = g^{(x \text{ div } P) \times P - (x \text{ div } P) \bmod p_i} = g^{(x \text{ div } (P \times p_i)) \times (P \times p_i)}$$

After the next computation, $G = \left(g^P\right)^{p_i} = g^{P \times p_i}$ and then

$$X = x \bmod P + P \times z = x \bmod P + P \times ((x \text{ div } P) \bmod p_i) = x \bmod P \times p_i$$

and finally
$$P = \prod_{\alpha=1}^{i-1} p_\alpha^{e_\alpha} \times p_i^{j-1} \times p_i = \prod_{\alpha=1}^{i-1} p_\alpha^{e_\alpha} \times p_i^{j}$$

The result X which is returned is $X = x \bmod \prod_{\alpha=1}^{i} p_\alpha^{e_\alpha}$.

The main computation is the evaluation of z on line "ii.". Its complexity is $O(\sqrt{p_i})$ so the global time complexity of the algorithm is $O\left(\sum_{i=1}^{\ell} e_i \times \sqrt{p_i}\right)$.

$\square$

Efficient Polynomial Operations in the Shared-Coefficients Setting

Payman Mohassel and Matthew Franklin

Department of Computer Science, University of California, Davis CA 95616
mohassel@cs.ucdavis.edu, franklin@cs.ucdavis.edu

Abstract. We study the design of efficient and private protocols for polynomial operations in the shared-coefficients setting. We propose efficient protocols for *polynomial multiplication, division with remainder, polynomial interpolation, polynomial gcd,* and a few other operations. All the protocols introduced in this paper are *constant-round*, and more efficient than the *general* MPC. The protocols are all composable, and can be combined to perform more complicated functionalities. We focus on using a *threshold additively homomorphic public key scheme* due to the applications of our protocols. But, our protocols can also be securely computed in the *information-theoretic* setting. Finally, we mention some applications of our protocols to *privacy-preserving set-operations*.

Keywords: secure multi-party computation, passive adversary, polynomial operations, threshold homomorphic encryption, privacy-preserving set operations.

1 Introduction

Secure multiparty computation (MPC) is an important and classic problem in the realm of *cryptography* and *distributed computing*. In this problem, a group of parties want to compute a function of their inputs while keeping their inputs private. The special case of two-party computation was first studied by Yao [Yao82, Yao86]. Classic works such as [GMW87], [BGW88], and [CCD88] give solutions for the more general case of multiparty computation. These works solve the problem of *general* multiparty computation by performing gate by gate secure computation of a *circuit* (boolean or arithmetic) that implements the desired function.

As the function being computed becomes more complicated, so does the circuit that computes such a function. This, in turn, makes the *general* MPC solutions inefficient. Therefore, researchers have turned to designing special-purpose protocols for specific functions in order to improve on the complexity of general MPC solutions.

Polynomials have turned out to be useful tools for designing efficient and secure distributed protocols for specific functionalities. [FNP04], [FIPR05], and [KS05] use polynomials to design efficient multiparty protocols. In these papers,

M. Yung et al. (Eds.): PKC 2006, LNCS 3958, pp. 44–57, 2006.

coefficients of polynomials are encrypted using an additively homomorphic cryptosystem. Then, different operations on polynomials such as *polynomial evaluation*, and *polynomial multiplication* are performed.

These works motivated us to take a closer look at different operations on polynomials. Furthermore, polynomials have appeared (and will continue to appear) in many schemes, or algorithms. Some of these schemes might have privacy concerns, and require a set of parties to securely perform some operations on the polynomials. Anywhere that such operations on polynomials are being performed and privacy is a concern, our protocols can be useful.

1.1 Our Contribution

We propose efficient protocols for *polynomial multiplication, division with remainder, polynomial interpolation, polynomial gcd*, and other polynomial operations. These protocols are composable and can be combined to perform more complicated functionalities. In this paper, we are concerned with both *communication* and *round* complexity of our protocols. Particularly, all protocols introduced in this paper have constant number of rounds, while we try to optimize their communication complexity wherever possible.

We propose several applications of our methods to *privacy-preserving set-operations*. In this setting, parties hold sets of data, and want to perform joint operations on their sets. These operations could be union, intersection, subtraction, or any other operation on sets. In many cases, sets are represented by polynomials. Different operations on polynomials lead to different set-operations. The coefficients of such polynomials are often encrypted using a *threshold additively-homomorphic public-key cryptosystem*. That is why we also use such a cryptosystem to distribute secrets among the parties and to operate on those secrets.

But, we would like to note that our protocols can be implemented using tools other than a threshold additively-homomorphic cryptosystem. For example, any *threshold linear secret-sharing scheme* can be used to replace such a cryptosystem.

For simplicity, and with slight abuse of terminology, we will use the single term *shared* throughout this paper to refer to both distribution methods: threshold additively-homomorphic encryption, and threshold linear secret-sharing. See Section 2.1 for more detail.

Our protocols are secure against a semi-honest (passive) adversary. Such an adversary will follow the steps of protocol but will try to learn extra information from the messages it receives during every round of the protocol. The security of our protocols are guaranteed as along as the underlying protocols (multiplication, addition, sharing random values, ...) that are discussed in section 2, can be performed securely. In the *computational setting*, we require that the threshold homomorphic cryptosystem used be *semantically* secure. This leads to secure implementation of the multiplication protocol described in section 2.1. The threshold version of Paillier's cryptosystem is semantically secure and is suited for this purpose. Similarly, in the *information-theoretic setting*, [BGW88] and [CCD88] provide such secure protocols.

1.2   Organization

In section 2, we describe all the tools we need for our protocols. In section 3, we describe an efficient protocol for multiplying two shared polynomials. A protocol for Division with remainder is described in section 4. Multiplying many shared polynomials in constant-round is explained in section 5. An efficient protocol for polynomial interpolation is give in section 6. In section 7, we design constant-round protocols for gcd of two and many shared polynomials. We also describe a protocol for determining if two shared polynomials are coprime or not.

2   Preliminaries

Throughout this paper, F is a finite field of size q. $F[x]$ is the ring of polynomials over F. $F[x]/f$ is the extension field where f is an irreducible polynomial.

In this paper, by a *shared* value, we mean a value that has been distributed among the parties using either (1) a threshold additively-homomorphic public key encryption scheme or (2) a threshold linear secret sharing scheme. The techniques described in this paper will not depend on which method is used. See Section 2.1 for more details.

Throughout this paper, by a *shared polynomial*, we mean a polynomial whose coefficients have been individually encrypted or shared using one of the methods mentioned in the preceding paragraph. A shared polynomial leaks an upper bound on the degree of the polynomial. For some of our protocols, the exact degrees of some shared polynomials may be leaked.

In this paper, by a *shared matrix*, we mean a matrix whose elements have been individually encrypted or shared using one of the methods described above.

We measure the complexity of our protocols by the number of multiplications of shared values that are necessary. This is a natural measure due to the fact that addition of shared values (for either of the two aforementioned methods) can be performed non-interactively. When the context is clear, we may refer to this complexity measure as simply *multiplications*.

2.1   Shared Values

In this paper, we assume that we either have a threshold additively-homomorphic public key encryption scheme or a threshold linear secret-sharing scheme. As noted above, we may use the term *shared value* to refer to a value that has been distributed according to either method.

Threshold Additively-Homomorphic Encryption. We use a threshold cryptosystem with homomorphic properties such as Paillier's cryptosystem [Pai00]. Paillier's cryptosystem is additively homomorphic, and supports threshold decryption [FP00]. Such a cryptosystem has the following four properties:

1. To share a value between the parties, a party can encrypt the value using the public key to the cryptosystem, and broadcast the ciphertext.

2. Parties can jointly reveal an encrypted value using the threshold decryption.
3. Given the ciphertexts, $E_{pk}(a)$, and $E_{pk}(b)$, and a public plaintext c, parties can compute $E_{pk}(a + b)$, and $E_{pk}(ca)$ non-interactively.
4. Given the ciphertexts $E_{pk}(a)$ and $E_{pk}(b)$ parties can securely compute $E_{pk}(ab)$ in constant number of rounds.

The first three properties are automatically satisfied by any threshold additively homomorphic cryptosystem. We give a simple constant-round protocol to satisfy the fourth property here[1]. Let's assume that parties are holding the ciphertexts $E_{pk}(a)$, and $E_{pk}(b)$. They want to compute $E_{pk}(ab)$. The protocol follows:

1. Party i broadcasts $E_{pk}(r_i)$ to all the parties, where r_i is a randomly chosen plaintext.
2. Parties compute $E_{pk}(a + \sum_i r_i)$, and decrypt the result to get $a' = a + \sum_i r_i$.
3. Each party computes $a' E_{pk}(b) = E_{pk}(a'b)$.
4. Party i computes $r_i E_{pk}(b) = E_{pk}(r_i b)$, and broadcasts it to other parties.
5. Parties compute $E_{pk}(a'b) - \sum_i E_{pk}(r_i b) = E_{pk}(ab)$.

One minor issue is that the domain of Paillier's cryptosystem is the ring Z_n, where n is the product of two large and secret primes. Note that Z_n has all of the properties of a finite field except that some of the non-zero elements in Z_n are not invertible. However, an extended gcd algorithm on x and n either finds the inverse of $x \bmod n$, or finds a non-trivial factor of n. So in practice we can describe computations in Z_n as if it were a finite field.

Threshold Linear Secret Sharing. We require a threshold linear secret-sharing scheme over a field with the following properties:

1. Parties can share a value in constant number of rounds.
2. Parties can reveal their shares in a constant number of rounds.
3. Given shares of values a and b, and a publicly known value c, parties can compute shares of $(a + b)$, and ca without any interaction.
4. Given shares of values a, and b, parties can compute shares of ab in constant number of rounds.

The secret-sharing scheme can be unconditionally or computationally secure. Shamir's polynomial-based threshold linear secret sharing scheme [Sha79] is unconditionally secure. One example of a secret-sharing scheme for the computational setting is given in [GRR98].

2.2   Existing Constant-Round Protocols

In this section, we review some of the existing protocols with constant number of rounds. We would like to remind the reader that the term *shared value* (and *shared polynomial* and *shared matrix*) is used throughout the remainder of this

---

[1] See [CDN01] for a similar protocol.

paper regardless of whether the underlying distribution method is by threshold additively-homomorphic encryption or by threshold linear secret sharing.

Shares of a polynomial P in $F[x]$, are simply the collection of shares of all of P's coefficients. In a similar way, shares of a matrix M over F are the collection of shares of all the elements in M.

We will use or refer to the following techniques throughout the paper. Most of these protocols have appeared in [BB89], and [CD01].

Sharing a Secret Random Field Element, Polynomial, or Matrix. A protocol in which parties generate shares of a random and secret value $r \in F$. This can be done by letting each party share a random value between the parties. Then, parties take the sum of all of those values as r. We can extend this protocol to share random polynomials in $F[x]$ or $F[x]/f$. In a similar way, we can also share random matrices over F.

Constant-Round Multiplication and Division. Consider the polynomials P_A and P_B in $F[x]$. If P_A, and P_B are both secret and shared among the parties, then the parties can use the basic polynomial multiplication to compute shares of $P_A P_B$ in constant-round. We will describe a more communication-efficient protocol for this task in Section 3. If at least one of the polynomials is publicly known, the multiplication does not need any interaction. The case of matrices is similar.

If P_A is shared, and P_B is publicly known, parties can compute shares of Q and R such that $P_A = QP_B + R$ and $deg(R) \leq P_B$. This can be done using the synthetic division, and does not require any interaction between the parties. In Section 4, we describe an efficient division protocol for the case where both P_A and P_B are secret and shared.

Sharing Secret Invertible Field Elements and Matrices. This is a protocol that generates a sharing of a secret, random non-zero field element, or an invertible matrix. The protocol securely generates two random elements (matrices), securely multiplies them, and reveals the result. If this is non-zero (invertible), one of the secret elements(matrices) is taken as the desired output of the protocol. The probability that a random n by n matrix is invertible is greater than $\frac{1}{4}$, and at least $1 - \frac{n}{q}$.

Constant-Round Inversion of Matrices and Field Elements. In this protocol, given shares of a field element (matrix) X, parties compute shares of the inverse of that element (matrix). As it is described in [BB89], parties first generate shares of a random non-zero (invertible) field element (matrix) R. Then, they compute shares of RX, and reveal the result. Parties compute $(RX)^{-1} = X^{-1}R^{-1}$ non-interactively. Finally, they compute $X^{-1}R^{-1}*R = X^{-1}$ non-interactively.

Unbounded Fan-In Multiplication in Constant-Round. Given shares of polynomially many field elements (matrices) $X_1, \ldots, X_l$, parties want to compute shares of their product. Parties generate shared random non-zero (invertible) field elements (matrices) $R_1, \ldots, R_l$. They compute $P_1 = X_1 R_1$, and $P_i = R_{i-1}^{-1} X_i R_i$ for $i \geq 2$. They publicly announce all the P_i values, compute $\prod_i P_i$, and multiply the result by R_l, all non-interactively. This gives them shares of $\prod_i X_i$.

Linear Algebra in Constant-Round. consider the following protocols: (1) Given shares of a matrix A, parties want to compute shares of $det(A)$ (2) Given shares of a matrix A, and shares of vector b, parties want to compute shares of solution(s) to the linear system $Ax = b$. [CD01] proposes efficient and constant-round protocols for these two problems, and others. These protocols are more elaborate, and we will not describe them here.

2.3   Privacy-Preserving Set-Operations

[KS05] uses polynomials to represent sets of data. The polynomial representation of a set S of elements in F is the polynomial $P = \prod_i (x - s_i)$, where $s_i \in S$. Then, different operations on polynomials lead to different operations on the underlying set. For instance, to compute the union of two disjoint sets, one can simply multiply the two polynomials.

By performing different operations on the polynomials, [KS05] designs privacy preserving operations on sets. These operations include, *set-intersection*, *set-union*, *element reduction*, and others. For these protocols to be private, coefficients of polynomials can be shared using either a threshold additively-homomorphic encryption scheme or a threshold linear secret-sharing scheme. In fact, the results in [KS05] are presented using only threshold additively-homomorphic encryption, but it is easy to translate their results to the threshold linear secret-sharing setting. For consistency we will use the single term *shared* (as discussed in Section 2.1) throughout this section to describe their results.

Their protocols gain efficiency compared to general multiparty solutions, due to the fact that the following operations can be performed without any interaction:

1. If a party knows the polynomial P_A, and is given the shared polynomial P_B, then he can compute shared polynomial $P_A P_B$ without any interaction.
2. A party can compute the derivative of a shared polynomial P without any interaction with other parties.

In case of polynomial multiplication, if both polynomials are shared, the most efficient solution is the general multiparty computation. An appropriate general MPC for this case is [CDN01]. For instance, the classic polynomial multiplication algorithm (polynomials of degree $O(n)$), gives us a circuit with $O(n^2)$ multiplication gates over a ring, each of which requires interaction between the parties. The most efficient polynomial multiplication algorithm has a circuit with $O(npolylog(n))$ gates.

Another interesting operation on polynomials that has *not* been considered in the privacy-preserving setting, is the division with remainder of polynomials.

Such a protocol leads to operations for set deletion/subtraction (when the element(s) is known to be in the set).

One can verify that if a party A knows polynomial P_A and is given the shared polynomial P_B, he can perform the synthetic division algorithm to compute the shared polynomials Q and R without any interaction with other parties, where $P_B = QP_A + R$, and $deg(R) \leq P_A$. But, if both polynomials are shared, the most efficient protocols are the general MPC protocols.

In later sections, we will propose protocols for these, and other tasks. Our protocols will be constant-round , and more efficient than the general MPC.

3   Multiplying Two Polynomials

Consider two shared polynomials $f(x), g(x) \in F[x]$, where F is a finite field, and $deg(f) = deg(g) = n$. Parties want to compute shares of the polynomial $h(x) = f(x)*g(x)$. The following is a simple and efficient constant-round protocol for computing the shared product polynomial, with communication complexity of $O(n)$ multiplications. To the best of our knowledge, this protocol has not been published previously.

1. Each party computes his/her share of $f(i)$ and $g(i)$ for all $0 \leq i \leq 2n$.
2. Parties engage in $2n$ multiplications to get their shares of $h(i) = f(i) * g(i)$.
3. Each party can perform the Lagrange Interpolation on its own to get his/her share of coefficients of $h(x)$.

In step 1, no interaction is necessary. All the i's are public, and therefore, parties are computing a linear function of shared coefficients. In step 2, parties perform $2n$ multiplications of shared elements in the field. Step 3 is also performed without any interaction between the parties. This leads to the communication complexity of $O(n)$ multiplications. This also provides an efficient privacy-preserving set union protocol for the setting of [KS05].

4   Division with Remainder

Let $f(x)$ and $g(x)$ be two polynomials in $F[x]$ where $deg(f) = n$, $deg(g) = m$, and $m \leq n$. Given shares of f and g, parties want to compute shares of q and r such that $f(x) = g(x)q(x) + r(x)$, and $deg(r) \leq deg(g)$. The synthetic polynomial division is sequential and does not directly lead to a constant-round protocol for polynomial division. Furthermore, it requires $O(n^2)$ multiplication of elements of a field. The fastest division algorithm still requires $O(npolylog(n))$ such multiplications.

Next, we give a constant-round protocol for the division with remainder of two shared polynomials. The communication complexity of our protocol is $O(n)$ multiplications. The idea is borrowed from a division algorithm using Newton's iteration (See chapter 9 of [GG03] for more information).

Consider the equation

$$f(x) = g(x)q(x) + r(x) \tag{1}$$

By substituting $\frac{1}{x}$ for the variable x in the polynomials, we have the following equation:

$$x^n f(1/x) = [x^{n-m} q(1/x)] * [x^m g(1/x)] + (x^{n-m+1}) * [x^{m-1} r(1/x)] \tag{2}$$

Let $rev_k(a) = x^k a(1/x)$ for an arbitrary polynomial $a(x)$. When $deg(a) = k$, this operation simply reverses the order of coefficients of $a(x)$. We can rewrite the above equation as:

$$rev_n(f) = rev_{n-m}(q) * rev_m(b) + x^{n-m+1} * rev_{m-1}(r) \Rightarrow$$
$$rev_n(f) = \qquad rev_{n-m}(q) * rev_m(g) \; mod \; x^{n-m+1} \qquad \Rightarrow$$
$$rev_{n-m}(q) = \qquad rev_n(f) * rev_m(g)^{-1} \; mod \; x^{n-m+1}$$

$$\tag{3}$$

If parties can compute shares of $rev_{n-m}(q)$ efficiently and in constant-round, they can also compute shares of $q(x)$, and $r(x) = f(x) - g(x)q(x)$ efficiently. Note that we already have an efficient protocol for multiplying two polynomials from section 3. The division algorithm follows:

1. Parties compute shares of $rev_n(f)$ and $rev_m(g)$ without any interaction.
2. Now, parties need to compute shares of $rev_m(g)^{-1} \; mod \; x^{n-m+1}$. We will give an efficient sub protocol for this operation later in this section.
3. They can use the protocol for multiplying two polynomials to compute shares of $rev_v(f) * rev_m(g)^{-1}$.
4. Parties reduce the result mod x^{n-m+1} and reverse the coefficients to get $q(x)$ shared without any interaction.
5. By performing another polynomial multiplication, parties compute shares of $g(x)q(x)$.
6. Parties compute shares of $r(x) = f(x) - g(x)q(x)$ without any interaction.

Note that division with remainder is reduced to two polynomial multiplications (step 3, 5) and one polynomial inversion (step 2). We already know how to do the polynomial multiplication in an efficient way. It suffices to give an efficient protocol for inverting an invertible polynomial f mod x^t, where t is known to all parties. It is important to note that $rev_m(g)$ is invertible mod x^t for any $t \geq 1$. To see that, note that $deg(g) = m$. This means that the leftmost coefficient of $g(x)$ is non-zero. Therefore, the free coefficient (constant term) of $rev_m(g)$ is also non-zero. This implies that $rev_m(g)$ is not divisible by x, and is invertible mod x^t for any $t \geq 1$. This observation implies that for our division algorithm to work properly, we need to guarantee that the given (maximum) degrees for the polynomials are in fact the exact degrees of those polynomials.

Consider the ring $F[x]/x^t$. Consider the multiplicative subgroup $(F[x]/x^t)^*$ that contains all the invertible polynomials in $F[x]/x^t$. To invert a polynomial $f \in (F[x]/x^t)^*$, we adapt the matrix inversion technique of [BB89].

1. Parties compute shares of a uniformly random polynomial s in $F[x]/x^t$.
2. Parties compute shares of $f(x) * s(x) \bmod x^t$, and publicly announce their shares.
3. Parties compute their shares of $g(x) = (f(x) * s(x))^{-1} \bmod x^t = s(x)^{-1} * f(x)^{-1} \bmod x^t$. We expect s to be invertible in $F[x]/x^t$, because $gcd(s, x^t) = 1$ with high probability $(1 - 1/q)$.
4. Parties compute their shares of $f(x)^{-1} \bmod x^t = s(x) * g(x) \bmod x^t$.

Step 2 requires a polynomial multiplication. Steps 3 and 4 do not require any interaction between the parties. Therefore, the communication complexity of this inversion is $O(n)$ multiplications.

Our division with remainder protocol also provides an efficient privacy preserving subset deletion protocol for the setting of [KS05].

5   Multiplying Many Polynomials

Let $f_1, f_2, \ldots, f_l$ be polynomials in $F[x]$, where $deg(f_i) = n_i$. Given shares of f_i for all $1 \leq i \leq l$, parties want to compute shares of $h(x) = \prod_{i=1}^{l} f_i(x)$. In this section, we will give an efficient constant-round protocol for this task.

We would like to use the technique of [BB89] for unbounded fan-in multiplication of elements in a field. But, note that F[x] is not a field. An appropriate field that contains all the f_i's and their product $h(x)$ is the extension field $F[x]/f$ where f is an irreducible polynomial of degree $n_1 + n_2 + \ldots + n_l + 1$. To multiply two polynomials in $F[x]/f$, parties can multiply the polynomials using the protocol in section 3, and compute the result mod f. Since f is a publicly known polynomial, the second step doesn't require any interaction. The protocol for multiplying many polynomials follows:

1. One party computes an irreducible polynomial f of degree $n_1 + \ldots + n_l + 1$, and announces it to other parties.
2. Parties share l random polynomials $r_1, \ldots, r_l$ in the field $F[x]/f$.
3. Parties compute shares of $r_i(x)^{-1}$ for all $i \in \{0..l\}$.
4. Parties compute and publicly announce $(f_1(x)r_1(x) \bmod f)$, $(r_1(x)^{-1}f_2(x)r_2(x) \bmod f)$, $(r_2(x)^{-1}f_3(x)r_3(x) \bmod f)$, $\ldots$, $(r_{l-1}(x)^{-1}f_l(x)r_l(x) \bmod f)$.
5. Parties compute the product of the l public polynomials, and multiply the result by $r_l(x)^{-1}$.
6. Parties reduce the result mod f to obtain shares of $h(x)$.

The above protocol is constant-round. The communication complexity is dominated by step 4, which requires $O(l(\sum_{i=1}^{l} n_i))$ multiplications.

6   Polynomial Interpolation

Let x_i and y_i be shared elements of the field F for $i \in \{1..n\}$. Parties would like to compute shares of the polynomial $f \in F[x]$ such that $f(x_i) = y_i$ for all $i \in \{1..n\}$.

A simple and constant-round protocol for this problem is possible based on the existing techniques. Consider the Vandermonde matrix:

$$
V = \begin{bmatrix}
1 & x_1 & x_1^2 & ... & x_1^n \\
1 & x_2 & x_2^2 & ... & x_2^n \\
. & . & . & . & . \\
. & . & . & . & . \\
. & . & . & . & . \\
1 & x_n & x_n^2 & ... & x_n^n
\end{bmatrix}
\tag{4}
$$

Parties can compute the matrix V, and solve the linear system $VX = [y_1, y_2, ..., y_n]^T$. The components of the solution to the linear system are the coefficients of f. If x_i's are distinct, the system will be non-singular, and solving the linear system is reduced to matrix inversion. [BB89] gives an efficient and constant-round algorithm for inverting matrices. The communication complexity of this method will be $O(n^3)$ multiplications.

Using the protocol from section 5 for multiplying many polynomials, we can improve on that, and achieve a constant-round protocol with communication complexity of $O(n^2)$ multiplications. The protocol follows:

1. Parties compute shares of the polynomial $P = (x - x_1)(x - x_2)...(x - x_n)$.
2. Parties compute shares of n polynomials $P_i = P/(x - x_i)$ for all $i \in \{1..n\}$.
3. Parties compute shares of $P_i(x_i)$ and $P_i(x_i)^{-1}$ for all $i \in \{1..n\}$.
4. Parties compute shares of the Lagrange coefficients, $\gamma_i = P_i(x) * P_i(x_i)^{-1}$ for all $i \in \{1..n\}$.
5. Parties compute shares of $f = \sum_{i=1}^{n} \gamma_i * y_i$.

The above protocol is constant round. For step 1, we will use the protocol for multiplying many polynomials which requires $O(n^2)$ multiplications. Step 2 requires n runs of polynomial division protocol, and also requires $O(n^2)$ multiplications. Step 3 consists of n polynomial evaluation (or equivalently, n runs of unbounded fan-in multiplication of n field elements), and n inversion of field elements. Therefore, it requires a total of $O(n^2)$ multiplications. It is easy to see that steps 4 and 5 also require $O(n^2)$ multiplications. Therefore, the above protocol has a total communication complexity of $O(n^2)$ multiplications.

7 Computing GCD of Polynomials

Given shares of $f(x)$, and $g(x)$ in $F[x]$, where $deg(f) = n$, $deg(g) = m$, and $n \geq m$, parties want to compute shares of $d(x) = gcd(f, g)$. Here, we assume that we leak the degree of the gcd (so that everyone learns number of coefficients of the gcd).

Euclid's Algorithm for computing the gcd of two polynomials is sequential in nature. Particularly, it requires the parties to perform $O(n)$ division protocols in a sequential manner. Furthermore, we cannot use the division algorithm we introduced in Section 4, to improve the communication complexity of a Euclid-based protocol. The reason is that, as we mentioned earlier, the division protocol assumes that the polynomials have non-zero coefficients for their highest degree. This might not be true during all the steps of Euclid's Algorithm. Therefore, we take a different approach to solving the polynomial gcd problem efficiently and in constant number of rounds.

7.1 Extended Euclidean Algorithm and Subresultants

Consider the Extended Euclidean Algorithm (EEA) below:

$$
\begin{array}{lll}
r_0 = f & s_0 = 1 & t_0 = 0 \\
r_1 = g & s_1 = 0 & t_1 = 1 \\
r_2 = r_0 - r_1 * q_1 & s_2 = s_0 - s_1 * q_1 & t_2 = t_0 - t_1 * q_1 \\
\;\;\;\;\;\;\; \cdot & \;\;\;\;\; \cdot & \;\;\;\; \cdot \\
\;\;\;\;\;\;\; \cdot & \;\;\;\;\; \cdot & \;\;\;\; \cdot \\
\;\;\;\;\;\;\; \cdot & \;\;\;\;\; \cdot & \;\;\;\; \cdot \\
r_{i+1} = r_{i-1} - r_i * q_i & s_{i+1} = s_{i-1} - s_i * q_i & t_{i+1} = t_{i-1} - t_i * q_i \\
\;\;\;\;\;\;\; \cdot & \;\;\;\;\; \cdot & \;\;\;\; \cdot \\
\;\;\;\;\;\;\; \cdot & \;\;\;\;\; \cdot & \;\;\;\; \cdot \\
\;\;\;\;\;\;\; \cdot & \;\;\;\;\; \cdot & \;\;\;\; \cdot \\
0 = r_{l-1} - q_l * r_l & s_{l+1} = s_{l-1} - q_l * r_l & t_{l+1} = t_{l-1} - q_l * r_l
\end{array}
\tag{5}
$$

One invariant of the EEA is that $r_i = s_i * f + t_i * g$ for all $i \in \{0..l\}$. Note that $d(x) = r_l(x)$, and $s_l(x)$, and $t_l(x)$ are the *Bezout coefficients*. We denote the degree sequence of EEA by $(n_0, n_1, n_2, \ldots, n_l)$, where $n_i = deg(r_i)$ for all $i \in \{0..l\}$.

Next, we review some of the properties of subresultants of two polynomials. These properties will help us design a constant-round protocol for polynomial gcd.

Some Properties of the Subresultants. Consider the polynomials $f(x) = \sum_{j=0}^{n} a_j x^j$ and $g(x) = \sum_{j=0}^{m} b_j x^j$. The subresultant matrix S_i (for $i \in \{0..m\}$) is a $(n + m - 2i) * (n + m - 2i)$ matrix of the form:

$$
S_i =
\begin{bmatrix}
a_n & & & b_m & & \\
a_{n-1} & a_n & & b_{m-1} & b_m & \\
\vdots & & \ddots & \vdots & & \ddots \\
a_{n-m+i+1} & \cdots & \cdots & a_n & b_{i+1} & \cdots & \cdots & b_m \\
\vdots & & & \vdots & \vdots & & & \ddots \\
a_{i+1} & \cdots & \cdots & a_m & b_{m-n+i+1} & \cdots & \cdots & \cdots & \cdots & b_m \\
\vdots & & & \vdots & \vdots & & & & \vdots \\
\vdots & & & \vdots & \vdots & & & & \vdots \\
a_{2i-m+1} & \cdots & \cdots & a_i & b_{2i-n+1} & \cdots & \cdots & \cdots & \cdots & b_i
\end{bmatrix}
\tag{6}
$$

All the entries in the S_i's are coefficients of f and g. The following two theorems about the subresultant matrices will be useful (please refer to [GG03] for proof details).

Theorem 1. *Integer k appears in the degree-sequence of EEA, iff $det(S_k) \neq 0$.*

Theorem 2. *If $k = n_i$, where n_i is the ith element in the degree sequence of EEA, the linear system $S_k * x = [0, ..., 0, 1]^T$ has a unique solution x such that $s_i = x[1...(m-k)]$, and $t_i = x[(m-k+1)...(m+n-2k)]$.*

7.2   Shared GCD of Two Polynomials

Here is the intuition behind our protocol for computing shares of the gcd of two shared polynomials. First, parties compute $p = deg(d(x)) = deg(r_l(x))$ without learning anything else. Note that based on Theorem 1, p is the only element in the degree sequence with the property that:

$$det(S_p) \neq 0, \text{ and } det(S_i) = 0 \text{ for all } 0 \leq i < p. \tag{7}$$

Parties then jointly solve a linear system (Theorem 2) to compute shares of the *Bezout* coefficients $s_l(x)$ and $t_l(x)$ from which shares of the gcd can be derived. The polynomial gcd protocol follows:

The Protocol

1. Parties compute shares of $det(S_i)$ for all $i \in \{0..m\}$.
2. Parties compute shares of non-zero random field elements $h_1, ..., h_m$.
3. Parties compute shares of $b_0, ..., b_m$ such that $b_k = \sum_{i=0}^{k} h_i * det(S_i)$ for all $k \in \{0..m\}$. (Note: $b_i = 0$ for all $0 \leq i < p$. $b_i \neq 0$ for all $p \leq i \leq m$, with high probability).
4. Parties generate shares of non-zero random elements $r_1, ..., r_m$ of the field.
5. Parties compute and announce shares of values $c_i = r_i * b_i$.
6. Note that $c_i = 0$ for all $0 \leq i < p$, and $c_i \neq 0$ for all $p \leq i \leq m$. By counting the non-zero c_i's, parties learn $p = deg(d(x))$ (Nothing else is learned, since all the non-zero c_i's are random).
7. Parties compute shares of the solution to the linear system $S_p * X = [0, ..., 1]^T$, and extract shares of the $s_l(x)$ and $t_l(x)$ from the unique shared solution (based on Theorem 2).
8. Parties compute shares of $d = f * s_l + g * t_l$. (Parties only consider the first $p + 1$ coefficients of the result).

All the steps of the protocol can be performed in constant number of rounds. [CD01] introduces an efficient, and constant-round algorithm for computing determinant of a shared matrix (step 1). Since S_p is always invertible, the linear system of step 7 can be solved using the matrix inversion protocol of [BB89].

The communication complexity of the protocol is dominated by step 1, in which determinants of $O(n)$ matrices are computed, and each matrix is $O(n)$ by

$O(n)$. In the computational setting, our protocol is not very appealing. In particular, the general MPC protocol of [BMR90] can compute the gcd of two polynomials in constant number of rounds and with communication complexity of $O(n^2)$ multiplications. Our protocol is more interesting in the *information-theoretic* setting. In the information-theoretic setting, we only know of general constant-round protocols for problems in NL (please see [FKN94],[IK97],[IK00]). It is unlikely that these general techniques would lead to the same communication-efficiency as our protocol for polynomial gcd.

7.3   Are Two Shared Polynomials Coprime?

Given shares of $f(x)$ and $g(x)$ in $F[x]$, parties want to compute shares of the bit b such that $b = 0$ if $gcd(f, g) = 1$, and $b = 1$ otherwise.

Let us consider the *Syslvester* matrix (S_0) of the two polynomials. The determinant of this matrix is also called the *resultant* of two polynomials. The following is a corollary of theorem 1:

Corollary 1. $gcd(f, g) = 1$ *iff* $det(S_0) \neq 0$.

This leads to the following protocol:

1. Parties compute shares of the determinant of S_0.
2. Parties compute shares of the bit b such that $b = 0$ if $det(S_0) = 0$ and $b = 1$ otherwise.

This reduces the problem to a protocol for testing equality of a shared value with zero. One can use the protocol given in [DFNT05] to implement such a functionality in constant-round.

7.4   Shared GCD of Many Polynomials

Given shares of polynomials $f_1, f_2, \ldots, f_t$ in $F[x]$, parties want to compute shares of $gcd(f_1, ..., f_t)$.

Let $g = f_2 + \sum_{3 \leq i \leq t} r_i f_i$, where r_i's are chosen independently at random from F. The following theorem shows that $gcd(f_1, \ldots, f_t) = gcd(g, f_1)$ with very high probability (see Chapter 6 of [GG03] for proof details).

Theorem 3. *The probability that* $gcd(f_1, \ldots, f_t) \neq gcd(g, f_1)$ *is less than* $(\max_{1 \leq i \leq t} deg(f_i))/q$.

This leads to the following protocol for computing the shared gcd of many shared polynomials:

1. Parties generate shares of random field elements r_i for all $i \in \{1..t\}$.
2. Parties compute shares of $g = f_2 + \sum_{3 \leq i \leq t} r_i f_i$.
3. Parties compute shares of $d = gcd(g, f_1)$ using the given constant-round polynomial gcd.

References

[BB89]   J. Bar-Ilan and D. Beaver. Non-cryptographic fault-tolerant computing in constant number of rounds of interaction. In *Proceedings of ACM PODC, pp. 201-209*, 1989.

[BGW88]   M. Ben-Or, S. Goldwasser, and A. Widgerson. Completeness theorems for non-cryptographic fault-tolerant distributed computation. In *Proceedings of ACM STOC, pages 1-10*, 1988.

[BMR90]   D. Beaver, S. Micali, P. Rogaway. The Round Complexity of Secure Protocols. In *Proceedings of 22nd ACM STOC, pp. 503-513*, 1990.

[CCD88]   D. Chaum, C. Crepeau, and I. Damgard. Multi-party unconditionally secure protocols. In *Proceedings of ACM STOC, pages 11-19*, 1988.

[CD01]   R. Cramer and I. Damgard. Secure distributed linear algebra in a constant number of rounds. In *Proceedings of Crypto, pages 119-136*, August 2001.

[CDN01]   R. Cramer, I. Damgard, and J. Nielsen. Multiparty computation from homomorphic encryption. In *Proceedings of Eurocrypt, pages 280-300*, 2001.

[DFNT05]   I. Damgård, M. Fitzi, J. Buus Nielsen, and T. Toft. How to split a shared secret into shared bits in constant-round. Cryptology ePrint Archive, Report 2005/140, 2005. `http://eprint.iacr.org/`.

[FIPR05]   M. Freedman, Y. Ishai, B. Pinkas, and O. Reingold. Keyword search and oblivious pseudorandom functions. In *Proceedings of Theory of Cryptography Conference*, 2005.

[FKN94]   U. Feige, J. Kilian, M. Naor. A Minimal Model for Secure Computation. In *Proceedings of ACM STOC '94, pp. 554-563*, 1994.

[FNP04]   M. Freedman, K. Nissim, and B. Pinkas. Efficient private matching and set intersection. In *Proceedings of Eurocrypt*, 2004.

[FP00]   P. Fouque and D. Pointcheval. Threshold cryptosystems secure against chosen-ciphertext attacks. In *Proceedings of Asiacrypt, pages 573-84*, 2000.

[GG03]   J. Von Zur Gathen and J. Gerhard. *Modern Computer Algebra*. University Press, Cambridge, 2nd edition, 2003.

[GMW87]   O. Goldreich, S. Micali, and A. Wigderson. How to play any mental game or a completeness theorem for protocols with honest majority. *Proceedings of the 19th Annual ACM symposium on Theory of Computing, pages 218-229*, 1987.

[GRR98]   R. Gennaro, M. Rabin, and T. Rabin. Simplified vss and fast-track multiparty computations with applications to threshold cryptography. In *Proceedings of ACM PODC, pages 101-111*, 1998.

[IK97]   Y. Ishai and E. Kushilevitz. Private Simultaneous Messages Protocols with Applications. In *Proceedings of 5th Israel Symposium on Theoretical Comp. Sc., pp. 174-183*, 1997.

[IK00]   Y. Ishai and E. Kushilevitz. Randomizing polynomials: A New Paradigm for Round-efficient Secure Computation. In *Proceedings of FOCS*, 2000.

[KS05]   Lea Kissner and Dawn Song. Privacy preserving set operations. In *Proceedings of CRYPTO '05*, August 2005.

[Pai00]   P. Paillier. Public-key cryptosystems based on composite degree residuosity classes. In *Proceedings of Asiacrypt, pages 573-84*, 2000.

[Sha79]   A. Shamir. How to share a secret. In *CACM, pages 612-613*, 1979.

[Yao82]   A. C. Yao. Protocols for secure computation. In *Proceedings of Focs, pp. 160-164*, 1982.

[Yao86]   A. C. Yao. How to generate and exchange secrets. In *Proceedings of 27th FOCS, pages 162-167*, 1986.

Generic On-Line/Off-Line Threshold Signatures

Chris Crutchfield, David Molnar, David Turner, and David Wagner

University of California, Berkeley
{cyc, dmolnar, dbturner, daw}@cs.berkeley.edu

Abstract. We present *generic on-line/off-line threshold signatures*, in which the bulk of signature computation can take place "off-line" during lulls in service requests [6]. Such precomputation can help systems using threshold signatures quickly respond to requests. For example, tests of the Pond distributed file system showed that computation of a threshold RSA signature consumes roughly 86% of the time required to service writes to small files [12]. We apply the "hash-sign-switch" paradigm of Shamir and Tauman [16] and the distributed key generation protocol of Gennaro et al. [7] to convert any existing secure threshold digital signature scheme into a threshold on-line/off-line signature scheme. We show that the straightforward attempt at proving security of the resulting construction runs into a subtlety that does not arise for Shamir and Tauman's construction. We resolve the subtlety and prove our signature scheme secure against a static adversary in the partially synchronous communication model under the one-more-discrete-logarithm assumption [2]. The on-line phase of our scheme is efficient: computing a signature takes one round of communication and a few modular multiplications in the common case.

Keywords: On-line/Off-line, Signature Schemes, Threshold Cryptography, Chameleon Hash Functions, Bursty Traffic.

1 Introduction

We present *generic on-line/off-line threshold signatures* to improve the performance of threshold signature schemes, and we show how to construct such signatures from existing threshold signature schemes. In a threshold signature scheme, given a group of n players, and a threshold $t < n$, no subset of the players of size at most t can generate a signature. In other words, unlike standard signature schemes — in which a single player must protect his or her secret key — at most t of the n players in a threshold signature scheme may be compromised without endangering the security of the signature scheme.

Threshold signatures have been applied in several areas to avoid concentrating trust in any single entity. For example, OceanStore [10, 12] is a large-scale distributed data storage system that requires the computation of threshold signatures by an "inner ring" of servers for performing a Byzantine agreement when writing a file. Latency tests in Pond [12], the OceanStore prototype, show that for a 4 KB write, 77.8 ms out of 90.2 ms total time to service the write operation is spent on computing Shoup's RSA threshold signature scheme [17]. Therefore,

M. Yung et al. (Eds.): PKC 2006, LNCS 3958, pp. 58–74, 2006.

computation is the dominant factor; although network communication and local file system access contribute to the time, the bulk of the contribution to service time comes from computing the threshold signatures [12].

Optimizing threshold signature computation is particularly important for distributed file systems because small file writes are common [14]. For example, Baker et al. found that for a file trace from the Sprite file system, 80% of all sequential transfers were less than 2300 bytes in length [1]. For larger files in Pond (2 MB), there is little change in the time spent computing the threshold signature; instead, the time spent on writing the file dominates the threshold signature time. Even so, because threshold signature computation takes up 86% of the time to service a small write in Pond, optimizing this computation improves the common case. Threshold signatures have also been applied as part of other applications, such as distributed certificate authorities, so increasing their performance can help these applications as well [20].

Our Approach. In an on-line/off-line scheme [6], servers can perform the bulk of the computation in an *off-line phase* before even seeing the message to be signed. The results of this precomputation are saved and then used in the *on-line phase* when a message must be signed. Because distributed systems often have "bursty" traffic, resources are available for such precomputation. For example, during the day and evening, traffic is high, but during the night and morning, traffic is low. Enabling threshold signatures to be computed off-line allows systems such as OceanStore to build up a stockpile of precomputed values while traffic is low. These values can be used to quickly sign messages later when traffic is high. Furthermore, other distributed file systems have been observed to have bursty traffic [15, 19], and so they can enjoy the benefits of our on-line/off-line threshold signature scheme. Although there do exist on-line/off-line schemes such as threshold DSS [8], our scheme has the advantage that any existing threshold signature scheme that is secure against random message attack can be used with our on-line/off-line scheme to create a threshold scheme that is secure against an adaptive chosen message attack.

The main idea of our scheme is to apply the "hash-sign-switch" paradigm of Shamir and Tauman [16] to a threshold signature scheme. In this paradigm, we make use of a *chameleon hash function,* which is a special type of two-argument hash function $CH_{HK}(m, r)$ endowed with a public and secret key [9]. Knowledge of the public key HK allows one to evaluate the hash function, while knowledge of the secret key allows one to find collisions. Shamir and Tauman show that any standard signature scheme can be converted to an on-line/off-line scheme as follows: for the off-line phase, compute a standard signature on $CH_{HK}(a, r)$, where a and r are chosen randomly. Then, at the on-line phase, given the message m, use the secret key to find an r' such that $CH_{HK}(m, r') = CH_{HK}(a, r)$. The signature on $CH_{HK}(a, r)$ together with r' then forms a signature on the message m; in a sense, we "switch" m for the random value a. We refer to the signed value of $CH_{HK}(a, r)$ as the *signature stamp.* If finding a collision in the chameleon hash is more efficient than signing the message directly (as is the case for several chameleon hash functions), this is a net performance win.

Overview of Our Construction. For our work, we focus on the specific chameleon hash function $CH_{HK}(m, r) = g^r h^m \bmod p$ with public key $HK = (p, g, h)$ and the secret key y is the discrete logarithm of h to the base g. We show how to use the discrete logarithm distributed key generation algorithm of Gennaro et al. [7] to perform chameleon hash key generation and computation of the signature stamp. We then show an efficient distributed algorithm for finding collisions with low overhead per player. We stress that *no trusted dealer* is required by our scheme; given an underlying threshold signature scheme with distributed key generation and distributed signing algorithms, we obtain a fully distributed signature scheme.

We also show methods for guaranteeing the robustness of our scheme using zero-knowledge proofs for verification. We provide two variants. The first is non-interactive and secure in the Random Oracle Model. The second uses an observation of Damgård and Dupont to obtain robustness at the cost of limited interaction but is secure without random oracles [4]. In both cases, instead of running verification each time a signature must be generated, we decide to forego this step and be *optimistic* because, as observed in [4], the signature shares will be correct almost always. If the signature created is not valid, then we can run the verification procedure in order to expose the corrupted players. The full details for our signature scheme appear in Sect. 3.

A Subtlety In The Proof. Surprisingly, the straightforward adaptation of the proof of Shamir and Tauman for non-threshold on-line/off-line signature schemes *fails* to establish security for our new on-line/off-line threshold scheme. The subtlety is that in our scheme, the "signature stamp" value $CH_{HK}(m, r)$ is disclosed to all players at the close of our off-line threshold phase, including the adversary. While m and r are not disclosed, the output of the chameleon hash must be broadcast to allow for "black-box" use of the underlying threshold signature scheme in creating the stamp. As a result, any attempt at simulating the adversary's view of a signature query is "pinned down" by the value of the chameleon hash encoded in the stamp. In contrast, Shamir and Tauman do not reveal any chameleon hash values associated with a message to the adversary until *after* a signing query for that message is made. Therefore, their reduction is not "pinned down" in the same way and can easily answer adversary signing queries by simply evaluating the chameleon hash function on the queried message. While this is not an attack on the threshold on-line/off-line scheme, it shows that a new idea appears necessary to prove the scheme secure.

We resolve this subtlety by first introducing a new assumption for chameleon hash functions, which we call the *one-more-r assumption*. Informally, the new assumption says that given a sequence of random "challenge" outputs $v_1, \ldots, v_n$ of the chameleon hash function, the adversary may adaptively pick values v_i, provide messages m_i, and then learn r_i such that $CH_{HK}(m_i, r_i) = v_i$. Then, even given this extra information, the adversary has negligible advantage at inverting the chameleon hash on any given challenge value not picked. We show that this new assumption is sufficient to prove security of our scheme. Then we justify the assumption in the case of the $g^r h^m \bmod p$ chameleon hash by showing it is implied by the *one-more-discrete-logarithm* assumption of Bellare et al [2]. This establishes the security of our scheme based on a standard assumption. The details for showing our scheme is existentially unforgeable and robust against a static adversary are in Sect. 5.

Performance Results. We analyze the performance of our scheme in Sect. 6. We show the cost of our off-line phase is dominated by the cost of the distributed discrete logarithm key generation protocol. While our off-line phase in consequence requires several rounds of communication and computation, we argue that this overhead uses resources that would otherwise sit idle. If a new request arrives at a server during a busy time, the servers can simply fall back to directly computing a threshold signature.

Finally, we show that our optimistic on-line phase obtains a factor of $\mathcal{O}\left(\frac{k}{t}\right)$ improvement in computation compared to Shoup's RSA threshold signature scheme, where k is a security parameter, while also requiring only one round of communication [17]. For example, with the parameters suggested for Pond, this is a factor of 1024 improvement. Our scheme does, however, make a tradeoff by incurring a larger cost in the off-line phase to obtain a quick on-line phase.

1.1 Previous Work

The first on-line/off-line signature scheme was developed by Even, Goldreich, and Micali [6]. This scheme allowed for the conversion of any standard signature scheme into a one-time on-line/off-line signature scheme. Their result, however, increased the size of the signature by a quadratic factor. In order to mitigate this, Shamir and Tauman [16] applied the results of Krawczyk and Rabin [9], using chameleon hash functions to construct a one-time on-line/off-line signature scheme that only increases the size of the signature by a factor of two. Although smart cards appear to be an important application of on-line/off-line signatures as noted in [6, 16], the application to bursty traffic has received little attention.

The origins of threshold signatures and threshold cryptography can be traced back to Desmedt and Frankel [5]. Some examples of threshold signatures include a robust threshold DSS signature scheme, which is an on-line/off-line scheme, by Gennaro et al. [8], and a robust, non-interactive threshold RSA signature scheme by Shoup [17]. The latter construction is the signature scheme implemented in Pond [12], a prototype version of the OceanStore [10] design, and partly our motivation for this paper.

1.2 Our Results

We compare our optimistic on-line/off-line threshold signature scheme with that of Shoup's signature scheme [17]. Shoup describes two variants of an RSA threshold signature scheme, and it is the first variant that we compare our scheme against. In both schemes, let n be the number of players, $t < \frac{n}{3}$ be the threshold[1], and $k \in \mathbb{N}$ be a security parameter. Our construction requires $2t+1$ players

---

[1] Shoup's RSA threshold signature scheme can actually tolerate a threshold of $t < \frac{n}{2}$ and only needs $t + 1$ players to generate a signature.

Table 1. Comparison between Shoup's Threshold RSA and our On-line/Off-line Threshold Scheme where in this paper $K_{\mathrm{DKG}} \in \mathcal{O}(tk^3)$

Threshold Sig. Schemes:	Shoup's RSA Scheme	Our On-line/Off-line Scheme
Key Generation	$\mathcal{O}(k^2 nt \log t + k^3) + K_{\mathrm{RSA}}$	$K_{\mathrm{On/Off}} + K_{\mathrm{DKG}}$
Off-line Phase	None	$3K_{\mathrm{DKG}} + \mathcal{O}(k^2) + \tau$
On-line Player	$\mathcal{O}(k^3)$	$\mathcal{O}(k^2)$
On-line Reconstruction	$\mathcal{O}(tk^3)$	$\mathcal{O}(t^2 k^2)$
On-line Rounds of Comm.	1	1

to construct a signature and tolerates the participation of at most t corrupted players. We analyze the bit complexity of both schemes using the following metrics and show the results in Table 1:

- Key Generation Complexity — Work done to perform key generation and distributing private key shares among the players. Let K_{RSA} denote the bit complexity for generating the RSA public and private keys, let $K_{\mathrm{On/Off}}$ denote the bit complexity for generating public and private keys in our scheme, and let K_{DKG} denote the bit complexity for distributed key generation.
- Off-line Phase Complexity — Work done to perform precomputation, meaning the computation performed for a signature before a message arrives. Furthermore, let τ be the bit complexity for generating a standard threshold signature.
- On-line Player Complexity — Work done by a player in computing its signature share when a message arrives. Note that all players compute their signature share in parallel.
- On-line Reconstruction Complexity — Work done by the players in combining all of the signature shares and creating a signature.
- On-line Rounds of Communication — Number of rounds the players need to generate a signature.

Note that Shoup's RSA signature scheme is not considered to be an on-line/off-line scheme because no precomputation is performed. Furthermore, an optimistic version of Shoup's scheme does not reduce its asymptotic complexity in the on-line phase. Finally, referring to Table 1, we see that both schemes only require one round of communication because all of the members of the group do not have to wait for each other when a message m arrives; instead, they can immediately compute their signature shares for m. Because we can set the modulus in both schemes to be of the same size, we can compare fairly based on the bit complexity. A more complete analysis that includes robustness can be found in Sect. 6.

2   Preliminaries

Definition 1 (Negligible Function). A function $\eta : \mathbb{N} \to \mathbb{R}$ is negligible if for all $c > 0$, $\eta(n) < \frac{1}{n^c}$ for all sufficiently large n.

Definition 2 (Discrete Logarithm Assumption). Let $p = 2q+1$ be a prime where q is a random k-bit prime, and let g be a generator for a subgroup of $\mathbb{Z}_p^*$ with order q. For all probabilistic polynomial time algorithms A, if x is chosen uniformly at random from $\mathbb{Z}_q$ and $h = g^x \pmod{p}$, then $\Pr[\mathsf{A}(p,q,g,h) = x] \leq \eta(k)$, where η is a negligible function.

Definition 3 (Chameleon Hash Function). Given a public key HK and a private key or *trapdoor* TK, which are generated with respect to a security parameter k, a message $m \in \mathcal{M}$, and a random $r \in \mathcal{R}$ where $\mathcal{M}$ is the message space, and $\mathcal{R}$ is some finite space, we denote a chameleon hash function [9] by $CH_{HK}(m,r)$, which is a hash function with the following properties:

- **Collision Resistance.** Given any probabilistic polynomial time malicious entity $\mathcal{A}$ that does not know the private key TK, but only the public key HK, define its *advantage* to be the probability of finding (m_1, r_1) and (m_2, r_2) such that $CH_{HK}(m_1, r_1) = CH_{HK}(m_2, r_2)$. We require the advantage of $\mathcal{A}$ to be negligible.
- **Trapdoor Collisions.** There exists a polynomial time algorithm A such that on inputs the pair (HK, TK), a pair $(m_1, r_1) \in \mathcal{M} \times \mathcal{R}$, and a message $m_2 \in \mathcal{M}$, then A outputs r_2 such that $CH_{HK}(m_1, r_1) = CH_{HK}(m_2, r_2)$.
- **Uniform Probability Distribution.** If $r_1 \in \mathcal{R}$ is distributed uniformly, $m_1 \in \mathcal{M}$, and $(m_2, r_2) \in \mathcal{M} \times \mathcal{R}$ such that $CH_{HK}(m_1, r_1) = CH_{HK}(m_2, r_2)$, then r_2 is computationally indistinguishable from uniform over $\mathcal{R}$.

Throughout the rest of this paper, we will work with a particular family of chameleon hash functions based on discrete logarithms. We do so because the discrete logarithm-based hash function is best suited for using Lagrange interpolation. There are also other chameleon hash functions, such as those based on factoring, for example, but the mathematics involved in the interpolation would not be as convenient.

Let $k \in \mathbb{N}$ be a security parameter. We begin by picking a k-bit Germain prime $p' \in \mathbb{N}$, which has the property that $p = 2p' + 1$ and p' are both primes. Although it is not known if there are infinitely many Germain primes, we will assume that we can find one of the appropriate size. Let g' be a generator for $\mathbb{Z}_p^*$. Now let $Q_p \subset \mathbb{Z}_p^*$ denote the subgroup of quadratic residues generated by $g \equiv (g')^2 \pmod{p}$, so that $|Q_p| = \frac{p-1}{2} = p'$. Finally, pick the private key $y \in \mathbb{Z}_{p'}^*$. Then we define our chameleon hash function $CH_{HK} : \mathbb{Z}_{p'} \times \mathbb{Z}_{p'} \to Q_p$ to be

$$CH_{HK}(m,r) = g^{r+ym} \equiv g^r h^m \pmod{p}$$

where $h \equiv g^y \pmod{p}$ and the public key is $HK = (p, g, h)$. Although we choose to work over the group $\mathbb{Z}_p^*$, one could also work with ECC groups or any other group of prime order.

Definition 4 (Signature Scheme). A signature scheme $\mathcal{S}$ is a triple of randomized algorithms (Key-Gen, Sig, Ver) where:

- Key-Gen: $1^* \to \mathcal{PK} \times \mathcal{SK}$ is a key generation algorithm such that on input 1^k, where $k \in \mathbb{N}$ is a security parameter, it outputs (PK, SK), such that $PK \in \mathcal{PK}$, the set of all public verification keys, and $SK \in \mathcal{SK}$, the set of all secret keys.
- Sig: $\mathcal{SK} \times \mathcal{M} \to \mathcal{SIGS}$ is a signing algorithm such that $\mathcal{M}$ is the message space and $\mathcal{SIGS}$ is the signature space. For shorthand, let $S_{SK}(m) = \mathsf{Sig}(SK, m)$ for all $m \in \mathcal{M}$.
- Ver: $\mathcal{PK} \times \mathcal{M} \times \mathcal{SIGS} \to \{\mathsf{Reject}, \mathsf{Accept}\}$ is a verification algorithm such that $\mathsf{Ver}(PK, m, \sigma) = \mathsf{Accept}$ if and only if σ is a possible output of $\mathsf{Sig}(SK, m)$. Again, for shorthand, let $V_{PK}(m, \sigma) = \mathsf{Ver}(PK, m, \sigma)$ for all $m \in \mathcal{M}$ and $\sigma \in \mathcal{SIGS}$.

Definition 5 (Threshold Signature Scheme). Given a signature scheme $\mathcal{S} = (\mathsf{Key\text{-}Gen}, \mathsf{Sig}, \mathsf{Ver})$, a threshold signature scheme $\mathcal{TS}$ for $\mathcal{S}$ is a triple of randomized algorithms $(\mathsf{Thresh\text{-}Key\text{-}Gen}, \mathsf{Thresh\text{-}Sig}, \mathsf{Ver})$ for a set of n players $\mathcal{P} = \{P_1, P_2, \ldots, P_n\}$ with threshold value t where:

- Thresh-Key-Gen is a distributed key generation algorithm used by the players to create $(PK, SK) \in \mathcal{PK} \times \mathcal{SK}$ such that each $P_i \in \mathcal{P}$ receives a share SK_i of the secret key SK.
- Thresh-Sig is a distributed signing algorithm used by the players to create a signature for a message $m \in \mathcal{M}$ such that the output of the algorithm is $S_{SK}(m)$. This algorithm can be decomposed into two algorithms: signature share generation and signature reconstruction.

In this paper, we assume that $\mathcal{TS}$ is *simulatable*, as defined in Gennaro et al. [8]. This means that there exists a simulator $\mathsf{SIM}_1^{\mathcal{TS}}$ which, on input PK, simulates the view of the adversary for a run of Thresh-Key-Gen that fixes the public key to be PK. In addition, there exists a simulator $\mathsf{SIM}_2^{\mathcal{TS}}$ for Thresh-Sig, such that on input the public key PK, the message v, the signature σ of v, and the key shares $x_{i_1}, x_{i_2}, \ldots, x_{i_t}$ of the servers controlled by the adversary, simulates the view of the adversary for a run of Thresh-Sig on v that produces σ.

Definition 6 (Signature Stamp). In an on-line/off-line signature scheme, we call the precomputed signature from the off-line phase a signature stamp.

Definition 7 (Distributed Key Generation). A Distributed Key Generation (DKG) protocol is often used in threshold signature schemes in order to construct the public key and private key. In a DKG protocol with n players, the public key is made known to all players, whereas the private key is known by none. Instead, each player receives a *key share*, from which they can — acting in concert — recover the private key. A DKG protocol is, of course, fully distributed, and requires no trusted dealer.

In this paper, we use a discrete logarithm-based DKG protocol (where the private key is y and the public key is $h = g^y$ for some g), namely the New-DKG protocol as defined by Gennaro et al. [7]. This protocol has the property that there exists a simulator $\mathsf{SIM}^{\mathrm{DKG}}$ that on input h can simulate the interactions of the DKG protocol with a set $\mathcal{P}_{\mathcal{A}} \subset \mathcal{P}$ of players controlled by the adversary $\mathcal{A}$, where $|\mathcal{P}_{\mathcal{A}}| \leq t$, such that the resulting public key produced is fixed to be h. In addition, as a result of this simulation, $\mathsf{SIM}^{\mathrm{DKG}}$ is able to recover the key shares held by the adversary's players $\mathcal{P}_{\mathcal{A}}$.

3   An On-Line/Off-Line Threshold Signature Scheme

We shall construct an optimistic, generic on-line/off-line threshold signature scheme $\mathcal{TS}^{\mathrm{On/Off}} = (\mathsf{On/Off\text{-}Thresh\text{-}Key\text{-}Gen}, \mathsf{Thresh\text{-}Sig\text{-}Off\text{-}line}, \mathsf{Thresh\text{-}Sig\text{-}On\text{-}line}, \mathsf{Ver})$ that does not require the use of a trusted dealer, and we show how existing threshold signature schemes can be used in performing a threshold computation of the signature stamp off-line. Furthermore, we use the New-DKG protocol from Gennaro et al. [7].

3.1   Key Generation (Done Once)

On/Off-Thresh-Key-Gen

Inputs: A threshold signature scheme $\mathcal{TS} = (\mathsf{Thresh\text{-}Key\text{-}Gen}, \mathsf{Thresh\text{-}Sig}, \mathsf{Ver})$, a set of n players $\mathcal{P} = \{P_1, P_2, \ldots, P_n\}$, a threshold $t < \frac{n}{3}$, and a security parameter $k \in \mathbb{N}$.
Public Output: A set of public keys.
Private Output: All players $P_i \in \mathcal{P}$ receive a set of private keys.

1. Run Thresh-Key-Gen on input 1^k to obtain $(PK, SK) \in \mathcal{PK} \times \mathcal{SK}$ and each $P_i \in \mathcal{P}$ receives the secret key share SK_i.
2. Create a random k bit Germain prime $p' \in \mathbb{N}$, where $p = 2p' + 1$ is also a prime, and let g be a generator for Q_p.
3. Use the DKG protocol to create $h = g^y$, where $y \in \mathbb{Z}_{p'}$ is the secret key and $P_i \in \mathcal{P}$ receives the share y_i for a degree t polynomial $p_y(x) \in \mathbb{Z}_{p'}[x]$ such that $p_y(0) = y$.
4. Check that $n < p'$ so that each player $P_i \in \mathcal{P}$ has index $i \in \mathbb{Z}_{p'}^*$. Otherwise abort.
5. Publish the public keys $(PK, HK = (p, g, h))$. All players $P_i \in \mathcal{P}$ retain (SK_i, y_i).

3.2   Off-Line Phase (Done Per Message)

In the off-line phase, we will show how to construct the chameleon hash function and create the signature stamp in a distributed manner.

Thresh-Sig-Off-line

Inputs: The same set of n players $\mathcal{P}$ and a threshold $t < \frac{n}{3}$.
Private Output: A signature stamp.

1. Use the DKG protocol to create g^r, where $r \in \mathbb{Z}_{p'}$ so that P_i receives the share r_i for another degree t polynomial $p_r(x) \in \mathbb{Z}_{p'}[x]$ such that $p_r(0) = r$.
2. Use the DKG protocol to create h^m where $m \in \mathbb{Z}_{p'}$. Each player P_i receives a share m_i for a degree t polynomial $p_m(x) \in \mathbb{Z}_{p'}[x]$ such that $p_m(0) = m$.
3. Finally, the DKG protocol is used to generate shares z_i for each $P_i \in \mathcal{P}$ of a degree $2t$ polynomial $p_0(x) \in \mathbb{Z}_{p'}[x]$ such that $p_0(0) = 0$.
4. Now g^r and h^m are both known to the players, so $CH_{HK}(r, m) = g^r h^m \pmod{p}$.
5. Use Thresh-Sig to compute the signature stamp $S_{SK}(CH_{HK}(r, m))$.

3.3   On-Line Phase (Done Per Message)

Thresh-Sig-On-line

Inputs: A subset $\mathcal{P}' \subset \mathcal{P}$ of size $2t + 1$ and a message $m' \in \mathbb{Z}_{p'}$.
Public Output: A signature for m'.

1. For each $P_i \in \mathcal{P}'$, define col-1$_i = r_i - y_i m'$ and col-2$_i = y_i m_i + z_i$, which are P_i's share of the trapdoor collision. Then, P_i broadcasts the pair (col-1$_i$, col-2$_i$) to all of the other players in $\mathcal{P}'$.
2. Define $f_i(x)$ to be $f_i(x) = \prod_{P_j \in \mathcal{P}' \setminus \{P_i\}} \frac{j-x}{j-i}$, as in the definition of Lagrange interpolation. Now use Lagrange interpolation on the shares to compute the trapdoor collision

$$
\begin{aligned}
r' &= \sum_{P_i \in \mathcal{P}'} (\text{col-1}_i + \text{col-2}_i) f_i(0) \\
&= \sum_{P_i \in \mathcal{P}'} (r_i + y_i m_i + z_i - y_i m') f_i(0) \\
&\equiv r + ym - ym' \pmod{p'}.
\end{aligned}
$$

3. In this way, the signature for message m' is

$$
(S_{SK}(CH_{HK}(m, r)), m', r').
$$

Notice that the definition of col-2$_i$ requires adding the share z_i. This is necessary because we have to multiply the secrets y and m, so each player computes $y_i m_i$ which becomes a share of a degree $2t$ polynomial that is not chosen uniformly at random; thus, adding the share z_i will make the polynomial random. Furthermore, this degree $2t$ polynomial is the reason for requiring $t < \frac{n}{3}$.

3.4 Verification (Done Per Message)

Given the signature (σ, m', r'), where $\sigma \in \mathcal{SIGS}$, simply check that

$$V_{PK}(CH_{HK}(m', r'), \sigma) = \mathsf{Accept}$$

holds true, as in the standard signature scheme.

3.5 Signature Share Verification (Performed If Necessary)

If $V_{PK}(CH_{HK}(m', r'), \sigma) = \mathsf{Reject}$, then some players are sending incorrect shares. In order to ensure robustness, we must be able to construct a valid signature. The naïve solution of trying all possible subsets of size $2t + 1$ to construct a valid signature is unacceptable because there are an exponential number of such subsets. Instead, we will identify and remove the corrupted players. To do so, we have each player in $\mathcal{P}$ check the validity of the pair $(\mathsf{col}\text{-}1_i, \mathsf{col}\text{-}2_i)$ for each player $P_i \in \mathcal{P}'$:

1. **Verifying** $\mathsf{col}\text{-}1_i$. Because g^{r_i} and g^{y_i} are known values from the DKG protocol, we can compute for each $P_i \in \mathcal{P}'$, $g^{r_i} \cdot (g^{y_i})^{-m'} = g^{r_i - y_i m'} \pmod{p}$ and confirm that $g^{\mathsf{col}\text{-}1_i} = g^{r_i - y_i m'}$ as desired.
2. **Verifying** $\mathsf{col}\text{-}2_i$. Although we have access to g^{z_i} from the DKG protocol, we do not have $g^{y_i m_i}$. Instead, what we will do is confirm that the discrete logarithm of $g^{\mathsf{col}\text{-}2_i} g^{-z_i} = g^{\mathsf{col}\text{-}2_i - z_i}$ to the base g^{m_i} is equal to the discrete logarithm of g^{y_i} to the base g. Now we can apply Chaum and Pedersen's ZKP for equality of discrete logarithms [3] with the Fiat-Shamir heuristic: Let $d = g^{y_i}, e = g^{m_i}$, and $f = g^{\mathsf{col}\text{-}2_i - z_i}$. Player $P_i \in \mathcal{P}'$ chooses $r \in \mathbb{Z}_{p'}$ uniformly at random and computes $H(g, d, e, f, g^r, e^r) = c$, where H is a random oracle and c is the challenge. P_i computes $v = y_i c + r$ and broadcasts the pair (c, v). Finally, all players compute and confirm that $H(g, d, e, f, g^v d^{-c}, e^v f^{-c}) = c$.

If any of the shares are deemed incorrect, then broadcast a *complaint* against P_i. If there are at least $t + 1$ complaints, then clearly P_i must be corrupt since with at most t malicious players, there can be at most t false complaints. Also, if P_i is corrupt, there will always be enough honest players to generate at least $t + 1$ complaints and P_i will surely be disqualified in this case. Once eliminated, P_i is removed from $\mathcal{P}'$ and is replaced with a new player, thus resulting in a new signature. As long as at most t players are corrupted, there will always be enough honest players to create a valid signature.

4 Security Model

4.1 Security Definitions

We define two assumptions that we will use in our proof. The first is the one-more-discrete-logarithm assumption introduced by Bellare et al. [2]

Definition 8 (One-More-Discrete-Logarithm Assumption). We let $p = 2q + 1$ be a prime where q is a random k-bit prime, and let g be a generator for a subgroup of $\mathbb{Z}_p^*$ with order q. We let $n : \mathbb{N} \to \mathbb{N}$ be a function of k. Now let $\left(x_1, x_2, \ldots, x_{n(k)}, x_{n(k)+1}\right)$ be elements of $\mathbb{Z}_q$ chosen uniformly at random, and for each $i \in \{1, 2, \ldots, n(k) + 1\}$, define $z_i = g^{x_i} \pmod{p}$. Now let the adversary $\mathcal{A}$ have access to a discrete log oracle DLog such that if $x \in \mathbb{Z}_q$, $z = g^x \pmod{p}$, then $\mathsf{DLog}(g, z) = x$. In the one-more discrete-logarithm problem [2], $\mathcal{A}^{\mathsf{DLog}}$ is given $\left(z_1, z_2, \ldots, z_{n(k)+1}\right)$ and must output $\left(x_1, x_2, \ldots, x_{n(k)+1}\right)$ by querying DLog at most $n(k)$ times. The assumption is $\Pr[\mathcal{A}^{\mathsf{DLog}}(g, z_1, z_2, \ldots, z_{n(k)+1}) = \left(x_1, x_2, \ldots, x_{n(k)+1}\right)] \leq \eta(k)$, where η is a negligible function.

We define a similar assumption that is related to finding collisions in a chameleon hash function. We will use this assumption to show our new scheme is secure. In Sect. 5.2, we show that this assumption is implied by the one-more-discrete-logarithm assumption for the chameleon hash function we use.

Definition 9 (One-More-R Assumption). As above, we let g be a generator for a subgroup of $\mathbb{Z}_p^*$ with order q, a k-bit prime. In addition, we let k' be randomly chosen from $\mathbb{Z}_q$ and let $h = g^{k'}$. We let $n : \mathbb{N} \to \mathbb{N}$ be a function of k. Now let $\left(v_1, v_2, \ldots, v_{n(k)}, v_{n(k)+1}\right)$ be randomly chosen elements in the range of $CH_{HK}(\cdot)$. Now we give the adversary $\mathcal{A}$ access to a $\mathsf{Get\text{-}An\text{-}R}(v, m)$ oracle, such that if v is an output of the chameleon hash function and $r = \mathsf{Get\text{-}An\text{-}R}(v, m)$, then $CH_{HK}(m, r) = v$. In the One-More-R problem, $\mathcal{A}^{\mathsf{Get\text{-}An\text{-}R}}$ is given $\left(v_1, v_2, \ldots, v_{n(k)+1}\right)$ and with at most $n(k)$ queries to $\mathsf{Get\text{-}An\text{-}R}$, must output $\left((m_1, r_1), (m_2, r_2), \ldots, (m_{n(k)+1}, r_{n(k)+1})\right)$ such that $v_i = CH_{HK}(m_i, r_i)$. The assumption is that $\Pr[\mathcal{A}^{\mathsf{Get\text{-}An\text{-}R}}(g, h, v_1, v_2, \ldots, v_{n(k)+1}) = \left((m_1, r_1), (m_2, r_2), \ldots, (m_{n(k)+1}, r_{n(k)+1})\right)] \leq \eta(k)$, where η is a negligible function.

4.2 Adversarial Model

We assume that there is a static adversary $\mathcal{A}$ that corrupts some subset of the players in $\mathcal{P}$ before beginning the threshold signature scheme. Furthermore, we can analyze two different types of static adversaries: one that compromises before the off-line phase and the other compromises after the off-line phase terminates. We assume the former case in our proof of existential unforgeability. As for the communication model, we assume that all players are connected by secure point-to-point channels. Furthermore, we will assume a partially synchronous communication model during the key generation and off-line phases for the purpose of using the DKG protocol of Gennaro et al. [7].

5 Proof of Security

5.1 Robustness

Theorem 1. *Suppose that an adversary corrupts at most* $t < \frac{n}{3}$ *players. Then, our on-line/off-line threshold signature scheme* $\mathcal{TS}^{\mathrm{On/Off}}$ *is robust.*

Proof. We need to show completeness, soundness, and zero knowledge simulatability of the signature share verification protocol when verifying col-2_i from player $P_i \in \mathcal{P}'$.

- **Completeness:** An honest player $P_i \in \mathcal{P}'$ should convince any verifier that the protocol was followed with high probability. In fact, if the signature share verification protocol is correctly followed, then the verifier will accept with probability 1.
- **Soundness:** No corrupted player $P_i \in \mathcal{P}'$ should be able to fool any verifier into accepting incorrect shares with high probability. Using the definitions for e, d, and f from Sect. 3.5, we require that both

$$
\begin{aligned}
g^v d^{-c} &\equiv g^r \pmod{p} \\
e^v f^{-c} &\equiv e^r \pmod{p}
\end{aligned} \quad .
$$

Therefore, $g^v d^{-c} \equiv g^{v-y_i c} \equiv g^r \pmod{p}$ if and only if $v \equiv y_i c + r \pmod{p'}$. In addition, $e^v f^{-c} \equiv g^{m_i v} g^{(\text{col-}2_i - z_i)(-c)} \equiv (g^{m_i})^r \pmod{p}$, which implies that $m_i v - c(\text{col-}2_i - z_i) \equiv m_i r \pmod{p'}$. By using $e^v f^{-c} \equiv e^r \pmod{p}$ from above, we see that $m_i y_i c \equiv c(\text{col-}2_i - z_i) \pmod{p'}$. If $c \not\equiv 0 \pmod{p'}$, then clearly col-2_i is the correct share. If $c \equiv 0 \pmod{p'}$, then col-2_i may be incorrect. By the Discrete Logarithm Assumption, no probabilistic polynomial time adversary can produce such a v with non-negligible probability.
- **Zero Knowledge Simulatability:** No cheating verifier should learn anything useful after running the protocol. We can easily construct a simulator S which simulates the view of the verifier when verifying P_i's col-2_i. To do so, S selects c and v uniformly at random and fixes $H(g, d, e, f, g^v d^{-c}, e^v f^{-c})$ to be c, since we are working in the Random Oracle model. Thus, S has recreated the view of the verifier without knowing P_i's secret key share y_i, so the signature share verification protocol has zero knowledge.

As a result, our on-line/off-line threshold signature scheme is robust. We sketch an alternative approach without random oracles in Sect. 7.   □

5.2   Existential Unforgeability

The proof of existential unforgeability will be in a similar style to the proof in Shamir and Tauman [16]. First we make use of the following Lemma to show that our One-More-R assumption is implied by a standard assumption:

Lemma 1. *Suppose that there exists an adversary $\mathcal{B}$ that breaks the One-More-R assumption for the discrete logarithm chameleon hash with advantage greater than ε. Then there exists an algorithm $\mathcal{A}$ that breaks the One-More-Discrete-Log assumption with advantage greater than ε.*

Proof. We let $\mathcal{A}$ respond to $\mathcal{B}$'s queries in the One-More-R problem. $\mathcal{A}$ is given as input g and $(z_1, z_2, \ldots, z_{n(k)+1})$. Let $\mathcal{A}$ be described as follows:

1. Pick y uniformly at random in $\mathbb{Z}_{p'}$.
2. Let $h = g^y$, and initialize $\mathcal{B}$ with g and h.
3. For $1 \leq i \leq n(k) + 1$, pick m_i uniformly in $\mathbb{Z}_{p'}$ and let $v_i = z_i h^{m_i}$.
4. Send $\mathcal{B}$ the tuple $\left(v_1, v_2, \ldots, v_{n(k)+1}\right)$.
5. Whenever $\mathcal{B}$ makes a Get-An-R(v, m) query, receive $t = \mathsf{DLog}(g, v)$. Return the value $t - ym$ to $\mathcal{B}$.
6. If $\mathcal{B}$ successfully outputs $\left((m'_1, r'_1), (m'_2, r'_2), \ldots, (m'_{n(k)+1}, r'_{n(k)+1})\right)$ where $CH_{HK}(m'_i, r'_i) = v_i$ for all i, $\mathcal{A}$ returns $\left(x_1, x_2, \ldots, x_{n(k)+1}\right)$ where $x_i = r'_i + y(m'_i - m_i)$. Otherwise, abort.

Clearly, we have $\varepsilon < \mathsf{Adv}\ \mathcal{B} \leq \mathsf{Adv}\ \mathcal{A}$.   □

Using the One-More-R assumption, we can prove that our on-line/off-line threshold signature scheme is secure against adaptive chosen message attack.

Theorem 2. *Let $\mathcal{TS} = $ (Thresh-Key-Gen, Thresh-Sig, Ver) be a given simulatable threshold signature scheme. Then we let $\mathcal{TS}^{\mathrm{On/Off}} = $ (On/Off-Thresh-Key-Gen, Thresh-Sig-Off-line, Thresh-Sig-On-line, Ver) be the resulting On-line/Off-line Threshold Signature scheme. If $\mathcal{TS}^{\mathrm{On/Off}}$ is existentially forgeable by an q-adaptive chosen message attack with success probability ε, then one of the following must hold:*

1. *There exists a probabilistic algorithm that breaks either the One-More-R assumption or the collision resistance of CH_{HK} with probability at least $\frac{\varepsilon}{2}$.*
2. *The underlying threshold signature scheme $\mathcal{TS}$ is existentially forgeable by a q-random message attack with probability at least $\frac{\varepsilon}{2}$.*

Proof. Suppose that an adversary $\mathcal{A}$ forges a signature in the $\mathcal{TS}^{\mathrm{On/Off}}$ scheme with a q-chosen message attack with probability ε. Now let $\{m_1, m_2, \ldots, m_q\}$ be the q messages chosen by $\mathcal{A}$ to be signed by the $\mathcal{TS}^{\mathrm{On/Off}}$ scheme. Let $\{(\sigma_1, m_1, r_1), \ldots, (\sigma_q, m_q, r_q)\}$ be the signatures produced in this fashion by the $\mathcal{TS}^{\mathrm{On/Off}}$ scheme. Then $\mathcal{A}$ outputs a signature forgery (σ, m, r) such that $V_{PK}(CH_{HK}(m, r), \sigma) = \mathsf{Accept}$ and $m \neq m_i$ for all i, with probability ε. Moreover, either there exists an i such that $CH_{HK}(m_i, r_i) = CH_{HK}(m, r)$ or there does not exist such an i. One of these cases occurs with probability at least $\frac{\varepsilon}{2}$.

If the first case holds with probability at least $\frac{\varepsilon}{2}$, then we define a simulator S that breaks the One-More-R assumption. S is given as input the public bases g and h, as well as the set of challenges $(v_1, v_2, \ldots, v_{n(k)+1})$.

S simulates the On/Off-Thresh-Key-Gen phase with $\mathcal{A}$. When the simulation gets to the point where h is to be generated by using the DKG protocol, S uses $\mathsf{SIM}^{\mathrm{DKG}}(h)$, the DKG simulator, to "fix" the result of the DKG run to be h.

On the ith run of the Thresh-Sig-Off-line phase, S simulates the phase as normal. However, when it reaches the point where h^m is to be generated using the DKG protocol, it uses $\mathsf{SIM}^{\mathrm{DKG}}(v_i g^{-r})$ to fix the value of h^m so that the resulting chameleon hash $g^r h^m$ equals the given v_i value. S then simulates the rest of the phase as normal.

On the jth run of the Thresh-Sig-On-line phase, with input m'_j specified by $\mathcal{A}$, S simulates the phase as normal. Suppose that the players involved are $\mathcal{P}' \subset \mathcal{P}$. Of the players in $\mathcal{P}'$, without loss of generality let $\mathcal{P}_{\mathcal{A}} = \{P_1, P_2, \dots, P_t\} \subset \mathcal{P}'$ be the players controlled by the adversary $\mathcal{A}$. Since S "controls" more than t players, it is able to reconstruct the values of $r_i, y_i, m_i,$ and z_i for all $P_i \in \mathcal{P}_{\mathcal{A}}$ from its own shares, since all were generated by the DKG protocol. Hence S is able to recover col-1_i and col-2_i for all $P_i \in \mathcal{P}_{\mathcal{A}}$. Now S fixes $P_l \in \mathcal{P}' \setminus \mathcal{P}_{\mathcal{A}}$. For each $P_i \in \mathcal{P}' \setminus (\mathcal{P}_{\mathcal{A}} \cup \{P_l\})$, S picks col-1_i and col-2_i uniformly at random and broadcasts them. In addition, S queries the Get-An-R oracle on m'_j and v_j to receive r'_j. With this information S can simply fix the value of (col-1_l, col-2_l) such that the interpolation of all the col-1_i + col-2_i values comes out to be r'_j.

At the end, $\mathcal{A}$ produces (σ, m, r) such that $V_{PK}(CH_{HK}(m,r), \sigma) = \textsf{Accept}$ and there exists an i such that $CH_{HK}(m, r) = v_i$. If v_i was not used by S in a run of Thresh-Sig-On-line, then S has produced One-More-R value, namely r. On the other hand, if v_i was used by S, then we have a collision with CH_{HK}.

If the second case holds with probability at least $\frac{\varepsilon}{2}$, then we define a simulator S that existentially forges a signature under a random message attack on the underlying threshold signature $\mathcal{TS}$. In addition, we let $\textsf{SIM}_1^{\mathcal{TS}}$ and $\textsf{SIM}_2^{\mathcal{TS}}$ be defined as in Definition 5.

S simulates the On/Off-Thresh-Key-Gen phase as normal, except during the execution of Thresh-Key-Gen. In this case, S uses $\textsf{SIM}_1^{\mathcal{TS}}$ to fix the public key for $\mathcal{TS}$ to be the public key for the signing oracle $\textsf{Sig}_{\mathcal{TS}}$.

On the ith run of the off-line phase, let S simulate it as normal, except for the computation of h^m and running Thresh-Sig. Let S query $\textsf{Sig}_{\mathcal{TS}}$, which outputs (v_i, σ_i), where v_i is chosen uniformly at random and $V_{PK}(v_i, \sigma_i) = \textsf{Accept}$. Next, use $\textsf{SIM}^{\text{DKG}}(v_i g^{-r})$ to fix h^m. Finally, S then uses $\textsf{SIM}_2^{\mathcal{TS}}$ to simulate a run of Thresh-Sig with S on input v_i, such that the output is fixed to σ_i. We can do this because our assumption is that Thresh-Sig is simulatable.

Each run of the on-line phase is simulated as normal by S. At the end, $\mathcal{A}$ produces (σ, m, r) such that $V_{PK}(CH_{HK}(m,r), \sigma) = \textsf{Accept}$ and for all i, $v_i \neq CH_{HK}(m, r)$. But in this case, S has forged a signature σ on a message $CH_{HK}(m, r)$ not queried to the signing oracle $\textsf{Sig}_{\mathcal{TS}}$. □

From this, we can derive the following theorem:

Theorem 3. *Suppose that a static adversary corrupts at most $t < \frac{n}{3}$ players before beginning the off-line phase. Then our on-line/off-line threshold signature scheme $\mathcal{TS}^{\text{On}/\text{Off}}$ is existentially unforgeable against adaptive chosen message attacks assuming that the underlying threshold signature scheme $\mathcal{TS}$ is existentially unforgeable against random message attacks.*

6 Evaluation

We analyze the number of bit operations required by our scheme, as previously shown in Table 1. First, in our scheme, is the threshold key generation. The bit complexity of Thresh-Key-Gen for $\mathcal{TS}$, as well as generating a Germain prime is included in $K_{\text{On/Off}}$. Afterwards, we invoke the **New-DKG** protocol [7] once, and an analysis shows that it requires $3t + 4$ exponentiations, so $K_{\text{DKG}} \in \mathcal{O}(tk^3)$ since an exponentiation requires $\mathcal{O}(k^3)$ bit operations over $\mathbb{Z}_p$. Thus, the key generation phase takes $K_{\text{On/Off}} + K_{\text{DKG}}$ bit operations.

Next, we analyze our off-line phase. First, we invoke the **New-DKG** protocol three times, so this gives $3K_{\text{DKG}}$. Next, we have g^r and h^m, so we multiply both terms to get $CH_{HK}(r, m)$. Moreover, a single multiplication requires $\mathcal{O}(k^2)$ bit operations over $\mathbb{Z}_p$. Finally, the signature stamp $S_{SK}(CH_{HK}(m, r))$ requires τ bit operations. Thus the off-line phases requires a total of $3K_{\text{DKG}} + \mathcal{O}(k^2) + \tau$ bit operations.

For our on-line complexity, we can separate a player's computational complexity for generating a signature share from the signature reconstruction complexity. Each player $P_i \in \mathcal{P}'$ performs two additions and two multiplications when computing col-1_i and col-2_i. The on-line signature reconstruction requires computing $f_i(0)$, which is $2t$ multiplications, and this is done for all $P_i \in \mathcal{P}'$, so we have a total of $(2t + 1)^2$ multiplications when we compute r'. Only addition of the $2(2t + 1)$ shares as well as performing $2t$ subtractions when computing $f_i(0)$ is required giving a total of $2t(2t + 1) + 2(2t + 1) - 1 = 4t^2 + 6t + 1$ additions. Furthermore, each addition over $\mathbb{Z}_p$ requires $\mathcal{O}(k)$ bit operations. Already we see that the number of multiplications in the on-line phase is substantially fewer than k since the threshold t is quite small when compared to a k bit prime. If verification of the signature shares is required, then each share requires six modular exponentiations. A summary of the number of operations performed appears in Table 2.

Table 2. Our On-line Phase Computational Complexity

Our On-line Phase Complexity	Additions	Multiplications	Exponentiations
Player Signature Share	2	2	0
Signature Reconstruction	$4t^2 + 6t + 1$	$4t^2 + 4t + 1$	0
Signature Share Verification	0	3	6

We review the complexity of Shoup's RSA threshold signature scheme [17], which was also shown in Table 1. The key generation phase of Shoup's signature scheme requires a trusted party, but asymptotically the computation cost is the same as our distributed key generation. In Shoup's on-line phase, the reconstruction complexity, once again, can be separated from the share verification complexity. The reconstruction of the signature requires t modular exponentiations, $t - 1$ modular multiplications, and one invocation of the extended Euclidean algorithm. Finally, verifying an individual signature share also requires six modular exponentiations and three modular multiplications. Although both threshold signature schemes have approximately the same signature share verification complexity, we have managed to avoid any modular exponentiations in the reconstruction complexity of our signature scheme.

7 Extensions

7.1 Using Merkle Trees for Batching

We explained earlier that computing a threshold signature when performing writes for small files in Pond [12] is expensive, while for large files, the time spent computing the threshold signature is negligible compared to the actual write. In the event that a threshold signature must be quickly computed on demand, our scheme immediately becomes attractive over other schemes. This is especially true for Pond when computing threshold signatures for small writes.

One way of improving performance is to batch messages, an idea due to Wong and Lam [18], by using Merkle hash trees [11]. Instead of signing messages one by one, we wait for n messages to arrive and then build a Merkle tree over these messages. If there are a total of n messages and the batch size is B, then a total of $\lceil \frac{n}{B} \rceil$ signature stamps are needed. This approach does trade latency for throughput, and it depends on how much time can be spent waiting for messages to arrive on-line. In fact, Merkle trees for batching has been applied to Shoup's scheme in OceanStore in order to increase throughput for small updates [13].

7.2 Eliminating Random Oracles

By using the techniques in [4], which eliminates the random oracle from the verification step in Shoup's RSA threshold scheme, we can eliminate the random oracle H, but at the cost of including interaction.

Acknowledgments

We thank Lea Kissner, Emil Ong, Naveen Sastry, Umesh Shankar, and Hoeteck Wee for providing helpful feedback on an earlier draft of this work, as well as the anonymous referees for their helpful comments. This research was supported by grant NSF CNS-0093337.

References

[1] Mary G. Baker, John H. Hartman, Michael D. Kupfer, Ken W. Shirriff, and John K. Ousterhout. Measurements of a Distributed File System. In *Proceedings of 13th ACM Symposium on Operating Systems Principles*, pages 198–212. Association for Computing Machinery SIGOPS, 1991.

[2] Mihir Bellare, Chanathip Namprempre, David Pointcheval, and Michael Semanko. The One-More-RSA-Inversion Problems and the Security of Chaum's Blind Signature Scheme. *Journal of Cryptology*, 16(3):185–215, 2003.

[3] David Chaum and Torben P. Pedersen. Wallet Databases with Observers. In *CRYPTO*, volume 740 of *Lecture Notes in Computer Science*, pages 89–105. Springer-Verlag, 1992.

[4] Ivan Damgård and Kasper Dupont. Efficient Threshold RSA Signatures with General Moduli and No Extra Assumptions. In *Public Key Cryptography*, volume 3386 of *Lecture Notes in Computer Science*, pages 346–361. Springer-Verlag, 2005.

[5] Yvo Desmedt and Yair Frankel. Threshold Cryptosystems. In *CRYPTO*, volume 435 of *Lecture Notes in Computer Science*, pages 307–315. Springer-Verlag, 1989.

[6] Shimon Even, Oded Goldreich, and Silvio Micali. On-Line/Off-Line Digital Schemes. In *CRYPTO*, volume 435 of *Lecture Notes in Computer Science*, pages 263–275. Springer-Verlag, 1989.

[7] Rosario Gennaro, Stanislaw Jarecki, Hugo Krawczyk, and Tal Rabin. Secure Distributed Key Generation for Discrete Logarithm Cryptosystems. To appear, *Journal of Cryptology*. http://www.research.ibm.com/security/dkg03.ps.

[8] Rosario Gennaro, Stanislaw Jarecki, Hugo Krawczyk, and Tal Rabin. Robust Threshold DSS Signatures. *Inf. Comput.*, 164(1):54–84, 2001.

[9] Hugo Krawczyk and Tal Rabin. Chameleon Signatures. In *Proceedings of the Network and Distributed System Security Symposium*, pages 143–154, 2000.

[10] John Kubiatowicz, David Bindel, Yan Chen, Steven Czerwinski, Patrick Eaton, Dennis Geels, Ramakrishna Gummadi, Sean Rhea, Hakim Weatherspoon, Westley Weimer, Chris Wells, and Ben Zhao. OceanStore: An Architecture for Global-Scale Persistent Storage. In *Proceedings of ACM Architectural Support for Programming Languages and Operating Systems*, Novemeber 2000.

[11] Ralph Merkle. Protocols for Public Key Cryptosystems. In *IEEE Symposium on Security and Privacy*, pages 122–134, April 1980.

[12] Sean Rhea, Patrick Eaton, Dennis Geels, Hakim Weatherspoon, Ben Zhao, and John Kubiatowicz. Pond: The OceanStore Prototype. In *Proceedings of the Conference on File and Storage Technologies*. USENIX, 2003.

[13] Sean Rhea and John Kubiatowicz. The OceanStore Write Path. http://roc.cs.berkeley.edu/retreats/summer_02/slides/srhea.pdf, June 2002.

[14] Mendel Rosenblum and John K. Ousterhout. The Design and Implementation of a Log-Structured File System. In *ACM Transactions on Computer Systems*, volume 10, pages 26–52, February 1992.

[15] Chris Ruemmler and John Wilkes. UNIX Disk Access Patterns. In *USENIX Winter 1993 Conference Proceedings*, January 1993.

[16] Adi Shamir and Yael Tauman. Improved Online/Offline Signature Schemes. In *CRYPTO*, volume 2139 of *Lecture Notes in Computer Science*, pages 355–367. Springer-Verlag, 2001.

[17] Victor Shoup. Practical Threshold Signatures. In *EUROCRYPT*, volume 1807 of *Lecture Notes in Computer Science*, pages 207–220. Springer-Verlag, 2000.

[18] Chung Kei Wong and Simon S. Lam. Digital Signatures for Flows and Multicasts. *IEEE/ACM Trans. Netw.*, 7(4):502–513, 1999.

[19] Zhiyong Xu, Yingwu Zhu, Rui Min, and Yiming Hu. Achieving Better Load Balance in Distributed Storage System. In *International Conference on Parallel and Distributed Processing Techniques and Applications*, June 2002.

[20] Lidong Zhou, Fred B. Schneider, and Robbert van Renesse. COCA: A Secure Distributed Online Certification Authority. *ACM Trans. Computer Systems*, 20(4):329–368, 2002.

Linear Integer Secret Sharing and Distributed Exponentiation

Ivan Damgård* and Rune Thorbek

BRICS**, Dept. of Computer Science, University of Aarhus

Abstract. We introduce the notion of Linear Integer Secret-Sharing (LISS) schemes, and show constructions of such schemes for any access structure. We show that any LISS scheme can be used to build a secure distributed protocol for exponentiation in any group. This implies, for instance, distributed RSA protocols for arbitrary access structures and with arbitrary public exponents.

1 Introduction

In a secret sharing scheme, a *dealer* distributes *shares* of a secret to a number of shareholders, such that only certain designated subsets of them - the *qualified sets* can reconstruct the secret, while other subsets have no information about it. The collection of qualified sets is called the *access structure*. In particular, the access structure consisting of all sets of cardinality greater than t is called a *threshold-t* structure.

Secret Sharing was first introduced[20] as a way to store critical information such that we get at the same time protection of privacy and security against loosing the information. Later, secret sharing has proved extremely useful, not just as a passive storage mechanism, but also as a tool in interactive protocols, for instance in threshold cryptography. Here, the private key in a public key scheme is secret shared among a set of servers, and the idea is that a qualified subset of the servers can use their shares to help a client to decrypt or sign an input message, but without having to reconstruct the private key in a single location. As long as an adversary cannot corrupt too large a subset of the servers, he cannot prevent the system from working, nor can he learn any information on the private key.

The central operation we need to perform securely in these applications is typically an exponentiation, that is, we are given some finite group G and an input $a \in G$, and we want to compute a^s, where s is a secret exponent which has been secret-shared among the servers. In some cases the group order is a public prime q. The problem is then straightforward to solve since we can use any standard linear secret sharing scheme over the field Z_q. The observation is

---

* FICS, Foundations in Cryptography and Security, center supported by the Danish research Council.
** Basic Research in Computer Science, Center of the Danish National research Foundation.

M. Yung et al. (Eds.): PKC 2006, LNCS 3958, pp. 75–90, 2006.

simply that for any linear scheme (such as Shamir's) over Z_q, the secret can be written as a linear combination $s = \sum_{i \in I} \alpha_i s_i \bmod q$, where I is any qualified set of servers holding shares $\{s_i \mid i \in I\}$, and where the α_i's can be computed from the index set I. Now, if the servers provide $a_i = a^{s_i}$ (and prove they did so correctly), we can compute $a^s = \prod_{i \in I} a_i^{\alpha_i}$. However, there are other cases where the group order is not prime and is not public (or even unknown to everyone), such as when G is Z_N^* for an RSA modulus N or when G is a class group. This leads to various problems: it would be natural to try to build a secret sharing scheme over Z_t where t is the order of G, but the standard constructions do not immediately work if t is not a prime. Matters are of course even worse if t is unknown to everyone.

The literature contains many techniques for getting around these problems. The techniques work in various particular scenarios, but they all have shortcomings in general. We give a short overview here:

- The black-box secret sharing schemes of [8, 13, 21] can be used to share a secret chosen from any Abelian group, including Z_t. This requires, of course, that the dealer knows t so he can do computations in Z_t. This is never the case if G is a class group, and if $G = Z_N^*$, the dealer must know the factorization of N. Note that in proactive threshold RSA schemes, each player typically has to reshare his share of the private key from time to time, however, we can of course not afford to reveal the factorization of N to every shareholder.
- In Shoup's threshold RSA protocol[22], the idea is to restrict the modulus N to be a safe prime product, which allows us to work in a subgroup of Z_N^* whose order is the product of two large primes. This is "close enough" to a prime so that standard Shamir sharing of s will work. This requires that the dealer knows the factorization. Moreover, for technical reasons, the protocol can only compute $a^{s \cdot n!}$ where n is the number of servers. This is solved by exploiting that we have the public exponent e available. Assuming e is relatively prime to $n!$, we can compute a^s efficiently. The problem in general is of course that we may not always be able to choose the group order as we like, and the inverse of s modulo the group order may not always be available or it may not be prime to $n!$. For instance, we cannot use small public exponents such as 3.[1]
- The secret sharing scheme of [15] which was also used in [12, 10] is a variant of Shamir's scheme, where we use polynomials over the integers. Using this to share s does not require any knowledge of the order of G. However, the scheme does not allow reconstruction of s by a linear combination of shares, instead one obtains the secret times some constant, typically $s \cdot n!$. This causes the protocol to produce $a^{s \cdot n!}$ as output, and we have the same problem as with Shoup's protocol.

---

[1] Shoup suggests an alternative solution where any public exponent can be used, but this requires that one additionally assumes that the DDH assumption holds in the RSA group.

– Finally, the method of Rabin [18] uses secret sharing in "two levels", i.e., the secret exponent s is shared additively, such that $s = s_1 + ... + s_n$ where server i knows s_i, and then s_i is itself secret shared among the servers. Schemes of this type require no knowledge of the group order to do the sharing since in principle, any secret-sharing scheme can be used to share the s_i's. On the other hand, shares become larger than with other schemes and extra rounds of interaction is needed (to reconstruct s_i) as soon as even one server i fails to participate correctly. Hence (in contrast to the other types of protocols) this approach cannot be made non-interactive, not even in the random oracle model.

A final issue with current state of the art of distributed exponentiation is that known solutions (except the two-level method) do not generalize to non-threshold access structures. The point of general structures is that when we secret share the private key according to a threshold structure, we are implicitly assuming that all servers are equally easy to break into, and so the only important parameter is the *number* of corrupted servers. In reality, some servers may well be more reliable than others, and so we may need to specify which sets should be qualified in a more flexible way, that is, we need a more general access structure.

1.1   Our Results

In this paper, we introduce a type of secret sharing scheme called *Linear Integer Secret-Sharing* (LISS). In a LISS scheme, the secret is an integer chosen from a (publically known) interval, and each share is computed as an integer linear combination of the secret and some random numbers chosen by the dealer. Reconstruction of the secret is also by computing a linear combination with integer coefficients of the shares in a qualified set.

LISS schemes are closely related to - but not the same as - the black-box secret sharing schemes (BBSS) mentioned earlier of Desmedt-Frankl[13] and Cramer-Fehr[8]. Whereas BBSS schemes are designed to secret share elements from any *finite* abelian group and use computations in this group to do it, our computations are done over the (infinite) ring of integers. This difference has a number of consequences that we return to below. LISS schemes are also different from the method in [15] based on integer polynomials, since they require a final division to get the secret while for LISS schemes we insist that linear combinations be sufficient.

Note that it was shown in [5,6] that perfect secret sharing and private computation over countably infinite domains (like the integers) is not possible. However, this does not rule out schemes of our type since we restrict our secrets to be chosen from a publically known interval and only aim for statistical rather than perfect privacy.

Cramer and Fehr introduce the concept of an integer span program (ISP) and use it to construct BBSS schemes. We show that any ISP can also be used to build a secure LISS scheme. Roughly speaking, an ISP is specified by a matrix with integer entries, and these entries are used as coefficients in the linear combinations that produce the shares from secret and randomness. In particular, the construction from [8] of an ISP for threshold-t access structures implies a LISS scheme for the same structure. Moreover, we revisit the well known construction of Benaloh and Leichter [1] based on monotone formulas that was originally conceived for a finite Abelian group, and we show that a LISS scheme can be built from any monotone formula. This implies that a LISS schemes exists for any access structure, though not necessarily an efficient one.

The ISP construction of Cramer and Fehr was shown to imply optimal threshold BBSS schemes. We show that this is not always the case for LISS schemes: if we base the Benaloh-Leichter construction on a monotone formula for the threshold function, we obtain threshold LISS schemes. It now turns out that, depending on how small a formula we can produce, this construction may produce a threshold LISS scheme with smaller shares or smaller randomness complexity than those coming from the Cramer-Fehr construction. With current of state of the art, this does not happen in general, but we find that for a fixed threshold and a large number of players, there are monotone formula constructions that produce smaller shares than Cramer-Fehr[2].

It is interesting to note that if the known lower bound on the montone formula size for the threshold function [3] turn out to be tight, this would make the Benaloh-Leichter construction more efficient in general than the Cramer-Fehr construction. While this may not seem likely with our current knowledge, it does mean that determining the efficiency of an optimal threshold LISS scheme remains an open question. The reason why BBSS schemes are different from LISS schemes in this respect is that when we use an ISP for building a BBSS scheme, the size of shares we get is independent of the size of the integers occurring in the description of the ISP, but this is no longer true when we build a LISS scheme.

Finally, we show that any LISS scheme can be used to build a distributed exponentiation protocol. The protocol does not use multilevel secret sharing. Thus, it can be made non-interactive using any of the known techniques for this purpose, such as the Fiat-Shamir heuristic (the random oracle model) or [7, 11, 16]. Furthermore, no player, including the dealer, needs to know the order of the group involved. This implies that we obtain the first non-interactive distributed exponentiation protocol that works for any group and any access structure.

We also look at the particular case of distributed RSA. We generalize the results of Damgård and Dupont[10] to arbitrary access structures, and thus obtain a distributed RSA signature scheme for any access structure, any public exponent and any modulus, efficiently and in constant-round without using random oracles or any assumptions other than the RSA assumption.

We emphasize that our result that all LISS schemes can be used for distributed exponentiation does not hold for BBSS schemes, not even if we assume that the dealer knows the group order[3]. The reason for this is that in order to do the proof

---

[2] Note that in a later paper[9], Cramer, Fehr and Stam propose a construction that they conjecture to be more efficient than[8], but so far, the asymptotic efficiency of the scheme remains unproved.

[3] We note that the BBSS constructions of [13, 8] are in fact applicable to distributed exponentiation, but this is due to special properties of those constructions.

of security for an exponentiation protocol using known simulation techniques, the secret sharing scheme needs to have the so called *share completion property:* given an unqualified set of shares and the secret, we can compute by linear combinations a *complete* set of shares consistent with what we were given. It is not known whether BBSS or LISS schemes have this property in general, in fact the answer is probably no. Here, we get around this problem by coming up with a different simulation technique where share completion is not needed. This technique always works with a LISS scheme, but fails with BBSS when the group order is not public.

2   Linear Integer Secret Sharing

First we formally define the required access structures.

Definition 1. *A* monotone access structure *on* $\{1, \ldots, n\}$ *is a non-empty collection* Γ *of sets* $A \subseteq \{1, \ldots, n\}$ *such that* $\emptyset \notin \Gamma$ *and such that for all* $A \in \Gamma$ *and for all sets* B *with* $A \subseteq B \subseteq \{1, \ldots, n\}$ *it holds that* $B \in \Gamma$.

Definition 2. *Let* t *and* n *be integers with* $0 < t < n$. *The* threshold-t access structure $T_{t,n}$ *is the collection of sets* $A \subseteq \{1, \ldots, n\}$ *with* $|A| > t$.

Let $P = \{1, \ldots, n\}$ denote the n shareholders (or players) and D the dealer. Let Γ be a monotone access structure on P. The dealer D wants to share a secret s from the publically known interval $[0..2^l]$ to the shareholders P over Γ, such that every set of shareholders $A \in \Gamma$ can reconstruct s, but such that a set of shareholders $A \notin \Gamma$ get no or little information on s. We call the sets which are allowed to reconstruct the secret *qualified* and the sets which should not be able to obtain any information about the secret *forbidden*.

For this purpose we use a *distribution matrix* $M \in Z^{d \times e}$ and a *distribution vector* $\boldsymbol{\rho} = (s, \rho_2, \ldots, \rho_e)^T$, where s is the secret, and the ρ_i's are uniformly random chosen integers in $[0..2^{l_0+k}]$ for $2 \leq i \leq e$, where k is the security parameter and l_0 is a constant that is part of the description of the scheme. The dealer D calculates shares by

$$M \cdot \boldsymbol{\rho} = (s_1, \ldots, s_d)^T, \tag{1}$$

where we denote each s_i as a *share unit* for $1 \leq i \leq d$. Let $\psi : \{1, \ldots, d\} \to P$ be a surjective function. The i'th share unit is then given to the $\psi(i)$'th shareholder, we say that $\psi(i)$ owns the i'th row in M. If $A \subseteq P$ is a set of shareholders, then M_A denotes the restriction of M to rows jointly owned by A. We denote d_A for the number of rows in M_A. Similarly, for $\boldsymbol{s} \in Z^d$ let $\boldsymbol{s}_A \in Z^{d_A}$ denote the restriction of $\boldsymbol{s}$ to the coordinates jointly owned by A. The share of shareholder j is then defined to be $\boldsymbol{s}_{\psi^{-1}(j)}$, which denotes all the entries in $\boldsymbol{s}$ which shareholder j owns, i.e., the share of shareholder j is the share units owned by j.

More formally, we let $[0..2^l]$ be the set of secrets, then each shareholder j is associated a positive integer $d_j = |\psi^{-1}(j)|$ for $1 \leq j \leq n$, such that the set of possible shares for shareholder j, is a subset $\mathcal{S}_j \subseteq Z^{d_j}$ of the Z-module Z^{d_j}. Each possible share for shareholder j is in the subset $\mathcal{S}_j$. The size of shareholder j share is defined to be the number of bits used to uniquely represent the share from $\mathcal{S}_j$. Note, that $d = \sum_{j=1}^{n} d_j$, where d is the number of share units. Then let $\mathcal{S} = \mathcal{S}_1 \times \ldots \times \mathcal{S}_n \subseteq Z^d$, which defines the subset of possible shares for the shareholders. Define the *expansion rate* to be $\mu = d/n$, where d is the number of share units and n is the number of shareholders. Note, that for a given distribution of a secret, the shares of the shareholdes can be considered as an element in the subset $\mathcal{S}$. If we use m bits to uniquely represent the shares in $\mathcal{S}$, then we define the *average share size* to be m/μ, which is the number of share bits each shareholder will get on average.

Definition 3. *A LISS scheme is* correct, *if the secret is reconstructed from shares $\{s_i \mid i \in A\}$ where A is a qualified set of shareholders, by taking an integer linear combination of the shares, with coefficient that depend only on the index set A.*

Definition 4. *A LISS scheme is* private, *if for any two secrets s, s', independent random coins r, r' and any forbidden set A of shareholders, the distribution of $\{s_i(s, r, k) \mid i \in A\}$ and $\{s_i(s', r', k) \mid i \in A\}$ are statistically indisinguishable. More precisely, the statistical distance between the two distributions is negligible in k.*

In the following we define the notion of an *Integer Span Program* (ISP, introduced in [8]) and show how any ISP can be used to build a correct and private LISS scheme.

Definition 5. $\mathcal{M} = (M, \psi, \varepsilon)$ *is called an* Integer Span Program *(ISP), if $M \in Z^{d \times e}$ and the d rows of M are labelled by a surjective function $\psi : \{1, \ldots, d\} \to \{1, \ldots, n\}$. Finally, $\varepsilon = (1, 0, \ldots, 0)^T \in Z^e$ is called the* target vector. *We define* $\text{size}(\mathcal{M}) = d$, *where d is the number of rows of M.*

Definition 6. *Let Γ be a monotone access structure and let $\mathcal{M} = (M, \psi, \varepsilon)$ be a integer span program. Then $\mathcal{M}$ is an ISP for Γ, if for all $A \subseteq \{1, \ldots, n\}$ the following holds.*

- *If $A \in \Gamma$, then there is a vector $\boldsymbol{\lambda} \in Z^d$ such that $M_A^T \boldsymbol{\lambda} = \boldsymbol{\varepsilon}$.*
- *If $A \notin \Gamma$, then there exists $\boldsymbol{\kappa} = (\kappa_1, \ldots, \kappa_e)^T \in Z^e$ such that $M_A \boldsymbol{\kappa} = \mathbf{0} \in Z^d$ with $\kappa_1 = 1$, which is called the* sweeping vector *for A.*

In other words, the rows owned by a qualified set must include the target vector in their span, while for a forbidden set, there must exist a sweeping vector which is orthogonal to all rows of the set, but has inner product 1 with the target vector. We also say that $\mathcal{M}$ computes Γ.

We define $\kappa_{\max} = \max\{|a| \mid a$ is an entry in some sweeping vector$\}$.

Note 1. In the case of a *span program*, which works over a field, the explicit requirement of a sweeping vector is not necessary. This is because the following holds for fiels, $\varepsilon \in \text{im}(M_A^T)$ if and only if there exists a sweeping vector. When working with the integers then only the "only if" implication is guaranteed.

If we have an ISP $\mathcal{M} = (M, \psi, \varepsilon)$ which computes Γ, we build a LISS scheme for Γ as follows: we use M as the distribution matrix, and set $l_0 = l + \lceil \log_2(\kappa_{\max}(e - 1)) \rceil + 1$, where as before l is the length of the secret.

Now, the first requirement in Definition 6 obviously makes the scheme correct, in that a qualified set A can compute the secret by taking a linear combination of their values, since there exsists $\boldsymbol{\lambda}_A \in Z^{d_A}$ such that $M_A^T \cdot \boldsymbol{\lambda}_A = \varepsilon$ which gives

$$\boldsymbol{s}_A^T \cdot \boldsymbol{\lambda}_A = (M_A \cdot \boldsymbol{\rho})^T \cdot \boldsymbol{\lambda}_A = \boldsymbol{\rho}^T \cdot (M_A^T \cdot \boldsymbol{\lambda}_A) = \boldsymbol{\rho}^T \cdot \varepsilon = s$$

The Lemma below shows that the second requirement is sufficient to make the scheme private.

Lemma 1. *If $s \in [0..2^l]$ and the ρ_i's are chosen uniformly at random in $[0..2^{l_0+k}]$ for all $2 \leq i \leq e$, then the LISS scheme derived from $\mathcal{M}$ is private.*

Proof. We have chosen $\boldsymbol{\rho} = (s, \rho_2, \ldots, \rho_e)^T$, with $\rho_i \in [0..2^{l_0+k}]$ as uniformly random numbers for $2 \leq i \leq e$, and the secret $s \in [0..2^l]$.

Let $s' \in [0..2^l]$ be arbitrary. We first observe, that $\boldsymbol{s}_A = M_A \boldsymbol{\rho}$ are shares that a subset A can see. If $A \notin \Gamma$, then we by definition know that there exists a sweeping vector $\boldsymbol{\kappa}$ such that $M_A \boldsymbol{\kappa} = \boldsymbol{0} \in Z^{d_A}$.

Define $\boldsymbol{s}' = M(\boldsymbol{\rho} + (s' - s)\boldsymbol{\kappa})$. We note that $\boldsymbol{s}'_A = \boldsymbol{s}_A$, i.e., the shareholders in A see the same shares, but the secret s' was shared instead of s. Define $\boldsymbol{\rho}$ to be *good* if $\boldsymbol{\rho}' = \boldsymbol{\rho} + (s' - s)\boldsymbol{\kappa}$ has entries in the specified range. Then the above implies that if we restrict the distribution of A's shares of s to the cases where $\boldsymbol{\rho}$ is good, the resulting distribution equals the one generated from s' and $\boldsymbol{\rho}'$.

It follows that the statistical distance between the distributions of A's shares of s and s' is at most twice the probability that $\boldsymbol{\rho}$ is not good, which we can estimate by the union bound as $e - 1$ times the probability that a single entry is out of range. So since $|s' - s| \leq 2^l$, the distance is at most

$$2 \cdot \frac{2^l \kappa_{\max}(e - 1)}{2^{l_0+k}} \leq 2^{-k}$$

3   Constructions

3.1   Benaloh-Leichter

In this section we show how to construct an ISP based on Benaloh and Leichter Generalized Secret Sharing scheme [1]. This scheme was already shown to work for secret sharing in any finite group, but to use it over the integers, we need to revisit the scheme to make sure that the required sweeping vectors exist and check the size of their coordinates.

As pointed out in [1], there is a one-to-one correspondence between monotone access structures and monotone formulas. Every monotone access structure can be described by a monotone formula, and every monotone formula describes a monotone access structure, where each variable in the formula is associated with a shareholder in P. A subset of the shareholders corresponds to an input to the formula by setting an input variable to 1 iff the corresponding shareholder is in the the subset. A subset is in the access structure represented by the formula if the formula accepts the corresponding setting of the variables. So it is enough to show how to construct an ISP from an arbitrary monotone formula f.

The details of this follow from Benaloh and Leichter's original construction and can be found in the full version of this paper [14]. Here, we only summarize the conclusions:

One can efficiently construct a distribution matrix $M \in Z^{d \times e}$ for the access structure representing monotone formula f, where d, e are at most the size of f. Moreover, each row has only 0 or 1 entries and there are at most $depth(f)$ 1's in every row. Finally, sweeping vectors have only $0, 1, -1$ as entries.

So when sharing a secret using M we need at most $d \cdot \text{depth}(f)$ additions to calculate all the d share units from (1). Each share unit is the result of adding at most of $\text{depth}(f)$ integers of $(l_0 + k)$-bit, i.e., each share unit is at most $l_0 + k + \log \text{depth}(f)$ bits long.

From [23] we have the existence of a monotone formula for the majority function of size $\mathcal{O}\left(n^{5.3}\right)$ and of depth $\mathcal{O}(\log n)$. A threshold-t function $T_{t,n}$ can be constructed from the majority function, by fixing some of the inputs of the majority function. This construction implies that we need a majority function of size at most $2n$ to construct the threshold-t function $T_{t,n}$, i.e. [23] gives the existence of a monotone formula for the threshold-t function $T_{t,n}$ of size $\mathcal{O}\left(n^{5.3}\right)$ and of depth $\mathcal{O}(\log n)$.

It follows from the above that each share unit is of size $\mathcal{O}(l_0 + k + \log \log n)$ and the time to compute all share units is $\mathcal{O}\left(n^{5.3} \log n(l_0 + k + \log \log n)\right)$, where we assume it takes $\mathcal{O}(b)$ time to add two b-bit numbers and $\mathcal{O}(b)$ time to generate a b-bit random integer. This implies that the average share size is $\mathcal{O}\left(n^{4.3}(l_0 + k + \log \log n)\right)$ bits.

Boppana, generalizing Valiant's result in [2], showed that every threshold t function $T_{t,n}$ can be represented by a monotone formula of size $\mathcal{O}\left(t^{4.3} n \log n\right)$. Each share unit size is still the same, hence the average share size becomes $\mathcal{O}\left(t^{4.3} \log n(l_0 + k + \log \log n)\right)$ bits. The total computation time of alle the shares is $\mathcal{O}\left(t^{4.3} n \log^2 n(l_0 + k + \log \log n)\right)$.

3.2 Cramer-Fehr

In this section we consider the ISP's constructed by Cramer and Fehr in [8].

As described, if we have an ISP $\mathcal{M} = (M, \psi, \varepsilon)$ we use $M \in Z^{d \times e}$ as the distribution matrix and we calculate the shares from (1). If we define $m_{\max}$ to be the maximal entry in the distribution matrix M. We need $d \cdot e$ multiplications of $\mathcal{O}(l_0 + k + m_{\max})$-bit numbers and $d \cdot (e-1)$ additions of $\mathcal{O}(l_0 + k + m_{\max} + e)$-bit numbers to calculate the shares.

From the proof of Corollary 1 in [8] we have that for a threshold-t access structure $T_{t,n}$ that

$$d = n(\lfloor \log n \rfloor + 2)$$
$$e = t(\lfloor \log n \rfloor + 2) + 1$$

We also know, that $m_{max} = \mathcal{O}\left(n^2\right)$. If we assume that we use $\mathcal{O}\left(b\right)$ time to choose a b-bit random number, $\mathcal{O}\left(b\right)$ time to add two b-bit numbers, and $\mathcal{O}\left(b\log^2 b\right)$ time to multiply two b-bit numbers. Then we need

$$\mathcal{O}\left(tn\log^2 n(l_0 + k + n^2)\log^2(l_0 + k + n^2) + tn\log^2 n(l_0 + k + n^2 + t\log n)\right)$$
$$= \mathcal{O}\left(tn\log^2 n(l_0 + k + n^2)\log^2(l_0 + k + n^2)\right)$$

time to compute the shares. Furthermore, we have that each share unit is of size $\mathcal{O}\left(l_0 + k + n^2 + \log(t\log n)\right) = \mathcal{O}\left(l_0 + k + n^2\right)$-bit, hence the average share size is $\mathcal{O}\left(\log n(l_0 + k + n^2)\right)$.

3.3 Comparison

In this section we compare the average share size, the number of random bits required to do the computations, and the computation complexity of the LISS scheme based on Benaloh-Leichter construction (BLc) with the scheme based on the Cramer-Fehr construction (CFc) in the threshold-t case.

First we make some observations. Recall that $l_0 = l + \lceil\log_2(\kappa_{max}(e-1))\rceil + 1$. For BLc we get that $l_0 = l + \lceil\log_2(n^{5.3}-1)\rceil + 1$, which asymptotically reduces to $l_0 \in \mathcal{O}\left(l + \log n\right)$. In the CFc we have that $\kappa_{max} = c2^n$ and $e = t(\lfloor\log n\rfloor + 2) + 1$, i.e., $l_0 = l\lceil\log_2(c2^n t(\lfloor\log n\rfloor + 2))\rceil + 1$, which asymptotically reduces to $l_0 \in \mathcal{O}\left(l + n\right)$.

First we will compare the results of the CFc with the BLc based on the threshold-t function build from Valiant [23] majority function. The results are compared in the table below, where we use l instead of the more scheme dependent l_0. Let ss denote the share size of each shareholder, rb the number of random bits used in the computation of the shares, and ct the computation time of the shares.

	CFc	BLc (Valiant)
ss	$\mathcal{O}\left((l + k + n^2)\log n\right)$	$\mathcal{O}\left((l + k + \log\log n)n^{4.3}\right)$
rb	$\mathcal{O}\left((l + k + n)t\log n\right)$	$\mathcal{O}\left((l + k + \log\log n)n^{5.3}\right)$
ct	$\mathcal{O}\left(tn\log^2 n(l + k + n^2)\log^2(l + k + n^2)\right)$	$\mathcal{O}\left(n^{5.3}\log n(l + k + \log\log n)\right)$

These results show a great advantage of the CFc if n is a dominating factor of the parameters, if this is not the case, the asymptotic bounds are of the same magnitude.

We may also base the BLc on the result from Boppana [2], which states that the size of the formula for the threshold function $T_{t,n}$ is $\mathcal{O}\left(t^{4.3}n\log n\right)$. We now compare it against the CFc and let t be fixed while n grows. This implies that the formula size is $\mathcal{O}\left(n\log n\right)$ for a fixed value of t. This can be a reasonable model in some cases: we may have a large number of share holders, while we believe that the adversary can only corrupt a small number of them. In the table below we compare the results to the CFc for a constant value of t,

	CFc	BLc (Boppana)
ss	$\mathcal{O}\left((l + k + n^2)\log n\right)$	$\mathcal{O}\left((l + k + \log\log n)\log n\right)$
rb	$\mathcal{O}\left((l + k + n)\log n\right)$	$\mathcal{O}\left((l + k + \log\log n)n\log n\right)$
ct	$\mathcal{O}\left(n\log^2 n(l + k + n^2)\log^2(l + k + n^2)\right)$	$\mathcal{O}\left(n\log^2 n(l + k + \log\log n)\right)$

Note that in this case, the BLc actually has a better share size and computation time complexity than the CFc. This indicates that the BLc with the current state of the art can compete with the CFc in special cases.

Results of Radhakrishnan [3] show that the lower bound for a monotone formula that computes the threshold-t function $T_{t,n}$ for $2 \leq t \leq \frac{n}{2}$, has size at least $\lfloor\frac{t}{2}\rfloor n \log(\frac{n}{t-1})$. As he notes, that in the monotone formulas model, the complexities of computing $T_{t,n}$ and $T_{n-t+1,n}$ are the same. Hence, the lower bound of $\lfloor\frac{t}{2}\rfloor n \log(\frac{n}{t-1})$ holds for the function $T_{n-t+1,n}$, $2 \leq t \leq \frac{n}{2}$, as well. This result is far below Valiants [23] and Boppana [2], so in particular BLc is in general better than CFc if the bound turns out to be tight.

To summarize the results of this section, we find that CFc seems better in the general case of the threshold-t function, but if n is small compared to the other factors, then the BLc can be just as good. Furthermore, for fixed t and large n, the BLc has an advantage over the CFc. The result of Radhakrishnan gives a big gab for improvements from the current state of the art of threshold functions, which would favor BLc. Finally, it must be stressed, of course, that the BLc has the advantage that it can be used over any monotone access structure. However, the BLc is only efficient if there is a polynomial-size monotone formula describing the access structure.

4   Distributed Exponentiation

In this section we will consider solutions to the the distributed exponentiation problem based on LISS. The set-up is as follows: we have n servers $P_1, ..., P_n$, an access structure Γ with an ISP $\mathcal{M} = (M, \psi, \varepsilon)$, and an adversary Adv who may corrupt any subset of servers not in Γ. The family of subsets not in Γ is called *the adversary structure* $\bar{\Gamma}$. Finally, we have a special player C called the client who may also be corrupted, independently of which servers are corrupt.

In this first solution we give, we consider non-adaptive corruption in the semi-honest model, i.e., the adversary must choose which players to corrupt before the protocol starts, he sees all internal data and communication of corrupt players, he may cause them to stop playing at any time, but all players follow the protocol as long as they participate. In order to solve the problem in this model, we must assume that the adversary structure is Q2, i.e., any set of form $A \cup B$, $A, B \in \bar{\Gamma}$ is strictly smaller than $\{P_1, ..., P_n\}$. This ensures that the set of honest servers is in Γ.

We will use Canetti's Universal Composability (UC) framework to state and prove our protocols. For details on this framework, refer to [4]. In order to focus on the actual protocol for exponentiation, we will assume a trusted dealer who chooses the group to use and secret-shares the exponent. In the UC framework, this means we assume a functionality representing the dealer is given, as detailed below. We assume for simplicity synchronous communication and also that the client C can broadcast information to all servers. But we do not assume any private channels so all communication between players is seen by the adversary.

Functionality F_{Deal}

1. Upon receiving "start" from all honest players, choose the group G to use and an exponent s (in principle any efficient algorithm for this could be used here).
2. Generate the distribution vector $\boldsymbol{\rho} = (s, \rho_2, \ldots, \rho_e)^T$ and calculate the shares from

$$M \cdot \boldsymbol{\rho} = (s_1, \ldots, s_d)^T,$$

   finally distributes the shares, such that s_i is sent privately to $P_{\psi(i)}$ for $1 \leq i \leq d$. Finally, send a description of G to all players and the adversary (information allowing to represent group elements and computing the group operation).

Such a functionality together with the protocol we give below will implement the following functionality

Functionality $F_{Deal-and-Exp}$

1. Upon receiving "start" from all honest players, choose the group G to use and an exponent s (same algorithm as used in F_{Deal}). Send a description of G (information allowing to represent group elements and computing the group operation) to all players and the adversary.
2. At any later time, upon receiving "Exponentiate a" for $a \in G$ from the client, send "Exponentiate a", to all players and the adversary. In the next round, send "Result a^s" to the client and the adversary.

The protocol proceeds as follows:

Protocol Exponentiate

1. Initially, each player sends "start" to F_{Deal}, and stores the description of G and shares of s received from F_{Deal}.
2. On input $a \in G$, C broadcasts a to the servers.
3. Each P_j sends to C $a_i = a^{s_i}$ for each component s_i of the share held by P_j.
4. Since $\bar{\Gamma}$ is Q2, C is guaranteed to receive valid contributions from a qualified set of players $A \in \Gamma$. C uses the entries in the reconstruction vector for A $\boldsymbol{\lambda} = (\lambda_1, \ldots, \lambda_{d_A})^T$ together with the contributions $(a_1 = a^{s_1}, \ldots, a_{d_A} = a^{s_{d_A}})$ to construct

$$a^s = \Pi_{i=1}^{d_A} a_i^{\lambda_i}.$$

Theorem 1. *The Exponentiate protocol when given access to F_{Deal} and a broadcast channel from C to the servers, securely implements $F_{Deal-and-Exp}$. The adversary is assumed to non-adaptively corrupt any set in Q2 structure $\bar{\Gamma}$ in a semi-honest fashion.*

Proof. Security is proved by constructing an ideal model adversary which works in a setting where it may communicate with ideal functionality $F_{Deal-and-Exp}$ and must simulate everything the real life adversary Adv would see in a real attack. This works by running internally a copy of Adv and proceeds as follows:

1. Let B be the set of servers corrupted by Adv. Having received the description of G from $F_{Deal-and-Exp}$, compute a sharing of 0 to simulate the action of F_{Deal}, i.e., the distribution vector is $\boldsymbol{\rho} = (0, \rho_2, \ldots, \rho_e)^T$ and the shares are

$$\boldsymbol{s} = (s_1, \ldots, s_d)^T = M \cdot \boldsymbol{\rho} \qquad (2)$$

Give to the Adv the shares from (2) belonging to the servers in B.

2. Upon receiving "Exponentiate a" and "Result a^s" from $F_{Deal-and-Exp}$, we must simulate the contributions that honest players send to C. To this end, note that if we had used $\boldsymbol{\rho}' = \boldsymbol{\rho} + s\boldsymbol{\kappa}_B$ as distribution vector in (2), then the corrupted servers in B would get the same shares, but the secret value would be s instead of 0.

   Now, let R be a row in the distribution matrix M belonging to honest server P_j, say the i'th row, and let s_i be the share unit we computed from this row in (2). Had we used $\boldsymbol{\rho}'$ instead of $\boldsymbol{\rho}$, then the share unit coming from R would have been $s_i' = (\boldsymbol{\rho} + s\boldsymbol{\kappa}_B) \cdot R = s_i + s\boldsymbol{\kappa}_B \cdot R$ instead. The observation is now that because we know a^s and s_i, we can compute $a^{s_i'}$ even though we do not know s. Concretely, we simulate the contribution from P_j by

$$a^{s_i}(a^s)^{\boldsymbol{\kappa}_B \cdot R} = a^{s_i + s\boldsymbol{\kappa}_B \cdot R}$$
$$= a^{s_i'}$$

Give all simulated contributions to Adv.

We now need to prove that no environment can distinguish between the real protocol and the simulated game. The is straightforward: First, the shares computed in step 1 of the simulation are statistically indistinguishable from the shares computed by F_{Deal} by privacy of the LISS scheme and since B in unqualified. Second, in both the simulated game and real protocol, honest players output always the correct value a^s, by definition of $F_{Deal-and-Exp}$, respectively correctness of the LISS scheme. Finally, given a, a^s, the simulated and real contributions from honest players are statistically indistinguishable, since the vector we use for the simulated sharing is $\boldsymbol{\rho}' = \boldsymbol{\rho} + s\boldsymbol{\kappa}_B$ which is statistically close to a uniformly chosen sharing vector for s. □

4.1   Active Adversaries and Distributed RSA

If we are not guaranteed that corrupted players follow the protocol, we can expand the Exponentiate protocol in a natural way by having players prove in zero-knowledge that their contributions are correct. Given any appropriate scheme for proving correctness of contributions, a corrupt player must either give correct information or be disqualified. Since this is equivalent to the semihonest model, security essentially follows from security of the zero-knowledge proofs and the proof we already gave above.

Depending on the structure of the group and the assumptions we are willing to make, there are many different ways to do the zero-knowledge proofs, see for instance [21, 19, 22, 7, 11, 10, 12, 16]. Most of the techniques can be made non-interactive in the random oracle model, or are already non-interactive given some set-up assumption. If all else fails, generic zero-knowledge techniques can be used[17].

However, a detailed account of all possibilities is out of scope of this paper. We concentrate instead on distributed RSA as a particularly interesting special case. The functionality for initial set-up and the functionality we want to implement are modified from the general case as follows:

Functionality $F_{RSA-Deal}$

1. Upon receiving "start" from all honest players, choose the modulus n to use, secret and public exponents s, e and a random square v in $G = Z_N^*$.
2. Generate the distribution vector $\boldsymbol{\rho} = (s, \rho_2, \dots, \rho_e)^T$ and calculate the shares from

$$M \cdot \boldsymbol{\rho} = (s_1, \dots, s_d)^T,$$

finally distributes the shares, such that s_i is sent privately to $P_{\psi(i)}$ for $1 \leq i \leq d$. Finally, send N, e, v and $v_i = v^{s_i} \bmod N$ for every share unit s_i to all players and the adversary .

Functionality F_{RSA}

1. Upon receiving "start" from all honest players, choose the modulus N to use, secret and public exponents s, e. Send N, e to all players and the adversary
2. At any later time, upon receiving "Exponentiate a" for $a \in Z_N^*$ from the client, send "Exponentiate a", to all players and "Exponentiate $a, a^s \bmod N$" to the adversary. Two rounds later, send "Result $a^s \bmod N$" to all players.

The protocol we will use is the Exponentiate protocol from the previous section, with the extension that C will check each contribution $a_i = a^{s_i} \bmod N$ from server P_j. We want to show that a sufficient check can be done in constant-round without using random oracles to ensure soundness and zero-knowledge, and regardless of which modulus and public exponent is used. To do this, we generalize the results from [10]. Concretely, we use the following well known protocol, which we will repeat in parallel $\lceil 2 + 2 \log_2 n \rceil$ times:

1. P_j chooses a random $k + max$- bit number r and sends to C $u_1 = a^r \bmod N, u_2 = v^r \bmod N$. Here, max is the maximal bitlength of any s_i that can occur.
2. C sends a random bit b to P_j.
3. P_j sends $z = r + bs_i$, and C checks that $a^z = u_1 a_i^b \bmod N, v^z = u_2 v_i^b \bmod N$.

The following Lemma is an easy consequence of corresponding results in [10]:

Lemma 2. *The above protocol is statistical zero-knowledge. Furthermore, if $a_i \neq a^s \bmod N$ then a polynomial time prover who can make C accept with probability more than $1/(4n^2)$ can compute efficiently a multiple of the order of v.*

Note that the last result in the lemma implies that if an adversary can cheat the protocol on input a random v, he can factor N by a standard reduction and hence also break RSA.

Even though the soundness error for this protocol is not negligible, we can show that checking the contributions in this way is sufficient to allow C to reconstruct the correct result efficiently. This is done by a generalization of the results from [10]. There it was observed that as long as the expected number of accepted incorrect contributions is small enough, C can reconstruct efficiently by searching exhaustively for a set of correct contribution. In [10], this was done for the case of a threshold access structure. Here we have to be more careful with the search algorithm and the analysis because we have no lower bound on the number of honest players for a general access structure.

Algorithm Reconstruct

1. On input public key $N, e, a \in Z_N^*$ and a set of contributions to finding $a^s \bmod N$, execute the protocol above with each server to check the correctness of each contribution.
2. Let the set of accepted contributions be Acc. Do the following for $j = 0, ..., |Acc|$:
3. For each subset $B \subset Acc$ of size $|Acc| - j$, run the reconstruction algorithm from the Exponentiate protocol on the contributions in B, attempting to compute $a^s \bmod N$. Let z be the result. If $z^e = a \bmod N$, output z and stop.

Lemma 3. *The expected number of subsets considered by Reconstruct is at most 2.*

Proof. Let m be the number of incorrect contributions submitted by corrupt players. Clearly, the worst case is if all corrupt players submit bad contributions, so we may assume that the number of honest players is $n - m$. Let p be the probability that an incorrect contribution is accepted. Then

$$p_i = Pr(i \text{ incorrect shares accepted}) = p^i (1-p)^i \binom{m}{i} \leq p^i m^i$$

Given that i incorrect shares are accepted, we have $n - m + i$ contributions, and we finish at the latest when we have searched all subsets of size $n - m$. This means checking a total of

$$\binom{n-m+i}{n-m+i} + \binom{n-m+i}{n-m+i-1} + ... + \binom{n-m+i}{n-m} \leq (i+1)\binom{n-m+i}{n-m}$$
$$= (i+1)\binom{n-m+i}{i}$$
$$\leq (i+1)(n-m+i)^i$$

subsets. It follows that the expected number of subsets we check is at most

$$\sum_{i=0}^{m} p^i m^i \cdot (i+1)(n-m+i)^i \leq \sum_{i=0}^{m} p^i m^i 2^i n^i \leq \sum_{i=0}^{m}(2pn^2)^i \leq \sum_{i=0}^{m} 2^{-i} \leq 2$$

using the above and the fact that $p \leq 1/(4n^2)$. $\square$

A final observation is that by choosing z at random in Z_N^*, and setting $v = z^{2e} \bmod N$, a simulator can easily create a random square v for which $v^s \bmod N$ is known (namely $z^2 \bmod N$). It is then easy to simulate the information $F_{RSA-Deal}$ sends to corrupt players. Using this, the proof of Theorem 1, Lemma 3 and Lemma 2, it is straightforward to show:

Theorem 2. *Under the RSA assumption, the Exponentiate protocol expanded with the above Reconstruction algorithm and given access to the $F_{RSA-deal}$ functionality implements the F_{RSA} functionality. The adversary may non-adaptively and actively corrupt any set in Q2 structure $\bar{\Gamma}$.*

We believe that the interest of this result is that it buys us full generality in access structure and choice of keys and no dependency on extra set-up or complexity assumptions. Since the number of servers n can be expected to be quite small in practice, the overhead compared to more standard solutions is moderate: a factor of $\log n$ in complexity and potentially 2 extra moves. However, in practice, faults are usually rare, so if the the client attempts to get the result from all contributions first and only asks to have the proofs completed if this fails, then the scheme will be non-interactive "almost always".

Acknowledgements

Thomas Mølhave, Peter Bro Miltersen, Gudmund Skovbjerg Frandsen, and the anonymous reviewers from the committee for helpful comments.

References

1. Josh Cohen Benaloh, Jerry Leichter: *Generalized Secret Sharing and Monotone Functions.* Proc. of CRYPTO 1988: 27-35
2. R. B. Boppana: *Amplification of Probabilistic Boolean Formulas.* Advances in Computing Research 5: 27-45 (1989)
3. Jaikumar Radhakrishnan: *Better Lower Bounds for Monotone Threshold Formulas.* J. Comput. Syst. Sci. 54(2): 221-226 (1997)
4. Ran Canetti: *Universally Composable Security: A New Paradigm for Cryptographic Protocols*, FOCS 2001: 136-145.
5. Benny Chor and Eyal Kushilevitz: *Secret Sharing Over Infinite Domains.*, J. Cryptology 6(2): 87-95 (1993)
6. Benny Chor, Mihály Geréb-Graus and Eyal Kushilevitz *Private Computations over the Integers.*, SIAM J. Comput. 24(2): 376-386 (1995)
7. Cramer and Damgård: *Secret-Key Zero-Knowlegde and Non-interactive Verifiable Exponentiation*, Proc. of TCC 04, Springer Verlag LNCS.

8. Ronald Cramer, Serge Fehr: *Optimal Black-Box Secret Sharing over Arbitrary Abelian Groups.* Proc. of CRYPTO 2002: 272-287

9. Cramer, Fehr and Stam: *Black-Box Secret Sharing from Primitve Sets in Algebraic Number Fields*, Proc. of Crypto 05, Springer Verlag LNCS.

10. Ivan Damgård, Kasper Dupont: *Efficient Threshold RSA Signatures with General Moduli and No Extra Assumptions.* Proc. of Public Key Cryptography 2005: 346-361

11. Damgård, Fazio and Nicolosi: *Non-Interactive Zero-Knowledge Proofs from Homomorphic Encryption* Proc. of TCC 06, Springer Verlag LNCS.

12. Ivan Damgård, Maciej Koprowski: *Practical Threshold RSA Signatures without a Trusted Dealer.* Proc. of EUROCRYPT 2001: 152-165

13. Yvo Desmedt, Yair Frankel: *Perfect Homomorphic Zero-Knowledge Threshold Schemes over any Finite Abelian Group.* SIAM J. Discrete Math. 7(4): 667-679 (1994)

14. Ivan Damgård and Rune Thorbek: *Linear Integer Secret Sharing and Distributed Exponentiation* (full version), the Eprint archive, www.iacr.org

15. Yair Frankel, Peter Gemmell, Philip D. MacKenzie, Moti Yung: *Optimal Resilience Proactive Public-Key Cryptosystems.* FOCS 1997: 384-393

16. Rosario Gennaro, Tal Rabin, Stanislaw Jarecki, and Hugo Krawczyk: *Robust and Efficient Sharing of RSA Functions.* J. Cryptology 2000 13(2): 273-300

17. Oded Goldreich, Silvio Micali, Avi Wigderson: *Proofs that Yield Nothing But Their Validity or All Languages in NP Have Zero-Knowledge Proof Systems* J. ACM 38(3): 691-729 (1991).

18. Tal Rabin: *A Simplified Approach to Threshold and Proactive RSA.* Proc. of CRYPTO 1998: 89-104

19. Claus-Peter Schnorr: *Efficient Signature Generation by Smart Cards.* J. Cryptology 4(3): 161-174 (1991)

20. Adi Shamir: *How to Share a Secret.* Commun. ACM 22(11): 612-613 (1979)

21. Alfredo De Santis, Yvo Desmedt, Yair Frankel, Moti Yung: *How to share a function securely. STOC 1994: 522-533*

22. Victor Shoup: *Practical Threshold Signatures.* Proc. of EUROCRYPT 2000: 207-220

23. Leslie G. Valiant: *Short Monotone Formulae for the Majority Function.* J. Algorithms 5(3): 363-366 (1984)

Encoding-Free ElGamal Encryption Without Random Oracles

Benoît Chevallier-Mames[1,2], Pascal Paillier[3], and David Pointcheval[2]

[1] Gemplus, Security Technology Department,
La Vigie, Avenue du Jujubier, ZI Athélia IV,
F-13705 La Ciotat Cedex, France
benoit.chevallier-mames@gemplus.com
[2] École Normale Supérieure,
Département d'Informatique, 45 rue d'Ulm,
F-75230 Paris 05, France
david.pointcheval@ens.fr
[3] Gemplus, Security Technology Department,
34 rue Guynemer,
F-92447 Issy-les-Moulineaux, France
pascal.paillier@gemplus.com

Abstract. ElGamal encryption is the most extensively used alternative to RSA. Easily adaptable to many kinds of cryptographic groups, ElGamal encryption enjoys homomorphic properties while remaining semantically secure providing that the DDH assumption holds on the chosen group. Its practical use, unfortunately, is intricate: plaintexts have to be encoded into group elements before encryption, thereby requiring awkward and ad hoc conversions which strongly limit the number of plaintext bits or may partially destroy homomorphicity. Getting rid of the group encoding (*e.g.*, with a hash function) is known to ruin the standard model security of the system.

This paper introduces a new alternative to group encodings and hash functions which remains *fully compatible* with standard model security properties. Partially homomorphic in customizable ways, our encryptions are comparable to plain ElGamal in efficiency, and boost the encryption ratio from about 13 for classical parameters to the optimal value of 2.

Keywords: Cryptography, ElGamal encryption, Diffie-Hellman, Residuosity classes, Group encodings.

1 Introduction

Since the discovery of public-key cryptography [7], very few practical cryptosystems have been suggested that sustain a strong evidence of security in the standard model.

FACTORING VS. DISCRETE-LOG ENCRYPTION SCHEMES. In brief, there exist two main families of provably secure cryptosystems. The first family relates to integer factoring (Rabin [21], RSA [22], Naccache-Stern [16], Okamoto-Uchiyama [18], Paillier [19]). The others are based on the discrete logarithm

M. Yung et al. (Eds.): PKC 2006, LNCS 3958, pp. 91–104, 2006.

or the Diffie-Hellman problems. Within this family, ElGamal encryption [8] is certainly the most extensively used for cryptographic applications.

Cryptosystems belonging to the first family support the encryption of messages without prior formatting in the sense that any fixed-size integer is a proper input of the encryption algorithm. However, all known discrete-log-based encryption schemes which feature standard-model security such as Cramer-Shoup encryption [5], are restricted to encrypt group elements.

This drawback, often overlooked, seems inherent to the nature of these cryptosystems. Variants and alternate designs either drastically degrade bandwidth and efficiency, or imply extra (and possibly questionable) assumptions in their security analysis.

Historically, the first designs suggested to work in the largest possible subgroup over which the encryption takes place. By virtue of the fact that invoking the DDH assumption requires to use a prime order subgroup (or at least a subgroup which order does not have small factors), the subgroup of quadratic residues in $\mathbb{Z}_p^*$ appears as the best choice in this respect. However, one then has to perform operations in the group of order $q = (p-1)/2$ which implies exponentiations with large exponents.

A standard lesser evil consists in applying a hash function to the Diffie-Hellman session key before masking the plaintext. The price to pay then amounts to making stronger assumptions, such as the Hash Diffie-Hellman assumption [1, 12] or the random oracle model [2].

OUR CONTRIBUTIONS. This paper introduces a novel encryption technique that does not require message encoding before encryption and enjoys strong security against chosen-plaintext attacks without any extra assumption *i.e.*, the security of our cryptosystems stands in the standard model. One-wayness and indistinguishability rely on the use of new specifically introduced integer-theoretic problems which we call the (computational/decision) Class Diffie-Hellman problems (CCDH, resp. DCDH).

Most interestingly, we provide a proof that CCDH is in fact *equivalent* to CDH, meaning that the one-wayness of our schemes is identical to the one of ElGamal encryption while providing an optimal encryption ratio of 2 instead of 13. The study of DCDH, however, remains a challenging open problem.

In terms of performance, the encryption and decryption procedures are equivalent to respectively 6 and 5 exponentiations in a subgroup of prime order q with *e.g.*, $\log q = 160$. No group encoding is required before encryption. Finally the ciphertext size is identical to an ElGamal ciphertext, although the encryption ratio reaches its optimum level: one may encrypt 1024-bit strings into a 2048-bit ciphertext while still relying on a 160-bit subgroup.

Our cryptosystems also provide a weak form of additive or multiplicative homomorphic property, in the sense that one can add a constant or multiply by a constant an encrypted value. However, one cannot re-randomize encryptions. This amounts to say that if two ciphertexts were created using this property (with the same random coins), every one may recover the difference or the ratio between the plaintexts, without any private material.

Our encryption schemes are based on the mathematical properties of integers modulo p^2 where p is a prime number. Interestingly, one would note that homomorphicity has often been achieved by relying on the properties of special moduli: Okamoto and Uchiyama [18] use properties of integers modulo $n = p^2 q$, while Paillier [19] and Bresson, Catalano and Pointcheval [3] rather employ moduli of the form n^2. Damgård and Jurik [6] use operations modulo n^s for $s > 2$. In all of these schemes, however, various forms of RSA moduli constitute basic scheme parameters and the trapdoor technique relates to factoring rather than to discrete-log problems. Our work, by opposition, makes exclusive use of prime-order groups.

OUTLINE OF THE PAPER. Our work is divided as follows. Section 2 reviews standard definitions and security notions for public-key encryption. Section 3 briefly recalls ElGamal encryption and variants thereof. In Section 4, we introduce the Class Diffie-Hellman problems, then proceed to define and comment on our encryption schemes. Their security is further discussed in Section 5. We finally provide extensions to $\mathbb{Z}_{p^k}$ in Section 6.

2   Preliminaries

2.1   Public-Key Encryption

We identify a public-key encryption scheme S to a tuple of probabilistic algorithms $\mathsf{S} = (\mathcal{K}, \mathcal{E}, \mathcal{D})$ defined as follows:

KEY GENERATION. Given a security parameter k, $\mathcal{K}(1^k)$ produces a pair $(\mathsf{pk}, \mathsf{sk})$ of public and private keys.

ENCRYPTION. Given a message m and a public key pk, $\mathcal{E}_{\mathsf{pk}}(m)$ produces a ciphertext c. If the procedure is probabilistic, we write $c = \mathcal{E}_{\mathsf{pk}}(m; r)$ where r denotes the randomness used by $\mathcal{E}$.

DECRYPTION. Given a ciphertext c and a private key sk, $\mathcal{D}_{\mathsf{sk}}(c)$ returns a plaintext m or possibly $\bot$ if the ciphertexts is invalid.

2.2   Security Notions for Encryption Schemes

ONE-WAYNESS. A most important security notion that one would expect from an encryption scheme to fulfil is the property of *one-wayness* (OW): an attacker should not be able to recover the plaintext matching a given ciphertext. We capture this notion more formally by saying that for any adversary $\mathcal{A}$, succeeding in inverting the effects of $\mathcal{E}$ on a ciphertext c should occur with negligible probability. $\mathcal{A}$ is said to (k, ε, τ)-break OW when

$$\mathsf{Succ}_{\mathsf{S}}^{\mathsf{ow}}(\mathcal{A}) = \Pr_{m, r}[(\mathsf{pk}, \mathsf{sk}) \leftarrow \mathcal{K}(1^k) \ : \ \mathcal{A}(\mathsf{pk}, \mathcal{E}_{\mathsf{pk}}(m; r)) = m] \geq \varepsilon \ ,$$

where the probability is taken over the random coins of the experiment and the ones of the adversary, and $\mathcal{A}$ halts after τ elementary steps. An encryption scheme is said to be one-way if no probabilistic algorithm (k, ε, τ)-breaks OW for $\tau \leq \mathsf{poly}\,(k)$ and $\varepsilon \geq 1/\mathsf{poly}\,(k)$.

SEMANTIC SECURITY. The notion of *semantic security* (IND) [13], *a.k.a.*, *indistinguishability of encryptions* captures a strong notion of privacy. Here, the attacker should not learn any information whatsoever about a plaintext given its encryption. The adversary $\mathcal{A} = (\mathcal{A}_1, \mathcal{A}_2)$ is said to (k, ε, τ)-break IND when

$$\mathsf{Adv}_S^{\mathsf{ind}}(\mathcal{A}) = 2 \times \Pr_{b,r}\left[\begin{array}{l} (\mathsf{pk}, \mathsf{sk}) \leftarrow \mathcal{K}(1^k), (m_0, m_1, s) \leftarrow \mathcal{A}_1(\mathsf{pk}), \\ c = \mathcal{E}_{\mathsf{pk}}(m_b; r) \ : \ \mathcal{A}_2(m_0, m_1, s, c) = b \end{array} \right] - 1 \geq \varepsilon,$$

where again the probability is taken over the random coins of the experiment as well as the ones the adversary. $\mathcal{A}$ must run in at most τ steps and it is imposed that $|m_0| = |m_1|$. An encryption scheme is said to be semantically secure or indistinguishable if no probabilistic algorithm can (k, ε, τ)-break IND for $\tau \leq \mathsf{poly}\,(k)$ and $\varepsilon \geq 1/\mathsf{poly}\,(k)$.

2.3   Computational Assumptions

We now briefly recall the definition of the discrete-log and related problems needed for the sake of this work. In what follows, $\mathbb{G}$ denotes an abelian group (denoted multiplicatively) of prime order q. We also consider a generator g of $\mathbb{G} = \langle g \rangle$.

Definition 1 (Discrete Logarithm – DL). *Given* $g^x \in \mathbb{G}$ *where* $x \leftarrow \mathbb{Z}_q$, *compute* x.

Definition 2 (Computational Diffie-Hellman – CDH). *Given* $g^x \in \mathbb{G}$ *and* $g^y \in \mathbb{G}$ *for* $x, y \leftarrow \mathbb{Z}_q$, *compute* $g^{xy} \in \mathbb{G}$.

Definition 3 (Decision Diffie-Hellman – DDH). *Let us consider the two distributions* $D = (g^x, g^y, g^{xy})$ *and* $R = (g^x, g^x, g^z)$ *for randomly distributed* $x, y, z \leftarrow \mathbb{Z}_q$. *Distinguish* D *from* R.

It is easily seen that $\mathsf{DDH} \Leftarrow \mathsf{CDH} \Leftarrow \mathsf{DL}$ where $\Leftarrow$ denotes polynomial reduction between computational problems. In most cryptographic applications, the structure of the group $\mathbb{G}$ is chosen in such a way that these three computational problems seem intractable. A typical example is to choose $\mathbb{G} \subseteq \mathbb{F}_p^*$ where q divides $(p-1)$ where classically, p is a 1024-bit prime and q a 160-bit prime. Another widely used family of groups is elliptic curves over large prime fields [15, 14].

3   The ElGamal Cryptosystem

ElGamal encryption was introduced by T. ElGamal in 1985 [8]. The algebraic framework requires a cryptographic group $\mathbb{G}$ of order q given with some generator g.

One generates a public-private key pair by randomly selecting $x \leftarrow \mathbb{Z}_q$ and computing $y = g^x$. The public key is then y while the private key is x. In order to encrypt a message m, one randomly selects $r \leftarrow \mathbb{Z}_q$ and computes $u = g^r$ and $v = y^r m$. The ciphertext is $c = (u, v)$. Using the private key x, the ciphertext $c = (u, v)$ can be decrypted as $m = v \cdot u^{-x}$.

The key point here resides in the definition of the message space $\mathcal{M}$. As defined originally in [8], the group $\mathbb{G}$ was chosen to be the set of integers modulo a large prime p (i.e., $\mathbb{G} = \mathbb{Z}_p$), q was set to $p - 1$ and $\mathcal{M}$ was identified to $\mathbb{Z}_p^*$. Unfortunately, using this definition, the cryptosystem is not indistinguishable: given a ciphertext $c = (u, v)$, an attacker can well decide with non negligible probability whether c encrypts a given message m_0. To this end, the attacker computes $v' = v \cdot m_0^{-1}$, and then computes $a = u^{(p-1)/2}$ and $b = v'^{(p-1)/2}$. If only one of the elements a or b is equal to 1, the adversary knows that c does not encrypt m_0. This simple attack actually checks the parity of the logarithms of u and v' with respect to g and y respectively: if $c = (u, v)$ encrypts m_0, it is needed that these parities be identical.

This attack against indistinguishability shows that the order of the group $\mathbb{G}$ must be relatively prime to any small integer (the attack described just above can be extended trivially for any small divisor of q), and most preferably, the order of group $\mathbb{G}$ must be chosen to be prime.

DESCRIPTION. Unfortunately, the above constraint translates into a restriction on the message space $\mathcal{M}$: it has to be embedded into the group $\mathbb{G}$. Hence, before encryption takes place, the message must be *encoded* into a group element, and this group encoding must be efficiently invertible in order to allow the original message to be recovered during the decryption process. Such an encoding may be time-consuming, and may also partially or totally destroy the inherent homomorphic property of the system. Also, using a group encoding remains incompatible with the optimization which consists in working in a small subgroup of $\mathbb{Z}_p^*$ of prime order q where q is a 160-bit prime, a setting in which group exponentiations are much faster.

Set up: Let p be an ℓ_p-bit prime and q an ℓ_q-bit prime so that q divides $(p-1)$. Let $\mathbb{G}$ be the subgroup of $\mathbb{Z}_p^*$ of order q, and g be a generator of $\mathbb{G}$. Let Ω be a one-to-one encoding map from $\mathbb{Z}_q$ onto $\mathbb{G}$.

Key generation: The private key is $x \leftarrow \mathbb{Z}_q$. The corresponding public key is $y = g^x$.

Encryption: To encrypt a message $m \in \mathbb{Z}_q$, one encodes m by computing $\omega = \Omega(m)$, randomly selects $r \leftarrow \mathbb{Z}_q$ and computes $(u, v) = (g^r, y^r \omega)$. The ciphertext is $c = (u, v)$.

Decryption: To decrypt a ciphertext $c = (u, v)$, one computes $\omega = v \cdot u^{-x}$ and recovers the original plaintext $m = \Omega^{-1}(\omega)$.

This cryptosystem is known to be one-way under the CDH assumption, and indistinguishability holds under the DDH assumption. These security notions are reached in the context of chosen-plaintext attacks, in the standard model.

3.1   The Hash-ElGamal Cryptosystem

In order to overcome the issue of group encoding, a hash variant of ElGamal encryption was suggested.

Set up: Let p be an ℓ_p-bit prime and q an ℓ_q-bit prime so that q divides $(p-1)$. Let $\mathbb{G}$ be the subgroup of order q of $\mathbb{Z}_p^*$, and g be a generator of $\mathbb{G}$. Let $\mathcal{H} : \mathbb{G} \to \{0,1\}^{\ell_m}$ be a hash function.

Key generation: The private key is again $x \leftarrow \mathbb{Z}_q$. The corresponding public key is $y = g^x$.

Encryption: To encrypt a message $m \in \{0,1\}^{\ell_m}$, one randomly selects $r \leftarrow \mathbb{Z}_q$ and computes $(u,v) = (g^r, \mathcal{H}(y^r) \oplus m)$. The ciphertext is $c = (u,v)$.

Decryption: To decrypt a ciphertext $c = (u,v)$, one computes $m = \mathcal{H}(u^x) \oplus v$.

This cryptosystem features one-wayness and indistinguishability under chosen plaintext attacks under the sole CDH assumption. The security proof, however, stands in the random oracle model. Alternatively, under the DDH assumption, one can apply a randomness extractor in place of the random oracle, in order to generate a truly random mask. But this either requires large groups, or drastically reduces the size of the mask [4].

4   Encoding-Free ElGamal Encryption

We now proceed to describe our new technique for encoding-free ElGamal encryption. Our cryptosystems enjoy performances similar to plain ElGamal but do not require group encoding, nor randomness extractors. Furthermore, their security holds in the standard model under new intractability assumptions that we introduce below. We start by providing definitions as well as the mathematical facts underlying our proposal.

4.1   The Class Function

Let p and q be prime numbers such that $q \mid p-1$. Let g be an integer of order pq modulo p^2 and $\mathbb{G} = \langle g \rangle$ the group formed by all elements of order pq modulo p^2. Hence $\mathbb{G}_p = \langle g \bmod p \rangle$ is the subgroup of order q in $\mathbb{Z}_p^*$. By the Chinese Remainder Theorem, there is a canonical mapping between $\mathbb{Z}_p \times \mathbb{Z}_q$ and $\mathbb{Z}_{pq}$. For any $x \in \mathbb{Z}_p$ and $y \in \mathbb{Z}_q$, $\langle x, y \rangle$ stands for the unique integer modulo pq such that $\langle x, y \rangle = x \bmod p$ and $\langle x, y \rangle = y \bmod q$.

Definition 4 (Class of an element of $\mathbb{G}$). *Each and every element w of $\mathbb{G}$ can be written as $w = g^{\langle x, y \rangle} \bmod p^2$ for a unique $x \in \mathbb{Z}_p$ and a unique $y \in \mathbb{Z}_q$. The integer $x = \llbracket w \rrbracket$ is said to be the* class *of w with respect to g.*

It is easily seen that if $w = g^{\langle x, y \rangle} \bmod p^2$, then $w = g^y \bmod p$. In other words, y is the discrete log of $w \bmod p$ with respect to $g \bmod p$. This means that, unless extracting discrete logs over $\mathbb{G}_p$ is easy, y cannot be easily computed from w. It appears, however, that computing the class of elements of $\mathbb{G}$ can be done publicly and efficiently.

Lemma 1. *Define over* $\mathbb{G}$ *the function* $\mathcal{L}(w) = (w^q - 1 \bmod p^2)/p$. *The class of* $w = g^{\langle x,\, y\rangle} \bmod p^2$ *can be computed as* $x = \mathcal{L}(w)\mathcal{L}(g)^{-1} \bmod p$.

This property is well-known and we refer the reader to [18, 19] for a proper proof. Now let a be an integer modulo q and consider $w = g^a \bmod p$. Since w can also be viewed as an element of $\mathbb{G}$, there exist integers x, y such that $w = g^{\langle x,\, y\rangle} \bmod p^2$. However, $g^{\langle x,\, y\rangle} = g^y \bmod p$ and therefore $y = a$ by unicity of y. It appears that the value of x can be recovered as a function of a:

Lemma 2. *Let us define*

$$\mathsf{Upper}(g^a) = \frac{g^a \bmod p^2 - g^a \bmod p}{p}$$

and

$$\Delta(g^a) = \frac{q}{\mathcal{L}(g)} \cdot \frac{\mathsf{Upper}(g^a)}{g^a} \bmod p \, .$$

Then

$$[\![g^a \bmod p]\!] = a - \Delta(g^a) \bmod p \, .$$

Proof. Noting $g^a = A + p \cdot \bar{A} \bmod p^2$ for $A, \bar{A} \in \mathbb{Z}_p$ with $A \neq 0$, and using the identity $1 + p \cdot \mathcal{L}(g) = g^{\langle q,\, 0\rangle} \bmod p^2$, we have

$$g^a = A\left(1 + p \cdot \frac{\bar{A}}{A}\right) = A\,(1 + p)^{\frac{\bar{A}}{A}} = A \cdot g^{\langle \frac{q}{\mathcal{L}(g)} \frac{\bar{A}}{A},\, 0\rangle} \bmod p^2 \, .$$

Taking the class of the left and right terms, we get $a \cdot [\![g]\!] = [\![A]\!] + \Delta(g^a)$ which leads to the above using the trivial fact that $[\![g]\!] = 1$. □

Lemma 3. *The mapping* $a \to [\![g^a \bmod p]\!]$ *is random self-reducible.*

Proof. Assume we want $[\![A]\!]$ for some given $A = g^a \bmod p$. We make use of the fact that for any $r \in \mathbb{Z}_q$, we have

$$[\![A^r \bmod p]\!] = [\![A^r \bmod p^2]\!] - \Delta(A^r) = r \cdot [\![A]\!] - \Delta(A^r) \bmod p \, .$$

If r is drawn uniformly at random from $\mathbb{Z}_q^*$, $A^r \bmod p$ is a random element of $\mathbb{G}_p$. Knowing $[\![A^r \bmod p]\!]$ and r, $[\![A]\!]$ is easily recovered as

$$[\![A]\!] = r^{-1}\left([\![A^r \bmod p]\!] + \Delta(A^r)\right) \bmod p \, .$$ □

4.2 The Class Diffie-Hellman Problems

We now turn to defining the computational problems over which we base the encryption schemes suggested in the forthcoming sections.

Definition 5 (Computational Class Diffie-Hellman). *Let* $\mathbb{G}_p = \langle g \bmod p\rangle$ *be defined as above. Given group elements* $g^a \bmod p$ *and* $g^b \bmod p$, *compute* $[\![g^{ab} \bmod p]\!]$.

Definition 6 (Decision Class Diffie-Hellman). *Distinguish the two distributions* $D = (g^a \bmod p, g^b \bmod p, [\![g^{ab} \bmod p]\!])$ *and* $R = (g^a \bmod p, g^b \bmod p, z)$ *for* $a, b \leftarrow \mathbb{Z}_q$ *and* $z \leftarrow \mathbb{Z}_p$.

We denote these problems CCDH and DCDH throughout the paper. As we shall now see, CCDH is in fact closely related to CDH.

Theorem 1. CCDH *and* CDH *are equivalent.*

Proof. [CCDH $\Leftarrow$ CDH]. Assume we are given a probabilistic algorithm $\mathcal{A}$ such that $\mathcal{A}(g^a \bmod p, g^b \bmod p)$ outputs $g^{ab} \bmod p$ with probability ε and time bound τ, the success probability being taken over the random variables of $\mathcal{A}$ and the random selections $a, b \leftarrow \mathbb{Z}_q$. Given $A, B \leftarrow \mathbb{G}_p$, we run $\mathcal{A}(A, B)$ to get DH(A, B) and deduce $[\![$DH$(A, B)]\!]$, thereby succeeding in solving CCDH with probability ε and no more than $\tau + \mathsf{poly}\,(\log p)$ steps.

[CDH $\Leftarrow$ CCDH]. Assume there exists a probabilistic algorithm $\mathcal{A}$ which solves CCDH. By virtue of Lemma 3, we may assume that the input distribution of $\mathcal{A}$ need not be uniform and that the success probability of $\mathcal{A}$ is overwhelming. We build a reduction algorithm $\mathcal{B}$ that computes $C = $ DH(A, B) for arbitrary elements $A, B \leftarrow \mathbb{G}_p$. $\mathcal{B}$ first runs $\mathcal{A}(A, B)$ to get $[\![C]\!]$. $\mathcal{B}$ now sets $A' = Ag \bmod p$ and runs $\mathcal{A}$ again to get $[\![C']\!] = \mathcal{A}(A', B)$ where $C' = $ DH$(A', B) = BC \bmod p$. We must have

$$[\![C']\!] = [\![BC \bmod p]\!] = [\![BC \bmod p^2]\!] - \Delta(BC) = [\![B]\!] + [\![C]\!] - \Delta(BC)$$

wherefrom $\Delta(BC) = [\![B]\!] + [\![C]\!] - [\![C']\!] \bmod p$. Since

$$BC = C' + p \cdot \mathsf{Upper}(BC) = C' \left(1 + p \cdot \frac{\mathcal{L}(g)}{q} \cdot \Delta(BC)\right) \bmod p^2 \,,$$

$\mathcal{B}$ now remains with the problem of finding a solution to the modular equation

$$\frac{C}{C'} = B^{-1}\left(1 + p \cdot \frac{\mathcal{L}(g)}{q} \cdot \left([\![B]\!] + [\![C]\!] - [\![C']\!]\right)\right) \bmod p^2 \qquad (1)$$

where the unknowns are $C, C' \in \mathbb{Z}_p$. Setting the right-hand term to $\mu < p^2$, $\mathcal{B}$ applies the extended Euclidean algorithm to μ and p^2 in order to find small solutions $C, C' < p$ satisfying $C/C' = \mu \bmod p^2$. The validity of C is easily checked by making sure that $C'C^{-1} \bmod p$ is equal to B. This stage finishes with probability one in time bounded by $\log^3 p$ resulting in that $C = $ DH(A, B) is found with no more than two calls to $\mathcal{A}$ and polynomial extra time. $\qquad \square$

So far, the study of DCDH remains a challenging open question. In particular, the relations between DCDH and DDH are somewhat unclear. Although we do not provide evidence of that fact, we suspect these two problems to be extremely closely connected. We will make the assumption that DCDH is intractable throughout the rest of this paper.

4.3   Encoding-Free Additive Encryption

As discussed above, our goal is to render ElGamal encryption truly practical by getting rid of intricate group encoding mechanisms while maintaining a security level in the standard model (in opposition to Hash-ElGamal encryption for instance). The basic idea, instead of embedding the message into a group element, consists in converting the session key output by the Diffie-Hellman exchange[1] into an integer modulo p using the class function.

Set up: Let p an ℓ_p-bit prime and q an ℓ_q-bit prime divisor of $p-1$. Let g be a generator of the subgroup $\mathbb{G}_p$ of order q of $\mathbb{Z}_p^*$.

Key generation: The private key is a random number $x \in \mathbb{Z}_q$. The corresponding public key is $y = g^x \bmod p$.

Encryption: To encrypt a message $m \in \mathbb{Z}_p$, one picks a random $r \in \mathbb{Z}_q$ and computes $u = g^r \bmod p$ and $v = [\![y^r \bmod p]\!] + m \bmod p$. The ciphertext is $c = (u, v)$.

Decryption: To decrypt a ciphertext $c = (u, v)$, one simply computes $m = v - [\![u^x \bmod p]\!] \bmod p$.

4.4   Encoding-Free Multiplicative Encryption

Since the message and the class of $g^{xy} \bmod p$ are both integers modulo p, encryption may also be performed using modular multiplication instead of modular addition.

Set up: Let p an ℓ_p-bit prime and q an ℓ_q-bit prime divisor of $p-1$. Let g be a generator of the subgroup $\mathbb{G}_p$ of order q of $\mathbb{Z}_p^*$.

Key generation: The private key is a random number $x \in \mathbb{Z}_q$. The corresponding public key is $y = g^x \bmod p$.

Encryption: To encrypt a message $m \in \mathbb{Z}_p^*$, one picks a random $r \in \mathbb{Z}_q$ and computes $u = g^r \bmod p$ and $v = [\![y^r \bmod p]\!] \cdot m \bmod p$. The ciphertext is $c = (u, v)$.

Decryption: To decrypt a ciphertext $c = (u, v)$, one simply computes $m = v[\![u^x \bmod p]\!]^{-1} \bmod p$.

4.5   Properties of Our Encryption Schemes

No conversion. Our encryption schemes do not require any conversion: the message space is *really* the ring $\mathbb{Z}_p$ (or the multiplicative subgroup $\mathbb{Z}_p^*$ in the multiplicative version.) Therefore, any string of bitlength lesser than k, where $p > 2^k$, can be encrypted directly. This is a strong property since we may have q much smaller than p without impact on the encryption and decryption procedures.

---

[1] ElGamal encryption can indeed be viewed as a Diffie-Hellman key exchange where the publication of the public-key y plays the role of the first pass.

EFFICIENCY. It is easily seen that ciphertexts have a similar size as with ElGamal encryption. The bandwidth is exactly $\frac{1}{2}$ (*i.e.*, the encryption ratio is exactly 2), by opposition to ElGamal encryption for which the bandwidth is $\frac{q}{2p}$. We recall that for $p = 1024$ and $q = 160$, the bandwidth of ElGamal is close to $\frac{1}{13}$).

From the viewpoint of computational performances, it appears that in addition to the two exponentiations that are inherent to ElGamal encryption, we require an additional exponentiation in $\mathbb{Z}_{p^2}$ with a ℓ_q-bit exponent. This amounts to four times the execution time of the same exponentiation in $\mathbb{Z}_p$. Totaling everything, we need 6 exponentiations vs. 2 exponentiations in ElGamal. However, no encoding is needed, which are basically done with exponentiations.

When decrypting an ElGamal encryption, an exponentiation of ℓ_q bits in $\mathbb{Z}_p$ is required, as well as a group decoding. In our schemes, however, we require an exponentiation in $\mathbb{Z}_{p^2}$ with an exponent of size ℓ_q and another exponentiation with an exponent of size ℓ_q. Finally, we require 5 exponentiations to be compared to the single exponentiation needed in ElGamal. Once again, no inverse of the encoding is needed.

MULTIPLICATIVE OR ADDITIVE HOMOMORPHISM. Last but not least, our schemes feature a partial homomorphic property over the ring of integers modulo p. We mean for instance that one could add some constant to an encrypted plaintext without needing the private key. Although these properties do forbid resistance against chosen-ciphertext attacks, these are perceived as most desirable in many cryptographic applications such as electronic voting, and we expect to see applications of our work in this regard. However, our schemes do not allow to re-randomize a ciphertext per se.

5   Security Analysis

We now proceed to assessing the security of our schemes. Obviously, one cannot prevent chosen-ciphertext attacks due to the partial malleability described above. However, generic conversions do exist to convert CPA-secure schemes into CCA-secure schemes (in the random oracle model)[9, 10, 11, 20, 17] when the context of use demands CCA security.

ONE-WAYNESS. Focusing on the additive version of our encoding-free encryption scheme, we state:

Theorem 2. *Let $\mathcal{A}$ be an adversary which can invert our cryptosystem with success probability ε under a chosen-plaintext attack within time τ. Then the Computational Class Diffie-Hellman problem can be solved with success probability ε within time similar to τ.*

Proof. Given a Computational Class Diffie-Hellman instance $(g, y = g^x \bmod p, w = g^s \bmod p)$, our goal is to compute $z = [\![g^{xs} \bmod p]\!]$. To this aim, we use the OW − CPA attacker $\mathcal{A}$ against our scheme, where g is the public generator, and set the public key to y. We submit to $\mathcal{A}$ the ciphertext $(u, v) = (w, a)$

for a randomly chosen $a \in \mathbb{Z}_p$. This is a truly random ciphertext of a random message, for which we have set $r = s$, and so $\mathcal{A}$ succeeds with probability ε to find the corresponding plaintext m. If $\mathcal{A}$ succeeds, we thus learn $[\![g^{xs} \bmod p]\!]$, our expected result $z = a - m \bmod p$.   □

It is easily seen that the same theorem holds for the multiplicative encryption scheme. One would simply note that the message space in this latter version is $\mathbb{Z}_p^*$, and not $\mathbb{Z}_p$, as one needs to compute the inverse $m^{-1} \bmod p$ to deduce z from a and m.

INDISTINGUISHABILITY. About indistinguishability, we state a similar result:

Theorem 3. *Let $\mathcal{A}$ be an adversary breaking the indistinguishability of our cryptosystem with advantage ε under a chosen-plaintext attack within time τ. Then the Decisional Class Diffie-Hellman problem can be solved with advantage $\varepsilon/2$ within time similar to τ.*

Proof. Assume we are given an instance $(g, y = g^x \bmod p, w = g^s \bmod p, z)$ of the Decisional Class Diffie-Hellman problem in $\mathbb{Z}_p$, and want to decide whether z is randomly selected in $\mathbb{Z}_p$ or whether $z = [\![g^{xs} \bmod p]\!]$.

As above, we make use an IND − CPA attacker $\mathcal{A}$ against our scheme, where g is the public generator, and set the public key to y. We let the adversary to choose two messages m_0 and m_1, pick a random bit b, and encrypt m_b as $(u, v) = (w, z + m_b \bmod p)$. Finally, we send this ciphertext to the $\mathcal{A}$ as the challenge ciphertext.

Clearly, if $z = [\![g^{xs} \bmod p]\!]$, c is a valid ciphertext of m_b, where we set $r = s$, and consequently the attacker $\mathcal{A}$ can guess the value b with advantage ε. On the contrary, if z is a random element of $\mathbb{Z}_p$, $z' = z + m_b \bmod p$ is also a random element of $\mathbb{Z}_p$, thereby making the ciphertext independent from the message m_b. The advantage of $\mathcal{A}$ is then necessarily zero.

Hence, to solve our decisional problem, we reply TRUE if the guess of $\mathcal{A}$ is correct, otherwise a random bit is replied. Our reduction solves DCDH with advantage at least $\varepsilon/2$.   □

6   Generalization to $\mathbb{Z}_{p^k}$

As the scheme suggested by Damgård-Jurik [6] is a generalization of Paillier encryption, we may generalize our systems using $\mathbb{Z}_{p^k}$ for any integer $k > 2$. For any integer $k > 2$, we denote naturally $\mathcal{L}_k$ the function defined by $X \mapsto \frac{X^q - 1 \bmod p^k}{p}$, and let the class of w as $[\![w]\!]_k = \mathcal{L}_k(w)\mathcal{L}_k(g)^{-1} \bmod p^{k-1}$. Then the generalization of our technique to $\mathbb{Z}_{p^k}$ is as follows:

Set up: Let p an ℓ_p-bit prime and q an ℓ_q-bit prime divisor of $(p-1)$. Let g be a generator of the subgroup $\mathbb{G}_p$ of order q of $\mathbb{Z}_p$.

Key generation: The private key is a random number $x \in \mathbb{Z}_q$. The corresponding public key is $y = g^x \bmod p$.

Encryption: To encrypt a message $m \in \mathbb{Z}_{p^{k-1}}$, one picks a random $r \in \mathbb{Z}_q$ and computes $u = g^r \bmod p$ and $v = [\![y^r \bmod p]\!]_k + m \bmod p^{k-1}$. The ciphertext is $c = (u, v)$.

Decryption: To decrypt a ciphertext $c = (u, v)$, one simply computes

$$m = v - [\![u^x \bmod p]\!]_k \bmod p^{k-1}.$$

We may equally well use modular multiplication instead of addition of course. In these cryptosystems, the encryption bandwidth is equal to $\frac{k-1}{k}$, and therefore can be made nearly optimal. Furthermore, the property of partial malleability is still a feature of the scheme. Regarding security, one refer the reader to [6] for proofs that the generalizations of CCDH and DCDH are equivalent to their version for $k = 2$. We then adapt the proof of the scheme in $\mathbb{Z}_{p^2}$ to show that the one-wayness and that indistinguishability of the generalized schemes are identical to the extended versions of CCDH and DCDH.

7   Conclusion and Open Issues

In this paper, we have proposed new cryptosystems based on new computational problems related to the Diffie-Hellman problems. Encryption does not require messages to be converted into group elements by opposition to all known discrete-log-based cryptosystem proven secure in the standard model.

Our cryptosystems feature a better encryption ratio (decreased by a factor 6.5 for common parameters), an identical ciphertext size, and remain comparable in speed with ElGamal encryption. Their security in the standard model under chosen-plaintext attacks is based on the CDH assumption for one-wayness, and on the assumption that the Decision Class Diffie-Hellman for indistinguishability.

Our encryption schemes are partially homomorphic, either additively or multiplicatively. To the best of our knowledge, this gives the only example of an additive encryption (even if partial) featuring standard-model security in the discrete-log setting.

An open research area would be to find a discrete-log-based cryptosystem that would provide a *fully* additive or multiplicative homomorphism. Another independent but challenging topic would be to provide a more accurate study on the connections between DCDH and DDH.

Acknowledgements

The first author would like to thank Jean-François Dhem and Philippe Proust, as well as his colleague Eric Brier for fruitful and enjoying discussions about the difficulty of the DCDH problem.

This work was funded in part by the European project ECRYPT and in part by the French RNRT project CRYPTO++.

References

1. M. Abdalla, M. Bellare, and P. Rogaway. DHAES: An Encryption Scheme Based on the Diffie-Hellman Problem. Submission to IEEE P1363a. September 1998. Available from http://grouper.ieee.org/groups/1363/.
2. M. Bellare and P. Rogaway. Optimal Asymmetric Encryption – How to Encrypt with RSA. In *Eurocrypt '94*, LNCS 950, pages 92–111. Springer-Verlag, Berlin, 1995.
3. E. Bresson, D. Catalano, and D. Pointcheval. A Simple Public-Key Cryptosystem with a Double Trapdoor Decryption Mechanism and its Applications. In *Asiacrypt '03*, LNCS 2894, pages 37–54. Springer-Verlag, Berlin, 2003.
4. O. Chevassut, P.-A. Fouque, P. Gaudry, and D. Pointcheval. The Twist-Augmented Technique for Key Exchange. In *PKC '06*, LNCS. Springer-Verlag, Berlin, 2006.
5. R. Cramer and V. Shoup. A Practical Public Key Cryptosystem Provably Secure against Adaptive Chosen Ciphertext Attack. In *Crypto '98*, LNCS 1462, pages 13–25. Springer-Verlag, Berlin, 1998.
6. I. Damgård and M. Jurik. A Generalisation, a Simplification and Some Applications of Paillier's Probabilistic Public-Key System. In *PKC '01*, LNCS 1992, pages 119–137. Springer-Verlag, Berlin, 2001.
7. W. Diffie and M. E. Hellman. New Directions in Cryptography. *IEEE Transactions on Information Theory*, IT–22(6):644–654, November 1976.
8. T. El Gamal. A Public Key Cryptosystem and a Signature Scheme Based on Discrete Logarithms. *IEEE Transactions on Information Theory*, IT–31(4):469–472, July 1985.
9. E. Fujisaki and T. Okamoto. How to Enhance the Security of Public-Key Encryption at Minimum Cost. In *PKC '99*, LNCS 1560, pages 53–68. Springer-Verlag, Berlin, 1999.
10. E. Fujisaki and T. Okamoto. Secure Integration of Asymmetric and Symmetric Encryption Schemes. In *Crypto '99*, LNCS 1666, pages 537–554. Springer-Verlag, Berlin, 1999.
11. E. Fujisaki and T. Okamoto. How to Enhance the Security of Public-Key Encryption at Minimum Cost. *IEICE Transaction of Fundamentals of Electronic Communications and Computer Science*, E83-A(1):24–32, January 2000.
12. R. Gennaro, H. Krawczyk, and T. Rabin. Secure Hashed Diffie-Hellman over Non-DDH Groups. In *Eurocrypt '04*, LNCS 3027, pages 361–381. Springer-Verlag, Berlin, 2004.
13. S. Goldwasser and S. Micali. Probabilistic Encryption. *Journal of Computer and System Sciences*, 28:270–299, 1984.
14. N. Koblitz. Elliptic Curve Cryptosystems. *Mathematics of Computation*, 48(177):203–209, January 1987.
15. V. Miller. Uses of Elliptic Curves in Cryptography. In *Crypto '85*, LNCS 218, pages 417–426. Springer-Verlag, Berlin, 1986.
16. D. Naccache and J. Stern. A New Public-Key Cryptosystem. In *Eurocrypt '97*, LNCS 1233, pages 27–36. Springer-Verlag, Berlin, 1997.
17. T. Okamoto and D. Pointcheval. REACT: Rapid Enhanced-security Asymmetric Cryptosystem Transform. In *CT – RSA '01*, LNCS 2020, pages 159–175. Springer-Verlag, Berlin, 2001.
18. T. Okamoto and S. Uchiyama. A New Public Key Cryptosystem as Secure as Factoring. In *Eurocrypt '98*, LNCS 1403, pages 308–318. Springer-Verlag, Berlin, 1998.

19. P. Paillier. Public-Key Cryptosystems Based on Composite-Degree Residuosity Classes. In *Eurocrypt '99*, LNCS 1592, pages 223–238. Springer-Verlag, Berlin, 1999.
20. D. Pointcheval. Chosen-Ciphertext Security for any One-Way Cryptosystem. In *PKC '00*, LNCS 1751, pages 129–146. Springer-Verlag, Berlin, 2000.
21. M. O. Rabin. Digitalized Signatures and Public Key Functions as Intractible as Factorization. Technical Report MIT/LCS/TR-212, Massachusetts Institute of Technology – Laboratory for Computer Science, January 1979.
22. R. Rivest, A. Shamir, and L. Adleman. A Method for Obtaining Digital Signatures and Public Key Cryptosystems. *Communications of the ACM*, 21(2):120–126, February 1978.

Parallel Key-Insulated Public Key Encryption

Goichiro Hanaoka[1], Yumiko Hanaoka[2], and Hideki Imai[1,3]

[1] Research Center for Information Security,
National Institute of Advanced Industrial Science and Technology,
1102 Akihabara Daibiru, 1-18-13 Sotokanda, Chiyoda-ku, Tokyo 101-0021, Japan
hanaoka-goichiro@aist.go.jp
[2] NTT DoCoMo, Inc.,
3-5 Hikarino-oka, Yokosuka 239-8536, Japan
hanaoka@nttdocomo.co.jp
[3] Institute of Industrial Science, University of Tokyo,
4-6-1 Komaba, Meguro-ku, Tokyo 153-8505, Japan
imai@iis.u-tokyo.ac.jp

Abstract. Security is constantly been infringed by inadvertent loss of
secret keys, and as a solution, Dodis, Katz, Xu, and Yung [11], in Eurocrypt 2002, proposed a new paradigm called key-insulated security
which provides tolerance against key exposures. Their scheme introduces
a "helper key" which is used to periodically update the decryption key.
The most attractive part of this scheme is that even if a decryption key
of a time period is exposed, the security of the rest of the periods are
unaffected. But how does this helper key managed? Can it be done efficiently? As, to alleviate the damage caused by key exposures, decryption
key has to be updated at very short intervals, although frequent updating
will, in contrary, increase the risk of helper key exposure. In this paper,
we propose *parallel key-insulated public key encryption* in which two distinct helper keys *alternately* update a decryption key. The helper key of
one system is independent from the other. Not only does it decrease the
chance of helper key exposures, it also allows frequent updating of the
decryption key, and over all, increases the security of the system.

1   Introduction

Background. The problem of key exposure is an important issue in practice,
regardless. No matter how strong the encryption scheme is, if the key is exposed,
we lose the security. Leaving it just under users' care and responsibility is too
high of a risk to take: Loss of important documents and personal information
that results from careless handling by humans happens nothing out of the ordinary, and the damage exerted, can be immeasurable. Classic approach was to
try to earn the time before system collapse, although not solving the problem
fundamentally, secret keys leaked eventually. Dodis, Katz, Xu and Yung looked
at this problem from a different prospective: Their idea was to minimize the
damage instead of just trying to gain time. Their proposed scheme was called,
key-insulated public-key encryption (KIPE) [11]. In their KIPE, a helper key
is introduced and is stored in the helper device which is kept isolated from the

M. Yung et al. (Eds.): PKC 2006, LNCS 3958, pp. 105–122, 2006.

network except for times it is used to update the decryption key. Encryption in KIPE is carried out using a fixed public key and time (e.g. date), and so, the need to announce new public key to others after each key updating (like what the certificate authority does in PKI) can be omitted. Regarding its security, security for all time periods except for time period exposed, both forward and backward security, are guaranteed.

Now, to increase the system tolerance against key exposures for KIPE system, the first thing that comes into mind is to update the decryption key at short timing (i.e. frequent intervals), however, this will, in turn, increase the frequency of helper device connection to the network and increase the risk of helper key exposure. This is due to that the KIPE assumes helper key exposures to less likely occur than decryption key exposures: Helper key and decryption key are managed independently and helper device can be stored in a physically much safer place as it is used only at key updates. Frequent updating of the decryption key will in turn put the helper key in a higher risk of exposure (as it will be connected to the network more often). So, a trade-off between decryption key and helper key exposures exists. For deeper understanding, let's consider the next example: Suppose you are a busy office worker who wishes to increase system tolerance by frequently updating the key. You think that updating twice each day is manageable. You decide to update the key once at home (at approx. midnight) and once at the office (at approx. noon). Since you leave the helper device at home, now, you will need to remind yourself not to forget to bring the device to work each day, or otherwise, make a copy of the device and leave one copy at your office for convenience. In either case, security of the decryption key is increased but the risk of helper key exposure is also increased (doubled). So, as we can see, unless the KIPE model is changed, it is impossible to increase the security of both decryption key and helper key simultaneously.

Our Results. In this paper, we propose *parallel key-insulated public key encryption* (PKIPE). Our PKIPE allows frequent updating of the decryption key, and at the same time, reduces the risk of helper key exposure. PKIPE differs from the original KIPE in that two distinct helper devices are introduced and each device is alternately used to update a single decryption key (so, you don't have to carry your helper device to-and-from work and office each day).

Initialization in PKIPE involves providing two auxiliary *helpers* H_1 and H_2 with master helper keys mst_1 and mst_2, respectively, and the user's terminal with a *stage 0 user secret key* usk_0. Similarly to the original KIPE, user's public encryption key pk is treated like that of an ordinary encryption scheme with regard to certification, but its lifetime is divided into stages $i = 1, 2, ..., N(= 2n)$ with encryption in stage i performed as a function of pk, i and the plaintext, and decryption in stage i performed by using a *stage i user secret key* usk_i obtained by the following key-update process performed at the beginning of stage i:

- If $i = 2k-1$ for $k \in \{1, 2, ..., n\}$, H_1 sends to the user's terminal over a secure channel, a *stage i helper key* hsk_i computed as a function of mst_1 and i,
- If $i = 2k$ for $k \in \{1, 2, ..., n\}$, similarly to the above, H_2 sends hsk_i computed as a function of mst_2 and i,

the user computes usk_i as a function of usk_{i-1} and hsk_i, and erases usk_{i-1}. Like the original KIPE, our PKIPE also address random access key update [11] in which the user computes an arbitrary stage user secret key (that could also be a past key).

The security intentions are:

1. If none of the helpers is compromised, similar to the original KIPE, exposure of any of user secret keys does not compromise the security of the non-exposed stages, and

2. even if one of H_1 and H_2 is compromised in addition to the exposure of any of user secret keys, it still does not compromise the security of the non-exposed stages except for the ones whose corresponding user secret keys can be trivially determined from the exposed keys.

For case **2.**, consider a situation where an adversary obtains mst_1, usk_{i_0} and usk_{i_1} such that i_0 and i_1 are even and odd, respectively. Obviously, stages i_0 and i_1 are compromised. The security of stage $i_0 + 1$ may also be compromised since usk_{i_0+1} is easily computable from usk_{i_0} and mst_1. Similarly, security of stage $i_1 - 1$, too, may be compromised. (Notice that we address random access key update and so we can recover past keys). On the other hand, for example, the security of stage $i_1 + 1$ is not compromised as usk_{i_1+1} is computed as a function of usk_{i_1} and mst_2, and not mst_1. So, in this case, security of all stages except for i_0, $i_0 + 1$, i_1 and $i_1 - 1$ remain secure. Furthermore, if only one of H_1 or H_2 is compromised but none of the user secret key is exposed, then all stages remain secure. In other words, even for the case when one of helper keys, mst_1 and mst_2 is exposed, the security of our PKIPE is guaranteed to maintain at least the security level of the original KIPE.

Similar to the original KIPE, we can further address the case when all of the helper keys are exposed:

3. Even if both helpers H_1 and H_2 are compromised, security of all stages remain secure as long as user secret key (of even one stage) is not compromised in addition to the helper keys.

Our proposed schemes are proven to be semantically secure in the random oracle model.

Related Works. Followed by the earlier proposal made by Dodis, Katz, Xu and Yung [11], Dodis, Franklin, Katz, Miyaji and Yung proposed an *intrusion-resilient public key encryption* (IRPKE) [13] which strengthened the forward security of KIPE. The security of IRPKE has enhanced, only, it became less convenient as it did not allow random access key update. There were proposal of signature schemes as well with the same intention to provide tolerance against key exposures: Key-insulated signature [12] and intrusion-resilient signature [17]. On the other hand, as an encryption scheme that allows key update, there is, the KIPE and also, *forward secure public key encryption* (FSPKE). FSPKE was introduced by Anderson [1] and the first efficient construction was proposed by Canetti, Halevi and Katz [10]. Dodis, Franklin, Katz, Miyaji and Yung showed that by using FSPKE with a homomorphic property, a generic IRPKE can be constructed [14]. Not to mention, many variations of *forward secure signatures* have also been introduced, e.g. [8, 2].

Identity-based encryption (IBE) [18, 5, 9] works as a crucial building block in the construction of KIPE. Bellare and Palacio showed in [7] that a KIPE (OT-KIPE)[1] which allows unlimited number of key updating is equivalent to an IBE, and so, constructing a provably secure OT-KIPE in the standard model with [3], [4] or [19] can be done also. In this paper, we show that [5] is used as a basic building block to construct PKIPE.

2 Definitions

First, we give the model of PKIPE and the security notion. We follow by showing the characteristics of bilinear maps and a related computational assumption.

2.1 Model: Parallel Key-Insulated Public Key Encryption

A PKIPE scheme $\mathcal{E}$ consists of five efficient algorithms (**KeyGen, Δ-Gen, Update, Encrypt, Decrypt**).

KeyGen: Takes a security parameter k and returns mst_1, mst_2, usk_0 and pk. Public key pk includes a description of finite message space $\mathcal{M}$, and description of finite ciphertext space $\mathcal{C}$.

Δ-Gen: Takes as inputs, mst_j and i, and returns stage i helper key hsk_i if $j = i \bmod 2$, or $\perp$ otherwise.

Update: Takes as inputs, usk_{i-1}, hsk_i and i, and returns stage i user secret key usk_i.

Encrypt: Takes as inputs, pk, i and $M \in \mathcal{M}$, and returns ciphertext $C \in \mathcal{C}$.

Decrypt: Takes as inputs, pk, usk_i and $C \in \mathcal{C}$, and returns $M \in \mathcal{M}$ or $\perp$.

These algorithms satisfy $\forall i \in \{1, ..., N\}$, $\forall M \in \mathcal{M}$, **Decrypt**$(pk, usk_i, C) = M$ where $C = $ **Encrypt**(pk, i, M).

2.2 Security Notion

Here, we define the notion of semantic security for PKIPE. This is based on the security definition in the original KIPE [11, 7]. It should be noticed that the definition in [7] looks simpler than in [11] but they are essentially the same.

We say that a PKIPE scheme $\mathcal{E}$ is *semantically secure against an adaptive chosen ciphertext attack under an adaptive chosen key exposure attack* (IND-KE-CCA) if no polynomially bounded adversary $\mathcal{A}$ has a non-negligible advantage against the challenger in the following IND-KE-CCA game:

Setup: The challenger takes a security parameter k and runs the **KeyGen** algorithm. He gives pk to $\mathcal{A}$ and keeps usk_0, mst_1 and mst_2 to himself.

---

[1] key-insulated public key encryption with optimum threshold.

Phase 1: $\mathcal{A}$ issues queries $q_1, \cdots, q_m$ where each of the queries q_i is one of:

- Exposure query $\langle j, \texttt{class} \rangle$: If $\texttt{class}$ = "user", the challenger responds by running the algorithms Δ-**Gen** and **Update** to generate usk_j and sends it to $\mathcal{A}$. If $\texttt{class}$ = "helper", the challenger sends mst_j to $\mathcal{A}$.
- Decryption query $\langle j, C \rangle$: The challenger responds by running the algorithms Δ-**Gen** and **Update** to generate usk_j. He then runs **Decrypt** to decrypt the ciphertext C using usk_j and sends the result to $\mathcal{A}$.

These queries may be asked adaptively, that is, each query q_i may depend on the replies to $q_1, \cdots, q_{i-1}$.

Challenge: Once $\mathcal{A}$ decides that Phase 1 is over, she outputs two equal length plaintexts $M_0, M_1 \in \mathcal{M}$ and $j^* \in \{1, 2, ..., N\}$ on which she wishes to be challenged. The challenger picks a random bit $\beta \in \{0, 1\}$ and sets $C^* = $ **Encrypt**(pk, j^*, M_β). The challenger sends C^* as the challenge to $\mathcal{A}$.

Phase 2: $\mathcal{A}$ issues additional queries $q_{m+1}, \cdots, q_{max}$ where each of the queries is one of:

- Exposure query $\langle j, \texttt{class} \rangle$: Challenger responds as in Phase 1.
- Decryption query $\langle j, C \rangle$: Challenger responds as in Phase 1.

These queries may be asked adaptively as in Phase 1.

Guess: Finally, $\mathcal{A}$ outputs $\beta' \in \{0, 1\}$. She wins the game if $\beta' = \beta$ and

1. $\langle j^*, C^* \rangle$ does not appear in Decryption queries,
2. $\langle j^*, \text{"user"} \rangle$ does not appear in Exposure queries,
3. both $\langle j^*-1, \text{"user"} \rangle$ and $\langle 2-(j^* \bmod 2), \text{"helper"} \rangle$ do not simultaneously appear in Exposure queries,
4. both $\langle j^*+1, \text{"user"} \rangle$ and $\langle (j^* \bmod 2)+1, \text{"helper"} \rangle$ do not simultaneously appear in Exposure queries,
5. both $\langle 1, \text{"helper"} \rangle$ and $\langle 2, \text{"helper"} \rangle$ do not simultaneously appear in Exposure queries.

We refer to such an adversary $\mathcal{A}$ as an IND-KE-CCA adversary. We define $\mathcal{A}$'s advantage in attacking the scheme $\mathcal{E}$ as $Adv_{\mathcal{E}, \mathcal{A}} = \Pr[\beta' = \beta] - 1/2$. The provability is over the random bits used by the challenger and $\mathcal{A}$. As usual, we can define chosen plaintext security similarly to the game above except that the adversary is not allowed to issue any Decryption queries. We call this adversary IND-KE-CPA *adversary*.

Definition 1. We say that a PKIPE system $\mathcal{E}$ is (t, ϵ)-*adaptive chosen ciphertext secure under adaptive chosen key exposure attacks* if for any t-time IND-KE-CCA adversary $\mathcal{A}$, we have $Adv_{\mathcal{E}, \mathcal{A}} < \epsilon$. As shorthand, we say that $\mathcal{E}$ is IND-KE-CCA *secure*. Also, we say that $\mathcal{E}$ is (t, ϵ)-*adaptive chosen plaintext secure under adaptive chosen key exposure attacks* if for any t-time IND-KE-CPA adversary $\mathcal{A}$, we have $Adv_{\mathcal{E}, \mathcal{A}} < \epsilon$. As shorthand, we say that $\mathcal{E}$ is IND-KE-CPA *secure*.

IND-KE-CCA is already a strong security notion, but its security can be enhanced further to cover the compromise of both the helper keys. Concretely, as a constraint on the above adversary's Exposure query, we can modify 5. so that:

5′. $\langle 1, \text{"helper"}\rangle$, $\langle 2, \text{"helper"}\rangle$, and $\langle j, \text{"user"}\rangle$ do not simultaneously appear in Exposure queries for any $j \in \{1, 2, ..., N\}$.

Such modification allows $\mathcal{A}$ to obtain both mst_1 and mst_2 if $\mathcal{A}$ doesn't ask any of user secret keys. Let this adversary be a *strong* IND-KE-CCA adversary. Similarly, we can define *strong* IND-KE-CPA *adversary*, and here as well, she is not allowed to issue any Decryption queries.

Definition 2. We say that a PKIPE system $\mathcal{E}$ is (t, ϵ)-*adaptive chosen ciphertext secure under strongly adaptive chosen key exposure attacks* if for any t-time strong IND-KE-CCA adversary $\mathcal{A}$, we have $Adv_{\mathcal{E},\mathcal{A}} < \epsilon$. As shorthand, we say that $\mathcal{E}$ is *strongly* IND-KE-CCA *secure*. Also, we say that $\mathcal{E}$ is (t, ϵ)-*adaptive chosen plaintext secure under strongly adaptive chosen key exposure attacks* if for any t-time strong IND-KE-CPA adversary $\mathcal{A}$, we have $Adv_{\mathcal{E},\mathcal{A}} < \epsilon$. As shorthand, we say that $\mathcal{E}$ is *strongly* IND-KE-CPA *secure*.

A Remark. In the discussion we had so far, it may seem like we may have overlooked the exposure of stage i helper key, but actually, we haven't. It is obvious that if hsk_i can be computed from usk_{i-1} and usk_i for any stage i, then exposure of hsk_i can be emulated by using the responses to the Exposure queries. So, the security definition so far given is sufficient as it is even against exposure of stage i helper keys for any i, if we assume that such property holds. As a matter of fact, all of our constructions satisfy this property.

2.3   Bilinear Maps and the CBDH Assumption

Throughout this paper, we let $\mathbb{G}_1$ and $\mathbb{G}_2$ be two multiplicative cyclic groups of prime order q, and g be a generator of $\mathbb{G}_1$. A *bilinear map* $e : \mathbb{G}_1 \times \mathbb{G}_1 \to \mathbb{G}_2$ satisfies the following properties: (i) For all $u, v \in \mathbb{G}_1$ and $a, b \in \mathbb{Z}$, $e(u^a, v^b) = e(u, v)^{ab}$. (ii) $e(g, g) \neq 1$. (iii) There is an efficient algorithm to compute $e(u, v)$ for all $u, v \in \mathbb{G}_1$. The *Computational Bilinear Diffie-Hellman (CBDH) problem* [5] in $\langle \mathbb{G}_1, \mathbb{G}_2, e \rangle$ is as follows: given a tuple $(g, g^a, g^b, g^c) \in (\mathbb{G}_1)^4$ as input, output $e(g, g)^{abc} \in \mathbb{G}_2$. An algorithm $\mathcal{A}_{cbdh}$ solves CBDH problem in $\langle \mathbb{G}_1, \mathbb{G}_2, e \rangle$ with the probability ϵ_{cbdh} if $\Pr[\mathcal{A}_{cbdh}(g, g^a, g^b, g^c) = e(g, g)^{abc}] \geq \epsilon_{cbdh}$, where the probability is over the random choice of generator $g \in \mathbb{G}_1 \backslash \{1\}$, and $a, b, c \in \mathbb{Z}_q$ and random coins consumed by $\mathcal{A}_{cbdh}$.

Definition 3. We say that the $(t_{cbdh}, \epsilon_{cbdh})$-*CBDH assumption* holds in $\langle \mathbb{G}_1, \mathbb{G}_2, e \rangle$ if no t_{cbdh}-time algorithm has advantage of at least ϵ_{cbdh} in solving the CBDH problem in $\langle \mathbb{G}_1, \mathbb{G}_2, e \rangle$.

3   Chosen Plaintext Secure Construction

In this section, we propose our PKIPE schemes and prove its security under CBDH assumption in the random oracle model. Intuitively, picture two independent Boneh-Franklin IBEs (BF-IBE) [5, 6] integrated to one another and the master key of one BF-IBE is free to leak. Applying a straightforward 2-out-of-2 threshold key generation of BF-IBE [5] is not the correct answer since then the master keys of both BF-IBEs will be required to update a decryption key. Instead, in our PKIPE schemes, master keys of the two independent BF-IBEs are *alternately* used to update a single key (so, only one master key is used at a time). Furthermore, interestingly, decryption key size, ciphertext size and computational cost for decryption in our PKIPE remain unchanged (and public key size and encryption cost is increased but only slightly for one element in $\mathbb{G}_1$ and one pairing computation, respectively) as in the original BF-IBE. In our schemes, we let $N = O(\mathsf{poly}(k))$.

3.1 Construction

Let $\mathbb{G}_1$ and $\mathbb{G}_2$ be two groups of order q of size k, and g be a generator of $\mathbb{G}_1$. Let $e : \mathbb{G}_1 \times \mathbb{G}_1 \to \mathbb{G}_2$ be a bilinear map. Let G, H be cryptographic hash functions $G : \mathbb{G}_2 \to \{0,1\}^n$ for some n, $H : \{0,1\}^* \to \mathbb{G}_1$, respectively. The message space is $\mathcal{M} = \{0,1\}^n$. The PKIPE1 scheme consists of the following algorithms:

PKIPE1: IND-KE-CPA CONSTRUCTION

KeyGen: Given a security parameter k, **KeyGen** algorithm:
1. generates $\mathbb{G}_1$, $\mathbb{G}_2$, g and e.
2. picks $s_1, s_2 \in \mathbb{Z}_q^*$ uniformly at random, and sets $h_1 = g^{s_1}$ and $h_2 = g^{s_2}$,
3. chooses cryptographic hash functions G and H,
4. computes $u_{-1} = H(-1)$ and $u_0 = H(0)$,
5. computes $d_{-1} = u_{-1}^{s_1}$ and $d_0 = u_0^{s_2}$,
6. outputs $pk = \langle q, \mathbb{G}_1, \mathbb{G}_2, e, n, g, h_1, h_2, G, H \rangle$, $mst_1 = s_1$, $mst_2 = s_2$ and $usk_0 = d_{-1} \cdot d_0$.

Δ-Gen: For given mst_j and $i \in \{1, 2, ..., N\}$, **Δ-Gen** algorithm:
1. outputs $\perp$ if $i \not\equiv j \bmod 2$,
2. computes $u_{i-2} = H(i-2)$ and $u_i = H(i)$,
3. computes $d_{i-2} = u_{i-2}^{s_j}$ and $d_i = u_i^{s_j}$,
4. outputs $hsk_i = d_{i-2}^{-1} \cdot d_i$.

Update: For given usk_{i-1}, hsk_i and i, **Update** algorithm:
1. computes $usk_i = usk_{i-1} \cdot hsk_i$,
2. deletes usk_{i-1} and hsk_i,
3. outputs usk_i.

Encrypt: For given pk, i and a message $M \in \{0,1\}^n$, **Encrypt** algorithm:
1. chooses random $r \in \mathbb{Z}_q^*$,
2. computes $u_{i-1} = H(i-1)$ and $u_i = H(i)$,
3. if $i = 0 \bmod 2$, computes $W = (e(h_1, u_{i-1}) \cdot e(h_2, u_i))^r$,
4. if $i = 1 \bmod 2$, computes $W = (e(h_1, u_i) \cdot e(h_2, u_{i-1}))^r$,
5. sets $C = \langle i, g^r, G(W) \oplus M \rangle$,
6. outputs C as a ciphertext.

Decrypt: For given pk, usk_i and $C = \langle i, c_0, c_1 \rangle$, **Decrypt** algorithm:
1. computes $W' = e(c_0, usk_i)$,
2. computes $M' = c_1 \oplus G(W')$,
3. outputs M' as a plaintext.

3.2 Security

Now, we prove that PKIPE1 is IND-KE-CPA under the CBDH assumption. For readers who are already familiar with KIPE and/or IBE, here we give an overview of the proof. PKIPE1 is based on [5, 6], so, a proof technique similar to [5, 6] can be applied. However, there are still some technical hurdles to overcome due to the peculiar key-updating mechanism using two different helper keys. Namely, embedding the given CBDH instance into the responses to the adversary's queries cannot be straightforwardly carried out since the keys are mutually dependent on one another, and that the simulation fails if inconsistency of the responses is noticed by the adversary. For example, suppose that the simulator embeds the given instance into $usk_\alpha (= d_{\alpha-1}d_\alpha)$ for some stage α. Here, the simulator does not know the value of usk_α but has to respond to any Exposure queries (except for usk_α) including $usk_{\alpha-1}(= d_{\alpha-2}d_{\alpha-1})$ and $usk_{\alpha+1}(= d_\alpha d_{\alpha+1})$. We notice that both factors of usk_α, i.e. $d_{\alpha-1}$ and d_α appear in $usk_{\alpha-1}$ or $usk_{\alpha+1}$, and so, responding to $usk_{\alpha-1}$ and $usk_{\alpha+1}$ without knowing usk_α is not easy.

Theorem 1. *Suppose $(t_{cbdh}, \epsilon_{cbdh})$-CBDH assumption holds in $\langle \mathbb{G}_1, \mathbb{G}_2, e \rangle$ and hash functions G and H are random oracles. Then, PKIPE1 is $(t_{pkipe}, \epsilon_{pkipe})$-IND-KE-CPA secure as long as $\epsilon_{pkipe} \leq \frac{3q_G N}{2} \epsilon_{cbdh}$ and $t_{pkipe} \leq t_{cbdh} + \Theta(\tau(2q_H + 3q_E))$, where IND-KE-CPA adversary $\mathcal{A}_{pkipe}$ issues at most q_H H-queries and q_E Exposure queries. Here, τ is the maximum time for computing an exponentiation in $\mathbb{G}_1, \mathbb{G}_2$, and pairing e.*

Proof. We show that we can construct an algorithm $\mathcal{A}_{cbdh}$ that can solve the CBDH problem in $\langle \mathbb{G}_1, \mathbb{G}_2, e \rangle$ by using an adversary $\mathcal{A}_{pkipe}$ that breaks IND-KE-CPA security of our scheme. The algorithm $\mathcal{A}_{cbdh}$ is given an instance $\langle g, g^a, g^b, g^c \rangle$ in $\mathbb{G}_1$ from the challenger and tries to output $e(g, g)^{abc}$ using $\mathcal{A}_{pkipe}$. Let $g_1 = g^a, g_2 = g^b, g_3 = g^c$. The algorithm $\mathcal{A}_{cbdh}$ works by interacting with $\mathcal{A}_{pkipe}$ in an IND-KE-CPA game as follows:

Before starting the simulation, $\mathcal{A}_{cbdh}$ flips a coin $\mathcal{COIN} \in \{0, 1\}$ such that we have $\Pr[\mathcal{COIN} = 0] = \delta$ for some δ which we will determine later. If $\mathcal{COIN} = 0$, $\mathcal{A}_{cbdh}$ simulates the responses to $\mathcal{A}_{pkipe}$'s queries expecting that $\mathcal{A}_{pkipe}$ will never submit $\langle j, \text{"helper"} \rangle$ as Exposure query for any j. If $\mathcal{COIN} = 1$, $\mathcal{A}_{cbdh}$ carries out the simulation expecting that $\mathcal{A}_{pkipe}$ will submit $\langle j, \text{"helper"} \rangle$ for some j.

If $\mathcal{COIN} = 0$, $\mathcal{A}_{cbdh}$ responses to $\mathcal{A}_{pkipe}$'s queries will be as follows:

Setup: $\mathcal{A}_{cbdh}$ picks a random $s \in \mathbb{Z}_q^*$. Also, $\mathcal{A}_{cbdh}$ gives $\mathcal{A}_{pkipe}$ the system parameter $pk = \langle q, \mathbb{G}_1, \mathbb{G}_2, e, n, g, h_1, h_2, G, H \rangle$, where $h_1 = g_1$ and $h_2 = g_1^s$, and random oracles G, H are controlled by $\mathcal{A}_{cbdh}$ as described below.

G-queries: $\mathcal{A}_{pkipe}$ issues up to q_G queries to the random oracle G. To respond to these queries algorithm, $\mathcal{A}_{cbdh}$ forms a list of tuples $\langle W, x \rangle$ as explained below. We call this list G_{list}. The list is initially empty. When $\mathcal{A}_{pkipe}$ gives $\mathcal{A}_{cbdh}$ a query W to the oracle G, $\mathcal{A}_{cbdh}$ responds as follows:

1. If the query W already appears on the G_{list} in a tuple $\langle W, x \rangle$, then outputs $G(W) = x$.

2. $\mathcal{A}_{cbdh}$ chooses a random $x \in \{0,1\}^n$.

3. $\mathcal{A}_{cbdh}$ adds the tuple $\langle W, x \rangle$ to the G_{list} and outputs $G(W) = x$.

H-**queries:** $\mathcal{A}_{cbdh}$ picks a random $\alpha \in \{1, ..., N\}$ in advance. $\mathcal{A}_{pkipe}$ issues up to q_H queries to the random oracle H. To respond to these queries algorithm, $\mathcal{A}_{cbdh}$ forms a list of tuples $\langle i, u_i, r_i \rangle$ as explained below. We call the list H_{list}. The list is initially empty. When $\mathcal{A}_{pkipe}$ gives $\mathcal{A}_{cbdh}$ a query i to the oracle H, $\mathcal{A}_{cbdh}$ responds as follows:

1. If the query i already appears on the H_{list} in a tuple $\langle i, u_i, r_i \rangle$, then outputs $H(i) = u_i$.

2. If $i = \alpha$, $\mathcal{A}_{cbdh}$ sets $u_i = g_2$ and $r_\alpha = 0$.

3. If $i < \alpha$, $\mathcal{A}_{cbdh}$ chooses a random $r_i \in \mathbb{Z}_q^*$ and sets $u_i = g^{r_i}$.

4. If $i > \alpha$, $\mathcal{A}_{cbdh}$ chooses a random $r_i \in \mathbb{Z}_q^*$ and sets $u_i = g_2^z \cdot g^{r_i}$, where
   - $z = 1$ if $i = \alpha \bmod 2$,
   - $z = -s$ if $i = 1 \bmod 2$ and $\alpha = 0 \bmod 2$,
   - $z = -s^{-1}$ if $i = 0 \bmod 2$ and $\alpha = 1 \bmod 2$, where s^{-1} is the inverse of $s \bmod q$,

5. $\mathcal{A}_{cbdh}$ adds the tuple $\langle i, u_i, r_i \rangle$ to the H_{list} and outputs $H(i) = u_i$.

Challenge: Once algorithm $\mathcal{A}_{pkipe}$ decides that Phase 1 is over, it outputs a target stage i^* and two messages M_0, M_1 on which it wishes to be challenged. Algorithm $\mathcal{A}_{cbdh}$ responds as follows:

1. $\mathcal{A}_{cbdh}$ sets $C^* = \langle i^*, c_0^*, c_1^* \rangle$ as $c_0^* = g_3$ and $c_1^* = \mu$, where $\mu \in_R \{0,1\}^n$.

2. $\mathcal{A}_{cbdh}$ gives $C^* = \langle i^*, c_0^*, c_1^* \rangle$ as the challenge ciphertext to $\mathcal{A}_{pkipe}$.

Exposure queries: $\mathcal{A}_{pkipe}$ issues up to q_E Exposure queries. When $\mathcal{A}_{pkipe}$ gives a query $\langle i, \text{class} \rangle$, $\mathcal{A}_{cbdh}$ responds as follows:

1. If $\text{class} = $ "helper" or $i = \alpha$, $\mathcal{A}_{cbdh}$ aborts the simulation.

2. $\mathcal{A}_{cbdh}$ runs the algorithm for responding to H-queries to obtain $\langle i, u_i, r_i \rangle$ and $\langle i-1, u_{i-1}, r_{i-1} \rangle$.

3. $\mathcal{A}_{cbdh}$ sets $usk_i = h_1^{r_{i-1}} \cdot h_2^{r_i}$ if $i = 0 \bmod 2$, or $usk_i = h_1^{r_i} \cdot h_2^{r_{i-1}}$ otherwise, and outputs usk_i to $\mathcal{A}_{pkipe}$. Observe that usk_i is the user secret key corresponding to the stage i. Especially, when $i > \alpha$,

$$u_{i-1}^{\log_g h_1} \cdot u_i^{\log_g h_2} = (g_2^{-s} \cdot g^{r_{i-1}})^a \cdot (g_2 \cdot g^{r_i})^{s \cdot a} = h_1^{r_{i-1}} h_2^{r_i}$$
$$(\text{if } i = 0 \bmod 2, \ \alpha = 0 \bmod 2)$$

$$= (g_2 \cdot g^{r_{i-1}})^a \cdot (g_2^{-s^{-1}} \cdot g^{r_i})^{s \cdot a} = h_1^{r_{i-1}} h_2^{r_i}$$
$$(\text{if } i = 0 \bmod 2, \ \alpha = 1 \bmod 2)$$

$$u_{i-1}^{\log_g h_2} \cdot u_i^{\log_g h_1} = (g_2 \cdot g^{r_{i-1}})^{s \cdot a} \cdot (g_2^{-s} \cdot g^{r_i})^a = h_2^{r_{i-1}} h_1^{r_i}$$
$$(\text{if } i = 1 \bmod 2, \ \alpha = 0 \bmod 2)$$

$$= (g_2^{-s^{-1}} \cdot g^{r_{i-1}})^{s \cdot a} \cdot (g_2 \cdot g^{r_i})^a = h_2^{r_{i-1}} h_1^{r_i}$$
$$(\text{if } i = 1 \bmod 2, \ \alpha = 1 \bmod 2)$$

Guess: When $\mathcal{A}_{pkipe}$ decides that Phase 2 is over, $\mathcal{A}_{pkipe}$ outputs its guess bit $\beta' \in \{0,1\}$. At the same time, algorithm $\mathcal{A}_{cbdh}$ terminates the simulation. Then, $\mathcal{A}_{cbdh}$ picks a tuple $\langle W, x \rangle$ uniformly at random from the G_{list}, and computes $T = (\frac{W}{e(g_1, g_3)^{r_{\alpha-1}}})^{s^{-1}}$ if $\alpha = 0 \bmod 2$, or $T = (\frac{W}{e(g_1, g_3)^{s \cdot r_{\alpha-1}}})$ if $\alpha = 1 \bmod 2$. Finally, $\mathcal{A}_{cbdh}$ outputs T.

Claim 1. *If $i^* = \alpha$ and $\mathcal{A}_{cbdh}$ does not abort, then $\mathcal{A}_{pkipe}$'s view is identical to its view in the real attack until $\mathcal{A}_{pkipe}$ submits W^* as a G-query, where $W^* = e(g_1, g_3)^{r_{\alpha-1}} \cdot e(g, g)^{s \cdot abc}$ if $\alpha = 0 \bmod 2$, or $W^* = e(g_1, g_3)^{s \cdot r_{\alpha-1}} \cdot e(g, g)^{abc}$ if $\alpha = 1 \bmod 2$.*

Proof. It is obvious that the responses to G and H are as in the real attack. Interestingly, the responses to Exposure queries are perfect if $\mathcal{A}_{cbdh}$ does not abort. Finally, we show that the response to Challenge is indistinguishable from the real attack until $\mathcal{A}_{pkipe}$ submits W^*. Let the response to Challenge be $C^* = \langle \alpha, c_0^*, c_1^* \rangle$. Then, c_0^* is uniformly distributed in $\mathbb{G}_1$ due to random $\log_g g_3 (= c)$, and therefore are as in the real attack. Also, since $c_1^* = M_\beta \oplus G(W^*)$, it is information-theoretically impossible to obtain any information on M_β unless $\mathcal{A}_{pkipe}$ asks $G(W^*)$. □

Next, let us define by E_1, an event assigned to be true if and only if $i^* = \alpha$. Similarly, let us define by E_2, an event assigned to be true if and only if a G-query coincides with W^*, and by E_{msk}, an event assigned to be true if and only if an Exposure query coincides with $\langle i, \text{"helper"} \rangle$ for any $i \in \{1, 2\}$.

Claim 2. *We have that $\Pr[\beta' = \beta | E_1, \neg E_{msk}] \geq \Pr[\beta' = \beta | \neg E_{msk}]$.*

Proof. It is clear that $\sum_{i \in \{1, \dots, N\}} \Pr[\beta' = \beta | i^* = i, \neg E_{msk}] \Pr[i^* = i | \neg E_{msk}] = \Pr[\beta' = \beta | \neg E_{msk}]$. Since α is uniformly chosen from $\{1, \dots N\}$ at random, we have $\Pr[\beta' = \beta | i^* = \alpha, \neg E_{msk}]] \Pr[i^* = \alpha | \neg E_{msk}] \geq \frac{1}{N} \Pr[\beta' = \beta | \neg E_{msk}]$. Therefore, we have $\Pr[\beta' = \beta | E_1, \neg E_{msk}] \geq \Pr[\beta' = \beta | \neg E_{msk}]$, which proves the claim. □

Claim 3. *We have that $\Pr[\beta' = \beta | E_1, \neg E_2, \neg E_{msk}] = 1/2$.*

Proof. Let C^* be $\langle \alpha, c_0^*, c_1^* \rangle$. Since $c_1^* = M_\beta \oplus G(W^*)$, it is impossible to obtain any information on M_β without asking W^* as a G-query. □

Claim 4. *We have that $\Pr[\mathcal{A}_{cbdh}(g, g^a, g^b, g^c) = e(g, g)^{abc} | \mathcal{COIN} = 0] \geq \frac{1}{q_G N} \cdot \Pr[E_2 | E_1, \neg E_{msk}] \Pr[\neg E_{msk}]$.*

Proof. If $i^* = \alpha$, then $e(g, g)^{abc}$ can easily be calculated from W^*, and W^* appears in G_{list} with probability $\Pr[E_2]$. We have $\Pr[E_2] \geq \Pr[E_2 | E_1, \neg E_{msk}] \cdot \Pr[E_1 | \neg E_{msk}] \cdot \Pr[\neg E_{msk}]$ and $\Pr[E_1 | \neg E_{msk}] = 1/N$. Hence, by choosing a tuple from G_{list} uniformly at random, $\mathcal{A}_{cbdh}$ can correctly output $e(g, g)^{abc}$ with probability of at least $1/q_G \cdot 1/N \cdot \Pr[E_2 | E_1, \neg E_{msk}] \Pr[\neg E_{msk}]$. □

Finally, we calculate $p_0 := \Pr[\mathcal{A}_{cbdh}(g, g^a, g^b, g^c) = e(g, g)^{abc} | \mathcal{COIN} = 0]$. Letting $\gamma := \Pr[\beta' = \beta | E_{msk}] - 1/2$, from Claims 1 and 2, we have

$$\Pr[\beta' = \beta] - \frac{1}{2} = \Pr[\beta' = \beta | \neg E_{msk}] \Pr[\neg E_{msk}] + \Pr[\beta' = \beta | E_{msk}] \Pr[E_{msk}] - \frac{1}{2}$$

$$= \Pr[\beta' = \beta | \neg E_{msk}](1 - \Pr[E_{msk}]) + (\frac{1}{2} + \gamma) \Pr[E_{msk}] - \frac{1}{2}$$

$$\leq \Pr[\beta' = \beta | E_1, \neg E_{msk}](1 - \Pr[E_{msk}]) + (\frac{1}{2} + \gamma) \Pr[E_{msk}] - \frac{1}{2}.$$

From $\Pr[\beta' = \beta | E_1, \neg E_{msk}] = \Pr[\beta' = \beta | E_1, E_2, \neg E_{msk}] \cdot \Pr[E_2 | E_1, \neg E_{msk}] + \Pr[\beta' = \beta | E_1, \neg E_2, \neg E_{msk}] \cdot \Pr[\neg E_2 | E_1, \neg E_{msk}]$ and Claim 3, we have

$$\Pr[\beta' = \beta] - \frac{1}{2} \leq (\Pr[E_2 | E_1, \neg E_{msk}] + \frac{1}{2}(1 - \Pr[E_2 | E_1, \neg E_{msk}]))(1 - \Pr[E_{msk}])$$
$$+ (\frac{1}{2} + \gamma) \Pr[E_{msk}] - \frac{1}{2}$$
$$= \frac{1}{2} \Pr[E_2 | E_1, \neg E_{msk}] \Pr[\neg E_{msk}] + \gamma \Pr[E_{msk}].$$

From Claim 4, we have $p_0 \geq \frac{2}{q_G N} (\epsilon_{pkipe} - \gamma \Pr[E_{msk}])$.

Next, we discuss for the $\mathcal{COIN} = 1$ case. If $\mathcal{COIN} = 1$, $\mathcal{A}_{cbdh}$ responses to $\mathcal{A}_{pkipe}$'s queries as follows:

Setup: $\mathcal{A}_{cbdh}$ picks random $s \in \mathbb{Z}_q^*$ and $\mathbf{b} \in \{1, 2\}$. Let $\bar{\mathbf{b}}$ be 1 (resp. 2) if $\mathbf{b} = 2$ (resp. 1). Also, $\mathcal{A}_{cbdh}$ gives $\mathcal{A}_{pkipe}$ the system parameter $pk = \langle q, \mathbb{G}_1, \mathbb{G}_2, e, n, g, h_1, h_2, G, H \rangle$, where $h_{\mathbf{b}} = g_1$ and $h_{\bar{\mathbf{b}}} = g^s$, and random oracles G, H are controlled by $\mathcal{A}_{cbdh}$ as described below.

G-queries: $\mathcal{A}_{pkipe}$ issues up to q_G queries to the random oracle G. To respond to these queries algorithm $\mathcal{A}_{cbdh}$ forms a list of tuples $\langle W, x \rangle$ as explained below. We call this list G_{list}. The list is initially empty. When $\mathcal{A}_{pkipe}$ gives $\mathcal{A}_{cbdh}$ a query W to the oracle G, $\mathcal{A}_{cbdh}$ responds as follows:

1. If the query W already appears on the G_{list} in a tuple $\langle W, x \rangle$, then outputs $G(W) = x$.
2. $\mathcal{A}_{cbdh}$ chooses a random $x \in \{0, 1\}^n$.
3. $\mathcal{A}_{cbdh}$ adds the tuple $\langle W, x \rangle$ to the G_{list} and outputs $G(W) = x$.

H-queries: $\mathcal{A}_{cbdh}$ picks a random $\alpha \in \{1, ..., N\}$ in advance. $\mathcal{A}_{pkipe}$ issues up to q_H queries to the random oracle H. To respond to these queries algorithm $\mathcal{A}_{cbdh}$ forms a list of tuples $\langle i, u_i, r_i \rangle$ as explained below. We call the list H_{list}. The list is initially empty. When $\mathcal{A}_{pkipe}$ gives $\mathcal{A}_{cbdh}$ a query i to the oracle H, $\mathcal{A}_{cbdh}$ responds as follows:

1. If the query i already appears on the H_{list} in a tuple $\langle i, u_i, r_i \rangle$, then outputs $H(i) = u_i$.
2. If $i = \alpha - 1$ and $\alpha \equiv \bar{\mathbf{b}} \bmod 2$, $\mathcal{A}_{cbdh}$ sets $u_i = g_2$ and $r_i = 0$.
3. If $i = \alpha$ and $\alpha \equiv \mathbf{b} \bmod 2$, $\mathcal{A}_{cbdh}$ sets $u_i = g_2$ and $r_i = 0$.
4. Else, $\mathcal{A}_{cbdh}$ chooses a random $r_i \in \mathbb{Z}_q^*$ and sets $u_i = g^{r_i}$.
5. $\mathcal{A}_{cbdh}$ adds the tuple $\langle i, u_i, r_i \rangle$ to the H_{list} and outputs $H(i) = u_i$.

Challenge: Once algorithm $\mathcal{A}_{pkipe}$ decides that Phase 1 is over, it outputs a target stage i^* and two messages M_0, M_1 on which it wishes to be challenged. Algorithm $\mathcal{A}_{cbdh}$ responds as follows:

1. $\mathcal{A}_{cbdh}$ sets $C^* = \langle i^*, c_0^*, c_1^* \rangle$ as $c_0^* = g_3$ and $c_1^* = \mu$, where $\mu \in_R \{0, 1\}^n$.
2. $\mathcal{A}_{cbdh}$ gives $C^* = \langle i^*, c_0^*, c_1^* \rangle$ as the challenge ciphertext to $\mathcal{A}_{pkipe}$.

Exposure queries: $\mathcal{A}_{pkipe}$ issues up to q_E Exposure queries. When $\mathcal{A}_{pkipe}$ gives a query $\langle i, \mathtt{class} \rangle$, $\mathcal{A}_{cbdh}$ responds as follows:

1. If $i = \mathbf{b}$ and $\mathtt{class} = $ "helper", $\mathcal{A}_{cbdh}$ aborts the simulation.
2. If $i = \bar{\mathbf{b}}$ and $\mathtt{class} = $ "helper", $\mathcal{A}_{cbdh}$ returns s to $\mathcal{A}_{pkipe}$.

3. If $i = \alpha$ and class = "user", $\mathcal{A}_{cbdh}$ aborts the simulation.
4. If $i = \alpha - 1$, class = "user" and $\alpha \equiv \bar{\mathbf{b}}$ mod 2, $\mathcal{A}_{cbdh}$ aborts the simulation.
5. If $i = \alpha + 1$, class = "user" and $\alpha \equiv \mathbf{b}$ mod 2, $\mathcal{A}_{cbdh}$ aborts the simulation.
6. Else[2], $\mathcal{A}_{cbdh}$ runs the algorithm for responding to H-queries to obtain $\langle i, u_i, r_i \rangle$ and $\langle i-1, u_{i-1}, r_{i-1} \rangle$, and sets $usk_i = h_1^{r_{i-1}} \cdot h_2^{r_i}$ if $i = 0$ mod 2, or $usk_i = h_1^{r_i} \cdot h_2^{r_{i-1}}$ otherwise. $\mathcal{A}_{cbdh}$ outputs usk_i to $\mathcal{A}_{pkipe}$.

Guess: When $\mathcal{A}_{pkipe}$ decides that Phase 2 is over, $\mathcal{A}_{pkipe}$ outputs the guess bit $\beta' \in \{0, 1\}$. At the same time, algorithm $\mathcal{A}_{cbdh}$ terminates the simulation. Then, $\mathcal{A}_{cbdh}$ picks a tuple $\langle W, x \rangle$ uniformly at random from the G_{list}, and computes $T = W \cdot e(g, g_3)^{-s \cdot r_\alpha}$ if $\alpha \equiv \bar{\mathbf{b}}$ mod 2, or $T = W \cdot e(g, g_3)^{-s \cdot r_{\alpha-1}}$ if $\alpha \equiv \mathbf{b}$ mod 2. Finally, $\mathcal{A}_{cbdh}$ outputs T.

Claim 5. *If $i^* = \alpha$, $\mathcal{A}_{pkipe}$ submits $\langle \bar{\mathbf{b}}, \text{"helper"} \rangle$ as an Extraction query, and $\mathcal{A}_{cbdh}$ does not abort, then $\mathcal{A}_{pkipe}$'s view is identical to its view in the real attack until $\mathcal{A}_{pkipe}$ submits W^* as a G-query, where $W^* = e(g, g_3)^{s \cdot r_\alpha} \cdot e(g, g)^{abc}$ if $\alpha \equiv \bar{\mathbf{b}}$ mod 2, or $W^* = e(g, g_3)^{s \cdot r_{\alpha-1}} \cdot e(g, g)^{abc}$ if $\alpha \equiv \mathbf{b}$ mod 2.*

Next, let us define by E_3, an event assigned to be true if and only if $i^* = \alpha$. Similarly, let us define by E_4, an event assigned to be true if and only if a G-query coincides with W^*, by E_5, an event assigned to be true if and only if an Exposure query coincides with $\langle \mathbf{b}, \text{"helper"} \rangle$, and by E_{msk}, an event assigned to be true if and only if an Exposure query coincides with $\langle i, \text{"helper"} \rangle$ for any $i \in \{1, 2\}$. Notice that E_{msk} is identical to that in the case of $\mathcal{COIN} = 0$.

Claim 6. *We have that $\Pr[\beta' = \beta | E_3, \neg E_5, E_{msk}] \geq \Pr[\beta' = \beta | E_{msk}]$.*

Claim 7. *We have that $\Pr[\beta' = \beta | E_3, \neg E_4, \neg E_5, E_{msk}] = 1/2$.*

Proofs of Claims 5, 6 and 7 are given in the full version of this paper.

Claim 8. *We have that $\Pr[\mathcal{A}_{cbdh}(g, g^a, g^b, g^c) = e(g, g)^{abc} | \mathcal{COIN} = 1] \geq \frac{1}{2 q_G N} \cdot \Pr[E_4 | E_3, \neg E_5, E_{msk}] \Pr[E_{msk}]$.*

Proof. If $i^* = \alpha$, then $e(g, g)^{abc}$ can easily be calculated from W^*, and W^* appears in G_{list} with probability $\Pr[E_4]$. We have $\Pr[E_4] \geq \Pr[E_4 | E_3, \neg E_5, E_{msk}] \cdot \Pr[E_3 | \neg E_5, E_{msk}] \cdot \Pr[\neg E_5, E_{msk}]$. Furthermore, we have $\Pr[E_3 | \neg E_5, E_{msk}] = 1/N$, and $\Pr[\neg E_5, E_{msk}] = 1/2 \cdot \Pr[E_{msk}]$. Hence, by choosing a tuple from G_{list} uniformly at random, $\mathcal{A}_{cbdh}$ can correctly output $e(g, g)^{abc}$ with probability of at least $1/q_G \cdot 1/N \cdot 1/2 \cdot \Pr[E_4 | E_3, \neg E_5, E_{msk}] \Pr[E_{msk}]$. $\square$

Finally, we calculate $p_1 := \Pr[\mathcal{A}_{cbdh}(g, g^a, g^b, g^c) = e(g, g)^{abc} | \mathcal{COIN} = 1]$. Letting $\eta := \Pr[\beta' = \beta | \neg E_{msk}] - 1/2$, from Claims 5 and 6, we have

---

[2] Notice that in this case, class is always "user".

$$\Pr[\beta' = \beta] - \frac{1}{2} = \Pr[\beta' = \beta | \neg E_{msk}] \Pr[\neg E_{msk}] + \Pr[\beta' = \beta | E_{msk}] \Pr[E_{msk}] - \frac{1}{2}$$

$$= (\frac{1}{2} + \eta) \Pr[\neg E_{msk}] + \Pr[\beta' = \beta | E_{msk}](1 - \Pr[\neg E_{msk}]) - \frac{1}{2}$$

$$\leq (\frac{1}{2} + \eta) \Pr[\neg E_{msk}]$$

$$+ \Pr[\beta' = \beta | E_3, \neg E_5, E_{msk}](1 - \Pr[\neg E_{msk}]) - \frac{1}{2}.$$

Since we have $\Pr[\beta' = \beta | E_3, \neg E_5, E_{msk}] = \Pr[\beta' = \beta | E_3, E_4, \neg E_5, E_{msk}] \cdot \Pr[E_4 | E_3, \neg E_5, E_{msk}] + \Pr[\beta' = \beta | E_3, \neg E_4, \neg E_5, E_{msk}] \cdot \Pr[\neg E_4 | E_3, \neg E_5, E_{msk}]$, from Claim 7, we have

$$\Pr[\beta' = \beta] - \frac{1}{2} \leq (\frac{1}{2} + \eta) \Pr[\neg E_{msk}]$$

$$+ (\Pr[E_4 | E_3, \neg E_5, E_{msk}] + \frac{1}{2}(1 - \Pr[E_4 | E_3, \neg E_5, E_{msk}]))$$

$$\cdot (1 - \Pr[\neg E_{msk}]) - \frac{1}{2}$$

$$= \frac{1}{2} \Pr[E_4 | E_3, \neg E_5, E_{msk}] \Pr[E_{msk}] + \eta \Pr[\neg E_{msk}].$$

From Claim 8, we have $p_1 \geq \frac{1}{q_G N}(\epsilon_{pkipe} - \eta \Pr[\neg E_{msk}])$.

Claim 9. *We have that* $\epsilon_{pkipe} \geq \gamma \Pr[E_{msk}] + \eta \Pr[\neg E_{msk}]$.

Proof. By the definitions of γ and η, we have $\gamma + 1/2 = \Pr[\beta' = \beta | E_{msk}]$ and $\eta + 1/2 = \Pr[\beta' = \beta | \neg E_{msk}]$, and consequently, $\epsilon_{pkipe} + \frac{1}{2} \geq \Pr[\beta' = \beta] = (\gamma + \frac{1}{2}) \Pr[E_{msk}] + (\eta + \frac{1}{2}) \Pr[\neg E_{msk}]$. Hence, we have $\epsilon_{pkipe} \geq \gamma \Pr[E_{msk}] + \eta \Pr[\neg E_{msk}]$, which proves the claim. □

Now, we calculate $\epsilon_{cbdh}(= \Pr[\mathcal{A}_{cbdh}(g, g^a, g^b, g^c) = e(g,g)^{abc}])$. From Claim 9, we have

$$\epsilon_{cbdh} = \delta \cdot p_0 + (1 - \delta) \cdot p_1$$

$$\geq \delta(\frac{2}{q_G N}(\epsilon_{pkipe} - \gamma \Pr[E_{msk}])) + (1 - \delta)(\frac{1}{q_G N}(\epsilon_{pkipe} - \eta \Pr[\neg E_{msk}]))$$

$$\geq \delta(\frac{2}{q_G N}(\epsilon_{pkipe} - \gamma \Pr[E_{msk}])) + (1 - \delta)(\frac{1}{q_G N}\gamma \Pr[E_{msk}])$$

$$\geq \frac{1}{q_G N}(2\delta \epsilon_{pkipe} + (1 - 3\delta)\gamma \Pr[E_{msk}])$$

By letting $\delta = 1/3$, we finally have $\epsilon_{cbdh} \geq \frac{2}{3q_G N} \epsilon_{pkipe}$.

From the above discussions, we can see that the claimed bound of the running-time of $\mathcal{A}_{cbdh}$ holds. This completes the proof of the theorem. □

3.3   Strongly IND-KE-CPA Scheme

We can build a construction of a strongly IND-KE-CPA scheme PKIPE2 by only slightly modifying PKIPE1. The PKIPE2 consists of the following algorithms:

PKIPE2: STRONGLY IND-KE-CPA CONSTRUCTION

KeyGen: Given a security parameter k, **KeyGen** algorithm does the same as that of PKIPE1 except that it:
    2. picks random, $s_1, s_2, s_3 \in \mathbb{Z}_q^*$, and sets $h_1 = g^{s_1 s_3}$ and $h_2 = g^{s_2 s_3}$,
    6. outputs $pk = \langle q, \mathbb{G}_1, \mathbb{G}_2, e, n, g, h_1, h_2, G, H \rangle$, $mst_1 = s_1$, $mst_2 = s_2$ and $usk_0 = \langle d_{-1}^{s_3} \cdot d_0^{s_3}, s_3 \rangle$.
Δ-Gen: Same as in PKIPE1.
Update: For given $usk_{i-1} = \langle usk'_{i-1}, s_3 \rangle$, hsk_i and i, **Update** algorithm:
    1. computes $usk'_i = usk'_{i-1} \cdot hsk_i^{s_3}$,
    2. deletes usk'_{i-1} and hsk_i,
    3. outputs $usk_i = \langle usk'_i, s_3 \rangle$.
Encrypt: Same as in PKIPE1.
Decrypt: For given $usk_i = \langle usk'_i, s_3 \rangle$ and $C = \langle i, c_0, c_1 \rangle$, **Decrypt** algorithm does the same as that of PKIPE1 except that it:
    1. computes $W' = e(c_0, usk'_i)$.

The security proof of PKIPE2 can be done similarly to PKIPE1. Here we briefly explain why both master keys, mst_1 and mst_2, can be exposed and still guarantee security. Since plaintext M is perfectly hidden by $G(e(g^r, usk'_i))$, it is necessary to compute $e(g^r, usk'_i)$ for compromising semantic security of PKIPE2. However, this is almost as difficult as the CBDH problem without knowing s_3 even if the adversary knows both mst_1 and mst_2. Hence, PKIPE2 is more secure than PKIPE1 against exposure of master helper keys.

4   Chosen Ciphertext Secure Construction

In this section, we construct chosen ciphertext secure PKIPE schemes by extending PKIPE1 and PKIPE2 with Fujisaki-Okamoto padding [15, 16]. It should be noticed that the proofs of security of our schemes cannot be straightforwardly done since the model of PKIPE significantly differs from the standard public key encryption.

4.1   Construction

Let F, G, H be cryptographic hash functions $F : \{1, ..., N\} \times \{0,1\}^n \times \{0,1\}^\ell \to \mathbb{Z}_q^*$, $G : \mathbb{G}_2 \to \{0,1\}^{n+\ell}$ for some n and ℓ, and $H : \{0,1\}^* \to \mathbb{G}_1$, respectively. The message space is $\mathcal{M} = \{0,1\}^n$. Except for the ones that are mentioned, the notions are the same as in PKIPE1. The PKIPE3 consists of the following algorithms:

PKIPE3: IND-KE-CCA Construction

KeyGen: Given a security parameter k, **KeyGen** algorithm does the same as that of PKIPE1 exceptthat it:

    3. chooses cryptographic hash functions F, G and H,

    6. outputs $pk = \langle q, \mathbb{G}_1, \mathbb{G}_2, e, n, g, h_1, h_2, F, G, H \rangle$, $mst_1 = s_1$, $mst_2 = s_2$ and $usk_0 = d_{-1} \cdot d_0$.

Δ-Gen: Same as in PKIPE1.

Update: Same as in PKIPE1.

Encrypt: For given pk, i and a message $M \in \{0,1\}^n$, **Encrypt** algorithm:

    1. chooses random $R \in \{0,1\}^\ell$,

    2. computes $\sigma = F(i, M, R)$,

    3. computes $u_{i-1} = H(i-1)$ and $u_i = H(i)$,

    4. if $i = 0 \bmod 2$, computes $W = (e(h_1, u_{i-1}) \cdot e(h_2, u_i))^\sigma$,

    5. if $i = 1 \bmod 2$, computes $W = (e(h_1, u_i) \cdot e(h_2, u_{i-1}))^\sigma$,

    6. sets $C = \langle i, \ g^\sigma, \ G(W) \oplus (M \| R) \rangle$,

    7. outputs C as a ciphertext.

Decrypt: For given pk, usk_i and $C = \langle i, c_0, c_1 \rangle$, **Decrypt** algorithm:

    1. outputs $\perp$ if $C \notin \mathbb{Z}_N \times \mathbb{G}_1 \times \{0,1\}^{n+\ell}$,

    2. computes $W' = e(c_0, usk_i)$,

    3. computes $(M' \| R') = c_1 \oplus G(W')$,

    4. outputs M' as a plaintext if $c_0 = g^{\sigma'}$, or $\perp$ otherwise, where $\sigma' = F(i, M', R')$.

4.2 Security

Now, we prove that PKIPE3 is IND-KE-CCA under the CBDH assumption.

Theorem 2. *Suppose $(t_{cbdh}, \epsilon_{cbdh})$-CBDH assumption holds in $\langle \mathbb{G}_1, \mathbb{G}_2, e \rangle$ and hash functions G and H are random oracles. Then, PKIPE3 is $(t_{pkipe}, \epsilon_{pkipe})$-IND-KE-CCA secure as long as $\epsilon_{pkipe} \leq \frac{3q_G N}{2}\epsilon_{cbdh} + \frac{2q_F}{2^\ell} + \frac{2q_D}{q}$ and $t_{pkipe} \leq t_{cbdh} + \Theta(\tau(5q_F + 2q_H + 3q_E + 5q_D))$, where IND-KE-CPA adversary $\mathcal{A}_{pkipe}$ issues at most q_F F-queries, q_H H-queries, q_D Decryption queries and q_E Exposure queries. Here, τ is the maximum time for computing an exponentiation in $\mathbb{G}_1$, $\mathbb{G}_2$, and pairing e.*

Proof. The proof of theorem is almost identical to Theorem 1 except that here, $\mathcal{A}_{cbdh}$ has to simulate responses to Decryption queries as well. For either the case for $\mathcal{COIN} = 0$ and 1, if $i \neq \alpha$, then it will be easy for $\mathcal{A}_{cbdh}$ to calculate usk_i on his own, so the decryption will be easily done as well. Therefore, we only need to consider the case for $i = \alpha$. Concretely, $\mathcal{A}_{cbdh}$'s responses to $\mathcal{A}_{pkipe}$'s queries can be simulated as follows:

F-queries: $\mathcal{A}_{pkipe}$ picks a random $R^* \in \{0,1\}^\ell$ in advance. $\mathcal{A}_{pkipe}$ issues up to q_F queries to the random oracle F. To respond to these queries, algorithm $\mathcal{A}_{cbdh}$ forms a list of tuples $\langle i, M, R, \sigma \rangle$ as explained below. We call this list F_{list}. The list is initially empty. When $\mathcal{A}_{pkipe}$ gives $\mathcal{A}_{cbdh}$ a query (i, M, R) to the oracle F, $\mathcal{A}_{cbdh}$ responds as follows:

1. If $R = R^*$, $\mathcal{A}_{cbdh}$ aborts the simulation.
2. If the query (i, M, R) already appears on the F_{list} in a tuple $\langle i, M, R, \sigma \rangle$, then outputs $F(i, M, R) = \sigma$.
3. $\mathcal{A}_{cbdh}$ chooses a random $\sigma \in \mathbb{Z}_q^*$.
4. $\mathcal{A}_{cbdh}$ adds the tuple $\langle i, M, R, \sigma \rangle$ to the F_{list} and outputs $F(i, M, R) = \sigma$.

Challenge: Once algorithm $\mathcal{A}_{pkipe}$ decides that Phase 1 is over, it outputs a target stage i^* and two messages M_0, M_1 on which it wishes to be challenged. Algorithm $\mathcal{A}_{cbdh}$ responds as follows:

1. $\mathcal{A}_{cbdh}$ sets $C^* = \langle i^*, c_0^*, c_1^* \rangle$ as $c_0^* = g_3$ and $c_1^* = \mu$, where $\mu \in_R \{0,1\}^{n+\ell}$.
2. $\mathcal{A}_{cbdh}$ gives $C^* = \langle i^*, c_0^*, c_1^* \rangle$ as the challenge ciphertext to $\mathcal{A}_{pkipe}$.

Decryption queries: $\mathcal{A}_{pkipe}$ issues up to q_D Decryption queries. When $\mathcal{A}_{pkipe}$ gives a query $C = \langle i, c_0, c_1 \rangle$, $\mathcal{A}_{cbdh}$ responds as follows:

1. If $i \neq \alpha$, $\mathcal{A}_{cbdh}$ runs the algorithm to respond to Exposure queries to obtain usk_i, decrypts C, and outputs the decryption result to $\mathcal{A}_{pkipe}$.
2. If $i = \alpha$, $\mathcal{A}_{cbdh}$ searches for a tuple $\langle \alpha, M, R, \sigma \rangle$ from F_{list} such that

$$
\begin{aligned}
c_0 &= g^\sigma, \\
c_1 &= G((e(h_1, u_{\alpha-1}) \cdot e(h_2, u_\alpha))^\sigma) \oplus (M||R) && \text{if } \alpha = 0 \bmod 2, \\
&= G((e(h_1, u_\alpha) \cdot e(h_2, u_{\alpha-1}))^\sigma) \oplus (M||R) && \text{if } \alpha = 1 \bmod 2.
\end{aligned}
$$

3. If there exists such a tuple, $\mathcal{A}_{cbdh}$ outputs M to $\mathcal{A}_{pkipe}$. Otherwise, $\mathcal{A}_{cbdh}$ outputs $\perp$.

Responses to G-queries, H-queries and Exposure queries can be simulated similarly to the proof in Theorem 1.

Next, let us define by F-$Fail$ an event assigned to be true if and only if there exists a F-query $\langle i, M, R \rangle$ such that $R = R^*$. Similarly, let us define by D-$Fail$ an event assigned to be true if and only if $\mathcal{A}_{cbdh}$ returns $\perp$ for a Decryption query which should not be rejected.

Using this, and following the proof of Theorem 1, we get the next inequalities:

$$
p_0 \geq \frac{2}{q_G N} (\epsilon_{pkipe} - \gamma \Pr[E_{msk}] - \Pr[F\text{-}Fail] - \Pr[D\text{-}Fail]),
$$

$$
p_1 \geq \frac{1}{q_G N} (\epsilon_{pkipe} - \eta \Pr[\neg E_{msk}] - \Pr[F\text{-}Fail] - \Pr[D\text{-}Fail]),
$$

where $p_w := \Pr[\mathcal{A}_{cbdh}(g, g^a, g^b, g^c) = e(g,g)^{abc} | \mathcal{COIN} = w]$ for $w \in \{0,1\}$, and q_G, γ, η and E_{msk} are denoted similarly as in Theorem 1.

We then calculate $\Pr[F\text{-}Fail]$ and $\Pr[D\text{-}Fail]$. Since it is information theoretically impossible to obtain any informaion on R^*, $\mathcal{A}_{pkipe}$ submits R^* as in one of F-queries with probability at most $q_F/2^\ell$. $\mathcal{A}_{cbdh}$ fails to respond to a Decryption query only when $\mathcal{A}_{pkipe}$ succeeds to generate a ciphertext $C = \mathbf{Encrypt}(pk, \alpha, M; R)$ without submitting a F-query $\langle \alpha, M, R \rangle$. Hence, $\Pr[D\text{-}Fail]$ will be at most q_D/q.

Finally, by letting $\delta = 1/3$, we have $\epsilon_{cbdh} \geq \frac{2}{3q_G N}(\epsilon_{pkipe} - \frac{2q_F}{2^\ell} - \frac{2q_D}{q})$.

From the above discussions, we can easily see that the claimed bound of the running-time of $\mathcal{A}_{cbdh}$ holds. This completes the proof of the theorem. $\square$

Strongly IND-KE-CCA Construction. We can build a strongly IND-KE-CCA scheme by combining the ideas of PKIPE2 and PKIPE3. A concrete construction of the scheme is given in the full version of this paper.

Acknowledgement

The authors would like to thank Nuttapong Attrapadung, Yang Cui, Yevgeniy Dodis, Jun Furukawa, Moti Yung, Rui Zhang, and anonymous referees for their comments and suggestions.

References

1. R. Anderson, "Two remarks on public key cryptology," Invited Lecture, ACM CCCS'97, available at http://www.cl.cam.ac.uk/users/rja14/.
2. M. Abdalla and L. Reyzin, "A new forward-secure digital signature scheme," Proc. of Asiacrypt'00, LNCS 1976, Springer-Verlag, pp. 116-129, 2000.
3. D. Boneh and X. Boyen, "Efficient selective-ID secure identity-based encryption without random oracles," Proc. of Eurocrypt'04, LNCS 3027, Springer-Verlag, pp.223-238, 2004.
4. D. Boneh and X. Boyen, "Secure identity based encryption without random oracles," Proc. of Crypto'04, LNCS 3152, Springer-Verlag, pp.443-459, 2004.
5. D. Boneh and M. Franklin, "Identity-based encryption from the Weil pairing," Proc. of Crypto'01, LNCS 2139, Springer-Verlag, pp.213-229, 2001.
6. D. Boneh and M. Franklin, "Identity-based encryption from the Weil pairing," SIAM J. of Computing, vol. 32, no. 3, pp.586-615, 2003 (full version of [5]).
7. M. Bellare and A. Palacio, "Protecting against key exposure: strongly key-insulated encryption with optimal threshold," available at http://eprint.iacr.org/2002/064/ .
8. M. Bellare and S.K. Miner, "A forward-secure digital signature scheme," Proc. of Crypto'99, LNCS 1666, Springer-Verlag, pp. 431-448, 1999.
9. C. Cocks, "An identity based encryption scheme based on quadratic residues," Proc. of IMA Int. Conf. 2001, Coding and Cryptography, LNCS 2260, Springer-Verlag, pp. 360-363, 2001.
10. R. Canetti, S. Halevi and J. Katz, "A forward secure public key encryption scheme," Proc. of Eurocrypt'03, LNCS 2656, Springer-Verlag, pp.255-271, 2003.
11. Y. Dodis, J. Katz, S. Xu and M. Yung, "Key-insulated public key cryptosystems," Proc. of Eurocrypt'02, LNCS 2332, Springer-Verlag, pp.65-82, 2002.
12. Y. Dodis, J. Katz, S. Xu and M. Yung, "Strong key-insulated signature schemes," Proc. of PKC'03, LNCS 2567, Springer-Verlag, pp.130-144, 2003.
13. Y. Dodis, M. Franklin, J. Katz, A. Miyaji and M. Yung, "Intrusion-resilient public-key encryption," Proc. of CT-RSA'03, LNCS 2612, Springer-Verlag, pp.19-32, 2003.

14. Y. Dodis, M. Franklin, J. Katz, A. Miyaji and M. Yung, "A generic construction for intrusion-resilient public-key encryption," Proc. of CT-RSA'04, LNCS 2964, Springer-Verlag, pp.81-98, 2004.
15. E. Fujisaki and T. Okamoto, "How to enhance the security of public-key encryption at minimum cost," Proc. of PKC'99, LNCS 1560, Springer-Verlag, pp.53-68, 1999.
16. E. Fujisaki and T. Okamoto, "Secure integration of asymmetric and symmetric encryption schemes," Proc. of Crypto'99, LNCS 1666, Springer-Verlag, pp.537-554, 1999.
17. G. Itkis and L. Reyzin, "SiBIR: signer-base intrusion-resilient signatures," Proc. of Crypto'02, LNCS 2442, Springer-Verlag, pp.499-514, 2002.
18. A. Shamir, "Identity-based cryptosystems and signature schemes," Proc. of Crypto'84, LNCS 196, Springer-Verlag, pp.47-53, 1985.
19. B. Waters, "Efficient identity based encryption without random oracles," Proc. of Eurocrypt'05, LNCS 3494, Springer-Verlag, pp.114-127, 2005.

Provably Secure Steganography with Imperfect Sampling

Anna Lysyanskaya and Mira Meyerovich

Brown University,
Providence RI 02912, USA
{anna, mira}@cs.brown.edu

Abstract. The goal of steganography is to pass secret messages by disguising them as innocent-looking covertexts. Real world stegosystems are often broken because they make invalid assumptions about the system's ability to sample covertexts. We examine whether it is possible to weaken this assumption. By modeling the covertext distribution as a stateful Markov process, we create a sliding scale between real world and provably secure stegosystems. We also show that insufficient knowledge of past states can have catastrophic results.

Keywords: Information hiding, steganography, digital signatures, Markov processes.

1 Introduction

The goal of steganography is to pass secret messages by sending innocuous data. The sender may give the receiver *covertexts* that are distributed according to a *covertext distribution*. A covertext is made up of multiple *documents*. For example, a digital camera can define a covertext distribution of photographs, in which pixels, tiles, or even entire pictures can be considered documents. A *stegosystem* transforms a secret message, called a *hiddentext*, into a *stegotext* that looks like a covertext.

Real-world stegosystems are broken because they make invalid assumptions about the covertext distribution. Often, this is an assumption about an *adversary's lack of knowledge* about the distribution. For example, for a long time, modifying the least significant bits of pixels values in bitmaps was considered a good idea because these bits looked random. Then Moskowitz, Longdon and Chang [MLC01] showed that there is a strong correlation between the least significant bit and the most significant bit (see Figures 7-10 in their paper for an instructive example).

Provably secure steganography attacks the problem by quantifying the *stegosystem's need for knowledge*. Anderson and Petitcolas [AP98] observe that every covertext can be compressed to generate a hiddentext. Therefore, to hide a message, we can "decompress" it into a stegotext. Le [Le03] and Le and Kurosawa [LK03] construct a provably secure compression-based stegosystem that assumes both the sender and receiver know the covertext distribution exactly.

M. Yung et al. (Eds.): PKC 2006, LNCS 3958, pp. 123–139, 2006.

Independently, Sallee [Sal03] implemented a compression-based stegosystem for JPEG images that lets the sender and receiver estimate the covertext distribution. Compression-based schemes need to know the exact probability of every possible covertext.

Cachin [Cac98] proposed using rejection-sampling to generate stegotexts that look like covertexts. A publicly known hash function assigns a bit value to documents. To send one bit, the stegosystem samples from the covertext distribution until it selects a document that evaluates to the message XOR K, where K is a session key both parties derive from their shared secret key. Sending multiple bits requires stringing several documents together. Cachin's scheme is secure if the hash function is unbiased. Because the stegosystem only needs to be able to sample from the covertext distribution, it is known as a *black-box* stegosystem. This paper examines the nature of the black-box required for steganography.

Hopper, Langford and von Ahn [HLvA02] improve on Cachin's results. They give the first rigorous definition of steganographic security by putting it in terms of computational indistinguishability from the covertext distribution. Their stegosystem uses Cachin's rejection-sampling technique, but generalizes it to be applicable to any distribution, assuming it (1) has sufficient entropy and (2) can be sampled perfectly based on prior history. Reyzin and Russell [RR03] improve the robustness and efficiency of the Hopper et al. scheme. Von Ahn and Hopper [vAH04] create a public-key provably secure stegosystem and Backes and Cachin [BC05] and Hopper [Hop05] consider chosen covertext attacks. Despite these improvements, the two assumptions necessary for provably secure steganography remain in the literature. The entropy assumption appears inherent to the problem. We address the possibility of weakening the sampling assumption.

Some prior work focuses on the performance measures of black-box stegosystems. In particular, there is the *rate* of a stegosystem, which measures how many bits of the message you can pack per document transmitted. There is also the *query complexity per document* which measures how many times you need to query the sampler in order to create a document of the stegotext. Notably, Dedic et al. [DIRR05] showed that if the rate is w, then the query complexity per document is 2^w. We do not worry about query complexity, but rather about the very nature of the sampler at the disposal of a stegosystem, so the underlying question is very different.

Black-box stegosystems [Cac98, HLvA02, RR03, vAH04, BC05, Hop05] assume that they have access to an *adaptive* sampler. The sampler must be able to take an arbitrary history of documents as input and output a document distributed according to the covertext distribution conditioned on the prior history. For example, if our covertext distribution consists of images of teddy-bears, and each document is an 8×8 pixel tile, then the sampler's input is the first $k - 1$ tiles of the image (say, the ears of the teddy bear), and the output is the kth tile of the image (say, the nose). The stegosystem needs to be able to query the sampler multiple times on the same input: it continues to sample until it gets a document that corresponds to the message it wants to hide. The sampler must output many noses that correspond to the same set of ears.

Sampling teddy-bear noses based on teddy-bear ears is an absurd example. We use it because in the real world there are no known naturally occuring distributions that can be sampled based on history.[1] Our work examines whether accurate adaptive sampling is really neccessary. We come to the somewhat unsurprising conclusion that a stegosystem must assume that the sampler it uses is accurate. Our chief contribution is to examine what it really means to have a bad sampler.

There are many ways to characterize the abilities of a sampler. It can be contextual: given documents $d_i, \ldots, d_{j-1}, d_{j+1}, \ldots, d_k$, it produces possible values for d_j. A special case of a context sampler is a history-based sampler: given $d_i, \ldots, d_{j-1}$, it produces possible values for d_j. Since history-based samplers are sufficient for secure steganography, we limit our examination to those. Past experience has shown that stegosystems are broken when there is a statistical correlation between documents of the covertext distribution. For example, the least-significant and most-significant bits in a bitmap are correlated, which leads to Moskowitz et al's [MLC01] attack. Therefore, a history-based sampler might make a mistake *when it does not consider some of the history* (usually, due to either ignorance or memory and computational limitations). This means we can characterize a history-based sampler by the length of history it considers. We call a sampler that considers only some of the history a *semi-adaptive* sampler, while one that ignores the history entirely is called *non-adaptive*.

Some samplers may be limited by the number of times they can be queried on the same input. For example, Hopper et al [HLvA02] point out that human beings have difficulty generating multiple independent samples of e-mails on the same topic. The distribution of the output of the sampler and the covertext distribution may gradually (or even sharply) diverge after several draws. This problem can be analyzed in terms of query complexity, which is discussed in [DIRR05]. We do not consider it further.

Semi-adaptive samplers lead us naturally to consider Markov processes. Suppose the actual covertext distribution is D. The distribution D' from which a semi-adaptive sampler draws is a Markov process. Since a stegosystem approximates the distribution it samples, security requires that D and D' are sufficiently close. We introduce the concept of an α-*memoryless distribution*, a distribution that is computationally indistinguishable from some Markov process of order α. We design the definition of α-memorylessness so that it is necessary and sufficient for secure black-box steganography with semi-adaptive sampling.

We have three results:

1. We analyze what happens to the von Ahn and Hopper public key stegosystem [vAH04] when the sampler only considers the last α documents of the history. We calculate how inaccuracy in the sampler translates into insecurity in the stegosystem. Our results show that assuming the covertext distribution is α-memoryless is neccessary and sufficient for maintaining security.

---

[1] Artificial distributions, such as the output of randomized algorithms and encryption functions, can be sampled perfectly. However, they tend to arouse suspicion, thus making them unsuitable for steganography.

2. We analyze the security of non-adaptive black-box stegosystems. Independently,[2] Petrowski et al. [PKSM] implemented a non-adaptive stegosystem for JPEG images, giving empirical evidence that memoryless distributions exist and can be used for secure steganography.

3. We construct a pathological α-memoryless high-entropy distribution for which black-box steganography is infeasible if the stegosystem's sampler considers only the last $\alpha - 1$ documents of the history (under the discrete logarithm assumption). An efficient adversary can detect any attempt at covert communication with overwhelming probability.

Organization: Section 2 presents notation and definitions. Section 3 analyzes the von Ahn and Hopper stegosystem [vAH04] in the context of semi-adaptive sampling. Section 4 examines non-adaptive stegosystems. Section 5 constructs a pathological covertext distribution for which black-box steganography is infeasible. Section 6 concludes. We have omitted some of the proofs; they can be found in the full paper [LM05].

2 Notation

We call a function $\nu\colon \mathbb{N} \to (0,1)$ *negligible* if for all $c > 0$ and for all sufficiently large k, $\nu(k) < 1/k^c$.

The hiddentext will always be in $\{0,1\}^*$. A covertext is composed of a sequence of documents. Each document comes from the alphabet $\mathbb{A}$; $|\mathbb{A}|$ may be exponential. We denote concatenation with the $\circ$ operator; a string s can be parsed to $s = s_1 \circ s_2 \circ ... \circ s_n$, where $|s| = n$. The symbol λ denotes the empty string.

Our main results measure the security of stegosystems; we calculate the probability of a stegosystem being broken in terms of the probability of an adversary breaking other cryptographic primitives. The term $\mathbf{Adv}_P^{\mathsf{game}}(A, k)$ refers to the probability of adversary A breaking the security of primitive P in the context of a scenario defined by game when the security parameter is k. For example, $\mathbf{Adv}_{\mathsf{DSA}}^{\mathsf{sig}}(A, 160)$ is the probability that A forges a 160-bit DSA signature. What we really care about is attacks by an a large class of adversaries, where each class defines the maximum amount of time and other resources an adversary can use. $\mathbf{InSec}_P^{\mathsf{game}}(class)$ is the maximum probability that any adversary in *class* can break the security of primitive P while in the scenario defined by game. For example, $\mathbf{InSec}_F^{\mathsf{owf}}(t, k)$ is the maximum probability of any adversary inverting the one-way function F if it runs in $t(k)$ time, where k is the security parameter. Therefore, if we say $3\mathbf{InSec}_\Sigma^{\mathsf{sig}}(t, q, k) \leq \mathbf{InSec}_F^{\mathsf{owf}}(t, k)$, this means that signature scheme Σ is three times as hard to break as one-way function F.

To define the probability of an attacker winning in a scenario, we need to consider the outcome of several events. The expression $Pf[e_1, e_2, \ldots, e_n : c]$ is the probability that condition c holds given that events $e_1, e_2, \ldots, e_n$ occured (and in that order). For example, let A be some algorithm that takes as input an integer

---

[2] We presented preliminary results of this work in August 2004 [LM04].

and outputs a single bit. The expression $Pr[x \leftarrow \mathbb{Z}; b \leftarrow A(x) : b = x \bmod 2]$ is the probability that $b = x \bmod 2$, given that first x was randomly chosen from $\mathbb{Z}$ and then b was generated by executing $A(x)$. In other words, it is the probability that A correctly calculates $x \bmod 2$ on a randomly chosen integer x.

We say that a function $f : \mathbb{A} \to \{0,1\}$ is ϵ-*biased* with respect to distribution D if $|Pr[d \leftarrow D : f(d) = 0] - 1/2| < \epsilon$. A $\epsilon(k)$-biased function is called an *unbiased* function if ϵ is a negligible function.[3] A covertext distribution that has sufficient minimum entropy for steganography is called *always informative* (see Hopper et al [HLvA02] for details).

We write $x \leftarrow D\langle h, n \rangle$ to denote sampling n documents from D conditioned on the prior history h; $D\langle h, n \rangle$ defines a distribution over $\mathbb{A}^n$. A semi-adaptive sampler samples one document from the distribution D conditioned only on the last α documents of h. $D^{\alpha}\langle h, n \rangle$ generates an n-document string by calling a semi-adaptive samper n times, each time appending the result to h. When we give a player sampling access to a distribution, we use $\cdot$ to denote the parameters that the player can pick. For example, the oracle $D\langle \cdot, 2 \rangle$ samples two documents from D based on a history supplied by the player.

An α-memoryless distribution is indistinguishable from a Markov process of order α. (A sequence of random variables $X_1, \ldots, X_n$ such that for $\alpha < i \leq n$, the conditional distribution $\{X_i \mid X_{i-\alpha}, \ldots, X_{i-1}\}$ is identical to the conditional distribution $\{X_i \mid X_1, \ldots, X_{i-1}\}$.) Since we require computational indistinguishability, we parameterize everything by k (e.g. D_k, a family of distributions).

Definition 1 (α-Memoryless). *Let D_k be a family of distributions indexed by a public parameter k and let D_k^{α} be the best Markov model of order α that approximates D_k. We define the advantage of an adversary A against the Markov model as:*

$$\mathbf{Adv}_{D,\alpha}^{\mathrm{mem}}(A, k) = |Pr[h \leftarrow D_k\langle \lambda, n(k) - 1 \rangle; x \leftarrow D_k^{\alpha}\langle h, 1 \rangle : A(h \circ x) = 1]$$
$$- Pr[x \leftarrow D_k\langle \lambda, n(k) \rangle : A(x) = 1]|$$

We let $\mathbf{InSec}_{D,\alpha}^{\mathrm{mem}}(t, n, k) = \max_{A \in \mathcal{A}(t,n,k)} \mathbf{Adv}_{D,\alpha}^{\mathrm{mem}}(A, k)$, where $\mathcal{A}(t, n, k)$ is the set of all adversaries that run in time $t(k)$ and get a sample $n(k)$ documents long. We say that D_k is α-memoryless if $\mathbf{InSec}_{D,\alpha}^{\mathrm{mem}}(t, n, k) \leq \nu(k)$ for some negligible function ν. D_k is strictly α-memoryless if $\mathbf{InSec}_{D,\beta}^{\mathrm{mem}}(t, n, k)$ is non-negligible for all $\beta < \alpha$.

Remark 1. This property is necessary and sufficient for steganography with semi-adaptive sampling.

The following definitions are either standard or come from von Ahn and Hopper [vAH04]. We assume that all adversaries are probabilistic polynomial-time Turing machines. However, the distributions we work with are arbitrary and may act as arbitrarily powerful adversaries. For example, someone who can adaptively sample a distribution might be able to use it to calculate discrete logarithms.

---

[3] The function f is typically chosen after we fix the distribution (and the security parameter). A universal hash function is often used in practice.

We define $\mathbf{InSec}_{X,Y}^{\mathsf{dist}}(t, n, k)$ as the maximum probability that an adversary can distinguish distribution X_k from Y_k if it runs in time $t(k)$ and gets a $n(k)$ document long sample. Steganography requires an IND$-CPA cryptosystem whose ciphertext is indistinguishable from random. $\mathbf{InSec}_{\mathcal{E}}^{\mathsf{cpa}}(t, q, n, k)$ is the insecurity of cryptosystem $\mathcal{E}$ against a chosen plaintext attack by an adversary that runs in $t(k)$ time, makes $q(k)$ queries and gets responses totaling $n(k)$ bits (see Hopper et al. [HLvA02] or full paper for details).

The standard specification [vAH04] of a public-key stegosystem is:

Definition 2 (Public Key Stegosystem). *A public key stegosystem is the triple* $\mathcal{S} = (SG, SE, SD)$. $SG(1^k)$ *generates a key-pair* (SK, PK). $SE(PK, m)$ *takes the public key* PK *and a message* $m \in \{0,1\}^*$, *and returns some stegotext* s. $SD(SK, s)$ *takes the secret key* SK *and stegotext* s *and returns a hiddentext* m. *For all* $m \in \{0,1\}^*$, *the probability that* $SD(SK, SE(PK, m))$ *fails to recover* m *should be negligible.*

Von Ahn and Hopper [vAH04] define the security of a public-key stegosystem against a chosen hiddentext attack. An adversary A queries an oracle with hiddentexts. The oracle responds either with stegotexts generated by $SE(PK, \cdot)$ or with covertexts of the appropriate length, generated by $D^*(\cdot)$. A should not be able to distinguish the two cases.

Definition 3 (SS-CHA). *The advantage of an adversary* A *against a public-key stegosystem* $\mathcal{S} = (SG, SE, SD)$ *in a chosen hiddentext attack (CHA) is:*

$$\mathbf{Adv}_{\mathcal{S},D}^{\mathsf{cha}}(A, k) = \left| Pr[PK \leftarrow SG(1^k) : A_k^{SE(PK,\cdot),D} = 1] - Pr[A_k^{D^*(\cdot),D} = 1] \right|$$

We let $\mathbf{InSec}_{\mathcal{S},D}^{\mathsf{cha}}(t, q, n, k) = \max_{A \in \mathcal{A}(t,q,n,k)} \mathbf{Adv}_{\mathcal{S},D}^{\mathsf{cha}}(A, k)$ *where* $\mathcal{A}(t, q, n, k)$ *is the set of all adversaries that run in* $t(k)$ *time, make* $q(k)$ *queries and get responses totaling* $n(k)$ *bits. A stegosystem is considered secure against a chosen hiddentext attack (SS-CHA) if* $\mathbf{InSec}_{\mathcal{S},D}^{\mathsf{cha}}(t, q, n, k) \leq \nu(k)$ *for some negligible function* ν.

Remark 2. We restrict the usual definition of security. Typically, the adversary is allowed to query the stegosystem with any history and message. In our model, we assume that an adaptive sampler does not exist. A stegosystem that is secure against such an attack is an adaptive sampler (see Hopper [Hop04] Section 3.3.2). We force the adversary to always query the stegosystem with history λ (the empty string).

3   Semi-adaptive Stegosystem

In this section we examine what happens to the von Ahn and Hopper [vAH04] public-key stegosystem when we replace the adaptive sampling oracle with a semi-adaptive one. We show that if the oracle samples based on the last α documents of the history, then an α-memoryless distribution is necessary and sufficent for maintaining security.

3.1   The vAH04 Stegosystem with Semi-adaptive Sampling

The von Ahn and Hopper stegosystem [vAH04] (Construction 2 in their paper) is a public-key provably secure stegosystem; See Algorithm 3.1. and 3.2 for the encoding and decoding algorithms (we have modified them slightly to fit our notation). Their stegosystem uses an IND\$-CPA public-key cryptosystem $\mathcal{E} = (G, E_{PK}, D_{SK})$ and a publicly known function $f : \Sigma \to \{0, 1\}$ that is ϵ-biased with respect to the covertext distribution D_k. The encoder first encrypts the message using E_{PK}. Next, for each bit b of ciphertext, the encoder samples the covertext distribution until it gets a document d such that $f(d) = b$. The encoder appends all of the resulting documents together to form the stegotext. The decoder extracts the ciphertext by evaluating f on every document of the stegotext and then decrypts the ciphertext.

Algorithm 3.1. Encode

Input: Public key PK, message m, number of times to sample T
step 1: Encrypt message
  $c \leftarrow E_{PK}(m)$;

step 2: Stegocode ciphertext
  parse c as $c_1 \circ c_2 \circ ... \circ c_n$;
  $h \leftarrow \lambda$;
  for $j \leftarrow 1$ **to** n **do**
    $i \leftarrow 1$;
    repeat
      $s_j \leftarrow D_k\langle h, 1\rangle$, increment i ;
    until $f(s_j) = c_j$ **or** $i > T$;
    $h \leftarrow h \circ s_j$;
  end
  $s \leftarrow s_1 \circ s_2 \circ ... \circ s_n$;
  return s ;

Algorithm 3.2. Decode

Input: Secret key SK, stegotext s
step 1: Extract ciphertext
  $c \leftarrow f(s_1) \circ f(s_2) \circ ... \circ f(s_n)$;

step 2: Decrypt message
  $m \leftarrow D_{SK}(c)$;
return m

For the remainder of Section 3, we will refer to the von Ahn and Hopper stegosystem as $\mathcal{S} = (SG, SE, SD)$ and assume that D_k is the covertext distribution. We define a length function $\mathcal{L} : \mathbb{Z} \to \mathbb{Z}$ that calculates the length of a ciphertext for a message m: $\mathcal{L}(|m|) = |E_{PK}(m)|$. Von Ahn and Hopper [vAH04] prove that their stegosystem is secure:

Theorem 1 ([vAH04]). *If D_k is an always informative distribution and f is ϵ-biased on D_k, then $\mathcal{S}$ is a SS-CHA secure stegosystem:*

$$\mathbf{InSec}^{\mathsf{cha}}_{\mathcal{S},D}(t,q,n,k) \leq \mathbf{InSec}^{\mathsf{cpa}}_{\mathcal{E}}(t + O(kn),q,n,k) + \mathcal{L}(n)\epsilon$$

Remark 3. What Theorem 1 really states is that the output of $\mathcal{S}$ is indistinguishable from the distribution it samples.

$\mathcal{S}$ uses a perfect sampler. We now consider the stegosystem $\mathcal{T} = (TG, TE, TD)^4$ that functions identically to $\mathcal{S}$, except that its only access to D_k is via D_k^α, an oracle that only considers the last α documents of the history. The main result of this section is the proof that $\mathcal{T}$ is correct and that $\mathcal{T}$ is secure if and only if D_k is α-memoryless.

3.2   Analysis of $\mathcal{T}$

Lemma 1. *Assume that D_k is an always informative α-memoryless distribution and f is an ϵ-biased function on D_k. For all hiddentexts $m \in \{0,1\}^*$, the probability that $\mathcal{T}$ fails to encode m is negligible:*

$$Pr[(PK, SK) \leftarrow TG(1^k); s \leftarrow TE(PK, m); m' \leftarrow TD(SK, s) : m' \neq m]$$
$$\leq \mathcal{L}(|m|)(1/2 + \epsilon + \mathbf{InSec}^{\mathsf{mem}}_{D,\alpha}(O(1), \mathcal{L}(|m|), k))^k$$

Proof. The probability of error is at most the length of the ciphertext multiplied by the probability that any individual bit of ciphertext is encoded incorrectly. See full paper for details.

Theorem 2. *If D_k is an always informative α-memoryless distribution and f is ϵ-biased on D_k, then $\mathcal{T}$ is a SS-CHA secure stegosystem:*

$$\mathbf{InSec}^{\mathsf{cha}}_{\mathcal{T},D}(t,q,n,k) \leq \mathbf{InSec}^{\mathsf{cpa}}_{\mathcal{E}}(t + O(kn),q,n,k)$$
$$+ n\mathbf{InSec}^{\mathsf{mem}}_{D,\alpha}(t + O(n),n,k) + \mathcal{L}(n)\epsilon$$

Proof. The probability that $\mathcal{T}$ can be broken is the probability that an adversary distinguishes the IND\$-CPA cryptosystem $\mathcal{E}$ from random plus the probability that an adversary can distinguish D_k from D_k^α; both these values are negligible. See full paper for details.

Theorem 3. *Let D_k be an always informative distribution and f an ϵ-biased function on D_k. If D_k is not α-memoryless then $\mathcal{T}$ is not a SS-CHA secure stegosystem:*

$$\mathbf{InSec}^{\mathsf{cha}}_{\mathcal{T},D}(t + O(1),1,n,k) \geq \mathbf{InSec}^{\mathsf{mem}}_{D,\alpha}(t,n,k)$$
$$- \mathbf{InSec}^{\mathsf{cpa}}_{\mathcal{E}}(t + O(kn),1,n,k) - n\epsilon$$

---

[4] As a mnemonic device, think of $\mathcal{S}$ as the stegosystem with a Standard sampler and $\mathcal{T}$ as having a sampler that considers only the Tail of the history.

Remark 4. Note that $\mathbf{InSec}_{D,\alpha}^{\text{mem}}(t, n, k)$ is not negligible because D_k is not α-memoryless. Any adversary that can distinguish D_k from D_k^{α} can be used to attack $\mathcal{T}$.

Proof. Assume D_k is not α-memoryless. By definition, there exists an adversary A such that $\mathbf{Adv}_{D,\alpha}^{\text{mem}}(A, k)$ is non-negligible. Let A run in time t and require a challenge sample of length n. We use A to create an adversary B that can tell whether it is querying an oracle representing $\mathcal{T}$ or D_k. B will ask its oracle for a single covertext of length n and pass the output to A. B will output whatever A outputs. B's advantage in distinguishing $\mathcal{T}$ from D_k is at least as much as A's advantage in distinguishing D_k^{α} from D_k minus the probability of distinguishing $\mathcal{T}$ from D_k^{α}:

$$\mathbf{Adv}_{\mathcal{T},D}^{\text{cha}}(B, k) \geq \mathbf{Adv}_{D,\alpha}^{\text{mem}}(A, k) - \mathbf{InSec}_{\mathcal{T},D^{\alpha}}^{\text{cha}}(t, 1, n, k)$$

Using Theorem 1, we get:

$$\mathbf{Adv}_{\mathcal{T},D}^{\text{cha}}(B, k) \geq \mathbf{Adv}_{D,\alpha}^{\text{mem}}(A, k) - \mathbf{InSec}_{\mathcal{E}}^{\text{cpa}}(t + O(kn), 1, n, k) - n\epsilon$$

B runs in time $t + O(1)$ and gets 1 challenge string of length n, therefore:

$$\mathbf{InSec}_{S,D}^{\text{cha}}(t + O(1), 1, n, k) \geq \mathbf{InSec}_{D,\alpha}^{\text{mem}}(t, n, k)$$
$$- \mathbf{InSec}_{\mathcal{E}}^{\text{cpa}}(t + O(kn), 1, n, k) - n\epsilon$$

This means that if D_k is not α-memoryless, then there exists an adversary that can launch a successful SS-CHA attack on $\mathcal{T}$ with non-negligible probability.

Remark 5. The above proof would probably work for any black-box stegosystem. However, because it is unclear how to deal with a stegosystem that somehow uses outside information (or how to rule out this possibility), we limit our analysis to the stegosystem $\mathcal{T}$.

4   Non-adaptive Stegosystems

In this section, we show how to apply public-key black-box steganography as proposed by von Ahn and Hopper [vAH04] to real world covertext distributions. (Independently, Petrowski et. al. [PKSM] implemented a similar system for JPEG images, but their work has no security analysis.) The key insight is that multiple digital photographs of a still scene are almost but not completely identical. We can break up each image into 8×8 pixel tiles.[5] A cryptographic hash function assigns a value to each tile. The stegosystem choses the appropriate tiles to create a composite photo that encodes the secret message. The scheme assumes each 8×8 pixel tile is independent of its neighbors.

This stegosystem is equivalent to using D_k^0 to sample D_k and assuming that the covertext distribution is 0-memoryless, as shown in Algorithm 4.1. Non-adaptive steganography can be applied to any digital image format, TCP time-stamp intervals, etc.

---

[5] The dimensions of the tile are an artifact of the JPEG compression algorithm.

Algorithm 4.1. Non-adaptive stegosystem

Input: Public key PK, message m, T covertexts $x^{(1)}, \ldots, x^{(T)}$ (each covertext
    $x^{(i)}$ is of length $|E_{PK}(m)|$
step 1: Encrypt message
  $c \leftarrow E_{PK}(m)$;

step 2: Stegocode ciphertext
  parse c as $c_1 \circ c_2 \circ \ldots \circ c_n$;
  for $j \leftarrow 1$ ***to*** n **do**
    $i \leftarrow 1$;
    repeat
      $s_j \leftarrow x_j^{(i)}$, increment i ;
    until $f(s_j) = c_j$ ***or*** $i > T$;
  end
  $s \leftarrow s_1 \circ s_2 \circ \ldots \circ s_n$;
  return s ;

The analysis of Algorithm 4.1 follows directly from Section 3. Correctness: The probability that the stegosystem fails to encode a hiddentext m is: $\mathcal{L}(|m|)(1/2 + \epsilon + \mathbf{InSec}^{\mathrm{mem}}_{D,0}(O(1), \mathcal{L}(|m|), k))^k$. Security: Algorithm 4.1 is secure if and only if D is 0-memoryless: an independent, but not necessarily identically distributed, sequence of random variables.

5   Pathological Covertext Distribution

In this section, we construct a pathological strictly α-memoryless distribution and prove that no computationally bounded algorithm can use it to hide messages without access to D_k^α. The distribution will publish a verification key that can be used by anyone to check if a covertext is legitimate. The probability that steganography will be detected is $1 - \nu(k)$, where ν is a negligible function.

We give a stegosystem a list of covertexts generated by $D\langle\lambda, \cdot\rangle$ and access to $D^{\alpha-1}\langle\cdot, 1\rangle$, a semi-adaptive oracle with insufficient memory. For example, a stegosystem might store a database of photographs (this corresponds to $D\langle\lambda, \cdot\rangle$) and maintain an internal Markov model about pixel color distributions based on the 8 adjacent pixels (this corresponds to $D^{\alpha-1}\langle\cdot, 1\rangle$, where $\alpha - 1 = 8$). We show that any stegotext produced by a stegosystem is really just a quote of a covertext in its database.

5.1   The Distribution

Our goal is to devise a covertext distribution where (1) each document depends on only the α documents that came before it (so it is α-memoryless); (2) a stegosystem cannot by itself compute the ith document d_i in a legitimate covertext; finally (3) it is very unlikely that the output of $D^{\alpha-1}\langle h, 1\rangle$ is a valid continuation of the last α documents of h.

The first construction that comes to mind is to make each document be a concatenation of a random number r_i and a signature on the previous α random numbers: $\sigma_i = \sigma(r_{i-\alpha}, \ldots, r_i)$. This will meet requirements (1) and (2). There is a subtle problem with this as far as requirement (3) is concerned. Suppose we are given $\alpha - 1$ documents $r_{n-\alpha+1}\sigma_{n-\alpha+1}, \ldots, r_{n-1}\sigma_{n-1}$. The signatures $\sigma_{n-\alpha+1}, \ldots, \sigma_{n-1}$ can leak partial information about the value $r_{n-\alpha}$. As a result, $D^{\alpha-1}\langle \cdot, 1 \rangle$, even though not explicitly given $d_{n-\alpha}$, may nevertheless calculate $r_{n-\alpha}$ and compute the correct signature $\sigma_n = \sigma(r_{n-\alpha}, \ldots, r_n)$.

In order to fix this problem, we need to construct a signature function σ for which the following property holds: We fix a sequence of $2\alpha - 1$ integers $r_1, \ldots, r_{2\alpha-1}$. Then the sequence of $\alpha - 1$ documents $r_{\alpha+1}\sigma_{\alpha+1}, \ldots, r_{2\alpha-1}\sigma_{2\alpha-1}$ should be information theoretically independent of r_α. This property ensures that $D^{\alpha-1}$ cannot learn r_α and so will be unable to compute the correct signature $\sigma_{2\alpha}$ based on the previous α documents of h, as required by (3) above.

Consider the following hash function $h : \mathbb{Z}_p^\alpha \to G$, where p is a k-bit prime and G is a group of order p. The hash function $h_{p,G,g_1,\ldots,g_{\alpha+1}}$ is parameterized by p, G and $\alpha + 1$ generators of G: $g_1, \ldots, g_{\alpha+1}$. (We will omit the subscript of h in the future). On input $(r_1, \ldots, r_{\alpha+1}) \in \mathbb{Z}_p^{\alpha+1}$ the hash function returns:

$$h(r_1, r_2, \ldots, r_{\alpha+1}) \doteq g_1^{r_1} \cdot g_2^{r_2} \cdots \cdots g_{\alpha+1}^{r_{\alpha+1}}$$

The hash function h has the information hiding property that we need because it reveals only a linear combination of its inputs (see the proof of Lemma 4 in the full paper).

We now formalize the above discussion. We define a secure stateless signature scheme, show how to combine it with h and prove the result is secure under the discrete logarithm assumption. Then we construct our pathological distribution.

Definition 4 (Stateless Signature Scheme). *A stateless signature scheme* $\Sigma = (G, \sigma, V)$ *is a triple of polynomial time algorithms where:* $G(1^k)$ *is the key generation algorithm,* $\sigma : \{0,1\}^k \times \mathcal{M}_k \to \{0,1\}^{poly(k)}$ *is a probabilitic algorithm that on input* (SK, m) *outputs a* $poly(k)$ *bit signature, and* $V : \{0,1\}^k \times \mathcal{M}_k \times \{0,1\}^{poly(k)} \to \{0,1\}$ *is the signature verification function that accepts valid signatures.*

We define $\mathbf{InSec}_\Sigma^{\text{sig}}(t, q, k)$ as the insecurity of signature scheme Σ against an adaptive chosen message attack by an adversary that runs in time $t(k)$ and makes $q(k)$ queries to the signing oracle (see Goldreich [Gol04] for details).

Goldreich [Gol04] shows that *stateless* signature schemes exist if one-way functions exist. It is also known that the discrete logarithm assumption implies one-way functions. Therefore, the discrete logarithm assumption also implies the existence of stateless signature schemes. We let $\mathbf{DL}(t, k)$ be the maximum probability that any algorithm running in time $t(k)$ can solve the discrete logarithm problem.

We construct a signature scheme using the hash function h:

Construction 1. *Let $\Sigma' = (G', \sigma', V')$ be a secure stateless signature scheme that takes messages in $\{0,1\}^{2k}$ and outputs signatures in $\{0,1\}^{poly(k)}$. We use (G', σ', V') and the hash function h to construct a new stateless signature scheme $\Sigma = (G, \sigma, V)$. We let $G = G'$.*

The signature function $\sigma : \{0,1\}^k \times (\mathbb{Z}_p^*)^{\alpha+1} \rightarrow \{0,1\}^{poly(k)}$:

$$\sigma(SK, r_1 \circ \cdots \circ r_{\alpha+1}) = \sigma'(SK, h(r_1, \ldots, r_{\alpha+1}))$$

The verification function $V : \{0,1\}^k \times (\mathbb{Z}_p^*)^{\alpha+1} \times \{0,1\}^{poly(k)} \rightarrow \{0,1\}$:

$$V(VK, s, r_1 \circ \cdots \circ r_{\alpha+1}) = V'(VK, s, h(r_1, \ldots, r_{\alpha+1}))$$

We further define σ on input from $(\mathbb{Z}_p^*)^{\beta}$, where $\beta < \alpha + 1$ as follows: $\sigma(r_1, \ldots, r_\beta) = \sigma'(h(0, \ldots, 0, r_1, \ldots, r_\beta))$. V extends in the obvious way.

Lemma 2. *$\Sigma = (G, \sigma, V)$ from Construction 1 is a secure stateless signature scheme under the discrete logarithm assumption:*

$$\mathbf{InSec}_\Sigma^{\mathsf{sig}}(t, q, k) \leq \mathbf{InSec}_{\Sigma'}^{\mathsf{sig}}(t + O(q), q, k) + \mathbf{DL}(t + O(q), k).$$

Proof. The intuition behind the proof is that any adversary that can attack Σ can be used to either attack the underlying signature scheme or calculate discrete logarithms. See full paper for details.

We use the signature scheme from Construction 1 to construct a distribution D_{VK} over the alphabet $\{\mathbb{Z}_p^* \times \{0,1\}^{poly(k)}\}^*$, where p is a k bit prime and $poly(k)$ is the length of a signature in Σ. Each document consists of an element in $\mathbb{Z}_p^*$ and a signature on the previous $\alpha + 1$ elements.

Construction 2 (Pathological Distribution D_{VK}). *Let $\Sigma = (G, \sigma, V)$ be a secure stateless signature scheme from Construction 1. We use G to generate the keys (SK, VK) and index distribution D_{VK} via the public verification key. If d_i is the ith document, then $d_i = r_i \sigma(SK, r_{i-\alpha} \circ \cdots \circ r_i)$, where r_i is chosen randomly from $\mathbb{Z}_p$. The output of $D_{VK}\langle \lambda, n \rangle$ looks like:*

$$D_{VK}\langle \lambda, n \rangle \rightarrow r_1 \sigma(SK, r_1)$$
$$\circ\, r_2 \sigma(SK, r_1 \circ r_2) \circ \cdots$$
$$\cdots \circ r_{\alpha+1} \sigma(SK, r_1 \circ r_2 \circ \cdots \circ r_{\alpha+1}) \circ \cdots$$
$$\cdots \circ r_n \sigma(SK, r_{n-\alpha} \circ \cdots \circ r_n)$$

We define $\sigma_i = \sigma(SK, r_{i-\alpha}, \ldots, r_i)$.

Definition 5 (Γ). *Suppose we query $D_{VK}\langle \lambda, n \rangle$ q times and record the result on tape Q. We define the probability that any one sequence $r_1, \ldots, r_d$ appears two or more times in Q as $\Gamma(d, n, q, k)$.*

Lemma 3. *$\Gamma(d, n, q, k)$ is a negligible function in k.*

Proof. The proof relies on the fact that $|\mathbb{Z}_p| = \Theta(2^k)$. See full paper for details.

5.2   Pathology of the Distribution

We now show that any computationally bounded stegosystem for D_{VK} is guaranteed to be caught with overwhelming probability.

Theorem 4. *Let S be an arbitrary probabilistic polynomial time stegosystem for distribution D_{VK} that has a database of q_1 covertexts of length n generated by $D_{VK}\langle\lambda,\cdot\rangle$ and is allowed to make q_2 queries to $D_{VK}^{\alpha-1}\langle\cdot,1\rangle$. Suppose it takes S time t to generate a stegotext of length $N > \alpha$. Then there exists an adversary that can distinguish S from D_{VK} with probability $1 - \nu(k)$, for a negligible function ν. The adversary uses only the verification key VK and $q_1 + 1$ samples from the oracle of length N each; it runs in time $O((t + N)(q_1 + 1))$.*

Remark 6. The stegosystem needs to forge signatures if it wants to generate more than q_1 distinct stegotexts. All the adversary does is ask for $q_1 + 1$ samples and checks them for duplicates and/or invalid signatures.

We will prove Theorem 4 in three steps. First we will construct an oracle $D*_{VK}^{\alpha-1}$ that is information theoretically indistinguishable from $D_{VK}^{\alpha-1}\langle\cdot,1\rangle$. Then we will show that a stegosystem whose only resource is $D*_{VK}^{\alpha-1}$ cannot create stegotexts longer than α with more than negligible probability. Finally, we will augment the stegosystem by giving it access to $D_{VK}\langle\lambda,\cdot\rangle$ and prove Theorem 4 by showing that it still cannot generate new stegotexts.

Algorithm 5.1. $D*_{VK}^{\alpha-1}\langle\cdot,1\rangle$ with oracle access to $\sigma(SK,\cdot)$

Input: history: $h = r_1\sigma_1,\dots,r_{n-1}\sigma_{n-1}$
If the history is more than $\alpha - 1$ documents long, $D*_{VK}^{\alpha-1}$ randomly
chooses $\hat{r}_n$ and $\hat{r}_{n-\alpha}$ and signs the result.
if $n \le \alpha - 1$ then return $D_{VK}\langle h,1\rangle$;
else
    $\hat{r}_n \leftarrow$ Random ;
    $\hat{r}_{n-\alpha} \leftarrow$ Random ;
    $\hat{u} \leftarrow h(\hat{r}_{n-\alpha}, r_{n-\alpha+1}, \dots, r_{n-1}, \hat{r}_n)$;
    $\hat{\sigma}_n \leftarrow \sigma(\hat{u})$;
end
return $\hat{r}_n\hat{\sigma}_n$;
We use $\hat{x}$ to signify that the value of x was assigned by $D*_{VK}^{\alpha-1}\langle\cdot,1\rangle$

Lemma 4. *Consider $D*_{VK}^{\alpha-1}\langle\cdot,1\rangle$ (Algorithm 5.1). $D*_{VK}^{\alpha-1}\langle\cdot,1\rangle = D_{VK}^{\alpha-1}\langle\cdot,1\rangle$.*

Proof. Lemma 4 follows from the information-theoretic hiding property of h, see full paper for proof.

Lemma 5. *D_{VK} is strictly α-memoryless.*

Proof. Lemma 5 follows from Lemma 4, see full paper for proof.

Lemma 6. *Let S be any stegosystem that has oracle access to $D_{VK}^{\alpha-1}\langle\cdot,1\rangle$, but with no direct access to D_{VK} - i.e. S does not know SK and has no oracle access to $\sigma(SK,\cdot)$. Suppose it takes S t time and q queries to $D_{VK}^{\alpha-1}\langle\cdot,1\rangle$ to output a stegotext $s = r_1\sigma_1 \circ \cdots \circ r_n\sigma_n$ of length $n > \alpha$. Then there exists an efficient adversary that can distinguish S from D_{VK} with overwhelming probability using only one sample of length α and running in time $O(t)$:*

$$\mathbf{InSec}_{S,D}^{\mathsf{cha}}(t,1,\alpha+1,k) \geq 1 - \mathbf{InSec}_{\Sigma}^{\mathsf{sig}}(t+O(1),q,k) - \mathbf{DL}(t+O(q),k)$$

Furthermore, $\forall i > \alpha$, the probability that an arbitrary signature σ_i is valid is at most:

$$\mathbf{InSec}_{\Sigma}^{\mathsf{sig}}(t+O(1),q,k) + \mathbf{DL}(t+O(q),k).$$

Proof. Assume we have a secure stegosystem S with no direct access to D_{VK}. We construct an adversary A that uses S to forge signatures or calculate discrete logs. A tells S to generate a single stegotext of any length $n > \alpha$. While S is working, A intercepts all of S's queries to $D_{VK}^{\alpha-1}\langle\cdot,1\rangle$ and redirects them to $D*_{VK}^{\alpha-1}\langle\cdot,1\rangle$. Finally, S outputs a stegotext $s = r_1\sigma_1 \circ r_2\sigma_2 \circ \cdots \circ r_n\sigma_n$.

Choose any $i > \alpha$. We have three cases to consider:

1. If σ_i is not a valid signature on $r_{i-\alpha}\circ\cdots\circ r_i$ then the stegosystem is insecure. The probability that this happens is $\mathbf{InSec}_{S,D}^{\mathsf{cha}}(t+O(1),1,n,k)$.
2. If σ_i is a valid signature on $r_{i-\alpha}\circ\cdots\circ r_i$ and it was not generated by $D*_{VK}^{\alpha-1}\langle\cdot,1\rangle$ then S violated the security of Σ. The probability that this happens is $\mathbf{InSec}_{\Sigma}^{\mathsf{sig}}(t+O(1),q,k)$.
3. If σ_i is a valid signature that was generated by $D*_{VK}^{\alpha-1}\langle\cdot,1\rangle$ then we use S and $D*_{VK}^{\alpha-1}\langle\cdot,1\rangle$ to calculate discrete logarithms. We set up a reduction algorithm

---

Algorithm 5.2. $D**_{VK}^{\alpha-1}\langle\cdot,1\rangle$ with oracle access to $\sigma(SK,\cdot)$

Input: history: $r_1\sigma_1,\ldots,r_{n-1}\sigma_{n-1}$
if $n < \alpha$ **then return** $D_{VK}\langle h,1\rangle$;
else
    $\hat{r}_n \leftarrow$ Random ;
    $\boxed{\hat{r} \leftarrow \text{ Random}}$;
    $\boxed{\hat{u} \leftarrow y \cdot g^{\hat{r}} \cdot h(1,r_{n-\alpha+1},\ldots,r_{n-1},\hat{r}_n)}$;
    $\hat{\sigma}_n \leftarrow \sigma(\hat{u})$;
end
return $\hat{r}_n\hat{\sigma}_n$;
$D**_{VK}^{\alpha-1}\langle h,1\rangle$ is almost identical to $D*_{VK}^{\alpha-1}\langle h,1\rangle$. We highlighted the differences.

---

that uses the stegosystem as a black box and controls the actions of $D_{VK}^{\alpha-1}\langle\cdot,1\rangle$. The reduction would get a challenge string $y = g^x$, where g is a generator of the group G and x is unknown. Next, the reduction would ask the stegosystem to generate a stegotext. Whenever the stegosystem queries $D_{VK}^{\alpha-1}\langle\cdot,1\rangle$, the reduction would redirect the call to $D * *_{VK}^{\alpha-1}\langle\cdot, 1\rangle$. Algorithm 5.2 shows how $D * *_{VK}^{\alpha-1}\langle\cdot, 1\rangle$ inserts y into every signature. $D * *_{VK}^{\alpha-1}\langle\cdot, 1\rangle$ ensures that the returned signature $\hat{\sigma}_n$ is valid only if $r_{n-\alpha} = \log_g (y \cdot g^{\hat{r}}) = \log_g (g^{x+\hat{r}}) = x + \hat{r}$, where $\hat{r}$ is chosen by $D * *_{VK}^{\alpha-1}\langle\cdot, 1\rangle$. Since the signature σ_i is generated by $D * *_{VK}^{\alpha-1}\langle\cdot, 1\rangle$, we know that $s_{i-\alpha} = x + \hat{r}$. The reduction outputs $s_{i-\alpha} - \hat{r}$, thereby calculating the discrete logarithm. As a result, the probability that this case occurs is $\mathbf{DL}(t + O(q), q, k)$.

Based on our case analysis, we see that $\mathbf{InSec}_{\mathcal{S},D}^{\mathsf{cha}}(t, 1, n, k) \geq 1 - \mathbf{InSec}_{\Sigma}^{\mathsf{sig}}(t + O(1), q, k) - \mathbf{DL}(t + O(q), k)$. Substituting $n = \alpha + 1$ proves the first part of Lemma 6. Furthermore, we've shown that $\forall i \geq 1$, the probability that an arbitrary signature σ_i is valid is at most $\mathbf{InSec}_{\Sigma}^{\mathsf{sig}}(t + O(1), q, k) + \mathbf{DL}(t + O(q), k)$.

Proof (Theorem 4). Assume a stegosystem $\mathcal{S}$ has a database of q_1 covertexts generated by $D_{VK}\langle\lambda, n\rangle$ and the ability to query $D_{VK}^{\alpha-1}\langle\cdot, 1\rangle$ q_2 times. We can create an adversary A that distinguishes the output of D_{VK} from $\mathcal{S}$. A gets VK as input and permission to query a mystery oracle that is either D_{VK} or $\mathcal{S}$. A will ask its oracle to generate $q_1 + 1$ covertexts of length N. A outputs 1 if the oracle returns any duplicate or invalid covertexts. If the oracle is $D_{VK}\langle\lambda, \cdot\rangle$, then A outputs 1 with probability $\Gamma(N, N, q_1 + 1, k)$ (the probability that duplicate covertexts occur). We examine what happens when the oracle is $\mathcal{S}$.

$\mathcal{S}$ can use its covertext database to generate stegotexts. Each covertext of length n can generate at most 1 valid stegotext of length N (the stegosystem can take an N document prefix). The stegosystem cannot take an arbitrary substring of a covertext because it would have to forge a signature on the new first integer and the α dummy arguments.

$\mathcal{S}$ gives A a list of $q_1 + 1$ stegotexts: $s^{(1)}, \ldots, s^{(q_1+1)}$. Each stegotext $s^{(i)}$ can be parsed as $r_1^{(i)}\sigma_1^{(i)} \circ \cdots \circ r_N^{(i)}\sigma_N^{(i)}$. $\mathcal{S}$ can easily create q_1 distinct stegotexts from its covertext dictionary. We examine how $\mathcal{S}$ generates the $q_1 + 1$st stegotext. There are 3 cases:

1. $\mathcal{S}$ has generated a new message signature pair that is not in the covertext database and that did not come from $D_{VK}^{\alpha-1}\langle\cdot, 1\rangle$. Then $\mathcal{S}$ has broken the security of the signature scheme Σ. $\mathcal{S}$ ran in $(q_1 + 1)t$ time and made $nq_1 + q_2$ queries to $\sigma(SK, \cdot)$ (via its queries to $D_{VK}\langle\lambda, \cdot\rangle$ and $D_{VK}^{\alpha-1}\langle\cdot, 1\rangle$). Therefore, this case occurs with probability at most $\mathbf{InSec}_{\Sigma}^{\mathsf{sig}}((q_1 + 1)t, nq_1 + q_2, k)$.

2. $\mathcal{S}$ used a signature generated by $D_{VK}^{\alpha-1}\langle\cdot, 1\rangle$. By Lemma 6, we know that $\forall i, j > \alpha$, $\mathcal{S}$ can use $D_{VK}^{\alpha-1}\langle\cdot, 1\rangle$ to generate a valid $\sigma_j^{(i)}$ with probability at most $\mathbf{InSec}_{\Sigma}^{\mathsf{sig}}(t + O(1), q_2, k) + \mathbf{DL}(t + O(q_2), k)$. Therefore, the probability that this case occurs is the total number of such signatures $(N - \alpha)(q_1 + 1)$ times the probability that any particular one was generated by $D_{VK}^{\alpha-1}\langle\cdot, 1\rangle$. This gives a total probability of: $(N-\alpha)(q_1+1)(\mathbf{InSec}_{\Sigma}^{\mathsf{sig}}(t + O(1), q_2, k) + \mathbf{DL}(t + O(q_2), k))$

3. The covertext database contains two identical sequences of α integers, thus letting $\mathcal{S}$ cut and paste two covertexts. This occurs with probability $\Gamma(\alpha, n, q_2, k)$.

Adding up the probabilities from the case analysis above, we get that

$$\mathbf{Adv}_{\mathcal{S},D}^{\mathsf{cha}}(A,k) \geq 1 - \Gamma(N,N,q_1+1,k) - \mathbf{InSec}_{\Sigma}^{\mathsf{sig}}((q_1+1)t, nq_1+q_2, k)$$
$$- (N-\alpha)(q_1+1)(\mathbf{InSec}_{\Sigma}^{\mathsf{sig}}(t+O(1), q_2, k) + \mathbf{DL}(t+O(q_2), k))$$
$$- \Gamma(\alpha, n, q_2, k)$$

A runs in $O((t+N)(q_1+1))$ time and makes q_1+1 queries of total length $N(q_1+1)$. Therefore, $\mathbf{InSec}_{\mathcal{S},D}^{\mathsf{cha}}(O((t+N)(q_1+1)), q_1+1, N(q_1+1)) \geq \mathbf{Adv}_{\mathcal{S},D}^{\mathsf{cha}}(A,k) \geq 1-\nu(k)$ for the negligible function ν defined above. This gives us the lower bound of $1-\nu(k)$ on the insecurity of $\mathcal{S}$.

6 Conclusion

Our results link current theoretical research to real world stegosystems. We show that a stegosystem must assume that its approximation of the covertext distribution is correct. A slight error, or a missed correlation, can lead to almost certain detection. It is impossible to leverage incomplete or incorrect information to somehow create properly distributed covertexts.

Acknowledgements

Anna Lysyanskaya is supported by NSF CAREER grant CNS-0374661. Mira Meyerovich is supported by a U.S. Department of Homeland Security (DHS) Fellowship under the DHS Scholarship and Fellowship Program and NSF grant CNS-0374661. The DHS Scholarship and Fellowship Program is administered by the Oak Ridge Institute for Science and Education (ORISE) for DHS through an interagency agreement with the U.S Department of Energy (DOE). ORISE is managed by Oak Ridge Associated Universities under DOE contract number DE-AC05-06OR23100. All opinions expressed in this paper are the authors' and do not necessarily reflect the policies and views of NSF, DHS, DOE, or ORISE.

References

[AP98]   Ross J. Anderson and Fabien AP Petitcolas. On the limits of steganography. *IEEE Journal on Selected Areas in Communications*, 16(4):474–481, May 1998.

[BC05]   Michael Backes and Christian Cachin. Public-key steganography with active attacks. In Joe Kilian, editor, *Theory of Cryptography Conference Proceedings*, volume 3378 of *LNCS*, pages 210–226. Springer Verlag, 2005.

[Cac98]   Christian Cachin. An information-theoretic model for steganography. In David Aucsmith, editor, *Proc. 2nd Information Hiding Workshop*, volume 1525 of *LNCS*, pages 306–318. Sprinter Verlag, 1998.

[DIRR05]   Nenad Dedić, Gene Itkis, Leonid Reyzin, and Scott Russell. Upper and lower bounds on black-box steganography. In Joe Kilian, editor, *Theory of Cryptography Conference Proceedings*, volume 3378 of *LNCS*, pages 227–244. Springer Verlag, 2005.

[Gol04]   Oded Goldreich. Foundations of cryptography: Volume 2, basic applications. 2004.

[HLvA02]   Nicholas J. Hopper, John Langford, and Louis von Ahn. Provably secure steganography. In Moti Yung, editor, *Advances in Cryptology - CRYPTO 2002, 22nd Annual International Cryptology Conference, Santa Barbara, California, USA, August 18-22, 2002, Proceedings*, volume 2442 of *LNCS*. Springer, 2002.

[Hop04]   Nicholas J. Hopper. Toward a theory of steganography. CMU Ph.D. Thesis, 2004.

[Hop05]   Nicholas J. Hopper. On steganographic chosen covertext security. In *ICALP 2005, 32nd Annual International Colloquium on Automata, Languages and Programming, Lisboa, Portugal, July 11-15 2005, Proceedings*, 2005.

[Le03]   Tri Van Le. Efficient provably secure public key steganography. Technical report, Florida State University, 2003. Cryptography ePrint Archive, http://eprint.iacr.org/2003/156.

[LK03]   Tri Van Le and Kaoru Kurosawa. Efficient public key steganography secure against adaptively chosen stegotext attacks. Technical report, Florida State University, 2003. Cryptography ePrint Archive, http://eprint.iacr.org/2003/244.

[LM04]   Anna Lysyanskaya and Mira Meyerovich. Steganography with imperfect sampling. At: CRYPTO 2004 Rump Session, August 2004, 2004.

[LM05]   Anna Lysyanskaya and Mira Meyerovich. Steganography with imperfect sampling. Technical Report ePrint Archive 2005/305, Brown University, 2005. Cryptography ePrint Archive, from http://eprint.iacr.org/2005/305.

[MLC01]   Ira S. Moskowitz, Garth E. Longdon, and LiWu Chang. A new paradigm hidden in steganography. In *Proceedings of the 2000 workshop on New Security Paradigms*. ACM Press, 2001.

[PKSM]   Kyle Petrowski, Mehdi Kharrazi, Husrev T. Sencar, and Nasir Memon. Psteg: steganographic embedding through patching. In *2005 IEEE International Conference on Acoustics, Speech, and Signal Processing*.

[RR03]   Leonid Reyzin and Scott Russell. Simple stateless steganography. Technical Report ePrint Archive 2003/093, Boston University, 2003. Cryptography ePrint Archive, from http://eprint.iacr.org/2003/093.

[Sal03]   Phil Sallee. Model-based steganography. In *IWDW*, pages 154–167, 2003.

[vAH04]   Louis von Ahn and Nicholas J. Hopper. Public-key steganography. In Christian Cachin and Jan Camenisch, editors, *Advances in Cryptology — EUROCRYPT 2004*, volume 3027 of *LNCS*, pages 323–341. Springer Verlag, 2004.

Collision-Resistant No More:
Hash-and-Sign Paradigm Revisited

Ilya Mironov

Microsoft Research (Silicon Valley Campus)
mironov@microsoft.com

Abstract. A signature scheme constructed according to the hash-and-sign paradigm—hash the message and then sign the hash, symbolically $\sigma(H(M))$—is no more secure than the hash function H against a collision-finding attack. Recent attacks on standard hash functions call the paradigm into question. It is well known that a simple modification of the hash-and-sign paradigm may replace the collision-resistant hash with a weaker primitive—a target-collision resistant hash function (also known as a universal one-way hash, UOWHF). The signer generates a random key k and outputs the pair $(k, \sigma(k||H_k(M)))$ as a signature on M. The apparent problem with this approach is the increase in the signature size. In this paper we demonstrate that for three concrete signature schemes, DSA, PSS-RSA, and Cramer-Shoup, the message can be hashed simultaneously with computing the signature, using one of the signature's components as the key for the hash function. We prove that our constructions are as secure as the originals for DSA and PSS-RSA in the random oracle model and for the Cramer-Shoup signature scheme in the standard model.

Keywords: TCR, UOWHF, collision-resistance, signatures, Cramer-Shoup, DSA, PSS-RSA.

1 Introduction

History of relation between cryptographically secure hash functions and digital signature schemes is one of co-evolution and divergence. Early constructions of dedicated hash functions were motivated by their applications to signature schemes [Riv91, NIS95]; by now the hash functions have extended their application domain to include MACs [BCK96] and public-key encryption [Sho00b]. In turn, unforgeability of many signature schemes crucially depends on security of the underlying hash function. This paper is concerned with divesting signature schemes of their reliance on collision-resistant hash functions by replacing them with a strictly weaker primitive. The general approach is well known; the novelty is in doing so without increasing the signature length.

Hash functions often play a dual role of a *domain extender* and a *random oracle* in constructions of signature schemes.

The first role, that of a domain extender, is due to the fact that it is much easier to design a scheme secure for signing messages of a fixed length than

M. Yung et al. (Eds.): PKC 2006, LNCS 3958, pp. 140–156, 2006.
© International Association for Cryptologic Research 2006

of unrestricted length. Consider, for example, the RSA signature defined as $\sigma_{\text{RSA}}(M) = M^d \mod N$. If the message domain were unrestricted, a forgery would be trivial since $\sigma_{\text{RSA}}(M) = \sigma_{\text{RSA}}(M + N)$. Virtually all practical signature schemes follow the hash-and-sign paradigm: apply a hash function to the message and sign the result, which we represent symbolically as $\sigma(H(M))$. The natural security requirement for H is that the hash function must be collision-resistant. Otherwise, if two messages have identical hashes $H(M_1) = H(M_2)$ a signature on one of them is a signature on the other. In light of recent attacks on standard hash functions, such as [WY05, WYY05a], feasibility of constructing efficient collision-resistant hash functions appears problematic; bypassing the requirement would make signatures more robust and may potentially increase their efficiency.

The following simple attack on the RSA function, whose domain is restricted to $1 \leq M < N$, motivates the second role of hash functions: $\sigma_{\text{RSA}}(M^2 \mod N) = \sigma_{\text{RSA}}(M)^2 \mod N$. Coincidentally, hashing the message before applying the RSA function thwarts this attack, at least in practice. Many practical signature schemes are vulnerable to similar attacks, which are remedied by a judicious application of a hash function. Thus, the Fiat-Shamir heuristic [FS87], which gives a generic way of transforming an identification scheme into a signature, and the full-domain hash [BR93], which is suitable for signatures based on a trapdoor permutation such as RSA or Rabin functions, elevated the status of the hash function from a technical prop to an indispensable element of the construction, in the same time upping the ante for design of the hash function. Not only must the hash be collision-resistant, it should be a real-world implementation of a certain idealized abstraction, called the random oracle. This methodology is adopted by many practical signatures, although there is evidence that it may never be proved secure in the standard model [DOP05, PV05].

By explicitly decoupling the two roles of the hash function we can have more transparent security proofs and more efficient designs of signature schemes. In this paper we relax the collision-resistant requirement, without addressing the need for a random oracle. For the basic Cramer-Shoup signature scheme [CS00], provable in the standard model, this means a strictly better signature scheme (computationally equivalent scheme which relies on a weaker assumption). For discussion of our result as applied to two signature schemes provably secure in the random oracle model, DSA and PSS-RSA, see Section 6.

The primitive, which we prefer to collision-resistant hash functions, is due to Naor and Yung [NY89]. Simultaneous with development of practical signature schemes offering only heuristic security, a series of seminal papers [GMR88, NY89, Rom90] established that provably secure signature schemes can be constructed from one-way functions. An intermediate step of this construction is a family of universal one-way hash functions, also called target-collision resistant (TCR) hashes. TCR hashes is a class of *keyed* hash functions formally defined in Section 2. Further validating this approach, Simon [Sim98] demonstrated that a collision-resistant hash is a fundamentally stronger primitive (and hence more difficult to construct) than a TCR function by proving impossibility of a black-box construction of a collision-resistant hash from a one-way function.

Moreover, a TCR hash may replace a collision-resistant function as the first step of the hash-and-sign signature scheme. Most importantly, it can be done via a little tweak of the hash-and-sign paradigm rather than by going through the theoretically secure but inefficient construction of [NY89]. Informally, if $\sigma(\cdot)$ is secure for signing fixed-length messages and $H_k(\cdot)$ is TCR, the hybrid scheme $(k, \sigma(k||H_k(M)))$, where key k is chosen uniformly at random by the signer, is secure as well. The obvious problem with the scheme is the increase in the signature length, since the key k becomes part of the signature (discussion of the length of the key is deferred to Section 6).

We observe that for many signature schemes, such as Cramer-Shoup, those based on Fiat-Shamir heuristic and probabilistic full-domain hash, the signature *already* includes some randomly generated data, which is independent of the message. We demonstrate that this data can double as the key of the TCR hash, thus eliminating the need for extra key material. The resulting schemes retain the signature length of the originals and are at least as secure.

Some schemes and results of this paper were independently discovered and presented by Halevi and Krawczyk [HK05a, HK05b].

2 Definitions

Our definitions of signature schemes and TCRs follow [GMR88] and [NY89] except that we recast the definitions in the language of exact security.

Signature scheme. A signature scheme $\mathcal{S}$ consists of a triple of algorithms:

- Key generation algorithm $KeyGen(1^k) = (\text{PK}, \text{SK})$, a randomized algorithm producing a public-private key pair for a given security parameter.
- Verification algorithm $Verify_{\text{PK}}(M, \sigma) \in \{\texttt{accept}, \texttt{reject}\}$. We say that σ is a valid signature on M if $Verify_{\text{PK}}(M, \sigma) = \texttt{accept}$.
- Signing algorithm $Sign_{\text{SK}}(M) = \sigma \in \{0,1\}^n$. The signing algorithm outputs a valid signature on M with an overwhelming probability taken over its own coin tosses.

A signature scheme $\mathcal{S}$ is (t, ε, q_S)-secure against existential forgery under adaptive chosen-message attack if the attacker running in time less than t and making no more than q_S signing queries cannot succeed with probability more than ε in producing a valid signature on a message M, which has not been previously signed by the signing oracle. In other words, the adversary obtains at most q_S valid signatures on adaptively chosen (queries may depend on the answers to the previous queries) messages. The adversary wins if he can compute a valid signature on a message not in the list of queries.

TCR. A (t, ε)-target collision-resistant hash function (TCR), also known as a universal one-way hash function (UWOHF) is a keyed hash function $H : \{0,1\}^k \times \{0,1\}^* \mapsto \{0,1\}^n$ such that no adversary running in time less than t can win the following game with probability more than ε:

Step 1. Output $X \in \{0,1\}^*$.

Step 2. Receive K randomly chosen from $\{0,1\}^k$.

Step 3. Produce Y so that $H_K(X) = H_K(Y)$.

As a warm-up exercise, we sketch a proof that combining a TCR hash with a signature scheme secure for signing fixed-length strings results in a signature scheme secure for messages of unrestricted length.

Proposition 1. *Assume a signature scheme* $\mathcal{S} = (KeyGen, Sign, Verify)$ *is* (t, ε_S, q_S)-*secure against existential forgery under an adaptive chosen-message attack where the messages are restricted to length* n. *Assume further that* $H : \{0,1\}^k \times \{0,1\}^* \mapsto \{0,1\}^{n-k}$ *is a* (t, ε_H)-*TCR. Then there exists a* $(t, \varepsilon_S + \varepsilon_H q_S, q_S)$-*secure signature scheme for arbitrary-length messages.*

Proof. Let the signature scheme $\mathcal{S}'$ be the following:

$Sign'$: $Verify'$:

Step 1. Generate $K \xleftarrow{\ \varepsilon\ } \{0,1\}^k$.   Step 1. Parse signature as (K, σ).

Step 2. $\sigma \leftarrow Sign_{\text{SK}}(K \| H_K(M))$.   Step 2. Run $Verify_{\text{PK}}(K \| H_K(M), \sigma)$.

Step 3. Output signature $K \| \sigma$.

($KeyGen$ is the same as in $\mathcal{S}$).

Assume that there exists an adversary capable of producing a valid signature $(M, (K, \sigma))$ having queried the signing oracle on messages $M_1, \ldots, M_{q_S}$, such that $M \neq M_i$ for $1 \leq i \leq q_S$. Let the signatures output by the oracle be $(K_1, \sigma_1), \ldots, (K_{q_S}, \sigma_{q_S})$. Two cases are possible. Either $K \| H_K(M) \neq K_i \| H_{K_i}(M_i)$ for all $i \in [1, q_S]$ or there is i such that $K \| H_K(M) = K_i \| H_{K_i}(M_i)$ and $M \neq M_i$. In the former case the adversary can be trivially used to forge a signature for the scheme $\mathcal{S}$. In the latter, draw a random index $j \in [1, q_S]$ and, when the adversary makes query M_j, send M_j as the first message of the TCR-game. Upon receiving key K', set $K_j = K'$. With probability $1/q_S$ the adversary outputs a message-signature pair so that $K \| H_K(M) = K' \| H_{K'}(M_j)$. Since the keys have fixed size k bits, it follows that $K = K'$ and we win the TCR-game by outputting M, which collides with M_j under key K'.

The probability that a t-time adversary forges a signature is less than the sum of ε_S—the probability that he succeeds in breaking the signature scheme $\mathcal{S}$—and $\varepsilon_H q_S$, where ε_H is the probability that it breaks H.   □

Pseudo-random generator. We say that a function $F : A \mapsto B$ is (t, ε, q_F)-pseudo-random generator if no adversary running in time less than t and making less than q_F queries of F can distinguish $F(x)$, where $x \xleftarrow{\ \varepsilon\ } A$, from the uniform distribution on B with probability more than ε. We relax the standard definition [BM82] by dropping the usual requirement that the function stretches its input (i.e., that $|A| < |B|$). Although compressing pseudo-random generators are trivial to construct, the assumption that a particular function, such as SHA-1, is a pseudo-random generator, is substantive.

3   DSA Scheme

We present the original DSA scheme together with our variant, which we call TCR-DSA, see Figure 1. The new signature scheme uses three hash functions: $H\colon \{0,1\}^{\ell_2} \times \{0,1\}^* \mapsto \{0,1\}^{\ell_1}$, which we assume to be a (t_H, ε_H)-TCR, and two functions $F_1\colon \mathbb{Z}_p \mapsto \{0,1\}^{\ell_2}$ and $F_2\colon \{0,1\}^{\ell_1+\ell_2} \mapsto \{0,1\}^n$, which we model as random oracles.

DSA   TCR-DSA

Key selection:

p, q—prime, $|p| = n$, $|q| = m$, $p|q-1$

$g \in \mathbb{Z}_q$, ord $g = p$

$a \xleftarrow{\mathfrak{c}} \mathbb{Z}_p$; $h = g^a \bmod q$

public key: p, q, g, h

private key: a

Hash functions:

$G\colon \{0,1\}^* \mapsto \{0,1\}^n$

$\left| \begin{array}{l} H\colon \{0,1\}^{\ell_2} \times \{0,1\}^* \mapsto \{0,1\}^{\ell_1} \text{—TCR} \\ F_2\colon \{0,1\}^{\ell_1+\ell_2} \mapsto \{0,1\}^n \\ F_1\colon \mathbb{Z}_p \mapsto \{0,1\}^{\ell_2} \end{array} \right\}$ random oracles

Signature generation:

$k \xleftarrow{\mathfrak{c}} \mathbb{Z}_p$

$r = (g^k \bmod q) \bmod p$

$\quad\quad\quad\quad\quad\quad\quad\quad\quad | \; k \xleftarrow{\mathfrak{c}} \mathbb{Z}_p$

$\quad\quad\quad\quad\quad\quad\quad\quad\quad | \; r = (g^k \bmod q) \bmod p$

$\quad\quad\quad\quad\quad\quad\quad\quad\quad | \; \boxed{r_1 = F_1(r)}$

$s = k^{-1}(\boxed{G(M)} + ra) \bmod p \quad | \; s = k^{-1}(\boxed{F_2(r_1, H_{r_1}(M))} + ra) \bmod p$

$\sigma = (r, s)$

$\quad\quad\quad\quad\quad\quad\quad\quad\quad | \; \sigma = (r, s)$

Signature verification:

$\quad\quad\quad\quad\quad\quad\quad\quad\quad \| \; \boxed{r_1 = F_1(r)}$

$u = g^{\boxed{G(M)}} h^r \bmod q \quad\quad u = g^{\boxed{F_2(r_1, H_{r_1}(M))}} h^r \bmod q$

$w = u^{s^{-1} \bmod p} \bmod q \quad\quad w = u^{s^{-1} \bmod p} \bmod q$

accept if $w \bmod p = r$ $\quad\quad\quad$ accept if $w \bmod p = r$

Fig. 1. DSA and TCR-DSA (differences are enclosed in boxes)

In this section we tie security of TCR-DSA to that of the DSA instantiated with any concrete function, which is a good $\{0,1\}^{2n} \mapsto \{0,1\}^n$ pseudo-random generator, and under the δ-min-entropy of r assumption (defined below) in the random oracle model.

First, we formulate an assumption on uniformity of r (in both schemes), also discussed in [Bro05].

Assumption of "δ-min-entropy of r". Define the min-entropy of distribution $\mathcal{D}$ as

$$H_\infty(\mathcal{D}) = -\log \max \Pr[x \in \mathcal{D}].$$

Let $\mathcal{R}$ be the distribution of $r = (g^k \mod q) \mod p$, where k is uniform in $\mathbb{Z}_p$. We assume that $H_\infty(\mathcal{R}) > \delta$.

[NS02, Lemma 10] proves that r has min-entropy $O(\delta \log p)$ for some δ that depends on $\log q / \log p$. In practice, we expect r to be distributed much smoother, having min-entropy of the order of $\log p - c \log \log p$ for some small c (consider the occupancy problem applied to p balls and 2^n bins).

Theorem 1. *Under the assumptions that*

- *DSA is $(t, \varepsilon_{\mathrm{DSA}}, q_S)$-secure for some $G \colon \{0,1\}^* \mapsto \{0,1\}^n$;*
- *G restricted to inputs of length $2n$ is (t, ε_G)-pseudo-random generator;*
- *H is (t, ε_H)-TCR;*
- *r has $(\log p - \delta)$-min-entropy;*
- *F_1, F_2 are modeled as random oracles, which together are queried no more than q_F times;*

then TCR-DSA is $(t, 2\varepsilon_{\mathrm{DSA}} + \varepsilon_G + \varepsilon_H q_S + (2^{-\delta} q_S p + q_F) 2^{-\delta} q_S, q_S)$-secure.

Proof. We demonstrate how to transform any forgery of TCR-DSA into either an attack on H as a TCR or a forgery of DSA instantiated with G. We do so by defining Game 0 that consists of the challenger interacting with the TCR-DSA adversary $\mathcal{A}$ and the DSA signing oracle. $\mathcal{A}$ queries F_1 and F_2, requests signatures, and attempts to forge a TCR-DSA signature. In the spirit of [Sho04] we describe a sequence of games that transforms the initial game to one whose success probability we can easily analyze.

Game 0. Obtain the public key for the DSA oracle and pass it on as the public key of TCR-DSA. We keep two lists L_1, L_2, initially empty, of inputs on which F_1 and F_2 are defined. Queries to F_1 are answered randomly; queries to F_2 are answered by randomly choosing $M' \xleftarrow{\math$} \{0,1\}^{2n}$ and returning $G(M')$ (M' is stored; if M' appeared previously, the process is repeated). Notice that under the assumption of computational indistinguishability of G's output, F_2 cannot be distinguished from a true random oracle with probability more than ε_G. Upon receiving a new signing query M do the following:

Step 1. Generate $M' \xleftarrow{\math$} \{0,1\}^{2n}$. Repeat if M' appeared previously.

Step 2. Obtain (r, s) by querying the DSA signing oracle on M'.

Step 3. Fail if $r \in L_1$. Define $r_1 = F_1(r)$ randomly, appending the result to L_1.

Step 4. Fail if $(r_1, H_{r_1}(M)) \in L_2$. Otherwise let $F_2(r_1, H_{r_1}(M)) = G(M')$, add $(r_1, H_{r_1}(M))$ to L_2 and store M' together with $r_1, H_{r_1}(M)$.

Step 5. Output (r, s) as a TCR-DSA signature on M.

Finally, if $\mathcal{A}$ outputs $M^*, (r^*, s^*)$ as a forgery of TCR-DSA, do the following:

Step 6. Compute $r_1^* = F_1(r^*)$.

Step 7. Fail if F_2 has not been queried on $(r_1^*, H_{r_1^*}(M^*))$.

Step 8. Fetch M_0^* such that $F_2(r_1^*, H_{r_1^*}(M^*)) = G(M_0^*)$.

Step 9. Fail if the DSA oracle has been queried on M_0^*.

Step 10. Output $M_0^*, (r^*, s^*)$ as a DSA forgery.

Observe that if Game 0 succeeds, the challenger aided by $\mathcal{A}$ queried the DSA oracle no more than q_S times and successfully forged a DSA signature. The probability of this event is no more than $\varepsilon_{\mathrm{DSA}}$. In order to complete the proof we shall bound the probability that Game 0 fails (Steps 3, 4, 7, 9).

To bound the failure probability of Step 3 of Game 0 we need the following lemma.

Lemma 1. *Let $\mathcal{D}$ be a distribution on set X. Let $\tau = 2^{-H_\infty(\mathcal{D})}|X|$. We claim that for any set $A \subset X$ and any $x_1, \dots, x_n \xleftarrow{\ \text{\tiny c}\ }_{\mathcal{D}} X$ (n elements chosen from X independently at random according to $\mathcal{D}$) the following holds:*

$$\Pr[\exists i, j (i \neq j, x_i = x_j) \bigvee \exists i (x_i \in A)] < (\tau^2 n^2)/|X| + \tau |A| n / |X|.$$

Proof. Observe that

$$\Pr[\exists i, j \colon i \neq j, x_i = x_j] \leq E[\#\{i < j \colon x_i = x_j\}] = \sum_{i<j} E[x_i = x_j] < n^2 \tau^2 / |X|. \quad (1)$$

To analyze the probability that $x_i \in A$ for some i, consider $p = \Pr[x \xleftarrow{\ \text{\tiny c}\ }_{\mathcal{D}} X \colon x \in A]$. Then, $\Pr[\exists i \colon x_i \in A] = 1 - (1 - p)^n < pn$. Further, $p = \sum_{a \in A} \Pr[x \xleftarrow{\ \text{\tiny c}\ }_{\mathcal{D}} X \colon x = a] < \tau |A| / |X|$, which, together with (1), completes the proof. $\square$(Lemma 1)

By applying Lemma 1 to the distribution of r and A defined as the set of inputs on which F_1 is queried directly, we obtain that Step 3 fails with probability at most $2^{-2\delta} q_S^2 p + 2^{-\delta} q_F q_S = (2^{-\delta} q_S p + q_F) 2^{-\delta} q_S$.

Since r_1 never repeats, the probability that Step 4 fails is at most $q_F^2 2^{-\ell_2}/2$.

If Step 7 fails, it means that the forger produced a valid signature (r^*, s^*) without knowing the value of $(r_1^*, H_{r_1^*}(M^*))$. Since the value is distributed randomly, same forger can be used against DSA. The probability of the failure is thus at most $\varepsilon_{\mathrm{DSA}}$.

Now we rewrite Step 3 of Game 0, replacing it with the following:

Step $3a'$. Submit M as the first move of the TCR game.

Step $3b'$. Obtain $\kappa \in \{0,1\}^{\ell_2}$ as the key. Set $r_1 = F_1(r) = \kappa$.

Step 9 fails if the DSA oracle has been previously called on M_0^*, which can only happen if $(r_1^*, H_{r_1^*}(M^*)) = (r_1', H_{r_1'}(M'))$ for some other M'. It implies that $r_1^* = r_1'$ and the result is obviously a collision under $H_{r_1}(\cdot)$, which we output by rewriting Step 9:

Step $9'$. If DSA oracle has been queried on M_0^*, fetch $(r_1', H_{r_1'}(M')) = (r_1^*, H_{r_1^*}(M^*))$. Find the game (started in Step $3a'$), where the M' was the first move and r_1' was the key. Complete the game by outputting M^*. Fail.

The new game fails with exactly the same probability as Game 0. To complete the proof we notice that Step 9' fails with probability at most $q_S \varepsilon_H$. $\square$[Theorem 1]

We proved that TCR-DSA signature scheme is as secure as DSA for *arbitrary G*, which can, in particular, be modeled as a random oracle, or be extremely slow and provably (under, say, the discrete-logarithm assumption) collision-resistant. Although a direct proof of security of TCR-DSA under some standard assumptions would be tempting, we are concerned with the *tightness* of the reduction. Best known reductions, even in the random oracle model, tie the forgery probability of DSA variants to the hardness of discrete logarithm with q_F (number of random oracle queries) factor [BPVY00]. In order to shave off the factor, we may either assume additionally that the underlying group can be accurately modeled in the generic group model [Bro05], or make some non-standard assumptions [PV05]. Our reduction is tight in respect to the forgery probability of DSA and loose with respect to the security of H. The latter is hardly a bottleneck, since neither the key nor the output length of H affects the length of the signature and therefore boosting security of H should only be constrained by efficiency considerations.

Our proof does rely on one non-standard assumption, that of δ-min entropy of r. For our result to be meaningful, δ should be sufficiently high (of the order of $\log p$), which ensures that all values of r are unique with high probability. Two points are in order. First, for $\delta \approx -\log \varepsilon$ the assumption can be derived from $(t, \varepsilon, 0)$-security of DSA, where t is the time required to do 2^δ DSA verifications. Second, the proof of Theorem 1 can be restructured to accommodate $\delta \approx -\log \varepsilon$. The proof will appear in the full version of the paper.

4 RSA-PSS Signature Scheme

RSA-based probabilistic signature scheme (PSS-RSA) was proposed by Bellare and Rogaway [BR96] as a strengthening of the full domain hash scheme [BR93]. PSS-RSA enjoys *tight security* reduction to the underlying hard problem—the RSA assumption—in the random oracle model. In other words, assuming that certain hash functions are ideal, forging PSS-RSA is computationally equivalent to inverting the RSA function. Later, Coron proved an even tighter reduction to the RSA assumption [Cor02], which we use as a basis for our security claim.

Strictly speaking, PSS-RSA does not follow the hash-and-sign paradigm, since the message is concatenated with some random *salt* and only then is hashed using a hash function, modeled as a random oracle. We propose to hash the message, whose length is unrestricted, using a conventional TCR function keyed with the salt, and hash the short TCR function's output with a conservatively designed "oracle" (see Section 6).

Security of TCR-PSS-RSA (see Figure 2) relies on the following:

(t, ε)-**RSA assumption.** No algorithm running in time less than t can solve $x^r = y \mod N$ for x with probability more than ε, where N is a random RSA modulus, $y \xleftarrow{\text{\$}} \mathbb{Z}_N^*$, and r is fixed.

RSA-PSS   TCR-RSA-PSS

Key selection:

p, q—prime, $|p| = |q| = n/2$, $N = pq$
$e, d \in Z_N$, $ed = 1 \pmod{N}$
public key: N, d
private key: e

Hash functions:

$$H\colon \{0,1\}^{k_0} \times \{0,1\}^* \mapsto \{0,1\}^{k_1}\text{—TCR}$$

$h\colon \boxed{\{0,1\}^*} \mapsto \{0,1\}^{k_1}$ $\quad h\colon \boxed{\{0,1\}^{k_0+k_2}} \mapsto \{0,1\}^{k_1}$
$g_1\colon \{0,1\}^{k_1} \mapsto \{0,1\}^{k_0}$ $\quad g_1\colon \{0,1\}^{k_1} \mapsto \{0,1\}^{k_0}$
$g_2\colon \{0,1\}^{k_1} \mapsto \{0,1\}^{n-k_0-k_1-1}$ $\quad g_2\colon \{0,1\}^{k_1} \mapsto \{0,1\}^{n-k_0-k_1-1}$

h, g_1, g_2—random oracles

Signature generation:

$r \xleftarrow{\varepsilon} \{0,1\}^{k_0}$ $\qquad r \xleftarrow{\varepsilon} \{0,1\}^{k_0}$
$\boxed{w = h(M\|r)}$ $\qquad \boxed{w = h(r\|H_r(M))}$
$r^* = g_1(w) \oplus r$ $\qquad r^* = g_1(w) \oplus r$
$y = 0\|w\|r^*\|g_2(w)$ $\qquad y = 0\|w\|r^*\|g_2(w)$
$\sigma = y^d \bmod N$ $\qquad \sigma = y^d \bmod N$

Signature verification:

$y = \sigma^e \bmod N$ $\qquad y = \sigma^e \bmod N$
check $y = b\|w\|r^*\|\gamma$ $\qquad$ check $y = b\|w\|r^*\|\gamma$
$r = r^* \oplus g_1(w)$ $\qquad r = r^* \oplus g_1(w)$

accept if $\begin{cases} \boxed{h(M\|r) = w} \\ g_2(w) = \gamma \\ b = 0 \end{cases}$ $\qquad$ accept if $\begin{cases} \boxed{h(r\|H_r(M)) = w} \\ g_2(w) = \gamma \\ b = 0 \end{cases}$

Fig. 2. PSS-RSA and TCR-PSS-RSA (differences are enclosed in boxes)

Theorem 2. *If all of the following hold:*

- *$(t, \varepsilon_{\mathrm{RSA}})$-RSA assumption;*
- *H is (t, ε_H)-TCR;*
- *h, g_1, g_2 are modeled as random oracles and queried no more than q_F times;*

then TCR-PSS-RSA is $(t, \varepsilon_{\mathrm{RSA}}(1 + 6q_S 2^{-k_0} + 2(q_S + q_F)^2 2^{-k_1} + \varepsilon_H q_S, q_S)$-secure.

Proof [sketch]. Let $M_1, \ldots, M_{q_S}$ be the signing queries made by the adversary, $r_1, \ldots, r_{q_S}$ be the r values from the corresponding signatures output by the signer, $M' \neq M_i$ for $1 \leq i \leq q_S$ be the message with forged signature, and r' be its r-value. The proof from [Cor02] of PSS-RSA applies virtually without any changes, where $H_r(M)$ replaces M. We have to make sure that Coron's proof also rules out "weak" forgeries (which corresponds to $H_{r'}(M') = H_{r_i}(M_i)$, and $r' \neq r_i$ for some i), which it does, and bound the probability that $H_{r_i}(M_i) = H_{r'}(M')$ and $r_i = r'$.

To bound the probability of the latter event, consider a simulator that knows the private key of the signature scheme. Upon receiving a signing query for M_i, it starts a TCR game, submitting M_i as the first message. It receives a random key r_i, which it uses in computing a signature on M_i. If the adversary succeeds in creating a collision, the simulator is able to complete one of the TCR games.   □

5   Cramer-Shoup Signature Scheme

Historically, the Cramer-Shoup signature scheme [CS00] was the first efficient signature scheme provably secure in the standard model (i.e., without random oracles). The scheme relies on the strong RSA assumption, introduced in [BP97].

The basic Cramer-Shoup signature scheme, which uses a collision-resistant hash function, was presented in [CS00] together with a variant, where the hash

CS	TCR-CS

Key selection:
p, q—strong primes, $|p| = |q| = \ell_1$, $n = pq$
$h, x \xleftarrow{\text{¢}} \text{QR}_n$; $e' \xleftarrow{\text{¢}} \mathbb{P}_{\ell+1}$
$k' \xleftarrow{\text{¢}} \{0,1\}^{\ell_2}$
public key: n, h, x, e', k'
private key: p, q

Hash function
$H\colon \{0,1\}^{\ell_2} \times \{0,1\}^* \mapsto \{0,1\}^\ell$—TCR
$\left\lfloor \mu\colon \{0,1\}^{\ell+1} \mapsto \{0,1\}^{\ell_2}\right.$—projection

Signature generation:

CS	TCR-CS
generate $e \in \mathbb{P}_{\ell+1}$, $e \neq e'$	generate $e \in \mathbb{P}_{\ell+1}$, $e \neq e'$
$y' \xleftarrow{\text{¢}} \text{QR}_n$	$y' \xleftarrow{\text{¢}} \text{QR}_n$
$\boxed{k \xleftarrow{\text{¢}} \{0,1\}^{\ell_2}}$	
$x' = (y')^{e'} h^{-\boxed{H_k(M)}}$	$x' = (y')^{e'} h^{-\boxed{H_{\mu(e)}(M)}}$
$y = \left(xh^{-\boxed{H_{k'}(k,x')}}\right)^{1/e}$	$y = \left(xh^{\boxed{H_{k'}(x')}}\right)^{1/e}$
$\boxed{\sigma = (e, y, y', k)}$	$\boxed{\sigma = (e, y, y')}$

Signature verification:

CS	TCR-CS
check e is odd, $|e| = \ell + 1$, $e \neq e'$	check e is odd, $|e| = \ell + 1$, $e \neq e'$
check $x' = (y')^e h^{-\boxed{H_k(M)}}$	check $x' = (y')^e h^{-\boxed{H_{\mu(e)}(M)}}$
check $x = y^e h^{-\boxed{H_{k'}(k,x')}}$	check $x = y^e h^{-\boxed{H_{k'}(x')}}$

Fig. 3. CS and TCR-CS (differences are enclosed in boxes). $\mathbb{P}_\ell$ is the set of prime numbers of length ℓ; QR_n is the set of quadratic residues modulo n. Function $\mu(\cdot)$ returns most significant ℓ_2 bits of the input.

function is presumed to be a TCR. Our scheme combines the short signature length of the former and security of the latter. The TCR-based variant (CS) and our scheme (TCR-CS) are compared in Figure 3.

CS scheme makes use of a TCR by applying the generic transformation, outlined in the introduction,—the TCR's key is generated by the signer and transmitted as part of the signature. We propose to derive the hash function's key from the randomly chosen prime number e, which is already included in the signature.

Our proof follows closely Cramer-Shoup's original proof [CS00]. The main technical difficulty in constructing the reduction, which is not present in the original proof, consists in incorporating the hash function's key into a prime with a special structure. We expand on it below.

In addition to standard modular arithmetic, in the CS scheme the signer generates a *fresh* $(l+1)$-bit prime e with each signature (following [CS00] we assume $\ell = 160$). The prime numbers need not be uniformly distributed; the only requirement is that the probability that the same prime number is generated twice be negligible. Efficiency of the scheme (especially relative to [GHR99], which is otherwise comparable in terms of security and signature length) critically depends on the signer's ability to generate primes quickly. To this end, [CS00] proposes to use primes of special structure, namely $e = 2PR + 1$, where P is a 53-bit prime, which can be tested for primality much faster than the average $(\ell + 1)$-bit integer. For TCR-CS to be as efficient, we would prefer to use the same procedure. On the other hand, our reduction technique prescribes taking a random key obtained as part of the TCR game and using it in the signature. If e were a random 161-bit prime, doing so would be trivial—a random 161-bit number is prime with probability approximately $1/112$, hence the reduction would only suffer a factor of 112. Primes of the special structure $2PR + 1$, where $|P| = 53$, are more rare (a random 161-bit number has this structure with probability no more than 2^{-13}), and testing for it is prohibitively expensive.

Instead of using e as a key, we solve the problem by taking $\mu(e)$, where $\mu : \{0, 1\}^{161} \mapsto \{0, 1\}^{106}$ is a projection function, which simply drops 55 least significant bytes of its input. To reverse the procedure, which is what the reduction is to do, we adapt the prime generation algorithm from [CS00]. For a given key $k \in \{0, 1\}^{106}$, generate a random prime P in the range $(2^{52}, 2^{53})$, take a random number R in the range $((k2^{55} - 1)/2P, (k+1)2^{55} - 2)/2P)$, and accept $e = 2PR + 1$ if e is prime. If the procedure completes, $\mu(e) = k$ trivially holds. [CS00] shows that the expected number of trials until P is prime is 64 (for the purpose of the reduction, a pool of 53-bit long primes can be precomputed), and for any fixed P the expected probability that e is prime is at least $1/128$.

Before can sketch the proof of the following theorem, whose exact security claim is based on [SS00], we introduce the strong RSA assumption.

(t, ε)-**strong RSA assumption.** No algorithm running in time less than t can solve $x^r = y \bmod N$ for x and $r > 1$ with probability more than ε given random RSA modulus N, and random $y \in \mathbb{Z}_N^*$.

Theorem 3. *Fix $\ell = 160$. Let T_e is the time required to do 161-bit exponentiation. If the following holds:*

- $(t + T_e q_S \log q_S, \varepsilon_{\text{RSA}})$-*RSA assumption;*
- $(t + T_e q_S \log q_S, \varepsilon_{\text{SRSA}})$-*strong RSA assumption;*
- *A concrete pseudo-random number generator used for generating e and y' is (t, ε_G)-secure;*
- *H is (t, ε_H)-TCR;*

then TCR-CS *is* $(t, q_S, \varepsilon_{\text{RSA}}(q_S+1)+\varepsilon_{\text{SRSA}}\cdot 1.01+\varepsilon_H q_S 128+\varepsilon_G+q_S^2 2^{-145}+2^{-80})$-*secure.*

Proof [sketch]. For a detailed proof we refer the reader to [CS00, SS00]. Consider an adversary that makes q_S signing queries M_i, obtains signatures $\sigma_i = (e_i, y_i, y'_i)$, and then forges a signature $\sigma = (e, y, y')$ on $M \neq M_i$ for $1 \leq i \leq q_S$. Let $x'_i = (y'_i)^e h^{-H_{\mu(e_i)}(M_i)}$ and $x' = (y')^e h^{-H_{\mu(e)}(M')}$. We distinguish between three kinds of forgeries:

Type I. There is $1 \leq i \leq q_S$, such that $e = e_i$ and $x' = x'_i$.
Type II. There is $1 \leq i \leq q_S$, such that $e = e_i$ and $x' \neq x'_i$.
Type III. For all $1 \leq i \leq q_S$, $e \neq e_i$.

Proof from [CS00, SS00] applies without change for Type II and III forgeries (it suffices to check that nowhere in the proof does the choice of e depend on the hash of the message). To invoke the original proof for Type I forgery we have to bound the probability that $H_{\mu(e)}(M) = H_{\mu(e)}(M')$. We argue that such a forgery cannot happen with probability more than $\varepsilon_H q_S 128$, where ε_H is the security parameter of H. The proof is analogous to Theorem 2, with the only difference being the embedding process, described earlier in the section, that is used to map a random TCR key to a prime of $2PR + 1$ form. □

Finally, we observe that our modification applies to Fischlin's variant of the Cramer-Shoup scheme [Fis03], which is optimized for the size of the signature.

6 Discussion

In this section we address two points often raised in discussions of using TCR hashes as a building block of signature schemes: the problem of hash function's keylength, which is message size-dependent, and the random oracle assumption, which directly implies existence of collision-resistant functions.

Keylength of TCR hash. Bellare and Rogaway observed in [BR97] that adapting the iterative Merkle-Damgård [Mer90, Dam90] paradigm for TCR construction is not straightforward. Namely, even the second iteration of a TCR hash may be insecure (in contrast with a composition of collision-resistant hash functions, which is provably collision-resistant). They proposed interleaving applications of the compression function with XORing the chaining variable with independent masking keys, which increases the key length logarithmically with the size of the message. Their method was improved by Shoup [Sho00a], whose scheme was shown to be optimal among a concrete class of algorithms in [Mir01, Sar03]. For example, the key length required to hash a 1Gb message by going through the Shoup method applied to a keyed variant of the SHA-1 compression function is more than 4.8Kb. The proofs of optimality are exact and hence leave no hope of reducing the keylength if we are to stay within the existing paradigm.

We emphasize that the proofs of optimality only apply to a specific class of "masking-based" domain extenders. There are two potential ways to beat the lower bounds: design a dedicated TCR function, whose security is not degraded by chaining, or demonstrate a provably secure generic way of composing TCR hashes without key expansion. Both approaches are reasonable (see, for instance, [HPL04] which strengthens the definition of TCR to allow application of the Merkle-Damgård construction), and we expect that the interest in TCR functions rekindled by recent attacks on collision-resistant hash functions will spur further research in this area.

Random oracles and TCR functions. Pondering on the difference between collision-resistant hash functions and TCRs might appear rather pointless in the presence of the random oracle paradigm. Indeed, if we assume that a concrete hash function instantiates a random oracle, it is implicit that the function is collision-resistant and its domain can be trivially extended by going through the Merkle-Damgård construction, hence obliterating the need for TCRs. We claim that although this reduction is sound in theory, it may not be practical and may lead to bad design choices.

Hash functions must work for message lengths ranging from a few bytes to several hundred megabytes, which forces hash function designers to make certain trade-offs and defend against new classes of attacks. Designing an "oracle-like" hash function that accepts long inputs is inherently more challenging than designing a short-input function (for theoretical analysis of some of the difficulties see [KS05, CDMP05], for practical attacks that span several blocks see [WY05, BCJ+05, WYY05b]). It suffices to point out that the latest generation of hash functions, such as SHA-256,512 or Whirlpool, works at a fraction of the speed of MD5 and is much slower than AES [NES03, NM02].

Constructing an "oracle"—a function that thoroughly but slowly hashes one block (0.5–1Kb long) is conceivable, but it would be inadequate as a general-purpose hash function. It is plausible that the trend towards slower hash functions can be reversed if, instead of designing one-size-fits-all collision-resistant hash functions, we settle for fast TCR functions able to handle long messages and relatively slow "oracles" for fixed-length inputs.

In support of our view we cite the performance characteristics of signature schemes and hash functions from the NESSIE report [NES03, Table 50]. For three signature schemes (Cramer-Shoup, ECDSA, and RSA-PSS) the speed of the sign and verify operations ranged from 1.6M (RSA-PSS verify) to 62M (RSA-PSS sign) CPU cycles on Pentium IV. For comparison, one-block SHA-256 evaluation, which takes about 1.5K CPU cycles [NM02], is faster by approximately three orders of magnitude. It means that the hash function (applied to one block!)

can be slowed down by two orders of magnitude without the schemes' overall performance taking notice.

Finally, we note that the "oracle" functions may find applications in practical solutions to the problem raised in the beginning of this section, namely the keylength of TCR functions. Shoup's masking-based solution to domain expansion requires a long key, which can be derived from a shorter key using an "oracle." The resulting scheme would be provably secure in the random oracle world and enjoy efficiency of a cheap TCR construction.

7 Conclusions

For any hash-and-sign signature scheme a collision-finding attack on the underlying hash function is devastating. Recent attacks on MD5 and SHA-1 [WY05, WYY05a] suggest that designing efficient collision-resistant hash functions is harder than it has been commonly thought.

TCR hashes provide a good alternative to collision-resistant hash functions in the context of digital signatures. Traditionally, replacing collision-resistant hashes with TCRs, which are by definition *keyed* hash functions, resulted in an increase in the signature size, which has to additionally accommodate the hash function's key. We argue that for specific signature schemes the key can be derived from the already present part of the signature. For the Cramer-Shoup signature scheme we prove in the standard model our variant of the scheme, which provides a shorter signature while offering the same security.

Security of signature schemes provable in the random oracle model relies on the assumption that some concrete hash functions are real-world implementations of a certain ideal functionality. We revisit two popular signature schemes, DSA and PSS-RSA, and propose their TCR-based variants, whose proofs of security, while still dependent on random oracles, only require short-input ones. We argue that a short-input oracle might be easier to construct, since it can afford to be much slower than a conventional hash function.

References

[BCJ+05]   Eli Biham, Rafi Chen, Antoine Joux, Patrick Carribault, Christophe Lemuet, and William Jalby. Collisions of SHA-0 and reduced SHA-1. In Cramer [Cra05], pages 36–57.

[BCK96]   Mihir Bellare, Ran Canetti, and Hugo Krawczyk. Keying hash functions for message authentication. In Neal Koblitz, editor, *Advances in Cryptology—CRYPTO '96*, volume 1109 of *Lecture Notes in Computer Science*, pages 1–15. Springer, 1996.

[BM82]   Manuel Blum and Silvio Micali. How to generate cryptographically strong sequences of pseudo random bits. In *23rd Annual Symposium on Foundations of Computer Science*, pages 112–117, Chicago, Illinois, 3–5 November 1982. IEEE.

[BP97]   Niko Barić and Birgit Pfitzmann. Collision-free accumulators and fail-stop signature schemes without trees. In Walter Fumy, editor, *Advances in Cryptology—EUROCRYPT '97*, volume 1233 of *Lecture Notes in Computer Science*, pages 480–494. Springer, 1997.

[BPVY00]   Ernest F. Brickell, David Pointcheval, Serge Vaudenay, and Moti Yung. Design validations for discrete logarithm based signature schemes. In Hideki Imai and Yuliang Zheng, editors, *Public Key Cryptography—PKC 2000*, volume 1751 of *Lecture Notes in Computer Science*, pages 276–292. Springer, 2000.

[BR93]   Mihir Bellare and Phillip Rogaway. Random oracles are practical: A paradigm for designing efficient protocols. In *ACM Conference on Computer and Communications Security*, pages 62–73, 1993.

[BR96]   Mihir Bellare and Phillip Rogaway. The exact security of digital signatures—how to sign with RSA and Rabin. In Ueli M. Maurer, editor, *Advances in Cryptology—EUROCRYPT '96*, volume 1070 of *Lecture Notes in Computer Science*, pages 399–416. Springer, 1996.

[BR97]   Mihir Bellare and Phillip Rogaway. Collision-resistant hashing: Towards making UOWHFs practical. In Burton S. Kaliski Jr., editor, *Advances in Cryptology—CRYPTO '97*, volume 1294 of *Lecture Notes in Computer Science*, pages 470–484. Springer, 1997.

[Bra90]   Gilles Brassard, editor. *Advances in Cryptology—CRYPTO '89, 9th Annual International Cryptology Conference, Santa Barbara, California, USA, August 20–24, 1989, Proceedings*, volume 435 of *Lecture Notes in Computer Science*. Springer, 1990.

[Bro05]   Daniel R. L. Brown. Generic groups, collision resistance, and ECDSA. *Designs, Codes and Cryptography*, 35(1):119–152, 2005.

[CDMP05]   Jean-Sébastien Coron, Yevgeniy Dodis, Cécile Malinaud, and Prashant Puniya. Merkle-Damgård revisited: How to construct a hash function. In Shoup [Sho05], pages 430–448.

[Cor02]   Jean-Sébastien Coron. Optimal security proofs for PSS and other signature schemes. In Knudsen [Knu02], pages 272–287.

[Cra05]   Ronald Cramer, editor. *Advances in Cryptology—EUROCRYPT 2005, 24th Annual International Conference on the Theory and Applications of Cryptographic Techniques, Aarhus, Denmark, May 22–26, 2005, Proceedings*, volume 3494 of *Lecture Notes in Computer Science*. Springer, 2005.

[CS00]   Ronald Cramer and Victor Shoup. Signature schemes based on the strong RSA assumption. *ACM Trans. on Information and System Security (TISSEC)*, 3(3):161–185, 2000.

[Dam90]   Ivan Damgård. A design principle for hash functions. In Brassard [Bra90], pages 416–427.

[DOP05]   Yevgeniy Dodis, Roberto Oliveira, and Krzysztof Pietrzak. On the generic insecurity of the full domain hash. In Shoup [Sho05], pages 449–466.

[Fis03]   Marc Fischlin. The Cramer-Shoup Strong-RSA signature scheme revisited. In Yvo Desmedt, editor, *Public Key Cryptography*, volume 2567 of *Lecture Notes in Computer Science*, pages 116–129. Springer, 2003.

[FS87]   Amos Fiat and Adi Shamir. How to prove yourself: Practical solutions to identification and signature problems. In Andrew M. Odlyzko, editor, *Advances in Cryptology—CRYPTO '86*, volume 263 of *Lecture Notes in Computer Science*, pages 186–194. Springer, 1987.

[GHR99]   Rosario Gennaro, Shai Halevi, and Tal Rabin. Secure hash-and-sign sig-
            natures without the random oracle. In Jacques Stern, editor, *Advances
            in Cryptology—EUROCRYPT '99*, volume 1592 of *Lecture Notes in Com-
            puter Science*, pages 123–139. Springer, 1999.
[GMR88]   Shafi Goldwasser, Silvio Micali, and Ronald L. Rivest. A digital signature
            scheme secure against adaptive chosen-message attacks. *SIAM Journal on
            Computing*, 17:281–308, 1988.
[HK05a]   Shai Halevi and Hugo Krawczyk. Strengthening digital signatures via
            randomized hashing. Internet-Draft, Crypto Forum Research Group, May
            2005.
[HK05b]   Shai Halevi and Hugo Krawczyk. Strengthening digital signatures via
            randomized hashing. Talk at Cryptographic Hash Workshop (NIST), Oct
            31–Nov 1. 2005.
[HPL04]   Deukjo Hong, Bart Preneel, and Sangjin Lee. Higher order universal one-
            way hash functions. In Pil Joong Lee, editor, *Advances in Cryptology—
            ASIACRYPT 2004*, volume 3329 of *Lecture Notes in Computer Science*,
            pages 201–213. Springer, 2004.
[Knu02]   Lars R. Knudsen, editor. *Advances in Cryptology—EUROCRYPT 2002,
            International Conference on the Theory and Applications of Cryptographic
            Techniques, Amsterdam, The Netherlands, April 28–May 2, 2002, Proceed-
            ings*, volume 2332 of *Lecture Notes in Computer Science*. Springer, 2002.
[KS05]   John Kelsey and Bruce Schneier. Second preimages on n-bit hash functions
            for much less than 2^n work. In Cramer [Cra05], pages 474–490.
[Mer90]   Ralph C. Merkle. One way hash functions and DES. In Brassard [Bra90],
            pages 428–446.
[Mir01]   Ilya Mironov. Hash functions: From Merkle-Damgård to Shoup. In Birgit
            Pfitzmann, editor, *Advances in Cryptology—EUROCRYPT 2001*, volume
            2045 of *Lecture Notes in Computer Science*, pages 166–181. Springer, 2001.
[NES03]   NESSIE Consortium. Performance of optimized implementations of the
            NESSIE primitives, version 2.0. Deliverable report D21, February 2003.
            NES/DOC/TEC/WP6/D21/2.
[NIS95]   NIST. Secure hash standard. FIPS PUB 180-1, National Institute of
            Standards and Technology, April 1995.
[NM02]   Junko Nakajima and Mitsuru Matsui. Performance analysis and parallel
            implementation of dedicated hash functions. In Knudsen [Knu02], pages
            165–180.
[NS02]   Phong Q. Nguyen and Igor E. Shparlinski. The insecurity of the digital sig-
            nature algorithm with partially known nonces. *J. Cryptology*, 15(3):151–
            176, 2002.
[NY89]   Moni Naor and Moti Yung. Universal one-way hash functions and their
            cryptographic applications. In *Proceedings of the Twenty First Annual
            ACM Symposium on Theory of Computing*, pages 33–43, 15–17 May 1989.
[Pre00]   Bart Preneel, editor. *Advances in Cryptology—EUROCRYPT 2000, In-
            ternational Conference on the Theory and Application of Cryptographic
            Techniques, Bruges, Belgium, May 14–18, 2000, Proceeding*, volume 1807
            of *Lecture Notes in Computer Science*. Springer, 2000.
[PV05]   Pascal Paillier and Damien Vergnaud. Discrete-log-based signatures
            may not be equivalent to discrete log. In Bimal Roy, editor, *Advances
            in Cryptology—ASIACRYPT 2005*, Lecture Notes in Computer Science,
            pages 1–20. Springer, 2005.

[Riv91]   Ronald L. Rivest. The MD4 message digest algorithm. In Alfred Menezes
             and Scott A. Vanstone, editors, *Advances in Cryptology—CRYPTO
             '90*, volume 537 of *Lecture Notes in Computer Science*, pages 303–311.
             Springer, 1991.

[Rom90]   John Rompel. One-way functions are necessary and sufficient for secure
             signatures. In *Proceedings of the Twenty Second Annual ACM Symposium
             on Theory of Computing*, pages 387–394, 14–16 May 1990.

[Sar03]   Palash Sarkar. Masking based domain extenders for UOWHFs: Bounds
             and constructions. Cryptology ePrint Archive, Report 2003/225, 2003.
             http://eprint.iacr.org/.

[Sho00a]   Victor Shoup. A composition theorem for universal one-way hash func-
             tions. In Preneel [Pre00], pages 445–452.

[Sho00b]   Victor Shoup. Using hash functions as a hedge against chosen ciphertext
             attack. In Preneel [Pre00], pages 275–288.

[Sho04]   Victor Shoup. Sequences of games: a tool for taming complexity in
             security proofs. Cryptology ePrint Archive, Report 2004/332, 2004.
             http://eprint.iacr.org/.

[Sho05]   Victor Shoup, editor. *Advances in Cryptology—CRYPTO 2005: 25th
             Annual International Cryptology Conference, Santa Barbara, California,
             USA, August 14–18, 2005, Proceedings*, volume 3621 of *Lecture Notes in
             Computer Science*. Springer, 2005.

[Sim98]   Daniel R. Simon. Finding collisions on a one-way street: Can secure hash
             functions be based on general assumptions? In Kaisa Nyberg, editor,
             Advances in Cryptology—EUROCRYPT '98, volume 1403 of *Lecture Notes
             in Computer Science*, pages 334–345. Springer, 1998.

[SS00]   Thomas Schweinberger and Victor Shoup. ACE: The advanced crypto-
             graphic engine. Manuscript, 2000. http://shoup.net/papers/ace.pdf.

[WY05]   Xiaoyun Wang and Hongbo Yu. How to break MD5 and other hash func-
             tions. In Cramer [Cra05], pages 19–35.

[WYY05a]   Xiaoyun Wang, Yiqun Lisa Yin, and Hongbo Yu. Finding collisions in the
             full SHA-1. In Shoup [Sho05], pages 17–36.

[WYY05b]   Xiaoyun Wang, Hongbo Yu, and Yiqun Lisa Yin. Efficient collision search
             attacks on SHA-0. In Shoup [Sho05], pages 1–16.

Higher Order Universal One-Way Hash Functions from the Subset Sum Assumption

Ron Steinfeld, Josef Pieprzyk, and Huaxiong Wang

Dept. of Computing, Macquarie University, North Ryde, Australia
{rons, josef, hwang}@comp.mq.edu.au
http://www.ics.mq.edu.au/acac/

Abstract. Universal One-Way Hash Functions (UOWHFs) may be used in place of collision-resistant functions in many public-key cryptographic applications. At Asiacrypt 2004, Hong, Preneel and Lee introduced the stronger security notion of higher order UOWHFs to allow construction of long-input UOWHFs using the Merkle-Damgård domain extender. However, they did not provide any provably secure constructions for higher order UOWHFs.

We show that the subset sum hash function is a kth order Universal One-Way Hash Function (hashing n bits to $m < n$ bits) under the Subset Sum assumption for $k = O(\log m)$. Therefore we strengthen a previous result of Impagliazzo and Naor, who showed that the subset sum hash function is a UOWHF under the Subset Sum assumption. We believe our result is of theoretical interest; as far as we are aware, it is the first example of a natural and computationally efficient UOWHF which is also a provably secure higher order UOWHF under the same well-known cryptographic assumption, whereas this assumption does not seem sufficient to prove its collision-resistance. A consequence of our result is that one can apply the Merkle-Damgård extender to the subset sum compression function with 'extension factor' $k+1$, while losing (at most) about k bits of UOWHF security relative to the UOWHF security of the compression function. The method also leads to a saving of up to $m \log(k+1)$ bits in key length relative to the Shoup XOR-Mask domain extender applied to the subset sum compression function.

Keywords: hash function, provable security, subset sum.

1   Introduction

Motivation. Universal One-Way Hash Functions (UOWHFs), introduced by Naor and Yung [14] (also known as 'Target Collision Resistant' functions), achieve weaker security than collision-resistant hash functions, but still suffice for important cryptographic applications – in particular they suffice for hashing long messages prior to signing with a digital signature scheme [14, 3, 16] (and even can be used to construct digital signature schemes).

A common methodology for designing hash functions consists of two stages. In the first stage, one designs an (efficient) *compression function* f which hashes a (relatively short) n-bit string to a shorter m-bit string (e.g. a compression

M. Yung et al. (Eds.): PKC 2006, LNCS 3958, pp. 157–173, 2006.

function may hash a $n = 600$ bit input to a $m = 400$ bit output, compressing by $n - m = 200$ bits). The compression function f is designed to achieve some well defined security property (such as UOWHF security). Then in the second stage, one specifies a *domain extender* algorithm, which uses the compression function f to build a hash function f' hashing ℓ-bit inputs (for $\ell > n$) to an m-bit output. The domain extender is designed to ensure that if f satisfies its security property, then the extended function f' will satisfy the desired security property (e.g. UOWHF security).

The simplest and most natural domain extender is the well-known Merkle-Damgård (MD) extender [11, 5]. It was shown in [11, 5] that the MD extender preserves the collision-resistance security of the compression function, i.e. the MD extended function f' is collision-resistant if the compression function f is collision-resistant. However, as pointed out in [3], efficient collision-resistant compression functions seem difficult to design, and weakening the security requirement on the compression function is desirable.

A typical example that we focus on in this paper is the *subset sum* compression function, a computationally efficient function which was shown in [9] to achieve UOWHF security under the well known subset sum assumption (while the collision-resistance of this function depends on a less known and potentially much easier 'weighted knapsack' problem). It is natural to attempt to apply the MD extender to the subset sum compression function, and hope that the resulting function also achieves UOWHF security. Unfortunately, it was shown in [3] that the MD extender is not guaranteed to preserve UOWHF security of a compression function. Thus the result of [9] does not guarantee the security of the MD extended subset sum hash function, even assuming the subset sum assumption. Although other domain extenders exist [14, 3, 16] which do preserve the UOWHF property of the compression function, they are less simple than the MD extender and also (at least slightly) increase the length of the hash function key depending on the extension input length ℓ.

A possible way to use the MD extender for building UOWHF functions was proposed at Asiacrypt 2004 by Hong, Preneel and Lee [7]. They defined a stronger security property for compression functions called *higher order* UOWHF security. The 0th order UOWHF property is just the normal UOWHF property, but for $k > 0$, a kth order UOWHF is a stronger requirement than UOWHF. They showed that if a compression function f has the stronger kth order UOWHF property, then the MD extended function f' is guaranteed to have the UOWHF property, as long as the MD 'extension factor' is at most $k + 1$. However, it is known that there exist UOWHFs which are not kth order UOWHFs for any $k > 0$, so it is dangerous in general to simply take an UOWHF and assume that it is also a higher order UOWHF - in particular, the security loss as a function of k is unknown. Motivated by this concern in applying this result to the MD extended subset sum function, we were led to the following natural questions: Does the subset sum compression function satisfy the kth order UOWHF property for some $k > 0$, assuming only the subset sum assumption? If so, can we give an upper bound on the security lost as a function of k?

Our Results. We show that the subset sum hash function is a kth order UOWHF family (hashing n bits to $m < n$ bits) under the Subset Sum assumption for $k = O(\log m)$. Thus our result strengthens the one of Impagliazzo and Naor [9], who showed that the subset sum hash function is a UOWHF (i.e. UOWHF of order $k = 0$) under the Subset Sum assumption. Concretely, we show that the function's security as a kth order UOWHF deteriorates by (at most) about k bits (relative to the UOWHF case $k = 0$). Combined with the result of [7], we conclude that one can apply the MD extension to the subset sum compression function with 'extension factor' $k + 1$, while losing (at most) about k bits of UOWHF security relative to the UOWHF security of the compression function (which is almost equivalent to the subset sum problem). We believe our result is of theoretical interest; in particular, as far as we are aware, our result is the first example of a natural UOWHF which is also a provably secure higher order UOWHF under the same well-known cryptographic assumption (while this assumption does not seem sufficient to prove its collision-resistance). In addition to showing that the natural MD extender can be applied to the subset sum compression function for small extension factors, our result also allows to shorten the key length of the extended hash function (compared with the total key length of the most efficient known UOWHF domain extender due to Shoup [16]).

Organization. The paper is organized as follows. In Section 2, we recall the definition of hash function security properties (in particular UOWHFs and higher order UOWHFs), and the construction of the subset sum compression function. Section 3 contains our main result on the kth order UOWHF security of the subset sum function. In Section 4, we discuss the application of our result to the extended subset sum function. Section 5 concludes the paper. Due to page limits, proofs of some claims in the paper were omitted – they can be found in the full version of the paper, available on the authors' web page.

2   Preliminaries

Collision-Resistant Hash Functions (CRHFs). Ideally, we would like a hash function to satisfy the strong security notion of collision-resistance, which is defined as follows.

Definition 1 (CRHFs). *A* (t, ϵ) *Collision-Resistant Hash Function (CRHF) family is a collection* $\mathcal{F}$ *of functions* $f_K : \{0, 1\}^n \to \{0, 1\}^m$ *indexed by a key* $K \in \mathcal{K}$ *(where* $\mathcal{K}$ *denotes the key space), and such that any attack algorithm* A *running in time* t *has success probability at most* ϵ *in the following game:*

- *Key Sampling. A uniformly random key* $K \in \mathcal{K}$ *is chosen and revealed to* A.
- A *Collides.* A *runs (on input* K*) and outputs a pair of hash function inputs* $s_1, s_2 \in \{0, 1\}^n$.

We say that A *succeeds in the above game if it finds a valid collision for* f_K, *i.e. if* $s_1 \neq s_2$ *but* $f_K(s_1) = f_K(s_2)$.

Universal One-Way Hash Functions (UOWHFs). Naor and Yung [14] (see also [3]) showed that for several important cryptographic applications (such as hashing prior to signing a message with a digital signature scheme) one can weaken the collision-resistance requirement on a hash function, to a notion called Universal One-Way Hash Function (UOWHF), which is defined as follows.

Definition 2 (UOWHFs). *A* (t, ϵ) *Universal One-Way Hash Function (UOWHF) family [14] is a collection* $\mathcal{F}$ *of functions* $f_K : \{0,1\}^n \to \{0,1\}^m$ *indexed by a key* $K \in \mathcal{K}$ *(where* $\mathcal{K}$ *denotes the key space), and such that any attack algorithm* A *running in time* t *has success probability at most* ϵ *in the following game:*

- *Key Sampling. A uniformly random key* $K \in \mathcal{K}$ *is chosen (but not yet revealed to* A*).*
- A *Commits. A runs (with no input) and outputs a hash function input* $s_1 \in \{0,1\}^n$.
- *Key Revealed: The key* K *is given to* A.
- A *Collides. A continues running and outputs a second hash function input* $s_2 \in \{0,1\}^n$.

We say that A *succeeds in the above game if it finds a valid collision for* f_K*, i.e. if* $s_1 \neq s_2$ *but* $f_K(s_1) = f_K(s_2)$.

Higher Order UOWHFs. Hong, Preneel and Song [7] strengthened the definition of UOWHFs (while still being weaker than the CRHF requirement) by allowing the attacker to query an oracle for the hash function k times before commiting to the first input. A function that is secure even under this stronger attack is called a kth order UOWHF.

Definition 3 (kth Order UOWHFs). *A* (t, ϵ) kth *order Universal One-Way Hash Function family [7] is a collection* $\mathcal{F}$ *of functions* $f_K : \{0,1\}^n \to \{0,1\}^m$ *indexed by a key* $K \in \mathcal{K}$ *(where* $\mathcal{K}$ *denotes the key space), and such that any attack algorithm* A *running in time* t *has success probability at most* ϵ *in the following game:*

- *Key Sampling. A uniformly random key* $K \in \mathcal{K}$ *is chosen (but not yet revealed to* A*).*
- *Oracle Queries. A runs (with no input) and makes* k *adaptive queries* $q_1, \ldots, q_k$ *(with* $q_i \in \{0,1\}^n$ *for* $i = 1, \ldots, k$*) to an oracle for* $f_K(\cdot)$*, receiving answers* $y_1, \ldots, y_k$ *(where* $y_i = f_K(q_i)$ *for* $i = 1, \ldots, k$*).*
- A *Commits. A outputs a hash function input* $s_1 \in \{0,1\}^n$.
- *Key Revealed: The key* K *is given to* A.
- A *Collides. A continues running and outputs a second hash function input* $s_2 \in \{0,1\}^n$.

We say that A *succeeds in the above game if it finds a valid collision for* f_K*, i.e. if* $s_1 \neq s_2$ *but* $f_K(s_1) = f_K(s_2)$.

Note that a 0th order UOWHF is just a UOWHF, and a kth order UOWHF is also a rth order UOWHF for any $r \leq k$, but a UOWHF is not necessarily a higher order UOWHF; indeed, there exist UOWHFs which are not even first order UOWHFs [3].

The Subset-Sum Problem. This is defined as follows.

Definition 4 (Subset Sum Problem $\mathsf{SubSum}(n, m, p)$). *Let n and $m < n$ be positive integers, and let p denote a positive integer satisfying $2^{m-1} < p \leq 2^m$. The $\mathsf{SubSum}(n, m, p)$ problem is the following: Given p, a vector of n uniformly random integers $\mathbf{a} = (\mathbf{a}[1], \ldots, \mathbf{a}[n]) \in_R \mathbb{Z}_p^n$ and an independent uniform target integer $T \in_R \mathbb{Z}_p$, find a subset $\mathbf{s} = (\mathbf{s}[1], \ldots, \mathbf{s}[n])$ with $\mathbf{s}[i] \in \{0, 1\}$ for $i = 1, \ldots, n$ such that $\sum_{i=1}^{n} \mathbf{s}[i] \cdot \mathbf{a}[i] \equiv T \pmod{p}$.*

We say that problem $\mathsf{SubSum}(n, m, p)$ is (t, ϵ)-hard if, any algorithm A for $\mathsf{SubSum}(n, m, p)$ having run-time at most t has success probability at most ϵ, where the probability is over the uniformly random choice of $\mathbf{a} \in \mathbb{Z}_p^n$, $T \in \mathbb{Z}_p$ and the random coins of A.

A related, but possibly easier problem than Subset Sum is the *Weighted Knapsack* problem.

Definition 5 (Weighted Knapsack Problem $\mathsf{WKnap}(n, m, p)$). *Let n and $m < n$ be positive integers, and let p denote a positive integer satisfying $2^{m-1} < p \leq 2^m$. The $\mathsf{WKnap}(n, m, p)$ problem is the following: Given p, a vector of n uniformly random integers $\mathbf{a} = (\mathbf{a}[1], \ldots, \mathbf{a}[n]) \in_R \mathbb{Z}_p^n$ and an independent uniform target integer $T \in_R \mathbb{Z}_p$, find a weight vector $\mathbf{s} = (\mathbf{s}[1], \ldots, \mathbf{s}[n])$ with $\mathbf{s}[i] \in \{-1, 0, 1\}$ for $i = 1, \ldots, n$ such that $\sum_{i=1}^{n} \mathbf{s}[i] \cdot \mathbf{a}[i] \equiv T \pmod{p}$.*

We say that problem $\mathsf{WKnap}(n, m, p)$ is (t, ϵ)-hard if, any algorithm A for $\mathsf{WKnap}(n, m, p)$ having run-time at most t has success probability at most ϵ, where the probability is over the uniformly random choice of $\mathbf{a} \in \mathbb{Z}_p^n$, $T \in \mathbb{Z}_p$ and the random coins of A.

A decision variant of the subset sum problem was one of the first problems to be proven NP Complete [10]. The problem is well known in cryptography (also known as the knapsack problem) due to its role in the early history of public-key cryptosystems. The security of the Merkle-Hellman public key cryptosystem [12] was intended to based on the hardness of subset sum, but was later broken [15] due to the special non-random choice of the knapsack integers $\mathbf{a}[1], \ldots, \mathbf{a}[n]$. Later attacks based on lattice reduction work even for random knapsack integers, but only when m is sufficiently larger than n (i.e. when the function is used in *expansion* mode). According to [9], the best known provable lattice attack of this type [4] succeeds with high probability over a random choice of $\mathbf{a}[1], \ldots, \mathbf{a}[n]$, assuming a perfect lattice shortest vector oracle is available, whenever $m > 1.0629 \cdot n$.

Let us make a few other remarks:

- We use $m < n$ in our hash functions, which avoids the above-mentioned direct lattice attacks. However, one can still pick the (say) first $n' \leq m/1.0629$

integers $\mathbf{a}[1], \ldots, \mathbf{a}[n']$ and try to use the method of [4] to find a solution involving only those integers (i.e. set the $n - n'$ remaining weights to zero). A solution involving only the first n' integers is expected to exist with probability $1/2^{m-n'}$, so to make this probability at most $2^{-\delta}$ we need $m - n' \geq \delta$. It follows that we need $m \geq (1.0629/0.0629)\delta$, e.g. for $\delta = 80$, we need $m \geq 1352$ bit.

- A series of papers, starting from [1,6] and up to the recent [13] have given reductions showing that the average-case weighted knapsack problem is as hard as various worst-case lattice problems, such as SVP approximation problems with a small polynomial approximation factor. However, although the average-case to worst-case connections exhibited in these papers are theoretically impressive, the concrete complexity of these 'polynomial approximation factor' lattice problems (even in the worst case) is currently unknown, and they may turn out to be substantially easier than subset sum due to the good performance of lattice reduction algorithms in practice.
- The Weighted knapsack problem may also be easier than the subset sum problem (see [2] for more discussion). Hence the subset sum hash function may not be as secure a collision-resistant function as it is as a UOWHF (or as we show, as a higher order UOWHF).

The Subset Sum Hash Function

Definition 6 (Subset Sum Hash Function Family $\mathcal{F}_{SS}(n,m,p)$). *Let n and $m < n$ be positive integers, and let p denote a positive integer satisfying $2^{m-1} < p \leq 2^m$. The subset sum hash function family $\mathcal{F}_{SS}(n,m,p)$ is defined as follows. The key space is $\mathcal{K} = \mathbb{Z}_p^n$. Given a key $\mathbf{a} = (\mathbf{a}[1], \ldots, \mathbf{a}[n]) \in \mathbb{Z}_p^n$, the associated hash function $f_\mathbf{a} : \{0,1\}^n \to \{0,1\}^m$ is defined by $f_\mathbf{a}(\mathbf{s}) = \sum_{i=1}^n \mathbf{s}[i] \cdot \mathbf{a}[i] \bmod p \in \{0,1\}^m$ for $\mathbf{s} = (\mathbf{s}[1], \ldots, \mathbf{s}[n]) \in \{0,1\}^n$.*

We observe that that the subset sum hash function is a *public coin* function (see [8]), since the key consists of uniformly random integers in $\mathbb{Z}_p$.

3   The Security of the Subset Sum Hash Function

It is easy to see that the subset sum hash function family $\mathcal{F}_{SS}(n,m,p)$ is a CRHF family assuming the hardness of the weighted knapsack problem $\mathsf{WKnap}(n,m,p)$. However, as discussed above, the problem $\mathsf{WKnap}(n,m,p)$ may be easier than the subset sum problem $\mathsf{SubSum}(n,m,p)$. It is therefore desirable to have a hash family whose security relies only on the hardness of $\mathsf{SubSum}(n,m,p)$. With this motivation, Impagliazzo and Naor [9] relaxed their requirement from CRHF to a UOWHF, and showed that the subset sum hash function family $\mathcal{F}_{SS}(n,m,p)$ is a UOWHF assuming only the hardness of the subset sum problem $\mathsf{SubSum}(n,m,p)$. When translated to our concrete notation, the result of [9] can be stated as follows.

Theorem 1 (Impagliazzo-Naor). *If the Subset Sum problem $\mathsf{SubSum}(n,m,p)$ is (t,ϵ)-hard, then the the Subset Sum hash function family $\mathcal{F}_{SS}(n,m,p)$ is a (t',ϵ') Universal One-Way Hash Function (UOWHF) family, where:*

$$t' = t - O(m \cdot n) \quad and \quad \epsilon' = 2n \cdot \epsilon.$$

In this section we strengthen Theorem 1 by showing that the subset sum hash function family $\mathcal{F}_{SS}(n, m, p)$ is actually a kth order UOWHF for small $k = O(\log m)$, still assuming only the hardness of the subset sum problem $\mathsf{SubSum}(n, m, p)$. More concretely, we bound the way the security of $\mathcal{F}_{SS}(n, m, p)$ as a kth order UOWHF deteriorates with increasing k.

To begin with, we observe that for $k \geq m+2$, the security of $\mathcal{F}_{SS}(n, m, p)$ as a kth order UOWHF already deteriorates to the hardness of a weighted knapsack problem, i.e. the collision resistance of a related subset sum function.

Proposition 1. *For $k \geq m+2$, if the subset sum hash family $\mathcal{F}_{SS}(n, m, p)$ is a (t, ϵ) kth order UOWHF then the weighted knapsack problem $\mathsf{WKnap}(\min(k, n) - 1, m, p)$ is (t', ϵ') hard, where:*

$$t' = t - O(n) \quad and \quad \epsilon' = \epsilon.$$

Proof. Let A' be an attacker for weighted knapsack problem $\mathsf{WKnap}(n', m, p)$ for $n' = \min(k, n) - 1$ with run-time/succ. prob. (t', ϵ'). Consider attacker A against the kth order UOWHF notion of the subset sum hash family $\mathcal{F}_{SS}(n, m, p)$ which runs as follows.

After a random key $\mathbf{a} = (\mathbf{a}[1], \ldots, \mathbf{a}[n]) \in \mathbb{Z}_p^n$ is chosen, A queries to $f_\mathbf{a}(.)$ the $\min(k, n)$ singleton subsets $\mathbf{q}_i$ for $i = 1, \ldots, n'+1$, where $\mathbf{q}_i[j] = 1$ if $j = i$ and $\mathbf{q}_i[j] = 0$ for $j \neq i$. Thus A obtains answers $y_i = \mathbf{a}[i]$ for $i = 1, \ldots, n'+1$. Now A runs A' on input modulus p, knapsack vector $\mathbf{a}' = (\mathbf{a}[1], \ldots, \mathbf{a}[n'])$ and target $T = \mathbf{a}[n'+1]$. After time t and with probability ϵ, A' returns $\mathbf{s} = (\mathbf{s}[1], \ldots, \mathbf{s}[n']) \in \{-1, 0, 1\}^{n'}$ satisfying $\sum_{i=1}^{n'} \mathbf{s}[i] \cdot \mathbf{a}[i] \equiv \mathbf{a}[n'+1] \pmod{p}$. So A has a collision $f_\mathbf{a}(\mathbf{s}_1) = f_\mathbf{a}(\mathbf{s}_2)$, where for $i = 1, \ldots, n'-1$, $\mathbf{s}_1[i] = 1$ if and only if $\mathbf{s}[i] = 0$, $\mathbf{s}_2[i] = 1$ if and only if $\mathbf{s}[i] = -1$, $(\mathbf{s}_1[n'], \mathbf{s}_2[n']) = (0, 1)$ (so $\mathbf{s}_1 \neq \mathbf{s}_2$) and for $i \geq n'+1$ we set $\mathbf{s}_1[i] = \mathbf{s}_2[i] = 0$. A outputs $\mathbf{s}_1$ and then $\mathbf{s}_2$ as his collision pair and breaks kth order UOWHF notion of $\mathcal{F}_{SS}(n, m, p)$. The attacker A has run-time $t = t' + O(n)$ and success probability $\epsilon = \epsilon'$. The proposition follows.   □

For $k \leq m+1$, the reduction of Proposition 1 continues to hold, but in this case the associated weighted knapsack instance $\mathsf{WKnap}(k - 1, m, p)$ has a solution with probability at most $3^{k-1}/p \leq 3^{k-1}/2^{m-1}$, which for fixed m decreases exponentially as k decreases towards 0. Thus for k sufficiently smaller than m we may hope that the subset sum hash family $\mathcal{F}_{SS}(n, m, p)$ is secure as a kth order UOWHF even if the weighted knapsack problem is easy to solve when a solution exists. Indeed, we next show that for $k = O(\log m)$ the subset sum hash function is a kth order UOWHF assuming only the hardness of subset sum. For technical reasons we also restrict in this result the modulus p to be *prime*.

Theorem 2. *Let n and $m < n$ be positive integers, let p denote a prime satisfying $2^{m-1} < p \leq 2^m$, and $k < \log_3(p) - 1$. If the Subset Sum problem $\mathsf{SubSum}(n, m, p)$ is (t, ϵ)-hard, then the Subset Sum hash function family*

$\mathcal{F}_{SS}(n, m, p)$ is a (t', ϵ') kth order Universal One-Way Hash Function (UOWHF) family, where:

$$t' = t - O(k^2 n T_M(p)) \quad and \quad \epsilon' = 2^{k+1} \cdot (n - k) \cdot \epsilon + \frac{3^{k+1}}{2^m},$$

and $T_M(p)$ denotes the time to perform a multiplication modulo p.

Proof. Let A' be a kth order UOWHF attacker against the subset sum hash function family $\mathcal{F}_{SS}(n, m, p)$ with run-time/succ. prob. (t', ϵ'). We show how to use A' to construct an attacker A against subset sum problem $\mathsf{SubSum}(n, m, p)$ with run time $t = t' + O(k^2 n T_M(p))$ and succ. prob. $\epsilon \geq \frac{1}{2^{k+1} \cdot (n-k)} \cdot (\epsilon' - \frac{3^{k+1}}{2^m})$, which establishes the claimed result.

The basic idea of the reduction at a high level and its relation to the one in [9] is as follows. Given its subset sum instance $(\mathbf{a}, T)$, A runs A', answering its oracle queries using key $\mathbf{a}$ to obtain the first colliding input $\mathbf{s}_1$, but then reveals a different key $\mathbf{a}' \equiv_p \mathbf{a} + \mathbf{d}$ to A'. The new key $\mathbf{a}'$ is chosen by A based on $\mathbf{s}_1$ and the target sum T. In the reduction of [9], $\mathbf{d}$ is chosen to have Hamming weight 1 (in a random bit position) and such that $\sum_i \mathbf{s}_1[i] \cdot \mathbf{a}'[i] \equiv_p T$. This implies that a successful colliding $\mathbf{s}_2$ will be a solution to subset sum instance $(\mathbf{a}, T)$ if $\mathbf{s}_2$ has a zero in the position where $\mathbf{d}$ is non-zero. The authors in [9] are able to argue that such a zero position in $\mathbf{s}_2$ will exist (and equal the randomly chosen non-zero position in $\mathbf{d}$ with probability $1/n$). In our case, however, $\mathbf{a}'$ must also be consistent with the k earlier oracle query answers. This implies that $\mathbf{d}$ is restricted to be a solution of a linear system of rank $k + 1$, so the minimum allowable Hamming weight of $\mathbf{d}$ increases to $k + 1$, and the proof of [9] seems difficult to extend – we need that certain $k + 1$ bits of $\mathbf{s}_2$ are *zero* (e.g. such bits may not exist). Instead, we use an alternative approach which only requires *guessing* the values (whatever they are) of the $k+1$ bits of $\mathbf{s}_2$ in positions where $\mathbf{d}$ is non-zero (hence we succeed with probability $1/2^{k+1}$). To do this, we choose $\mathbf{d}$ of weight $k+1$ such that $\sum_i \mathbf{s}_1[i] \cdot (\mathbf{a}[i] + \mathbf{d}[i]) \equiv_p T + \sum_i \widehat{\mathbf{s}}_2[i] \cdot \mathbf{d}[i]$ (where we use our guesses $\widehat{\mathbf{s}}_2$ for the $k+1$ bits of $\mathbf{s}_2$ on the right hand side) – note that this requirement is equivalent to equation (4) in the proof below. Then a colliding $\mathbf{s}_2$ gives $\sum_i \mathbf{s}_2[i] \cdot (\mathbf{a}[i] + \mathbf{d}[i]) \equiv_p T + \sum_i \widehat{\mathbf{s}}_2[i] \cdot \mathbf{d}[i]$ which implies that $\mathbf{s}_2$ is a solution to instance $(\mathbf{a}, T)$ if our guesses of $k+1$ bits of $\mathbf{s}_2$ were right (note the simplified discussion above ignores some other issues handled by the proof).

We now present the detailed reduction game.

1. **Subset Sum Instance Generation.** A random subset sum instance $(\mathbf{a}, T)$ (where $\mathbf{a} \in_R \mathbb{Z}_p^n$ and $T \in_R \mathbb{Z}_p$) is generated and given to A.
2. **Oracle Queries.** A runs A' with no input. When A' makes its ith oracle query $\mathbf{q}_i \in \{0, 1\}^n$, A responds with answer $y_i = f_{\mathbf{a}}(\mathbf{q}_i) = \sum_{j=1}^n \mathbf{q}_i[j] \cdot \mathbf{a}[j] \bmod p$ (for $i = 1, \ldots, k$). A also stores the queries $\mathbf{q}_1, \ldots, \mathbf{q}_k$ for later use.
3. **A' Commits.** A' outputs hash function input $\mathbf{s}_1 \in \{0, 1\}^n$.
4. **Key Revealed.** A samples a difference vector $\mathbf{d} \in \mathbb{Z}_p^n$ (using the algorithm detailed below) and gives A' the key $\mathbf{a}' = \mathbf{a} + \mathbf{d} \bmod p$. The difference vector $\mathbf{d}$ is sampled by A as follows:

(a) A uses the stored queries of A′ to build a $k \times n$ matrix Q having $\mathbf{q}_i$ as its ith row for $i = 1, \ldots, k$. *Remark*: The difference vector $\mathbf{d}$ will satisfy the matrix equation $Q \cdot \mathbf{d} \equiv \mathbf{0}$ (mod p), which implies that $Q \cdot \mathbf{a}' \equiv Q \cdot \mathbf{a}$ (mod p), i.e. $\mathbf{a}'$ is consistent with the answers to queries $\mathbf{q}_1, \ldots, \mathbf{q}_k$.

(b) A performs Gaussian elimination on the matrix Q (by performing $O(k^2)$ elementary row operations over the field $\mathbb{Z}_p$ and $O(k)$ column swapping operations). Let $\widehat{Q}$ be the resulting $k \times n$ matrix (with entries in $\mathbb{Z}_p$) which is in reduced row echelon form:

$$\widehat{Q} = \begin{pmatrix} 1 \, 0 \cdots 0 \; \mathbf{q}_1'[k+1] \; \cdots \; \mathbf{q}_1'[n] \\ 0 \, 1 \cdots 0 \; \mathbf{q}_2'[k+1] \; \cdots \; \mathbf{q}_2'[n] \\ \vdots \; \vdots \; \ddots \; \vdots \qquad \vdots \qquad \cdots \qquad \vdots \\ 0 \, 0 \ldots 1 \; \mathbf{q}_k'[k+1] \; \cdots \; \mathbf{q}_k'[n] \end{pmatrix}. \tag{1}$$

A also keeps track of the column swapping operations to compute the corresponding column permutation $\pi : \{1, \ldots, n\} \rightarrow \{1, \ldots, n\}$ such that $\mathbf{d} \in \mathbb{Z}_p^n$ satisfies $Q\mathbf{d} \equiv 0$ (mod p) if and only if $\widehat{\mathbf{d}} = (\mathbf{d}[\pi(1)], \ldots, \mathbf{d}[\pi(n)])^T$ satisfies $\widehat{Q}\widehat{\mathbf{d}} \equiv 0$ (mod p). *Remark*: We assume, without loss of generality, that the k query vectors $\mathbf{q}_1, \ldots, \mathbf{q}_k$ are linearly independent over $\mathbb{Z}_p$ – If some query vector $\mathbf{q}_i$ of A′ is a linear combination of the $i - 1$ previous query vectors (the linear combination coefficients can be efficiently computed by Gaussian elimination over $\mathbb{Z}_p$), A′ can itself answer the query by the same linear combination of the $i - 1$ previous query answers. Hence we can always modify A′ so that it always makes k linearly independent queries, without affecting the success probability of A′.

(c) A picks a uniformly random integer $\ell \in_R \{k+1, \ldots, n\}$, and $k + 1$ independent uniformly random bits $(\widehat{\mathbf{s}}[1], \ldots, \widehat{\mathbf{s}}[k]) \in \{0, 1\}^k$ and $\widehat{\mathbf{s}}[\ell] \in \{0, 1\}$. A defines $\widehat{\mathbf{s}}[j] = 0$ for $j \notin \{1, \ldots, k\} \cup \{\ell\}$ and computes (as detailed later) the unique vector $\mathbf{d} \in \mathbb{Z}_p^n$ (if it exists) satisfying

$$\mathbf{d}[\pi(j)] = 0 \text{ for } j \in \{k+1, \ldots, n\} \setminus \{\ell\}. \tag{2}$$

and

$$Q \cdot \mathbf{d} \equiv \mathbf{0} \quad (\text{mod } p) \tag{3}$$

and

$$\sum_{j=1}^{n} (\widehat{\mathbf{s}}[j] - \mathbf{s}_1[\pi(j)]) \cdot \mathbf{d}[\pi(j)] \equiv T' - T \quad (\text{mod } p), \tag{4}$$

where $T' = \sum_{j=1}^{n} \mathbf{s}_1[j] \cdot \mathbf{a}[j] \bmod p$. If no solution $\mathbf{d} \in \mathbb{Z}_p^n$ satisfying (2), (3) and (4) exists or if the solution exists but is not unique (because $T' - T \equiv 0$ (mod p)), then A sets $\mathbf{d} = \mathbf{0}$.

5. **A′ Collides.** A′ continues running and outputs a second hash function input $\mathbf{s}_2 \in \{0, 1\}^n$.

6. **A Output.** A outputs $\mathbf{s}_2$ as its solution to the subset sum instance $(\mathbf{a}, T)$.

This completes the description of A. For clarity, and also for reference in later analysis, we now give more details on how A efficiently computes a unique $\mathbf{d} \in \mathbb{Z}_p^n$ satisfying (2), (3) and (4) (or determines that such $\mathbf{d}$ does not exist or is not unique). Using (1), the conditions (3) and (4) are equivalent to requiring that $\widehat{\mathbf{d}} = (\mathbf{d}[\pi(1)], \ldots, \mathbf{d}[\pi(n)])^T$ satisfies the $(k+1) \times n$ linear system

$$\widehat{Q}' \cdot \widehat{\mathbf{d}} \equiv \mathbf{t} \pmod{p}, \tag{5}$$

where $\widehat{Q}'$ is the $(k+1) \times n$ matrix having $\widehat{Q}$ as its first k rows and the row vector $\mathbf{s}' = (\widehat{\mathbf{s}}[1] - \mathbf{s}_1[\pi(1)], \ldots, \widehat{\mathbf{s}}[n] - \mathbf{s}_1[\pi(n)])$ as the $(k+1)$th row, and $\mathbf{t} = (0, 0, \ldots, 0, T' - T)^T$. By adding the multiple $-(\widehat{\mathbf{s}}[j] - \mathbf{s}_1[\pi(j)])$ of row j to row $k+1$ for $j = 1, \ldots, k$, A transforms the linear system (5) to the equivalent system

$$\widehat{Q}'' \cdot \widehat{\mathbf{d}} \equiv \mathbf{t} \pmod{p}, \tag{6}$$

where $\widehat{Q}''$ is a $(k+1) \times n$ matrix having $\widehat{Q}$ as its first k rows and its last row $\mathbf{s}''$ has its first k entries equal to 0 (i.e. $\mathbf{s}''[j] = 0$ for $j = 1, \ldots, k$). Now there are two cases. In the case $\mathbf{s}''[\ell] \equiv 0 \pmod{p}$, clearly either there are no solutions to (6) satisfying (2) (if $T' - T \not\equiv 0 \pmod{p}$), or the solution is not unique (if $T' - T \equiv 0 \pmod{p}$), so A sets $\mathbf{d} = \mathbf{0}$. In the second case $\mathbf{s}''[\ell] \not\equiv 0 \pmod{p}$, A uses back substitution to compute the unique solution $\mathbf{d}$ to (6) satisfying (2), i.e from the $(k+1)$th row of (6):

$$\mathbf{d}[\pi(\ell)] = \mathbf{s}''[\ell]^{-1} \cdot (T' - T) \bmod p \tag{7}$$

and from the first k rows:

$$\mathbf{d}[\pi(j)] = -\mathbf{q}_j'[\ell] \cdot \mathbf{d}[\pi(\ell)] \bmod p \text{ for } j = 1, \ldots, k. \tag{8}$$

The running-time of A is $t = t' + O(k^2 n T_M(p))$ as claimed. Now we analyse the success probability ϵ of A. Let us define several events in the above game:

1. SucA': A' succeeds, i.e. $\mathbf{s}_2 - \mathbf{s}_1 \neq 0$ and

$$\sum_{i=1}^n (\mathbf{s}_2[i] - \mathbf{s}_1[i]) \cdot \mathbf{a}'[i] \equiv 0 \pmod{p}. \tag{9}$$

2. SucA$_1'$: SucA' occurs and $\mathbf{s}_2 - \mathbf{s}_1$ is linearly independent of $\{\mathbf{q}_1, \ldots, \mathbf{q}_k\}$ over $\mathbb{Z}_p$.
3. SucA$_2'$: SucA' occurs and $\mathbf{s}_2 - \mathbf{s}_1$ is a linear combination of $\{\mathbf{q}_1, \ldots, \mathbf{q}_k\}$ over $\mathbb{Z}_p$.

Notice that events SucA$_1'$ and SucA$_2'$ partition the event SucA' so

$$\Pr[\text{SucA}'] = \Pr[\text{SucA}_1'] + \Pr[\text{SucA}_2']. \tag{10}$$

Claim 1. *If event* SucA$_1'$ *occurs then there exist 'good' values* $(\ell^*, \widehat{\mathbf{s}}^*, \widehat{\mathbf{s}}^*[\ell^*]) \in \{k+1, \ldots, n\} \times \{0,1\}^k \times \{0,1\}$ *such that if* A *correctly guessed those values when choosing its random variables* $(\ell, \widehat{\mathbf{s}}, \widehat{\mathbf{s}}[\ell])$ *(i.e. if* $(\ell, \widehat{\mathbf{s}}, \widehat{\mathbf{s}}[\ell]) = (\ell^*, \widehat{\mathbf{s}}^*, \widehat{\mathbf{s}}^*[\ell^*])$) *then* A *succeeds in solving its subset sum instance (i.e.* $\sum_{i=1}^n \mathbf{s}_2[i] \cdot \mathbf{a}[i] \equiv T \pmod{p}$).*

Proof. If SucA_1' occurs, then substituting $\mathbf{a}' \equiv \mathbf{a} + \mathbf{d} \pmod{p}$ and the definition of T' in (9) we obtain

$$\sum_{i=1}^{n} \mathbf{s}_2[i] \cdot \mathbf{a}[i] - T' \equiv \sum_{i=1}^{n} -(\mathbf{s}_2[i] - \mathbf{s}_1[i]) \cdot \mathbf{d}[i].$$

Hence if $\mathbf{d}$ satisfies

$$\sum_{i=1}^{n} (\mathbf{s}_2[i] - \mathbf{s}_1[i]) \cdot \mathbf{d}[i] \equiv T' - T \pmod{p} \tag{11}$$

then $\sum_{i=1}^{n} \mathbf{s}_2[i] \cdot \mathbf{a}[i] \equiv T \pmod{p}$ and A succeeds as claimed.

Now consider the equations (2),(3) and (4) and suppose for a moment that we had $\widehat{\mathbf{s}}[i] = \mathbf{s}_2[\pi(i)]$ for *all* $i = 1, \ldots, n$ (i.e. A correctly guessed *all* the n bits of $\mathbf{s}_2$). Because $\mathbf{s}_2 - \mathbf{s}_1$ is linearly independent of $\{\mathbf{q}_1, \ldots, \mathbf{q}_k\}$ over $\mathbb{Z}_p$, we know that the last row $\mathbf{s}''$ of the reduced matrix $\widehat{Q}''$ in (6) has a non-zero entry $\mathbf{s}''[\ell^*] \neq 0 \pmod{p}$ where $\ell^* \in \{k+1, \ldots, n\}$, so if $\ell = \ell^*$ then a unique solution $\mathbf{d} = \mathbf{d}^*$ satisfying (2),(3) and (4) exists. Now observe that because of (2), the solution $\mathbf{d}^*$ depends only on ℓ^* and a subset of $k + 1$ bits of $\mathbf{s}_2$, namely the bits $\mathbf{s}_2[\pi(1)], \ldots, \mathbf{s}_2[\pi(k)]$ and $\mathbf{s}_2[\pi(\ell^*)]$. So if A correctly guesses just those values (i.e. $\ell = \ell^*$ and $\widehat{\mathbf{s}}[i] = \mathbf{s}_2[\pi(i)]$ for $i \in \{1, \ldots, k\} \cup \{\ell^*\}$ with $\widehat{\mathbf{s}}[i] = 0$ for all other values of i) then $\mathbf{d} = \mathbf{d}^*$ is still a unique solution satisfying (2),(3) and (4) which is computed by A' (using (7) and (8)), so from (2) and (4) we conclude that (11) is satisfied and A succeeds as claimed. This completes the proof of the claim. $\square$

Claim 2. *In the above game, A perfectly simulates the distribution of the view of A' as in the real kth order UOWHF attack game. Furthermore, the simulated view of A' is statistically independent of the random choices $(\ell, \widehat{\mathbf{s}}, \widehat{\mathbf{s}}[\ell])$ made by A.*

Proof. See full version of the paper.

From the above Claims we obtain the following lower bound on the success probability ϵ of A:

$$\epsilon \geq \Pr[\mathsf{SucA}_1' \wedge (\ell, \widehat{\mathbf{s}}, \widehat{\mathbf{s}}[\ell]) = (\ell^*, \widehat{\mathbf{s}}^*, \widehat{\mathbf{s}}^*[\ell^*])] \text{ using Claim 1}$$

$$\geq \frac{1}{(n-k)2^{k+1}} \cdot \Pr[\mathsf{SucA}_1'] \text{ using independence Claim 2}$$

$$\geq \frac{1}{(n-k)2^{k+1}} \cdot (\epsilon' - \Pr[\mathsf{SucA}_2']) \text{ using (10) and Claim 2.} \tag{12}$$

The following claim therefore completes the proof of the theorem's lower bound on the success probability of A. It is obtained by an information theoretic argument based on the fact that the answers y_i to the oracle queries of A' are independent and uniformly random in $\mathbb{Z}_p$ (over the random choice of $\mathbf{a}$).

Claim 3. $\Pr[\mathsf{SucA}_2'] \leq \frac{3^{k+1}}{2^m}$.

Proof. See full version of the paper.

Plugging the bound of Claim 3 in (12) establishes the claimed lower bound $\epsilon \geq \frac{1}{(n-k)2^{k+1}} \cdot \left(\epsilon' - \frac{3^{k+1}}{2^m}\right)$ on A's success probability, completing the proof of the theorem. $\square$

4   Application to Construction of Long-Input UOWHFs

In this section we discuss the application of our result to constructing UOWHFs used to hash long messages using a subset-sum compression function, in conjunction with the results of [7].

Let us suppose we wish to use the compression function family $\mathcal{F}_{SS}(n, m, p)$ (hashing n bits to $m < n$ bits) to construct a hash function family $\mathcal{F}'_{SS}(\ell, m)$ hashing a long l-bit message to m bits, where ℓ could be much larger than n. We want to ensure that $\mathcal{F}'_{SS}(\ell, m)$ is a UOWHF family, assuming that the underlying family $\mathcal{F}_{SS}(n, m, p)$ is a UOWHF family (or a higher order UOWHF family). A well-known and natural 'domain-extension' method is the Merkle-Damgård (MD) transform [11, 5], which works as follows. We assume for simplicity that $\ell = m + \mathcal{L} \cdot (n - m)$ for a positive integer $\mathcal{L}$. Then the MD family $\mathcal{F}'_{SS}(\ell, m)$ is defined as follows. A key $\mathbf{a} \in \mathbb{Z}_p^n$ of $\mathcal{F}'_{SS}(\ell, m)$ is just a uniformly random key of $\mathcal{F}_{SS}(n, m, p)$. An input message $M \in \{0, 1\}^\ell$ is hashed using $f'_{\mathbf{a}}$ as follows:

1. Split $M \in \{0, 1\}^\ell$ into one m-bit block $x_0 \in \{0, 1\}^m$ and $\mathcal{L} = (\ell - m)/(n - m)$ $(n - m)$-bit blocks $(M[0], \dots, M[\mathcal{L} - 1])$.
2. For $i = 0, \dots, \mathcal{L} - 1$, compute $x_{i+1} = f_{\mathbf{a}}(x_i, M[i])$. Return $x_{\mathcal{L}} \in \{0, 1\}^m$.

It has been proved in [11, 5] that if the compression family $\mathcal{F}_{SS}(n, m, p)$ is collision-resistant, then so is the MD family $\mathcal{F}'_{SS}(\ell, m)$. However, as discussed above, the collision-resistance of $\mathcal{F}_{SS}(n, m, p)$ relies on the hardness of the weighted knapsack problem $\mathsf{WKnap}(n, m, p)$, which may be substantially easier than the subset sum problem $\mathsf{SubSum}(n, m, p)$. So, using the fact that UOWHF security is enough for many hashing applications, and in order to rely only on the hardness of $\mathsf{SubSum}(n, m, p)$, one could hope to use Theorem 1, which shows that $\mathcal{F}_{SS}(n, m, p)$ is a (0th order) UOWHF family assuming only the hardness of $\mathsf{SubSum}(n, m, p)$. Unfortunately, as shown in [3], the MD construction does not preserve the UOWHF property in general, i.e. the fact that $\mathcal{F}_{SS}(n, m, p)$ is a UOWHF family does not imply that $\mathcal{F}'_{SS}(\ell, m)$ is a UOWHF family.

However, Hong, Preneel and Lee [7] have shown that if $\mathcal{F}_{SS}(n, m, p)$ is a (t, ϵ) kth order UOWHF for some $k > 0$ and $\mathcal{L} \leq k + 1$, then the MD family $\mathcal{F}'_{SS}(\ell, m)$ is approximately a $(t, \mathcal{L} \cdot \epsilon)$ UOWHF. Combined with our result (Theorem 2), we conclude that for $k = O(\log m)$, the MD family $\mathcal{F}'_{SS}(\ell, m)$ is a UOWHF for $\mathcal{L} \leq k + 1$, assuming only the hardness of $\mathsf{SubSum}(n, m, p)$. More precisely, if subset sum problem $\mathsf{SubSum}(n, m, p)$ is (t, ϵ)-hard for some large time bound t, then $\mathcal{F}'_{SS}(\ell, m)$ is approximately a $(t, 2^{k+1}(n - k)\mathcal{L} \cdot \epsilon)$-UOWHF. Comparing with Theorem 1, we see that the proven kth order UOWHF security of $\mathcal{F}_{SS}(n, m, p)$ (defined as the log of attacker's run-time/success probability ratio) is at most about $k + \log(\mathcal{L})$ bits lower than the proven UOWHF security of $\mathcal{F}_{SS}(n, m, p)$ (which in turn, by Theorem 1, is essentially equivalent to the hardness of $\mathsf{SubSum}(n, m, p)$).

4.1   Comparison with Shoup XOR-Mask UOWHF Domain Extender

Besides the basic MD construction, several other domain extenders for UOWHF hash families are known [14, 3, 16] which do preserve the UOWHF security of the underlying compression family; however, unlike the MD extension above, they all have the property that the length of key increases with the length of the message. The most efficient (in terms of key length) known extender of this type is the Shoup XOR-Mask variant of MD [16]. Let us denote this construction (hashing $\ell = m + \mathcal{L} \cdot (n - m)$ bits to m bits for a positive integer $\mathcal{L}$) by $= \mathcal{F}''_{SS}(\ell, m)$. It is built from the compression family $\mathcal{F}_{SS}(n, m, p)$ as follows. A key for family $\mathcal{F}''_{SS}(\ell, m)$ consists of a key $\mathbf{a} \in \mathbb{Z}^n_p$ for $\mathcal{F}_{SS}(n, m, p)$ and $\lfloor \log(\mathcal{L}) \rfloor + 1$ random 'masks' $\mathbf{K}^* = (K^*[0], \ldots, K^*[\lfloor \log(\mathcal{L}) \rfloor])$, where $K^*[i] \in \{0, 1\}^m$ for all i and $\mathcal{L} = (\ell - m)/(n - m)$. To hash an input message $M \in \{0, 1\}^\ell$ using $f''_{\mathbf{a}, \mathbf{K}^*}$,

1. Split $M \in \{0, 1\}^\ell$ into one m-bit block $x_0 \in \{0, 1\}^m$ and $\mathcal{L} = (\ell - m)/(n - m)$ blocks of $(n - m)$-bit each, $(M[0], \ldots, M[\mathcal{L} - 1])$.
2. For $i = 0, \ldots, \mathcal{L} - 1$, compute $x_{i+1} = f_{\mathbf{a}}(x_i \oplus K^*[\nu_2(i+1)], M[i])$, where $\nu_2(i)$ denotes the largest integer ν such that 2^ν divides i. Return $x_{\mathcal{L}} \in \{0, 1\}^m$.

Hence, for $\mathcal{L} \leq k + 1$, the key length for the Shoup XOR-Mask extension $\mathcal{F}''_{SS}(\ell, m)$ is $len_{\mathcal{F}''} = n \cdot m + (\lfloor \log(\mathcal{L}) \rfloor + 1) \cdot m$ compared to $len_{\mathcal{F}'} = n \cdot m$ for the MD extension discussed above, so the MD extension achieves a saving of up to $(\lfloor \log(k + 1) \rfloor + 1) \cdot m$ bits by taking advantage of our result (Theorem 2). The MD extension method is also simpler. On the other hand, because the key length $n \cdot m$ for the compression family $\mathcal{F}_{SS}(n, m, p)$ dominates, the relative saving in *total* key length is small, and is only about $\frac{(\lfloor \log(k+1) \rfloor + 1)}{n}$. However, as we explain in the next section, the total key length is not so important in applications and more significant relative savings in *per use* key length can be achieved in certain cases by combining our result with the 'XOR Mask Transform'.

Hashing Longer Messages. One can also take advantage of our result for hashing longer messages of arbitrary length $\ell > (k + 1) \cdot (n - m)$. To do so (still assuming only the kth order UOWHF security of the compression family $\mathcal{F}_{SS}(n, m, p)$), it is possible to combine the MD extension with the Shoup extension. Namely, first apply the MD extension to $\mathcal{F}_{SS}(n, m, p)$ to construct the UOWHF family $\mathcal{F}'_{SS}((k+1) \cdot (n-m) + m, m)$ (hashing $(k+1) \cdot (n-m) + m$ bits to m bits), then apply the Shoup XOR-Mask extension to the compression family $\mathcal{F}'_{SS}(\ell, m)$ to hash ℓ bits to m bits. Compared to applying the Shoup extension directly to $\mathcal{F}_{SS}(n, m, p)$, this 'combined' method reduces the number of blocks in the Shoup extension by a factor of $k + 1$, leading to a saving in key length by an additive amount of $\log(k + 1) \cdot m$ bits.

4.2 Using the 'Semi-Public Key' XOR Mask Transform

In this section we show that more significant relative savings in UOWHF key length can be achieved in certain cases by combining our result with the 'Semi-Public Key XOR Mask Transform'.

The Semi-Public Key XOR Mask Transform. As remarked in [9], UOWHF hash families have the following useful property, namely that the UOWHF property is preserved by what we call the 'Semi-Public Key XOR-Mask Transform'. First, let us define the 'XOR-Mask Transform'.

Definition 7 ('XOR-Mask Transform'). *Let $\mathcal{F}(n,m)$ be a hash family (hashing n bits to m bits). Define the XOR-Mask Ttransform hash family $\mathcal{F}'(n,m)$ (hashing n bits to m bits) as follows. A key of $\mathcal{F}'(n,m)$ consists of a key $\mathbf{a}$ of $\mathcal{F}(n,m)$ and a random 'mask' $K \in \{0,1\}^n$. An input $M \in \{0,1\}^n$ is hashed using key $(\mathbf{a}, K)$ as follows $f'_{\mathbf{a},K}(M) = f_{\mathbf{a}}(M \oplus K)$.*

We call the XOR-Mask Transform a 'Semi-public Key' transform, if the portion $\mathbf{a}$ of the key $(\mathbf{a}, K)$ of $f'_{\mathbf{a},K}$ is published before the attacker commits to its first collision input. Then we have the following simple but useful result.

Lemma 1. *['Semi-public Key XOR-Mask Transform' Preserves UOWHF Security] Let $\mathcal{F}(n,m)$ be a hash family (hashing n bits to m bits), and let $\mathcal{F}'(n,m)$ denote the corresponding XOR-Mask transform of $\mathcal{F}(n,m)$. If $\mathcal{F}(n,m)$ is a (0th order) UOWHF family, then $\mathcal{F}'(n,m)$ is a (0th order) UOWHF family, even against 'Semi-Public Key' UOWHF attacks on $\mathcal{F}'(n,m)$, in which the random key $\mathbf{a}$ of $\mathcal{F}(n,m)$ is given to the attacker before committing to the first colliding input $\mathbf{s}_1 \in \{0,1\}^n$ (i.e. only the 'XOR-Mask' $K \in \{0,1\}^n$ is kept hidden from the attacker until he commits to $\mathbf{s}_1$).*

As remarked in [9], the practical implication of Lemma 1 for hash function applications (e.g. hashing a message prior to signing with a digital signature scheme) is that one can publish the long key $\mathbf{a}$ of $\mathcal{F}(n,m)$ once and for all (e.g. in the public key of a signature scheme, or in a hashing standard document), and then each use of the hash function (e.g. hashing and signing a message) only requires appending (to the signature) a relatively short fresh 'mask key' $K \in \{0,1\}^n$.

Key Savings with the XOR Mask Transform. To construct a long ℓ-bit input UOWHF function (with $\ell = m + \mathcal{L} \cdot (n-m)$ for integer $\mathcal{L}$) from the subset sum compression family $\mathcal{F}(n,m,p)$ using the XOR Mask Transform, the standard method is to apply the Semi-Public Key XOR-Mask transform to $\mathcal{F}(n,m,p)$ (with mask key length n bit) and then the Shoup XOR-Mask domain extender from the previous section. Note that an m-bit part of the XOR transform mask key K can be 'absorbed' into the Shoup mask keys. Hence the result is a UOWHF family $\mathcal{F}'(\ell,m)$ mapping $\{0,1\}^l$ to $\{0,1\}^m$ with 'per-use' key length $l' = (\lfloor \log(\mathcal{L}) \rfloor + 1) \cdot m + (n-m) = n + \lfloor \log(\mathcal{L}) \rfloor \cdot m$. In terms of provable security, combining the reduction in [16] with Theorem 1, we obtain that if subset sum problem $\mathsf{SubSum}(n,m,p)$ is (t,ϵ)-hard, then $\mathcal{F}'(\ell,m)$ is approximately a $(t, 2n\mathcal{L} \cdot \epsilon)$ UOWHF.

We now show that one can shorten the 'per use' key length of the standard method using our result, if the compression ratio $\tau = n/m$ of the building block subset sum compression function family $\mathcal{F}(n,m,p)$ is close to 1 (the relative saving increases as τ gets close to 1 and decreases with increasing message length). We remark that the hardness of subset sum can only improve as τ gets close to 1, and indeed some efficient attacks are known which exploit a large value of $\tau > 1$ (see [9]); therefore the use of τ close to 1 may be necessary to achieve sufficient security.

Assume that $k + 1$ is a divisor of $\mathcal{L}$ so $\mathcal{L} = \mathcal{L}' \cdot (k + 1)$ for positive integer $\mathcal{L}'$. We first apply the MD extender with extension factor $k + 1$ to $\mathcal{F}(n, m, p)$ to obtain a UOWHF family $\mathcal{F}^2$ mapping $\{0, 1\}^{m+(k+1)\cdot(n-m)}$ to $\{0, 1\}^m$. Next we apply the Semi-Public XOR Mask Transform to $\mathcal{F}^2$ to obtain UOWHF $\mathcal{F}^3$ with same domain and range and XOR mask key length $m + (k + 1) \cdot (n - m)$ bit. Finally we apply the Shoup XOR-Mask extender with $\mathcal{L}'$ blocks to $\mathcal{F}^3$ obtain UOWHF $\mathcal{F}''(\ell, m)$ mapping $\{0, 1\}^{\ell = m + \mathcal{L} \cdot (n-m)}$ to $\{0, 1\}^m$, with 'per-use' key length $l'' = (\lfloor \log(\mathcal{L}') \rfloor + 1) \cdot m + (k + 1) \cdot (n - m) = n + \lfloor \log(\mathcal{L}') \rfloor \cdot m + k \cdot (n - m)$. In terms of provable security, we combine the reductions in [16] and [7] with our Theorem 2 to obtain that if subset sum problem $\mathsf{SubSum}(n, m, p)$ is (t, ϵ)-hard then $\mathcal{F}''(\ell, m)$ is approximately a $(t, 2^{k+1}(n - k)\mathcal{L} \cdot \epsilon)$ UOWHF, so our method's provable security is about 2^k times lower than the standard method.

The relative saving $S(k) \stackrel{\text{def}}{=} (l' - l'')/l'$ in 'per use' key length of our method over the standard method is

$$S(k) = \frac{(\lfloor \log(\mathcal{L}' \cdot (k + 1)) \rfloor - \lfloor \log(\mathcal{L}') \rfloor) \cdot m - k \cdot (n - m)}{n + \lfloor \log(\mathcal{L}) \rfloor \cdot m}. \tag{13}$$

Dropping the floor functions and using $\tau = n/m$, we obtain the continuous approximation

$$S(k) \approx \frac{\log(k + 1) - (\tau - 1) \cdot k}{\log(\mathcal{L}) + \tau}.$$

It is clear that for fixed $\mathcal{L}$ and τ close to 1, there is an optimum choice k_o for k which maximises $S(k)$. Using the continuous approximation for $S(k)$ above it is easy to show that the optimum values are given by

$$k_o \approx \frac{1}{\ln(2)(\tau - 1)} - 1, \quad S(k_o) \approx \frac{\log(\frac{1}{\ln(2)(\tau-1)}) + \tau - 1 - 1/\ln(2)}{\log(\frac{\mathcal{L}'}{\ln(2)(\tau-1)}) + \tau}, \tag{14}$$

corresponding to an absolute additive saving in 'per use' key length of $l' - l'' \approx (\log(\frac{1}{\ln(2)(\tau-1)}) + \tau - 1 - 1/\ln(2)) \cdot m$ bits. Because the total 'per use' key length l' of the Shoup method increases only logarithmically with the message length, this constant additive saving remains significant even for quite long message lengths. On the other hand, the above comparison does not take into account that the proven security of our method is lower than the standard method by a factor of about 2^k relative to the subset sum problem. Let $T(\tau, m)$ denote the security (run time to success probability ratio) of subset sum problem $\mathsf{SubSum}(\tau \cdot m, m, p)$. To compare the key length at equal proven security level, we may assume a larger modulus length $m' > m$ in our method (but same compression ratio $\tau = n'/m' = n/m$) chosen such that $T(\tau, m') = 2^k \cdot T(\tau, m)$. Assuming $T(\tau, m) = C(\tau) \cdot 2^{c \cdot m}$ for some function $C(\tau)$ and constant $c > 0$ (e.g. $c = 0.0629/(1.0629) \approx 0.059$ may be reasonable as discussed in Section 2), we obtain $m' = m + k/c$. This leads to a reduced relative key length saving (for equal length messages)

$$S'(k) \geq \left(1 + \frac{k/c}{m}\right) S(k) - \frac{k/c}{m}. \tag{15}$$

This relative saving is still significant for short messages when m is sufficiently large compared to k/c, although the saving decreases (and actually becomes negative) for very long messages. Table 1 shows an example of the achievable savings.

Table 1. Example of savings in 'per use' key length using our method combined with the Shoup method ('our' column), compared to the Shoup method alone ('std' column). The savings have been corrected for equal provable security as explained in the text, assuming parameter values $m = 2000$, $\tau = 1.07$, $k = 19$, $c = 0.059$, $m' = 2321$.

Msg Len (kbit)	Key Len std (kbit)	Key Len our (kbit))	Savings (%)
5.6	10.1	5.6	45.2
8.8	12.1	7.9	35.1
15.3	14.1	10.2	27.8
106	20.1	17.2	14.8
1661	28.1	26.5	6.0
6637	32.1	31.1	3.3

One could obtain slightly greater savings with our method if Lemma 1 could be generalized to higher order UOWHFs. However we point out that this is not true in general, and in particular, the kth order UOWHF property of the subset sum function is not preserved by the 'Semi-Public Key XOR-Mask Transform' – we refer the reader to the full version of the paper for more details.

5   Conclusion

We have shown that the subset sum hash function is a kth order UOWHF for $k = O(\log m)$. Concretely, we have shown that its security as a kth order UOWHF is at most about k bits lower than its security as a (0th order) UOWHF (which in turn is almost equivalent to the subset sum problem), and showed an application of this result to shortening the key length of long-input UOWHFs built from the subset sum compression function using the Shoup XOR-mask domain extender. An interesting research problem is to find other applications for higher order UOWHFs (for which UOWHFs are not sufficient).

Acknowledgements. This work was supported by Australian Research Council Discovery Grants DP0345366 and DP0451484.

References

1. M. Ajtai. Generating Hard Instances of Lattice Problems. In *Proc. 28th STOC*, pages 99–108, New York, 1996. ACM Press.
2. M. Bellare and D. Micciancio. A New Paradigm for Collision-free Hashing: Incrementality at Reduced Cost. In *EUROCRYPT '97*, volume 1233 of *LNCS*, pages 163–192, Berlin, 1997. Springer-Verlag.

3. M. Bellare and P. Rogaway. Collision-Resistant hashing: Towards making UOWHFs Practical. In *CRYPTO '97*, volume 1294 of *LNCS*, pages 470–484, Berlin, 1997. Springer-Verlag.
4. M.J. Coster, B.A. LaMacchia, A.M. Odlyzko, and C.P. Schnorr. An Improved Low-Density Subset Sum Algorithm. In *EUROCRYPT '91*, volume 547 of *LNCS*, pages 54–67, Berlin, 1991. Springer-Verlag.
5. I. Damgård. A Design Principle for Hash Functions. In *CRYPTO '89*, volume 435 of *LNCS*, pages 416–427, Berlin, 1989. Springer-Verlag.
6. O. Goldreich, S. Goldwasser, and S. Halevi. Collision-free hashing from lattice problems. Technical Report TR96-056, Electronic Colloquium on Computational Complexity (ECCC), 1996.
7. D. Hong, B. Preneel, and S. Lee. Higher Order Universal One-Way Hash Functions. In *ASIACRYPT 2004*, volume 3329 of *LNCS*, pages 201–213, Berlin, 2004. Springer-Verlag.
8. C. Hsiao and L. Reyzin. Finding Collisions on a Public Road, or Do Secure Hash Functions Need Secret Coins? In *CRYPTO '04*, volume 3152 of *LNCS*, pages 92–105, Berlin, 2004. Springer-Verlag.
9. R. Impagliazzo and M. Naor. Efficient Cryptographic Schemes Provably as Secure as Subset Sum. *Journal of Cryptology*, 9:199–216, 1996.
10. R. M. Karp. Reducibility among Combinatorial Problems. In R. E. Miller and J.W. Thatcher, editors, *Complexity of Computer Computation*. Plenum, New York, 1972.
11. R. Merkle. One Way Hash Functions and DES. In *CRYPTO '89*, volume 435 of *LNCS*, pages 428–446, Berlin, 1989. Springer-Verlag.
12. R. Merkle and M. Hellman. Hiding Information and Signatures in Trapdoor Knapsacks. *IEEE Trans. on Information Theory*, 24:525–530, 1978.
13. D. Micciancio and O. Regev. Worst-Case to Average-Case Reductions based on Gaussian Measures. In *Proc. FOCS 2004*, pages 372–381. IEEE Computer Society Press, 2004.
14. M. Naor and M. Yung. Universal One-Way Hash Functions and their Cryptographic Significance. In *Proc. 21st STOC*, pages 33–43, New York, 1989. ACM Press.
15. A. Shamir. A Polynomial Time Algorithm for Breaking the Basic Merkle-Hellman Cryptosystem. *IEEE Trans. on Information Theory*, 30:699–704, 1984.
16. V. Shoup. A Composition Theorem for Universal One-Way Hash Functions. In *EUROCRYPT 2000*, volume 1807 of *LNCS*, pages 445–452, Berlin, 2000. Springer-Verlag.

An Algorithm to Solve the Discrete Logarithm Problem with the Number Field Sieve

An Commeine[1] and Igor Semaev[2]

[1] Katholieke Universiteit Leuven, Departement Wiskunde, Afdeling Algebra,
Celestijnenlaan 200B, B-3001 Leuven, Belgium
[2] Universitetet i Bergen, Institutt for informatikk, HIB - Thormhlensgt. 55,
N-5020 Bergen, Norway

Abstract. Recently, Shirokauer's algorithm to solve the discrete logarithm problem modulo a prime p has been modified by Matyukhin, yielding an algorithm with running time $L_p[\frac{1}{3}, 1.9018\ldots]$, which is, at the present time, the best known estimate of the complexity of finding discrete logarithms over prime finite fields and which coincides with the best known theoretical running time for factoring integers, obtained by Coppersmith. In this paper, another algorithm to solve the discrete logarithm problem in $\mathbb{F}_p^*$ for p prime is presented. The global running time is again $L_p[\frac{1}{3}, 1.9018\ldots]$, but in contrast with Matyukhins method, this algorithm enables us to calculate individual logarithms in a separate stage in time $L_p[\frac{1}{3}, 3^{1/3}]$, once a $L_p[\frac{1}{3}, 1.9018\ldots]$ time costing pre-computation stage has been executed. We describe the algorithm as derived from [6] and estimate its running time to be $L_p[\frac{1}{3}, (\frac{64}{9})^{1/3}]$, after which individual logarithms can be calculated in time $L_p[\frac{1}{3}, 3^{1/3}]$.

Keywords: Discrete Logarithms, Number Field Sieve.

1 Introduction

Given a prime p and integers a and b, the discrete logarithm of b to the base a in the multiplicative group of the finite field $\mathbb{F}_p$ is defined as the smallest nonnegative integer x such that $a^x \equiv b \pmod{p}$, if it exists.

The security of many, widely used public key cryptosystems, as the well-known Diffie-Hellman key exchange algorithm and the ElGamal Digital signature algorithm, depends on the assumption that for suitably chosen primes, discrete logs are hard to compute. As such, one of the most stimulating factors in research on the complexity of discrete logs is the fact that fast discrete logarithm algorithms could easily undermine these cryptosystems ([12],[13] for a survey).

General methods that can also be applied in other groups than $\mathbb{F}_p^*$, are Shanks deterministic "baby steps, giant steps" attack ([14]) and two other randomized algorithms due to Pollard ([16]), such as the Pollard ρ-method. For both methods, the number of operations to compute a discrete logarithm roughly equals $q^{1/2}$, where q is the largest prime factor of $p-1$, but Pollards methods use almost no space in contrast with Shanks method, which has space requirement $q^{1/2}$. Moreover, the Pollard ρ-method was parallelized in 1993 by van Oorschot

M. Yung et al. (Eds.): PKC 2006, LNCS 3958, pp. 174–190, 2006.

and Wiener ([23]) in such a way that the expected number of steps that each processor performs to obtain a discrete logarithm is about $q^{1/2}/t$, where t is the number of processors. These attacks have an exponential worst case complexity, since the largest prime factor of $p-1$ can be almost as large as p.

Making use of additional knowledge of the underlying group, index calculus methods, based on an idea of Kraitchik ([11]), provide subexponential algorithms. These methods typically consist of three phases: generating relations, solving equations and computing individual logarithms using the results of the first two steps. The first two steps, called the pre-computation stage, determine the running time of the algorithm. Once the pre-computation stage is finished for a prime p, individual logarithms modulo that prime can be computed more efficiently. Running time bounds of the earliest index calculus algorithms are of the form $L_p[\frac{1}{2}, c]$ for some constant $c > 0$. Large c however yield impractical algorithms, so many researchers tried to lower this value c during 1970s and 1980s ([11],[14] for references). Both the Linear Sieve Method and the Gaussian Integer Method ([4]), where the use of an imaginary quadratic number field was introduced, achieved the value $c = 1$. In 1998, work on the latter allowed Joux and Lercier to compute discrete logs modulo a 90-digit prime number in [6]. The asymptotic running time bound with $c = 1$ was a record value for a long time.

Speeding up the pre-computation stage was possible due to advances in linear algebra, namely solving sparse systems with n unknowns in not much more than n^2 steps ([15]). This is achieved by the Wiedemann algorithm ([24]), based on the Berlekamp-Massey algorithm and the Cayley-Hamilton theorem and, by adaptations of the finite field version of Lanczos and conjugate gradient algorithms ([4],[14]), that can be combined with structured Gauss Elimination ([14]).

In 1988, Pollard found a new approach for factoring integers. This technique was developed into the special number field sieve by Hendrik Lenstra. It factors integers of special forms in time $L_N[\frac{1}{3}, c]$ with $c = (\frac{32}{9})^{1/3} = 1.5262\ldots$, where N is the number to be factored. Later the method was extended to factor arbitrary integers in time $L_N[\frac{1}{3}, c]$ with $c = (\frac{64}{9})^{1/3} = 1.9229\ldots$ in the general number field sieve, that arose through a collaboration of several researchers ([8] for details). The value of c was improved to $c = 1.9018\ldots$ by Coppersmith in [3].

The general number field sieve was adapted to the computation of discrete logs modulo a prime by Gordon in [5] in 1992. He obtained running time $L_p[\frac{1}{3}, c]$ with $c = 2.0800\ldots$. The value of c was lowered by Shirokauer in [19] to $c = (\frac{64}{9})^{1/3} = 1.9229\ldots$ in 1993. Adapting this algorithm following the ideas of Coppersmith, Matyukhin in [10] achieved the same constant as Coppersmith in [3], thus $c = 1.9018\ldots$. With the latter two algorithms however, it's impossible to efficiently compute individual logarithms, since the linear algebra must be redone for every new logarithm. For special prime numbers, this deficiency was overcome by Semaev in [21], moreover yielding a running time of $L_p[\frac{1}{3}, (\frac{32}{9})^{1/3}]$ and $L_p[\frac{1}{3}, \frac{1+2\sqrt{2}}{18^{1/3}}] = L_p[\frac{1}{3}, 1.4608\ldots]$ for an individual logarithm. Joux and Lercier were able to separate the pre-computation stage and the computation of individual logarithms for primes lacking any special structure in [6], which formed the base of their computation of discrete logs modulo a 130-digits prime, the current record for general primes ([7]). Since their objective was to describe the main ideas behind their C-implementation, they didn't write down the actual algorithm they used to compute individual logarithms nor performed an asymptotic time analysis however.

To achieve a separate individual logarithm stage, we adapt the method in [6] for the pre-computation part and modify the individual logarithm algorithm of [21]. Instead of working with real numbers, we choose to work with a 'logarithmic map' as in [19], though an approach developed in [21] apparently gives the same asymptotic results. The improvements of Coppersmith in [3] are taken into account, to achieve a global running time of $L_p[\frac{1}{3}, 1.9018\ldots]$. In contrast with Matyukhin however, individual logarithms can be calculated separately in time $L_p[\frac{1}{3}, 3^{1/3}] = L_p[\frac{1}{3}, 1.44225\ldots]$ after a $L_p[\frac{1}{3}, 1.9018\ldots]$-time costing precomputation stage. In order to compare the method in [6] with ours, we give a precise theoretical description of the algorithm as we've understood and built it out of the ideas given in [6]. A running time analysis of this algorithm is performed, using the theoretical settings developed in the analysis of our algorithm. We show that the optimal cost for this algorithm is $L_p[\frac{1}{3}, (\frac{64}{9})^{1/3}]$, with the possibility to calculate individual logarithms separately in time $L_p[\frac{1}{3}, 3^{1/3}]$.

The core idea, which allows us to achieve this running time for the individual logarithm stage, is expressing logarithms of medium-sized prime numbers into logarithms of smaller numbers and the reduction of first degree prime ideals into first degree prime ideals with smaller norm. Inspiration for this was found in [2]. This idea of reducing unknown into known information is also applicable in the one-polynomial variant of the Number Field Sieve, yielding a very similar separate individual logarithm algorithm, again with running time $L_p[\frac{1}{3}, 3^{1/3}]$, not changing the pre-computation time of $L_p[\frac{1}{3}, (\frac{64}{9})^{1/3}]$. (The most expensive reduction will take more time in this setting however; see Remark, Section 4.2.)

We want to remark that running times of all recent algorithms of the form $L_p[\frac{1}{3}, c]$, as the one presented in this paper, are based on heuristic assumptions. There's no proof that they'll run fast. It's possible to obtain rigorous probabilistic algorithms, with running time bounded by $L_p[\frac{1}{2}, c]$ with high probability ([18]).

2 Preliminaries

Definition 1. *An integer n is B-smooth if and only if $q \leq B$ for all (natural) prime numbers q that divide n.*

When assessing a running time analysis of the algorithm, we make use of the complexity-function

$$L_p[t, s] = e^{s(1+o(1))(\ln p)^t (\ln \ln p)^{1-t}},$$

where $o(1)$ denotes a function tending to 0 as $p \to \infty$. The expression $o(1)$ in the exponent hides a lot: this notation is meant as a first order approximation to the real computational complexity.

The following theorem gives an estimation of the probability that a number smaller or equal to x is y-smooth in terms of the above complexity function.

Theorem 1. *Let* $0 < y_1 < x_1 \leq 1$ *and* $y_2, x_2 > 0$. *Let* $x = L_p[x_1, x_2]$ *and* $y = L_p[y_1, y_2]$, *then*

$$\frac{\psi(x, y)}{x} = L_p[x_1 - y_1, -\frac{x_2}{y_2}(x_1 - y_1)] \; ,$$

where $\psi(x, y) =$ *the number of natural numbers smaller or equal to* x *which are* y-*smooth.*

This follows from a more general theorem of Canfield, Erdös and Pomerance:

Theorem 2. *([1]) If* $x \geq 10$ *and* $y > \ln x$, *then it holds that*

$$\psi(x, y) = x u^{-u(1+o(1))} \text{ with } u = \frac{\log x}{\log y} \; ,$$

where the limit implicit in the $o(1)$ *is for* $x \to \infty$.

We recall some useful results from algebraic number theory. Let $f = X^d + f_1 X^{d-1} + \cdots + f_d$ be a monic, irreducible polynomial of degree d with root α. We denote the field $\mathbb{Q}(\alpha) = K$ and ϑ_K the ring of algebraic integers of K. Following propositions are useful:

Proposition 1. *([21]) If* q *does not divide* $[\vartheta_K : \mathbb{Z}[\alpha]]$ *and*

$$f(X) = \prod_i h_i^{e_i}(X) \text{ in } \mathbb{F}_q[X] \; ,$$

where $h_i(X)$ *are distinct irreducible polynomials in* $\mathbb{F}_q[X]$, *then*

$$q\vartheta_K = \prod_i \mathcal{U}_i^{e_i} \; ,$$

for distinct prime ideals $\mathcal{U}_i = h_i(\alpha)\vartheta_K + q\vartheta_K$ *in* ϑ_K *and* $Norm(\mathcal{U}_i) = q^{\deg h_i(X)}$.

This proposition suggests making a distinction between prime ideals in ϑ_K.

Definition 2. *A prime ideal* $\mathcal{P}$ *of* ϑ_K *of degree 1 is* bad *if its norm divides the index* $[\vartheta_K : \mathbb{Z}[\alpha]]$. *All other prime ideals of degree 1 are called* good.

Good prime ideals appear in factorizations as mentioned below.

Proposition 2. *([21]) If* $a, b \neq 0$ *are coprime integers such that*

$$b^d f\left(\frac{a}{b}\right) = a^d + f_1 b a^{d-1} + \cdots + f_d b^d$$

is coprime to $[\vartheta_K : \mathbb{Z}[\alpha]]$, *then*

$$(a - b\alpha)\vartheta_K = \mathcal{U}_1^{l_1} \mathcal{U}_2^{l_2} \ldots \mathcal{U}_s^{l_s} \; ,$$

where $\mathcal{U}_i$ *are distinct good prime ideals of* ϑ_K *for* $i = 1, \ldots, s$ *and* $Norm(\mathcal{U}_i) = q_i$ *for distinct* q_i. *Moreover,*

$$\left| b^d f\left(\frac{a}{b}\right) \right| = \prod_{i=1}^{s} q_i^{l_i} \; .$$

For ease of exposition, suppose $p - 1 = 2q$ with q a large prime that doesn't ramify in K. Let $\Gamma_K = \{\gamma \in \vartheta_K \mid \gcd(\mathrm{Norm}(\gamma), q) = 1\}$. We use a map l as in [19]: set $\epsilon_K = \mathrm{lcm}\left\{\left|(\vartheta_K/\mathcal{Q})^*\right| \mid \mathcal{Q} \text{ prime ideal in } \vartheta_K \text{ lying above } q\right\}$, then

$$l : \Gamma_K \longrightarrow q\vartheta_K/q^2\vartheta_K$$
$$\gamma \longmapsto (\gamma^{\epsilon_K} - 1) + q^2\vartheta_K .$$

Consider $q\vartheta_K/q^2\vartheta_K$ as a $\mathbb{Z}/q\mathbb{Z}$-vectorspace. We generate a sequence of length a little more than the unity rank of ϑ_K of random units $u \in \vartheta_K^*$ and calculate the images $l(u)$. The linear independent vectors amongst these images $l(u)$ span the subspace $l(\vartheta_K^*) \subseteq q\vartheta_K/q^2\vartheta_K$ with high probability. Assume they form a basis $\{qb_j + q^2\vartheta_K \mid j = 1, \ldots, t_K\}$ of $l(\vartheta_K^*)$. Expand this basis to a basis $\{qb_j + q^2\vartheta_K \mid j = 1, \ldots, d\}$ of the whole $\mathbb{Z}/q\mathbb{Z}$-vectorspace $q\vartheta_K/q^2\vartheta_K$. Denote

$$\lambda_{K,j} : \Gamma_K \longrightarrow \mathbb{Z}/q\mathbb{Z}$$
$$\gamma \longmapsto \lambda_{K,j}(\gamma)$$

such that $l(\gamma) = \sum_{j=1}^d \lambda_{K,j}(\gamma)(qb_j + q^2\vartheta_K)$. Remark that $l(\gamma\gamma') = l(\gamma) + l(\gamma')$, such that $\lambda_{K,j}(\gamma\gamma') = \lambda_{K,j}(\gamma) + \lambda_{K,j}(\gamma')$ for $j = 1, \ldots, d$.

The largest contribution to the time needed for the practical determination of all $\lambda_{K,j}(\gamma)$ for $\gamma \in \Gamma_K$, comes from the exponentiation to the power $\epsilon_K < q^d$ in the ring $\mathbb{Z}[X]/(f, q^2)$, costing $O(d^3 \ln^3 p)$ bit operations.

3   The Algorithm

3.1   Needs and Assumptions

Choose two natural numbers $d = \delta(1+o(1))\,(\ln p/\ln\ln p)^{1/3}$ and $m = p^{(1+o(1))/d}$, both depending on p, where the limit implicit in the $o(1)$ is for $p \to \infty$. The parameter δ will be defined later. Suppose f is an irreducible polynomial of degree d with coefficients bounded by m, such that $f(m) \equiv 0 \bmod p$, obtained as in the Number Field Sieve setting (NFS). Remark that use of polynomials as in [6], namely a degree $d + 1$-polynomial with small coefficients and having a root μ modulo p and a degree d-polynomial with the same root μ modulo p, having coefficients of the order $p^{1/(d+1)}$, is thought of giving the best practical results.

For simplicity, we assume $f = f_0$ to be monic. We work with polynomials

$$f_i(X) = f_0(X) + i(X - m) \quad \text{for } i = 1, \ldots, V$$

that are irreducible and such that neither p nor q divide their discriminants. These conditions are easily checked ([5]). For simplicity, we assume all values of i determine valid polynomials. Remark that the coefficients of these polynomials get somewhat larger, becoming $\leq (V + 1)m = VL_p[\frac{2}{3}, \frac{1}{\delta}]$ in first order estimate.

Let α_i be a root of f_i, $K_i = \mathbb{Q}(\alpha_i)$ an algebraic number field of degree d over $\mathbb{Q}$ and ϑ_{K_i} the ring of algebraic integers of K_i. Remark that α_i is an algebraic integer in K_i by the assumption that f_i is monic. The number p doesn't divide the discriminant of the polynomial f_i, hence it doesn't divide $[\vartheta_{K_i} : \mathbb{Z}[\alpha_i]]$. According to Proposition 1, $\mathcal{P}_i = (\alpha_i - m)\vartheta_{K_i} + p\vartheta_{K_i}$ then is a first degree prime ideal, and we denote $\pi_i(\varepsilon) = \overline{\varepsilon}$ for π_i the projection-map

$$\pi_i : \vartheta_{K_i} \longrightarrow \frac{\vartheta_{K_i}}{\mathcal{P}_i}\,(\cong \mathbb{F}_p)\ ,\ \overline{\alpha_i} = m\ . \tag{1}$$

For every field K_i, we denote the maps $\lambda_{K_i,j}$ and the set Γ_{K_i}, defined as above, as $\lambda_{i,j}$ and Γ_i respectively. Let r_i be the torsion free rank of $\vartheta_{K_i}^*$. Since q doesn't divide the discriminant of f_i, $\vartheta_{K_i}^*$ contains no primitive q'th roots of unity. This implies that the dimension t_{K_i} of the $\mathbb{Z}/q\mathbb{Z}$-subspace $l(\vartheta_{K_i}^*) \subseteq q\vartheta_{K_i}/q^2\vartheta_{K_i}$ is less then or equal to r_i. We assume that $\gcd(h_{K_i}, q) = 1$ and $\{u \in \vartheta_{K_i}^* \mid u \equiv 1 \bmod q^2\} \subseteq (\vartheta_{K_i}^*)^q$ for every i. One can check that, under these conditions, the well-defined homomorphisms

$$\overline{\lambda}_i : \vartheta_{K_i}^*/(\vartheta_{K_i}^*)^q \longrightarrow (\mathbb{Z}/q\mathbb{Z})^{r_i}$$
$$\gamma(\vartheta_{K_i}^*)^q \longmapsto (\lambda_{i,1}(\gamma), \ldots, \lambda_{i,r_i}(\gamma))$$

are isomorphisms (thus $t_{K_i} = r_i$).

3.2   The Algorithm

Choose bounds $E = L_p[\frac{1}{3}, \epsilon]$, $B_1 = L_p[\frac{1}{3}, \beta]$ and $B_2 = L_p[\frac{1}{3}, \gamma]$, where ϵ, β, γ are parameters with $\beta \geq \gamma$.

Finding Relations

1. Let S_i be the set of good prime ideals in ϑ_{K_i} with norm $\leq B_2$ and coprime to q. As in the modified number field sieve due to Coppersmith, we set $V = \pi(B_1)/(\pi(B_2) + d) = L_p[\frac{1}{3}, \beta - \gamma]$ and determine triples (a, b, i) with $|a| \leq E$, $1 \leq b \leq E$, called good, such that, for q_j ranging over prime numbers $\leq B_1$ and $\mathcal{U}_i$ ranging over prime ideals in S_i, it holds that

$$a - bm = \pm \prod_{q_j \leq B_1} q_j^{e_{abj}} \tag{2}$$

$$(a - b\alpha_i)\vartheta_{K_i} = \prod_{\mathcal{U}_i \in S_i} \mathcal{U}_i^{n_{ab\mathcal{U}_i}}\ . \tag{3}$$

To achieve about $2(|S_i| + r_i)$ triples per field K_i, we take $\epsilon = (3\gamma^2\delta\beta + \gamma + \beta)/((6\gamma - \delta)\delta\beta)$ and $6\gamma - \delta > 0$. It is shown in [3] that finding appropriate triples takes time

$$L_p[\frac{1}{3}, \max\{\beta, 2\epsilon\}] + L_p[\frac{1}{3}, 2\epsilon - \frac{1}{3\delta\beta} + \beta - \gamma]\ . \tag{4}$$

2. Since $\overline{\lambda}_i$ are isomorphisms for $i = 0, \ldots, V$, it follows from [20] that there exist unique elements $\mathcal{X}_{\mathcal{U}_i}, \mathcal{X}_{i,j} \in \mathbb{Z}/q\mathbb{Z}$, not depending on the set S_i of ideals, such that for all triples (a, b, i) collected, it holds that

$$\log_g \pi_i(a - b\alpha_i) \equiv \sum_{\mathcal{U}_i \in S_i} \mathcal{X}_{\mathcal{U}_i} n_{ab\mathcal{U}_i} + \sum_{j=1}^{r_i} \mathcal{X}_{i,j} \lambda_{i,j}(a - b\alpha_i) \pmod{q},$$

using (3). Together with (2) and taking into account that $\log_g \pm 1 \equiv 0 \pmod{q}$, this equivalence leads to the equation

$$-\sum_{q_j \le B_1} e_{abj} \log_g q_j + \sum_{\mathcal{U}_i \in S_i} \mathcal{X}_{\mathcal{U}_i} n_{ab\mathcal{U}_i} + \sum_{j=1}^{r_i} \mathcal{X}_{i,j} \lambda_{i,j}(a - b\alpha_i) \equiv 0 \pmod{q}.$$

To establish these equations, we only need to evaluate $\lambda_{i,j}(a - b\alpha_i)$ for $j = 1, \ldots, r_i$ for all good triples (a, b, i). This takes asymptotic time $O(d^3 \ln^3 p) \left(\sum_{i=0}^{V} 2(|S_i| + r_i) \right) \approx O(d^3 \ln^3 p) 2(V + 1)(\pi(B_2) + d) = \pi(B_1)$.

Solving the System. Through finding relations as above, we get a homogeneous system of about $\sum_{i=0}^{V} 2(|S_i| + r_i) \approx 2(V + 1)(\pi(B_2) + d) \approx 2\pi(B_1)$ equations, which has to be solved for $\pi(B_1) + \sum_{i=0}^{V} (|S_i| + r_i) \approx \pi(B_1) + (\pi(B_2) + d)(V + 1) \approx 2\pi(B_1)$ unknowns $\log_g q_j$ and $\mathcal{X}_{\mathcal{U}_i}, \mathcal{X}_{i,j}$. In order to get a unique non-zero solution to the system, take g a B_1-smooth number $g = \prod_{q_j \le B_1} q_j^{e_{gj}}$, generating $\mathbb{F}_p^*$, what can be done under the assumption of the Extended Riemann Hypothesis ([22]), and expand the system with the equation

$$\sum_{q_j \le B_1} e_{gj} \log_g q_j \equiv \log_g g \equiv 1 \pmod{q}.$$

Let U be the matrix with blocks $U_i = (e_{abij})_{(a,b,i),j}$ on its rows, where $e_{abij} = e_{abj}$ in (2) for a good triple (a, b, i) and let P, respectively L, be matrices with blocks $P_i = (n_{ab\mathcal{U}_i})_{(a,b,i),\mathcal{U}_i}$, respectively $L_i = (\lambda_{i,j}(a - b\alpha_i))_{(a,b,i),j}$, on the diagonal for i from 0 to V. The rows of these matrices run over good triples (a, b, i). Let U_g be the rowvector $(e_{gj})_j$, then the matrix of the system has layout:

$$\begin{pmatrix} 1, & -U_g, & 0, & 0 \\ 0, & -U, & P, & L \end{pmatrix} = \begin{pmatrix} 1 & -U_g & 0 & 0 & \cdots & 0 & 0 & 0 & \cdots & 0 \\ 0 & -U_0 & P_0 & 0 & \cdots & 0 & L_0 & 0 & \cdots & 0 \\ 0 & -U_1 & 0 & P_1 & \cdots & 0 & 0 & L_1 & \cdots & 0 \\ \vdots & \vdots & & & \ddots & & & & \ddots & \\ 0 & -U_V & 0 & 0 & \cdots & P_V & 0 & 0 & \cdots & L_V \end{pmatrix}.$$

This sparse system can be solved combining structured Gaussian elimination with a sparse matrix technique, such as Wiedemann's algorithm ([24]) or Lanczos and conjugate gradient methods ([4],[14]). According to [15], asymptotical time cost to solve the system is

$$O(\pi(B_1)^2) = L_p[\frac{1}{3}, 2\beta]. \tag{5}$$

As stated in [20], we can choose whatever 'logarithmic' maps $\mu_{i,j}$ instead of the mappings $\lambda_{i,j}$ used here (as in [19], see above). In this way we can make the system more sparse, so sparse matrix techniques to solve the system work faster. We've for example found maps $\mu_{i,j}$ such that each L_i contained at most $r_i(|S_i| + 1)$ non-zero entries. However, one has to make sure that the advantage of having a sparser system doesn't get lost by the cost of evaluating the mappings $\mu_{i,j}$. This still has to be examined.

3.3   Running Time Analysis Pre-computation

With running time considerations (4),(5), and taking $\gamma \leq \beta$, ϵ as above and $6\gamma - \delta > 0$, total pre-computation time becomes

$$L_p[\frac{1}{3}, \max\{2\epsilon, 2\epsilon - \frac{1}{3\delta\beta} + \beta - \gamma, 2\beta\}] \ ,$$

which has optimal value $L_p[\frac{1}{3}, 2\beta] = L_p[\frac{1}{3}, 1.9018\ldots]$ as in [3], by taking

$$\beta = \left(\frac{46 + 13\sqrt{13}}{108}\right)^{\frac{1}{3}} \ , \quad \gamma = \beta\left(\frac{\sqrt{13} - 1}{3}\right) \ , \quad \delta = \beta\left(\frac{4\sqrt{13} - 10}{3}\right) .$$

4   The Individual Logarithm

4.1   The Algorithm

In this section we determine $\log_a b \ (\bmod\ p - 1)$ for a generator a of $\mathbb{F}_p^*$ by making use of the $\log_g q_k$, $\mathcal{X}_{\mathcal{U}_i}$ and $\mathcal{X}_{i,j}$ calculated in the former section.

Use the procedure below to calculate $\log_g z \ (\bmod\ p - 1)$ for $z = a$ and $z = b$. Once these logarithms are calculated, the asked for $\log_a b$ is found as $\log_a b \equiv \log_g b / \log_g a \ (\bmod\ p - 1)$.

1. Let $Q \leq B_1$ be the largest prime number in the factorbase for which the logarithm is known. Factor $Q^h z$ using the Elliptic Curve Method (ECM) ([9]) for random integers $h \in \{1, \ldots, p - 1\}$, until you find one for which $Q^h z \bmod p$ is $L_p[\frac{2}{3}, (\frac{1}{3})^{1/3}]$-smooth. Thus

$$Q^h z \equiv q_1^{n_1} \ldots q_r^{n_r} (\bmod\ p) \ , \ q_i \text{ prime numbers} \leq L_p[\frac{2}{3}, (\frac{1}{3})^{\frac{1}{3}}] \ . \quad (6)$$

To check for factors $\leq L_p[\frac{2}{3}, (\frac{1}{3})^{1/3}]$, each application of ECM takes asymptotic time $L_p[\frac{1}{3}, 2(\frac{1}{3})^{2/3}]$ ([10]), such that the total time to find a good h is

$$L_p[\frac{1}{3}, \left(\frac{1}{3}\right)^{\frac{2}{3}}] L_p[\frac{1}{3}, 2\left(\frac{1}{3}\right)^{\frac{2}{3}}] = L_p[\frac{1}{3}, 3^{\frac{1}{3}}] = L_p[\frac{1}{3}, 1.44225\ldots] \ ,$$

where we estimate the probability for a number $< p$ to be $L_p[\frac{2}{3}, (\frac{1}{3})^{1/3}]$-smooth as $L_p[\frac{1}{3}, -(\frac{1}{3})^{2/3}]$, using Theorem 1.

2. For all $q_i(> B_1)$ in (6), we need to find $\log_g q_i$. This is done by expressing these logarithms in terms of known logarithms by means of reductions, which are described in the next subsection.
3. Calculate $\log_g z \equiv -h \log_g Q + \sum_{i=1}^{r} n_i \log_g q_i \pmod{q}$ as a sum of known logarithms. Then, compute $\log_g z \pmod{p-1}$ as $(\log_g z \bmod q) + \phi q$, testing whether $\phi = 0$ or $\phi = 1$ using modular exponentiation.

The computation $\log_a b \equiv \log_g b / \log_g a \pmod{p-1}$ after applying the procedure to $z = a, b$, together with the above calculations, take time $O(\ln^3 p)$.

4.2   Reductions

We explain how to reduce a number and a prime ideal. Time for whatever reduction is of the form $L_p[\frac{1}{3}, c]$, with $c \leq 3^{1/3}$ for a good choice of parameters.

Reduction of a Number l'. We need to reduce numbers l' with $B_1 < l' \leq L_p[\frac{2}{3}, (\frac{1}{3})^{1/3}]$. Depending on the largeness of the number that needs to be reduced, we use different parameters. Let $M = L_p[\frac{2}{3}, c_M]$ for some constant c_M. If $l' \in [B_1, M]$, we use a parameter ν_1 with $\delta/(6\beta) = 0.2456\ldots < \nu_1 < 1$ and set $e_1 = (\frac{3\nu_1\beta}{6\nu_1\beta - \delta})(\frac{2}{3\nu_1\delta\beta} + \frac{\delta}{6\nu_1} - \beta + \gamma)$; for larger l' we use a parameter ν_2 with $0 < \nu_2 < 1$ and set $e_2 = (\gamma - \beta)/2 + \delta/(12\nu_2)$.

Choose a pair of coprime integers (a, b) with $|a|, |b| \leq L_p[\frac{1}{3}, e_i] l'^{1/2}$ in the lattice generated by $(m, 1)$ and $(l', 0)$, which implies that l' divides $a - bm$. We expect about $L_p[\frac{1}{3}, 2e_i]$ such couples. If $|a - bm/l'|$ is l'^{ν_i}-smooth, check whether $|\text{Norm}(a - b\alpha_j)| = |b^d f_j(a/b)|$ is l'^{ν_i}-smooth, for j such that $\text{Norm}(a - b\alpha_j)$ is simultaneously coprime with q and $[\vartheta_{K_j} : \mathbb{Z}[\alpha_j]]$. If so, Proposition 2 implies that we have a couple (a, b) and j such that at the same time

$$a - bm = l' \prod_l l^{e_{l',l}} \qquad l \leq l'^{\nu_i}, \text{ prime} \tag{7}$$

$$(a - b\alpha_j)\vartheta_{K_j} = \prod_{\mathcal{U}_j} \mathcal{U}_j^{m_{l',\mathcal{U}_j}} \qquad \text{Norm}(\mathcal{U}_j) \leq l'^{\nu_i}, \mathcal{U}_j \text{ good prime ideal}. \tag{8}$$

This allows us to express $\log_g l'$ in terms of $\log_g l$ with $l \leq l'^{\nu_i}$ and $\mathcal{X}_{\mathcal{U}_j}$ for good prime ideals $\mathcal{U}_j$ with $\text{Norm}(\mathcal{U}_j) \leq l'^{\nu_i}$ as follows. Equality (8) implies that

$$\log_g \pi_j(a - b\alpha_j) \equiv \sum_{\mathcal{U}_j} \mathcal{X}_{\mathcal{U}_j} m_{l',\mathcal{U}_j} + \sum_{k=1}^{r_j} \mathcal{X}_{j,k} \lambda_{j,k}(a - b\alpha_j) \pmod{q} ,$$

where $\mathcal{U}_j$ runs over ideals as in (8). Combining this equivalence with (7) yields

$$\log_g l' \equiv \sum_{\mathcal{U}_j} \mathcal{X}_{\mathcal{U}_j} m_{l',\mathcal{U}_j} + \sum_{k=1}^{r_j} \mathcal{X}_{j,k} \lambda_{j,k}(a - b\alpha_j) - \sum_{l \leq l'^{\nu_i}} e_{l',l} \log_g l \pmod{q} , \tag{9}$$

where l runs over prime numbers as in (7) and $\mathcal{U}_j$ are prime ideals as in (8).

Using Theorem 2, one can check that the probability for the number $|(a - bm)/l'|$, respectively $|b^d f_j(a/b)|$, to be l'^{ν_i}-smooth can be estimated to be at least $\mathcal{P}_{11} = L_p[\frac{1}{3}, -\frac{1}{3\delta\nu_1\beta}]$, respectively $\mathcal{P}_{21} = L_p[\frac{1}{3}, -(\frac{1}{3\nu_1\delta\beta} + \frac{e_1\delta}{3\nu_1\beta} + \frac{\delta}{6\nu_1})]$ for

$l' \in [B_1, M]$ and at least $\mathcal{P}_{12} = L_p[\frac{1}{6}, -\frac{1}{6\delta\nu_2 c_M}]$, respectively $\mathcal{P}_{22} = L_p[\frac{1}{3}, \frac{-\delta}{6\nu_2}]$ for larger l'. Remark that $L_p[\frac{1}{3}, 2e_i]\mathcal{P}_{1i}V \geq 1/\mathcal{P}_{2i}$ for $i = 1, 2$, so enough pairs (a, b) are considered to finish the procedure with a successful triple (a, b, j).

To find a good triple (a, b, j), we have to test $L_p[\frac{1}{3}, 2e_i]$ values $|(a - bm)/l'|$ and $1/\mathcal{P}_{2i}$ values $|b^d f_j(a/b)|$ for l'^{ν_i}-smoothness, using ECM. According to [10], this takes time at most $L_p[\frac{1}{4}, \sqrt{\nu_1 c_M}]$ for a number $l' \in [B_1, M]$, while for larger l' it costs time $L_p[\frac{1}{3}, 2\sqrt{\nu_2}(\frac{1}{3})^{2/3}]$. Using the fact that $1/(3\nu_1\delta\beta) - \beta + \gamma > 0$ since $1/(3\delta\beta(\beta - \gamma)) = 2$, reducing a number $l' \in [B_1, M]$ takes time at most

$$L_p[\frac{1}{3}, 2e_1] + L_p[\frac{1}{3}, \frac{1}{3\nu_1\delta\beta} + \frac{e_1\delta}{3\nu_1\beta} + \frac{\delta}{6\nu_1}] = L_p[\frac{1}{3}, 2e_1] .$$

For a choice $0.6942\ldots = \frac{4+\delta^2\beta+3^{1/3}\delta^2}{6\delta\beta(\beta-\gamma+3^{1/3})} \leq \nu_1 < 1$, this won't exceed $L_p[\frac{1}{3}, 3^{1/3}]$. For larger numbers l' time cost will be at most

$$L_p[\frac{1}{3}, 2e_2 + 2\sqrt{\nu_2}\left(\frac{1}{3}\right)^{\frac{2}{3}}] + L_p[\frac{1}{3}, \frac{\delta}{6\nu_2} + 2\sqrt{\nu_2}\left(\frac{1}{3}\right)^{\frac{2}{3}}] = L_p[\frac{1}{3}, \frac{\delta}{6\nu_2} + 2\sqrt{\nu_2}\left(\frac{1}{3}\right)^{\frac{2}{3}}] ,$$

which has minimal value $L_p[\frac{1}{3}, 1.1338\ldots]$ for a choice $\nu_2 = \left(\delta^2/(3^{\frac{2}{3}}4)\right)^{1/3} < 1$.

Remark that for a choice $(1 >)\nu_1 \geq \frac{4+\delta^2\beta+x\delta^2}{6\delta\beta(\beta-\gamma+x)} = 0.7406\ldots$ with $x = 1.1338\ldots$, reducing a number $l' \in [B_1, M]$ takes time $\leq L_p[\frac{1}{3}, 1.1338\ldots]$.

Reduction of a Prime Ideal in the Ring ϑ_{K_j}. In expression (9), there can appear $\mathcal{X}_{\mathcal{U}'_j}$ with $B_2 < \text{Norm}(\mathcal{U}'_j) = k' \leq L_p[\frac{2}{3}, \nu_2/3^{1/3}]$. To determine such an unknown number, we reduce the ideal $\mathcal{U}'_j$, which is, according to Proposition 1, generated by $\alpha_j - \alpha_{j,k'}$ and k', for $0 \leq \alpha_{j,k'} < k'$ a root of $f_j(X) \equiv 0 \pmod{k'}$.

As with reducing numbers, we distinguish between $k' \in [B_2, M]$ and larger k', with M as in the reduction of numbers. Likewise we introduce parameters $\tilde{\nu}_1$ with $0.28287\ldots = \delta/(6\gamma) < \tilde{\nu}_1 < 1$ and set $\tilde{e}_1 = \left(\frac{3\gamma\tilde{\nu}_1}{6\gamma\tilde{\nu}_1 - \delta}\right)\left(\frac{2}{3\gamma\tilde{\nu}_1\delta} + \frac{\delta}{6\tilde{\nu}_1}\right)$, and $\tilde{\nu}_2$ with $0 < \tilde{\nu}_2 < 1$ and set $\tilde{e}_2 = \delta/(6\tilde{\nu}_2)$.

Choose a pair of coprime integers (a, b) with $|a|, |b| \leq L_p[\frac{1}{3}, \tilde{e}_i]k'^{1/2}$, subject to the usual restriction that $|b^d f_j(a/b)|$ is simultaneously coprime with q and $[\vartheta_{K_j} : \mathbb{Z}[\alpha_j]]$ and the new restriction that $\mathcal{U}'_j$ divides $(a - b\alpha_j)\vartheta_{K_j}$, by taking couples in the lattice spanned by $(\alpha_{j,k'}, 1)$ and $(k', 0)$. When both $|b^d f_j(a/b)|/k'$ and $|a - bm|$ are $k'^{\tilde{\nu}_i}$-smooth, which can be checked using ECM, we have a couple (a, b) such that simultaneously

$$a - bm = \prod_l l^{e_{\mathcal{U}'_j, l}} \qquad l \leq k'^{\tilde{\nu}_i} \text{ prime numbers}, \tag{10}$$

$$(a - b\alpha_j)\vartheta_{K_j} = \mathcal{U}'_j \prod_{\mathcal{U}_j} \mathcal{U}_j^{m_{\mathcal{U}'_j, \mathcal{U}_j}} \quad \text{Norm}(\mathcal{U}_j) \leq k'^{\tilde{\nu}_i}, \mathcal{U}_j \text{ good prime ideals.} \tag{11}$$

Similarly as before, equality (11) implies that

$$\log_g \pi_j(a - b\alpha_j) \equiv \mathcal{X}_{\mathcal{U}'_j} + \sum_{\mathcal{U}_j} \mathcal{X}_{\mathcal{U}_j} m_{\mathcal{U}'_j, \mathcal{U}_j} + \sum_{k=1}^{r_j} \mathcal{X}_{j,k}\lambda_{j,k}(a - b\alpha_j) \pmod{q} ,$$

where $\mathcal{U}_j$ runs over ideals as in (11). Combining this with (10) yields

$$\mathcal{X}_{\mathcal{U}_j'} \equiv \sum_l e_{\mathcal{U}_j',l} \log_g l - \sum_{\mathcal{U}_j} \mathcal{X}_{\mathcal{U}_j} m_{\mathcal{U}_j',\mathcal{U}_j} - \sum_{k=1}^{r_j} \mathcal{X}_{j,k} \lambda_{j,k}(a - b\alpha_j) \pmod{q},$$

with l prime numbers as in (10) and $\mathcal{U}_j$ prime ideals as in (11).

Deduced as with the reduction of numbers, time-cost of a reduction for ideals with norm $k' \in [B_2, M]$ is $L_p[\frac{1}{3}, \frac{2}{3\gamma\tilde{\nu}_1\delta} + \frac{\tilde{e}_1\delta}{3\gamma\tilde{\nu}_1} + \frac{\delta}{6\tilde{\nu}_1}]$, which doesn't exceed $L_p[\frac{1}{3}, 3^{1/3}]$ for a choice $0.9308\ldots = \frac{4+\delta^2\gamma+3^{1/3}\delta^2}{6\delta\gamma 3^{1/3}} \leq \tilde{\nu}_1 < 1$. For ideals with larger norm the reduction takes time $L_p[\frac{1}{3}, \frac{\delta}{6\tilde{\nu}_2} + 2\sqrt{\nu_2\tilde{\nu}_2}\left(\frac{1}{3}\right)^{2/3}]$, which is minimal for $\tilde{\nu}_2 = \left(\delta^2/(12\nu_2 b_2)\right)^{1/3} < 1$, and time-cost is then equal to $L_p[\frac{1}{3}, 0.9658\ldots]$.

Remark that for a choice $(1 >)\tilde{\nu}_1 \geq \frac{4+\delta^2\gamma+x\delta^2}{6\delta\gamma x} = 0.9967\ldots$ with $x = 1.1338\ldots$, time for the reduction of an ideal with norm $k' \in [B_2, M]$ will be $\leq L_p[\frac{1}{3}, 1.1338\ldots]$.

Remark. This strategy of 'reducing' can also be used with the classical Number Field Sieve setting, where only one polynomial is used at the algebraic side. In a similar way as above, one can show that the reduction of a number l or a prime ideal $\mathcal{U}$ with $\text{Norm}(\mathcal{U}) = l$ takes time $L_p[\frac{1}{3}, (\frac{3}{2})^{1/3}] = L_p[\frac{1}{3}, 1.1447\ldots]$ if $L_p[\frac{1}{2}, c_m] \leq l < L_p[\frac{2}{3}, (\frac{1}{3})^{1/3}]$ by taking $\nu = (1/2)^{2/3}$. Since for smaller medium-sized l time needed for a reduction can be made less than $L_p[\frac{1}{3}, (\frac{3}{2})^{1/3}]$ by taking $(1 >)\nu \geq (2^{1/3}6 + 6^{1/3}8 + 24^{1/3}3)/36$, this is the most time consuming reduction. We've shown above that the most time-consuming reduction in our many polynomial case has time cost $L_p[\frac{1}{3}, 1.1338\ldots]$. Hence, the most expensive reduction in the one polynomial variant takes more time than the most expensive reduction in our case. The algorithm to separately compute individual logarithms after the pre-computation is done with the original Number Field Sieve setting, using the idea of reductions, is the same as the one above and has the same running time, namely $L_p[\frac{1}{3}, 3^{1/3}]$. Thus, asymptotically there is no difference in time-usage between the one or more polynomial setting to calculate individual logarithms once the pre-computation has been executed (recall however that the pre-computation is more expensive with the one polynomial setting!).

Reductions: An Example. Suppose we want to find discrete logarithms in $\mathbb{F}_{83}^*$ to the base $g = 2$. Take $d = 2$ and $m = 30$. Set $f(X) = X^2 + 13$, since for this irreducible polynomial, we have $f(30) \equiv 0 \pmod{83}$ and neither $p = 83$ nor $q = 41$ divide the discriminant -52 of f. Hence, we work in the extension field $\mathbb{Q}(\sqrt{-13})$, for which it is known that $\vartheta = \vartheta_{\mathbb{Q}(\sqrt{-13})} = \mathbb{Z} + \sqrt{-13}\mathbb{Z}$, such that $[\vartheta, \mathbb{Z}[\sqrt{-13}]] = 1$. The unity rank of ϑ is 0, such that no maps λ_j are needed. Note that in fact $\vartheta^* = \{-1, 1\}$, such that it holds that $\{u \in \vartheta^* \mid u \equiv 1 \bmod 41^2\} \subseteq (\vartheta^*)^{41}$. Further on, we have $h_{\mathbb{Q}(\sqrt{-13})} = 2$, thus $h_{\mathbb{Q}(\sqrt{-13})}$ is co-prime with 41.

Let $\bar{t} = t + p\mathbb{Z} \in \mathbb{F}_p$ for every $t \in \mathbb{Z}$. Denote with $\mathcal{U}_{l,r}$ the degree one prime ideal generated by the prime number l and $-r + \sqrt{-13}$ for $r \in \mathbb{N}$. We take smoothness-bound $B_1 = 19$ at the rational side, and smoothness-bound $B_2 = 17$

at the algebraic side. Let S be the set of all good degree one prime ideals with norm ≤ 17. Suppose the pre-computation stage is executed.

Suppose we have to calculate $\log_g \overline{71}$. We use a reduction of the number 71. Take $\nu = 0.91$. For the coprime integers $a = 1, b = -26$, we have that

$$(1 + 26 \times 30)/71 = 11 \quad \text{and} \quad \text{Norm}(1 + 26\sqrt{-13}) = 1 + 13 \times 26^2 = 11 \times 17 \times 47$$

are simultaneously $71^{0.91}$-smooth. The conditions for $\text{Norm}(1 + 26\sqrt{-13})$ to be coprime with 41 and $[\vartheta, \mathbb{Z}[\sqrt{-13}]]$ are fulfilled, so Proposition 2 implies that

$$1 + 26 \times 30 = 71 \times 11,$$
$$(1 + 26\sqrt{-13})\vartheta = \mathcal{U}_{11,8}\mathcal{U}_{17,15}\mathcal{U}_{47,9},$$

simultaneously. This leads to the result that

$$\log_g \overline{71} \equiv \mathcal{X}_{\mathcal{U}_{11,8}} + \mathcal{X}_{\mathcal{U}_{17,15}} + \mathcal{X}_{\mathcal{U}_{47,9}} - \log_g \overline{11} \pmod{41}. \tag{12}$$

In this expression for $\log_g \overline{71}$, $\mathcal{X}_{\mathcal{U}_{47,9}}$ is (the only) unknown.

Let $\nu' = 0.8$. Applying the Gaussian Algorithm, we find a short vector $(2, -5)$ in the lattice spanned by $(9, 1)$ and $(47, 0)$, for which we know $\mathcal{U}_{47,9}$ divides $(a - b\sqrt{-13})\vartheta$ for elements (a, b). Since $\text{Norm}(2 + 5\sqrt{-13})$ is coprime with 41 and $[\vartheta, \mathbb{Z}[\sqrt{-13}]]$ and since $\text{Norm}(2 + 5\sqrt{-13})/47 = (2^2 + 13 \times 5^2)/47 = 7$ and $2 + 5 \times 30 = 2^3 \times 19$ are both $47^{0.8}$-smooth, we use $(2, -5)$ to reduce $\mathcal{U}_{47,9}$. Proposition 2 implies that simultaneously

$$2 + 5 \times 30 = 2^3 \times 19,$$
$$(2 + 5\sqrt{-13})\vartheta_{\mathbb{Q}(\sqrt{13})} = \mathcal{U}_{7,1}\mathcal{U}_{47,9},,$$

what results in the expression

$$\mathcal{X}_{\mathcal{U}_{47,9}} \equiv 3\log_g \overline{2} + \log_g \overline{19} - \mathcal{X}_{\mathcal{U}_{7,1}}$$
$$\equiv 3 + 6 - 32 \equiv 18 \pmod{41},$$

where $\mathcal{X}_{\mathcal{U}_{7,1}} \equiv 32 \pmod{41}$ and $\log_g \overline{19} \equiv 6 \pmod{41}$ were pre-computed.

Getting back to computation (12) of $\log_g \overline{71}$, we see that

$$\log_g \overline{71} \equiv 34 + 5 + 18 - 24 \equiv 33 \pmod{41},$$

where $\mathcal{X}_{\mathcal{U}_{11,8}} \equiv 34$, $\mathcal{X}_{\mathcal{U}_{17,15}} \equiv 5$, $\log_g \overline{11} \equiv 24 \pmod{41}$ were pre-computed. One can check that indeed $2^{33} \equiv 71 \pmod{83}$. Remark that the above expression for $\log_g \overline{71}$ is exactly expression (9) for this particular case.

4.3   Running Time Analysis Individual Logarithm

We analyze the time needed to perform step 2 of the algorithm. Set $\nu = \max \{\nu_1, \nu_2, \tilde{\nu}_1, \tilde{\nu}_2\}$. When a number or a prime ideal is reduced, (7) or respectively (10) introduces $O((\ln p/ \ln \ln p)^{1/3})$ new medium-sized prime numbers $B_1 \leq l < L_p[\frac{2}{3}, (\frac{1}{3})^{1/3}]$ with unknown logarithms. Via (8) or (11), any reduction will also invoke $O((\ln p/\ln \ln p)^{2/3})$ new medium-sized prime ideals $\mathcal{U}_j$ (ideals for which $B_2 \leq \text{Norm}(\mathcal{U}_j) < L_p[\frac{2}{3}, (\frac{1}{3})^{1/3}])$ for which $\mathcal{X}_{\mathcal{U}_j}$ is unknown. Let Z be the maximal number of the total of new unknowns induced by one reduction, thus $Z = O((\ln p/\ln \ln p)^{2/3})$. To calculate $\log_g q_i$ for q_i as in (6), $1 + Z + Z^2 + \ldots + Z^{\tilde{w}-1} \leq Z^{\tilde{w}}$ reduction-steps will be needed to get all $\log_g l$ and $\mathcal{X}_{\mathcal{U}_j}$ in the original factorbase, where $\tilde{w}$ is a natural number such that $q_i^{\nu^{\tilde{w}}} \leq B_2$. Since $q_i \leq L_p[\frac{2}{3}, (\frac{1}{3})^{1/3}]$, it suffices to find $\tilde{w}$ such that $L_p[\frac{2}{3}, (\frac{1}{3})^{1/3}]^{\nu^{\tilde{w}}} \leq B_2$ or, in other words, such that $\nu^{\tilde{w}} \ln L_p[\frac{2}{3}, (\frac{1}{3})^{1/3}] \leq \ln B_2$. Since this holds for $\tilde{w} \geq \frac{1}{\ln \nu} \ln \frac{\ln B_2}{\ln L_p[\frac{2}{3}, (\frac{1}{3})^{1/3}]} = O(\ln \ln p)$, we can take $\tilde{w} = O(\ln \ln p)$. Hence, the number of reductions won't exceed

$$O((\ln p/\ln \ln p)^{2/3})^{O(\ln \ln p)} = e^{O((\ln \ln p)^2)} .$$

Combining all results of the reductions into the value $\log_g q_i \pmod{q}$ uses time $O((\ln p)^3)e^{O((\ln \ln p)^2)} \approx e^{O((\ln \ln p)^2)}$.

Let c be the constant such that time cost for the most expensive reduction is $L_p[\frac{1}{3}, c]$. It takes time at most

$$L_p[\frac{1}{3}, c]e^{O((\ln \ln p)^2)} + e^{O((\ln \ln p)^2)} = L_p[\frac{1}{3}, c]$$

to compute $\log_g q_i$ for a medium-sized number q_i, so all desired unknown logarithms in (6) can be determined in time $O((\ln p/\ln \ln p)^{\frac{2}{3}})L_p[\frac{1}{3}, c] = L_p[\frac{1}{3}, c]$.

We conclude that the total running time for the individual logarithm algorithm is $L_p[\frac{1}{3}, \max\{3^{1/3}, c\}]$. By choosing parameters as described above, c can be taken not to exceed $3^{1/3}$. Hence, given the results of the pre-computation stage, a calculation of an individual logarithm takes time $L_p[\frac{1}{3}, 3^{1/3}] = L_p[\frac{1}{3}, 1.44225\ldots]$.

5   The Algorithm of Joux and Lercier

To make a running time analysis of the method in [6], we describe the algorithm as we understood it, using the theoretical background we developed before, introducing constants $s_d, s_\alpha, s_\beta, s_l, s_k, c_d, c_\alpha, c_\beta, c_l, c_k \in \mathbb{R}$, which we determine to get a minimal running time. Assume that the optimal degree d behaves as $d = c_d(1 + o(1))(\ln p/\ln \ln p)^{s_d}$.

Choose d such that $d + 1$ is a prime number. Let f_β be an irreducible polynomial of degree $d + 1$ with root μ in $\mathbb{F}_p$ and coefficients of order $O(1)$, such that its Galois group has order $d + 1$. Take f_α an irreducible polynomial of degree d such that $f_\alpha(\mu) \equiv 0 \pmod{p}$. By construction, the coefficients of this polynomial are of order $p^{1/(d+1)} = L_p[1 - s_d, 1/c_d]$. In general, f_α isn't monic. For ease of exposition however, we assume f_α and f_β to be monic. Let α and β be roots of f_α, f_β respectively. The ring of algebraic integers in $\mathbb{Q}(\alpha)$, respectively $\mathbb{Q}(\beta)$, is denoted as ϑ_α, respectively ϑ_β. Let r_α, respectively r_β, be the torsion-free rank of ϑ_α^*, respectively ϑ_β^*. At the side of f_α, respectively f_β, we work with smoothness-bound $B_\alpha = L_p[s_\alpha, c_\alpha]$, respectively $B_\beta = L_p[s_\beta, c_\beta]$. Let S_α, respectively S_β, denote the set of degree one prime ideals in ϑ_α, respectively ϑ_β, with norm less then B_α, respectively B_β. Denote $\lambda_{\mathbb{Q}(\alpha),j} = \lambda_j$. Let g denote a generator of $\mathbb{F}_p^*$.

Let $L = L_p[s_l, c_l]$. Sieving coprime pairs (a, b) with $|a| \leq L$, $1 \leq b \leq L$, appropriate for the algorithm in [6], takes asymptotic time ([10],[19])

$$L_p[s_\alpha, c_\alpha] + L_p[s_\beta, c_\beta] + L_p[s_l, 2c_l] \quad,$$

and results in pairs (a, b) such that simultaneously

$$(a + b\alpha)\vartheta_\alpha = \prod_{P \in S_\alpha} P^{e_{(a,b),P}} \quad, \tag{13}$$

$$(a + b\beta)\vartheta_\beta = \prod_{Q \in S_\beta} Q^{e_{(a,b),Q}} \quad. \tag{14}$$

Since, using Theorem 1, the probability for $|\text{Norm}(a - b\beta)|$ to be B_β-smooth, for $|\text{Norm}(a - b\alpha)|$ to be B_α-smooth respectively, is estimated as $L_p[s_l + s_d - s_\beta, -(s_l+s_d-s_\beta)c_d c_l/c_\beta]$ and as $L_p[s_1 - s_\alpha, -(s_1-s_\alpha)c_1/c_\alpha]$ respectively, where $s_1 = \max\{1 - s_d, s_l + s_d\}$ and $c_1 = 1/c_d, c_d c_l + 1/c_d$ or $c_d c_l$ if respectively $s_l <, =$ or $> 1 - 2s_d$, the condition to have $|S_\alpha| + |S_\beta| + r_\alpha + r_\beta + O(1)$ surviving pairs, becomes the following on the parameters s:

$$s_l \geq s_\alpha \ , \ s_l \geq s_\beta \ , \ s_l \geq s_l + s_d - s_\beta \ , \ s_l \geq 1 - s_d - s_\alpha \ , \ s_l \geq s_l + s_d - s_\alpha \ . \tag{15}$$

Once these parameters are determined, we get conditions on the constants c.

Assume conditions as in [20] are fulfilled. Let $\mathcal{X}_P$, $\mathcal{X}_j$ be the so called virtual logarithms. According to [20] and using (13), every couple (a, b) invokes an immediate congruence

$$\log_g(a + b\mu) \equiv \sum_{P \in S_\alpha} e_{(a,b),P} \mathcal{X}_P + \sum_{j=1}^{r_\alpha} \lambda_j(a + b\alpha)\mathcal{X}_j \pmod{q} \ . \tag{16}$$

Since the polynomial f_β has very small coefficients, it is assumed that the resulting number field has a simple structure, namely that the class field number is 1, and that all fundamental units of ϑ_β can be computed. A similar approach as in [17] can then be used. (Note however that if this approach would run too slowly, one can continue as on the f_α-side, as shown in [20].) For every Q in S_β, let $Q = \gamma_Q \vartheta_\beta$ with $\gamma_Q \in \vartheta_\beta$ and U the set of fundamental units in ϑ_β. Expression (14) leads to

$$\log_g(a + b\mu) \equiv \sum_{u \in U} e_{(a,b),u} \log_g \overline{u} + \sum_{Q \in S_\beta} e_{(a,b),Q} \log_g \overline{\gamma_Q} \pmod{q} \ . \tag{17}$$

Combining (16) and (17) now yields $|S_\alpha| + |S_\beta| + r_\alpha + r_\beta + O(1)$ equations

$$\sum_{P \in S_\alpha} e_{(a,b),P} \mathcal{X}_P + \sum_{j=1}^{r_\alpha} \lambda_j(a - b\alpha)\mathcal{X}_j \equiv$$
$$\sum_{u \in U} e_{(a,b),u} \log_g \overline{u} + \sum_{Q \in S_\beta} e_{(a,b),Q} \log_g \overline{\gamma_Q} \pmod{q}$$

in unknowns $\mathcal{X}_P$, $\mathcal{X}_j$, $\log_g \overline{\gamma_Q}$ and $\log_g \overline{u}$. This sparse system is solved for its unknowns in time $L_p[s_\alpha, 2c_\alpha] + L_p[s_\beta, 2c_\beta]$, using a sparse matrix technique. In order to get a unique non-zero solution of the system, we set $\log_g \overline{\gamma_Q} = 1$ for a $Q \in S_\beta$ such that $\overline{\gamma_Q}$ is a generator in $\mathbb{F}_p^*$. This ends the pre-computation stage. The running time for this stage is optimal for parameters $s_\alpha = s_\beta = s_d = s_l = \frac{1}{3}$, $c_\alpha = c_\beta = c_l = \left(\frac{8}{9}\right)^{1/3}$, $c_d = \left(\frac{3}{8}\right)^{1/3}$ and then equals $L_p[\frac{1}{3}, \left(\frac{64}{9}\right)^{1/3}]$.

Set $K = L_p[s_k, c_k]$. To find an individual logarithm $\log_a b \pmod{p-1}$ for $a, b \in \mathbb{F}_p^*$ and a a generator of $\mathbb{F}_p^*$, the following procedure for $y = a$ and $y = b$ is executed. Let s be the largest small prime whose logarithm can be computed from the factor bases. Set $z = s^i y \mod p$ for $i = 1$. (Increase i if no good representation can be found.) Use lattice basis reduction to find quotients

$$z \equiv \frac{a_0 + a_1\mu + \cdots + a_d\mu^d}{b_0 + b_1\mu + \cdots + b_d\mu^d} \pmod{p}, \tag{18}$$

where $a_0, a_1, \ldots, a_d, b_0, b_1, \ldots, b_d$ are integers of size $O(p^{1/(2d+2)})$ such that $\gcd(a_0, a_1, \ldots, a_d) = \gcd(b_0, b_1, \ldots, b_d) = 1$. Check whether both $|\mathrm{Norm}(a_0 + a_1\beta + \cdots + a_d\beta^d)|$ and $|\mathrm{Norm}(b_0 + b_1\beta + \cdots + b_d\beta^d)|$ are coprime with the index $[\vartheta_\beta, \mathbb{Z}[\beta]]$ and K-smooth, using a $L_p[\frac{s_k}{2}, \sqrt{2s_k c_k}]$-costing ECM-test. From Proposition 2 of [21], applied for $h_1(X) = a_0 + a_1 X + \cdots + a_d X^d$ and $h_2(X) = b_0 + b_1 X + \cdots + b_d X^d$, it follows that both norms are $\leq L_p[s_d, \frac{3s_d c_d}{2}]L_p[1, \frac{1}{2}] = L_p[1, \frac{1}{2}]$. Using Theorem 1, we see that the probability for these numbers to be simultaneously K-smooth is $L_p[1 - s_k, -\frac{1-s_k}{c_k}]$. Since the lattice-reduction only costs time $L_p[0, 3]$, we conclude that finding a good representation of z takes time $L_p[1 - s_k, \frac{1-s_k}{c_k}]L_p[\frac{s_k}{2}, \sqrt{2s_k c_k}]$, which is minimal for $s_k = 2/3$, $c_k = (1/3)^{1/3}$ and then equals $L_p[\frac{1}{3}, 3^{1/3}]$. We show that the time needed to execute the rest of the individual logarithm algorithm is less.

One can easily show that the ideals $(a_0 + a_1\beta + \cdots + a_d\beta^d)\vartheta_\beta$ and $(b_0 + b_1\beta + \cdots + b_d\beta^d)\vartheta_\beta$ split completely into first degree prime ideals. Thus,

$$(a_0 + a_1\beta + \cdots + a_d\beta^d)\vartheta_\beta = \prod_{Q \in \tilde{S}_\beta} Q^{v_Q} ,$$
$$(b_0 + b_1\beta + \cdots + b_d\beta^d)\vartheta_\beta = \prod_{Q \in \tilde{S}_\beta} Q^{w_Q} ,$$

for $\tilde{S}_\beta$ a set of degree one prime ideals in ϑ_β with norm less then K. These equalities imply the equations

$$\log_g(a_0 + a_1\mu + \cdots + a_d\mu^d) \equiv \sum_{u \in U} e_{v,u} \log_g \overline{u} + \sum_{Q \in \tilde{S}_\beta} v_Q \log_g \overline{\gamma_Q} \pmod{q} ,$$
$$\log_g(b_0 + b_1\mu + \cdots + b_d\mu^d) \equiv \sum_{u \in U} e_{w,u} \log_g \overline{u} + \sum_{Q \in \tilde{S}_\beta} w_Q \log_g \overline{\gamma_Q} \pmod{q} .$$

Remark that $\log_g \overline{\gamma_Q}$ is unknown for all $Q \in \tilde{S}_\beta \setminus S_\beta$. To find these unknown logarithms, we reduce the ideal Q in a similar way as described above, searching numbers a, b in an appropriate lattice such that $| b^{d+1} f_\beta(a/b) | / \mathrm{Norm}(Q)(\in \mathbb{Z})$ and $| b^d f_\alpha(a/b) |$ are simultaneously $\mathrm{Norm}(Q)^\nu$- smooth for a $\nu < 1$. Medium-sized prime ideals at the f_α-side are reduced similarly. One can check that the asymptotical running time for the reduction of prime ideals Q (at any side) with $L_p[\frac{1}{2}, c_m] < \mathrm{Norm}(Q) \leq L_p[\frac{2}{3}, (\frac{1}{3})^{1/3}]$ is minimal for $\nu = (1/2)^{2/3}$ and then equals $L_p[\frac{1}{3}, (\frac{3}{2})^{1/3}]$. By taking $\nu \geq (4 + 4^{1/3})/256^{1/3}$, time for the reduction of an ideal Q (at any side) with $B_\alpha = B_\beta < \mathrm{Norm}(Q) \leq L_p[\frac{1}{2}, c_m]$ is less then $L_p[\frac{1}{3}, (\frac{3}{2})^{1/3}]$, where c_m is a constant. Following an analogous reasoning as in Section 4.3, one can then see that all unknown $\log_g \overline{\gamma_Q}$ in the above equalities can be determined in time $L_p[\frac{1}{3}, (\frac{3}{2})^{1/3}]$.

Finally, compute $\log_g y$ as

$$\log_g y \equiv -i \log_g s + \log_g (a_0 + a_1 \mu + \cdots + a_d \mu^d) - \log_g (b_0 + b_1 \mu + \cdots + b_d \mu^d) \ (\bmod \ q),$$

(see (18)) and then determine the asked for $\log_a b \ (\bmod \ p - 1)$ in the same way as in the former individual logarithm algorithm, thus costing time $O(\ln^3 p)$.

We conclude that a seperate individual logarithm stage takes asymptotic time $L_p[\frac{1}{3}, 3^{1/3}]$, after a $L_p[\frac{1}{3}, (\frac{64}{9})^{1/3}]$-costing pre-computation stage .

Acknowledgement

The paper was partially written when Professor I.Semaev was staying at the Department of Mathematics, Section Algebra, Catholic University of Leuven under the project Flanders FWO G.0186.02.

We want to thank the anonymous referees for their very detailed and valuable comments.

References

1. Canfield, E., Erdös, P., Pomerance, C.: On a problem of Oppenheim concerning "factorisatio numerorum". J.Number Theory **17** (1983) 1–28
2. Coppersmith, D.: Fast Evaluation of Logarithms in Fields of Characteristic Two. IEEE Transactions on Information Theory IT-30 (1984) 587–594
3. Coppersmith, D.: Modifications to the Number Field Sieve. J. Cryptology **6** (1993) 169–180
4. Coppersmith, D., Odlyzko, A., Schroeppel, R.: Discrete logarithms in $GF(p)$. Algorithmica **1** (1986) 1–15
5. Gordon, D.: Discrete logarithms in $GF(p)$ using the number field sieve. SIAM Journal of Discrete Mathematics **6** (1993) 124–138
6. Joux, A., Lercier, R.: Improvements to the general Number Field Sieve for discrete logarithms in prime fields. Mathematics of Computation **72** (2003) 953–967
7. Joux, A., Lercier, R.: Calcul de logarithmes discrets dans $GF(p)$ — 130 chiffres. CRYPTO Mailing List (6/2005)
8. Lenstra, A., Lenstra, H. (eds): The Development of the Number Field Sieve. Lecture Notes in Mathematics **1554** , Springer-Verlag, 1993
9. Lenstra, H.: Factoring integers with elliptic curves. Annals of Mathematics **126** (1987) 649–673
10. Matyukhin, D.: On asymptotic complexity of computing discrete logarithms over $GF(p)$. Discrete Mathematics and Applications **13** (2003) 27–50
11. McCurley, K.: The discrete logarithm problem, in: Pomerance,C. (ed): Cryptography and Computational Number Theory. Proc. Symp.Appl.Math. **42**, Amer. Math. Soc.,1990, 49–74

12. Odlyzko, A.: Discrete logarithms: The past and the future. Designs, Codes and Cryptography **19** (2000), 129–145.
13. Odlyzko, A.: Discrete Logarithms and Smooth Polynomials, in: Mullen, G., Shiue, P. (eds): Finite Fields: Theory, Applications and Algorithms. Contemporary Math **168**, Amer. Math. Soc.,1994, 269–278
14. Odlyzko, A.: Discrete logarithms in finite fields and their cryptographic significance, in: Beth, T.,Cot, N., Ingemarsson, I. (eds): Advances in Cryptology: Proceedings of Eurocrypt '84. Lecture Notes in Computer Science **208**, Springer-Verlag,1985,224–314
15. Odlyzko, A.: On the complexity of Computing Discrete Logarithms and Factoring Integers, in: Cover,T. and Gopinath,B. (eds.): Open Problems in Communication and Computation. Springer, 1987, 113-116
16. Pollard, J.: Monte Carlo methods for index computations mod p. Mathematics of Computation **32** (1978) 918–924
17. Pollard, J.: Factoring with cubic integers, in:[8].Springer-Verlag, 1993, 4–10
18. Pomerance, C.: Fast, rigorous factorization and discrete logarithm algorithms, in: Nozaki, N., Johnson, D., Nishizaki, T.,Wilf, H.(eds): Discrete Algorithms and Complexity. Academic Press, 1987, 119–143
19. Schirokauer, O.: Discrete logarithms and local units. Philosophical Transactions of the Royal Society of London (A) **345** (1993) 409–423
20. Schirokauer, O.: Virtual Logarithms. Journal of Algorithms **57** (2005) 140–147
21. Semaev, I.: Special prime numbers and discrete logs in prime finite fields. Mathematics of Computation **71** (2002) 363–377
22. Shoup, V.: Searching for primitive roots in finite fields. Mathematics of Computation **58** (1992) 918–924
23. van Oorschot, P., Wiener, M.: Parallel collision search with cryptanalytic applications. J. Cryptology **12** (1999) 1–28
24. Wiedemann, D.: Solving sparse linear equations over finite fields. IEEE Trans.Inform. Theory **32** (1986) 54–62

Efficient Scalar Multiplication
by Isogeny Decompositions

Christophe Doche[1], Thomas Icart[2], and David R. Kohel[3]

[1] Department of Computing,
Macquarie University, Australia
doche@ics.mq.edu.au
[2] Laboratoire d'Informatique de l'École Polytechnique, France
thomas.icart@polytechnique.org
[3] School of Mathematics and Statistics, University of Sydney, Australia
kohel@maths.usyd.edu.au

Abstract. On an elliptic curve, the degree of an isogeny corresponds essentially to the degrees of the polynomial expressions involved in its application. The multiplication–by–ℓ map $[\ell]$ has degree ℓ^2, therefore the complexity to directly evaluate $[\ell](P)$ is $O(\ell^2)$. For a small prime $\ell (= 2, 3)$ such that the additive binary representation provides no better performance, this represents the true cost of application of scalar multiplication. If an elliptic curve admits an isogeny φ of degree ℓ then the costs of computing $\varphi(P)$ should in contrast be $O(\ell)$ field operations. Since we then have a product expression $[\ell] = \hat{\varphi}\varphi$, the existence of an ℓ-isogeny φ on an elliptic curve yields a theoretical improvement from $O(\ell^2)$ to $O(\ell)$ field operations for the evaluation of $[\ell](P)$ by naïve application of the defining polynomials. In this work we investigate actual improvements for small ℓ of this asymptotic complexity. For this purpose, we describe the general construction of families of curves with a suitable decomposition $[\ell] = \hat{\varphi}\varphi$, and provide explicit examples of such a family of curves with simple decomposition for [3]. Finally we derive a new tripling algorithm to find complexity improvements to triplication on a curve in certain projective coordinate systems, then combine this new operation to non-adjacent forms for ℓ-adic expansions in order to obtain an improved strategy for scalar multiplication on elliptic curves.

Keywords: Elliptic curve cryptography, fast arithmetic, efficiently computable isogenies, efficient tripling, ℓ-adic NAF$_w$.

1 Introduction

Given an elliptic curve E/K, together with a point $P \in E(K)$ and an integer k, the efficient computation of the scalar multiple $[k]P$ is central in elliptic curve cryptography. Many ways to speed up this computation have been actively researched. For instance, one can cite

- the use of alternative representations for the scalar multiple k (non-adjacent forms [MO90, CMO97, TYW04], ternary/binary approach [CJLM05], or the Dual Base Number System [DJM99, CS05]).

M. Yung et al. (Eds.): PKC 2006, LNCS 3958, pp. 191–206, 2006.

- the improvement of existing operations by use of other systems of coordinates (projective , weighted projective [CMO98]) and the introduction of new basic operations like $[2]P \pm Q$, $[3]P$, $[3]P \pm Q$, $[4]P$, $[4P] \pm Q$ (see [CJLM05, DIM05]).
- the use of endomorphisms (first on a singular curve that appeared to be insecure [MV90], later with Koblitz curves [Kob92, Sol00, Lan05] and GLV curves [GLV01, CLSQ03]).

See [ACD+05, chaps. 9, 13, and 15] and [HMV03] for a more comprehensive description of all the techniques involved.

The purpose of this article is to investigate new and more efficient ways to compute the multiplication–by–ℓ map. Our method relies on the use of isogenies but is different from the one developped in [BJ03]. Indeed, given an integer $\ell \geqslant 2$, it is possible in some cases and for well chosen families of curves to split the map $[\ell]$ as the product of two isogenies. A direct computation of $[\ell]P$ involves the evaluation of rational polynomials of degree ℓ^2. The interest of this approach is that the isogenies φ and $\hat{\varphi}$ such that $[\ell] = \hat{\varphi}\varphi$ will be both of degree ℓ. Therefore it should be possible to obtain more efficient formulas to compute $[\ell]$ this way. We investigate this idea for small values of ℓ, especially 2 and 3 and obtain a more efficient tripling leading to a very fast scalar multiplication algorithm.

2   Splitting Multiplication by ℓ

In this section we describe the definitions and background results for existence and construction of an ℓ-isogeny φ such that $[\ell] = \hat{\varphi}\varphi$.

2.1   Subgroup (Schemes) Defined over K

Let E be an elliptic curve over a field K, with defining equation

$$F(x,y) = y^2 + (a_1 x + a_3)y - (x^3 + a_2 x^2 + a_4 x + a_6) = 0.$$

We give an elementary background on concepts and conditions for torsion subgroups to be defined over the base field K.

Definition 2.1. *Let N be an integer greater than 1 and let $E[N]$ be the group of N-torsion points in $\overline{K}$. A torsion subgroup G of $E[N]$ is said to be defined over K or to be K-rational if $G\backslash\{O\}$ is the zero set of a finite set of polynomials $\{f_1(x,y), \ldots, f_n(x,y)\}$ in $K[x,y]/\big(F(x,y)\big)$.*

A torsion subgroup can be specified by two polynomials, one of which is the polynomial $\psi_G(x)$ whose roots are the x-coordinates of the points $P = (x,y)$ in G. If N is odd, then this polynomial suffices to define the torsion subgroup. If N is even, then the full ideal of polynomials which have zeros on G cannot be specified as a single polynomial in x. As an example, if $G = \{O, (x_0, y_0)\}$, where (x_0, y_0) is a 2-torsion point, then G is determined as the zero set of the polynomial $x - x_0$, but both $y - y_0$ and $2y + a_1 x + a_3$ are zero on $\{(x_0, y_0)\}$, but are not in the ideal $(x - x_0)$.

From the odd case, we see that the condition for a subgroup to be K-rational is not that the points have coefficients in K, but that the symmetric functions in these coefficients must lie in K. Since every finite subgroup G of $E(\overline{K})$ is the kernel of an isogeny $\varphi_G : E \to E'$, the question of whether the subgroup can be defined over K, is related to the K-rationality of the isogeny φ_G. The following classical theorem states that these concepts are equivalent.

Theorem 2.1. *A finite subgroup G of E is K-rational if and only if G is the kernel of an isogeny $\psi : E \to E'$ defined over K.*

Since the subgroup $E[N]$ of $E(\overline{K})$ is the kernel of the scalar multiplication $[N]$, which is defined over K, we obtain:

Corollary 2.1. *Every torsion subgroup $E[N]$ is K-rational.*

The defining polynomials for the N-torsion subgroups are the *division polynomials* $\psi_N(x, y)$, which are computable by explicit recursive formulas.

Corollary 2.2. *Let G and H be two finite K-rational subgroups of E. Then $G \cap H$ and $G + H$ are K-rational subgroups of E.*

Proof 2.1. The intersection property holds immediately since if G and H are the zero sets of $S = \{g_1, \ldots, g_r\}$, and $T = \{h_1, \ldots, h_s\}$, respectively, then $G \cap H$ is the zero set of $S \cup T$. To prove that $G + H$ is K-rational we apply the theorem to the isogeny $\varphi_{H'} \circ \varphi_G$ where $H' = \varphi_G(H)$.

Combining the previous two corollaries we obtain:

Corollary 2.3. *Suppose that E admits an isogeny $E \to E'$ with cyclic kernel of order N. Then $E[\ell]$ contains a rational subgroup of order ℓ for every ℓ dividing N.*

These corollaries permit us to find a product decomposition for any isogeny, or its defining kernel subgroup, into scalar multiplications $[\ell]$ (determined by $E[\ell]$) and isogenies of prime degree (given by a rational subgroup G of order ℓ), for primes ℓ dividing the degree of the isogeny. Since efficient algorithms for scalar multiplication $[\ell]$ by small primes have been well-investigated, in the next section we focus on isogenies of prime order ℓ which "split" the isogeny $[\ell]$ into a product of isogenies φ and $\hat{\varphi}$.

2.2   Parameterizations of Cyclic ℓ-Torsion Subgroups

The theory of modular curves gives a means of achieving explicit parameterizations of families of elliptic curves with the structure of an isogeny of degree ℓ. We describe the general background to this construction to motivate the examples.

It is well-known that the j-invariant of an elliptic curve E over any field K determines the isomorphism class of that curve over $\overline{K}$. Conversely, any value $j \neq 0, 12^3$ is the j-invariant of an elliptic curve

$$E_j : y^2 + xy = x^3 - \frac{36}{j - 12^3}x - \frac{1}{j - 12^3}.$$

The j-invariant can be identified with a generator of the function field $K(X(1))$ of the modular curve $X(1)$, classifying elliptic curves up to isomorphism. We view the above equation E_j as a family of elliptic curves over the "j-line" $X(1)\backslash\{0,1,\infty\} \cong \mathbb{A}^1\backslash\{0,1\}$.

In order to determine similar models for elliptic curves which admits an ℓ-isogeny, or equivalently a K-rational cyclic subgroup G of $E[\ell]$, we use the modular curves $X_0(\ell)$ covering $X(1)$.

For the values $\ell = 2, 3, 5, 7$, and 13 the curve $X_0(\ell)$ has genus 0, which means that there exists a modular function u on $X_0(\ell)$ such that $K\big(X_0(\ell)\big) = K(u)$. The covering $X_0(\ell) \to X(1)$ is determined by an inclusion of function fields $K\big(X(1)\big) \to K\big(X_0(\ell)\big)$, which means that we can express j as a rational function in u.

For the above values of ℓ, we may use quotients of the Dedekind η function on the upper half plane

$$u(q) = \left(\frac{\eta(\tau)}{\eta(\ell\tau)}\right)^r = q^{-1} \prod_{n=1}^{\infty} \left(\frac{1-q^n}{1-q^{n\ell}}\right)^r$$

where $r = 24/\gcd(12, \ell - 1)$ and $q = \exp(2\pi i\tau)$, to find a relation with the q-expansion $j(q)$ for the j-function to solve for the expression for the j-function. Substituting into the above equations we then twist the curve or make a change of variables to simplify the resulting equation to obtain the models for which the ℓ-torsion contains a parameterized rational subgroup of order ℓ (over $K(u)$ or over K for any particular value of u in K). The models used in the isogeny decompositions which follow may be derived by this technique, with the kernel polynomial determined by factorization of the ℓ-division polynomial of this curve.

2.3   Parameterized Models

Applying these ideas, we have built families of curves for which [2] or [3] splits into 2 isogenies of degree respectively 2 and 3. For instance, an elliptic curve defined over a field of characteristic different from 2 and 3 with a rational 3-torsion subgroup can be expressed in the form (up to twists):

$$E : y^2 = x^3 + 3u(x + 1)^2$$

with the 3-torsion subgroup defined by $x = 0$; we note that the curve E does not necessarily have a point of order 3. The image curve, under a certain 3-isogeny to be specified below, is defined by an equation:

$$E_t : y^2 = x^3 - u(3x - 4u + 9)^2.$$

Note that the same thing holds in characteristic 2. In fact, an elliptic curve with a rational 3-torsion subgroup can be expressed in the form (up to twists):

$$E : y^2 + (x + u)y = x^3.$$

It has a rational 3-torsion subgroup defined by $x = 0$. The image curve is defined by an equation:

$$E_t : y^2 + (x + u + 1)y = x^3 + x^2 + (u + 1)(x + u + 1).$$

Explicit formulas of the curves and isogenies to split [2] in characteristic greater than 2 and to split [3] in characteristic greater than 3 can be found in Section 3.

2.4   On Special Versus Generic Elliptic Curves

Since we propose curves of a particular form, it is relevant to make a distinction between curves of a special form and generic curves.

A family of elliptic curves is a parameterized equation of different elliptic curves $E/K(u_1, \ldots, u_t)$ in indeterminates $u_1, \ldots, u_t$. We say that a family of elliptic curves is *geometrically special* if, for $(u_1, \ldots, u_t) \in \overline{K}^n$, there exists a finite set of j-invariants of curves in the family. Otherwise, we say that the family is *geometrically general*. Standard examples of families are the family of elliptic curves $y^2 = x^3 + ax + b$, over $K(a, b)$ which is geometrically general, or the family of Koblitz curves $y^2 + xy = x^3 + ax^2 + 1$ over $\mathbb{F}_2(a)$ which are geometrically special.

Any family of curves obtained by the CM construction are geometrically special because there exists only a finite set of j-invariants for each fixed discriminant D. Even if D is allowed to vary, in practice there are only a finite set of candidates D with $|D|$ bounded by the time to compute a class polynomial for D. Similarly, any family of supersingular elliptic curves is geometrically special, since there are only finitely many j-invariants of supersingular elliptic curves.

The curves that we introduce lie in geometrically general families because their invariants give infinitely many j-invariants $j = j(u)$, and conversely, every j-invariant arises as $j(u)$ for some u in $\overline{K}$.

We say that a family is *arithmetically special* if the properties of the curves in the family are in some way special with respect to a random curve over K. This is more imprecise, but to make it more precise one should speak of an arithmetic invariant, like group order or discriminant of the endomorphism ring which can distinguish curves in the family and those outside of it. Every special construction will be arithmetically special. For instance, Jao et al. [JMV05] observe that curves produced by CM construction are arithmetically special and distinguished by properties of the discriminant of their endomorphism rings. By construction we build curves that are arithmetically special, since they all have a cyclic ℓ-isogeny. In contrast, a curve over a finite field has a 50% chance of such a rational ℓ-isogeny, and a curve with such a rational isogeny over a number field is exceptional. Supersingular elliptic curves are arithmetically special with respect to existence of rational isogenies: over a finite degree extension L/K, all $\ell + 1$ cyclic ℓ-isogenies for all ℓ become simultaneously L-rational.

Despite the fact that our families have arithmetically special ℓ-torsion, by virtue of the criterion by which they are constructed, for any prime $n \neq \ell$, the n-torsion and n-isogenies follow the general behavior, and we have no reason to expect any special properties of the group orders $|E(K)|$ for curves in our families, apart from the potential factors of ℓ which arise.

3   Efficiently Applicable Isogenies

Let us investigate at present how the multiplications by [2] and [3] can be efficiently split as a product of 2 isogenies in practice.

3.1   Elliptic Curves with Degree 2 Isogenies

An elliptic curve defined over a field $\mathbb{F}_q$ of characteristic $\neq 2$ with a rational 2-torsion subgroup can be expressed in the form (up to twists):

$$E : y^2 = x^3 + ux^2 + 16ux$$

with a 2-torsion point $(0,0)$. The corresponding isogeny of degree 2 is:

$$(x_1, y_1) \mapsto (x_t, y_t) = \left(x_1 + u\left(1 + \frac{16}{x_1}\right), \; y_1\left(1 - \frac{16u}{x_1^2}\right) \right),$$

to an image curve defined by an equation:

$$E_t : y^2 = x^3 - 2ux^2 + u(u - 64)x.$$

The isogeny dual to the first isogeny is given by

$$(x_t, y_t) \mapsto (x_2, y_2) = \left(\frac{1}{2^2}\left(x_t - 2u + \frac{u(u - 64)}{x_t}\right), \; \frac{1}{2^3}y_t\left(1 - \frac{u(u - 64)}{x_t^2}\right) \right).$$

The composition of these maps gives the multiplication–by–2 map on E.

A general quadratic twist of E can be put in the standard Weierstraß form by a change of variables (x, y) to $(x - \lambda u/3, y)$:

$$y^2 = x^3 + \lambda ux^2 + 16\lambda^2 ux \longrightarrow y^2 = x^3 - \lambda^2\frac{u(u - 48)}{3}x + \lambda^3\frac{u^2(2u - 144)}{27},$$

over any field of characteristic different form 2 or 3. Conversely, the elliptic curve $y^2 = x^3 + ax + b$ has j-invariant $j = 6912a^3/(4a^3 + 27b^2)$. The corresponding values for (λ, u) are $\lambda = -9b(u - 48)/\bigl(au(2u - 144)\bigr)$, where u is a root of the cubic polynomial $(u - 48)^3 - j(u - 64)$.

Effective scalar multiplication by splitting [2]. To take advantage of this splitting, let us introduce a new system of coordinates. Since they are similar to López-Dahab coordinates $(\mathcal{LD})$ introduced in characteristic 2, cf. [LD98], let us call them *modified López-Dahab coordinates* $(\mathcal{LD}^m)$. A point (x_1, y_1) in affine coordinates $(\mathcal{A})$ on the elliptic curve E will be represented by (X_1, Y_1, Z_1, Z_1^2) where $x_1 = X_1/Z_1$ and $y_1 = Y_1/Z_1^2$. It is a simple exercise to check that (X_2, Y_2, Z_2, Z_2^2) corresponding to $(x_2, y_2) = [2](x_1, y_1)$ is given by

$$
\begin{aligned}
A &= X_1^2, & B &= X_1^2 - 16uZ_1^2, & Y_t &= Y_1 \times B, \\
X_2 &= B^2, & Z_2 &= 4Y_1^2, & C &= X_1^2 \times uZ_1^2, \\
D &= Z_2^2, & E &= u(Z_2 - 4C), & Y_2 &= Y_t\bigl(2X_2 + E + 256C\bigr).
\end{aligned}
$$

The number of elementary operations needed to obtain (X_2, Y_2, Z_2, Z_2^2) is thus $5M + 4S$, where M and S respectively denotes the cost of a multiplication and a squaring in the field $\mathbb{F}_q$. However, if u is chosen so that a multiplication by u is negligible, the costs for a doubling drop to $3M + 4S$. Note that it is sufficient to choose u to fit in a word, or to have a low Hamming weight representation in order to achieve this property. Clearly, the number of suitable values of u for a given p is extremely large and therefore this assumption has a limited impact on the rest of the system.

Note also that the fastest system of coordinates for doubling corresponds to modified Jacobian coordinates $\mathcal{J}^m$ (see for instance [CMO98]) where a point (x_1, y_1) is represented by (X_1, Y_1, Z_1, aZ_1^4) with $x_1 = X_1/Z_1^2$ and $y_1 = Y_1/Z_1^3$. Indeed, to perform a double on the curve $y^2 = x^3 + ax + b$, one needs only 4M+4S. It is to be noted that choosing a special value for a does not change the overall complexity, except when $a = -3$. Note that in that particular case, Bernstein showed how to perform a doubling in Jacobian coordinates using 3M + 5S. His method also saves one field reduction [Ber01]. The addition $\mathcal{J}^m + \mathcal{J}^m = \mathcal{J}^m$ needs 13M + 6S whereas the mixed addition $\mathcal{J}^m + \mathcal{A} = \mathcal{J}^m$ only 9M + 5S. Again this complexity is independent of the value of the parameters so that no advantage can be obtained from a special choice of a curve in modified Jacobian coordinates.

Now, let us give addition formulas for $\mathcal{LD}^m$. We will only address the mixed coordinates case, since it is the most important in practice. So let $(X_1, Y_1, 1)$ in $\mathcal{A}$ and (X_2, Y_2, Z_2, Z_2^2) in $\mathcal{J}^m$ be two points on E. Again it is a simple exercise to check that (X_3, Y_3, Z_3, Z_3^2) is given that:

$$A = Y_1 \times Z_2^2 - Y_2, \quad B = X_1 \times Z_2 - X_2, \quad C = B \times Z_2,$$
$$Z_3 = C^2, \quad D = X_1 \times Z_3, \quad E = A^2,$$
$$F = X_2 \times B \times C, \quad X_3 = E - uZ_3 - D - F, \quad G = Z_3^2,$$
$$H = A \times C, \quad Y_3 = H \times (D - X_3) - Y_1 \times G.$$

These computations require 9M + 3S if a multiplication by u is negligible. So, choosing a special value for u provides an improvement and makes modified López–Dahab coordinates faster than modified Jacobian coordinates. At present let us generalize the concept to the multiplication–by–[3] map.

3.2   Elliptic Curves with Degree 3 Isogenies

As mentioned earlier, an elliptic curve defined over a field of characteristic different from 2 and 3 with a rational 3-torsion subgroup can be expressed in the form (up to twists):
$$E : y^2 = x^3 + 3u(x + 1)^2$$

with the 3-torsion subgroup defined by $x = 0$; we note that the curve E does not necessarily have a point of order 3. The corresponding isogeny of degree 3 is:

$$(x_1, y_1) \mapsto (x_t, y_t) = \left(x_1 + 4u + 12u\frac{x_1 + 1}{x_1^2}, y_1\left(1 - 12u\frac{x_1 + 2}{x_1^3}\right)\right).$$

The image curve is defined by an equation:
$$E_t : y^2 = x^3 - u(3x - 4u + 9)^2$$

which subsequently has a 3-torsion subgroup defined by $x = 0$, defining the kernel of the dual isogeny. This isogeny takes form

$$(x_t, y_t) \mapsto (x_3, y_3) = \left(\frac{1}{3^2} \left(x_t - 12u + \frac{12u(4u-9)}{x_t} - \frac{4u(4u-9)^2}{x_t^2} \right), \right.$$
$$\left. \frac{1}{3^3} y_t \left(1 - \frac{12u(4u-9)}{x_t^2} + \frac{8u(4u-9)^2}{x_t^3} \right) \right).$$

The composition of these maps gives the multiplication–by–3 map on E.

A general quadratic twist of E can be put in the standard Weierstraß form by a change of variables (x, y) to $(x - \lambda u, y)$:

$$y^2 = x^3 + 3\lambda u(x + \lambda)^2 \longrightarrow y^2 = x^3 - 3\lambda^2 u(u-2)x + \lambda^3 u(2u^2 - 6u + 3).$$

Conversely, the elliptic curve $y^2 = x^3 + ax + b$ has j-invariant $j = 6912a^3/(4a^3 + 27b^2)$. The corresponding values for (λ, u) are determined by $\lambda = -3b(u - 2)/(a(2u^2 - 6u + 3))$, where u is a root of the quartic polynomial $6912u(u - 2)^3 - j(4u - 9)$.

Effective scalar multiplication by splitting [3]. As above, to take advantage of this splitting, we will use weighted projective coordinates. More precisely let us represent the affine point $P_1 = (x_1, y_1)$ by (X_1, Y_1, Z_1, Z_1^2) where $x_1 = X_1/Z_1^2$ and $y_1 = Y_1/Z_1^3$. These coordinates are called *new Jacobian* and are denoted by $\mathcal{J}^n$. We will also describe doublings and mixed additions for this system. The term Z_1^2 will contribute to make the mixed addition more efficient. First let us give the formulas to compute $[3]P_1 = (X_3, Y_3, Z_3, Z_3^2)$:

$$A = (X_1 + 3Z_1^2)^2, \qquad B = uZ_1^2 \times A, \qquad X_t = Y_1^2 + B,$$
$$Y_t = Y_1 \times (Y_1^2 - 3B), \qquad Z_t = X_1 \times Z_1, \qquad C = Z_t^2,$$
$$D = \left((4u - 9)C - X_t\right)^2, \qquad E = -3uC \times D, \qquad X_3 = (Y_t^2 + E),$$
$$Y_3 = Y_t(X_3 - 4E), \qquad Z_3 = 3X_t \times Z_t, \qquad Z_3^2.$$

It is easy to see that 6M + 6S are needed to obtain $[3]P_1$ in $\mathcal{J}^n$ when u is suitably chosen so that a multiplication by u is negligible. Otherwise, 8M+6S are necessary.

Now let us see how a doubling can be efficiently obtained in that system. In fact, it is sufficient to slightly modify the formulas existing for Jacobian coordinates. We have:

$$A = Y_1 \times Z_1, \qquad Z_2 = 2A, \qquad B = 4Y_1^2 \times X_1,$$
$$C = B + 6uA^2, \qquad Z_2^2 = 4A^2, \qquad D = 3X_1^2,$$
$$E = D + 6uZ_1^2 \times (Z_1^2 + X_1), \qquad X_2 = -2B + E^2, \qquad Y_2 = -8Y_1^4 + E \times (B - X_2).$$

Thus a doubling in $\mathcal{J}^n$ requires 4M + 5S as long as we neglect multiplications by u, otherwise a doubling can be obtained with 6M + 4S.

Finally, let us detail the addition of an affine point $(X_1, Y_1, 1)$ and a point (X_2, Y_2, Z_2, Z_2^2) in $\mathcal{J}^n$. Again, they slightly differ from the ones for the addition in Jacobian coordinates, see [ACD+05].

$$A = X_1 \times Z_2^2, \qquad B = Y_1 \times Z_2^2 \times Z_2, \qquad C = X_2 - A,$$
$$D = Y_2 - B, \qquad Z_3 = Z_2 \times C, \qquad E = Z_3^2,$$
$$F = C^2, \qquad G = C \times F, \qquad H = A \times F,$$
$$X_3 = -G - 3uE - 2H + D^2, \quad Y_3 = -B \times G + D \times (H - X_3).$$

In total, one needs $8M + 3S$ to compute an addition. If u is a random element in the field, then an extra multiplication is required. Note that the extra element Z_2^2 in $\mathcal{J}^n$ allows to save one squaring in the addition above.

Comparison with other algorithms. Direct tripling formulas have been introduced by Ciet et al. [CJLM05]. The general idea is to avoid computing intermediate values for the doubling. This allows to get rid of one inversion at the cost of more multiplications. Recently, Dimitrov et al. succeeded in totally avoid using inversions [DIM05]. Usually, no special value for the parameters of the curve is considered, probably because this has a limited impact anyway on the complexity of the operations. In our case, important savings can be made if the parameter u of the curve is specially chosen, as suggested by the next table comparing the complexities of different operations in different coordinate systems. Note that we only require that a multiplication by u is trivial so that a very large scope of values are still available, like a small u or more generally u with a low Hamming weight expansion.

System	This work	[DIM05]	[CJLM05]
Equation	$y^2 = x^3 + 3u(x+1)^2$	$y^2 = x^3 + ax + b$	$y^2 = x^3 + ax + b$
Coordinates	New Jacobian $\mathcal{J}^n$	Jacobian $\mathcal{J}$	Affine $\mathcal{A}$
Tripling	$8M + 6S$	$10M + 6S$	$I + 7M + 4S$
special u or a	$6M + 6S$	$9M + 6S$	—
Doubling	$6M + 4S$	$4M + 6S$	$I + 2M + 2S$
special u or a	$4M + 5S$	$4M + 5S$	—
$a = -3$	NA	$4M + 4S$	—
Mixed Addition	$9M + 3S$	$8M + 3S$	$I + 2M + S$
special u or a	$8M + 3S$	—	—

Note also that there exist formulas to directly compute $[2]P \pm Q$ and $[3]P \pm Q$ with respectively $I + 9M + 2S$ and $2I + 9M + 3S$; see [CJLM05] for details.

Since we have a very efficient tripling algorithm, it is natural to consider the expansion of k in base 3 leading to a "triple and add algorithm" as well as other generalizations, like expansions in non-adjacent form. We discuss this at present.

4 Non-adjacent Forms for ℓ-Adic Expansions

Given two integers k and $\ell \geqslant 2$, it is well-known that k can be expressed in a unique way in base ℓ. For computer applications, ℓ is usually chosen to be 2 or a power of 2. In the context of multiplication and of exponentiation/scalar multiplication other representations have been considered, for instance the binary non-adjacent form and width-w non-adjacent form, respectively denoted by NAF and NAF$_w$, see [ACD+05].

Recently, Takagi et al. [TYW04] have generalized the concept of width-w non-adjacent form to any radix ℓ and introduced an ℓ-NAF$_w$.

Definition 4.1. *Let ℓ and w be two integers greater than 1. Let k be a positive integer, then a signed-digit expansion of the form*

$$k = \sum_{i=0}^{m} k_i \ell^i$$

where

- *there is at most 1 nonzero digit among any w adjacent coefficients*
- *k_i belongs to $\{0, \pm 1, \pm 2, \dots, \pm \lfloor \frac{\ell^w - 1}{2} \rfloor\} \setminus \{\pm r, \pm 2r, \dots, \pm \lfloor \frac{\ell^{w-1} - 1}{2} \rfloor r\}$*
- *the leftmost nonzero digit is positive*

is called a width-w *non-adjacent expansion in basis ℓ, ℓ-NAF$_w$ for short, and is denoted by $(k_m \dots k_0)_{\ell\text{-}NAF_w}$.*

It can be shown that such an expansion always exists for any positive integer. In fact, it is trivial to derive an algorithm to compute the ℓ-NAF$_w$ generalizing the one existing for the NAF$_w$.

Algorithm 1. ℓ-NAF$_w$ representation

INPUT: A positive integer k, a radix $\ell \geqslant 2$ and a parameter $w > 1$.
OUTPUT: The ℓ-NAF$_w$ representation $(k_m \dots k_0)_{\ell\text{-}NAF_w}$ of k.

---

1. $i \leftarrow 0$

2. **while** $k > 0$ **do**

3.   **if** $k \not\equiv 0 \pmod{\ell}$ **then**

4. $k_i \leftarrow k \bmod \ell^w$

5.   **if** $k_i > \ell^w/2$ **then** $k_i \leftarrow k_i - \ell^w$

6. $k \leftarrow k - k_i$

7.   **else** $k_i \leftarrow 0$

8. $k \leftarrow k/\ell$ and $i \leftarrow i + 1$

9. **return** $(k_m \dots k_0)_{\ell\text{-}NAF_w}$

Remarks

- The classical NAF corresponds to the choice $\ell = w = 2$.
- Takagi *et al.* [TYW04] proved that this expansion is unique and that it has the smallest Hamming weight among all signed representations for k having digits k_i's such that $|k_i| < \ell^w/2$.

It is well-known that the density of the classical NAF_w is $1/(w+1)$. This result can be generalized to $\ell\text{-NAF}_w$, as shown in [TYW04]. See also [HT05] for further results.

Proposition 4.1. *The average density of the ℓ-NAF_w is equal to* $\dfrac{\ell - 1}{(\ell - 1)w + 1}$.

Proof 4.1. *For that matter, we compute the average length $E(\ell, w)$ of running 0's between two nonzero coefficients. From the definition, it is clear that there are at least $w - 1$ consecutive zeroes between two nonzero coefficients in the ℓ-NAF_w expansion.*

Assuming that $k \not\equiv 0 \pmod{\ell}$ then $k_i \neq 0$ and $k \leftarrow k - k_i$ is now a multiple of ℓ^w. Let $t = k/\ell^w$. There are different possibilities for the integer t which can take any value. If t is not a multiple of ℓ, there will be exactly $w - 1$ consecutive zeroes until the next nonzero coefficient is found. Now the probability that t is not a multiple of ℓ is $(\ell - 1)/\ell$. In the same way, there will be exactly $w - 2 + i$ consecutive zeroes until the next nonzero coefficient is found if and only if t is a multiple of ℓ^{i-1} but not a multiple of ℓ^i. This event occurs with a probability equal to $(\ell - 1)/\ell^i$, namely $\ell - 1$ choices $(\ell^{i-1}, 2\ell^{i-1}, \ldots, (\ell - 1)\ell^{i-1})$ out of ℓ^i possible residues. This implies that the average length of running zeroes is

$$E(\ell, w) = w - 2 + \sum_{i \geq 1} i(\ell - 1)/\ell^i$$

and a simple computation gives $E(\ell, w) = w - 2 + \ell/(\ell - 1)$. Since the average density of the ℓ-NAF_w is $1/\big(E(\ell, w) + 1\big)$, we obtain the expected result.

5   Experiments

In the following, we count the number of elementary operations needed to perform a scalar multiplication on an elliptic curve (with generic or special parameters) defined over a finite field $\mathbb{F}_p$ of size respectively 160 and 200 bits with various methods. More precisely we investigate

- the double and add, also known as the binary method and denoted by Bin.
- the $\ell\text{-NAF}_w$ for $\ell = 2$ and $w = 2, 3, 4,$ and 5.
- the triple and add, also known as the ternary method and denoted by Tern.
- the 3-NAF_2.
- the sextuple and add method, denoted by Sext.

Table 1. Complexities with a 160bit size for a random curve

Method	#$\mathcal{P}$	δ	A.	B.	I/M	C.	I/M
Bin.	—	1/2	2384M	80I + 1552M	10.4	160I + 1136M	7.8
NAF	—	1/3	2076M	53I + 1503M	10.8	160I + 947M	7.1
NAF$_3$	2	1/4	1928M	40I + 1480M	11.2	160I + 856M	6.7
NAF$_4$	4	1/5	1837M	32I + 1466M	11.6	160I + 800M	6.5
NAF$_5$	8	1/6	1780M	27I + 1457M	12	160I + 765M	6.3
Tern.	—	2/3	2057M	134I + 1321M	5.5	168I + 1164M	5.3
3-NAF$_2$	2	2/5	1749M	80I + 1391M	4.5	141I + 1110M	4.5
3-NAF$_3$	8	2/7	1623M	58I + 1419M	3.5	130I + 1088M	4.1
Sext.	—	5/6	1957M	52I + 1557M	7.7	124I + 1220M	5.9
6-NAF$_2$	6	5/11	1683M	28I + 1514M	6.1	124I + 1052M	5.1
Tern./bin.	—	—	1773M	36I + 1507M	7.4	127I + 1067M	5.6
DBNS	—	—	1883M	45I + 1519M	8.1	129I + 1113M	6

- the 6-NAF$_2$.
- the ternary/binary approach [CJLM05], denoted by Tern./bin.
- the Dual Base Number System (DBNS) as explained in [DIM05]. Note however that we did not try to tune the values of b_{max} and t_{max}, i.e. the biggest possible values for the powers of 2 and 3 in the expansion of k. This would certainly lead to big improvements.

In each case, we give the number #$\mathcal{P}$ of precomputations needed to compute $[k]P$ when combined with a left-to-right approach. The density δ of the obtained expansion is also given. The different situations under scrutiny are:

A. Curve: $y^2 = x^3 + u(x + 1)^3$ defined over a finite field of odd characteristic. Operations:
  - tripling map [3] obtained as the composition of 2 isogenies expressed in new Jacobian coordinates
  - doubling and addition in new Jacobian coordinates
B. Curve: $y^2 = x^3 + ax + b$ defined over a finite field of odd characteristic. Operations:
  - direct tripling formulas explained in [DIM05].
  - direct $[2]P \pm Q$ and $[3]P \pm Q$ explained in [CJLM05] whenever it is possible.
C. Same curve and same operations as in B. except that the direct tripling formulas come from [CJLM05].

We assume that the cost of a squaring is 0.8M. This allows us to express the complexity only in terms of inversions and multiplications. All the complexities

Table 2. Complexities with a 160bit size for a special curve

Method	#$\mathcal{P}$	δ	A.	B.	I/M	C.	I/M
Bin.	—	1/2	2112M	80I + 1424M	8.6	160I + 1136M	6.1
NAF	—	1/3	1831M	53I + 1332M	9.4	160I + 947M	5.5
NAF$_3$	2	1/4	1696M	40I + 1288M	10.2	160I + 856M	5.2
NAF$_4$	4	1/5	1613M	32I + 1261M	11	160I + 800M	5.1
NAF$_5$	8	1/6	1561M	27I + 1244M	11.7	160I + 765M	5
Tern.	—	2/3	1788M	134I + 1287M	3.7	168I + 1164M	3.7
3-NAF$_2$	2	2/5	1507M	80I + 1330M	2.2	141I + 1110M	2.8
3-NAF$_3$	8	2/7	1392M	58I + 1347M	0.8	130I + 1088M	2.3
Sext.	—	5/6	1706M	52I + 1479M	4.4	124I + 1220M	3.9
6-NAF$_2$	6	5/11	1457M	28I + 1397M	2.1	124I + 1052M	3.3
Tern./bin.	—	—	1541M	36I + 1394M	4.1	127I + 1067M	3.7
DBNS	—	—	1643M	45I + 1415M	5	129I + 1113M	4.1

Table 3. Complexities with a 200bit size for a random curve

Method	#$\mathcal{P}$	δ	A.	B.	I/M	C.	I/M
Bin.	—	1/2	2980M	100I + 1940M	10.4	200I + 1420M	7.8
NAF	—	1/3	2604M	67I + 1881M	10.8	200I + 1189M	7.1
NAF$_3$	2	1/4	2410M	50I + 1850M	11.2	200I + 1070M	6.7
NAF$_4$	4	1/5	2296M	40I + 1832M	11.6	200I + 1000M	6.5
NAF$_5$	8	1/6	2216M	33I + 1819M	12	200I + 951M	6.3
Tern.	—	2/3	2570M	168I + 1646M	5.5	210I + 1453M	5.3
3-NAF$_2$	2	2/5	2183M	100I + 1735M	4.5	176I + 1385M	4.5
3-NAF$_3$	8	2/7	2023M	72I + 1771M	3.5	162I + 1357M	4.1
Sext.	—	5/6	2424M	64I + 1932M	7.7	154I + 1511M	5.9
6-NAF$_2$	6	5/11	2093M	35I + 1880M	6.1	154I + 1308M	5.1
Tern./bin.	—	—	2221M	45I + 1887M	7.4	159I + 1337M	5.6
DBNS	—	—	2378M	58I + 1905M	8.1	162I + 1403M	6

are obtained in a theoretical way except for the ternary/binary and the DBNS approaches. In these cases, an average over 10^4 exponents has been computed. In each case, we provide the ratio between a multiplication and an inversion so that the complexities of this work and [DIM05] (resp. [CJLM05]) are equal. Thus, if

Table 4. Complexities with a 200bit size for a special curve

Method	#$\mathcal{P}$	δ	A.	B.	I/M	C.	I/M
Bin.	—	1/2	2640M	100I + 1780M	8.6	200I + 1420M	6.1
NAF	—	1/3	2297M	67I + 1668M	9.4	200I + 1189M	5.5
NAF$_3$	2	1/4	2120M	50I + 1610M	10.2	200I + 1070M	5.2
NAF$_4$	4	1/5	2016M	40I + 1576M	11	200I + 1000M	5.1
NAF$_5$	8	1/6	1943M	33I + 1552M	11.8	200I + 951M	5
Tern.	—	2/3	2234M	168I + 1604M	3.7	210I + 1453M	3.7
3-NAF$_2$	2	2/5	1881M	100I + 1659M	2.2	176I + 1385M	2.8
3-NAF$_3$	8	2/7	1735M	72I + 1681M	0.7	162I + 1357M	2.3
Sext.	—	5/6	2113M	64I + 1835M	4.4	154I + 1511M	3.9
6-NAF$_2$	6	5/11	1812M	35I + 1736M	2.2	154I + 1308M	3.3
Tern./bin.	—	—	1933M	45I + 1743M	4.2	159I + 1332M	3.8
DBNS	—	—	2077M	58I + 1777M	5.1	162I + 1404M	4.2

I/M is bigger than the indicated value, our method will be more efficient. See Tables 1, 2, 3, and 4 for details.

6 Conclusion

We have described a family of elliptic curve defined over a prime field of large characteristic for which the multiplication–by–3 map, can be decomposed into the product of 2 isogenies. Explicit formulas indicate that a tripling can be done with 8M + 6S, and even 6M + 6S if the parameter of the curve is suitably chosen. Since 3 plays an major role, we also tested generalizations of the width-w NAF expansion to deal with ℓ-adic expansions. We then tested our new tripling algorithm in different situations. When there is no memory constraints, the 3-NAF$_2$, 6-NAF$_2$, and 3-NAF$_3$ give excellent results for respectively only 2, 6 and 8 precomputed values and outclass their binary counterparts. Also, this system performs better than those described in [CJLM05] and [DIM05] for most methods (especially the most efficient ones) under very realistic assumptions concerning the ratio I/M (typically I/M is between 4 and 10). For that range of ratio, if we precompute and store two values, the 3-NAF$_2$ combined with our method on a special curve will give an improvement of 9 to 30% over [DIM05] for both sizes 160 and 200bit.

Of course, it would be desirable to extend this work and different directions are of interest. Indeed, the same study should be carried out in characteristic 2 and bigger values of ℓ should be investigated, the first candidate being 5. Also, the Dual Base Number System (DBNS) when combined with this new tripling method should give very good results with appropriate settings that need to be found. Also, designing direct formulas for $[2]P \pm Q$ and $[3]P \pm Q$ in new Jacobian coordinates would lead to further improvements.

References

[ACD+05]   R. M. Avanzi, H. Cohen, C. Doche, G. Frey, T. Lange, K. Nguyen, and F. Vercauteren, *Handbook of Elliptic and Hyperelliptic Curve Cryptography*, CRC Press, Inc., 2005.

[Ber01]   D. J. Bernstein, *A software implementation of NIST P-224*, slides of a talk given at ECC 2001.

[BJ03]   É. Brier and M. Joye, *Fast point multiplication on elliptic curves through isogenies*, Applied Algebra, Algebraic Algorithms and Error-Correcting Codes – AAECC 2003, Lecture Notes in Comput. Sci., vol. 2643, Springer-Verlag, Berlin, 2003, pp. 43–50.

[CJLM05]   M. Ciet, M. Joye, K. Lauter, and P. L. Montgomery, *Trading inversions for multiplications in elliptic curve cryptography*, Des. Codes Cryptogr. (2005), To appear. Also available from Cryptology ePrint Archive.

[CLSQ03]   M. Ciet, T. Lange, F. Sica, and J.-J. Quisquater, *Improved algorithms for efficient arithmetic on elliptic curves using fast endomorphisms*, Advances in Cryptology – Eurocrypt 2003, Lecture Notes in Comput. Sci., vol. 2656, Springer-Verlag, Berlin, 2003, pp. 388–400.

[CMO97]   H. Cohen, A. Miyaji, and T. Ono, *Efficient elliptic curve exponentiation*, Information and Communication Security – ICICS 1997, Lecture Notes in Comput. Sci., vol. 1334, Springer-Verlag, Berlin, 1997, pp. 282–290.

[CMO98]   ———, *Efficient elliptic curve exponentiation using mixed coordinates*, Advances in Cryptology – Asiacrypt 1998, Lecture Notes in Comput. Sci., vol. 1514, Springer-Verlag, Berlin, 1998, pp. 51–65.

[CS05]   M. Ciet and F. Sica, *An Analysis of Double Base Number Systems and a sublinear scalar multiplication algorithm*, Progress in Cryptology – Mycrypt 2005, Lecture Notes in Comput. Sci., vol. 3715, Springer-Verlag, Berlin, 2005, pp. 171–182.

[DIM05]   V. S. Dimitrov, L. Imbert, and P. K. Mishra, *Efficient and secure elliptic curve point multiplication using double-base chains*, Advances in Cryptology – Asiacrypt 2005, Lecture Notes in Comput. Sci., vol. 3788, Springer-Verlag, Berlin, 2005, pp. 59–78.

[DJM99]   V. S. Dimitrov, G. A. Jullien, and W. C. Miller, *Theory and applications of the double-base number system*, IEEE Trans. on Computers **48** (1999), no. 10, 1098–1106.

[GLV01]   R. P. Gallant, R. J. Lambert, and S. A. Vanstone, *Faster point multiplication on elliptic curves with efficient endomorphisms*, Advances in Cryptology – Crypto 2001, Lecture Notes in Comput. Sci., vol. 2139, Springer-Verlag, Berlin, 2001, pp. 190–200.

[HMV03]   D. Hankerson, A. J. Menezes, and S. A. Vanstone, *Guide to elliptic curve cryptography*, Springer-Verlag, Berlin, 2003.

[HT05]   D.-G. Han and T. Takagi, *Some analysis of radix-r representations*, preprint, 2005. See http://eprint.iacr.org/2005/402/

[JMV05]   D. Jao, S. D. Miller, and R. Venkatesan, *Do all elliptic curves of the same order have the same difficulty of discrete log?*, Advances in Cryptology – Asiacrypt 2005, Lecture Notes in Comput. Sci., vol. 3788, Springer-Verlag, Berlin, 2005, pp. 21–40.

[Kob92]   N. Koblitz, *CM-curves with good cryptographic properties*, Advances in Cryptology – Crypto 1991, Lecture Notes in Comput. Sci., vol. 576, Springer-Verlag, Berlin, 1992, pp. 279–287.

[Lan05]   T. Lange, *Koblitz curve cryptosystems*, Finite Fields Appl. **11** (2005), no. 2, 220–229.

[LD98]   J. López and R. Dahab, *Improved algorithms for elliptic curve arithmetic in GF(2^n)*, Tech. Report IC-98-39, Relatório Técnico, October 1998.

[MO90]   F. Morain and J. Olivos, *Speeding up the computations on an elliptic curve using addition-subtraction chains*, Inform. Theory Appl. **24** (1990), 531–543.

[MV90]   A. J. Menezes and S. A. Vanstone, *The implementation of elliptic curve cryptosystems*, Advances in Cryptology – Auscrypt 1990, Lecture Notes in Comput. Sci., vol. 453, Springer-Verlag, Berlin, 1990, pp. 2–13.

[Sol00]   J. A. Solinas, *Efficient arithmetic on Koblitz curves*, Des. Codes Cryptogr. **19** (2000), 195–249.

[TYW04]   T. Takagi, S.-M. Yen, and B.-C. Wu, *Radix-r non-adjacent form*, Information Security Conference – ISC 2004, Lecture Notes in Comput. Sci., vol. 3225, Springer-Verlag, Berlin, 2004, pp. 99–110.

Curve25519: New Diffie-Hellman Speed Records

Daniel J. Bernstein*

djb@cr.yp.to

Abstract. This paper explains the design and implementation of a high-security elliptic-curve-Diffie-Hellman function achieving record-setting speeds: e.g., 832457 Pentium III cycles (with several side benefits: free key compression, free key validation, and state-of-the-art timing-attack protection), more than twice as fast as other authors' results at the same conjectured security level (with or without the side benefits).

Keywords: Diffie-Hellman, elliptic curves, point multiplication, new curve, new software, high conjectured security, high speed, constant time, short keys.

1 Introduction

This paper introduces and analyzes Curve25519, a state-of-the-art elliptic-curve-Diffie-Hellman function suitable for a wide variety of cryptographic applications. This paper uses Curve25519 to obtain new speed records for high-security Diffie-Hellman computations.

Here is the high-level view of Curve25519: Each Curve25519 user has a 32-byte secret key and a 32-byte public key. Each set of two Curve25519 users has a 32-byte shared secret used to authenticate and encrypt messages between the two users.

Medium-level view: The following picture shows the data flow from secret keys through public keys to a shared secret.

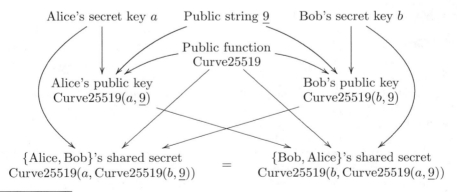

* Thanks to Tanja Lange for her extensive comments. Date of this document: 2006.02.09. Permanent ID of this document: 4230efdfa673480fc079449d90f322c0. This document is final and may be freely cited.

M. Yung et al. (Eds.): PKC 2006, LNCS 3958, pp. 207–228, 2006.

A hash of the shared secret $\mathrm{Curve25519}(a, \mathrm{Curve25519}(b, 9))$ is used as the key for a secret-key authentication system (to authenticate messages), or as the key for a secret-key authenticated-encryption system (to simultaneously encrypt and authenticate messages).

Low-level view: The Curve25519 function is $\mathbf{F}_p$-restricted x-coordinate scalar multiplication on $E(\mathbf{F}_{p^2})$, where p is the prime number $2^{255} - 19$ and E is the elliptic curve $y^2 = x^3 + 486662x^2 + x$. See Section 2 for further details.

Conjectured security level. Breaking the Curve25519 function—for example, computing the shared secret from the two public keys—is conjectured to be extremely difficult. Every known attack is more expensive than performing a brute-force search on a typical 128-bit secret-key cipher.

The general problem of elliptic-curve discrete logarithms has been attacked for two decades with very little success. Generic discrete-logarithm algorithms break prime groups that are not sufficiently large, but the prime group used in this paper has size above 2^{252}. Elliptic curves with certain special algebraic structures can be broken much more quickly by non-generic algorithms, but $E(\mathbf{F}_{p^2})$ does not have those structures. See Section 3 of this paper for more detailed comments on the security of the Curve25519 function.

If large quantum computers are built then they will break Curve25519 and all other short-key discrete-logarithm systems. See [56] for details of a general elliptic-curve-discrete-logarithm algorithm. The ramifications of this observation are orthogonal to the topic of this paper and are not discussed further.

Efficiency. My public-domain Curve25519 software provides several efficiency features, thanks in large part to the choice of the Curve25519 function:

- **Extremely high speed.** My software computes Curve25519 in just 832457 cycles on a Pentium III, 957904 cycles on a Pentium 4, 640838 cycles on a Pentium M, and 624786 cycles on an Athlon. Each of these numbers is a new speed record for high-security Diffie-Hellman functions. I am working on implementations for the UltraSPARC, PowerPC, etc.; I expect to end up with similar cycle counts.
- **No time variability.** Most speed reports in the cryptographic literature are for software without any protection against timing attacks. See [12], [51], and [50] for some successful attacks. Adding protection can dramatically slow down the computation. In contrast, my Curve25519 software is already immune to timing attacks, including hyperthreading attacks and other cache-timing attacks. It avoids all input-dependent branches, all input-dependent array indices, and other instructions with input-dependent timings.
- **Short secret keys.** The Curve25519 secret key is only 32 bytes. This is typical for high-security Diffie-Hellman functions.
- **Short public keys.** The Curve25519 public key is only 32 bytes. Typical elliptic-curve-Diffie-Hellman functions use 64-byte public keys; those keys can be compressed to half size, as suggested by Miller in [46], but the time for decompression is quite noticeable and usually not reported.
- **Free key validation.** Typical elliptic-curve-Diffie-Hellman functions can be broken if users do not validate public keys; see, e.g., [14, Section 4.1] and [3].

The time for key validation is quite noticeable and usually not reported. In contrast, every 32-byte string is accepted as a Curve25519 public key.

- **Short code.** My software is very small. The compiled code, including all necessary tables, is around 16 kilobytes on each CPU, and can easily fit alongside other networking tools in the CPU's instruction cache.

The new speed records are the highlight of this paper. Sections 4 and 5 explain the computation of Curve25519 in detail from the bottom up.

One can improve speed by choosing functions at lower security levels; for example, dropping from 255 bits down to 160 bits. But—as discussed in Section 3—I can easily imagine an attacker with the resources to break a 160-bit elliptic curve in under a year. Users should not expose themselves to this risk; they should instead move up to the comfortable security level of Curve25519.

Of course, when users exchange large volumes of data, their bottleneck is a secret-key cryptosystem, and the Curve25519 speed no longer matters.

Comparison to previous work. There is an extensive literature analyzing the speed of various implementations of various Diffie-Hellman functions at various conjectured security levels.

In particular, there have been some reports of high-security elliptic-curve scalar-multiplication speeds: [17, Table 8] reports 1920000 cycles on a 400 MHz Pentium II for field size $2^{256} - 2^{224} + 2^{192} + 2^{96} - 1$; [33, Table 7] reports 1740000 cycles on a 400 MHz Pentium II for field size 2^{283} using a subfield curve; [4, Table 4] reports 3086000 cycles on a 1000 MHz Athlon for a random 256-bit prime field. At a lower security level: [7, Table 3] reports 2650000 cycles on a 233 MHz Pentium MMX for field size $(2^{31} - 1)^6$; [58, Table 4] reports 4500000 cycles on a 166 MHz Pentium Pro for field size $(2^{31} - 19)^6$; [26, Table 6] reports 1720000 cycles on an 800 MHz Pentium III for field size 2^{233}.

The Curve25519 timings are more than twice as fast as the above reports. The comparison is actually even more lopsided than this, because the Curve25519 timings include free key compression, free key validation, and state-of-the-art timing-attack protection, while the above reports do not.

I have previously reported preliminary implementation work achieving about half of this speedup using a standard NIST curve. The other half of the speedup relies on switching to a better-designed curve. This paper covers both halves of the speedup.

At a lower level, designing and implementing an elliptic-curve-Diffie-Hellman function means making many choices that affect speed. Making a few bad choices can destroy performance. In the design and implementation of Curve25519 I have tried to globally optimize the entire sequence of choices:

- Use large characteristic, not characteristic 2.
- Use curve shape $y^2 = x^3 + Ax^2 + x$, with $(A - 2)/4$ small, rather than $y^2 = x^3 - 3x + a_6$.
- Use x as a public key, not (x, y).
- Use a secure curve that also has a secure twist, rather than taking extra time to prohibit keys on the twist.

- Use x/z inside scalar multiplication, not $(x/z, y/z)$ or $(x/z^2, y/z^3)$.
- Convert variable array indexing into arithmetic.
- Use a fixed position for the leading 1 in the secret key.
- Multiply the secret key by a small power of 2 to account for cofactors in the curve group and the twist group.
- Use a prime field, not an extension field.
- Use a prime extremely close to 2^b for some b.
- Use radix $2^{b/w}$ for some w, even if b/w is not an integer.
- Allow coefficients slightly larger than the radix, rather than reducing each coefficient as soon as possible.
- Put coefficients into floating-point registers, not integer registers. Choose w accordingly.

See Sections 4 and 5 for details and credits. Beware that these choices interact across many levels of design and implementation: for example, there are other curve shapes and prime shapes for which $(x/z^2, y/z^3)$ is better than x/z. This type of interaction makes the optimal sequence of choices difficult to identify even when all possible choices are known.

2 Specification

This section defines the Curve25519 function. Readers not familiar with rings, fields, and elliptic curves should consult Appendix A for definitions and for a proof of Theorem 2.1.

Theorem 2.1. *Let p be a prime number with $p \geq 5$. Let A be an integer such that $A^2 - 4$ is not a square modulo p. Define E as the elliptic curve $y^2 = x^3 + Ax^2 + x$ over the field $\mathbf{F}_p$. Define $X_0 : E(\mathbf{F}_{p^2}) \to \mathbf{F}_{p^2}$ as follows: $X_0(\infty) = 0$; $X_0(x, y) = x$. Let n be an integer. Let q be an element of $\mathbf{F}_p$. Then there exists a unique $s \in \mathbf{F}_p$ such that $X_0(nQ) = s$ for all $Q \in E(\mathbf{F}_{p^2})$ such that $X_0(Q) = q$.*

In particular, define p as the prime $2^{255} - 19$. Define $\mathbf{F}_p$ as the prime field $\mathbf{Z}/p = \mathbf{Z}/(2^{255} - 19)$. Note that 2 is not a square in $\mathbf{F}_p$; define $\mathbf{F}_{p^2}$ as the field $(\mathbf{Z}/(2^{255} - 19))[\sqrt{2}]$. Define $A = 486662$. Note that $486662^2 - 4$ is not a square in $\mathbf{F}_p$. Define E as the elliptic curve $y^2 = x^3 + Ax^2 + x$ over $\mathbf{F}_p$. Define a function $X_0 : E(\mathbf{F}_{p^2}) \to \mathbf{F}_{p^2}$ as follows: $X_0(\infty) = 0$; $X_0(x, y) = x$. Define a function $X : E(\mathbf{F}_{p^2}) \to \{\infty\} \cup \mathbf{F}_{p^2}$ as follows: $X(\infty) = \infty$; $X(x, y) = x$.

At this point I could say that, given $n \in 2^{254} + 8\{0, 1, 2, 3, \ldots, 2^{251} - 1\}$ and $q \in \mathbf{F}_p$, the Curve25519 function produces s in Theorem 2.1. However, to match cryptographic reality and to catch the types of design error explained by Menezes in [45], I will instead define the inputs and outputs of Curve25519 as sequences of bytes.

The set of **bytes** is, by definition, $\{0, 1, \ldots, 255\}$. The encoding of a byte as a sequence of bits is not relevant to this document. Write $s \mapsto \underline{s}$ for the standard little-endian bijection from $\{0, 1, \ldots, 2^{256} - 1\}$ to the set $\{0, 1, \ldots, 255\}^{32}$ of 32-byte strings: in other words, for each integer $s \in \{0, 1, \ldots, 2^{256} - 1\}$, define $\underline{s} = (s \bmod 256, \lfloor s/256 \rfloor \bmod 256, \ldots, \lfloor s/256^{31} \rfloor \bmod 256)$.

The set of Curve25519 **public keys** is, by definition, $\{0, 1, \ldots, 255\}^{32}$; in other words, $\{\underline{q} : q \in \{0, 1, \ldots, 2^{256} - 1\}\}$. The set of Curve25519 **secret keys** is, by definition, $\{0, 8, 16, 24, \ldots, 248\} \times \{0, 1, \ldots, 255\}^{30} \times \{64, 65, 66, \ldots, 127\}$; in other words, $\{\underline{n} : n \in 2^{254} + 8\{0, 1, 2, 3, \ldots, 2^{251} - 1\}\}$.

Now Curve25519 : {Curve25519 secret keys} $\times$ {Curve25519 public keys} $\rightarrow$ {Curve25519 public keys} is defined as follows. Fix $q \in \{0, 1, \ldots, 2^{256} - 1\}$ and $n \in 2^{254} + 8\{0, 1, 2, 3, \ldots, 2^{251} - 1\}$. By Theorem 2.1, there is a unique integer $s \in \{0, 1, 2, \ldots, 2^{255} - 20\}$ with the following property: $s = X_0(nQ)$ for all $Q \in E(\mathbf{F}_{p^2})$ such that $X_0(Q) = q \bmod 2^{255} - 19$. Finally, Curve25519$(\underline{n}, \underline{q})$ is defined as $\underline{s}$. Note that Curve25519 is not surjective: in particular, its final output bit is always 0 and need not be transmitted.

3 Security

This section discusses attacks on Curve25519. The bottom line is that all known attacks are extremely expensive.

Responsibilities of the user. The legitimate users are assumed to generate independent uniform random secret keys. A user can, for example, generate 32 uniform random bytes, clear bits $0, 1, 2$ of the first byte, clear bit 7 of the last byte, and set bit 6 of the last byte.

Large deviations from uniformity can eliminate all security. For example, if the first 16 bytes of the secret key $\underline{n}$ were instead chosen as a public constant, then a moderately large computation would deduce the remaining bytes of $\underline{n}$ from the public key Curve25519$(\underline{n}, 9)$. This is not Curve25519's fault; the user is responsible for putting enough randomness into keys.

Legitimate users are also assumed to keep their secret keys secret. This means that a secret key $\underline{n}$ is not used except to compute the public key Curve25519$(\underline{n}, 9)$ and to compute the shared-secret hash $H(\text{Curve25519}(\underline{n}, \underline{q}))$ given $\underline{q}$.

Users are *not* assumed to throw $\underline{n}$ away after a single $\underline{q}$. Diffie-Hellman secret keys can—and, for efficiency, should—be reused with many public keys, as in [23, Section 3]. Each user's secret key $\underline{n}$ is combined with many other users' public keys $\underline{q_1}, \underline{q_2}, \underline{q_3}, \ldots$, producing shared-secret hashes $H(\text{Curve25519}(\underline{n}, \underline{q_1}))$, $H(\text{Curve25519}(\underline{n}, \underline{q_2}))$, $H(\text{Curve25519}(\underline{n}, \underline{q_3}))$, $\ldots$.

Choice of key-derivation function. There are no theorems guaranteeing the safety of any particular key-derivation function H with, e.g., 512-bit output. Some silly choices of H are breakable. As an extreme example, if H outputs just 64 bits followed by all zeros, then an attacker can perform a brute-force search for those 64 bits.

On the other hand, from the perspective of a secret-key cryptographer, it seems very easy to design a safe function H. A small amount of mixing, far less than necessary to make a safe secret-key cipher, stops all known attacks.

For concreteness I will define $H(x_0, x_1, x_2, x_3, x_4, x_5, x_6, x_7)$ as the 64-byte string Salsa20$(c_0, x_0, 0, x_1, x_2, c_1, x_3, 0, 0, x_4, c_2, x_5, x_6, 0, x_7, c_3)$. Here Salsa20 is the function defined in [13, Section 8]; (c_0, c_1, c_2, c_3) is "Curve25519output" in ASCII; and each x_i has 4 bytes.

If fewer than 64 bytes are needed then the Salsa20 output can simply be truncated. If more than 64 bytes are needed then Salsa20 can be invoked again with $(c_0, x_0, 1, x_1, \ldots)$ to produce another 64 bytes.

Powers of the attacker. An attacker sees public keys $q_1 = \text{Curve25519}(\underline{n_1}, \underline{9})$, $q_2 = \text{Curve25519}(\underline{n_2}, \underline{9})$, ... generated from the legitimate users' independent uniform random secret keys $n_1, n_2, \ldots$.

The attacker also sees messages protected by a secret-key cryptosystem C where the keys for C are the shared-secret hashes $H(\text{Curve25519}(\underline{n_i}, q_i)) = H(\text{Curve25519}(\underline{n_j}, q_i))$ for various sets $\{i, j\}$. The attacker's goal is to decrypt or forge these messages.

The attacker can also compute a public key $q' \notin \{q_1, q_2, \ldots\}$ and—by using q' in the Diffie-Hellman protocol—see messages protected by C where the keys for C are $H(\text{Curve25519}(\underline{n_1}, q'))$, $H(\text{Curve25519}(\underline{n_2}, q'))$, ... This would be pointless if the attacker generated q' in the normal way, but the attacker is not required to generate q' in the normal way; legitimate users are *not* assumed to check that q' was generated from a secret key, let alone a secret key known to the attacker. The attacker might take $q' = \underline{1}$, for example, or $q' = q_1 \oplus \underline{1}$. The attacker can adaptively generate many public keys q'.

Of course, security depends on the choice of secret-key cryptosystem C. One could make a poor choice of C, allowing messages to be decrypted or forged without any weakness in Curve25519. But standard choices of C are conjectured to be safe. Further discussion of the choice of C is outside the scope of this document.

Simplified attack notions. There are many papers using simpler models of Diffie-Hellman attackers, and proving theorems of the form "a fast attack in complicated-security-model implies a fast attack in simplified-security-model." The reader might wonder why I am not using one of these simplified notions.

Example: Bentahar in [10], improving an algorithm by Muzereau, Smart, and Vercauteren in [48] based on an idea by Maurer in [44], showed that one can evaluate discrete logarithms on typical elliptic curves using roughly 2^{13} calls to a reliable oracle for the function $(mQ, nQ) \mapsto mnQ$. Bentahar then repeated the standard conjecture that computing discrete logarithms on a typical 256-bit elliptic curve costs at least 2^{128} (never mind the question of exactly what "cost" means), and deduced the conjecture that computing $(mQ, nQ) \mapsto mnQ$ costs at least 2^{115}. Why, then, should one make a conjecture regarding the difficulty of computing $(mQ, nQ) \mapsto mnQ$, rather than a simplified conjecture regarding the difficulty of computing discrete logarithms?

Answer: A standard conjecture says that computing $(mQ, nQ) \mapsto mnQ$ costs at least 2^{128}. This conjecture is quantitatively stronger than anything that can be obtained by applying Bentahar's theorem to a simplified conjecture.

Similar comments apply to other theorems of this type; see, e.g., [39, Section 3.2]. Often the theorems are so weak that they say nothing about any real-world system. To focus attention on the security properties that applications actually need, I have chosen to make a complicated but strong conjecture about security, rather than a simplified but weak conjecture.

Generic discrete logarithms by the rho and kangaroo methods. The attacker can expand Curve25519($\underline{n}$, $\underline{9}$) into a point (x, y) on $E(\mathbf{F}_{p^2})$, namely the nth multiple of the base point $(9, \ldots)$. The attacker can then use Pollard's rho method or Pollard's kangaroo method to compute the discrete logarithm of this point, namely n. The main cost in either method is the cost of performing a huge number of additions of elliptic-curve points; both methods are almost perfectly parallelizable, with negligible communication costs. See [63], [55], [61], and [60].

The number of additions here is about the square root of the length of the n interval: in this case, about 2^{125}. The computation can finish after far fewer additions, but the success chance is at most (and conjecturally at least) about $a^2/2^{251}$ after a additions.

How many elliptic-curve additions can an attacker perform? The traditional estimate is roughly 2^{70} elliptic-curve additions: a modern CPU costs about 2^6 dollars; a modern CPU cycle is about 2^{-31} seconds; each elliptic-curve addition in the rho or kangaroo method costs about 2^{10} CPU cycles for roughly 2^2 field multiplications that each cost 2^8 cycles; the attacker is willing to spend a year, i.e., 2^{25} seconds; the attacker can afford to spend 2^{30} dollars.

I don't agree with the traditional estimate. I agree that modern circuitry takes about 2^{-21} seconds for a single rho/kangaroo step; but it is a huge error to assume that this circuitry costs as much as 2^6 dollars. One can fit many parallel rho/kangaroo circuits into the same amount of circuitry as a modern CPU. A reasonable estimate for "many" is 2^{10}; see [28] for a fairly detailed chip design, and [28, Section 5.2] for the estimate. By switching to this chip, the attacker can perform roughly 2^{80} elliptic-curve additions. The attacker has an excellent chance of computing a 160-bit discrete logarithm, but only about a 2^{-90} chance of computing a 251-bit discrete logarithm.

Of course, one must adjust these estimates as chip technology improves. It is not enough to account for increases in cycle speed and for decreases in chip cost; one must also account for increases in chip size. However, the Curve25519 security level will remain comfortable for the foreseeable future.

Batch discrete logarithms. Silverman and Stapleton observed, and Kuhn and Struik proved in [41, Section 4] assuming standard conjectures, that the rho method can compute u discrete logarithms using about $\sqrt{u}$ times as much effort as computing a single discrete logarithm.

For example, given public keys Curve25519($\underline{n_1}$, $\underline{9}$), ..., Curve25519($\underline{n_u}$, $\underline{9}$), the attacker can discover most of the secret keys $\underline{n_1}, \ldots, \underline{n_u}$ using only about $2^{125}\sqrt{u}$ additions, i.e., about $2^{125}/\sqrt{u}$ additions per key.

This does not mean, however, that one of the keys will be found within the first $2^{125}/\sqrt{u}$ additions. On the contrary: the attacker is likely to wait for 2^{125} additions before finding the first key, then another $2^{125}(\sqrt{2} - 1)$ additions before finding the second key, etc. Curve25519 is at a comfortable security level where finding the first key is, conjecturally, far out of reach, so the reduced cost of finding subsequent keys is not a threat. The attacker can perform only $2^{125}\epsilon$

additions for small ϵ, so the attacker's chance of success—of finding *any* keys—is only about ϵ^2.

Generic discrete logarithms are often claimed to be about as difficult as brute-force search for a half-size key. But brute-force search computes a batch of u keys with about the *same* effort as computing a single key. Furthermore, brute-force search has probability roughly $u\epsilon$ of finding some key after the first ϵ of the computation, whereas discrete logarithms have only an ϵ^2 chance. Evidently generic discrete logarithms are *more* difficult than brute-force search for a half-size key: $u\epsilon$ is much larger than ϵ^2, except in the extreme case where u and ϵ are both close to 1.

Small-subgroup attacks. If the subgroup of $E(\mathbf{F}_{p^2})$ generated by the base point $(9,\ldots)$ has non-prime order then the attacker can use the Pohlig-Hellman method to save time in computing discrete logarithms. See, e.g., [5, Section 19.3].

This attack fails against Curve25519. The order of the base point is a prime, namely $2^{252} + 27742317777372353535851937790883648493$.

An active attacker has more options. Say there is a point $(x,y) \in E(\mathbf{F}_{p^2})$ of order b, with $x \in \mathbf{F}_p$ and with b not very large. The attacker can issue a public key $\underline{x}$. The legitimate user will then authenticate and encrypt data under $H(\text{Curve25519}(\underline{n},\underline{x})) = H(X_0(n(x,y))) = H(X_0((n \bmod b)(x,y)))$; the attacker can compare the results to all possibilities for $n \bmod b$, presumably determining $n \bmod b$.

The active attack also fails against Curve25519. The group $\{\infty\} \cup (E(\mathbf{F}_{p^2}) \cap (\mathbf{F}_p \times \mathbf{F}_p))$ has size $8p_1$, where $p_1 = 2^{252} + \cdots$ is the prime number displayed above. The "twist" group $\{\infty\} \cup (E(\mathbf{F}_{p^2}) \cap (\mathbf{F}_p \times \sqrt{2}\mathbf{F}_p))$ has size $2(p+1) - 8p_1 = 4p_2$, where p_2 is the prime $2^{253} - 55484635555474470707170387558176729 6995$. Consequently, the only possibilities for b below 2^{252} are $1, 2, 4, 8$. Secret keys $\underline{n}$ by definition have $n \bmod 8 = 0$ and thus $n \bmod b = 0$.

History: Lim and Lee in [42] pointed out active attacks on Diffie-Hellman in the group $\mathbf{F}_p^*$. They recommended in [42, Section 4] that, rather than taking the time to test that public keys are in a particular subgroup of prime order q, one choose a prime p such that "each prime factor of $(p-1)/2q$ is larger than q." Biehl, Meyer, and Müller in [14, Section 4.1] pointed out analogous attacks on elliptic curves when public keys are represented as pairs (x,y); they did not propose any workaround other than testing keys. In a November 2001 sci.crypt posting I wrote "You can happily skip both the y transmission and the square root. In fact, if both the curve and its twist have nearly prime order, then you can even skip square testing."

Other attacks. The kangaroo method actually searches simultaneously for $n/8$ and $p_1 - n/8$ in an interval. The range of $n/8$ is $\{2^{251}, \ldots, 2^{252} - 1\}$, so either $n/8$ or $p_1 - n/8$ is in the range $\{(p_1+1)/2, \ldots, 2^{252} - 1\}$. However, p_1 is only marginally above 2^{252}, so this range has length only marginally below 2^{251}.

More generally, when a group G has an easily computed automorphism φ of small order b, one can apply the kangaroo method to the orbits of φ, using only about $\sqrt{\#G/b}$ steps rather than $\sqrt{\#G}$ steps. See, e.g., [5, Section 19.5.5]. But my elliptic curve has no structure of this type other than negation. In fact, it has no complex endomorphisms of small norm. To prove this, compute the trace $t = p + 1 - 8p_1$, and observe that $t^2 - 4p$ is not a small multiple of a square: it is divisible once by the prime 83129560545462778877481, for example.

My elliptic curve also resists the transfer attacks surveyed in [30, Chapter 22]. The primes p_1 and p_2 do not equal the field characteristic p. The order of p modulo p_1 is not small: in fact, it is $(p_1 - 1)/6$. The order of p modulo p_2 is not small: in fact, it is $p_2 - 1$. Weil descent simply splits $E(\mathbf{F}_{p^2})$ into the subgroup $E(\mathbf{F}_p)$, of order $8p_1$, and the twist, of order $4p_2$; there are no proper subfields of $\mathbf{F}_p$ to exploit.

4   Fast Arithmetic Modulo $2^{255} - 19$

This section explains one way to use common CPU instructions, specifically floating-point instructions, to quickly multiply and add in the field $\mathbf{F}_p$ where $p = 2^{255} - 19$. I will focus on the Pentium M for concreteness, but the same techniques work well for a wide variety of CPUs. This section also discusses the choice of field structure and the choice of prime.

In this section, "floating-point" is abbreviated "fp."

Representing integers modulo $2^{255} - 19$. Define R as the ring of polynomials $\sum_i u_i x^i$ where u_i is an integer multiple of $2^{\lceil 25.5i \rceil}$. One way to see that R is a ring is to observe that it is the intersection of the subrings $\mathbf{Z}[x]$ and $\overline{\mathbf{Z}}[2^{25.5}x]$ of $\overline{\mathbf{Z}}[x]$, where $\overline{\mathbf{Z}}$ is the ring of algebraic integers in $\mathbf{C}$.

Elements of R represent elements of $\mathbf{Z}/(2^{255} - 19)$: each polynomial represents its value at 1. Often a polynomial is chosen to meet two restrictions:

- The polynomial degree is small, to limit the number of coefficients that need to be multiplied as part of polynomial multiplication. Specifically, **reduced-degree** polynomials have degree at most 9.
- Each coefficient u_i is a small multiple of $2^{\lceil 25.5i \rceil}$, to limit the effort of multiplying coefficients. Specifically, **reduced-coefficient** polynomials have $u_i/2^{\lceil 25.5i \rceil} \in \{-2^{25}, -2^{25} + 1, \ldots, -1, 0, 1, \ldots, 2^{25} - 1, 2^{25}\}$.

To summarize: A reduced-degree reduced-coefficient polynomial is a polynomial $u_0 + u_1 x + \cdots + u_9 x^9$ with $u_0/2^0$, $u_1/2^{26}$, $u_2/2^{51}$, $u_3/2^{77}$, $u_4/2^{102}$, $u_5/2^{128}$, $u_6/2^{153}$, $u_7/2^{179}$, $u_8/2^{204}$, $u_9/2^{230}$ all in $\{-2^{25}, -2^{25} + 1, \ldots, -1, 0, 1, \ldots, 2^{25} - 1, 2^{25}\}$. This polynomial represents the integer $u_0 + u_1 + \cdots + u_9$.

Note that integers are not converted to a unique "smallest" representation until the end of the Curve25519 computation. Producing reduced representations is generally much faster than producing "smallest" representations.

Representing coefficients inside CPUs. The Pentium M has eight "fp registers," each of which holds a real number $2^e f$ for integers e and f with $f \in \{-2^{64}, \ldots, 2^{64}\}$ and with e in an adequate range for all the computations discussed here. My computations hold polynomial coefficients in fp registers to the extent possible, as in [11, Section 4].

The Pentium M has many more "L1-cache doublewords" that can hold $2^e f$ with f limited to the range $\{-2^{53}, \ldots, 2^{53}\}$; e.g., reduced coefficients. To perform arithmetic on numbers in L1-cache doublewords, the Pentium M must take time to copy ("load") the numbers into registers; but this is not a big problem, because these loads can be overlapped with arithmetic if they are not too frequent.

Why split 255-bit integers into ten 26-bit pieces, rather than nine 29-bit pieces or eight 32-bit pieces? Answer: The coefficients of a polynomial product do not fit into the Pentium M's fp registers if pieces are too large. The cost of handling larger coefficients outweighs the savings of handling fewer coefficients. The overall time for 29-bit pieces is sufficiently competitive to warrant further investigation, but so far I haven't been able to save time this way. I'm sure that 32-bit pieces, the most common choice in the literature, are a bad idea.

Of course, the same question must be revisited for each CPU. The Pentium 1, Pentium MMX, Pentium Pro, Pentium II, Pentium III, Pentium 4, Athlon, and Athlon XP work well with 26-bit pieces; on the Athlon 64 and Opteron, 32-bit pieces might be slightly better. On the UltraSPARC and PowerPC, fp registers use $\{-2^{53}, \ldots, 2^{53}\}$ rather than $\{-2^{64}, \ldots, 2^{64}\}$, and I recommend twelve 22-bit pieces. The UltraSPARC and PowerPC can overlap fp additions with fp multiplications, so I expect them to end up with comparable cycle counts to the Pentium M despite the larger number of pieces.

Given that there are 10 pieces, why use radix $2^{25.5}$ rather than, e.g., radix 2^{25} or radix 2^{26}? Answer: My ring R contains $2^{255}x^{10} - 19$, which represents 0 in $\mathbf{Z}/(2^{255} - 19)$. I will reduce polynomial products modulo $2^{255}x^{10} - 19$ to eliminate the coefficients of x^{10}, x^{11}, etc. With radix 2^{25}, the coefficient of x^{10} could not be eliminated. With radix 2^{26}, coefficients would have to be multiplied by $2^5 \cdot 19$ rather than just 19, and the results would not fit into an fp register.

Using floating-point operations. The Pentium M has circuits for three fast operations on numbers stored in fp registers: sum, difference, and product. These are exact operations if the results fit into the 64-bit fp precision; otherwise the results are rounded to the nearest fp numbers.

The Pentium M can perform, at best, one fp operation per cycle. About 92% of the cycles in my Curve25519 computation (589825 out of 640838) are occupied by fp operations. One can understand the cycle counts fairly well by simply counting the fp operations. Similar comments apply to other CPUs, although the details depend on the CPU.

Warning: Writing an fp program in the C programming language, and feeding the result to a C compiler, often produces machine language that takes 3 or more Pentium M cycles for each fp operation. Further discussion of this phenomenon is outside the scope of this paper. My Curve25519 software is actually written in qhasm, a new programming language designed for high-speed computations.

Beware that a few CPUs have input-dependent fp timings. An old example is the Sun microSPARC-IIep. A newer example is the IBM PowerPC RS64 IV, which takes an extra cycle to multiply by 0. Fast constant-time computations on these CPUs need extra effort.

Adding integers modulo $2^{255} - 19$. If two integers are represented by two polynomials u and v then the sum of the two integers is represented by $u + v$. Similarly, the difference of the two integers is represented by $u - v$.

If u and v are reduced-degree reduced-coefficient polynomials then computing $u + v$ (or $u - v$) involves 10 additions (or subtractions) of fp numbers. Note that the sum is reduced-degree but usually not reduced-coefficient. In a long chain of sums one would occasionally have to take extra time to reduce the coefficients. This is never necessary in the Curve25519 computation: every sum (and difference) is used solely as input to products, as Appendix B illustrates.

Statistics: Each addition or subtraction takes 10 fp operations. There are 8 additions and subtractions, totalling 80 fp operations, in each iteration of the Curve25519 main loop. There are 2040 additions and subtractions, totalling 20400 fp operations, in the entire Curve25519 computation.

Multiplying integers modulo $2^{255} - 19$. If two integers are represented by polynomials u and v then their product is represented by the polynomial product uv. If u and v are reduced-degree reduced-coefficient polynomials, or sums of two such polynomials, then computing uv in the simplest way involves 100 fp multiplications and 81 fp additions; I am experimenting with other polynomial-multiplication algorithms and expect to end up with slightly better results. The product uv is then replaced by a reduced-degree reduced-coefficient polynomial:

- The coefficients of $x^{10}, x^{11}, \ldots, x^{18}$ in uv are eliminated by reduction modulo $2^{255}x^{10} - 19$. For example, the coefficient of x^{18} is multiplied by $19 \cdot 2^{-255}$ and added to the coefficient of x^8. Each reduction involves 1 fp multiplication and 1 fp addition.

- The "high" part of each coefficient is subtracted from that coefficient and added ("carried") to the next coefficient. The high part is, by definition, the nearest multiple of the power of 2 for the next coefficient. One carry involves 4 fp additions: 2 to identify the high part (by a rounded addition and then subtraction of a large constant), 1 to subtract, and 1 to add.

Starting from uv, I carry from x^8 to x^9, then from x^9 to x^{10}; then I eliminate coefficients of $x^{10}, x^{11}, \ldots, x^{18}$; then I carry from x^0 to x^1, from x^1 to x^2, $\ldots$, from x^7 to x^8, and once more from x^8 to x^9. Note that the coefficient of x^9 is a multiple of 2^{230}, and is between -2^{254} and 2^{254} after subtraction of its original high part, so the final carry from x^8 to x^9 produces reduced coefficients. Overall there are 18 fp operations to eliminate 9 coefficients, and 44 fp operations for 11 carries. There are many other reasonable carry sequences; on some CPUs it might be a good idea to have two parallel carry chains, decreasing latency at the expense of an extra carry.

Squaring is easier than general multiplication, because polynomial squaring is easier than general polynomial multiplication. Overall a squaring eliminates $9^2 + 9$ coefficient multiplications at the expense of 9 initial coefficient doublings; note that doubling coefficients at the beginning is slightly better than doubling products later. Multiplication by a small constant is also easier than general multiplication, because the constant is represented by a polynomial of degree 0.

Statistics: Each multiplication by a small constant takes 55 fp operations. Each squaring takes 162 fp operations. Each general multiplication takes 243 fp operations. Each iteration of the Curve25519 main loop has 1 multiplication by a small constant, using 55 fp operations; 4 squarings, using 648 fp operations; and 5 general multiplications, using 1215 fp operations; in total 10 multiplications, using 1918 fp operations. The Curve25519 computation has 255 multiplications by small constants, using 14025 fp operations; 1274 squarings, using 206388 fp operations; and 1286 general multiplications, using 312498 fp operations; in total 2815 multiplications, using 532911 fp operations.

Note that the squaring-to-multiplication floating-point-operation ratio is only $162/243 = 2/3$, far below the 0.8 ratio often used in the literature for estimating the costs of elliptic-curve operations.

Selecting integers. Consider the problem of computing $x[b]$, where $x[0], x[1]$ are integers modulo $2^{255} - 19$ and b is an input-dependent bit. Using b as an array index—without taking extra time for preloads, interrupt elimination, etc.—could allow hyperthreading attacks and other cache-timing attacks; see [12, Sections 8–15]. I instead compute $x[b]$ as $(1-b)x[0]+bx[1]$. Similarly, if I need to compute the pair $(x[b], x[1-b])$, I compute $(x[0] - b(x[0] - x[1]), x[1] + b(x[0] - x[1]))$.

Statistics: Each iteration of the Curve25519 main loop has 2 fp operations inside computing b and $1 - b$; 2 paired selections, taking 80 fp operations; and 2 more selections, taking 60 more fp operations. The total is 142 fp operations. The entire Curve25519 computation spends 36210 fp operations, about 6% of the total, on selection. Of course, these operations could be eliminated if timing attacks were not a concern.

Why this field? CPUs include fast integer-multiplication circuits (usually buried inside fp-multiplication circuits aimed at the large fp market) but not circuits for fast multiplication of polynomials modulo 2. Characteristic-2 fields allow several other speedups—see, e.g., [35, Section 3.4] and [25, Section 15.1]— but I can't see any way for them to set speed records on existing CPUs.

"Optimal extension fields," such as degree-10 extensions of prime fields of size around 2^{26}, are advertised in [7] and [6] as allowing faster multiplication and much faster inversion, perhaps so fast as to make affine-coordinate elliptic-curve computations faster than projective-coordinate elliptic-curve computations. My current assessment is that these fields have some slight advantages: there are no carry chains, so operations are easier to reorder; there are 10 reductions modulo a prime, rather than 11 carries, although one reduction is usually slightly more expensive than one carry; inversion is faster, although not fast enough to make affine coordinates worthwhile; and, most importantly, degree 9 might fit into 64-bit fp. Unfortunately, these fields have a huge disadvantage: even if they are slightly faster on some CPUs, they are much slower on other CPUs. A 255-bit integer can be split into 4 or 8 or 10 or 12 pieces to accommodate the capabilities of different processors; an "optimal extension field" is tied to a particular number of pieces.

So I selected a prime field. Prime fields also have the virtue of minimizing the number of security concerns for elliptic-curve cryptography; see, e.g., [29] and [22].

I chose my prime $2^{255} - 19$ according to the following criteria: primes as close as possible to a power of 2 save time in field operations (as in, e.g, [9]), with no effect on (conjectured) security level; primes slightly below $32k$ bits, for some k, allow public keys to be easily transmitted in 32-bit words, with no serious concerns regarding wasted space; $k = 8$ provides a comfortable security level. I considered the primes $2^{255} + 95$, $2^{255} - 19$, $2^{255} - 31$, $2^{254} + 79$, $2^{253} + 51$, and $2^{253} + 39$, and selected $2^{255} - 19$ because 19 is smaller than $31, 39, 51, 79, 95$.

5   Fast Curve25519 Computation

This section explains fast x-coordinate point addition on my elliptic curve $y^2 = x^3 + 486662x^2 + x$; explains fast x-coordinate scalar multiplication, i.e., fast computation of Curve25519; and compares this curve to other elliptic curves.

Recall that Section 2 defines two x-coordinate functions. One function X_0 maps ∞ to 0; the other function X maps ∞ to ∞. Curve25519 is defined using X_0, but inside the computation it is convenient to use X until the last moment.

Addition. Montgomery in [47, Section 10.3.1] published formulas to compute $X(2Q)$ given $X(Q)$, and to compute $X(Q + Q')$ given $X(Q), X(Q'), X(Q - Q')$, assuming that $Q \neq \infty$, $Q' \neq \infty$, $Q - Q' \neq \infty$, $Q + Q' \neq \infty$. It turns out that Montgomery's formulas also work for ∞, provided that $Q - Q' \notin \{\infty, (0,0)\}$, so the Curve25519 computation can avoid checking for ∞. See Appendix B of this paper.

Montgomery's formulas represent each X value as a fraction x/z, replacing divisions with multiplications. Montgomery commented that, when d is large, one can perform d divisions in $\mathbf{F}_p$ at about the same cost as $4d$ multiplications in $\mathbf{F}_p$, so dividing x by z may be a good idea when there are many separate elliptic-curve computations to perform at once; I have not implemented this option yet.

The formula for $X(2Q)$ involves 2 squarings, 1 multiplication by $121665 = (486662 - 2)/4$, and 2 more multiplications. The formula for $X(Q + Q')$ involves 2 squarings and 3 more multiplications when z_1 in Theorem B.2, the denominator of $X(Q - Q')$, is known to be 1; otherwise it involves 2 squarings and 4 more multiplications. The Curve25519 computation always has $z_1 = 1$.

Scalar multiplication. Montgomery suggested using his formulas to obtain $X(nQ + Q), X(nQ), X(Q)$ given $X(\lfloor n/2 \rfloor Q + Q), X(\lfloor n/2 \rfloor Q), X(Q)$: if n is even then $nQ = 2\lfloor n/2 \rfloor Q$ and $nQ + Q = (\lfloor n/2 \rfloor Q + Q) + (\lfloor n/2 \rfloor Q)$; if n is odd then $nQ + Q = 2(\lfloor n/2 \rfloor Q + Q)$ and $nQ = (\lfloor n/2 \rfloor Q + Q) + (\lfloor n/2 \rfloor Q)$. Either case involves one doubling and one addition.

The formulas, repeated k times, produce $X(nQ + Q), X(nQ), X(Q)$ with k doublings and k additions starting from $X(\lfloor n/2^k \rfloor Q + Q), X(\lfloor n/2^k \rfloor Q), X(Q)$. I compute $X(nQ)$ for any $n \in 2^{254} + 8\{0, 1, \ldots, 2^{251} - 1\}$ with 255 doublings and

255 additions starting from $X(Q), X(0), X(Q)$. The first and last few iterations could be simplified.

The final $X(nQ)$, like other X values, is represented as a fraction x/z. I compute $X_0(nQ) = xz^{p-2}$ using a straightforward sequence of 254 squarings and 11 multiplications. This is about 7% of the Curve25519 computation. An extended-Euclid inversion of z, randomized to protect against timing attacks, might be faster, but the maximum potential speedup is very small, while the cost in code complexity is large.

Theorems B.1 and B.2 justify the above procedure if $X_0(Q) \neq 0$. The same formulas also work for $X_0(Q) = 0$: every computed fraction has denominator 0, so the final output is 0 as desired.

Other addition chains. Montgomery pointed out that one can replace the addition chain $\{\lfloor n/2^k \rfloor\} \cup \{\lfloor n/2^k \rfloor + 1\}$ with any differential addition chain (any "Lucas chain"), i.e., any addition chain where each sum is already accompanied by a difference. One can find such a chain with only about 384 elements, as discussed in [59, Section 5]. On the other hand, most of the additions then require $z_1 \neq 1$ in Theorem B.2, costing extra multiplications in $\mathbf{F}_p$. It is also not clear how easily these addition chains can be protected against cache-timing attacks. Further investigation is required.

A more common strategy is to drop the difference requirement, compensate by computing more coordinates of each multiple of Q (Jacobian coordinates, for example, or Chudnovsky coordinates), and use an addition chain with only about 320 elements. See, e.g., [17] or [4]. Unfortunately, even if A is selected so that $y^2 = x^3 + Ax^2 + x$ is isomorphic to a curve $y^2 = x^3 - 3x - a_6$, each doubling in known coordinate systems takes at least 8 field multiplications, and each general addition takes even more. All of my experiments with this strategy have ended up using more field operations, more floating-point operations, and more cycles than the x-coordinate strategy.

One can save a large fraction of the time for computing Curve25519($\underline{n}, \underline{q}$) when q is fixed—in particular, for computing public keys Curve25519($\underline{n}, \underline{9}$)—by precomputing various multiples of $(q, \ldots)$. An essentially optimal algorithm, published by Pippenger in [52] in 1976, computes u public keys with only about $256/\lg 8u$ additions per key. This speedup is negligible in the Diffie-Hellman context (and is not provided by my current software), since each key is used many times; but the speedup is useful for other applications of elliptic curves.

Why this curve? I chose the curve shape $y^2 = x^3 + Ax^2 + x$, as suggested by Montgomery, to allow extremely fast x-coordinate point operations. Curves of this shape have order divisible by 4, requiring a marginally larger prime for the same conjectured security level, but this is outweighed by the extra speed of curve operations. I selected $(A - 2)/4$ as a small integer, as suggested by Montgomery, to speed up the multiplication by $(A - 2)/4$; this has no effect on the conjectured security level.

To protect against various attacks discussed in Section 3, I rejected choices of A whose curve and twist orders were not $\{4 \cdot \text{prime}, 8 \cdot \text{prime}\}$; here $4, 8$ are minimal since $p \in 1 + 4\mathbf{Z}$. The smallest positive choices for A are 358990, 464586, and 486662. I rejected $A = 358990$ because one of its primes is slightly *smaller* than 2^{252}, raising the question of how standards and implementations should handle the theoretical possibility of a user's secret key matching the prime; discussing this question is more difficult than switching to another A. I rejected 464586 for the same reason. So I ended up with $A = 486662$.

Special curves with small complex automorphisms have potential benefits, as discussed in [31], and are worth further investigation, but so far I have not succeeded in saving time using them.

References

1. — (no editor), *17th annual symposium on foundations of computer science*, IEEE Computer Society, Long Beach, California, 1976. MR 56:1766. See [52].
2. Kazimierz Alster, Jerzy Urbanowicz, Hugh C. Williams (editors), *Public-key cryptography and computational number theory: proceedings of the international conference held in Warsaw, September 11–15, 2000*, Walter de Gruyter, Berlin, 2001. ISBN 3–11–017046–9. MR 2002h:94001. See [60].
3. Adrian Antipa, Daniel Brown, Alfred Menezes, René Struik, Scott Vanstone, *Validation of elliptic curve public keys*, in [21] (2003), 211–223. MR 2171928. Citations in this paper: §1.
4. Roberto M. Avanzi, *Aspects of hyperelliptic curves over large prime fields in software implementations*, in [36] (2004), 148–162. Citations in this paper: §1, §5.
5. Roberto M. Avanzi, *Generic algorithms for computing discrete logarithms*, in [19] (2005), 477–494. MR 2162735. Citations in this paper: §3, §3.
6. Roberto M. Avanzi, Preda Mihăilescu, *Generic efficient arithmetic algorithms for PAFFs (processor adequate finite fields) and related algebraic structures (extended abstract)*, in [43] (2004), 320–334. Citations in this paper: §4.
7. Daniel V. Bailey, Christof Paar, *Efficient arithmetic in finite field extensions with application in elliptic curve cryptography*, Journal of Cryptology **14** (2001), 153–176. ISSN 0933–2790. Citations in this paper: §1, §4.
8. Mihir Bellare (editor), *Advances in cryptology—CRYPTO 2000: proceedings of the 20th Annual International Cryptology Conference held in Santa Barbara, CA, August 20–24, 2000*, Lecture Notes in Computer Science, 1880, Springer-Verlag, Berlin, 2000. ISBN 3–540–67907–3. MR 2002c:94002. See [14].
9. Andreas Bender, Guy Castagnoli, *On the implementation of elliptic curve cryptosystems*, in [16] (1990), 186–192. MR 91d:11154. Citations in this paper: §4.
10. Kamel Bentahar, *The equivalence between the DHP and DLP for elliptic curves used in practical applications, revisited* (2005). URL: http://eprint.iacr.org/2005/307. Citations in this paper: §3.
11. Daniel J. Bernstein, *The Poly1305-AES message-authentication code*, in [32] (2005), 32–49. URL: http://cr.yp.to/papers.html#poly1305. ID 0018d9551b5 546d97c340e0dd8cb5750. Citations in this paper: §4.
12. Daniel J. Bernstein, *Cache-timing attacks on AES* (2005). URL: http://cr.yp.to/papers.html#cachetiming. ID cd9faae9bd5308c440df50fc26a517b4. Citations in this paper: §1, §4.
13. Daniel J. Bernstein, *Salsa20 specification* (2005). URL: http://cr.yp.to/snuffle.html. Citations in this paper: §3.

14. Ingrid Biehl, Bernd Meyer, Volker Müller, *Differential fault attacks on elliptic curve cryptosystems (extended abstract)*, in [8] (2000), 131–146. URL: `http://lecturer.ukdw.ac.id/vmueller/publications.php`. Citations in this paper: §1, §3.

15. Colin Boyd (editor), *Advances in cryptology—ASIACRYPT 2001: proceedings of the 7th international conference on the theory and application of cryptology and information security held on the Gold Coast, December 9–13, 2001*, Lecture Notes in Computer Science, 2248, Springer-Verlag, Berlin, 2001. ISBN 3–540–42987–5. MR 2003d:94001. See [59].

16. Gilles Brassard (editor), *Advances in cryptology—CRYPTO '89*, Lecture Notes in Computer Science, 435, Springer-Verlag, Berlin, 1990. ISBN 0–387–97317–6. MR 91b:94002. See [9].

17. Michael Brown, Darrel Hankerson, Julio López, Alfred Menezes, *Software implementation of the NIST elliptic curves over prime fields* (2000); see also newer version [18]. URL: `http://www.cacr.math.uwaterloo.ca/techreports/2000/corr2000-56.ps`. Citations in this paper: §1, §5.

18. Michael Brown, Darrel Hankerson, Julio López, Alfred Menezes, *Software implementation of the NIST elliptic curves over prime fields*, in [49] (2001), 250–265; see also older version [17]. MR 1907102.

19. Henri Cohen, Gerhard Frey (editors), *Handbook of elliptic and hyperelliptic curve cryptography*, CRC Press, 2005. ISBN 1–58488–518–1. See [5], [24], [25], [30].

20. Yvo Desmedt (editor), *Advances in cryptology—CRYPTO '94*, Lecture Notes in Computer Science, 839, Springer-Verlag, Berlin, 1994. See [44].

21. Yvo Desmedt, *Public Key Cryptography—PKC 2003, 6th international workshop on theory and practice in public key cryptography, Miami, FL, USA, January 6–8, 2003, proceedings*, Lecture Notes in Computer Science, 2567, Springer, Berlin, 2003. ISBN 3–540–00324–X. See [3].

22. Claus Diem, *The GHS attack in odd characteristic*, Journal of the Ramanujan Mathematical Society **18** (2003), 1–32. MR 2004a:14030. URL: `http://www.math.uni-leipzig.de/~diem/preprints`. Citations in this paper: §4.

23. Whitfield Diffie, Martin Hellman, *New directions in cryptography*, IEEE Transactions on Information Theory **22** (1976), 644–654. ISSN 0018–9448. MR 55:10141. URL: `http://cr.yp.to/bib/entries.html#1976/diffie`. Citations in this paper: §3.

24. Christophe Doche, Tanja Lange, *Arithmetic of elliptic curves*, in [19] (2005), 267–302. MR 2162729. Citations in this paper: §A.

25. Christophe Doche, Tanja Lange, *Arithmetic of special curves*, in [19] (2005), 355–387. MR 2162731. Citations in this paper: §4.

26. Kenny Fong, Darrel Hankerson, Julio López, Alfred Menezes, *Field inversion and point halving revisited* (2003); see also newer version [27]. URL: `http://www.cacr.math.uwaterloo.ca/techreports/2003/tech_reports2003.html`. Citations in this paper: §1.

27. Kenny Fong, Darrel Hankerson, Julio López, Alfred Menezes, *Field inversion and point halving revisited*, IEEE Transactions on Computers **53** (2004), 1047–1059; see also older version [26]. ISSN 0018–9340.

28. Jens Franke, Thorsten Kleinjung, Christof Paar, Jan Pelzl, Christine Priplata, Martin Simka, Colin Stahlke, *An efficient hardware architecture for factoring integers with the elliptic curve method*, Workshop Record of SHARCS 2005 (2005), 51–62. URL: `http://www.best.tuke.sk/simka/pub.html`. Citations in this paper: §3, §3.

29. Gerhard Frey, *How to disguise an elliptic curve (Weil descent)* (1998). URL: `http://www.cacr.math.uwaterloo.ca/conferences/1998/ecc98/slides.html`. Citations in this paper: §4.

30. Gerhard Frey, Tanja Lange, *Transfer of discrete logarithms*, in [19] (2005), 529–543. MR 2162738. Citations in this paper: §3.
31. Robert P. Gallant, Robert J. Lambert, Scott A. Vanstone, *Faster point multiplication on elliptic curves with efficient endomorphisms*, in [38] (2001), 190–200. MR 2003h:14043. Citations in this paper: §5.
32. Henri Gilbert, Helena Handschuh (editors), *Fast software encryption: 12th international workshop, FSE 2005, Paris, France, February 21–23, 2005, revised selected papers*, Lecture Notes in Computer Science, 3557, Springer, 2005. ISBN 3–540–26541–4. See [11].
33. Darrel Hankerson, Julio Lopez Hernandez, Alfred Menezes, *Software implementation of elliptic curve cryptography over binary fields* (2000); see also newer version [34]. URL: http://www.cacr.math.uwaterloo.ca/techreports/2000/corr2000-42.ps. Citations in this paper: §1.
34. Darrel Hankerson, Julio Lopez Hernandez, Alfred Menezes, *Software implementation of elliptic curve cryptography over binary fields*, in [40] (2000), 1–24; see also older version [33].
35. Darrel Hankerson, Alfred Menezes, Scott Vanstone, *Guide to elliptic curve cryptography*, Springer, New York, 2004. ISBN 0–387–95273–X. MR 2054891. Citations in this paper: §4.
36. Marc Joye, Jean-Jacques Quisquater (editors), *Cryptographic hardware and embedded systems—CHES 2004: 6th international workshop, Cambridge, MA, USA, August 11–13, 2004, proceedings*, Lecture Notes in Computer Science, 3156, Springer, 2004. ISBN 3–540–22666–4. See [4].
37. Burton S. Kaliski Jr. (editor), *Advances in cryptology—CRYPTO '97: 17th annual international cryptology conference, Santa Barbara, California, USA, August 17–21, 1997, proceedings*, Lecture Notes in Computer Science, 1294, Springer, 1997. ISBN 3–540–63384–7. MR 99a:94041. See [42].
38. Joe Kilian (editor), *Advances in cryptology: CRYPTO 2001, 21st annual international cryptology conference, Santa Barbara, California, USA, August 19–23, 2001, proceedings*, Lecture Notes in Computer Science, 2139, Springer, 2001. ISBN 3–540–42456–3. MR 2003d:94002. See [31].
39. Neal Koblitz, Alfred J. Menezes, *Another look at "provable security"* (2004). URL: http://www.cacr.math.uwaterloo.ca/~ajmeneze/publications/provable.pdf. Citations in this paper: §3.
40. Çetin Kaya Koç, Christof Paar, *Cryptographic hardware and embedded systems— CHES 2000: Proceedings of the 2nd International Workshop held in Worcester, MA, USA, August 2000*, Lecture Notes in Computer Science, Springer, 2000. ISBN 3–540–42521–7. See [34].
41. Fabian Kuhn, Rene Struik, *Random walks revisited: extensions of Pollard's rho algorithm for computing multiple discrete logarithms*, in [64] (2001), 212–229. URL: http://www.distcomp.ethz.ch/publications.html. Citations in this paper: §3.
42. Chae Hoon Lim, Pil Joong Lee, *A key recovery attack on discrete log-based schemes using a prime order subgroup*, in [37] (1997), 249–263. URL: http://dasan.sejong.ac.kr/~chlim/english_pub.html. Citations in this paper: §3, §3.
43. Mitsuru Matsui, Robert Zuccherato (editors), *Selected areas in cryptography: 10th annual international workshop, SAC 2003, Ottawa, Canada, August 14–15, 2003, revised papers*, Lecture Notes in Computer Science, 3006, Springer, 2004. ISBN 3–540–21370–8. See [6].
44. Ueli M. Maurer, *Towards the equivalence of breaking the Diffie-Hellman protocol and computing discrete logarithms*, in [20] (1994), 271–281. URL: http://www.crypto.ethz.ch/~maurer/publications.html. Citations in this paper: §3.

45. Alfred Menezes, *Another look at HMQV* (2005). URL: `http://eprint.iacr.org/2005/205`. Citations in this paper: §2.

46. Victor S. Miller, *Use of elliptic curves in cryptography*, in [65] (1986), 417–426. MR 88b:68040. Citations in this paper: §1.

47. Peter L. Montgomery, *Speeding the Pollard and elliptic curve methods of factorization*, Mathematics of Computation **48** (1987), 243–264. ISSN 0025-5718. MR 88e:11130. URL: `http://cr.yp.to/bib/entries.html#1987/montgomery`. Citations in this paper: §5.

48. A. Muzereau, Nigel P. Smart, Frederik Vercauteren, *The equivalence between the DHP and DLP for elliptic curves used in practical applications*, LMS Journal of Computation and Mathematics **7** (2004), 50–72. URL: `http://www.lms.ac.uk/jcm/7/lms2003-034/`. Citations in this paper: §3.

49. David Naccache (editor), *Topics in cryptology—CT-RSA 2001: Proceedings of the Cryptographers' Track at the RSA Conference held in San Francisco, CA, April 8–12, 2001*, Lecture Notes in Computer Science, 2020, Springer, 2001. ISBN 3-540-41898-9. MR 2003a:94039. See [18].

50. Dag Arne Osvik, Adi Shamir, Eran Tromer, *Cache atacks and countermeasures: the case of AES (extended version)* (2005). URL: `http://www.wisdom.weizmann.ac.il/~tromer/`. Citations in this paper: §1.

51. Colin Percival, *Cache missing for fun and profit* (2005). URL: `http://www.daemonology.net/hyperthreading-considered-harmful/`. Citations in this paper: §1.

52. Nicholas Pippenger, *On the evaluation of powers and related problems (preliminary version)*, in [1] (1976), 258–263; newer version split into [53] and [54]. MR 58:3682. URL: `http://cr.yp.to/bib/entries.html#1976/pippenger`. Citations in this paper: §5.

53. Nicholas Pippenger, *The minimum number of edges in graphs with prescribed paths*, Mathematical Systems Theory **12** (1979), 325–346; see also older version [52]. ISSN 0025-5661. MR 81e:05079. URL: `http://cr.yp.to/bib/entries.html#1979/pippenger`.

54. Nicholas Pippenger, *On the evaluation of powers and monomials*, SIAM Journal on Computing **9** (1980), 230–250; see also older version [52]. ISSN 0097-5397. MR 82c:10064. URL: `http://cr.yp.to/bib/entries.html#1980/pippenger`.

55. John M. Pollard, *Kangaroos, Monopoly and discrete logarithms*, Journal of Cryptology **13** (2000), 437–447. ISSN 0933-2790. Citations in this paper: §3.

56. John Proos, Christof Zalka, *Shor's discrete logarithm quantum algorithm for elliptic curves* (2003). URL: `http://www.cacr.math.uwaterloo.ca/techreports/2003/tech_reports2003.html`. Citations in this paper: §1.

57. Nigel P. Smart, *A comparison of different finite fields for use in elliptic curve cryptosystems* (2000); see also newer version [58]. URL: `http://www.cs.bris.ac.uk/Publications/pub_info.jsp?id=1000458`.

58. Nigel P. Smart, *A comparison of different finite fields for elliptic curve cryptosystems*, Computers and Mathematics with Applications **42** (2001), 91–100; see also older version [57]. MR 2002c:94033. Citations in this paper: §1.

59. Martijn Stam, Arjen K. Lenstra, *Speeding up XTR*, in [15] (2001), 125–143. MR 2003h:94049. Citations in this paper: §5.

60. Edlyn Teske, *Square-root algorithms for the discrete logarithm problem (a survey)*, in [2] (2001), 283–301. MR 2003c:11156. URL: `http://www.cacr.math.uwaterloo.ca/~eteske/publications.html`. Citations in this paper: §3.

61. Edlyn Teske, *Computing discrete logarithms with the parallelized kangaroo method* (2001); see also newer version [62]. URL: `http://www.cacr.math.uwaterloo.ca/techreports/2001/tech_reports2001.html`. Citations in this paper: §3.
62. Edlyn Teske, *Computing discrete logarithms with the parallelized kangaroo method*, Discrete Applied Mathematics **130** (2003), 61–82; see also older version [61]. MR 2004h:11112.
63. Paul C. van Oorschot, Michael Wiener, *Parallel collision search with cryptanalytic applications*, Journal of Cryptology **12** (1999), 1–28. ISSN 0933–2790. URL: `http://members.rogers.com/paulv/papers/pubs.html`. Citations in this paper: §3.
64. Serge Vaudenay, Amr M. Youssef (editors), *Selected areas in cryptography: 8th annual international workshop, SAC 2001, Toronto, Ontario, Canada, August 16–17, 2001, revised papers*, Lecture Notes in Computer Science, 2259, Springer, 2001. ISBN 3–540–43066–0. MR 2004k:94066. See [41].
65. Hugh C. Williams (editor), *Advances in cryptology: CRYPTO '85*, Lecture Notes in Computer Science, 218, Springer, Berlin, 1986. ISBN 3–540–16463–4. See [46].

A   Appendix: Rings, Fields, and Curves

This appendix reviews elliptic curves at the level of generality of Theorem 2.1. See [24, Chapter 13] for much more information about elliptic curves.

The base field. Let p be a prime number with $p \geq 5$. Define $\mathbf{F}_p$ as the set $\{0, 1, \ldots, p-1\}$. Define a binary operation $+$ on $\mathbf{F}_p$ as addition mod p. Define a binary operation $\cdot$ on $\mathbf{F}_p$ as multiplication mod p. Define a unary operation $-$ on $\mathbf{F}_p$ as negation mod p.

$\mathbf{F}_p$ is a commutative ring under $0, 1, -, +, \cdot$. This means that it satisfies every $0, 1, -, +, \cdot$ identity satisfied by $\mathbf{Z}$; e.g., the identity $a(b+c+1) = ab + ac + a$. Furthermore, because p is prime, $\mathbf{F}_p$ is a field: every nonzero element of $\mathbf{F}_p$ has a reciprocal in $\mathbf{F}_p$.

Squares in the base field. Squaring is a 2-to-1 map on the nonzero elements of $\mathbf{F}_p$, so there are exactly $(p-1)/2$ non-squares in $\mathbf{F}_p$. Find the smallest $\delta \in \{1, 2, \ldots, p-1\}$ such that δ is not a square in $\mathbf{F}_p$.

Fermat's little theorem implies that $\alpha^{(p-1)/2} = 1$ if α is a nonzero square in $\mathbf{F}_p$; $\alpha^{(p-1)/2} = -1$ if α is a non-square in $\mathbf{F}_p$; and $\alpha^{(p-1)/2} = 0$ if $\alpha = 0$. Consequently, if α is a non-square in $\mathbf{F}_p$, then α/δ is a nonzero square in $\mathbf{F}_p$.

The extension field. Define $\mathbf{F}_{p^2}$ as the set $\mathbf{F}_p \times \mathbf{F}_p$. Define a unary operation $-$ on $\mathbf{F}_{p^2}$ by $-(c, d) = (-c, -d)$. Define a binary operation $+$ on $\mathbf{F}_{p^2}$ by $(a, b) + (c, d) = (a+c, b+d)$. Define a binary operation $\cdot$ on $\mathbf{F}_{p^2}$ by $(a, b) \cdot (c, d) = (ac + \delta bd, ad + bc)$.

$\mathbf{F}_{p^2}$ is a commutative ring under $0, 1, -, +, \cdot$. Furthermore, each nonzero $(a, b) \in \mathbf{F}_{p^2}$ has a reciprocal $(a/(a^2 - \delta b^2), -b/(a^2 - \delta b^2)) \in \mathbf{F}_{p^2}$.

The injection $a \mapsto (a, 0)$ from $\mathbf{F}_p$ to $\mathbf{F}_{p^2}$ is a ring morphism: it preserves $0, 1, -, +, \cdot$. Thus $(a, 0)$ is abbreviated a without risk of confusion. The element $(0, 1)$ of $\mathbf{F}_{p^2}$ is abbreviated $\sqrt{\delta}$; it satisfies $\sqrt{\delta}^2 = (\delta, 0) = \delta$.

The elliptic curve. Let A be an integer such that $A^2 - 4 \bmod p$ is not a square in $\mathbf{F}_p$. Define $E(\mathbf{F}_{p^2})$ as $\{\infty\} \cup \{(x, y) \in \mathbf{F}_{p^2} : y^2 = x^3 + Ax^2 + x\}$.

Define a unary operation $-$ on $E(\mathbf{F}_{p^2})$ as follows: $-\infty = \infty$; $-(x, y) = (x, -y)$. Define a binary operation $+$ on $E(\mathbf{F}_{p^2})$ as follows:

- $\infty + \infty = \infty$.
- $\infty + (x, y) = (x, y)$.
- $(x, y) + \infty = (x, y)$.
- $(x, y) + (x, -y) = \infty$.
- If $y \neq 0$ then $(x, y) + (x, y) = (x'', y'')$ where $\lambda = (3x^2 + 2Ax + 1)/2y$, $x'' = \lambda^2 - A - 2x = (x^2 - 1)^2/4y^2$, and $y'' = \lambda(x - x'') - y$. Here $/$ refers to division in $\mathbf{F}_{p^2}$.
- If $x' \neq x$ then $(x, y) + (x', y') = (x'', y'')$ where $\lambda = (y' - y)/(x' - x)$, $x'' = \lambda^2 - A - x - x'$, and $y'' = \lambda(x - x'') - y$.

Standard (although lengthy) calculations show that $E(\mathbf{F}_{p^2})$ is a commutative group under $\infty, -, +$. This means that every $0, -, +$ identity satisfied by $\mathbf{Z}$ is also satisfied by $E(\mathbf{F}_{p^2})$ when 0 is replaced by ∞.

Note that the following three sets are subgroups of $E(\mathbf{F}_{p^2})$:

- $\{\infty, (0, 0)\}$. Indeed, $\infty + \infty = \infty$; $(0, 0) + (0, 0) = \infty$; and $(0, 0) + \infty = (0, 0)$.
- $\{\infty\} \cup (E(\mathbf{F}_{p^2}) \cap (\mathbf{F}_p \times \mathbf{F}_p))$. Indeed, if $x, y, x', y' \in \mathbf{F}_p$ then the quantities λ, x'', y'' defined above are in $\mathbf{F}_p$.
- $\{\infty\} \cup (E(\mathbf{F}_{p^2}) \cap (\mathbf{F}_p \times \sqrt{\delta}\mathbf{F}_p))$. This time λ is a ratio of an element of $\mathbf{F}_p$ and an element of $\sqrt{\delta}\mathbf{F}_p$, and is therefore an element of $\sqrt{\delta}\mathbf{F}_p$, producing $x'' \in \mathbf{F}_p$ and $y'' \in \sqrt{\delta}\mathbf{F}_p$.

Note also that if $x^3 + Ax^2 + x = 0$ in $\mathbf{F}_p$ then $x = 0$. (Otherwise $A^2 - 4 = (x - 1/x)^2$ in $\mathbf{F}_p$, so $A^2 - 4 \bmod p$ is a square in $\mathbf{F}_p$, contradiction.) In other words, $(x, 0) \notin E(\mathbf{F}_{p^2})$ if $x \neq 0$.

Proof of Theorem 2.1. Let n be an integer. Let q be an element of $\mathbf{F}_p$. Define $\alpha = q^3 + Aq^2 + q$. Define $X_0 : E(\mathbf{F}_{p^2}) \to \mathbf{F}_{p^2}$ as follows: $X_0(\infty) = 0$; $X_0(x, y) = x$.

I will show that there are exactly two $Q \in E(\mathbf{F}_{p^2})$ such that $X_0(Q) = q$, that both of them have the same value of $X_0(nQ)$, and that the value is in $\mathbf{F}_p$. Here nQ means the nth multiple of Q under the above group operations on $E(\mathbf{F}_{p^2})$.

Case 1: $\alpha = 0$. Then $q = 0$. The only square root of 0 in $\mathbf{F}_{p^2}$ is 0, so $\{Q \in E(\mathbf{F}_{p^2}) : X_0(Q) = q\}$ is exactly the group $\{\infty, (0, 0)\}$. Thus each $Q \in E(\mathbf{F}_{p^2})$ with $X_0(Q) = q$ has $nQ \in \{\infty, (0, 0)\}$; i.e., $X_0(nQ) = 0$.

Case 2: α is a nonzero square in $\mathbf{F}_p$. Select a square root r. Now $q \neq 0$, and the only square roots of $q^3 + Aq^2 + q$ in $\mathbf{F}_{p^2}$ are $\pm r$, so $\{Q \in E(\mathbf{F}_{p^2}) : X_0(Q) = q\} = \{(q, r), (q, -r)\}$. Define $s = X_0(n(q, r))$. The group $\{\infty\} \cup (E(\mathbf{F}_{p^2}) \cap (\mathbf{F}_p \times \mathbf{F}_p))$ contains (q, r), so it contains $n(q, r)$, so $s \in \{0, 1, 2, 3, \ldots, p - 1\}$. Furthermore $n(q, -r) = n(-(q, r)) = -n(q, r)$, so $X_0(n(q, -r)) = X_0(n(q, r)) = s$. Thus $X_0(nQ) = s$ for all $Q \in E(\mathbf{F}_{p^2})$ such that $X_0(Q) = q$.

Case 3: α is a non-square in $\mathbf{F}_p$. Then α/δ is a nonzero square in $\mathbf{F}_p$. Select a square root r. Now $q \neq 0$, and the only square roots of $q^3 + Aq^2 + q$ in

$\mathbf{F}_{p^2}$ are $\pm r\sqrt{\delta}$, so $\{Q \in E(\mathbf{F}_{p^2}) : X_0(Q) = q\} = \{(q, r\sqrt{\delta}), (q, -r\sqrt{\delta})\}$. Define $s = X_0(n(q, r\sqrt{\delta}))$. The group $\{\infty\} \cup (E(\mathbf{F}_{p^2}) \cap (\mathbf{F}_p \times \sqrt{\delta}\mathbf{F}_p))$ contains $(q, r\sqrt{\delta})$, so it contains $n(q, r\sqrt{\delta})$, so $s \in \{0, 1, 2, 3, \ldots, p-1\}$. Furthermore $n(q, -r\sqrt{\delta}) = n(-(q, r\sqrt{\delta})) = -n(q, r\sqrt{\delta})$, so $X_0(n(q, -r\sqrt{\delta})) = X_0(n(q, r\sqrt{\delta})) = s$. Thus $X_0(nQ) = s$ for all $Q \in E(\mathbf{F}_{p^2})$ such that $X_0(Q) = q$. $\qquad\square$

B   Appendix: Montgomery's Double-and-Add Formulas

This appendix states Montgomery's x-coordinate double-and-add formulas, and proves that the formulas work whenever $Q - Q' \notin \{\infty, (0,0)\}$.

The following diagram summarizes Montgomery's formulas in the case $z_1 = 1$. As in Theorems B.1 and B.2, x/z and x'/z' are the x-coordinates of points Q, Q'; x_2/z_2 is the x-coordinate of $2Q$; x_1 is the x-coordinate of $Q - Q'$; and x_3/z_3 is the x-coordinate of $Q + Q'$.

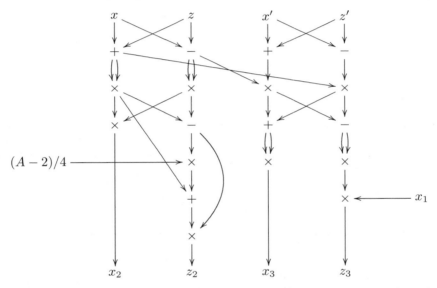

One can see at a glance that there are 4 squarings, 1 multiplication by $(A-2)/4$, and 5 other multiplications; and that there are 8 additions/subtractions, none of which produce input to another addition/subtraction.

Theorem B.1. *Let p be a prime number with $p \geq 5$. Let A be an integer such that $A^2 - 4$ is not a square modulo p. Define E as the elliptic curve $y^2 = x^3 + Ax^2 + x$ over the field $\mathbf{F}_p$. Define $X : E(\mathbf{F}_{p^2}) \to \{\infty\} \cup \mathbf{F}_{p^2}$ as follows: $X(\infty) = \infty$; $X(x, y) = x$. Fix $x, z \in \mathbf{F}_p$ with $(x, z) \neq (0, 0)$. Define*

$$x_2 = (x^2 - z^2)^2 = (x - z)^2(x + z)^2,$$
$$z_2 = 4xz(x^2 + Axz + z^2)$$
$$= ((x+z)^2 - (x-z)^2)\left((x+z)^2 + \frac{A-2}{4}((x+z)^2 - (x-z)^2)\right).$$

Then $X(2Q) = x_2/z_2$ for all $Q \in E(\mathbf{F}_{p^2})$ such that $X(Q) = x/z$.

Here x/z means the quotient of x and z in $\mathbf{F}_p$ if $z \neq 0$; it means ∞ if $x \neq 0$ and $z = 0$; it is undefined if $x = z = 0$.

Proof. Case 1: $z = 0$. Then $x_2 = x^4 \neq 0$ and $z_2 = 0$. Also $X(Q) = x/0 = \infty$ so $Q = \infty$ so $2Q = \infty$ so $X(2Q) = \infty = x_2/0 = x_2/z_2$.

Case 2: $z \neq 0$ and $x = 0$. Then $x_2 = z^4 \neq 0$ and $z_2 = 0$. Also $X(Q) = 0/z = 0$ so $Q = (0,0)$ so $2Q = \infty$ so $X(2Q) = \infty = x_2/0 = x_2/z_2$.

Case 3: $z \neq 0$ and $x \neq 0$. Then $Q = (x/z, y)$ for some $y \in \mathbf{F}_{p^2}$ satisfying $y^2 = (x/z)^3 + A(x/z)^2 + (x/z)$ and thus $4y^2z^4 = 4(x^3z + Ax^2z^2 + xz^3) = z_2$. The non-squareness of $A^2 - 4$ implies that $y \neq 0$; hence $z_2 \neq 0$. Also $X(2Q) = ((x/z)^2 - 1)^2/4y^2$ by definition of doubling; thus $z_2 X(2Q) = z^4((x/z)^2 - 1)^2 = (x^2 - z^2)^2 = x_2$.   □

Theorem B.2. *In the context of Theorem B.1, fix $x, z, x', z', x_1, z_1 \in \mathbf{F}_p$ with $(x, z) \neq (0,0)$, $(x', z') \neq (0,0)$, $x_1 \neq 0$, and $z_1 \neq 0$. Define*

$$x_3 = 4(xx' - zz')^2 z_1 = ((x - z)(x' + z') + (x + z)(x' - z'))^2 z_1,$$
$$z_3 = 4(xz' - zx')^2 x_1 = ((x - z)(x' + z') - (x + z)(x' - z'))^2 x_1.$$

Then $X(Q+Q') = x_3/z_3$ for all $Q, Q' \in E(\mathbf{F}_{p^2})$ such that $X(Q) = x/z$, $X(Q') = x'/z'$, and $X(Q - Q') = x_1/z_1$.

Proof. Case 1: $Q = Q'$. Then $X(Q - Q') = X(\infty) = \infty$, so $z_1 = 0$, contradiction.

Case 2: $Q = \infty$. Then $z = 0$ and $x \neq 0$; also $X(Q-Q') = X(-Q') = X(Q')$, so $x_1/z_1 = x'/z'$, so $x' \neq 0$ and $z' \neq 0$. Finally $x_3 = 4(xx')^2 z_1$ and $z_3 = 4(xz')^2 x_1$ so $x_3/z_3 = (x'/z')^2 z_1/x_1 = x'/z' = X(Q') = X(Q + Q')$.

Case 3: $Q' = \infty$. Then $z' = 0$ and $x' \neq 0$; also $X(Q - Q') = X(Q)$, so $x_1/z_1 = x/z$, so $x \neq 0$ and $z \neq 0$. Finally $x_3 = 4(xx')^2 z_1$ and $z_3 = 4(zx')^2 x_1$ so $x_3/z_3 = (x/z)^2 z_1/x_1 = x/z = X(Q) = X(Q + Q')$.

Case 4: $Q = -Q'$. Then $X(Q') = X(Q)$ so $x/z = x'/z'$ so $xz' = zx'$ so $z_3 = 0$. Suppose that $x_3 = 0$. Then $(x - z)(x' + z') + (x + z)(x' - z') = 0$ and $(x-z)(x'+z') - (x+z)(x'-z') = 0$, so $(x-z)(x'+z') = 0$ and $(x+z)(x'-z') = 0$. If $x + z \neq 0$ then $x' - z' = 0$ so $x' + z' = 2x' \neq 0$ so $x - z = 0$; i.e., $X(Q) = 1$ and $X(Q') = 1$. Otherwise $x = -z$ so $x - z = 2x \neq 0$ so $x' = -z'$; i.e., $X(Q) = -1$ and $X(Q') = -1$. Either way $X(Q - Q') = X(2Q) = (X(Q)^2 - 1)^2/\cdots = (1 - 1)^2/\cdots = 0$ by definition of doubling, so $x_1 = 0$, contradiction.

Thus $x_3 \neq 0$, and $x_3/z_3 = \infty = X(\infty) = X(Q + Q')$.

Case 5: $Q \neq \infty$; $Q' \neq \infty$; $Q \neq Q'$; and $Q \neq -Q'$. Then $z \neq 0$, $z' \neq 0$, and $x/z \neq x'/z'$, so $z_3 \neq 0$. Find $y, y' \in \mathbf{F}_{p^2}$ such that $Q = (x/z, y)$ and $Q' = (x'/z', y')$. Write $\alpha = x'/z' - x/z$ and $\beta = A + x/z + x'/z'$. Then $X(Q+Q') = ((y' - y)/\alpha)^2 - \beta$ and $X(Q - Q') = ((-y' - y)/\alpha)^2 - \beta$ by definition of $Q \pm Q'$, so $X(Q+Q')X(Q-Q') = \beta^2 - 2\beta((y')^2 + y^2)/\alpha^2 + ((y')^2 - y^2)^2/\alpha^4$. Substitute $y^2 = (x/z)^3 + A(x/z)^2 + (x/z)$ and $(y')^2 = (x'/z')^3 + A(x'/z')^2 + (x'/z')$ and simplify to see that $X(Q+Q')X(Q-Q') = (xx' - zz')^2/(xz' - x'z)^2$; this is what Montgomery did. Finally $X(Q+Q') = (xx' - zz')^2 z_1/(xz' - x'z)^2 x_1 = x_3/z_3$.   □

Strongly Unforgeable Signatures Based on Computational Diffie-Hellman

Dan Boneh[1,*], Emily Shen[1], and Brent Waters[2]

[1] Computer Science Department, Stanford University, Stanford, CA
{dabo, emily}@cs.stanford.edu
[2] SRI International, Palo Alto, CA
bwaters@csl.sri.com

Abstract. A signature system is said to be strongly unforgeable if the signature is existentially unforgeable and, given signatures on some message m, the adversary cannot produce a new signature on m. Strongly unforgeable signatures are used for constructing chosen-ciphertext secure systems and group signatures. Current efficient constructions in the standard model (i.e. without random oracles) depend on relatively strong assumptions such as Strong-RSA or Strong-Diffie-Hellman. We construct an efficient strongly unforgeable signature system based on the standard Computational Diffie-Hellman problem in bilinear groups.

1 Introduction

A digital signature system is said to be secure if it is existentially unforgeable under a chosen-message attack [20]. Roughly speaking, this means that an adversary who is given a signature for a few messages of his choice should not be able to produce a signature for a new message. For a variety of applications, however, a stronger security property called *strong unforgeability* is needed [1]. Strong unforgeability ensures the adversary cannot even produce a new signature for a previously signed message. In other words, suppose an adversary obtains a message-signature pair (m, σ) along with other message-signature pairs of his choice. The signature system is strongly unforgeable if the adversary cannot produce a new signature $\hat{\sigma}$ for m. We give a precise definition in the next section.

Strongly unforgeable signatures have a number of applications. They are useful for building chosen-ciphertext secure encryption systems [14,8] as well as group signatures [2,5]. To see the relation to chosen-ciphertext security recall that chosen-ciphertext secure systems in the standard model often incorporate a (one-time) signature in the ciphertext. This signature is generated by the encryptor and is a signature on the ciphertext. Strong unforgeability is needed to ensure that the adversary cannot somehow modify the signature in the challenge ciphertext and come up with an alternate valid signature on the same ciphertext. This alternate signature would give the adversary a valid ciphertext that is different from the challenge ciphertext. The adversary could then issue a decryption query for this new ciphertext and break the system. Consequently,

---

* Supported by NSF and the Packard Foundation.

M. Yung et al. (Eds.): PKC 2006, LNCS 3958, pp. 229–240, 2006.
© International Association for Cryptologic Research 2006

a signature system that is existentially unforgeable but not strongly unforgeable would result in an insecure encryption system. A similar issue comes up in several group signature constructions.

Several existing signature systems are strongly unforgeable. In the random oracle model, constructions based on the full domain hash [3, 9, 6] and other methods [3, 18, 26] are strongly unforgeable.

Without random oracles, several constructions can be shown to be strongly unforgeable; however, they typically depend on relatively strong assumptions:

- Gennaro, Halevi, and Rabin [17] and Cramer and Shoup [11] construct strongly unforgeable signatures based on the Strong-RSA assumption.
- Boneh and Boyen [4] construct a strongly unforgeable signature based on the Strong-Diffie-Hellman assumption.
- A Verifiable Unpredictable Function (VUF) gives a signature system where each message has a unique signature. Such signatures are clearly strongly unforgeable. VUFs were defined by Micali, Rabin, and Vadhan [25] where they give a proof-of-concept construction based on the (large exponent) RSA assumption. A different VUF was proposed by Lysyanskaya [23] using the Many-Diffie-Hellman assumption (a.k.a. the n-party Diffie-Hellman assumption) in bilinear groups. This construction was extended by Dodis [13] to obtain a Verifiable Random Function under a much stronger assumption.
- Tree-based signatures [20, 19, 27, 15, 10, 7] can be proven secure without random oracles and based on standard assumptions. However, they generally tend to be less efficient than signatures presented in this paper.

Our contribution. In this paper we construct a strongly unforgeable signature system (without random oracles) based on the *standard Computational Diffie-Hellman* (CDH) problem in bilinear groups. The system is simple, efficient, and produces signatures that are only 2 group elements plus a short string.

Currently, the only (efficient) signature that is known to be existentially unforgeable based on CDH (in the standard model) is due to Waters [28]. This signature, however, is not strongly unforgeable — given a signature on some message m it is easy to derive many other signatures on the same message. Nevertheless, we use the Waters signature scheme as our starting point. We show how to strengthen the signature to obtain a strongly unforgeable signature based on the standard CDH. We actually do a little more — we provide a general transformation that converts any unforgeable signature of a certain type into a strongly unforgeable signature. We then apply this transformation to the Waters signature to obtain a strongly unforgeable signature based on CDH.

2   Preliminaries

Before presenting our construction we briefly review the security definitions, a few facts about bilinear maps, and our complexity assumptions.

2.1   Strong Existential Unforgeability

A signature system consists of three algorithms: *KeyGen*, *Sign*, and *Verify*. Strong existential unforgeability under an adaptive chosen-message attack is defined using the following game:

Setup. The challenger runs *KeyGen*. It gives the adversary the resulting public key PK and keeps the private key SK to itself.

Signature Queries. The adversary issues signature queries $m_1, \ldots, m_q$. To each query m_i the challenger responds by running *Sign* to generate a signature σ_i of m_i and sending σ_i to the adversary. These queries may be asked adaptively so that each query m_i may depend on the replies to $m_1, \ldots, m_{i-1}$.

Output. Finally the adversary outputs a pair (m, σ). The adversary wins if σ is a valid signature of m according to *Verify* and (m, σ) is not among the pairs (m_i, σ_i) generated during the query phase.

We define the advantage of an adversary $\mathcal{A}$ in attacking the signature scheme as the probability that $\mathcal{A}$ wins the above game, taken over the random bits of the challenger and the adversary.

Definition 1. *A signature scheme is (t, q, ϵ)-strongly existentially unforgeable under an adaptive chosen-message attack if no t-time adversary $\mathcal{A}$ making at most q signature queries has advantage at least ϵ in the above game.*

2.2   Existential Unforgeability

We will also use the traditional security property of (weak) existential unforgeability under an adaptive chosen-message attack [20]. It is defined using the following game.

Setup and Signature Queries. Same as in the strong unforgeability game.

Output. The adversary outputs a pair (m, σ). The adversary wins if σ is a valid signature of m according to *Verify* and m is not among the messages m_i queried during the query phase.

We define the advantage of an adversary $\mathcal{A}$ in weakly attacking a signature scheme as the probability that $\mathcal{A}$ wins the above game, taken over the random bits of the challenger and the adversary.

Definition 2. *A signature scheme is (t, q, ϵ)-existentially unforgeable under an adaptive chosen-message attack if no t-time adversary $\mathcal{A}$ making at most q signature queries has advantage at least ϵ in the above game.*

2.3   Bilinear Groups

We use the following notation:

1. $\mathbb{G}$ and $\mathbb{G}_1$ are two (multiplicative) cyclic groups of prime order p;
2. g is a generator of $\mathbb{G}$;

3. e is a computable map $e : \mathbb{G} \times \mathbb{G} \to \mathbb{G}_1$ with the following properties:
   - Bilinear: for all $u, v \in \mathbb{G}$ and $a, b \in \mathbb{Z}$, $e(u^a, v^b) = e(u, v)^{ab}$.
   - Non-degenerate: $e(g, g) \neq 1$.

We say that $\mathbb{G}$ is a bilinear group [21] if the group operation in $\mathbb{G}$ is efficiently computable and there exists a group $\mathbb{G}_1$ and an efficiently computable bilinear map $e : \mathbb{G} \times \mathbb{G} \to \mathbb{G}_1$ as above.

2.4   Computational Diffie-Hellman (CDH) Assumption

The computational Diffie-Hellman problem in a cyclic group $\mathbb{G}$ of order p is defined as follows. Given $g, g^a, g^b \in \mathbb{G}$, output $g^{ab} \in \mathbb{G}$. We say that algorithm $\mathcal{A}$ has advantage ϵ in solving CDH in $\mathbb{G}$ if

$$\Pr[\mathcal{A}(g, g^a, g^b) = g^{ab}] \geq \epsilon \ ,$$

where the probability is over the random choice of generator $g \in \mathbb{G}$, the random choice of $a, b \in \mathbb{Z}_p$, and the random bits of $\mathcal{A}$.

Similarly, we say that algorithm $\mathcal{A}$ has advantage ϵ in solving discrete log in $\mathbb{G}$ if
$$\Pr[\mathcal{A}(g, g^a) = a] \geq \epsilon \ ,$$

where the probability is over the random choice of generator $g \in \mathbb{G}$, the random choice of $a \in \mathbb{Z}_p$, and the random bits of $\mathcal{A}$.

Definition 3. *The (t, ϵ)-CDH assumption holds in $\mathbb{G}$ if no t-time adversary has advantage at least ϵ in solving CDH in $\mathbb{G}$. Similarly, the (t, ϵ)-Dlog assumption holds in $\mathbb{G}$ if no t-time adversary has advantage at least ϵ in solving discrete log.*

2.5   Collision-Resistant Hashing

Let $\mathcal{H} = \{H_k\}$ be a keyed hash family of functions $H_k : \{0, 1\}^* \to \{0, 1\}^n$ indexed by $k \in \mathcal{K}$. We say that algorithm $\mathcal{A}$ has advantage ϵ in breaking the collision-resistance of $\mathcal{H}$ if

$$\Pr[\mathcal{A}(k) = (m_0, m_1) \ : \ m_0 \neq m_1, \ H_k(m_0) = H_k(m_1)] \geq \epsilon \ ,$$

where the probability is over the random choice of $k \in \mathcal{K}$ and the random bits of $\mathcal{A}$.

Definition 4. *A hash family $\mathcal{H}$ is (t, ϵ)-collision-resistant if no t-time adversary has advantage at least ϵ in breaking the collision-resistance of $\mathcal{H}$.*

Our construction makes use of collision-resistant hashing. We note, however, that collision-resistant hashing can be easily built based on the CDH assumption [12]. Therefore, in theory, assuming the existence of collision-resistant functions does not strengthen the complexity assumption we are making. In practice, of course, one would use a standard hash function such as SHA-256 and assume that it is collision-resistant.

3 From Weak Unforgeability to Strong Unforgeability

Our goal is to construct a strongly unforgeable signature based on CDH. We begin by presenting a general transformation that converts any *partitioned* unforgeable signature (defined below) into a strongly unforgeable signature. In the next section we apply this transformation to the Waters signature.

Definition 5. *We say that a signature system is* partitioned *if it satisfies two properties:*

- **Property 1.** *The signing algorithm can be broken into two deterministic algorithms F_1 and F_2 so that a signature on a message m using secret key SK is computed as follows:*
  1. *Select a random r in $\mathcal{R}$.*
  2. *Set $\sigma_1 \leftarrow F_1(m, r, SK)$ and $\sigma_2 \leftarrow F_2(r, SK)$.*
  3. *Output the signature $\sigma \leftarrow (\sigma_1, \sigma_2)$.*
- **Property 2.** *Given m and σ_2 there is at most one σ_1 so that (σ_1, σ_2) verifies as a valid signature on m under PK.*

In other words, a signature is partitioned if half the signature, namely σ_2, does not depend on m. Furthermore, given m and σ_2 the signature is fully determined. Many standard discrete-log-based signature systems in the literature can be partitioned. For example, for DSS [24] using x to denote the secret key, the functions F_1, F_2 are:

$$F_1(m, r, x) = r^{-1}\big(m + xF_2(r, x)\big) \bmod q$$
$$F_2(r, x) = (g^r \bmod p) \bmod q$$

We note, however, that property 2 may not hold for DSS.

Next, we present our transformation. Let $\mathbb{G}$ be a group of prime order p and let $\mathcal{H} = \{H_k\}$ be a collision-resistant hash family of functions $H_k : \{0,1\}^* \to \{0,1\}^n$ indexed by $k \in \mathcal{K}$. We assume $p \geq 2^n$ so that hash outputs can be viewed as elements of $\mathbb{Z}_p$. Furtheremore, we assume that each element of $\mathbb{Z}_p$ has a unique encoding, say as an integer in $[0, p)$. In describing the system we use the notation $x\|y$ to denote the marked concatenation of the two strings x and y.

Let $\Sigma = (KeyGen, Sign, Verify)$ be a partitioned signature where the signing algorithm is partitioned using functions F_1 and F_2. Suppose the randomness for signature generation is picked from some set $\mathcal{R}$. We build a new strongly unforgeable signature system $\Sigma_{\text{new}} = (KeyGen_{\text{new}}, Sign_{\text{new}}, Verify_{\text{new}})$ as follows:

***KeyGen*$_{\text{new}}$.** To generate the public key, select random generators $g, h \in \mathbb{G}$ and a random hash key $k \in \mathcal{K}$. Next, run *KeyGen* to obtain a secret key SK and public key PK. The public and secret keys for the new system are:

$$\text{PK}' = (\text{PK}, g, h, k) \qquad \text{and} \qquad \text{SK}' = (\text{SK})$$

***Sign*$_{\text{new}}$(SK, M).** A signature on a message $M \in \{0,1\}^\ell$ is generated as follows.
  1. Select a random exponent $s \in \mathbb{Z}_p$ and a random $r \in \mathcal{R}$.

    2. Set $\sigma_2 \leftarrow F_2(r, \mathrm{SK})$.

    3. Compute $t \leftarrow H_k(M\|\sigma_2) \in \{0,1\}^n$ and view t as an element of $\mathbb{Z}_p$.

    4. Compute $m \leftarrow g^t h^s \in \mathbb{G}$.

    5. Compute $\sigma_1 \leftarrow F_1(m, r, \mathrm{SK})$ and output the signature $\sigma \leftarrow (\sigma_1, \sigma_2, s)$.

Verify$_{\mathbf{new}}(\mathbf{PK}, M, \sigma)$. A signature $\sigma = (\sigma_1, \sigma_2, \sigma_3)$ on a message M is verified as follows:

    1. Compute $\tilde{t} \leftarrow H_k(M\|\sigma_2)$ and view $\tilde{t}$ as an element of $\mathbb{Z}_p$.

    2. Compute $\tilde{m} \leftarrow g^{\tilde{t}} h^{\sigma_3}$.

    3. Output $Verify(\mathrm{PK}, \tilde{m}, (\sigma_1, \sigma_2))$.

The basic idea. To give some intuition for signature generation, note that in Step 4 we derive a new message m that is then signed by the underlying signature system in Step 5. This m is derived from the original message M and from σ_2. The σ_2 is derived from the randomness r. Hence, in effect, the signer is signing both the message M and the secret randomness r that is used to create the signature. The adversary, as a result, cannot "re-randomize" a given signature without invalidating the signature. This may suggest that the resulting signature scheme is strongly unforgeable. Unfortunately, in creating this circularity — making the message m being signed depend on the randomness r — we break the proof of security for the underlying signature. Because of Steps 3 and 4 we can no longer prove that the system is secure.

To repair the damage we introduce an additional hashing step (Step 4) where we hash again using a chameleon hash [22]. The extra randomness s of the chameleon hash lets us break the circularity in the proof of security. This lets us repair the proof and prove strong unforgeability based strictly on the weak unforgeability of the underlying system. In particular, the randomness of the chameleon hash is crucial for responding to signature queries from a Type III adversary in the proof of security below.

In summary, the high level structure of the signing algorithm is as follows: (1) first, hash $M\|\sigma_2$ using a chameleon hash to obtain a new message m, (2) then, use the underlying signature to sign m with randomness r, (3) finally, output the resulting signature along with the randomness s of the chameleon hash. The proof of security in the next subsection shows that the resulting signature is strongly unforgeable.

3.1   Security

Let $\Sigma = (KeyGen, Sign, Verify)$ be a partitioned signature scheme and let $\Sigma_{\mathrm{new}} = (KeyGen_{\mathrm{new}}, Sign_{\mathrm{new}}, Verify_{\mathrm{new}})$ be the signature system resulting from the transformation described above. The following theorem proves strong unforgeability of Σ_{new}.

Theorem 1. *The signature scheme Σ_{new} is (t, q, ϵ)-strongly existentially unforgeable assuming the underlying signature scheme Σ is $(t, q, \epsilon/3)$-existentially unforgeable, the $(t, \epsilon/3)$-Dlog assumption holds in $\mathbb{G}$, and $\mathcal{H}$ is $(t, \epsilon/3)$-collision-resistant.*

Proof. Suppose $\mathcal{A}$ is a forger that (t, q, ϵ)-breaks strong unforgeability of Σ_{new}. Forger $\mathcal{A}$ is first given a public key (PK, g, h, k).

Forger $\mathcal{A}$ asks for signatures on messages $M_1, \ldots, M_q$ and is given signatures $\sigma_i = (\sigma_{i,1}, \sigma_{i,2}, s_i)$ for $i = 1, \ldots, q$ on these messages. Let $t_i = H_k(M_i \| \sigma_{i,2})$ and $m_i = g^{t_i} h^{s_i}$ for $i = 1, \ldots, q$. Let $(\hat{M}, \hat{\sigma} = (\hat{\sigma}_1, \hat{\sigma}_2, \hat{s}))$ be the forgery produced by $\mathcal{A}$, let $\hat{t} = H_k(\hat{M} \| \hat{\sigma}_2)$, and let $\hat{m} = g^{\hat{t}} h^{\hat{s}}$. We distinguish among three types of forgeries:

Type I. A forgery where $\hat{m} = m_i$ and $\hat{t} = t_i$ for some $i \in \{1, \ldots, q\}$.
Type II. A forgery where $\hat{m} = m_i$ and $\hat{t} \neq t_i$ for some $i \in \{1, \ldots, q\}$.
Type III. Any other forgery ($\hat{m} \neq m_i$ for all $i \in \{1, \ldots, q\}$).

A successful forger must output a forgery of Type I, Type II, or Type III. We show that a Type I forgery can be used to break the collision-resistance of $\mathcal{H}$, a Type II forgery can be used to solve discrete log in $\mathbb{G}$, and a Type III forgery can be used to break existential unforgeability of the underlying signature scheme Σ. Our simulator can flip a coin at the beginning of the simulation to guess which type of forgery the adversary will produce and set up the simulation appropriately. In all three cases the simulation is perfect. We start by describing how to use a Type III forgery which is the more interesting case.

Type III forger: Suppose algorithm $\mathcal{A}$ is a Type III forger that (t, q, ϵ)-breaks strong unforgeability of Σ_{new}. We construct a simulator $\mathcal{B}$ that (t, q, ϵ)-breaks existential unforgeability of Σ. $\mathcal{B}$ is given a public key PK. $\mathcal{B}$'s goal is to produce a pair (m, σ) where σ is a valid signature on m and m is not among $\mathcal{B}$'s chosen message queries. $\mathcal{B}$ runs $\mathcal{A}$ as follows.

Setup. Algorithm $\mathcal{B}$ generates the public key PK' as follows.
1. Select a random generator $g \in \mathbb{G}$.
2. Select a random exponent $a \in \mathbb{Z}_p^*$ and set $h \leftarrow g^a$.
3. Select a random hash key $k \in \mathcal{K}$.
4. Provide the public key PK' $\leftarrow (\text{PK}, g, h, k)$ to $\mathcal{A}$.
Signature Queries. Algorithm $\mathcal{A}$ issues up to q signature queries. Algorithm $\mathcal{B}$ responds to a query on a message M as follows.
1. Select a random exponent $w \in \mathbb{Z}_p$ and set $m \leftarrow g^w$.
2. Ask $\mathcal{B}$'s challenger for a signature on message m. Obtain a signature (σ_1, σ_2) on m.
3. Compute $t \leftarrow H_k(M \| \sigma_2)$.
4. Set $s \leftarrow (w - t)/a$.
5. Return $\sigma \leftarrow (\sigma_1, \sigma_2, s)$ to $\mathcal{A}$.
Indeed, $m = g^w = g^{as+t} = g^t h^s$ and s is uniform in $\mathbb{Z}_p$ as required. Hence, σ is a valid signature on M.
Output. Finally, algorithm $\mathcal{A}$ outputs a forgery $(\hat{M}, (\hat{\sigma}_1, \hat{\sigma}_2, \hat{s}))$. Algorithm $\mathcal{B}$ produces a weak forgery on the underlying scheme as follows.
1. Compute $\hat{t} \leftarrow H_k(\hat{M} \| \hat{\sigma}_2)$.
2. Compute $\hat{m} \leftarrow g^{\hat{t}} h^{\hat{s}}$.
3. Output $(\hat{m}, (\hat{\sigma}_1, \hat{\sigma}_2))$.

Note that $\hat{m} \notin \{m_1, \ldots, m_q\}$ because if $\hat{m} = m_i$ for some $i \in \{1, \ldots, q\}$ then, either $\hat{t} = t_i$ (a Type I forgery) or $\hat{t} \neq t_i$ (a Type II forgery). Therefore $\mathcal{B}$ produces a forgery on some new message $\hat{m}$ for the underlying scheme whenever $\mathcal{A}$ produces a Type III forgery, as required.

Type I forger: Next we show how to use a Type I forger. Suppose $\mathcal{A}$ is a Type I forger that (t, q, ϵ)-breaks strong unforgeability of Σ_{new}. We construct an algorithm $\mathcal{B}$ that (t, ϵ)-breaks the collision-resistance of $\mathcal{H}$. Algorithm $\mathcal{B}$ is given a random key $k' \in \mathcal{K}$. $\mathcal{B}$'s goal is to output a pair of messages (m_1, m_2) such that $m_1 \neq m_2$ and $H_{k'}(m_1) = H_{k'}(m_2)$. $\mathcal{B}$ runs $\mathcal{A}$ as follows.

Setup. Algorithm $\mathcal{B}$ sets $k \leftarrow k'$ and generates the remaining elements of the public key and the private key according to $KeyGen_{\text{new}}$. $\mathcal{B}$ gives $\mathcal{A}$ the resulting public key $\text{PK}' = (\text{PK}, g, h, k)$ and keeps the secret key SK'.

Signature Queries. $\mathcal{A}$ issues up to q signature queries. $\mathcal{B}$ responds to a query on a message M_i by running $Sign_{\text{new}}(\text{SK}', M_i)$ and returning the signature σ_i to $\mathcal{A}$.

Output. $\mathcal{A}$ outputs a forgery $\left(\hat{M}, \ \hat{\sigma} = (\hat{\sigma}_1, \hat{\sigma}_2, \hat{s})\right)$ such that

$$(\hat{M}, \hat{\sigma}) \notin \{(M_1, \sigma_1), \ldots, (M_q, \sigma_q)\} \quad \text{and} \quad \hat{m} = m_i \quad \text{and} \quad \hat{t} = t_i$$

for some $i \in \{1, \ldots, q\}$. More precisely, $\hat{t} = t_i$ means that $H_k(\hat{M} \| \hat{\sigma}_2) = H_k(M_i \| \sigma_{i,2})$. Similarly, $\hat{m} = m_i$ means that $g^{\hat{t}} h^{\hat{s}} = g^{t_i} h^{s_i}$.

Then $\mathcal{B}$ outputs the pair $(\hat{M} \| \hat{\sigma}_2, \ M_i \| \sigma_{i,2})$ as a collision on H_k.

We show that algorithm $\mathcal{B}$ succeeds in producing an H_k-collision whenever $\mathcal{A}$ produces a Type I forgery. Since $H_k(\hat{M} \| \hat{\sigma}_2) = H_k(M_i \| \sigma_{i,2})$ we only need to show that $\hat{M} \| \hat{\sigma}_2 \neq M_i \| \sigma_{i,2}$.

Suppose towards a contradiction that $\hat{M} = M_i$ and $\hat{\sigma}_2 = \sigma_{i,2}$. Since $\hat{t} = t_i$ and $\hat{m} = m_i$ we know that $\hat{s} = s_i$. (We require that any exponent $s \in \mathbb{Z}_p$ has a unique encoding.) Furthermore, since $\hat{\sigma}_2 = \sigma_{i,2}$ and $\hat{m} = m_i$, the second property of partitioned signatures implies that $\hat{\sigma}_1 = \sigma_{i,1}$. Hence, we have just shown that $\hat{M} = M_i$ and $\hat{\sigma} = \sigma_i$ which contradicts the fact that $(\hat{M}, \hat{\sigma})$ is a strong existential forgery. Therefore, $\hat{M} \| \hat{\sigma}_2 \neq M_i \| \sigma_{i,2}$, implying that whenever $\mathcal{A}$ produces a Type I forgery, $\mathcal{B}$ produces an H_k-collision.

Type II forger: Finally, we show how to use a Type II forger. Suppose $\mathcal{A}$ is a Type II forger that (t, q, ϵ)-breaks strong unforgeability of Σ_{new}. We construct an algorithm $\mathcal{B}$ that (t, ϵ)-solves discrete log in $\mathbb{G}$. Algorithm $\mathcal{B}$ is given a random pair (g', h') and its goal is to output a such that $h' = (g')^a$. $\mathcal{B}$ runs $\mathcal{A}$ as follows.

Setup. Algorithm $\mathcal{B}$ sets $g \leftarrow g'$, $h \leftarrow h'$, and generates the remaining elements of the public key and the private key according to $KeyGen_{\text{new}}$. $\mathcal{B}$ gives $\mathcal{A}$ the resulting public key $\text{PK}' = (\text{PK}, g, h, k)$ and keeps the private key SK'.

Signature Queries. $\mathcal{A}$ issues up to q signature queries. $\mathcal{B}$ responds to a query on a message M_i by running $Sign_{\text{new}}(\text{SK}', M_i)$ and returning the signature σ_i to $\mathcal{A}$.

Forgery. $\mathcal{A}$ outputs a forgery $(\hat{M}, \hat{\sigma} = (\hat{\sigma}_1, \hat{\sigma}_2, \hat{s}))$ such that $\hat{m} = m_i$ and $\hat{t} \neq t_i$ for some $i \in \{1, \ldots, q\}$. Then we have $g^{\hat{t}} h^{\hat{s}} = g^{t_i} h^{s_i}$, which can be written as $g^{\hat{t}}(g^a)^{\hat{s}} = g^{t_i}(g^a)^{s_i}$. Then $\mathcal{B}$ computes $a = (t_i - \hat{t})/(\hat{s} - s_i) \in \mathbb{Z}_p$ and outputs a in response to its discrete log challenge. Note that $\hat{s} - s_i \neq 0$ since $\hat{s} = s_i$ and $g^{\hat{t}} h^{\hat{s}} = g^{t_i} h^{s_i}$ imply $\hat{t} = t_i$.

Algorithm $\mathcal{B}$ succeeds in solving its discrete log challenge whenever $\mathcal{A}$ produces a Type II forgery, as required.

In summary, we showed how to use all three forgery types to break existential unforgeability of the underlying signature scheme, collision-resistance of $\mathcal{H}$, or discrete log. This completes the proof of Theorem 1. □

4 A Concrete Construction: Strong Unforgeability from CDH

We now apply Theorem 1 to the Waters signature which is based on CDH without random oracles. It is straightforward to verify that the Waters signature is partitioned. The functions F_1 and F_2 are:

$$F_1(m, r, \mathrm{SK}) = \mathrm{SK} \cdot \left(u' \prod_{i=1}^{n} u_i^{m_i}\right)^r \quad \in \mathbb{G}$$

$$F_2(r, \mathrm{SK}) = g^r \quad \in \mathbb{G}$$

where $u', u_1, \ldots, u_n \in \mathbb{G}$ are part of the public key and $m = m_1 \ldots m_n \in \{0,1\}^n$. The second property of partitioned signatures holds since given m and $\sigma_2 = F_2(r, \mathrm{SK})$ there is only one σ_1 for which the verification equation will hold. Note that we are assuming that each element $g \in \mathbb{G}$ has a unique encoding (otherwise an attacker can invalidate property 2 by simply changing the encoding of a group element).

Thus, applying Theorem 1 to the Waters signature system we obtain a strongly unforgeable scheme based on CDH without random oracles. The resulting system is as follows. Let $\mathbb{G}$ be a bilinear group of prime order p and let $e : \mathbb{G} \times \mathbb{G} \rightarrow \mathbb{G}_1$ denote the bilinear map and g be the corresponding generator. Let $\mathcal{H} = \{H_k\}$ be a collision-resistant hash family of functions $H_k : \{0,1\}^* \rightarrow \{0,1\}^n$ indexed by $k \in \mathcal{K}$. We assume $p \geq 2^n$ so that hash outputs can be viewed as elements of $\mathbb{Z}_p$.

KeyGen. To generate the public key, select a random generator $g \in \mathbb{G}$ and a random $\alpha \in \mathbb{Z}_p$ and set $g_1 = g^\alpha$. Next, select random $g_2, h \in \mathbb{G}$. Select random $u', u_1, \ldots, u_n \in \mathbb{G}$ and let $U = (u_1, \ldots, u_n)$. Finally, select a random hash key $k \in \mathcal{K}$. The public and secret keys are:

$$\mathrm{PK} = (g, g_1, g_2, h, u', U, k) \qquad \text{and} \qquad \mathrm{SK} = (g_2^\alpha)$$

Note that the secret key is a single group element, but the public key contains $n + 5$ group elements where n is the hash output size.

Sign. A signature on a message $M \in \{0,1\}^{\ell}$ is generated as follows.
1. Select random exponents $r, s \in \mathbb{Z}_p$.
2. Set $\sigma_2 \leftarrow g^r \in \mathbb{G}$.
3. Compute $t \leftarrow H_k(m \| \sigma_2) \in \{0,1\}^n$ and view t as an element of $\mathbb{Z}_p$.
4. Compute $m \leftarrow H_k(g^t h^s)$ and write m as $m_1 \ldots m_n \in \{0,1\}^n$.
5. Compute $\sigma_1 \leftarrow g_2^{\alpha} \cdot (u' \prod_{i=1}^n u_i^{m_i})^r$ and output the signature (σ_1, σ_2, s).

Verify. A signature $\sigma = (\sigma_1, \sigma_2, \sigma_3)$ on a message M is verified as follows:
1. Compute $\tilde{t} \leftarrow H_k(M \| \sigma_2)$ and view $\tilde{t}$ as an element of $\mathbb{Z}_p$.
2. Compute $\tilde{m} \leftarrow H_k(g^{\tilde{t}} h^{\sigma_3})$ and write $\tilde{m}$ as $\tilde{m}_1 \ldots \tilde{m}_n \in \{0,1\}^n$.
3. Check that

$$e(\sigma_1, g) \stackrel{?}{=} e(\sigma_2, u' \prod_{i=1}^n u_i^{\tilde{m}_i}) \cdot e(g_1, g_2) .$$

Accept if this holds and reject otherwise.

Corollary 1. *The signature system above is (t, q, ϵ)-strongly existentially unforgeable assuming the $(t, \epsilon/24(n+1)q)$-CDH assumption holds in $\mathbb{G}$, and $\mathcal{H}$ is $(t, \epsilon/3)$-collision-resistant.*

Proof. The Waters system is known to be (t, q, ϵ)-existentially unforgeable assuming $(t, \epsilon/8(n+1)q)$-CDH holds in $\mathbb{G}$. It follows that the system is $(t, q, \epsilon/3)$-existentially unforgeable assuming $(t, \epsilon/24(n+1)q)$-CDH holds in $\mathbb{G}$. When $(t, \epsilon/3)$-CDH holds in $\mathbb{G}$ then $(t, \epsilon/3)$-Dlog must also hold in $\mathbb{G}$. Hence, since the system is partitioned, all the requirements of Theorem 1 are satisfied. Consequently, the signature system above is strongly unforgeable.

Efficiency. Our signature system is only slightly worse than the Waters signature system in terms of performance. The signing operation in our scheme takes four exponentiations and $n/2 + 2$ group operations in $\mathbb{G}$ on average. The verification algorithm consists of two pairings, two exponentiations, $n/2 + 1$ group operations in $\mathbb{G}$ and one group operation in $\mathbb{G}_1$ on average. Like the Waters signature scheme public keys are approximately n group elements. However, we note that the values $u', U = (u_1, \ldots, u_n)$ can actually come from a common reference string and be shared by all users in a system. If this is the case each user's public key can be short.

5 Conclusions

We constructed a strongly unforgeable signature system based on the standard Computational Diffie-Hellman problem in bilinear groups. The signature is efficient and contains only two group elements (plus a short random string). The public key size is proportional to the output size of the hash function used. We presented the construction in two steps. First, we showed a general mechanism for transforming any partitioned (weakly) unforgeable system into a strongly unforgeable system. We then applied this transformation to a specific system.

Surprisingly, our signature system does not seem to naturally extend to give an efficient threshold signature [16]. In fact, the only known efficient strongly unforgeable threshold signatures (in the standard model) appear to be the unique signatures of Lysyanskaya [23] and Dodis [13]. Thresholdizing these signatures, however, requires multiple rounds of interaction with the signing servers and the resulting signatures are somewhat long. We leave as an open problem the question of constructing a threshold unforgeable signature based on a standard assumption.

References

1. J. An, Y. Dodis, and T. Rabin. On the security of joint signature and encryption. In L. R. Knudsen, editor, *Proceedings of Eurocrypt 2002*, volume 2332 of *LNCS*, pages 83–107. Springer-Verlag, 2002.
2. G. Ateniese, J. Camenisch, M. Joye, and G. Tsudik. A practical and provably secure coalition-resistant group signature scheme. In M. Bellare, editor, *Proceedings of Crypto 2000*, volume 1880 of *LNCS*, pages 255–70. Springer-Verlag, Aug. 2000.
3. M. Bellare and P. Rogaway. The exact security of digital signatures: How to sign with RSA and Rabin. In U. Maurer, editor, *Proceedings of Eurocrypt '96*, volume 1070 of *LNCS*, pages 399–416. Springer-Verlag, 1996.
4. D. Boneh and X. Boyen. Short signatures without random oracles. In C. Cachin and J. Camenisch, editors, *Proceedings of Eurocrypt 2004*, volume 3027 of *LNCS*, pages 56–73. Springer-Verlag, 2004. Full version at: http://eprint.iacr.org/2004/171.
5. D. Boneh, X. Boyen, and H. Shacham. Short group signatures. In M. Franklin, editor, *Proceedings of Crypto 2004*, volume 3152 of *LNCS*, pages 41–55. Springer-Verlag, 2004.
6. D. Boneh, B. Lynn, and H. Shacham. Short signatures from the Weil pairing. *J. of Cryptology*, 17(4):297–319, 2004. Early version in Asiacrypt '01.
7. D. Boneh, I. Mironov, and V. Shoup. A secure signature scheme from bilinear maps. In M. Joye, editor, *Proceedings of RSA-CT '03*, volume 2612 of *LNCS*, pages 98–110. Springer-Verlag, 2003.
8. R. Canetti, S. Halevi, and J. Katz. Chosen-ciphertext security from identity-based encryption. In C. Cachin and J. Camenisch, editors, *Proceedings of Eurocrypt 2004*, LNCS, pages 207–222. Springer-Verlag, 2004. http://eprint.iacr.org/2003/182/.
9. J.-S. Coron. On the Exact Security of Full Domain Hash. In M. Bellare, editor, *Proceedings of Crypto 2000*, volume 1880 of *Lecture Notes in Computer Science*, pages 229–235. Springer-Verlag, 2000.
10. R. Cramer and I. Damgård. New generation of secure and practical rsa-based signatures. In N. Koblitz, editor, *Proceedings of Crypto '96*, volume 1109 of *LNCS*, pages 173–185. Springer-Verlag, 1996.
11. R. Cramer and V. Shoup. Signature schemes based on the strong RSA assumption. *ACM TISSEC*, 3(3):161–185, 2000. Extended abstract in Proc. 6th ACM CCS, 1999.
12. I. Damgård. Collision free hash functions and public key signature schemes. In D. Chaum and W. L. Price, editors, *Proceedings of Eurocrypt '87*, volume 304 of *LNCS*, pages 203–216. Springer-Verlag, 1987.

13. Y. Dodis. Efficient construction of (distributed) verifiable random functions. In Y. Desmedt, editor, *Workshop on Public Key Cryptography (PKC)*, volume 2567 of *LNCS*, pages 1–17. Springer-Verlag, 2003.
14. D. Dolev, C. Dwork, and M. Naor. Non-malleable cryptography. *SIAM J. of Computing*, 30(2):391–437, 2000.
15. C. Dwork and M. Naor. An efficient existentially unforgeable signature scheme and its applications. *J. of Cryptology*, 11(2):187–208, 1998. Early version in Crypto '94.
16. P. Gemmel. An introduction to threshold cryptography. *RSA CryptoBytes*, 2(3):7–12, 1997.
17. R. Gennaro, S. Halevi, and T. Rabin. Secure hash-and-sign signatures without the random oracle. In J. Stern, editor, *Proceedings of Eurocrypt 1999*, volume 1592 of *LNCS*, pages 123–139. Springer-Verlag, 1999.
18. E.-J. Goh and S. Jarecki. A signature scheme as secure as the Diffie-Hellman problem. In E. Biham, editor, *Proceedings of Eurocrypt 2003*, volume 2656 of *LNCS*, pages 401–415. Springer-Verlag, 2003.
19. O. Goldreich. Two remarks concerning the goldwasser-micali-rivest signature scheme. In A. M. Odlyzko, editor, *Proceedings of Crypto'86*, volume 263 of *LNCS*, pages 104–110. Springer-Verlag, 1987.
20. S. Goldwasser, S. Micali, and R. Rivest. A digital signature scheme secure against adaptive chosen-message attacks. *SIAM J. Computing*, 17(2):281–308, 1988.
21. A. Joux. A one round protocol for tripartite Diffie-Hellman. In W. Bosma, editor, *Proceedings of ANTS IV*, volume 1838 of *LNCS*, pages 385–94. Springer-Verlag, 2000.
22. H. Krawczyk and T. Rabin. Chameleon signatures. In *Proceedings of NDSS 2000*. Internet Society, 2000. http://eprint.iacr.org/1998/010/.
23. A. Lysyanskaya. Unique signatures and verifiable random functions from the DH-DDH separation. In M. Yung, editor, *Proceedings of Crypto 2002*, volume 2442 of *LNCS*, pages 597–612. Springer-Verlag, 2002.
24. A. J. Menezes, P. C. Van Oorschot, and S. A. Vanstone. *Handbook of Applied Cryptography*. CRC Press, 1997.
25. S. Micali, M. Rabin, and S. Vadhan. Verifiable random functions. In *Proceedings of the 40th Annual Symposium on the Foundations of Computer Science*, pages 120–130, New York, NY, October 1999. IEEE.
26. S. Micali and L. Reyzin. Improving the exact security of digital signature schemes. *J. of Cryptology*, 15(1):1–18, 2002.
27. M. Naor and M. Yung. Universal one-way hash functions and their cryptographic applications. In *Proceedings of STOC'89*, pages 33–43, 1989.
28. B. Waters. Efficient identity-based encryption without random oracles. In R. Cramer, editor, *Proceedings of Eurocrypt 2005*, volume 3494 of *LNCS*, pages 114–127. Springer-Verlag, 2005.

Generalization of the Selective-ID Security Model for HIBE Protocols

Sanjit Chatterjee and Palash Sarkar

Applied Statistics Unit, Indian Statistical Institute,
203, B.T. Road, Kolkata, India 700108
{sanjit_t, palash}@isical.ac.in

Abstract. We generalize the selective-ID security model for HIBE by introducing two new security models. Both these models allow the adversary to commit to a set of identities and in the challenge phase choose any one of the previously committed identities. Two constructions of HIBE are presented which are secure in the two models. One of the HIBE constructions supports an unbounded number of levels, i.e., the maximum number of levels does not need to be specified during the set-up. Further, we show that this HIBE can be modified to obtain a multiple receiver IBE which is secure in the selective-ID model without the random oracle assumption.

1 Introduction

Identity based encryption (IBE) was introduced by Shamir [16]. This is a public key encryption protocol where the public key can be any string. The corresponding private key is generated by a private key generator (PKG) and provided to the user in an offline phase. The notion of IBE can simplify many applications of public key encryption (PKE) and is currently an active research area.

The notion of the IBE was later extended to hierarchical IBE (HIBE) [14, 15]. In an IBE, the PKG has to generate the private key for any identity. The notion of the HIBE reduces the workload of the PKG by delegating the private key generation task to lower level entities, i.e., entities who have already obtained their private keys. Though a HIBE by itself is an interesting cryptographic primitive, it can also be used to construct other primitives like forward secure encryption and broadcast encryption protocols.

The first efficient construction of an IBE was provided by Boneh and Franklin [9]. This paper also introduced an appropriate security model for IBE. The proof of security in [9] used the so-called random oracle assumption. This started a search for constructions which can be proved to be secure without the random oracle assumption. The first such construction of a HIBE was given in [11]. However, the HIBE in [11] can only be proved to be secure in a weaker model (the selective-ID model) as opposed to the full model considered in [9]. Later Boneh and Boyen [4] presented a more efficient construction of HIBE which is also secure in the selective-ID (sID) model without the random oracle assumption.

M. Yung et al. (Eds.): PKC 2006, LNCS 3958, pp. 241–256, 2006.

The full security model in [9] allows an adversary to adaptively ask the PKG for private keys of identities of its choosing. (The security model also allows decryption queries, which we ignore for the present.) Then it submits two messages M_0, M_1 and an identity v^* and is given an encryption of M_γ under v^*, where γ is a randomly chosen bit. The identity v^* can be any identity other than those for which the adversary has already obtained the private key or can easily obtain the private key from the information it has received. The main difficulty in obtaining an efficient construction of a HIBE which is secure in this model is the wide flexibility of the adversary in choosing v^*.

The sID model attempts to curb the adversary's flexibility in the following manner. In the game between the adversary and the simulator, the adversary has to commit to an identity even before the HIBE protocol is set-up by the simulator. The simulator then sets up the HIBE. This allows the simulator to set-up the HIBE based on the identity committed by the adversary. In the actual game, the adversary cannot ask for the private key of the committed identity (or of any of its prefix, in the case of HIBE). During the challenge stage, the adversary submits two messages M_0, M_1 as usual and is given an encryption of M_γ under the previously fixed identity v^*. Note that this is significantly more restrictive than the full model since the adversary has to commit to an identity even before it sees the public parameters of the HIBE.

Our Contributions: In this paper, we generalize the sID model and introduce two new models of security for HIBE protocols. The basic idea is to modify the security game so as to allow the adversary to commit to a set of identities (instead of one identity in the sID model) before set-up. During the game, the adversary can execute key extraction queries on any identity not in the committed set. In the challenge stage, the challenge identity is chosen by the adversary from among the set that it has previously committed to.

For IBE, this is a strict generalization of the sID model, since we can get the sID model by enforcing the size of the committed set of identities to be one. On the other hand, for HIBE, there are two ways to view this generalization leading to two different security models $\mathcal{M}_1$ and $\mathcal{M}_2$.

In $\mathcal{M}_1$, the adversary commits to a set $\mathcal{I}^*$. It can then ask for the private key of any identity $v = (v_1, \ldots, v_\tau)$ as long as all the v_is are not in $\mathcal{I}^*$. Further, during the challenge stage, it has to submit an identity all of whose components are in $\mathcal{I}^*$. If we restrict the adversary to only single component identities (i.e., we are considering only the IBE protocols), then this is a clear generalization of the sID model for IBE. On the other hand, in the case of HIBE, we cannot fix the parameters of this model to obtain the sID model for HIBE.

The second model, $\mathcal{M}_2$, is an obvious generalization of the sID model for HIBE. In this case, the adversary specifies τ sets $\mathcal{I}_1^*, \ldots, \mathcal{I}_\tau^*$. Then it can ask for private key of any identity v as long as there is an i such that the ith component of v is not in $\mathcal{I}_i^*$. In the challenge stage, the adversary has to submit an identity such that for all i, the ith component of the identity is in $\mathcal{I}_i^*$.

Even though $\mathcal{M}_2$ generalizes the sID model for HIBE, we think $\mathcal{M}_1$ is also an appropriate model for a HIBE protocol. The adversary would be specifying a set of "sensitive" keywords to be $\mathcal{I}^*$. It can then ask for the private key of any identity as long as one component of the identity is not sensitive and in the challenge stage has to submit an identity all of whose components are sensitive. The added flexibility in $\mathcal{M}_2$ is that the adversary can specify different sets of sensitive keywords for the different levels of HIBE. In practice, this flexibility might not be required since keywords like root, admin, dba, etcetera will be sensitive for all levels.

We present two constructions of HIBE denoted by $\mathcal{H}_1$ and $\mathcal{H}_2$. $\mathcal{H}_1$ is proved to be secure in the model $\mathcal{M}_1$ under the DBDH assumption while $\mathcal{H}_2$ is proved to be secure in the model $\mathcal{M}_2$ also under the DBDH assumption. Our constructions and proofs of security are very similar to that of the Boneh-Boyen HIBE (BB-HIBE) [4]. The actual technical novelty in the proofs is the use of a polynomial, which in the case of the BB-HIBE is of degree one. The use of an appropriate polynomial of degree greater than one allows us to prove security in the more general models $\mathcal{M}_1$ and $\mathcal{M}_2$. However, this flexibility comes at a cost. In the case of $\mathcal{H}_2$, the number of required scalar multiplications increases linearly with the size of the committed set of identities.

One interesting feature about $\mathcal{H}_1$ is that it can support unbounded number of levels. In other words, the set-up for $\mathcal{H}_1$ does not specify the maximum number of levels of the HIBE. This is an added advantage and to the best of our knowledge is not present in any of the previous HIBE constructions.

The situation for $\mathcal{H}_1$ is also interesting in another aspect. If we consider only IBE, then the number of scalar multiplications increases with the size of the committed set of identities. On the other hand, in the case of BB-HIBE, the number of scalar multiplications increases linearly with the depth of the HIBE. Since $\mathcal{H}_1$ can support HIBE of unbounded depth, this feature is not present in $\mathcal{H}_1$.

Multiple receiver IBE (MR-IBE) is an interesting concept which was introduced by Baek, Safavi-Naini and Susilo [1]. In an MR-IBE, an encryptor can encrypt a message in such a way that any one of a set of identities can decrypt the message. A trivial way to achieve this is to separately encrypt the message several times. It turns out that the efficiency can be improved. A more efficient construction of MR-IBE was presented in [1]. The proof of security was in the sID model under the *random oracle* assumption.

We show that the HIBE $\mathcal{H}_1$ when restricted to IBE can be easily modified to obtain an efficient MR-IBE. Our MR-IBE is proved to be secure in the sID model *without* the random oracle assumption and to the best of our knowledge this is the first of such kind.

2   Security Model for HIBE

2.1   HIBE Protocol

Following [15, 14] a hierarchical identity based encryption (HIBE) scheme is specified by four algorithms: Setup, Key Generation, Encryption and Decryption.

Setup: It takes input a security parameter and returns the system parameters together with the master key. The system parameters are publicly known while the master key is known only to the private key generator (PKG).

The system parameters include a description of the message space, the ciphertext space and the identity space. The system parameters may also specify a positive integer h, which denotes the maximum number of levels that are allowed in the HIBE. *If h is not specified, then the HIBE can support an unbounded number of levels.* An identity of depth τ is a tuple $(v_1, \ldots, v_\tau)$, where each v_j is an element of a set $\mathcal{I}$. From an application point of view, we would like $\mathcal{I}$ to be the set of all binary strings. On the other hand, for construction purposes, this is too general and one usually requires $\mathcal{I}$ to have an algebraic structure. The two requirements are met by assuming that a collision resistant hash function maps an arbitrary string to the set $\mathcal{I}$ having an algebraic structure.

A special case of a HIBE protocol arises when only single component identities are allowed. In this case, the protocol is said to be simply an identity based encryption (IBE) protocol.

Key Generation: The task of this algorithm is to assign a private key D_v for an identity v of depth τ. To this end, it takes as input an identity $v = (v_1, \ldots, v_\tau)$ of depth τ and the private key $D_{|\tau-1}$ corresponding to the identity $v_{|\tau-1} = (v_1, \ldots, v_{\tau-1})$ and returns D_v. In the case $\tau = 1$, the private key $D_{|\tau-1}$ is the master key of the PKG and the key generation is done by the PKG. In the case $\tau > 1$, the private key corresponding to $v = (v_1, \ldots, v_\tau)$ is done by the entity whose identity is $v_{|\tau-1} = (v_1, \ldots, v_{\tau-1})$ and who has already obtained his/her private key $D_{|\tau-1}$.

Encryption: It takes as input the identity v and a message from the message space and produces a ciphertext in the cipher space.

Decryption: It takes as input the ciphertext and the private key of the corresponding identity v and returns the message or **bad** if the ciphertext is not valid.

2.2   Security Model

The security model for HIBE is defined as an interactive game between an adversary and a simulator. Currently, there are two security models for HIBE – the selective-ID (sID) model and the full model. We will be interested in defining two new security models. We present the description of the interactive game in a manner which will help in obtaining a unified view of the sID, full and the new security models that we define.

In the game, the adversary is allowed to query two oracles – a decryption oracle $\mathcal{O}_d$ and a key-extraction oracle $\mathcal{O}_k$. The game has several stages.

Adversary's Commitment: In this stage, the adversary commits to two sets $\mathcal{S}_1$ and $\mathcal{S}_2$ of identities. The commitment has the following two consequences as we will define later.

1. The adversary is not allowed to query $\mathcal{O}_k$ on any identity in $\mathcal{S}_1$.
2. In the challenge stage, the adversary has to choose one of the identitites from the set $\mathcal{S}_2$.

There is a bit of technical difficulty here. Note that the adversary has to commit to a set of identities even before the HIBE protocol has been set-up. On the other hand, the identity space is specified by the set-up algorithm of the HIBE protocol. In effect, this means that the adversary has to commit to identities even before it knows the set of identities. Clearly, this is not possible.

One possible way out is to allow the adversary to commit to binary strings and later when the set-up program has been executed, these binary strings are mapped to identities using a collision resistant hash functions. Another solution is to run the set-up program in two phases. In the first phase, the identity space is specified and is made available to the adversary; then the adversary commits to $\mathcal{S}_1$ and $\mathcal{S}_2$; and after obtaining $\mathcal{S}_1$ and $\mathcal{S}_2$ the rest of the set-up program is executed.

The above two approaches are not necessarily equivalent and may have different security consequences. On the other hand, note that if $\mathcal{S}_1 = \emptyset$ and $\mathcal{S}_2$ is the set of all identities (as is true in the full model), then this technical difficulty does not arise.

Set-Up: The simulator sets up the HIBE protocol and provides the public parameters to the adversary and keeps the master key to itself. Note that at this stage, the simulator knows $\mathcal{S}_1, \mathcal{S}_2$ and could possibly set-up the HIBE based on this knowledge. However, while doing this, the simulator must ensure that the probability distribution of the public parameters remains the same as in the specification of the actual HIBE protocol.

Phase 1: The adversary makes a finite number of queries where each query is addressed either to $\mathcal{O}_d$ or to $\mathcal{O}_k$. In a query to $\mathcal{O}_d$, it provides the ciphertext as well as the identity under which it wants the decryption. The simulator has to provide a proper decryption. Similarly, in a query to $\mathcal{O}_k$, it asks for the private key of the identity it provides. This identity cannot be an element of $\mathcal{S}_1$. Further, the adversary is allowed to make these queries adaptively, i.e., any query may depend on the previous queries as well as their answers.

Certain queries are useless and we will assume that the adversary does not make such queries. For example, if an adversary has queried $\mathcal{O}_k$ on any identity, then it is not allowed to present the same identity to $\mathcal{O}_d$ as part of a decryption query. The rationale is that since the adversary already has the private key, it can itself decrypt the required ciphertext.

Challenge: The adversary chooses an identity $\mathsf{v}^* \in \mathcal{S}_2$ with the restriction that it has not queried $\mathcal{O}_k$ for the private key of v^* or any of its prefixes and two messages M_0, M_1 and provides these to the simulator. The simulator randomly chooses a $\gamma \in \{0, 1\}$ and returns the encryption of M_γ under v^* to the adversary.

Phase 2: The adversary issues additional queries just as in Phase 1, with the (obvious) restriction that it cannot ask $\mathcal{O}_d$ for the decryption of C^* under v^* nor $\mathcal{O}_k$ for the private key of any prefix of v^*.

Guess: The adversary outputs a guess γ' of γ.

Adversary's Success: The adversary wins the game if it can successfully guess γ, i.e., if $\gamma = \gamma'$. The advantage of an adversary $\mathcal{A}$ in attacking the HIBE scheme is defined as:
$$\mathsf{Adv}_{\mathcal{A}}^{\mathsf{HIBE}} = 2|\Pr[(\gamma = \gamma')] - 1/2|$$

The quantity $\mathsf{Adv}^{\mathsf{HIBE}}(t, q_{\mathsf{ID}}, q_{\mathsf{C}})$ denotes the maximum of $\mathsf{Adv}_{\mathcal{A}}^{\mathsf{HIBE}}$ where the maximum is taken over all adversaries running in time at most t and making at most q_{C} queries to $\mathcal{O}_d$ and at most q_{ID} queries to $\mathcal{O}_k$.

A HIBE protocol is said to be secure if $\mathsf{Adv}^{\mathsf{HIBE}}(t, q_{\mathsf{ID}}, q_{\mathsf{C}})$ is negligible. Any HIBE protocol secure against such an adversary is said to be secure against chosen ciphertext attack (CCA). A weaker version of security does not allow the adversary to make decryption queries, i.e., the adversary is not given access to $\mathcal{O}_d$. A HIBE protocol secure against such a weaker adversary is said to be secure against chosen plaintext attack (CPA). $\mathsf{Adv}^{\mathsf{HIBE}}(t, q)$ in this context denotes the maximum advantage where the maximum is taken over all adversaries running in time at most t and making at most q queries to the key-extraction oracle. There are several generic as well as non-generic methods for converting a CPA-secure HIBE into a CCA-secure HIBE. Hence, in this paper, we will only consider construction of CPA-secure HIBE.

2.3 Full Model

Suppose $\mathcal{S}_1 = \emptyset$ and $\mathcal{S}_2$ is the set of all identities. By the rules of the game, the adversary is not allowed to query $\mathcal{O}_k$ on any identity in $\mathcal{S}_1$. Since $\mathcal{S}_1$ is empty, this means that the adversary is actually allowed to query $\mathcal{O}_k$ on any identity. Further, since $\mathcal{S}_2$ is the set of all identities, in the challenge stage the adversary is allowed to choose any identity. In effect, this means that the adversary does not really commit to anything before set-up and hence in this case, the commitment stage can be done away with. This particular choice of $\mathcal{S}_1$ and $\mathcal{S}_2$ is called the full model and is currently believed to be the most general notion of security for HIBE.

Note that the other restriction that the adversary has not asked for the private key for any prefix of the challenge identity as well as the restriction in Phase 2 still applies.

2.4 Selective-ID Model

Let $\mathcal{S}_1 = \mathcal{S}_2$ be a singleton set. This means that the adversary commits to one particular identity; never asks for its private key; and in the challenge phase is given the encryption of M_γ under this particular identity. This model is significantly weaker than the full model and is called the selective-ID model.

2.5   New Security Models

We introduce two new security models by suitably defining the sets $\mathcal{S}_1$ and $\mathcal{S}_2$. In our new models, (as well as the sID model), we have $\mathcal{S}_1 = \mathcal{S}_2$. (Note that in the full model, $\mathcal{S}_1 = \overline{\mathcal{S}_2}$.)

Model $\mathcal{M}_1$: Let $\mathcal{I}^*$ be a set. We define $\mathcal{S}_1 = \mathcal{S}_2$ to be the set of all tuples $(\mathsf{v}_1, \ldots, \mathsf{v}_\tau)$, $(\tau \geq 1)$, such that each $\mathsf{v}_i \in \mathcal{I}^*$. First consider the case of IBE, i.e., where only single component identities are allowed. Then, we have $\mathcal{S}_1 = \mathcal{S}_2 = \mathcal{I}^*$. Let $|\mathcal{I}^*| = n$. If we put $n = 1$, then we obtain the sID model for IBE as discussed in Section 2.4. In other words, for IBE protocol, $\mathcal{M}_1$ is a strict generalization of sID model.

Let us now see what this means. In the commit phase, the adversary commits to the set of identities $\mathcal{I}^*$; never asks for the private key of any of these identities; and during the challenge phase presents one of these identities to the simulator. This is the generalization of the sID model, where instead of a single identity, the adversary may choose one from a set of identities.

In the case of HIBE, the situation is different. Model $\mathcal{M}_1$ is no longer a strict generalization of the usual sID model for HIBE. We cannot restrict the parameters of the model $\mathcal{M}_1$ in any manner and obtain the sID model for HIBE. Thus, in this case, $\mathcal{M}_1$ must be considered to be a new model. We later discuss the interpretation of this model as well as the other ones.

Model $\mathcal{M}_2$: Let $\mathcal{I}_1^*, \ldots, \mathcal{I}_\tau^*$ be sets and $|\mathcal{I}_j^*| = n_j$ for $1 \leq j \leq \tau$. We set

$$\mathcal{S}_1 = \mathcal{S}_2 = \mathcal{I}_1^* \times \cdots \times \mathcal{I}_\tau^*.$$

This model is a strict generalization of the sID model for HIBE. This can be seen by setting $n_1 = \cdots = n_\tau = 1$, i.e., $\mathcal{I}_1^*, \ldots, \mathcal{I}_\tau^*$ to be singleton sets.

3   Interpreting Security Models

The full security model is currently believed to provide the most general security model for HIBE. In other words, it provides any entity (having any particular identity) in the HIBE with the most satisfactory security assurance that the entity can hope for. The notion of security based on indistinguishability is derived from the corresponding notion for public key encryption and the security assurance provided in that setting also applies to the HIBE setting.

The additional consideration is that of identity and the key extraction queries to $\mathcal{O}_k$. We may consider the identity present during the challenge stage to be a target identity. In other words, the adversary wishes to break the security of the corresponding entity. In the full model, the target identity can be any identity, with the usual restriction that the adversary does not know the private key corresponding to this identity or one of its prefixes.

From the viewpoint of an individual entity $\mathbf{e}$ in the HIBE structure, the adversary's behaviour appears to be the following. The adversary can possibly corrupt any entity in the structure, but as long as it is not able to corrupt that particular entity **e** or one of its ancestors, then it will not be able to succeed in an attack where the target identity is that of **e**. In other words, obtaining the private keys corresponding to the other identities does not help the adversary. Intuitively, that is the maximum protection that any entity **e** can expect from the system.

Let's reflect on the sID model. In this model, the adversary commits to an identity even before the set-up of the HIBE is done. The actual set-up can depend on the identity in question. Now consider the security assurance obtained by an individual entity **e**. Entity **e** can be convinced that if the adversary had targeted its identity and then the HIBE structure was set-up, in that case the adversary will not be successful in attacking it. Alternatively, **e** can be convinced that the HIBE structure can be set-up so as to protect it. Inherently, the sID model assures that the HIBE structure can be set-up to protect any identity, but only one.

Suppose that a HIBE structure which is secure in the sID model has already been set-up. It has possibly been set-up to protect one particular identity. The question now is what protection does it offer to entities with other identities? The model does not assure that other identities will be protected. Of course, this does not mean that other identities are vulnerable. The model simply does not say anything about these identities.

The system designer's point of view also needs to be considered. While setting up the HIBE structure, the designer needs to ensure security. The HIBE is known to be secure in the sID model and hence has a proof of security. The designer will play the role of the simulator in the security game. In the game, the adversary commits to an identity and then the HIBE is set-up so as to protect this identity. However, since the actual set-up has not been done, there is no real adversary and hence no real target identity. Thus, the designer has to assume that the adversary will probably be targetting some sensitive identity like root. The designer can then set-up the HIBE so as to protect this identity. However, once the HIBE has been set-up, the designer cannot say anything about the security of other possible sensitive identities like sysadmin. This is a serious limitation of the sID model.

This brings us to the generalization of the sID model that we have introduced. First consider the model $\mathcal{M}_1$ as it applies to IBE. In this model, the designer can assume that the adversary will possibly attack one out of a set of sensitive identities like {root, admin, dba, sysadmin}. It can then set-up the IBE so as to protect this set of identities. This offers a strictly better security than the sID model.

Now consider the model $\mathcal{M}_1$ as it applies to HIBE. In this case, the set $\mathcal{I}^*$ can be taken to be a set of sensitive keywords such as {root, admin, dba, sysadmin}. The adversary is not allowed to obtain private keys corresponding to identities all of whose components lie in $\mathcal{I}^*$. For the above example, the adversary cannot obtain the private key of (root, root), or (admin, root, dba). On the other hand, it is allowed to obtain keys corresponding to identities like (root, abracadabra).

Thus, some of the components of the identities (on which key extraction query is made) may be in $\mathcal{I}^*$; as long as all of them are not in $\mathcal{I}^*$, the adversary can obtain the private key. On the other hand, all the components of the target identity have to be sensitive keywords, i.e., elements of $\mathcal{I}^*$. Clearly, model $\mathcal{M}_1$ provides an acceptable security notion for HIBE. Intuitively, it provides better security than the sID model for HIBE, though we cannot fix the parameters of $\mathcal{M}_1$ so that it collapses to the sID model for HIBE.

The model $\mathcal{M}_2$ is a clear generalization of the usual sID model for HIBE. The adversary fixes the sensitive keywords for each level of the HIBE upto the level it wishes to attack. It cannot make a key extraction query on an identity of depth τ, such that for $1 \leq i \leq \tau$, the ith component of the identity is among the pre-specified sensitive keywords for the ith level of the HIBE. Further, the target identity must be such that each of its component is a sensitive keyword for the corresponding HIBE level. As mentioned earlier, by fixing exactly one keyword for each level of the HIBE, we obtain the sID model.

The difference between models $\mathcal{M}_1$ and $\mathcal{M}_2$ is that from a technical point of view, in $\mathcal{M}_2$, for each level of the HIBE, the adversary is allowed to indepedently choose the set of possible values which the corresponding component of the target identity may take. In $\mathcal{M}_1$, the set of possible values for all components are the same. It is due to this difference, that we cannot collapse $\mathcal{M}_1$ to the sID model. On the other hand, in practical applications, the sensitive keywords for all levels are likely to be the same. In such a situation, $\mathcal{M}_1$ provides a more cleaner notion of security. Of course, this is still much less comprehensive than the full security model.

4   Constructions

We present two HIBE protocols $\mathcal{H}_1$ and $\mathcal{H}_2$. The HIBE $\mathcal{H}_1$ can be proved to be secure in model $\mathcal{M}_1$, whereas the HIBE $\mathcal{H}_2$ can be proved to be secure in model $\mathcal{M}_2$.

4.1   Cryptographic Bilinear Map

Let G_1 and G_2 be cyclic groups of same prime order p and $G_1 = \langle P \rangle$, where we write G_1 additively and G_2 multiplicatively. A mapping $e : G_1 \times G_1 \rightarrow G_2$ is called a cryptographic bilinear map if it satisfies the following properties:

- Bilinearity : $e(aP, bQ) = e(P, Q)^{ab}$ for all $P, Q \in G_1$ and $a, b \in Z_p$.
- Non-degeneracy : If $G_1 = \langle P \rangle$, then $G_2 = \langle e(P, P) \rangle$.
- Computability : There exists an efficient algorithm to compute $e(P, Q)$ for all $P, Q \in G_1$.

Since $e(aP, bP) = e(P, P)^{ab} = e(bP, aP)$, $e()$ also satisfies the symmetry property. Modified Weil pairing [8] and Tate pairing [2, 13] are examples of cryptographic bilinear maps.

4.2 HIBE $\mathcal{H}_1$

Set-Up: The identity space consists of all tuples $(\mathsf{v}_1, \ldots, \mathsf{v}_\tau)$, where each $\mathsf{v}_i \in Z_p$. Note that we do not fix a upper bound on τ. The message space is G_2. (In practical applications, the protocol will be converted into a hybrid encryption scheme where the message can be any binary string.) The ciphertext corresponding to an identity $(\mathsf{v}_1, \ldots, \mathsf{v}_\tau)$ is a tuple $(A, B, C_1, \ldots, C_\tau)$, where $A \in G_2$ and $B, C_1, \ldots, C_\tau \in G_1$.

Randomly choose $x \in Z_p$ and set $P_1 = xP$. Randomly choose P_2, P_3, $Q_1, \ldots, Q_n$ from G_1 where n is a parameter of the model. The public parameters are $(P, P_1, P_2, P_3, Q_1, \ldots, Q_n)$ and the master secret key is xP_2. Note that, the public parameter size does not depend on the levels of the HIBE. In other words, potentially $\mathcal{H}_1$ can support unbounded number of levels. Since, P_1, P_2 are not directly required in Encryption or Decryption, we may replace them in the public parameters by $e(P_1, P_2)$. This will save the pairing computation during the encryption.

Key Generation: Let $\mathsf{v} = (\mathsf{v}_1, \ldots, \mathsf{v}_\tau)$ be an identity. For any $y \in Z_p$ define

$$V(y) = y^n Q_n + \cdots + y Q_1.$$

Let $V_i = P_3 + V(\mathsf{v}_i)$. The private key d_v corresponding to v is defined to be

$$(xP_2 + r_1 V_1 + \ldots + r_\tau V_\tau, r_1 P, \ldots, r_\tau P) = (d_0, d_1, \ldots, d_\tau)$$

where $r_1, \ldots, r_\tau$ are random elements of Z_p. It is standard [4] to verify that the knowledge of a random private key corresponding to the tuple $(\mathsf{v}_1, \ldots, \mathsf{v}_{\tau-1})$ allows the generation of a random private key corresponding to v.

Encryption: Suppose a message M is to be encrypted under the identity $\mathsf{v} = (\mathsf{v}_1, \ldots, \mathsf{v}_\tau)$. Choose a random $t \in Z_p$. The ciphertext is $(A, B, C_1, \ldots, C_\tau)$, where

$$A = M \times e(P_1, P_2)^t; \quad B = tP; \quad C_i = tV_i, \text{ for } 1 \le i \le \tau.$$

Decryption: Suppose $(A, B, C_1, \ldots, C_\tau)$ is to be decrypted using the private key $(d_0, d_1, \ldots, d_\tau)$ corresponding to the identity $\mathsf{v} = (\mathsf{v}_1, \ldots, \mathsf{v}_\tau)$. Compute

$$A \times \frac{\prod_{i=1}^{\tau} e(d_i, C_i)}{e(d_0, B)}.$$

Again, it is standard to verify that the above computation yields M.

4.3 HIBE $\mathcal{H}_2$

The description of $\mathcal{H}_2$ is similar to that of $\mathcal{H}_1$. The only differences are in the specification of the maximum depth of the HIBE, the public parameters and the definition of V_i's.

1. Define the maximum depth of the HIBE to be h. Additionally, a tuple $(n_1, \ldots, n_h)$ of positive integers is required.
2. Replace P_3 in $\mathcal{H}_1$, by the tuple $(P_{3,1}, \ldots, P_{3,h})$ where each $P_{3,i}$ is an element of G_1. Also the points Q_i's $(1 \leq i \leq n)$ are replaced by the points $Q_{i,j}$'s, where $1 \leq i \leq h$ and $1 \leq j \leq n_i$.
3. Define $V(i, y) = y^{n_i} Q_{i,n_i} + \ldots + y Q_{i,1}$. Given an identity $\mathsf{v} = (\mathsf{v}_1, \ldots, \mathsf{v}_\tau)$, define $V_i = P_{3,i} + V(i, \mathsf{v}_i)$.

With these differences, the rest of set-up, key generation, encryption and decryption algorithms remain the same.

5 Security Reduction

In this section, we show that the breaking of $\mathcal{H}_1$ amounts to solving the DBDH problem and similarly for $\mathcal{H}_2$.

5.1 Hardness Assumption

Assume the bilinear map notation from Section 4.1. The DBDH problem in $G_1, G_2, e()$ [9] is as follows: Given a tuple $\langle P, aP, bP, cP, Z \rangle$, where $Z \in G_2$, decide whether $Z = e(P, P)^{abc}$ which we denote as Z is real or Z is random. The advantage of a probabilistic algorithm $\mathcal{B}$, which takes as input a tuple $\langle P, aP, bP, cP, Z \rangle$ and outputs a bit, in solving the DBDH problem is defined as

$$\mathsf{Adv}_\mathcal{B}^{\mathsf{DBDH}} = |\Pr[\mathcal{B}(P, aP, bP, cP, Z) = 1 | Z \text{ is real}]$$
$$-\Pr[\mathcal{B}(P, aP, bP, cP, Z) = 1 | Z \text{ is random}]|$$

where the probability is calculated over the random choice of $a, b, c \in Z_p$ as well as the random bits used by $\mathcal{B}$. The quantity $\mathsf{Adv}^{\mathsf{DBDH}}(t)$ denotes the maximum of $\mathsf{Adv}_\mathcal{B}^{\mathsf{DBDH}}$ where the maximum is taken over all adversaries running in time at most t.

5.2 Security Reduction for $\mathcal{H}_1$

The security reduction is to show that if there is an adversary which can break $\mathcal{H}_1$ then one obtains an algorithm to solve DBDH. The heart of such an algorithm is a simulator which is constructed as follows. On given an instance of DBDH as input, the simulator plays the security game with an adversary for $\mathcal{H}_1$. The adversary executes the commitment stage; then the simulator sets up the HIBE based on the adversary's commitment as well as the DBDH instance. The simulator gives the public parameters to the adversary and continues the game by answering all queries made by the adversary. In the process it guesses the bit γ and encrypts M_γ using the DBDH instance provided as input. Finally, the adversary outputs γ'. Based on the value of γ and γ', the simulator decides whether the instance it received is real or random. Intuitively, if the adversary has an advantage in breaking the HIBE protocol, the simulator also has a good advantage in distinguishing between real and random instances. This leads to an upper bound on the advantage of the adversary in terms of the advantage of the simulator in solving DBDH. The details of the reduction are given below.

DBDH Instance: The simulator receives an instance $(P, P_1 = aP, P_2 = bP, Q = cP, Z) \in G_1^4 \times G_2$ of DBDH. It has to decide whether $Z = e(P, P)^{abc}$ (i.e., Z is real) or whether Z is random. Note that it does not know a, b, c.

The simulator now starts the security game for model $\mathcal{M}_1$. This consists of several stages which we describe below. We will consider security against chosen plaintext attacks and hence the adversary will only have access to the key extraction oracle $\mathcal{O}_k$.

Adversary's Commitment: The adversary commits to a set $\mathcal{I}^*$. We will assume that the elements of $\mathcal{I}^*$ are elements of Z_p. Alternatively, if these are bit strings, then (as is standard) they will be hashed using a collision resistant hash function into elements of Z_p. We write $\mathcal{I}^* = \{v_1^*, \dots, v_n^*\}$.

Set-Up: Define a polynomial in $Z_p[x]$ by

$$F(x) = (x - v_1^*) \cdots (x - v_n^*) \tag{1}$$
$$= x^n + a_{n-1}x^{n-1} + \cdots + a_1 x + a_0 \tag{2}$$

where the coefficients a_i's are in Z_p and are obtained from the values $\{v_1^*, \dots, v_n^*\}$. (Since $F(x)$ is a polynomial of degree n over Z_p and $v_1^*, \dots, v_n^*$ are its n distinct roots, we have $F(v) \neq 0$ for any $v \in Z_p \setminus \{v_1^*, \dots, v_n^*\}$.) Note that, these coefficients depend on the adversary's input and one cannot assume any distribution on these values. For notational convenience, we define $a_n = 1$. Randomly choose $b_0, \dots, b_n$ from Z_p and define another polynomial

$$J(x) = b_n x^n + b_{n-1}x^{n-1} + \cdots + b_1 x + b_0 \tag{3}$$

Define $P_3 = a_0 P_2 + b_0 P$ and for $1 \leq i \leq n$, define $Q_i = a_i P_2 + b_i P$. Note that, Q_is are random elements of G_1. Now note that for $y \in Z_p$,

$$V(y) = P_3 + yQ_1 + y^2 Q_2 + \cdots + y^n Q_n$$
$$= F(y)P_2 + J(y)P.$$

The public parameters are $(P, P_1, P_2, P_3, Q_1, \dots, Q_n)$ which has the same distribution as the public parameters in the protocol specification. These are given to the adversary. The master secret is aP_2, which is not known to the simulator.

Phase 1: In this stage, the adversary can make queries to $\mathcal{O}_k$, all of which have to be answered by the simulator. Suppose the adversary queries $\mathcal{O}_k$ on an identity $v = (v_1, \dots, v_\tau)$. By the constraint of model $\mathcal{M}_1$ all the v_i's cannot be in $\mathcal{I}^*$. Suppose $\imath$ is such that $v_\imath$ is not in $\mathcal{I}^*$. Then $F(v_\imath) \neq 0$.

As in the protocol, define $V_i = P_3 + V(\mathsf{v}_i)$. Choose $r_1, \ldots, r_{i-1}, r'_i, r_{i+1}, \ldots,$ r_τ randomly from Z_p. Define $W = \sum_{i=1, i \neq \iota}^{\tau} r_i V_i$. The first component d_0 of the secret key for $\mathsf{v} = (\mathsf{v}_1, \ldots, \mathsf{v}_\tau)$ is computed in the following manner.

$$d_0 = -\frac{J(v_\iota)}{F(v_\iota)} P_1 + r'_\iota (F(v_\iota) P_2 + J(v_\iota) P) + W.$$

The following computation shows that d_0 is a properly formed.

$$d_0 = \pm a P_2 - \frac{J(v_\iota)}{F(v_\iota)} P_1 + r'_\iota (F(v_\iota) P_2 + J(v_\iota) P) + W$$

$$= a P_2 + (r'_\iota - \frac{a}{F(v_\iota)})(F(v_\iota) P_2 + J(v_\iota) P) + W$$

$$= a P_2 + \sum_{i=1}^{\tau} r_i V_i$$

where $r_\iota = r'_\iota - a/F(v_\iota)$. Since r'_ι is random, so is r_ι. The quantities $d_1, \ldots, d_\tau$ are computed in the following manner.

$$d_i = r_i P \qquad\qquad 1 \le i \le \tau,\ i \neq \iota;$$
$$= r'_\iota P - \tfrac{1}{F(v_\iota)} P_1 = r_\iota P\ i = \iota.$$

This technique is based on the algebraic techniques introduced by Boneh and Boyen [4]. The generalization is in the definition of $F()$ and $J()$. Here we take these to be polynomials, which allows us to tackle the case of adversary committing to more than one identity. In case the polynomials are of degree one, then we get exactly the Boneh-Boyen HIBE [4].

Challenge Generation: The adversary submits messages M_0, M_1 and an identity $\mathsf{v} = (\mathsf{v}_1, \ldots, \mathsf{v}_\tau)$. By the rules of model $\mathcal{M}_1$, each $\mathsf{v}_i \in \mathcal{I}^*$ and so $F(\mathsf{v}_i) = 0$ for $1 \le i \le \tau$. Consequently, $V_i = F(\mathsf{v}_i) P_2 + J(\mathsf{v}_i) P = J(\mathsf{v}_i) P$ and $cV_i = cJ(\mathsf{v}_i) P = J(\mathsf{v}_i)(cP) = J(\mathsf{v}_i) Q = W_i$ (say), where $Q = cP$ was supplied as part of the DBDH instance. Note that it is possible to compute cV_i even without knowing c. The simulator now randomly chooses a bit γ and returns

$$(M_\gamma \times Z, Q, W_1, \ldots, W_\tau)$$

to the adversary. This is a proper encryption of M_γ under the identity v.

Phase 2: The key extraction queries in this stage are handled as in Phase 1.

Guess: The adversary outputs a guess γ'. The simulator outputs 1 if $\gamma = \gamma'$, else it outputs 0.

If $Z = e(P, P)^{abc}$, then the simulator provides a perfect simulation of the $\mathcal{M}_1$ game. On the other hand, if Z is random, the adversary receives no information about the message M_γ from the challenge ciphertext. Formalizing this argument in the standard manner shows that $\mathsf{Adv}_{\mathcal{A}}^{\mathcal{H}_1}(t, q) \le \mathsf{Adv}_{\mathcal{B}}^{\mathrm{DBDH}}(t + O(\sigma nq))$ where σ is the time for scalar multiplication in G_1 and q is the maximun number of queries allowed to the adversary.

5.3 Security Reduction for $\mathcal{H}_2$

The security reduction for $\mathcal{H}_2$ in model $\mathcal{M}_2$ is similar to that of $\mathcal{H}_1$ in model $\mathcal{M}_1$. We mention only the differences.

Adversary's Commitment: Following model $\mathcal{M}_2$, the adversary commits to sets $\mathcal{I}_1^*, \ldots, \mathcal{I}_\tau^*$, where $|\mathcal{I}_i^*| = n_i$.

Set-Up: The simulator defines polynomials $F_1(x), \ldots, F_\tau(x)$, and $J_1(x), \ldots, J_\tau(x)$ where

$$F_i(x) = \prod_{\mathsf{v} \in \mathcal{I}_i} (x - \mathsf{v})$$
$$= x^{n_i} + a_{i,n_i-1}x^{n_i-1} + \cdots + a_{i,1}x + a_{i,0};$$
$$J_i(x) = b_{i,n_i}x^{n_i} + b_{i,n_i-1}x^{n_i-1} + \cdots + b_{i,1}x + b_{i,0}$$

where $b_{i,j}$'s are random elements of Z_p. For notational convenience, we define $a_{i,n_i} = 1$. For $1 \leq i \leq \tau$, define $P_{3,i} = a_{i,0}P_2 + b_{i,0}P$ and $Q_{i,j} = a_{i,j}P_2 + b_{i,j}P$, $1 \leq j \leq n_i$.

Key Extraction Query: Suppose the private key of $\mathsf{v} = (\mathsf{v}_1, \ldots, \mathsf{v}_\nu)$ is required. According to model $\mathcal{M}_2$, there is at least one i such that $\mathsf{v}_i \notin \mathcal{I}_i^*$. Then this i can be used to generate the private key in a manner similar to the key generation by the simulator for $\mathcal{H}_1$ in model $\mathcal{M}_1$.

Challenge Generation: Suppose the challenge identity is $\mathsf{v}^* = (\mathsf{v}_1^*, \ldots, \mathsf{v}_\nu^*)$. Then by the constraint of $\mathcal{M}_2$ for each i, $\mathsf{v}_i^* \in \mathcal{I}_i^*$ and consequently $F_i(\mathsf{v}_i^*) = 0$. This allows the generation of a proper ciphertext as in the simulation of $\mathcal{H}_1$ in model $\mathcal{M}_1$.

Finally, we obtain the following result.

$$\mathsf{Adv}_{\mathcal{A}}^{\mathcal{H}_2}(t,q) \leq \mathsf{Adv}_{\mathcal{B}}^{\mathrm{DBDH}}(t + O(\sigma \sum_{i=1}^{h} n_i q)).$$

6 Multi-Receiver IBE

A multi-receiver IBE (MR-IBE) is an extension of the IBE, which allows a sender to encrypt a message in such a way that it can be decrypted by any one of a particular set of identities. In other words, there is one encryptor but more than one valid receivers. In IBE, the number of valid receivers is one. One trivial way to realize an MR-IBE from an IBE is to encrypt the same message several times. A non-trivial construction attempts to reduce the cost of encryption.

This notion was introduced in [1] and a non-trivial construction based on the Boneh-Franklin IBE (BF-IBE) was provided. The construction was proved to be secure in the *selective*-ID model under the *random oracle* assumption. Note that the BF-IBE is secure in the full model under the random oracle assumption.

We show that $\mathcal{H}_1$ restricted to IBE can be modified to obtain an MR-IBE. The required modifications to the protocol are as follows.

1. The encryption is converted into a hybrid scheme. Instead of multiplying the message with the "mask" $Z = e(P_1, P_2)^t$, the value Z is provided as input to a pseudorandom generator and the message (considered to be a bit string) is XORed with the resulting keystream.
2. The private key corresponding to an identity v is $d_v = (xP_2 + rV_v, rP)$, where $V_v = P_3 + V(v)$ as defined in in Section 4.2.
3. Suppose the intended set of receivers is $\{v_1, \ldots, v_\tau\}$. Then the ciphertext consists of the encryption of the message as mentioned above plus a header of the form $(tP, tV_1, \ldots, tV_\tau)$, where V_i is as defined in the construction of $\mathcal{H}_1$ in Section 4.2 and t is a random element of Z_p.
4. The receiver possessing the secret key d_{v_i} $(1 \leq i \leq \tau)$ can compute $e(P_1, P_2)^t$ in the standard manner and hence obtain the input to the pseudorandom generator. Thus it can decrypt the message.

The MR-IBE described above can be proved to be secure in the selective-ID model *without* the random oracle assumption. The security model for MR-IBE is the following. In the commitment stage, the adversary commits to a set of identities; does not ask for the private key of these identities in the key extraction queries and finally asks for the encryption under this set of identities. Note that this is very similar to the model $\mathcal{M}_1$ restricted to IBE. The only difference is that during the generation of the challenge ciphertext, in $\mathcal{M}_1$, the adversary supplies only one identity out of the set of identities it had previously committed to, whereas in the model for MR-IBE, the adversary asks for the encryption under the whole set of these identities.

This difference is easily tackled in our proof in Section 5.2 which shows that $\mathcal{H}_1$ is secure in model $\mathcal{M}_1$. Recall that the construction of the polynomial $F(x)$ is such that $F(v) = 0$ for all $v \in \mathcal{I}^*$, where $\mathcal{I}^*$ is the set of committed identities. In the challenge stage of the security proof for $\mathcal{H}_1$ as an IBE, we use this fact for only one identity (the identity given by the adversary). In the proof for MR-IBE, we will need to generate cV_i for all $v \in \mathcal{I}^*$. Since $F(v) = 0$ for any such v, this can be done in the standard fashion.

The above argument does not provide any security degradation. Hence, we obtain an MR-IBE which can be proved to be secure in the selective-ID model *without* the random oracle assumption.

7   Conclusion

In this paper, we have generalized the notion of *selective*-ID secure HIBE. Two new security models $\mathcal{M}_1$ and $\mathcal{M}_2$ have been introduced. In the security game, both these models allow an adversary to commit to a set of identities (as opposed to a single identity in the sID model) before the set-up. During the challenge stage, the adversary can choose any one of the previously committed identities as a challenge identity. We provide two HIBE constructions $\mathcal{H}_1$ and $\mathcal{H}_2$ which are secure in the models $\mathcal{M}_1$ and $\mathcal{M}_2$ respectively. Interestingly, the HIBE $\mathcal{H}_1$ allows delegation of an unbounded number of levels, i.e., the maximum number of delegation levels is not fixed during the protocol set-up. Further, we also show that $\mathcal{H}_1$ can be modified to obtain an MR-IBE protocol which is secure in the sID model *without* random oracles. The only previous construction of MR-IBE is secure in the sID model under the random oracle assumption.

Acknowledgement

The authors express their sincere gratitude to the anonymous reviewers of PKC 2006.

References

1. J. Baek, R. Safavi-Naini and W. Susilo. Efficient Multi-Receiver Identity-Based Encryption and Its Application to Broadcast Encryption. PKC 2005, LNCS 3386, pp 380–397, 2005.
2. P. S. L. M. Barreto, H. Y. Kim, B. Lynn and M. Scott. Efficient Algorithms for Pairing-Based Cryptosystems. CRYPTO 2002, LNCS 2442, pp. 354–368, 2002.
3. M. Bellare and P. Rogaway. Random Oracles are Practical: A Paradigm for Designing Efficient Protocols. In ACM Conference on Computer and Communications Security - CCS 1993, pp 62–73, 1993.
4. D. Boneh, X. Boyen. Efficient Selective-ID Secure Identity Based Encryption Without Random Oracles, EUROCRYPT 2004, LNCS 3027, pp 223–238, 2004.
5. D. Boneh, X. Boyen. Secure Identity Based Encryption without Random Oracles. CRYPTO 2004, LNCS 3152, pp 443–459, 2004.
6. D. Boneh, X. Boyen, E. Goh, Hierarchical Identity Based Encryption with Constant Size Ciphertext, EUROCRYPT 2005, LNCS 3494, pp 440-456, 2005.
7. D. Boneh, R. Canetti, S. Halevi, and J. Katz. Chosen-Ciphertext Security from Identity-Based Encryption. Journal Submission. Available from D. Boneh's website.
8. D. Boneh, M. Franklin. Identity Based Encryption from the Weil Pairing. CRYPTO 2001, LNCS 2139, pp. 213–229, 2001.
9. D. Boneh, M. Franklin. Identity Based Encryption from the Weil Pairing. SIAM J. of Computing, Vol. 32, No. 3, pp. 586–615, 2003.
10. D. Boneh and J. Katz. Improved Efficiency for CCA-Secure Cryptosystems Built Using Identity Based Encryption. RSA-CT 2005, LNCS 3376, pp. 87-103, 2005.
11. R. Canetti, S. Halevi and J. Katz. A Forward-Secure Public-Key Encryption Scheme. EUROCRYPT 2003, LNCS 2656, pp 255-271. 2003.
12. R. Canetti, S. Halevi and J. Katz. Chosen-ciphertext Security from Identity Based Encryption. EUROCRYPT 2004. LNCS 3027, pp 207–222, 2004.
13. S. Galbraith, K. Harrison and D. Soldera. Implementing the Tate Pairing. ANTS V, LNCS 2369, pp. 324-337, 2002.
14. C. Gentry and A. Silverberg, Hierarchical ID-Based Cryptography, ASIACRYPT 2002, LNCS 2501, pp 548–566, 2002.
15. J. Horwitz and B. Lynn. Towards Hierarchical Identity-Based Encryption. EUROCRYPT 2002, LNCS 2332, pp 466–481, 2002.
16. A. Shamir. Identity-based Cryptosystems and Signature Schemes. CRYPTO 1984, LNCS 196, pp 47–53, 1985.
17. B. Waters. Efficient Identity-Based Encryption without Random Oracles. EUROCRYPT 2005, LNCS 3494, pp 114–127, 2005. Also available from Cryptology ePrint Archive, Report 2004/180, http://eprint.iacr.org/2004/180/.

Identity-Based Aggregate Signatures

Craig Gentry[1,*] and Zulfikar Ramzan[2]

[1] Stanford University
cgentry@cs.stanford.edu
[2] DoCoMo Communications Laboratories USA, Inc.
ramzan@docomolabs-usa.com

Abstract. An *aggregate signature* is a single short string that convinces any verifier that, for all $1 \leq i \leq n$, signer S_i signed message M_i, where the n signers and n messages may all be distinct. The main motivation of aggregate signatures is compactness. However, while the aggregate signature itself may be compact, aggregate signature verification might require potentially lengthy additional information – namely, the (at most) n distinct signer public keys and the (at most) n distinct messages being signed. If the verifier must obtain and/or store this additional information, the primary benefit of aggregate signatures is largely negated.

This paper initiates a line of research whose ultimate objective is to find a signature scheme in which the *total information needed to verify* is minimized. In particular, the verification information should preferably be as close as possible to the theoretical minimum: the complexity of describing which signer(s) signed what message(s). We move toward this objective by developing *identity-based* aggregate signature schemes. In our schemes, the verifier does not need to obtain and/or store various signer public keys to verify; instead, the verifier only needs a description of who signed what, along with two constant-length "tags": the short aggregate signature and the single public key of a Private Key Generator. Our scheme is secure in the random oracle model under the computational Diffie-Hellman assumption over pairing-friendly groups against an adversary that chooses its messages and its target identities adaptively.

1 Introduction

Authentication is crucial for many cryptographic applications. Improving the performance of building blocks, like digital signatures, that provide a means for authentication is therefore an essential goal. While time complexity is a well-known traditional measure for evaluating performance, communication complexity is becoming increasingly important for two reasons. First, consider wireless devices (e.g., PDAs, cell phones, RFID chips, and sensors). Here battery life is often more of a limiting bottleneck than processor speed. Communicating a single bit of data consumes several orders of magnitude more power than executing a basic 32-bit arithmetic instruction [BA05]. Second, consider wireless network scenarios (e.g., MANETS, cellular networks, tactical networks, and sensor nets).

---

* This research was conducted while the author was at DoCoMo Labs, USA.

M. Yung et al. (Eds.): PKC 2006, LNCS 3958, pp. 257–273, 2006.

Here reliable bandwidth may be more of a limiting factor than computation. In these cases it would be preferable to limit the communication requirements (i.e., the size) of a digital signature. An *aggregate signature* is one technique towards achieving this aim.

AGGREGATE SIGNATURES. In an aggregate signature scheme [BGLS03], multiple signatures can be aggregated into a compact "aggregate signature," even if these signatures are on (many) different documents and were produced by (many) different signers. This is useful in many real-world applications. For example, certificate chains in a hierarchical PKI of depth n consist of n signatures by n different CAs on n different public keys; by using an aggregate signature scheme, this chain can be compressed down to a single aggregate certificate. Another application is secure routing. In Secure BGP [KLS00], each router successively signs its segment of a path in the network, and forwards the collection of signatures associated with the path to the next router; forwarding these signatures entails a high transmission overhead that could be reduced by using aggregate signatures. Aside from compactness, aggregate signatures have other advantages. For example, in scenarios such as database outsourcing [MNT04] and dynamic content distribution [SRF+04] one may want to prevent a malicious party from removing a signature from a collection of signatures without being detected. An aggregate signature scheme makes this possible, since a signature that has been aggregated cannot (under certain conditions) be separated.

Currently, two aggregate signature schemes exist. The first [BGLS03] uses bilinear maps and supports flexible aggregation – i.e., given n individual signatures $\sigma_1, \ldots, \sigma_n$, *anyone* can aggregate them in *any order* into an aggregate signature σ. The second [LMRS04] uses a weaker assumption – namely, certified trapdoor permutations – but it permits only *sequential* aggregation – i.e., the n-th signer must aggregate its own signature into the aggregate signature formed by the first $n - 1$ signers.

For both schemes above, the aggregate signature is compact (i.e., its size is independent of n). However, the total information $\mathcal{V}$ needed to verify the aggregate signature – namely, the aggregate signature itself, the public keys of the individual signers, and a description of the respective messages that they signed – is not necessarily compact at all. Of course, $\mathcal{V}$ must (information-theoretically) contain a description $\mathcal{D}$ of what signer signed what message, since the verification information must *convince* the verifier that certain signers signed certain messages. But $|\mathcal{D}|$ can grow slowly with the number of individual signatures n; e.g., in a routing application, one can use IP addresses as identities, and we can reduce communication further since the higher-order bits of the IP addresses of consecutive routers may be identical, so only need to be transmitted once.

Beyond this information-theoretic minimum, however, $\mathcal{V}$ in current aggregate signature schemes must also contain individual signer public keys, whose length is dictated by the security parameter of the signature scheme (not by basic information-theoretic considerations). Theoretically, this means that $|\mathcal{V}| - |\mathcal{D}|$ grows linearly with n. Practically speaking, this means that current aggregate signature schemes may not perform significantly better than traditional signature schemes in situations where verifiers cannot be expected to already have the signers' public keys – e.g., in a dynamic multi-hop network in which a node is unlikely to have a prior relationship with a neighboring node. Clearly, it would be preferable if $\mathcal{V}$ could specify the signers by their identities rather than by their individual public keys.

IDENTITY-BASED SIGNATURES. In identity-based cryptography (IBC) [Sha84], the central idea is to simplify public-key and certificate management by using a user's "identity" (e.g., its email address) as its public key. For this to be possible, the IBC system requires a trusted third party, typically called a "Private Key Generator" (PKG), to generate user private keys from its "master secret" and the user's identity. Only the PKG has a traditional "random-looking" public key. In an identity-based encryption (IBE) scheme, the sender encrypts a message using the recipient's identity and the PKG's public key; it need not obtain the recipient's public key and certificate before encrypting, since the recipient has no traditional public key and since the sender knows that the recipient (or an attacker) will not be able to decrypt unless it has received an identity-based private key from the PKG (in effect, an implicit certificate). In an identity-based signature (IBS) scheme, the verifier verifies a signature by using the signer's identity and PKG's public key; the verification information does not include any certificate or any individual public key for the signer.

Research on IBS has experienced a revival in the wake of the discovery – independently by Boneh and Franklin [BF03] and by Cocks [Coc01] – of practical IBE schemes. (Early schemes include [Sha84, FS86, GQ88]; recent schemes and analyses include [CC03, Boy03, LQ04, BNN04].) Unfortunately, IBS does not have the significant infrastructural advantages over traditional public-key signing that IBE has over traditional public-key encryption. In IBE, the fact that the sender does not need to obtain the recipient's public key and certificate before encrypting means that no infrastructure (i.e., public-key infrastructure (PKI)) needs to be deployed to distribute such information to third parties (including non-clients); rather, the authority (the PKG) only needs infrastructure to distribute private keys directly to its clients. On the other hand, IBS and public-key signing (PKS) are analogous infrastructurally: in IBS (resp. PKS), the PKG (resp. CA) sends a private key (resp. certificate) to each client. Thus, the main advantage of IBS over PKS, at least abstractly, turns out to be communication-efficiency, since (unlike PKS) the signer does not need to send an individual public key and certificate with its signature.

This advantage of IBS becomes more compelling when we consider multiple signers, all of which are clients of the same PKG. In this setting, the verifier needs only one traditional public key (the PKG's) to verify multiple identity-based signatures on multiple documents. Unfortunately, current identity-based signatures are not aggregable. Interestingly, multiple-signer IBS therefore has precisely the opposite problem of aggregate signing: for IBS, the public key is (in some sense) aggregable, while the individual signatures are not.

GOALS AND CHALLENGES. Our goal is simple: a signature scheme (allowing distinct signers to sign distinct documents) in which the total verification information is minimized. We cannot do better than the information-theoretic lower bound of describing who signed what, but we would like to get as close to this lower bound as possible.

Based on the above discussion, one natural approach is to construct an "identity-based aggregate signature" (IBAS) scheme – i.e., a scheme in which the verification information (apart from the required description of who signed what) consists only of a single aggregate signature and a single public key (of the PKG). In a sense, identity-based aggregate signatures would really address the motivating applications considered first in the context of regular (non ID-based) aggregate signatures.

However, there certainly does not appear to be any generic way of combining an aggregate signature scheme with an IBS scheme to achieve this desideratum. To see the difficulty, note that each of the current aggregate signature schemes are deterministic, and with good reason; if each successive signer contributed randomness to the aggregate signature in a trivial way, this randomness would cause the size of the signature to grow linearly with n – hence the signature would not be compact. On the other hand, identity-based signature schemes tend to be randomized; typically, the signer uses the Fiat-Shamir heuristic (which involves choosing a random commitment and treating the output of a hash function as the challenge to which the signer responds) to prove knowledge of the authority's signature on its identity. In short, current approaches for constructing aggregate signatures appear to be fundamentally at odds with current approaches for constructing identity-based signatures. To construct an IBAS scheme, it seems we must somehow find a way to "aggregate the randomness" provided by the multiple signers.

OUR RESULTS. Our first contribution is a formal definition of identity-based aggregate signatures and a corresponding formal security model. Second, we describe, as a stepping stone, an identity-based multi-signature scheme (which may be of independent interest). Third, we present a concrete IBAS scheme that meets our definition. As desired, our scheme allows multiple signers to sign multiple documents in such a way that the total verification information, apart from a description of who signed what, consists only of a short aggregate signature (which consists of only 2 group elements and a short (e.g., 160-bit) string) and the PKG's public key (which is also short – about the same size as the PKG's public key in Boneh-Franklin). Our scheme is also very efficient computationally. In fact, it allows more efficient verification than the aggregate signature scheme of [BGLS03], since verification requires only three pairing computations, regardless of the value of n, while [BGLS03] uses $\mathcal{O}(n)$ pairing computations. (Note: verification in our scheme uses $\mathcal{O}(n)$ elliptic curve scalar multiplications, but these can be computed quite quickly.) Later we describe certain extensions and additional benefits of our scheme.

Our scheme is provably secure in the random oracle model, assuming the hardness of computational Diffie-Hellman over groups with bilinear maps. In our security model, the adversary can make q_E adaptive key extraction queries (wherein he receives the signing key corresponding to any ID of his choice), q_S adaptive signature queries (wherein he receives the signature on any message of his choice), and q_H hash queries (wherein he receives the output of a hash function, modeled as a random oracle, on inputs of his choice). The adversary succeeds if he constructs a single non-trivial forgery. The concrete security loss in our scheme is roughly $q_E \cdot q_H \cdot q_S$. While one would prefer a smaller loss, it is worth noting that typical ID-based signature schemes usually suffer from a concrete security loss of roughly $q_E \cdot q_S$ because the simulator usually has to guess the ID and message that will be used in the forgery. We further note that such a quadratic loss is also inherent in schemes where security is proved using the forking lemma [PS96],[PS00]).

We remark that in our scheme all signers must use the same (unique) random string w when signing – this step seems necessary to enable signature aggregation. Choosing such a w may be straightforward in certain settings. For example, if the signers have access to loosely synchronized clocks, then w could be chosen based on the current time. Further, if w is sufficiently long (i.e., accounting for birthday bounds), then it will be statistically unique. In order to alleviate any cost incurred in choosing w, we describe a simple extension of our scheme that allows a signer to securely re-use the same w a constant number of times.

Aside from requiring a common value of w, aggregation in our scheme is very flexible. Anybody can aggregate individual identity-based signatures into an identity-based aggregate signature, and aggregate smaller aggregates into larger aggregates. Moreover, our scheme permits aggregation across multiple trusted authorities; i.e., signers under different PKGs can aggregate their signatures. As a stepping stone to IBAS, we also describe an identity-based multisignature (in which all signers sign the same message) that may be of independent interest.

OTHER RELATED WORK. Aggregate signatures are related to, but more flexible than, multisignatures [Oka98, OO99, MOR01, Bol03]. Although the term "multisignature" has been used in the literature to denote a variety of different types of schemes, we will use the term to denote an aggregate signature in which all users sign the same message. Aggregate signatures are also tenuously related to threshold signatures [Sho00]. Recall that, in a threshold signature scheme, t signature components from any t signers can be combined into a single signature, for some threshold $t \leq n$. The signers must undergo a large setup cost, they all sign the same message, and the verifier cannot tell which signers contributed components to a complete threshold signature. Secure identity-based threshold signature schemes are known [BZ04].

Subsequent to our work, a recent paper claimed an ID-based aggregate signature construction [CLW05]. However, "identity-based aggregate signatures" may not be the best term to describe this result since each signer S_i that participates in the creation of a signature must first generate a random scalar r_i and *broadcast* $r_i P$ (for a certain elliptic curve point P) to all of the other signers so that they can each compute $(\sum r_i)P$. Signer S_i then inputs $(\sum r_i)P$ and its message m_i into a hash function to obtain a signature scheme via the Fiat-Shamir heuristic. Later, individual signatures can be aggregated. However, because of the large setup cost (in which the users essentially broadcast their key shares) and the fact that the signature cannot be verified until all of the signers contribute, this scheme actually bears some resemblance to an identity-based *threshold* signature scheme. Also subsequent to our work, Herranz [Her05] describes a Schnorr-based IBAS scheme that permits "partial" aggregation – that is, signatures can only be aggregated if they all come from the same signer.

ORGANIZATION OF THE PAPER. After providing some preliminaries in Section 2, we propose a definition of identity-based aggregate signatures in Section 3, together with the security model. Next, as a stepping stone to our IBAS construction, we give a simple identity-based multisignature scheme in Section 4. We provide our IBAS construction in Section 5 and describe the security proof in Section 6. Finally, we conclude and mention open problem in Section 7.

2   Preliminaries

Let λ denote the security parameter, which will be an an implicit input to the algorithms in our scheme. For a set S, we let $|S|$ denote the number of elements in S, and $x \xleftarrow{D} S$ denote the experiment of choosing $x \in S$ according to probability distribution D.

2.1   Bilinear Maps

Our IBAS scheme uses a bilinear map, which is often called a "pairing." Typically, the pairing used is a modified Weil or Tate pairing on a supersingular elliptic curve or abelian variety. However, we describe bilinear maps and the related mathematics in a more general format here.

Let $\mathbb{G}_1$ and $\mathbb{G}_2$ be two cyclic groups of some large prime order q. We write $\mathbb{G}_1$ additively and $\mathbb{G}_2$ multiplicatively.

Admissible pairings: We will call $\hat{e}$ an *admissible pairing* if $\hat{e} : \mathbb{G}_1 \times \mathbb{G}_1 \to \mathbb{G}_2$ is a map with the following properties:

1. Bilinear: $\hat{e}(aQ, bR) = \hat{e}(Q, R)^{ab}$ for all $Q, R \in \mathbb{G}_1$ and all $a, b \in \mathbb{Z}$.
2. Non-degenerate: $\hat{e}(Q, R) \neq 1$ for some $Q, R \in \mathbb{G}_1$.
3. Computable: There is an efficient algorithm to compute $\hat{e}(Q, R)$ for any $Q, R \in \mathbb{G}_1$.

Notice that $\hat{e}$ is also symmetric – i.e., $\hat{e}(Q, R) = \hat{e}(R, Q)$ for all $Q, R \in \mathbb{G}_1$ – since $\hat{e}$ is bilinear and $\mathbb{G}_1$ is a cyclic group.

2.2   Computational Assumptions

The security of our schemes is based on the assumed hardness of the computational Diffie-Hellman (CDH) problem in $\mathbb{G}_1$.

Definition 1 (Computational Diffie-Hellman Problem in $\mathbb{G}_1$ (CDH$_{\mathbb{G}_1}$ Problem)). *Given $P, aP, bP \in \mathbb{G}_1$, as well as an admissible pairing $\hat{e} : \mathbb{G}_1 \times \mathbb{G}_1 \to \mathbb{G}_2$, compute abP (for unknown randomly chosen $a, b \in \mathbb{Z}/q\mathbb{Z}$).*

An algorithm $\mathcal{A}$ has an advantage ϵ in solving $\text{CDH}_{\mathbb{G}_1}$ if $\Pr[\mathcal{A}(P, aP, bP) = abP] \geq \epsilon$, where the probability is over the choice of P in $\mathbb{G}_1$, the random scalars a and b in $\mathbb{Z}_q$, and the random bits used by $\mathcal{A}$. Our computational assumption is now formally defined as follows.

Definition 2 (Computational Diffie-Hellman Assumption in $\mathbb{G}_1$ ($\text{CDH}_{\mathbb{G}_1}$ Assumption)). *We say that the* (t, ϵ)-*$CDH_{\mathbb{G}_1}$ Assumption holds if no t-time algorithm $\mathcal{A}$ has advantage ϵ in solving the $CDH_{\mathbb{G}_1}$ Problem.*

We may occasionally refer to the $\text{CDH}_{\mathbb{G}_1}$ Assumption without specifying t or ϵ. The $\text{CDH}_{\mathbb{G}_1}$ Assumption underlies the security of numerous cryptosystems (e.g., [BLS01, BGLS03, CC03]), and is weaker than other commonly-used assumptions relating to bilinear maps, such as the "Bilinear Diffie-Hellman" assumption used in Boneh-Franklin (given $P, aP, bP, cP \in \mathbb{G}_1$ and the bilinear map $\hat{e} : \mathbb{G}_1 \times \mathbb{G}_1 \rightarrow \mathbb{G}_2$, it is hard to compute $\hat{e}(P, P)^{abc} \in \mathbb{G}_2$).

3   Identity-Based Aggregate Signatures

We now define the procedures involved in an IBAS scheme, and thereafter specify what it means for IBAS scheme to be secure.

3.1   Components of an Identity-Based Aggregate Signature

An IBAS scheme is composed of five algorithms: key generation by the PKG, private key extraction by the PKG for individual users, signing by an individual user, aggregation of multiple individual signatures or aggregates of signatures, and verification of an identity-based aggregate signature:

- KeyGen takes 1^λ as input and outputs a suitable key pair (Pk,Sk).
- KeyExt takes Sk and a user identity ID_i as input and outputs a user private key USk_i.
- Sign takes USk_i, message m_i and possibly some state information w as input and outputs an individual identity-based signature σ_i.
- Agg takes as input Pk, w, two sets of identity-message pairs S_1 and S_2, and two identity-based (aggregate) signatures σ_{S_1} and σ_{S_2} on the identity-message pairs contained in sets S_1 and S_2 respectively; if Verify(Pk, w, S_1, σ_{S_1}) = Accept and Verify(Pk, w, S_2, σ_{S_2}) = Accept, it outputs the identity-based aggregate signature $\sigma_{S_1 \cup S_2}$ on the identity-message pairs in $S_1 \cup S_2$ (where identity-message pairs may be repeated).
- Verify takes as input Pk, w, an identity-based aggregate signature σ_S, and a description of the identity-message pairs in set S, and outputs Accept if and only if σ_S could be a valid output of Sign or Agg for Pk, w and S.

Remark 1. Depending on the instantiation, the state information w may be empty. Also, it is possible that Sign and Agg may be inseparably combined into a single step in certain instantiations – e.g., if the IBAS scheme permits only *sequential* aggregation.

3.2   Security Model

An IBAS scheme should be secure against existential forgery under an adaptive-chosen-message and an adaptive-chosen-identity attack. Informally, existential forgery here means that the adversary attempts to forge an identity-based aggregate signature on identities and messages of his choice.

We formalize the identity-based aggregate signature model as follows. The adversary's goal is the existential forgery of an aggregate signature. We give the adversary the power to choose the identities on which it wishes to forge a signature, the power to request the identity-based private key on all but one of these identities, and the power to choose the state w used in its forgery. The adversary is also given access to a signing oracle on any desired identity. The adversary's advantage $\mathsf{AdvIBAS}_{\mathcal{A}}$ is defined as its probability of success (taken over the coin tosses of the key-generation algorithm and of $\mathcal{A}$) in the following game.

Setup: The adversary $\mathcal{A}$ is given the public key Pk of the PKG, an integer n, and any other needed parameters.

Queries: Proceeding adaptively, $\mathcal{A}$ may choose identities ID_i and request the private key USk_i. Also, $\mathcal{A}$ may request an identity-based aggregate signature σ_S on $(\mathsf{Pk}, w, S, \{m_i\}_{i=1}^{k-1})$ where $S = \{\mathsf{ID}_i\}_{i=1}^{k-1}$. We require that $\mathcal{A}$ has not made a query $(\mathsf{Pk}, w, S', \{m_i'\}_{i=1}^{k-1})$ where $ID_i \in S \cap S'$ and $m_i' \neq m_i$.

Response: For some $(\mathsf{Pk}, \{\mathsf{ID}_i\}_{i=1}^{l}, \{m_i\}_{i=1}^{l})$ for $l \leq n$, $\mathcal{A}$ outputs an identity-based aggregate signature σ_l.

$\mathcal{A}$ wins if σ_l is a valid signature on $(\mathsf{Pk}, \{\mathsf{ID}_i\}_{i=1}^{l}, \{m_i\}_{i=1}^{l})$, and the signature is nontrivial – i.e., for some i, $1 \leq i \leq l$, $\mathcal{A}$ did not request the private key for ID_i and did not request a signature including the pair (ID_i, m_i).

Definition 3. *An IBAS adversary $\mathcal{A}$ $(t, \epsilon, n, q_H, q_E, q_S)$-breaks an IBAS scheme in the above model if: for integer n as above, $\mathcal{A}$ runs in time at most t; $\mathcal{A}$ makes at most q_H hash function queries, at most q_E private key extraction queries and at most q_S signing oracle queries; and $\mathsf{AdvIBAS}_{\mathcal{A}}$ is at least ϵ.*

Definition 4. *An IBAS scheme is $(t, \epsilon, n, q_H, q_E, q_S)$-secure against existential forgery if no adversary $(t, \epsilon, n, q_H, q_E, q_S)$-breaks it.*

4   An Identity-Based Multisignature Scheme

Before presenting our construction of an IBAS scheme, we address, as a stepping stone, the simpler problem of constructing an identity-based ad-hoc multisignature scheme. In this scheme, all signers sign the same message, possibly in a completely decentralized fashion. Thereafter, *any subset* of the individual identity-based signatures on the message can be aggregated by anyone in any order. We use the term "ad hoc" to stress this flexibility.

Interestingly, the individual signatures in this identity-based multisignature scheme are very similar to one-level hierarchical identity-based signatures as presented by Gentry and Silverberg [GS02]. We modify their scheme slightly by hashing the message by itself, rather than together with the signer's identity, to enable aggregation; this makes our security reduction slightly looser. This construction will be instructive as to how one can "aggregate the randomness" provided by multiple signers. The scheme is as follows.

Setup: The Private Key Generator (PKG) generates parameters and keys essentially as in [GS02]. Specifically, it:

1. generates groups $\mathbb{G}_1$ and $\mathbb{G}_2$ of prime order q with admissible pairing $\hat{e}$: $\mathbb{G}_1 \times \mathbb{G}_1 \to \mathbb{G}_2$;
2. chooses an arbitrary generator $P \in \mathbb{G}_1$;
3. picks a random $s \in \mathbb{Z}/q\mathbb{Z}$ and sets $Q = sP$;
4. chooses cryptographic hash functions $H_1, H_2 : \{0,1\}^* \to \mathbb{G}_1$.

The PKG's public key is $(\mathbb{G}_1, \mathbb{G}_2, \hat{e}, P, Q, H_1, H_2)$; its secret is $s \in \mathbb{Z}/q\mathbb{Z}$.

Private key extraction: The client with identity ID_i receives the value sP_i from the PKG as its private key, where $P_i = H_1(\mathsf{ID}_i) \in \mathbb{G}_1$.

Individual Signing: To sign m, the signer with identity ID_i:

1. computes $P_m = H_2(m) \in \mathbb{G}_1$;
2. generates random $r_i \in \mathbb{Z}/q\mathbb{Z}$;
3. computes its signature (S_i', T_i'), where $S_i' = r_i P_m + sP_i$ and $T_i' = r_i P$.

Aggregation: Anyone can aggregate a collection of individual signatures (on the same m) into a multisignature. In particular, individual signatures (S_i', T_i') for $1 \leq i \leq n$ can be aggregated into (S_n, T_n), where $S_n = \sum_{i=1}^{n} S_i'$ and $T_n = \sum_{i=1}^{n} T_i'$.

Verification: Let (S_n, T_n) be the multisignature (where n is the number of signers). The verifier checks that:

$$\hat{e}(S_n, P) = \hat{e}(T_n, P_m)\hat{e}(Q, \sum_{i=1}^{n} P_i) \ ,$$

where $P_i = H_1(\mathsf{ID}_i)$ and $P_m = H_2(m)$.

Notice how, although each of the individual identity-based signatures is randomized, the randomness is "aggregated" into the scalar coefficient of P_m, the element of $\mathbb{G}_1$ corresponding to the common message being signed. Notice also that aggregation is perfectly flexible. Users generate their signatures in a decentralized fashion; later, anyone can aggregate them. The users do not need to maintain any state. Verification requires only three pairing computations (and n point *additions*).

In the full version [GR06], we give a proof of the following theorem.

Theorem 1. *Let $\mathcal{A}$ be an adversary that $(t, \epsilon, n, q_E, q_S)$-breaks the identity-based multisignature scheme. Then, there exists an algorithm $\mathcal{B}$ that solves $CDH_{\mathbb{G}_1}$ in time $O(t) + O(\log^3 q)$ with probability at least $\epsilon(1 - 1/q)/64(q_E + q_S)^2$.*

5   Construction of an Identity-Based Aggregate Signature Scheme

In our identity-based multisignature scheme, we were able to aggregate the randomness contributed by the individual signers into the scalar coefficient of the common message point P_m. However, for IBAS, signers may sign distinct messages, and aggregating the signers' randomness seems difficult. Our solution to this problem, at a high level, is simply to create a "dummy message" w that is mapped to an element P_w of $\mathbb{G}_1$ whose scalar coefficient provides a place where individual signers can aggregate their randomness, and to embed messages into individual signatures using a different mechanism. The details follow.

Setup: The Private Key Generator (PKG) generates parameters and keys essentially as above. Specifically, it:

1. generates groups $\mathbb{G}_1$ and $\mathbb{G}_2$ of prime order q and an admissible pairing $\hat{e}$: $\mathbb{G}_1 \times \mathbb{G}_1 \to \mathbb{G}_2$;
2. chooses an arbitrary generator $P \in \mathbb{G}_1$;
3. picks a random $s \in \mathbb{Z}/q\mathbb{Z}$ and sets $Q = sP$;
4. chooses a cryptographic hash functions $H_1, H_2 : \{0,1\}^* \to \mathbb{G}_1$ and $H_3 : \{0,1\}^* \to \mathbb{Z}/q\mathbb{Z}$.

The system parameters are $params = (\mathbb{G}_1, \mathbb{G}_2, \hat{e}, P, Q, H_1, H_2, H_3)$. The root PKG's secret is $s \in \mathbb{Z}/q\mathbb{Z}$.

Private key generation: The client with identity ID_i receives from the PKG the values of $sP_{i,j}$ for $j \in \{0,1\}$, where $P_{i,j} = H_1(\mathrm{ID}_i, j) \in \mathbb{G}_1$.

Individual Signing: The first signer chooses a string w that it has never used before. Each subsequent signer checks that it has not used the string w chosen by the first signer. (Alternatively, different signers may arrive at the same w independently – e.g., if they issue signatures according to a pre-established schedule.) To sign m_i, the signer with identity ID_i:

1. computes $P_w = H_2(w) \in \mathbb{G}_1$;
2. computes $c_i = H_3(m_i, \mathrm{ID}_i, w) \in \mathbb{Z}/q\mathbb{Z}$;
3. generates random $r_i \in \mathbb{Z}/q\mathbb{Z}$;
4. computes its signature (w, S_i', T_i'), where $S_i' = r_i P_w + sP_{i,0} + c_i sP_{i,1}$ and $T_i' = r_i P$.

Aggregation: Anyone can aggregate a collection of individual signatures that use the same string w. For example, individual signatures (w, S_i', T_i') for $1 \le i \le n$ can be aggregated into (w, S_n, T_n), where $S_n = \sum_{i=1}^n S_i'$ and $T_n = \sum_{i=1}^n T_i'$. Our security proof does not permit the aggregation of individual (or aggregate) signatures that use different w's.

Verification: Let (w, S_n, T_n) be the identity-based aggregate signature (where n is the number of signers). The verifier checks that:

$$\hat{e}(S_n, P) = \hat{e}(T_n, P_w)\hat{e}(Q, \sum_{i=1}^{n} P_{i,0} + \sum_{i=1}^{n} c_i P_{i,1}) \ ,$$

where $P_{i,j} = H_1(\mathrm{ID}_i, j)$, $P_w = H_2(w)$ and $c_i = H_3(m_i, \mathrm{ID}_i, w)$, as above.

Remark 2. This scheme is reasonably efficient. Unlike the BGLS [BGLS03] aggregate signature, this scheme requires a constant number of pairing computations for verification (though the total work is still linear in the number of signers).

Remark 3. If we were to just set the signature to be $sP_{i,0} + c_1 sP_{i,1}$, then after two signatures an adversary will likely be able to recover the values of $sP_{i,0}$ and $sP_{i,1}$ using linear algebra. The purpose of the one-time-use P_w is to disturb this linearity, while providing a place where all the signers can "aggregate their randomness."

Remark 4. To allow each signer to produce k individual identity-based signatures with a single value of w, we can change private key generation so that the client with identity ID_i receives from the PKG the values of $sP_{i,j}$ for $j \in [0, k]$, where $P_{i,j} = H_1(\mathrm{ID}_i, j) \in \mathbb{G}_1$. To sign, the signer computes $c_{ij} = H_3(m_i, \mathrm{ID}_i, w, j)$ for $1 \le i \le k$, and sets $S'_i = r_i P_w + sP_{i,0} + \sum_{j=1}^{k} c_{ij} sP_{i,j}$. The result of the signing procedure is the same, and verification is modified in the obvious fashion.

Remark 5. It is possible to aggregate individual identity-based signatures even if the signers have different PKGs, and the security proof goes through. However, to verify such a multiple-PKG identity-based aggregate signature, the verifier needs the public key of every PKG. Thus, from a bandwidth perspective, the single-PKG case is optimal.

6   The Security of Our IBAS Construction

We start by providing some intuition for how an algorithm $\mathcal{B}$ can solve a computational Diffie-Hellman problem – i.e., compute sP' from P, sP, and P' – by interacting with an algorithm $\mathcal{A}$ that breaks our IBAS scheme. The security proof for the multisignature scheme in the full version [GR06] provides additional intuition. During the interaction, $\mathcal{B}$ must either respond correctly to $\mathcal{A}$'s queries, or abort. $\mathcal{A}$ can make several types of queries:

1. H_1 **and Extraction Queries:** $\mathcal{A}$ can ask for the identity-based private keys $sP_{i,j}$ for $j \in \{0, 1\}$ that correspond to identity ID_i. $\mathcal{B}$ handles these queries through its control of the H_1 oracle. In particular, it usually generates $P_{i,j}$ in such a way that it knows $b_{i,j} = \log_P P_{i,j}$; then, it can compute $sP_{i,j} = b_{i,j} sP$. However, $\mathcal{B}$ occasionally sets $P_{i,j} = b_{i,j} P + b'_{i,j} P'$. In this case, $\mathcal{B}$ cannot respond to an extraction query on ID_i, but if $\mathcal{A}$ later chooses ID_i as a target identity, $\mathcal{A}$'s forgery may help $\mathcal{B}$ solve its computational Diffie-Hellman problem.

2. H_2 **queries:** $\mathcal{B}$, through its control over the H_2 oracle, will usually generate P_w in such a way that it knows $d_w = \log_{P'} P_w$, but occasionally generates P_w so that it knows $c_w = \log_P P_w$ instead.
3. H_3 **and signature queries:** $\mathcal{B}$'s control over the H_2 and H_3 oracles helps it to respond to signature queries regarding the tuple $(\mathsf{ID}_i, m_j, w_k)$ when it cannot even extract the private key corresponding to ID_i. How can $\mathcal{B}$ generate valid and consistent values of $P_{i,0}$, $P_{i,1}$, P_{w_k}, $d_{i,j,k} = H_3(\mathsf{ID}_i, m_j, w_k)$, $S'_i = rP_{w_k} + sP_{i,0} + d_{ijk}sP_{i,1}$ and $T'_i = rP$ in such a situation? In particular, how can it generate S'_i, which seems to require that $\mathcal{B}$ know sP'? If $\mathcal{B}$ knows $\log_{P'} P_w$, it can compute the value of r' such that $r'sP_w$ "cancels out" the multiple of sP' that comes from the final two terms; it then sets T'_i to be $r'sP$. If $\mathcal{B}$ doesn't know $\log_{P'} P_w$, it has one more trick it can use; occasionally, $\mathcal{B}$ sets d_{ijk} to be the unique value in $\mathbb{Z}/q\mathbb{Z}$ that causes the multiples of sP' in the final two terms to cancel. In this case, $\mathcal{B}$ can produce a valid signature. Once this unique value is revealed for a given ID_i, it cannot use this trick again (otherwise, the simulation will not be convincing to $\mathcal{A}$).

If $\mathcal{B}$ is lucky, its simulation does not abort and $\mathcal{A}$ produces a forgery on a tuple $(\mathsf{ID}_i, m_j, w_k)$ for which it does not know $\log_P P_{i,j}$, does know $\log_P P_w$, and where d_{ijk} was not chosen using the trick above. In this case, $\mathcal{A}$'s forgery gives $\mathcal{B}$ the value of sP' with extremely high probability.

The following theorem characterizes the security of our IBAS scheme.

Theorem 2. *Let $\mathcal{A}$ be an adversary that $(t, \epsilon, n, q_{H_3}, q_E, q_S,)$-breaks the IBAS scheme. Then, there exists an algorithm $\mathcal{B}$ that solves $CDH_{\mathbb{G}_1}$ in time $O(t) + O(\log^3 q)$ with success probability at least $\epsilon/1024 q_E q_S (q_{H_3} - q_S)$.*

Proof: Algorithm $\mathcal{B}$ is given an instance $(P, Q, P', \hat{e})$ (for $Q = sP$) of the $CDH_{\mathbb{G}_1}$ problem, and will interact with algorithm $\mathcal{A}$ as follows in an attempt to compute sP'.

Setup: $\mathcal{B}$ sets the public key of the PKG to be $(\mathbb{G}_1, \mathbb{G}_2, \hat{e}, P, Q, H_1, H_2, H_3)$, and it transmits this key to $\mathcal{A}$. Here the H_i's are random oracles controlled by $\mathcal{B}$.

Hash Queries: $\mathcal{A}$ can make an H_1-query, H_2-query, or H_3-query at any time. $\mathcal{B}$ gives identical responses to identical queries, maintaining lists relating to its previous hash query responses for consistency. $\mathcal{B}$ also maintains H_3-list2, which addresses certain special cases of the H_3 simulation. $\mathcal{B}$ responds to $\mathcal{A}$'s H_1-query on (ID_i, j) as follows:

For $\mathcal{A}$'s H_1-query on (ID_i, j) for $j \in \{0, 1\}$:

1. If ID_i was in a previous H_1-query, $\mathcal{B}$ recovers $(b_{i0}, b'_{i0}, b_{i1}, b'_{i1})$ from its H_1-list.
2. Else, $\mathcal{B}$ generates a random $H_1\text{-}coin_i \in \{0, 1\}$ so that $\Pr[H_1\text{-}coin_i = 0] = \delta_1$ for δ_1 to be determined later. If $H_1\text{-}coin_i = 0$, $\mathcal{B}$ generates random $b_{i0}, b_{i1} \in \mathbb{Z}/q\mathbb{Z}$ and sets $b'_{i0} = b'_{i1} = 0$; else, it generates random $b_{i0}, b'_{i0}, b_{i1}, b'_{i1} \in \mathbb{Z}/q\mathbb{Z}$. $\mathcal{B}$ logs $(\mathsf{ID}_i, H_1\text{-}coin_i, b_{i0}, b'_{i0}, b_{i1}, b'_{i1})$ in its H_1-list.
3. $\mathcal{B}$ responds with $H_1(\mathsf{ID}_i, j) = P_{ij} = b_{ij}P + b'_{ij}P'$.

For $\mathcal{A}$'s H_2-query on w_k:

1. If w_k was in a previous H_2-query, $\mathcal{B}$ recovers c_k from its H_2-list.
2. Else, $\mathcal{B}$ generates a random H_2-$coin_k \in \{0,1\}$ so that $\Pr[H_1\text{-}coin_i = 0] = \delta_2$ for δ_2 to be determined later. $\mathcal{B}$ generates a random $c_k \in (\mathbb{Z}/q\mathbb{Z})^*$. It logs $(w_k, H_2\text{-}coin_k)$ in its H_2-list.
3. If H_2-$coin_k = 0$, $\mathcal{B}$ responds with $H_2(w_k) = P_{w_k} = c_k P'$; otherwise, it responds with $H_2(w_k) = P_{w_k} = c_k P$.

For $\mathcal{A}$'s H_3-query on $(\mathsf{ID}_i, m_j, w_k)$:

1. If $(\mathsf{ID}_i, m_j, w_k)$ was in a previous H_3-query, $\mathcal{B}$ recovers d_{ijk} from its H_3-list.
2. Else, $\mathcal{B}$ runs an H_1-query on $(\mathsf{ID}_i, 0)$ to recover b'_{i0} and b'_{i1} from its H_1-list. $\mathcal{B}$ generates a random H_3-$coin_{ijk} \in \{0,1\}$ so that $\Pr[H_3\text{-}coin_{ijk} = 0] = \delta_3$ for δ_3 to be determined later.
   (a) If H_1-$coin_i = 1$, H_2-$coin_k = 1$, and H_3-$coin_{ijk} = 0$, $\mathcal{B}$ checks whether H_3-list2 contains a tuple $(\mathsf{ID}_{i'}, m_{j'}, w_{k'}) \neq (\mathsf{ID}_{i'}, m_{j'}, w_{k'})$ with $\mathsf{ID}_{i'} = \mathsf{ID}_i$. If so, $\mathcal{B}$ aborts. If not, it puts $(\mathsf{ID}_i, m_j, w_k)$ in H_3-list2 and sets $d_{ijk} = -b'_{i0}/b'_{i1} (\mathrm{mod} q)$.
   (b) If H_1-$coin_i = 0$, H_2-$coin_k = 0$, or H_3-$coin_{ijk} = 1$, $\mathcal{B}$ generates a random $d_{ijk} \in (\mathbb{Z}/q\mathbb{Z})^*$.
   (c) $\mathcal{B}$ logs $(\mathsf{ID}_i, m_j, w_k, H_3\text{-}coin_{ijk}, d_{ijk})$ in its H_3-list.
3. $\mathcal{B}$ responds with $H_3(\mathsf{ID}_i, m_j, w_k) = d_{ijk}$.

Extraction Queries: When $\mathcal{A}$ requests the private key corresponding to ID_i, $\mathcal{B}$ recovers $(H_1\text{-}coin_i, b_{i0}, b'_{i0})$. If H_1-$coin_i = 0$, $\mathcal{B}$ responds with $(sP_{i,0}, sP_{i,1}) = (b_{i0}Q, b_{i1}Q)$. If H_1-$coin_i = 1$, $\mathcal{B}$ aborts.

Signature Queries: When $\mathcal{A}$ requests a (new) signature on $(\mathsf{ID}_i, m_j, w_k)$, $\mathcal{B}$ first confirms that $\mathcal{A}$ has not previously requested a signature by ID_i on w_k (otherwise, it is an improper query). Then, $\mathcal{B}$ proceeds as follows:

1. If H_1-$coin_i = H_2$-$coin_k = H_3$-$coin_{ijk} = 1$, $\mathcal{B}$ aborts.
2. If H_1-$coin_i = 0$, $\mathcal{B}$ generates random $r \in \mathbb{Z}/q\mathbb{Z}$ and outputs the signature (w_k, S'_i, T'_i), where $S'_i = sP_{i,0} + d_{ijk}sP_{i,1} + rP_{w_k} = b_{i0}Q + d_{ijk}b_{i1}Q + rP_{w_k}$ and $T'_i = rP$.
3. If H_1-$coin_i = 1$ and H_2-$coin_k = 0$, $\mathcal{B}$ generates random $r \in \mathbb{Z}/q\mathbb{Z}$ and outputs the signature (w_k, S'_i, T'_i), where

$$S'_i = sP_{i,0} + d_{ijk}sP_{i,1} + (r - (b'_{i0} + d_{ijk}b'_{i1})sc_k^{-1})P_{w_k}$$
$$= b_{i0}Q + b'_{i0}sP' + d_{ijk}b_{i1}Q + d_{ijk}b'_{i1}sP' + rc_kP' - (b'_{i0} + d_{ijk}b'_{i1})sP'$$
$$= b_{i0}Q + d_{ijk}b_{i1}Q + rc_kP', \text{ and}$$
$$T'_i = (r - (b'_{i0} + d_{ijk}b'_{i1})sc_k^{-1})P = rP - (b'_{i0} + d_{ijk}b'_{i1})c_k^{-1}Q .$$

4. If H_1-$coin_i = H_2$-$coin_k = 1$ and H_3-$coin_{ijk} = 0$, $\mathcal{B}$ generates random $r \in \mathbb{Z}/q\mathbb{Z}$ and outputs the signature (w_k, S'_i, T'_i), where $T'_i = rP$, and

$$S'_i = sP_{i,0} + d_{ijk}sP_{i,1} + rP_{w_k}$$
$$= b_{i0}Q + b'_{i0}sP' + d_{ijk}b_{i1}Q - (b'_{i0}/b'_{i1})b'_{i1}sP' + rc_kP$$
$$= b_{i0}Q + d_{ijk}b_{i1}Q + rc_kP .$$

$\mathcal{A}$'s **Response:** Finally, with probability at least ϵ, $\mathcal{A}$ outputs $\{\mathsf{ID}_i\}_{i=1}^l$ and $\{m_j\}_{j=1}^l$ with $l \leq n$, and string w_K, such that there exists $I, J \in [1, l]$ such that it has not extracted the private key for ID_I or requested a signature for $(\mathsf{ID}_I, m_J, w_K)$. In addition, it also outputs an identity-based aggregate signature (w_K, S_l, T_l) satisfying the equation

$$\hat{e}(S_l, P) = \hat{e}(T_l, P_{w_K})\hat{e}(sP, \sum_{i=1}^l P_{i,0} + \sum_{i=1}^l c_i P_{i,1}) \ ,$$

where $P_{i,b} = H_1(\mathsf{ID}_i, b)$, $P_{w_K} = H_2(w_K)$ and $c_i = H_3(m_j, \mathsf{ID}_i, w_K)$ as required.

$\mathcal{B}$'s **Final Action:** If it is not the case that the above (I, J, K) can satisfy H_1-$coin_I = H_2$-$coin_J = H_3$-$coin_{IJK} = 1$, then $\mathcal{B}$ aborts. Otherwise, it can solve its instance of CDH$_{\mathbb{G}_1}$ with probability $1 - 1/q$ as follows.

$\mathcal{A}$'s forgery has the form (S_l, T_l), where $T_l = rP$ and $S_l = rP_{w_K} + \sum_{i=1}^l sP_{i,0} + c_i sP_{i,1}$, where we let $c_i = H_3(\mathsf{ID}_i, m_j, w_K)$ be the hash of the tuple "signed" by the entity with identity ID_i. Since H_2-$coin_k = 1$, $\mathcal{B}$ knows the discrete logarithm c_K of P_{w_K} with respect to P. It can therefore compute:

$$S_l - c_K T_l = \sum_{i=1}^l sP_{i,0} + c_i sP_{i,1} = s\left(\sum_{i=1}^l b_{i,0}P + b_{i,0}'P' + c_i(b_{i,1}P + b_{i,1}'P')\right)$$
$$= s\left(\sum_{i=1}^l (b_{i,0} + c_i b_{i,1})\right) P + s\left(\sum_{i=1}^l (b_{i,0}' + c_i b_{i,1}')\right) P' \ .$$

If H_1-$coin_i = H_3$-$coin_{ijk} = 1$ for at least one of the signed tuples, then the probability that $\sum_{i=1}^l (b_{i,0}' + c_i b_{i,1}') \neq 0$ is $1 - 1/q$; if $\sum_{i=1}^l (b_{i,0}' + c_i b_{i,1}') \neq 0$, $\mathcal{B}$ can easily derive sP' from the expression above.

We now demonstrate that the above simulation is perfect. The analysis assumes that $\mathcal{A}$ makes no redundant queries and that $\mathcal{A}$ must make an H_3 query on a tuple $(\mathsf{ID}_i, m_j, w_k)$ before making a signature query on it. Let $\mathcal{E}$ represent the set of extraction query responses that $\mathcal{B}$ has made up to a specified point in the simulation; similarly, let $\mathcal{S}$ be the set of signature query responses, and $\mathcal{H}_i$ be the set of H_i query responses for $i \in \{1, 2, 3\}$. Let $E_{1,*,*}$ be the event that H_1-$coin_i = 1$; here, "*" means that H_2-$coin_k$ and H_3-$coin_{ijk}$ may each be 0 or 1. Let $E_{1,1,*}$, $E_{1,1,1}$ and $E_{1,1,0}$ denote the corresponding events in the obvious way.

Perfect Simulation: We claim that, if $\mathcal{B}$ does not abort, $\mathcal{A}$'s view is the same as in the "real" attack. In the "real" attack, each of the hash functions H_i behave like random functions. Then, given the values of $P_{i,j} = H_1(\mathsf{ID}_i, j)$, $P_{w_k} = H_2(w_k)$, and $d_{ijk} = H_3(\mathsf{ID}_i, m_j, w_k)$, we choose a signature uniformly from:

$$\{(w_k, S_i', T_i') : S_i' = sP_{i,0} + d_{ijk}sP_{i,1} + rP_w, T_i' = rP, r \in \mathbb{Z}/q\mathbb{Z}\}.$$

Similarly, in the simulation, we choose a signature uniformly from $\{(w_k, S_i', T_i') : S_i' = sP_{i,0} + d_{ijk}sP_{i,1} + rP_w, T_i' = rP, r \in \mathbb{Z}/q\mathbb{Z}\}$ given values of $P_{i,j} = H_1(\mathsf{ID}_i, j)$, $P_{w_k} = H_2(w_k)$, and $d_{ijk} = H_3(\mathsf{ID}_i, m_j, w_k)$. Also, the H_i behave like random functions – i.e., they are one-to-one and the outputs are chosen with uniform distribution. The only case in which this may not be obvious is when $H_1\text{-}coin_i = H_2\text{-}coin_k = 1$ and $H_3\text{-}coin_{ijk} = 0$. In this case, unless $\mathcal{A}$ has made a previous H_3 query on $(\mathsf{ID}_i, m_{j'}, w_{k'}) \neq (\mathsf{ID}_i, m_j, w_k)$ for which $H_1\text{-}coin_i = H_2\text{-}coin_{k'} = 1$ and $H_3\text{-}coin_{ij'k'} = 0$ (in which case $\mathcal{B}$ aborts), $\mathcal{B}$ sets $H_3(\mathsf{ID}_i, m_j, w_k)$ to be $-b'_{i0}/b'_{i1}(\mathrm{mod} q)$ (rather than choosing the H_3 output uniformly randomly).

However, the value of $-b'_{i0}/b'_{i1}(\mathrm{mod} q)$ is itself uniformly random. More specifically, given $\mathcal{A}$'s view up until the H_3 query on $(\mathsf{ID}_i, m_j, w_k)$ – namely, the sets $\mathcal{E}$, $\mathcal{S}$, and $\{H_i\}$ – we have that

$$\Pr[H_3(\mathsf{ID}_i, m_j, w_k) = c \mid \mathcal{E}, \mathcal{S}, \mathcal{H}_1, \mathcal{H}_2, \mathcal{H}_3, E_{1,1,0}] = 1/q$$

for every $c \in \mathbb{Z}/q\mathbb{Z}$, as long as $\mathcal{B}$ does not abort. Most surprisingly, the value $H_3(\mathsf{ID}_i, m_j, w_k) = -b'_{i0}/b'_{i1}(\mathrm{mod} q)$ is independent of an H_1 query response on ID_i even though $H_1(\mathsf{ID}_i, j) = b_{ij}P + b'_{ij}P'$, since, given $H_1(\mathsf{ID}_i, 0) = b_{i0}P + b'_{i0}P'$, the pairs (b_{i0}, b'_{i0}) with $b'_{i0} = \log_{P'}(H_1(\mathsf{ID}_i, 0)) - b_{i0}\log_{P'}(P)$ are equally likely. It should be clear that the value of $H_3(\mathsf{ID}_i, m_j, w_k)$ is also independent of H_1 queries on identities other than ID_i, all extraction query responses (since they are completely dependent on H_1 query responses), all H_2 queries, all H_3 queries on tuples other than $(\mathsf{ID}_i, m_j, w_k)$ (again, assuming $\mathcal{B}$ does not abort), and all signature queries on tuples other than $(\mathsf{ID}_i, m_j, w_k)$.

To complete the proof, we need to bound from below the probability that $\mathcal{B}$ aborts. The details are provided in the full version [GR06].

7   Summary and Open Problems

We presented an IBAS scheme which allows distinct signers to sign distinct documents in such a way that the total information needed to verify the signatures is about as close as possible to the information-theoretic minimum. The aggregate signature can be generated in a completely decentralized fashion, without requiring a complicated setup procedure. Our scheme was quite efficient - requiring only 4 elliptic curve scalar multiplications and 2 point additions for signature generation; 2 extra point additions for aggregation; and 3 pairing computations *(independent of the number of signers)*, 1 point multiplication, $2n-1$ point additions, and n scalar multiplication (where n is the number of signatures that are aggregated) for verification. Verification in our scheme is much faster than the BGLS aggregate signature scheme [BGLS03] which requires $O(n)$ pairing computations. Further, our scheme allows aggregation even if the signers have different PKGs. Finally, our scheme is provably secure in the random oracle model under Computational Diffie-Hellman against an adversary who could choose both its target identities and messages adaptively.

It may be possible to construct practical IBAS schemes using different approaches and assumptions – e.g., based on strong RSA – but, again, aggregating individual signer randomness is a problem. With strong RSA, one might even consider a deterministic scheme, roughly as follows. The PKG publishes a modulus N, a base $a \in \mathbb{Z}_N^*$, and hash functions $H_1 : \{0,1\}^* \to \{0,1\}^d$ (e.g., $d = 160$)

and $H_2 : \{0,1\}^* \to \mathcal{P}$ (where $\mathcal{P}$ is a suitable set of prime numbers). To a user with identity ID_i who wants to generate up to t signatures, the PKG gives the value $a^{1/P_i}(\mathrm{mod}N)$, where $P_i = \prod_{j \in [1,t]}^{k \in [1,d]} H_2(\mathsf{ID}_i, j, k)$. To sign m for its j-th signature, the user computes $a^{1/P_{i,j,m}}(\mathrm{mod}N)$ for

$$P_{i,j,m} = \prod^{k \in [1,d]} H_2(\mathsf{ID}_i, j, k)^{H_1(\mathsf{ID}_i,j,m)_k},$$

where $H_1(\mathsf{ID}_i, j, m)_k$ is the k-th bit of $H_1(\mathsf{ID}_i, j, m)$. With this approach the "de-accumulation" that a user performs is computationally-intensive if t is reasonably large. One could amortize the expense of de-accumulation by using tree-traversal (pebbling-type) techniques – e.g., as described in [Szy04] – but this restricts the users to using the j-values in order, which makes it less likely that distinct users will use the same j, which increases the amount of verification information.

References

[BA05]   K.C. Barr and K. Asanovic. Energy aware lossless data compression. In *Proc. of Mobisys 2005*, 2005.

[BF03]   D. Boneh and M. Franklin. Identity-based encryption from the Weil pairing. *SIAM J. of Computing*, 32(3):586–615, 2003.

[BGLS03] D. Boneh, C. Gentry, B. Lynn, and H. Shacham. Aggregate and verifiably encrypted signatures from bilinear maps. In *Proc. of Eurocrypt 2003*, volume 2656 of *LNCS*, pages 416–432. Springer-Verlag, 2003.

[BLS01]   D. Boneh, B. Lynn, and H. Shacham. Short signatures from the weil pairing. In *Proc. of Asiacrypt 2001*, volume 2248 of *LNCS*, pages 514–532. Springer-Verlag.

[BNN04]   Mihir Bellare, Chanathip Namprempre, and Gregory Neven. Security proofs for identity-based identification and signature schemes. In *Proc. of Eurocrypt 2004*, volume 3027 of *LNCS*, pages 268–286. Springer-Verlag, 2004.

[Bol03]   A. Boldyreva. Efficient threshold signature, multisignature and blind signature schemes based on the gap-Diffie-Hellman-group signature scheme. In *Proc. of PKC 2003*, volume 2567 of *LNCS*, pages 31–46. Springer-Verlag, 2003.

[Boy03]   X. Boyen. Multipurpose identity-based signcryption (a swiss army knife for identity-based cryptography). In *Proc. of Crypto 2003*, volume 2729 of *LNCS*, pages 383–399. Springer-Verlag, 2003.

[BZ04]   J. Baek and Y. Zheng. Identity-based threshold signature scheme from the bilinear pairings. In *Proc. of ITCC (1)*, pages 124–128, 2004.

[CC03]   J.C. Cha and J.H. Cheon. An identity-based signature from gap diffie-hellman groups. In *Proc. of PKC 2003*, volume 2567 of *LNCS*, pages 18–30.

[CLW05]   X. Cheng, J. Liu, and X. Wang. Identity-based aggregate and verifiably encrypted signatures from bilinear pairing. In *Proc. of ICCSA 2005*, pages 1046–1054, 2005.

[Coc01]   C. Cocks. An identity based encryption scheme based on quadratic residues. In *Proc. of IMA Int. Conf. 2001*, volume 2260 of *LNCS*, pages 360–363.

[FS86]   A. Fiat and A. Shamir. How to prove yourself: Practical solutions to iden-
             tification and signature problems. In *Proc. of Crypto 1986*, volume 263 of
             LNCS, pages 186–194. Springer, 1986.
[GR06]   C. Gentry and Z. Ramzan. Identity-Based Aggregate Signatures. Full
             Version. *Cryptology E-print Archive, 2006.*
[GQ88]   L.C. Guillou and J.-J. Quisquater. A "paradoxical" identity-based sig-
             nature scheme resulting from zero-knowledge. In *Proc. of Crypto 1988*,
             volume 403 of *LNCS*, pages 216–231. Springer-Verlag, 1988.
[GS02]   C. Gentry and A. Silverberg. Hierarchical ID-based cryptography. In *Proc.
             of Asiacrypt 2002*, volume 2501 of *LNCS*, pages 548–566. Springer-Verlag,
             2002.
[Her05]   J. Herranz. Deterministic identity-based signatures for partial aggre-
             gation. Cryptology ePrint Archive, Report 2005/313, 2005. http://
             eprint.iacr.org/.
[KLS00]   S. Kent, C. Lynn, and K. Seo. Secure border gateway protocol (secure-bgp).
             IEEE J. Selected Areas in Comm., 19(4):582–592, 2000.
[LMRS04]   A. Lysyanskaya, S. Micali, L. Reyzin, and H. Shacham. Sequential aggre-
             gate signatures from trapdoor permutations. In *Proc. of Eurocrypt 2004*,
             volume 9999 of *LNCS*, pages 74–90. Springer-Verlag, 2004.
[LQ04]   B. Libert and J.-J. Quisquater. Identity based undeniable signatures. In
             Proc. of CT-RSA 2004, pages 112–125, 2004.
[MNT04]   E. Mykletun, M. Narasimha, and G. Tsudik. Signature bouquets: Im-
             mutability for aggregated/condensed signatures. In *Proc. of ESORICS
             2004*, pages 160–176, 2004.
[MOR01]   S. Micali, K. Ohta, and L. Reyzin. Accountable subgroup multisignatures
             (extended abstract). In *Proc. of CCS 2001*, pages 245–54. ACM Press,
             2001.
[Oka98]   T. Okamoto. A digital multisignature scheme using bijective public-key
             cryptosystems. *ACM Trans. Computer Systems*, 6(4):432–441, 1998.
[OO99]   K. Ohta and T. Okamoto. Multisignature schemes secure against active
             insider attacks. *IEICE Trans. Fundamentals*, E82-A(1):21–31, 1999.
[PS96]   D. Pointcheval and J. Stern. Security proofs for signature schemes. In *Proc.
             of Eurocrypt.* Springer-Verlag, 1996.
[PS00]   D. Pointcheval and J. Stern. Security arguments for digital signatures and
             blind signatures. *Journal of Cryptology*, 13(3):361–396, 2000.
[Sha84]   A. Shamir. Identity-based cryptosystems and signature schemes. In *Proc.
             of Crypto 1984*, volume 196 of *LNCS*, pages 47–53. Springer-Verlag, 1984.
[Sho00]   V. Shoup. Practical threshold signatures. In *Proc. of Eurocrypt 2000*,
             volume 1807 of *LNCS*, pages 207–220. Springer-Verlag, 2000.
[SRF$^+$04] T. Suzuki, Z. Ramzan, H. Fujimoto, C. Gentry, T. Nakayama, and R. Jain.
             A system for end-to-end authentication of adaptive multimedia content. In
             Proc. of Conference on Communications and Multimedia Security, 2004.
[Szy04]   M. Szydlo. Merkle tree traversal in log space and time. In *Proc. of Euro-
             crypt*, volume 3027 of *LNCS*, pages 541–554. Springer-Verlag, 2004.

On the Limitations of the Spread of an IBE-to-PKE Transformation

Eike Kiltz

CWI Amsterdam, The Netherlands
kiltz@cwi.nl
http://kiltz.net

Abstract. By a generic transformation by Canetti, Halevi, and Katz (CHK) every Identity-based encryption (IBE) scheme implies a chosen-ciphertext secure public-key encryption (PKE) scheme. In the same work it is claimed that this transformation maps the two existing IBE schemes to two *new and different* chosen-ciphertext secure encryption schemes, each with individual advantages over the other.

In this work we reconsider one of the two specific instantiations of the CHK transformation (when applied to the "second Boneh/Boyen IBE scheme"). We demonstrate that by applying further simplifications the resulting scheme can be proven secure under a weaker assumption than the underlying IBE scheme.

Surprisingly, our simplified scheme nearly converges to a recent encryption scheme due to Boyen, Mei, and Waters which itself was obtained from the other specific instantiation of the CHK transformation (when applied to the "first Boneh/Boyen IBE scheme"). We find this particularly interesting since the two underlying IBE schemes are completely different.

The bottom line of this paper is that the claim made by Canetti, Halevi, and Katz needs to be reformulated to: the CHK transformation maps the two known IBE schemes to nearly one single encryption scheme.

1 Introduction

CHOSEN-CIPHERTEXT SECURE ENCRYPTION SCHEMES. One of the main fields of interest in cryptography is the design and the analysis of the security of encryption schemes in the public-key setting. In this work we consider such schemes for which one can provide theoretical proofs of security (without relying on heuristics such as the random oracle), but which are also efficient and practical.

The notion of chosen-ciphertext security was introduced by Naor and Yung [13] and developed by Rackoff and Simon [14], and Dolev, Dwork, and Naor [9]. In a chosen ciphertext attack, the adversary is given access to a decryption oracle that allows him to obtain the decryptions of ciphertexts of his choosing. Intuitively, security in this setting means that an adversary obtains (effectively) no information about encrypted messages, provided the corresponding ciphertexts are never submitted to the decryption oracle. For different reasons, the notion of chosen-ciphertext security has emerged as the "right" notion of security for encryption schemes.

M. Yung et al. (Eds.): PKC 2006, LNCS 3958, pp. 274–289, 2006.

As an example of an encryption scheme that meets this strong security property in the standard model we have the scheme from Cramer and Shoup [7, 8] which was recently improved by Kurosawa and Desmedt [11]. Until 2004 the Cramer-Shoup scheme and its variants remained basically the only practical schemes with such strong security properties that could be proved secure in the standard model (under a reasonable complexity-theoretic assumption).

FROM IDENTITY-BASED ENCRYPTION TO CHOSEN-CIPHERTEXT SECURE ENCRYPTION. One of the recent celebrated applications of *identity-based encryption* (IBE) is the work due to Canetti, Halevi, and Katz [6, 2] showing an elegant black-box transformation from any IBE (plus a one-time signature) into an encryption scheme without giving up its efficiency. We will refer to this as the *CHK transformation*. If the IBE scheme is weakly (selective-identity) chosen-plaintext secure then the resulting encryption scheme is chosen-ciphertext secure. Efficient constructions of IBE schemes in the standard model were recently developed by Boneh and Boyen [1] so the CHK transformation provides further alternative instances of chosen-ciphertext secure encryption schemes in the standard model.

Boneh and Katz [4] later improve the efficiency of the CHK transformation by basically replacing the one-time signature by a message authentication code (MAC). The latter BK transformation results in shorter ciphertexts and more efficient encryption/decryption.

SPECIFIC INSTANTIATIONS OF THE CHK TRANSFORMATION. Until now there are only two different identity-based encryption schemes known, both due to Boneh and Boyen [1]. The CHK transformation maps each individual IBE scheme to a new chosen-ciphertext secure encryption scheme [6]. In particular, in Chapter 7 of [2] the following two encryption schemes are proposed:

1. IBE-to-PKE[BB1]: the first Boneh/Boyen IBE scheme [1] plugged into the CHK-transformation
2. IBE-to-PKE[BB2]: the second Boneh/Boyen IBE scheme [1] plugged into the CHK-transformation

It is claimed in [6, 4, 2] that the two encryption schemes have different properties. In particular, the second scheme offers more efficient decryption while relying on a stronger assumption.

REVISITING THE IBE-TO-PKE[BB1] SCHEME. Boyen, Mei, and Waters [5] recently revisited the IBE-to-PKE[BB1] scheme, i.e. the encryption scheme obtained from the CHK transformation instantiated with the first IBE scheme from [1]. By avoiding the CHK transformation they show how to make the resulting scheme more efficient in terms of computational time and ciphertext expansion. In particular, they come up with a chosen-ciphertext secure encryption scheme with security based on the *Bilinear Decisional Diffie-Hellman* (BDDH) assumption in the standard model.

1.1   Our Results

REVISITING THE IBE-TO-PKE[BB2] SCHEME. In this work we reconsider the IBE-to-PKE[BB2] scheme, i.e. the encryption scheme obtained by the

CHK-transformation instantiated with the second IBE scheme from Boneh and Boyen. Similar to the work from [5] we obtain a direct construction avoiding the CHK transformation. The resulting scheme is again simple and practical.

We can prove security of the resulting encryption scheme with respect to a weaker assumption than the security assumption needed for the IBE scheme. In particular, our scheme can be proved secure under the new *square Bilinear Decisional Diffie-Hellman* (square-BDDH) assumption, whereas the original IBE scheme can only be proved secure under the *q-Bilinear Decisional Diffie-Hellman* (*q*-BDDHI) assumption.[1] (We stress that unfortunately our results do not imply that the underlying IBE scheme can be proved secure under this weaker assumption).

COMPARISON WITH THE ENCRYPTION SCHEME FROM BOYEN, MEI, AND WATERS. Surprisingly, our simplified IBE-to-PKE[BB2] encryption scheme turns out to be (nearly) equivalent to the encryption scheme from Boyen, Mei, and Waters [5] which itself was a simplification of the IBE-to-PKE[BB1] scheme.

Our **main result** can be formulated as follows: In contrast to what was claimed in [6, 4, 2] for the two different IBE schemes BB1 and BB2, we have

$$\text{IBE-to-PKE[BB1]} \approx \text{IBE-to-PKE[BB2]} ,$$

where "$\approx$" reads "nearly converges to" and will be further explained below. In other words, the CHK IBE-to-PKE transformation does not seem to spread the IBE schemes well over all encryption schemes, i.e. the transformation maps the two different IBE schemes from Boneh and Boyen to nearly the same encryption scheme.

We stress that the equivalence is not obtained by "simplifying away" all possible differences between the two schemes. In fact, the "core" of the two schemes is the same and already the raw schemes IBE-to-PKE[BB1] and IBE-to-PKE[BB2] can be shown to be equivalent by removing the unnecessary overhead of the two respective decryption algorithms.

We now explain the meaning of the above "$\approx$". There is only a small difference between the two simplified schemes "hidden" in the respective key generation algorithms. Intuitively, in the BMW construction key generation involves the generation of one more independent random element (let's call it y), whereas our scheme "recycles" the randomness. More precisely, this value y contains some redundant information and therefore depends on some other element from the key.

COMPLEXITY THEORETIC ASSUMPTIONS. We study the relations between all mentioned assumptions, in particular showing the (assumption-wise) hierarchy *q*-BDDHI (for any $q \geq 1$) implies square-BDDH implies BDDH.

DISCUSSION. We study the spread of the CHK transformation, i.e. how well the CHK transformation spreads different IBE schemes over the set of all encryption schemes. Our results indicate that the CHK transformation maps the two

---

[1] Here q is an upper bound on the decryption queries made by an adversary attacking the choosen-ciphertext security of the scheme.

different IBE schemes to one single encryption scheme. Unfortunately these two
IBE schemes are the only IBE schemes we know until today.

In light of the number of different encryption schemes secure against chosen-
ciphertext attacks in the standard model the implication of our result is purely
destructive. Due to its similarities we propose to "remove" the IBE-to-PKE[BB2]
scheme from our toolbox of *different* practical encryption schemes: instead of two
we only get one new scheme from identity-based techniques.

From a theoretical side we find it interesting that two completely different
identity-based encryption schemes finally lead to very similar encryption schemes
after applying the CHK transformation and some simplifications. Again we stress
that this does not imply that the two different IBE schemes from [1] also converge
to one (and there are reasons that they don't).

PRESENTATION. To simplify our presentation all schemes will be described as key
encapsulation mechanisms rather than full public-key encryption schemes. We
remark that since a secure key encapsulation mechanism plus a secure symmetric
encryption scheme implies secure public-key encryption this is a more general
concept.

In Section 2 we formally define the concept of a key encapsulation mechanism.
Next, in Section 3 we state all relevant complexity-theoretic assumptions and clas-
sify them by their strength. The two schemes, the original one by Canetti, Halevi,
and Katz, and our proposed simplification are presented in Section 4. We conclude
this paper with an efficiency comparison of the two schemes in Section 5.

2   Notation and Definitions

If x is a string, then $|x|$ denotes its length, while if S is a set then $|S|$ denotes
its size. If $k \in \mathbb{N}$ then 1^k denotes the string of k ones. If S is a set then $s \stackrel{\$}{\leftarrow} S$
denotes the operation of picking an element s from S uniformly at random.
We write $\mathcal{A}(x, y, \ldots)$ to indicate that $\mathcal{A}$ is an algorithm with inputs $x, y, \ldots$
and by $z \stackrel{\$}{\leftarrow} \mathcal{A}(x, y, \ldots)$ we denote the operation of running $\mathcal{A}$ with inputs
$(x, y, \ldots)$ and letting z be the output. We write $\mathcal{A}^{\mathcal{O}_1, \mathcal{O}_2, \cdots}(x, y, \ldots)$ to indicate
that $\mathcal{A}$ is an algorithm with inputs $x, y, \ldots$ and access to oracles $\mathcal{O}_1, \mathcal{O}_2, \ldots$ and
by $z \stackrel{\$}{\leftarrow} \mathcal{A}^{\mathcal{O}_1, \mathcal{O}_2, \cdots}(x, y, \ldots)$ we denote the operation of running $\mathcal{A}$ with inputs
$(x, y, \ldots)$ and access to oracles $\mathcal{O}_1, \mathcal{O}_2, \ldots$, and letting z be the output.

We now formally introduce the notions of a key-encapsulation mechanism
together with a security definition.

2.1   Public Key Encapsulation Schemes

A *public-key encapsulation mechanism* (KEM) $\mathcal{KEM}$ = (KEMkg, KEMencaps,
KEMdecaps) with key-space KeySp(k) consists of three polynomial-time
algorithms. Via $(pk, sk) \stackrel{\$}{\leftarrow}$ KEMkg(1^k) the randomized key-generation algorithm
produces keys for security parameter $k \in \mathbb{N}$; via $(K, C) \stackrel{\$}{\leftarrow}$ KEMencaps(pk)
a key $K \in$ KeySp(k) together with a corresponding ciphertext C is created;

via $K \leftarrow$ KEMdecaps(sk, C) the possessor of secret key sk decrypts ciphertext C to get back a key. For consistency, we require that for all $k \in \mathbb{N}$, and all $(K, C) \xleftarrow{\$}$ KEMencaps(pk) we have $\Pr[\text{KEMdecaps}(sk, C) = K] = 1$, where the probability is taken over the choice of $(pk, sk) \xleftarrow{\$}$ KEMkg(1^k), and the coins of all the algorithms in the expression above.

Formally, we associate with an adversary $\mathcal{A}$ the following experiment:

$$\textbf{Experiment Exp}_{\mathcal{KEM},\mathcal{A}}^{kem\text{-}cca}(k)$$

$(pk, sk) \xleftarrow{\$}$ KEMkg(1^k)

$K_0^* \xleftarrow{\$}$ KeySp(k) ; $(K_1^*, C^*) \xleftarrow{\$}$ KEMencaps(pk)

$\delta \xleftarrow{\$} \{0, 1\}$

$\delta' \xleftarrow{\$} \mathcal{A}^{\text{Dec}}(pk, K_\delta^*, C^*)$

If $\delta \neq \delta'$ then return 0 else return 1

where the oracle $\text{Dec}(C)$ returns $K \xleftarrow{\$}$ KEMdecaps(sk, C) with the restriction that $\mathcal{A}$ is not allowed to query oracle $\text{Dec}(\cdot)$ for the target ciphertext C^*. We define the advantage of $\mathcal{A}$ in the experiment as

$$\textbf{Adv}_{\mathcal{KEM},\mathcal{A}}^{kem\text{-}cca}(k) = \left| \Pr\left[\textbf{Exp}_{\mathcal{KEM},\mathcal{A}}^{kem\text{-}cca}(k) = 1 \right] - \frac{1}{2} \right| .$$

A KEM scheme $\mathcal{KEM}$ is said to be *secure against adaptively-chosen ciphertext attacks* if the advantage function $\textbf{Adv}_{\mathcal{KEM},\mathcal{A}}^{kem\text{-}cca}(k)$ is a negligible function in k for all polynomial-time adversaries $\mathcal{A}$.

2.2   Target Collision Resistant Hash Functions

Let $(\text{CR}_s)_{s \in S}$ be a family of hash functions for security parameter k and with seed $s \in S = S(k)$. $\mathcal{F}$ is said to be *collision resistant* if, for a hash function $\text{CR} = \text{CR}_s$ (where the seed is chosen at random from S), it is infeasible for any polynomial-time adversary to find two distinct values $x \neq y$ such that $\text{CR}(x) = \text{CR}(y)$.

A weaker notion is that of *target collision resistant hash functions*. Here it should be infeasible for a polynomial-time adversary to find, given a randomly chosen element x and a randomly drawn hash function $\text{TCR} = \text{TCR}_s$, a distinct element $y \neq x$ such that $\text{TCR}(x) = \text{TCR}(y)$. (In collision resistant hash functions the value x may be chosen by the adversary.) Such hash functions are also called *universal one-way hash functions* [12] and can be built from arbitrary one-way functions [12, 15]. We define

$$\textbf{Adv}_{\text{TCR},\mathcal{A}}^{\text{hash-tcr}}(k) = \Pr[\mathcal{A} \text{ finds a collision}].$$

Hash function family TCR is said to be a *target collision resistant* if the advantage function $\textbf{Adv}_{\text{TCR},\mathcal{A}}^{\text{hash-tcr}}$ is a negligible function in k for all polynomial-time adversaries $\mathcal{A}$.

3   Assumptions

In this section we give a parameter generating algorithm for bilinear groups and pairings and state our complexity assumptions.

3.1 Parameter Generation Algorithms for Bilinear Groups

The scheme will be parameterized by a *bilinear parameter generator*. This is a polynomial-time algorithm BilinGen that on input 1^k returns the description of a multiplicative cyclic group $\mathbb{G}_1$ of prime order p, where $2^k < p < 2^{k+1}$, the description of a multiplicative cyclic group $\mathbb{G}_T$ of the same order, a random element g that generates $\mathbb{G}_1$, and a bilinear pairing $\hat{e}\colon \mathbb{G}_1 \times \mathbb{G}_1 \to \mathbb{G}_T$. This bilinear pairing should be efficiently computable and satisfy the conditions below.

Bilinear: For all $g, h \in \mathbb{G}_1, x, y \in \mathbb{Z}$, $\hat{e}(g^x, h^y) = \hat{e}(g, h)^{xy}$
Non-degenerate: $\hat{e}(g, g) \neq 1_{\mathbb{G}_2}$

We use $\mathbb{G}_1^*$ to denote $\mathbb{G}_1 \setminus \{0\}$, i.e. the set of all group elements except the neutral element. Throughout the paper we use $\mathcal{BG} = (\mathbb{G}_1, \mathbb{G}_T, p, \hat{e}, g)$ (obtained by running BilinGen) as shorthand for the description of bilinear groups.

3.2 The Square BDDH Assumption

Let $\mathcal{BG}$ be the description of bilinear groups and let $g \in \mathbb{G}_1$ be a random element from group $\mathbb{G}_1$. Consider the following problem: Given $(g, g^a, g^b, W) \in \mathbb{G}_1^3 \times \mathbb{G}_T$ as input, output yes if $W = \hat{e}(g, g)^{a^2 b}$ and no otherwise. More formally we associate with an adversary $\mathcal{B}$ the following experiment:

> **Experiment $\mathbf{Exp}_{\mathsf{BilinGen}, \mathcal{B}}^{\mathrm{sbddh}}(1^k)$**
> $\mathcal{BG} \xleftarrow{\$} \mathsf{BilinGen}(1^k)$
> $a, b, w \xleftarrow{\$} \mathbb{Z}_p^*$
> $\gamma \xleftarrow{\$} \{0, 1\}$; if $\gamma = 0$ then $W \leftarrow \hat{e}(g, g)^{a^2 b}$ else $W \leftarrow \hat{e}(g, g)^w$
> $\gamma' \xleftarrow{\$} \mathcal{B}(1^k, \mathcal{BG}, g, g^a, g^b, W)$
> If $\gamma \neq \gamma'$ then return 0 else return 1

We define the advantage of $\mathcal{B}$ in the above experiment as

$$\mathbf{Adv}_{\mathsf{BilinGen}, \mathcal{B}}^{\mathrm{sbddh}}(k) = \left| \Pr\left[\mathbf{Exp}_{\mathsf{BilinGen}, \mathcal{B}}^{\mathrm{sbddh}}(1^k) = 1 \right] - \frac{1}{2} \right|.$$

We say that the *Square Bilinear Decision Diffie-Hellman (square BDDH) assumption relative to generator* BilinGen holds if $\mathbf{Adv}_{\mathsf{BilinGen}, \mathcal{B}}^{\mathrm{sbddh}}$ is a negligible function in k for all polynomial-time adversaries $\mathcal{B}$.

3.3 The BDDH Assumption

Let $\mathcal{BG}$ be the description of bilinear groups and let $g \in \mathbb{G}_1$ be a random element from group $\mathbb{G}_1$. Consider the following problem formalized by Boneh and Franklin [3]: Given $(g, g^a, g^b, g^c, W) \in \mathbb{G}_1^4 \times \mathbb{G}_T$ as input, output yes if $W = \hat{e}(g, g)^{abc}$ and no otherwise. The corresponding BDDH assumption can be formalized the same way as the square BDDH assumption in the last paragraph.

3.4 The q-BDDHI Assumption

Let $\mathcal{BG}$ be as above and let $z \in \mathbb{G}_1$ be a random element from group $\mathbb{G}_1$. For a function $q = q(k) \geq 1$ polynomial in the security parameter k consider the following problem introduced by Boneh and Boyen [1]: Given $(z, z^y, z^{(y^2)}, \ldots, z^{(y^q)}, W) \in \mathbb{G}_1^{q+1} \times \mathbb{G}_T$ as input, output yes if $W = \hat{e}(z, z)^{1/y}$ and no otherwise.

3.5   Relation Between the Assumptions

The next lemma classifies the strength of the different assumptions we intro-duced. Here "A $\leq$ B" means that assumption B implies assumption A, i.e. as-sumption B is a stronger assumption than A.

Lemma 1. *BDDH $\leq$ square BDDH $\leq$ 1-BDDHI $\leq$ 2-BDDHI ...*

In partiuclar this means that square BDDH is a stronger assumption than BDDH, but weaker than q-BDDHI (for any $q \geq 1$). The simple proof of Lemma 1 is postponed until Appendix B.

4   Key Encapsulation Based on the Second Boneh/Boyen IBE Scheme

In this section we revisit the encryption scheme from [6, 4] obtained by applying the CHK transformation to the second Boneh/Boyen IBE scheme from [1]. As already mentioned in the Introduction the scheme is presented as a key encap-sulation mechanism (KEM) instead of an encryption scheme as in the original paper. After reminding the reader of the original scheme we then move on to present our simplifications.

For both schemes let the global system parameters be $\mathcal{BG} = (\mathbb{G}_1, \mathbb{G}_T, p, \hat{e}, g)$, a random bilinear group obtained by running BilinGen(1^k).

4.1   CHK2: The Original Scheme from [6]

In this construction, we use a one-time signature scheme $\mathcal{OTS} = (\mathsf{Skg}, \mathsf{Sign}, \mathsf{Vfy})$. The key generation algorithm Skg is run to obtain a random pair of verifica-tion/signing keys $(v, s) \xleftarrow{\$} \mathsf{Skg}(1^k)$; the signing key s is used to sign a message M to obtain a signature $\sigma \xleftarrow{\$} \mathsf{Sign}_s(M)$ on a message M; using the public veri-fication key v, a signature σ can be verified by running $\mathsf{Vfy}_v(M, \sigma)$. We require that this scheme be secure in the sense of *strong unforgeability*, see [6] for exact definitions and constructions (details can be skipped here).

The key encapsulation mechanism proposed by Canetti, Halevi, and Katz [6] which we will denote by CHK2 is given in Fig. 1 (in order to simplify the com-parison, compared to [6] we made some slight change of variables). It is straight-forward to verify the correctness of the scheme. In terms of security the following theorem was derived in [6]:

Theorem 2. *Assuming the q-BDDHI assumption holds relative to the generator* BilinGen, *$\mathcal{OTS}$ is a strong, one-time signature scheme, then the KEM from Fig. 1 is chosen-ciphertext secure. Here $q = q(k)$ is an upper bound on the decapsulation queries made by an adversary attacking the scheme.*

$$\boxed{\begin{array}{l}
\qquad\qquad\quad\mathsf{KEMkg}(1^k) \\
\qquad\quad x_1, x_2 \xleftarrow{\$} \mathbb{Z}_p^* \\
\qquad\quad h_1 \leftarrow g^{x_1} \; ; \; h_2 \leftarrow g^{x_2} \; ; \; z \leftarrow \hat{e}(h_2, h_2) \\
\qquad\quad pk \leftarrow (h_1, h_2, z) \; ; \; sk \leftarrow (x_1, x_2) \\
\qquad\quad \text{Return } (pk, sk)
\end{array}}$$

$$\boxed{\begin{array}{ll}
\mathsf{KEMencaps}(pk) & \quad \mathsf{KEMdecaps}(sk, C) \\
r \xleftarrow{\$} \mathbb{Z}_p^* \; ; \; c_1 \leftarrow g^r & \quad \text{Parse } C \text{ as } (c_1, c_2, v, \sigma) \\
(v, s) \xleftarrow{\$} \mathsf{Skg}(1^k) \; ; \; c_2 \leftarrow h_1^r \cdot h_2^{v \cdot r} & \quad \text{If } \mathsf{Vfy}_v(c_1 \| c_2, \sigma) = \texttt{reject} \\
K \leftarrow z^r & \qquad \text{then return } \texttt{reject}. \\
 & \quad \text{Else} \\
\sigma \xleftarrow{\$} \mathsf{Sign}_s(c_1 \| c_2) & \qquad r' \xleftarrow{\$} \mathbb{Z}_p \\
C \leftarrow (c_1, c_2, v, \sigma) & \qquad K \leftarrow \hat{e}\left(c_1^{r'} c_2, h_2^{1/(v + x_1/x_2 + r'/x_2)}\right) \\
\text{Return } (K, C) &
\end{array}}$$

Fig. 1. The original CHK2 scheme

4.2   CHK2': An Equivalent Depcapsulation Algorithm

A closer inspection of the decapsulation algorithm of the CHK2 scheme from Fig. 1 shows that it *implicitly rejects* inconsistent ciphertexts (i.e., ciphertexts that were not obtained running the encapsulation algorithm with the correct public key) by returning a random session key in that case. Once consistency of the ciphertext is established, recovering the session key can be greatly improved.

For a value $v \in \mathbb{Z}_p$ we have

$$c_1^{x_1 + x_2 v} = c_2 \Leftrightarrow \hat{e}(g, c_1^{x_1 + x_2 v}) = \hat{e}(g, c_2)$$

$$\Leftrightarrow \hat{e}(g^{x_1 + x_2 v}, c_1) = \hat{e}(g, c_2)$$

$$\Leftrightarrow \hat{e}(h_1 h_2^v, c_1) = \hat{e}(g, c_2).$$

Therefore it can be publicly verified (using the public key only) if $c_1^{x_1 + x_2 v} = c_2$ by checking if $\hat{e}(h_1 h_2^v, c_1) = \hat{e}(g, c_2)$. A tuple (c_1, c_2) meeting this property is dubbed to be *consistent with* v. Note that any tuple (c_1, c_2) correctly generated by the encapsulation algorithm is always consistent with its verification key v. (A correctly generated ciphertext has the form $C = (c_1, c_2, v, \sigma) = (g^r, h_1^r \cdot h_2^{vr}, v, \sigma)$. Therefore $c_1^{x_1 + x_2 v} = (g^r)^{x_1 + x_2 v} = (g^{x_1})^r (g^{x_2 v})^r = h_1^r \cdot h_2^{rv}$.)

An equivalent way to compute the session key K, given that the signature was successfully verified, is as follows: First, a random key K is returned if (c_1, c_2) is not consistent with v, i.e. if $c_1^{x_1 + x_2 \cdot v} \neq c_2$ which can be checked as described above. Otherwise, the key is recovered as $K = \hat{e}(h_2^{x_2}, c_1)$.

We claim that this decapsulation algorithm is equivalent to the one from CHK2 (Fig. 1). It is easy to verify that

$$\hat{e}(c_1^{r'} c_2, h_2^{1/(v + x_1/x_2 + r'/x_2)}) = \hat{e}(h_2^{x_2}, c_1)^{\Delta(r')},$$

where $\Delta(r') = (r' + \log_{c_1} c_2)/(r' + x_1 + v \cdot x_2)$ is a random element from $\mathbb{Z}_p$ if $c_1^{x_1 + x_2 v} \neq c_2$ (i.e., if (c_1, c_2) is not consistent with v) and $\Delta(r') = 1$ otherwise. We have seen that if (c_1, c_2) is consistent with v decapsulation computes the key K as

$$= \hat{e}(h_2^{x_2}, g^r)^1$$
$$= \hat{e}(h_2, g^{x_2})^r$$
$$= \hat{e}(h_2, h_2)^r = z^r \, ,$$

as the key computed in the encapsulation algorithm. This shows correctness.

We note that, equivalently, instead of returning a random key K the decapsulation algorithm could as well reject the ciphertext.

4.3   CHK2": Our Simplification

In this section we show how to avoid the one-time signature scheme by replacing it with a (determinstic) target collision resistant hash function applied to parts of the ciphertext. We note that the usage of the hash function is somewhat reminiscent of the Cramer/Shoup scheme [7].

Let $\mathsf{TCR} : \mathbb{G}_1 \to \mathbb{Z}_p$ be a target collision resistant hash function. Our simplification of the above construction is depicted in Fig. 2. Correctness of decapsulation follows from the correctness of the last scheme.

KEMkg(1^k)
$x_1, x_2 \overset{\$}{\leftarrow} \mathbb{Z}_p^*$
$h_1 \leftarrow g^{x_1}$; $h_2 \leftarrow g^{x_2}$; $z \leftarrow \hat{e}(h_2, h_2)$
$pk \leftarrow (h_1, h_2, z)$; $sk \leftarrow (x_1, x_2, y = h_2^{x_2})$
Return (pk, sk)

KEMencaps(pk)
$r \overset{\$}{\leftarrow} \mathbb{Z}_p^*$; $c_1 \leftarrow g^r$
$v \leftarrow \mathsf{TCR}(c_1)$; $c_2 \leftarrow h_1^r \cdot h_2^{v \cdot r}$
$K \leftarrow z^r$
$C \leftarrow (c_1, c_2)$
Return (C, K)

KEMdecaps(sk, C)
Parse C as (c_1, c_2)
$v \leftarrow \mathsf{TCR}(c_1)$
If $c_1^{x_1 + x_2 \cdot v} \neq c_2$ then reject
Else $K \leftarrow \hat{e}(y, c_1)$
Return K

Fig. 2. CHK2": Our simplification of CHK2

Let $C = (c_1, c_2)$ be an arbitrary ciphertext and let $v = \mathsf{TCR}(c_1)$. We call C *consistent* if it passes the verification check in the decapsulation algorithm, i.e. if $c_1^{x_1 + x_2 v} = c_2$. By the discussion above we note that our KEM allows for public verification of the consistency of a ciphertext by testing if $\hat{e}(h_1 h_2^v, c_1) = \hat{e}(g, c_2)$. This public consistency check will play a crucial role in the proof of security. We note that the original CHK2 scheme from Fig. 1 already has a similar public verification property (using the one-time signature scheme).

4.4   Security

Theorem 3. *Assume* TCR *is a target collision resistant hash function. Under the square BDDH assumption relative to the generator* $\mathsf{BilinGen}$ *the KEM from Fig. 2 is secure against chosen-ciphertext attacks.*

The security reduction is tight. The proof of Theorem 3 is given in Appendix A. We will try to provide some intuition instead.

SECURITY OF THE SCHEME CHK2'. Let $C^* = (c_1^*, c_2^*, v^*, \sigma^*)$ be the challenge ciphertext output by the simulator in the security experiment. It is clear that, without any decryption oracle queries, the value of the bit δ remains hidden to the adversary. This is so because (c_1^*, c_2^*) comes from a chosen-plaintext secure encryption scheme, v^* is independent of the message, and σ^* is the result of applying the one-time signing algorithm to $c_1^* \| c_2^*$.

We claim that decryption oracle queries cannot further help the adversary in guessing the value of δ. Consider an arbitrary ciphertext query $(c_1, c_2, v, \sigma) \neq (c_1^*, c_2^*, v^*, \sigma^*)$ made by the adversary during the experiment. If $v = v^*$ then $(c_1, c_2, \sigma) \neq (c_1^*, c_2^*, \sigma^*)$ and the decryption oracle will answer reject since the adversary is unable to forge a new valid signature σ with respect to v^*. Now let $v \neq v^*$. Intuitively, a query with $v \neq v^*$ does not help the adversary since the underlying IBE scheme is *selective-identity secure*. In a nutshell, this IBE security property exactly translates to what we need here. I.e, any decryption query made for the "identity" v distinct from "target identity" v^* (which is is completely independent of the adversary's view until it sees the target ciphertext; therefore the simulator may as well choose v^* in the beginning of the experiment) does not help the adversary further. Details will be given in the proof.

SECURITY OF THE SCHEME CHK2". To argue for security we again claim that decryption oracle queries cannot further help the adversary in guessing the value of δ. If $v \neq v^*$ we can still argue as in the CHK2' scheme. If $v = v^*$ then by the target collision resistance of TCR we may assume $c_1 = c_1^*$. In this case consistency implies $c_2^* = c_2$ and therefore $C^* = C$.

5   Comparison and Efficiency

5.1   Relation Between CHK2 and CHK2"

In terms of functionality of the CHK2" scheme we note that the element $y = h_2^{x_2}$ is contained in the secret key for the sole reason of improving efficiency of decapsulation when recovering the key as $K = \hat{e}(h_2^{x_2}, c_1) = \hat{e}(y, c_1)$. Apart from that, key-generation is equivalent to the CHK2 scheme from Section 4.1.

The value y gives rise to a tradeoff between the length of the secret key and decryption speed. In particular, the secret value $y = h_2^{x_2}$ can always be reconstructed by the owner of the secret key on-line during decapsulation. This variant makes the secret-key one element shorter with the drawback of one more exponentiation during decapsulation.

Every IBE scheme can be viewed as a more general concept, a *tag-based encryption* (TBE) scheme. It was recently shown [10] that TBE is already sufficient for the CHK transformation to obtain a chosen-ciphertext secure encryption scheme. We note that the TBE scheme implied by the BB2 IBE scheme already can be proved secure under the (weaker) square BDDH assumption meaning that the original CHK2 scheme is also secure under square BDDH. To be more precise, in the transformation chain IBE $\Rightarrow$ TBE $\Rightarrow$ "chosen-ciphertext secure encryption", the security improvement is already obtained after the first implication.

5.2   Relation Between CHK1" and CHK2"

As we instantly notice, our CHK2" scheme from Section 4.3 is very similar to the scheme from Boyen, Mei, and Waters [5] which we will refer to as CHK1". (For completeness we remind the reader of CHK1" in Appendix C.) Let us point out the differences.

The only difference is that the key generation algorithm of CHK1" chooses (in an information theoretical sense) a new independent secret value y. In contrast, our scheme derives the secret value $y = h_2^{x_2}$ from h_2 and x_2, i.e. the secret key contains some redundant information. (The sole reason the value y is included in our scheme is to save one exponentiation in the decapsulation algorithm.) This dependence of y is the reason why we need a stronger assumption to prove security. Performance of the two KEMs is exactly the same.

5.3   Relation Between CHK1 and CHK2

We denote by CHK1 the scheme obtained by plugging the first Boneh/Boyen IBE scheme into the CHK transformation. We note that the CHK1 scheme (which for completeness is also presented in Appendix C) is already equivalent to the CHK2 scheme.

Similar to our scheme CHK2' between CHK2 and CHK2" from Section 4.4 (which was equivalent to CHK2) we can also build a scheme CHK1' between CHK1 and simple CHK1 scheme that still uses the one-time signature but simplifies decryption by equivalently replacing the original randomized decryption by a consistency check plus a deterministic computation of the key. Again this scheme CHK1' can be shown to be equivalent to CHK1.

Both schemes, CHK1' and CHK2' already give nearly the same schemes with the same small difference as the two schemes CHK1" and CHK2".

5.4   Efficiency

We summarize our results and present a quick efficiency comparison of our proposed scheme with the original scheme from Canetti, Halevi, and Katz [6].

The scheme CHK2 is the scheme obtained from the second Boneh/Boyen IBE scheme plugged into the CHK transformation from Section 4.1. We give the performance values for the more MAC-based BK transformation [4]. The scheme CHK2" from Section 4.3 is our simplified version of CHK2. For comparison the schemes CHK1 and its simplified variant CHK1" are given in Appendix C. For comparison we borrowed some figures from [2, 5]. Ciphertext overhead represents the difference (in bits) between the ciphertext length and the message length, and $|p|$ is the length of a group element.

Scheme	Assumption	Encapsulation #pairings + #[multi,reg]-exp + ...	Decapsulation	Ciphertext Overhead	Keysize (pk, sk)
CHK2"	square-BDDH	$0 + [1,2] + $ TCR	$1 + [0,1] + $ TCR	$2|p|$	$(3,3)$
CHK2	q-BDDHI	$0 + [1,2] + $ MAC	$1 + [0,2] + $ MAC	$2|p| + 768$	$(3,2)$
CHK1" [5]	BDDH	$0 + [1,2] + $ TCR	$1 + [0,1] + $ TCR	$2|p|$	$(3,3)$
CHK1	BDDH	$0 + [1,2] + $ MAC	$1 + [1,0] + $ MAC	$2|p| + 768$	$(3,3)$

6 Conclusion

We have shown that, after removing an unnecessary decryption overhead, CHK1 is nearly the same scheme as CHK2. Furthermore, their respective simplifications CHK1" [5] and CHK2" are also nearly the same. This contradicts the statement from [6, 4, 2] that the two schemes are different schemes, with different performance and security properties. In our point of view the fact that the CHK IBE-to-PKE transformation maps two different IBE schemes to nearly the same encryption scheme is very surprising.

For any new IBE scheme, even though it seems to be very different from the two known IBE schemes, care should be taken when claiming that the CHK transformation applied to it yields a new encryption scheme.

Acknowledgments

We thank Ronald Cramer for proposing the title and the anonymous PKC referees for their detailed comments. This research was supported by the research program Sentinels (http://www.sentinels.nl). Sentinels is being financed by Technology Foundation STW, the Netherlands Organization for Scientific Research (NWO), and the Dutch Ministry of Economic Affairs.

References

1. D. Boneh and X. Boyen. Efficient selective-id secure identity based encryption without random oracles. In C. Cachin and J. Camenisch, editors, *EUROCRYPT 2004*, volume 3027 of *LNCS*, pages 223–238. Springer-Verlag, May 2004.
2. D. Boneh, R. Canetti, S. Halevi, and J. Katz. Chosen-ciphertext security from identity-based encryption. Accepted to *SIAM Journal on Computing*, January 2006.
3. D. Boneh and M. K. Franklin. Identity based encryption from the Weil pairing. *SIAM Journal on Computing*, 32(3):586–615, 2003.
4. D. Boneh and J. Katz. Improved efficiency for CCA-secure cryptosystems built using identity-based encryption. In A. Menezes, editor, *CT-RSA 2005*, volume 3376 of *LNCS*, pages 87–103. Springer-Verlag, Feb. 2005.
5. X. Boyen, Q. Mei, and B. Waters. Simple and efficient CCA2 security from IBE techniques. In *ACM Conference on Computer and Communications Security—CCS 2005*, pages 320–329. New-York: ACM Press, 2005.

6. R. Canetti, S. Halevi, and J. Katz. Chosen-ciphertext security from identity-based encryption. In C. Cachin and J. Camenisch, editors, *EUROCRYPT 2004*, volume 3027 of *LNCS*, pages 207–222. Springer-Verlag, May 2004.
7. R. Cramer and V. Shoup. A practical public key cryptosystem provably secure against adaptive chosen ciphertext attack. In H. Krawczyk, editor, *CRYPTO'98*, volume 1462 of *LNCS*, pages 13–25. Springer-Verlag, Aug. 1998.
8. R. Cramer and V. Shoup. Design and analysis of practical public-key encryption schemes secure against adaptive chosen ciphertext attack. *SIAM Journal on Computing*, 33(1):167–226, 2003.
9. D. Dolev, C. Dwork, and M. Naor. Non-malleable cryptography. In *23rd ACM STOC*, pages 542–552. ACM Press, May 1991.
10. E. Kiltz. Chosen-ciphertext security from tag-based encryption. In S. Halevi and T. Rabin, editors, *TCC 2006*, volume 3876 of *LNCS*, pages 581–600. Springer-Verlag, Mar. 2006.
11. K. Kurosawa and Y. Desmedt. A new paradigm of hybrid encryption scheme. In M. Franklin, editor, *CRYPTO 2004*, volume 3152 of *LNCS*, pages 426–442. Springer-Verlag, Aug. 2004.
12. M. Naor and M. Yung. Universal one-way hash functions and their cryptographic applications. In *21st ACM STOC*, pages 33–43. ACM Press, May 1989.
13. M. Naor and M. Yung. Public-key cryptosystems provably secure against chosen ciphertext attacks. In *22nd ACM STOC*. ACM Press, May 1990.
14. C. Rackoff and D. R. Simon. Non-interactive zero-knowledge proof of knowledge and chosen ciphertext attack. In J. Feigenbaum, editor, *CRYPTO'91*, volume 576 of *LNCS*, pages 433–444. Springer-Verlag, Aug. 1991.
15. J. Rompel. One-way functions are necessary and sufficient for secure signatures. In *22nd ACM STOC*, pages 387–394. ACM Press, May 1990.

A   Proof of Theorem 3

Suppose there exists a polynomial time adversary $\mathcal{A}$ that breaks the chosen-ciphertext security of the encapsulation scheme with (non-negligible) advantage $\mathbf{Adv}_{\mathcal{KEM},\mathcal{A}}^{kem\text{-}cca}(k)$. We show that there exists an adversary $\mathcal{B}$ that runs in about the same time as $\mathcal{A}$ and runs adversary $\mathcal{A}$ as a subroutine to solve a random instance of the square BDDH problem with advantage

$$\mathbf{Adv}_{\mathcal{G},\mathcal{B}}^{sbddh}(k) \geq \mathbf{Adv}_{\mathcal{KEM},\mathcal{A}}^{kem\text{-}cca}(k) - \mathbf{Adv}_{\mathsf{TCR},\mathcal{H}}^{hash\text{-}tcr}(k) . \tag{1}$$

Now Eqn. (1) proves the Theorem.

We now give the description of adversary $\mathcal{B}$. Adversary $\mathcal{B}$ inputs an instance of the square BDDH problem, i.e. $\mathcal{B}$ inputs the values $(1^k, \mathcal{BG}, g, g^a, g^b, W)$. $\mathcal{B}$'s goal is to determine whether $W = \hat{e}(g,g)^{a^2 b}$ or W is a random element in $\mathbb{G}_T$. Adversary $\mathcal{B}$ runs adversary $\mathcal{A}$ simulating its view as in the original KEM security experiment as follows:

Key Generation and Challenge. Initially adversary $\mathcal{B}$ picks a random value $d \in \mathbb{Z}_p^*$ and defines the target ciphertext

$$C^* = (\ c_1^* = g^b, \quad c_2^* = (g^b)^d\ ) . \tag{2}$$

and the challenge key as $K^* = W$. We denote $v = \mathsf{TCR}(c_1^*)$ as the target tag (associated with the target ciphertext). The public key $pk = (h_1, h_2)$ is defined as

$$pk = (\ h_1 = (g^a)^{-v^*} \cdot g^d),\quad h_2 = g^a,\quad z = \hat{e}(g^a, g^a)\ ). \tag{3}$$

This implicitly defines the secret key $sk = (x_1, x_2, v)$ as $x_2 = a$, $x_1 = \log_g(h_1) = -v^*a + d$, and $v = h_2^{x_2} = g^{(a^2)}$ where x_1, x_2 and v are not known to adversary $\mathcal{B}$. Note that the public key is identically distributed as in the original KEM.

With each ciphertext $C = (c_1, c_2)$ we associate a tag $v = \mathsf{TCR}(c_1)$. Recall that we call a ciphertext consistent (i.e., it passes the consistency test in the decapsulation algorithm) if $c_1^{x_1 + x_2 \cdot v} = c_2$. Note that the way the keys are setup this condition can be rewritten as

$$c_2 = c_1^{x_1 + x_2 v} = c_1^{x_2 v - v^* x_2 + d} = (c_1^{x_2})^{v - v^*} \cdot c_1^d. \tag{4}$$

Given a consistent ciphertext $C = (c_1, c_2)$ with associated tag $v \neq v^*$ the session key $K = \hat{e}(y, c_1)$ can alternatively be computed by Eqn. (4) as

$$K = \hat{e}(y, c_1) = \hat{e}(h_2^{x_2}, c_1) = \hat{e}(h_2, c_1^{x_2}) = \hat{e}(h_2, c_2/c_1^d)^{(v - v^*)^{-1}}. \tag{5}$$

By Eqn. (4) and since $v^* = \mathsf{TCR}(c_1^*)$ the challenge ciphertext $C^* = (c_1^*, c_2^*) = (g^b, (g^b)^d) = (c_1^*, (c_1^*)^d)$ is consistent. If $W = \hat{e}(g, g)^{a^2 b}$ then it follows by Eqn. (3) (since $x_2 = a$ and $h_2 = g^{x_2}$) that $C^* = (g^b, (g^b)^d)$ is a correct ciphertext of key $K^* = W = \hat{e}(g, g)^{a^2 b} = \hat{e}(g^a, g^a)^b = z^b$, distributed as in the original experiment. On the other hand, when W is uniform and independent in $\mathbb{G}_T$ then C^* is independent of $K^* = W$ in the adversary's view.

Adversary $\mathcal{B}$ runs $\mathcal{A}$ on input (pk, K^*, C^*) answering to its queries as follows:

Decryption Queries. The KEM decapsulation queries are simulated by $\mathcal{B}$ as follows: Let $C = (c_1, c_2)$ be an arbitrary ciphertext submitted to the decapsulation oracle $\mathsf{Dec}(\cdot)$. First $\mathcal{B}$ performs a consistency check as explained in Section 4.3, i.e. it checks if $\hat{e}(h_1 h_2^v, c_1) = \hat{e}(g, c_2)$ using the bilinear map from $\mathcal{BG}$. If C is not consistent then $\mathcal{B}$ returns reject. Otherwise, if the ciphertext is consistent $\mathcal{B}$ computes $v = \mathsf{TCR}(c_1)$ and distinguishes the following three cases:

Case 1. $v = v^*$ and $c_1 = c_1^*$: adversary $\mathcal{B}$ rejects the query. In this case consistency (c.f. Eqn. (4)) implies $c_2 = c_1^d = (c_1^*)^d = c_2^*$ and hence $C = C^*$ and the query made by $\mathcal{A}$ is illegal. Therefore it may be rejected by $\mathcal{B}$.

Case 2. $v = v^*$ and $c_1 \neq c_1^*$: adversary $\mathcal{B}$ found a collision $c_1 \neq c_1^*$ in TCR with $\mathsf{TCR}(c_1) = \mathsf{TCR}(c_1^*)$. In that case $\mathcal{B}$ returns the collision and aborts.

Case 3. $v \neq v^*$: adversary $\mathcal{B}$ computes the correct session key by Eqn. (5) as $K \leftarrow \hat{e}(h_2, c_2/c_1^d)^{(v - v^*)^{-1}}$.

This completes the description of the decapsulation oracle.

We have shown that unless $\mathcal{B}$ finds a collision in TCR (Case 2) the simulation of the decapsulation oracle is always perfect, i.e. the output of oracle $\mathsf{Dec}(C)$ is identically distributed as the output of $\mathsf{KEMdecaps}(sk, C)$.

Guess. Eventually, $\mathcal{A}$ outputs a guess $\delta' \in \{0,1\}$ where $\delta' = 1$ means that K^* is the correct key. Algorithm $\mathcal{B}$ concludes its own game by outputting $\gamma' = \delta'$ where $\gamma' = 1$ means that $W = \hat{e}(g,g)^{a^2 b}$ and $\gamma' = 0$ means that W is random.

This completes the description of adversary $\mathcal{B}$.

ANALYSIS. We have shown that as long as there is no hash collision in TCR found by $\mathcal{B}$, adversary $\mathcal{A}$'s view in the simulation is identically distributed to its view in the real attack game.

Note that c_1^* is a random element from $\mathbb{G}_1$ (provided from outside of $\mathcal{B}$'s view), therefore finding a value c_1 with $\mathsf{TCR}(c_1) = \mathsf{TCR}(c_1^*)$ really contradicts to the security property of the *target* collision resistant hash function. The probability that $\mathcal{B}$ finds a collision in the hash function TCR is bounded by $\mathbf{Adv}_{\mathsf{TCR},\mathcal{H}}^{\mathrm{hash\text{-}tcr}}(k)$, where $\mathcal{H}$ is an adversary against the target collision resistance of TCR, running in about the same time as $\mathcal{B}$.

Define "$\mathcal{B}$ WINS" to be the event that $\mathcal{B}$ wins its square BDDH game, i.e. it outputs $\delta' = 1$ if $W = \hat{e}(g,g)^{a^2 b}$ and $\delta' = 0$ if W is random in $\mathbb{G}_T$. Assume there was no hash collision found by $\mathcal{B}$. On the one hand, if W is uniform and independent in $\mathbb{G}_T$ then the challenge ciphertext C^* is independent of $K^* = W$ in the adversary's view. In that case we have $\Pr[\mathcal{B} \text{ WINS}] = \Pr[\delta' = 0] = \frac{1}{2}$. On the other hand, when $W = \hat{e}(g,g)^{a^2 b}$ then C^* is a correct ciphertext of the challenge key K^*, distributed as in the original experiment. Then, by our assumption, $\mathcal{A}$ must make a correct guess $\delta' = 1$ with advantage at least $\mathbf{Adv}_{\mathcal{KEM},\mathcal{A}}^{kem\text{-}cca}(k)$ and we have $|\Pr[\mathcal{B} \text{ WINS}] - \frac{1}{2}| = |\Pr[\delta' = 1] - \frac{1}{2}| \geq \mathbf{Adv}_{\mathcal{KEM},\mathcal{A}}^{kem\text{-}cca}(k)$.

Therefore, adversary $\mathcal{B}$'s advantage in the square BDDH game is bounded by $\mathbf{Adv}_{\mathcal{G},\mathcal{B}}^{\mathrm{sbddh}}(k) \geq \mathbf{Adv}_{\mathcal{KEM},\mathcal{A}}^{kem\text{-}cca}(k) - \mathbf{Adv}_{\mathsf{TCR},\mathcal{H}}^{\mathrm{hash\text{-}tcr}}(k)$ which proves Eqn. (1) and completes the proof of the theorem.

B   Proof of Lemma 1

The implications BDDH $\leq$ square BDDH and 1-BDDHI $\leq$ 2-BDDHI $\leq$ 3-BDDHI $\leq$ ... are obvious. To prove "square BDDH assumption $\leq$ 1-BDDHI assumption", assume there exists a polynomial-time adversary $\mathcal{A}$ that breaks the square BDDH assumption with non-negliglible probability of success. We show that then there exists a polynomial-time adversary $\mathcal{B}$ with oracle access to $\mathcal{A}$ that breaks the 1-BDDHI assumption. Let $(h, h^z, W) \in \mathbb{G}_1^2 \times \mathbb{G}_T$ be an input instance of the 1-BDDHI problem given to $\mathcal{B}$. $\mathcal{B}$'s goal is to decide whether $W = \hat{e}(h,h)^{1/z}$ or W is random. $\mathcal{B}$ picks two random values x_0, y_0 and define its output as the bit $\gamma := \gamma'$, where γ' is input from $\mathcal{A}$ as

$$\gamma' \leftarrow \mathcal{A}(h^z, h^{x_0}, h^{y_0}, W' = W^{x_0^2 y_0}).$$

Defining $g = h^z$ (and hence $h = g^{1/z}$), $x = x_0/z$, and $y = y_0/z$ we have $(h^z, h^{x_0}, h^{y_0}) = (g, (g^{1/z})^{x_0}, (g^{1/z})^{y_0}) = (g, g^x, g^y)$. If $W = \hat{e}(h,h)^{1/z}$ then

$$W' = W^{x_0^2 y_0} = \hat{e}(h,h)^{1/z \cdot x_0^2 y_0} = \hat{e}(g,g)^{1/z^3 \cdot x_0^2 y_0} = \hat{e}(g,g)^{x^2 y}.$$

If W is a random element, so is W'. Therefore $\mathcal{B}$ solves 1-BDDHI with the same success probability as $\mathcal{A}$ solves square BDDH, which was non-negliglible by assumption. This proves the lemma.

C   The Schemes CHK1 and CHK1"

For completeness we include the complete description of the schemes CHK1 [6] and CHK1" [5] in Fig. 3 and Fig. 4, respectively.

$\mathsf{KEMkg}(1^k)$
$\quad x, x_1, x_2, \xleftarrow{\$} \mathbb{Z}_p^*$
$\quad h_1 \leftarrow g^{x_1} \;;\; h_2 \leftarrow g^{x_2} \;;\; y \leftarrow g^x \;;\; z \leftarrow \hat{e}(g, y)$
$\quad pk \leftarrow (h_1, h_2, z) \;;\; sk \leftarrow (x_1, x_2, x)$
$\quad$ Return (pk, sk)

$\mathsf{KEMencaps}(pk)$
$\quad r \xleftarrow{\$} \mathbb{Z}_p^* \;;\; c_1 \leftarrow g^r$
$\quad (v, s) \xleftarrow{\$} \mathsf{Skg}(1^k) \;;\; c_2 \leftarrow h_1^r \cdot h_2^{v \cdot r}$
$\quad K \leftarrow z^r$
$\quad \sigma \xleftarrow{\$} \mathsf{Sign}_s(c_1 \| c_2)$
$\quad C \leftarrow (c_1, c_2, v, \sigma)$
$\quad$ Return (K, C)

$\mathsf{KEMdecaps}(sk, C)$
$\quad$ Parse C as (c_1, c_2, v, σ)
$\quad$ If $\mathsf{Vfy}_v(c_1 \| c_2, \sigma) = \mathtt{reject}$
$\quad\quad$ then return $\mathtt{reject}$.
$\quad$ Else
$\quad\quad r' \xleftarrow{\$} \mathbb{Z}_p$
$\quad\quad K \leftarrow \hat{e}\left(c_1^{x + r'(x_1 + x_2 \cdot v)} \cdot c_2^{-r'}, g\right)$

Fig. 3. The CHK1 scheme from [6]

Theorem 4 ([6]). *Assume $\mathcal{OTS}$ is a strong, one-time signature scheme. Under the BDDH assumption relative to generator $\mathcal{G}$, the CHK1 scheme from Fig. 3 is secure against chosen-ciphertext attacks.*

Theorem 5 ([5]). *Under the BDDH assumption relative to generator $\mathcal{G}$, the CHK1" scheme from Fig. 4 is secure against chosen-ciphertext attacks.*

$\mathsf{KEMkg}(1^k)$
$\quad x_1, x_2, x \xleftarrow{\$} \mathbb{Z}_p^*$
$\quad h_1 \leftarrow g^{x_1} \;;\; h_2 \leftarrow g^{x_2} \;;\; y \leftarrow g^x \;;\; z \leftarrow \hat{e}(g, y)$
$\quad pk \leftarrow (h_1, h_2, z) \;;\; sk \leftarrow (x_1, x_2, y)$
$\quad$ Return (pk, sk)

$\mathsf{KEMencaps}(pk)$
$\quad r \xleftarrow{\$} \mathbb{Z}_p^* \;;\; c_1 \leftarrow g^r$
$\quad v \leftarrow \mathsf{TCR}(c_1) \;;\; c_2 \leftarrow h_1^r \cdot h_2^{v \cdot r}$
$\quad K \leftarrow z^r$
$\quad C \leftarrow (c_1, c_2)$
$\quad$ Return (C, K)

$\mathsf{KEMdecaps}(sk, C)$
$\quad$ Parse C as (c_1, c_2)
$\quad v \leftarrow \mathsf{TCR}(c_1)$
$\quad$ If $c_1^{x_1 + x_2 \cdot v} \neq c_2$ then $\mathtt{reject}$
$\quad$ Else $K \leftarrow \hat{e}(y, c_1)$
$\quad$ Return K

Fig. 4. The CHK1" scheme from [5]

Inoculating Multivariate Schemes
Against Differential Attacks

Jintai Ding and Jason E. Gower

Department of Mathematical Sciences,
University of Cincinnati,
Cincinnati, OH 45221-0025, USA
ding@math.uc.edu, gowerj@math.uc.edu

Abstract. We demonstrate how to prevent differential attacks on multivariate public key cryptosystems using the Plus (+) method of external perturbation. In particular, we prescribe adding as few as 10 Plus polynomials to the Perturbed Matsumoto-Imai (PMI) cryptosystem when $g = 1$ and $r = 6$, where θ is the Matsumoto-Imai exponent, n is the message length, $g = \gcd(\theta, n)$, and r is the internal perturbation dimension; or as few as $g + 10$ when $g \neq 1$. The external perturbation does not significantly decrease the efficiency of the system, and in fact has the additional benefit of resolving the problem of finding the true plaintext among several preimages of a given ciphertext. We call this new scheme the Perturbed Matsumoto-Imai-Plus (PMI+) cryptosystem.

Keywords: multivariate, public key, cryptography, Matsumoto-Imai, perturbation, plus, differential.

1   Introduction

Though number theory based cryptosystems such as RSA are currently nearly ubiquitous, they are not appropriate for all implementations. Most notably, such schemes are not well-suited for use in small devices with limited computing resources. Multivariate public key cryptography provides one alternative since computations in small finite fields can be faster than working with large numbers. Furthermore, solving systems of multivariate quadratic polynomial equations over a finite field appears to be a difficult problem (analogous to integer factorization, though it is unknown precisely how difficult either problem actually is), so it seems reasonable to expect that we will be able to build secure multivariate public key cryptosystems and signature schemes from systems of quadratic polynomials that appear to be randomly chosen. Indeed, such systems may even resist future quantum computer attacks. In the last ten years, there has been significant effort put into realizing practical implementations, such as Matsumoto-Imai, HFE, HFEv, Sflash, Oil & Vinegar, Quartz, TTM, and TTS, to name but a few. So far the most secure encryption scheme seems to be HFE [13], though such an implementation with 2^{80} security would be very slow. On the other hand,

M. Yung et al. (Eds.): PKC 2006, LNCS 3958, pp. 290–301, 2006.

Sflash [1] has been recommended by the New European Schemes for Signatures, Integrity, and Encryption (NESSIE, [11]) as a signature scheme for constrained environments.

Internal perturbation was recently introduced by Ding [3] as a general method to improve the security of multivariate public key cryptosystems. Roughly speaking, the idea is to "internally perturb" the system using a randomly chosen subspace of small dimension to create "noise" to be added to the system so that the resulting system still works efficiently and is much more difficult to break. The first application of this method was to the Matsumoto-Imai (MI) cryptosystem [10], a system that is otherwise vulnerable to the linearization attack [12]. The resulting system, called the perturbed Matsumoto-Imai cryptosystem (PMI), is slower as one needs to go through a search process on the perturbation space, though it is much faster than a 1024-bit implementation of RSA [15]. However, the recent attack of Fouque, Granboulan, and Stern [8] has shown that PMI is insecure. The basic idea of this attack is to use differentials to create a test for membership in the subset $\mathcal{K}$ of plaintexts that produce no noise. Once $\mathcal{K}$ is known, one can effectively "denoise" the system and thereby eliminate the internal perturbation. The linearization attack can then be applied to break the system as in the case of MI.

1.1 Our Results

In this paper we will show that PMI is easily protected from this attack by adding a small amount of external perturbation in the form of Plus (+) polynomials [14]. To put things in more concrete terms, let $g = \gcd(\theta, n)$, where θ is the Matsumoto-Imai exponent and n is the message length. Then by adding as few as 10 Plus polynomials to PMI when $g = 1$ and $r = 6$, or as few as $g + 10$ when $g \neq 1$, we will have a new scheme that resists the differential attack. The resulting scheme, called the Perturbed Matsumoto-Imai-Plus (PMI+) cryptosystem, uses the externally added random quadratic polynomials to create a situation in which almost all plaintexts satisfy the test for membership used in the differential attack on PMI. Not only is PMI+ then protected from the differential attack, we can use the theory of Markov chains to pick an optimal amount of perturbation so that the resulting efficiency degradation is slight. Moreover, the extra Plus polynomials can be used to solve the problem of finding the true plaintext from among several preimages of a given ciphertext.

1.2 Outline of the Paper

The remainder of this paper is organized as follows. After briefly recalling MI and PMI in Section 2.2, we describe the differential attack on PMI in Section 3. We show how to protect PMI from the differential attack in Section 4, and discuss how to use the theory of Markov chains to choose the optimal amount of external perturbation in the form of Plus polynomials. We conclude the paper in Section 5.

2   Matsumoto-Imai and Perturbed Matsumoto-Imai

In this section we provide a brief description of the Matsumoto-Imai cryptosystem, its variant, the Perturbed Matsumoto-Imai cryptosystem, and the most serious non-differential attacks on each.

2.1   Matsumoto-Imai

Let k be a finite field of size q and characteristic two, and fix an irreducible polynomial of $g(x) \in k[x]$ of degree n. Then $K = k[x]/(g(x))$ is an extension of degree n over k. We also have a k-vector space isomorphism $\phi : K \longrightarrow k^n$ defined by $\phi(a_0 + \cdots + a_{n-1}x^{n-1}) = (a_0, \ldots, a_{n-1})$. Fix θ so that $\gcd(1 + q^\theta, q^n - 1) = 1$ and define $F : K \longrightarrow K$ by

$$F(X) = X^{1+q^\theta}.$$

Then F is invertible and $F^{-1}(X) = X^t$, where $t(1 + q^\theta) \equiv 1 \bmod q^n - 1$. Define the map $\tilde{F} : k^n \longrightarrow k^n$ by $\tilde{F}(x_1, \ldots, x_n) = \phi \circ F \circ \phi^{-1}(x_1, \ldots, x_n) = (\tilde{F}_1, \ldots, \tilde{F}_n)$. In this case, the $\tilde{F}_i(x_1, \ldots, x_n)$ are quadratic polynomials in the variables $x_1, \ldots, x_n$. Finally, let L_1 and L_2 be two randomly chosen invertible affine transformation over k^n and define $\bar{F} : k^n \longrightarrow k^n$ by

$$\bar{F}(x_1, \ldots, x_n) = L_1 \circ \tilde{F} \circ L_2\,(x_1, \ldots, x_n) = (\bar{F}_1, \ldots, \bar{F}_n).$$

The public key of the Matsumoto-Imai cryptosystem (referred to as C^* or MI) consists of the polynomials $\bar{F}_i(x_1, \ldots, x_n)$. See [10] for more details.

2.2   Perturbed Matsumoto-Imai

Fix a small integer r and randomly choose r invertible affine linear functions $z_1, \ldots, z_r$, written

$$z_j(x_1, \ldots, x_n) = \sum_{i=1}^{n} \alpha_{ij} x_i + \beta_j,$$

for $j = 1, \ldots, r$. This defines a map $Z : k^n \longrightarrow k^r$ by $Z(x_1, \ldots, x_n) = (z_1, \ldots, z_r)$. Randomly choose n quadratic polynomials $f_1, \ldots, f_n$ in the variables $z_1, \ldots, z_r$. The f_i define a map $f : k^r \longrightarrow k^n$ by $f(z_1, \ldots, z_r) = (f_1, \ldots, f_n)$. Define $\tilde{f} : k^n \longrightarrow k^n$ by $\tilde{f} = f \circ Z$, and $\bar{\bar{F}} : k^n \longrightarrow k^n$ by

$$\bar{\bar{F}} = \tilde{F} + \tilde{f}.$$

The map $\bar{\bar{F}}$ is called the perturbation of $\tilde{F}$ by $\tilde{f}$, and as with MI, its components are quadratic polynomials in the variables $x_1, \ldots, x_n$. Finally, define the map $\hat{F} : k^n \longrightarrow k^n$ by

$$\hat{F}(x_1, \ldots, x_n) = L_1 \circ \bar{\bar{F}} \circ L_2(x_1, \ldots, x_n) = (y_1, \ldots, y_n),$$

where the L_i are randomly chosen invertible affine maps on k^n. The public key of the Perturbed Matsumoto-Imai (PMI) cryptosystem consists of the components y_i of $\hat{F}$. See [3] for more details.

Although for MI there is a bijective correspondence between plaintext and ciphertext, PMI does not enjoy this property. Indeed, for a given ciphertext $c \in k^n$, $\hat{F}^{-1}(c)$ may have as many as q^r elements, though we may add some redundancy to the plaintext in order to distinguish it from the other preimages.

2.3 Non-differential Attacks on MI and PMI

Patarin's linearization attack [12] is the most successful attack against MI, and it is clear that it cannot be used to attack a general PMI with a reasonable r. However, Gröbner bases algorithms, such as Faugère's F_4 [6], can be used to attack any multivariate scheme. Though the exact running time complexity is unknown, there is evidence [5] which strongly suggests that PMI is resistant to attacks using F_4. More specifically, experiments from [5] indicate that within a reasonably range of n, a polynomial model is appropriate for predicting the security of PMI with $r < 6$, while an exponential model is appropriate for $r \geq 6$. For example, the exponential model is used to predict a security level of 2^{160} against F_4 for instances of PMI with parameters $(q, n, r, \theta) = (2, 136, 6, 40)$.

In the next section we will recall the new differential attack of Fouque, Granboulan, and Stern [8]. Both MI and PMI as previously described are susceptible to this attack. In particular, it is claimed that this attack applied to PMI will have a computation complexity of at most 2^{49} binary operations.

3 Differential Attack on PMI

We begin by establishing the notation used in the sequel; see [8] for proofs of quoted results. For each plaintext message $v \in k^n$, define the differential

$$L_v(x) = \hat{F}(x + v) + \hat{F}(x) + \hat{F}(v) + \hat{F}(0),$$

for a given instance of PMI. It is straightforward to show that L_v is linear in x.

Let $\mathcal{K}$ be the "noise kernel," the kernel of the linear part of the affine transformation $Z \circ L_2$. Then it can also be shown that

$$v \in \mathcal{K} \implies \dim(\ker(L_v)) = \gcd(\theta, n).$$

The differential attack amounts to computing a basis for $\mathcal{K}$, followed by q^r MI-type attacks, each attack being against PMI restricted to one of the q^r affine planes parallel to $\mathcal{K}$. For the MI-type attack to begin, $\mathcal{K}$ must be computed. In order to more clearly see how to thwart this attack, we now recall the particulars of this computation.

3.1 Testing for Membership in $\mathcal{K}$

For each $v \in k^n$, define the function T by

$$T(v) = \begin{cases} 1, & \text{if } \dim(\ker(L_v)) \neq \gcd(\theta, n); \\ 0, & \text{otherwise.} \end{cases}$$

Let $\alpha = P[T(v) = 0]$ and $\beta = P[v \in \mathcal{K}] = q^{-r}$; in other words, α is the probability that $T(v) = 0$, and β is the probability that $v \in \mathcal{K}$. We can use T to devise a test for detecting whether or not a given v is very likely to be in $\mathcal{K}$, assuming the following proposition: If for many different v_i' such that $T(v_i') = 0$ we have $T(v + v_i') = 0$, then $v \in \mathcal{K}$ with high probability. Suppose we pick N vectors $v_1', \ldots, v_N'$ such that $T(v_i') = 0$. Define $p(v) = P[T(v + v_i') = 0 \,|\, T(v_i') = 0]$. If v is chosen at random, then $p(v) = \alpha$; otherwise, $p(v) = \frac{\beta}{\alpha} + \frac{(\alpha - \beta)^2}{\alpha(1 - \beta)}$. In this latter case it is not hard to show that $\frac{p(v)}{\alpha} - 1 = \frac{\beta}{1 - \beta}(\frac{1}{\alpha} - 1)^2 \doteq \beta(\frac{1}{\alpha} - 1)^2$, where $\frac{\beta}{1 - \beta} = \beta + \beta^2 + \beta^3 + \cdots \doteq \beta$ if β is very small. Thus we have the approximation $p(v) \doteq \alpha + \alpha\beta(\frac{1}{\alpha} - 1)^2$ whenever $v \in \mathcal{K}$. It follows that one way to decide whether or not $v \in \mathcal{K}$ is to approximate $p(v)$ and decide whether it is closer to α or $\alpha + \alpha\beta(\frac{1}{\alpha} - 1)^2$.

At this point we note that it seems more natural to consider the function $T'(v + v_i') = \frac{1 - T(v + v_i')}{\alpha} - 1$, which has expected value $E[T'(v + v_i')] = \frac{p(v)}{\alpha} - 1$, and then consider the average $\frac{1}{N}\sum_{i=1}^{N} T'(v + v_i')$, which we expect to be close to $\frac{p(v)}{\alpha} - 1$, for large enough N by the Central Limit Theorem (see [7]). Then our task would be to determine whether this average is closer to 0 or $\beta(\frac{1}{\alpha} - 1)^2$.

The new function T' is defined as above in terms of T, and is such that

$$T'(v + v_i') = \begin{cases} \frac{1}{\alpha} - 1, & \text{with probability } p(v); \\ -1, & \text{with probability } 1 - p(v). \end{cases}$$

Also $\mu = E[T'(v + v_i')] = \frac{p(v)}{\alpha} - 1$ and $\sigma^2 = Var[T'(v + v_i')] = \frac{p(v)(1 - p(v))}{\alpha^2}$. Let X_i be independent and identically distributed random variables with the same distribution as T', and define $S_N = \sum_{i=1}^{N} X_i$. Then the Central Limit Theorem states that

$$P\left[\frac{S_N - N\mu}{\sigma\sqrt{N}} < x\right] \longrightarrow \mathfrak{N}(x) \quad \text{as} \quad N \longrightarrow \infty,$$

where

$$\mathfrak{N}(x) = \frac{1}{\sqrt{2\pi}}\int_{-\infty}^{x} e^{-y^2/2}\, dx$$

is the standard normal distribution function. In other words, the Central Limit Theorem implies that the following approximation is valid for large N:

$$A_N \approx \mu + \frac{\sigma}{\sqrt{N}}\chi,$$

where $A_N = \frac{1}{N}S_N$ and χ is a random variable with standard normal distribution.

3.2   Efficiency of the Test

Suppose $v \in K$. In this case $\mu = \frac{p(v)}{\alpha} - 1 = \beta(\frac{1}{\alpha} - 1)^2$, and $\sigma^2 = \frac{p(v)(1 - p(v))}{\alpha^2}$, which can be computed in terms of α and β. We also take $N = \frac{1}{(\alpha\beta)^2}$, as in [8].

We first consider the probability that the question "$A_N > \beta(\frac{1}{\alpha} - 1)^2$?" will return true. Equivalently, we consider the probability that

$$\mu + \frac{\sigma}{\sqrt{N}} \chi > \beta \left(\frac{1}{\alpha} - 1 \right)^2 = \mu,$$

which is the probability that $\chi > 0$. But this probability is $1 - \mathfrak{N}(0) = 1 - 0.5 = 0.5$. In other words, the "efficiency" of this test is such that it detects a vector $v \in \mathcal{K}$ (which is actually in $\mathcal{K}$) roughly half of the time. If we are to collect $n - r$ linearly independent vectors in $\mathcal{K}$, then we must perform on average $2(n - r)q^r$ tests.

3.3 Reliability of the Test

Let us now compute the probability that this question returns a false-positive; i.e., the question "$A_N > \beta(\frac{1}{\alpha} - 1)^2$?" returns true for $v \notin \mathcal{K}$. Here we must consider the probability that

$$\mu + \frac{\sigma}{\sqrt{N}} \chi > \beta \left(\frac{1}{\alpha} - 1 \right)^2, \tag{1}$$

where now $\mu = 0$ and $\sigma^2 = \frac{1-\alpha}{\alpha}$. For example, if we take $\alpha = 0.59$ and $\beta = 2^{-6}$ as in the examples given in [8], then this is the probability that $\chi > 0.9819$, which is $1 - \mathfrak{N}(0.9819) \doteq 1 - 0.8369 = 0.1631$. This quantity gives us a measure of the "reliability" of this test in the sense that it tells us that roughly 16% of the $n - r$ vectors that our test leads us to believe are in $\mathcal{K}$ actually are *not* in $\mathcal{K}$. Though this might seem like a serious problem, it can be remedied by repeating the test a few times, each time with a different set of vectors $v'_1, \ldots, v'_N$. In the example above, by taking $8N$ vectors v'_i, performing the test 8 times with a new set of N vectors each time, and rejecting the vector v if any of the 8 tests fails, the probability that we correctly conclude that $v \in \mathcal{K}$ is $1 - (.1631)^8 \doteq 0.9999995$. This in turn means that the probability that there are no false-positives among our final set of $n - r$ vectors is $(1 - (.1631)^8)^{130} \doteq 0.9999349$. Therefore, if we perform 8 tests on $\frac{2(n-r)q^r}{0.1631}$ vectors, then the probability that we have $n - r$ vectors in $\mathcal{K}$ is 0.9999349.

We note that the above is a description of a modified version of Technique 1 for which a much higher degree of reliability is obtained. The authors in [8] do not necessarily require such a high level of reliability from Technique 1 since they also use Technique 2, which we have not yet addressed, as a filter to find those elements from Technique 1 which are actually in $\mathcal{K}$. Later in this paper we will show that Technique 2 will not be practical once we add external perturbation in the form of the Plus method. Therefore, we have presented Technique 1 is it must be implemented to be used without filters.

4 Preventing Differential Attacks on PMI

One way to prevent the differential attack is to perturb the system so that the dimension of the kernel of the differential L_v is the same for nearly every vector in k^n. This can be achieved by adding a sufficient number of randomly chosen quadratic polynomials according to the Plus method [14].

4.1   Perturbed Matsumoto-Imai-Plus

We now present the Perturbed Matsumoto-Imai-Plus cryptosystem. We will use the same notation as before. In particular, let L_2 and $\bar{\bar{F}}$ be as defined in Section 2.2. Randomly pick a quadratic polynomials $q_i(x_1, \ldots, x_n)$ and define the map $\bar{\bar{F}}^+ : k^n \longrightarrow k^{n+a}$

$$\bar{\bar{F}}^+ = \left(\bar{\bar{F}}_1, \bar{\bar{F}}_2, \ldots, \bar{\bar{F}}_n, q_1, \ldots, q_a \right).$$

Let $\hat{L}_1$ be a randomly chosen invertible affine map on k^{n+a} and define the map $\hat{F}^+ : k^n \longrightarrow k^{n+a}$ by

$$\hat{F}^+(x_1, \ldots, x_n) = \hat{L}_1 \circ \bar{\bar{F}}^+ \circ L_2(x_1, \ldots, x_n) = (\hat{y}_1, \ldots, \hat{y}_{n+a}),$$

The public key of the Perturbed Matsumoto-Imai-Plus (PMI+) cryptosystem consists of the $n + a$ quadratic polynomial components $\hat{y}_i$ of $\hat{F}$. Clearly PMI+ is simply PMI with a additional random quadratic polynomials (externally) mixed into the system by $\hat{L}_1$.

To decrypt, we must first invert $\hat{L}_1$. After we set aside the last a components, we can then apply the decryption process for the associated PMI. We note that the extra a components can be used to determine the true plaintext from among the (possibly q^r) preimages of the given ciphertext. We now study the effect that the Plus polynomials have on the computation of $\mathcal{K}$ using the differential attack.

4.2   PMI+ and the Effect on $\mathcal{K}$

We begin with the case where $\gcd(\theta, n) = 1$. Here $\dim(\ker(L_v)) = 1$ for every $v \in \mathcal{K}$. The fact that $\dim(\ker(L_v)) \neq 1$ for many $v \notin \mathcal{K}$ is the very fact that Technique 1 exploits in computing $\mathcal{K}$. So our task is to perturb PMI so that $\dim(\ker(L_v)) = 1$ for nearly every $v \notin \mathcal{K}$.

Consider the effect on the linear differential $L_v(x)$ upon adding Plus polynomials. We write $M_{v,a}$ for the matrix associated with the linear differential obtained after adding a Plus polynomials, and in particular, $M_{v,0}$ for the matrix associated with the linear differential L_v with no Plus polynomials. Let $R(a)$ be the rank of the matrix $M_{v,a}$. Note that $R(a) < n$, since $M_{v,a} v^T = 0$ for any a.

Suppose we add one more Plus polynomial (increase a by one). What is the probability that $R(a + 1) = R(a) + 1$? Note that if $R(a) = n - 1$, then this probability is zero since $R(a) < n$. So let's assume $R(a) = n - i$, where $i = 2, 3, \ldots, n - 1$. This probability is equivalent to the probability that we choose a new row-vector to be added to form $M_{v,a+1}$ from $M_{v,a}$, which is orthogonal to v and is not in the span of the row-vectors of $M_{v,a}$. The space of vectors orthogonal to v is of dimension $n - 1$, and the span of the row-vectors of $M_{v,a}$ is of dimension $n - i$, hence the probability that $R(a + 1) = R(a) + 1$ will be

$1 - 2^{1-i}$, where $i = 2, 3, \ldots, n - 1$. Thus, if $n_{\delta,a}$ is the number of vectors v with $\dim\left(\ker\left(M_{v,a}\right)\right) = \delta$, for a given a and $\delta = 1, 2, \ldots, n - 1$, then we expect:

$$n_{\delta,a+1} = n_{\delta,a} \cdot 2^{1-\delta} + n_{\delta+1,a} \cdot \left(1 - 2^{-\delta}\right)$$

In order to obtain the distribution for $n_{\delta,a}$ when $a = 0$, and to predict how large we must choose a in order to protect PMI+ from the differential attack, we will use the language of Markov chains [9]. Let $P = (p_{ij})$ be the $n \times n$ matrix with entries given by:

$$p_{ij} = \begin{cases} 2^{-i+1}, & \text{if } i = j; \\ 1 - 2^{-i+1}, & \text{if } i = j + 1; \\ 0, & \text{otherwise.} \end{cases}$$

Then for a fixed vector $v \in k^n$, p_{ij} gives the 1-step transition probability from state s_i to s_j upon appending a randomly chosen row vector to $M_{v,a}$, where state s_i corresponds to nullity$(M_{v,a}) = i$. Here s_1 is an absorbing state and for all other $i \neq 1$, s_i is a transient state.

Let $\mathcal{M}_v$ be the matrix associated with MI for a given v. Without loss of generality, assume that L_2 is chosen so the the perturbation Z is a function only of r variables, say $x_1, \ldots, x_r$. Adding the perturbation then is analogous to removing the first r columns of $\mathcal{M}_v$ and replacing them with r randomly chosen column vectors. Deleting r columns will increase the nullity to either $r + 1$ with probability $\binom{n-1}{r}/\binom{n}{r} = 1 - \frac{r}{n}$, or r with probability $\binom{n-1}{r-1}/\binom{n}{r} = \frac{r}{n}$. If we then add r random column vectors to this matrix one at a time, the nullity will increase according to r-step transition probability matrix P_r^r, where P_r is the top-left $(r + 1) \times (r + 1)$ submatrix of P. In particular, if we let $\pi_0 = (0, 0, \ldots, 0, \frac{r}{n}, 1 - \frac{r}{n})$ be the initial state distribution vector, then $\pi_0 P_r^r$ can be used to calculate the probability that nullity$(M_{v,0}) = i$. For example, if $n = 31$ and $r = 6$, then these probabilities are given by:

$$\pi_0 P_6^6 = \begin{pmatrix} 0.350125 \\ 0.539086 \\ 0.106813 \\ 3.94582 \times 10^{-3} \\ 3.01929 \times 10^{-5} \\ 4.67581 \times 10^{-8} \\ 1.17354 \times 10^{-11} \end{pmatrix}$$

Finally, to obtain the probability that nullity$(M_{v,a}) = i$, we let $\pi' = \pi_0 P_r^r$ and compute $\pi' P^a$

We performed experiments to test the validity of our model. Each experiment was characterized by an instance of PMI defined by the parameters (q, n, r, θ), the number of Plus polynomials a, and κ randomly chosen test vectors. For each test vector v, we computed $\dim\left(\ker\left(M_{v,a}\right)\right)$. Tables 1 and 2 report the observed (predicted) values of $n_{\delta,a}$ for two experiments performed with parameters $(q, n, r, \theta, \kappa) = (2, 31, 6, 2, 2^{15})$ and $(2, 36, 6, 4, 2^{15})$, respectively, each with $a = 0, 1, 2, \ldots, 11$. The predictions for $a = 0$ are obtained from the matrix

Table 1. Observed (predicted) values of $n_{\delta,a}$ for $(q,n,r,\theta,\kappa) = (2,31,6,2,2^{15})$ and $a = 0,1,\ldots,11$

	$v \notin \mathcal{K}$				$v \in \mathcal{K}$
a	$\delta = 1$	$\delta = 2$	$\delta = 3$	$\delta = 4$	$\delta = 1$
0	19003 (11304)	12182 (17404)	1081 (3448)	19 (127)	483
1	25081 (25094)	6906 (6902)	298 (287)	0 (2)	483
2	28548 (28534)	3660 (3676)	77 (74)	0 (0)	483
3	30366 (30378)	1896 (1888)	23 (19)	0 (0)	483
4	31334 (31314)	944 (965)	7 (6)	0 (0)	483
5	31810 (31806)	473 (477)	2 (2)	0 (0)	483
6	32040 (32046)	244 (238)	1 (0)	0 (0)	483
7	32154 (32162)	130 (123)	1 (0)	0 (0)	483
8	32208 (32219)	77 (66)	0 (0)	0 (0)	483
9	32246 (32246)	39 (38)	0 (0)	0 (0)	483
10	32263 (32266)	22 (20)	0 (0)	0 (0)	483
11	32278 (32274)	7 (11)	0 (0)	0 (0)	483

Table 2. Observed (predicted) values of $n_{\delta,a}$ for $(q,n,r,\theta,\kappa) = (2,36,6,4,2^{15})$ and $a = 0,1,\ldots,11$

	$v \notin \mathcal{K}$					$v \in \mathcal{K}$			
a	$\delta = 1$	$\delta = 2$	$\delta = 3$	$\delta = 4$	$\delta = 5$	$\delta = 1$	$\delta = 2$	$\delta = 3$	$\delta = 4$
0	14602 (101)	14942 (2274)	2610 (16272)	120 (1865)	2 (37)	0	0	0	492
1	21975 (22073)	9550 (9428)	722 (758)	28 (17)	1 (0)	0 (0)	0 (0) (0)	433 (430)	59 (62)
2	26693 (26750)	5367 (5316)	210 (205)	6 (4)	0 (0)	0 (0)	322 (325)	165 (160)	5 (7)
3	29380 (29376)	2838 (2841)	58 (58)	0 (1)	0 (0)	167 (161)	273 (285)	52 (46)	0 (1)
4	30810 (30799)	1457 (1462)	9 (14)	0 (0)	0 (0)	295 (304)	180 (176)	17 (13)	0 (0)
5	31519 (31538)	756 (735)	1 (2)	0 (0)	0 (0)	383 (385)	106 (103)	3 (4)	0 (0)
6	31916 (31897)	359 (379)	1 (0)	0 (0)	0 (0)	433 (436)	57 (55)	2 (1)	0 (0)
7	32095 (32096)	181 (180)	0 (0)	0 (0)	0 (0)	460 (462)	30 (30)	2 (0)	0 (0)
8	32205 (32186)	71 (90)	0 (0)	0 (0)	0 (0)	470 (475)	21 (16)	1 (0)	0 (0)
9	32246 (32240)	30 (36)	0 (0)	0 (0)	0 (0)	481 (480)	11 (11)	0 (0)	0 (0)
10	32258 (32261)	18 (15)	0 (0)	0 (0)	0 (0)	487 (486)	5 (6)	0 (0)	0 (0)
11	32270 (32267)	6 (9)	0 (0)	0 (0)	0 (0)	490 (490)	2 (2)	0 (0)	0 (0)

$\pi' = \pi_0 P_r^r$, while the predictions for $a > 0$ are obtained by using the observed distribution from $a - 1$ and the 1-step transition matrix P_r.

We note that although the predictions for $a = 0$ are not as accurate as those for $a > 0$, this is likely due to the fact that we chose the perturbation variables $z_1, \ldots, z_r$ in a simplified way for the experiments.

It remains to predict how large a must be in order to protect PMI+ against a differential attack. As was previously stated, the effect of adding Plus polynomials is to increase the value of α. In the example given in [8] $\alpha \doteq 0.59$ and so the question "$A_N > \beta(\frac{1}{\alpha} - 1)^2$?" is answered with a false-positive with the probability that $\chi > 0.9819$, which is 0.1631. Now suppose the attacker is willing to do as much as 2^{2w} work to correctly decide the answer to this test with this same probability. Then Inequality (1) becomes

$$\chi > \frac{\sqrt{N}}{\sigma} \left[\beta \left(\frac{1}{\alpha} - 1 \right)^2 - \mu \right] = 2^{w-r} \left(\frac{1-\alpha}{\alpha} \right)^{3/2}.$$

If we assume that we are using Technique 1 as described in Section 4, then our total work (for the entire attack) will be

$$8N \cdot \frac{n^3}{6} \cdot \frac{2(n-r)q^r}{0.1631} \doteq 2^{2w+38.32},$$

which if we want less than 2^{80} then we must have $w < 20.84$. This implies that we must take $2^{14.84} \left(\frac{1-\alpha}{\alpha} \right)^{3/2} < 0.9819$, or $\alpha > 0.998962$ if we wish to thwart this attack. To compute the value of a necessary to insure $\alpha > 0.998962$, we use the matrix P. In particular, we must compute a so that the first entry of $\pi' P^a$ is greater than 0.998962. If we take $n = 136$, $r = 6$, and $\gcd(\theta, n) = 1$, then we must take $a \geq 10$.

Finally, we consider $\gcd(\theta, n) \neq 1$. Let $g = \gcd(\theta, n)$. If $v \in \mathcal{K}$, then nullity $(M_{v,0}) = g$; otherwise nullity$(M_{v,0}) \in \{g - r, \ldots, g + r\}$. We must now add roughly g Plus polynomials just to get to a situation similar to the $g = 1$ case. Thus, by taking $a \doteq g + 10$, we can protect the special case of $g \neq 1$ from the differential attack.

4.3   Using Filters with the Differential Attack and Other Security Concerns

We now address Technique 2 of [8]. The idea of this technique is to look for a maximal clique in the graph with vertices $v \in k^n$ such that $T(v) = 0$, where two vertices v, v' are connected if $T(v + v') = 0$. Since $\mathcal{K}$ is a subspace of k^n, the elements of $\mathcal{K}$ form a clique. The hypothesis underlying Technique 2 is that if we look at a big enough subgraph then the maximal clique in this subgraph will consist almost exclusively of vectors from $\mathcal{K}$. However, by increasing the value of α near one, this clique is now very likely to have many elements *not* in $\mathcal{K}$ (in fact almost *every* element of k^n is in the clique) and therefore membership in this clique cannot be used as a filter to Technique 1.

We must be careful not to add too many extra polynomials since otherwise we may create a weakness to Gröbner bases attacks [2, 16]. From [5], we know that if we choose $r = 6$ and $n > 83$, then we can expect the PMI cryptosystem to have the security of 2^{80} against such an attack using F_4. In order to create a secure PMI+ scheme from these parameters, we suggest $(q, n, r, \theta) = (2, 84, 6, 4)$ and $a = 14$. Since we have added relatively very few extra polynomials, the attack complexity of F_4 will be essentially the same as it is for the corresponding PMI. Other secure implementations include the now-salvaged scheme $(q, n, r, \theta) = (2, 136, 6, 8)$ with $a = 18$, or any (q, n, r, θ) with $a = 11$, $g = 1$, $r = 6$ and $n > 84$. In summary, when designing PMI+, one must be careful with the choice of $g = \gcd(\theta, n)$, as $g + 10$ extra polynomials will be needed in order to defend against the differential attack, but if g is too large the extra polynomials may increase the vulnerability to a Gröbner basis attack.

Of course, it may also be possible to attack PMI+ by looking for ways to somehow separate the PMI polynomials from the Plus polynomials. If this was possible, the differential attack could then proceed as with PMI alone. However this approach has yet to be successfully applied to the MI-Minus-Plus cryptosystem [14], as we have no such method to differentiate between MI polynomials and random polynomials. Therefore, it seems unlikely that such an approach will be successfully applied to PMI+.

As we mentioned before, the extra Plus polynomials can be used to identify the true plaintext from among all preimages of a given ciphertext. Though the Plus polynomials slightly decrease the efficiency and increase the key sizes of the scheme, they do serve to both protect against the differential attack and aid in finding the true plaintext during the decryption process.

Recently, the perturbation method was also applied to the HFE cryptosystem to improve its security and efficiency [4]. Our preliminary experiments suggest that the differential analysis attack cannot be used to attack HFE, though further experiments and theoretical arguments are needed to confirm this hypothesis.

5   Conclusion

We have presented a method for preventing differential attacks against multivariate schemes. In particular, we have shown that by externally adding as few as 10 Plus polynomials in the case where $\gcd(\theta, n) = 1$, we create a new scheme (PMI+) which is resistant to the differential attack. Since very few extra polynomials are needed, the threat posed by Gröbner bases attacks is not significantly increased. If $g = \gcd(\theta, n) \neq 1$, then as few as $g + 10$ Plus polynomials will be needed to protect PMI+, though we do not claim PMI+ will be secure against Gröbner bases attacks if g is large. In any case, as long as the external perturbation is not too large, the efficiency of PMI+ will not be significantly degraded. In fact, the extra Plus polynomials can be used to identify the true plaintext from among all pre-images of a given ciphertext. For use in practical implementations, which will enjoy a security level of 2^{80}, we suggest that $n \geq 83$, $r = 6$ and $a = 14$ whenever $g \leq 4$. In particular the scheme $(q, n, r, \theta) = (2, 136, 6, 8)$ with $a = 18$ will be both very efficient and have a security level of 2^{80}. Sizes for the public keys of these implementations are roughly 41 kilobytes and 175 kilobytes, respectively.

References

1. M.-L. Akkar, N. T. Courtois, R. Duteuil, and L. Goubin. *A Fast and Secure Implementation of Sflash*. In *PKC 2003*, LNCS 2567:267–278.
2. N. Courtois, A. Klimov, J. Patarin, and A. Shamir. *Efficient Algorithms for Solving Overdefined Systems of Multivariate Polynomial Equations*. In *Eurocrypt 2000*, LNCS 1807:392–407.

3. Jintai Ding. *A New Variant of the Matsumoto-Imai Cryptosystem Through Perturbation.* In *PKC 2004*, LNCS 2947:305–318.
4. J. Ding and D. Schmidt. *Cryptanalysis of HFEv and Internal Perturbation of HFE.* In *PKC 2005*, LNCS 3386:288–301.
5. J. Ding, J. E. Gower, D. Schmidt, C. Wolf, and Z. Yin. *Complexity Estimates for the F_4 Attack on the Perturbed Matsumoto-Imai Cryptosystem.* In the proceedings of the *Tenth IMA International Conference on Cryptography and Coding*, LNCS, 3796:262–277.
6. Jean-Charles Faugère. *A New Efficient Algorithm for Computing Gröbner Bases (F_4).* In *Journal of Applied and Pure Algebra*, 139:61–88, June 1999.
7. William Feller. An Introduction to Probability Theory and Its Applications. Third edition, vol. I, Wiley & Sons, 1968.
8. P.-A. Fouque, L. Granboulan, and J. Stern. *Differential Cryptanalysis for Multivariate Schemes.* In *Eurocrypt 2005*, LNCS 3494:341–353.
9. J. G. Kemeny and J. L. Snell. Finite Markov Chains. D. Van Nostrand Company, Inc., 1960.
10. T. Matsumoto and H. Imai. *Public Quadratic Polynomial-Tuples for Efficient Signature-Verification and Message-Encryption.* In *Eurocrypt 1988*, LNCS 330: 419–453.
11. NESSIE. European project IST-1999-12324 on New European Schemes for Signature, Integrity and Encryption. http://www.cryptonessie.org.
12. Jacques Patarin. *Cryptanalysis of the Matsumoto and Imai Public Key Scheme of Eurocrypt'88.* In *Crypto 1995*, LNCS 963:248–261.
13. Jacques Patarin. *Hidden Fields Equations (HFE) and Isomorphisms of Polynomials (IP): Two New Families of Asymmetric Algorithms.* In *Eurocrypt 1996*, LNCS 1070:33–48. Extended version: http://www.minrank.org/hfe.pdf.
14. J. Patarin, L. Goubin, and N. Courtois. C^{*}_{-+} *and HM: Variations Around Two Schemes of T. Matsumoto and H. Imai.* In *Asiacrypt 1998*, LNCS 1514:35–50.
15. B.-Y. Yang, J.-M. Chen, and Y.-H. Chen. Private communication.
16. B.-Y. Yang, J.-M. Chen, and N. Courtois. *On Asymptotic Security Estimates in XL and Gröbner Bases-Related Algebraic Cryptanalysis.* In *ICICS 2004*, LNCS 3269:410–413.

Random Subgroups of Braid Groups: An Approach to Cryptanalysis of a Braid Group Based Cryptographic Protocol

Alexei Myasnikov[1,*], Vladimir Shpilrain[2,*], and Alexander Ushakov[3]

[1] Department of Mathematics, McGill University, Quebec H3A 2T5, Montreal
alexeim@math.mcgill.ca
[2] Department of Mathematics, The City College of New York, NY 10031, New York
shpilrain@yahoo.com
[3] Department of Mathematics, Stevens Institute of Technology, NJ 07030, Hoboken
aushakov@mail.ru

Abstract. Motivated by cryptographic applications, we study subgroups of braid groups B_n generated by a small number of random elements of relatively small lengths compared to n. Our experiments show that "most" of these subgroups are equal to the whole B_n, and "almost all" of these subgroups are generated by positive braid words. We discuss the impact of these experimental results on the security of the Anshel-Anshel-Goldfeld key exchange protocol [2] with originally suggested parameters as well as with recently updated ones.

1 Introduction

Braid group cryptography has attracted a lot of attention recently due to several suggested key exchange protocols (see [2], [11]) using braid groups as a platform. We refer to [3], [5] for more information on braid groups.

Here we start out by giving a brief description of the Anshel-Anshel-Goldfeld key exchange protocol [2] (subsequently called the AAG protocol) to explain our motivation.

Let B_n be the group of braids on n strands and $X_n = \{x_1, \ldots, x_{n-1}\}$ the set of standard generators. Thus,

$$B_n = \langle x_1, \ldots, x_{n-1}; \ x_i x_{i+1} x_i = x_{i+1} x_i x_{i+1}, \ x_i x_j = x_j x_i \text{ for } |i - j| > 1 \rangle.$$

Let $N_1, N_2 \in \mathbb{N}$, $1 \leq L_1 \leq L_2$, and $L \in \mathbb{N}$ be preset parameters. The AAG protocol [2] is the following sequence of steps:

(1) Alice randomly generates an N_1-tuple of braid words $\bar{a} = \{a_1, \ldots a_{N_1}\}$, each of length between L_1 and L_2, such that each generator of B_n non-trivially occurs in $\bar{a}$. The tuple $\bar{a}$ is called *Alice's public set*.

(2) Bob randomly generates an N_2-tuple of braid words $\bar{b} = \{b_1, \ldots b_{N_2}\}$, each of length between L_1 and L_2, such that each generator of B_n is non-trivially involved in $\bar{b}$. The tuple $\bar{b}$ is called *Bob's public set*.

---

* Partially supported by the NSF grant DMS-0405105.

M. Yung et al. (Eds.): PKC 2006, LNCS 3958, pp. 302–314, 2006.

(3) Alice randomly generates a product $A = a_{s_1}^{\varepsilon_1} \ldots a_{s_L}^{\varepsilon_L}$, where $1 \leq s_i \leq N_1$ and $\varepsilon_i = \pm 1$ (for each $1 \leq i \leq L$). The word A is called *Alice's private key*.

(4) Bob randomly generates a product $B = b_{t_1}^{\delta_1} \ldots b_{t_L}^{\delta_L}$, where $1 \leq t_i \leq N_2$ and $\delta_i = \pm 1$ (for each $1 \leq i \leq L$). The word B is called *Bob's private key*.

(5) Alice computes $b_i' = D(A^{-1}b_i A)$ $(1 \leq i \leq N_2)$ and transmits them to Bob. Here $D(w)$ denotes Dehornoy's form of a braid word w (see the beginning of the next Section 2).

(6) Bob computes $a_i' = D(B^{-1}a_i B)$ $(1 \leq i \leq N_1)$ and transmits them to Alice.

(7) Alice computes $K_A = A^{-1}a_{s_1}'^{\varepsilon_1} \ldots a_{s_L}'^{\varepsilon_L}$. It is straightforward to see that $K_A = A^{-1}B^{-1}AB$ in the group B_n.

(8) Bob computes $K_B = b_{t_L}'^{-\delta_L} \ldots b_{t_1}'^{-\delta_1} B$. Again, it is easy to see that $K_B = A^{-1}B^{-1}AB$ in the group B_n.

Thus, Alice and Bob end up with the same element $K = K_A = K_B = A^{-1}B^{-1}AB$ of the group B_n. This K is now their common secret key.

Note that for an intruder to get the common secret key K, it is sufficient to find any element $C = a_{r_1}^{\tau_1} \ldots a_{r_m}^{\tau_m}$ such that $\overline{b}' = C^{-1}\overline{b}C$ in the group B_n (see e.g. [11], [15]). Finding such an element is an instance of the following problem (call it *subgroup-restricted conjugacy search problem* for future reference):

> Let G be a group, A a subgroup of G generated by some $\{a_1, \ldots a_r\}$, and let $\overline{g} = (g_1, \ldots g_k)$, $\overline{h} = (h_1, \ldots h_k)$ be two tuples of elements of G. Find $x \in A$, as a word in $\{a_1, \ldots a_r\}$, such that $\overline{h} = x^{-1}\overline{g}x$, provided that at least one such x exists.

Without the restriction $x \in A$, this would be a well-known (multiple simultaneous) *conjugacy search problem*. While the latter problem for braid groups is not known to have polynomial-time solution, some important recently made inroads [7], [12] suggest that it may be solved quite efficiently by a deterministic algorithm for at least some inputs, e.g. if one of the tuples $\overline{g}$ or $\overline{h}$ consists of positive braid words only. Thus, having the above subgroup $A \leq B_n$ significantly different from B_n should be important for the security of the AAG protocol.

In the present paper, we experimentally show that the parameters

$$N = 80, \ N_1 = 20, \ N_2 = 20, \ L_1 = 5, \ L_2 = 8, \ L = 100$$

for the AAG protocol suggested in [1] may not provide sufficient level of security because the relevant subgroup $A \leq B_n$ is either the whole B_n or is "very close" to the whole B_n.

> More specifically, out of 100 experiments that we performed, a randomly selected tuple $\overline{a} = (a_1, \ldots, a_{N_1})$ with parameters as above (see our Section 5 for details on producing random tuples) generated the whole group B_n in 63 experiments. In the remaining 37 experiments, the subgroups were "close" to the whole group B_n, and in 36 of them, the subgroups were generated by positive braid words. See Section 4 for more details.

Similar results were obtained in [9] using homomorphisms of braid groups onto permutation groups. In this paper we go further and extend these results to recently suggested greater parameter values; this is discussed later in this section. Our approach to cryptanalysis of the AAG protocol (we call it the "subgroup attack") is rather general and can be used in cryptanalysis of commutator key exchange schemes based on other groups.

In the AAG protocol, there are two subgroups $\bar{a} = (a_1, \ldots, a_{N_1})$ and $\bar{b} = (b_1, \ldots, b_{N_2})$ each of which is generated independently of the other. The following procedure can be used to attack the AAG protocol:

(1) Given two tuples $\bar{a}$ and $\bar{b}$, simplify them using the procedure(s) in our Section 3.

(2) Both simplified tuples will consist of positive braid words with probability 98% (99% each), see the list in the beginning of our Section 4. In that case, the corresponding multiple simultaneous conjugacy search problem can be efficiently solved by the method of [12] (using super summit sets).

(3) With probability 98% (99% each), the centralizer of Alice's and Bob's subgroup coincides with the center of B_n. Therefore, any solution of the multiple simultaneous conjugacy search problem obtained by using, say, the method of [12] mentioned above, will differ from the actual Alice's (Bob's) private key by a factor lying in the center of B_n. This will yield the correct common secret key K because K is the commutator $K = A^{-1}B^{-1}AB$, and therefore its value does not change if either A or B or both are multiplied by elements from the center of the ambient group B_n. Thus, one does not have to solve the subgroup-restricted conjugacy search problem in this case.

The above claim that the centralizer of any subgroup (except the last one) on the list in the beginning of Section 4 coincides with the center of B_n, follows from the following fact: any element in the group B_n that commutes with x_i^k for some positive k, also commutes with x_i. This, in turn, follows from the results of [8].

Thus, it appears that with probability at least $98\% \cdot 98\% \approx 96\%$, the AAG protocol (with parameters as in [1]) can be successfully attacked by the procedure outlined above.

We note that by increasing the crucial parameters L_1 and L_2 (and therefore increasing the lengths of the private keys), it is probably possible to downsize the relevant subgroup so that the method of [12] would not work. However, for public sets with longer elements, length-based attacks, as described in [6], [9], [10], may become a threat, although it seems that the existing experimental base is insufficient to draw any definitive conclusions on using longer keys in the AAG protocol.

Another possible way of improving security of the AAG protocol might be increasing the rank of the ambient braid group. However, we have run similar experiments with $N = 150$, $N_1 = 20$, $N_2 = 20$, $L_1 = 10$, $L_2 = 13$, $L = 100$

and arrived at similar results: with probability at least 92%, the AAG protocol with these parameters can be successfully attacked by our procedure.

The arrangement of the paper is as follows. In Section 2, we introduce some more notation and describe an algorithm from [13] producing a shorter word representing a given braid word. In Section 3, we describe a heuristic procedure which allows us to simplify a given set of generators of a subgroup in B_n. In Section 4, we describe results of our experiments. In Section 5, we explain how these experimental results affect the security of the AAG protocol. Finally, in Section 5, we describe our procedure for producing random subgroup generators as in the AAG protocol.

2   Preliminaries

Let $F(X_n)$ be the free group generated by X_n. An element of $F(X_n)$ is a reduced word over $X_n^{\pm 1}$ referred to as a *braid word*. For a braid word $w = w_1 \ldots w_k \in F(X_n)$ we will denote by $|w|$ its length k and by $|w|_{B_n}$ the length of a shortest braid word w' defining the same element of B_n as w does. There is no efficient way to compute $|w|_{B_n}$; in [14] the authors prove that the problem of computing a geodesic for a braid word is co-NP-complete. We will employ Algorithm 1 from [13] to obtain a shorter word representing a given braid word w; description of this algorithm is given below, for the sake of completeness. For relatively short words w considered in this paper, one almost always has $|Shorten(w)| = |w|_{B_n}$ (where $|Shorten(w)|$ is the output of Algorithm 1 in [13]; see [13] for more information).

By Dehornoy's form of a braid we mean a braid word without any "handles", i.e. a completely reduced braid word in the sense of [4]. The procedure that computes Dehornoy's form for a given word chooses a specific ("permitted") handle inside of the word and removes it (see [1] or [4]). This can introduce new handles but the main result about Dehornoy's forms states that any sequence of handle reductions eventually terminates. Of course, the result depends on how one chooses the handles at every step. Let us fix any particular strategy for selecting handles. For a word $w = w(X_n)$ we denote by $D(w)$ the corresponding Dehornoy's form (i.e., the result of handle reductions where handles are chosen by the fixed strategy).

Now we describe Algorithm 1 from [13]. This algorithm tries to minimize a given braid word. It uses the property of Dehornoy's form that for a "generic" braid word one has $|D(w)| < |w|$.

Algorithm 1. *(Minimization of braids)*
SIGNATURE. $w' = Shorten(w)$.
INPUT. *A word $w = w(x_1, \ldots, x_{n-1})$ in generators of the braid group B_n.*
OUTPUT. *A word w' such that $|w'| \leq |w|$ and $w' = w$ in B_n.*
INITIALIZATION. *Put $w_0 = w$ and $i = 0$.*
COMPUTATIONS.

A. *Increment i.*
B. *Put $w_i = D(w_{i-1})$.*
C. *If $|w_i| < |w_{i-1}|$ then*
    1) Put $w_i = w_i^{\Delta}$.
    2) Goto A.
D. *If i is even then output w_{i+1}^{Δ}.*
E. *If i is odd then output w_{i+1}.*

3   Subgroup Simplification

In this section we describe a heuristic procedure which allows us to simplify a given set of generators of a subgroup in B_n.

3.1   Reducing Generating Sets

Let S be a set of words in the alphabet X_n. We say that the set S is *reduced* if:

1) $|w| = |w|_{B_n}$ for each $w \in S$, i.e., each word from S is geodesic in B_n.
2) For each pair of words $u, v \in S$ and any numbers $\varepsilon, \delta \in \{-1, 1\}$, one has

$$|u^{\varepsilon} v^{\delta}|_{B_n} > ||u|_{B_n} - |v|_{B_n}|.$$

(Otherwise, the total length of elements of S can be reduced by replacing the longer of the words u, v by $u^{\varepsilon} v^{\delta}$.)

Let $\langle S \rangle$ denote the subgroup generated by S. We say that two sets $S, T \subseteq B_n$ are *equivalent* if $\langle S \rangle = \langle T \rangle$ in B_n.

The following algorithm tries to reduce a given set S, i.e., tries to find a reduced set equivalent to S. As mentioned above, the problem of finding a geodesic for a given braid word is computationally hard. Instead, we are using here the procedure *Shorten* (Algorithm 1 in [13]) to minimize the length of braid words. Thus, in general, the output of Algorithm 2 may not be a reduced set of braid words, but for generating sets meeting the requirements in [1], this is usually the case.

Algorithm 2. *(Reduction of a generating set)*
SIGNATURE. $T = Reduce(S)$.
INPUT. *A finite set S of braid words.*
OUTPUT. *A finite reduced set T of braid words which is equivalent to S.*
INITIALIZATION. *Put $T = S$.*
COMPUTATIONS.

A. *For each word $w \in T$, replace w with the word $Shorten(w)$ (cf. Algorithm 1 in [13]). Remove the empty word if produced.*
B. *For each pair of words $u, v \in T$ and numbers $\varepsilon, \delta \in \{-1, 1\}$, compute $w = Shorten(u^{\varepsilon} v^{\delta})$.*
    1) If $|w| = ||u| - |v|| = 0$ then remove v from the current set T.
    2) If $|w| = ||u| - |v|| \neq 0$ then remove from T the longer of the words u, v and add w to T.

C. *When all pairs of words $u, v \in T$ are handled (including the new words) output the current set T.*

Proposition 1. *Algorithm 2 terminates on any finite subset S of $F(X_n)$. Furthermore, if $T = Reduce(S)$, then $\langle T \rangle = \langle S \rangle$.*

Proof. Since each reduction decreases the total length of the generating set, the number of reductions Algorithm 2 performs is finite and limited by $L(S)$, the total length of elements of S.

To prove the second statement observe that the transformations used in Algorithm 2 are Nielsen transformations; they do not change the subgroup generated by a given set.

Let $(\bar{a}, \bar{a}')$ be a pair of conjugate tuples of braid words and $(\bar{z}, \bar{z}')$ be a pair of conjugate tuples of braid words. We say that tuples $(\bar{a}, \bar{a}')$ and $(\bar{z}, \bar{z}')$ are equivalent if the following conditions hold:

(E1) The tuples $\bar{a}$ and $\bar{z}$ define the same subgroup (i.e., $\langle \bar{a} \rangle = \langle \bar{z} \rangle$).
(E2) For any braid word $x \in B_n$ $x^{-1} \bar{a} x = \bar{a}'$ if and only if $x^{-1} \bar{z} x = \bar{z}'$.

Observe that from (E1), (E2), and the fact that tuples are conjugate follows that $\langle \bar{a}' \rangle = \langle \bar{z}' \rangle$.

Now assume that we have two conjugate tuples $\bar{a}$ and $\bar{a}'$ of braid words as in the AAG protocol. The next algorithm reduces the pair $(\bar{a}, \bar{a}')$.

Algorithm 3. *(Reduction of conjugate tuples)*
SIGNATURE. $(\bar{z}, \bar{z}') = Reduce(\bar{a}, \bar{a}')$.
INPUT. *Conjugate tuples $\bar{a} = \{a_1, \ldots, a_{N_1}\}$ and $\bar{a}' = \{a'_1, \ldots, a'_{N_1}\}$ of braid words.*
OUTPUT. *Conjugate tuples $(\bar{z}, \bar{z}')$ equivalent to $(\bar{a}, \bar{a}')$.*
INITIALIZATION. *Put $\bar{z} = \bar{a}$ and $\bar{z}' = \bar{a}'$.*
COMPUTATIONS.

A. *Replace each word $z_i \in \bar{z}'$ with the word $Shorten(z_i)$ (cf. Algorithm 1 in [13]) and each $z'_i \in \bar{z}'$ with $Shorten(z'_i)$. Remove empty words if produced.*
B. *For each pair of words $z_i, z_j \in \bar{z}$ ($i \neq j$) and numbers $\varepsilon, \delta \in \{-1, 1\}$, compute $w = Shorten(z_i^\varepsilon z_j^\delta)$.*
  1) *If $|w| = ||z_j| - |z_i|| = 0$, then remove z_i from $\bar{z}$ and remove z'_i from $\bar{z}'$.*
  2) *If $|w| = |z_j| - |z_i| > 0$, then replace $z_j \in \bar{z}$ with w and replace $z'_j \in \bar{z}'$ with $Shorten(z_i'^\varepsilon z_j'^\delta)$.*
C. *Repeat Step B. while applicable (i.e., while the set S' keeps changing).*
D. *Output the obtained set S'.*

Proposition 2. *Let $(\bar{a}, \bar{a}')$ be a pair of conjugate tuples. Algorithm 3 terminates on $(\bar{a}, \bar{a}')$. Furthermore, if $(\bar{z}, \bar{z}') = Reduce(\bar{a}, \bar{a}')$, then $(\bar{z}, \bar{z}')$ is equivalent to $(\bar{a}, \bar{a}')$.*

Proof. The transformations used in Algorithm 3 are Nielsen transformations; they do not change the subgroup generated by a given set. Hence (E1) holds. Furthermore, by transforming $z_i \in \bar{z}$, we transform $z'_i \in \bar{z}'$ the same way. Thus, the property (E2) holds and the output $(\bar{z}, \bar{z}')$ is equivalent to the input $(\bar{a}, \bar{a}')$.

3.2   Extending Generating Sets

We say that a set $S \cup S'$ is an *extension* of S. The next algorithm heuristically
extends a reduced set of generators S by adding words (one at a time) of length
2 from the subgroup $\langle S \rangle$, and then reduces the set. Basically, the algorithm
generates words from $\langle S \rangle$ using a few patterns and, in case a new word has
length 2, adds it to the current set and reduces the result.

Algorithm 4. *(Extension of a generating set)*
SIGNATURE. $T = Extend(S)$.
INPUT. *A set S of braid words.*
OUTPUT. *A reduced set S' of braid words equivalent to S.*
INITIALIZATION. *Put $T = S$.*
COMPUTATIONS.

A. *For each pair of words $(u, v) \in T$, and each pair of numbers $\varepsilon, \delta \in \{-1, 1\}$:*
   1) *Compute $w = Shorten(v^{2\varepsilon} u^{\delta} v^{-\varepsilon} u^{-\delta} v^{-\varepsilon})$ and $T' = Reduce(T \cup \{w\})$. If $|w| = 2$ and $T \neq T'$, then put $T = T'$.*
   2) *Compute $w = Shorten(v^{\varepsilon} u^{\delta})$ and $T' = Reduce(T \cup \{w\})$. If $|w| = 2$ and $T \neq T'$, then put $T = T'$.*
B. *When all pairs of words $u, v \in T$ are handled (including the new ones), output the current set T.*

Proposition 3. *Algorithm 4 terminates on any finite set S of braid words and, if $T = Extend(S)$, then $\langle S \rangle = \langle T \rangle$.*

Proof. The latter statement is obviously true by Proposition 1 and since each
braid word we add to T defines an element of $\langle S \rangle$.

   Note that Algorithm 4 extends the current set T with braid words w of length
2 only. Moreover, a word $w = x_i^{\varepsilon} x_j^{\delta}$ of length 2 cannot be added twice (the second
time $T' = T$). Thus, Algorithm 4 can add at most $4n^2$ new words to T.

Now assume that we have two conjugate tuples $\overline{a}$ and $\overline{a}'$ of braid words as in
the AAG protocol. The next algorithm computes an extended conjugated pair
of tuples $(\overline{z}, \overline{z}')$ equivalent to $(\overline{a}, \overline{a}')$. In Algorithm 5, for a tuple $\overline{a} = (a_1, \ldots, a_k)$
and a braid word w, by $\overline{a} \cup w$ we denote a tuple $(a_1, \ldots, a_k, w)$.

Algorithm 5. *(Extension of conjugate tuples)*
SIGNATURE. $(\overline{z}, \overline{z}') = Extend(\overline{a}, \overline{a}')$.
INPUT. *Conjugate tuples $\overline{a} = \{a_1, \ldots, a_k\}$ and $\overline{a}' = \{a'_1, \ldots, a'_k\}$ of braid words.*
OUTPUT. *Conjugate "extended" tuples $(\overline{z}, \overline{z}')$ equivalent to $(\overline{a}, \overline{a}')$.*
INITIALIZATION. *Put $\overline{z} = \overline{a}$ and $\overline{z}' = \overline{a}'$.*
COMPUTATIONS.

A. *For each distinct pair of words $(z_i, z_j) \in \overline{a}$, and each pair of numbers $\varepsilon, \delta \in \{-1, 1\}$:*
   1) *Perform the following:*
      – *Compute $w = Shorten(z_i^{2\varepsilon} z_j^{\delta} z_i^{-\varepsilon} z_j^{-\delta} z_i^{-\varepsilon})$.*

- Compute $w' = Shorten(z_i'^{2\varepsilon} z_j'^{\delta} z_i'^{-\varepsilon} z_j'^{-\delta} z_i'^{-\varepsilon})$.
- Compute $(\overline{y}, \overline{y}') = Reduce(\overline{z} \cup \{w\}, \overline{z}' \cup \{w'\})$. If $|w| = 2$ and $(\overline{z}, \overline{z}') \neq (\overline{y}, \overline{y}')$, then put $(\overline{z}, \overline{z}') = (\overline{y}, \overline{y}')$.

2) Perform the following:
- Compute $w = Shorten(z_i^{\varepsilon} z_j^{\delta})$.
- Compute $w' = Shorten(z_i'^{\varepsilon} z_j'^{\delta})$.
- Compute $(\overline{y}, \overline{y}') = Reduce(\overline{z} \cup \{w\}, \overline{z}' \cup \{w'\})$. If $|w| = 2$ and $(\overline{z}, \overline{z}') \neq (\overline{y}, \overline{y}')$, then put $(\overline{z}, \overline{z}') = (\overline{y}, \overline{y}')$.

B. When all pairs of words $z_i, z_j \in S$ are handled (including the new words), output the current pair $(\overline{z}, \overline{z}')$.

Proposition 4. Let $(\overline{a}, \overline{a}')$ be a pair of conjugate tuples. Algorithm 5 terminates on $(\overline{a}, \overline{a}')$. Furthermore, if $(\overline{z}, \overline{z}') = Extend(\overline{a}, \overline{a}')$, then $(\overline{z}, \overline{z}')$ is equivalent to $(\overline{a}, \overline{a}')$.

Proof. Each time we extend the tuples $(\overline{z}, \overline{z}')$ with elements w, w' which follows from the tuples (i.e., $w \in \langle \overline{z} \rangle$ and $w' \in \langle \overline{z}' \rangle$). So, now the property (E1) follows from Proposition 2. Furthermore, braid words w and w' were obtained the same way. Thus, the property (E2) holds and the output $(\overline{z}, \overline{z}')$ is equivalent to the input $(\overline{a}, \overline{a}')$.

We therefore have

Proposition 5. Let $(\overline{a}, \overline{a}')$ and $(\overline{b}, \overline{b}')$ be two pairs of conjugated tuples as in AAG-protocol. Let $(\overline{y}, \overline{y}') = Extend(\overline{a}, \overline{a}')$ and $(\overline{z}, \overline{z}') = Extend(\overline{b}, \overline{b}')$. Then to break the AAG protocol with $(\overline{a}, \overline{a}')$ and $(\overline{b}, \overline{b}')$ it is sufficient to break AAG-protocol with $(\overline{y}, \overline{y}')$ and $(\overline{z}, \overline{z}')$.

Proof. Obvious.

The main point of Proposition 5 is that the obtained instance $(\overline{y}, \overline{y}')$ and $(\overline{z}, \overline{z}')$ of the AAG protocol is easier to break than the original $(\overline{a}, \overline{a}')$ and $(\overline{b}, \overline{b}')$. (It will be clear from the experimental results described in the next section.) Furthermore, $(\overline{y}, \overline{y}')$ and $(\overline{z}, \overline{z}')$ can be computed quite efficiently.

4   Experimental Results

We performed a series of 100 experiments with randomly generated subgroups of B_{80}. In each experiment we

1) Generated Alice's and Bob's public and private keys $\overline{a}$, $\overline{b}$, A, B (as described in the Introduction).
2) Computed $\overline{a}'$ and $\overline{b}'$.
3) Computed $(\overline{y}, \overline{y}') = Extend(\overline{a}, \overline{a}')$.

The obtained sets of results are as follows:

1) In 63 cases, $\overline{y} = (x_1, \ldots, x_{79})$.
2) In 25 cases, $\overline{y} = (x_1, \ldots, x_{i-1}, x_i^2, x_{i+1}, \ldots, x_{79})$ for some i.

3) In 5 cases, $\overline{y} = (x_1, \ldots, x_{i-1}, x_i^2, x_{i+1}, \ldots, x_{j-1}, x_j^2, x_{j+1}, \ldots, x_{79})$ for some i, j.

4) In 5 cases, $\overline{y} = (x_1, \ldots, x_{i-1}, x_i^2, x_i x_{i+1}^2 x_i, x_{i+2}, \ldots, x_{79})$ for some i.

5) In 1 case,
$\overline{y} = (x_1, \ldots, x_{i-1}, x_i^2, x_i x_{i+1}^2 x_i, x_{i+1}, \ldots, x_{j-1}, x_j^3, x_{j+1}, \ldots, x_{79})$ for some i, j.

6) In 1 case, $\overline{y} = (x_1, \ldots, x_{i-1}, x_i^{-1} x_{i+1} x_i, x_{i+2} \ldots, x_{79})$ for some i.

Thus, randomly generated tuples of braid words $\overline{a}$ and $\overline{b}$ of "AAG-type" generate either the whole B_n or a subgroup which is "close" to the whole group B_n.

To explain this phenomenon, consider two particular braid words in B_{80}:

$$w_1 = x_{71} x_{47} x_{11} x_{45}^{-1} x_9 x_6 x_{72}^{-1} \quad \text{and} \quad w_2 = x_{64} x_{32}^{-1} x_{39}^{-1} x_{17} x_8 x_{26} x_{31}^{-1} x_{78}.$$

It is easy to check that $w_1^2 w_2 w_1^{-1} w_2^{-1} w_1^{-1} = x_9^2 x_8 x_9^{-1} x_8^{-1} x_9^{-1} = x_9 x_8^{-1}$. This happens, basically, because all generators in w_1 commute with all generators in w_2 except x_8 which does not commute with x_9.

In general, if we pick two random braid words w_1 and w_2 (of length $5 - 8$ over the alphabet $\{x_1, \ldots, x_{79}\}$) in $\overline{a}$ such that w_1 contains some fixed generator $x_i^{\pm 1}$ and w_2 contains $x_{i+1}^{\pm 1}$, then there is a big chance that all other generators that occur in w_1 or w_2 commute with each other and with x_i and x_{i+1}. In other words, for each $1 \leq i \leq 79$, with significant probability, there are two words w_1 and w_2 such that

1. $w_1 = w_1' x_i^{\pm 1} w_1''$;
2. $w_2 = w_2' x_{i+1}^{\pm 1} w_2''$;
3. x_i commutes with w_1', w_2', w_1'', and w_2'';
4. x_{i+1} commutes with w_1', w_2', w_1'', and w_2'';
5. w_1' commutes with w_2' and w_2'', and w_1'' commutes with w_2' and w_2''.

In this case, for some $\varepsilon, \delta \in \{-1, 1\}$, we have $w_1^{2\varepsilon} w_2^{\delta} w_1^{-\varepsilon} w_2^{-\delta} w_1^{-\varepsilon} = x_i^{\varepsilon} x_{i+1}^{-\varepsilon}$.

Somewhat informally, Algorithm 5 works as follows. First, a lot of words of the form $x_i^{\varepsilon} x_{i+1}^{-\varepsilon}$ are being produced (using the pattern $v^{2\varepsilon} u^{\delta} v^{-\varepsilon} u^{-\delta} v^{-\varepsilon}$). Then, using generators of the form $x_i^{\varepsilon} x_{i+1}^{-\varepsilon}$, Algorithm 4 produces all kinds of generators of the form $x_i^{\varepsilon} x_j^{\delta}$ (using the pattern $v^{\varepsilon} u^{\delta}$). Finally, after sufficient number of words of length 2 is produced, the algorithm reduces the initial subgroup generators to generators of the whole group B_n.

Remark 1. We note that increasing the parameters L_1 and L_2 decreases the probability for pairs of words w_1, w_2 to satisfy the properties (1)–(5) above. However, if the increase is moderate, then it is quite likely that w_1 and w_2 will contain two pairs of non-commuting generators, say, x_i, x_j in w_1 and $x_{i\pm 1}$, $x_{j\pm 1}$ in w_2. Then, for some $\varepsilon, \delta \in \{-1, 1\}$, we have $w_1^{2\varepsilon} w_2^{\delta} w_1^{-\varepsilon} w_2^{-\delta} w_1^{-\varepsilon} = x_i^{\varepsilon} x_{i\pm 1}^{-\varepsilon} x_j^{\varepsilon} x_{j\pm 1}^{-\varepsilon}$ which is a word of length 4. In this case, performance of the algorithm 5 can be improved by allowing to add words of length 4 to the generating set (at the cost of somewhat reducing the speed of computation). As the parameter values L_1 and L_2 are increased further, the pattern $w_1^{2\varepsilon} w_2^{\delta} w_1^{-\varepsilon} w_2^{-\delta} w_1^{-\varepsilon}$ produces longer and longer words, and for some of these words the algorithm may fail to prove that the relevant subgroup is the whole group B_n (sometimes the subgroup may actually be different from B_n).

We used this modification of the algorithm to test the following parameters: $N = 80$, $N_1 = 20$, $N_2 = 20$, and $L_1 = 11$, $L_2 = 13$. Even with the generators that long, many subgroups do generate the whole B_N. As we have mentioned before, further increase of the length of the generators can make the protocol vulnerable to length-based attacks.

5 The Impact of the Experimental Results on the Security of the AAG Protocol

As described in the previous section, our experiments show that with the choice of parameters for the AAG protocol suggested in [1], the subgroups generated by $\bar{a}$ and $\bar{b}$ tend to have the following properties:

(G1) They are either the whole group B_n or "almost" the whole B_n.
(G2) They have cyclic centralizer which coincides with the center of B_n. (The latter is generated by the element Δ^2.)
(G3) They are generated by short (of length up to 3) positive braid words.

Furthermore, Algorithm 5 efficiently transforms an initial generating tuple into a simplified generating tuple of type (G1)–(G3). In this section, we explain how these results affect the security of the AAG protocol. The techniques used in this section were developed by S. J. Lee and E. Lee in [12] and by J. Gonzalez-Meneses in [7]. We refer the reader to these two papers for more information on the algorithms; here we just recall some notation that we need.

For $a \in B_n$, the number $\inf(a)$ denotes the maximum integer k such that $a = \Delta^k p$ in the group B_n, where $\Delta \in B_n$ is the half-twist braid and p is a positive braid. For an r-tuple of braids $\bar{a} = (a_1, \ldots, a_r)$, denote by $C^{inf}(S)$ the set of all r-tuples $(b_1, \ldots, b_r) \in B_n^r$ such that $\inf(b_i) \geq \inf(a_i)$ $(i = 1, \ldots, r)$ and there exists $w \in B_n$ such that $\bar{b} = w^{-1}\bar{a}w$.

The following algorithm combines two ingredients: the subgroup simplification algorithm of the present paper and the summit attack of [7], [12] into one attack on Alice's (or Bob's) key.

Algorithm 6. *(Attack on AAG-protocol)*
SIGNATURE. $w = GetConjugator(\bar{a}, \bar{a}')$.
INPUT. *Conjugate tuples* $(\bar{a}, \bar{a}')$ *of AAG-type.*
OUTPUT. *A braid word w such that $\bar{a}' = w^{-1}\bar{a}w$.*
COMPUTATIONS.

A. *Compute* $(\bar{a}_1, \bar{a}_1') = Extend(\bar{a}, \bar{a}')$.
B. *Using technique from [12], compute* $(\bar{a}_2, \bar{a}_2')$, u, *and* v *satisfying the following properties:*
  1) $\bar{a}_2 \in C^{inf}(\bar{a}_2') \subseteq C^{inf}(\bar{a}_1')$ *and* $\bar{a}_2' \in C^{inf}(\bar{a}_2) \subseteq C^{inf}(\bar{a}_1)$.

2) $\bar{a}_2 = u^{-1}\bar{a}_1 u$.

3) $\bar{a}_2' = v^{-1}\bar{a}_1' v$.

C. *Using technique from [7], compute a braid word s such that* $\bar{a}_2 = s^{-1}\bar{a}_2' s$.

D. *Output* $us^{-1}v^{-1}$.

By Theorem 2 of [12], the step B of Algorithm 6 can be performed very efficiently (by a polynomial time algorithm). The time complexity of the step C is proportional to the size of $C^{inf}(\bar{a}_1)$ which is large in general, but for all subgroups obtained in our experiments these sets were small. For instance, if the tuple $\bar{a}$ consists of all generators of B_n, then $|C^{inf}(\bar{a}_1)| = 2$ as shown in the next proposition.

Proposition 6. *Let* $\bar{x} = (x_1, \ldots, x_{n-1})$. *Then* $C^{inf}(\bar{x}) = \{\bar{x}, \Delta^{-1}\bar{x}\Delta\}$.

Proof. Let $c_0 \in B_n$ be such that $c_0^{-1}\bar{x}c_0 \in C^{inf}(\bar{x})$. Then for each $i = 1, \ldots, n-1$ one has

$$c_0^{-1}x_i c_0 = x_{s_i}$$

for some $1 \le s_i \le n - 1$. Since conjugation is an automorphism, it is easy to see that either $(s_1, \ldots, s_{n-1}) = (1, \ldots, n-1)$ or $(s_1, \ldots, s_{n-1}) = (n-1, \ldots, 1)$ which proves the proposition.

For other generating tuples obtained in our experiments the sizes of the summit set $C^{inf}(\bar{x})$ are small, too. Therefore, we can say that Algorithm 6 is efficient on a randomly generated subgroup as described in the AAG protocol. We should mention that the obtained conjugator may not be exactly Alice's (Bob's) private key; we compute it up to the centralizer of Bob's (Alice's) subgroup. However, since in almost all examples the centralizer is generated by the element Δ^2 (i.e., coincides with the center of B_n), this is not a problem. We would like to point out that without the first step the attack may not be efficient since the size of the summit set would be huge.

Now, with Algorithm 6 it is easy to find the shared key obtained by Alice and Bob in the AAG protocol:

Algorithm 7. *(Attack on the AAG protocol)*

SIGNATURE. $w = GetSharedKey(\bar{a}, \bar{a}', \bar{b}, \bar{b}')$.

INPUT. *Conjugate tuples* $(\bar{a}, \bar{a}')$ *and* $(\bar{b}, \bar{b}')$ *of as in the AAG protocol.*

OUTPUT. *The shared key K.*

COMPUTATIONS.

A. *Let* $w_a = GetConjugator(\bar{a}, \bar{a}')$.

B. *Let* $w_b = GetConjugator(\bar{b}, \bar{b}')$.

C. *Output* $w_a^{-1}w_b^{-1}w_a w_b$.

References

1. I. Anshel, M. Anshel, B. Fisher, D. Goldfeld, *New Key Agreement Protocols in Braid Group Cryptography.* In: Progress in Cryptology – CT-RSA 2001, 13–27. Lecture Notes Comp. Sc., vol. 2020. Berlin Heidelberg New York Tokyo: Springer 2001.

2. I. Anshel, M. Anshel, D. Goldfeld, *An algebraic method for public-key cryptography*, Math. Res. Lett. **6** (1999), 287–291.
3. J. S. Birman, *Braids, links and mapping class groups*, Ann. Math. Studies **82**, Princeton Univ. Press, 1974.
4. P. Dehornoy, *A fast method for comparing braids*, Adv. Math. **125** (1997), 200–235.
5. D. B. A. Epstein, J. W. Cannon, D. F. Holt, S. V. F. Levy, M. S. Paterson, W. P. Thurston, *Word processing in groups*. Jones and Bartlett Publishers, Boston, MA, 1992.
6. D. Garber, S. Kaplan, M. Teicher, B. Tsaban, U. Vishne, *Probabilistic solutions of equations in the braid group*, preprint. http://arxiv.org/abs/math.GR/0404076
7. J. Gonzalez-Meneses, *Improving an algorithm to solve Multiple Simultaneous Conjugacy Problems in braid groups*, Contemp. Math., Amer. Math. Soc. **372** (2005), 35–42.
8. J. Gonzalez-Meneses and B. Wiest, *On the structure of the centraliser of a braid*, Ann. Sci. École Norm. Sup. **37** (5) (2004), 729–757.
9. Hofheinz, D., Steinwandt, R., *A practical attack on some braid group based cryptographic primitives*. In: Public Key Cryptography, 6th International Workshop on Practice and Theory in Public Key Cryptography, PKC 2003 Proceedings, 187–198 (Y. G. Desmedt, ed., Lecture Notes Comp. Sc., vol. 2567) Berlin Heidelberg New York Tokyo: Springer 2002.
10. Hughes, J., Tannenbaum, A., *Length-based attacks for certain group based encryption rewriting systems*. In: Workshop SECI02 Securitè de la Communication sur Intenet, September 2002, Tunis, Tunisia. http://www.network.com/~hughes/
11. K. H. Ko, S. J. Lee, J. H. Cheon, J. W. Han, J. Kang, C. Park, *New public-key cryptosystem using braid groups*. In: Advances in cryptology – CRYPTO 2000 (Santa Barbara, CA), 166–183 (Lecture Notes Comp. Sc., vol. 1880) Berlin Heidelberg New York Tokyo: Springer 2000.
12. S. J. Lee, E. Lee, *Potential Weaknesses of the Commutator Key Agreement Protocol Based on Braid Groups*. In: Advances in cryptology – EUROCRYPT 2002, 14–28 (Lecture Notes Comp. Sc., vol. 2332) Berlin Heidelberg New York Tokyo: Springer 2002.
13. A. Myasnikov, V. Shpilrain, A. Ushakov, *A practical attack on some braid group based cryptographic protocols*. In: Advances in cryptology – CRYPTO 2005 (Santa Barbara, CA). Lecture Notes Comp. Sc. **3621** (2005), 86–96.
14. M. Paterson, A. Razborov, *The set of minimal braids is co-NP-complete*, J. Algorithms **12** (1991), 393–408.
15. V. Shpilrain and A. Ushakov, *The conjugacy search problem in public key cryptography: unnecessary and insufficient*, Applicable Algebra in Engineering, Communication and Computing, to appear. http://eprint.iacr.org/2004/321/

Appendix: Generating Random Subgroups

The question of how one could produce a random generating set of a required type for a subgroup of B_n is by no means trivial. We used the following procedure for producing random subgroup generators as in the AAG protocol. In the description of the algorithm below, when we say "uniformly choose an integer" from a given interval, that means all integers from this interval are selected with equal probabilities.

Algorithm 8. *(Subgroup generator)*
INPUT. *The rank n of the braid group, the rank k of a subgroup, and numbers L_1, L_2 such that $L_1 < L_2$.*
OUTPUT. *Braid words $w_1, \dots, w_k$ over X_n such that $L_1 \leq |w_i| \leq L_2$ and each generator $x \in X_n$ non-trivially occurs in at least one of the w_i's.*
COMPUTATIONS.

A. *For each $1 \leq i \leq k$, uniformly choose an integer l_i, $L_1 \leq l_i \leq L_2$, and compute $L = \sum_{i=1}^{k} l_i$.*
B. *Construct a sequence $\{a_1, \dots, a_L\} \in (X^{\pm 1})^*$ the following way:*
   1) *For each $1 \leq i \leq n-1$, uniformly choose $\varepsilon_i \in \{-1, 1\}$ and put $a_i = x_i^{\varepsilon_i}$.*
   2) *For each $n \leq i \leq L$, uniformly choose $j_i \in \{1, \dots, n-1\}$ and $\varepsilon_i \in \{-1, 1\}$, and put $a_i = x_{j_i}^{\varepsilon_i}$.*
C. *Randomly permute elements in $\{a_1, \dots, a_L\}$.*
D. *For each $1 \leq j \leq k$, compute $s_j = \sum_{i=1}^{j-1} l_i$ and put $w_j = Shorten(a_{(s_j)+1} \cdots a_{s_{(j+1)}})$.*
E. *If some braid generator x_i does not occur in the obtained sequence $w_1, \dots, w_k$, then repeat all the steps.*

Note that, in theory, Algorithm 8 might go into an infinite loop if the subgroup generators $\{w_1, \dots, w_k\}$ do not involve some braid generator x_i. But in real life, such a situation is extremely rare. In fact, the greatest number of iterations Algorithm 8 performed in our experiments was 5.

High-Order Attacks Against the Exponent Splitting Protection

Frédéric Muller[1] and Frédéric Valette[2]

[1] HSBC-France
Frederic.Muller@m4x.org
[2] CELAR, RENNES, France
Frederic.Valette@m4x.org

Abstract. Exponent splitting is a classical technique to protect modular exponentiation against side-channel attacks. Although it is rarely implemented due to efficiency reasons, it is widely considered as a highly-secure solution. Therefore it is often used as a reference to benchmark new countermeasure proposals.

In this paper, we make new observations about the statistical behavior of the splitting of the exponent. We look at the correlations between the two shares, and show an important imbalance. Later, we show how to use this imbalance in higher-order attacks (mostly based on address-bit, safe-error and fault analysis). We also present experimental results to estimate their feasibility.

1 Introduction

Modular exponentiation is frequently used by public-key cryptosystems, for example RSA [17] or DSA [16]. However, data manipulated during these computations should generally be kept secret, since any leakage of information (even only a few bits of secret information) may be useful to an attacker. For example, during the generation of an RSA signature by a cryptographic device, the secret exponent is used to transform an input related to the message into a digital signature via modular exponentiation.

In recent years, many methods have been proposed to attack these algorithms, using a physical source of information, instead of the usual cryptographic inputs and outputs. The first important result was due to Kocher who suggested to use timing information to retrieve secret keys manipulated by the cryptographic operations [14]. Another interesting idea was proposed by Boneh *et al.* who suggested to modify the physical environment of a cryptographic device to create a fault during the computations [3]. Faulty results sometimes leak information about the secret key.

These attacks, generally called **side-channel attacks**, may represent an important threat for systems. Indeed it is often assumed that cryptographic devices are tamper-resistant, while naive implementations often leak information about the secrets stored and manipulated by the device. Many attacks, either passive (like Kocher's timing attack) or active (like Boneh *et al.*'s fault attack), have been

M. Yung et al. (Eds.): PKC 2006, LNCS 3958, pp. 315–329, 2006.

studied, and some generic countermeasures were proposed. Among the possible protection methods, an interesting direction [4], inspired by the well-known secret sharing techniques [18] consists in splitting the secret data in two (or more) shares. Then two (or more) separate computations are performed (one on each share), such that the actual output can be retrieved from the different results. This idea, initially introduced by Chari *et al.* in [4] was further developed by Clavier and Joye in the case of modular exponentiation [6]. Similar methods also exist for secret-key algorithms [10] and for scalar multiplication on elliptic curves [19].

For modular exponentiation, it is called **the exponent splitting method** and is widely considered as a secure solution to thwart side-channel attacks. However its inefficiency (it roughly doubles the execution time) is an important limitation in practice. Recent countermeasures (see [5] for instance) often use the exponent splitting method as a reference to evaluate the security level they achieve.

In this paper, we make new observations about the statistical behavior of the sharing method. As a result, the two separate modular exponentiations have strong correlations. Later, we exploit these correlations in higher-order side-channel attacks, *i.e.* attacks that analyse simultaneously the physical information at two different instants in the computation. More precisely, we describe 4 new higher-order attacks against this countermeasure. They work when all the exponentiation are protected against Simple Power Analysis (SPA), and can even defeat some extra randomization countermeasures. Three of the four attacks are active attacks, and as such require the injection of faults during the cryptographic computations.

Our paper is constructed as follows : first, we remind the Exponentiation Splitting method, as well as several popular side-channel attack techniques in this context. Then, we describe our new results : we start by our new statistical observations, and we continue by suggesting three new high-order fault attacks.

2   The Exponent Splitting Countermeasure

The idea to share a secret in several parts was first introduced by Shamir in [18] for a cryptographic purpose. Later, Chari *et al.* suggested to split a cryptographic computation in several shares [4], in such a way that :

- The actual output can be retrieved from the outputs of each partial computation.
- One needs to attack the scheme as many times as the number of shares in order to retrieve the secret.

In particular, they argued that this approach was a reasonable countermeasure against side-channel attacks. For instance, randomizing the splitting algorithm allows to counter attacks based on statistical analysis.

More specifically in the case of modular exponentiation, Clavier and Joye introduced the idea of **exponent splitting** to thwart side-channel attacks [6]. Similar ideas were described in [19] in the case of scalar exponentiation on elliptic curves. Besides the switching from multiplicative to additive notation, the idea of both methods is essentially the same.

2.1 Definition

Let us consider a secret exponent, noted

$$d = \sum_{i=0}^{n-1} d_i.2^i$$

In many cryptographic algorithms (RSA for instance), one needs to raise some input M to the power d, modulo some large number N. The result is noted :

$$S = M^d \bmod N = \prod_{i=0}^{n-1} M^{d_i.2^i} \bmod N$$

The main idea of the splitting technique is to pick a random r (smaller than d)[1] and to compute the value $r^* = d - r$. Then, one computes separately ($S_r = M^r \bmod N$) and ($S_{r^*} = M^{r^*} \bmod N$) from which it is easy to recover S by :

$$S = S_r \cdot S_{r^*} = M^{(r+r^*)} \bmod N = M^d \bmod N$$

A natural idea is that, since any of the two exponentiations consists in basically raising M to a random exponent, it is sufficient to protect one of the two exponentiations against side-channel attacks.

2.2 Alternative Solutions

Because r is purely random, it seems that this countermeasure offers a very high level of security. Alternative protection methods can be grouped in two classes :

- Those based on randomizing the input data (either M or d), prior to the exponentiation algorithm [7, 14].
- Those based on randomizing the exponentiation algorithm itself (see [5, 11]).

For many of these countermeasures used alone, some problems have been identified [8]. So it is customary to combine several countermeasures in implementations, provided it does not affect too badly the performances.

No attack is known against the exponent splitting method, even without additional countermeasure (some basic SPA-protection is still needed, as shown in the next Section). However, the exponent splitting is much less efficient than the alternative propositions, since it doubles the length of the computation. The goal of some recent proposals (see [5] for instance) is to reach the same level of security than exponent splitting, at a more reasonable cost.

---

[1] One could think of picking a random r smaller than $\varphi(N)$. Although this does not totally thwart our attacks, it changes the analysis as pointed out in Section 5.4.

3   Some Usual Side-Channel Attacks

In this section, we describe some popular side-channel attacks against modular exponentiations. In general, one distinguishes between **passive attacks** where an attacker observes some physical variable in the environment, and **active attacks** where the physical environment is modified by the attacker.

Attacks can also be sorted according to which physical mean is used. As an example, many papers focus on power attacks, where the source of information is the power consumption of the cryptographic device. Regarding active attacks (*e.g.* fault attacks), it is not always specified which mean is used to inject a fault. Popular methods used in practice include light and power glitches.

3.1   SPA

Modular exponentiation is generally implemented using a sequence of squaring and multiplication modulo N. Simple Power Analysis (SPA) [15] is based on the natural idea that multiplication and squaring may not result in the same power consumption. It is therefore a passive attack, where one monitors power traces of a cryptographic device executing a modular exponentiation[2]. One expects to retrieve the sequence of squaring and multiplication that was actually executed, from the power traces.

In a naive implementation of modular exponentiation, the multiplication at step i is executed if and only if $d_i = 1$. Therefore **an attacker learns if $d_i = 1$ by simply looking if a multiplication was executed at step i**. It is quite simple to thwart SPA by always executing the squaring and the multiplication at step i. When $d_i = 0$, the multiplication is a useless operation, so the *"square-and-multiply always"* algorithm, as depicted in Figure 1 is slightly slower than a naive implementation. It is a very popular algorithm, often implemented in practice

---

Input: a message M, an n-bit integer $d = \sum_{i=0}^{n-1} d_i 2^i$
Output: M^d
$Q[0] = 1$
for i from $n - 1$ down to 0
    $Q[0] = Q[0]^2$
    $Q[1] = Q[0] \times M$
    $Q[0] = Q[d_i]$
return $Q[0]$

Fig. 1. "Square-and-multiply always" algorithm, resistant against SPA

(sometimes in addition to other countermeasures). This SPA-protection remains a requirement for the security of Exponent Splitting. Otherwise an attacker can learn separately r and r^* by running the SPA twice and then reconstruct

---

[2] SPA has been primarily developed as a power attack, however it adapts very simply to other physical sources of information, like electromagnetic radiations.

$$d = r + r^*$$

However it may seem sufficient to protect only one of the two exponentiations if one considers only SPA. Indeed, since r is random, an attacker learns basically nothing about d if he obtains only r or $d - r$. However, protecting only one of the two modular exponentiations is not a very natural solution.

3.2   Fault Attacks

Cryptographic devices are often sensitive to perturbations of their environment [3]. Fault attacks are based on the assumption that the normal execution of the modular exponentiation can be modified by such physical perturbation. This goal is generally reached by light or power glitches, or temperature variations.

For instance, assume that an attacker is able to flip the value of the bit d_i during the exponentiation of the input M. Then, instead of the correct result S, the attacker obtains the "faulty" result :

$$S' = S \cdot M^{2^i}$$

if $d_i = 0$ and

$$S' = S \cdot M^{-2^i}$$

if $d_i = 1$. Therefore an attacker **learns one bit of the secret exponent, by comparing one correct and one faulty modular exponentiation**.

3.3   Safe Errors Attacks

Safe errors attacks can be viewed as an enhancement of fault attacks, adapted to thwart some countermeasures. The attacker uses the fact that some of the operations that are executed can be useless. For instance, in the "square-and-multiply always" algorithm of Figure 1, the multiplication is useless when $d_i = 0$.

If a fault is injected at this step of the computation, the result of the exponentiation will be $S' = S$ when $d_i = 0$ and an invalid value otherwise. Like for a basic fault attack, comparing one correct and one faulty modular exponentiation allows an attacker to learn one bit of d. Moreover, the underlying assumptions are much lighter : **it is easier to inject an arbitrary fault, than a fault that specifically flips one bit of the exponent**.

Both faults and safe-error attacks do not apply to exponent splitting, because learning one bit of r (or r^*) does not provide any information about d.

3.4   Address-Bit Attacks

The address-bit attack is a specific attack to target algorithms like the "square-and-multiply always" of Figure 1, where the fact that d_i is 0 or 1 does not affect the intermediate **values** that are computed, but affects instead the **addresses** that are manipulated. For instance, when $d_i = 1$, $Q[1]$ will be manipulated at the last stage of round i, while it is $Q[0]$ otherwise.

Power attacks [15] or ElectroMagnetic (EM) analysis [9] are often based on a correlation between the **manipulated data** and the physical source of information. However, it is also known that **addresses of manipulated registers** can affect the power dissipation or the EM radiation. Address-bit attacks have been developed to take advantage of such properties [12]. Suppose we use EM as the physical source of information and that our probe is physically closer to register A than register B. If a group of experiments all read the register A, their EM signature will be significantly different from a group of experiments reading register B.

This idea has been used to break the basic "square-and-multiply-always" algorithm : since there is no extra randomization, the address-bit is always d_i at step i. Therefore the EM signature at this stage of the computation depends on d_i. However this attack no longer works for the exponent splitting method, since the address-bits are randomized at each execution.

3.5   Impact on Exponent Splitting

We observed that, taken separately, none of this well-known attack techniques allows to break the Exponent Splitting protection. Indeed, each exponentiation uses a random exponent, so attacks requiring some degree of randomization are not possible.

In addition, provided at least one of the exponentiation is SPA-protected, SPA does not work against the Exponent Splitting. However, in practice, it is better to **protect both exponentiations against SPA**. Otherwise, an attacker could mount a **combined attack** : apply SPA to the unprotected exponentiation to learn (for instance) r, then attack the remaining SPA-protected exponentiation by other means.

For instance, one could think of an address-bit attack on M^{r^*}, assuming prior knowledge of r : the attacker repeats several time the computation for a fixed given M. He makes an assumption about the i Least Significant Bits (LSB) of the secret d. From this guess and from r, he gets one candidate for the i LSB's of r^* of each computation. Then he looks at the i-th step of M^{r^*} and performs an address-bit attack, as described in Section 3.4. If the guess is right, he will observe two groups with significantly different EM signatures. Otherwise, he will just observe some random data. So he learns the i LSB's of d and it is straightforward to repeat the process to learn more bits of d.

To summarize, it is recommended to **protect both exponentiations against SPA**, in order to thwart combined attacks. With this assumption, no attack is known against the exponent splitting protection. In particular no additional countermeasure (like exponent randomization for instance) is needed.

4   New Attacks Against the Exponent Splitting

We focus on some statistical properties of the exponent splitting, at the bit level. Since r is randomly drawn, it does not leak information about d when considered alone[3]. However, the pair (r, r^*) is not uniformly distributed, since it always satisfies

$$r + r^* = d$$

We explore the statistical impact of this relation at the bit-level. Later, we use the observed imbalance to mount side-channel attacks.

4.1   Statistical Properties of the Exponent Splitting

Although each bit of r and r^* takes the values 0 or 1 with probability 0.5, there is a bias in the distribution of the i-th bits of the pair (r, r^*). We denote respectively by r_i, r_i^* and d_i the i-th bits of r, r^* and d. Besides, the i-th carry bit in the addition $r + r^* = d$ is noted c_i. At the bit level, the following relation is satisfied :

$$c_i + r_i + r_i^* = d_i + 2.c_{i+1} \qquad (1)$$

In particular, we have

$$c_i \oplus r_i \oplus r_i^* = d_i \qquad (2)$$

Let also p_i denote the probability that $c_i = 0$. The probability is taken over all the possible choices of r and r^*. Initially, $p_0 = 1$.

Suppose that $d_i = 0$. Since r_i is drawn at random, when $c_i = 0$, we get from (2) that :

$$(r_i, r_i^*) = (0, 0)$$

with probability 0.5 and

$$(r_i, r_i^*) = (1, 1)$$

with probability 0.5. In the first case, we obtain from (1) that $c_{i+1} = 0$, while in the second case $c_{i+1} = 1$.

Similarily, when $c_i = 1$, it is equaly likely that (r_i, r_i^*) is equal to $(0, 1)$ or $(1, 0)$. In both cases, we get $c_{i+1} = 1$. Therefore, the transition rule for these probabilities can be summarized as in Table 1. In the case $d_i = 1$, we obtain another rule for probability transitions which is given in Table 2.

Table 1. Probability transition when $d_i = 0$

$$\Pr[(r_i, r_i^*) = (0, 0)] = 0.5 \times p_i$$
$$\Pr[(r_i, r_i^*) = (0, 1)] = 0.5 \times (1 - p_i)$$
$$\Pr[(r_i, r_i^*) = (1, 0)] = 0.5 \times (1 - p_i)$$
$$\Pr[(r_i, r_i^*) = (1, 1)] = 0.5 \times p_i$$
$$p_{i+1} = 0.5 \times p_i$$

From these equations, we can observe that the two bits (r_i, r_i^*) are not uniformly distributed (unless $p_i = 0.5$) and that the imbalance depends on the

---

[3] Actually, it is not true : r is generally drawn at random in the interval $[0, d]$ which is not exactly equivalent to drawing at random an n-bit integer. This results in (small) imbalances that have already been used for cryptanalysis purpose [1].

Table 2. Probability transition when $d_i = 1$

$$\Pr[(r_i, r_i^*) = (0,0)] = 0.5 \times (1 - p_i)$$
$$\Pr[(r_i, r_i^*) = (0,1)] = 0.5 \times p_i$$
$$\Pr[(r_i, r_i^*) = (1,0)] = 0.5 \times p_i$$
$$\Pr[(r_i, r_i^*) = (1,1)] = 0.5 \times (1 - p_i)$$
$$p_{i+1} = (0.5 \times (1 - p_i)) + p_i = 0.5 \times (1 + p_i)$$

value of the bits from 0 to i of the secret exponent. Acutally, what we have is a **Markov chain** where the bit-level probabilities of step i can be derived from those of step $i - 1$ using one of the two previous probability transition rules.

4.2 An Example

To illustrate our ideas, we have drawn at random an exponent d of length 24 bits and repeated the splitting method a large number of times. We computed experimentally the probability distribution of (r_i, r_i^*) for all steps i. Table 3 summarizes these results.

Table 3. An example of bit-level imbalance for a 24-bit secret d

	d_0	d_1	d_2	d_3	d_4	d_5	d_6	d_7	d_8	d_9	d_{10}	d_{11}	d_{12}	d_{13}	d_{14}	d_{15}	d_{16}	d_{17}	d_{18}	d_{19}	d_{20}	d_{21}	d_{22}	d_{23}
(r_i, r_i^*)	0	1	0	1	0	1	0	0	0	0	0	0	1	0	0	1	0	0	0	1	1	1	1	1
$(0,0)$	50	25	38	31	35	33	34	16	8	4	2	1	50	25	13	45	28	14	8	47	23	11	5	2
$(1,0)$	0	25	12	19	15	17	16	34	41	46	48	49	0	25	37	5	22	36	42	3	27	39	45	48
$(0,1)$	0	25	13	18	15	17	16	33	42	46	49	49	0	25	36	6	22	36	43	4	28	40	46	49
$(1,1)$	50	25	37	32	35	33	34	17	9	4	1	1	50	25	14	44	28	14	7	46	22	10	4	1

Intuitively, when the secret exponent has a long run of bits equal to 0 or 1, it is very likely that the bits of r and r^* are different. In the case of a run of 0's, we can see that p_i becomes very close to 0, so there is generally no carry bit. However, after a long run of 1's, p_i gets close to 1, so a carry bit is likely to propagate. In the next section, we show applications of these bit-level observations to mount safe-error attacks, fault attacks and address-bit attacks. We assume that an **attacker can infer the value of the bits of d from the probability distribution of (r_i, r_i^*)**. This problem (called the Hidden Markov Problem) has already been handled by Karlof and Wagner in [13]. We also mention that the paper [8] deals with a similar problem to break the Ha-Moon countermeasure [11].

4.3 Application to Safe Error Attack

In this section, we assume that an attacker is able to create faults with enough precision to target a specific step in the "square-and-multiply always" algorithm. We consider a **second-order safe-error attack**, *i.e.* the attacker injects two faults during the same computation and observes if the result remains valid or not.

Suppose the attacker injects a fault during the multiplication at step i of the exponentiation M^r, and a fault during the multiplication at step i of the exponentiation M^{r^*}. These two faults have no effect on the final computation, as long as $(r_i, r_i^*) = (0, 0)$.

By repeating the process, the attacker obtains an estimation of the probability $\Pr[(r_i, r_i^*) = (0, 0)]$ for the positions i of his choice. We have seen in Section 4.1 that, this probability is strongly correlated with the value of the bits d_i (see Table 3 for a concrete example). This observation allows the attacker to learn the secret exponent (refer to Section 5 for further analysis).

4.4 Application to Fault Attacks

In this section, we use an idea similar to the previous attack, although we are not specifically focusing on safe-errors, *i.e.* faults which will keep the output of the exponentiation unchanged. We suppose that an attacker is able to "flip" the value of the bit r_i by fault injection, like in the usual fault attack (see Section 3.2).

Depending on the value of the bit r_i, the output can be modified to $S \cdot M^{2^i}$ (if $r_i = 0$) or $S \cdot M^{-2^i}$ (if $r_i = 1$). Since r_i is random, this provides no information about d. However, suppose that we consider a **second-order fault attack** where we simultaneously flip the bit r_i and the bit r_i^*. Depending on the value of these two bits, the observed result can take 4 values :

$$\text{if } (r_i, r_i^*) = (0, 0) \text{ then we get } S \cdot M^{2^{i+1}}$$
$$\text{if } (r_i, r_i^*) = (0, 1) \text{ then we get } S$$
$$\text{if } (r_i, r_i^*) = (1, 0) \text{ then we get } S$$
$$\text{if } (r_i, r_i^*) = (1, 1) \text{ then we get } S \cdot M^{-2^{i+1}}$$

Like in the previous section, we obtain a safe-error in 2 of the 4 cases. This allows us to tell when $r_i \neq r_i^*$, although we cannot tell between the two cases $(0, 1)$ and $(1, 0)$. In addition, we can also detect here the case $(0, 0)$ and $(1, 1)$ because we obtained specific faults in the output of the modular exponentiation.

By repeating the process over several experiments, we get much more information than in the previous section, since we learn estimates for

- $\Pr[(r_i, r_i^*) = (0, 0)]$
- $\Pr[(r_i, r_i^*) = (1, 1)]$
- $\Pr[(r_i, r_i^*) = (0, 1) \text{ or } (1, 0)]$

This information makes the analysis of the Hidden Markov Model [13] easier, however the injected faults need to specifically flip one bit of the exponent. This is more difficult to obtain in practice than an arbitrary fault on the multiplication. Therefore it is not clear that our second-order fault attack will require less messages than the second-order safe-error attack, although it provides a better statistical information.

4.5 Application to Address-Bit Attack

In this section, we suggest to mount a **statistical address-bit attack**. The idea is similar to the usual address-bit attacks, although here we only know probabistically if the two address-bits are equal or not.

Suppose that we already know the $i - 1$ less significant bits of d. Therefore we know that the carry bit c_i is equal to 0 with a probability p_i, that can be computed using the rules given in Section 4.1.

If $d_i = 0$ then $r_i = r_i^*$ with probability p_i.
If $d_i = 1$ then $r_i = r_i^*$ with probability $1 - p_i$.

This observation allows us to learn the bit d_i (using EM radiations for instance, as described in Section 3.4), by comparing the addresses manipulated at stage i of both modular exponentiations. Suppose, for example, that $p_i > 0.5$. Then the address-bits should be equal more often if and only if $d_i = 0$. Clearly, the "bad case" here is when $p_i = 0.5$, since we are unable to determine the value of d_i. However, such bad cases remain unlikely, as illustrated in Table 3. The advantage of this address-bit attack is that it is a passive attack. See Section 5 for more details about implementation of this attack.

4.6   Combining Safe-Error and Address-Bit Attacks

The efficiency of the previous safe-error attack can be improved, by combining it with fault attacks. We want to improve the prediction of the carry bit c_i, so we inject one fault at step $i - 1$, while we simultaneously monitor the EM radiations of step i. This might look complicated, but it is not necessarily more difficult than injecting two faults during the same cryptographic computation.

In order to predict the carry bit c_i, we need some information about the step $i - 1$. So, we inject an arbitrary fault during the multiplication at round $i - 1$, for any one of the two modular exponentiations. If the result remains valid, we learn that $r_{i-1} = 0$. Otherwise $r_{i-1} = 1$.

- In the case $d_{i-1} = 1$. We inject a fault at the $(i - 1)$-th step until we find an exponentiation where $r_{i-1} = 0$. Then from relation (1) we see that necessarily, $c_i = 0$. Therefore the address bits r_i and r_i^* are equal if and only if $d_i = 0$. This allows to apply the usual address-bit attack, as described in Section 3.4.
- In the case $d_{i-1} = 0$, we inject a fault until we find an exponentiation where $r_{i-1} = 1$. Then, we see that necessarily, $c_i = 1$. Therefore the address bits r_i and r_i^* are equal if and only if $d_i = 1$.

The advantage of this combined attack is that it no longer requires any Markov model analysis, so the number of required message is much smaller.

4.7   Summary

We proposed a variety of attacks against the exponent splitting countermeasure, based on statistical properties of the sharing method, at the bit-level. We proposed a passive attack based on **statistical address-bit analysis** and several active attacks, either based on **faults** or **safe-errors**. See Table 4 for a summary of our proposed attacks.

Table 4. Summary of our proposed attacks. The number of faults is given per sample.

Type of attack	Needs Markov analysis ?	Active ?	Number of Faults
Safe-error	yes	yes	2
Fault	yes	yes	2
Address-bit	yes	no	0
Combined	no	yes	1

5   Experimental Results

In this Section, we implemented software simulations for the safe-error attack and the statistical address-bit attack. Both are based on a Markov model analysis, where one wants to retrieve d_i from partial information about the distribution of (r_i, r_i^*). We want to obtain a more accurate estimation of the real cost of this analysis. As we have seen previously, some problem will arise. For instance, when $p_i = 0.5$, it is impossible to tell whether d_i is equal to 0 or 1. In particular, such problems happen after a long run of consecutive 0's or 1's. We want to estimate the impact of this "difficult" positions.

Besides, we did not implement the fault attack, since it relies essentially on the same principle than the safe-error attack, although the underlying assumptions are much stronger (we need the ability to inject faults that specifically flip the value of some exponent bits). We did not implement the combined attack either, since it is an improvement of the statistical address-bit attack. Besides, there is no Markov model analysis in this attack (see Table 4), so its complexity depends on the quality of our address-bit observations : in theory, 2 observations per bit of the secret exponent should be sufficient.

5.1   Safe-Error Attack

Let $q_i = \Pr[(r_i, r_i^*) = (0,0)]$. From the probability transition rules of Table 1 and 2, we obtain :

$$
\begin{array}{lll}
\text{if } d_{i-1} = d_i = 0 & \text{then} & q_i = 0.5 \cdot q_{i-1} \\
\text{if } d_{i-1} = d_i = 1 & \text{then} & q_i = 0.5 \cdot q_{i-1} \\
\text{if } d_{i-1} = 0 \text{ and } d_i = 1 & \text{then} & q_i = 0.5 \cdot (1 - q_{i-1}) \\
\text{if } d_{i-1} = 1 \text{ and } d_i = 0 & \text{then} & q_i = 0.5 \cdot (1 - q_{i-1})
\end{array}
$$

Then, we adopt a recursive approach : we learn d_i from d_{i-1}, by testing whether the probability q_i is closer to $0.5 \cdot q_{i-1}$ or from $0.5 \cdot (1 - q_{i-1})$. Clearly, the only problem arises when $q_{i-1} \simeq 0.5$ where it is very difficult to make a decision. The following Table 5 summarizes our experimental results, where L denotes the exponent length and D the number of experiments, *i.e.* the number of fault injections here. Besides, this process must be repeated for each bit of the scalar, so the number of experiments is about $L \times D$ in total. Actually, the parameter D was chosen such that we could derive the value of the most

Table 5. Experimental results for the safe-error attacks

L	D	Errors	Unable to decide
40	20	3.93	5.21
40	100	2.22	2.40
160	100	8.48	6.79
160	300	6.06	1.81
160	1000	3.58	1.22
1024	100	52.25	39.90
1024	1000	7.26	37.48

"difficult" bits. For many positions, the value of d_i is easy to determine with much less than D faults. This was not taken into account in our evaluation of the cost. To average these figures, we repeated the attack several hundred times, for randomly chosen exponents. To conclude, if one wants to remove most errors and "no decision" cases, one needs about 100 faults for a 160-bit scalar, and 1000 faults for a 1024-bit scalar.

5.2   Statistical Address-Bit Attack

We implemented the statistical address-bit attack. We suppose that the i LSB's of the scalar are known and try to determine if the next bit is 0 or 1 by looking at the equality of the address-bits r_i and r_i^*. The results are summarized in Table 6. We observe that these figures are slightly better than those of Table 5. Besides, the attack does not need to be repeated for each bit of the scalar, since we can monitor the N steps of the exponentiation algorithm. So this attack is actually much more efficient than the safe-error attack. However, these two attacks rely on different physical assumptions : the safe-error attack is active, although the underlying assumption is much weaker than for fault attacks (where one bit of the exponent needs specifically to be flipped). On the other hand, the address-bit attack is passive.

Table 6. Experimental results for the statistical address-bit attack

l	D	Errors	Unable to decide
40	20	2.57	1.83
40	100	1.65	0.40
160	100	5.78	1.64
160	300	3.82	0.49
160	1000	2.35	0.12
1024	100	35.90	9.52
1024	1000	12.49	1.10

5.3   Dealing with Errors and the "Unable to Decide" Case

In the previous statistical attacks, it occured that we were unable to make a decision between $d_i = 0$ and $d_i = 1$. In particular, this occurs after long runs of 0 or 1's, where the statistical behavior is quite special.

Actually, it is not necessarily a problem if some bits of the secret scalar remain unknown at the end of the attack. Indeed, there are some mathematical solutions to deal with it. First, if the number of unknowns is small, we can simply guess these bits. Secondly, there exist some algorithms to take advantage of (even relatively small) partial key exposure for an RSA exponent (see the paper by Blömer and May, for instance [2]). Therefore, we may retrieve the "missing" bits by mathematical means, once several bits have been leaked using side-channels.

5.4   Additional Countermeasures

A natural question is to tell whether such attacks can be thwarted by putting more countermeasures (in addition to the SPA countermeasures).

- Countermeasures based on **randomizing the message** will not work here. Indeed, our attacks do not exploit the actual values that are manipulated during the exponentiations. So it does not matter that the message is initially randomized.
- There is **another way to initially split the secret exponent** : draw at random r in the interval $[0, \varphi(N)]$, then compute $r^* = d - r \mod \varphi(N)$. This is not likely to be implemented, because $\varphi(N)$ is not always known by the device (although it could be recomputed from d and e). The problem with this alternative splitting is that we could face two possible targets instead of one :
$$ r + r^* = d \text{ and } r + r^* = d' = d + \varphi(N) $$
  It is better if d is far from $\frac{\varphi(N)}{2}$, because one of the two targets is over-represented, and the other one just acts as noise. So we would recover, either d or $d + \varphi(N)$, but in both cases this is equivalent to the secret key. The tricky case is when $d \simeq \frac{\varphi(N)}{2}$, because d and d' occur equally often. An open problem is to propose a dedicated analysis, in order to recover two such exponents simultaneously.
- However, as soon as the device knows $\varphi(N)$, it is very likely that the **exponent randomization** would be implemented. The idea of this countermeasure is to draw a random x for each exponentiation, and to perform each exponentiation with exponent $d + x \cdot \varphi(N)$ instead of the actual exponent d. Implementing this protection apparently thwarts our attacks.
- Countermeasures based on **randomizing the exponentiation algorithm itself** (see [5] for a nice example) seem also to thwart our attacks.

6   Conclusion

Contrarily to a widespread belief, the exponent splitting countermeasure does not offer, by itself, a satisfying level of security against side-channel attacks.

Although analyzing a single modular exponentiation is useless, attacks become possible as soon as one considers both exponentiations together.

We described statistical weaknesses of the countermeasure at the bit-level, which show that the i-th stages of both modular exponentiations are strongly correlated. We showed a variety of attacks that break the exponent splitting countermeasure (safe-error, fault, address-bit, combined attacks). All of them are higher-order attacks, *i.e.* they require to exploit simultaneously both exponentiations. There are some technical difficulties to realize second-order attacks (like injecting two faults in the same cryptographic computations), however it is unreasonable for the security to rely on this difficulty only. Therefore, we recommand not to use the exponent splitting protection alone. One should either combine it with additional countermeasures like the randomization of the exponent, or use some of the recent alternative, like [5], which has the advantage of being much more efficient.

References

1. D. Bleichenbacher. On the Generation of DSA One-time Keys. Presented at the *Workshop on Elliptic Curve Cryptography – ECC'02*, 2002.
2. J. Blömer and A. May. New Partial Key Exposure Attacks on RSA. In D. Boneh, editor, *Advances in Cryptology – CRYPTO'03*, volume 2729 of *Lectures Notes in Computer Science*, pages 27–43. Springer, 2003.
3. D. Boneh, R. DeMillo, and R. Lipton. On the Importance of Checking Cryptographic Protocols for Faults (Extended Abstract). In W. Fumy, editor, *Advances in Cryptology – Eurocrypt'97*, volume 1233 of *Lectures Notes in Computer Science*, pages 37–51. Springer, 1997.
4. S. Chari, C. Jutla, J. Rao, and P. Rohatgi. Towards Sound Approaches to Counteract Power-Analysis Attacks. In M. Wiener, editor, *Advances in Cryptology – CRYPTO'99*, volume 1666 of *Lectures Notes in Computer Science*, pages 398–412. Springer, 1999.
5. B. Chevallier-Mames. Self-Randomized Exponentiation Algorithms. In T.Okamoto, editor, *CT-RSA 2004*, volume 2964 of *Lectures Notes in Computer Science*, pages 2.3–249. Springer, 2004.
6. C. Clavier and M. Joye. Universal Exponentiation Algorithm. In Ç. Koç, D. Naccache, and C. Paar, editors, *Cryptographic Hardware and Embedded Systems (CHES) – 2001*, volume 2162 of *Lectures Notes in Computer Science*, pages 300–308. Springer, 2001.
7. J-S. Coron. Resistance Against Differential Power Analysis for Elliptic Curve Cryptosystems. In Ç. Koç and C. Paar, editors, *Cryptographic Hardware and Embedded Systems (CHES) – 1999*, volume 1717 of *Lectures Notes in Computer Science*, pages 292–302. Springer, 1999.
8. P-A. Fouque, F. Muller, G. Poupard, and F. Valette. Defeating Countermeasures Based on Randomized BSD Representations. In M. Joye and J-J. Quisquater, editors, *Cryptographic Hardware and Embedded Systems (CHES) – 2004*, volume 3156 of *Lectures Notes in Computer Science*, pages 312–327. Springer, 2004.
9. K. Gandolfi, C. Mourtel, and F. Olivier. Electromagnetic Analysis : Concret Results. In Ç. Koç, D. Naccache, and C. Paar, editors, *Cryptographic Hardware and Embedded Systems (CHES) – 2001*, volume 2162 of *Lectures Notes in Computer Science*, pages 251–261. Springer, 2001.

10. L. Goubin and J. Patarin. DES and Differential Power Analysis, The "Duplication" Method. In Ç. Koç and C. Paar, editors, *Cryptographic Hardware and Embedded Systems (CHES) – 1999*, volume 1717 of *Lectures Notes in Computer Science*, pages 158–172. Springer, 1999.
11. J. Ha and S. Moon. Randomized signed-scalar Multiplication of ECC to resist Power Attacks. In B. Kaliski, Ç. Koç, and C. Paar, editors, *Cryptographic Hardware and Embedded Systems (CHES) – 2002*, volume 2523 of *Lectures Notes in Computer Science*, pages 551–563. Springer, 2002.
12. K. Itoh, T. Izu, and M. Takenaka. Address-Bit Differential Power Analysis of Cryptographic Schemes OK-ECDH and OK-ECDSA. In B. Kaliski, Ç. Koç, and C. Paar, editors, *Cryptographic Hardware and Embedded Systems (CHES) – 2002*, volume 2523 of *Lectures Notes in Computer Science*, pages 129–143. Springer, 2002.
13. C. Karlof and D. Wagner. Hidden Markov Model Cryptanalysis. In C. Walter, Ç. Koç, and C. Paar, editors, *Cryptographic Hardware and Embedded Systems (CHES) – 2003*, volume 2779 of *Lectures Notes in Computer Science*, pages 17–34. Springer, 2003.
14. P. Kocher. Timing Attacks on Implementations of Diffie-Hellman, RSA, DSS, and Others Systems. In N. Koblitz, editor, *Advances in Cryptology – Crypto'96*, volume 1109 of *Lectures Notes in Computer Science*, pages 104–113. Springer, 1996.
15. P. Kocher, J. Jaffe, and B. Jun. Differential Power Analysis. In M. Wiener, editor, *Advances in Cryptology – Crypto'99*, volume 1666 of *Lectures Notes in Computer Science*, pages 388–397. Springer, 1999.
16. National Institute of Standards and Technology (NIST). Digital Signature Standard (DSS) FIPS Publication 186-2, February 2000. Available at http://csrc.nist.gov/publications/fips/fips186-2/fips186-2-change1.pdf.
17. R. Rivest, A. Shamir, and L. Adleman. A method for obtaining digital signatures and public-key cryptosystems. In *Communications of the ACM 21(2)*, pages 120–126, 1978.
18. A. Shamir. How to Share a Secret. *Communications of the ACM (CACM)*, 22(11):612–613, November 1979.
19. E. Trichina and A. Bellezza. Implementation of Elliptic Curve Cryptography with Built-In Counter Measures against Side Channel Attacks. In B. Kaliski, Ç. Koç, and C. Paar, editors, *Cryptographic Hardware and Embedded Systems (CHES) – 2002*, volume 2523 of *Lectures Notes in Computer Science*, pages 98–113. Springer, 2002.

New Online/Offline Signature Schemes Without Random Oracles

Kaoru Kurosawa[1] and Katja Schmidt-Samoa[2]

[1] Department of Computer and Information Sciences, Ibaraki University, Japan
[2] Fachbereich Informatik, Technische Universität Darmstadt, Germany

Abstract. In this paper, we propose new signature schemes provably secure under the strong RSA assumption in the standard model. Our proposals utilize Shamir-Tauman's generic construction for building EF-CMA secure online/offline signature schemes from trapdoor commitments and less secure basic signature schemes. We introduce a new natural intractability assumption for hash functions, which can be interpreted as a generalization of second pre-image collision resistance. Assuming the validity of this assumption, we are able to construct new signature schemes provably secure under the strong RSA assumption without random oracles. In contrast to Cramer-Shoup's signature scheme based on strong RSA in the standard model, no costly generation of prime numbers is required for the signer in our proposed schemes. Moreover, the security of our schemes relies on weaker assumptions placed on the hash function than Gennaro, Halevi and Rabin's solution.

Keywords: Online/offline signatures, trapdoor hash, strong RSA assumption, division intractability.

1 Introduction

Digital signatures are intended to replace handwritten signatures in the electronic world. The security goal here is authenticity, *e.g.*, the proof of authorship of messages. Besides obvious applications in electronic commerce, digital signatures are important building blocks for various kinds of cryptographic protocols, and traditional public key infrastructures rely on digital signatures for certifying public keys.

Until 1999, all provably secure solutions for efficient digital signature schemes relied on the random oracle methodology [BR93]. In the random oracle model (ROM), all parties (the legitimate ones as well as the adversary) have black-box access to functions which behave like truly random functions. Under this idealized assumption it became possible to develop cryptosystems that are both efficient and provably secure. In concrete implementations, however, truly random functions are out of reach and the random oracles are replaced by concrete objects like cryptographic hash functions. Thus it is obvious that even a rigorously analyzed security proof in the random oracle model does not guaranty security in the real world. As a real world adversary may exploit some weaknesses of the hash functions used, a proof in the ROM can only exclude *generic*

M. Yung et al. (Eds.): PKC 2006, LNCS 3958, pp. 330–346, 2006.

attacks against the scheme. Even worse, recently published results show separations between the random oracle scenario and standard model as there exist cryptosystems provably secure in the ROM that nevertheless are breakable when implemented with any concrete realization [CGH98, CGH04].

Then, in 1999, Cramer and Shoup on the one hand and Gennaro, Halevi and Rabin on the other hand independently came up with practical solutions for digital signature schemes provably secure without random oracles, *i.e.*, in the standard model [CS99, GHR99]. Interestingly, the security of both proposals relies on the same intractability assumption, namely the hardness of the flexible RSA problem, also known as the strong RSA assumption. However, none of these solutions is free from disadvantages. The major drawback of the Cramer-Shoup scheme—referred to as CS scheme in the following—is that the signer is required to generate a prime number for producing a signature. According to heuristics given in [CS99], the costs for prime number generation are one third of the total signing costs on average. The most crucial disadvantage of the Gennaro-Halevi-Rabin scheme—referred to as GHR scheme in the following—is that its security relies on a strong non-standard assumption placed on the hash function used. Gennaro *et al.* prove the existence of suitable hash functions under the strong RSA assumption by constructing a concrete implementation, however, when utilizing this fully proved hash function the entire system becomes less efficient than the CS scheme. Our aim in this paper is to overcome both drawbacks.

On the first glance, the CS scheme and the GHR scheme seem quite different. But in the light of more recent results about generic constructions of provably secure signature schemes, one may observe a common design principle (here, we consider the fully proved GHR scheme): In both cases, first a commitment to the message is constructed, followed by signing the commitment with a "weak" signature scheme. For the first step a *trapdoor* commitment scheme is utilized, which enables the simulator in the security proof to answer signature queries based on previously computed commitments. Although the weak basic signature schemes are different in CS and GHR, both make use of prime numbers to permit the reduction of the flexible RSA problem to the security of the basic signature scheme[1]. In 2001, Shamir and Tauman universalized this approach and proposed a generic construction for online/offline signature schemes [ST01]. As now the mechanisms to enhance the security of "weak" signature schemes by the means of trapdoor commitments are better understood, it seems worthwhile to revisit the CS and GHR schemes.

Our goal is to get rid off the need for prime number generation as well as off the strong assumption placed on the hash function. Therefore, the GHR basic signature scheme seems to be a more promising candidate to start with because

---

[1] In the GHR scheme, the hash function used in the basic signature scheme has to satisfy a rather strong assumption. Gennaro *et al.* show that a trapdoor commitment scheme combined with a collision resistant hash function producing prime digests only is a possible implementation for the hash function. Thus, formally the task of prime number generation is assigned to the hash function here.

prime number generation is incorporated directly in its CS pendant. An analysis of this scheme reveals that the weak security conditions necessary for a Shamir-Tauman-like construction can be fulfilled if the utilized hash function possesses a property that is similar but intuitively less demanding than its analog in the in the GHR framework. To be more concrete, Gennaro *et al.* introduced the notion of a *division-intractable* family of hash functions $\mathcal{H}$, which briefly states that given $H \in \mathcal{H}$, it is infeasible to find values $X_1, \ldots, X_n, Y$ such that $H(Y)$ divides the product $\prod_{i=1}^{n} H(X_i)$. In contrast, our construction only requires what we call *weak division-intractability*, meaning that given $H \in \mathcal{H}$ and $X_1, \ldots, X_n$, it is infeasible to find Y such that $H(Y)$ divides the product $\prod_{i=1}^{n} H(X_i)$. Thus, the values X_i are not longer under the attacker's control. Note that our newly defined property relaxes Gennaro *et al.*'s notion of (strong) division intractability in exactly the same way as second pre-image resistance relaxes collision resistance.

2   Preliminaries

Throughout this paper, we use the following notations: For any positive integer N we write $\mathbb{Z}_N$ for the ring of residue classes modulo N, and $\mathbb{Z}_N^\times$ for its multiplicative group. $|N|_2$ denotes the bit-length of N, and we write $[N]^k$ for the integer corresponding to the k most significant bits of N. As usual, a probability $\Pr(k)$ is called *negligible* if $\Pr(k)$ decreases faster than the inverse of any polynomial in k, *i.e.* $\forall c \exists k_c (k > k_c \Rightarrow \Pr(k) < k^{-c})$. In contrast, a probability $\Pr(k)$ is called *overwhelming*, if $1 - \Pr(k)$ is negligible.

We abbreviate *probabilistic polynomial time* by PPT.

2.1   Digital Signature Schemes

A digital signature scheme is denoted by $\Omega = (\mathsf{G}_{sign}, \mathsf{Sign}, \mathsf{Verify})$. G_{sign} is a PPT algorithm which on input a security parameter generates (sk, vk), where vk and sk are the secret signing and the public verification key, respectively. Sign is a PPT algorithm which produces a signature σ on input a message m and the secret key sk. Verify is a polynomial time algorithm which checks the validity of (m, σ) by using vk, say $\mathsf{Verify}(\mathrm{vk}, m, \sigma) = \mathsf{valid}$ or $\mathsf{invalid}$. It is required that $\mathsf{Verify}(\mathrm{vk}, m, \sigma) = \mathsf{valid}$ holds if and only if σ is a possible outcome of $\mathsf{Sign}(\mathrm{sk}, m)$. For brevity, we also write $\mathsf{Sign}_{\mathrm{sk}}(m)$ instead of $\mathsf{Sign}(\mathrm{sk}, m)$ and $\mathsf{Verify}_{\mathrm{vk}}(m, \sigma)$ instead of $\mathsf{Verify}(\mathrm{vk}, m, \sigma)$.

In the following, we review security notions for digital signature schemes. All the notions below have been introduced by Goldwasser, Micali and Rivest [GMR88].

The standard security notion of signature schemes is existential unforgeability under adaptive chosen message attacks (EF-CMA). Here, the attacker is allowed to query the signing oracle adaptively.

Definition 1 (EF-CMA). *A digital signature scheme* $\Omega = (\mathsf{G}_{sign}, \mathsf{Sign}, \mathsf{Verify})$ *is said to be* existential unforgeable under adaptive chosen message attacks *if for any PPT adversary* $\mathcal{A}$ *the following probability is negligible in* ℓ:

$$\Pr \left[\begin{array}{l} (\text{sk}, \text{vk}) \hookleftarrow \mathsf{G}_{sign}(1^\ell), \\ FOR\ i = 1, \dots, k: \\ \quad \{m_i \hookleftarrow \mathcal{A}(\text{vk}, m_1, \sigma_1, \dots, m_{i-1}, \sigma_{i-1});\ \sigma_i \hookleftarrow \mathsf{Sign}_{\text{sk}}(m_i)\}, \\ (m^*, \sigma^*) \hookleftarrow \mathcal{A}(\text{vk}, m_1, \sigma_1, \dots, m_k, \sigma_k): \\ m^* \notin \{m_1, \dots, m_t\} \wedge \mathsf{Verify}_{\text{vk}}(m^*, \sigma^*) = \mathsf{valid} \end{array} \right].$$

In this paper, we call a signature scheme is *adaptively secure* if it is EF-CMA.

A much weaker security notion is existential unforgeability against random message attacks, *a.k.a.* known message attacks (EF-KMA). Here, the adversary is just given the verification key and a list of randomly generated valid message/signature pairs without any control over the messages.

Definition 2 (EF-KMA). *A digital signature scheme* $\Omega = (\mathsf{G}_{sign}, \mathsf{Sign}, \mathsf{Verify})$ *is said to be* existentially unforgeable under known message attacks *if for any PPT adversary* $\mathcal{A}$ *the following probability is negligible in* ℓ:

$$\Pr \left[\begin{array}{l} (\text{sk}, \text{vk}) \hookleftarrow \mathsf{G}_{sign}(1^\ell), \\ FOR\ i = 1, \dots, k: \{m_i \hookleftarrow \mathcal{M},\ \sigma_i \hookleftarrow \mathsf{Sign}_{\text{sk}}(m_i)\}, \\ (m^*, \sigma^*) \hookleftarrow \mathcal{A}(\text{vk}, m_1, \sigma_1, \dots, m_k, \sigma_k): \\ m^* \notin \{m_1, \dots, m_t\} \wedge \mathsf{Verify}_{\text{vk}}(m^*, \sigma^*) = \mathsf{valid} \end{array} \right].$$

In this paper, we call EF-KMA secure signature schemes *weakly secure*.

2.2 Trapdoor Commitment Schemes

A trapdoor commitment scheme is defined by $\mathcal{TC} = (\mathsf{G}_{TC}, \mathsf{Tcom}, \mathsf{Topen})$, where Topen is Twopen or Tsopen as shown below. G_{TC} is a PPT algorithm which generates (pk, tk), where pk is the public key and tk is the trapdoor. Associated to $\mathcal{TC}$ are the spaces of messages $\mathcal{M}$, randomness $\mathcal{R}$ and commitments $\mathcal{C}$.

Tcom is the algorithm that computes a commitment to m as $x = \mathsf{Tcom}(\text{pk}, m, r)$, where $r \in \mathcal{R}$ is a random nonce. To open the commitment x, the sender reveals m, r and the receiver recomputes x.

Twopen is the algorithm that weakly opens a commitment in any desired way with the trapdoor tk. For given m, r and a target message m', it outputs $r' = \mathsf{Twopen}(\text{tk}, m, r, m')$ such that $x = \mathsf{Tcom}(\text{pk}, m, r) = \mathsf{Tcom}(\text{pk}, m', r')$.

Hence, the trapdoor holder is able to create a "dummy commitment" and later open this commitment to any message of his choice.

However, for some applications a strictly stronger property turns out to be useful; namely, the owner of the trapdoor key should be able to open a commitment arbitrarily even without knowledge of the pre-image values r, m. We call this mechanism *strong trapdoor opening*[2] and the corresponding schemes *strong*. In such a strong trapdoor commitment scheme there exists an algorithm Tsopen such that for a given commitment x and a target message m it outputs $r = \mathsf{Tsopen}(\text{tk}, m, x)$ with $x = \mathsf{Tcom}(\text{pk}, m, r)$.

The existence of (strong or weak) trapdoor opening algorithms Topen implies that the receiver cannot obtain any information about m given x.

---

[2] In [ST01], this property is referred to as *inversion property*.

The security of trapdoor commitment schemes requires that without knowledge of the trapdoor key it should be hard to find collisions. Moreover, randomness r obtained by invoking the trapdoor opening algorithm should be indistinguishable from properly generated r. Again, we simplify the notation by writing the keys as indices.

Definition 3. *We say that a trapdoor commitment scheme* $\mathcal{TC} = (\mathsf{G}_{TC}, \mathsf{Tcom},$ $\mathsf{Topen})$ *is secure if the following properties hold:*

Collision resistance: *For any PPT* $\mathcal{A}$ *the following probability is negligible in* ℓ:

$$\Pr\left[\begin{array}{l}(\text{pk}, \text{tk}) \leftarrow \mathsf{G}_{TC}(1^{\ell}), \mathcal{A}(\text{pk}) = (r, m, r', m'),\\ m \neq m' \wedge \mathsf{Tcom}_{\text{pk}}(r, m) = \mathsf{Tcom}_{\text{pk}}(r', m')\end{array}\right].$$

Uniformity: *The outcome of* Topen *is computationally indistinguishable from uniform in* $\mathcal{R}$ *provided that*
  - *in case of weak altering the input r is uniformly distributed in $\mathcal{R}$, resp.*
  - *in case of strong altering the following holds: for any $m \in \mathcal{M}$ the distribution of the input x is computationally indistinguishable from the distribution of* $\mathsf{Tcom}_{\text{pk}}(m, r)$, *where r is uniformly distributed in $\mathcal{R}$.*

2.3 Hash Functions

A hash function is an efficiently computable procedure that maps strings of arbitrary length to strings of fixed length. The sequence $\mathcal{H} = (H_k)_{k \in \mathbb{N}}$ is called a family of hash functions if each H_k is a collection of hash functions with output length k. Analog to signature and trapdoor commitment schemes, collections of hash functions can also be defined via a key generation algorithm, but for better readability, we utilize less formal notations below. Within the scope of this paper, the most important security properties of hash functions are the standard requirements (second pre-image) collision resistance (dating back to Damgård [Dam87]) and the non-standard ones weak/strong division intractability (the strong version introduced by Gennaro, Halevi and Rabin [GHR99], the weak version introduced and defined below in the present paper).

Definition 4 ((Second pre-image) collision resistance). *A family* $\mathcal{H} = (H_k)_{k \in K}$ *of hash functions is said to be*

collision resistant *if for any PPT adversary* $\mathcal{A}$, *the following probability is negligible in k:*

$$\Pr_{H \in H_k}[\mathcal{A}(H) = (X, Y) : X \neq Y \wedge H(X) = H(Y)],$$

second pre-image collision resistant *if for any PPT adversary* $\mathcal{A}$, *the following probability is negligible in k:*

$$\Pr_{H \in H_k, X}[\mathcal{A}(H, X) = (Y) : X \neq Y \wedge H(X) = H(Y)].$$

It is obvious that collision resistance implies second pre-image collision resistance.

Definition 5 (Weak/strong division intractability). *A family $\mathcal{H} = (H_k)_{k \in \mathbb{N}}$ of hash functions is said to be*

strongly division intractable *if for any PPT adversary $\mathcal{A}$, the following probability is negligible in k:*

$$\Pr_{H \in H_k} \left[\begin{array}{l} \mathcal{A}(H) = (X_1, X_2, \dots, X_n, Y) : \\ Y \notin \{X_1, X_2, \dots, X_n\} \wedge H(Y) \ divides \ \prod_{i=1}^{n} H(X_i) \end{array} \right],$$

weakly division intractable *if for any PPT adversary $\mathcal{A}$, the following probability is negligible in k for any n which is polynomially bounded by k:*

$$\Pr_{H \in H_k, X_1, \dots, X_n} \left[\begin{array}{l} \mathcal{A}(H, X_1, X_2, \dots, X_n) = Y : \\ Y \notin \{X_1, X_2, \dots, X_n\} \wedge H(Y) \ divides \ \prod_{i=1}^{n} H(X_i) \end{array} \right].$$

Note that our newly defined property of weak division intractability relaxes Gennaro *et al.*'s notion of (strong) division intractability in exactly the same way as second pre-image collision resistance lessens full collision resistance. Moreover, while division intractability obviously implies collision resistance, it is also easy to see that weak division intractability implies second pre-image collision resistance. The opposite directions, however, are not true. We will discuss the relationship between strong and weak division intractability further in Section 5.

2.4 Intractability Assumptions

Our proposed online/offline signature schemes rely on the following standard intractability assumptions:

Claim (Blum Factorization Assumption). Given $N = pq$ for two random primes p, q with $|p|_2 \approx |q|_2$ and $p = q = 3 \bmod 4$, it is hard to factor N.

The integer N from the preceeding assumption is called a *Blum integer*. If N is a Blum integer, then squaring is a permutation on the group $\mathrm{QR}(N)$ of quadratic residues modulo N.

Claim (p^2q Factorization Assumption). Given $N = p^2q$ for two random primes p, q with $|p|_2 \approx |q|_2$, it is hard to factor N.

The following assumption has been first described by Barić and Pfitzmann [BP97].

Claim (Strong RSA Assumption). Given $N = pq$ for two random primes p, q and a randomly chosen $s \in \mathbb{Z}_N^\times$, it is hard to find values $r \in \mathbb{Z}_N^\times$ and $e > 1$ such that $r^e = s \bmod N$.

In the preceeding claim, the tuple (N, s) is called an *instance of the flexible RSA problem*. In the rest of this paper, we sometimes use special moduli such as Blum integers or products of safe primes[3]. In this case, the Strong RSA Assumption has to be understood with respect to these kind of moduli.

We now state a useful lemma, which is proved, for example, in [CL02].

---

[3] A prime p is called a *safe prime* if $(p-1)/2$ is also prime.

Lemma 1. *Let $N = pq$ be the product of two distinct safe primes $p = 2p'+1, q = 2q' + 1$. Given $s, t \in \mathrm{QR}(N)$ along with $0 < a < b$ such that $s^b = t^a \bmod N$ and $\gcd(a, b) < a$, one can efficiently compute values $r, e > 1$ such that $r^e = s \bmod N$.*

Proof. By using extended Euclidean algorithm, we can efficiently find $u, v \in \mathbb{Z}$ such that $au + bv = \gcd(a, b) =: c$. In particular, we have $(a/c)u + (b/c)v = 1$.

Without loss of generality, we may assume $\gcd(c, p'q') = 1$, because otherwise we can factor N (either directly from the knowledge of p' resp. q', or by applying Miller's algorithm [Mil75] on a multiple of $\varphi(N) = 4p'q'$). Therefore, from $s^b = t^a \bmod N$, we conclude $s^{b/c} = t^{a/c} \bmod N$, leading to

$$s = s^{(a/c)u+(b/c)v} = s^{(a/c)u}t^{(a/c)v} = (s^u t^v)^{(a/c)} \bmod N.$$

Hence, we obtain $e = a/c$ and $r = s^u t^v \bmod N$. □

Note that as one quarter of the elements of $\mathbb{Z}_N^\times$ are quadratic residues, we have that if the Strong RSA Assumption is true at all, then it is also true for instances (N, s) where s is randomly chosen from $\mathrm{QR}(N)$. Thus efficiently finding t, a, b given N, s as in Lemma 1 above violates the Strong RSA Assumption.

2.5   Online/Offline Signature Schemes

The notion of online/offline signatures was introduced by Even *et al.* [EGM96]. In such schemes, the online phase of the signing algorithm is made very fast due to the precomputation performed in the offline phase before the message actually to be signed is known.

In 2001, Shamir and Tauman improved this generic construction [ST01]. Informally, their new approach can be described as using the well-known hash-then-sign paradigm, where the ordinary hash function is replaced by a trapdoor commitment scheme: Let $\Omega = (\mathsf{G}_{sign}, \mathsf{Sign}, \mathsf{Verify})$ and $\mathcal{TC} = (\mathsf{G}_{TC}, \mathsf{Tcom}, \mathsf{Topen})$ be a weakly secure signature scheme and a trapdoor commitment scheme, respectively. The key generation algorithm of the entire online/offline signature scheme runs both individual key generation algorithms $\mathsf{G}_{sign}, \mathsf{G}_{TC}$, and the signer is given the secret signing key sk as well as the secret trapdoor key tk. The public key is (vk, pk), where vk is the verification key of Ω and pk is the public key of $\mathcal{TC}$.

Offline phase: Choose a dummy message $\tilde{m}$ and a random number $\tilde{r}$. Compute hash $= \mathsf{Tcom}_{\mathrm{pk}}(\tilde{m}, \tilde{r})$, $\sigma = \mathsf{Sign}_{\mathrm{sk}}(\mathrm{hash})$ and store $(\tilde{m}, \tilde{r}, \sigma)$.
Online phase: Given a message m, first retrieve $(\tilde{m}, \tilde{r}, \sigma)$ from memory. Then, by using tk, find r such that $\mathsf{Tcom}_{\mathrm{pk}}(m, r) = \mathsf{Tcom}_{\mathrm{pk}}(\tilde{m}, \tilde{r})$ holds. Output (σ, r) as the signature of m.

Verification is straightforward, as by construction σ is a valid hash-then-sign signature of m.

Fortunately, this generic construction also enhances the security of the basic signature scheme: If Ω is existentially unforgeable against generic message attacks (EF-GMA), then the online-offline scheme as described above is adaptively secure (EF-CMA). Moreover, if $\mathcal{TC}$ also allows *strongly* trapdoor opening, then Ω is only required to be existentially unforgeable under known message attacks (EF-KMA).

Therefore, Shamir and Tauman's construction might also be useful in environments where the distinction between online and offline costs is not an issue. In this case, the composed signature algorithm simply consists of committing to the message and signing the commitment, and there is no need for the signer to know the trapdoor key. The ability of arbitrarily opening commitments is only required in the security proof to enable the simulator to respond to the signature queries. In the following, we call this construction the *commit-then-sign approach*. As mentioned in the Introduction, the CS scheme also follows this design principle[4].

Remark 1. The technique of commiting to a message with a trapdoor commitment scheme and signing the commitment has also been used by Krawczyk and Rabin for introducing chameleon signatures [KR00]. In contrast to the approach above, in a chameleon signature scheme the *recipient* is the trapdoor holder. Whilst in case of Shamir/Tauman, the intended goal is efficient online signing and a security enhancement of the basic signature scheme, the aim of chameleon signatures is to distract the receiver of a signature from revealing the signed message to any third party.

3   The Primitives

In this section, we present the building blocks for our proposed full signature schemes. As noted above, the basic primitives are a (strong) trapdoor commitment scheme and a weakly secure signature scheme.

3.1   A Trapdoor Commitment Scheme with Strongly Trapdoor Opening Based on Factoring

We propose a factorization-based trapdoor commitment scheme $\mathcal{TC}_{2^k} = (\mathsf{G}_{TC}, \mathsf{Tcom}, \mathsf{Topen})$ resting on the 2^k identification scheme of Shoup [Sho99] as follows:

G_{TC}: Let ℓ be a security parameter. Choose two ℓ-bit prime numbers p and q such that $p = q = 3 \bmod 4$. Let $N = pq$. Pick $v \in QR(N)$ randomly and define a parameter k such that 2^k grows faster than any polynomial in ℓ. The public key consists of (N, v, k) and the trapdoor key is (p, q).

Tcom: To commit to a message $m \in \{0, \ldots, 2^{k-1} - 1\}$, the commiter chooses a random value $r \in \mathbb{Z}_N^\times$ and computes $\mathsf{Tcom}_{\mathsf{pk}}(r, m) = r^{2^k} v^m \bmod N$.

Topen: Given a target message m and a commitment x, the strong trapdoor opening algorithm computes $r \in \mathbb{Z}_N^\times$ such that $x = r^{2^k} v^m \bmod N$. Weak trapdoor opening is realized by $\mathsf{Twopen}_{\mathsf{tk}}(m, r, m') = r' = rv^{(m-m')2^{-k}} \bmod N$.

---

[4] In fact, Cramer and Shoup also proposed an online/offline version of their scheme by providing the signer with the trapdoor key. Thus, Shamir and Tauman's idea is not new.

We have the following theorem:

Theorem 1. *Under the Blum Factorization Assumption the above construction* $\mathcal{TC}_{2^k}$ *is a strong trapdoor commitment scheme secure in the sense of Definition 3.*

Proof. The correctness of the trapdoor opening algorithms is obvious.

To prove the collision resistance, we assume that $\mathcal{A}$ is a PPT collision finder. We then construct a PPT algorithm I which can factor Blum integers N as follows: On input N, I chooses a such that

$$\left(\frac{a}{N}\right) = -1$$

randomly, where $\left(\frac{\cdot}{\cdot}\right)$ denotes the Jacobi symbol. I computes $v = a^2 \bmod N$ and runs $\mathcal{A}$ on input (N, v). $\mathcal{A}$ eventually outputs $(m, r), (m', r')$ such that $m \neq m'$, $\mathsf{Tcom}(r, m) = \mathsf{Tcom}(r', m')$. It holds that

$$r^{2^k} v^m = r'^{2^k} v^{m'} \bmod N.$$

Therefore, we obtain that

$$(r/r')^{2^k} = v^{m'-m} \bmod N.$$

Wlog, assume that $m' > m$ and let $m' - m = u2^t$, where u is odd. Then $t < k-1$. Let $z = r/r' \bmod N$. Now

$$z^{2^k} = v^{u2^t} = (a^2)^{u2^t} \bmod N.$$

Since $p = q = 3 \bmod 4$, we have

$$(z^{2^{k-t-1}})^2 = (a^u)^2 \bmod N.$$

From $k - t - 1 > 0$, we have

$$\left(\frac{z^{2^{k-t-1}}}{N}\right) = 1.$$

On the other hand,

$$\left(\frac{a^u}{N}\right) = -1$$

because u is odd. Therefore, we can factor N with probability 1 by computing $\gcd(a^u - z^{2^{k-t-1}}, N)$.

Finally, we note that for each message $m \in \{0, \ldots, 2^{k-1} - 1\}$ and for each commitment $x \in \mathrm{QR}(N)$ there are exactly four $r \in \mathbb{Z}_N^\times$ with $x = \mathsf{Tcom}(r, m)$. Consequently, uniformity holds for both trapdoor opening algorithms. $\square$

Remark 2. If weak altering is sufficient, we define $v^{2^{-k}} \bmod N$ as the trapdoor key.

As we will see, combined with a weakly secure signature scheme, $\mathcal{TC}_{2^k}$ yields an adaptively secure commit-then-sign scheme as described in Section 2.5. However, as the opening algorithms require a modular exponentiation, it is not reasonable to use $\mathcal{TC}_{2^k}$ as a building block for a full online/offline signature scheme.

For the construction of schemes with real online/offline properties, trapdoor commitments with extremely fast weak trapdoor opening are required. A variant of the following scheme $\mathcal{TC}_{p^2q} = (\mathsf{G}_{TC}, \mathsf{Tcom}, \mathsf{Topen})$ has recently been proposed by Schmidt-Samoa and Takagi [SST05]:

G_{TC}: Let ℓ be a security parameter. Randomly choose two ℓ-bit primes p, q with $p \nmid q - 1, q \nmid p - 1$ and compute $N = p^2 q$. Define a parameter k minimal with respect to $2^k > pq\sqrt{p}$, and a parameter l maximal with respect to $lpq < 2^k$. The public key is $\mathrm{pk} = (N, k)$, and the trapdoor key is $\mathrm{tk} = (p, q, l)$.

Tcom: To commit to a message $m \in \{0, \ldots, [N]^{|N|_2 - k} - 1\}$, a value $r \in \{0, \ldots, 2^k - 1\}$ is chosen uniformly at random and $\mathsf{Tcom}(r, m) = (2^k m + r)^N \bmod N$ is computed, where $[N]^{|N|_2 - k}$ stands for the integer corresponding to the $|N|_2 - k$ most significant bits of N.

Topen: Given a target message m and a commitment x, the strong trapdoor opening algorithm first computes $aux = x^{1/N} - 2^k m \bmod pq$. Then, $0 \leq s < l$ is chosen uniformly at random, and the output r is computed as $r = aux + spq$.

Weak trapdoor opening on the input m, r, m' is realized by first computing $aux = 2^k(m - m') + r \bmod pq$, and then proceeding as before.

Theorem 2 ([SST05]). $\mathcal{TC}_{p^2q} = (\mathsf{G}_{TC}, \mathsf{Tcom}, \mathsf{Topen})$ *is a secure trapdoor commitment scheme in the sense of Definition 3.*

Remark 3. In the original scheme from [SST05], the randomness is chosen from $\mathbb{Z}_{pq}$. In this case, however, a polynomial number of trapdoor openings reveals a logarithmic number of the most significant bits of the secret pq. Although this is not a thread in the light of current factoring achievements (lattice methods like [Cop97] require the knowledge of the $\mathcal{O}((pq)^{1/3})$ most significants bit of pq to factor p^2q), we slightly modified the scheme as described above. Now, the randomness is sampled from the set $\{0, \ldots, 2^k - 1\}$, and the r constructed by the opening algorithms Topen is uniformly distributed over the set $\{0, \ldots, lpq - 1\}$. These distributions are statistically close (a simple computation shows that the distance is upperbounded by $2/\sqrt{p}$). This modification also ensures that the simulator in the commit-then-sign security proof is able to compute commitments properly.

Note that weak trapdoor opening only requires a modular addition, a short integer multiplication, and a bit-shift, and therefore can be computed extremely fast.

3.2   A Weakly Secure Signature Scheme Based on Strong-RSA

In this section, we analyze a simple RSA-type hash-then-sign signature scheme. The proposed scheme is essentially the same as Gennaro, Halevi and Rabin introduced in [GHR99]. In that paper, Gennaro *et al.* proved that when instantiated with a so-called *suitable* hash function, their scheme is adaptively secure (EF-CMA) under the Strong RSA Assumption. The most crucial demands on a suitable hash function are (strong) division intractability, which can be achieved by forcing the output to be a prime, and the property that collision finding does not help solving the flexible RSA problem, *i.e.*, the two associated intractability assumptions should be unrelated in a sense. The latter requirement is dealt with by implementing the hash function as a trapdoor commitment scheme. In the following, we prove that if we relax the hash requirement to *weak* division intractability, then the signature scheme is still weakly secure.

Let us now describe the basic signature scheme $\Omega_{\mathsf{S-RSA}} = (\mathsf{G}_{sign}, \mathsf{Sign}, \mathsf{Verify})$.

G_{sign}: On input a security parameter ℓ, choose two safe ℓ-bit primes p, q. Set $N = pq$ and randomly select $y \in \mathrm{QR}(N)$. Finally, pick a weakly division intractable hash function H from a family of hash functions. We assume that H always outputs odd integers[5]. The public key consists of N, y and H; the secret key is p, q.

Sign: To sign a message $m \in \{0,1\}^*$, first compute the hash $e = H(m)$. Then, with knowledge of p and q, compute an e-th root of y modulo N:

$$\sigma = y^{\frac{1}{e}} \bmod N.$$

Then, σ is the signature of m.

Verify: Given (m, σ), output valid if $\sigma^{H(m)} = y \bmod N$ holds and invalid, otherwise.

Note that the signing algorithm can compute an appropriate root modulo N with overwhelming probability because N is a product of safe primes. Namely, four is the only small factor of $\varphi(N)$ and thus, any odd element not co-prime with $\varphi(N)$ reveals the factorization of N.

Theorem 3. *Provided the Strong RSA Assumption is valid, the basic signature scheme* $\Omega_{\mathsf{S-RSA}}$ *above is existentially unforgeable under known message attacks (EF-KMA).*

Proof. Let $\mathcal{F}$ be a EF-KMA adversary against $\Omega_{\mathsf{S-RSA}}$. We construct an attacker $\mathcal{A}$ against the Strong RSA Assumption, which uses $\mathcal{F}$ as a subroutine. $\mathcal{A}$ is given a quadratic instance (N, s) of the flexible RSA problem for safe moduli, *i.e.*, N is a product of two safe primes and s is a quadratic residue modulo N. $\mathcal{A}$ picks dummy messages $m_1, \ldots, m_k$ at random and defines

$$y = s^{\prod_{i=1}^{k} H(m_i)} \bmod N.$$

Moreover, $\mathcal{A}$ computes

$$\sigma_j = s^{\prod_{i=1, i \neq j}^{k} H(m_i)} \bmod N$$

---

[5] This can be easily achieved by setting the least significant output bit to one.

for $j = 1, \ldots, k$. Observe that, by construction, σ_j is a valid signature on m_j. $\mathcal{A}$ gives the forger $\mathcal{F}$ the public key N, y as well as the signature/message pairs $(m_1, \sigma_1), \ldots, (m_k, \sigma_k)$. Eventually, $\mathcal{F}$ outputs a forgery (m, σ). Validity of this forgery implies

$$\sigma^{H(m)} = y = s^{\prod_{i=1}^{k} H(m_i)} \bmod N.$$

As H is weakly division intractable and $m \notin \{m_1, \ldots, m_k\}$, we must have $\gcd(\prod_{i=1}^{k} H(m_i), H(m)) < H(m)$. Thus, by applying Lemma 1, $\mathcal{A}$ can efficiently find values $r, e > 1$ with $r^e = s \bmod N$. Consequently, $\mathcal{A}$ could break the Strong RSA Assumption if the advantage of $\mathcal{F}$ were non-negligible.   □

4   New Adaptively Secure Signatures Based on Strong-RSA

In this section, we eventually combine the primitives described in the section above using Shamir-Tauman's approach. As mentioned before, we utilize the trapdoor commitment $\mathcal{TC}_{2^k}$ to enhance the weak security of the basic signature scheme $\Omega_{\mathsf{S-RSA}}$ to full adaptive security, whereas the usage of $\mathcal{TC}_{p^2 q}$ additionally provides online/offline functionality. The reason why we have introduced $\mathcal{TC}_{2^k}$ is that its underlying intractability assumption (Blum Factorization) is implied by the Strong RSA Assumption, and thus we can base the entire construction on the latter only.

In the following, we assume that H is a hash function that always outputs odd integers. Our first proposal is as follows:

G_{sign}: Choose two safe primes p_1, q_1 as well as two primes p_2, q_2 with $p_2 = q_2 = 3 \bmod 4$. Set $N_1 = p_1 q_1$, $N_2 = p_2 q_2$ and randomly select $y \in \mathrm{QR}(N_1)$, $v \in \mathrm{QR}(N_2)$. Define a parameter k such that 2^k grows faster than any polynomial in the security parameter. The public key consists of N_1, N_2, y, v, k; the secret key is p_1, q_1.

Sign: To sign a message $m \in \{0, \ldots, 2^{k-1} - 1\}$, first commit to m by choosing a random value $r \in \mathbb{Z}_{N_2}^{\times}$ and computing $x = r^{2^k} v^m \bmod N_2$. Then build the hash $e = H(x)$. Finally, with knowledge of p_1 and q_1, construct an e-th root of y modulo N_1:

$$\sigma = y^{\frac{1}{e}} \bmod N_1.$$

Output (σ, r) as the signature of m.

Verify: Given (m, σ, r), first compute $x = r^{2^k} v^m \bmod N_2$. Output valid if $\sigma^{H(x)} = y \bmod N_1$ holds and invalid, otherwise.

Theorem 4. *If H is weakly division intractable and the Strong RSA Assumption is valid, then the signature scheme above is existentially unforgeable under adaptive chosen message attacks (EF-CMA).*

Proof. From Theorem 1 we have that the commitment scheme utilized in the construction above is a secure trapdoor commitment scheme which allows strongly trapdoor opening. Theorem 1 states that the basic signature scheme used to sign the commitments is weakly secure under the Strong RSA Assumption. The generation of different moduli ensures that the underlying problems are unrelated, *i.e.*, even with knowledge of p_2, q_2, which enables to open the commitments in any desired way, it is still assumed to be infeasible to solve the flexible RSA problem with respect to N_1. Thus, from the results of Shamir and Tauman [ST01], the assertion follows.

A direct proof without using the result from Shamir and Tauman is given in the full version of this paper [KSS06]. □

Now we replace the commitment scheme to achieve online/offline functionality.

G_{sign}: Choose two safe primes p_1, q_1 as well as two primes p_2, q_2 with $p_2 \nmid q_2 - 1, q_2 \nmid p_2 - 1$. Set $N_1 = p_1 q_1$, $N_2 = p_2^2 q_2$ and randomly select $y \in QR(N_1)$. Define a parameter k minimal with respect to $2^k > pq\sqrt{p}$, and a parameter l maximal with respect to $lpq < 2^k$. The public key consists of N_1, N_2, y, k; the secret key is p_1, q_1, p_2, q_2, l.

Sign: 1. Offline phase: Pick a dummy message $\tilde{m} \in \{0, \ldots, [N_2]^{|N_2|_2 - k} - 1\}$, and commit to $\tilde{m}$ by choosing a random value $\tilde{r} \in \mathbb{Z}_{p_2 q_2}$ and computing $x = (2^k \tilde{m} + \tilde{r})^{N_2} \bmod N_2$. Then build the hash $e = H(x)$. Finally, with knowledge of p_1 and q_1, construct an e-th root of y modulo N_1:

$$\sigma = y^{\frac{1}{e}} \bmod N_1.$$

Store $\sigma, \tilde{m}, \tilde{r}$.

2. Online phase: To finish the signature generation when the message m to be signed is known, first retrieve $\sigma, \tilde{m}, \tilde{r}$ from memory. Then compute $aux = 2^k(\tilde{m} - m) + \tilde{r} \bmod p_2 q_2$. Finally, $0 \le s < l$ is chosen uniformly at random, and r is computed as $r = aux + spq$. Output (σ, r) as the signature of m.

Verify: Given (m, σ, r), first compute $x = (2^k m + r)^{N_2} \bmod N_2$. Output valid if $\sigma^{H(x)} = y \bmod N_1$ holds and invalid, otherwise.

The following theorem can be proved exactly as the theorem above because the commitment scheme utilized in the construction above is a secure trapdoor commitment scheme [SST05] which allows strongly trapdoor opening.

Theorem 5. *Assume the Strong RSA Assumption and the p^2q Factorization Assumption are valid. If H is weakly division intractable, then the signature scheme above is existentially unforgeable under adaptive chosen message attacks (EF-CMA).*

Remark 4. In the schemes above, we restricted the message spaces according to the requirements of the trapdoor commitment schemes. Extensions to arbitrary message spaces are possible when utilizing families of collision-resistant hash functions.

5   Comparison

In this section, we compare our proposals with the CS and GHR schemes[6]. Under the assumption that weak, resp. strong division intractable hash functions exist, neither GHR nor our proposals require the signer to perform costly prime number generations as in (modified) CS.

We next discuss why we regard weak division intractability as more reasonable than its strong pendant. First note that a random oracle is weakly as well as strongly division intractable. Assuming a hash function behaving like a random oracle, Coron and Naccache analyzed the complexity of an attack against strong division intractability [CN00]. The outline of their proposed attack is to find a smooth hash value first, and then, for each of its (small) prime divisors p, to search for another hash value divisible by p. Based on theoretical results on the density of smooth numbers, Coron and Naccache show that the running time of this attack is sub-exponential in the digest length. Thus, they recommend a digest length of at least 1024 bits, which is twice as large as suggested by Gennaro et al. in [GHR99]. We want to point out that this attack does not work against weak division intractability where the adversary has no control over the hash values that should be divided.

Table 1. Experiments on weak division intractability

$n\backslash k$	20			40			60			80			100$^{(+)}$		
k	1	56	1	41	21555	606	2256	18490671	93702	—			—		
$k^{1.5}$	<1	9	1	3	415	4	105	33631	229	5566	3141452	14240	—		
k^2	<1	3.5	1	<1	44	1	5	941	11	208	28883	431	10823	493263	13613
$k^{2.5}$	<1	2.2	1	<1	14	1	<1	135	2	8	1383	7	342	13749	1289
k^3	<1	1.5	1	<1	5	1	—			—					

We conducted some experiments to investigate weak division intractability (of random oracles) heuristically. For each pair (n, k), we performed 200 experiments: n k-bit numbers were chosen uniformly at random, and we counted the number of random k-bit numbers x to pick, until x divides the product of the others. The measured data suggests that the expected value of numbers x to pick is lower bounded by $n^{-1.5}2^{k/3}$ for n chosen polynomial in k. Table 1 shows the results of some of these experiments. For each pair (n, k), the table contains three entries: the first one is the evaluation of $n^{-1.5}2^{k/3}$, the second one is the mean of all performed experiments, and the third one is the second-smallest number appearing in the 200 experiments (an entry "-" indicates that no experiments have been performed at all, whilst the index "+" denotes that the respective data is based on less than 200 experiments).

---

[6] In [CL02], Camenisch and Lysyanskaya also propose a signature scheme based on strong RSA in the standard model. As their scheme is less efficient as CS–it has other qualities instead–we exclude it from our considerations.

344 K. Kurosawa and K. Schmidt-Samoa

If the assumed bound $n^{-1.5}2^{k/3}$ is correct, than the probability that for n fixed uniformly distributed k-bit integers a randomly chosen k-bit integer divides the product of the others is upperbounded by $n^{1.5}2^{-k/3}$. That is, asymptotically this probability is independent from n (provided that n is polynomial in k). For a more practical-oriented interpretation, recall that in our schemes the number n describes the number of the adversary's signature queries. It is common to upperbound this number by 2^{30}. Therefore, we assume that moderate digest lengths, say 256-512 bits, are reasonable for our proposals. We leave the theoretical investigation of weak division-intractability as further work.

Gennaro *et al.* showed how to build strongly division intractable hash functions from collision resistant hash functions essentially by forcing the output to be a prime. Although this approach is not of practical relevance (because in this case CS is clearly more efficient), note that to achieve weak division intractability in that way only second pre-image collision resistant hash functions instead of collision resistant ones were required.

We finally compare the computational efficiency. For a fair comparison, in case of GHR we refer to the variant where suitability of the hash function is achieved by combining a division intractable hash function with a trapdoor commitment scheme. Referring to the computational costs for the modular exponentiations, the differences between all schemes are within a small margin. There is one full modular exponentiation needed for signing in the basic signature scheme, but this task can be significantly sped up by using standard techniques like Chinese remaindering and efficient exponentiation based on precomputation. For the latter, comb methods like [LL94] can be applied because the base of the exponentiation is fixed (this is immediate in our proposals and in the GHR scheme, whilst it requires appropriately chosen verification keys and additional secret keys in the CS scheme and in its modification proposed by Fischlin [Fis03]). In addition, all schemes require a short exponentiation for commiting to the message[7]. In Fischlin's modification of CS, this short exponentiation is eliminated at the expense of a slightly more costly full exponentiation and an increased length of the verification key. Verification requires two short exponentiation in CS, one short plus one short double exponentiation in Fischlin's modified CS and in our first proposal, and one short plus one full exponentiation in our second proposal. The verification costs for GHR depend on the trapdoor commitment used.

6 Conclusion

In this paper we utilized a Shamir-Tauman-like framework to construct new signature schemes based on the strong RSA assumption. Our proposals are existentially unforgeable under adaptive chosen message attacks in the standard model. As in the well-known Gennaro-Halevi-Rabin scheme, we utilized a hash function with a special property, namely division intractability. However, we significantly relaxed this requirement such that for our proposal *weak* division intractability

---

[7] This exponentiation is full in our second proposal, but there only the offline costs are affected.

is sufficient. The relation between weak and strong division intractability can be compared to the relation between second pre-image resistance and collision resistance. This newly defined property may be of independent interest. In contrast to the Cramer-Shoup signature scheme based on strong RSA, in our schemes there is no need for the signer to generate a fresh prime number for each message to be signed.

Acknowledgments

The authors wish to thank anonymous referees for useful comments. The second author was supported by the Japanese Society for Promotion of Science (JSPS) for doing research in Japan.

References

[BP97]   N. Barić and B. Pfitzmann. Collision-free accumulators and fail-stop signature schemes without trees. In Walter Fumy, editor, *EUROCRYPT*, volume 1233 of *Lecture Notes in Computer Science*, pages 366 – 377, Berlin, 1997. Springer-Verlag.

[BR93]   M. Bellare and P. Rogaway. Random oracles are practical: A paradigm for designing efficient protocols. In *Proc. of the 1st ACM Conference on Computer and Communications Security (CCS)*, pages 62–73. ACM Press, 1993.

[CGH98]   R. Canetti, O. Goldreich, and S. Halevi. The random oracle methodology, revisited (preliminary version). In *Proc. of the 30th Annual ACM Symposium on Theory of Computing (STOC '98)*, pages 209–218, New York, NY, USA, 1998. ACM Press.

[CGH04]   R. Canetti, O. Goldreich, and S. Halevi. On the random-oracle methodology as applied to length-restricted signature schemes. In Moni Naor, editor, *TCC*, volume 2951 of *Lecture Notes in Computer Science*, pages 40–57. Springer, 2004.

[CL02]   J. Camenisch and A. Lysyanskaya. A signature scheme with efficient protocols. In Stelvio Cimato, Clemente Galdi, and Giuseppe Persiano, editors, *SCN*, volume 2576 of *Lecture Notes in Computer Science*, pages 268–289. Springer, 2002.

[CN00]   J.-S. Coron and D. Naccache. Security analysis of the Gennaro-Halevi-Rabin signature scheme. In Bart Preneel, editor, *EUROCRYPT*, volume 1807 of *Lecture Notes in Computer Science*, pages 91–101. Springer, 2000.

[Cop97]   D. Coppersmith. Small solutions to polynomial equations, and low exponent rsa vulnerabilities. *J. Cryptology*, 10(4):233–260, 1997.

[CS99]   R. Cramer and V. Shoup. Signature schemes based on the strong RSA assumption. In *ACM Conference on Computer and Communications Security*, pages 46–51, 1999.

[Dam87]   I. Damgård. Collision free hash functions and public key signature schemes. In David Chaum and Wyn L. Price, editors, *EUROCRYPT*, volume 304 of *Lecture Notes in Computer Science*, pages 203–216. Springer, 1987.

[EGM96]   S. Even, O. Goldreich, and S. Micali. On-line/off-line digital signatures. *Journal of Cryptology*, 9(1):35–67, 1996.

[Fis03]   M. Fischlin. The Cramer-Shoup strong-RSA signature scheme revisited. In Yvo Desmedt, editor, *Public Key Cryptography*, volume 2567 of *Lecture Notes in Computer Science*, pages 116–129. Springer, 2003.

[GHR99]   R. Gennaro, S. Halevi, and T. Rabin. Secure hash-and-sign signatures without the random oracle. In Jacques Stern, editor, *EUROCRYPT*, volume 1592 of *Lecture Notes in Computer Science*, pages 123–139. Springer, 1999.

[GMR88]   S. Goldwasser, S. Micali, and R. L. Rivest. A digital signature scheme secure against adaptive chosen-message attacks. *SIAM J. Comput.*, 17(2):281–308, 1988.

[KR00]   H. Krawczyk and T. Rabin. Chameleon signatures. In *Proc. of the Symposium on Network and Distributed Systems Security (NDSS)*. The Internet Society, 2000.

[KSS06]   K. Kurosawa and K. Schmidt-Samoa. New online/offline signature schemes without random oracles. Cryptology ePrint Archive, 2006. http://eprint.iacr.org/.

[LL94]   C. H. Lim and P. J. Lee. More flexible exponentiation with precomputation. In Yvo Desmedt, editor, *CRYPTO*, volume 839 of *Lecture Notes in Computer Science*, pages 95–107. Springer, 1994.

[Mil75]   G. L. Miller. Riemann's hypothesis and tests for primality. In *Proc. of the 7th annual ACM symposium on Theory of computing (STOC '75)*, pages 234–239, New York, NY, USA, 1975. ACM Press.

[Sho99]   Victor Shoup. On the security of a practical identification scheme. *J. Cryptology*, 12(4):247–260, 1999.

[SST05]   K. Schmidt-Samoa and T. Takagi. Paillier's cryptosystem modulo p^2q and its applications to trapdoor commitment schemes. In Ed Dawson and Serge Vaudenay, editors, *Mycrypt*, volume 3715 of *Lecture Notes in Computer Science*, pages 296–313. Springer, 2005.

[ST01]   A. Shamir and Y. Tauman. Improved online/offline signature schemes. In Joe Kilian, editor, *CRYPTO*, volume 2139 of *Lecture Notes in Computer Science*, pages 355–367. Springer, 2001.

Anonymous Signature Schemes

Guomin Yang[1], Duncan S. Wong[1,*], Xiaotie Deng[1], and Huaxiong Wang[2]

[1] Department of Computer Science,
City University of Hong Kong,
Hong Kong, China
{csyanggm, duncan, deng}@cs.cityu.edu.hk
[2] Department of Computing,
Macquarie University, Australia
hwang@ics.mq.edu.au

Abstract. Digital signature is one of the most important primitives in public key cryptography. It provides authenticity, integrity and non-repudiation to many kinds of applications. On signer privacy however, it is generally unclear or suspicious of whether a signature scheme itself can guarantee the anonymity of the signer. In this paper, we give some affirmative answers to it. We formally define the signer anonymity for digital signature and propose some schemes of this type. We show that a signer anonymous signature scheme can be very useful by proposing a new anonymous key exchange protocol which allows a client Alice to establish a session key with a server Bob securely while keeping her identity secret from eavesdroppers. In the protocol, the anonymity of Alice is already maintained when Alice sends her signature to Bob in clear, and no additional encapsulation or mechanism is needed for the signature. We also propose a method of using anonymous signature to solve the collusion problem between organizers and reviewers of an anonymous paper review system.

1 Introduction

Digital signature is one of the most important primitives in public key cryptography. It is a very useful tool for providing authenticity, integrity and non-repudiation while it has seldom been considered to provide user privacy by its own. In many applications such as e-voting, e-auction, authentication protocols, and many others, we need to protect a signer's identity from being known by eavesdroppers or other parties in a system. For example, in an anonymous electronic transaction processing system [11] or an anonymous key exchange protocol [18], additional mechanisms or encapsulation techniques such as extra layers of encryption are applied onto their underlying signature schemes for protecting the signer's identity. In some other examples such as [6], several requirements for the signer anonymity of a signature scheme are informally given. However,

---

* The work was supported by a grant from the Research Grants Council of the Hong Kong Special Administrative Region, China (RGC Ref. No. CityU 1161/04E) and a grant from CityU (Project No. 9360087).

M. Yung et al. (Eds.): PKC 2006, LNCS 3958, pp. 347–363, 2006.

among these solutions or discussions, they usually require significant increase of system complexities or lack formal methodologies for analyzing the level of anonymity being provided to signers. Although it is widely believed that a signature scheme by itself may provide a certain degree of anonymity to its signers, there is no formal treatment on this subject. It is still generally unclear on exactly what conditions that a signature itself can provide anonymity of its signer. Comparing with the progress on the decryptor identity exposure issue of public key encryption schemes [2], it has been far lagged behind on the research of the signer anonymity of signature schemes themselves.

Consider the following example (Fig. 1) which is a key transport protocol proposed by Boyd and Park [6] for a mobile client A to transport a session key σ to a server B. The protocol is also targeted to provide client anonymity by protecting A's identity ID_A from being known by eavesdroppers.

$$A \rightarrow B : PKE_B(ID_A, \sigma, count)$$
$$A \leftarrow B : Enc_\sigma(count, r_B)$$
$$A \rightarrow B : Sig_A(ID_B, h(count, \sigma, r_B))$$

Fig. 1. Boyd-Park Authenticated Key Transport Protocol

In the first message of the protocol, A encrypts ID_A, σ and a field *count* under B's public key encryption function PKE_B which is assumed to be publicly known. This protects A's identity from being known by eavesdroppers. In the third message of the protocol however, A also needs to generate and send a signature to B in clear. Obviously, to hide the identity of A, this signature should not provide any meaningful information about A's identity to eavesdroppers.

To illustrate some subtleties of making a signature signer anonymous, we describe several potential attacking techniques which can be used to compromise a signer's identity.

Redundant Structure Attack. As remarked by the authors in [6], it is important to make sure that the signature does not contain any "redundant" structure, which can be revealed during the signature verification procedure and does not require the signed message to be known, while such a redundant structure may help an eavesdropper identify the mobile client. For example, a *recoverable* signature scheme [5] allows the message to be recovered and verified from the redundant structure of such a signature once the correct signature verification function is given. Hence if the signature scheme Sig_A in the protocol above is recoverable, an eavesdropper can find out the identity of A by trying the signature verification functions of all mobile clients one by one until a message starting with ID_B is recovered and verified.

Different Domain Attack. In order to prevent Redundant Structure Attack, a signature scheme which appears to be immune from such an attack, an ElGamal or Schnorr [16] type signature scheme was chosen for this key transport protocol [6]. However, we notice that an eavesdropper may still be able to identify the mobile client by examining the signature from another aspect: simply from *the length of a signature*. Suppose there are two mobile clients in the system and one of them is communicating with the server using this anonymous key transport protocol. When Schnorr signature scheme is used, the two mobile clients may select their own keys in different groups that could have different sizes. By examining the length of the signature in the protocol, the eavesdropper can tell which mobile client is communicating with the server.

Sparse Message Attack. For signature schemes where redundant structure does not exist and all signers have the same signature domain, an adversary may still be able to find out the signer from just the given signature. Below is an example.

Consider a trapdoor one-way permutation family indexed by signers' public keys (e.g. RSA [15]), a signature of a message is generated by computing the permutation inverse of the message using a signer's private signing key (i.e. a trapdoor information). If the message space is sparse in the image of the permutation family (e.g. the image of the permutation family contains only a few meaningful messages), the adversary is able to find out who the actual signer is. Given a signature, the adversary can find out the actual signer's identity using the following elimination method: For a trial signer, the adversary computes the one-way permutation of the signature indexed by the signer's public key and checks if the result is in the corresponding message space. If it is not, then the adversary is sure that this signer is not the actual signer of the signature. The adversary will simply repeat this elimination procedure until a signer is found.

Contributions. We formally introduce signer anonymous digital signature and define two security models subsequently for it. The first one is *static*, it provides an intuitive way to screen off signatures which do not have the anonymity property; the second one, a stronger model, combines the static model with the adaptive chosen message attack, and this *adaptive* model is then used in the security analyses of the signer anonymity of our proposed schemes.

Some commonly used signature schemes are examined. We show that the basic RSA signature scheme [15] is in general not signer anonymous, except in a special case where some restrictive assumptions are applied. We then show that PSS [5] is not signer anonymous even with those restrictive assumptions. We also show that Schnorr and ElGamal signature schemes are not signer anonymous, except all signers are choosing keys under a common domain.

To transform those signature schemes to signer anonymous versions, we propose some extensions of them and show that they are signer anonymous even under our adaptive model. We also propose a new anonymous key exchange protocol which allows a client Alice to establish a session key with a server Bob securely while keeping her identity secret from eavesdroppers. In the protocol Alice sends her signer anonymous signature to Bob in clear, while the anonymity of Alice is already maintained. As another application, we propose a method of using anonymous signature to solve the collusion problem between organizers and reviewers of an anonymous paper review system.

Paper Organization. In Sec. 2, we review some related work. This is followed by Sec. 3 in which we introduce a security model for signer anonymous signature. In Sec. 4, we review some commonly used signature schemes and show that they are not signer anonymous. In Sec. 5, we introduce a stronger model for signer anonymous signature and call it the adaptive model. In Sec. 6, we propose some modifications of the signature schemes reviewed in Sec. 4 and show their anonymity under the stronger adaptive model. In Sec. 7, we apply our anonymous signature schemes on the design of anonymous key establishment protocols and the construction of an anonymous paper review system which solves the collusion problem between organizers and reviewers.

2   Related Work

For the counterpart of digital signature in public key cryptography, the public key encryption with key privacy was introduced and first formalized by Bellare et al. in [2]. In their model, a secure key-privacy-enabled encryption scheme not only ensures that an encrypted message is semantically secure against adaptive chosen-ciphertext attacks but also prevents the public from getting the decryptor's identity from the encrypted message. Several techniques were also proposed in [2] for converting a conventional encryption scheme to a key-privacy-enabled encryption scheme. However, these techniques cannot be simply applied to digital signature schemes for converting them to anonymous version. The main challenge of constructing an anonymous signature scheme is that signature schemes are not designed for hiding messages. It is different from a public key encryption scheme. For a secure key-privacy-enabled encryption scheme, an attacker (i.e. the one who wants to find out the identity of the decryptor) has access to both the message and the corresponding ciphertext (and of course the public keys of all decryptors in a system). For constructing a secure anonymous signature scheme, on the other hand, we need to consider the impacts of messages to the anonymity of signatures more carefully. For example, if a signature and the corresponding message are given, it is impossible to have a signature scheme be anonymous because the signature is publicly verifiable and the number of public keys in a system is usually limited. Another example, if the message of a challenge signature is not given but the message space is small, it would still be easy to find out the identity of the signer by searching over all the possible messages for each possible signer.

Notice that signer anonymity is not the same as *sender anonymity* while the latter is not new. In signcryption schemes with key privacy [7,17], or in designated verifier signature schemes [12,13], the identity of the sender is protected (i.e. sender anonymity) using the intended decryptor/verifier's public key. Their techniques are similar to that of key-privacy-enabled encryption schemes [2]. An anonymous signature scheme, on the other hand, does not have an intended recipient when a signature is generated. It solely focuses on the signer anonymity of a signature scheme itself.

3   A Static Security Model for Signer Anonymity

Definition 1. *A digital signature scheme is a tuple of four algorithms denoted by* $(\mathcal{K}, \mathcal{M}, \mathcal{S}, \mathcal{V})$.

1. *The key generation algorithm* $\mathcal{K}$ *is a randomized algorithm which on input* 1^k, *where* $k \in \mathbb{N}$ *is a security parameter, returns in polynomial time a pair* (pk, sk) *of matching public and secret keys.*
2. *The message space generator* $\mathcal{M}$ *is an algorithm which on input a public key* pk *returns in polynomial time a set* M *(called the message space with respect to* pk). *Formally, the output is a description of* M *and for simplicity, we denote* M *by* $\mathcal{M}(pk)$.
3. *The signing algorithm* $\mathcal{S}$ *is a (possibly randomized) algorithm which on input* 1^k, *a message* m *and the secret key* sk *returns in polynomial time a signature* σ *for* m.
4. *The verification algorithm* $\mathcal{V}$ *is a deterministic algorithm which on input* 1^k, *a message* m, *the public key* pk, *and a candidate signature* σ *for* m *returns in polynomial time a bit indicating the validity of the signature.*

(*Correctness.*) We require that $\mathcal{V}(1^k, m, pk, \mathcal{S}(1^k, m, sk)) = 1$ for any $(pk, sk) \leftarrow \mathcal{K}(1^k)$ and $m \in \mathcal{M}(pk)$.

In the following, we specify a basic model which captures our fundamental notion of signer anonymity. For simplicity, we omit the expression of 1^k from the inputs of $\mathcal{S}$ and $\mathcal{V}$ in the rest of the paper.

3.1   Static Model

Definition 2. *Let* $\mathcal{SD} = (\mathcal{K}, \mathcal{M}, \mathcal{S}, \mathcal{V})$ *be a digital signature scheme. Suppose the key generation algorithm is run twice with the security parameter* k, *and* $(pk_0, sk_0) \leftarrow \mathcal{K}(1^k)$ *and* $(pk_1, sk_1) \leftarrow \mathcal{K}(1^k)$ *are generated.* $\mathcal{SD}$ *is said to produce computationally indistinguishable signatures (or signatures with signer anonymity in the static model) if for every probabilistic polynomial time (PPT) algorithm* $\mathcal{D}$, *every positive polynomial* $p(\cdot)$, *and all sufficiently large* k's,

$$|\Pr[\mathcal{D}(1^k, pk_0, pk_1, \sigma_0) = 1] - \Pr[\mathcal{D}(1^k, pk_0, pk_1, \sigma_1) = 1]|$$
$$< \frac{1}{p(k)}$$

where $\sigma_0 \leftarrow \mathcal{S}(m_0, sk_0)$, $\sigma_1 \leftarrow \mathcal{S}(m_1, sk_1)$ *and* $m_0 \in_R \mathcal{M}(pk_0)$, $m_1 \in_R \mathcal{M}(pk_1)$.

By $x \in_R X$, we mean that an element x is randomly chosen from a set X.

3.2   Discussions

A *message-recoverable* signature scheme, such as PSS-R [5], allows the message of each of its signatures to be recovered directly from the signature once the corresponding public key is given while having negligible chance to have a message recovered from the signature if an incorrect public key is supplied. In Def. 2, since public keys are known to $\mathcal{D}$, we can see that a *message-recoverable* signature scheme cannot be anonymous.

Although messages m_0 and m_1 are unknown to the distinguisher $\mathcal{D}$, the corresponding message spaces are publicly known (since $\mathcal{M}$, pk_0 and pk_1 are known). Hence for satisfying Def. 2, it is required that all message spaces should be sufficiently large so that it is negligible for $\mathcal{D}$ to guess correctly the message. One may consider that every message space should have at least 2^k messages. We will give a more precise specification to the message space. One should also note that the size of the message space is a necessary requirement to the anonymity of a signature scheme, but it is not sufficient.

On the signature spaces, Def. 2 also indicates that $\mathcal{D}$ should not be able to distinguish computationally a signature from one space to another. As a counterexample, if the signature space correlates to the length of the corresponding public key (mentioned earlier in the introduction section), $\mathcal{D}$ may be able to compromise the anonymity of a signature from this information.

4   Signature Signatures That Are Not Signer Anonymous

4.1   The Basic RSA Signature Scheme

In the following, we show that unless intentionally specified, the basic RSA signature scheme [15] (the primitive one without using hash function), in its general use, is not signer anonymous according to Def. 2.

Consider two signers $Signer_0$ and $Signer_1$ with RSA moduli N_0 and N_1, respectively. Without loss of generality, let $N_0 > N_1$. If the two moduli are of different length, it is obvious that signatures generated by the two signers can easily be identified by checking the length of a given signature. Even if N_0 and N_1 are of equal length, we can still distinguish signatures for most of the cases. In the following, we elaborate this in detail.

Let us evaluate the probability that a signature of $Signer_0$ falls into the range of $\mathbb{Z}_{N_0} - \mathbb{Z}_{N_1}$. Let $\Delta = N_0 - N_1$. The probability that a signature of $Signer_0$ falls into $\{N_1, \cdots, N_0 - 1\}$ will be Δ/N_0. This value is upper bounded by $\Delta/2^{k-1}$ if $|N_0| = k$. Hence if $|\Delta|$ is in the order of $\log(k)$, then the probability will be negligible for sufficiently large k. This is the case when we say that N_0 and N_1 are "very close" to each other. In this case, the basic RSA signature scheme may be anonymous. However, this is true only if all message spaces in the system are *dense* in the corresponding ranges, for example, every element in $\mathbb{Z}_{N_i}$, $i = 0, 1$, is valid/meaningful. On the other hand, if the message space of $Signer_0$ or $Signer_1$ is *sparse* in $\mathbb{Z}_{N_i}$, $i = 0/1$, that is, there are only a few elements in $\mathbb{Z}_{N_i}$ that are valid (or meaningful) messages. Then the scheme cannot be anonymous.

For example, suppose a signature $\sigma = m_0^{d_0} \bmod N_0$ is given where d_0 is the private exponent of $Signer_0$, the distinguisher $\mathcal{D}$ can determine if $Signer_1$ is the actual signer by computing $m' = \sigma^{e_1} \bmod N_1$, where e_1 is the public exponent of $Signer_1$ and then determining if m' is in the message space of $Signer_1$. Since the message space of $Signer_1$ in $\mathbb{Z}_{N_1}$ is sparse, it will have a non-negligible chance that m' is not in the message space, which allows $\mathcal{D}$ to find out the actual signer with non-negligible advantage.

All of the above are concerning about special cases. In the general case where N_0 and N_1 are generated by following a *conventional procedure*, that is, each of N_0 and N_1 is a product of two randomly chosen equal-length primes and $|N_0| = |N_1| = k$, the following theorem implies that with at least a constant probability that a RSA signature can be distinguished successfully (i.e. not signer anonymous under Def. 2).

Theorem 1. *If N_0 and N_1 are generated by following the conventional procedure, then the probability that $|N_0 - N_1| \geq 2^{k-2}$ is at least $\frac{1}{400}$.*

Due to page limitation, readers please refer to our full paper [19] for the proof.

PSS. Based on the results above, we can see that PSS [5] is not signer anonymous either. Due to page limitation, readers please refer to our full paper [19] for details.

4.2 Schnorr Signature Scheme [16]

On input a security parameter 1^k, the key generation algorithm $\mathcal{K}$ returns a public key pk which consists of a set of group parameters $\mathcal{I} = (p, q, g, G, h)$ and an element $y \in G$, and a secret key sk which is a random element $x \in_R \mathbb{Z}_q$, such that $y = g^x \bmod p$. In $\mathcal{I}$, p, q are two large primes chosen randomly such that $q|p-1$, G is a subgroup of $\mathbb{Z}_p^*$ with order q, g is a generator of G so that computing discrete logarithms to the base g is difficult, and $h : \{0,1\}^* \rightarrow \{0, 1, \cdots, 2^k - 1\}$ is a hash function where $2^k < q$.

In the original Schnorr signature scheme, the message space can be arbitrarily specified as any subset of $\{0,1\}^*$. For allowing us to specify the minimum size of the message space that an anonymous Schnorr signature scheme should be in the later part of this paper, we quantify the message space. We define the message space generator $\mathcal{M}$ such that on input pk, which is generated by $\mathcal{K}(1^k)$, $\mathcal{M}(pk)$ outputs the description of a message space $M^{Schnorr}$ such that $|M^{Schnorr}| \geq 2^k$. Below are the signature generation and verification algorithms.

Signing algorithm. On input a message $m \in M^{Schnorr}$ and a secret key x, $\mathcal{S}(m,x)$ is computed as follows:
1. Choose a random $w \in_R \mathbb{Z}_q$ and compute $t = g^w \bmod p$.
2. Compute $r = h(t, m)$.
3. Compute $s = w - xr \bmod q$.
The signature for m is the pair (r, s).

> **Verification algorithm.** To verify a signature (r, s) for message m under public key $(\mathcal{I}, y)$, compute $t = g^s y^r \bmod p$ and output 1 if $r = h(t, m)$, otherwise output 0.

Since signers generate their public key pairs independently, it is pretty likely that different signers have their keys under different sets of group parameters. We can see that the scheme is not signer anonymous as identity information will be leaked from the value of s by applying similar arguments to that in Sec. 4.1. Interestingly, in a special case where all signers are sharing a common set of group parameters, the scheme can actually be shown to provide signer anonymity under the random oracle model [4] without any modification. The proof technique is similar to that for Lemma 2.

5   An Adaptive Security Model for Signer Anonymity

Def. 2 is static as the distinguisher cannot adaptively acquire additional information about the challenging signature from the environment. In the following, we define a stronger model which allows the distinguisher to adaptively obtain signatures generated by the entity who generates the challenging signature.

Definition 3 (SA-CMA). *Let k be a security parameter. A digital signature scheme $\mathcal{SD}$ is signer anonymous against chosen message attack (SA-CMA) if for all sufficiently large k, no PPT adversary (or distinguisher) $\mathcal{D}$ can win the following game with a probability non-negligibly larger than $\frac{1}{2}$. The game is simulated by a challenger.*

1. *(Key Generation Phase.) The challenger runs $\mathcal{K}(1^k)$ multiple times for generating polynomially many public and secret key pairs. All the public keys are accessible by $\mathcal{D}$.*
2. *(Training Phase.) $\mathcal{D}$ adaptively queries the challenger with a public key pk_i and a message $m \in \mathcal{M}(pk_i)$. The challenger produces $\sigma \leftarrow \mathcal{S}(m, sk_i)$ and replies $\mathcal{D}$ with σ if pk_i is generated in the Key Generation Phase; otherwise, a '$\perp$' is returned indicating that signature generation has failed.*
3. *(Key Selection Phase I.) $\mathcal{D}$ picks two public keys from the public keys generated in the Key Generation Phase. We denote these two key pairs by (pk_0, sk_0) and (pk_1, sk_1).*
4. *(Key Selection Phase II.) The challenger gives all the secret keys to $\mathcal{D}$ except sk_0 and sk_1.*
5. *(Challenge Phase.) The challenger tosses a random coin $\varpi \xleftarrow{R} \{0,1\}$, then uniformly picks a message $m \in \mathcal{M}(pk_\varpi)$, and returns a challenge signature $\sigma \leftarrow \mathcal{S}(m, sk_\varpi)$ to $\mathcal{D}$.*
6. *(Cracking Phase.) $\mathcal{D}$ can still adaptively make signing queries as in the Training Phase but the associated public key with each query can only be pk_0 or pk_1.*
7. *(Output Phase.) At the end of the game, $\mathcal{D}$ outputs a bit ϖ' and wins if $\varpi' = \varpi$.*

$\mathcal{D}$'s advantage is defined as $\mathbf{Adv}^{\mathsf{sa-cma}} = \Pr[\varpi' = \varpi] - \frac{1}{2}$ and $\Pr[\varpi' = \varpi]$ is the probability that $\mathcal{D}$ wins the game. The probability is taken over the coin tosses of both $\mathcal{D}$ and the challenger, including the coin toss for ϖ.

If a scheme satisfies this definition, we say that the scheme is SA-CMA secure. Note that in the *Cracking Phase* we only allow the distinguisher to query with public key pk_0 or pk_1, since the secret keys corresponding to all other public keys have already been given to the distinguisher.

As the distinguisher $\mathcal{D}$ of the adaptive model has an additional signing oracle to access, the model is obviously stronger than the static one given in Def. 2. Another seemingly "stronger" definition is to let $\mathcal{D}$ perform the Challenge Phase and the Cracking Phase in the following way:

Definition 4.   ...
5. *The challenger tosses a random coin $\varpi \xleftarrow{R} \{0,1\}$.*
6. *$\mathcal{D}$ can adaptively perform the following queries:*
   (a) *$\mathcal{D}$ performs signing queries as in the Training Phase except that now the allowable public keys are pk_0 and pk_1 only.*
   (b) *$\mathcal{D}$ queries a special oracle called challenging oracle. The challenging oracle uniformly picks a message $m \in \mathcal{M}(pk_\varpi)$, and returns $\sigma \leftarrow \mathcal{S}(m, sk_\varpi)$ to $\mathcal{D}$.*

...

But the following result shows that Def. 3 and Def. 4 are equivalent.

Theorem 2. *If there exists no PPT algorithm that has a non-negligible advantage in winning the game in Def. 3, then there exists no PPT algorithm that has a non-negligible advantage in winning the game in Def. 4.*

Due to page limitation, readers please refer to our full paper [19] for the proof.

6   Modified Signature Schemes for Signer Anonymity

In this section, we propose some modifications on the schemes described in Sec. 4 and show that they are signer anonymous under the adaptive model (i.e. SA-CMA in Def. 3). We start with Schnorr signature scheme and provide the full proof for its signer anonymity. Then we modify the basic RSA signature scheme and subsequently the PSS. Due to page limitation, readers please refer to our full paper [19] for the discussions of the last two schemes.

Extended Schnorr Signature Scheme for Signer Anonymity. The key generation algorithm $\mathcal{K}$ and the message space generator $\mathcal{M}$ are almost the same as the original Schnorr signature scheme described in Sec. 4.2, except that the public key now also contains an additional parameter denoted by $b \in \mathbb{N}$. Let q_{min} and q_{max} denote the lower bound and upper bound of the group orders of all signers, respectively. Let 2^b be an integer which is ℓ bits longer than q_{max} and $\ell = k + 1$. One may imagine $k = 160$ and hence $\ell = 161$. Let $h : \{0,1\}^* \to \{0, 1, \cdots, 2^k - 1\}$ be a hash function where $2^k < q_{min}$.

For a signer with public key $pk = (\mathcal{I}, b, y)$ and secret key x generated by $\mathcal{K}(1^k)$ where $\mathcal{I} = (p, q, g, G, h)$ and $y = g^x \bmod p$, the signature generation and verification algorithms are as follows. Let n be the largest integer such that $nq < 2^b$.

Signing algorithm. On input a message $m \in \mathcal{M}(pk)$ and secret key x, $\mathcal{S}(m, x)$ is computed as follows:
1. Choose a random $w \in \mathbb{Z}_q$ and compute $t = g^w \bmod p$.
2. Compute $r = h(t, m)$ and then $s = w - xr \bmod q$.
3. Choose a number $\lambda \xleftarrow{R} \{0, 1, \cdots, n-1\}$ and compute $s' = s + \lambda q$

The signature for m is the pair (r, s').

Verification algorithm. To verify signature (r, s') for message m and public key $(\mathcal{I}, y)$, compute $s = s' \bmod q$ and $t = g^s y^r \bmod p$, and output 1 if $r = h(t, m)$, otherwise, output 0.

Consider two arbitrary signers $Signer_i$ and $Signer_j$ whose sets of group parameters are denoted by $\mathcal{I}_i = (p_i, q_i, g_i, G_i, h)$ and $\mathcal{I}_j = (p_j, q_j, g_j, G_j, h)$, respectively. Let n_i and n_j be the largest integers such that $n_i q_i < 2^b$ and $n_j q_j < 2^b$, respectively. Without loss of generality, we assume $n_i q_i < n_j q_j$.

Lemma 1. *For the extended Schnorr signature scheme above, if signer $Signer_i$ generates a signature (r_i, s'_i) and signer $Signer_j$ generates a signature (r_j, s'_j), then the probability that s'_j is in $\Delta = \{n_i q_i, \cdots, n_j q_j - 1\}$ is at most 2^{-k}.*

Proof. First, note that s'_i and s'_j are uniformly distributed on $\{0, 1, \cdots, n_i q_i - 1\}$ and $\{0, 1, \cdots, n_j q_j - 1\}$, respectively. Second, since $n_j q_j < 2^b$ and $n_i q_i \geq 2^b - q_i$, $n_j q_j - n_i q_i < 2^b - (2^b - q_i) = q_i \leq q_{max}$. Hence,

$$\Pr[s'_j \in \Delta] < q_{max}/(2^b - q_{max}) < 1/2^{l-1} = 1/2^k. \qquad \square$$

In the following, we assume that h behaves like a random oracle [4]. If an algorithm $\mathcal{A}$ runs in time at most t and completes successfully with probability at least $\epsilon > 0$, then $\mathcal{A}$ is said to be a (t, ϵ)-algorithm. The probability is taken over the input domain and the coin tosses of $\mathcal{A}$.

Lemma 2. *In the extended Schnorr signature scheme above, suppose for any pair of signers $Signer_i$ and $Signer_j$, $q_i = q_j$. Then if there exists a $(t, \epsilon + \frac{1}{2})$-algorithm (distinguisher) $\mathcal{D}$ which wins the game of Def. 3 after performing at most q_H hash queries and q_S signing queries, there exists a (t', ϵ')-algorithm $\mathcal{F}$ which existentially forges under the chosen message attack [9] a signature after performing at most $q_H + q_S$ hash queries and q_S signing queries, where $t' \leq t + q_K c$ and $\epsilon' \geq (1 - \frac{q_H + q_S}{2^k})(1 - \frac{q_S}{2^k})\frac{\epsilon}{q_K}$ for q_K being some polynomial in k and c being the time required for generating one key pair in the extended Schnorr signature scheme.*

Proof. We construct an algorithm $\mathcal{F}$ which runs $\mathcal{D}$ under a simulated environment of Def. 3 and forges a Schnorr signature.

At the beginning of the simulation, $\mathcal{F}$ is given a security parameter k, a set of group parameters $\mathcal{I} = (p, q, g, G, h)$, a challenge element $\mathsf{y} \in G$, an auxiliary parameter $b \in \mathbb{N}$ and a message space $M^{Schnorr}$ such that $|M^{Schnorr}| \geq 2^k$. $\mathcal{F}$ is to forge a signature $\sigma^* = (r^*, s^*)$ with message $m^* \in M^{Schnorr}$ such that $r^* = h(g^{s^*} \mathsf{y}^{r^*} \bmod p, \ m^*)$ where h is provided as a random oracle by the unforgeability game simulator of $\mathcal{F}$. Note that $\mathcal{F}$ has access to the random oracle of h and a signing oracle corresponding to the challenge public key y. The signing oracle, on input a message $m \in M^{Schnorr}$, returns a signature $\sigma = (r, s)$ such that $r = h(g^s \mathsf{y}^r \bmod p, \ m)$. We denote the random oracle for h by $\mathcal{HO}$ and the signing oracle by $\mathcal{SO}$.

In the Key Generation Phase of the game defined in Def. 3, $\mathcal{F}$ randomly generates $q_K{-}1$ public key pairs where q_K is some polynomial in k. For each of the public key pairs, say the i-th, the set of group parameters $\mathcal{I}_i = (p_i, q_i, g_i, G_i, h)$ is generated such that $q_i = q$, $q_i | p_i{-}1$, and g_i is the generator of G_i whose order is q_i. Also an element y_i is generated as $g_i^{x_i} \bmod p_i$ where x_i is randomly chosen from $\mathbb{Z}_{q_i}$. The public key of i-th public key pair is set to $pk_i = (\mathcal{I}_i, b, y_i)$ and the corresponding secret key is x_i. Let $\mathcal{L} = \{pk_i\}_{1 \leq i \leq q_K}$ be the set of public keys generated in this phase except pk_j, which instead is assigned to $(\mathcal{I}, b, \mathsf{y})$. The value of j is chosen randomly from 1 to q_K.

In the Training Phase and the Cracking Phase, $\mathcal{F}$ answers all oracle queries made by $\mathcal{D}$. For a hash query, the query is relayed by $\mathcal{F}$ to $\mathcal{HO}$ for an answer. The answer is then relayed back to $\mathcal{D}$. $\mathcal{F}$ also maintains a list Ψ of queried values and their returns. For a signature query with message m in the corresponding message space, there are two cases. Case 1: if the public key is not y, $\mathcal{F}$ follows the signing algorithm of the scheme to generate a signature. This can be done as $\mathcal{F}$ knows the corresponding signing key (or secret key). Case 2: if the public key is y, $\mathcal{F}$ relays the query to $\mathcal{SO}$ and relays the signature back to $\mathcal{D}$. Note that the list Ψ should also be updated for hash values. In addition to these steps, in the Cracking Phase, we will see shortly that $\mathcal{F}$ needs to carry out a few more checkings when relaying queries and answers between $\mathcal{D}$ and the oracles $\mathcal{HO}$, $\mathcal{SO}$ to and fro.

In the Key Selection Phase I, if $\mathcal{D}$ picks two public keys such that none of the keys is y, $\mathcal{F}$ fails and halts. Let the two public keys be $(\hat{\mathcal{I}}_0, b, \hat{y}_0)$, $(\hat{\mathcal{I}}_1, b, \hat{y}_1)$. Suppose $\mathcal{F}$ does not fail and proceeds successfully to the Challenge Phase, $\mathcal{F}$ sets the challenge signature $\sigma^* = (r^*, s^*)$ by randomly picks $r^* \xleftarrow{R} \{0, 1\}^k$ and $s^* \xleftarrow{R} \{0, 1, \cdots, nq{-}1\}$ where n is the largest integer so that $nq < 2^b$. If r^* is already in the list Ψ as a queried hash oracle answer, $\mathcal{F}$ fails and halts (we will see below that this event is called $\mathbf{E}_2$). Otherwise, an entry $(\top, r^*)$ is added into the list Ψ, where $\top$ represents some hash input whose value is not known yet but its hash value has been given as r^*.

The simulation proceeds until $\mathcal{D}$ reaches the Output Phase. When $\mathcal{D}$ outputs and halts, $\mathcal{F}$ also halts and outputs nothing. That means $\mathcal{F}$ has failed to forge a signature. However during the Cracking Phase, whenever $\mathcal{D}$ makes a hash query, $\mathcal{F}$ checks if the answer of $\mathcal{HO}$ is r^*. If this is the case and at the same time the hash evaluation is of the form $h(g^s \mathsf{y}^{r^*} \bmod p, \ m^*)$ where $m^* \in M^{Schnorr}$

and m^* is not involved in a signing query in the Training phase, $\mathcal{F}$ outputs the forged signature $\sigma^* = (r^*, s^*)$ and message m^*, and halts. In addition, during the Cracking Phase, whenever $\mathcal{D}$ makes a signing query with some message $m^* \in M^{Schnorr}$ under y, $\mathcal{F}$ first queries $\mathcal{HO}$ for the value of $h(g^{s^*} y^{r^*} \bmod p, m^*)$. If the hash value is equal to r^* and m^* is not involved in a signing query in the Training Phase, $\mathcal{F}$ outputs the forged signature $\sigma^* = (r^*, s^*)$ and message m^*, and halts; if the hash value is not r^*, $\mathcal{F}$ then relays the query to $\mathcal{SO}$ and continues the simulation as described above. Note that if m^* turns out to have been queried in some signing query during the Training Phase, $\mathcal{F}$ fails and halts (we will see below that this event is called $\mathbf{E}_3$).

Analysis. First of all, it is easy to see that the running time of $\mathcal{F}$ is in polynomial of that of $\mathcal{D}$ and $\mathcal{F}$ perfectly simulates the game of Def. 3 except during the Challenge Phase. In this phase, the challenger in a real game (that is, $\mathcal{F}$ in the simulated game described above) should have randomly picked a key among two given public keys, then picked a message randomly from the message space corresponding to the chosen public key and generated a challenge signature accordingly.

First, we investigate the distribution of the messages which produce a signature (r^*, s^*) with respect to each of $(\hat{\mathcal{I}}_0, b, \hat{y}_0)$ and $(\hat{\mathcal{I}}_1, b, \hat{y}_1)$. For each of $(\hat{\mathcal{I}}_{\varpi^*}, b, \hat{y}_{\varpi^*})$, $\varpi^* = 0, 1$, define two sets

$$M_{\varpi^*} = \{m \, : \, r^* \leftarrow h(g_{\varpi^*}^{s^*} \hat{y}_{\varpi^*}^{r^*} \bmod p_{\varpi^*}, m), \ m \in M_{\varpi^*}^{Schnorr}\}.$$

Under the assumption that h is a random function [4], M_{ϖ^*} is uniformly distributed, and the expected number of messages in M_{ϖ^*} is equal to $|M_{\varpi^*}^{Schnorr}|/2^k$. From the fact that $\log_2(|M_{\varpi^*}^{Schnorr}|) \geq k$, we have at least half chance (derived from $1 - (1 - 2^{-k})^{|M^{Schnorr}\varpi^*|} \geq 1/2$) that the challenge signature $\sigma^* = (r^*, s^*)$, generated by $\mathcal{F}$ in the Challenge Phase of the simulated game above, is a valid signature of some message in $M_{\varpi^*}^{Schnorr}$.

Let $\mathbf{E}_1$ be the event that the hash evaluation

$$r^* \leftarrow h(g_{\varpi^*}^{s^*} \hat{y}_{\varpi^*}^{r^*} \bmod p_{\varpi^*}, \ m^*) \tag{1}$$

is carried out during the cracking phase where $\varpi^* = 0/1$. If event $\mathbf{E}_1$ does not occur, it is indistinguishable from $\mathcal{D}$'s point of view between the Challenge Phase of a real game and that of the simulated game by $\mathcal{F}$. By the random oracle assumption, it is unknown on which message m^* will make Eq. (1) hold. Hence $\mathcal{D}$ has no advantage in winning the game.

Since the position of $(\mathcal{I}, b, \mathsf{y})$ in $\mathcal{L}$ is randomly chosen, the probability of selecting $(\mathcal{I}, b, \mathsf{y})$ in Key Selection Phase I is $2/q_K$. Due to the same reason, in event $\mathbf{E}_1$, the chance that $\hat{y}_{\varpi^*} = \mathsf{y}$ is $1/2$. Note that $\Pr[\mathcal{D} \text{ wins}] \geq \epsilon + 1/2$. Let $\Pr[\mathcal{D} \text{ wins} \,|\mathbf{E}_1] = \lambda + 1/2$. We have

$$\epsilon + \frac{1}{2} \leq \Pr[\mathcal{D} \text{ wins}]$$

$$= (\lambda + \frac{1}{2})\Pr[\mathbf{E}_1] + \Pr[\mathcal{D} \text{ wins} \,|\overline{\mathbf{E}_1}]\Pr[\overline{\mathbf{E}_1}]$$

$$= (\lambda + \frac{1}{2})\Pr[\mathbf{E_1}] + \frac{1}{2}\Pr[\overline{\mathbf{E_1}}].$$

Hence $\lambda \Pr[\mathbf{E_1}] \geq \epsilon$. Since $\epsilon > 0$, we have $0 < \lambda \leq 1/2$. Therefore $\Pr[\mathbf{E_1}] \geq 2\epsilon$.

To find out the lower bound of the winning probability of $\mathcal{F}$, we only have two events left to evaluate, that is, the chance that $\mathcal{F}$ fails due to the following two events.

Event $\mathbf{E_2}$: During the Challenge Phase, r^* is found to be in the list of Ψ.

Event $\mathbf{E_3}$: During the Cracking Phase, if evaluation $r^* \leftarrow h(g^{s^*} \mathsf{y}^{r^*} \bmod p, m^*)$ occurs while m^* has been involved in a signing query during the Training Phase.

Since r^* is randomly chosen from $\{0,1\}^k$ and h is a random function, we have $\Pr[\mathbf{E_2}] \leq \frac{q_H + q_S}{2^k}$. Similarly, we have $\Pr[\mathbf{E_3}] \leq \frac{q_S}{2^k}$.

Combining all the events above, they include the case that y is one of $\hat{y}_0$ and $\hat{y}_1$, the case that (r^*, s^*) is a valid signature of y, $\mathbf{E_1}$ occurs, the case that y is involved in the event $\mathbf{E_1}$, the case that r^* is not in the list Ψ during the Challenge Phase (i.e. $\overline{\mathbf{E_2}}$), and the case that the forged message m^* has not been involved in any signing query during the Training Phase (i.e. $\overline{\mathbf{E_3}}$), we have

$$\Pr[\mathcal{F} \text{ wins}] \geq (1 - \frac{q_H + q_S}{2^k})(1 - \frac{q_S}{2^k})\frac{\epsilon}{q_K}.$$

On the running time of $\mathcal{F}$, we can see that besides running $\mathcal{D}$, $\mathcal{F}$ needs to generates $q_K - 1$ key pairs during the Key Generation Phase and at most q_S additional hash queries during the Cracking Phase. Let c be the time required for generating one key pair. The running time of $\mathcal{F}$ is at most $t + q_K c$. Also $\mathcal{F}$ performs at most $q_H + q_S$ hash queries and q_S signing queries. $\qquad\square$

Theorem 3. *The extended Schnorr signature scheme described above is SA-CMA secure.*

Proof. Without loss of generality, suppose in the game of Def. 3, the distinguisher $\mathcal{D}$ picks the public keys corresponding $Signer_i$ and $Signer_j$ in the Key Selection Phase I, and $Signer_j$ is picked by the challenger in the Challenge Phase. We follow the notations used above and in the proof of Lemma 1, we assume that $n_i q_i < n_j q_j$. Let $\mathbf{E}$ be the event that $s'_j \notin \Delta$. In other words, $\mathbf{E}$ is the event that $s'_j \in \{0, 1, \cdots, n_i q_i - 1\}$, that is, in the same domain as $Signer_i$ has been picked by the challenger. According to Lemma 2, we have $\Pr[\mathcal{D} \text{ wins the game } |\mathbf{E}] \leq \frac{1}{2} + \epsilon(k)$ under the assumption that the extended Schnorr signature scheme is existentially unforgeable [9], where ϵ is a negligible function. Since $\Pr[\mathbf{E}] \leq 1$, we have

$$\Pr[\mathcal{D} \text{ wins the game } \wedge \mathbf{E}] \leq \frac{1}{2} + \epsilon(k) \qquad (2)$$

According to Lemma 1, we have $\Pr[\overline{\mathbf{E}}] \leq 2^{-k}$. Since $\Pr[\mathcal{D} \text{ wins the game } |\overline{\mathbf{E}}] \leq 1$, we have

$$\Pr[\mathcal{D} \text{ wins the game } \wedge \overline{\mathbf{E}}] \leq 2^{-k} \qquad (3)$$

Combining Eq. (2) and (3), we have

$$\Pr[\mathcal{D} \text{ wins the game }] \leq \frac{1}{2} + \epsilon(k) + 2^{-k} \qquad \qquad \square$$

The extended Schnorr signature scheme still maintains existential unforgeability against adaptive chosen message attack (euf-cma) [9], namely, given a signing oracle, an adversary cannot forge a signature for a message m which has not been queried to the signing oracle before. However, the extended scheme does not satisfy the strong unforgeability [3, 1], namely, given a signing oracle, an adversary cannot forge a valid pair of message m and signature σ which has not been a query output of the signing oracle for m before.

7   Applications

7.1   Anonymous Key Exchange

As shown in Fig. 1 and discussed in the introduction section, the protocol cannot provide client anonymity if the Different Domain Attack is feasible. In order to make it client anonymous, we modify the last message flow from A to B by using an anonymous signature scheme and change the message to

$$A \rightarrow B \ : \ Sig_A(h(ID_B, count, \sigma, r_B))$$

where $h : \{0,1\}^* \rightarrow \{0,1\}^k$ is a hash function which behaves like a random oracle.

The example above is an anonymous key transport protocol. Next, we construct an anonymous key *exchange* protocol which not only ensures the anonymity of the client but also allows the client and the server to establish a session key from both of their session key contributions. The protocol is based on a key exchange protocol called "SIG-DH" [8] which is a signature-based variation of the Diffie-Hellman key exchange protocol with provable security against various active attacks defined in the Canetti-Krawczyk model [8].

Let k be a security parameter. Let G be a group generated by g with large prime order q so that computing discrete logarithms to be base g is difficult. Let $H : \{0,1\}^* \rightarrow \{0,1\}^{3k}$ be a hash function. Each party has a secret signing key for a signature algorithm Sig. By $Sig_A(m)$, we mean the signature on message m generated by party A with identity $ID_A \in \{0,1\}^k$. Assume the public keys of all parties in the system are publicly known. Let E be a block cipher (e.g. AES [14]) of block size k. Suppose a client (the initiator) A and a server (the responder) B already have a session-id s shared. We will explain shortly on how the session-id s is established. The following protocol is carried out between them.

1. A randomly chooses a temporal identity $alias \in_R \{0,1\}^k$, $x \in_R \mathbb{Z}_q$, and sends $(alias, s, \alpha = g^x)$ to B.
2. Upon receipt of $(alias, s, \alpha)$, B randomly chooses $y \in_R \mathbb{Z}_q$, then computes $\kappa_1 \| \kappa_2 \| \kappa_3 \leftarrow H(\alpha^y)$ such that $|\kappa_i| = k$ for $i = 1, 2, 3$, erases y, and sends to A the message $(B, s, \beta = g^y)$ together with $SIG_B(B, s, \beta, \alpha, alias)$.

3. Upon receipt of $(B, s, \beta = g^y)$ and B's signature, A computes $\kappa'_1 \| \kappa'_2 \| \kappa'_3 \leftarrow H(\beta^x)$, erases x, and verifies the signature. If the signature is valid, A sends to B the message $(alias, s, C_1 = E_{\kappa_1}(A))$ together with its signature $\sigma = Sig_A(h(alias, A, s, \alpha, \beta, B, \kappa'_2))$ where $h : \{0, 1\}^* \rightarrow \{0, 1\}^k$ is a hash function. A outputs the session key κ'_3 under session-id s.
4. Upon receipt of $(alias, s, C_1)$ and a signature σ, B computes $A' = E_{\kappa_1}^{-1}(C_1)$, and verifies the identity A' (e.g. for access control) and signature σ. If all verifications are passed, B outputs the session key κ_3 under session-id s.

A $\hspace{10cm}$ B

$$alias, s, \alpha = g^x$$
$$\xrightarrow{\hspace{8cm}}$$

$$B, s, \beta = g^y, Sig_B(B, s, \beta, \alpha, alias)$$
$$\xleftarrow{\hspace{8cm}}$$

$$alias, s, E_{\kappa_1}(A), Sig_A(h(alias, A, s, \alpha, \beta, B, \kappa'_2))$$
$$\xrightarrow{\hspace{8cm}}$$

Fig. 2. Anonymous SIG-DH Protocol

(*Analysis.*) The protocol described above (Fig. 2) supports anonymity of the client A if Sig is an anonymous signature scheme. In the protocol, all hash functions are assumed to behave like random oracles. The session-id s should also be randomly selected each time for ensuring A's anonymity. As suggested by the authors of [8], in practice, the session-id s can be a pair (s_1, s_2) where s_1 is a value randomly chosen by A such that it is different from the values in other of A's sessions and s_2 is randomly chosen by B in a similar way. These values can be exchanged by the parties as a prologue [10]. Alternatively, s_1 can be included by A in the first message of the protocol, and s_2 be included by B in the second message.

The protocol assumes that the signature verification keys of all parties are publicly known. In practice, we can add the client's certificate into the encryption in the third message provided that the certificates of all clients are of the same length. Also, we assume that the server does not know the client at the beginning of the communication. In case it is already known, the encryption operation in the third message can be removed from the protocol.

Comparing with the original "SIG-DH" protocol [8], the anonymous version proposed above has an additional message component κ'_2 in the signature of A. κ'_2 is used for satisfying the anonymity requirement of an anonymous signature scheme, that is, preventing an adversary from compromising A's anonymity by searching through the list of all possible 'messages' of the signature.

7.2   Anonymous Paper Review

In a conventional anonymous paper review system for a conference, authors separate their authorship information from the paper bodies before submitting them to the conference organizer. The paper bodies are required to be fully anonymous, that is, no author name, affiliation, acknowledgement, or obvious reference should appear in them. The organizer then keeps the authorship information of the papers secret from the reviewers and only sends those anonymized paper bodies to reviewers to review. One problem of the current system is that the anonymity of the papers will be compromised once the authorship information of the papers is leaked to the reviewers from the organizer. The organizer or some insider in the organizing institute, for example a graduate student who is responsible for maintaining the paper submission server, may leak the authorship information of the papers to the reviewers. In the following, we describe a method which uses anonymous signature to solve this collusion problem.

Consider the paper submission server is now a bulletin board which posts and timestamps any message received. Once posted, the message cannot be altered. Let $Paper_A$ be a paper which is fully anonymous. Let A be the identity of the paper's author and assume that each author already has his public key (for signature verification) published. To submit the paper $Paper_A$, the author randomly picks a long binary string $r \in \{0,1\}^k$ where k is the security parameter, and generates a signature $\sigma_A = \mathsf{AnonSig}_A(h(Paper_A, r))$ using his anonymous signature generation algorithm denoted by $\mathsf{AnonSig}_A$ on the message $h(Paper_A, r)$ where $h : \{0,1\}^* \to \{0,1\}^k$ is a hash function which behaves like a random oracle. The author posts $Paper_A$ and σ_A onto the bulletin board for review. When all the reviews are completed and the acceptance decision on each paper has been made, the decision will be posted on the bulletin board. If $Paper_A$ is accepted, the author A will reveal the value of r for claiming his authorship on $Paper_A$. From this point on, everyone is able to verify his authorship using σ_A, $(Paper_A, r)$ and A's public key.

Discussions: In the review stage, no author has given out any authorship information and the secrecy of r prevents anyone from identifying the signer of σ_A. This new system can also let the public access the bulletin board instead of restricting its access to reviewers only. In this way, everyone can access those papers once they are posted. Since every paper is timestamped when it is first submitted and posted to the bulletin board, this helps paper authors to claim that they are the first ones who obtained those new results described in their papers without compromising the process of anonymous review. In addition, it will also help discover parallel submissions.

References

1. J.H. An, Y. Dodis, and T. Rabin. On the security of joint signature and encryption. In *Proc. EUROCRYPT 2002*, pages 83–107. Springer-Verlag, 2002. LNCS 2332.
2. M. Bellare, A. Boldyreva, A. Desai, and D. Pointcheval. Key-privacy in public-key encryption. In *Proc. ASIACRYPT 2001*, pages 566–582. Springer-Verlag, 2001. LNCS 2248.
3. M. Bellare and C. Namprempre. Authenticated encryption: Relations among notions and analysis of the generic composition paradigm. In *Proc. ASIACRYPT 2000*, pages 531–545. Springer-Verlag, 2000. LNCS 1976.
4. M. Bellare and P. Rogaway. Random oracles are practical: A paradigm for designing efficient protocols. In *First ACM Conference on Computer and Communications Security*, pages 62–73, Fairfax, 1993. ACM.

5. M. Bellare and P. Rogaway. The exact security of digital signatures - how to sign with RSA and Rabin. In *Advances in Cryptology - Eurocrypt'96*, pages 399–416. Springer-Verlag, 1996. LNCS 1070.
6. C. Boyd and D. Park. Public key protocols for wireless communications. *The 1st International Conference on Information Secuirty and Cryptology (ICISC'98)*, pages 47–57, 1998.
7. X. Boyen. Multipurpose identity-based signcryption: A swiss army knife for identity-based cryptography. In *Proc. CRYPTO 2003*, pages 383–399. Springer-Verlag, 2003. LNCS 2729.
8. R. Canetti and H. Krawczyk. Analysis of key-exchange protocols and their use for building secure channels. In *Proc. EUROCRYPT 2001*, pages 453–474. Springer-Verlag, 2001. LNCS 2045. http://eprint.iacr.org/2001/040/.
9. S. Goldwasser, S. Micali, and R. Rivest. A digital signature scheme secure against adaptive chosen-message attack. *SIAM J. Computing*, 17(2):281–308, April 1988.
10. D. Harkins, C. Kaufman, and R. Perlman. The internet key exchange (IKE) protocol <draft-ietf-ipsec-ikev2-00.txt>. INTERNET-DRAFT, November 2001.
11. E. Van Herreweghen. Secure anonymous signature-based transactions. In *ESORICS '00: Proc. of the 6th European Symposium on Research in Computer Security*, pages 55–71. Springer-Verlag, 2000. LNCS 1895.
12. M. Jakobsson, K. Sako, and R. Impagliazzo. Designated verifier proofs and their applications. In *Proc. EUROCRYPT 96*, pages 143–154, 1996. LNCS 1070.
13. F. Laguillaumie and D. Vergnaud. Designated verifier signatures: Anonymity and efficient construction from any bilinear map. In *Proc. of the 4th Intl. Conference on Security in Communication Networks (SCN 2004)*, pages 105–119, 2004. LNCS 3352.
14. NIST FIPS PUB 197. *Announcing the ADVANCED ENCRYPTION STANDARD (AES)*, November 2001.
15. R. Rivest, A. Shamir, and L. Adleman. A method for obtaining digital signatures and public-key cryptosystems. *Communications of the ACM*, 21(2):120–126, February 1978.
16. C. Schnorr. Efficient identification and signatures for smart cards. In *Proc. CRYPTO 89*, pages 239–252. Springer, 1990. LNCS 435.
17. G. Yang, D. Wong, and X. Deng. Analysis and improvement of a signcryption scheme with key privacy. In *Proc. of the 8th Information Security Conference (ISC '05)*, pages 218–232. Springer-Verlag, 2005. LNCS 3650.
18. G. Yang, D. Wong, and X. Deng. Efficient anonymous roaming and its security analysis. In *Proc. of the 3rd International Conference on Applied Cryptography and Network Security (ACNS 2005)*, pages 334–349. Springer-Verlag, 2005. LNCS 3531.
19. G. Yang, D. S. Wong, X. Deng, and H. Wang. Anonymous signature schemes. Cryptology ePrint Archive, Report 2005/407, 2005. http://eprint.iacr.org/.

The Power of Identification Schemes

Kaoru Kurosawa[1] and Swee-Huay Heng[2]

[1] Department of Computer and Information Sciences,
Ibaraki University,
4-12-1 Nakanarusawa, Hitachi, Ibaraki 316-8511, Japan
kurosawa@mx.ibaraki.ac.jp
[2] Faculty of Information Science and Technology,
Multimedia University,
Jalan Ayer Keroh Lama, 75450 Melaka, Malaysia
shheng@mmu.edu.my

Abstract. In this paper, we show that identification schemes (ID-schemes) are very powerful in some areas of cryptography. We first prove an equivalence between non-interactive trapdoor commitment schemes and a natural class of identification schemes. We next propose a more efficient on-line/off-line signature transformation than Shamir-Tauman. As an application, we present a variant of Boneh-Boyen (BB) signature scheme which is not only on-line/off-line but also has a smaller public key size than the original BB scheme. Finally, we present the first identity-based ID-scheme which is secure against concurrent man-in-the-middle attack without random oracles by using our variant of BB signature scheme.

Keywords: Identification scheme, signature scheme, trapdoor commitment scheme, on-line/off-line, identity-based.

1 Introduction

1.1 Background

A commitment scheme consists of two phases: in the commit phase, a sender commits to a message, while in the decommit phase, the sender reveals the committed message. A trapdoor commitment scheme admits a trapdoor whose knowledge allows to open a commitment in any possible way. Gennaro generalized trapdoor commitment schemes to multi-trapdoor commitment schemes [12]. A multi-trapdoor commitment scheme is a family of secure trapdoor commitment schemes such that it admits a master trapdoor whose knowledge allows to open any commitment in the family in any possible way. He also showed a compiler which transforms any proof of knowledge (identification scheme) into one which is secure against the concurrent man-in-the-middle attack, where the compiler needs a multi-trapdoor commitment scheme and a strong one-time signature scheme in addition. We can thus have the following relationship:

ID-scheme + multi-trapdoor commitment + strong one-time signature
→ ID-scheme secure against concurrent man-in-the-middle attack.

M. Yung et al. (Eds.): PKC 2006, LNCS 3958, pp. 364–377, 2006.

On the other hand, the notion of on-line/off-line signature schemes was introduced by Even et al. [9]. The on-line phase of this kind of signatures can be made very fast due to the pre-computation of the off-line phase. Shamir and Tauman showed how to transform a non-adaptively secure signature scheme to an adaptively secure on-line/off-line signature scheme by using trapdoor commitment schemes [25]. That is,

Non-adaptive signature + trapdoor commitment →Adaptive on-line/off-line signature

(1)

This result is important because there exist only a few adaptively secure signature schemes in the standard model: Cramer-Shoup scheme [8] and Gennaro-Halevi-Rabin scheme [13] under the strong RSA assumption, and Boneh-Boyen scheme [1] under the strong Diffie-Hellman assumption.

Meanwhile, the idea of identity (ID)-based cryptography was formulated by Shamir [24] in 1984. An ID-based scheme is an asymmetric system wherein the public key is effectively replaced by a user's publicly available identity information or any arbitrary string which derived from the user's identity. It enables any pair of users to communicate securely without exchanging public or private keys and without keeping any key directories. Many ID-based schemes appeared in the literature since then, for example ID-based encryption schemes [4, 2, 3], ID-based signature schemes [21, 16, 7], etc.

The notion of ID-based identifications was formalized in Kurosawa and Heng [18] and Bellare et al. [6] independently. All the ID-based ID-schemes presented in the above two papers are provably secure in the random oracle model only. Provably secure ID-based ID-schemes in the standard model were first appeared in [19], but they are not secure against concurrent man-in-the-middle attack. In this paper, we propose the first ID-based ID-scheme which is provably secure against concurrent man-in-the-middle attack in the standard model.

1.2   Our Contributions

In this paper, we show that identification schemes (ID-schemes) are very powerful in some areas of cryptography.

We first prove an equivalence between non-interactive trapdoor commitment schemes and a natural class of identification schemes. This class includes Schnorr scheme [23], GQ scheme[15], Fiat-Shamir scheme [11] and the 2^ℓ-th root scheme [26].

Next, we show a more efficient transformation from a non-adaptively secure signature to an adaptively secure on-line/off-line signature than equation (1) by *directly* employing the canonical ID-scheme as a tool. The proposed transformation requires lesser memory in the off-line phase than Shamir-Tauman transformation [25] which is indicated by equation (1)).

Additionally, we present an on-line/off-line variant of Boneh-Boyen signature scheme (BB scheme) [1] as an example of the above transformation. The proposed scheme is not only on-line/off-line, but also the public key size is smaller than that of the original BB scheme. Although a similar scheme can be obtained by applying Shamir-Tauman transformation, our scheme, however, requires lesser memory in the off-line phase.

Finally, we present the first ID-based ID-scheme which is provably secure against concurrent man-in-the-middle attack in the standard model, deriving from our proposed variant of BB signature scheme.

All our results hold without relying on the random oracle heuristic. In the random oracle model, it is well-known that a canonical identification scheme can be transformed to a signature scheme by using the Fiat and Shamir technique [11]. Many signature schemes are obtained by this transformation [10, 15, 23, 20].

1.3   Organization

The rest of this paper is organized as follows. In Section 2, we briefly review some preliminaries. In Section 3, we prove the equivalence between identification scheme and trapdoor commitment scheme. In Section 4, we present a general transformation from any non-adaptively secure signature to the adaptively secure on-line/off-line signature by employing a canonical ID-scheme as a tool. In Section 5, we exhibit a concrete example by applying the above transformation to Boneh-Boyen signature scheme. In Section 6, we propose the first ID-based ID-scheme which is secure against concurrent man-in-the-middle attack in the standard model. Finally, we conclude this paper in Section 7.

2   Preliminaries

Throughout this paper, ℓ denotes the security parameter and a PPT algorithm denotes a probabilistic polynomial time algorithm.

2.1   Identification Scheme

In an identification scheme (ID-scheme), a prover P proves to a verifier V that she knows a *witness* s_I related to a public *instance* p_I. A canonical ID-scheme can be formalized by $\mathcal{ID} = (\mathsf{G}_{ID}, \mathsf{Commit}, \mathsf{Response}, \mathsf{Check})$, where G_{ID} is a PPT algorithm which generates (p_I, s_I). Commit , $\mathsf{Response}$ and Check are algorithms which specify the protocol (P, V) as follows.

Step 1. P chooses r at random from a certain domain CMT and computes $x = \mathsf{Commit}(r)$. P then sends x to V.

Step 2. V chooses a challenge c at random from a certain set CHA and sends it to P.

Step 3. P computes a response $y = \mathsf{Response}(s_I, r, c)$ and sends y to V. Let RES denote the set of possible y for p_I.

Step 4. V checks if

$$x = \mathsf{Check}(p_I, c, y). \qquad (2)$$

V accepts P if and only if equation (2) holds.

The above protocol (P, V) is often called a Σ-protocol. We say that (x, c, y) is a valid transcript for p_I if it satisfies equation (2).

Definition 1. *We say that $\mathcal{ID}$ is a Σ-ID-scheme if the following holds:*

Completeness. $\Pr(\text{equation (2) holds}) = 1$.

Special Soundness. *It is hard to compute two valid transcripts (x, c, y) and (x, c', y') such that $c \neq c'$ on input p_I.*

y-Uniformity. *For any fixed (s_I, c), $y = \mathsf{Response}(s_I, r, c)$ is uniformly distributed over RES if r is uniformly distributed over CMT.*

It is easy to see that y-uniformity implies that the protocol (P, V) is honest-verifier zero-knowledge. All the important identification schemes in cryptographic applications are Σ-ID-schemes.

2.2 Trapdoor Commitment Scheme

A trapdoor commitment scheme is defined by $\mathcal{TC} = (\mathsf{G}_{TC}, \mathsf{Tcom}, \mathsf{Topen})$. G_{TC} is a PPT algorithm which generates (pk, tk), where pk is the public key and tk is the trapdoor.

Tcom is the algorithm that computes a commitment on m as $x = \mathsf{Tcom}(pk, m, r)$, where r is a random number. To open the commitment x, the sender reveals m, r and the receiver recomputes x.

Topen is the algorithm that opens a commitment in any possible way with the trapdoor tk. For given m, r and $m' \neq m$, it outputs $r' = \mathsf{Topen}(tk, m, r, m')$ such that $x = \mathsf{Tcom}(pk, m, r) = \mathsf{Tcom}(pk, m', r')$.

This implies that the receiver has no information on m given x. We require that the sender cannot find a collision such as follows.

Definition 2. *We say that a trapdoor commitment scheme $\mathcal{TC}$ is secure if it is hard to compute (m, r) and (m', r') such that $\mathsf{Tcom}(m, r) = \mathsf{Tcom}(m', r')$ on input pk where $m \neq m'$.*

An example of trapdoor commitment scheme under the discrete logarithm assumption [22] is shown in Appendix A.

2.3 Signature Scheme

A signature scheme is denoted by $\Omega = (\mathsf{G}_{sign}, \mathsf{Sign}, \mathsf{Verify})$. G_{sign} is a PPT algorithm which generates (vk, sk), where vk is a verification key and sk is the secret key. Sign is a PPT algorithm which generates a signature σ on input a message m and the secret key sk. Verify is a polynomial time algorithm which checks the validity of (m, σ) by using vk, say $\mathsf{Verify}(vk, m, \sigma) = accept$ or $reject$.

Adaptive Security. The standard security notion of signature schemes is existential unforgeability against adaptive chosen message attack [14]. It is defined using the following game between a challenger and an adversary A:

1. The challenger runs G_{sign} to obtain (vk, sk). A is given vk.
2. A queries some message m_i to the challenger for $i = 1, \ldots, t$ adaptively. The challenger responds to each query with a signature $\sigma_i = \mathsf{Sign}(sk, m_i)$.

368   K. Kurosawa and S.-H. Heng

We say that Ω is adaptively secure if $\Pr(A \text{ wins})$ is negligible for any PPT adversary A as shown above.

Non-adaptive Security. A much weaker security notion is existential unforgeability against weak non-adaptive chosen message attack. It is defined using the following game between a challenger and an adversary A:

1. On input the security parameter 1^ℓ, the adversary A submits messages m_1, $\ldots, m_t$ (non-adaptively) to the challenger.
2. The challenger generates (vk, sk) randomly and computes the signatures $\sigma_1, \ldots, \sigma_t$. He then sends $vk, \sigma_1, \ldots, \sigma_t$ to A.
3. A outputs a forgery (m^*, σ^*). A wins the game if $m^* \notin \{m_1, \ldots, m_t\}$ and $\mathsf{Verify}(vk, m^*, \sigma^*) = accept$.

We say that Ω is non-adaptively secure if $\Pr(A \text{ wins})$ is negligible for any PPT adversary A as shown above.

There is another notion called one-time signature, informally this means that the adversary A is given the verification key vk and the signature σ on a message m of her choice (chosen after seeing vk), then it is infeasible for A to compute the signature of a different message, say (m^*, σ^*) such that $m^* \neq m$.

A *strong* one-time signature scheme means that it is infeasible for A to also generate (m^*, σ^*) such that $(m^*, \sigma^*) \neq (m, \sigma)$.

3   Equivalence Between $\mathcal{ID}$ and $\mathcal{TC}$

We say that a Σ-ID-scheme is *reversible* if there exists a polynomial time algorithm $\mathsf{Reverse}$ which computes r such that

$$x = \mathsf{Commit}(r) = \mathsf{Check}(p_I, c, y)$$

from p_I, s_I, c and y. All the important identification schemes in cryptographic applications are *reversible* Σ-ID-schemes.

For example, we have a look at the famous Schnorr ID-scheme [23]. Suppose that the Schnorr ID-scheme is defined as $\mathcal{ID} = (\mathsf{G}_{ID}, \mathsf{Commit}, \mathsf{Response}, \mathsf{Check})$. Let G be a group of prime order q and g be the generator of G. G_{ID} is a PPT algorithm which generates $(p_I, s_I) = (g^s, s)$ where s is randomly chosen from Z_q. Commit , $\mathsf{Response}$ and Check are algorithms which specify the protocol (P, V) as follows.

Step 1. P chooses r at random from Z_q and computes $x = \mathsf{Commit}(r) = g^r$. P then sends x to V.

Step 2. V chooses a challenge c at random from Z_q and sends it to P.

Step 3. P computes a response

$$y = \mathsf{Response}(s, r, c) = r + cs \bmod q \tag{3}$$

and sends y to V.

Step 4. V checks if
$$x = \mathsf{Check}(g^s, c, y).$$
More precisely, V checks whether $x = g^r = g^y/(g^s)^c$. V accepts P if and only if the above equation holds.

Thus, it is not difficult to see that the Schnorr ID-scheme is a Σ-ID-scheme since it satisfies all the conditions in Definition 1. It is also a reversible Σ-ID-scheme since there exists a polynomial time algorithm $\mathsf{Reverse}$ which computes r such that
$$x = \mathsf{Commit}(r) = \mathsf{Check}(g^s, c, y),$$
given g^s, s, c and y. That is, r can be computed from equation (3) via
$$r = y - cs \bmod q.$$

Next, we prove that non-interactive trapdoor commitment schemes are equivalent to *reversible* Σ-ID-schemes.

Theorem 1. *If there exists a reversible Σ-ID-scheme, then there exists a trapdoor commitment scheme.*

Proof. We first prove that a reversible Σ-ID-scheme implies a trapdoor commitment scheme. Suppose that there exists a reversible Σ-ID-scheme. We then construct a trapdoor commitment scheme $\mathcal{TC} = (\mathsf{G}_{TC}, \mathsf{Tcom}, \mathsf{Topen})$ as follows. Let H be a collision-resistant hash function. Let $\mathsf{G}_{TC} = \mathsf{G}_{ID}$. That is, the key pair of $\mathcal{TC}$ is given by $(pk, tk) = (p_I, s_I)$, where $(p_I, s_I) \leftarrow \mathsf{G}_{ID}(1^\ell)$.

(Commitment). For a message m, let $x = \mathsf{Tcom}(pk, m, y) = \mathsf{Check}(p_I, H(m), y)$, where y is chosen at random. That is, we consider an execution of $\mathcal{ID}$ on input p_I such that x is a commit, $H(m)$ is a challenge and y is a response.

(Trapdoor). Suppose that m, y and $m' \neq m$ are given. Then we compute y' such that $x = \mathsf{Check}(p_I, H(m), y) = \mathsf{Check}(p_I, H(m'), y')$ as follows. By using $\mathsf{Reverse}$, compute r such that $x = \mathsf{Commit}(r)$ from $p_I, s_I, H(m)$ and y. Then let $y' = \mathsf{Response}(s_I, r, H(m'))$.

(Security). The above $\mathcal{TC}$ is secure from the special soundness of $\mathcal{ID}$. □

Theorem 2. *If there exists a trapdoor commitment scheme, then there exists a reversible Σ-ID-scheme.*

Proof. We prove that a trapdoor commitment scheme implies a reversible Σ-ID-scheme. Suppose that there exists a trapdoor commitment scheme $\mathcal{TC} = (\mathsf{G}_{TC}, \mathsf{Tcom}, \mathsf{Topen})$. We then construct a reversible Σ-ID-scheme as follows. Let H be a collision-resistant hash function.

Let $\mathsf{G}_{ID} = \mathsf{G}_{TC}$. That is, let $(p_I, s_I) = (pk, tk)$. Let $x = \mathsf{Commit}(R) = \mathsf{Tcom}(p_I, m, r)$, where $R = (m, r)$ is randomly chosen.

From $R = (m, r)$ and a given challenge c, compute y such that
$$\mathsf{Tcom}(p_I, c, y) = \mathsf{Tcom}(p_I, m, r)$$
by using the trapdoor key tk. Let $\mathsf{Response}(tk, R, c) = y$.

Define $\mathsf{Check}(p_I, c, y) = \mathsf{Tcom}(p_I, c, y)$.

We show that the above scheme is a reversible Σ-ID-scheme. It is easy to see that $\Pr(\text{equation (2) holds}) = 1$. The special soundness holds from the security of $\mathcal{TC}$. The y-uniformity is clearly satisfied. Finally, we need to show Reverse which computes $R = (m, r)$ such that

$$x = \mathsf{Commit}(T) = \mathsf{Check}(p_I, c, y)$$

from tk, c and y. From our definition of Commit and Check, the above equation is written as

$$\mathsf{Tcom}(p_I, m, r) = \mathsf{Tcom}(p_I, c, y).$$

Next, Reverse chooses r at random and computes r which satisfies the above equation by using tk. This completes the proof. □

4   New On-Line/Off-Line Signature Scheme

The notion of on-line/off-line signature schemes was introduced by Even et al. [9]. In these schemes, the on-line phase of the signing algorithm is made very fast due to the pre-computation in the off-line phase. Shamir and Tauman showed how to transform a non-adaptively secure signature scheme to an on-line/off-line signature scheme which is adaptively secure by using trapdoor commitment schemes [25].

In this section, we show a more efficient transformation which requires lesser memory than Shamir-Tauman transformation by *directly* using Σ-ID-schemes instead of using our equivalence of Section 3 (see Table 1).

4.1   Proposed Transformation

Let $\Omega = (\mathsf{G}_{sign}, \mathsf{Sign}, \mathsf{Verify})$ be a non-adaptively secure signature scheme.

Let $\mathcal{ID} = (\mathsf{G}_{ID}, \mathsf{Commit}, \mathsf{Response}, \mathsf{Check})$ be a Σ-ID-scheme, where CHA is the set of challenges and RES is the set of responses. Let $H : \{0,1\}^* \to \mathrm{CHA}$ be a collision-resistant hash function.

Then our on-line/off-line signature scheme is constructed as follows.

Key generation. Run G_{sign} to generate (vk, sk), and run G_{ID} to generate (p_I, s_I). The verification key is $vk' = (vk, p_I)$ and the secret key is $sk' = (sk, s_I)$.

Signing. The signing algorithm operates as follows.

1. Off-line phase: Choose $r \in \mathrm{CMT}$ randomly and compute $x = \mathsf{Commit}(r)$. For x, compute $\sigma = \mathsf{Sign}(sk, x)$ and store (r, σ).
2. On-line phase: Given a message $m \in \{0,1\}^*$, the on-line phase proceeds as follows. Retrieve (r, σ) from the memory. Compute $y = \mathsf{Response}(s_I, r, H(m))$. Let $\sigma' = (\sigma, y)$ be a signature of m.

Note that $(x, H(m), y)$ is a valid transcript of $\mathcal{ID}$.

Verification. For m and $\sigma' = (\sigma, y)$, first compute $x = \mathsf{Check}(p_I, H(m), y)$. Next accept (m, σ') if and only if (x, σ) is a valid message-signature pair under vk, that is, $\mathsf{Verify}(vk, x, \sigma) = accept$.

Note that the on-line phase is efficient because it computes only $y = $ Response $(s_I, r, H(m))$.

Theorem 3. *The above signature scheme Ω' is adaptively secure if Ω is non-adaptively secure and $\mathcal{ID}$ is a Σ-ID-scheme.*

Proof. Suppose that there exists a PPT adversary A for Ω' such that $\Pr(A$ wins$)$ is non-negligible in the adaptive chosen message attack. Then we show that Ω is not non-adaptively secure or $\mathcal{ID}$ is not a Σ-ID-scheme.

The challenger gives $vk' = (vk, p_I)$ to A as the verification key. Assume that A queries messages m_i to the challenger and the challenger returns signature $\sigma' = (\sigma_i, y_i)$ for $i = 1, \ldots, t$. Eventually, A outputs a forgery m^* and $z = (\sigma^*, y^*)$. Let $x^* = $ Check$(p_I, H(m^*), y^*)$ and $x_i = $ Check$(p_I, H(m_i), y_i)$ for $i = 1, \ldots, t$.

We then distinguish two types of forgeries, Type-1 in which $x^* = x_j$ for some j, and Type-2 in which $x^* \neq x_i$ for any i. Type-1 forgery or type-2 forgery occurs with non-negligible probability.

(Type-1 forgery). In this case, we show a PPT algorithm M which breaks the special soundness of $\mathcal{ID}$. On input p_I, M behaves as follows.

1. M runs G_{sign} to obtain (vk, sk). M then acts as a challenger and sends $vk' = (vk, p_I)$ to A.
2. M simulates the challenger of A as follows. Suppose that A asks for a signature on m_i. Then M chooses $y_i \in$ RES randomly and computes $x_i = $ Check$(p_I, H(m_i), y_i)$. M next computes $\sigma_i = $ Sign(sk, x_i) by using sk and returns a signature $\sigma'_i = (\sigma_i, y_i)$ to A.
3. Eventually, A returns a valid forgery m^* and $z = (\sigma^*, y^*)$ such that $m^* \neq m_j$ and $x^* = x_j$ for some j.

M then outputs two valid transcripts $(x^*(= x_j), H(m^*), y^*)$ and $(x_j, H(m_j), y_j)$ for p_I. Note that $H(m^*) \neq H(m_j)$ with overwhelming probability because $m^* \neq m_j$ and H is collision-resistant. This means that M breaks the special soundness of $\mathcal{ID}$.

(Type-2 forgery). In this case, we show a PPT adversary B that breaks Ω by non-adaptive chosen message attack. On input 1^ℓ, B behaves as follows.

1. M runs G_{ID} to obtain (p_I, s_I). For $i = 1, \ldots, t$, B chooses $r_i \in$ CMT randomly and computes $x_i = $ Commit(r_i). B sends $x_1, \ldots, x_t$ as messages to its challenger.
2. The challenger runs G_{sign} to obtain (vk, sk). It computes $\sigma_i = $ Sign(sk, x_i) for $i = 1, \ldots, t$. It then returns $vk, \sigma_1, \ldots, \sigma_t$ to B.
3. B runs A on input $vk' = (vk, p_I)$.
4. M simulates the challenger of A as follows. Suppose that A asks for a signature on m_i. Then B computes $y_i = $ Response$(s_I, r_i, H(m_i))$ by using s_I and returns a signature $\sigma'_i = (\sigma_i, y_i)$ to A.
5. Eventually, A returns a valid forgery m^* and $z = (\sigma^*, y^*)$ such that $x^* \neq x_i$ for any i because it is a type-2 forgery.

B then outputs a forgery (x^*, σ^*). Now B wins because $x^* \neq x_i$ for any i and σ^* is a valid signature on x^*.

This completes the proof. $\qquad\qquad\qquad\qquad\qquad\qquad\qquad\qquad\qquad\square$

4.2 Comparison

Shamir-Tauman [25] showed a transformation using trapdoor commitment schemes $\mathcal{TC} = (\mathsf{G}_{TC}, \mathsf{Tcom}, \mathsf{Topen})$ as follows.

Let $\Omega = (\mathsf{G}_{sign}, \mathsf{Sign}, \mathsf{Verify})$ be a non-adaptively secure signature scheme. A secret key of the on-line/off-line signature scheme is (sk, tk), where sk is a secret key of Ω and tk is a trapdoor key of $\mathcal{TC}$. The public key is (vk, pk), where vk is a verification key of Ω and pk is a public key of $\mathcal{TC}$.

1. Off-line phase: Choose a random message m' and a random number r'. Compute $hash = \mathsf{Tcom}(pk, m', r')$ and $\sigma = \mathsf{Sign}(sk, hash)$. Then store (m', r', σ).
2. On-line phase: Given a message m, the on-line phase proceeds as follows. Retrieve (m', r', σ) from the memory. By using tk, find r such that $\mathsf{Tcom}(pk, m, r) = \mathsf{Tcom}(pk, m', r')$. Let $\sigma' = (\sigma, r)$ be a signature of m.

Now in Shamir-Tauman scheme, the off-line phase must store (m', r', σ). On the other hand, our off-line phase stores only (r, σ). Hence our memory size is smaller if $|r| = |r'|$.

Table 1. On-line/Off-line Signature Transformation

	Tool	Memory
Shamir-Tauman [25]	trapdoor commitment	(m', r', σ)
Proposed	Σ-ID-scheme	(r, σ)

5   Application to BB Signature Scheme

Boneh and Boyen showed a signature scheme under the strong Diffie-Hellman assumption in the standard model [1].

In this section, we show an on-line/off-line variant of BB signature scheme as an application of our transformation. The proposed scheme is not only on-line/off-line, but also the public key size is smaller than that of BB scheme while the other parameters are of the same size. A similar scheme can be obtained by using Shamir-Tauman transformation. Our scheme, however, requires lesser memory in the off-line phase as shown in Table 1.

5.1   BB Signature Scheme

Let (G_1, G_2) be bilinear groups such that $|G_1| = |G_2| = p$, where p is a prime. Let $e : G_1 \times G_2 \rightarrow G_T$ be a pairing, where $|G_T| = p$. Let g_1 be a generator of G_1 and g_2 be a generator of G_2. Let $H : \{0,1\}^* \rightarrow Z_p^*$ be a collision-resistant hash function.

The basic BB scheme is non-adaptively secure under the strong DH assumption. A verification key is $v(= g_2^\alpha)$, where $\alpha \in Z_q$ is the secret key. For a message $m \in \{0,1\}^*$, a signature is given by $\sigma = g_1^{\frac{1}{\alpha + H(m)}}$. Given (m, σ), verify that

$$e(\sigma, v \cdot g_2^{H(m)}) = e(g_1, g_2).$$

The full BB scheme is adaptively secure under the same assumption. A verification key is $u(= g_2^\alpha)$ and $v(= g_2^\beta)$, where $\alpha, \beta \in Z_q$ are the secret key. For a message $m \in \{0,1\}^*$, a signature is given by $(\sigma = g_1^{\frac{1}{\alpha + H(m) + \beta r}}, r)$, where $r \in Z_q$ is randomly chosen by the signer. Given (m, σ, r), verify that

$$e(\sigma, u \cdot g_2^{H(m)} \cdot v^r) = e(g_1, g_2).$$

5.2   Proposed On-Line/Off-Line Signature Scheme

We now apply our transformation of Section 4.1 to the basic BB scheme Ω and Schnorr identification scheme. Let $H : \{0,1\}^* \to Z_p^*$ and $\widetilde{H} : G_1 \to Z_p^*$ be two collision-resistant hash functions.

Key generation. Choose $\alpha \in Z_p$ randomly and compute $v = g_2^\alpha$. Let $\widetilde{g_1}$ be a generator of G_1. Choose $s \in Z_p$ randomly and compute $w = \widetilde{g_1}^{-s}$. Let (v, w) be a verification key and (α, s) be the secret key. Note that (v, α) is a key-pair of the basic BB scheme and (w, s) is a key-pair of Schnorr identification scheme.

Signing.

1. Off-line phase: Choose $r \in Z_p$ randomly and compute $x = \widetilde{g_1}^r$. For x, compute $\sigma = g_1^{\frac{1}{\alpha + \widetilde{H}(x)}}$ and store (r, σ). (Note that σ is a signature on x in the basic BB scheme.)
2. On-line phase: Given a message $m \in \{0,1\}^*$, the on-line phase proceeds as follows. Retrieve (r, σ) from the memory. Compute $y = r + sH(m) \bmod p$. Let $\sigma' = (\sigma, y)$ be a signature of m.

Verification. Given (m, σ, y), first compute $x = \widetilde{g_1}^y w^{H(m)}$. Next by using x, verify that

$$e(\sigma, v \cdot g_2^{\widetilde{H}(x)}) = e(g_1, g_2). \tag{4}$$

Theorem 4. *The above on-line/off-line signature scheme is adaptively secure under strong DH assumption in the standard model.*

Proof. The basic BB scheme is non-adaptively secure under strong DH assumption [1] and Schnorr scheme is a Σ-ID-scheme under the discrete logarithm assumption. Therefore, from Theorem 3, the above signature scheme is adaptively secure under strong DH assumption. $\qquad\square$

Note that the on-line phase computes only $y = r + sH(m) \bmod p$. Hence it is very efficient. Moreover, our scheme has a smaller verification key as shown below. In [5], it is suggested to use an elliptic curve over $GF(3^\ell)$ for G_1 and one over $GF(3^{6\ell})$ for G_2. Hence in our scheme, the verification key size is approximately a half of the full BB signature scheme as shown in the following table.

Table 2. BB Scheme and Our Variant

	verification key	secret key	signature
Full BB scheme [1]	$u, v \in G_2$	$\alpha, \beta \in Z_p$	$\sigma \in G_1, r \in Z_p$
Our scheme	$v \in G_2,\ w \in G_1$	$\alpha, s \in Z_p$	$\sigma \in G_1, y \in Z_p$

6   ID-Based ID-Scheme Without Random Oracles

The main differences of ID-based identification schemes from the usual identification schemes are that: (1) The adversary can choose a target identity ID of her choice to impersonate as opposed to a random public key; (2) The adversary can possess private keys of some users which she has chosen. The formal model of ID-based identification scheme was formalized in [18, 6].

In this section, we show the first ID-based ID-scheme which is provably secure against man-in-the-middle attack in the standard model by using our variant of BB signature scheme in Section 5.2. By applying Gennaro's technique [12] to the BB on-line/off-line *signature scheme*, we manage to transform it to an ID-based *ID-scheme* secure against concurrent man-in-the-middle attack under the strong DH assumption.

Gennaro [12]: Σ-ID-scheme $\rightarrow$ Very secure ID-scheme
Proposed: BB signature scheme $\rightarrow$ Very secure ID-based ID-scheme

6.1   Another Tool

We adopt the strong DH-based multi-trapdoor commitment scheme introduced by Gennaro into our construction since our BB on-line/off-line signature scheme is also based on the strong DH assumption.

The master key generation algorithm selects a random $\mu \in Z_p$ which will be the master trapdoor. The master public key will be the pair (g, g') where $g' = g^{\mu}$ in G. Each commitment in the family will be identified by a specific public key which is simply an element $n \in Z_p$. The specific trapdoor of this scheme is the value f_n in G such that $f_n^{\mu+n} = g$. To commit a message $m \in Z_p$ with public key n, the sender runs Pedersen's commitment [22] with bases g, h_n, where $h_n = g^n \cdot g'$. That is, it selects a random $\gamma \in Z_p$ and computes $\mathsf{com} = g^m h_n^{\gamma}$. The commitment to m is the value com. To open a commitment, the sender reveals m and $F = g^{\gamma}$. The receiver accepts the opening if $(g, F, g^n \cdot g', \mathsf{com} \cdot g^{-m})$ is a DH-tuple.

We also use a strong one-time signature scheme $\Omega = (\mathsf{G}_{sign}, \mathsf{Sign}, \mathsf{Verify})$.

6.2   Proposed ID-Based ID-Scheme

Let $\mathcal{IBI} = (\mathcal{S}, \mathcal{E}, \mathcal{P}, \mathcal{V})$ be four PPT algorithms known as setup, extract, and the identification protocol $(\mathcal{P}, \mathcal{V})$. Basically, our proposed scheme employs the key generation algorithm of BB on-line/off-line signature scheme as the setup algorithm and its signing algorithm as the extract algorithm.

Let (G_1, G_2) be bilinear groups where $|G_1| = |G_2| = p$ for some prime p. As usual, g_1 is a generator of G_1 and g_2 is a generator of G_2. Our proposed construction is as follows.

Setup. Choose $\alpha \in Z_p$ randomly and compute $v = g_2^\alpha$. Let $\widetilde{g_1}$ be a generator of G_1. Choose $s \in Z_p$ randomly and compute $w = \widetilde{g_1}^{-s}$. Choose two collision-resistant hash functions $H : \{0,1\}^* \to Z_p^*$ and $\widetilde{H} : G_1 \to Z_p^*$.

We also need the following extra common reference string: $g_1' = g_1^\mu$ for a random $\mu \in Z_p$ and a collision-resistant hash function H' with output in Z_p. The system parameters params is $(g_1, g_1', \widetilde{g_1}, g_2, v, w, H, \widetilde{H}, H')$ and the master-key is (α, s).

Extract. Given a master-key (α, s) and an identity $\mathsf{ID} \in \{0,1\}^*$, pick a random $r \in Z_p^*$ and compute $x = \widetilde{g_1}^r$. For x, compute $\sigma = g_1^{\frac{1}{\alpha + \widetilde{H}(x)}} \in G_1$. Next, compute $y = r + sH(\mathsf{ID}) \bmod p$. The user private key is (σ, y).

Protocol $(\mathcal{P}, \mathcal{V})$.

1. $\mathcal{P}$ first computes $(vk, sk) \leftarrow \mathsf{G}_{sign}(1^\ell)$ (run the key generation of the strong one-time signature scheme) and computes $n = H(vk)$, where n is a specific public key of the multi-trapdoor commitment scheme.
   It next chooses $R \in G_1$ randomly and computes $X = e(R, v \cdot g_2^{\widetilde{H}(x)})$. It also does the following: sets $h_n = g_1^n g_1'$; chooses $\gamma \in Z_p$ randomly and computes the commitment $\mathsf{com} = g_1^{H'(X)} h_n^\gamma$. It finally sends (y, com, vk) to $\mathcal{V}$.
2. $\mathcal{V}$ chooses $c \in Z_p$ randomly and sends c to $\mathcal{P}$.
3. $\mathcal{P}$ computes $S = R + c\sigma$ and $\mathsf{sig} = \mathsf{Sign}(sk, \mathsf{ID}, v, w, \mathsf{com}, c, X, \gamma, S)$. It then sends $(X, \gamma, S, \mathsf{sig})$ to $\mathcal{V}$.
4. $\mathcal{V}$ first computes $x = \widetilde{g_1}^y w^{H(\mathsf{ID})}$. $\mathcal{V}$ accepts if and only if $\mathsf{com} = g_1^{H'(X)} h_n^\gamma$, $\mathsf{Verify}(vk, \mathsf{ID}, v, w, \mathsf{com}, c, X, \gamma, S) = accept$ and $e(S, v \cdot g_2^{\widetilde{H}(x)}) = X \cdot e(g_1, g_2)^c$.

Note that (v, w) is a verification key, (α, s) is a secret key and (σ, y) is a signature on a message ID of our variant of BB signature scheme. In the basic Σ-ID-scheme, the prover reveals y at step 1, and then proves that it knows σ satisfying equation (4), where (X, c, S) is a valid transcript of the Σ-ID-scheme.

W can prove the following theorem even if the prover reveals y at step 1.

Theorem 5. *The above scheme is an ID-based ID-scheme which is secure against concurrent man-in-the-middle attack under the strong DH assumption.*

The above theorem can be proven similarly to Theorem 2 of the full version of [12] by adapting the proof for the identity-based setting.

7 Conclusion

We proved an equivalence between non-interactive trapdoor commitment schemes and a natural class of identification schemes. We also showed an efficient transformation from any non-adaptively secure signature to an adaptively secure on-line/off-line signature by using a canonical ID-scheme as a tool. For instance, we applied the above transformation to Boneh-Boyen signature scheme and we managed to obtain an on-line/off-line signature scheme with smaller public key size than that of the original Boneh-Boyen scheme. Finally, we presented the first ID-based ID-scheme which is provably secure against concurrent man-in-the-middle attack in the standard model.

References

1. D. Boneh and X. Boyen. Short signatures without random oracles. *Advances in Cryptology — EUROCRYPT '04*, LNCS 3027, pp. 56–73, Springer-Verlag, 2004.
2. D. Boneh and X. Boyen. Efficient selective-ID secure identity-based encryption without random oracles. *Advances in Cryptology — EUROCRYPT '04*, LNCS 3027, pp. 223–238, Springer-Verlag, 2004.
3. D. Boneh and X. Boyen. Secure identity based encryption without random oracles. *Advances in Cryptology–CRYPTO '04*, LNCS 3152, pp.443–459, Springer-Verlag, 2004.
4. D. Boneh and M. Franklin. Identity-based encryption from the Weil pairing. *Advances in Cryptology — CRYPTO '01*, LNCS 2139, pp. 213–229, Springer-Verlag, 2001.
5. D. Boneh, B. Lynn and H. Shacham. Short signatures from the Weil pairing. *Advances in Cryptology — ASIACRYPT '01, LNCS 2248,* pp. 514–532, Springer-Verlag, 2001.
6. M. Bellare, C. Namprempre and G. Nevan. Security proofs for identity-based identification and signature schemes. *Advances in Cryptology — EUROCRYPT '04*, LNCS 3027, pp. 268–286, Springer-Verlag, 2004.
7. J. C. Cha and J. H. Cheon. An identity-based signature from gap Diffie-Hellman groups. *Public Key Cryptography — PKC '03*, LNCS 2567, pp. 18–30, Springer-Verlag, 2003.
8. R. Cramer and V. Shoup. Signature schemes based on the strong RSA assumption. *ACM Transactions on Information and System Security — ACM TIDSEC '00*, vol. 3, no. 3, 2000. Extended abstract in *Proc. 6th ACM CCS*, 1999.
9. S. Even, O. Goldreich and S. Micali. On-line/Off-line digital signatures. *Journal of Cryptology*, vol. 9, no. 1, pp. 35–67, Springer-Verlag, 1996.
10. U. Feige, A. Fiat and A. Shamir. Zero-knowledge proofs of identity. *Journal of Cryptology*, vol. 1, pp. 77–94, Springer-Verlag, 1988.
11. A. Fiat and A. Shamir. How to prove yourself: practical solutions to identification and signature problems. *Advances in Cryptology — CRYPTO '86*, LNCS 263, pp. 186–194, Springer-Verlag, 1987.
12. R. Gennaro. Multi-trapdoor commitments and their applications to proofs of knowledge secure under concurrent man-in-the-middle attacks. *Advances in Cryptology — CRYPTO '04*, LNCS 3152, pp. 220–236, Springer-Verlag, 2004. Full version is available from IACR ePrint archive Report 2003/114 at http://eprint.iacr.org/2003/214.
13. R. Gennaro, S. Halevi and T. Rabin. Secure hash-and-sign signatures without the random oracle. *Advances in Cryptology — EUROCRYPT '99*, LNCS 1592, pp. 123–139, Springer-Verlag, 1999.

14. S. Goldwasser, S. Micali and R. Rivest. A digital signature scheme secure against adaptive chosen-message attacks. *SIAM Journal of Computing*, vol. 17, no. 2, pp. 281–308, 1988.

15. L. Guillou and J. Quisquater. A practical zero-knowledge protocol fitted to security microprocessors minimizing both transmission and memory. *Advances in Cryptology — EUROCRYPT '88*, LNCS 330, pp. 123–128, Springer-Verlag, 1989.

16. F. Hess. Efficient identity based signature schemes based on pairings. *Selected Areas in Cryptography — SAC '02*, LNCS 2595, pp. 310–324, Springer-Verlag, 2002.

17. E. van Heyst and T. P. Pedersen. How to make efficient fail-stop signatures. *Advances in Cryptology — EUROCRYPT '92*, LNCS 658, pp. 366–377, Springer-Verlag, 1992.

18. K. Kurosawa and S.-H. Heng. From digital signature to ID-based identification/signature. *Public Key Cryptography — PKC '04*, LNCS 2947, pp. 248–261, Springer-Verlag, 2004.

19. K. Kurosawa and S.-H. Heng. Identity-based identification without random oracles. *Information Security and Hiding — ISH '05 (in conjuction with ICCSA '05)*, LNCS 3481, pp. 603–613, Springer-Verlag, 2005.

20. T. Okamoto. Provably secure and practical identification schemes and corresponding signature schemes. *Advances in Cryptology — CRYPTO '92*, LNCS 740, pp. 31–53, Springer-Verlag, 1993.

21. K. G. Paterson. ID-based signatures from pairings on elliptic curves. *Electronic Letters*, vol. 38, no. 18, pp. 1025–1026, 2002.

22. T. P. Pedersen. Non-interactive and information-theoretic secure verifiable secret sharing. *Advances in Cryptology — CRYPTO '91*, LNCS 576, pp. 129–140, Springer-Verlag, 1992.

23. C. Schnorr. Efficient signature generation by smart cards. *Journal of Cryptology*, vol. 4, pp. 161–174, Springer-Verlag, 1991.

24. A. Shamir. Identity-based cryptosystems and signature schemes. *Advances in Cryptology — CRYPTO '84*, LNCS 0196, pp. 47–53, Springer-Verlag, 1985.

25. A. Shamir and Y. Tauman. Improved online/offline signature schemes. *Advances in Cryptology — CRYPTO '01*, LNCS 2139, pp. 355–367, Springer-Verlag, 2001.

26. V. Shoup. On the security of a practical identification scheme. *Journal of Cryptology*, vol. 12, no. 4, pp. 247–260, Springer-Verlag, 1999.

A   DLOG-Based Trapdoor Commitment

The public key consists of a group G of prime order p and its two generators g_1 and $g_2 = g_1^t$, where t is the trapdoor key. Let $\mathsf{Tcom}(m, r) = g_1^m g_2^r$. From m, r and $m' \neq m$, it is easy to compute r' such that $\mathsf{Tcom}(m, r) = \mathsf{Tcom}(m', r')$ by using t. Just solve

$$m + tr = m' + tr' \bmod p. \tag{5}$$

On the other hand, if one can find such a collision pair, then he can compute the discrete logarithm t of g_2 on base g_1 by solving equation (5) on t.

Security Analysis of KEA Authenticated Key Exchange Protocol

Kristin Lauter[1] and Anton Mityagin[2]

[1] Microsoft Research, One Microsoft Way, Redmond, WA 98052
klauter@microsoft.com
[2] Department of Computer Science, University of California, San Diego,
9500 Gilman Dr., La Jolla, CA 92037
amityagin@cs.ucsd.edu

Abstract. KEA is a Diffie-Hellman based key-exchange protocol developed by NSA which provides mutual authentication for the parties. It became publicly available in 1998 and since then it was neither attacked nor proved to be secure. We analyze the security of KEA and find that the original protocol is susceptible to a class of attacks. On the positive side, we present a simple modification of the protocol which makes KEA secure. We prove that the modified protocol, called KEA+, satisfies the strongest security requirements for authenticated key-exchange and that it retains some security even if a secret key of a party is leaked. Our security proof is in the random oracle model and uses the Gap Diffie-Hellman assumption. Finally, we show how to add a key confirmation feature to KEA+ (we call the version with key confirmation KEA+C) and discuss the security properties of KEA+C.

1 Introduction

AUTHENTICATED KEY EXCHANGE. Generally, key exchange protocols allow 2 parties who share no secret information to compute a secret key via public communication. Authenticated key exchange (AKE) not only allows parties to compute the shared key but also ensures authenticity of the parties. A party can compute a shared key only if it is the one it claims to be. AKE protocols operate in a public key infrastructure and the parties use each other's public keys to construct a shared secret.

NATURAL SOLUTION: SIGNED DIFFIE-HELLMAN. One possible solution for authenticated key exchange is to execute a Diffie-Hellman key exchange and to sign all the communication sent between the parties. Such an AKE protocol is sometimes referred to as Signed Diffie-Hellman. Let G be a group of prime order and denote by g a generator of G. Assume that the parties have secret/public keys for some digital signature scheme SIG and that parties know each other's registered public keys. Denote the signature of a message M under the secret key of a party $\mathbb{A}$ as $SIG_{\mathbb{A}}(M)$.

The protocol has 2 passes. First, an initiator $\mathbb{A}$ picks an ephemeral secret key x at random and sends to a responder $\mathbb{B}$ a tuple $\{g^x, SIG_{\mathbb{A}}(g^x, \mathbb{B})\}$. The responder

M. Yung et al. (Eds.): PKC 2006, LNCS 3958, pp. 378–394, 2006.
© International Association for Cryptologic Research 2006

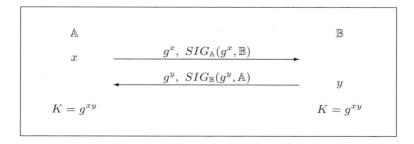

Fig. 1. Signed Diffie-Hellman authenticated key-exchange

$\mathbb{B}$ picks an ephemeral secret key y and replies with a tuple $\{g^y,\ SIG_{\mathbb{B}}(g^y, \mathbb{A})\}$. Parties then verify each other's signatures and if accepted, compute a shared session key $K = g^{xy}$. The protocol is depicted in Figure 1. This protocol was formally analyzed by Shoup [17] and it is proven to be secure (we will discuss below in detail what security means) against an adversary who can reveal session keys of honest key-exchange sessions but who cannot reveal ephemeral secret keys.

It is worth noting that Signed Diffie-Hellman AKE can be broken if an adversary can reveal ephemeral secret keys of the parties. Exposure of ephemeral secret keys can occur in practical implementations of AKE protocols if ephemeral keys are precomputed or if they are stored in insecure storage. If an adversary $\mathbb{M}$ reveals an ephemeral secret key x used by $\mathbb{A}$ in some session with $\mathbb{B}$, then $\mathbb{M}$ can impersonate $\mathbb{A}$ to $\mathbb{B}$ by starting a session with $\mathbb{B}$ and sending the same tuple $\{g^x, SIG_{\mathbb{A}}(g^x, \mathbb{B})\}$. $\mathbb{B}$ will accept this tuple because the signature is valid and then $\mathbb{M}$ can compute a session key using the knowledge of x.

SECURITY OF AUTHENTICATED KEY EXCHANGE. For AKE protocols there are a surprisingly large number of possible attack scenarios and there is no single security definition. We sketch 3 security notions which seem to capture all possible attacks, and give their precise definitions in Section 2:

1. The main security requirement (we will call it AKE security) as introduced by Bellare and Rogaway [4] and further refined by Bellare, Pointcheval and Rogaway [3] and by Canetti and Krawczyk [9], considers a multi-party experiment with unauthenticated communication channels (called the AKE experiment). The adversary controls all the communication and can corrupt some of the parties. Moreover, the adversary selects honest parties to participate in key-exchange sessions. The adversary must select an uncorrupted session called a test session and then he is given a challenge, which is either the session key of the test session or a randomly selected key. The goal of the adversary is to distinguish between these 2 cases.

2. One of the properties not captured by AKE security is Perfect Forward Secrecy (PFS). Perfect Forward Secrecy says that an adversary in the AKE experiment who corrupted one of the parties (that is, revealed the long-term secret key), should not be able to reveal session keys of past sessions executed by that

party. Krawzcyk [11] shows that no 2-pass AKE protocol can achieve perfect forward secrecy. Alternatively, he presents a notion of weak perfect forward secrecy (wPFS). Weak perfect forward secrecy guarantees security only for those previous sessions executed without the adversary's intrusion.

3. The last security requirement is resistance to key compromise imperson- ation (KCI). An adversary who reveals a long-term secret key of some party $\mathbb{A}$ should be unable to impersonate other parties to $\mathbb{A}$ (still, an adversary can impersonate $\mathbb{A}$ to anyone else).

All these security notions can involve either a "weak" or a "strong" adversary: a weak adversary can reveal session keys of sessions executed by honest parties while a strong adversary can reveal both session keys and ephemeral secret keys. Both adversaries can also do total corruptions, i.e. take full control over honest parties. We assume that a certificate authority (CA), upon registering a public key, doesn't require a party to prove knowledge of the corresponding secret key. That is, a certificate authority will register arbitrary public keys presented by parties, even ones matching existing public keys of other parties. In contrast, proof of knowledge of the secret key is required by many existing AKE protocols, but these checks are rarely done in practice.

KEA PROTOCOL. KEA authenticated key exchange [15] was designed by NSA in 1994 and originally its design was kept secret. It was declassified and became available to the public in 1998. KEA involves 2 parties, $\mathbb{A}$ and $\mathbb{B}$, with respec- tive secret keys a and b and public keys g^a and g^b. We assume that parties know each other's registered public keys. The protocol first executes a standard Diffie-Hellman communication: parties select ephemeral secret keys x and y at random and exchange ephemeral public keys g^x and g^y. Then each party com- putes g^{ay} and g^{bx} and computes a session key K by applying a hash function F to $g^{ay} \oplus g^{bx}$. The original description of KEA specifies F to be a certain function built on the SKIPJACK block cipher [15]. The design of KEA closely resembles Protocol 4 from Blake-Wilson et al. [5]. They suggest computing a session key as $H(g^{ay}, g^{bx})$, where H is a cryptographic hash function. Blake-Wilson et al. conjectured (without proof) the security of their protocol provided H is modeled by a random oracle.

ATTACKS ON KEA. We observe that AKE security of KEA (even against a weak adversary) can be violated if an adversary can register arbitrary public keys. Consider the following adversary $\mathbb{M}$. $\mathbb{M}$ registers a public key g^a of some honest party $\mathbb{A}$ as $\mathbb{M}$'s own public key. Then $\mathbb{M}$ intercepts a key-exchange session between $\mathbb{A}$ and some other honest party $\mathbb{B}$ and at the same time starts a session between $\mathbb{M}$ and $\mathbb{B}$. Now $\mathbb{M}$ forwards ephemeral public key g^x from $\mathbb{A}$ to $\mathbb{B}$ and ephemeral public key g^y from $\mathbb{B}$ to $\mathbb{A}$. Since $\mathbb{M}$ has the same public key as $\mathbb{A}$, both $\mathbb{A}$ and $\mathbb{B}$ will compute identical session keys, however they participate in two different key-exchange sessions. $\mathbb{B}$ participates in a session with $\mathbb{M}$ while $\mathbb{A}$ participates in a session with $\mathbb{B}$. Finally, $\mathbb{M}$ reveals a session key of one of the sessions and announces the other session as a test session. Given a challenge key, $\mathbb{M}$ compares it to the revealed key. If they are the same, $\mathbb{M}$ decides that the challenge is a correct key for the test session and if different, $\mathbb{M}$ decides that the challenge key was chosen at random. The demonstrated attack breaks AKE security against a weak adversary (who can only reveal session keys). This attack is often called as Unknown Key Share (UKS) attack.

One possible counter-measure to the above attack is not to allow 2 parties to have the same public key, and this check can be done by a certificate authority. We note that this counter-measure also wouldn't work. In the previous attack's scenario, an adversary can pick any exponent k, register a public key g^{ak} and instead of sending g^y as a response to $\mathbb{A}$, send a value g^{yk}. This way, both $\mathbb{A}$ and $\mathbb{B}$ will again have the same session key $H(g^{ayk} \oplus g^{bx})$.

SECURITY FIX: KEA+. We present a modified version of the KEA protocol, called KEA+, which is resistant to the above attacks. We prove that no such attacks on KEA+ are possible and that KEA+ satisfies the strongest known security requirement. The main idea behind KEA+ is to incorporate parties' identities in the computation of a session key. Interestingly, this simple feature of the protocol turns out to be crucial in the security analysis and avoids the proof-of-possession requirement.

The KEA+ protocol proceeds as follows. First, parties $\mathbb{A}$ and $\mathbb{B}$ randomly select ephemeral secret keys x and y and exchange ephemeral public keys g^x and g^y. Then parties verify that the received ephemeral public keys are in the group G and compute a session key K as $H(g^{ay}, g^{bx}, \mathbb{A}, \mathbb{B})$, where H can be an arbitrary cryptographic hash function. In the security analysis we model H by a random oracle. Figure 2 depicts actions performed by the parties. We note that verifying that the ephemeral public keys are in the group G is essential for the security of the protocol. Otherwise, the protocol is vulnerable to a so-called "small subgroup" attack.

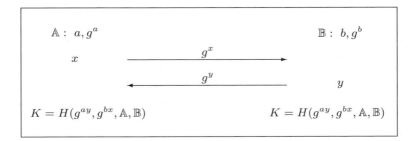

Fig. 2. New KEA+ protocol

We prove that KEA+ protocol satisfies AKE security, weak perfect forward secrecy and security against KCI attacks. All these results involve a strong adversary who can reveal ephemeral secret keys of the parties as well as session keys. The results hold under either the standard Gap Diffie-Hellman (GDH) assumption in a group G, as defined by Okamoto and Pointcheval [16], or under a stronger Pairing Diffie-Hellman (PDH) assumption. The latter assumption means hardness of the computational Diffie-Hellman problem, where a solver is given access to a bilinear pairing oracle. The reason for having two reductions (one to GDH and one to PDH) lies in the concrete security analysis. The reduction to PDH achieves better concrete security compared to the reduction to GDH.

We stress that KEA+ does not require parties to prove possession of secret keys upon key registration. Parties can register arbitrary public keys, even ones matching somebody else's keys. Moreover, an adversary can register keys for corrupted parties at any time in the experiment. Our security results imply that these powers do not allow the adversary to break the security of KEA+.

KEY CONFIRMATION: KEA+C. The 2-pass KEA+ protocol is optimized for communication and has exactly the same communication as the original Diffie-Hellman protocol. While satisfying the strongest security requirement, it doesn't provide delivery guarantees which might be desirable for some applications. Namely, KEA+ doesn't provide assurance that the other party actually completed the session. To address this issue, we add one more pass of communication to KEA+ to obtain a protocol called KEA+C, or KEA+ with key confirmation.

KEA+C involves a message authentication code to construct a confirmation message. KEA+C achieves a key confirmation property [11], namely it assures that the other party is able to compute the session key. As well, KEA+C satisfies the full perfect forward secrecy requirement lacking in KEA+. Finally, results of Canetti and Krawczyk [9] imply that KEA+C satisfies Universally Composable security defined by [6], which ensures that KEA+C can be securely executed concurrently with arbitrary other protocols.

HISTORY AND RELATED WORK. Defining security of authenticated key exchange dates back to the work Bellare and Rogaway [4] from 1993. Following work of Bellare, Pointcheval and Rogaway [3] and Shoup [17], the current security definition was formulated by Canetti and Krawczyk [9]. We refer the reader to [7] for a comparison and a discussion of existing security definitions for authenticated key exchange.

To date, a great number of AKE protocols have been proposed and many of them were subsequently broken. Currently, there exist a number of protocols that satisfy AKE security against adversaries who cannot reveal ephemeral secret keys (weak adversaries), and only a few protocols which are secure against strong adversaries. AKE protocols proved to be secure against strong adversaries include SIG-DH from [9], SIGMA [10] and HMQV [11].

We compare our KEA+ protocol with the recent HMQV protocol [11], which combines great efficiency with the highest security level. KEA+ and HMQV are both proven to achieve AKE security, security against KCI and wPFS[1]. However, the security of HMQV relies on the knowledge of the exponent assumption[2] [2]

---

[1] In fact, the wPFS requirement from [11] is stronger than ours. They allow an adversary to reveal long-term keys of both parties, while we only allow revealing the long-term key of at most one of the parties.

[2] We remark that in the analysis of HMQV this assumption is only needed to ensure security against strong adversaries (who can reveal ephemeral secret keys).

and doesn't have a concrete security analysis. As noted by Menezes [14], the concrete security reduction of [11] appears to be inefficient. Our security proof doesn't employ the knowledge of exponent assumption and provides a tight security reduction (under the Pairing Diffie-Hellman assumption). Our protocol requires the same number of exponentiations as HMQV (although one of the exponentiations in HMQV involves half-size exponents).

After submitting our paper we discovered the parallel independent work of Kudla and Paterson [13]. They use very similar techniques to prove the security of a modification of Protocol 4 from Blake-Wilson et al [5], which can be viewed as the KEA+ protocol where identities of the parties are excluded from the key computation. We want to highlight some differences between our work and theirs. First, their protocol is vulnerable to the UKS attack. This attack is not captured by their security analysis, as the security model of [13] requires that all parties (even ones controlled by the adversary) do key-generation properly. Second, they only prove security against weak adversaries (which cannot reveal ephemeral keys) and their security proof doesn't contain a concrete security analysis. Finally, we discuss a key-confirmation property and analyze the security of our KEA+C protocol.

2   Definitions

NOTATION. All protocols in the paper use a mathematical group G of a known prime order q where the Diffie-Hellman problem is computationally infeasible. The group G can be implemented either as a multiplicative subgroup of a finite field or as a group of points on an elliptic curve. We denote by g a generator of G and write the group operation in a multiplicative manner.

Throughout the paper, we will apply hash functions and signature schemes to lists of several arguments. In these cases, we write function arguments separated by commas, for example $H(X, Y, Z)$. Doing that, we assume that we have a collision-free encoding which maps lists of arguments to binary strings. Also, we assume that parties' identities are arbitrary binary strings.

GAP DIFFIE-HELLMAN (GDH). A computational Diffie-Hellman (CDH) problem is, given g^x and g^y (for randomly chosen x and y) to compute g^{xy}. A Decisional Diffie-Hellman (DDH) Oracle DDH takes input a triple $(g^x, g^y, Z) \in G^3$ and outputs 1 if $Z = g^{xy}$ and 0 otherwise. The Gap-Diffie-Hellman [16] problem is the CDH problem, where the solver algorithm is additionally given access to a DDH oracle. The advantage of such a solver $\mathbb{M}$, denoted as $\mathbf{Adv}^{\mathrm{GDH}}(\mathbb{M})$, is $\mathbb{M}$'s winning probability in the CDH problem. We say that G satisfies the Gap-Diffie-Hellman (GDH) assumption if no feasible adversary exists to solve the CDH problem, even provided with a DDH-oracle. Gap Diffie-Hellman is a standard cryptographic assumption which was used to establish the security of several key agreement protocols [1, 18, 12].

PAIRING DIFFIE-HELLMAN (PDH). Let G' be another mathematical group of the same order as G with efficiently computable group operation. A function

$e : G \times G \to G'$ is a bilinear pairing if it is non-degenerate and if for any pair $g^a, g^b \in G$, $e(g^a, g^b) = e(g, g)^{ab}$. A pairing oracle P associated with the pairing function e and the group G' takes two elements $X, Y \in G$ and returns $e(X, Y)$. The Pairing Diffie-Hellman problem is the CDH problem, where the solver is additionally given access to the pairing oracle P. The advantage $\mathbf{Adv}^{PDH}(\mathbb{M})$ of a PDH solver $\mathbb{M}$ is the probability of $\mathbb{M}$ solving the CDH problem. We say that G satisfies the PDH assumption if no feasible adversary exists to solve the CDH problem provided with an arbitrary PDH-oracle.

In the groups which have a bilinear pairing, PDH problem is equivalent to the original CDH problem. As well, one can consider PDH problem in the groups where no efficient pairing operation is known. We find the Pairing Diffie-Hellman assumption to be as justified as GDH since the only known way to compute DDH in groups where CDH is hard is via a pairing function.

AKE SECURITY. The AKE experiment involves multiple honest parties and an adversary $\mathbb{M}$ connected via an unauthenticated network. The adversary selects parties to execute key-exchange sessions and selects an order of the sessions. It can also corrupt some of the parties. An adversary has full control over the communications and he can delay/cancel/modify any message.

There is a special party, $\mathbb{CA}$, called the certificate authority, who registers the public keys of the parties. We model a $\mathbb{CA}$ as a trusted directory. The $\mathbb{CA}$ registers arbitrary keys (even those matching keys of other parties) with the only restriction that no party can have more than one registered public key. In the beginning of the AKE experiment all honest parties generate their public keys and register them with the $\mathbb{CA}$. The adversary can register public keys of adversary-controlled parties at any time in the experiment, even during the execution of an AKE session. That is, the adversary is allowed to mount the Unknown Key Share attack and related attacks.

To start an AKE session, the adversary activates an honest party and specifies that party's role in the exchange (initiator or responder) and the identity of the other participant. We identify an AKE session by a 4-tuple $(\mathbb{A}, \mathbb{B}, role, Comm)$, where $\mathbb{A}$ is the executing party, $\mathbb{B}$ is the other party, $role \in \{initiator, responder\}$ is $\mathbb{A}$'s role in the protocol and $Comm$ consists of all messages sent and received by $\mathbb{A}$. We stress that an AKE session is executed by a single party: since all communication is controlled by an adversary, a party executing a session cannot know for sure whom it is talking to. We call the session which is supposed to be executed by the other party as the matching AKE session. For example the session $(\mathbb{A}, \mathbb{B}, initiator, Comm)$ matches $(\mathbb{B}, \mathbb{A}, responder, Comm)$ and vice versa. A party completes the session when it receives the last message from the other party and computes the session key.

An adversary can corrupt honest parties as well as reveal session information. When an adversary corrupts a party (often referred to as a CORRUPT query), he learns the long-term secret key of that party and gets full control of that party from that moment on. Revealing session information (often referred to as a REVEAL query) only affects a single AKE session. We distinguish between 2 reveal scenarios. First, an adversary can learn only a session key of a completed session. We call it a session key reveal and we call an adversary who only makes session key reveals (in addition to total corruptions) a "weak" adversary. A second type of adversary, called a "strong" adversary, is also allowed to reveal an ephemeral secret key of a party executing a session.

We say that a completed session is "clean" if this session as well as its matching session (if it exists) is not corrupted (neither session key nor ephemeral secret key were revealed by $\mathbb{M}$) and if none of the participating parties is corrupted.

Eventually an adversary should select a clean completed session ($\mathbb{A}$, $\mathbb{B}$, *role*, *Comm*), which is called a test session. A challenger tosses a coin to obtain $b \in \{0, 1\}$; if $b = 0$ he sets K_C to be the session key of the test session and otherwise he sets K_C to be a random string of the same length. A challenger gives the challenge K_C to the adversary. After receiving the challenge, the adversary continues the experiment, but is not allowed to corrupt the test session nor any of the parties involved in the test session. The experiment ends when the adversary outputs a guess bit b'.

The advantage of the adversary $\mathbb{M}$ participating in the above AKE experiment against AKE protocol Π is defined as

$$\mathbf{Adv}_{\Pi}^{\mathrm{AKE}}(\mathbb{M}) = Pr[b = b'] - \frac{1}{2}.$$

We say that an AKE protocol is secure if no feasible AKE adversary has more than a negligible advantage in the AKE experiment.

PERFECT FORWARD SECRECY (PFS). The Perfect Forward Secrecy property of an AKE protocol guarantees that an adversary who corrupts a party cannot gain any information about session keys of previous AKE sessions. We formally define PFS by modifying the AKE experiment as follows. Now we allow the adversary to corrupt at most one of the two participants of the test session after the test session is completed. As in the original AKE experiment, the adversary must distinguish between the session key of the test session and a random key.

Krawczyk [11] observed that no 2-pass AKE protocol can achieve full PFS in a presence of strong adversaries. To address forward secrecy of 2-pass protocols, he suggests a relaxed notion, called weak PFS (wPFS). Weak PFS only guarantees security of those AKE sessions executed without active adversarial intrusion. We define weak PFS by limiting the set of clean sessions to only those executed without active adversarial intrusion. That is, the adversary is only allowed to forward communications in the test session and its matching session and is not allowed to cancel or modify them.

We remark that our definitions of PFS and wPFS are weaker than the ones by Krawczyk [11]. Krawczyk's definitions allow an adversary to corrupt both participants of the test session, while our definition only allows corruption of at most one of the participants.

SECURITY AGAINST KEY COMPROMISE IMPERSONATION (KCI). KCI security considers a scenario when an adversary reveals a long-term secret key of some party $\mathbb{A}$ without corrupting $\mathbb{A}$ (that is, without taking full control over $\mathbb{A}$). Note that in this case an adversary can impersonate $\mathbb{A}$ to anyone else. KCI security

386   K. Lauter and A. Mityagin

guarantees that an adversary should be unable to impersonate other parties to $\mathbb{A}$.

We define KCI security by the following modification of the AKE experiment. We allow an adversary to make a new type of corruption: to reveal a long-term secret key of a party without taking control over it. Now, a test session is allowed to be a clean session, where the party running the session had its long-term secret key revealed. Still, an adversary is not allowed to corrupt or reveal the long-term secret key of the other party.

3   Security of KEA+

AKE SECURITY OF KEA+. We show that the KEA+ protocol with a hash function modeled as a random oracle satisfies AKE security against a strong adversary under the GDH or PDH assumptions in a group G.

REDUCTION TO A FORGING ATTACK. Assume by contradiction that there exists some efficient adversary $\mathbb{M}$ against the KEA+ protocol. Let $(\mathbb{A}, \mathbb{B}, \textit{initiator}, X, Y)$ be a test session in some AKE experiment. Let A be the public key of $\mathbb{A}$ and B be the public key of $\mathbb{B}$. Denote by $CDH(\cdot, \cdot)$ the computational Diffie-Hellman function. We observe that since the session key of a test session is computed as a hash value of a 4-tuple $\{CDH(A, Y), CDH(B, X), \mathbb{A}, \mathbb{B}\}$, the adversary $\mathbb{M}$ has only 2 ways to distinguish K from a random string:

1. Forging attack. At some point $\mathbb{M}$ queries H on the tuple

$$\sigma = (CDH(A, Y), CDH(B, X), \mathbb{A}, \mathbb{B}).$$

2. Key-replication attack. $\mathbb{M}$ succeeds in forcing the establishment of a session that has the same signature (and subsequently, the same session key) as the test session. In this case $\mathbb{M}$ can learn the test-session key by simply making a reveal query on the session with the same key, without having to learn the value of the test signature.

We denote a 4-tuple $\sigma = (g^{ay}, g^{bx}, \mathbb{A}, \mathbb{B})$ as the "signature" of a key exchange session. Recall that the key for the test session is the value of a random oracle H on the test signature σ. Since H is a truly random function, an adversary has only 2 ways of learning $H(\sigma)$: $\mathbb{M}$ can either query σ to H himself or σ can be queried to H by some honest party and $\mathbb{M}$ can reveal $H(\sigma)$ by corrupting that party. Otherwise, $\mathbb{M}$ cannot distinguish information-theoretically between $H(\sigma)$ and a random string. Note that these cases correspond to a forging attack and a key-replication attack respectively. If $\mathbb{M}$ doesn't mount either of these attacks, then it cannot win the experiment with probability any better than $1/2$.

Let's see that a key-replication attack is impossible. In that case, if an adversary finds some session with the same signature σ as the test session, then this session must be executed by the same 2 parties, $\mathbb{A}$ and $\mathbb{B}$. Let the ephemeral public keys of this session be X' and Y'. Since the session has the same signature as the test session, $CDH(A, Y')$ must be equal to $CDH(A, Y)$ and

$CDH\ (B, X')$ – equal to $CDH(B, X)$. This implies that $X' = X$ and $Y' = Y$, and thus the sessions must be identical.

We're left to show impossibility of a forging attack. We are going to show that given an efficient forging adversary against KEA+, we can construct an adversary which efficiently solves the GDH problem. We first establish a reduction to GDH and then show how to modify it to obtain an improved reduction to PDH.

SECURITY AGAINST A SIMPLISTIC ADVERSARY. First we show how the reduction works in the simplistic case of a certain (very limited) adversary and then proceed to the general case. Assume that the AKE experiment only involves 2 honest parties $\mathbb{A}$ and $\mathbb{B}$ and that the adversary $\mathbb{M}$ passively observes a single AKE session executed by these parties and selects it as a test session. In this case the reduction to the GDH problem is natural: given a GDH challenge (X_0, Y_0) the GDH solver $\mathbb{S}$ runs the AKE experiment with parties $\mathbb{A}$ and $\mathbb{B}$ and the adversary $\mathbb{M}$. $\mathbb{S}$ sets the first challenge value X_0 to be the long-term public key of $\mathbb{A}$ and selects keys for $\mathbb{B}$ in the usual way. When $\mathbb{A}$ and $\mathbb{B}$ execute a test session, $\mathbb{A}$ picks a random x and sends g^x to $\mathbb{B}$, while $\mathbb{B}$ responds with Y_0. Note that a view of $\mathbb{M}$ in this simulated AKE experiment is distributed identically to a view of $\mathbb{M}$ in a true AKE experiment and thus $\mathbb{M}$ wins with the same probability. As we justified earlier, if $\mathbb{M}$ wins, he should query H a signature $\sigma = (CDH(X_0, Y_0), g^{bx}, \mathbb{A}, \mathbb{B})$. Note that in this case σ contains $CDH(X_0, Y_0)$, which is a solution to the original CDH problem.

IDEA OF THE GENERAL-CASE REDUCTION. The idea of the reduction is very similar to the simple case with the difference that $\mathbb{S}$ selects at random a party $\mathbb{A}$ (to put a first challenge value in $\mathbb{A}$'s public key) and a session executed by $\mathbb{A}$ and some other party $\mathbb{B}$ (to put a second challenge value in $\mathbb{B}$'s ephemeral public key). The complication that arises in the general case is how to handle session-corrupt queries involving the selected party $\mathbb{A}$. Since $\mathbb{S}$ doesn't know a secret key for $\mathbb{A}$'s public key, it cannot compute a signature (nor a session key) for such a session. We handle this case by picking a session key at random without computing a signature. Then $\mathbb{S}$ uses the DDH oracle to test if $\mathbb{M}$ queries H with a signature for such a session and if "yes", returns the previously selected session key. We proceed with a formal description and analysis of the reduction.

CONSTRUCTION OF A GDH SOLVER $\mathbb{S}$. Let $\mathbb{M}$ be an AKE adversary against KEA+. Consider the following GDH adversary $\mathbb{S}$:
$\mathbb{S}$ takes input a pair $(X_0, Y_0) \in G^2$. $\mathbb{S}$ is also given access to a DDH oracle DDH. $\mathbb{S}$ creates an AKE experiment which includes a number of honest parties and an adversary $\mathbb{M}$. We assume that the experiment involves at most n parties and that each party participates in at most k AKE sessions. $\mathbb{S}$ randomly selects one of the honest parties (say, this is a party $\mathbb{A}$) and sets the public key of $\mathbb{A}$ to be X_0. All the other parties compute their keys normally. $\mathbb{S}$ picks a number i_k at random from $\{1, \ldots, k\}$ and initializes the counter at $i = 1$ (i counts sessions that

A participates in). $\mathbb{S}$ runs an AKE experiment with adversary $\mathbb{M}$ and handles queries made by $\mathbb{M}$ as follows:

1. When $\mathbb{M}$ queries a hash function H on a string v, return the value of $\text{HSIM}(v)$. The procedure $\text{HSIM}(\cdot)$ which simulates a random oracle H is described later on.
2. When $\mathbb{M}$ starts a session $(\mathbb{B}, \mathbb{C}, role)$ between parties $\mathbb{B}$ and $\mathbb{C}$ both different from a selected party $\mathbb{A}$, $\mathbb{S}$ follows the protocol for KEA+. Denote $\mathbb{B}$'s secret key as b, $\mathbb{B}$'s public key as $B = g^b$ and $\mathbb{C}$'s public key as C. If $role = initiator$, $\mathbb{B}$ picks a random exponent x, returns $X = g^x$, waits for the reply Y and computes a session key $K = \text{HSIM}(Y^b, C^x, \mathbb{B}, \mathbb{C})$. If $role = responder$, $\mathbb{B}$ waits for $\mathbb{C}$'s initiating message X, picks a random exponent y, replies with g^y and computes a session key $K = \text{HSIM}(C^y, X^b, \mathbb{C}, \mathbb{B})$.
3. When $\mathbb{M}$ starts a session $(\mathbb{A}, \mathbb{C}, role)$ (here $\mathbb{A}$ is the special party whose public key is a GDH challenge X_0), $\mathbb{S}$ cannot follow the protocol since it doesn't know a secret for $\mathbb{A}$'s public key. Denote $\mathbb{C}$'s public key as C. If $\mathbb{A}$ is an initiator, it picks a random exponent x, sends g^x to $\mathbb{C}$ and waits for the reply Y. Now it sets a session key to be $\text{HSPEC}(1, Y, C^x, \mathbb{A}, \mathbb{C})$, see the description of the procedure HSPEC below. If $\mathbb{A}$ is the responder, it waits for an initiating message X, picks a random exponent y, replies with g^y and computes a session key $K = \text{HSPEC}(2, X, C^y, \mathbb{C}, \mathbb{A})$.
4. When $\mathbb{M}$ starts a session $(\mathbb{B}, \mathbb{A}, role)$ for some party $\mathbb{B}$, where the second party is the selected party $\mathbb{A}$, $\mathbb{S}$ first checks if $i = i_k$. If "no", $\mathbb{S}$ increments the counter i and behaves according to the rule for Query 2. If the check succeeds, $\mathbb{S}$ declares $(\mathbb{B}, \mathbb{A}, role)$ to be a "special session". In a special session, $\mathbb{B}$ outputs a message Y_0 (which is the second part of the GDH challenge) and doesn't compute a session key.
5. When $\mathbb{M}$ makes a session key-reveal or ephemeral secret key-reveal query against some session (different from the special session), $\mathbb{S}$ returns to $\mathbb{M}$ a session key or an ephemeral secret key for this session (which was computed previously in Queries 2, 3 or 4). If $\mathbb{M}$ tries to reveal a session key or an ephemeral secret key of the special session, $\mathbb{S}$ declares failure and stops the experiment.
6. When $\mathbb{M}$ makes a corruption on some party $\mathbb{C}$ (different from $\mathbb{A}$ and $\mathbb{B}$), $\mathbb{S}$ returns the secret key of $\mathbb{C}$ as well as ephemeral secret keys of all current AKE sessions executed by $\mathbb{C}$ and gives $\mathbb{M}$ full control over $\mathbb{C}$. If $\mathbb{M}$ tries to corrupt $\mathbb{A}$ or $\mathbb{B}$ (after a special session is selected), $\mathbb{S}$ declares failure.

When $\mathbb{M}$ stops, $\mathbb{S}$ goes over all random oracle queries made by $\mathbb{M}$ and checks (using a DDH oracle DDH) if any of them includes the value of $CDH(X_0, Y_0)$. If "yes", return $CDH(X_0, Y_0)$ to the GDH challenger. If "no", $\mathbb{S}$ declares failure.

Function $\text{HSIM}(Z_1, Z_2, \mathbb{B}, \mathbb{C})$. This function implements a random oracle on valid signatures of the KEA+ protocol. The function proceeds as follows:

- If the value of the function on that input has been previously defined, return it.
- If not defined, go over all the previous calls to $\text{HSPEC}(\cdot)$ and for each previous call of the form $\text{HSPEC}(i, Y, Z, \mathbb{B}', \mathbb{C}') = v$ check if

$$\mathbb{B} = \mathbb{B}', \quad \mathbb{C} = \mathbb{C}', \quad Z = Z_{3-i} \text{ and } \text{DDH}(X_0, Y, Z_i) = 1.$$

If all these conditions hold, return v.
- If not found, pick a random w from $\{0,1\}^l$, define $\text{HSIM}(Z_1, Z_2, \mathbb{B}, \mathbb{C}) = w$ and return w.

Function $\text{HSPEC}(i, Y, Z, \mathbb{B}, \mathbb{C})$. Informally, HSPEC implements a random oracle on signatures which are not known to $\mathbb{S}$. Specifically, the input corresponds to a signature $(Z_1, Z_2, \mathbb{B}, \mathbb{C})$, where $Z_i = CDH(X_0, Y)$ (here X_0 is a part of the GDH challenge) and $Z_{3-i} = Z$. This signature is not known to $\mathbb{S}$ since $\mathbb{S}$ cannot compute $CDH(X_0, Y)$. The function proceeds as follows:

- If the value of the function on that input has been previously defined, return it.
- If not defined, go over all the previous calls to $\text{HSIM}(\cdot)$ and for each previous call of the form $\text{HSIM}(Z_1, Z_2, \mathbb{B}', \mathbb{C}') = v$ check if

$$\mathbb{B} = \mathbb{B}', \quad \mathbb{C} = \mathbb{C}', \quad Z = Z_{3-i} \text{ and } \text{DDH}(X_0, Y, Z_i) = 1.$$

If all these conditions hold, return v.
- If the check failed for all the calls, pick a random w from $\{0,1\}^l$, define $\text{HSPEC}(i, Y, Z, \mathbb{B}, \mathbb{C})$ to be w and return w.

ANALYSIS OF $\mathbb{S}$. The the running time of $\mathbb{S}$ is the time needed to run an AKE experiment and $\mathbb{M}$ plus the time needed to handle H-queries. Each call to HSIM or HSPEC requires $\mathbb{S}$ to pass over all the previously made queries. Thus, time needed to handle H-queries is proportional to a squared number of queries. Since the number of H-queries is upper-bounded by the running time of $\mathbb{M}$, we can bound the running time of $\mathbb{S}$ by $O(t^2)$, where t is the running time of $\mathbb{M}$.

We are now going to show that if $\mathbb{M}$ doesn't corrupt $\mathbb{A}$ and doesn't reveal a session key or an ephemeral secret key for the special session, then the simulation of an AKE experiment is perfect. That is, the view of $\mathbb{M}$ in the experiment run by $\mathbb{S}$ is identically distributed to the view of $\mathbb{M}$ in an authentic experiment. To be precise, the view of $\mathbb{M}$ consists of public keys of all the parties, secret keys of the corrupted parties, ephemeral public keys of all the sessions, ephemeral secret keys and session keys of the corrupted sessions and of the random oracle's responses.

We start by observing that secret/public key pairs of all honest parties except $\mathbb{A}$ are distributed correctly. A public key of $\mathbb{A}$ is also distributed correctly, however $\mathbb{S}$ doesn't know the secret key for it. By assumption, $\mathbb{M}$ doesn't corrupt $\mathbb{A}$ and thus $\mathbb{M}$ wouldn't notice that. Similarly, ephemeral secret/public values of all sessions except the test session are distributed as in the original protocol. The ephemeral public key Y_0 in the test session is also distributed correctly, although $\mathbb{S}$ doesn't know a secret for it. Again, we assume that $\mathbb{M}$ doesn't corrupt the test session and so $\mathbb{S}$ wouldn't have to reveal it.

The adversary can obtain the random oracle's responses either by querying H directly or by revealing session keys from honest parties. Without loss of generality, we can assume that the adversary queries a random oracle only on tuples of the form $(Z_1, Z_2, \mathbb{B}_1, \mathbb{B}_2)$, where $Z_1, Z_2 \in G$ and B_1 and B_2 are identities of some parties. To ensure that the simulation is perfect, we need to verify that i) the oracle responses are selected at random and ii) if the same argument is queried several times, the same value is returned.

Recall that $\mathbb{S}$ handles two types of queries differently. Queries of the first type are fully specified 4-tuples and such queries are made both by $\mathbb{M}$ and by honest parties. They are handled by the function HSIM. Queries of the second type are made only by $\mathbb{A}$ and such queries have one of the components unspecified. That is, a value Z_i (for some $i = 1, 2$) is unknown and it is specified by $Y \in G$ such that $Z_i = CDH(X_0, Y)$. These queries are handled by HSPEC. Note that distinct HSPEC arguments correspond to distinct queries to H.

In our construction of HSIM and HSPEC, a new random value of H is chosen every time the argument wasn't found in the record of previous queries. Thus, condition i) is satisfied and we only need to show that by querying the same argument several times, $\mathbb{M}$ always receives the same answers. If the same query is made for the second time either to HSIM or to HSPEC, the same answer is returned. The only conflicts can arise if a query previously handled by HSIM is queried again to HSPEC or vice versa. That is, HSIM was called on a tuple $(Z_1, Z_2, \mathbb{B}, \mathbb{C})$ and HSPEC — on $(i, Y, Z, \mathbb{B}, \mathbb{C})$ where $Z_i = CDH(X_0, Y)$ and $Z_{3-i} = Z$. Note that one can check whether these queries correspond to identical signatures by checking that $Z_{3-i} = Z$ and that $DDH(X_0, Y, Z_i) = 1$. Whichever of the functions was called first, on the second call (to the other function) $\mathbb{S}$ will go over all previous calls to the first function and do such a check. If a match is found, the previously defined value is returned. This guarantees that condition ii) is also satisfied.

We showed that, provided $\mathbb{M}$ doesn't corrupt $\mathbb{A}$ or the special session, the simulation of the AKE experiment is perfect. Since the party $\mathbb{A}$ and the special session are chosen at random, a test session selected by $\mathbb{M}$ matches the special session with probability $1/nk$ (recall that n is the number of parties in the experiment and k is the maximal number of sessions any party can participate in). In this case, the simulation is perfect since $\mathbb{M}$ doesn't corrupt the test session. We know that a successful adversary must reveal the signature of the test session. Whenever $\mathbb{M}$ wins in the AKE experiment and the test session was guessed correctly, $\mathbb{S}$ reveals the signature of the test session which contains $CDH(X_0, Y_0)$, and therefore wins in the GDH experiment. To summarize the lengthy proof, for any AKE adversary $\mathbb{M}$ running in time t we constructed a GDH solver $\mathbb{S}$ which runs in time $O(t^2)$ such that

$$\mathbf{Adv}^{\mathrm{GDH}}(\mathbb{S}) \geq \frac{1}{nk}\mathbf{Adv}^{\mathrm{AKE}}_{\mathrm{KEA}+}(\mathbb{M}).$$

IMPROVING CONCRETE SECURITY REDUCTION. The above reduction transforms a time t AKE adversary to a GDH solver which runs in time $O(t^2)$ and makes $O(t^2)$ calls to a DDH oracle, which is fairly inefficient. We observe that given access to a pairing oracle, we can solve the CDH problem in time $O(t \log t)$ by making $O(t)$ calls to a pairing oracle.

The construction of the solver $\mathbb{S}$ remains the same except for the HSIM and HSPEC functions. We create an array T and implement HSIM and HSPEC as follows:

Function HSIM$(Z_1, Z_2, \mathbb{B}, \mathbb{C})$:

- Compute $\delta = (\mathrm{P}(g, Z_1), \mathrm{P}(g, Z_2), \mathbb{B}, \mathbb{C})$.
- Look up δ in T.
- If T contains a record (δ, v), return v.
- If not, pick w at random, add a record (δ, w) to T and return w.

Function HSPEC$(i, Y, Z, \mathbb{B}, \mathbb{C})$.

- Compute $Z_i' = \mathrm{P}(X_0, Y)$, $Z_{3-i}' = \mathrm{P}(g, Z)$ and set $\delta = (Z_1', Z_2', \mathbb{B}, \mathbb{C})$.
- Look up δ in T.
- If T contains a record (δ, v), return v.
- If not, pick w at random, add a record (δ, w) to T and return w.

First, note that the queries to HSIM and HSPEC which correspond to the same arguments to a random oracle will be mapped to the same values of δ. Thus a random oracle will be perfectly simulated and $\mathbb{S}$ will win the CDH experiment with the same probability as in the original proof.

Second, each call to HSIM or HSPEC requires only one oracle call to P. Moreover, if T is implemented as a balanced search tree indexed by values of δ, each search and insert operation in T takes logarithmic time in the size of T. Thus the processing of each call to HSIM or HSPEC takes at most $O(\log t)$ time, where t is the maximal running time of $\mathbb{M}$.

For any AKE adversary $\mathbb{M}$ running in time t we have a PDH solver $\mathbb{S}$ which runs in time $O(t \log t)$ and makes $O(t)$ oracle queries such that

$$\mathbf{Adv}^{\mathrm{PDH}}(\mathbb{S}) \geq \frac{1}{nk} \mathbf{Adv}^{\mathrm{AKE}}_{\mathrm{KEA}+}(\mathbb{M}).$$

WEAK PFS. We observe that our proof of AKE security can be modified to establish wPFS security of KEA+. Consider the same party $\mathbb{S}$ who runs an AKE experiment with an adversary $\mathbb{M}$. Consider the test session selected by $\mathbb{M}$ and its matching session. By the definition of wPFS, $\mathbb{M}$ did not cancel or modify communications sent between the parties involved in these sessions. The test session (as well as its matching session) must be clean at the time of completion. After the test session and its matching session are completed, $\mathbb{M}$ can corrupt either one of the involved parties but not both of them. Now consider that session, (out of the test session and its matching session), where the executing party can be corrupted and the other party is not corrupted. We observe that with probability $1/nk$ this session matches the special session $(\mathbb{B}, \mathbb{A}, role)$, which is randomly selected by $\mathbb{S}$.

Since $\mathbb{S}$ knows the long-term secret key of the party $\mathbb{B}$ executing the special session, $\mathbb{S}$ can handle corruptions of $\mathbb{B}$ which are made after the test session is completed. When $\mathbb{M}$ launches a corruption of $\mathbb{B}$, $\mathbb{S}$ hands to $\mathbb{M}$ the long-term secret key of $\mathbb{B}$ and ephemeral secret keys of all current sessions being executed by $\mathbb{B}$. Since the test session is already completed, $\mathbb{B}$ will know all the ephemeral secret keys for the current session (provided that the test session matches the special session). Therefore, the simulation of an AKE experiment remains perfect and the GDH/PDH solver $\mathbb{S}$ has the same advantage.

KCI SECURITY. The same proof of AKE security can be used to show that KEA+ also satisfies KCI security. The only difference is that now $\mathbb{S}$ has to handle long-term secret key reveals made by $\mathbb{M}$. Since $\mathbb{S}$ knows the long-term secret keys of all the parties other than $\mathbb{A}$, $\mathbb{S}$ can answer all such long-term secret key reveals anytime. We note that in the event that the special session matches the test session, $\mathbb{M}$ is not allowed to reveal the long-term secret key of $\mathbb{A}$. Therefore, in this case the simulation remains perfect and the GDH/PDH solver $\mathbb{S}$ has the same advantage in a CDH experiment.

4 Key Confirmation: KEA+C

PROTOCOL DESCRIPTION. We assume that both parties know each other's registered public keys. Let H be an arbitrary cryptographic hash function and MAC be an arbitrary message authentication code.

The KEA+C protocol is illustrated in Figure 3. First, $\mathbb{A}$ selects a random ephemeral secret key x and sends an ephemeral public key g^x to $\mathbb{B}$. In turn, $\mathbb{B}$ verifies that $g^x \in G$, selects a random ephemeral secret key y and computes a verification key $L = H(0, g^{ay}, g^{bx}, \mathbb{A}, \mathbb{B})$. $\mathbb{B}$ then sends back to $\mathbb{A}$ an ephemeral public key g^y together with a key confirmation value $sig_{\mathbb{B}} = MAC_L(0)$. On receipt of the tuple $(g^y, sig_{\mathbb{B}})$, the party $\mathbb{A}$ first verifies that $g^y \in G$ and if accepted, computes a verification key $L = H(0, g^{ay}, g^{bx}, \mathbb{A}, \mathbb{B})$, checks that $sig_{\mathbb{B}}$ is valid, sends to $\mathbb{B}$ a key confirmation value $sig_{\mathbb{A}}$ and computes a session key $K = H(1, g^{ay}, g^{bx}, \mathbb{A}, \mathbb{B})$. Finally, $\mathbb{B}$ verifies the validity of $sig_{\mathbb{A}}$ and if accepted, computes a session key $K = H(1, g^{ay}, g^{bx}, \mathbb{A}, \mathbb{B})$. The session key K should be used as a shared key between the parties while the confirmation key L as well as

$\mathbb{A} : a, g^a$		$\mathbb{B} : b, g^b$
x	g^x $\longrightarrow$	y
$L = H(0, g^{ay}, g^{bx}, \mathbb{A}, \mathbb{B})$ $sig_{\mathbb{B}} \stackrel{?}{=} MAC_L(0)$	$g^y,\ sig_{\mathbb{B}}$ $\longleftarrow$	$L = H(0, g^{ay}, g^{bx}, \mathbb{A}, \mathbb{B})$ $sig_{\mathbb{B}} = MAC_L(0)$
$sig_{\mathbb{A}} = MAC_L(1)$	$sig_{\mathbb{A}}$ $\longrightarrow$	$sig_{\mathbb{A}} \stackrel{?}{=} MAC_L(1)$
$K = H(1, g^{ay}, g^{bx}, \mathbb{A}, \mathbb{B})$		$K = H(1, g^{ay}, g^{bx}, \mathbb{A}, \mathbb{B})$

Fig. 3. KEA+C protocol

all the intermediate information (except possibly ephemeral secret keys) should be erased immediately after completion of a session. We remark that despite the visible similarity, the keys K and L are computationally independent. In a practical implementation, one might alternatively derive them from a 4-tuple $(g^{ay}, g^{bx}, \mathbb{A}, \mathbb{B})$ by applying 2 independent hash functions. When a hash function is modeled by a random oracle $H(0, \cdot)$ and $H(1, \cdot)$ are independent random oracles.

SECURITY ANALYSIS. We show that KEA+C has key confirmation, AKE security against a strong adversary, full PFS, KCI security and is also secure in the Universally Composable model as defined by Canetti and Krawczyk [9].

First of all, we observe that repeating the proof of security for KEA+ we obtain the same security guarantees for KEA+C, namely AKE security against a strong adversary, weak PFS and KCI security. Universally Composable security [6, 9] ensures that a key-exchange protocol can securely run concurrently with arbitrary other applications. In fact, UC-security of KEA+C automatically follows from the result of Canetti and Krawczyk [9]. They establish UC security of authenticated key exchange provided that the protocol satisfies AKE security and also enjoys the so-called "ACK property". The latter requires that at the time when the initiator party outputs its session key, the other party's state can be "simulated" given only the session key and public information in the protocol. We observe that Claim 15 in [9] implies that KEA+C has this property, thus establishing UC security of KEA+C. Finally, we observe that the full Perfect Forward Secrecy property follows from UC security.

Acknowledgements

The work for this paper was done while the second author was visiting Microsoft Research. The authors thank Josh Benaloh, Brian LaMacchia, Gideon Yuval and anonymous reviewers for helpful comments and suggestions.

References

1. M. Abdalla, O. Chevassut and D. Pointcheval, *One-Time Verifier-Based Encrypted Key Exchange*, Public Key Cryptography — PKC '05, pp. 47–64, Springer-Verlag, 2005
2. M. Bellare, A. Palacio, *The Knowledge-of-Exponent Assumptions and 3-Round Zero-Knowledge Protocols*, Advances in Cryptology — CRYPTO '04, pp. 273–289, Springer-Verlag, 2004
3. M. Bellare, D. Pointcheval, P. Rogaway, *Authenticated Key Exchange Secure Against Dictionary Attacks*, Advances in Cryptology — Eurocrypt '00, pp. 139–155, Springer-Verlag, 2000
4. M. Bellare and P. Rogaway, *Entity Authentication and Key Distribution*, Advances in Cryptology — CRYPTO '93, pp. 110–125, Springer-Verlag, 1993
5. S. Blake-Wilson, D. Johnson, and A. Menezes, *Key Agreement Protocols and their Security Analysis*, 6th IMA International Conference on Cryptography and Coding, LNCS 1355, pp. 30-45, Springer-Verlag, 1997

6. R. Canetti, *Universally Composable Security: A New Paradigm for Cryptographic Protocols*, FOCS '01: Proceedings of the 42nd IEEE symposium on Foundations of Computer Science, IEEE Computer Society, 2001

7. K.-K. R. Choo, C. Boyd and Y. Hitchcock, *Examining Indistinguishability-Based Proof Models for Key Establishment Protocols*, to appear in Advances in Cryptology — Asiacrypt '05, Springer-Verlag, 2005

8. I. R. Jeong, J. Katz, D. H. Lee, *One-Round Protocols for Two-Party Authenticated Key Exchange*, ACNS '04, 2004

9. R. Canetti and H. Krawczyk, *Analysis of Key-Exchange Protocols and Their Use for Building Secure Channels*, Advances in Cryptology — EUROCRYPT '01, pp. 453–474, Springer-Verlag, 2001

10. H. Krawczyk, *SIGMA: The "SIGn-and-MAc" Approach to Authenticated Diffie-Hellman and Its Use in the IKE Protocols*, Advances in Cryptology — CRYPTO '03, LNCS 2729, pp. 400–425, Springer-Verlag, 2003

11. H. Krawczyk, *HMQV: A High-Performance Secure Diffie-Hellman Protocol*, Advances in Cryptology — CRYPTO '05, LNCS 3621, pp. 546–566, Springer-Verlag, 2005

12. M. Jakobsson and D. Pointcheval, *Mutual Authentication for Low-Power Mobile Devices*, Financial Cryptography '01, pp. 178–195, Springer-Verlag, 2001

13. C. Kudla and K. G. Paterson, *Modular Security Proofs for Key Agreement Protocols*, Advances in Cryptology — ASIACRYPT '05, pp. 549–565, Springer-Verlag, 2005

14. A. Menezes, *Another look at HMQV*, IACR Eprint archive, http://eprint.iacr.org/2005/205, 2005

15. NIST, *SKIPJACK and KEA Algorithm Specification*, http://csrc.nist.gov/encryption/skipjack/skipjack.pdf, 1998

16. T. Okamoto and D. Pointcheval, *The Gap Problems: A New Class of Problems for the Security of Cryptographic Schemes*, Public Key Cryptology — PKC '01, LNCS 1992, pp. 104–118, Springer-Verlag, 2001

17. V. Shoup, *On Formal Models for Secure Key Exchange*, Theory of Cryptography Library, http://www.shoup.net/papers/skey.ps, 1999

18. Y. S. T. Tin, C. Boyd and J. M. González Nieto, *Provably Secure Mobile Key Exchange: Applying the Canetti-Krawczyk Approach*, ACISP '03, pp. 166–179, Springer-Verlag, 2003

SAS-Based Authenticated Key Agreement

Sylvain Pasini and Serge Vaudenay

EPFL, CH-1015 Lausanne, Switzerland
http://lasecwww.epfl.ch

Abstract. Key agreement protocols are frequently based on the Diffie-Hellman protocol but require authenticating the protocol messages in two ways. This can be made by a cross-authentication protocol. Such protocols, based on the assumption that a channel which can authenticate short strings is available (SAS-based), have been proposed by Vaudenay. In this paper, we survey existing protocols and we propose a new one. Our proposed protocol requires three moves and a single SAS to be authenticated in two ways. It is provably secure in the random oracle model. We can further achieve security with a generic construction (e.g. in the standard model) at the price of an extra move. We discuss applications such as secure peer-to-peer VoIP.

1 The SAS-Based Authenticated Key Agreement Problem

Secure communication channels are usually set up by authenticated key agreement protocols. This can be performed by relying on a public-key infrastructure, e.g. based on RSA [RSA78] or the Diffie-Hellman protocol [DH76]. Clearly, this is not well suited to the advent of mobile ad-hoc communications where ephemeral or bootstrap connections are needed "at once": we certainly would not like to register a certificate to connect a PDA to a cell phone or to print to the neighbor available printer device. Secure communications can also be manually set up. For instance, peer-to-peer links using PGP can be set up by checking the digest of a public key over the telephone. Wireless devices can be securely connected by having the user to manually check a hashed value as well. To save the human user load, the string to be manually checked must be as short as possible. Recently, protocols based on Short Authenticated Strings (SAS) have been studied by Vaudenay [Vau05]. It was shown how to design and analyze a protocol to authenticate an arbitrary string assuming that we can authenticate a short one over a dedicated secure channel. Those protocols are based on commitment schemes. It was also briefly proposed how to design message cross-authentication protocols, namely protocols to authenticate arbitrary strings in two ways.

A SAS-based Authenticated Key Agreement (AKA) protocol can be easily designed by running the Diffie-Hellman protocol over an insecure channel, then by authenticating the digest of the protocol transcript using a SAS-based message cross-authentication protocol. This typically results in a 5-move protocol in addition to the bidirectional SAS transmission. In the present work, we show how to decrease the interaction cost. Namely, we design a generic construction which can use a 4-move protocol in addition to the bidirectional SAS exchange. This construction can rely on the standard model

M. Yung et al. (Eds.): PKC 2006, LNCS 3958, pp. 395–409, 2006.

(without random oracles). We also design an optimal 3-move protocol which is provably secure (with tight reduction) in the random oracle model.[1]

2 Preliminaries

We adopt the security model from [Vau05, Vau06, PV06] based on the one from Bellare-Rogaway [BR93]. We consider a network of participants which are located at some nodes. A participant at node n is associated to a given identity ID_n. He locally maintains a database of (K_j, ID_j) pairs meaning that he can use the symmetric key K_j to securely communicate with ID_j in a private and authenticated way. Participants can run concurrent protocols. A protocol specifies a sequence of steps which consist of receiving a message and sending a response. An internal short-term state keeps track on previously completed steps. Once the protocol is completed, the short-term state is removed. A protocol starts with some specified inputs and an initial state (in terms of database content). It ends with some specified outputs (or an error message) and a final state. The difference between an input (resp. output) and an initial (resp. final) state is that the adversary has control on the first one but not on the second one, except if the node was corrupted or some information leaked. Protocol instances on a node n are denoted by a unique tag π_n^i. (Note that the state of a protocol related to a given tag changes with time as new steps are made.)

Nodes can communicate through an insecure broadband channel. In addition, they have access to peer-to-peer narrowband channels which can be used to authenticate short messages. A node receiving a message from one of these channels is ensured that this message was sent at some time in the past by a node whose identity is specified by the channel itself. In this paper, we concentrate on key agreement and cross-authentication protocols, so we assume that nodes share no prior exchanged keys.

2.1 Adversarial Model

By default, the adversary is assumed to have a full control on which node makes a new step of a given protocol instance, on the insecure channel, can influence the delivery of messages (without modifying them) over the authenticated channels, can choose the inputs of the protocols, and has access to the outputs. Occasionally, the adversary can violate the privacy of the internal state of a given node or even corrupt the node so that his behavior with respect to future runs of any protocol is no longer guaranteed. More formally, the adversary has access to the following oracles.

Launch. launch(n, role, x) launches a new protocol instance on node n playing role (e.g. either Alice or Bob) with input x. It returns a new instance tag π_n^i. Note that the instance inherits of the current node state as its input state.

Send. send(π, y) sends an incoming message y to the instance π. It returns an outgoing message z, or the final output of the protocol if it completed.

---

[1] After the present paper was submitted, a preprint was posted by Laur, Asokan, and Nyberg [LAN05]. This paper includes another 3-move protocol which is provably secure based on a generic commitment (e.g. in the standard model) but not optimal.

Test. test(n, k, ID) tells whether (k, ID) is an entry of the database of node n. In practice, this oracle may be implemented by an active adversary trying to impersonate node n to communicate with ID. If the attempt succeeds, it means that k was the right key to use.

Remove. remove(n, ID) removes any (k, ID) entry in the database of node n. In practice, this oracle may be implemented by an adversary making denial-of-services attacks in the communication link between n and ID so that n decides not to trust this connection anymore and to remove it.

Reveal. reveal(n) reveals the full current state of node n. This models side channels or careless uses.

Corrupt. corrupt(n) injects a malicious code in node n so that its behavior is no longer guaranteed.

The *attack cost* is measured by

- the number Q of launched instances of Alice or Bob, i.e. the *online complexity*.
- the additional complexity C, i.e. the *offline complexity*.
- the probability of success p.

We call *one-shot attacks* the attacks which launch only two instances in total, i.e. $Q = 2$.

By convention, we describe protocols by putting a *hat* on the notation for messages received by a node (i.e. inputs of the send oracle) which are not authenticated since they can differ from messages which were sent (i.e. outputs of the receive oracle) in the case of an active attack. A message m from a node of identity ID over an authenticated channel is denoted authenticate$_{\mathsf{ID}}(m)$.

2.2 Key Agreement, Cross-Authentication, and Mutual Authentication

Authenticated key agreement. An Authenticated Key Agreement (AKA) protocol between Alice and Bob starts with no input, is independent from the current state, and ends with no output but a final state specifying an entry (k, ID) to be inserted in the database: Alice of identity ID_A ends with (k, ID_B) and Bob of identity ID_B ends with (k, ID_A). An attack is successful if a test(n, k, ID) query positively answered where n and ID correspond to nodes on which no reveal nor corrupt query was made. For simplicity, we do not consider attacks making Alice and Bob end on some inconsistent states. Namely, *mutual authentication* is assumed to be (implicitly or explicitly) made by further communications.

To construct AKA protocols, we use the following building blocks.

Message cross-authentication. A Message Cross-Authentication (MCA) protocol between Alice and Bob of identity ID_A and ID_B starts with inputs m_A and m_B and ends with outputs (m_B, ID_B) and (m_A, ID_A), respectively. An adversary is successful if some instance ended on an incorrupted node with a pair (m, ID) but no instance on the node of identity ID with input m was launched. Note that test, remove, and reveal oracles are not relevant in this case.

Message mutual-authentication. A Message Mutual-Authentication (MMA) protocol between Alice and Bob of identity ID_A and ID_B starts with inputs m_A and m_B and ends with outputs ID_B and ID_A, respectively. A honest run of an MMA protocol must have

$m_A = m_B$. An adversary is successful if some instance on an incorrupted node started with any m and ended with any ID such that no instance on the node of identity ID with input m was launched. As for MCA protocols, test, remove, and reveal oracles are not relevant. Obviously, we can transform an MCA protocol into an MMA protocol by just checking that the output message is equal to the input one on both sides.

MCA from MMA. We can also transform an MMA protocol with at least one move over the insecure channel into an MCA protocol at the price of an extra move: Bob of identity ID_B first sends his input message m_B and Alice of identity ID_A initiates an MMA protocol with input $m_A||\hat{m}_B$ by sending m_A together with the first MMA protocol message. Bob then follows the MMA protocol with input $\hat{m}_A||m_B$. The final outputs of Alice and Bob are $(\hat{m}_B, ID_B)$ and $(\hat{m}_A, ID_A)$ respectively.

To compare protocols we focus on the number of message moves over the insecure channel and on the length of authenticated messages. Furthermore, a protocol with two equal SAS to be sent in both directions (called symmetric SAS) will be considered as better than a protocol with two SAS of similar length (but not necessarily equal) to be exchanged. Indeed, some authentication channels may provide symmetric authentication at no extra cost.

2.3   Equivocable Commitment and Random Oracle Commitment

In this paper, we consider (tag-based) equivocable commitment schemes as defined by two algorithms commit and open and three oracles setup, simcommit, and equivocate.

Setup. $K_P \leftarrow$ setup generates a public key K_P to be used as a common reference string and a secret key K_S to set up the simcommit and equivocate oracles. The public key K_P is implicitly used by all other algorithms and oracles but omitted in the notations for simplicity.

Commit. $(c,d) \leftarrow$ commit(m,r) generates a commit value c and a decommit value d for a key r with a tag m. We assume that the distribution of the generated c is independent from r: the commitment is *perfectly hiding*.

Open. $r \leftarrow$ open(m,c,d) yields r if (c,d) is a possible output for commit(m,r).

Simcommit. $(c,i) \leftarrow$ simcommit(m) simulates a commit value c for a tag m and produces extra information ξ to be used later. The distribution of c should be the same as for the distribution of c generated by any commit(m,r). It also creates a unique identifier i (a nounce) and inserts (i,m,c,ξ) in a database. This oracle uses the secret key K_S and should be secured. Access to the database must be restricted to this oracle and equivocate.

Equivocate. $d \leftarrow$ equivocate(i,r) yields d such that $r =$ open(m,c,d) where (i,m,c,ξ) is in the database of simcommit. This entry is further removed. (Namely, a simulated c can be equivocated only once.)

Access to simcommit and equivocate oracles is restricted depending on the application. The normal usage of the commitment scheme should be limited to commit and open but we stress that our security model assumes that the adversary may cheat on *some* commitments by having access to simcommit and equivocate oracles. Indeed, our notion of equivocable commitment relates to the notion of *simulation-sound* commitment [MY04].

The *hiding game* between a challenger C and an adversary $\mathcal{A}$ runs as follows.

1. C runs setup and sends K_P to $\mathcal{A}$
2. $\mathcal{A}$ sends a tag m to C
3. C commits to a random key with tag m and sends a commit value c to $\mathcal{A}$
4. $\mathcal{A}$ computes some r and sends it to C
5. C releases a decommit value d and $\mathcal{A}$ wins if $r \leftarrow \mathrm{open}(m,c,d)$

In that case, the adversary has access to the simcommit and equivocate oracles but cannot query simcommit with the selected tag m. Since the commitment is perfectly hiding, no adversary can win this game with a probability larger than 2^{-k} where k is the length of the key r.

The *binding game* between a challenger C and an adversary $\mathcal{A}$ runs as follows.

1. C runs setup and sends K_P to $\mathcal{A}$
2. $\mathcal{A}$ sends a tag m and a commit value c to C
3. C picks a random r and sends it to $\mathcal{A}$
4. $\mathcal{A}$ produces a decommit value d and wins if $r \leftarrow \mathrm{open}(m,c,d)$

We say that the commitment with k-bit keys r is (T,ε)-secure is any adversary with complexity limited to T has a wining probability of at most $2^{-k} + \varepsilon$. In that case, the adversary has access to the simcommit and equivocate oracles but cannot query simcommit with the selected tag m.

Secure equivocable commitment schemes can be easily constructed based on simulation-sound trapdoor commitments by MacKenzie-Yang [MY04] as detailed in [Vau05]. Constructions can be in the standard model with a common reference string, e.g. based on the security of DSA signatures [DSS00] or Cramer-Shoup signatures [CS02]. We can also build an efficient equivocable commitment scheme based on the random oracle model.

Random oracle commitment scheme. Let ℓ_c, ℓ_e, and k be three integers. The setup algorithm is unused, but we assume that we can use three oracles:

H. $c \leftarrow H(e,r,m)$ queried with an ℓ_e-bit string e and a k-bit string r, looks whether an entry (e,r,m,c) in a list exist. If not, the oracle creates one with a random ℓ_c-bit string c. In any case, the oracle answers c.

Simcommit. $(c,i) \leftarrow \mathrm{simcommit}(m)$ simply picks a random ℓ_c-bit string c and a nounce i and stores (i,c,m) in a list.

Equivocate. $d \leftarrow \mathrm{equivocate}(i,r)$ gets (i,c,m) and removes it form the list. The oracle then picks a random ℓ_e-bit string e. If $(e,r,m,\cdot)$ exists in the H list, the oracle fails. Otherwise, (e,r,m,c) is inserted. Clearly, if the number of oracle accesses to H and simcommit is limited by q, the probability that the oracle fails at least once is less than $q^2 \times 2^{-\ell_e - 1}$.

The algorithm $\mathrm{commit}(m,r)$ simply picks e at random, queries $H(e,r,m)$ and outputs $d = (e,r)$. The algorithm $\mathrm{open}(m,c,d)$ simply checks that $H(d,m) = c$ and parses

$d = (e,r)$ to yield r. Unless equivocate fails, this scheme is clearly an equivocable commitment scheme as previously defined. Since all commit values c are generated in an independent way, there are no collisions with probability at least $1 - q^2 \times 2^{-\ell_c-1}$. Clearly, being able to decommit any c to two values would lead H to a collision. Hence, the scheme is $(q, 2^{-k} + q^2 \times 2^{-\ell_e-1} + q^2 \times 2^{-\ell_c-1})$-secure. In practice, simcommit and equivocate are unused. So, we can just instantiate H by a standard hash function, provided that instantiation of that kind of random oracle makes sense [CGH98].

3   Previous SAS-Based Key Agreement Protocols

A classical authenticated Diffie-Hellman [DH76] protocol over a multiplicative group spanned by a generator g consists, for Alice (resp. Bob) of picking a random integer x_A (resp. x_B), sending the Diffie-Hellman public keys, $y_A = g^{x_A}$ (resp. $y_B = g^{x_B}$) over the authenticated channel, computing $z_A = y_B^{x_A}$ (resp. $z_B = y_A^{x_B}$) and ending with state (z_A, ID_B) (resp. (z_B, ID_A)). In this case, authenticated messages are pretty long, but authentication is necessary to thwart man-in-the-middle attacks.

We first informally present an AKA protocol from Hoepman [Hoe04]. It is based on the Diffie-Hellman protocol and it uses an authenticated channel for the authentication of each Diffie-Hellman value. This protocol runs in three steps: commitment, authentication, and opening. (The original protocol has a fourth step: the key validation.) Instead of revealing its Diffie-Hellman public key, each party first commits on it, keeping it hidden. In the next step, each participant authenticates a piece of its Diffie-Hellman public key. Finally, they open their commitments and check their respective commitment and authenticated string before completing the regular Diffie-Hellman protocol.

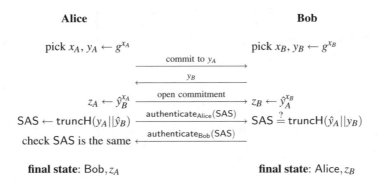

Fig. 1. PGPfone 1995 Key Agreement Protocol

Another AKA protocol, depicted on Fig. 1, was used by Zimmermann for the PGP-fone in 1995[2]. Its advantage is to reduce the number of moves in the insecure channel and to make both authenticated strings equal. In this protocol, only the first participant Alice commits to its public key. The commitment is immediately opened when the other

---

[2] Personal communication.

public key is received. Finally, the authenticated string is a piece of the digest (denoted truncH on Fig. 1) of the Diffie-Hellman protocol transcript.

For both the Hoepman and the PGPfone protocols, the security is not formally proven ([Hoe04] only provides a sketch of argument for the security). Another approach consists of authenticating the transcript of a classical key agreement protocol by using an MMA protocol. The MANA protocols by Gehrmann-Mitchell-Nyberg [GMN04, GN01, GN04] illustrates this. Finally, we study in what follows a generic construction reducing the amount of authenticated bits in AKA protocols. Using it with the Diffie-Hellman key agreement protocol and the MCA protocol of [Vau05], we obtain the DH-SC protocol of Čagalj-Čapkun-Hubaux [ČČH06]. Using an optimized MCA protocol we can save one protocol move. In what follows we describe the generic construction, analyze it, and study 3-move MMA and MCA protocols with symmetric SAS.

4   Reducing Key Agreement to Message Authentication

We can build an AKA protocol by exchanging Diffie-Hellman keys through a message cross-authentication protocol.

We propose a generic SAS-based construction for an AKA protocol that we call the constructed AKA protocol or simply *the* AKA protocol. For this, we use an initial AKA protocol (with longer strings to be authenticated), that we call the AKA_0 protocol, and an MCA protocol with short SAS. Consider that the AKA_0 protocol requires $n_k \geq 2$ moves, the $n_k - 1$-th being from Alice to Bob, and the MCA protocol requires $n_a \geq 2$ moves over the insecure channel, the first one being from Alice to Bob. In the AKA protocol, the $n_k - 2$ first moves of the AKA_0 are performed over the insecure channel. Then, both participants assembles his view on the protocol transcript τ by concatenating all protocol messages (sent and received ones). Then, an MCA protocol starts. Alice wishes to authenticate τ concatenated with her $n_k - 1$-th message α in the AKA_0 protocol. Bob wishes to authenticate the same $\tau \| \alpha$ concatenated with his last message β in the AKA_0 protocol. (Note that Bob selects the message to be authenticated after receiving Alice's first message in the MCA protocol.) At the end, both participants use the authenticated messages to complete the AKA_0 protocol and end with final states as specified in the AKA_0 protocol. We have $n_k + n_a - 2$ moves in total.

Note that MCA can have $n_a < 2$. (For instance the trivial MMA protocol exchanging authenticated digests has no move and thus we can build an MCA with only one move.) In that case, we augment the MCA protocol by virtual moves and we obtain n_k moves in total. However, MCA protocols with $n_a < 2$ must have pretty large SAS to exchange the messages.

We can make a similar construction based on an n_a'-move MMA protocol instead of an MCA protocol. In that case, we can only encapsulate the last move β of the AKA_0 protocol in the MMA protocol, leading us to $\max(n_k, n_k + n_a' - 1)$ moves in total.

Theorem 1. *Let us consider an n_k-move AKA protocol (the AKA_0 protocol) and an n_a-move MCA protocol. The generic construction is essentially an AKA protocol with $\max(n_k, n_k + n_a - 2)$ moves in which the structure of authenticated messages is similar as in the MCA protocol. There exists a constant μ such that for any T, if ε_1 resp. ε_2 denotes the best success probability of an adversary bounded by T against the AKA_0*

protocol resp. the MCA protocol, then any adversary bounded by $T \times \mu$ against the AKA protocol has probability of success at most $\varepsilon_1 + \varepsilon_2$.

Using the Diffie-Hellman protocol and an n_a-move MCA protocol leads us to a max $(2, n_a)$-move AKA protocol in which the structure of authenticated messages is similar as in the MCA protocol. With the construction based on an MMA protocol, we obtain $\max(2, n'_a + 1)$ moves. In the case where we want to achieve small SAS, we must have $n_a \geq 2$, leading us to n_a moves using MCA protocols and $n'_a + 1$ moves using MMA protocols. Since $(n'_a + 1)$-move MCA protocols can be made from n'_a-move protocols, we may decrease the total number of moves in AKA protocols by starting from MCA protocols directly.

Proof. For each instance of Alice, we let τ_A be the constructed transcript of the $n_k - 2$ first messages in the AKA protocol and we let α_A be her last message, i.e. the $n_k - 1$-th message in the protocol. We further let $\hat{\tau}_B || \hat{\alpha}_B || \hat{\beta}$ be the accepted message from Bob at the end of the MCA protocol. Similarly, for each instance of Bob, we let τ_B be the constructed transcript of the $n_k - 2$ first messages in the AKA protocol, $\hat{\tau}_A || \hat{\alpha}_A$ be the accepted message at the end of the MCA protocol, and β be his last message in the AKA$_0$ protocol assuming that Alice's last one is $\hat{\alpha}_A$. We let $\alpha_B = \hat{\alpha}_A$. Bob's message to be authenticated is $\tau_B || \alpha_B || \beta$.

Given an adversary $\mathcal{A}$ against the AKA protocol, we construct a simulator $\mathcal{B}$ interacting with $\mathcal{A}$ and attacking the MCA protocol. We simply simulate instances running the AKA$_0$ protocol and launch the MCA protocol instances when appropriate. test, remove, reveal and corruct queries can easily be simulated. Clearly, the attack against the MCA protocol does not succeed with probability at least $1 - \varepsilon$. In those cases, we have $\tau_B = \hat{\tau}_B$, $\tau_A = \hat{\tau}_A$, $\alpha_A = \hat{\alpha}_A = \alpha_B = \hat{\alpha}_B$, and $\beta = \hat{\beta}$, just as if the instance of Alice and Bob had the AKA$_0$ protocol run over an authenticated channel.

We construct a simulator C interacting with $\mathcal{A}$ and attacking the AKA$_0$ protocol over an authenticated channel. The simulator simply replaces inputs to the send oracle by authenticated ones when possible, or fails, and simulates the MCA protocol. Clearly, running $\mathcal{A}$ in parallel with $\mathcal{B}$ and C with the same random source, we derive that whenever $\mathcal{A}$ succeeds, either $\mathcal{B}$ or C succeed. □

A trivial MMA protocol consists of authenticating the digest of the input message from a collision-resistant hash function. This protocol can be transformed into an MCA protocol by using 2 moves (to exchange m_A and m_B) plus the authentication of a SAS in two ways as for the construction in Section 2.2. We obtain a 2-move AKA protocol with symmetric SAS, but the length of the SAS is quite long (typically, 160 bits).

A SAS-based cross-authentication protocol was proposed in [Vau05] by interleaving two SAS-based message authentication protocols. It is a 4-move MCA protocol with symmetric SAS and can thus be transformed into a 4-move AKA protocol with symmetric SAS based on Diffie-Hellman.

5   A New SAS-Based Message Mutual-Authentication Protocol

We propose a new protocol improving the number of exchanged messages. As depicted on Fig. 2, and without any attack, Alice and Bob start with the same message, i.e.

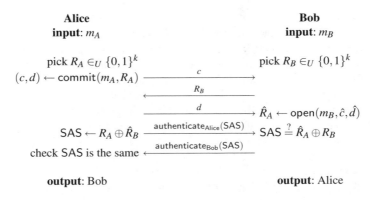

Fig. 2. A New SAS-Based Message Mutual-Authentication Protocol

$m_A = m_B$. Each participant chooses a k-bit random value R_A and R_B, respectively. Alice starts by committing on her random value R_A by sending c, keeping it hidden. Bob sends the random value R_B. Then, Alice opens her value by sending the decommit value d. Finally, both authenticate the SAS which has been computed using a simple XOR function. Using the generic construction with Diffie-Hellman we obtain a 4-move AKA protocol with symmetric SAS.

Theorem 2. *We consider adversaries against the MMA protocol of Fig. 2 who are bounded by complexity T, Q_A instances of Alice, and Q_B instances of Bob. We assume that we have an (T_C, ε)-secure equivocable commitment scheme. There exists a (small) constant μ such that any adversary wins either with probability limited to $Q_A \cdot (Q_A + Q_B)(2^{-k} + \varepsilon)$ or with complexity $T \geq T_C - \mu$.*

Proof. Any adversary which would attack an instance of either Alice or Bob needs one SAS to send her/him so that she/he can complete. This required SAS can easily be obtained from any instance of Alice since she does not need any prior authenticated message. It can also be obtained from any instance of Bob in which case he must be sent another SAS before. The output SAS by Bob is equal to the sent one. Indeed, a successful adversary interaction defines the first attacked instance and a prior sequence initiated by one instance of Alice followed by a chain (possibly empty) of instances of Bob and ended by the attacked instance. Every (unattacked) instance of Bob in this sequence is sending a SAS identical to the received one to the next instance. Every intermediate instance of Bob terminates with an output message which must be equal to the input message of the previous instance in the sequence (otherwise, they would be successfully attacked). However, the final instance in the sequence outputs a message which is different than the input of the previous instance. Hence, every instance in the sequence but the final one has the same input message and all instances yield the same SAS. Clearly, sending the output SAS from the leading Alice to the tailing instance produces a successful attack with no intermediate instance of Bob.

Let $\mathcal{A}_0$ be an adversary who launches at most Q_A instances of Alice and Q_B instances of Bob. We transform it into an adversary $\mathcal{A}$ who launches an instance of Alice and a single target instance (of either Alice or Bob) as follows:

1. $\mathcal{A}$ first picks two random numbers I, J such that $1 \leq I \leq Q_A$ and $1 \leq J < Q_A + Q_B$.
2. We initialize counters i and j to 0 and run $\mathcal{A}_0$ step by step.
   - Every time $\mathcal{A}_0$ would like to make a launch query to launch an instance of Alice, we increment i. If $i = I$, we really launch it and call the instance Alice π. Otherwise, we increment j and if $j = J$, we really launch it and call the target instance π'. Otherwise, we simulate the oracle call.
   - Every time $\mathcal{A}_0$ would like to make a launch query to launch an instance of Bob, we increment j. If $j = J$, we really launch it and call the target instance π'. Otherwise, we simulate the oracle call.
   - If we have to send a SAS to π, we just simulate the oracle call.
   - If we have to send a SAS to π' and we already got a SAS from π which is equal to the expected one, we just send it. Otherwise, the attack fails.

Due to the previous discussion, if $\mathcal{A}_0$ succeeds, if π' is the first attacked instance for $\mathcal{A}_0$ and if π is the leading instance of Alice in the sequence, then $\mathcal{A}$ succeeds. Hence, the probability of success of $\mathcal{A}$ is at least $\frac{1}{Q_A(Q_A+Q_B-1)}$ times the probability of success p of $\mathcal{A}_0$.

We now have an adversary $\mathcal{A}$ with Alice and a target instance. We assume that the adversary complexity is bounded by $T_C - \mu$ for some constant overhead μ to be determined by the following reductions. We consider two cases: attacks targeting an instance of Bob and attacks targeting an instance of Alice. Let p_A resp. p_B be the probability of a target Alice resp. Bob and q_A resp. q_B be the success probability conditioned to both cases, respectively. The success probability of $\mathcal{A}$ is $p = q_A p_A + q_B p_B$ and we have $p_A + p_B = 1$.

In both cases, we define a simulator $\mathcal{B}$ who simulates the two instances as follows. We first pick a random k-bit SAS. When an instance of Alice is launched for the first time by the adversary $\mathcal{A}$, we simulate a commitment c by using simcommit. Then the corresponding $\hat{R}_B$ is sent to this instance of Alice, the commit value is equivocated so that it opens to the key SAS $\oplus \hat{R}_B$. This simulation of Alice is perfect and has the

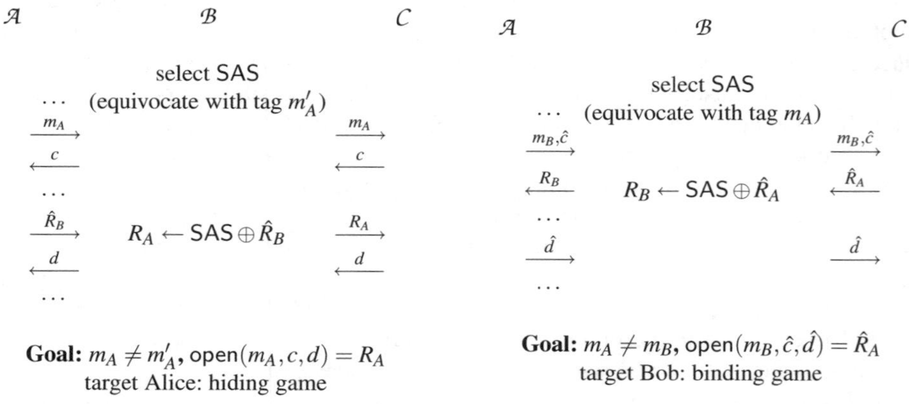

Goal: $m_A \neq m_A'$, open$(m_A, c, d) = R_A$
target Alice: hiding game

Goal: $m_A \neq m_B$, open$(m_B, \hat{c}, \hat{d}) = \hat{R}_A$
target Bob: binding game

Fig. 3. Simulator Playing the Hiding/Binding Game

property to determine the final SAS at the beginning. If the attack succeeds, the other instance will have to deal with a commit value with a different tag. Depending on whether the other instance is an Alice or a Bob, we simulate it so that we can win the hiding game or the binding game against a challenger C as depicted on Fig. 3. In the case of a target Alice, the adversary succeeds if $\hat{R}_B$ leads the target instance to derive SAS. In that case we can correctly derive R_A and win the hiding game. Since the equivocable commitment is always perfectly hiding, we deduce $q_A = 2^{-k}$. We could have played the binding game in a trivial way and won with the same probability 2^{-k}. In the case of a target Bob, the adversary succeeds if $\hat{d}$ decommits to a key which leads Bob to the right SAS, thus to the key $\hat{R}_A$. In that case, we win the binding game with probability q_B. To summarize, we made an adversary playing the binding game with probability of success p. Therefore, $p \leq 2^{-k} + \varepsilon$. $\qquad\square$

6   A New SAS-Based Message Cross-Authentication Protocol

We propose a new protocol based on the previous one, but improving the number of exchanged messages through the broadband insecure channel. Our protocol uses an almost strongly universal hash function family h [Sti91, Sti94]. In practice, one can use $h_K(x) = \mathrm{trunc}(\mathrm{hash}(K\|x))$ where hash is a collision-resistant hash function and trunc truncates to the leading ρ bits. Our protocol also uses a commitment scheme to commit on a κ-bit key K. Contrarily to our previous protocol, the committed key K can now be pretty large. Using the generic construction with Diffie-Hellman we obtain a 3-move AKA protocol with symmetric SAS. Note that we added an identity test on Alice's side to avoid trivial reflection attacks.

Theorem 3. *Let ℓ_e, ℓ_c be the parameters of the random oracle commitment scheme. Let q be the upper bound on the number of H queries. Let $\varepsilon = q^2 2^{-\ell_e} + q^2 2^{-\ell_c}$. Let h be an ε_h-almost strongly universal hash function family with ρ-bit digests, i.e. $\Pr[h_K(a) =$*

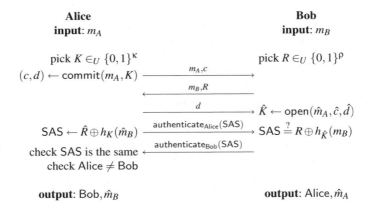

Fig. 4. A New SAS-Based Message Cross-Authentication Protocol

$\alpha, h_K(b) = \beta] \leq 2^{-2\rho} + 2^{-\rho}\varepsilon_h$ *for any* a, b, α, β *such that* $a \neq b$ *with a random K.*[3]
*We consider adversaries against the message cross authentication protocol of Fig. 4
who are bounded by Q instances of Alice or Bob and by q queries to H. The success
probability is limited by* $\frac{Q(Q-1)}{2}(2^{-\rho} + \varepsilon + \varepsilon_h)$.

By launching Q instances of either Alice or Bob with pairwise different input messages
and by picking independent uniformly distributed $\hat{R}$, all SAS are independent and uniformly distributed so we have one matching with probability $1 - 2^{-Q\rho} \cdot 2^{\rho}!/(2^{\rho} - Q)!$
which is roughly $\frac{Q(Q-1)}{2}2^{-\rho}$ when $Q \ll 2^{\frac{\rho}{2}}$. Hence, this bound is essentially tight. Note
that the above attack can apply to any MCA protocol of similar structure (see [PV06]),
so our protocol is optimal.

Proof. We let $\varepsilon_1 = \varepsilon_2 = \varepsilon_h$ (h is almost uniform). We have $\Pr[h_K(a) = \alpha] \leq 2^{-\rho} +$
ε_1 and $\Pr[h_K(a) \oplus h_K(b) = \alpha] \leq 2^{-\rho} + \varepsilon_2$ for any a, b, α such that $a \neq b$ and with K
uniformly distributed (h is ε-almost XOR universal [Kra94]). In what follows, only
those properties will be used. Namely, we could replace the condition on h by those
two properties.

We define a new character: the flipped Bob who proceeds as Bob but first issues a
SAS equal to $R \oplus h_{\hat{R}}(m_B)$ then receives a SAS for verification. In a new protocol, Alice
and the flipped Bob can interact with two crossing SAS exchange.

We consider an adversary successfully running his attack with many instances for
the original MCA protocol. We say that a given instance is attacked if it completed the
protocol during which a SAS was received, with an output which is not consistent with
the input of the instance who issued the received SAS. (Note that a successful adversary must have an attacked instance.) An attacked (target) instance (of either Alice or
Bob) must receive one SAS from a (sending) instance. Note that those two instances
must be different. (Indeed, no instance of Bob can send a SAS to himself otherwise it
would have to be received before being sent. Similarly, no instance of Alice can accept
a SAS coming from herself.) Clearly, both instances must agree on the SAS to complete. Hence, if the SAS sent by the target instance is forwarded to the sending instance
then both instances fully interact. We can guess the pair of instances with probability
$2/(Q(Q-1))$. Hence, we can simulate all instances except the two guessed ones. Since
the SAS verification phase is the last step on both instances, there is no trouble to make
the two instances exchange their SAS. We thus transform the initial adversary against
the MCA protocol with success probability p into a one-shot adversary against our new
protocol with success probability at least $2p(Q(Q-1))^{-1}$.

The interaction of the transformed adversary with an instance of Alice consists of
two steps

A_1 sending her her message m_A (for the launch query) and getting her commit value c
(for the first send query)

A_2 giving her Bob's alleged message $\hat{m}_B$ and random value $\hat{R}$ and getting her decommit
value d.

---

[3] Note that this definition of almost strongly universal hashing is slightly different from [Sti91,
Sti94] in the sense that perfect uniformity is not required.

Alice's SAS equals $\hat{R} \oplus h_K(\hat{m}_B)$ where K is the result of open(m_A, c, d). The second step must be performed after the first one.

The interaction of the adversary with an instance of Bob consists of two steps

B_1 sending him his message m_B (for the launch query) and Alice's alleged message $\hat{m}_A$ and commit value $\hat{c}$ and getting his random value R (for the first send query)

B_2 giving him Alice's alleged decommit value $\hat{d}$.

The adversary wins if the two instances complete and compute the same SAS and if the input message of one instance is different from the output message of the other instance.

In what follows we show that all cases can be simulated so that we can win a hard game, proving that the probability of success is at most $2^{-p} + \varepsilon + \max(\varepsilon_1, \varepsilon_2)$.

Cases Alice-Alice. We number 2 the instance of Alice whose A_2 step is the last. Since the commitment is perfectly hiding, this Alice leaks no information about K^2 (variable K for Alice number 2) until this very last step. Hence, K^2 is independent from the rest and $\hat{R}^1 \oplus \hat{R}^2 \oplus h_{K^1}(\hat{m}_B^1) = h_{K^2}(\hat{m}_B^2)$ with probability at most $2^{-p} + \varepsilon_1$.

On Bob's Incoming $\hat{c}$ (Step B_1). In the random oracle commitment model, we only consider the event where no collision occurred. Hence, a commit value $\hat{c}$ issued by the adversary for an instance of Bob is either a real output by H and can only be opened in a single way, or no output from H. In the latter case, we can consider $(\perp, \perp, \perp, \hat{c})$ as a new entry in the H list and count it as an extra oracle call. This way, $\hat{c}$ can never be opened. Hence, with probability at least $1 - (q+1)(q+2)2^{-\ell_e - 1} - (q+1)(q+2)2^{-\ell_c - 1}$, which is larger than $1 - \varepsilon$, the commit value(s) $\hat{c}$ by the adversary are either openable in a single fixed way or not openable. If they are not openable, the adversary fails. If openable $\hat{c}$ are issued by an oracle call to H by the adversary, we can thus virtually replace the adversary release of $\hat{c}$ by an adversary release of $\hat{K}$ and step B_2 can be ignored. If openable $\hat{c}$ are issued by other oracle calls to H, it can only be by a simulation of Alice, leading us to $c = \hat{c}$, thus $\hat{K} = K$ and $m_A = \hat{m}_A$.

Cases Bob-Bob. We number 2 the instance of Bob whose B_1 step is the last one. Those cases produce no oracle calls to H by Alice, so $\hat{K}^1$ and $\hat{K}^2$ are selected by the adversary before the B_1^2 step. Note that R^1 is already released. The attack succeeds if $R^2 = R^1 \oplus h_{\hat{R}^1}(m_B^1) \oplus h_{\hat{R}^2}(m_B^2)$ where R^2 is independent of the righthand term and selected at random by the second Bob. Clearly, this succeeds with probability 2^{-p}.

Cases Alice-Bob. Without loss of generality, we can assume that B_2 is the last step.

In cases $A_1 A_2 B_1 B_2$, R is selected in step B_1 so the adversary succeeds with probability 2^{-p}.

In cases $A_1 B_1 A_2 B_2$ with $c \neq \hat{c}$ or in cases $B_1 A_1 A_2 B_2$ (necessarily with $c \neq \hat{c}$), the adversary has no information about K until step A_2 and succeeds when $\hat{R} \oplus R \oplus h_{\hat{K}}(m_B) = h_K(\hat{m}_B)$. Hence succeeds with probability at most $2^{-p} + \varepsilon_1$.

In cases $A_1 B_1 A_2 B_2$ with $c = \hat{c}$, we must have $m_A = \hat{m}_A$. This can only be an attack for $m_B \neq \hat{m}_B$. The adversary has no information about K until step A_2 and succeeds when $\hat{R} \oplus R = h_K(m_B) \oplus h_K(\hat{m}_B)$, hence with probability at most $2^{-p} + \varepsilon_2$. $\square$

With the same analysis as in [Vau05], in a network of N participants, each limited to R runs of the protocol, and a maximal attack probability *at large* p, we should use $\rho \approx \log_2 \frac{N^2 R^2}{2p}$. When p is the probability to attack a target node, we should use $\rho \approx \log_2 \frac{NR^2}{2p}$. With $N \approx 2^{20}$, $R \approx 2^{10}$, and $p \approx 2^{-10}$, we obtain $\rho \approx 49$. In an ATM-like environment, we can take $N = 2$, $R = 3$, and $p = 3 \cdot 10^{-4}$, leading us to $\rho \approx 15$. In between, we believe that $\rho = 20$ bits provides enough security in a small community of human users.

7   Conclusion

We have shown how to construct efficient SAS-based AKA protocols based on existing ones and SAS-based MMA or MCA protocols. We have proposed a new 3-move MMA protocol using a generic commitment scheme. It can make a secure and efficient SAS-based AKA protocol with 4 moves over the insecure channel. We have also proposed a new 3-move MCA protocol using random oracle commitments. It can make a secure and efficient SAS-based AKA protocol with 3 moves in the random oracle model. For both constructions, we can have e.g. a SAS of 20 bits. Note that our two constructions use the same authenticated strings in both directions.

Applications of such protocols can be traditional key agreement, but run in an ad-hoc way. For instance, it can be used to exchange PGP public keys to be authenticated by a human-to-human telephone conversation. It can also be used to secure peer-to-peer VoIP communications. Other straightforward applications can be the Bluetooth-like establishment of symmetric key between associated wireless devices, e.g. for wireless USB.

References

[BR93]   Mihir Bellare and Phillip Rogaway. Entity authentication and key distribution. In Douglas R. Stinson, editor, *Advances in Cryptology – CRYPTO '93: 13th Annual International Cryptology Conference*, volume 773 of *Lecture Notes in Computer Science*, pages 232–249, Santa Barbara, California, U.S.A., 1993. Springer-Verlag.

[ČČH06]   Mario Čagalj, Srdjan Čapkun, and Jean-Pierre Hubaux. Key agreement in peer-to-peer wireless networks. *Proceedings of the IEEE, Special Issue in Security and Cryptography*, 94(2):467–478, 2006.

[CGH98]   Ran Canetti, Oded Goldreich, and Shai Halevi. The random oracle methodology revisited (preliminary version). In *STOC '98: Proceedings of the thirtieth annual ACM symposium on Theory of computing*, pages 209–218, New York, NY, USA, May 1998. ACM Press.

[CS02]   Ronald Cramer and Victor Shoup. Universal hash proofs and a paradigm for adaptive chosen ciphertext secure public-key encryption. In Lars R. Knudsen, editor, *Advances in Cryptology – EUROCRYPT '02: International Conference on the Theory and Applications of Cryptographic Techniques*, volume 2332 of *Lecture Notes in Computer Science*, Amsterdam, The Netherlands, April 2002. Springer-Verlag.

[DH76]   Whitfield Diffie and Martin E. Hellman. New directions in cryptography. *IEEE Transactions on Information Theory*, IT–22(6):644–654, November 1976.

[DSS00]   Digital signature standard (DSS). Federal Information Processing Standard, Publication 186-2, U.S. Department of Commerce, National Institute of Standards and Technology, 2000.

[GMN04] Christian Gehrmann, Chris J. Mitchell, and Kaisa Nyberg. Manual authentication for wireless devices. *RSA Cryptobytes*, 7(1):29–37, January 2004.

[GN01]   Christian Gehrmann and Kaisa Nyberg. Enhancements to Bluetooth baseband security. In *Nordsec '01*, Copenhagen, Denmark, November 2001.

[GN04]   Christian Gehrmann and Kaisa Nyberg. Security in personal area networks. *Security for Mobility*, pages 191–230, 2004.

[Hoe04] Jaap-Henk Hoepman. The ephemeral pairing problem. In Ari Juels, editor, *Financial Cryptography: the 8th International Conference (FC '04)*, volume 3110 of *Lecture Notes in Computer Science*, pages 212–226, Key West, FL, USA, February 2004. Springer-Verlag.

[Kra94] Hugo Krawczyk. LFSR-based hashing and authentication. In Yvo Desmedt, editor, *Advances in Cryptology – CRYPTO '94: 11th Annual International Cryptology Conference*, volume 839 of *Lecture Notes in Computer Science*, pages 129–139, Santa Barbara, California, U.S.A., August 1994. Springer-Verlag.

[LAN05] Sven Laur, N. Asokan, and Kaisa Nyberg. Efficient mutual data authentication using manually authenticated strings. Cryptology ePrint Archive, Report 2005/424, 2005. http://eprint.iacr.org/.

[MY04]   Philip MacKenzie and Ke Yang. On simulation-sound trapdoor commitments. In Christian Cachin and Jan Camenisch, editors, *Advances in Cryptology – EURO-CRYPT '04 : International Conference on the Theory and Applications of Cryptographic Techniques*, volume 3027 of *Lecture Notes in Computer Science*, pages 382–400, Interlaken, Switzerland, May 2004. Springer-Verlag.

[PV06]   Sylvain Pasini and Serge Vaudenay. An optimal non-interactive message authentication protocol. In David Pointcheval, editor, *Topics in Cryptology – CT-RSA '06: The Cryptographers' Track at the RSA Conference 2006*, volume 3860 of *Lecture Notes in Computer Science*, pages 280–294, San Jose, California, U.S.A., February 2006. Springer-Verlag.

[RSA78] Ronald L. Rivest, Adi Shamir, and Leonard M. Adleman. A method for obtaining digital signatures and public-key cryptosystems. *Communications of the ACM*, 21(2):120–126, Februar 1978.

[Sti91] Douglas Stinson. Universal hashing and authentication codes. In Joan Feigenbaum, editor, *Advances in Cryptology – CRYPTO '91: 11th Annual International Cryptology Conference*, volume 576 of *Lecture Notes in Computer Science*, pages 74–85, Santa Barbara, California, U.S.A., August 1991. Springer-Verlag.

[Sti94] Douglas Stinson. Universal hashing and authentication codes. *Designs, Codes and Cryptography*, 4:369–380, 1994.

[Vau05] Serge Vaudenay. Secure communications over insecure channels based on short authenticated strings. In Victor Shoup, editor, *Advances in Cryptology – CRYPTO '05: The 25th Annual International Cryptology Conference*, volume 3621 of *Lecture Notes in Computer Science*, pages 309–326, Santa Barbara, California, U.S.A., August 2005. Springer-Verlag.

[Vau06] Serge Vaudenay. On Bluetooth repairing: Key agreement based on symmetric-key cryptography. In Dengguo Feng, Dongdai Lin, and Moti Yung, editors, *Information Security and Cryptology: First SKLOIS Conference, CISC'05*, volume 3822 of *Lecture Notes in Computer Science*, pages 1–9, Beijing, China, December 2006. Springer-Verlag.

The Twist-AUgmented Technique
for Key Exchange

Olivier Chevassut[1], Pierre-Alain Fouque[2],
Pierrick Gaudry[3], and David Pointcheval[2]

[1] Lawrence Berkeley National Lab. – Berkeley, CA, USA
OChevassut@lbl.gov
[2] CNRS-École normale supérieure – Paris, France
{Pierre-Alain.Fouque, David.Pointcheval}@ens.fr
[3] CNRS-LORIA – Nancy, France
Pierrick.Gaudry@loria.fr

Abstract. Key derivation refers to the process by which an agreed upon large random number, often named master secret, is used to derive keys to encrypt and authenticate data. Practitioners and standardization bodies have usually used the random oracle model to get key material from a Diffie-Hellman key exchange. However, formal proofs in the standard model require *randomness extractors* to formally extract the entropy of the random master secret into a seed prior to deriving other keys. Whereas this is a quite simple tool, it is not easy to use in practice –or it is easy to misuse it–.

In addition, in many standards, the acronym PRF (Pseudo-Random Functions) is used for several tasks, and namely the randomness extraction. While randomness extractors and pseudo-random functions are *a priori* distinct tools, we first study whether such an application is correct or not. We thereafter study the case of $\mathbb{Z}_p^\star$ where p is a safe-prime and the case of elliptic curve since in IPSec for example, only these two groups are considered. We present *very efficient* and *provable* randomness extraction techniques for these groups under the DDH assumption. In the special case of elliptic curves, we present a new technique —the so-called *'Twist-AUgmented'* technique— which exploits specific properties of some elliptic curves, and avoids the need of any randomness extractor. We finally compare the efficiency of this method with other solutions.

1 Introduction

Key exchange is an important problem in practice and several schemes have been designed to solve it since the seminal work of Diffie and Hellman [13]. Recently, different works have been published in order to analyze the security of those schemes in various settings (password, public-key, hybrid setting) and security models (random oracle, common reference string, standard model). But for several years, efficiency and security in the standard model have become the main goals to achieve in cryptography. The most widely used network security protocols nowadays are TLS [34], a.k.a SSL, SSH, and the Internet Key Exchange (IKE) protocols [18, 24] from the IPSec standard of the IETF. In all the descriptions, the

M. Yung et al. (Eds.): PKC 2006, LNCS 3958, pp. 410–426, 2006.

extraction of the master-key from a common (random) secret element is performed using a PRF, which is often instantiated by HMAC [5] (this is for example the case in IKE). However, it is well-known that such a primitive is not *a priori* well-suited for such a task [15], and the formal analysis requires unusual assumptions.

1.1 The Key Derivation Problem

Diffie-Hellman (DH) based key exchanges establish a secure communication channel between two parties by securely negotiating a large random element in a given cyclic group, called pre-master secret. Then, this secret is used to derive keys for encrypting and authenticating data. These keys must be bit-strings of some specific length uniformly distributed and used as input parameters to symmetric ciphers (for privacy), message authentication codes (for authentication), and pseudo-random functions (for expansion of a seed into a longer bit-string). However, they cannot be initialized with the *simple* bit-string encoding of the pre-master secret. Even though this secret is indistinguishable from a random element in the cyclic group under some classical computational assumptions, such as the Decisional Diffie-Hellman assumption (DDH), its encoding is not indistinguishable from a random bit-string with a uniform distribution. The entropy of the bit-string encoded secret is indeed high but not high enough to immediately obtain an *almost* uniformly distributed random bit-string: pseudo-entropy generators are not pseudo-random generators even when only considering the property of computational indistinguishability [19].

Most of the cryptographic protocols do not take into account this practical problem since it only appears during the implementation. Cryptographers indeed use "elements in sets" when designing their algorithms while standardization bodies represent and encode these elements. Engineers are left clueless when elements in a given set do not necessarily admit a compact encoding —in bijection with a set of ℓ-bit strings— even for a well-chosen ℓ. Practitioners have no choice but to make educated guesses on which encoding to use and so, may introduce security breaches. This is the case of the Diffie-Hellman version of the SSL protocol [34] where the binary encoding of the random element is used as it. IKE raises this problem too. It explicitly deals with the extraction issue via a mechanism analyzed in [15], and follows the general framework described below.

1.2 Randomness Extraction and Key Derivation

In order to correctly derive several keys from a common (random) secret element —the so-called pre-master key—, two steps are required, with two different tools:

Randomness Extraction – in a first stage, one uses a family of functions $\mathcal{F}$ keyed by *random and public nonces* and applies it to the pre-master secret, to get the master key;

Key Derivation – in the second stage, the output is used as a key to a family of functions $\mathcal{G}$, with known inputs in order to derive further key material to create a secure channel.

This two-phase protocol also appears in the random generator architecture of Barak and Halevi [2]. The aim of the randomness extractor phase is to generate a short seed concentrating the entropy of the source and then in the key derivation, this seed will be used to generate keys. It is important to separate these stages, since different cryptographic primitives are needed. However, in many specifications, $\mathcal{F}$ and $\mathcal{G}$ are asked to be Pseudo-Random Function Families (with the same notation prf, such as in IKE [18, 24]).

Before going into more details, let us review informally the main difference between randomness extractors and PRF. A PRF is a family of functions, from a set D on a set R, such that it is computationally hard to distinguish the inputs/outputs of a function taken at random from the set of all functions from D to R and of a function taken at random in the PRF family. It is important to note that the key, or the index of the function taken in the PRF family, must be kept secret, otherwise the distinction becomes easy. A randomness extractor has the property that the output distribution is close to the uniform one, if the input distribution has enough entropy. If the index is known, the randomness extractor is called a *strong* randomness extractor. Hereafter, we only look at strong randomness extractors, where the index is implicitly made public, and we thus simply call them randomness extractors.

As a consequence, one can easily note that the notation prf has two different purposes: (1) first stage, prf is used as a randomness extractor, with a public and random key and a high-entropy input (but not as a PRF); (2) second stage, prf is used as a PRF, to build a PRG. The HMAC function [5], designed and analyzed as a secure MAC, is furthermore the default prf in several standards.

In this article, we primarily focus on the randomness extraction phases for DH-based protocol and we show efficient and provable techniques for this task. The key derivation phases can be solved by using techniques coming from the random oracle methodology (see the recently proposed internet draft by Dang and Polk in [12]) or by using a PRP in the counter mode.

1.3   HMAC as a Randomness Extractor

HMAC, as well as some other constructions, have been recently studied as randomness extractors by Dodis *et al.* in [15]. This is the first formal analysis of practical randomness extractors. They namely prove that variants of these constructions are almost universal hash functions under various assumptions. They basically show how to construct a variable-input length almost universal hash function family from a fixed-input length almost universal hash function family (or even random functions/permutations). Thereafter, a little modification of the Leftover Hash Lemma (LHL) [20] with a *randomly chosen function* from a family of (almost) universal hash functions can be used to extract the entropy of a random source.

Therefore, if the key of the (almost) universal hash function is correctly chosen (not biased by the adversary), the whole construction is correct. But the latter remark is important and not trivial in practice, since this key is not always (cannot always be) authenticated [10]. Finally, although this solution can be proven in the standard model, it is overkill compared with our solutions.

1.4   Randomness Extractors

The notion of a randomness extractor is thus very important from a practical point of view and is often ignored or misused by cryptographers, since solutions are quite theoretical and requirements are strong.

In complexity theory, randomness extraction from a distribution has been extensively studied (see [28] for a survey). For certain random sources, it has been shown that it is impossible to extract even one bit of randomness [26]. One way to solve this last problem is to use a small number of uniformly random bits as a *catalyst* in addition to the bits from the weak random source as in the LHL as said in [23]. However, in some cases, we can eliminate the need for the random catalyst by restricting the class of weak random sources. Trevisan and Vadhan and later Dodis [35, 14] have called such functions *deterministic extractors*. In cryptography, randomness extractors have been studied under different adversaries to construct truly random generators [3], and deterministic extractors have been used to built All-Or-Nothing-Transforms (AONTs) schemes and Exposure-Resilient Functions (ERF) [9, 16].

In the key exchange setting, the problem is to transform the random common secret of small entropy rate into a common secret of entropy rate 1, where the entropy rate is the ratio k/n of a random source of block-length n and of min-entropy k (basically the number of random bits). For example, under the DDH assumption in a 160-bit prime order q subgroup in $\mathbb{Z}_p^\star$, we know that the input random source (in a DH-based key exchange protocol) has 160 bits of min-entropy. So, for a 1024-bit prime p, the entropy rate of the initial source is $160/1024$. Because of the specific structure of the source, deterministic extractors (which exploit the algebraic structure) may be used to derive cryptographic keys. They would avoid problems with probabilistic randomness extractors if the key of a universal hash function can be controlled by the adversary. On the other hand, as we will see, large groups may be required, which would make the overall protocol too inefficient. We will thus introduce a new technique to avoid extractors, which takes advantage of the specific structure of elliptic curves.

1.5   Contribution and Organization

In this paper, we first focus on various techniques to derive a uniformly distributed bit-string from a high-entropy bit-string source. We explain their advantages and drawbacks. Then, we apply Kaliski's technique [22], with quadratic twists of elliptic curves, to avoid them. It is quite well-suited to authenticated key exchange, since it already works on cyclic groups. Therefore, it is more efficient than the Leftover Hash Lemma while retaining the same security attributes (and namely, no additional assumption).

The basic idea is to run twice in parallel, an authenticated Diffie-Hellman protocol on an elliptic curve $\mathbb{E}$ and on the quadratic twist $\tilde{\mathbb{E}}$ of $\mathbb{E}$. This produces two points K and $\tilde{K}$ uniformly distributed on $\mathbb{E}$ and $\tilde{\mathbb{E}}$ respectively. With well-chosen elliptic curves, the random choice of the abscissa of either K or $\tilde{K}$ is an ℓ-bit long random string. Randomness extractors are thus not needed anymore.

This "Twist AUgmented" (TAU) technique is provably secure assuming only the intractability of the decisional Diffie-Hellman problem on elliptic curves.

Even though quadratic twists were previously introduced in the literature [7, 8] in other contexts or with binary curves, we also show here that appropriate prime order curves can be efficiently generated.

2   The Leftover Hash Lemma

In this section, we focus on the most well-known randomness extractor, which makes use of the Leftover Hash Lemma [21, 20]. It provides a probabilistic extractor, which is optimal in general. Whereas in theory, (almost) universal hash functions (AUH) should be used, in practice, one often asks for pseudo-random functions (PRF). Let us see whether the practical way to do it is correct or not, from a theoretical point of view. The definitions are given in the full version [11].

Lemma 1 (LHL [21]). *Let $\mathcal{D}$ be a probabilistic distribution over $\{0,1\}^n$ with min-entropy at least σ. Let e be an integer and $m = \sigma - 2e$. Let $\mathcal{H} = \{h_k\}_k$, with $h_k \in \mathcal{F}_{n,m}$ for any $k \in \{0,1\}^\ell$, be an almost universal hash function family. Let H be a random variable uniformly distributed on $\mathcal{H}$, X denotes a random variable taking value in $\{0,1\}^n$, and H, X are independent. Then, $(H, H(X))$ is $2^{-(e+1)}$-uniform on $\mathcal{H} \times \{0,1\}^m$.*

Impagliazzo and Zuckerman in [21] prove the lemma with an almost universal hash function where $\varepsilon = 1/2^n$. In [15], it is proved for any ε-almost universal hash function family for $\varepsilon \ll 1/2^m$. See also [31] for a proof. Therefore, combined with the analysis of NMAC as an ε-AUH function, this may justify the design of IKE when HMAC is used under a specific assumption on the independence of the two keys in NMAC. We show in the following that the same result holds for some PRFs provided ε be taken into account to estimate the size of the output. However, we begin to prove a slight generalization of the LHL, similar to [15].

Lemma 2 (LHL with ε-AUH). *Let $\mathcal{D}$ be a probabilistic distribution over $\{0,1\}^n$ with min-entropy at least σ. Let e be an integer and $m \leq \alpha - 2e$ where $\alpha = \min(\sigma, \log_2(1/\varepsilon))$. Let $\mathcal{H} = \{h_k\}_k$, with $h_k \in \mathcal{F}_{n,m}$ for any $k \in \{0,1\}^\ell$, be a ε-almost universal hash function family. Let H be a random variable uniformly distributed on $\mathcal{H}$, X denotes a random variable taking value in $\{0,1\}^n$, and H, X are independent. Then, $(H, H(X))$ is 2^{-e}-uniform on $\mathcal{H} \times \{0,1\}^m$.*

Proof. The proof relies on two claims. The first one comes from [31]. It applies to a random variable X distributed according to a distribution $\mathcal{D}$, taking values on the finite set S and of collision probability $\kappa = \kappa(X)$. If X is δ-uniform on S, then $\kappa \geq (1 + 4\delta^2)/|S|$.

The second claim studies the collision probability $\kappa = \kappa(H, H(X))$ where H denotes a random variable with uniform probability on $\mathcal{H}$, X denotes a random variable on the set $\{0,1\}^n$, and H and X are independent. We can easily adapt the proof of [31] to prove that the statistical distance between the distribution of $(H, H(X))$ and the uniform distribution on $\mathcal{H} \times \{0,1\}^m$ is δ, which is at most $(1/2) \cdot \sqrt{2^m \cdot (\kappa + \varepsilon)}$. So it can be upper-bounded by $(1/2) \cdot \sqrt{2^m \cdot (2^{-\sigma} + \varepsilon)}$, since the collision probability κ is less than the guessing probability γ as noted in [11]. If we denote by $\alpha = \min(\sigma, \log_2(1/\varepsilon))$, then we can upper-bound δ by $(1/2) \cdot \sqrt{2^m \cdot 2 \cdot 2^{-\alpha}}$ and so if we want a bias of 2^{-e} we need $m \leq \alpha - 2e$. $\square$

Remark 3. This requires $\varepsilon \ll 1/2^m$ as it is observed in [15], but $\varepsilon \leq 1/2^{m+2e}$ is enough. Anyway, this definitely excludes function families where the key-length is the same as the output-length (as compression functions), unless they are completely balanced, with $\varepsilon = 0$, which is quite a strong assumption.

2.1   Pseudo-random Functions vs. Almost Universal Hash Functions

We have already discussed the practical meaning of the universal hashing property for compression functions. However, many standards (such as IKE [18, 24]) use the acronym `prf` at several places, for different purposes: randomness extractors and actual PRF. Let us recall here the *crucial* difference between pseudo-random functions and randomness extractors: the former use random *secret* keys, while the latter use random *but known* keys. We thus show below that the *strong* assumption of PRF implies the almost universal hashing property. Therefore, the Leftover Hash Lemma 2 applied with some PRF (namely keyed with uniform random bit-strings and with advantage sufficiently small) provides a good randomness extractor.

Theorem 4. *If a family of functions $\mathcal{F}$ is a $(2, \varepsilon, 2T_f)$-PRF in $\mathcal{F}_{n,m}$, then it is an ε-AUH function family, where T_f denotes the maximal time to evaluate an instance of $\mathcal{F}$ for all $x \in \{0,1\}^n$.*

Proof. We want to show that if the hash function family $\mathcal{F}$ is not $\varepsilon - $ AUH, *i.e.* there exist x, y such that $\Pr_k[f_k(x) = f_k(y)] > 1/2^m + \varepsilon$, then there exists an adversary against the PRF property with advantage at least ε.

Let us consider the following family of distinguishers, $\mathcal{D}_{x,y}$ for each pair (x, y) of elements in $\{0,1\}^n$. The distinguisher $\mathcal{D}_{x,y}$ queries the oracle (either f_k for a random k or a random function) to get $X = f(x)$ and $Y = f(y)$, and simply answers 1 if $X = Y$ and 0 otherwise.

Suppose that $\mathcal{F}$ is not an ε-AUH function family. It means there exists a pair (x, y) for which $\Pr_k[f_k(x) = f_k(y)] > 1/2^m + \varepsilon$. Let us consider the advantage of the corresponding distinguisher $\mathcal{D}_{x,y}$: if f is a truly random function in $\mathcal{F}_{n,m}$, the set of all functions from $\{0,1\}^n$ to $\{0,1\}^m$, then $\Pr[\mathcal{D}_{x,y} = 1] = 1/2^m$; if f is a randomly chosen f_k in $\mathcal{F}$, then $\Pr[\mathcal{D}_{x,y} = 1] > 1/2^m + \varepsilon$. As a consequence, the advantage of $\mathcal{D}_{x,y}$ is not less than ε, which is in contradiction with the above PRF property. $\square$

Therefore, we have the following corollary by combining lemma 2 with the previous theorem.

Corollary 5. *Let $\mathcal{F}$ be a family of functions in $\mathcal{F}_{n,m}$, and T_f denote the maximal time to evaluate an instance of $\mathcal{F}$ on any $x \in \{0,1\}^n$. If $\mathcal{F}$ is a $(2, \varepsilon, 2T_f)$-PRF, when applied on a random source with min-entropy at least σ, then it is a good randomness extractor, of bias bounded by $1/2^e$, as soon as*

$$m \leq \min(\sigma, \log_2(1/\varepsilon)) - 2e.$$

Remark 6. This result is not in contradiction with the example described in [15], since if $\varepsilon = 1/2^m$ with m bits of output, then clearly $\min(\sigma, \log_2(1/\varepsilon)) \leq m$. The above corollary just claims that the bias is less than 1. As a consequence, we cannot extract m bits.

2.2   The Leftover Hash Lemma in Practice

Even if there exist efficient universal hash functions, practitioners and designers usually apply pseudo-random functions, or HMAC, which are clearly less efficient than a simple linear operation. Anyway, a correct application would be valid in both cases (according to the analysis for HMAC [15] — incomplete because of the above problem with compression functions). However, the Leftover Hash Lemma requires the key of the function family to be uniformly distributed, which is not an easy task, since it may be (partly) chosen by a malicious user. This is the case in IKEv1 [18], for compatibility reasons, and thus nothing can be formally proved.

A simple way to guarantee such a uniform distribution is for the users to sign this key (as done in IKEv2). However, such a signature is not always possible, or available, according to the context such as in password-based authenticated key exchange.

Another solution to cope with the randomness extraction error is, as noticed by Shoup [31] and also by Barak *et al.* in [3], to use the same "certified key" or the same hard-coded key in the software. Indeed, they suggest an extension of the LHL which allows the derivation of many random bit-strings with a *unique random* key, and thus a *public and fixed* hash function. However, the quality of the extracted randomness decreases linearly with the number of extractions – due to the hybrid technique. Nevertheless, this is often the unique solution.

3   Deterministic Randomness Extractors

Other alternatives to the LHL are also available, namely when no certification is available, as in the password-based setting, by using deterministic randomness extractors. Several of them exist in the literature and have already been employed by standardization bodies to convert a random element of a group into a random bit-string as in [29].

3.1   Hash-Diffie-Hellman

The simplest one, and perfectly reasonable in practice, is the use of a cryptographic hash function. In the random oracle model [6], this gives a perfect random bit-string, under the so-called computational Diffie-Hellman assumption. In the standard model, a weaker assumption has been defined, the Hash Diffie-Hellman assumption [1, 17]. But this assumption is, in some sense, the assumption that a hash function is perfectly suited to this goal, while this is not the applications that designers of hash functions have in mind. Everybody may agree on the practical validity of such a construction, but it definitely requires non-standard assumptions, from a theoretical point of view. We would thus prefer to avoid this solution.

3.2   A Simple Deterministic Extractor

Basically, when we want an extractor of the entropy from a random (uniformly distributed) element in a cyclic group $\mathbb{G}$ of order q, a bijection from $\mathbb{G}$ to $\mathbb{Z}_q$ would do the job, since it would transfer the uniform distribution $\mathbb{G}$ into a uniform distribution in $\mathbb{Z}_q$ (an appropriate choice for q thereafter allows the truncation to the $\log q$-rightmost bits to get an almost uniformly distributed bit-string). Let us briefly review such a well-known bijection in the specific case where $\mathbb{G}$ is the group of the quadratic residues modulo p, for a safe prime p, close enough to a power of 2. This result is in the folklore, but some lemmas are useful for the following, we thus briefly review the whole technique.

Theorem 7. *There is an efficient bijection from a subgroup $\mathbb{G}$ of prime order q in $\mathbb{Z}_p^\star$ to $\mathbb{Z}_q$, when $p = 2q + 1$.*

Proof. Let us use a finite field $\mathbb{Z}_p$, with $p = 2q + 1$ (a safe prime) and work in the cyclic group of order q: the group $\mathbb{G}$ of the quadratic residues modulo p. Since $p = 3 \bmod 4$, this is a Blum prime, and thus -1 does not lie in $\mathbb{G}$.

We can define the following extractor, for any $y \in \mathbb{G}$: if $y \leq q$, then $f(y) = f_1(y) = y$, else $f(y) = f_2(y) = p - y$. Since -1 is not in $\mathbb{G}$, and $p - y = -y = (-1) \times y \bmod p$, f_1 maps $\mathbb{G}$ to $\mathbb{G}$ (the identity function) and f_2 maps $\mathbb{G}$ to $\mathbb{Z}_p \backslash \mathbb{G}$. Therefore, f is an injective mapping and for $y \in \mathbb{G}$, $f_1(y), f_2(y)$ are in $\mathbb{Z}_q$. A simple counting argument proves that this is a bijection.   □

The following lemma analyzes the security when truncation is used in order to get ℓ bits uniformly distributed. The proof of the lemma is done in the full version [11].

Lemma 8. *Let us denote by $\mathcal{U}_q$ the uniform distribution on the space $\mathbb{Z}_q$ and by $\mathcal{U}_{2^\ell}$ the uniform distribution on the space $\{0, 1\}^\ell \sim \{0, \dots, 2^\ell - 1\}$. If $|q| = \ell$ and $|q - 2^\ell| \leq 2^{\ell/2}$, then the statistical distance is bounded by $1/\sqrt{2^\ell}$.*

Therefore, the truncation of f gives a deterministic randomness extractor from $\mathbb{G}$ onto $\mathbb{Z}_q$. However, this requires the use of a safe prime, and thus quite large groups, which make DH-protocols quite inefficient.

4   The "Twist-AUgmented" Technique

In this section, we describe a new mechanism which excludes all the above drawbacks: it does not require any authenticated random value (needed for probabilistic extractors); it is provably secure in the standard model, under classical assumptions; it works in small groups (contrary to the above deterministic example.)

In the early 90's, Kaliski [22] used elliptic curves and their twists for making a random permutation from a random function. This construction can be used to make a uniform distribution in $\mathbb{Z}_{2q}$ from points uniformly distributed on a curve or its quadratic twist, both on the finite field $\mathbb{F}_q$. More recently, quadratic twists have also been used in the context of password-authenticated key exchange [8]. The goal was to make the Bellovin et al.'s encrypted key exchange protocol [4] immune to partition attacks but did not explain how to specify the key-derivation function. It has also been applied to the context of public-key encryption [7].

We can take advantage of elliptic curves and their quadratic twists, as done by Kaliski [22], to come up with a technique that does not require stronger assumptions. This technique, called "Twist-AUgmented" (TAU), uses the fact that a random point on a curve over $\mathbb{F}_p$ has an abscissa uniformly distributed in a set E and that a random point over its twist has an abscissa uniformly distributed in the set $\tilde{E}$ as well, i.e. it is the complementary set of E in $\mathbb{F}_p$. Therefore by choosing one of the two abscissae at random, we will get an element almost uniformly distributed in $\mathbb{F}_p$. For well-chosen fields, we thus efficiently get an almost uniformly distributed bit-string, which may be 256 bits long: it is enough to derive two keys (for privacy and for authentication) without any pseudo-random function by simply splitting this bit-string. As a consequence, it avoids the requirement of randomness extractors, and even pseudo-random functions, since we directly get a uniformly distributed *bit-string*, large enough.

4.1   Quadratic Twist of an Elliptic Curve

Let $p > 3$ be a prime number. An elliptic curve is a set of points $\mathbb{E} = \mathbb{E}_{a,b} = \{(x, y) : y^2 = x^3 + ax + b\} \cup \{\infty_{\mathbb{E}}\}$, where a and b are elements of $\mathbb{F}_p$ and $\infty_{\mathbb{E}}$ is a symbol for the point at infinity. It is well known that an elliptic curve $\mathbb{E}$ can be equipped with a group law —the so-called chord and tangent group law— such that the computational and decisional Diffie-Hellman problems are believed to be hard problems in general.

Let c be a quadratic non-residue in $\mathbb{F}_p$, and define the **quadratic twist** of $\mathbb{E}_{a,b}$ to be the curve given by the following equation: $\tilde{\mathbb{E}}_{a,b} = \{(x, y) : cy^2 = x^3 + ax + b\} \cup \{\infty_{\tilde{\mathbb{E}}}\}$.

The change of variables $x' = cx$ and $y' = c^2 y$ transforms the equation of $\tilde{\mathbb{E}}_{a,b}$ into $y'^2 = x'^3 + ac^2 x' + bc^3$. This demonstrates that $\tilde{\mathbb{E}}_{a,b}$ is isomorphic to an elliptic curve and can therefore be equipped with a group law. The main interest of the introduction of the quadratic twist here follows directly from the definition: if x is not the abscissa of a point of $\mathbb{E}_{a,b}$, then $x^3 + ax + b$ is not a square in $\mathbb{F}_p$ and therefore $(x^3 + ax + b)/c$ is a square in $\mathbb{F}_p$. Then it is the abscissa of a point of $\tilde{\mathbb{E}}_{a,b}$. The converse is also true.

Note 9. In the cryptographic application we have in mind, this is crucial to keep the equation of $\tilde{\mathbb{E}}$ in the non-Weierstrass form. For the internal computations, of course, we apply the above-mentioned transformation so that we can use the classical algorithms, but the result of any computation should be transformed back to the previous representation before usage in cryptographic primitives.

Cardinalities. Hasse-Weil's theorem gives a good bound on the group order of an elliptic curve [33]. Let us write $q = \#\mathbb{E} = p + 1 - t$, then we have $|t| < 2\sqrt{p}$. We could apply the same result to $\tilde{\mathbb{E}}$, but in fact the number of points of a curve and its twist are far from being independent. Starting with the fact that a scalar is either a point on $\mathbb{E}$ or a point on $\tilde{\mathbb{E}}$, it is easy to derive that $\tilde{q} = \#\tilde{\mathbb{E}} = p + 1 + t$. For maximal security, it is desirable that the group orders are prime numbers. Hence, since p is odd, this implies that t is odd. Then both q and $\tilde{q}$ are odd.

Choice of the Prime Field. We have restricted ourselves to curves defined over prime fields. The notion of a quadratic twist of an elliptic curve also exists for more general finite fields and in particular for fields of characteristic 2. However, they are of less interest in our context where we want to use the property that the abscissae of the points of the groups we are dealing with cover the whole finite field. In characteristic 2, all the non-super-singular curves have a group order that is divisible by (at least) 2. Hence keeping the covering property would imply to work with non-prime order groups. Even if it looks feasible to patch the protocol for that situation, it is certainly less elegant than using a prime-order group with curves over prime fields.

To achieve our goal, we need that the abscissa of a point taken randomly in $\mathbb{E}$ or in $\tilde{\mathbb{E}}$ behaves like a random bit-string of length ℓ. Since all the elements of $\mathbb{F}_p$ are obtainable as abscissae of points of $\mathbb{E}$ and $\tilde{\mathbb{E}}$, we will be able to show that the random abscissa in $\mathbb{E}$ or $\tilde{\mathbb{E}}$ gives a random element in $\mathbb{F}_p$ (see Lemma 10, the proof appears in the full version [11].) To convert this element to a bit-string of length ℓ without any further device and keeping the randomness unbiased, it is necessary to have p very close to 2^ℓ. Hence we propose to use a prime p which can be written $p = 2^\ell - \varepsilon$, where ε is an integer less than $2^{\ell/2}$ (see previous Lemma 8, which proof appears in the full version [11].)

This extra-condition on p is not a practical inconvenience. In fact, the primes that are used in practice are almost always of this form, because they allow a faster arithmetic than more general primes. For instance, the curves proposed by the NIST are defined over a finite field with primes which are often suitable to our case (the prime field, not the curves!).

Finding a Suitable Elliptic Curve and Twist. The basic approach for constructing a curve $\mathbb{E}$ over $\mathbb{F}_p$ such that both q and $\tilde{q}$ are primes is to pick random curves, count their cardinalities with the SEA algorithm, and keep only the good ones. With this strategy, if numbers of points were completely independent and behaved like random numbers in the Hasse-Weil interval, we would expect to have to have to build $O(\log^2 p)$ curves before finding a good one. If $\log p \approx 200$, it means that we have to run the SEA algorithm about 20000 times to construct a good curve, which is prohibitive.

Fortunately, the SEA algorithm [27] is suited for this kind of search, since it computes the order of $\mathbb{E}$ modulo small primes and recombines the group order by

Chinese Remaindering. Hence as soon as we know the order of $\mathbb{E}$ modulo a small prime ℓ, we abort the computation if this is zero. Furthermore, the group order of $\tilde{\mathbb{E}}$ modulo ℓ is readily deduced from $\#\mathbb{E} \bmod \ell$, and similar abortion can be played also with the twist. As a consequence, most of the curves are very quickly detected as bad curves, because either the curve or its twist has a non-prime group order.

In fact, the situation is more tricky, since the order of the curve and of its twist are not independent. For instance, imagine that $p \equiv 2 \bmod 3$, then the condition $\#\mathbb{E} \equiv 0 \bmod 3$ is equivalent to $t \equiv 0 \bmod 3$, which in turn is equivalent to $\#\tilde{\mathbb{E}} \equiv 0 \bmod 3$. A rigorous estimation of the running time of the SEA algorithm equipped with the early-abort strategy is out of the scope of this work. We just propose some numerical experiments to justify the claim that the construction of secure pairs of curve and twist is easily feasible on a reasonable computer.

We picked randomly about 30000 200-bit primes, and for each of them we picked a random curve and computed its cardinality and the cardinality of its twist. In the following table, we summarize the percentage of the curves for which both number of points are not divisible by all primes up to P_{max}.

P_{max}	1	2	3	5	7	11	13	17	19
remaining curves	100 %	33 %	12 %	7.2 %	4.9 %	3.9 %	3.3 %	3.0 %	2.7 %

From this data, we see that for 97.3 % of the curves, the SEA algorithm will be stopped at a very early stage, thus spending only a tiny fraction of the running time of the whole computation. With usual reasonable heuristics, it is expected that about 500 full computations are required on average before finding a good pair of curve and twist. A single full SEA computation takes about 20 seconds for this size on a personal computer, hence in about 3 hours, we expect to build good parameters for a key-size of 200 bits. An example curve is given in Appendix A.

If there is a need to construct the curves in a constraint environment, then it is probably a better idea to use the theory of Complex Multiplication. We will not give the details here, since the construction is well described both in the literature and in the standards. For our purpose, it suffices to choose a group order and a twisted group order which are both primes.

4.2   TAU Distribution

Now, we show that the distribution of the master secret key K, if we take it at random either on the curve $\mathbb{E}$ or $\tilde{\mathbb{E}}$, is uniformly distributed on $\{0,1\}^{\ell}$, in a statistical way. On the one hand, we prove that it is statistically indistinguishable from the uniform distribution on $\{0, \ldots, p-1\}$ and then that the latter distribution is statistically indistinguishable from the uniform distribution on $\{0,1\}^{\ell}$ by using lemma 8 by replacing q by p. The proofs of the following lemmas are done in the full version [11]. Let us denote by $\mathcal{D}$ the distribution of K:

$$\mathcal{D} = \{K = [\mathbf{R}_b]_{\mathsf{abs}} \big| b \xleftarrow{R} \{0,1\}, \mathbf{R}_0 \xleftarrow{R} \mathbb{E}, \mathbf{R}_1 \xleftarrow{R} \tilde{\mathbb{E}}\}$$
$$= \{K = x_b \big| b \xleftarrow{R} \{0,1\}, x_0 \xleftarrow{R} [\mathbb{E}]_{\mathsf{abs}}, x_1 \xleftarrow{R} [\tilde{\mathbb{E}}]_{\mathsf{abs}}\}.$$

Lemma 10. *The distribution $\mathcal{D}$ is statistically close to the uniform distribution $\mathcal{U}_p$ in $\mathbb{F}_p \sim \mathbb{Z}_p$:*

$$\delta = \frac{1}{2} \times \sum_{x \in \mathbb{F}_p} \left| \Pr_{K \overset{R}{\leftarrow} \mathcal{U}_p} [K = x] - \Pr_{K \overset{R}{\leftarrow} \mathcal{D}} [K = x] \right| \leq \frac{1}{\sqrt{2^{\ell-1}}}.$$

Corollary 11. *The statistical distance between the uniform distribution on $\mathcal{U}_\ell$ and the TAU technique if $|p - 2^\ell| \leq 2^{\ell/2}$, is upper bounded by $(1 + \sqrt{2})/\sqrt{2^\ell}$ according to Lemmas 10 and 8.*

Note 12. However, in an actual scheme, the bit b many not be perfectly uniformly distributed, but biased in a negligible way. Anyway, it will be important to show that such a bias will not impact much the distribution of the key (see the proof of Theorem 13.)

4.3 Working Using Abscissae Only

In the basic description, even if only the abscissa of a point is used at the end to derive the key, we worked all along with points on the elliptic curves. In fact, this is not necessary. Let $\mathbf{P}$ be a point on an elliptic curve, then to compute the abscissa of a multiple of $\mathbf{P}$, only the abscissa of $\mathbf{P}$ is required. This is a very classical result, that is used for instance in fast versions of the ECM factoring algorithm [25].

As a consequence, it is possible to improve the TAU protocol as follows (see figure 1): each time there is a point on a curve, we replace it by just its abscissa. In particular, now X_0, X_1, Y_0 and Y_1 are just elements of $\mathbb{F}_p$ which are abscissae of points on the curve or on the twist. We then denote by $x \circ X$ the abscissa of the point $\mathbf{Y}$ which is x times a point $\mathbf{X}$ whose abscissa is X. The space saving is tiny (namely just the one bit that was used to code the ordinate), but this has the advantage to put in light the fact that ordinate's role is irrelevant in the TAU protocol. Furthermore, this improves the time complexity by more than 30%, at least from Bob's view point. Indeed, while in the basic Diffie-Hellman protocol both Alice and Bob have to compute 2 exponentiations, in the TAU version, Alice has to compute 3.5 on average (an additional cost of 75%), and Bob still 2 only (just a negligible additional cost due to the computation with abscissae only.) The use of the 2 coordinates of the points would require an additional square root computation, and thus an exponentiation in the field. Such an operation is much less expensive than the computation of the multiple of a point in the curve, but its cost is not negligible.

Note that not all EC-based protocols can be transformed to work only with abscissae. For instance, El-Gamal signatures involve additions in the elliptic curve, and this cannot be done only with the input of abscissae of the points; only an exponentiation is feasible. TAU can use this improved technique.

4.4 Efficient and Unconditionally Secure Pseudo-random Functions

Roughly, our TAU technique runs twice the basic scheme (but with an actual cost of only 37% more), and provides a long bit-string which is uniformly distributed, under the Elliptic Curve Decisional Diffie-Hellman assumption. Such a long bit-string K allows an efficient and secure key re-generation, to get both a key confirmation k_m and a session/master key sk, without any additional assumption about pseudo-random functions: K can be simply split into k_m and sk, with convenient sizes.

For the same security level, the LHL would require a group of order around q^2, and thus with a complexity exactly twice as much as the basic scheme. With the above improved technique using abscissae, our technique does not double the whole basic scheme, but the complexity is just increased by a factor 1.38. We thus get an average improvement of 30% if we compare to the LHL.

5   The "Twist-AUgmented" Authenticated Diffie-Hellman Protocol

5.1   Description

Using the properties of "Twist-AUgmented" deterministic randomness extractor, we then convert any Diffie-Hellman-like protocol, which provides a random element in a cyclic group, into a protocol which provides a random bit-string, without any additional assumptions. See figure 1 for the description, which implements the above improvement using abscissae only.

5.2   Semantic Security

On Figure 1, we present the TAU-enhancement of a classical authenticated Diffie-Hellman key exchange: basically, some flows are doubled, on each curve. However, Bob randomly chooses the curve which will be used for the Diffie-Hellman computation, and compute correct values on this curve only. For the other part, he plays randomly. This protocol achieves the property of semantic security under the elliptic-curve decisional Diffie-Hellman assumption and does not use ideal-hash functions. In order to prove this claim (the full proof is postponed to the the full version [11]) we consider games that have distances that can be measured easily. We use Shoup's lemma to bound the probability of events in successive games [30, 32]. The first game $\mathbf{G}_1$ goes back to the less efficient, but equivalent, protocol using abscissae and ordinates, and the second game $\mathbf{G}_2$ allows us to avoid active attacks, granted signatures, so that in the following games we only have to worry about replay attacks. Proving the claim boils down to coming up with the appropriate games $\mathbf{G}_3$ through $\mathbf{G}_8$, in which we obtain a random master key K uniformly distributed in $\{0, \ldots, 2^\ell - 1\}$. The game $\mathbf{G}_9$, providing random session keys, is then easy to come up with and therefore the proof of the claim easily follows. In the last game $\mathbf{G}_9$, the adversary has indeed clearly no means to get any information about the random bit involved in the Test-query except to flip a coin.

Alice   *Bob*

Common twisted curves $\mathbb{E}_0, \mathbb{E}_1$ over the finite field $\mathbb{F}_p$
of respective prime orders q_0, q_1
$\mathcal{X}_i = [\mathbb{E}_i = \langle \mathbf{P}_i \rangle]_{\mathsf{abs}} = \langle P_i \rangle_{\mathsf{abs}}$, where $P_i = [\mathbf{P}_i]_{\mathsf{abs}}$, for $i = 0, 1$

Signing Key : sk_A Signing Key : sk_B
Verification Key : vk_A Verification Key : vk_B
accept $\leftarrow$ false   accept $\leftarrow$ false
terminate $\leftarrow$ false   terminate $\leftarrow$ false

$s \xleftarrow{R} \{0,1\}^\star, x_0 \xleftarrow{R} \mathbb{Z}_{q_0}, X_0 = x_0 \circ P_0$
$x_1 \xleftarrow{R} \mathbb{Z}_{q_1}, X_1 = x_1 \circ P_1$
$\sigma_A = \mathsf{AUTH.Sign}(\mathsf{sk}_A; (s, X_0, X_1))$ $\xrightarrow[\;X_0, X_1, \sigma_A\;]{Alice, s}$ Check σ_A
$\beta \xleftarrow{R} \{0,1\}$
$y_\beta \xleftarrow{R} \mathbb{Z}_{q_\beta}, Y_\beta = y_\beta \circ P_\beta$
$Y_{1-\beta} \xleftarrow{R} \mathcal{X}_{1-\beta}$
$K_\beta = y_\beta \circ X_\beta,$
$k_m = \mathsf{MacKey}(K_\beta)$
$\sigma_B = \mathsf{AUTH.Sign}(\mathsf{sk}_B; (s, X_0, X_1, Y_0, Y_1))$
Check σ_B $\xleftarrow[\;Y_0, Y_1, \sigma_B, \mu_B\;]{Bob, s}$ $\mu_B = \mathsf{MAC.Sign}(k_m; (\text{"1"}, s, Bob))$
$d \xleftarrow{R} \{0,1\}, K = x_d \circ Y_d$
$k_m = \mathsf{MacKey}(K)$
Try to check μ_B : in case of failure
$\quad d = 1 - d, K = x_d \circ Y_d$
$\quad k_m = \mathsf{MacKey}(K)$
Check μ_B
$\mu_A = \mathsf{MAC.Sign}(k_m, (\text{"0"}, s, Alice))$
accept $\leftarrow$ true $\xrightarrow[\;\sigma_A, \mu_A\;]{s}$ Check μ_A
accept $\leftarrow$ true
terminate $\leftarrow$ true   terminate $\leftarrow$ true

$\mathsf{sk} = \mathsf{SessionKey}(K)$
$\mathsf{sid} = s, Alice, Bob, X_0, X_1, Y_0, Y_1, \sigma_A, \sigma_B, \mu_A, \mu_B$

where $\mathsf{SessionKey}(K) = \mathsf{PRF}_K(0), \mathsf{MacKey}(K) = \mathsf{PRF}_K(1)$
$[\mathbf{R}]_{\mathsf{abs}}$ is the abscissa of the point $\mathbf{R}$ in $\mathbb{F}_p$
$x \circ P$ is the abscissa of x times a point $\mathbf{P}$ whose abscissa is P
and when a check fails whithout being caught, one stops the
execution: terminate $\leftarrow$ true

Fig. 1. An honest execution of the "Twist-AUgmented" Authenticated Diffie-Hellman protocol

Theorem 13. *For any adversary $\mathcal{A}$ running within time bound t, with less than q_s different sessions*

$$\mathsf{Adv}_{\mathsf{TAU}}^{\mathsf{ake}}(\mathcal{A}) \leq 4 \cdot \mathsf{Succ}_{\mathsf{AUTH}}^{\mathsf{euf-cma}}(2t, q_s, q_s) + 10 \cdot \mathsf{Succ}_{\mathsf{MAC}}^{\mathsf{euf-cma}}(2t, 1, 0)$$
$$+ 2 \cdot \mathsf{Adv}_{\mathbf{P}, \langle \mathbf{P} \rangle}^{\mathsf{ecddh}}(t') + 2 \cdot \mathsf{Adv}_{\mathbf{Q}, \langle \mathbf{Q} \rangle}^{\mathsf{ecddh}}(t')$$
$$+ 2q_s \mathsf{Adv}_{\mathcal{F}}^{\mathsf{prf}}(t', 2) + 20 \mathsf{Adv}_{\mathcal{F}}^{\mathsf{prf}}(2t, 1) + \frac{20 + 5q_s}{\sqrt{2^\ell}},$$

where $t' \leq t + 8 \times q_s T_m$, and T_m is an upper-bound on the time to compute the multiplication of a point by a scalar.

6   Conclusion

This paper presents a new technique in order to get an appropriate session key with Diffie-Hellman key exchanges. It provides the best efficiency, since it is more than 30% more efficient than using the Leftover Hash Lemma, while it does not require any authenticated randomness.

Acknowledgement

The work described in this paper has been supported in part by the European Commission through the IST Programme under Contract IST-2002-507932 ECRYPT. The first author is supported by the Director, Office of Science, Office of Advanced Scientific Computing Research, Mathematical Information and Computing Sciences Division, of the U.S. Department of Energy under Contract No. DE-AC03-76SF00098. This document is report LBNL-54709. Disclaimer available at http://www-library.lbl.gov/disclaimer.

References

1. M. Abdalla, M. Bellare, and P. Rogaway. The Oracle Diffie-Hellman Assumptions and an Analysis of DHIES. In *CT – RSA '01*, LNCS 2020, pages 143–158. Springer-Verlag, 2001.
2. B. Barak and S. Halevi. An architecture for robust pseudo-random generation and applications to /dev/random. In *Proc. of ACM CCS*, ACM, 2005.
3. B. Barak, R. Shaltiel and E. Tromer. True Random Number Generators Secure in a Changing Environment. In *CHES '03*, pages 166–180. LNCS 2779, 2003.
4. S. M. Bellovin and M. Merritt. Encrypted Key Exchange: Password-Based Protocols Secure against Dictionary Attacks. In *Proc. of the Symposium on Security and Privacy*, pages 72–84. IEEE, 1992.
5. M. Bellare, R. Canetti and H. Krawczyk. Keying Hash Functions for Message Authentication. In *Crypto '96*, LNCS 1109, pages 1–15. Springer-Verlag, 1996.
6. M. Bellare and P. Rogaway. Random Oracles Are Practical: a Paradigm for Designing Efficient Protocols. In *Proc. of ACM CCS*, pages 62–73. ACM Press, 1993.
7. B. Möller. A Public-Key Encryption Scheme with Pseudo-Random Ciphertexts. In *ESORICS '04*, LNCS 3193, pages 335–351. Springer-Verlag, Berlin, 2004.
8. C. Boyd, P. Montague, and K. Nguyen. Elliptic Curve Based Password Authenticated Key Exchange Protocols. In *ACISP '01*, LNCS 2119, pages 487–501. Springer-Verlag, 2001.
9. R. Canetti, Y. Dodis, S. Halevi, E. Kushilevitz and A. Sahai. Exposure-Resilient Functions and All-Or-Nothing Transforms. In *Eurocrypt '00*, LNCS 1807, pages 453–469. Springer-Verlag, 2000.
10. O. Chevassut, P. A. Fouque, P. Gaudry, and D. Pointcheval. Key Derivation and Randomness Extraction. ePrint Report 2005/061. Available at http://eprint.iacr.org/.

11. O. Chevassut, P. A. Fouque, P. Gaudry, and D. Pointcheval. The Twist-Augmented Technique for Key Exchange. Full version available at http://www.di.ens.fr/users/pointche/pub.php.
12. Q. Dang and T. Polk. Hash-Based Key Derivation. draft-dang-nistkdf-00.txt. Available at http://www.ietf.org/internet-drafts/.
13. W. Diffie and M. E. Hellman. New Directions in Cryptography. *IEEE Transactions on Information Theory*, IT–22(6):644–654, November 1976.
14. Y. Dodis. Exposure-Resilient Cryptography. *PhD Thesis*, MIT, August 2000.
15. Y. Dodis, R. Gennaro, J. Håstad, H. Krawczyk, and T. Rabin. Randomness Extraction and Key Derivation Using the CBC, Cascade and HMAC Modes. In *Crypto '04*, LNCS, pages 494–510. Springer-Verlag, 2004.
16. Y. Dodis, A. Sahai, A. Smith. On perfect and adaptive security in exposure-resilient cryptography. In *Eurocrypt '01*, LNCS 2405, pages 301–324. Springer-Verlag, 2001.
17. R. Gennaro, H. Krawczyk, and T. Rabin. Secure Hashed Diffie-Hellman over Non-DDH Groups. In *Eurocrypt '04*, LNCS 3027, pages 361–381. Springer-Verlag, 2004.
18. D. Harkins and D. Carrel. The Internet Key Exchange (IKE). RFC 2409, 1998.
19. J. Håstad, R. Impagliazzo, L. Levin, and M. Luby. A Pseudorandom Generator from any One-Way Function. *SIAM Journal of Computing*, 28(4):1364–1396, 1999.
20. I. Impagliazzo, L. Levin, and M. Luby. Pseudo-Random Generation from One-Way Functions. In *Proc. of the 21st STOC*, pages 12–24. ACM Press, New York, 1989.
21. I. Impagliazzo and D. Zuckerman. How to Recycle Random Bits. In *Proc. of the 30th Annual IEEE FOCS*, pages 248–253, 1989.
22. B. Kaliski. One-Way Permutations on Elliptic Curves. *Journal of Cryptology*, 3(3):187–199, 1991.
23. J. Kamp and D. Zuckerman. Deterministic Extractors for Bit-Fixing Sources and Exposure-Resilient Cryptography. In *Proc. of the 44th Annual IEEE Symposium on Foundations of Computer Science*, 2003.
24. C. Kaufman. The Internet Key Exchange (IKEv2) Protocol. INTERNET-DRAFT draft-ietf-ipsec-ikev2-17.txt, September 23, 2004. Available at http://www.ietf.org/internet-drafts/draft-ietf-ipsec-ikev2-17.txt
25. P. L. Montgomery. *An FFT Extension of the Elliptic Curve Method of Factorization.* PhD thesis, University of California – Los Angeles, 1992.
26. M. Santha and U. V. Vazirani. Generating quasi-random sequences from semi-random sources. In *J. of Computer and System Sciences*, 63:612–626, 1986.
27. R. Schoof. Counting Points on Elliptic Curves over Finite Fields. In *J. Théor. Nombres Bordeaux*, 7:219–254, 1995.
28. R. Shaltiel. Recent developments in Extractors. In *Bulletin of the European Association for Theoretical Computer Science*, Volume 77, June 2002, pages 67–95. Available at http://www.wisdom.weizmann.ac.il/~ronens/papers/survey.ps, 2002.
29. V. Shoup. A Proposal for an ISO Standard for Public-Key Encryption, december 2001. ISO/IEC JTC 1/SC27.
30. V. Shoup. OAEP Reconsidered. In *Crypto '01*, LNCS 2139, pages 239–259. Springer-Verlag, Berlin, 2001.
31. V. Shoup. A Computational Introduction to Number Theory Algebra. In *Cambridge University Press*, 2005. Freely available at http://www.shoup.net/ntb/.
32. V. Shoup. Sequences of Games: A Tool for Taming Complexity in Security Proofs. Available at http://www.shoup.net/papers/, 2004.
33. J. H. Silverman. *The Arithmetic of Elliptic Curves*, volume 106 of *Graduate Texts in Mathematics*. Springer-Verlag, 1986.

34. T. Dierks and C. Allen. The TLS Protocol Version 1.0. RFC 2246, January 1999. OpenSSL. version 0.9.7e
35. L. Trevisan and S. Vadhan. Extracting Randomness from Samplable Distributions. In *Proc. of the 41st Annual IEEE FOCS*, 2000.

A   An Example 200-Bit Pair of Curve and Twist

We give a pair of curve and twist suitable for implementing the TAU protocol. This curve was produced using the method sketched in Section 4.1. We choose a curve with $a = -3$, to allow the use of the fast projective group law.

Let $\ell = 200$, and let $p = 2^\ell - 978579$. Let b in $\mathbb{F}_p$ be given by

$$b = 386119362724722930774569388602676779780560253666503462427823.$$

The trace of the curve $\mathbb{E}$ of equation $y^2 = x^3 - 3x + b$, is

$$t_\mathbb{E} = -1864972684066157296039917581949.$$

Hence, the group orders of $\mathbb{E}$ and of its twist $\tilde{\mathbb{E}}$ are $p + 1 \pm t_\mathbb{E}$, which are both prime numbers.

Password-Based Group Key Exchange in a Constant Number of Rounds

Michel Abdalla, Emmanuel Bresson, Olivier Chevassut, and David Pointcheval

[1] Departement d'Informatique, École normale supérieure,
45 Rue d'Ulm, 75230 Paris Cedex 05, France
{Michel.Abdalla, David.Pointcheval}@ens.fr
http://www.di.ens.fr/~{mabdalla, pointche}
[2] Cryptology Department, CELAR, 35174 Bruz, France
Emmanuel.Bresson@polytechnique.org
http://www.di.ens.fr/~bresson
[3] Lawrence Berkeley National Laboratory, Berkeley, CA 94720, USA
OChevassut@lbl.gov
http://www.dsd.lbl.gov/~chevassu

Abstract. With the development of grids, distributed applications are spread across multiple computing resources and require efficient security mechanisms among the processes. Although protocols for authenticated group Diffie-Hellman key exchange protocols seem to be the natural mechanisms for supporting these applications, current solutions are either limited by the use of public key infrastructures or by their scalability, requiring a number of rounds linear in the number of group members. To overcome these shortcomings, we propose in this paper the first provably-secure password-based constant-round group key exchange protocol. It is based on the protocol of Burmester and Desmedt and is *provably-secure* in the random-oracle and ideal-cipher models, under the Decisional Diffie-Hellman assumption. The new protocol is very efficient and fully scalable since it only requires four rounds of communication and four multi-exponentiations per user. Moreover, the new protocol avoids intricate authentication infrastructures by relying on passwords for authentication.

Keywords: Password-based Authentication, Group Key Exchange.

1 Introduction

Motivation. Modern distributed applications often need to maintain consistency of replicated information and coordinate the activities of many processes. Collaborative applications and distributed computations are both examples of these types of applications. With the development of grids [12], distributed computations are spread across multiple computing resources requiring efficient security mechanisms between the processes. Although protocols for group Diffie-Hellman key exchange [5, 7, 6, 8] provide a natural mechanism for supporting these applications, these protocols are limited in their scalability due to a number

M. Yung et al. (Eds.): PKC 2006, LNCS 3958, pp. 427–442, 2006.

of rounds linear in the number of group members. An alternative is to use a protocol for group key exchange that runs in a constant number or rounds [11, 15, 16]. The two measures of a protocol's efficiency are the computational cost per member and the communication complexity (number of protocol rounds) of the given protocol. Since the Moore's laws has told us that computing power grows faster than communication power, it is therefore natural to trade communication power for computing power in a group key exchange protocol.

A password is the ideal authentication means to exchange a session key in the absence of public-key infrastructures or pre-distributed symmetric keys. In a group, the sharing of a password among the members greatly simplifies the setup of distributed applications [7, 11]. An example of distributed applications could simply be the networking of all the devices attached to a human. Low-entropy passwords are easy for humans to remember, but cannot of course guarantee the same level of security as high-entropy secrets such as symmetric or asymmetric keys. The most serious attack against a password-based protocol is the so-called *dictionary attack*: the attacker recovers the password and uses it to impersonate the legitimate user. The low-entropy feature makes the job of the attacker easier since the attacker (off-line) runs through all the possible passwords in order to obtain partial information and to maximize his success probability. The minimum required from a protocol is security against this attack.

Contributions. In the present paper, we study the problem of scalable protocols for authenticated group Diffie-Hellman key exchange. Many researchers have studied and found solutions to this problem in the context of a Public-Key Infrastructure (PKI), yet a (secure) solution had to be found in the context of a (short) password shared among the members of the group. Two attempts in this direction are due to Dutta and Barua [11] and to Lee, Hwang, and Lee [17]. Unfortunately, adding authentication services to a group key exchange protocol is a not trivial since redundancy in the flows of the protocol can open the door to different forms of attacks. In fact, in Section 3, we briefly describe attacks against the schemes of Dutta and Barua [11] and of Lee, Hwang, and Lee [17]. Then, in Section 4, we show how to add password-authentication services to the Burmester and Desmedt scheme [9, 10]. Our protocol is *provably secure* in the random-oracle [4] and ideal-cipher models [3] under the Decisional Diffie-Hellman assumption.

Related Work. Following the work of Bresson et al. on the group Diffie-Hellman key exchange problem [5, 7, 6, 8], several researchers have developed similar protocols but that run in a constant number of rounds. Katz and Yung [15] added authentication services to the original Burmester and Desmedt's protocol [9, 10]. Later, Kim, Lee and Lee extended the work of Katz and Yung to take into account the notion of dynamicity in the membership [16]. The problem of adding password-authentication services followed shortly after. In [7], Bresson et al. proposed the first solution to the group Diffie-Hellman key exchange problem in the password-based scenario. Their protocol, however, has a total number of rounds which is linear in the total number of players in the group. In [11, 17], two different password-based versions of Burmester-Desmedt protocol were proposed along with proofs in the random-oracle and ideal-cipher models. Unfortunately, the latter two schemes are not secure.

Outline of the paper. The paper is organized as follows. In Section 2, we recall the security model usually used for password-based group Diffie-Hellman key exchange. This model was previously defined in [7], but also takes advantage of [1]. In Section 3 we recall Burmester-Desmedt scheme and describe attacks against the schemes of Dutta and Barua [11] and of Lee, Hwang, and Lee [17]. In Section 4, we describe the mechanics behind our protocol. In Section 5, we show that our protocol is *provably-secure* in the random-oracle and ideal-cipher models under the Decisional Diffie-Hellman assumption.

2   Security Model

2.1   Password-Based Authentication

In the password-based authentication setting, we assume each player holds a password pw drawn uniformly at random from the dictionary Password of size N. This secret of low-entropy (N is often assumed to be small, *i.e.* typically less than a million) will be used to authenticate the parties to each other

Unfortunately, one cannot prevent an adversary to choose randomly a password in the dictionary and to try to impersonate a player. However such on-line exhaustive search (even if N is not so large) can easily be *limited* by requiring a minimal time interval between successive failed attempts or locking an account after a threshold of failures. Security against such active attacks is measured in the number of passwords the adversary can "erase" from the candidate list after a failure.

On the other hand, off-line exhaustive search cannot be limited by such practical behaviors or computational resources considerations. Hopefully, they can be *prevented* if the protocol is carefully designed and ensures that no information about the password can leak from passively eavesdropped transcripts, but also from active attacks.

2.2   Formal Definitions

We denote by $U_1, \ldots, U_n$ the parties that can participate in the key exchange protocol P. Each of them may have several *instances* called oracles involved in distinct, possibly concurrent, executions of P. We denote U_i instances by U_i^j. The parties share a low-entropy secret pw which is uniformly drawn from a small dictionary Password of size N.

The key exchange algorithm P is an interactive protocol between the U_i's that provides the instances with a session key sk. During the execution of this protocol, the adversary has the entire control of the network, and tries to break the privacy of the key.

Remark 1. In the "constant-round" protocols that we will study, simultaneous broadcasts are intensively used. However we do not make any assumption about the correctness of the latter primitive: it is actually a multi-cast, in which the adversary may delay, modify, or cancel the message sent to each recipient independently.

In the usual security model [7], several queries are available to the adversary to model his capability. We however enhance it with the Real-or-Random notion for the semantic security [1] instead of the Find-then-Guess. This notion is strictly stronger in the password-based setting. And actually, since we focus on the semantic security only, we can assume that each time a player accepts a key, the latter is revealed to the adversary, either in a real way, or in a random one (according to a bit b). Let us briefly review each query:

- Send(U_i^j, m): This query enables to consider active attacks by having $\mathcal{A}$ sending a message to any instance U_i^j. The adversary $\mathcal{A}$ gets back the response U_i^j generates in processing the message m according to the protocol P. A query Send(Start) initializes the key exchange algorithm, and thus the adversary receives the initial flows sent out by the instance.
- Test$^b(U_i^j)$: This query models the misuse of the session key by instance U_i (*known-key attacks*). The query is only available to $\mathcal{A}$ if the attacked instance actually "holds" a session key. It either releases the actual key to $\mathcal{A}$, if $b = 1$ or a random one, if $b = 0$. The random keys must however be consistant between users in the same session. Therefore, a random key is simulated by the evaluation of a random function on the view a user has of the session: all the partners have the same view, they thus have the same random key (but independent of the actual view.)

Remark 2. Note that it has been shown [1] that this query is indeed enough to model *known-key attacks* —where Reveal queries, which always answer with the real keys, are available—, and makes the model even stronger. Even though their result has only been proven in the two-party and three-party scenarios, one should note that their proof can be easily extended to the group scenario.

As already noticed, the aim of the adversary is to break the privacy of the session key (a.k.a., semantic security). This security notion takes place in the context of executing P in the presence of the adversary $\mathcal{A}$. One first draws a password pw from Password, flips a coin b, provides coin tosses to $\mathcal{A}$, as well as access to the Test^b and Send oracles.

The goal of the adversary is to guess the bit b involved in the Test queries, by outputting this guess b'. We denote the **AKE advantage** as the probability that $\mathcal{A}$ correctly guesses the value of b. More precisely we define $\mathsf{Adv}_P^{\mathsf{ake}}(\mathcal{A}) = 2\Pr[b = b'] - 1$. The protocol P is said to be (t, ϵ)-**AKE-secure** if $\mathcal{A}$'s advantage is smaller than ϵ for any adversary $\mathcal{A}$ running with time t.

2.3 On the Simplification of the Model

In previous models, Execute queries were introduced to model passive eavesdropping. However, they can easily be simulated using the Send queries. In our analysis, we refine the way to deal with the adversary possible behaviors. We will denote by q_{active} the number of messages the adversary produced by himself (thus without including those he has just forwarded). This number upper-bounds the number of on-line "tests" the adversary performs to guess the password. And we denote by q_{session} the total number of sessions the adversary has initiated: nq_{session}, where n is the size of the group, upper-bounds the total number of messages the adversary has sent in the protocol (including those he has built and those he has just forwarded). We emphasize that this is stronger than considering only Execute and Send queries: while being polynomially equivalent, the two models are not tightly equivalent, since the adversary does not need to know in advance if he will forward all the flows, or be active when a new session starts. Moreover, suppressing the Execute queries makes the model even simpler.

The best we can expect with such a scheme is that the adversary erases no more than 1 password for each *session* in which he plays actively (since there exists attacks which achieve that in any password-based scheme.) However, in our quite efficient scheme, we can just prevent the adversary from erasing more than 1 password for each *player* he tries to impersonate (we will even show our proof is almost optimal.)

3 Preliminaries

The best starting point for an efficient password-based group key exchange, and namely if one wants a constant-round protocol, is the scheme proposed by Burmester and Desmedt [9, 10] at Eurocrypt 94 and later formally analyzed by Katz and Yung in 2003 [15].

3.1 The Burmester and Desmedt Protocol

In the Burmester-Desmedt scheme, one considers a cyclic group $\mathbb{G}$ generated by g, in which the Decisional Diffie-Hellman (DDH) assumption holds. The protocol works as follows, where all the indices are taken modulo n (between 1 and n), and n is the size of the group:

- Each player U_i chooses a random exponent x_i and broadcasts $z_i = g^{x_i}$;
- Each player computes the $Z_i = z_{i-1}^{x_i}$ and $Z_{i+1} = z_i^{x_{i+1}} = z_{i+1}^{x_i}$, and broadcasts $X_i = Z_{i+1}/Z_i$;
- Each player computes his session key as $K_i = Z_i^n X_i^{n-1} X_{i+1}^{n-2} \cdots X_{i+n-2}$.

It is easy to see that for any i, we have $K_i = \prod_{j=1}^{j=n} Z_j = g^{x_1 x_2 + x_2 x_3 + \cdots + x_n x_1}$.

3.2 A Naive Password-Based Approach

We immediately note that encrypting values in the second round would lead to a trivial dictionary attack, since the product of all values is equal to 1. One may want to enhance the Burmester and Desmedt's protocol by using a password pw

to "mask" the first round only. One then comes up to the simple protocole, using a mask of the form h^{pw}, where h is another generator of the group $\mathbb{G}$, whose discrete logarithm in the base g is unknown [2]:

- Each player U_i chooses a random exponent x_i, computes $z_i = g^{x_i}$ and broadcasts $z_i^\star = z_i h^{pw}$;
- Each player extracts z_{i-1} and z_{i+1}, and computes the $Z_i = z_{i-1}^{x_i}$ and $Z_{i+1} = z_{i+1}^{x_{i+1}} = z_{i+1}^{x_i}$. He then broadcasts $X_i = Z_{i+1}/Z_i$;
- Each player computes his secret as $K_i = Z_i^n X_i^{n-1} X_{i+1}^{n-2} \cdots X_{i+n-2}$.

Thereafter, one can add any key confirmation and/or any intricate key extraction (even in the random oracle model, such as $sk_i = \mathcal{H}(\mathsf{View}, K_i)$), but it does not help. Indeed, the homomorphic property of this "masking" technique allows active attacks from the adversary: Assume that the adversary impersonates players U_1 and U_3 and sends for the first round $z_1^\star = g^{u_1}$ and $z_3^\star = g^{u_3}$, for known values u_1 and u_3. On the second round, the adversary waits for receiving X_2 from player U_2:

$$X_2 = \left(\frac{z_3}{z_1}\right)^{x_2} = g^{x_2(u_3 - u_1)} = \left(\frac{z_2}{h^{pw}}\right)^{u_3 - u_1}.$$

Then one knows that $h^{pw} = z_2/X_2^{(u_1 - u_3)^{-1}}$, which can be easily checked off-line: a dictionary attack.

Furthermore, one can be easily convinced that any mechanism such as proof of knowledge, commitments, etc. to "enforce" the adversary to properly construct his values are useless against this attack, since in the above attack, the adversary plays "honestly".

3.3   The Dutta and Barua Protocol

Dutta and Barua [11] proposed a variant of the Kim-Lee-Lee protocol [16] presented at Asiacrypt '04. It makes use of the ideal-cipher model, instead of a simple mask as above, and is claimed to be secure against dictionary attacks:

- Each player U_i chooses a random exponent x_i, as well as a random key k_i, computes $z_i = g^{x_i}$, and broadcasts $z_i^\star = \mathcal{E}_{pw}(z_i)$;
- Each player extracts z_{i-1} and z_{i+1}, and computes the $K_i^L = \mathcal{H}(z_{i-1}^{x_i}) = \mathcal{H}(g^{x_{i-1}x_i})$ and $K_i^R = \mathcal{H}(z_{i+1}^{x_i}) = \mathcal{H}(z_{i+1}^{x_i}) = \mathcal{H}(g^{x_i x_{i+1}})$. For $i = 1, \ldots, n-1$, U_i computes $X_i = K_i^L \oplus K_i^R$, while U_n computes $X_n = k_n \oplus K_n^R$; For $i = 1, \ldots, n-1$, U_i broadcasts $\mathcal{E}'_{pw}(k_i \| X_i)$, while U_n broadcasts $\mathcal{E}''(X_n)$;
- After decryption, they can all recover all the k_i, and then the common session key is set as $sk = \mathcal{H}(k_1 \| \ldots \| k_n)$.

Unfortunately, their protocol contains another source of redundancy that can be exploited by an attacker: the encryption algorithm of all users use the password as their encryption key. Therefore, a simple attack against their scheme runs as follows: the adversary plays the role of user U_3, with honest users U_1

and U_2. When the adversary receives $z_1^\star = \mathcal{E}_{pw}(z_1)$ and $z_2^\star = \mathcal{E}_{pw}(z_2)$, he sets $z_3^\star = Z_1^\star$, sends it to users U_1 and U_2, and waits for their responses. Note that setting $z_3^\star = Z_1^\star$ implicitly sets $x_3 = x_1$. At this point, the adversary knows that $K_2^L = \mathcal{H}(g^{x_1 x_2})$ and $K_2^R = \mathcal{H}(g^{x_2 x_3}) = \mathcal{H}(g^{x_1 x_2})$, and thus $X_2 = 0^k$ (where k is the output length of the function $\mathcal{H}$). Upon receiving $\mathcal{E}'_{pw}(k_2 \| X_2)$ from U_2, he can perform an off-line dictionary attack that immediately leads to the correct password, since this will be the only one decrypting this value to $k_2 \| 0^k$.

This confirms the fact that converting a provably-secure scheme into a password-based protocol is not a simple task. The main problem we observe with the above scheme is the unique way in which the initial messages of all users are encrypted, allowing attacks where one player can easily replay messages from another player. Thus, to avoid problems such as these, one should at least make sure that the encryption key used by each user is unique to that user. In fact, this is one of the features of the protocol that we present in the next section.

3.4 The Lee-Hwang-Lee Protocol

In [17], Lee, Hwang, and Lee proposed another password-based version of the Burmester-Desmedt protocol, which makes use of the random-oracle and ideal-cipher models. Let $\mathcal{E}$ be an ideal cipher and let $\mathcal{H}$ and $\mathcal{H}'$ be random oracles. Their protocol works as follows:

- Each player U_i chooses a random exponent x_i, computes $z_i = g^{x_i}$, and broadcasts $(U_i, z_i^\star = \mathcal{E}_{pw}(z_i))$;
- Each player U_i extracts z_{i-1} and z_{i+1}, computes $K_i = \mathcal{H}(z_{i+1}^{x_i}) = \mathcal{H}(g^{x_i x_{i+1}})$, $K_{i-1} = \mathcal{H}(z_{i-1}^{x_i}) = \mathcal{H}(g^{x_{i-1} x_i})$, $w_i = K_{i-1} \oplus K_i$, and broadcasts (U_i, w_i).
- Each player U_i first computes the values $K_j = \mathcal{H}(g^{x_{j-1} x_j})$ for $j = 1, \dots, n$, using the values w_j that were broadcasted in the second round. Next, each player U_i sets $sk = \mathcal{H}'(\mathcal{H}(g^{x_1 x_2}) \| \dots \| \mathcal{H}(g^{x_{n-1} x_n}) \| \mathcal{H}(g^{x_n x_1}))$ as the common session key.

To show that the protocol above is not secure, we present the following simple attack against the semantic security of the session key. First, we start two sessions with player U_1 using $\{U_1, \dots, U_4\}$ as the group. Let x_1 and x_1' be the corresponding values chosen by the two instances of player U_1 in each of these sessions and let $(U_1, z_1^\star = \mathcal{E}_{pw}(g^{x_1}))$ and $(U_1, z_1'^\star = \mathcal{E}_{pw}(g^{x_1'}))$ be the corresponding values outputted by these instances. For the instance that outputted $(U_1, z_1^\star)$, we provide to it the values $(U_2, z_1'^\star)$, $(U_3, z_1^\star)$, and $(U_4, z_1'^\star)$, as the first-round messages of players U_2, U_3, and U_4. This implicitly makes $K_1 = K_2 = K_3 = K_4 = \mathcal{H}(g^{x_1' x_1})$. Likewise, for the instance that outputted $(U_1, z_1'^\star)$, we provide to it the values $(U_2, z_1^\star)$, $(U_3, z_1'^\star)$, and $(U_4, z_1^\star)$, as the first-round messages of players U_2, U_3, and U_4. This implicitly makes $K_1' = K_2' = K_3' = K_4' = \mathcal{H}(g^{x_1' x_1})$. As a result, $w_1 = w_2 = w_3 = w_4 = 0$ and $w_1' = w_2' = w_3' = w_4' = 0$ and, thus, we can easily compute the appropriate second-round messages for players U_2, U_3, and U_4 in both sessions. Moreover, the session keys of these two sessions are the same. Thus, we can ask test queries to both instances of player U_1 and check whether we get back the same value. This should be the case whenever the output of test oracle is the actual session key.

4   Our Protocol

As above, we use the ideal-cipher model. The latter considers a family of random permutations $\mathcal{E}_k : \mathbb{G} \to \mathbb{G}$ indexed by a $\ell_{\mathcal{H}}$-bit key k which are accessible (as well as their inverses) through oracle queries ($\mathcal{E}$ and $\mathcal{D}$). Here we use the password, together with nonces, and the index of the user, to encrypt the values in the first round. Other values are sent in the clear. Also a preliminary round is used during which each player chooses random nonces to be used. This will be crucial to define sessions, and then link the encrypted values all together.

Key generations (for the symmetric encryption $\mathcal{E}$, and for the session key) will make use of hash functions $\mathcal{H} : \{0,1\}^\star \to \{0,1\}^{\ell_{\mathcal{H}}}$ and $\mathcal{G} : \{0,1\}^\star \to \{0,1\}^{\ell_{\mathcal{G}}}$. Key confirmations will apply the function $\mathcal{A}uth : \{0,1\}^\star \to \{0,1\}^{\ell_{\mathcal{A}uth}}$.

4.1   Description

The protocol runs as follows:

1. Each player U_i chooses a random nonce N_i and broadcasts (U_i, N_i);
2. The session $S = U_1\|N_1\|\ldots\|U_i\|N_i\ldots\|U_n\|N_n$ is then defined, in which each player has a specific index i, and a specific symmetric key $k_i = \mathcal{H}(S, i, pw)$. Each player U_i chooses a random exponent x_i and broadcasts $z_i^\star = \mathcal{E}_{k_i}(z_i)$, where $z_i = g^{x_i}$;
3. Each player extracts $z_{i-1} = \mathcal{D}_{k_{i-1}}(z_{i-1}^\star)$ and $z_{i+1} = \mathcal{D}_{k_{i+1}}(z_{i+1}^\star)$, and computes the $Z_i = z_{i-1}^{x_i}$ and $Z_{i+1} = z_i^{x_{i+1}} = z_{i+1}^{x_i}$. He then broadcasts $X_i = Z_{i+1}/Z_i$;
4. Each player computes his secret as $K_i = Z_i^n X_i^{n-1} X_{i+1}^{n-2} \cdots X_{i+n-2}$, and broadcasts his key confirmation $\mathcal{A}uth_i = \mathcal{A}uth(S, \{z_j^\star, X_j\}_j, K_i, i)$.
5. After having received and checked all the key confirmations, each player defined is session key as $sk_i = \mathcal{G}(S, \{z_j^\star, X_j, \mathcal{A}uth_j\}_j, K_i)$.

4.2   Security Theorem

Here we present the main security result of this paper, whose proof appears in Section 5.

Theorem 3. *Let P the above protocol in which the password is chosen in a dictionary of size N. Then for any adversary $\mathcal{A}$ running in time t, that makes at most q_{active} attempts within at most $q\mathsf{Session}$ sessions, his advantage in breaking the semantic security of the session key, in the ideal-cipher model, is upper-bounded by:*

$$\mathsf{Adv}_P^{\mathsf{ake}}(t) \leq \frac{2q_{\mathsf{active}}}{N} + 4q_{\mathsf{session}} n \mathsf{Adv}_{\mathbb{G}}^{\mathsf{ddh}}(t) + \frac{2q_{\mathcal{G}}^2}{2^{\ell_{\mathcal{G}}}} + \frac{2q_{\mathcal{A}uth}^2}{2^{\ell_{\mathcal{A}uth}}}$$

$$+ \frac{8q_{\mathcal{G}} + 2q_{\mathcal{A}uth} + 2q_{\mathcal{D}} + 2nq_{\mathcal{E}}q_{\mathsf{session}} + (q_{\mathcal{E}} + q_{\mathcal{D}})^2}{|\mathbb{G}|} + \frac{2q_{\mathcal{H}}(q_{\mathcal{H}} + q_{\mathcal{D}})}{2^{\ell_{\mathcal{H}}}}$$

where $q_{\mathcal{G}}, q_{\mathcal{H}}, q_{\mathcal{A}uth}, q_{\mathcal{E}}, q_{\mathcal{D}}$ denote the number of oracle queries the adversary is allowed to make to the random oracles $\mathcal{G}$, $\mathcal{H}$ and $\mathcal{A}uth$, and to the ideal-cipher oracles $\mathcal{E}$ and $\mathcal{D}$, respectively.

This theorem states that the security of the session key is protected against dictionary attacks: the advantage of the adversary essentially grows linearly with the number of *active attempts* that the adversary makes (i.e., the number of messages that the adversary builds by himself). While the number of *sessions* includes both active attacks and passive ones (i.e., the session transcripts $\mathcal{A}$ passively eavesdropped), the theorem shows that these passive attacks are essentially negligible: a honest transcript does not help a computationally bounded adversary in guessing the password.

4.3   On the Tightness of Theorem 3

Clearly, Theorem 3 ensures that when building a message by himself, the adversary cannot "test" more than one password per message. Actually, in the proof, we use q_{active} to upper-bound the number of players the adversary tries to impersonate and thus the number of different passwords he can inject. Hence, we achieve a stronger security result than the one claimed in Theorem 3. However, it leaves open the possibility of whether an adversary can test several passwords in the same session. Since one may wonder whether a security proof with a tighter reduction could be found, here we present an online dictionary attack against our scheme that shows that this is not the case. More precisely, we exhibit an online dictionary attack in which the adversary can test several passwords in the same session (but still no more than one password for each message!). The idea behind the attack is to create a session in which the number of dishonest players (whose roles are played by the adversary) is twice the number of honest players and to surround each of the honest players with two dishonest players.

Let k be the number of honest players. The attack works as follows. First, the adversary starts a session in which all the honest players have indices of the form $3(i-1)+2$ for $i = 1, \ldots, k$. Then, let $\{pw_1, \ldots, pw_k\}$ be a list of candidate passwords that an adversary wants to try and let $i' = 3(i-1)$. To test whether pw_i for $i = 1, \ldots, k$ is the correct password, the adversary plays the role of players $U_{i'+1}$ and $U_{i'+3}$ and follows the protocol using pw_i as the password. That is, he chooses random exponents $x_{i'+1}$ and $x_{i'+3}$, computes the values $z_{i'+1} = g^{x_{i'+1}}$ and $z_{i'+3} = g^{x_{i'+3}}$, and then computes $z^{\star}_{i'+1}$ and $z^{\star}_{i'+3}$ from $z_{i'+1}$ and $z_{i'+3}$ using pw_i as the password. Let $X_{i'+2}$ be the value that the honest user $U_{i'+2}$ outputs in the third round of our protocol. To verify if his guess pw_i for the password is the correct one, the adversary computes $z_{i'+2}$ from $z^{\star}_{i'+2}$ using pw_i as the password and checks whether $z_{i'+2}^{x_{i'+3}-x_{i'+1}} = X_{i'+2}$. This should be the case whenever pw_i is equal to the actual password.

4.4   Computational Assumptions

Decisional Diffie-Hellman assumption (DDH). The DDH assumption states (roughly) that the distributions (g^u, g^v, g^{uv}) and (g^u, g^v, g^w) are computationally indistinguishable when u, v, w are indices chosen uniformly at random. This can be made more precise by defining two experiments, $\mathsf{DDH}^{\star}$ and $\mathsf{DDH}^{\$}$.

In experiment $\mathsf{DDH}^\star$, the inputs given to the adversary are $U = g^u$, $V = g^v$, and $W = g^{uv}$, where u and v are two random indices. In experiment $\mathsf{DDH}^\$$, the inputs given to the adversary are $U = g^u$, $V = g^v$, and $W = g^w$, where u, v, and w are random indices. The goal of the adversary is to guess a bit indicating the experiment he thinks he is in. A (t, ϵ)-distinguisher against DDH for $\mathbb{G}$ is a probabilistic Turing machine Δ with time-complexity t, which is able to distinguish these two distributions with an advantage $\mathsf{Adv}_\mathbb{G}^{\mathsf{ddh}}(\Delta)$ greater than ϵ. The **advantage function** $\mathsf{Adv}_\mathbb{G}^{\mathsf{ddh}}(t)$ for the group $\mathbb{G}$ is then defined as the maximum value of $\mathsf{Adv}_\mathbb{G}^{\mathsf{ddh}}(\Delta)$ over all Δ with time-complexity at most t.

Parallel Decisional Diffie-Hellman assumption (PDDH). We define a variant of the DDH problem, we name it the *Parallel Decisional Diffie-Hellman* problem, which is equivalent to the usual DDH problem. To this aim, we define the two following distributions:

$$\mathsf{PDH}_n^\star = \{g^{x_1}, \ldots, g^{x_n}, g^{x_1 x_2}, \ldots, g^{x_{n-1} x_n}, g^{x_n x_1} \mid x_1, \ldots, x_n \in_R \mathbb{Z}_q\},$$

$$\mathsf{PDH}_n^\$ = \{g^{x_1}, \ldots, g^{x_n}, g^{y_1}, \ldots, g^{y_n} \mid x_1, \ldots, x_n, y_1, \ldots, y_n \in_R \mathbb{Z}_q\}.$$

A (t, ϵ)-distinguisher against PDDH_n for $\mathbb{G}$ is a probabilistic Turing machine Δ with time-complexity t, which is able to distinguish these two distributions with an advantage $\mathsf{Adv}_\mathbb{G}^{\mathsf{pddh}_n}(\Delta)$ greater than ϵ. The **advantage function** $\mathsf{Adv}_\mathbb{G}^{\mathsf{pddh}_n}(t)$ for the group $\mathbb{G}$, is then defined as the maximum value of $\mathsf{Adv}_\mathbb{G}^{\mathsf{pddh}_n}(\Delta)$ over all Δ with time-complexity at most t.

Lemma 4 (Equivalence between PDDH_n and DDH). *For any group $\mathbb{G}$ and any integer n, the PDDH_n and the DDH problems are equivalent: for any time bound T,*

$$\mathsf{Adv}_\mathbb{G}^{\mathsf{ddh}}(T) \leq \mathsf{Adv}_\mathbb{G}^{\mathsf{pddh}_n}(T) \leq n \, \mathsf{Adv}_\mathbb{G}^{\mathsf{ddh}}(T).$$

Proof. We omit the proof of this lemma in this version of the paper as it follows from a standard hybrid argument [13, 14] with $n+1$ hybrid experiments, in which the first i DDH values are replaced by random ones in the i-th hybrid experiment for $i \in \{0, \ldots, n\}$. In fact, a proof of this lemma was implicitly made in the proceedings version of the paper by Katz and Yung in Crypto 2003 [15] when showing an upper bound for the probability distance between the experiments Fake_n and Real. Moreover, in the full version of their paper, they provide an even tighter security reduction between these two problems.

In our security analysis, we will need a challenger that outputs a new tuple either from $\mathsf{PDH}_n^\star$ or $\mathsf{PDH}_n^\$$, according to an input bit. That is, we have a fixed bit β, and for any new query S, $\mathsf{Chall}^\beta(S)$ outputs a new tuple from $\mathsf{PDH}_n^\star$ if $\beta = 0$, or from $\mathsf{PDH}_n^\$$ if $\beta = 1$. If the same S is queried again, then the same output tuple is returned. It is a well-known result that after q queries to the challenger, any adversary in time t cannot guess the bit β with advantage larger than $q \times \mathsf{Adv}_\mathbb{G}^{\mathsf{pddh}_n}(t) \leq qn \times \mathsf{Adv}_\mathbb{G}^{\mathsf{ddh}}(t)$.

5   Proof of Theorem 3

We proceed by defining several experiments (or *games*), the first one being the real-world experiment (in which the success of the adversary in outputting $b' = b$ — denoted by event S — is larger than $(1 + \mathsf{Adv}^{\mathsf{ake}}(\mathcal{A}))/2$ by definition), the last one being a *trivially secure* experiment in which the success of the adversary is straightforwardly $1/2$.

Game $\mathbf{G}_0$: This is the real attack game, in the random-oracle and ideal-cipher models.

Game $\mathbf{G}_1$: We simulate the random oracles $\mathcal{G}$, $\mathcal{H}$ and $\mathcal{A}uth$ in a classical way using the lists $\Lambda_{\mathcal{G}}$, $\Lambda_{\mathcal{H}}$ and $\Lambda_{\mathcal{A}uth}$, with a random value for any new query, and we cancel executions (by halting the simulation and declaring the adversary successful) in which a collision occurs in the output of hash functions. The probability of such bad event is upper-bounded by the birthday paradox.

$$| \Pr[\mathsf{S}_1] - \Pr[\mathsf{S}_0]| \leq \frac{q_{\mathcal{G}}^2}{2^{\ell_{\mathcal{G}}}} + \frac{q_{\mathcal{H}}^2}{2^{\ell_{\mathcal{H}}}} + \frac{q_{\mathcal{A}uth}^2}{2^{\ell_{\mathcal{A}uth}}}.$$

Game $\mathbf{G}_2$: In this game, we start to control the simulation of the ideal cipher by maintaining a list Λ that keeps track of the previous queries-answers and that links each query to a specific user. Members of the list Λ are of the form $(type, S, i, \alpha, k, z, z^{\star})$, where $type \in \{\mathsf{enc}, \mathsf{dec}\}$. Such record means that $\mathcal{E}_k(z) = z^{\star}$, and $type$ indicates which kind of queries generated the record. The index i indicates which player is associated with the key k, while S indicates the session with which we are dealing. These values are both set to $\bot$ if k does not come from a $\mathcal{H}$ query of the form $(S, i, *)$ with $i \in \{1, \ldots, n\}$, and S of any form. The element α will be explained later.

- On encryption query $\mathcal{E}_k(z)$, we look for a record $(\cdot, \cdot, \cdot, \cdot, k, z, *)$ in Λ. If such a record exists, we return its last component. Otherwise, we choose uniformly at random $z^{\star} \in \mathbb{G}$, add $(\mathsf{enc}, \bot, \bot, \bot, k, z, z^{\star})$ to Λ, and return $z^{\star}$.
- On decryption query $\mathcal{D}_k(z^{\star})$, we look for a record $(\cdot, \cdot, \cdot, \cdot, k, *, z^{\star})$ in Λ. If such a record exists, we return its sixth component. Otherwise, we distinguish two sub-cases, by looking up in Λ_H if k has been returned to a hash query of the form $(S, i, *)$: if it the case, we choose z at random in $\mathbb{G}^{\star} = \mathbb{G}\backslash\{0\}$ and update the list Λ with $(\mathsf{dec}, S, i, \bot, k, z, z^{\star})$; otherwise, we choose z at random in $\mathbb{G}^{\star}$ and update the list Λ with $(\mathsf{dec}, \bot, \bot, \bot, k, z, z^{\star})$. In both cases, the decryption query on $z^{\star}$ is answered with z.

Such a simulation is perfect, except for the following three points. First, collisions may appear that contradict the permutation property of the ideal-cipher: the probability can be upper-bounded by $(q_{\mathcal{E}} + q_{\mathcal{D}})^2/2|\mathbb{G}|$. Second, we avoided z being equal to 1 in the decryption queries. Finally, in the case of the decryption query simulation, one will cancel executions (by halting the simulation and declaring the the adversary successful) if the value k (involved in a decryption query) is output later by $\mathcal{H}$. Fortunately, this happens with probability at most $q_H/2^{\ell_{\mathcal{H}}}$ for each decryption query. Intuitively, as it will become clear in the next games, we indeed want to make sure that, for any k involved in a decryption query, if k comes from a $\mathcal{H}$ query, we know the corresponding pair (S, i). All being considered, such bad events are unlikely:

$$\left| \Pr[\mathsf{S}_2] - \Pr[\mathsf{S}_1] \right| \leq \frac{(q_{\mathcal{E}} + q_{\mathcal{D}})^2}{2|\mathbb{G}|} + \frac{q_{\mathcal{D}}}{|\mathbb{G}|} + \frac{q_{\mathcal{H}} q_{\mathcal{D}}}{2^{\ell_{\mathcal{H}}}}.$$

Game G_3: In this game, we change the simulation of the decryption queries, and make use of our challenger to embed an instance of the PDH problem in the protocol simulation. In this game, we set $\beta = 0$, so that our challenger $\mathsf{Chall}^\beta(\cdot)$ output tuples $(\zeta_1, \ldots, \zeta_n, \gamma_1, \ldots, \gamma_n)$ according to the $\mathsf{PDH}_n^\star$ distribution. We use these $(2n)$-tuples to properly simulate the decryption queries.

More precisely, we issue a new tuple each time a new session S appears in a decryption query. But if several queries are asked with the same S, the challenger outputs the same tuple, so we will derive many related instances, granted the random self-reducibility. The latter tells us that, given one tuple outputted by the challenger, then for any randomly chosen $(\alpha_1, \ldots, \alpha_n)$, the tuple $(\zeta_1^{\alpha_1}, \ldots, \zeta_n^{\alpha_n}, \gamma_1^{\alpha_1 \alpha_2}, \ldots, \gamma_n^{\alpha_n \alpha_1})$ has the same distribution as the original one.

We make use of this property as follows, by modifying the first sub-case previously considered for *new* decryption queries.

– On a new decryption query $\mathcal{D}_k(z^\star)$, such that $k = \mathcal{H}(S, i, *)$ was previously obtained from $\mathcal{H}$ for some valid index i, we query $\mathsf{Chall}^\beta(S)$ in order to get a tuple $(\zeta_1, \ldots, \zeta_n, \gamma_1, \ldots, \gamma_n)$. We then randomly choose $\alpha \in \mathbb{Z}_q^\star$, add $(\mathsf{dec}, S, i, \alpha, k, z = \zeta_i^\alpha, z^\star)$ to Λ, and return z.

Above, we have defined the list Λ whose elements are of the form $(type, S, i, \alpha, k, z, z^\star)$. The component '$\alpha$' now comes into play. This element is an exponent indicating how we applied the random self-reducibility of the PDDH problem, to the instance generated by the challenger upon the request S: $X = \zeta_i^\alpha$. Here, the element α can only be defined if S and i are known (in order to know which tuple, and which ζ_i, we are working with.) If α is unknown to the simulator, we set $\alpha = \perp$.

This change does not modify the view of the adversary, so: $\Pr[\mathsf{S}_3] = \Pr[\mathsf{S}_2]$.

Game G_4: We are now ready to simulate the Send queries in a different way, but only in the second and third rounds: when the session S is defined, user i computes the symmetric keys as before $k_j = \mathcal{H}(S, j, pw)$, for all j. We thus know we are working with the tuple $(\zeta_1, \ldots, \zeta_n, \gamma_1, \ldots, \gamma_n)$.

In the second round, U_i randomly chooses a value $z_i^\star \in \mathbb{G}$ to be broadcasted, and asks $z_i = \mathcal{D}_{k_i}(z_i^\star)$, using the above simulation (which leads to add α_i to the list Λ, unless $z_i^\star$ already appeared as an encryption result. But the latter event cannot happen with probability greater than $q_{\mathcal{E}}/|\mathbb{G}|$.)

In the third round, U_i recovers $z_{i-1} = \mathcal{D}_{k_{i-1}}(z_{i-1}^\star)$ and $z_{i+1} = \mathcal{D}_{k_{i+1}}(z_{i+1}^\star)$. But then, two situations may appear:

– $z_{i-1}^\star$ and $z_{i+1}^\star$ have been simulated according to the above simulation of the second round, and then one gets α_{i-1} and α_{i+1} in the list Λ such that $z_{i-1} = \zeta_{i-1}^{\alpha_{i-1}}$ and $z_{i+1} = \zeta_{i+1}^{\alpha_{i+1}}$;

– one of the $z_j^\star$ has been previously answered by the encryption oracle in response to an attacker query $\mathcal{E}_k(z^\star)$, where $k = \mathcal{H}(S, j, pw)$ is the correct key for player U_j in session S. We denote such an event by Encrypt. In such a case, we stop the simulation, letting the adversary win.

If everything runs smoothly, one gets

$$z_i = \zeta_i^{\alpha_i} \quad z_{i-1} = \zeta_{i-1}^{\alpha_{i-1}} \quad z_{i+1} = \zeta_{i+1}^{\alpha_{i+1}}.$$

One can then correctly compute

$$Z_i = \mathsf{CDH}(z_{i-1}, z_i) = \gamma_{i-1}^{\alpha_{i-1}\alpha_i} \quad Z_{i+1} = \mathsf{CDH}(z_i, z_{i+1}) = \gamma_i^{\alpha_i\alpha_{i+1}}.$$

One then broadcasts $X_i = Z_{i+1}/Z_i$. After this final round, everybody can compute the session key as before. The simulation is still perfect, unless the above bad events happen:

$$\big|\Pr[\mathsf{S}_4] - \Pr[\mathsf{S}_3]\big| \leq \frac{q_\mathcal{E} q_{\mathsf{passive}}}{|\mathbb{G}|} + \Pr[\mathsf{Encrypt}_4] \leq \frac{n q_\mathcal{E} q_{\mathsf{session}}}{|\mathbb{G}|} + \Pr[\mathsf{Encrypt}_4].$$

Game G_5: Since it is clear that the security of the above scheme still relies on the DDH assumption, we now flip the bit β to 1, in order to receive tuples $(\zeta_1, \ldots, \zeta_n, \gamma_1, \ldots, \gamma_n)$ according to the $\mathsf{PDH}_n^\$$ distribution (in which the y_i's denote the values $\log_g \gamma_i$).

$$\big|\Pr[\mathsf{S}_5] - \Pr[\mathsf{S}_4]\big| \leq q_{\mathsf{session}} \mathsf{Adv}_{\mathbb{G}}^{\mathsf{pddh}_n}(t)$$

$$\big|\Pr[\mathsf{Encrypt}_5] - \Pr[\mathsf{Encrypt}_4]\big| \leq q_{\mathsf{session}} \mathsf{Adv}_{\mathbb{G}}^{\mathsf{pddh}_n}(t).$$

Game G_6: In order to stop active attacks, where the adversary forges flows, we modify the computation of the key confirmations: we replace the function $\mathcal{A}uth$ by a private one $\mathcal{A}uth'$: $\mathcal{A}uth_i = \mathcal{A}uth'(S, \{z_j^\star, X_j\}_j, K_i, i)$, where

$$K_i = Z_i^n X_i^{n-1} X_{i+1}^{n-2} \cdots X_{i+n-2} = \gamma_{i-1}^{n\alpha_{i-1}\alpha_i} X_i^{n-1} X_{i+1}^{n-2} \cdots X_{i+n-2}$$

$$= g^{n(\alpha_{i-1}\alpha_i y_{i-1})} X_i^{n-1} X_{i+1}^{n-2} \cdots X_{i+n-2}.$$

Let us list all the information a (powerful) adversary may have, from all the X_j sent by U_j in the S-th session:

$$\log X_j = y_j(\alpha_j\alpha_{j+1}) - y_{j-1}(\alpha_{j-1}\alpha_j) = A_j y_j - A_{j-1} y_{j-1}.$$

As explained in [15], this does not leak any information about y_{i-1}, since the above system contains only $n - 1$ independent equations with n unknowns. Any value for y_{n-1} is thus possible and would determine all the other values.

Therefore, after this modification, the probability for the adversary to see the difference between the current and the previous experiments is to query $\mathcal{A}uth(S, \{z_j^\star, X_j\}_j, K_i, i)$, which is upper-bounded by $q_{\mathcal{A}uth}/|\mathbb{G}|$.

$$\big|\Pr[\mathsf{S}_6] - \Pr[\mathsf{S}_5]\big| \leq \frac{q_{\mathcal{A}uth}}{|\mathbb{G}|} \qquad \big|\Pr[\mathsf{Encrypt}_6] - \Pr[\mathsf{Encrypt}_5]\big| \leq \frac{q_{\mathcal{A}uth}}{|\mathbb{G}|}.$$

Game G_7: Finally, we now derive the session keys using a private random oracle $\mathcal{G}'$: $sk_i = \mathcal{G}'(S, \{z_j^\star, X_j, \mathcal{A}uth_j\}_j)$. As above, after the modification of the derivation of the session key, the probability for the adversary to see the difference between the current and the previous experiments is to query $\mathcal{G}(S, \{z_j^\star, X_j, \mathcal{A}uth_j\}_j, K_i)$. Since the previous game, we know that inside each session, all the honest users have the same view, and thus theses queries are identical: the probability of such an event can also be upper-bounded by $q_\mathcal{G}/|\mathbb{G}|$, since no information has been leaked about K_i (except it does not correspond to the $\mathcal{A}uth$ queries asked above.)

$$\big|\Pr[S_7] - \Pr[S_6]\big| \leq \frac{q_\mathcal{G}}{|\mathbb{G}| - q_{\mathcal{A}uth}} \leq \frac{2q_\mathcal{G}}{|\mathbb{G}|}$$

$$\big|\Pr[\mathsf{Encrypt}_7] - \Pr[\mathsf{Encrypt}_6]\big| \leq \frac{q_\mathcal{G}}{|\mathbb{G}| - q_{\mathcal{A}uth}} \leq \frac{2q_\mathcal{G}}{|\mathbb{G}|}.$$

Furthermore, because the private oracle $\mathcal{G}'$ is private to the simulator, it is clear that

$$\Pr[S_7] = \frac{1}{2}.$$

Game G_8: In order to conclude the proof, we need to upper-bound the event $\mathsf{Encrypt}_7$. One can note that the password pw is only used in the simulation of the second and third rounds, to compute z_i, z_{i-1} and z_{i+1} (using the elements ζ_i, ζ_{i-1} and ζ_{i+1}), but eventually, we output X_i only, which are computed from the γ_{i-1} and γ_i. The latter is totally independent of the former.

We can thus simplify the simulation of the second and third rounds: In the second round, U_i randomly chooses $z_i^\star \in \mathbb{G}$, and sends it (this is exactly as before.) However no decryption is needed. In the third round, U_i simply computes and sends $X_i = \gamma_i/\gamma_{i-1}$ (this is just to make sure that the product of the X_i is equal to 1, but we just need random elements satisfying this relation, since they do not appear anywhere else.) This is a perfect simulation, since one does not need anymore to compute K_i.

At this point, the password is never used, and can thus be chosen at the very end only, which makes clear that probability of the $\mathsf{Encrypt}$ event is less than the number of first flows manufactured by the adversary, divided by N. The latter part is upper-bounded by q_{active}:

$$\Pr[\mathsf{Encrypt}_7] = \Pr[\mathsf{Encrypt}_8] \leq q_{\mathsf{active}}/N.$$

In the above, we used the fact that collisions in the output of $\mathcal{H}$ have been eliminated in previous games.

Putting all equations together, one easily gets the announced bound.

6   Conclusion

We described a constant-round password-based key exchange protocol for group, derived from the Burmester-Desmedt scheme. The protocol is proven secure against dictionary attacks under the DDH assumption, in the ideal-cipher and random oracle models. It remains an open problem to find a scheme whose security depends on the number of active sessions rather than on the number of manufactured flows.

Acknowledgements

The first and fourth authors were supported in part by France Telecom R&D as part of the contract CIDRE, between France Telecom R&D and École normale supérieure. The third author was supported by the Director, Office of Science, Office of Advanced Scientific Computing Research, Mathematical Information and Computing Sciences Division, of the U.S. Department of Energy under Contract No. DE-AC03-76SF00098. This document is report LBNL-59542. See http://www-library.lbl.gov/disclaimer.

References

1. Michel Abdalla, Pierre-Alain Fouque, and David Pointcheval. Password-based authenticated key exchange in the three-party setting. In Serge Vaudenay, editor, *PKC 2005: 8th International Workshop on Theory and Practice in Public Key Cryptography*, volume 3386 of *Lecture Notes in Computer Science*, pages 65–84, Les Diablerets, Switzerland, January 23–26, 2005. Springer-Verlag, Berlin, Germany.
2. Michel Abdalla and David Pointcheval. Simple password-based encrypted key exchange protocols. In Alfred Menezes, editor, *Topics in Cryptology – CT-RSA 2005*, volume 3376 of *Lecture Notes in Computer Science*, pages 191–208, San Francisco, CA, USA, February 14–18, 2005. Springer-Verlag, Berlin, Germany.
3. Mihir Bellare, David Pointcheval, and Phillip Rogaway. Authenticated key exchange secure against dictionary attacks. In Bart Preneel, editor, *Advances in Cryptology – EUROCRYPT 2000*, volume 1807 of *Lecture Notes in Computer Science*, pages 139–155, Bruges, Belgium, May 14–18, 2000. Springer-Verlag, Berlin, Germany.
4. Mihir Bellare and Phillip Rogaway. Optimal asymmetric encryption: How to encrypt with RSA. In Alfredo De Santis, editor, *Advances in Cryptology – EUROCRYPT'94*, volume 950 of *Lecture Notes in Computer Science*, pages 92–111, Perugia, Italy, May 9–12, 1994. Springer-Verlag, Berlin, Germany. http://www-cse.ucsd.edu/users/mihir.
5. Emmanuel Bresson, Olivier Chevassut, and David Pointcheval. Provably authenticated group Diffie-Hellman key exchange – the dynamic case. In Colin Boyd, editor, *Advances in Cryptology – ASIACRYPT 2001*, volume 2248 of *Lecture Notes in Computer Science*, pages 290–309, Gold Coast, Australia, December 9–13, 2001. Springer-Verlag, Berlin, Germany.
6. Emmanuel Bresson, Olivier Chevassut, and David Pointcheval. Dynamic group Diffie-Hellman key exchange under standard assumptions. In Lars R. Knudsen, editor, *Advances in Cryptology – EUROCRYPT 2002*, volume 2332 of *Lecture Notes in Computer Science*, pages 321–336, Amsterdam, The Netherlands, April 28 – May 2, 2002. Springer-Verlag, Berlin, Germany.

7. Emmanuel Bresson, Olivier Chevassut, and David Pointcheval. Group Diffie-Hellman key exchange secure against dictionary attacks. In Yuliang Zheng, editor, *Advances in Cryptology – ASIACRYPT 2002*, volume 2501 of *Lecture Notes in Computer Science*, pages 497–514, Queenstown, New Zealand, December 1–5, 2002. Springer-Verlag, Berlin, Germany.

8. Emmanuel Bresson, Olivier Chevassut, David Pointcheval, and Jean-Jacques Quisquater. Provably authenticated group Diffie-Hellman key exchange. In *ACM CCS 01: 8th Conference on Computer and Communications Security*, pages 255–264, Philadelphia, PA, USA, November 5–8, 2001. ACM Press.

9. Mike Burmester and Yvo Desmedt. A secure and efficient conference key distribution system (extended abstract). In Alfredo De Santis, editor, *Advances in Cryptology – EUROCRYPT'94*, volume 950 of *Lecture Notes in Computer Science*, pages 275–286, Perugia, Italy, May 9–12, 1994. Springer-Verlag, Berlin, Germany.

10. Mike Burmester and Yvo Desmedt. A secure and scalable group key exchange system. *Information Processing Letters*, 94(3):137–143, May 2005.

11. Ratna Dutta and Rana Barua. Password-based encrypted group key agreement. *International Journal of Network Security*, 3(1):30–41, July 2006. http://isrc.nchu.edu.tw/ijns.

12. Ian T. Foster and Carl Kesselman. *The Grid 2: Blueprint for a New Computing Infrastructure*. Morgan Kaufmann, 2004.

13. Oded Goldreich. *Foundations of Cryptography: Basic Applications*, volume 2. Cambridge University Press, Cambridge, UK, 2004.

14. Shafi Goldwasser and Silvio Micali. Probabilistic encryption. *Journal of Computer and System Sciences*, 28(2):270–299, 1984.

15. Jonathan Katz and Moti Yung. Scalable protocols for authenticated group key exchange. In Dan Boneh, editor, *Advances in Cryptology – CRYPTO 2003*, volume 2729 of *Lecture Notes in Computer Science*, pages 110–125, Santa Barbara, CA, USA, August 17–21, 2003. Springer-Verlag, Berlin, Germany.

16. Hyun-Jeong Kim, Su-Mi Lee, and Dong Hoon Lee. Constant-round authenticated group key exchange for dynamic groups. In Pil Joong Lee, editor, *Advances in Cryptology – ASIACRYPT 2004*, volume 3329 of *Lecture Notes in Computer Science*, pages 245–259, Jeju Island, Korea, December 5–9, 2004. Springer-Verlag, Berlin, Germany.

17. Su-Mi Lee, Jung Yeon Hwang, and Dong Hoon Lee. Efficient password-based group key exchange. In Sokratis K. Katsikas, Javier Lopez, and Günther Pernul, editors, *TrustBus 2004: Trust and Privacy in Digital Business, 1st International Conference*, volume 3184 of *Lecture Notes in Computer Science*, pages 191–199, Zaragoza, Spain, August 30 – September 1, 2004. Springer-Verlag, Berlin, Germany.

Conditional Oblivious Cast*

Cheng-Kang Chu and Wen-Guey Tzeng

Department of Computer Science,
National Chiao Tung University,
Hsinchu, Taiwan 30050
{ckchu, tzeng}@cis.nctu.edu.tw

Abstract. We introduce a new notion of *conditional oblivious cast* (COC), which involves three parties: a sender S and two receivers A and B. Receivers A and B own their secrets x and y, respectively, and the sender S holds the message m. In a COC scheme for the predicate Q (Q-COC), A and B send x and y in a masked form to S, and then S sends m to A and B such that they get m if and only if $Q(x, y) = 1$. Besides, the secrets x and y can not be revealed to another receiver nor the sender. We also extend COC to 1-out-of-2 COC (COC_2^1) in which S holds two messages m_0 and m_1, and A and B get m_1 if $Q(x, y) = 1$ and m_0 otherwise. We give the definitions for COC and COC_2^1, and propose several COC and COC_2^1 schemes for "equality", "inequality", and "greater than" predicates. These are fundamental schemes that are useful in constructing more complex secure interactive protocols. Our schemes are efficiently constructed via homomorphic encryption schemes and proved secure under the security of these encryption schemes.

Keywords: oblivious cast, conditional oblivious transfer, secure computation.

1 Introduction

Oblivious transfer (OT) is an important cryptographic primitive proposed by Rabin [18]. It involves two parties: the sender S and the receiver R, where S sends a bit of which R gets it with probability $\frac{1}{2}$. After Rabin's work, OT was developed in several types, such as 1-out-of-2 OT [11], 1-out-of-n OT [5, 16, 21], k-out-of-n OT [8, 14, 15], conditional OT (COT) [3, 10], etc. In Q-COT, S owns a secret x and a message m, and R owns a secret y such that R gets m from S if and only if the condition $Q(x, y)$ is evaluated as true.

Oblivious cast (OC) [12] is a generalization of OT to the three-party case: one sender S and two receivers A and B. The bit is received by exactly one of A and B, each with probability $\frac{1}{2}$. We generalize OC and introduce a new notion of *conditional oblivious cast* (COC), where A and B own their secrets x and y, respectively, and the sender S holds the message m. In a COC scheme for the predicate Q (Q-COC), A and B send x and y in a masked form to S, and

---

* Research supported in part by National Science Council grants NSC-94-2213-E-009-116, Taiwan, ROC.

M. Yung et al. (Eds.): PKC 2006, LNCS 3958, pp. 443–457, 2006.

then S sends m to A and B such that they get m if and only if $Q(x, y) = 1$. Furthermore, the secrets x and y can not be revealed to another receiver nor the sender. We also extend COC to 1-out-of-2 COC (COC_2^1) in which S holds two messages m_0 and m_1, and A and B get m_1 if $Q(x, y) = 1$ and m_0 otherwise.

There are two cases for the message receiving: A and B both get m, or only one of them gets m. The schemes we propose in this paper are all designed for the first case. However, in some applications only one receiver, determined by the condition, is allowed to get the message, and S can not know who gets the message. We have a general transformation of our COC_2^1 schemes to suit this kind of model (Section 4.3).

In this paper, we give the definitions for COC and COC_2^1, and propose several COC and COC_2^1 schemes for "equality", "inequality", and "greater than" predicates. These are fundamental schemes that are useful in constructing more complex secure interactive protocols. Our schemes are efficiently constructed via homomorphic encryption schemes and proved secure.

COC not only covers all functionalities of COT, but also broadens the range of its applications. We provide three examples:

- *Priced oblivious transfer*: Aiello et al. [1] introduced the notion of "priced oblivious transfer", which protects the privacy of a customer's purchase from a vendor. In their setting, the buyer needs to deposit an amount in each vendor. This is not very practical if a buyer wants to purchase various goods from many vendors. By using our COC schemes, we can construct a generalized priced OT such that the buyer can deposit the money in one bank only. When the buyer wants to buy an item from a vendor, he sends the corresponding price and the bank sends the buyer's current balance in the encryption form to the vendor. The vendor then sends the item such that the buyer can get it if the price does not exceed his balance.
- *Oblivious two-bidder system*: A party S has a secret for selling, and A and B are two bidders. The winner can obtain the secret from S directly. At the end, S has no idea who the winner is. This system can be constructed from COC for the "greater than" predicate (in the second message-receiving case) immediately.
- *Oblivious authenticated information retrieval*: A can get some information from S if he passes the authentication procedure provided by B. For instance, consider a mobile news subscription service provided by an independent agent. We assume that a mobile phone has no extra memory to store the subscription information but only an IMSI (International Mobile Subscriber Identity) in the SIM card. Users can pay the subscription fee to their mobile phone company, and the company provides an encrypted subscription list of IMSIs to the news provider. When a user wants to read news on the bus, his mobile phone sends the encrypted IMSI to the news provider. The news provider then sends news to the user if the IMSI is in the subscription list. In this case, the user's identity (IMSI) is anonymous to the news provider. The scheme can be constructed by COC for the "membership" predicate discussed in Section 5.2.

Related works. COT was first proposed by Di Crescenzo et al. [10]. In their definition of COT, the focus is to provide "all-or-nothing" transfer of the message from S to R by the condition. Blake et al. [3] strengthened COT to strong COT (SCOT), which provides "1-out-of-2" message transfer from S to R by the condition and adds more security requirements for S.

The notion of our COC is to separate the role of the secret holder from S. The main difference in design techniques is that, in COT and SCOT, the secure computation is done by S with a masked input and a plain input, whereas the secure computation in our COC and COC_2^1 is done by S with two masked inputs. A COC scheme that meets the requirements of our definitions can be easily transferred to a COT or SCOT scheme.

2   Definitions and Preliminaries

In this section we give formal definitions for COC and COC_2^1 and introduce useful tools and notations.

2.1   Conditional Oblivious Cast

Informally speaking, a COC scheme for predicate Q (Q-COC) has the following three properties:

- Correctness: both of A and B get m from S if $Q(x, y) = 1$.
- Sender's security: A and B cannot get any information about m if $Q(x, y) = 0$.
- Receiver's security: after running the protocol, x is kept secret from B and S, and y is kept secret from A and S.

The definition for Q-COC is as follows:

Definition 1 (Q-COC). *Let k be the security parameter, and A, B and S be all polynomial-time probabilistic Turing machines (PPTMs). Let $\langle A, B, S \rangle(\cdot)$ denote the communication transcript. We say that a three-party interactive system $\Pi = (A, B, S)$ is a secure Q-COC scheme if it satisfies the following requirements for some constant c:*

1. *Correctness: For any $x, y, m \in \{0, 1\}^{k^c}$ with $Q(x, y) = 1$,*
   $$\Pr[\mu \leftarrow \{0, 1\}^{k^c}; tr \leftarrow \langle A(x), B(y), S(m) \rangle(\mu) :$$
   $$\text{``} A(x, \mu, tr) = m \text{''} \wedge \text{``} B(y, \mu, tr) = m \text{''}] = 1.$$
2. *Sender's security: For any PPTM A', B' and any $x, y, m, m' \in \{0, 1\}^{k^c}$ with $Q(x, y) = 0$, A' and B' cannot distinguish the following probability ensembles with non-negligible advantage, respectively:*
   - $V_{A'B'}^\Pi = (x, \mu \leftarrow \{0, 1\}^{k^c}, tr \leftarrow \langle A'(x), B'(y), S(m) \rangle(\mu)),$
   - $R_{A'B'}^\Pi = (x, \mu \leftarrow \{0, 1\}^{k^c}, tr \leftarrow \langle A'(x), B'(y), S(m') \rangle(\mu)),$
   and
   - $V_{B'A'}^\Pi = (y, \mu \leftarrow \{0, 1\}^{k^c}, tr \leftarrow \langle A'(x), B'(y), S(m) \rangle(\mu)),$
   - $R_{B'A'}^\Pi = (y, \mu \leftarrow \{0, 1\}^{k^c}, tr \leftarrow \langle A'(x), B'(y), S(m') \rangle(\mu)).$

3. *Receiver's security:*

   (a) *For any PPTM A', B', S' and any $x, x', y, y', m \in \{0,1\}^{k^c}$ with $Q(x,y) = Q(x,y') = Q(x',y)$, S' cannot distinguish the following probability ensembles with non-negligible advantage:*

      $- V_{S'A'}^{\Pi} = (m, \mu \leftarrow \{0,1\}^{k^c}, tr \leftarrow \langle A'(x), B(y), S'(m) \rangle (\mu)),$

      $- S_{S'A'}^{\Pi} = (m, \mu \leftarrow \{0,1\}^{k^c}, tr \leftarrow \langle A'(x), B(y'), S'(m) \rangle (\mu)),$

     and

      $- V_{S'B'}^{\Pi} = (m, \mu \leftarrow \{0,1\}^{k^c}, tr \leftarrow \langle A(x), B'(y), S'(m) \rangle (\mu)),$

      $- S_{S'B'}^{\Pi} = (m, \mu \leftarrow \{0,1\}^{k^c}, tr \leftarrow \langle A(x'), B'(y), S'(m) \rangle (\mu)).$

   (b) *For any PPTM A', B', S' and any $x, x', y, y', m \in \{0,1\}^{k^c}$ with $Q(x,y) = Q(x,y') = Q(x',y)$, A' and B' cannot distinguish the following probability ensembles with non-negligible advantage, respectively:*

      $- V_{A'S'}^{\Pi} = (x, \mu \leftarrow \{0,1\}^{k^c}, tr \leftarrow \langle A'(x), B(y), S'(m) \rangle (\mu)),$

      $- S_{A'S'}^{\Pi} = (x, \mu \leftarrow \{0,1\}^{k^c}, tr \leftarrow \langle A'(x), B(y'), S'(m) \rangle (\mu)),$

     and

      $- V_{B'S'}^{\Pi} = (y, \mu \leftarrow \{0,1\}^{k^c}, tr \leftarrow \langle A(x), B'(y), S'(m) \rangle (\mu)),$

      $- S_{B'S'}^{\Pi} = (y, \mu \leftarrow \{0,1\}^{k^c}, tr \leftarrow \langle A(x'), B'(y), S'(m) \rangle (\mu)).$

2.2   1-Out-of-2 Conditional Oblivious Cast

In COC_2^1, the message sender S holds two messages m_0 and m_1. A Q-COC_2^1 scheme must satisfy the following three properties:

- Correctness: both of A and B get m_1 from S if $Q(x,y) = 1$, and m_0 if $Q(x,y) = 0$.
- Sender's security: A and B get exactly one message from S.
- Receiver's security: after running the protocol, x is kept secret from B and S, and y is kept secret from A and S.

The definition for Q-COC_2^1 is as follows.

Definition 2 (Q-COC_2^1). *Let k be the security parameter, and A, B and S be all PPTMs. Let $\langle A, B, S \rangle (\cdot)$ denote the communication transcript. We say that a three-party interactive system $\Pi = (A, B, S)$ is a secure Q-COC_2^1 scheme if it satisfies the following requirements for some constant c:*

1. *Correctness:*

   (a) *For any $x, y, m_0, m_1 \in \{0,1\}^{k^c}$ with $Q(x,y) = 0$,*

     $\Pr[\mu \leftarrow \{0,1\}^{k^c}; tr \leftarrow \langle A(x), B(y), S(m_0, m_1) \rangle (\mu) :$

                "$A(x, \mu, tr) = m_0$" $\wedge$ "$B(y, \mu, tr) = m_0$"$] = 1.$

   (b) *For any $x, y, m_0, m_1 \in \{0,1\}^{k^c}$ with $Q(x,y) = 1$,*

     $\Pr[\mu \leftarrow \{0,1\}^{k^c}; tr \leftarrow \langle A(x), B(y), S(m_0, m_1) \rangle (\mu) :$

                "$A(x, \mu, tr) = m_1$" $\wedge$ "$B(y, \mu, tr) = m_1$"$] = 1.$

2. *Sender's security: For any PPTM A', B' and any $x, y, m_0, m_1, m_1' \in \{0,1\}^{k^c}$ with $Q(x,y) = 0$, A' and B' cannot distinguish the following probability ensembles with non-negligible advantage, respectively:*

     $- V_{A'B'}^{\Pi} = (x, \mu \leftarrow \{0,1\}^{k^c}, tr \leftarrow \langle A'(x), B'(y), S(m_0, m_1) \rangle (\mu)),$

     $- R_{A'B'}^{\Pi} = (x, \mu \leftarrow \{0,1\}^{k^c}, tr \leftarrow \langle A'(x), B'(y), S(m_0, m_1') \rangle (\mu)),$

and
  - $V^{II}_{B'A'} = (y, \mu \leftarrow \{0,1\}^{k^c}, tr \leftarrow \langle A'(x), B'(y), S(m_0, m_1)\rangle(\mu))$,
  - $R^{II}_{B'A'} = (y, \mu \leftarrow \{0,1\}^{k^c}, tr \leftarrow \langle A'(x), B'(y), S(m_0, m_1')\rangle(\mu))$.
  The similar requirements is met $Q(x, y) = 1$.
3. *Receiver's security:*
   (a) *For any PPTM A', B', S' and any $x, x', y, y', m_0, m_1 \in \{0,1\}^{k^c}$ with $Q(x, y) = Q(x, y') = Q(x', y)$, S' cannot distinguish the following probability ensembles with non-negligible advantage:*
       - $V^{II}_{S'A'} = (m_0, m_1, \mu \leftarrow \{0,1\}^{k^c}, tr \leftarrow \langle A'(x), B(y), S'(m_0, m_1)\rangle(\mu))$,
       - $S^{II}_{S'A'} = (m_0, m_1, \mu \leftarrow \{0,1\}^{k^c}, tr \leftarrow \langle A'(x), B(y'), S'(m_0, m_1)\rangle(\mu))$,
       and
       - $V^{II}_{S'B'} = (m_0, m_1, \mu \leftarrow \{0,1\}^{k^c}, tr \leftarrow \langle A(x), B'(y), S'(m_0, m_1)\rangle(\mu))$,
       - $S^{II}_{S'B'} = (m_0, m_1, \mu \leftarrow \{0,1\}^{k^c}, tr \leftarrow \langle A(x'), B'(y), S'(m_0, m_1)\rangle(\mu))$.
   (b) *For any PPTM A', B', S' and any $x, x', y, y', m_0, m_1 \in \{0,1\}^{k^c}$ with $Q(x, y) = Q(x, y') = Q(x', y)$, A' and B' cannot distinguish the following probability ensembles with non-negligible advantage, respectively:*
       - $V^{II}_{A'S'} = (x, \mu \leftarrow \{0,1\}^{k^c}, tr \leftarrow \langle A'(x), B(y), S'(m_0, m_1)\rangle(\mu))$,
       - $S^{II}_{A'S'} = (x, \mu \leftarrow \{0,1\}^{k^c}, tr \leftarrow \langle A'(x), B(y'), S'(m_0, m_1)\rangle(\mu))$,
       and
       - $V^{II}_{B'S'} = (y, \mu \leftarrow \{0,1\}^{k^c}, tr \leftarrow \langle A(x), B'(y), S'(m_0, m_1)\rangle(\mu))$,
       - $S^{II}_{B'S'} = (y, \mu \leftarrow \{0,1\}^{k^c}, tr \leftarrow \langle A(x'), B'(y), S'(m_0, m_1)\rangle(\mu))$.

Remark. For clarity and simplicity, we will first assume that all parties in our COC and COC^1_2 schemes are semi-honest (honest-but-curious), that is, they follow the procedure step by step, but try to get extra information about the secrets or messages by extra computation. We also assume that A, B and S operates independently. No two parties will collude against the third one. Then we provide some techniques to transform the schemes into ones that are secure against malicious parties and their collusion in Section 5.1.

2.3 Homomorphic Encryption Schemes

Multiplicatively homomorphic encryption scheme. An encryption scheme (G, E, D) is multiplicatively homomorphic if for any m_0 and m_1, $D(E(m_0) \otimes E(m_1)) = D(E(m_0 \cdot m_1))$, where $\otimes$ is an operation defined on the image of E.

The ElGamal encryption scheme as follows is multiplicatively homomorphic.
  - $G(1^k) = (p, q, g, \alpha, \beta)$, where p is a k-bit prime, and $q = \frac{p-1}{2}$ is also a prime, $\mathbb{G}_q$ is the subgroup of $\mathbb{Z}_p^*$ with order q, g is a generator of $\mathbb{G}_q$, and $\beta = g^\alpha \bmod p$ for $\alpha \in \mathbb{G}_q$. Let $PK = (p, q, g, \beta), SK = (p, q, g, \alpha)$. All relevant computations are under group $\mathbb{G}_q$.
  - $E(m) = (g^r, m\beta^r)$, where $m \in \mathbb{G}_q, r \in_R \mathbb{Z}_q$.
  - $D(c) = c_2/c_1^\alpha$, where $c = (c_1, c_2)$.

For $E(m_0) = (g^{r_0}, m_0\beta^{r_0})$ and $E(m_1) = (g^{r_1}, m_1\beta^{r_1})$, the operation $E(m_0) \times E(m_1) = (g^{r_0} \cdot g^{r_1}, m_0\beta^{r_0} \cdot m_1\beta^{r_1})$ is multiplicatively homomorphic since

$$D(E(m_0) \times E(m_1)) = D(g^{r_0} \cdot g^{r_1}, m_0\beta^{r_0} \cdot m_1\beta^{r_1})$$
$$= D(g^{r_0+r_1}, m_0m_1\beta^{r_0+r_1})$$
$$= D(E(m_0 \cdot m_1)).$$

We can compute $E(m^c)$ from $E(m)$ via repeated multiplication for a constant c.

Additively homomorphic encryption scheme. An encryption scheme (G, E, D) is additively homomorphic if for any m_0 and m_1, $D(E(m_0) \oplus E(m_1)) = D(E(m_0 + m_1))$, where $\oplus$ is an operation defined on the image of E.

The Paillier encryption scheme [17] as follows is additively homomorphic.

- $G(1^k) = (p, q, N, \alpha, g)$, where $N = pq$ is a k-bit number, p and q are two large primes, g is an integer of order $\alpha N \mod N^2$ for some integer α. Let $PK = (g, N), SK = \lambda(N) = \text{lcm}(p - 1, q - 1)$.
- $E(m) = g^m r^N \mod N^2$, where $m \in \mathbb{Z}_N, r \in_R \mathbb{Z}_N$.
- $D(c) = \frac{L(c^{\lambda(N)} \mod N^2, N)}{L(g^{\lambda(N)} \mod N^2, N)} \mod N$, where $L(u, N) = \frac{u-1}{N}$.

For $E(m_0) = g^{m_0} r_0^N \mod N^2, E(m_1) = g^{m_1} r_1^N \mod N^2$, the operation $E(m_0) \cdot E(m_1) = (g^{m_0} r_0^N) \cdot (g^{m_1} r_1^N)$ is additively homomorphic since

$$\begin{aligned} D(E(m_0) \cdot E(m_1)) &= D((g^{m_0} r_0^N) \cdot (g^{m_1} r_1^N)) \\ &= D((g^{m_0+m_1}(r_0 r_1)^N)) \\ &= D(E(m_0 + m_1)). \end{aligned}$$

We can compute $E(cm)$ from $E(m)$ via repeated addition for a constant c.

Note that ElGamal and Paillier encryption schemes are proved semantically secure if and only if the Decisional Diffie-Hellman and the Computational Composite Residuosity assumptions hold, respectively [20, 17].

2.4   0-Encoding and 1-Encoding

In our COC scheme for "greater than" predicate, we use two types of encoding to reduce the "greater than" problem to the set intersection problem [13]. Let $s = s_n s_{n-1} \ldots s_1 \in \{0, 1\}^n$ be a binary string of length n. The 0-encoding of s is

$$\hat{S}_s^0 = \{s_n s_{n-1} \ldots s_{i+1} 1 | s_i = 0, 1 \leq i \leq n\}.$$

and 1-coding of s is

$$\hat{S}_s^1 = \{s_n s_{n-1} \ldots s_i | s_i = 1, 1 \leq i \leq n\}.$$

For two binary strings x, y of the same length, we have that $x > y$ if and only if there is exact one common element in $\hat{S}_x^1$ and $\hat{S}_y^0$.

If we compare strings in $\hat{S}_x^1$ and $\hat{S}_y^0$ one against one, it would be quite inefficient since we need $O(n^2)$ comparisons. Because each element in $\hat{S}_s^0$ (or $\hat{S}_s^1$) has a different length, we compare the elements of the same length in the two sets only. We define the *ordered* sets for $b \in \{0, 1\}, 1 \leq i \leq n$:

$$S_s^b[i] = \begin{cases} z_i & \text{if } \exists z_i \in \hat{S}_s^b \text{ and } |z_i| = i; \\ r_i^b & \text{otherwise,} \end{cases}$$

where $S_s^b[i]$ denotes the i-th element in S_s^b, and r_i^b is an arbitrary binary string with length $i+1+b$. Therefore, because of different lengths, r_i^b must not be equal to the string $S_s^{1-b}[i]$. Thus we just need to test if $S_x^1[i] = S_y^0[i]$ for each $i \in \{1, 2, \ldots, n\}$.

2.5   Setup and Notations

In the setup phase of our schemes for semi-honest adversary, A and B need to agree on a public/secret key pair (PK, SK) of the homomorphic encryption scheme privately. There are several ways to accomplish this work. For example, if A and B have their own public/secret key pairs, one party generates (PK, SK) first, and securely sends it to the other party. This common key pair allows S to compute the predicate on their secrets by the homomorphic encryption scheme. Also, S need choose a key pair (PK_S, SK_S) (for any semantically secure public key encryption scheme) such that A and B can send their secrets to S privately (against the other party).

Let $\mathbb{G}_q$ be the group of the multiplicatively homomorphic encryption scheme and $\mathbb{Z}_N$ be the group of the additively homomorphic encryption scheme. For key pair (PK, SK), E_{PK} and D_{SK} represent encryption and decryption for the underlying encryption scheme.

We use x_i to denote the i-th bit of the value $x = x_n x_{n-1} \cdots x_1$. Let $X[i]$ denote the i-th element of the ordered set X. Let $x \in_R X$ mean that x is chosen from X uniformly and independently. Let $|x|$ be the length (in bits) of x. To encrypt a vector $v = \langle v_1, v_2, \ldots, v_n \rangle$, we write $E(v) = \langle E(v_1), E(v_2), \ldots, E(v_n) \rangle$.

In some schemes, A and B need to "identify" the correct message from a set of decrypted ciphertexts. This can be achieved by some padding technique (e.g. OAEP [2]) such that receivers can check the integrity of a message. If a decryption contains the valid padding, it is the correct message with overwhelming probability.

3   Conditional Oblivious Cast

We provide COC schemes for three basic predicates: "equality", "inequality", and "greater than".

3.1   COC for "Equality" Predicate

To determine if $x = y$, we compute x/y via the multiplicatively homomorphic encryption scheme. If $x/y = 1$, A and B get the message m; otherwise, they get nothing. The scheme EQ-COC is described in Figure 1.

Theorem 1. *The EQ-COC scheme has the correctness property, unconditional sender's security, and computational receiver's security if the underlying homomorphic encryption scheme has semantic security.*

Proof. For correctness, if $x = y$, A and B compute m by

$$
\begin{aligned}
D_{SK}(e) &= D_{SK}(E_{PK}(m) \otimes (E_{PK}(x) \otimes E_{PK}(y)^{-1})^r) \\
&= D_{SK}(E_{PK}(m) \otimes (E_{PK}(1)^r)) \\
&= D_{SK}(E_{PK}(m)) \\
&= m.
\end{aligned}
$$

- System parameters: (p, q, g).
- Message sender S has a message m and a key pair (PK_S, SK_S).
- Receiver A has a secret x, and receiver B has a secret y, where $x, y \in \mathbb{G}_q$.
- Receiver A and B have a common key pair (PK, SK)

1. A and B send $E_{PK_S}(E_{PK}(x))$ and $E_{PK_S}(E_{PK}(y))$ to S respectively.
2. S decrypts the received messages to get $E_{PK}(x)$ and $E_{PK}(y)$. S computes

$$e = E_{PK}(m) \otimes (E_{PK}(x) \otimes E_{PK}(y)^{-1})^r$$

and sends it to A and B, where $r \in_R \mathbb{Z}_q$.
3. A and B compute $\hat{m} = D_{SK}(e)$ and identify whether $\hat{m}$ is valid.

Fig. 1. COC scheme for "Equality" predicate: EQ-COC

For sender's security, we show that if $x \neq y$, m is unconditionally secure to A and B. Since $e = E_{PK}(m) \otimes (E_{PK}(x) \otimes E_{PK}(y)^{-1})^r) = E_{PK}(m \cdot (x/y)^r), r \in_R \mathbb{Z}_q$, for any possible m', there is another $r' \in \mathbb{Z}_q$ such that $e = E_{PK}(m' \cdot (x/y)^{r'})$. As long as $x \neq y$, e can be decrypted to any possible message in $\mathbb{G}_q$. This ensures unconditional security of S's message m.

For receiver's security, it is easy to see that S gets no information about x and y due to semantic security of the encryption scheme. Since A and B are symmetric, we only prove the security of B against A. We construct a simulator S_A for A's real view

$$V_A(PK, SK, PK_S, x) = (PK, SK, PK_S, x, E_{PK_S}(E_{PK}(x)), E_{PK_S}(E_{PK}(y)), e).$$

The simulator S_A on input $(PK, SK, PK_S, x, \hat{m})$ is as follows, where $\hat{m}$ (may be a valid message or a random value) is the output of a real execution:

1. Choose a random value $y^* \in \mathbb{G}_q$.
2. Compute $e^* = E_{PK}(\hat{m})$.
3. Output $(PK, SK, PK_S, x, E_{PK_S}(E_{PK}(x)), E_{PK_S}(E_{PK}(y^*)), e^*)$.

By semantic security of the encryption scheme, A cannot distinguish the ciphertexts $E_{PK_S}(E_{PK}(y^*))$ and $E_{PK_S}(E_{PK}(y))$. Furthermore, since e^* is identically distributed as e, the output of S_A is indistinguishable from V_A. Therefore, A gets no information about y except those computed from x and $\hat{m}$. $\qquad \square$

In the scheme, we assume $x, y \in \mathbb{G}_q$. If the length of x (or y) is longer than $|p|$, A and B compare $h(x)$ and $h(y)$, where h is a collision-resistant hash function. This technique is applied to later schemes whenever necessary.

3.2   COC for "Inequality" Predicate

COC for the "inequality" predicate is more complicated than that for the "equality" predicate. A and B need to send the ciphertexts of their secrets bit by bit. We use additively homomorphic encryption schemes in this scheme, which is depicted in Figure 2.

- System parameters: n.
- Message sender S has a message m and a key pair (PK_S, SK_S).
- Receiver A has a secret x, and receiver B has a secret y, where $|x| = |y| = n$.
- Receiver A and B have a common key pair (PK, SK), where $PK = (g, N)$.

1. A and B send $E_{PK_S}(E_{PK}(x_i))$ and $E_{PK_S}(E_{PK}(y_i))$ to S respectively, $1 \le i \le n$.
2. For each $i \in \{1, 2, \ldots, n\}$, S decrypts the received messages to get $E_{PK}(x_i)$ and $E_{PK}(y_i)$, and computes the following values via homomorphic encryption:
   (a) $d_i = x_i - y_i$, $d_i' = x_i + y_i - 1$.
   (b) $e_i = 2e_{i+1} + d_i$, where $e_{n+1} = 0$.
   (c) $c_i = m + r_i(e_i - d_i + d_i')$, where $r_i \in_R \mathbb{Z}_N$
3. S sends $E_{PK}(c)$ in a random order to A and B, where $c = \langle c_1, c_2, \ldots, c_n \rangle$.
4. A and B decrypt the received messages and identify the correct message if existent.

Fig. 2. COC scheme for "Inequality" predicate: INE-COC

In the scheme, $d_i = x_i - y_i$ and $d_i' = x_i - \bar{y}_i$ are 0, 1 or -1. If $x_i = y_i$, $d_i = 0$; otherwise, $d_i' = 0$. Let l be the leftmost different bit between x and y, i.e. the largest i such that $d_i \ne 0$. We have $e_i = 0$ if $i > l$, $e_i \ne 0$ if $i < l$, and $e_i = d_i$ if $i = l$.

If $x \ne y$, the message m is embedded into the index i at which x_i and y_i are distinct. However, we have to avoid leaking information of the number of distinct bits. So S masks m with random values on all indices except the index l. It leaves only one copy of m in c_i's:

- For $i = l$, since $e_l = d_l$ and $d_l' = x_l - \bar{y}_l = 0$, $(e_l - d_l + d_l') = 0$. Therefore, $c_l = m$.
- For $1 \le i < l$, c_i would be a random value because $e_i - d_i + d_i' = 2e_{i+1} + d_i' \ne 0$ and $r_i \in_R \mathbb{Z}_N$.
- For $l < i \le n$, c_i is also a random value because $e_i = d_i = 0$, $d_i' \ne 0$ and $r_i \in_R \mathbb{Z}_N$.

Theorem 2. *The INE-COC scheme has the correctness property, unconditional sender's security, and computational receiver's security if the underlying homomorphic encryption scheme has semantic security.*

Proof. (sketch) Let l be the index of the first different bit of x and y (from the most significant bit). We see that $d_l = e_l = x_l - y_l = 1$ or -1, and $d_l' = x_j - \bar{y}_j = 0$. Therefore, $c_l = m + r_l(e_l - d_l + d_l') = m + r_l \cdot 0 = m$. Thus, A and B get m from the permutation of the encryptions.

For sender's security, we see that if $x = y$, all d_i's and e_i's are 0, and all d_i''s are not 0 (in fact, $+1$ or -1). Thus, for each index i, $c_i = m + r_i(0 \pm 1) = m \pm r_i$. Since for any possible $\tilde{m}$, there exists an $\tilde{r}_i$ such that $c_i = \tilde{m} + \tilde{r}_i$, m is unconditionally secure to A and B.

For receiver's security, S gets no information about x and y by the semantic security of the encryption scheme. As in the proof of EQ-COC, for each of A and B, we can construct a simulator such that the adversary cannot distinguish the real view and the simulated view. Therefore the receiver's security holds. $\square$

- System parameters: (p, q, g).
- Message sender S has a message m and a key pair (PK_S, SK_S).
- Receiver A has a secret x, and receiver B has a secret y, where $x, y \in \mathbb{G}_q, |x| = |y| = n$.
- Receiver A and B have a common key pair (PK, SK)

1. A encodes x as S_x^1, and sends $E_{PK_S}(E_{PK}(S_x^1[i]))$ to S, $1 \le i \le n$.
2. B encodes y as S_y^0, and sends $E_{PK_S}(E_{PK}(S_y^0[i]))$ to S, $1 \le i \le n$.
3. S decrypts the received messages and computes

$$e_i = E_{PK}(m) \otimes (E_{PK}(S_x^1[i]) \otimes E_{PK}(S_y^0[i])^{-1})^{r_i},$$

   where $r_i \in_R \mathbb{G}_q$, $1 \le i \le n$. S sends e_i's to A and B in a random order.
4. A and B search $\hat{m}_i = D_{SK}(e_i)$, $1 \le i \le n$, to identify the correct m if existent.

Fig. 3. COC scheme for "Greater Than" predicate: GT-COC

3.3   COC for "Greater Than" Predicate

For the "greater than" predicate, we use the encoding methods mentioned in Section 2.4. A encodes x via 1-encoding and B encodes y via 0-encoding. The problem is then reduced to the "equality" problem immediately. When S receives encrypted S_x^1 and S_y^0, he checks equality for corresponding strings. The scheme is presented in Figure 3. The security argument is the same as the proof of the EQ-COC scheme. This method is more efficient than the GT-COC$_2^1$ scheme (in the next section, by setting m_0 as a random number).

4   1-Out-of-2 Conditional Oblivious Cast

In this section, we present COC$_2^1$ schemes for the "equality" ("inequality") and "greater than" predicates.

4.1   COC$_2^1$ for "Equality" Predicate

Our COC$_2^1$ scheme for the equality predicate is naturally extended from the EQ-COC and INE-COC schemes. Intuitively, if $x = y$, A and B get m_1 by the EQ-COC scheme and, otherwise, they get m_0 by the INE-COC scheme. For better integration, we modify the EQ-COC scheme to use additively homomorphic encryption schemes. The scheme is shown in Figure 4. It is almost the same as the INE-COC scheme except that S sends an extra ciphertext c_{eq} to A and B.

Theorem 3. *The EQ-COC$_2^1$ scheme has the correctness property, unconditional sender's security, and computational receiver's security if the underlying homomorphic encryption scheme has semantic security.*

Proof. (sketch) We see that if $x = y$, all d_i's are equal to 0, and c_{eq} is equal to m_1. The opposite case holds by the same arguments in the proof of Theorem 2. This ensures the correctness property.

- System parameters: n.
- Message sender S has messages: (m_0, m_1) and a key pair (PK_S, SK_S).
- Receiver A has a secret x, and receiver B has a secret y, where $|x| = |y| = n$.
- Receiver A and B have a common key pair (PK, SK), where $PK = (g, N)$.

1. A and B send $E_{PK_S}(E_{PK}(x_i))$ and $E_{PK_S}(E_{PK}(y_i))$ to S respectively, $1 \leq i \leq n$.
2. For each $i \in \{1, 2, \ldots, n\}$, S decrypts the received messages to get $E_{PK}(x_i)$ and $E_{PK}(y_i)$, and computes the following values via homomorphic encryption:
   (a) $d_i = x_i - y_i, d'_i = x_i + y_i - 1$.
   (b) $e_i = 2e_{i+1} + d_i$, where $e_{n+1} = 0$.
   (c) $c_{eq} = m_1 + \sum_{i=1}^{n} r_i d_i,\ c'_i = m_0 + r'_i(e_i - d_i + d'_i)$, where $r_i, r'_i \in_R \mathbb{Z}_N$
3. S sends $E_{PK}(c_{eq}), E_{PK}(c')$ to A and B in a random order, where $c' = \langle c'_1, c'_2, \ldots, c'_n \rangle$.
4. A and B decrypt the received messages and identify the correct message

Fig. 4. 1-out-of-2 COC scheme for "Equality" predicate: EQ-COC$_2^1$

For sender's security, let $r = \sum_{i=1}^{n} r_i d_i$. Since $r_i \in_R \mathbb{Z}_N$, if $x \neq y$, there is a $d_i \neq 0$ such that r is uniformly distributed, and thus m_1 is unconditionally secure to A and B. If $x = y$, by the proof of Theorem 2, m_0 is unconditionally secure to A and B.

For receiver's security, S gets no information about x and y by the semantic security of the encryption scheme. For each of A and B, we can construct a simulator such that the adversary cannot distinguish the real view and the simulated view. The receiver's security holds. $\square$

4.2 COC$_2^1$ for "Greater Than" Predicate

It is obvious that we can apply the GT-COC scheme twice to achieve a GT-COC$_2^1$ scheme. One invocation is for testing $x > y$ and the other one is for testing $x \leq y$. But, this approach costs twice as much as the GT-COC scheme. Our scheme for GT-COC$_2^1$ in Figure 5 is more efficient. It costs an extra ciphertext (for the case $x = y$) from S to A and B only.

Let l be the leftmost different bit between x and y. For $i < l$ and $i > l$, e_i and e'_i would be random values in $\mathbb{Z}_N$, respectively. When $i = l$, we have $e_i = d_i$ and $e'_i = 0$. Therefore, f_i is a random value when $i \neq l$ and $f_l = d_l$. If $x > y$, $f_l = 1$ and thus $c_l = m_1$; if $x < y$, $f_l = -1$ and thus $c_l = m_0$. For the case $x = y$, we use an extra value c_{eq} to embed m_0 like scheme EQ-COC$_2^1$.

Theorem 4. *The GT-COC$_2^1$ scheme has the correctness property, unconditional sender's security, and computational receiver's security if the underlying homomorphic encryption scheme has semantic security.*

Proof. (sketch) For correctness, consider the following three cases:

- $x > y$: let l be the index of the first different bit of x and y (from the most significant bit), we have $e_l = d_l = 1, e'_l = d'_l = 0$, and thus $f_l = e_l + e'_l = 1$. Therefore $c_l = \frac{m_1 - m_0}{2} \cdot 1 + \frac{m_1 + m_0}{2} = m_1$.

- System parameters: n.
- Message sender S has messages: (m_0, m_1) and a key pair (PK_S, SK_S).
- Receiver A has a secret x, and receiver B has a secret y, where $|x| = |y| = n$.
- Receiver A and B have a common key pair (PK, SK), where $PK = (g, N)$.

1. A and B send $E_{PK_S}(E_{PK}(x_i))$ and $E_{PK_S}(E_{PK}(y_i))$ to S respectively, $1 \leq i \leq n$.
2. For each $i \in \{1, 2, \ldots, n\}$, S decrypts the received messages to get $E_{PK}(x_i)$ and $E_{PK}(y_i)$, and computes the following values via homomorphic encryption:
    (a) $d_i = x_i - y_i$, $d_i' = x_i + y_i - 1$
    (b) $e_i = r_i e_{i+1} + d_i$, $e_i' = r_i' d_i'$, where $e_{n+1} = 0$, $r_i, r_i' \in_R \mathbb{Z}_N$
    (c) $f_i = e_i + e_i'$
    (d) $c_i = \frac{m_1 - m_0}{2} f_i + \frac{m_1 + m_0}{2}$, $c_{eq} = m_0 + \sum_{i=1}^{n} r_i'' d_i$, where $r_i'' \in_R \mathbb{Z}_N$.
3. S sends $E_{PK}(c), E_{PK}(c_{eq})$ in a random order to A and B, where $c = \langle c_1, c_2, \ldots, c_n \rangle$.
4. A and B decrypt the received messages and identify the correct message.

Fig. 5. 1-out-of-2 COC scheme for "Greater Than" predicate: GT-COC$_2^1$

- $x < y$: similarly, since $f_l = e_l = d_l = -1$ in this case, we have $c_l = \frac{m_1 - m_0}{2} \cdot (-1) + \frac{m_1 + m_0}{2} = m_0$.
- $x = y$: by the same argument in the proof of Theorem 3, A and B get m_0 from c_{eq}.

For sender's security, we see that if $x \neq y$, then for all $i \neq l$, f_i is uniformly distributed in $\mathbb{Z}_N$. That is, all c_i's except c_l are uniformly distributed in $\mathbb{Z}_N$. For index l, according to the above argument, $c_l = m_0$ if $x < y$ and $c_l = m_1$ if $x > y$. Moreover, by the proof of Theorem 3, $c_{eq} = m_0$ if $x = y$, and c_{eq} is uniformly distributed if $x \neq y$. Therefore, m_0 is unconditionally secure to A and B if $x > y$, and m_1 is unconditionally secure to A and B if $x \leq y$.

For receiver's security, S gets no information about x and y by the semantic security of the encryption scheme. As in the previous proofs, for each of A and B, we can construct a simulator such that the adversary cannot distinguish the real view and the simulated view. Therefore, the receiver's security holds. □

4.3   A General Transformation

We provide a general transformation from COC$_2^1$ to the second case mentioned in Section 1 for COC. We use the GT-COC$_2^1$ scheme as an example. The alternative model for COC is that when $x > y$, only A gets the message m and when $x \leq y$, only B gets the message. We modify our GT-COC$_2^1$ scheme to meet this requirement. In the beginning, A and B choose their own public/secret key pairs, namely, (PK_A, SK_A) and (PK_B, SK_B). Then S lets $m_1 = E_{PK_A}(m)$ and $m_0 = E_{PK_B}(m)$, and performs the scheme as usual. We see that if $x > y$, both A and B get $m_1 = E_{PK_A}(m)$. But, only A can decrypt it to get the message m. Similarly, if $x \leq y$, only B gets the message.

5   Extensions

In this section we introduce how to modify our COC schemes against malicious parties and collusion. We also discuss the construction of other predicates. The details of these modifications and extensions are left to the full version of this paper.

5.1   Schemes Secure Against Malicious Parties and Collusion

We can make our COC schemes secure against malicious parties and their collusion by using the threshold version of homomorphic cryptosystems. At the initial stage, each party gets a secret key share (from a dealer or a distributed key generation protocol). If the number of collusive parties does not exceed the threshold, they get nothing about the message. Since all parties (including the sender) exchange messages in encrypted form, all computation can be publicly verified. After the final result in encrypted form is obtained, all parties perform the threshold decryption for the result.

We need some non-interactive zero-knowledge proof systems for verification in the corresponding schemes (assuming PK is the common public key):

- Proof of plaintext knowledge. The prover proves that he knows the plaintext x for the encryption $E_{PK}(x)$ he created.
- Proof of one-bit plaintext. The prover proves that x is 0 or 1 for the encryption $E_{PK}(x)$ he created.
- Proof of correct exponentiation. Given (multiplicatively homomorphic) $E_{PK}(x)$, the prover outputs $E_{PK}(a)$ and $E_{PK}(x^a)$, and proves that $E_{PK}(x^a)$ is indeed the encryption of x^a.
- Proof of correct multiplication. Given (additively homomorphic) $E_{PK}(x)$, the prover outputs $E_{PK}(a)$ and $E_{PK}(ax)$, and proves that $E_{PK}(ax)$ is indeed the encryption of ax.

We can find such proof systems for the ElGamal and Paillier homomorphic encryption schemes [7, 19, 6, 9]. For the schemes INE-COC, EQ-COC$_2^1$ and GT-COC$_2^1$, the receivers need to prove that the encrypted messages they send are indeed the encryptions of 0 or 1. Boneh et al. [4] provide a verification gadget for this type of checking. Thus we can avoid using the proof system of one-bit plaintext.

5.2   Other Predicates

In addition to the basic predicates, we can design COC (COC$_2^1$) schemes for many other interesting predicates. For these predicates, the sender may need perform multiplication on two messages encrypted by an additively homomorphic encryption scheme. However, there is no known encryption scheme with both additive and multiplicative homomorphism properties. Fortunately, Boneh et al. [4] introduced an additively homomorphic encryption scheme which can perform multiplication on two ciphertexts one time. In the setting of using threshold cryptosystem, the sender can even perform multiplication on two ciphertexts arbitrary times via some interactions [9].

In fact, our COC can be designed for any predicate based on the evaluation of bivariable polynomial $f(x,y)$. For example, to compute a public polynomial $f(x,y) = a_2x^2y^2 + a_1x^2y + a_0y$, the receivers send the encryptions of x, x^2 and y, y^2 to the sender respectively. The sender then computes the polynomial by the following steps.

1. Perform the multiplication on the encrypted messages [4] such that $z_2 = x^2y^2$ and $z_1 = x^2y$.
2. Perform the constant multiplication: a_2z_2, a_1z_1 and a_0y.
3. Perform $f(x,y) = a_2z_2 + a_1z_1 + a_0y$.

After computing $f(x,y)$, the sender can embed messages into the result.

Alternatively, we can assume that one receiver holds the polynomial f and the other holds the secret x, and the sender embeds messages into the result of $f(x)$. For example, for the "membership" predicate, one receiver first encodes his set of secrets as a k-degree polynomial such that $f(x) = 0$ iff x belongs to the set, and the other receiver computes $x, x^2, \ldots, x^k$ for his secret x. The sender then sends the message to the receivers such that they get it iff $f(x) = 0$. This "membership" predicate can be used in our oblivious authenticated information retrieval application described in Section 1.

6   Conclusion

We introduce a new notion of *conditional oblivious cast*, which extends conditional oblivious transfer to the three-party case. The definitions of this notion are given. We also provide some implementations for some basic predicates such as "equality", "inequality", and "greater than" predicates. We believe this new notion will be an useful primitive of cryptographic protocols.

References

1. William Aiello, Yuval Ishai, and Omer Reingold. Priced oblivious transfer: How to sell digital goods. In *Proceedings of Advances in Cryptology - EUROCRYPT '01*, volume 2045 of *LNCS*, pages 119–135. Springer-Verlag, 2001.
2. Mihir Bellare and Phillip Rogaway. Optimal asymmetric encryption. In *Proceedings of Advances in Cryptology - EUROCRYPT '94*, volume 950 of *LNCS*, pages 92–111. Springer-Verlag, 1994.
3. Ian F. Blake and Vladimir Kolesnikov. Strong conditional oblivious transfer and computing on intervals. In *Proceedings of Advances in Cryptology - ASIACRYPT '04*, volume 3329 of *LNCS*, pages 515–529. Springer-Verlag, 2004.
4. Dan Boneh, Eu-Jin Goh, and Kobbi Nissim. Evaluating 2-dnf formulas on ciphertexts. In *Proceedings of the 2nd Theory of Cryptography Conference (TCC 2005)*, volume 3378 of *LNCS*, pages 325–341. Springer-Verlag, 2005.
5. Gilles Brassard, Claude Crépeau, and Jean-Marc Robert. All-or-nothing disclosure of secrets. In *Proceedings of Advances in Cryptology - CRYPTO '86*, volume 263 of *LNCS*, pages 234–238. Springer-Verlag, 1986.

6. Jan Camenisch and Markus Stadler. Proof systems for general statements about discrete logarithms. Technical Report 260, Institute for Theoretical Computer Science, ETH Zurich, Mar 1997.
7. David Chaum, Jan-Hendrik Evertse, Jeroen van de Graaf, and Rene Peralta. Demonstrating possession of a discrete logarithm without revealing it. In *Proceedings of Advances in Cryptology - CRYPTO '86*, volume 263 of *LNCS*, pages 200–212. Springer-Verlag, 1986.
8. Cheng-Kang Chu and Wen-Guey Tzeng. Efficient k-out-of-n oblivious transfer schemes with adaptive and non-adaptive queries. In *Proceedings of the Public Key Cryptography (PKC '05)*, volume 3386 of *LNCS*, pages 172–183. Springer-Verlag, 2005.
9. Ronald Cramer, Ivan Damgård, and Jesper Buus Nielsen. Multiparty computation from threshold homomorphic encryption. In *Proceedings of Advances in Cryptology - EUROCRYPT '01*, volume 2045 of *LNCS*, pages 280–299. Springer-Verlag, 2001.
10. Giovanni Di Crescenzo, Rafail Ostrovsky, and Sivaramakrishnan Rajagopalan. Conditional oblivious transfer and timed-release encryption. In *Proceedings of Advances in Cryptology - EUROCRYPT '99*, volume 1592 of *LNCS*, pages 74–89. Springer-Verlag, 1999.
11. Shimon Even, Oded Goldreich, and Abraham Lempel. A randomized protocol for signing contracts. *Communications of the ACM*, 28(6):637–647, 1985.
12. Matthias Fitzi, Juan A. Garay, Ueli Maurer, and Rafail Ostrovsky. Minimal complete primitives for secure multi-party computation. In *Proceedings of Advances in Cryptology - CRYPTO '01*, volume 2139 of *LNCS*, pages 80–100. Springer-Verlag, 2001.
13. Hsiao-Ying Lin and Wen-Guey Tzeng. An efficient solution to the millionaires' problem based on homomorphic encryption. In *Proceedings of Applied Cryptography and Network Security 2005 (ACNS '05)*, volume 3531 of *LNCS*, pages 456–466. Springer-Verlag, 2005.
14. Yi Mu, Junqi Zhang, and Vijay Varadharajan. m out of n oblivious transfer. In *Proceedings of the 7th Australasian Conference on Information Security and Privacy (ACISP '02)*, volume 2384 of *LNCS*, pages 395–405. Springer-Verlag, 2002.
15. Moni Naor and Benny Pinkas. Oblivious transfer and polynomial evaluation. In *Proceedings of the 31st Annual ACM Symposium on the Theory of Computing (STOC '99)*, pages 245–254. ACM, 1999.
16. Moni Naor and Benny Pinkas. Efficient oblivious transfer protocols. In *Proceedings of the 12th Annual Symposium on Discrete Algorithms (SODA '01)*, pages 448–457. ACM/SIAM, 2001.
17. Pascal Paillier. Public-key cryptosystems based on composite degree residuosity classes. In *Proceedings of Advances in Cryptology - EUROCRYPT '99*, volume 1592 of *LNCS*, pages 223–238. Springer-Verlag, 1999.
18. Michael O. Rabin. How to exchange secrets by oblivious transfer. Technical Report TR-81, Aiken Computation Laboratory, Harvard University, 1981.
19. Claus Peter Schnorr. Efficient signature generation by smart cards. *Journal of Cryptology*, 4(3):161–174, 1991.
20. Yiannis Tsiounis and Moti Yung. On the security of ElGamal based encryption. In *Proceedings of the Public-Key Cryptography (PKC '98)*, volume 1431 of *LNCS*, pages 117–134. Springer-Verlag, 1998.
21. Wen-Guey Tzeng. Efficient 1-out-n oblivious transfer schemes. In *Proceedings of the Public-Key Cryptography (PKC '02)*, pages 159–171. Springer-Verlag, 2002.

Efficiency Tradeoffs for Malicious Two-Party Computation

Payman Mohassel and Matthew Franklin

Department of Computer Science, University of California, Davis CA 95616
mohassel@cs.ucdavis.edu, franklin@cs.ucdavis.edu

Abstract. We study efficiency tradeoffs for secure two-party computation in presence of malicious behavior. We investigate two main approaches for defending against malicious behavior in *Yao's garbled circuit* method: (1) *Committed-input* scheme, (2) *Equality-checker* scheme. We provide asymptotic and concrete analysis of communication and computation costs of the designed protocols. We also develop a weaker definition of security (*k-leaked model*) for malicious two-party computation that allows for disclosure of some information to a malicious party. We design more efficient variations of *Yao's* protocol that are secure in the proposed model.

Keywords: secure two-party computation, secure function evaluation, Yao's garbled circuit, malicious adversary.

1 Introduction

General two-party secure computation was an early success of modern cryptography. *Yao's garbled circuit* protocol [Yao86] is a classic and elegant solution to this problem. Thanks to Lindell and Pinkas [LP04] (building on Goldreich [Gol04] and others), we now have a careful proof of Yao's protocol in a suitable formal framework.

It is well-known that Yao's protocol is vulnerable to malicious behavior by its participants. The classic solution to this issue is the *zero-knowledge* compilation of Goldreich et al. [GMW86, GMW87, Gol04]. This paradigm is of great theoretical interest, but is not efficient in practice. For this reason, various alternative methods for protecting Yao's protocol against malicious behavior have been suggested [Pin03, MNPS04].

The general approach is based on *cut-and-choose* techniques that tend to gain efficiency at the cost of increased risk of undetected cheating. We cite in particular, the impressive Fairplay system of Malkhi et al. [MNPS04], which has made a major step forward in bringing Yao's protocol to practice, and which was the starting point for our work.

Although these cut-and-choose ideas are intuitive and natural, they have some hidden subtleties and complexities. Indeed, we show that one of the protocols in the Fairplay paper has a subtle bug that allows one of the parties to cheat undetectably. This suggests that cut-and-choose designs for protecting Yao's protocol from malicious behavior deserve a closer look.

M. Yung et al. (Eds.): PKC 2006, LNCS 3958, pp. 458–473, 2006.

Another reason to take a closer look at this design space is that the tradeoffs of efficiency vs. undetected cheating are not immediately apparent (especially when combined with other cryptographic techniques). We find some nice constructions with attractive balances of the relevant parameters. We are not claiming that the best possible tradeoffs have been found. In fact, the design space is so rich that we suspect that more work remains to be done in this area. This is especially true when the parameter tradeoffs includes the number of bits of secret information leaked to a malicious party (a setting we explore in Section 4).

1.1   Related Work

We mention some of the work in the literature that deals (in rather different ways from ours) with information leakage in two-party protocols. The original paper on zero-knowledge allowed for some information *leakage* to the verifier [GMR89]. This notion was further explored by Goldreich and Petrank [GP99].

Two-party protocols for fair exchange have a problem of early termination by a malicious party. One goal is to design protocols that minimize the *advantage* of the early terminator over the honest party, measured as the difference between the number of bits of recovered messages by each party. Of course, the progress of two-party fair exchange research has primarily focused on increased inefficiency to achieve *less leakage* to the early terminator. This is backwards from our motivation. For examples, refer to [lMR83, Cle89].

Some two-party protocols for computing specific functions allowed some leakage of information [FNW96]. Bar-Yehuda et al. [BYCKO93] consider tradeoffs of information leakage and round complexity for two-party secure computation where the parties are computationally unbounded but non-malicious. Abadi et al. [AFK87] give a model for information leakage to allow a computationally bounded party to compute a function privately, with the help of a computationally unbounded party.

1.2   Outline of the Paper

We study *Yao's garbled circuit* protocol in the presence of malicious behavior. We show that the Fairplay scheme of [MNPS04] is still vulnerable to a type of malicious behavior, and suggest a simple way of fixing it. Then, we introduce two different schemes for preventing malicious behavior (1) *Committed-input* scheme, (2) *Equality-checker* scheme. Both constructions have exponentially small error probabilities. We provide and compare communication and computation cost for the designed protocols, both asymptotically and with more concrete measurements. Then, we develop a weaker definition of security for two-party computation that allows for leakage of some information. We then design efficient variations of *Yao's* protocol that are secure in the weaker model. We hope that this weaker definition of security suggests a reasonable tradeoff between efficiency and security, and allows for more efficient and practical implementations of secure two-party protocols.

In Section 2, we review some preliminary concepts. We also give a description of *Fairplay* scheme of [MNPS04]. In Section 3, we mention a vulnerability (against malicious behavior) in Fairplay, and describe our *Committed-input* and *Equality-checker* schemes. In Section 4, we introduce our *k-leaked* model of security, and suggest several efficient constructions that are secure in that model.

2 Preliminaries

Two-Party Computation

A two-party computation is cast by specifying a random process that maps pairs of inputs (one input per each party) to pairs of outputs (one for each party). We refer to such a process as the desired functionality, denoted $f : \{0,1\}^* \times \{0,1\}^* \to \{0,1\}^* \times \{0,1\}^*$ where $f = (f_1, f_2)$. For every pair of input $x, y \in \{0,1\}^n$, the output-pair is a random variable $(f_1(x,y), f_2(x,y))$ ranging over pairs of strings. The first party wishes to obtain $f_1(x,y)$ and the second party wishes to obtain $f_2(x,y)$.

The security definition for two-party computation varies depending on whether the adversary is *malicious*, or *semi-honest*. A semi-honest (honest-but-curious) adversary follows the steps of the protocol, but does not hesitate to learn more information using the transcripts of messages it receives. On the other hand, a malicious party can behave in an arbitrary way. In this paper, we are concerned with computationally bounded *malicious* adversaries. The definitions we use are according to [Gol04]. These definitions compare the adversaries in the *real-model* with those in an *ideal-model* in which the parties have a *trusted party* at their disposal. Loosely speaking, a two-party protocol is secure if for any admissible pair of parties (A, B) in the *real-model*, there is an admissible pair of parties (A', B') in the *ideal model* where the outputs of the two executions are indistinguishable. A pair is admissible if at least one of the parties in the pair is *honest*. Intuitively, a secure protocol is required to work *correctly*, and to provide *privacy* for the honest participant.

In Section 4, we will present a tweaked version of these definitions that allows a malicious party to learn k bits of extra information.

Oblivious transfer is a special two-party protocol introduced by Rabin [Rab81]. We need the *1-out-of-2* oblivious transfer where $x = (z_0, z_1)$, $y = \sigma$, $f_1(x,y) = empty$, and $f_2(x,y) = z_\sigma$. Several oblivious transfer protocols that are secure in presence of *malicious* or *semi-honest* adversaries exist.

Yao's Garbled Circuit Protocol

Yao's garbled circuit [Yao86] is the first general purpose protocol designed for secure two-party computation. In this protocol, the function being computed is a polynomial size circuit. The first party computes the garbled form of the circuit in the following way:

He assigns two random strings $K_{j,0}$ and $K_{j,1}$ to every wire j in the circuit. These random strings correspond to values 0 and 1, respectively. He then computes a garbled truth table for every gate in the circuit. For this purpose, he uses the random strings as keys to a symmetric encryption scheme, to encrypt the corresponding key for the output wire. He also creates a table that translates the garbled form of the output wires to their actual values (0, or 1). He sends the garbled circuit, and the garbled strings corresponding to his input, to the second party. The second party learns the garbled form of his input bits through a series of oblivious transfers. The second party computes the garbled circuit, gate by gate, and obtains the output in the garbled form. He can then use the translation table to find the actual value of his output. We refer the reader to [LP04] for a complete description of *Yao's protocol* and the proof of its security in the *semi-honest* case.

Yao's protocol, in this form, is not secure when the parties are malicious. Classical ways of making two-party protocols secure against malicious adversaries exist [Gol04] (based on the zero-knowledge compilation technique of [GMW87], and [GMW86]). In particular, the circuit garbler would need to accompany the garbled circuit with a zero-knowledge proof that the circuit is built correctly, and that it computes the desired functionality. Furthermore, the circuit evaluator would need to accompany his final message with a zero-knowledge proof that the output is the result of performing the desired functionality on the inputs exchanged in previous steps of protocol. The general zero-knowledge proofs are quite inefficient and no efficient alternative zero-knowledge proofs are designed for this purpose.

Fairplay Scheme

One of the main sources of malicious behavior in Yao's garbled circuit protocol is the ability of the circuit garbler to garble and send a wrong circuit. Malkhi et al. [MNPS04] use a simple cut-and-choose construction which reduces the probability of making the wrong garbled circuit to $\frac{1}{m}$, where m is number of circuits sent by circuit garbler (Bob) to circuit evaluator (Alice).

The following is the Fairplay scheme described in [MNPS04]. We only consider the steps after both parties know the description of the circuit they want to compute.

1. Bob constructs m garbled/encrypted circuits and sends them to Alice. Alice randomly chooses one of the circuits that will be evaluated.
2. Bob exposes the secrets of the other $m - 1$ garbled/encrypted circuits, and Alice verifies them against her reference circuit.
3. Bob specifies his inputs and sends them to Alice in garbled form. Alice inserts Bob's inputs in the garbled/encrypted circuits she chose to evaluate.
4. Alice specifies her inputs, and then Alice and Bob engage in oblivious transfers (OTs) in order for Alice to receive her inputs (in garbled form) from Bob. Bob learns nothing about Alice's inputs.
5. Alice evaluates the chosen garbled/encrypted circuit, finds the garbled outputs of both her and Bob, and sends the relevant outputs to Bob.
6. Each party interprets his or her garbled outputs and prints the result.

In this scheme, the probability that Bob sends the wrong circuit and does not get caught is $\frac{1}{m}$. However, Alice is still vulnerable to a different type of malicious behavior from Bob. We will describe this vulnerability in the following section.

3   Preventing Malicious Behavior in Yao's Protocol

A Vulnerability in Fairplay, and How to Correct It

In step 4 of the Fairplay protocol, parties engage in oblivious transfers in order for Alice to get the garbled form of her inputs. In any of the oblivious transfers, Bob can change the order of two random strings corresponding to 0 and 1. Note that changing the order of strings is not a malicious behavior in an oblivious transfer, but becomes a malicious behavior in the above protocol.

To state the vulnerability more formally, note that Bob can *flip* any of Alice's input bits without Alice's detection. Let $x_1, x_2, \ldots, x_n$ be the bit values associated with input wires. Let W_A be the input wires owned by Alice, and let W_B be the input wires owned by Bob: $W_A \cup W_B = [1..n]$ while $W_A \cap W_B = \phi$. For any $S \subseteq [1..n]$, let $flip_S(x_1, \ldots, x_n) = (y_1, y_2, \ldots, y_n)$, where $y_i = 1 - x_i$ for all $i \in S$, and $y_i = x_i$ for all $i \notin S$. Then Bob can fool Alice into computing $f(flip_S(x_1, \ldots, x_n))$ for any $S \subseteq W_A$. It is important to note that this behavior is not allowed in the *ideal model*.

There is a simple solution to this problem. We will require Bob to include a commitment $z_{j,i,b}$ of the tuple $(j, i, b, K_{i,b}^{(j)})$ for every circuit copy $j \in [1..m]$, and every input wire $i \in W_A$, and every input value $b \in \{0, 1\}$, where $K_{i,b}^{(j)}$ denotes the random string corresponding to bit value b of wire i in circuit j (let $w_{j,i,b}$ be the corresponding witnesses for decommittal). The purpose of these commitments is to bind the random key strings with their corresponding bit values (0 or 1). Bob reveals the witnesses for all of the commitments except for those corresponding to the one circuit copy chosen by Alice. Alice can verify that the exposed commitments are correctly computed. For the remaining circuit s, Bob will obliviously transfer $(K_{i,0}^{(s)}, w_{s,i,0})$ or $(K_{i,1}^{(s)}, w_{s,i,1})$ for all $i \in W_A$. Alice can use the witnesses to verify that she has received the correct key string. Bob can only cheat with probability $\frac{1}{m}$.

Now, we want to make the cheating probability exponentially small in m. The idea mentioned in [Pin03] is that Alice chooses a fraction of circuits randomly. Bob exposes the secrets of those circuits. Alice evaluates the rest of the circuits and accepts the majority output as the correct output of the protocol. For the cut-and-choose protocols to work properly, Bob must be forced to give the same input to *most* of the circuits evaluated by Alice. Pinkas [Pin03] suggests the use of proofs of partial knowledge to achieve this goal, but defers the detail of the actual construction.

Next, we design two schemes for making the cheating probability exponentially small in m. In the following two protocols, we assume that only Alice needs to see the output of the protocol. Based on this assumption, both schemes are secure in presence of *malicious* adversaries.

3.1   Committed-Input Scheme

In this scheme, we will use *proof of equality* of discrete-log commitments [Ped91]. To commit to a value x, one generates a random value r and calculates $g^x h^r$, where g is a generator of group G and h is a random element of G. The commiter should not know the discrete-log of h base g. To prove that $g^x h^{r_1}$ and $g^y h^{r_2}$ are commitments to the same value, the commiter sends $r_2 - r_1$ to the verifier. The verifier can calculate $\frac{g^y h^{r_2}}{g^x h^{r_1}}$ and verify that the result of division is in fact $h^{r_2 - r_1}$. Please refer to [Ped91] for more detail. Note that any commitment scheme with an efficient *proof-of-equality* can be used in our construction. We focus on the Pedersen commitments for simplicity, and to help with our concrete complexity analysis in Section 3.3.

In the *Committed-input* scheme, Bob computes $K_{i,b}^{(j)} = g^b h^{r_{i,b}^{(j)}}$ for random $r_{i,b}^{(j)}$, for every $j \in [1..m]$, for every input wire $i \in W_B$ owned by Bob, and for every input value $b \in \{0,1\}$.[1] Bob chooses random keys for all of the other wires, including Alice's input wires. He also includes the commitment $z_{j,i,b}$ of the tuple $(j, i, b, K_{i,b}^{(j)})$ for all of Alice's input wire keys (let $w_{j,i,b}$ be the corresponding witness for decommittal). The protocol follows:

1. Bob and Alice agree on a group G, and a generator g. Alice sends a random element $h \in G$ to Bob.
2. Bob sends the garbled circuits $C^{(j)}$ for every $j \in [1..m]$ (including the translation tables of output wires.) He also sends $(j, i, z_{j,i,0}, z_{j,i,1})$ for every $j \in [1..m]$ and every input wire $i \in W_A$ (commitments in random order).
3. Alice randomly chooses a subset $S \subset [1..m]$, where $|S| = \frac{m}{2}$.
4. Bob exposes all the secrets of circuit $C^{(j)}$ for all $j \in S$. Then, he sends witnesses $r_{i,0}^{(j)}, r_{i,1}^{(j)}$ for every $j \in S$, and $i \in W_B$. He also sends witnesses $w_{j,i,0}, w_{j,i,1}$ for every $j \in S$ and every $i \in W_A$.
5. Alice verifies that all the exposed garbled circuits and commitments were computed correctly. In addition, she verifies that the commitments to 0's were used in the circuit as garbled forms of 0 and commitments to 1 were used as garbled forms of 1.
6. Renumber the remaining garbled circuits as $C^{(1)}, \ldots, C^{(\frac{m}{2})}$. Bob sends to Alice $K_{i,b_i}^{(j)}$ for every $j \in [1..(m/2)]$ and every $i \in W_B$. He also sends $\delta_i^{(j+1)} = r_{i,b_i}^{(j+1)} - r_{i,b_i}^{(j)}$ for every $j \in [1..(m/2)-1]$ and every $i \in W_B$, where b_i is Bob's input for wire i.
7. Alice verifies that $K_{i,b_i}^{(1)}, \ldots, K_{i,b_i}^{(m/2)}$ are all commitments to the same value: $K_{i,b_i}^{(j+1)} / K_{i,b_i}^{(j)} = h^{\delta_i^{j+1}}$ for all $j \in [1..(m/2)-1]$. She does so for all $i \in W_B$.
8. Alice specifies her input. Alice and Bob engage in oblivious transfers in order for Alice to receive her input bits in garbled form. Bob uses a single oblivious transfer to give Alice one of the two tuples
$(K_{i,0}^{(1)}, w_{1,i,0}, K_{i,0}^{(2)}, w_{2,i,0}, \ldots, K_{i,0}^{(m/2)}, w_{m/2,i,0})$ or
$(K_{i,1}^{(1)}, w_{1,i,1}, K_{i,1}^{(2)}, w_{2,i,1}, \ldots, K_{i,1}^{(m/2)}, w_{m/2,i,1})$
depending on whether her value for input wire i is 0 or 1. This Oblivious Transfer is done for every $i \in W_A$.

---

[1] If the length of these commitments does not match the length chosen for the random strings, we can use a hash function to map the commitments to strings of the required length.

9. Alice verifies that these received input wire values and witnesses are consistent. Then, Alice executes all $m/2$ garbled circuits and outputs the majority value of the outputs.

Proof of Security

We assume the basic building blocks for Yao's garbled circuit protocol: secure 1-out-of-2 oblivious transfer and secure symmetric encryption. In addition, we assume the security of Pedersen commitments (discrete log assumption).

Lemma 1. *With probability more than* $1 - (\frac{1}{2})^{\frac{m}{4}}$*, the majority of evaluated circuits are correct and have the same input, or Bob will get caught.*

Proof of lemma: The probability that more than half of the remaining $\frac{m}{2}$ circuits were wrong, and were not detected by Alice, is less than $\binom{3m/4}{m/2} / \binom{m}{m/2} < (\frac{1}{2})^{\frac{m}{4}}$. Therefore, the majority of circuits are correct with high probability, which means that the disc-log commitments corresponding to those circuits are also correct. Hence, Bob has to give the same input for those circuits or he will get caught during the verification (step 7).

The following two claims complete the security argument. Due to lack of space, proofs of the following two claims are not included in this extended abstract.

Claim 1. *The* Committed-input *scheme is secure when Bob (circuit garbler) is malicious (inverse exponential probability of undetected cheating).*

Claim 2. *The* Committed-input *scheme is secure when Alice (circuit evaluator) is malicious.*

3.2 Equality-Checker Scheme

In this scheme, we will avoid any *exponentiation* other than the ones computed for OTs. Before describing the scheme, lets define the equality-checkers used in the scheme. Let $z_{j,j',i,b}$ be Bob's commitment to the tuple $(j, j', K_{i,b}^{(j)}, K_{i,b}^{(j')})$ and let $w_{j,j',i,b}$ be the corresponding witness for decommittal. Bob computes these commitments for every j, j' such that $1 \leq j < j' \leq m$, for every $i \in W_B$, and for every $b \in \{0,1\}$. The idea is that a correctly built commitment binds the two random key strings that correspond to the same bit value for the same input wire, but in two different circuits. Alice can verify that Bob's input to two circuits $C^{(j)}$ and $C^{(j')}$ are equal if she is given the witnesses to the commitments z_{j,j',i,b_i} for every $i \in W_B$, where b_i is Bob's input bit for wire i. An *equality-checker* between circuits $C^{(j)}$ and $C^{(j')}$ is the collection of $z_{j,j',i,b}$ for all $i \in W_B$ and $b \in \{0,1\}$. Working with equality-checkers instead of individual commitments makes the proofs simpler.

1. Bob constructs m garbled/encrypted circuits and sends them to Alice. He also sends the $z_{j,i,b}$ commitments and the $m(m-1)/2$ equality-checkers described above.

2. Alice randomly chooses a subset $S \subset [1..m]$, where $|S| = \frac{m}{2}$ and sends S to Bob.
3. Bob exposes the secrets of circuits $C^{(j)}$ for all $j \in S$. Then, he sends witnesses $w_{j,i,b}$ for all $j \in S$, all $i \in W_A$, and all $b \in \{0,1\}$. He also sends witnesses $w_{j,j',i,b}$ for all $j, j' \in S$, all $i \in W_B$, and all $b \in \{0,1\}$ (these are the $(\frac{m}{2})(\frac{m}{2}-1)/2$ equality-checkers corresponding to pairs of revealed circuits). Alice verifies that the garbled circuits and commitments were computed correctly.
4. Renumber the remaining garbled circuits as $C^{(1)}, \ldots, C^{(m/2)}$. Bob sends the keys $K_{i,b_i}^{(j)}$ for every $j \in [1..\frac{m}{2}]$ and $i \in W_B$. He also sends witnesses w_{j,j',i,b_i} for every $1 \leq j < j' \leq \frac{m}{2}$, and every $i \in W_B$, where b_i is his input for wire i.
5. Alice uses the witnesses w_{j,j',i,b_i} to verify that Bob's input to all the circuits are the same.
6. Alice and Bob engage in oblivious transfers in order for Alice to receive her input bits in garbled form. Bob uses a single oblivious transfer to give Alice one of the two tuples $(K_{i,0}^{(1)}, K_{i,0}^{(2)}, \ldots, K_{i,0}^{(m/2)})$ or $(K_{i,1}^{(1)}, K_{i,1}^{(2)}, \ldots, K_{i,1}^{(m/2)})$ (depending on whether her value for input wire i is 0 or 1). This Oblivious Transfer is done for every $i \in W_A$.
7. Alice will evaluate the $\frac{m}{2}$ garbled circuits and print the majority output as the correct output.

Proof of Security

We assume the basic building blocks for Yao's garbled circuit protocol: secure 1-out-of-2 oblivious transfer and secure symmetric encryption. We also assume the security of the commitment scheme (which can be built from one way functions).

Lemma 2. *With probability more than* $1 - (1/2)^{\frac{m}{6}}$, *more than* $\frac{2}{3}$ *of the* $\frac{m}{2}$ *circuits are correct, or Bob will get caught.*

Proof of Lemma: (by contradiction) Let's assume that at most $\frac{2}{3}$ of the $\frac{m}{2}$ circuits are correct. This means that at least $\frac{m}{6}$ of the circuits are wrong. The probability that Alice doesn't detect those $\frac{m}{6}$ is less than $\binom{5m/6}{m/2} / \binom{m}{m/2} < (\frac{1}{2})^{\frac{m}{6}}$.

Lemma 3. *With probability more than* $1 - (1/2)^{\frac{m}{6}}$, *at least* $\frac{5}{6}$ *of Bob's* $\frac{m}{2}$ *inputs are the same, or Bob will get caught.*

Proof: See Appendix for the proof.

Claim 3. *The* Equality-checker *scheme is secure when Bob (circuit garbler) is malicious (inverse exponential probability of undetected cheating).*

Proof sketch: Now we know that Lemmas 2 and 3 are correct. In other words, at least $\frac{5}{6}$ of inputs are the same, and more than $\frac{2}{3}$ of circuits are correct with high probability. This implies that more than $\frac{2}{3} - \frac{1}{6} = \frac{1}{2}$ of the circuits are correct and have the same inputs, and hence, the majority output is the correct output. according to the union-bound this will happen with probability greater than $1 - (1/2)^{\frac{m}{6}} + 1 - (1/2)^{\frac{m}{6}} - 1 = 1 - 2(1/2)^{\frac{m}{6}}$.

Consider a strategy B for Bob in the real model. If Alice aborts the protocol, we are done (Bob is caught and he doesn't learn anything). But if Alice doesn't abort, she will respond with the majority output O which is equal to $f(x_a, x_{maj})$ with high probability. Here, x_a is Alice's input to the circuit, and x_{maj} is Bob's input to majority of the circuits. Bob's view of the protocol includes the OTs, and output O. Since he doesn't learn anything about Alice's input during the OTs, he can simulate them on his own using a simulator S_1.

The adversary B' in the ideal model will send the input x_{maj} to the *trusted-party* and get back $f(x_a, x_{maj})$ as the output. He can use the simulator S_1 to simulate the OTs, and emulate B's strategy step by step, and the view of the protocol will be indistinguishable.

The following claim completes the security argument (Proof is omitted due to lack of space).

Claim 4. *The* Equality-checker *scheme is secure when Alice (circuit evaluator) is malicious.*

3.3   Communication and Computation Analysis

To measure the communication and computation complexity of the schemes, we introduce the parameters m, I, O and g. m is number of garbled/encrypted circuits sent to Alice. I and O are the number of input and output bits respectively (Bob and Alice combined). g denotes the number of gates in the circuit. Whenever we want to consider one party's input or output, we will use the proper subscript.

Asymptotic Analysis

We will measure the communication and computation cost where the goal is to achieve an error probability as small as ϵ. To measure the computation cost, we split the computation into two types of operations: (1) exponentiations, and (2) everything else. In our protocols, OTs and disc-log commitments are from the first category, while the symmetric encryptions and other commitments used in the protocol are in the second category.

In the Fairplay scheme (with the vulnerability fixed as suggested), to achieve the required error probability, we need $m = \frac{1}{\epsilon}$ circuits. But for the Committed-input scheme and Equality-checker scheme, $m = O(ln(\frac{1}{\epsilon}))$. We summarize the communication and computation complexities in table 1. Note that $t = O(ln(\frac{1}{\epsilon}))$ is the security parameter (for a successful cheating probability of ϵ).

Table 1. Computation and Communication complexities

Scheme	Symmetric Enc.	Exponentiations	Communication Complexity
Fairplay	$O(\frac{1}{\epsilon}g)$	$O(I)$	$O(2^t g)$
Committed-input	$O(ln(\frac{1}{\epsilon})g)$	$O(ln(\frac{1}{\epsilon})I)$	$O(tg)$
Equality-checker	$O(ln(\frac{1}{\epsilon})g + ln(\frac{1}{\epsilon})^2 I)$	$O(I)$	$O(tg + t^2 I)$

More Concrete Analysis

We will try to measure the computational cost of all three constructions more precisely. We take into account all the encryptions, commitments and exponentiations, and include even the constant factors. We will measure the computational cost for 4 different circuits (AND[2], Billionaires[3], PIR[4], Median[5]). We borrow the circuits and their sizes from [MNPS04].

Fairplay: In the Fairplay scheme, to achieve an error probability ϵ, the total number of cryptographic operations are: $\frac{1}{\epsilon}(4g + 2O + 2I_A)$ symmetric encryptions and $2I_A$ exponentiations.

Committed-input: To achieve an error probability of ϵ, the total number of cryptographic operations are: $\frac{4}{ln(2)}ln(\frac{1}{\epsilon})(4g + 2O + 2I_A)$ symmetric encryptions and $2I_A + \frac{8}{ln(2)}ln(\frac{1}{\epsilon})I_B$ exponentiations.

Equality-checker: We have $\frac{6}{ln(2)}ln(\frac{1}{\epsilon})(4g + 2O + 2I_A) + \frac{72}{ln(2)^2}(ln(\frac{1}{\epsilon}))^2I_B$ symmetric encryptions, and $2I_A$ exponentiations.

Tables 2, 3 and 4 give the computational costs for the four mentioned circuits, for four different error probabilities. Each entry includes two integers, representing the number of symmetric encryptions and exponentiations, respectively.

Table 2. Computational cost for Fariplay scheme

Error probability	And	Billionaires	PIR	Median
$\frac{1}{100}$	$(176 * 10^2, 16)$	$(1092 * 10^2, 64)$	$(4976 * 10^2, 12)$	$(17916 * 10^2, 320)$
$\frac{1}{1000}$	$(176 * 10^3, 16)$	$(1092 * 10^3, 64)$	$(4976 * 10^3, 12)$	$(17916 * 10^3, 320)$
$\frac{1}{10000}$	$(176 * 10^4, 16)$	$(1092 * 10^4, 64)$	$(4976 * 10^4, 12)$	$(17916 * 10^4, 320)$
$\frac{1}{1000000}$	$(176 * 10^6, 16)$	$(1092 * 10^6, 64)$	$(4976 * 10^6, 12)$	$(17916 * 10^6, 320)$

Table 3. Computational cost for Committed-input scheme

Error probability	And	Billionaires	PIR	Median
$\frac{1}{100}$	$(4677, 441)$	$(29020, 1764)$	$(132239, 25524)$	$(476125, 8824)$
$\frac{1}{1000}$	$(7015, 653)$	$(43530, 2615)$	$(198358, 38280)$	$(714187, 13076)$
$\frac{1}{10000}$	$(9354, 866)$	$(58040, 3465)$	$(264478, 51036)$	$(952250, 17328)$
$\frac{1}{1000000}$	$(14031, 1291)$	$(87061, 5166)$	$(396717, 76549)$	$(1428375, 25832)$

Since *Equality-checker* and *Fairplay* have the same number of exponentiations, it is easy to compare their computational cost. You can see that for all four circuits, if we require an error probability of $\frac{1}{1000}$ or smaller, the computational cost of *Equality-checker* scheme is lower. However, if an error probability

---

[2] Performs bit-wise AND on two inputs of size 8. The circuit has 32 gates.

[3] Compares two 32-bit integers. The circuit has 256 gates.

[4] Bob's input size is 480 bits and Alice's input size is 6 bit. The circuit has 1229 gates.

[5] finds the median of two sorted arrays. The input for both Alice and Bob are ten 16-bit numbers. The circuit size is 4383 gates.

Table 4. Computational cost for Equality-checker scheme

Error probability	And	Billionaires	PIR	Median
$\frac{1}{100}$	$(19700, 16)$	$(94380, 64)$	$(961112, 12)$	$(968439, 320)$
$\frac{1}{1000}$	$(39100, 16)$	$(179708, 64)$	$(2013733, 12)$	$(1643347, 320)$
$\frac{1}{10000}$	$(64882, 16)$	$(290462, 64)$	$(3447731, 12)$	$(2445380, 320)$
$\frac{1}{1000000}$	$(135460, 16)$	$(588243, 64)$	$(7459858, 12)$	$(4430824, 320)$

of $\frac{1}{100}$ or larger is enough, Fairplay is a better choice. Therefore, the choice of efficient construction seems to depend on the likelihood of malicious behavior and the magnitude of damage it can have in the environment the protocol is being employed.

David Woodruff [Woo06] has proposed a modification to the Equality-checker scheme using expander graphs. Bob associates his m circuits with the vertices of an expander graph, and then commits only to those pairs of circuits that correspond to edges of this graph. There are explicit constructions of expander graphs for which this saves a factor of $\Theta(m)$ in the communication complexity, while preserving the security properties of the protocol. This is a nice asymptotic improvement, although it is unclear what the savings would be for the small values of m that might be used in practice.

4   How to Leak Information

The idea explored in this section is to weaken the notion of security by allowing a *malicious* party to learn k bits of information about the other party's input, in addition to the output of protocol. A *semi-honest* party should still only learn the output of the protocol.

Loosely speaking, a two-party protocol π between two parties A and B for computing $f(x_a, x_b)$, leaks only k bits of information if all the malicious party A (symmetrically, B) can learn from protocol π, it can also learn given the output $f(x_a, x_b)$ and an additional value $g(x_b)$ for a g of her choice in G, where G is a family of functions and $G \subseteq \{g|g : \{0,1\}^* \to \{0,1\}^k\}$.

The definition of security of a two-party protocol (refer to [Gol04]), compares the execution of admissible adversaries in the *real-model* and *ideal-model*. In order to formally incorporate the leakage of information in our definition of security, we need to change the definition of *ideal-model*. We call this new model the *k-leaked model*.

k-Leaked Model

In this model of computation, parties have a *semi-trusted* party at their disposal. Execution in the *k-leaked model* proceeds as follows:

- **Inputs:** Each party obtains an input denoted u.
- **Sending inputs to the semi-trusted party:** An honest party always sends u to the semi-trusted party. A malicious party may, depending on u (as well

as an auxiliary input and its coin tosses), either abort or send some other $u' \in \{0,1\}^{|u|}$ to the semi-trusted party.

- **Malicious party asks for k bits of information:** In case either party has aborted, the *semi-trusted party* replies to both parties with a special symbol, denoted $\perp$. Otherwise, the *semi-trusted party* has an input pair (x, y). A malicious party can choose a function $g \in G$, where $G \subseteq \{g | g : \{0,1\}^* \to \{0,1\}^k\}$, and ask the *semi-trusted party* for the value of g at the other party's input. The *semi-trusted party* answers accordingly.
- **The semi-trusted party answers the first party:** The semi-trusted party answers the first party with $f_1(x, y)$.
- **The semi-trusted party answers the second party:** In case the first party is malicious, it may, depending on its input and the answer it received, decide to *stop* the semi-trusted party. In this case the semi-trusted party sends $\perp$ to the second party. Otherwise (i.e. if not stopped), the semi-trusted party sends $f_2(x, y)$ to the second party.
- **Outputs:** An honest party always outputs the message it has obtained from the semi-trusted party. A malicious party may output an arbitrary function of its initial input and the message it has obtained from the semi-trusted party.

Note that we borrowed the definition of *ideal-model* from [Gol04] and made the necessary adjustments to obtain a definition for *k-leaked model*. Now, we can easily obtain a definition for our weakened notion of security by replacing the *ideal-model* by the *k-leaked model* in the security definition of [Gol04].

Loosely speaking, for any admissible pair of parties (A, B) in the *real-model*, there is an admissible pair of parties (A', B') in the *k-leaked model* where the outputs of the two executions are indistinguishable. A pair is admissible if at least one of the parties in the pair is *honest*. We will take advantage of this fact when designing our protocols.

4.1   How to Use the New Definition

In this section, we will describe a method for making *Yao's garbled-circuit* protocol secure against malicious behavior in the *1-leaked model*, where $G = \{g | g : \{0,1\}^* \to \{0,1\}\}$. Note that we have already designed two protocols for making *Yao's protocol* secure against malicious behavior. Our new construction is interesting because it is simple, generic, and more efficient. Particularly, it has the same communication and computation complexity as *Yao's garbled-circuit* protocol for semi-honest parties (Proof of security in the *1-leaked* model is omitted from this extended abstract).

The Protocol

The protocol takes place between Alice and Bob who want to compute $f(x_a, x_b)$ where x_a is Alice's input and x_b is Bob's.[6]

---

[6] Please note that the following protocol only considers the case where both parties share the same output. This doesn't effect the generality of the protocol since any two-party computation in which parties have different outputs can be solved using protocols in which both parties share the same output (please refer to [LP04]).

1. Alice creates a garbled circuit for computing f. She sends the garbled circuit, her garbled input, and a translation table for output wires to Bob.
2. Alice and Bob engage in a series of oblivious transfer protocols so that Bob learns the garbled form of his inputs.
3. Bob computes the circuit and translates the output strings to their actual value using the translation table. Lets call this output O_1.
4. Bob creates a garbled circuit for computing f. He sends the garbled circuit, his garbled input, and a translation table for output wires to Alice.
5. Alice and Bob engage in a series of oblivious transfer protocols so that Alice learns the garbled form of her inputs.
6. Alice computes the circuit and translates the output strings to their actual value, using the translation table. Lets call this value O_2.
7. Alice and Bob engage in a secure protocol (against malicious behavior) that returns 1 if $O_1 = O_2$ and 0 otherwise (This is where a malicious party can learn one extra bit). Bob and Alice need to prove to each other that they actually use O_1 and O_2 as their input to this sub-protocol.
8. If the answer is 0, parties output $\perp$, and abort.
9. Bob and Alice output O_1 and O_2 respectively.

Instantiating Step 7 of the Protocol

The sub-protocol in step 7 needs to return 0 if the inputs are not the same. In addition, any party using an input different from O_1 or O_2 should get caught. It is in fact easy to achieve the latter by requiring the parties to incorporate in the sub-protocol, the garbled form of the output they received. Note that if the translation tables are carefully constructed, a party computing a garbled circuit can only learn the garbled strings corresponding to its own output bits and not the complements. Hence, it is easy for the other party, who created the garbled circuit in first place, to verify the correctness of it. We need a conditional disclosure protocol as described in [AIR01].

In the following protocol, O_1 is the output received by Bob (in binary) and $W_b = w_1 || w_2 \ldots || w_n$ is the garbled form of O_1. Furthermore, the output received by Alice is O_2 with the garbled form $W_a = w_1 || w_2 \ldots || w_n$. Then, the protocol, at a high level, is as follows:

1. Alice discloses W_a to Bob if $O_1 = O_2$, and a random value $r_a \in \{0,1\}^{|W_a|}$ otherwise.
2. Bob calculates his own version of W_a using O_1 and the garbled strings corresponding to the output wires (Bob created the garbled circuit). He verifies that his calculated version is equal to the value he received from Alice. If not, he aborts.
3. Bob discloses W_b to Alice if $O_1 = O_2$, and a random value $r_b \in \{0,1\}^{|W_b|}$ otherwise.
4. Alice verifies the equality in a way similar to (step 2).

Table 5. Computational-cost of the scheme

symmetric Enc.	exponentiations	And	Billionaires	PIR	Median
$O(g)$	$O(I)$	$(352, 34)$	$(2184, 130)$	$(9952, 26)$	$(35832, 642)$

Computational-Cost. Note that by leaking one extra bit, we made the protocol much more efficient. We decreased the communication cost to only twice that of *Yao's garbled circuit* for semi-honest parties. The same is true regarding the cost of computation. Below is a measure of how the protocol performs, both asymptotically and in more concrete terms. As before, for the concrete measurements, the first component shows number of symmetric encryptions while the second component counts number of exponentiations performed. Comparing this table with Tables 2, 3,and 4 shows the dramatic improvement in the computation cost.

Non-interactive Computations

The protocol we used above to make *Yao's garbled-circuit* protocol secure against malicious behavior is generic enough that it can be used in different contexts as well. Particularly, any *non-interactive*[7] two-party protocol which is secure against semi-honest adversaries can use our scheme to make the protocol secure against malicious behavior in the *1-leaked model*. More generally, any non-interactive two-party protocol that is secure in the *semi-honest* version of the *k-leaked model*, can be made secure in the malicious version of *(k+1)-leaked model*. It is important to note that step 7 of the protocol should be instantiated appropriately.

Acknowledgements

We would like to thank David Woodruff and the anonymous reviewers for their helpful suggestions.

References

[AFK87]   M. Abadi, J. Feigenbaum, and J. Kilian. On hiding information from an oracle. In *STOC '87: Proceedings of the nineteenth annual ACM conference on Theory of computing*, pages 195–203. ACM Press, 1987.

[AIR01]   W. Aiello, Y. Ishai, and O. Reingold. Priced oblivious transfer: How to sell digital goods. *Eurocrypt*, 2001.

[BYCKO93] R. Bar-Yehuda, B. Chor, E. Kushilevitz, and A. Orlitsky. Privacy, additional information, and communication. *IEEE Transactions on Information Theory*, 1993.

[Cle89]   R. Cleve. Controlled gradual disclosure schemes for random bits and their applications. In *CRYPTO '89: Proceedings on Advances in cryptology*, pages 573–588. Springer-Verlag, 1989.

---

[7] We call a protocol non-interactive if one party sends his input (in some form) to the second party. Then, the second party computes the functionality on his own (no interaction here).

[FNW96]   R. Fagin, M. Naor, and P. Winkler. Comparing information without leaking it. *Commun. ACM*, 39(5):77–85, 1996.

[GMR89]   S. Goldwasser, S. Micali, and C. Rackoff. The knowledge complexity of interactive proof systems. *SIAM J. Comput.*, 18(1):186–208, 1989.

[GMW86]   O. Goldreich, S. Micali, and A. Wigderson. Proofs that yield nothing but their validity or all languages in np have zero-knowledge proofs. *Proceedings of of the 27th FOCS, pages 174-187*, 1986.

[GMW87]   O. Goldreich, S. Micali, and A. Wigderson. How to play any mental game or a completeness theorem for protocols with honest majority. *In proceedings of 19th Annual ACM Symposium on Theory of Computing, pages 218-229*, 1987.

[Gol04]   O. Goldreich. Foundations of cryptography - volume 2, ch. 7. 2004.

[GP99]   O. Goldreich and E. Petrank. Quantifying knowledge complexity. *Computational Complexity*, 8:50–98, 1999.

[lMR83]   M. luby, S. Micali, and C. Rackoff. How to simultaneously exchange a secret bit by flipping a symmetrically-biased coin. *FOCS*, 1983.

[LP04]   Y. Lindell and B. Pinkas. A proof of yao's protocol for secure two-party computation. *eprint archive*, 2004.

[MNPS04]   D. Malkhi, N. Nisan, B. Pinkas, and Y. Sella. Fairplay– a secure two-party computation system. *Proceedings of Usenix security*, 2004.

[Ped91]   T. P. Pederson. Non-interactive and information-theoritic secure verifiable secret-sharing. 1991.

[Pin03]   Benny Pinkas. Fair secure two-party computation. *Eurocrypt, LNCS 2656, Springer-Verlag, pp. 87-105*, 2003.

[Rab81]   M. Rabin. How to exchange secrets by oblivious transfer. *Technical Report Tech., Memo. TR-81, Aiken Computation Labratory, Harvard University*, 1981.

[Woo06]   D. Woodruff. unpublished manuscript, 2006.

[Yao86]   A. C. Yao. How to generate and exchange secrets. *In Proceedings of the 27th IEEE symposioum on Foundations of Computer science,pages 162-167*, 1986.

A   Proof of Lemma 3

Bob sends $\frac{m}{2}$ garbled inputs for the $\frac{m}{2}$ circuits that Alice will evaluate. Lets denote the set of these inputs I_B, where $|I_B| = \frac{m}{2}$. Let L be the largest subset of I_B with equal inputs, where $|L| = k$. In other words, all other subsets of equal inputs have sizes smaller or equal to k. We want to prove that, with high probability, k is greater than $\frac{5}{6}.\frac{m}{2} = \frac{5m}{12}$.

Note that Alice has $(\frac{m}{2})(\frac{m}{2}-1)/2$ equality-checkers that compare the $\frac{m}{2}$ inputs with each other. Some of these equality-checkers might be wrong (malicious Bob), and therefore verify the equality of two inputs that are not equal. We call two equality-checkers *distinct* if they compare the inputs to four different circuits. The next two Claims imply Lemma 3:

Claim A: If $k \leq \frac{5m}{12}$, at least $\frac{m}{12}$ of the distinct equality-checkers used by Alice for verification were wrong.

Claim B: If Bob sends $\frac{m}{12}$ wrong distinct equality-checkers to Alice, the probability that they are not detected by Alice, and are used by her to verify that Bob's inputs are the same, is less than $(1/2)^{\frac{m}{6}}$.

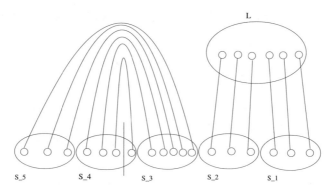

Fig. 1. Nodes represent inputs and edges represent equality-checkers

Proof of Claim A: We know that $|L| = k \leq \frac{5m}{12}$. We consider the following two case:

Case 1: ($\frac{m}{6} \leq k \leq \frac{5m}{12}$) This implies that $min(|L|, |I_B - L|) = min(k, \frac{m}{2} - k) \geq \frac{m}{2} - \frac{5m}{12} = \frac{m}{12}$. Therefore, there are at least $\frac{m}{12}$ distinct equality-checkers among those that compare the inputs in $(I_B - L)$ with those in L. These $\frac{m}{12}$ equality-checkers must have been wrong not to detect that the compared inputs are not the same.

Case 2: ($k \leq \frac{m}{6}$) Consider the partition $(S_1, S_2, ..., S_l, L)$ of the set I_B where each subset S_i and L only contain equal inputs (Fig 1.). Note that $S_1 \cup S_2 \ldots \cup S_l \cup L = I_B$, and all the subsets are pairwise disjoint. Lets denote $|S_i| = k_i$ for all $1 \leq i \leq l$. The fact that $k_1 + ... + k_l + k = \frac{m}{2}$, and ($k \leq \frac{m}{6}$) implies that $k_1 + k_2 + ... + k_l \geq k$. Hence, there are k distinct equality-checkers that compare the k inputs in L with inputs in $S_1, S_2, ..., S_j$ for some $1 \leq j < l$ (Fig 1.). This might only cover portions of set S_j. These k equality-checkers must have been wrong not to detect that their two inputs weren't equal. But there is more.

We insert the remaining portion of S_j and all of $S_{j+1}, ..., S_l$ in a list (in the same order). We cut the list in half, and pair up each input on the right side of the cut with its counterpart on the left (Fig. 1). In worst case, the cut is in the middle of a subset S_t ($j + 1 \leq t \leq l$). This means that at most $\frac{k_t}{2} < \frac{k}{2}$ of these pairs might include equal inputs (in the same subset). The equality-checkers corresponding to the rest of the pairs compare unequal inputs and must have been wrong not to detect the inequalities. Therefore, there is an additional $(\frac{m}{2} - k - k - k_t)/2 > (\frac{m}{2} - 3k)/2$ wrong equality-checkers. This makes the total number of wrong distinct equality-checkers at least $k + (\frac{m}{2} - 3k)/2 = \frac{m}{4} - \frac{k}{2} > \frac{m}{12}$.

Based on Case 1 and Case 2, if less than $\frac{5}{6}$ of the inputs are the same, and all the equality-checkers confirm the equality of inputs, there are at least $\frac{m}{12}$ wrong distinct equality-checkers among them.

Proof of Claim B: Lets assume that $\frac{m}{12}$ distinct equality-checkers are wrong and are used by Alice for verification. The probability that no two endpoints of any of the $m/12$ equality-checkers was exposed in the previous step is less than $(\frac{1}{2})^{\frac{m}{6}}$.

On Constructing Certificateless Cryptosystems from Identity Based Encryption

Benoît Libert* and Jean-Jacques Quisquater

UCL, Microelectronics Laboratory, Crypto Group,
Place du Levant, 3, B-1348, Louvain-La-Neuve, Belgium
{benoit.libert, jean-jacques.quisquater}@uclouvain.be

Abstract. Certificateless cryptography (CL-PKC) is a concept that aims at enjoying the advantages of identity based cryptography without suffering from its inherent key escrow. Several methods were recently suggested to generically construct a certificateless encryption (CLE) scheme by combining identity based schemes with ordinary public key cryptosystems. Whilst the security of one of these generic compositions was proved in a relaxed security model, we show that all them are insecure against chosen-ciphertext attacks in the strongest model of Al-Riyami and Paterson. We show how to easily fix these problems and give a method to achieve generic CLE constructions which are provably CCA-secure in the random oracle model. We finally propose a new efficient pairing-based scheme that performs better than previous proposals without pre-computation. We also prove its security in the random oracle model.

Keywords: Certificateless encryption, provable security, bilinear maps.

1 Introduction

In 2003, Al-Riyami and Paterson [2] invented a paradigm called certificateless public key cryptography (CL-PKC) which is intermediate between identity-based [27, 12] and traditional PKI-supported cryptography. The concept was introduced to suppress the inherent key-escrow property of identity-based cryptosystems (ID-PKC) without losing their most attractive advantage which is the absence of digital certificates and their important management overhead.

Independently of [2] and a bit earlier, Gentry [22] introduced a different but related concept named certificate based encryption (CBE) for which a signature analogue was studied in [24]. This approach is closer to the context of a traditional PKI model as it involves a certification authority (CA) providing an efficient implicit certification service for clients' public keys.

Although very different at first glance, the CBE and CLE concepts were first argued [2] to be closely related and both constructions of [2, 22] use the properties of pairings. A subsequent work of Yum and Lee considered the relations between identity-based (IBE), certificate based (CBE) and certificateless encryption schemes (CLE) and established a result of essential equivalence [31] between

---

* This author thanks the DGTRE's First Europe Program in Belgium.

M. Yung et al. (Eds.): PKC 2006, LNCS 3958, pp. 474–490, 2006.

the three primitives but this result does not hold for the strongest security model developed in [2] for CLE schemes. The same authors also proposed generic constructions of certificateless signatures [30] and encryption schemes [29] but only established the security of their designs in security models that are seemingly undermined w.r.t. the original model considered in [2] for the public key encryption case.

A more recent work [3] thoroughly investigated the connections between the CLE and CBE paradigms by proposing a simplified definition and a revised security model for certificate based encryption before proving that any secure certificateless encryption (CLE) scheme can be turned into a secure CBE in the amended model.

Among other related results, we mention a paper [16] describing a somewhat similar scheme to [3], another work [9] that investigates identity-based and certificateless extensions of key encapsulation mechanisms. Both works [9, 16] considered a model of security which is noticeably weaker (albeit realistic in practice) than the original one [2]. A very recent paper by Baek et al. [4] also showed how to devise a certificateless encryption scheme without pairings. The latter construction enjoys a better efficiency than pairing-based proposals [2, 3, 16] but is supported by a weaker security model and prevents users from generating their public key independently from the system's authority. Finally, Dent and Kudla [17] investigated the feasibility of provably secure CLE schemes in the standard model and ruled out the use of some particular proof techniques for achieving this purpose in accordance with intuitive arguments given in [16].

The contribution of the present paper to the area of certificateless cryptography is two-fold. It first identifies some weaknesses in generic constructions independently considered in [1] and [29]. It shows that one of these flaws is also present in the second provably secure CLE scheme of Al-Riyami and Paterson [3] where it can be very easily fixed. The paper then explains how to obtain generic constructions which are provably secure in the random oracle model. It does so by first giving a generic random oracle-using conversion to turn any CLE scheme which is only secure against chosen-plaintext attacks into an IND-CCA scheme in the full model of Al-Riyami and Paterson [2].

The second contribution of the paper is to describe a new efficient pairing-based scheme yielding some advantages over previous constructions [2, 3, 16, 9]: its encryption operation does not require to compute a pairing (only the decryption algorithm does) and is thus generally faster than in previous proposals [2, 3, 16, 9]. The security proof of the new scheme is nevertheless obtained under a stronger computational assumption than for previous schemes in the literature.

In the forthcoming sections of this paper, we first review the formal definition and adversarial model of CLE schemes in section 2. Section 3 illustrates the power of their security model by showing how several generic constructions studied so far are insecure in it. We explain in section 4 how to repair them and we prove the security of the fixed constructions in the random oracle model. Our new certificateless cryptosystem is then depicted in section 5 where security proofs in the random oracle model are detailed.

2   Preliminaries

We now recall the components of a certificateless encryption scheme before detailing the relevant formal security model [2].

2.1   Definition of Certificateless Encryption (CLE)

Definition 1. *A certificateless encryption scheme (CLE) is a 7-tuple of algorithms which are the following:*

Setup: *is a probabilistic algorithm run by a Key Generation Center (KGC), that, given a security parameter k, returns a randomly chosen master key* mk *and a list of public parameters* params.

Partial-Private-Key-Extract: *is a possibly probabilistic algorithm, run by the KGC, that takes as input a user's identifier* ID_A *and the master key* mk *to return his/her partial private key* d_A.

Set-Secret-Value: *is a probabilistic algorithm that, given a list of public parameters* params, *returns a randomly chosen secret value* x_A *for that user. This algorithm and the next two are performed by the user himself.*

Set-Private-Key: *is a deterministic private key generation algorithm that, given public parameters* params, *a user's partial private key* d_A *and secret value* x_A, *outputs a private key* S_A.

Set-Public-Key: *is a deterministic public key generation algorithm that, given public parameters* params *and a user's secret value* x_A, *computes his/her public key* pk_A. *The latter's well-formedness (i.e. its belonging to a specific group or set) must be publicly verifiable given* params.

Encrypt: *is a probabilistic algorithm taking as input a plaintext m, parameters* params, *a receiver's identity* ID_A *and his public key* pk_A *to produce a ciphertext* $C = \mathsf{Encrypt}(m, \mathsf{params}, \mathsf{ID}_A, \mathsf{pk}_A)$.

Decrypt: *is a deterministic algorithm that, given a ciphertext C, a list of public paramaters* params *and user* ID_A*'s private key, outputs a plaintext m or a distinguished symbol* $\perp$.

For completeness, it is obviously required that $\mathsf{Decrypt}(C, \mathsf{params}, S_A) = m$ *whenever* $C = \mathsf{Encrypt}(m, \mathsf{params}, \mathsf{ID}_A, \mathsf{pk}_A)$ *for all messages* $m \in \mathcal{M}$ *and public keys* $\mathsf{pk}_A = \mathsf{Set\text{-}Public\text{-}Key}(\mathsf{params}, x_A)$ *for which the matching private key is* $S_A = \mathsf{Set\text{-}Private\text{-}Key}(\mathsf{params}, \mathsf{Partial\text{-}Private\text{-}Key\text{-}Extract}(\mathsf{ID}_A), x_A)$ *and the secret value is* $x_A = \mathsf{Set\text{-}Secret\text{-}Value}(\mathsf{params})$.

Unlike Setup and Partial-Private-Key-Extract that are run by a Key Generation Center (KGC), algorithms Set-Secret-Value, Set-Private-Key and Set-Public-Key are executed by the user whose private key remains hidden from the KGC.

The recent pairing-free scheme of Baek et al. [4] fits a slightly different model where users have to obtain their partial private key and a partial public key before generating their full public key. This approach is closer to the "self-certified" paradigm [23] which is another approach suggested by Girault in 1991 to use public key cryptography without traditional digital certificates and without involving an escrow authority.

2.2   Security Model

In [2], two kinds of adversaries are distinguished against CLE schemes. A Type I adversary ignores the KGC's master key but can replace public keys of arbitrary identities with other public keys of her choosing. Such an adversarial behavior seems natural as, in the absence of digital certificates, anyone can alter public directories by replacing public keys without being caught or detected. As attackers against IBE schemes (recalled in appendix A), Type I adversaries can also obtain partial and full private keys of arbitrary identities.

In contrast, a Type II adversary knows the KGC's master key (and does not need a partial key exposure oracle) and may still obtain full private keys for arbitrary identities but is disallowed to replace public keys during the game.

For both types of adversaries, depending on the strength of the attack, we may or may not provide them with an oracle decrypting arbitrary ciphertexts using the private key associated with arbitrary identities.

In the chosen-ciphertext scenario, the authors of [2] consider decryption oracles that should be able (thanks to suitable knowledge extractors) to output consistent answers even for identities whose public key has been replaced and for which they do not know the new private key. The latter requirement might look too strong but it may be argued that decryption queries involving identities of replaced public key are far more useful to a Type I attacker (especially when the latter does not know the private key associated with the new public key).

In the security analysis of generic constructions in section 3.1, we will illustrate the importance of considering adversaries who replace public keys instead of merely corrupting their owner and learning his/her secret value.

Definition 2. *A CLE scheme is IND-CCA secure if no probabilistic polynomial time (PPT) adversary $\mathcal{A}$ of Type I or II has a non-negligible advantage in the following game:*

1. *Given a security parameter k, the challenger runs* Setup(k) *and then delivers the resulting parameters* params *to $\mathcal{A}$ who also receives the master key* mk *if she is of Type II. Otherwise,* mk *is kept secret.*
2. *$\mathcal{A}$ is given access to*
   - *a public key broadcast oracle* Public-Key-Broadcast *taking as input identities and returning the matching public keys.*
   - *a partial key exposure oracle* Partial-Private-Key-Extract *(if she is of Type I as such an oracle is useless otherwise) returning partial private keys associated with users' identities.*
   - *a private key exposure oracle* Private-Key-Extract *revealing private keys of entities whose public key was not replaced.*
   - *a decryption oracle* Decrypt *which, given a ciphertext and an identity (C, ID), returns the decryption of C using the private key corresponding to the current value of entity* ID*'s public key.*

If $\mathcal{A}$ is of Type I, she has also access to a public key replacement oracle Public-Key-Replace *which, given an identifier* ID *and a valid public key* pk$'$, *replaces user* ID*'s public key with* pk$'$.

478   B. Libert and J.-J. Quisquater

A outputs messages m_0, m_1 together with an identity ID^* of uncorrupted private key. If $\mathcal{A}$ is of Type I, ID^* may not have been submitted to both oracles Public-Key-Replace *and* Partial-Private-Key-Extract. *She gets a ciphertext $C^* = \mathsf{Encrypt}(m_b, \mathsf{params}, \mathsf{ID}^*, \mathsf{pk}^*)$ where $b \xleftarrow{R} \{0,1\}$ and pk^* is the public key currently associated with ID^*.*

4. *She then issues a new sequence of queries but is not permitted to ask for the decryption of C^* for the combination $(\mathsf{ID}^*, \mathsf{pk}^*)$ under which m_b was encrypted at step 3. Moreover no private key exposure query can be made on ID^* at any time and, in a Type I attack, ID^* may not be submitted to both oracles* Public-Key-Replace *and* Partial-Private-Key-Extract.

5. *A eventually outputs a bit b' and wins if $b' = b$. As usual, her advantage is $Adv_{CLE}^{\mathsf{ind-cca}}(\mathcal{A}) := 2 \times Pr[b' = b] - 1$.*

The above definition captures a chosen-ciphertext scenario. The weaker chosen-plaintext security (or IND-CPA security) notion is formalized by a similar game where attackers have no decryption oracles.

The security models considered in [4, 16, 29] are weaker in that they disallow Type I attackers to ever extract the partial private key of the target entity. In contrast, the above model allows them to do so as long as they do not additionally replace the associated public key. Besides, the models of [16, 29] only require challengers to correctly handle decryption queries for entities whose public key was not replaced. From here on, we will stick to the model of definition 2.

3   On the Power of Public Key Replacement Oracles

This section underlines the strength of the security model captured by definition 2. We first explain simple attacks that compromise the security of some generic constructions of certificateless encryption. We then exemplify that allowing decryption queries even for entities whose public keys have been replaced also harms the security of the scheme proposed by Al-Riyami and Paterson published in [3]. We also show how to very easily fix the problem.

3.1   The Case of Generic Constructions

In [1] and [29], generic constructions of certificateless encryption were independently proposed. Their idea is basically to combine strongly secure identity-based and traditional public key encryption schemes in a sequential or parallel fashion. More precisely, let $\Pi^{IBE} = (\mathsf{Setup}^{IBE}, \mathsf{Extract}^{IBE}, \mathcal{E}^{IBE}, \mathcal{D}^{IBE})$ be an IBE scheme (see appendix A for details on the formal syntax of such a primitive) and $\Pi^{PKE} = (\mathcal{K}^{PKE}, \mathcal{E}_{pk}^{PKE}, \mathcal{D}_{sk}^{PKE})$ denote a traditional public key encryption scheme (the latter being made of a key generation algorithm $\mathcal{K}^{PKE}$, a probabilistic encryption algorithm $\mathcal{E}_{pk}^{PKE}$ and the deterministic decryption algorithm $\mathcal{D}_{sk}^{PKE}$), a CLE scheme Π^{CLE} can be obtained with the present sequential composition. Its security was proved by Yum and Lee [29] in a model where adversaries are restricted not to issue a partial key exposure query on the target identity ID^* (recall that such a query is allowed in the strong model if entity ID^*'s public key is never replaced) nor to require the correct decryption of ciphertexts encrypted under identities of replaced public keys.

Setup: is an algorithm running the setup algorithm of Π^{IBE}. The message space of Π^{CLE} is the message space of Π^{PKE} while its ciphertext space is the one of Π^{IBE}. Both schemes have to be compatible in that the plaintext space of Π^{IBE} must contain the ciphertext space of Π^{PKE}.

Partial-Private-Key-Extract: is the private key generation algorithm of Π^{IBE}.

Set-Secret-Value and Set-Public-Key: run the key generation procedure of Π^{PKE} to obtain a private key sk and a public key pk. The former is the secret value and the latter becomes the public key.

Set-Private-Key: returns $S_A := (d_A, \mathsf{sk}_A)$ where d_A is obtained by running the key generation algorithm of Π^{IBE} for the identity ID_A and sk_A is entity A's secret value obtained from Π^{PKE}'s key generation algorithm.

Encrypt: to encrypt $m \in \mathcal{M}^{PKE}$ using the identifier $\mathsf{ID}_A \in \{0,1\}^*$ and the public key pk_A,

1. Check that pk_A has the right shape for Π^{PKE}.
2. Compute and output the ciphertext $C = \mathcal{E}^{IBE}_{\mathsf{ID}_A}(\mathcal{E}^{PKE}_{\mathsf{pk}_A}(m))$ where $\mathcal{E}^{IBE}_{\mathsf{ID}_A}$ and $\mathcal{E}^{PKE}_{\mathsf{pk}_A}$ respectively denote the encryption algorithms of Π^{IBE} and Π^{PKE} for the identity ID_A and the public key pk_A.

Decrypt: to decrypt C using $S_A = (d_A, \mathsf{sk}_A)$,

1. Compute $\mathcal{D}^{IBE}_{d_A}(C)$ using the decryption algorithm of Π^{IBE}. If the result is $\perp$, return $\perp$ and reject the ciphertext.
2. Otherwise, compute $\mathcal{D}^{PKE}_{\mathsf{sk}_A}(\mathcal{D}^{IBE}_{d_A}(C))$ using the decryption algorithm of Π^{PKE} and return the result.

This construction is insecure against Type I attacks in the full model of definition 2 even if its building blocks Π^{IBE} and Π^{PKE} are each IND-CCA secure in their model. We show it using simple arguments such as those given in [18, 32] against the security of naive multiple-encryptions. Let $C^* = \mathcal{E}^{IBE}_{\mathsf{ID}^*}(\mathcal{E}^{PKE}_{\mathsf{pk}^*}(m_b^*))$ be the challenge ciphertext in the game of definition 2 where m_b^* (for a random bit $b \in \{0,1\}$) denotes one of the messages produced by the adversary $\mathcal{A}_I$ in her challenge request. Assume that $\mathcal{A}_I$ never replaces the public key of ID^* but rather extracts the partial private key d_{ID^*} after the challenge phase. She then obtains $\mathcal{E}_1 = \mathcal{D}^{IBE}_{d_{\mathsf{ID}^*}}(C^*) = \mathcal{E}^{PKE}_{\mathsf{pk}^*}(m_b)$ and she may compute another encryption $C' = \mathcal{E}^{IBE}_{\mathsf{ID}^*}(\mathcal{E}_1) \neq C^*$ of the same plaintext and obtain m_b^*.

This does not contradict the result of [29] that considers a weaker model where attackers may not extract the partial private key for the target identity.

In [1], a reverse-ordered composition (that we call Generic-CLE-2) where ciphertexts have the form $C = \mathcal{E}^{PKE}_{\mathsf{pk}_A}(\mathcal{E}^{IBE}_{\mathsf{ID}}(m))$ is suggested. This composition is vulnerable against an attacker replacing the target entity's public key before the challenge phase. Knowing the secret value sk^* in the challenge phase, the adversary obtains $\mathcal{E}^{IBE}_{\mathsf{ID}^*}(m_b)$ that is re-encrypted into $C' = \mathcal{E}^{PKE}_{\mathsf{pk}^*}(\mathcal{E}^{IBE}_{\mathsf{ID}^*}(m_b)) \neq C^*$ which may be submitted to the decryption oracle even though entity ID^*'s public key was replaced in the model of [2].

In [1], a 'parallel' construction (that we will call Generic-CLE-3) was also considered. It encrypts a plaintext m into

$$C = \langle \mathcal{E}_{\mathsf{pk}_A}^{PKE}(m_1), \mathcal{E}_{\mathsf{ID}}^{IBE}(m_2) \rangle$$

where m_1 and m_2 are subject to the constraint $m = m_1 \oplus m_2$. This parallel approach is vulnerable to a similar attack to those outlined by Dodis and Katz [18] or Zhang et al. [32] against multiple-encryption schemes: if $C^* = \langle \mathcal{E}_1^*, \mathcal{E}_2^* \rangle$ is the challenge ciphertext in the IND-CCA game, both kinds of adversaries $\mathcal{A}_I$ or $\mathcal{A}_{II}$ may first request the decryption of $C_1' = \langle \mathcal{E}_1^*, \mathcal{E}_{\mathsf{ID}}^{IBE}(0^{IBE}) \rangle$ and then the decryption of $C_2' = \langle \mathcal{E}_{\mathsf{pk}}^{PKE}(0^{PKE}), \mathcal{E}_2^* \rangle$, where 0^{PKE} and 0^{IBE} are plaintexts made of zeros in Π^{IBE} and Π^{PKE}. By combining the results m_1' and m_2' of both decryption requests into $m_1' \oplus m_2'$, the adversary $\mathcal{A}_I$ gets back the plaintext encrypted in C^*. This attack works even if Π^{IBE} and Π^{PKE} are both IND-CCA secure and it does not even require $\mathcal{A}_I$ to replace any public key. Unlike the previous two attacks, it also works in the weaker models of [16, 29].

In [18], Dodis and Katz gave generic techniques to counteract such attacks and build IND-CCA secure (possibly parallel) multiple-encryption schemes from public key encryption schemes which are individually IND-CCA. They showed that their methods apply to the design of certificate-based encryption schemes [22] without resorting to the random oracle model. Because of the strong constraint imposed on decryption oracles in definition 2, those techniques do not seem to directly apply in the present context (although they do so in the relaxed models considered in [16, 29]). In security proofs, the difficulty is that the simulator does not know the secret value of entities whose public key was replaced.

3.2   The Second Al-Riyami-Paterson Scheme

In [3], the inventors of the certificateless paradigm proposed a variant (named FullCLE*) of their original scheme that is significantly more efficient. It again uses *bilinear map groups* which are groups $(\mathbb{G}_1, \mathbb{G}_2)$ of prime order q for which there exists a bilinear map $\hat{e} : \mathbb{G}_1 \times \mathbb{G}_1 \to \mathbb{G}_2$ satisfying the following properties:

1. Bilinearity: $\forall \, P, Q \in \mathbb{G}_1, \, \forall \, a, b \in \mathbb{Z}_p^*$, we have $\hat{e}(P^a, Q^b) = \hat{e}(P, Q)^{ab}$.
2. Non-degeneracy: if P generates $\mathbb{G}_1$, then $\hat{e}(P, P)$ generates $\mathbb{G}_2$.
3. Computability: $\forall \, P, Q \in \mathbb{G}_1, \, \hat{e}(P, Q)$ can be efficiently computed.

In FullCLE*, public keys are made of a single group element $Y_A = x_A P \in \mathbb{G}_1$, for a secret value $x_A \in \mathbb{Z}_q^*$, and checking their validity only requires an elliptic curve scalar multiplication. The plaintext is actually scrambled twice using two distinct superposed one-time masks. In some sense, this scheme may be regarded as an optimized composition of the Boneh-Franklin IBE [12] with an ElGamal-like cryptosystem [21]. In order to achieve the security in the sense of definition 2, the authors of [3] again applied the Fujisaki-Okamoto conversion [20].

In more details, the KGC has a master key $s \in \mathbb{Z}_q^*$ and a master public key $P_{pub} = sP$. It computes partial private keys as $d_A = sh_1(\mathsf{ID}_A)$, where $h_1 : \{0, 1\}^* \to \mathbb{G}_1^*$ maps public identifiers onto the group $\mathbb{G}_1$, while end-users' private keys consist of a secret value x_A and a partial private key d_A. In accordance with the Fujisaki-Okamoto construction, messages m are encrypted into

$$C = \langle U, V, W \rangle = \langle rP, \sigma \oplus h_2(\hat{e}(P_{pub}, h_1(\mathsf{ID}_A))^r) \oplus h_2'(rY_A), m \oplus h_4(\sigma) \rangle$$

where $r = h_3(\sigma, m)$ for a random string $\sigma \xleftarrow{R} \{0,1\}^{k_1}$ (for some $k_1 \in \mathbb{N}$) and hash functions $h_2 : \mathbb{G}_2 \to \{0,1\}^{k_1}$, $h_2' : \mathbb{G}_1 \to \{0,1\}^{k_1}$, $h_3 : \{0,1\}^{n+k_1} \to \mathbb{Z}_q^*$, $h_4 : \{0,1\}^{k_1} \to \{0,1\}^n$.

It turns out that the original Fujisaki-Okamoto padding [20] does not suffice to achieve the security level modelled in definition 2. We find that a Type I adversary $\mathcal{A}_I$ can break the non-malleability of FullCLE* in the scenario of definition 2 by replacing twice the target identity's public key. If the challenge ciphertext is $C^* = \langle U^*, V^*, W^* \rangle$ and x^* denotes the secret value of the target identity ID^* (which is known to a Type I adversary $\mathcal{A}$ replacing entity ID^*'s public key before the challenge phase), the attacker can replace entity ID^*'s public key with $x'P$ after the challenge phase and then ask for the decryption of $C' = \langle U^*, V^* \oplus h_2'(x^*U^*) \oplus h_2'(x'U^*), W^* \rangle$ (which is an encryption of the same plaintext as C^* for the combination $(\mathsf{ID}^*, x'P)$). Since decryption queries remain allowed even for entities of a replaced public key, $\mathcal{A}_I$ can issue a decryption query on $C' \neq C$ for the identity ID' and recover the plaintext.

Fortunately, such an attack is easily defeated by hashing the recipient's public key along with his identity and the pair (σ, m) when computing r in the encryption algorithm. A variant of FullCLE* independently proposed by Cheng and Comley [16] is immune to the latter attack because it scrambles σ with a hash value of both rY_A and $\hat{e}(P_{pub}, Q_{\mathsf{ID}_A})^r$ instead of using separate masks.

These observations shed new lights on the power of attackers replacing entities' public keys instead of merely obtaining their secret value. Indeed, the FullCLE* scheme remains secure in a model where attackers cannot replace public keys but are rather provided with an oracle returning secret values of arbitrary identities. The latter model is thus strictly weaker than the one of [2].

4   Secure Combinations in the Random Oracle Model

We now explain how to obtain generic constructions that withstand the attacks outlined in section 3.1 and that are provably secure in the random oracle model.

We first show a generic random oracle-based transformation that turns any IND-CPA certificateless encryption scheme into a secure CLE system in the chosen-ciphertext scenario of definition 2. We then show that all the generic compositions recalled in section 3.1 are IND-CPA if they start from chosen-plaintext secure IBE and public key encryption schemes.

4.1   From Chosen-Plaintext to Chosen-Ciphertext Security

This transformation is a modification of the first Fujisaki-Okamoto conversion [19] which provides IND-CCA secure public key encryption schemes from IND-CPA ones. Our modification is to include the recipient's identity and public key among the inputs of the hash function deriving random coins from the message and a random string in the encryption algorithm.

To handle decryption queries of the chosen-ciphertext attacker, the strategy of the plaintext extractor is essentially the following: for every new random oracle query on a string $(m||\sigma||\mathsf{pk}||\mathsf{ID})$, it returns a random value r and runs the encryption algorithm of the weakly secure CLE scheme with the identity ID and the public key pk (that may have been replaced or not) to encrypt $(m||\sigma)$ using the randomness r. The resulting ciphertext C is stored in a list. By doing so, the simulator anticipates subsequent decryption queries, knowing that any valid ciphertext submitted in a decryption query was previously computed and stored in the list with all but negligible probability. The latter strategy allows us to handle decryption queries even when the relevant public key was replaced. It is a *generic knowledge extractor* (in the random oracle model) while previous works [2, 3, 4] that considered the treatment of this kind of decryption requests only used knowledge extractors that were specific to their schemes.

Theorem 1. *Let Π^{CLE} be an IND-CPA certificateless encryption scheme and suppose that*

$$\mathcal{E}^{\mathsf{params}}_{ID,\mathsf{pk}}(M, R) \quad and \quad \mathcal{D}^{\mathsf{params}}_{S_{ID}}$$

are its encryption and decryption algorithms where ID and pk respectively denote the recipient's identity and his public key, M is a message of $n + k_0$ bits, R is a random string of ℓ bits while S_{ID} is the recipient's private decryption key. Then, an IND-CCA certificateless scheme $\overline{\Pi}^{CLE}$ can be obtained using modified encryption and decryption algorithms

$$\overline{\mathcal{E}}^{\mathsf{params}}_{ID,\mathsf{pk}}(m, \sigma) = \mathcal{E}^{\mathsf{params}}_{ID,\mathsf{pk}}(m||\sigma, H(m||\sigma||\mathsf{pk}||\mathsf{ID}))$$

where $H : \{0,1\}^* \rightarrow \{0,1\}^\ell$ is a random oracle, $m \in \{0,1\}^n$ is the plaintext and $\sigma \in \{0,1\}^{k_0}$ is a random string. The modified decryption algorithm is

$$\overline{\mathcal{D}}^{\mathsf{params}}_{S_{ID}}(C) = m \quad if \quad C = \mathcal{E}^{\mathsf{params}}_{ID,\mathsf{pk}}(m||\sigma, H(m||\sigma||\mathsf{pk}||\mathsf{ID}))$$

$$and \perp otherwise$$

where $(m||\sigma) = \mathcal{D}^{\mathsf{params}}_{S_{ID}}(C)$.

More precisely, assume that a Type I (resp. Type II) IND-CCA attacker $\mathcal{A}$ has advantage ϵ over $\overline{\Pi}^{CLE}$ when running in time τ, making q_D decryption queries and q_H random oracle queries. It implies a Type I (resp. Type II) IND-CPA attacker $\mathcal{B}$ with advantage

$$\epsilon' > (\epsilon - q_H/2^{k_0-1})(1 - 2^{-\ell_0})^{q_D}$$

over Π^{CLE} when running in time $\tau' < \tau + O(q_H \tau_{\mathcal{E}})$, where $\tau_{\mathcal{E}}$ is the the cost the original encryption algorithm and

$$\ell_0 = \log_2 \left(\min_{\substack{m \in \{0,1\}^{n+k_0} \\ ID,\mathsf{pk}}} [\#\{\mathcal{E}^{\mathsf{params}}_{ID,\mathsf{pk}}(m, r)|r \in \{0,1\}^\ell\}] \right)$$

is the logarithm of the cardinality of the smallest set of encrypted values that can be obtained for fixed plaintext, identity and public key.

Proof. The proof is quite similar to the one of theorem 3 in [19] but we have to show that the adapted conversion generically works in our context. We outline how $\mathcal{B}$ uses $\mathcal{A}$ to succeed in a chosen-plaintext attack against her challenger $\mathcal{CH}$. $\mathcal{B}$ starts by forwarding to $\mathcal{A}$ the public parameters (together with the KGC's master key in the scenario of a Type II attack) she obtains from $\mathcal{CH}$. Recall that Π^{CLE} can be itself a random oracle-using scheme. All random oracles pertaining to Π^{CLE} are thus controlled by $\mathcal{CH}$. The chosen-ciphertext attacker $\mathcal{A}$ also has access to a decryption oracle and an additional random oracle H that are simulated by $\mathcal{B}$ as follows:

- random oracle queries related to Π^{CLE} as well as public key broadcast, public key replacement (in the case of Type I attacks) and partial/full private key exposure queries are passed to $\mathcal{CH}$ whose answers are relayed to $\mathcal{A}$.
- Whenever $\mathcal{A}$ submits a string $(m||\sigma||\mathsf{pk}||\mathsf{ID})$ to the H oracle, $\mathcal{B}$ first checks if H was previously queried on the same input and returns the previously answered value if it was. Otherwise, $\mathcal{B}$ returns a randomly chosen $r \xleftarrow{R} \mathbb{Z}_q^*$. She then runs the encryption algorithm of Π^{CLE} to compute

$$C = \mathcal{E}_{\mathsf{ID},\mathsf{pk}}^{\mathsf{params}}(m||\sigma, r)$$

which is a $\overline{\Pi}^{CLE}$ encryption of m under the public key pk and the identity ID using the randomness $\sigma \in \{0,1\}^{k_0}$ (as well as a Π^{CLE} encryption of $(m||\sigma)$ for the randomness r). In order to anticipate subsequent decryption queries, a record containing the input $(m||\sigma||\mathsf{pk}||\mathsf{ID})$, the output r and the ciphertext C is stored in a list L_H. Note that $\mathcal{B}$ might need $\mathcal{CH}$ to answer queries for random oracles related to Π^{CLE} to be able to compute C.
- Decryption queries for a ciphertext C and an identity ID: $\mathcal{B}$ first recovers the public key pk currently associated with ID (by issuing a public key query to $\mathcal{CH}$). She then searches in list L_H for a tuple of the form $((m||x||\mathsf{pk}||\mathsf{ID}), r, C)$ in order to return the corresponding m if such a tuple exists and $\perp$ otherwise.

When $\mathcal{A}$ decides that phase 1 is over, she outputs messages (m_0, m_1) and an identity ID^* (whose private key was not exposed and that was not submitted to both the Public-Key-Replace and Partial-Private-Key-Extract oracles). At that point, $\mathcal{B}$ obtains the current value pk^* of entity ID^*'s public key (by issuing a Public-Key-Broadcast query to $\mathcal{CH}$) before randomly choosing two strings $\sigma_0, \sigma_1 \xleftarrow{R} \{0,1\}^{k_0}$ and in turn sending her challenge request $(M_0 = (m_0||\sigma_0), M_1 = (m_1||\sigma_1), \mathsf{ID}^*)$ to $\mathcal{CH}$. The latter then returns a Π^{CLE} encryption C^* of $M_b = (m_b||\sigma_b)$ for the identity ID^* and the current public key pk^* using some randomness $r^* \xleftarrow{R} \mathbb{Z}_q^*$.

As in the proof of theorem 2 in [19], if $\mathcal{A}$ ever queries H on the input $(m_d||\sigma_d||\mathsf{pk}^*||\mathsf{ID}^*)$ for $d \in \{0,1\}$, $\mathcal{B}$ halts and outputs the corresponding bit d as a result which is very likely to be correct in this case: since $\mathcal{A}$ has absolutely no information on $\sigma_{\bar{b}}$ ($\bar{b}$ being the complement bit of b), one can show as in [19] that $\mathcal{A}$ only asks for the hash value $H(m_{\bar{b}}||\sigma_{\bar{b}}||\mathsf{pk}^*||\mathsf{ID}^*)$ with probability $q_H/2^{k_0}$ throughout the game). On the other hand, if such an H-query never occurs, $\mathcal{B}$ outputs exactly the same result b' as $\mathcal{A}$ and obviously succeeds against $\mathcal{CH}$ if $\mathcal{A}$ yields a correct guess $b' = b$.

The probability for $\mathcal{B}$ to wrongly reject a ciphertext during the game is smaller than $1 - (1 - 2^{-\ell_0})^{q_D}$. Indeed, for a given decryption query on a ciphertext C and an identity ID, assume that $(m||\sigma) = \mathcal{D}_{S_{\text{ID}}}^{\text{params}}(C)$ and does not figure (together with ID and pk) in list L_H. The probability that $H(m||\sigma||\text{pk}||\text{ID})$ takes a value encrypting $(m||\sigma)$ into C is at most $2^{-\ell_0}$ (as at most $2^{\ell - \ell_0}$ distinct random values $r \in R$ may encrypt a given ciphertext into the same ciphertext by the definition of ℓ_0) .

It comes that $\mathcal{B}$'s advantage against $\mathcal{CH}$ is at least

$$\epsilon' > (\epsilon - q_H/2^{k_0 - 1})(1 - 2^{-\ell_0})^{q_D}$$

and that her running time is bounded by $\tau' < \tau + O(q_H \tau_{\mathcal{E}})$ where $\tau_{\mathcal{E}}$ is the time complexity of the encryption algorithm of the basic scheme Π^{CLE}. She also has to issue $q_D + 1$ public key broadcast oracle queries to $\mathcal{CH}$ and q_H queries to random oracles pertaining to Π^{CLE}.   □

4.2   Generic IND-CPA Secure Compositions

From now, we only have to consider constructions that are only secure against chosen-plaintext attacks. By applying to them the random oracle-using conversion, we end up with provably secure constructions in the random oracle model.

Let $\Pi^{IBE} = (\text{Setup}^{IBE}, \text{Extract}^{IBE}, \mathcal{E}^{IBE}, \mathcal{D}^{IBE})$ be an IBE scheme and $\Pi^{PKE} = (\mathcal{K}^{PKE}, \mathcal{E}_{pk}^{PKE}, \mathcal{D}_{sk}^{PKE})$ be a traditional public key encryption scheme.

Theorem 2. *If Π^{IBE} is IND-ID-CPA and Π^{PKE} is IND-CPA, then the Generic-CLE-1 is IND-CPA.*

The proof of the above theorem (detailed in the full paper) separately consider Type I and Type II adversaries.

Lemma 1. *A Type I IND-CPA adversary $\mathcal{A}_I$ having an advantage ϵ over Generic-CLE-1 implies either an IND-ID-CPA adversary with advantage $\epsilon/(2q_{\text{ID}})$ over Π^{IBE} or an IND-CPA adversary with advantage $\epsilon/(2q_{\text{ID}})$ over Π^{PKE}, where q_{ID} is the total number of distinct identities involved in $\mathcal{A}_I$'s requests.*

Lemma 2. *A Type II IND-CPA adversary $\mathcal{A}_{II}$ with advantage ϵ over Generic-CLE-1 implies an IND-CPA adversary $\mathcal{B}$ with advantage ϵ/q_{ID} over Π^{PKE}, where q_{ID} is the total number of distinct identities involved in $\mathcal{A}_{II}$'s requests.*

The proofs of chosen-plaintext security of Generic-CLE-2 and Generic-CLE-3 are very similar. In lemmas 1 and 2, q_{ID} can be the number of random oracle queries for hash functions mapping identifiers onto cyclic subgroups or finite fields if we assume that any query involving a given identity comes after a hash query on it.

This shows how to obtain a secure generic construction in the random oracle model. In the case of Generic-CLE-1, if the encryption schemes of Π^{PKE} and Π^{IBE} use distinct sets of randomness R_1 and R_2, the enhanced CLE scheme may use a random oracle $H : \{0,1\}^* \rightarrow R_1 \times R_2$ so that an encryption of a plaintext m using the random string σ is given by

$$\overline{\mathcal{E}}_{\mathsf{ID},\mathsf{pk}}^{CLE}(m||\sigma) = \mathcal{E}_{\mathsf{ID}}^{IBE}(\mathcal{E}_{\mathsf{pk}}^{PKE}(m||\sigma, r_1), r_2)$$

where $(r_1||r_2) = H(m||\sigma||\mathsf{pk}||\mathsf{ID})$. In the case of Generic-CLE-3, we have

$$\overline{\mathcal{E}}_{\mathsf{ID},\mathsf{pk}}^{CLE}(m||\sigma) = \langle \mathcal{E}_{\mathsf{pk}}^{PKE}(m_1, r_1), \mathcal{E}_{\mathsf{ID}}^{IBE}(m_2, r_2) \rangle$$

with $m_1 \oplus m_2 = m||\sigma$.

5   A New Efficient Construction

We present here our new efficient certificateless encryption scheme that we call NewFullCLE. Its security relies on the intractability of the following problem that was introduced in [10] by Boneh and Boyen.

Definition 3 ([10]). *The* **p-Bilinear Diffie-Hellman Inversion problem** *(p-BDHI) is, given* $\langle P, \alpha P, \alpha^2 P, \dots, \alpha^p P \rangle \in \mathbb{G}_1^{p+1}$*, to compute* $\hat{e}(P, P)^{1/\alpha} \in \mathbb{G}_2$*.*

5.1   The Scheme

Similarly to FullCLE*, NewFullCLE may be viewed as an optimized combination of an IBE with a traditional ElGamal-like [21] cryptosystem.

Setup: given security parameters k, k_0 so that k_0 is polynomial in k, this algorithm chooses a k-bit prime number q, bilinear map groups $(\mathbb{G}_1, \mathbb{G}_2)$ of order q, a generator $P \in \mathbb{G}_1$ and hash functions $h_1 : \{0,1\}^* \to \mathbb{Z}_q^*$, $h_2 : \mathbb{G}_2^2 \to \{0,1\}^{n+k_0}$, $h_3 : \{0,1\}^* \to \mathbb{Z}_q^*$. A master key $\mathsf{mk} := s \xleftarrow{R} \mathbb{Z}_q^*$ and a public key $P_{pub} = sP \in \mathbb{G}_1$ are also chosen. The group element $g = \hat{e}(P, P) \in \mathbb{G}_2$ is also included among the public parameters which are

$$\mathsf{params} := \{q, k, k_0, \mathbb{G}_1, \mathbb{G}_2, P, P_{pub}, g, \hat{e}, h_1, h_2, h_3, n, \mathcal{M}, \mathcal{C}\}$$

where $\mathcal{M} := \{0,1\}^n$, $\mathcal{C} := \mathbb{G}_1 \times \{0,1\}^{n+k_0}$ respectively denote cleartext and ciphertext spaces.

Partial-Private-Key-Extract: takes as input entity A's identifier $\mathsf{ID}_A \in \{0,1\}^*$ and extracts A's partial private key $d_A = \frac{1}{s+h_1(\mathsf{ID}_A)} P \in \mathbb{G}_1$.

Set-Secret-Value: given params and A as inputs, this algorithm picks $x_A \xleftarrow{R} \mathbb{Z}_q^*$ which is returned as user A's secret value.

Set-Private-Key: given params, user A's partial private key $d_A \in \mathbb{G}_1$ and his secret value $x_A \in \mathbb{Z}_q^*$, this algorithm returns the pair $S_A = (x_A, d_A) \in \mathbb{Z}_q^* \times \mathbb{G}_1$ as a private key.

Set-Public-Key: takes as input params and entity A's secret value $x_A \in \mathbb{Z}_q^*$ and produces A's public key $\mathsf{pk}_A := y_A = g^{x_A} \in \mathbb{G}_2$.

Encrypt: to encrypt $m \in \{0,1\}^n$ using the identifier $\mathsf{ID}_A \in \{0,1\}^*$ and the public key $\mathsf{pk}_A = y_A = g^{x_A}$, the sender

1. Checks that $y_A^q = 1_{\mathbb{G}_2}$.
2. Picks $\sigma \xleftarrow{R} \{0,1\}^{k_0}$, computes $r = h_3(m||\sigma||\mathsf{pk}_A||\mathsf{ID}_A) \in \mathbb{Z}_q^*$ and the ciphertext is

$$C = \langle c_1, c_2 \rangle = \langle rh_1(\mathsf{ID}_A)P + rP_{pub}, (m||\sigma) \oplus h_2(g^r||y_A^r) \rangle.$$

Decrypt: given $C = \langle c_1, c_2 \rangle$, the receiver computes $\omega = \hat{e}(c_1, d_A)$ and then $(m||\sigma) = c_2 \oplus h_2(\omega||\omega^{x_A}) \in \{0,1\}^{n+k_0}$. The message is accepted iff $c_1 = r(h_1(\mathsf{ID}_A)P + P_{pub})$ with $r = h_3(m||\sigma||\mathsf{pk}_A||\mathsf{ID}_A) \in \mathbb{Z}_q^*$.

In this construction, partial private keys are signatures computed using a signature scheme independently considered in [11] and [33]. The NewFullCLE scheme is constructed on the Sakai-Kasahara IBE [26, 14, 15] which bears itself similarities with the second IBE scheme that was proved to be selective-ID secure [13, 10] without random oracles by Boneh and Boyen [10]. As for the Cheng-Chen [14] variant of the Sakai-Kasahara IBE, its security proof holds in the random oracle model [8]. The consistency of the construction is easy to check as we have

$$\hat{e}\big(rh_1(\mathsf{ID}_A)P + rP_{pub}, \frac{1}{s + h_1(\mathsf{ID}_A)}P\big) = \hat{e}(P, P)^r.$$

Including g^r among the inputs of h_2 in step 2 of the encryption algorithm is necessary to achieve a security reduction under the p-BDHI assumption. The string $(m||\sigma)$ could be hidden by a hash value of only y_A^r but the security would have to rely on a newly defined fancy assumption.

Interestingly, hashing g^r along with y_A^r is no longer necessary if the scheme is transformed into a certificate-based encryption scheme [22]. This is due to particularities of the certificate-based security model which is not detailed here.

5.2   Efficiency Issues

As for the FullCLE* scheme proposed by Al-Riyami and Paterson [3], the validity of the public key can be checked very efficiently. As in [3], assuming that the bilinear map groups $(\mathbb{G}_1, \mathbb{G}_2)$ are chosen by a higher level authority and commonly used by several distinct KGCs, end-users may generate their public key independently of any authority in the system.

The encryption algorithm only entails two exponentiations in $\mathbb{G}_2$ and a multi-exponentiation in $\mathbb{G}_1$. It has a comparable efficiency to the pairing-free scheme of [4]. The receiver has to compute a pairing, an exponentiation in $\mathbb{G}_2$ beside a multi-exponentiation in $\mathbb{G}_1$. The decryption operation may be optimized by the receiver who can pre-compute and store $h_1(\mathsf{ID}_A)P + P_{pub}$ in such a way that a simple scalar multiplication in $\mathbb{G}_1$ suffices to verify the validity of the ciphertext. Such a pre-computation also enables a speed up the encryption operation for senders who encrypt several messages under the same public key.

From a computational point of view, NewFullCLE has the same efficiency as FullCLE* [3] if pre-computations are used in both schemes (although NewFullCLE might be more efficient on curves of embedding degree 2 as an exponentiation in $\mathbb{G}_T$ is cheaper than a scalar multiplication in $\mathbb{G}_1$ in this case) as the pairing can be computed in advance for each identity in FullCLE*. However, our construction performs better in the absence of pre-computations as its encryption procedure does not compute any pairing. The encryption algorithm is also faster than its counterpart in schemes of [16, 9] for similar parameters and without pre-computations. Moreover, NewFullCLE does not need a special (and much less efficient) hash function mapping strings onto a cyclic group (and it thus benefits from a faster partial private key generation algorithm) while all schemes have comparable decryption complexities.

Regarding key sizes, users' public keys lie in $\mathbb{G}_2$ and thus have longer representations (typically 1024 bits without optimizations) than elements in $\mathbb{G}_1$. However, pairing compression techniques due to Barreto and Scott [7] allow them to be compressed to a third (say 342 bits) of their original length on supersingular curves in characteristic 3 or even to $1/6$ of their length using ordinary curves such as those of Barreto and Naehrig [6]. Those compression techniques additionally increase the speed of exponentiations in $\mathbb{G}_2$.

The version of the scheme depicted in section 5.1 uses symmetric pairings (and thus supersingular curves). However, it can be implemented with asymmetric pairings as well. In environments where bandwidth is of primary concern, the size of ciphertexts can be minimized at the expense of a longer system-wide public key (which is less likely to transit across the network). In such a setting, asymmetric pairings $e : \mathbb{G}_1 \times \mathbb{G}_2 \to \mathbb{G}_T$ and ordinary curves such as MNT curves or BN curves [25, 6] should be used as long as a publicly computable but non-necessarily invertible isomorphism $\psi : \mathbb{G}_2 \to \mathbb{G}_1$ is available.

Regarding the latter criterion, NewFullCLE seems to be more suitable than previous proposals [2, 3, 16, 9] for an implementation with asymmetric pairings. Indeed, Smart and Vercauteren [28] recently underlined the hardness of finding ordinary pairing-friendly groups[1] ($\mathbb{G}_1, \mathbb{G}_2$) equipped with a publicly computable isomorphism $\psi : \mathbb{G}_2 \to \mathbb{G}_1$ as well as an efficient algorithm to hash onto $\mathbb{G}_2$. Our scheme avoids these problems as it does not require to hash onto $\mathbb{G}_2$ or $\mathbb{G}_1$. Concretely, users' public keys have lie in $\mathbb{G}_T$ while the system-wide public key and entities' partial private keys should respectively be $P_{pub} = sP_2$ and $d_A = 1/(h_1(\mathsf{ID}_A) + s)P_2$ for generators $P_2 \in \mathbb{G}_2$ and $P_1 = \psi(P_2) \in \mathbb{G}_1$. In that bandwidth-optimized version of the scheme, users' public keys can be about 512-bit long on MNT curves [25] or even shorter on BN curves [6]. Ciphertexts are 331 bits longer than plaintexts if $k_0 = 160$.

5.3 Security Results

We give a security statement (formally proven in the full version of the paper) under the p-Bilinear Diffie-Hellman Inversion assumption.

Theorem 3. *In the random oracle model, the NewFullCLE scheme is secure in the sense of definition 2 under the p-BDHI assumption.*

---

[1] More precisely, we mean groups allowing the use of the most efficient implementation techniques for ordinary curves [5].

6   Conclusion

This paper investigated the problem of generically constructing a certificateless cryptosystem which is secure in the strongest model by combining secure IBE schemes with a traditional public key cryptosystem.

It pinpointed security problems in three simple generic constructions and fixed them using a generic random oracle-using conversion (which extends the Fujisaki-Okamoto transformation) ensuring the security in the strongest sense given any scheme only withstanding chosen-plaintext attacks. We finally described a new scheme offering computational advantages over previous pairing-based constructions.

The feasibility of a CLE scheme provably fitting the model of [2] without random oracles still remains a challenging open problem.

References

1. S. S. Al-Riyami. Cryptographic schemes based on elliptic curve pairings. PhD thesis, University of London, 2004.
2. S. S. Al-Riyami and K. Paterson. Certificateless public key cryptography. In *Asiacrypt'03*, volume 2894 of *LNCS*, pages 452–473. Springer, 2003.
3. S. S. Al-Riyami and K. Paterson. CBE from CL-PKE: A generic construction and efficient schemes. In *PKC'05*, volume 3386 of *LNCS*, pages 398–415. Springer, 2005.
4. J. Baek, R. Safavi-Naini, and W. Susilo. Certificateless public key encryption without pairing. In *ISC'05*, volume 3650 of *LNCS*, pages 134–148. Springer, 2005.
5. P. S. L. M. Barreto, B. Lynn, and M. Scott. On the selection of pairing-friendly groups. In *SAC'03*, volume 3006 of *LNCS*, pages 17–25. Springer, 2003.
6. P. S. L. M. Barreto and M. Naehrig. Pairing-friendly elliptic curves of prime order. In *SAC'05*. To Appear.
7. P. S. L. M. Barreto and M. Scott. Compressed pairings. In *Crypto'04*, volume 3152 of *LNCS*, pages 140–156. Springer, 2004.
8. M. Bellare and P. Rogaway. Random oracles are practical: A paradigm for designing efficient protocols. In *1st ACM Conference on Computer and Communications Security*, pages 62–73, ACM Press, 1993.
9. K. Bentahar, P. Farshim, J. Malone-Lee, and N. P. Smart. Generic construction of identity-based and certificateless KEMs. Cryptology ePrint Archive, Report 2005/058, 2005. http://eprint.iacr.org/2005/058.
10. D. Boneh and X. Boyen. Efficient selective-ID secure identity based encryption without random oracles. In *Eurocrypt'04*, volume 3027 of *LNCS*, pages 223–238. Springer, 2004.
11. D. Boneh and X. Boyen. Short signatures without random oracles. In *Eurocrypt'04*, volume 3027 of *LNCS*, pages 56–73. Springer, 2004.
12. D. Boneh and M. Franklin. Identity-based encryption from the Weil pairing. In *Crypto'01*, volume 2139 of *LNCS*, pages 213–229. Springer, 2001.
13. R. Canetti, S. Halevi, and J. Katz. A forward secure public key encryption scheme. In *Eurocrypt'03*, volume 2656 of *LNCS*, pages 254–271. Springer, 2003.
14. L. Chen and Z. Cheng. Security proof of Sakai-Kasahara's identity-based encryption scheme. In *IMA Int. Conf. 2005*, volume 3796 of *LNCS*, pages 442–459. Springer, 2005. Also available from http://eprint.iacr.org/2005/226.

15. L. Chen, Z. Cheng, J. Malone-Lee, and N. P. Smart. An efficient ID-KEM based on the Sakai–Kasahara key construction. Cryptology ePrint Archive, Report 2005/224, 2005. http://eprint.iacr.org/2005/224.

16. Z. Cheng and R. Comley. Efficient certificateless public key encryption. Cryptology ePrint Archive, Report 2005/012, 2005. http://eprint.iacr.org/2005/012.

17. A. Dent and C. Kudla. On Proofs of Security for Certificateless Cryptosystems. Cryptology ePrint Archive, Report 2005/348, 2005. http://eprint.iacr.org/2005/348.

18. Y. Dodis and J. Katz. Chosen-ciphertext security of multiple encryption. In TCC'05, volume 3378 of LNCS, pages 188–209. Springer, 2005.

19. E. Fujisaki and T. Okamoto. How to enhance the security of public-key encryption at minimum cost. In PKC'99, volume 1560 of LNCS, pages 53–68. Springer, 1999.

20. E. Fujisaki and T. Okamoto. Secure integration of asymmetric and symmetric encryption schemes. In Crypto'99, volume 1666 of LNCS, pages 537–554. Springer, 1999.

21. T. E. Gamal. A public key cryptosystem and a signature scheme based on discrete logarithms. In Crypto'84, volume 196 of LNCS, pages 10–18. Springer, 1985.

22. C. Gentry. Certificate-based encryption and the certificate revocation problem. In Eurorypt'03, volume 2656 of LNCS, pages 272–293. Springer, 2003.

23. M. Girault. Self-certified public keys. In Eurocrypt'91, volume 547 of LNCS, pages 490–497. Springer, 1991.

24. G. Kang and S. H. H. J. H. Park. A certificate-based signature scheme. In CT-RSA'04, volume 2964 of LNCS, pages 99–111. Springer, 2004.

25. A. Miyaji, M. Nakabayashi, and S. Takano. New explicit conditions of elliptic curve traces for FR-reduction. IEICE Transactions on Fundamentals, E84-A(5):1234–1243, 2001.

26. R. Sakai and M. Kasahara. ID-based cryptosystems with pairing on elliptic curve. In SCIS'03, Hamamatsu, Japan, 2003. http://eprint.iacr.org/2003/054.

27. A. Shamir. Identity based cryptosystems and signature schemes. In Crypto'84, volume 196 of LNCS, pages 47–53. Springer, 1984.

28. N. P. Smart and F. Vercauteren. On computable isomorphisms in efficient pairing based systems. Cryptology ePrint Archive, Report 2005/116, 2005. http://eprint.iacr.org/2005/116.

29. D. H. Yum and P. J. Lee. Generic construction of certificateless encryption. In ICCSA'04, volume 3043 of LNCS, pages 802–811. Springer, 2004.

30. D. H. Yum and P. J. Lee. Generic construction of certificateless signature. In ACISP'04, volume 3108 of LNCS, pages 200–211. Springer, 2004.

31. D. H. Yum and P. J. Lee. Identity-based cryptography in public key management. In EuroPKI'04, volume 3093 of LNCS, pages 71–84. Springer, 2004.

32. R. Zhang, G. Hanaoka, J. Shikata and H. Imai. On the Security of Multiple Encryption or CCA-security+CCA-security=CCA-security? In PKC'04, volume 2947 of LNCS, pages 360–374. Springer, 2004.

33. F. Zhang, R. Safavi-Naini, and W. Susilo. An efficient signature scheme from bilinear pairings and its applications. In PKC'04, volume 2947 of LNCS, pages 277–290. Springer, 2004.

Appendix: Formal Model of Identity Based Encryption

We recall here the formalism introduced in [12] for identity based encryption. Such a primitive is described by the following definition.

Definition 4. *An identity based encryption (IBE) scheme consists of a 4-uple of algorithms ($\mathsf{Setup}^{IBE}, \mathsf{Extract}^{IBE}, \mathcal{E}^{IBE}, \mathcal{D}^{IBE}$) with the following specifications.*

Setup^{IBE}: *is a probabilistic algorithm run by a private key generator (PKG) that takes as input a security parameter to output a set of public parameters params including the master public key P_{pub} of the PKG. The algorithm also outputs the PKG's master key mk that is kept secret.*

$\mathsf{Extract}^{IBE}$: *is a key generation algorithm run by the PKG on input of a master key mk and a user's identity ID to return the user's private key d_{ID}.*

$\mathcal{E}^{IBE}$: *this probabilistic algorithm takes as input a plaintext M, a recipient's identity ID and the set of public parameters params to output a ciphertext C.*

$\mathcal{D}^{IBE}$: *is a deterministic decryption algorithm taking as input a ciphertext C, the system-wide parameters params and the private decryption key d_{ID} to return a plaintext M or a distinguished symbol $\perp$ if C is not a valid ciphertext.*

For consistency purposes, it is required that $M = \mathcal{D}^{IBE}(C, d_{ID}, \mathsf{params})$ if $C = \mathcal{E}^{IBE}(M, ID, \mathsf{params})$ for all messages M whenever $d_{ID} = \mathsf{Extract}^{IBE}(\mathsf{mk}, ID)$.

The models of chosen-plaintext and chosen-ciphertext security were extended to the IBE setting by Boneh and Franklin themselves [12]. Their model considers a "find-then-guess" game between a challenger and an adversary who may adaptively choose the identity on which she will be challenged after having seen private keys for several arbitrary identities.

Definition 5. *An IBE scheme is **IND-ID-CCA secure** if no PPT adversary has a non-negligible advantage in the following game.*

1. *The challenger runs the Setup algorithm on input of a security parameter k and sends the domain-wide parameters params to the adversary $\mathcal{A}$.*
2. *In a find stage, $\mathcal{A}$ starts probing the following oracles:*
   - *Key extraction oracle: given an identity ID, it returns the extracted private key associated with it.*
   - *Decryption oracle: given an identity $ID \in \{0,1\}^*$ and a ciphertext C, it generates the private key d_{ID} for ID and returns either a plaintext M or a distinguished symbol $\perp$ indicating that the ciphertext was ill-formed.*
   $\mathcal{A}$ can present her queries adaptively. At some point, she produces two plaintexts $M_0, M_1 \in \mathcal{M}$ and an identity ID^* for which she has not requested the private key in stage 2. The challenger computes $C = \mathcal{E}^{IBE}(M_b, ID^*, \mathsf{params})$, for a random hidden bit $b \xleftarrow{R} \{0,1\}$, which is sent to $\mathcal{A}$.
3. *In the guess stage, $\mathcal{A}$ asks new queries but is restricted not to issue a key extraction request on the identity ID^* nor to submit C to the decryption oracle for the identity ID^*. Eventually, $\mathcal{A}$ outputs a bit b' and wins if $b' = b$.*

$\mathcal{A}$'s advantage is defined as $Adv(\mathcal{A}) := 2 \times Pr[b' = b] - 1$.

Building Better Signcryption Schemes with Tag-KEMs

Tor E. Bjørstad[1] and Alexander W. Dent[2]

[1] The Selmer Center, Department of Informatics,
University of Bergen, Norway
[2] Royal Holloway, University of London,
Egham, Surrey, UK
tor.bjorstad@ii.uib.no, a.dent@rhul.ac.uk

Abstract. Signcryption schemes aim to provide all of the advantages of simultaneously signing and encrypting a message. Recently, Dent [8, 9] and Bjørstad [4] investigated the possibility of constructing provably secure signcryption schemes using hybrid KEM-DEM techniques [7]. We build on this work by showing that more efficient insider secure hybrid signcryption schemes can be built using tag-KEMs [1]. To prove the effectiveness of this construction, we will provide several examples of secure signcryption tag-KEMs, including a brand new construction based on the Chevallier-Mames signature scheme [5] which has the tightest known security reductions for both confidentiality and unforgeability.

1 Introduction

The signcryption primitive was introduced by Zheng in 1997 [13] to study asymmetric schemes that offer most or all the benefits provided by public-key encryption and signature schemes. Signcryption schemes must provide message authenticity, confidentiality and integrity, and may also offer a way to provide non-repudiation. As such, a signcryption scheme provides a secure, authenticated channel for message transmission. Although Zheng only considered schemes that are more computationally efficient than a direct composition of encryption and signature schemes, the definition of signcryption is normally expanded to include any asymmetric scheme that provides this functionality, regardless of efficiency. Direct composition of public-key encryption and signatures has been studied by An *et. al.* [2].

In order to obtain efficient encryption schemes in practice, hybrid techniques are commonly used. The practice of combining symmetric and asymmetric schemes to encrypt and transmit long messages efficiently has been common knowledge for many years. However, formal analysis was first performed by Cramer and Shoup in the late 1990s [7]. The usual construction paradigm, known as the KEM-DEM construction, consists of two parts: a key encapsulation mechanism (KEM) and a data encapsulation mechanism (DEM). The KEM uses asymmetric techniques to encrypt a symmetric key, while the DEM uses a symmetric cipher to encrypt the message payload using the key from the

M. Yung et al. (Eds.): PKC 2006, LNCS 3958, pp. 491–507, 2006.

KEM. The main benefit of the KEM-DEM construction paradigm is that the security of KEM and DEM may be analyzed separately.

The use of hybrid techniques to build signcryption schemes has been studied by Dent [8, 9, 10] and Bjørstad [4]. This has provided a useful perspective for analysis of those classes of signcryption schemes that use hybrid techniques. However, previous efforts have yielded complex verification-decryption (unsigncryption) algorithms, stemming from the need to verify a link between message, key and encapsulation. This article will examine a way to simplify the hybrid construction through use of tag-KEMs [1]. We show that adapting the tag-KEM + DEM construction to signcryption yields simpler scheme descriptions and better generic security reductions than previous efforts.

To demonstrate the usefulness of this new paradigm, we construct several signcryption schemes based on signcryption tag-KEMs. The first is a simple modification of Zheng's original signcryption scheme [13]. This scheme has become baseline standard for judging the efficiency and security of any new signcryption scheme or construction method. The second is a new signcryption scheme based on the Chevallier-Mames signature scheme [5]. As far as the authors are aware, this new signcryption scheme has the tightest known security bounds.

2   Preliminaries

2.1   Signcryption

The signcryption primitive was introduced in 1997 by Zheng [13].

Definition 1 (Signcryption). *A signcryption scheme* $SC = (Com, Key_S, Key_R, SC, USC)$ *is defined as tuple of five algorithms.*

- *A probabilistic common parameter generation algorithm, Com. It takes as input a security parameter 1^k, and returns all the global information I needed by users of the scheme, such as choice of groups or hash functions.*
- *A probabilistic sender key generation algorithm, Key_S. It takes as input the global information I, and outputs a private/public keypair (sk_S, pk_S) that is used to send signcrypted messages.*
- *A probabilistic receiver key generation algorithm, Key_R. It takes as input the global information I, and outputs a private/public keypair (sk_R, pk_R) that is used to receive signcrypted messages.*
- *A probabilistic signcryption algorithm SC. It takes as input the private key of the sender sk_S, the public key of the receiver pk_R, and a message m. It outputs a signcryptext σ.*
- *A deterministic unsigncryption algorithm USC. It takes as input the public key of the sender pk_S, the private key of the receiver sk_R, and a signcryptext σ. It outputs either a message m or the unique error symbol $\perp$.*

For a signcryption scheme to be sound, it is required that $m = USC(pk_S, sk_R, SC(sk_S, pk_R, m))$ for (almost) all fixed keypairs (sk_S, pk_S) and (sk_R, pk_R).

For a signcryption scheme to be useful, it is necessary that it also satisfies well-defined notions of security corresponding to the design goals of confidentiality and authenticity/integrity. Formally, the probability of an adversary breaking the security of signcryption should be *negligible* as a function of the security parameter 1^k.

Definition 2 (Negligible Function). *A function $f : \mathbb{N} \to \mathbb{R}$ is negligible if, for every polynomial p, there exists a $n_0 \in \mathbb{N}$ such that $|f(n)| \leq 1/|p(n)|$ for all $n \geq n_0$.*

Security models are commonly phrased in terms of games played between a hypothetical *challenger* and an *adversary*, who are both modelled as probabilistic Turing machines. The canonical notion of confidentiality for signcryption is that of indistinguishability of signcryptions (IND-CCA2). This is adapted directly from the corresponding security notion for encryption schemes: an adversary should not, even when given adaptive access to signcryption and unsigncryption oracles, be able to distinguish between the signcryption of two messages of his own choice. This security notion may be expressed by a game played between the challenger and a two-stage adversary $\mathcal{A} = (\mathcal{A}_1, \mathcal{A}_2)$. For a given security parameter 1^k, the game proceeds as follows:

1. The challenger generates a set of global parameters $I = Com(1^k)$, a sender keypair $(sk_S, pk_S) = Key_S(I)$ and a receiver keypair $(sk_R, pk_R) = Key_R(I)$.
2. The adversary runs $\mathcal{A}_1$ on the input (I, pk_S, pk_R). During its execution, $\mathcal{A}_1$ is given access to signcryption and unsigncryption oracles. The signcryption oracle takes a message m as input, and returns $SC(sk_S, pk_R, m)$. The unsigncryption oracle takes a signcryptext σ as input, and returns $USC(pk_S, sk_R, \sigma)$. $\mathcal{A}_1$ terminates by outputting two messages (m_0, m_1) of equal length, and some state information *state*.
3. The challenger computes a challenge signcryption by generating a random bit $b \in \{0, 1\}$ and computing $\sigma = SC(sk_S, pk_R, m_b)$.
4. The adversary runs $\mathcal{A}_2$ on the input $(state, \sigma)$. During its execution, $\mathcal{A}_2$ has access to signcryption and unsigncryption oracles as above, with the restriction that the challenge signcryptext σ may not be asked to the unsigncryption oracle. $\mathcal{A}_2$ terminates by outputting a guess b' for the value of b.

The adversary wins the game whenever $b = b'$. The advantage of $\mathcal{A}$ is defined as $|Pr[b = b'] - 1/2|$.

With regards to the authenticity and integrity of signcryption, the notion of existential forgery (UF-CMA) is adapted from analysis of signature schemes. It is however necessary to distinguish between different types of such forgery. In an *outsider-secure* signcryption scheme, the adversary is given access to signcryption and unsigncryption oracles, and the public keys of the sender and receiver. For the stronger notion of *insider security*, the unsigncryption oracle is replaced by giving the adversary direct access to the receiver's *private* key. This article will focus on insider-secure signcryption only. Efficient and secure hybrid signcryption scheme against outsider adversaries have been constructed by Dent [10].

It is also necessary to specify what it means for the adversary to win the security game. We use the notion of *strong* existential unforgeability (sUF-CMA). Here an adversary wins if it outputs a valid message/signcryption pair (m, σ) and the signcryption σ was not returned by the signcryption oracle when queried on the message m. Given a security parameter 1^k, a game for the sUF-CMA insider security of a signcryption scheme proceeds as follows:

1. The challenger generates a set of global parameters $I = Com(1^k)$, a sender keypair $(sk_S, pk_S) = Keys_S(I)$ and a receiver keypair $(sk_R, pk_R) = Key_R(I)$.
2. The adversary $\mathcal{A}$ is run on the input (I, pk_S, sk_R, pk_R). During its execution, $\mathcal{A}$ is given access to a signcryption oracle, which takes a message m as input and returns $SC(sk_S, pk_R, m)$. $\mathcal{A}$ terminates by outputting a message m and a signcryptext σ.

The adversary wins the game if $m = USC(pk_S, sk_R, \sigma)$ and the signcryption oracle never returned σ when queried on the message m. The advantage of $\mathcal{A}$ is defined as $Pr[\mathcal{A}$ wins].

2.2   Tag-KEMs

In the traditional KEM-DEM framework for hybrid encryption, the KEM uses public key methods to encrypt and transmit the symmetric key used by the DEM. Formally, a KEM consists of an asymmetric key generation algorithm that outputs a private/public keypair, an encapsulation algorithm that encrypts a random symmetric key using public-key techniques, and a decapsulation algorithm that uses the corresponding private key to decrypt said symmetric key from its encapsulation. This paradigm for building hybrid encryption schemes was extended in early 2005, when Abe *et. al.* [1] showed that one might build more efficient hybrid schemes by replacing the KEM with what they call a *tag-KEM*.

Definition 3 (Tag-KEM). *A tag-KEM TKEM = (Gen, Sym, Encap, Decap) is defined as a tuple of four algorithms:*

- *A probabilistic key generation algorithm, Gen. It takes as input a security parameter 1^k, and outputs a private key sk and a public key pk. The public key contains all specific choices used by the scheme, such as choice of groups.*
- *A probabilistic symmetric key generation algorithm, Sym. It takes as input a public key pk, and outputs a symmetric key K and some internal state information ω.*
- *A probabilistic encapsulation algorithm, Encap. It takes as input the state information ω together with an arbitrary string τ, which is called a tag, and outputs an encapsulation E.*
- *A deterministic decapsulation algorithm, Decap. It takes a private key sk, an encapsulation E and a tag τ as input, and outputs a symmetric key K.*

For a tag-KEM to be sound, the decapsulation algorithm Decap must output the correct key K when run with a correctly formed encapsulation E of K, and the corresponding private key and tag.

Tag-KEMs as such may be viewed as a generalisation of regular KEMs: if the tag τ is a fixed string, the *Sym* and *Encap* algorithms together make up the encapsulation algorithm of the traditional model.

Definition 4 (DEM). *A data encapsulation mechanism $DEM = (Enc, Dec)$ is defined as a pair of algorithms:*

- *A symmetric encryption algorithm Enc, that takes a symmetric key $K \in \mathcal{K}$ and a message m as input, and returns a ciphertext $C = Enc_K(m)$. The set $\mathcal{K}$ is called the keyspace of the DEM.*
- *A symmetric decryption algorithm Dec, that takes a symmetric key $K \in \mathcal{K}$ and a ciphertext c as input, and returns a message $m = Dec_K(C)$.*

For soundness, the encryption and decryption algorithms should be each other's inverses under a fixed key K. Notationally, $m = Dec_K\big(Enc_K(m)\big)$.

For the purposes of this paper, it is only required that DEMs are secure with respect to indistinguishability against *passive* attackers (IND-PA). Formally, this security notion is captured by the following game, played between a challenger and a two-stage adversary $\mathcal{A} = (\mathcal{A}_1, \mathcal{A}_2)$:

1. The challenger generates a random symmetric $K \in \mathcal{K}$.
2. The adversary runs $\mathcal{A}_1$ with the security parameter 1^k as input. $\mathcal{A}_1$ terminates by outputting two equal length messages m_0 and m_1, as well as some state information *state*.
3. The challenger generates a random bit $b \in \{0, 1\}$ and computes the challenge ciphertext $C = Enc_K(m_b)$.
4. The adversary runs $\mathcal{A}_2$ on the input $(state, C)$. $\mathcal{A}_2$ terminates by returning a guess b' for the value of b.

The adversary wins the game whenever $b = b'$. The advantage of $\mathcal{A}$ is defined as $|Pr[b = b'] - 1/2|$.

A tag-KEM may be combined with a DEM to form a hybrid encryption scheme in a similar way as a regular KEM. However, in [1] this is done in a novel manner, by using the ciphertext output by the DEM as the tag. The explicit construction is shown in Figure 1.

$Encr(pk, m)$:
$(K, \omega) \xleftarrow{R} Sym(pk)$.
$C \leftarrow Enc_K(m)$.
$E \xleftarrow{R} Encap(\omega, C)$.
$\sigma \leftarrow (E, C)$.
Return σ.

$Decr(sk, \sigma)$:
$(E, C) \leftarrow \sigma$.
$K \leftarrow Decap(sk, E, C)$.
$m \leftarrow Dec_K(C)$.
Return m.

$Key(1^k)$:
$(sk, pk) \xleftarrow{R} Key(1^k)$.
Return (sk, pk).

Fig. 1. Construction of asymmetric encryption scheme from a tag-KEM and DEM

The main result of Abe *et. al.* [1] is that the construction of Figure 1 is IND-CCA2 secure, provided that the DEM is secure against passive attackers (IND-PA), and it is not possible for an adversary, given a pair (E, K), to determine whether K is the key encapsulated by E, or a random key of the correct length. This contrasts with the traditional KEM-DEM construction, in which the DEM is required to be secure against an active attack for the resulting hybrid encryption scheme to be IND-CCA2.

3   Signcryption Tag-KEMs

3.1   Basic Definition

We define Signcryption Tag-KEMs (SCTK) by direct analogy to the previous definition of tag-KEMs for encryption.

Definition 5 (Signcryption Tag-KEM). *A signcryption tag-KEM SCTK =* (*Com*, *Keys*, *Key$_R$*, *Sym*, *Encap*, *Decap*) *is defined as a tuple of six algorithms.*

- *A probabilistic common parameter generation algorithm, Com. It takes as input a security parameter 1^k, and returns all the global information I needed by users of the scheme, such as choice of groups or hash functions.*
- *A probabilistic sender key generation algorithm, Keys. It takes as input the global information I, and outputs a private/public keypair (sk_S, pk_S) that is used to send signcrypted messages.*
- *A probabilistic receiver key generation algorithm, Key$_R$. It takes as input the global information I, and outputs a private/public keypair (sk_R, pk_R) that is used to receive signcrypted messages.*
- *A probabilistic symmetric key generation algorithm, Sym. It takes as input the private key of the sender sk_S and the public key of the receiver pk_R, and outputs a symmetric key K together with internal state information ω.*
- *A probabilistic key encapsulation algorithm, Encap. It takes as input the state information ω and an arbitrary tag τ, and returns an encapsulation E.*
- *A deterministic decapsulation/verification algorithm, Decap. It takes as input the sender's public key pk_S, the receiver's private key sk_R, an encapsulation E and a tag τ. The algorithm returns either a symmetric key K or the unique error symbol $\bot$.*

For the SCTK to be sound, the decapsulation/verification algorithm must return the correct key K whenever the encapsulation E is correctly formed and the corresponding keys and tag are supplied.

The basic idea behind a signcryption tag-KEM is that the key encapsulation algorithm provides what amounts to a signature on the tag τ. Signcryption tag-KEMs may thus be combined with regular DEMs to form a hybrid signcryption scheme as shown in Figure 2, using the SCTK to provide a signature on the symmetric ciphertext c and encapsulate the symmetric key K.

Previous discussion of hybrid signcryption schemes have discussed efficient hybrid signcryption as a variant of the "Encrypt-and-Sign" [2] paradigm. A

$Com(1^k)$:

$I \overset{R}{\leftarrow} Com(1^k)$.

Return I.

$Key_S(I)$:

$(sk_S, pk_S) \overset{R}{\leftarrow} Key_S(I)$.

Return (sk_S, pk_S).

$Key_R(I)$:

$(sk_R, pk_R) \overset{R}{\leftarrow} Key_R(I)$.

Return (sk_R, pk_R).

$SC(sk_S, pk_R, m)$:

$(K, \omega) \overset{R}{\leftarrow} Sym(sk_S, pk_R)$.

$C \leftarrow Enc_K(m)$.

$E \overset{R}{\leftarrow} Encap(\omega, C)$.

$\sigma \leftarrow (E, C)$.

Return σ.

$USC(pk_S, sk_R, \sigma)$:

$(E, C) \leftarrow \sigma$.

If $\perp \leftarrow Decap(pk_S, sk_R, E, C)$:

Return $\perp$ and terminate.

Else $K \leftarrow Decap(pk_S, sk_R, E, C)$.

$m \leftarrow Dec_K(C)$.

Return m.

Fig. 2. Construction of hybrid signcryption scheme from SCTK and DEM

straightforward approach is to encrypt the message to be sent with a symmetric cipher, while combining the features of key encapsulation and digital signatures into one efficient operation [8, 9, 4]. Using signcryption tag-KEMs in the construction yields something more akin to a "Encrypt-then-Sign" based scheme, since the signature is made on the ciphertext "tag".

Another feature of the signcryption tag-KEM construction is that it automatically supports the sending of associated data with a message. In particular, one may submit a tag $\tau = (C, l)$ to the encapsulation algorithm, consisting of the ciphertext C as well as a label l containing any associated data that is to be bound to C by the encapsulation. As the encapsulation acts as a signature on the input tag, the authenticity and integrity of both ciphertext and associated data is provided. The only requirement for doing this is that the tag τ must be formatted in such a way that $(C, l) \leftarrow \tau$ may be parsed in a deterministic and unambiguous manner. A standard application of this feature is the common practice of "binding" the sender's and receiver's public key to any signcryption sent between them. Many signcryption schemes explicitly do this, in order to provide some degree of multi-user security. Of course, a similar effect can be achieved by computing the signcryption of a combination of the message and a hash of the associated data. This provides similar results but requires either slightly greater bandwidth or a slightly reduced message space.

3.2 Security Models

For a signcryption tag-KEM to be considered secure, it must fulfill well-defined security notions with respect to confidentiality and authenticity/integrity. The tag-KEM confidentiality model used in [1] may easily adapted to the signcryption setting, and the notion of strong existential unforgeability is adapted to provide authenticity/integrity.

In the IND-CCA2 game for a signcryption tag-KEM, the adversary attempts to distinguish whether a given symmetric key is the one embedded in an encapsulation. The adversary $\mathcal{A} = (\mathcal{A}_1, \mathcal{A}_2, \mathcal{A}_3)$ runs in three stages, with each stage having access to oracles that fascilitate both adaptive encapsulation and decapsulation queries. For a given security parameter 1^k, this may be expressed by the following game:

1. The challenger generates a set of global parameters $I = Com(1^k)$, a sender keypair $(sk_S, pk_S) = Keys_S(I)$ and a receiver keypair $(sk_R, pk_R) = Key_R(I)$.
2. The adversary runs $\mathcal{A}_1$ on the input (I, pk_S, pk_R). Durings its execution, $\mathcal{A}_1$ is given access to three oracles, corresponding to each of the algorithms Sym, $Encap$ and $Decap$:
   - The symmetric key generation oracle does not take any input, and computes $(K, \omega) = Sym(sk_S, pk_R)$. It then stores the value ω (hidden from the view of the adversary, and overwriting any previously stored values), and returns the symmetric key K.
   - The key encapsulation oracle takes an arbitrary tag τ as input, and checks whether there exists a stored value ω. If there is not, it returns $\bot$ and terminates. Otherwise it erases the value from storage, and returns $Encap(\omega, \tau)$.
   - The decapsulation/verification oracle takes an encapsulation E and a tag τ as input, and returns $Decap(pk_S, sk_R, E, \tau)$.
   $\mathcal{A}_1$ terminates by returning state information $state_1$.
3. The challenger computes $(K_0, \omega) = Sym(sk_S, pk_R)$, and generates a random symmetric key $K_1 \in \mathcal{K}$ as well as a random bit $b \in \{0, 1\}$.
4. The adversary runs $\mathcal{A}_2$ on the input $(state_1, K_b)$. During its execution, $\mathcal{A}_2$ may access the same oracles as previously. $\mathcal{A}_2$ terminates by returning state information $state_2$ and a tag τ.
5. The challenger computes a challenge encapsulation $E = Encap(\omega, \tau)$.
6. The adversary runs $\mathcal{A}_3$ on the input $(state_2, E)$. During its execution, $\mathcal{A}_3$ may access the same oracles as previously, with the restriction that (E, τ) may not be asked to the decapsulation oracle. $\mathcal{A}_3$ terminates by returning a guess b' for the value of b.

The adversary wins the game whenever $b = b'$. The advantage of $\mathcal{A}$ is defined as $|Pr[b = b'] - 1/2|$. A signcryption tag-KEM is said to be *IND-CCA2 secure* if, for any adversary $\mathcal{A}$, the advantage of $\mathcal{A}$ in the IND-CCA2 game is negligible with respect to the security parameter 1^k.

It is important to notice the interaction between the symmetric key generation and encapsulation oracles. This is done to allow the adversary to perform completely adaptive encapsulations, without having access to the internal information stored in ω. The IND-CCA2 game ensures that a SCTK fulfills several necessary properties with regards to malleability and information hiding, and replaces the notions of IND-CCA2 and INP-CCA2 used by Dent [8, 9] for regular signcryption KEMs.

With respect to authenticity and integrity, an adversary should not be able to find encapsulation/tag-pairs (E, τ) such that $Decap(pk_S, sk_R, E, \tau) \neq \bot$, except by the way of oracles. Since the encapsulation algorithm should provide a signature on the tag τ, this is closely tied to forging the underlying signature scheme. An attack game corresponding to the sUF-CMA security of a SCTK may thus be specified as follows:

1. The challenger generates a set of global parameters $I = Com(1^k)$, a sender keypair $(sk_S, pk_S) = Keys_S(I)$ and a receiver keypair $(sk_R, pk_R) = Key_R(I)$.
2. The adversary $\mathcal{A}$ is run on the input (I, pk_S, sk_R, pk_R). During its execution, $\mathcal{A}$ may access the symmetric key generation and encapsulation oracles as were defined in the previous game. $\mathcal{A}$ terminates by returning an encapsulation E and a tag τ.

The adversary wins the game if $\perp \neq Decap(pk_S, sk_R, E, \tau)$ and the encapsulation oracle never returned E when queried on the tag τ. The advantage of $\mathcal{A}$ is defined as $Pr[\mathcal{A}$ wins$]$. A signcryption tag-KEM is said to be sUF-CMA secure if, for any adversary $\mathcal{A}$, the advantage of $\mathcal{A}$ in the sUF-CMA game is negligible with respect to the security parameter 1^k.

Definition 6 (Secure Signcryption Tag-KEM). *A signcryption tag-KEM SCTK is said to be secure if it is IND-CCA2 and sUF-CMA secure.*

3.3   Generic Security of Hybrid Signcryption

If the SCTK+DEM construction is to be of any use, the resulting signcryption scheme must be provably secure.

Theorem 1. *Let SC be a hybrid signcryption scheme constructed from a signcryption tag-KEM and a DEM. If the signcryption tag-KEM is IND-CCA2 secure and the DEM is IND-PA secure, then SC is IND-CCA2 secure.*

Proof. Let Game 0 be the regular IND-CCA2 game for signcryption, as specified in Section 2.1. In the following game, the hybrid signcryption procedure is altered to use a random key when generating the challenge signcryptext, rather than the real key output by Sym. We refer to the resulting game as Game 1:

1. The challenger generates a set of global parameters $I = Com(1^k)$, a sender keypair $(sk_S, pk_S) = Keys_S(I)$ and a receiver keypair $(sk_R, pk_R) = Key_R(I)$.
2. The adversary runs $\mathcal{A}_1$ on the input (I, pk_S, pk_R). During its execution, $\mathcal{A}_1$ has access to signcryption and unsigncryption oracles. The signcryption oracle takes a message m as input, and returns $SC(sk_S, pk_R, m)$. The unsigncryption oracle takes a signcryptext σ as input, and returns $USC(pk_S, sk_R, \sigma)$. $\mathcal{A}_1$ terminates by outputting two messages (m_0, m_1) and some state information $state$.
3. The challenger computes $(K, \omega) = Sym(sk_S, pk_R)$, and generates a random key $K' \in \mathcal{K}$, as well as a random bit $b \in \{0, 1\}$. He then computes $C = Enc_{K'}(m_b)$ and $E = Encap(\omega, C)$, and sets $\sigma = (E, C)$.
4. The adversary runs $\mathcal{A}_2$ on the input $(state, \sigma)$. During its execution, $\mathcal{A}_2$ may access signcryption and unsigncryption oracles as above, with the restriction that σ may not be asked to the unsigncryption oracle. $\mathcal{A}_2$ terminates by outputting a guess b' for the bit b.

$\mathcal{D}_1(I, pk_S, pk_R; \mathcal{O}_S, \mathcal{O}_E, \mathcal{O}_D)$:
$(m_0, m_1, s) \xleftarrow{R} \mathcal{A}_1(I, pk_S, pk_R; \mathcal{O}_{SC}, \mathcal{O}_{USC})$.
$state_1 \leftarrow (m_0, m_1, s)$.
Return $state_1$.

$\mathcal{D}_2(state_1, K; \mathcal{O}_S, \mathcal{O}_E, \mathcal{O}_D)$:
$b \xleftarrow{R} \{0,1\}$.
$C \leftarrow Enc_K(m_b)$.
$state_2 \leftarrow (state_1, b, C)$.
Return $(state_2, C)$.

$\mathcal{D}_3(state_2, E; \mathcal{O}_S, \mathcal{O}_E, \mathcal{O}_D)$:
$(m_0, m_1, s, b, C) \leftarrow state_2$.
$\sigma \leftarrow (E, C)$.
$b' \xleftarrow{R} \mathcal{A}_2(s, \sigma; \mathcal{O}_{SC}, \mathcal{O}_{USC})$.
If $b = b'$: Return 1.
Else: Return 0.

$\mathcal{O}_{SC}(m)$:
$K \xleftarrow{R} \mathcal{O}_S$.
$C \leftarrow Enc_K(m)$.
$E \xleftarrow{R} \mathcal{O}_E(C)$.
$\sigma \leftarrow (E, C)$.
Return σ.

$\mathcal{O}_{USC}(\sigma)$:
$(E, C) \leftarrow \sigma$.
If $\perp \leftarrow \mathcal{O}_D(E, C)$:
Return $\perp$ and terminate.
Else $K \leftarrow \mathcal{O}_D(E, C)$.
$m \leftarrow Dec_K(C)$.
Return m.

Fig. 3. Distinguisher algorithm $\mathcal{D}$

Let X_0 and X_1 be the events that $b = b'$ in Game 0 and Game 1, respectively. It is well known that any substantial difference in the advantage of the adversary $\mathcal{A}$ in Game 0 and Game 1 can be used to produce a distinguishing algorithm for the signcryption tag-KEM.

Figure 3 gives a complete specification of such a distinguishing algorithm $\mathcal{D}$. It plays the IND-CCA2 game against SCTK, using $\mathcal{A}$ as a subroutine. Oracle queries made by $\mathcal{A}$ are simulated by $\mathcal{D}$. It uses the subroutines $\mathcal{O}_{SC}$ to simulate signcryption oracle queries, and $\mathcal{O}_{USC}$ to simulate unsigncryption queries. The symmetric key generation, encapsulation and decapsulation/verification oracles accessible by $\mathcal{D}$ are referred to as $\mathcal{O}_S$, $\mathcal{O}_E$ and $\mathcal{O}_D$, respectively. We denote the execution of an algorithm $\mathcal{A}$ that takes input values $\alpha, \ldots$ and has access to oracles $\mathcal{O}, \ldots$ as $\mathcal{A}(\alpha, \ldots; \mathcal{O}, \ldots)$. A well-known derivation gives $|Pr[X_0] - Pr[X_1]| \leq 2\epsilon_{SCTK}$, where ϵ_{SCTK} is the advantage that $\mathcal{D}$ has in attacking the IND-CCA2 security of the SCTK.

We proceed to show that the advantage of $\mathcal{A}$ in Game 1 is bounded by that of a passive attacker against the DEM. Figure 4 specifies an adversary $\mathcal{B}$ against the IND-PA security of the DEM, that uses $\mathcal{A}$ as a subroutine. In the game described in Figure 4, $\mathcal{B}$ simulates the environment of $\mathcal{A}$ in Game 1 perfectly. Furthermore, $\mathcal{B}$ wins every time $\mathcal{A}$ would have won Game 1. Hence, they have the same advantage. It follows that

$$\epsilon_{SC} \leq 2\epsilon_{SCTK} + \epsilon_{DEM}, \tag{1}$$

where ϵ_{SC}, ϵ_{SCTK} and ϵ_{DEM} are the advantages of adversaries against IND-CCA2 security of the hybrid signcryption scheme, the IND-CCA2 security of the signcryption tag-KEM and the IND-PA security of the DEM, respectively.

$\square$

$\mathcal{B}_1$:
$I \xleftarrow{R} Com(1^k)$.
$(sk_S, pk_S) \xleftarrow{R} Keys_S(I)$.
$(sk_R, pk_R) \xleftarrow{R} Key_R(I)$.
$(m_0, m_1, s) \xleftarrow{R} \mathcal{A}_1(I, pk_S, pk_R; \mathcal{O}_{SC}, \mathcal{O}_{USC})$.
$state \leftarrow (I, sk_S, pk_S, sk_R, pk_R, m_0, m_1, s)$.
Return $(m_0, m_1, state')$.

$\mathcal{B}_2(state, C)$:
$(I, sk_S, pk_S, sk_R, pk_R, m_0, m_1, s) \leftarrow state$.
$(K, \omega) \xleftarrow{R} Sym(sk_S, pk_R)$.
$E \xleftarrow{R} Encap(\omega, C)$.
$\sigma \leftarrow (C, E)$.
$b \xleftarrow{R} \mathcal{A}_2(s, \sigma; \mathcal{O}_{SC}, \mathcal{O}_{USC})$.
Return b.

$\mathcal{O}_{SC}(m)$:
$(K, \omega) \xleftarrow{R} Sym(sk_S, pk_R)$.
$C \leftarrow Enc_K(m)$.
$E \xleftarrow{R} Encap(\omega, C)$.
$\sigma \leftarrow (E, C)$.
Return σ.

$\mathcal{O}_{USC}(\sigma)$:
$(E, C) \leftarrow \sigma$.
If $\perp \leftarrow Decap(pk_S, sk_R, E, C)$:
Return $\perp$ and terminate.
Else $K \leftarrow Decap(pk_S, sk_R, E, C)$.
$m \leftarrow Dec_K(C)$.
Return m.

Fig. 4. IND-PA adversary against the DEM

Remark 1. This reduction is significantly tighter than those found for regular hybrid signcryption in [8, 4]. In the original approach to hybrid signcryption, the confidentiality proof relies on four terms: the indistinguishability of the symmetric keys the KEM produces, the unforgeability of the KEM, the ability of the KEM to disguise the messages and the passive security of the DEM. This is particularly inefficient as many proofs of unforgeability contain weak security reductions. We see this improved security result, and the comparative simplicity of proving the security of a signcryption tag-KEM, as the main advantages of the SCTK paradigm.

Theorem 2. *Let SC be a hybrid signcryption scheme constructed from a signcryption tag-KEM and a DEM. If the signcryption tag-KEM is sUF-CMA secure, then SC is also sUF-CMA secure.*

Proof. Since every valid forgery of SC implies a valid encapsulation, it is reasonably straightforward to show that forgery of SC implies forgery of the underlying SCTK. Figure 5 specifies an adversary $\mathcal{B}$, which uses a black-box adversary $\mathcal{A}$ against the UF-CMA security of SC to win the corresponding sUF-CMA game against SCTK. In the above scenario, $\mathcal{A}$ wins the forgery game against SC whenever the returned σ unsigncrypts to m and m has not been queried to the signcryption oracle $\mathcal{O}_{SC}$. If this is the case, then $\mathcal{B}$ wins the sUF-CMA game against SCTK.

To see this, note that $\mathcal{B}$ wins whenever it returns a pair (E, C) that does not decapsulate to $\perp$ and such that E was never a response from $\mathcal{O}_E$ to a query C. Since σ is a valid ciphertext, the former condition is always fulfilled. Furthermore, one may note that the ciphertext σ is associated deterministically to m through the decapsulation algorithm. Hence, σ has been returned by $\mathcal{O}_{SC}$ if and only if

$\mathcal{B}(I, pk_S, sk_R, pk_R; \mathcal{O}_S, \mathcal{O}_E)$:	$\mathcal{O}_{SC}(m)$:
$(m, \sigma) \xleftarrow{R} \mathcal{A}(I, pk_S, sk_R, pk_R; \mathcal{O}_{SC})$.	$K \xleftarrow{R} \mathcal{O}_S$.
$(E, C) \leftarrow \sigma$.	$C \leftarrow Enc_K(m)$.
Return (E, C).	$E \xleftarrow{R} \mathcal{O}_E(C)$.
	$\sigma \leftarrow (E, C)$.
	Return σ.

Fig. 5. Construction of a sUF-CMA adversary against SCTK

m was ever queried. This implies that (E, C) was a query/response pair from $\mathcal{O}_{SC}$ if and only if (m, σ) was a query/response pair from $\mathcal{O}_E$. Hence, $\mathcal{B}$ wins every time $\mathcal{A}$ does.

It follows that

$$\epsilon_{SC} \leq \epsilon_{SCTK}, \qquad (2)$$

where ϵ_{SC} is the advantage of the UF-CMA adversary against SC, and ϵ_{SCTK} is the advantage of the resulting sUF-CMA adversary against SCTK. $\square$

4 Sample Schemes

4.1 Zheng Signcryption Revisited

Zheng's original signcryption scheme [13] has become somewhat of a canonical reference when hybrid signcryption is discussed [8, 4]. It is therefore natural to see whether it can be adapted to fit the generic tag-KEM framework as well. Since Zheng's original scheme essentially uses a KEM to sign the plaintext message, this requires only minor alterations. Figure 6 gives a complete specification of a signcryption tag-KEM that, when combined with a DEM as per Figure 2, yields something very similar to Zheng's original scheme. The only difference between the schemes is that the tag τ used by *Encap* is the ciphertext $C \leftarrow Enc_K(m)$, rather than m itself. It is well established that both Zheng's signcryption scheme and its associated signcryption KEM are secure [3, 8, 4], and it is therefore no surprise that the signcryption tag-KEM specified in Figure 6 is secure as well.

Theorem 3. *Zheng-SCTK, as specified in Figure 6, is a secure signcryption tag-KEM.*

A full version of the proof is given in the full version of the paper. The security bounds for Zheng's signcryption scheme in this framework are comparable to those of the original scheme-specific reduction [3]. This was not the case in generic models for hybrid signcryption [8, 4] based on regular KEMs. In the full version of the paper, we show that an attacker who attempts to break the confidentiality of the full signcryption scheme using at most q_E queries to the signcryption oracle, q_D queries to the unsigncryption oracle, q_G queries to

```
Com(1^k):                          Sym(sk_S, pk_R):
Pick a k-bit prime p.              n ←R Z/qZ.
Pick a large prime q that divides p − 1.   κ ← pk_R^n  mod p.
Pick g ∈ Z_q^* of order q.         bind ← pk_S || pk_R.
Pick cryptographic hash functions:  K ← G(κ).
G : {0,1}^* → K.                   ω ← (sk_S, n, κ, bind).
H : {0,1}^* → Z/qZ.               Return (K, ω).
I ← (p, q, g, G, H).
Return I.                          Encap(ω, τ):
                                   (sk_S, n, κ, bind) ← ω.
Keys_S(I):                         r ← H(τ || bind || κ).
sk_S ←R Z/qZ.                     s ← n/(sk_S + r)  mod q.
pk_S ← g^{sk_S}  mod p.           E ← (r, s).
Return (sk_S, pk_S).              Return E.

Key_R(I):                          Decap(pk_S, sk_R, E, τ):
sk_R ←R Z/qZ.                     (r, s) ← E.
pk_R ← g^{sk_R}  mod p.           κ ← (pk_S · g^r)^{s·sk_R}  mod p.
Return (sk_R, pk_R).             r' ← H(τ || bind || κ).
                                   If r ≠ r':
                                   Return ⊥ and terminate.
                                   Else K ← G(κ).
                                   Return K.
```

Fig. 6. The Zheng signcryption tag-KEM

the random oracle representing the hash function G and q_H queries to the random oracle representing the hash function H has an advantage bounded[1] by

$$2Adv_{GDH} + Adv_{DEM}$$

where Adv_{GDH} is a related attacker's probability of solving a Gap Diffie-Hellman problem and Adv_{DEM} is the advantage that a related attacker has in breaking the passive security of the DEM. If we compare this to the results of Bjørstad [4], then we find that an attacker who attempts to break the confidentiality of Zheng's scheme in Dent's hybrid model [9] has an advantage which is bounded above by

$$4Adv_{GDH} + Adv_{DEM} + 2q_H\sqrt{Adv_{DL}}$$

where Adv_{DL} is a related attacker's probability of solving a discrete logarithm problem. This demonstrates the usefulness of the new construction, as it gives significantly tighter security bounds.

Other existing signcryption schemes may also be representable as signcryption tag-KEMs. For example, it appears likely that the hybrid signcryption scheme of Malone-Lee [11] could also be adapted to the signcryption tag-KEM paradigm, along with its corresponding proof of security.

---

[1] For simplicity, we disregard the constant terms in the following expressions.

4.2   The CM Signcryption Tag-KEM

As discussed in [13, 4], the Zheng signcryption scheme is constructed by modifying an existing signature scheme. By making the randomiser κ computed during signature verification dependent on the receiver's key sk_S, an efficient signcryption scheme can be constructed at a very low additional cost. This trick may be applied to other signature schemes as well. In this section, we propose a new signcryption tag-KEM, built from a recent signature scheme due to Chevallier-Mames [5]. The resulting construction has tight security reductions with respect to the Computational Diffie-Hellman and Gap Diffie-Hellman problems. This is of practical interest, since previous hybrid signcryption schemes have had relatively loose security reductions with respect to unforgeability. Figure 7 gives a complete specification of the CM signcryption tag-KEM.

$Com(1^k)$:
Pick a large prime q.
Let G be a cyclic group of order q, such that the representation of the elements of G is included in $\{0,1\}^k$.
Pick a generator g of G.
Pick cryptographic hash functions:
$\mathcal{G} : \{0,1\}^* \times G^6 \to \mathbb{Z}_q$.
$\mathcal{H} : G \to G$.
$KDF : G \to \mathcal{K}$.
$I \leftarrow (q, G, g, \mathcal{G}, \mathcal{H}, KDF)$.
Return I.

$Key_S(I)$:
$sk_S \xleftarrow{R} \mathbb{Z}_q$.
$pk_S \leftarrow g^{sk_S}$.
Return (sk_S, pk_S).

$Key_R(I)$:
$sk_R \xleftarrow{R} \mathbb{Z}_q$.
$pk_R \leftarrow g^{sk_R}$. Return (sk_R, pk_R).

$Sym(sk_S, pk_R)$:
$n \xleftarrow{R} \mathbb{Z}_q$.
$u \leftarrow pk_R{}^n$.
$K \leftarrow KDF(u)$.
$\omega \leftarrow (sk_S, pk_R, n, u)$.
Return (K, ω).

$Encap(\omega, \tau)$:
$(sk_S, pk_R, n, u) \leftarrow \omega$.
$h \leftarrow \mathcal{H}(u)$.
$z \leftarrow h^{sk_S}$.
$v \leftarrow h^n$.
$c \leftarrow \mathcal{G}(\tau||pk_R, pk_S, g, z, h, u, v)$.
$s \leftarrow n + c \cdot sk_S, \mod q$.
$E \leftarrow (z, c, s)$.

$Decap(pk_S, sk_R, E, \tau)$:
$u \leftarrow (g^s \cdot pk_S{}^{-c})^{sk_R}$.
$h \leftarrow \mathcal{H}(u)$.
$v \leftarrow h^s \cdot z^{-c}$.
If $c \neq \mathcal{G}(\tau||pk_R, pk_S, g, z, h, u, v)$:
Return $\perp$.
Else $K \leftarrow KDF(u)$.
Return K.

Fig. 7. The CM signcryption tag-KEM

Theorem 4. *The CM signcryption tag-KEM specified in Figure 7 is a secure signcryption tag-KEM.*

A full proof is given in full version of the paper. The proof uses techniques that are directly analogous to those used in the security proofs for Zheng's scheme [3, 4]. However, this scheme has a better security reduction for authenticity/

integrity, since the security of the underlying signature scheme does not rely on a "forking lemma" argument [12]. To the authors' knowledge, this gives this scheme the best known security reductions.

As a side note, we remark that, in order to prove the integrity/authenticity of the CM signcryption tag-KEM, it was necessary to prove that the Chevallier-Mames signature scheme was strongly unforgeable. A proof of this fact was developed independently by Chevallier-Mames [6].

5   Building Better Key Agreement Mechanisms with Signcryption Tag-KEMs

The idea that signcryption KEMs can be used as key agreement mechanisms was first investigated by Dent [10]. Dent notes that whilst an encryption KEM provides a basic mechanism for agreeing a symmetric key between two parties, it does not provide any form of authentication or freshness guarantee. Moreover, he notes that signcryption KEMs (with outsider security) can be used to agree a symmetric key with authentication. A simple protocol key agreement protocol is then proposed, wherein freshness is guaranteed by the computing the MAC of a timestamp or nonce using the newly agreed symmetric key. However, as the paper remarks, this protocol is susceptible to a known key attack and should not be used in practice.

In this section we propose that signcryption tag-KEMs can be used as practical key agreement mechanisms, with the SCTK providing both the authentication and freshness components of the protocol in a simple way. Consider the following protocol which allows Alice and Bob to agree a key for a session with an ID SID between them:

1. Alice generates a random nonce r_A of an agreed length, and sends r_A to Bob.
2. Bob computes $(K, \omega) = Sym(sk_{Bob}, pk_{Alice})$ and $E = Encap(\omega, \tau)$ using the (unique) tag $\tau = r_A \| SID$. Bob accepts K as the shared secret key, and sends C to Alice.
3. Alice computes $K = Decap(pk_{Bob}, sk_{Alice}, E, \tau)$ using the tag $\tau = r_A \| SID$, and accepts K as the shared key providing $K \neq \bot$.

We argue that this protocol has the following attributes:

- **Implicit key authentication to both parties.** If both parties obtain the other's correct public key, then no attacker can distinguish between a session's correct public key and a randomly generated key without breaking the confidentiality criterion for the SCTK.
- **Resistance to known key attacks.** It is easy to see that an attacker that gains a key from any earlier protocol execution (or, indeed, in a later protocol execution) between Alice and Bob gains no advantage in breaking the scheme. This is because this "session corruption" is equivalent to making a signcryption oracle query with a random tag. Since the SCTK remains secure in this situation, so does the key agreement protocol.

– **Key confirmation from Bob to Alice.** Since no party (including Alice) can forge a signcryptext that purports to come from Bob, if Alice recovers a key K from C, then that key K *must* have been produced by Bob in the correct way. Therefore, Alice can have confidence that Bob knows the correct key. However, an extra round of interaction will be required if Alice wishes to give Bob key confirmation.

We argue that this derivation is useful because it finally gives a secure way to use KEMs for key establishment. Of course, a secure signcryption scheme can always be used as a key transport mechanism; however, it was not previously known if signcryption-style techniques could be used for key agreement. The afore-mentioned protocol settles this question. Whether an individual signcryption tag-KEM should be regarded as a key transport or key agreement mechanism depends upon its individual characteristics.

6   Conclusions

We have shown that there is a natural extension of the concept of a tag-KEM to the signcryption setting and proven that secure signcryption tag-KEMs can be combined with passively secure DEMs to provide signcryption schemes with full insider security. This vastly simplifies and improves upon the KEM-DEM model insider secure signcryption schemes proposed by Dent [9]. To show that this construction is viable, we have given several examples of signcryption tag-KEMs, including a brand new construction based on the Chevallier-Mames signature scheme with very tight security bounds.

Acknowledgements

Tor Bjørstad wishes to thank the ECRYPT project and the Norwegian Research Council for their generous financial support. Alexander Dent wishes to think the ECRYPT project and the EPSRC's Junior Research Fellowship programme for their generous financial support. Both authors wish to thank the PKC 2006 anonymous reviewers for their comments.

References

1. A. Abe, R. Gennaro, K. Kurosawa, and V. Shoup. Tag-KEM/DEM: A new frame-work for hybrid encryption and a new analysis of Kurosawa-Desmedt KEM. In *Advances in Cryptology – EUROCRYPT 2005*, volume 3494 of *Lecture Notes in Computer Science*, pages 128–146. Springer–Verlag, 2005.
2. J. H. An, Y. Dodis, and T. Rabin. On the security of joint signature and encryption. In *Advances in Cryptology – EUROCRYPT 2002*, volume 2332 of *Lecture Notes in Computer Science*, pages 83–107. Springer–Verlag, 2002.
3. J. Baek, R. Steinfeld, and Y. Zheng. Formal proofs for the security of signcryption. In *Proceedings of PKC 2002*, volume 2274 of *Lecture Notes in Computer Science*, pages 80–98. Springer–Verlag, 2002.

4. T. E. Bjørstad. Provable security of signcryption. Master's thesis, Norwegian University of Technology and Science, 2005. http://www.ii.uib.no/~tor/pdf/msc_thesis.pdf.
5. B. Chevallier-Mames. An efficient CDH-based signature scheme with a tight security reduction. In *Advances in Cryptology – CRYPTO 2005*, volume 3621 of *Lecture Notes in Computer Science*, pages 511–526. Springer–Verlag, 2005.
6. B. Chevallier-Mames. Personal correspondence, 2005.
7. R. Cramer and V. Shoup. Design and analysis of practical public-key encryption schemes secure against adaptive chosen ciphertext attack. *SIAM Journal on Computing*, 33(1):167–226, 2004.
8. A. W. Dent. Hybrid cryptography. Cryptology ePrint Archive, Report 2004/210, 2004. http://eprint.iacr.org/2004/210/.
9. A. W. Dent. Hybrid signcryption schemes with insider security. In *Proceedings of ACISP 2005*, volume 3574 of *Lecture Notes in Computer Science*, pages 253–266. Springer–Verlag, 2005.
10. A. W. Dent. Hybrid signcryption schemes with outsider security. In *Proceedings of ISC 2005*, volume 3650 of *Lecture Notes in Computer Science*, pages 203–217. Springer–Verlag, 2005.
11. J. Malone-Lee. Signcryption with non-interactive non-repudiation. Technical Report CSTR-02-004, Department of Computer Science, University of Bristol, 2004. http://www.cs.bris.ac.uk/Publications/Papers/1000628.pdf.
12. D. Pointcheval and J. Stern. Security proofs for signature schemes. In *Advances in Cryptology - EUROCRYPT '96*, volume 1070, pages 387–398. Springer–Verlag, 1996.
13. Y. Zheng. Digital signcryption or how to achieve cost (signature & encryption) << cost (signature) + cost (encryption). In *Advances in Cryptology – CRYPTO '97*, volume 1294 of *Lecture Notes in Computer Science*, pages 165–179. Springer–Verlag, 1997. Unpublished full version (47 pages), dated 1999, available through the author's home page http://www.sis.uncc.edu/~yzheng/papers/signcrypt.pdf.

Security-Mediated Certificateless Cryptography

Sherman S.M. Chow[1,*], Colin Boyd[2], and Juan Manuel González Nieto[2]

[1] Department of Computer Science,
Courant Institute of Mathematical Sciences,
New York University, NY 10012, USA
`schow@cs.nyu.edu`
[2] Information Security Institute,
Queensland University of Technology,
GPO Box 2434, Brisbane, QLD 4001, Australia
{`c.boyd, j.gonzaleznieto`}`@qut.edu.au`

Abstract. We introduce the notion of security-mediated certificateless (SMC) cryptography. This allows more lightweight versions of mediated cryptography while maintaining the ability for instantaneous revocation of keys. Moreover, our solutions avoid key escrow, which has been used in all previous mediated cryptography algorithms. We provide a model of security against a fully-adaptive chosen ciphertext attacker, who may be a rogue key generation centre or any coalition of rogue users. We present a generic construction and also a concrete algorithm based on bilinear pairings. Our concrete scheme is more efficient than the identity-based mediated encryption scheme of Baek and Zheng in PKC 2004 which is provably secure in a comparable security model. In addition, our proposals can be easily extended to support distributed security mediators.

Keywords: security-mediated cryptography, certificateless cryptography.

1 Introduction

During the 1980s and 1990s elaborate schemes for certification of public keys, including many standardised solutions, seemed to be moving towards a worldwide public key infrastructure (PKI). However, in recent years it has been widely recognised that this infrastructure has more problems than was at first realised. Business confidence in public key infrastructure has faltered. Apart from the many commercial, legal and political issues, a recurring dilemma has been how best to manage the processing, storage and revocation of public key certificates.

PUBLIC KEY REVOCATION. The need to be able to revoke public keys was recognised early in the development of public key infrastructure. It seems inevitable that on occasions some private keys will become compromised and in such a case

---

* Major part of the research is done while the author was a visiting scholar of the Information Security Institute (ISI), Queensland University of Technology (QUT). His visit is sponsored by Endeavour Australia Cheung Kong Award 2005.

M. Yung et al. (Eds.): PKC 2006, LNCS 3958, pp. 508–524, 2006.

it is no longer safe to use the corresponding public key. Initial solutions relied on certificate revocation lists (CRLs) similar to the idea of black lists for credit cards. The difficulty of managing CRLs has led to alternative revocation solutions [7, 12], many of which rely on some on-line checking. As modern networks become more widely available and reliable, use of on-line servers becomes much more realistic than it was several years ago.

Mediated cryptography was designed by Boneh, Ding and Tsudik [7] as a method to allow immediate revocation of public keys. They suggest that such a scheme is particularly useful in government, corporate or military environments, where there may be an unexpected and immediate requirement to revoke a key when a user suspects key compromise, or when a user is removed from a position of authority. Previous revocation techniques cannot satisfy this requirement. The basic idea of mediated cryptography is to use an on-line mediator for every transaction. This on-line mediator is referred to as a SEM (SEcurity Mediator) since it provides a control of security capabilities. If the SEM does not cooperate then no transactions with the public key are possible any longer. Once the SEM is notified that a user's key is to be revoked its use can be immediately stopped.

IDENTITY-BASED CRYPTOGRAPHY. Many recent research proposals have focussed on developing public key systems that avoid the use of certificates altogether. The impetus for this trend has largely come from the realisation that the use of pairings on elliptic curves opens up many new options that were not available before. The primary step in this direction was taken by Boneh and Franklin [8] who showed that identity-based cryptography could be practically achieved through use of pairings. Instead of using public keys and certificates, any identity string can take the place of both. Anyone can encrypt a message intended for the entity described by the identity string.

Identity-based cryptography does not solve the revocation problem. Indeed, in some sense it can be argued to make the situation worse since how can a person revoke his own identity? A pragmatic way to deal with this problem is to notice that the identity string can include any additional information, including a validity period. To manage revocation in identity-based cryptosystems, short validity periods may be encoded into the identity string. However, this does not fit an environment where immediate revocation may be required. Ding and Tsudik [10] therefore proposed a combined scheme providing both identity-based key and security-mediated feature.

ESCROW PROBLEM. A major drawback of all identity-based and security-mediated cryptosystems so far proposed is that they require a trusted third party to generate keys for all entities. This is widely known as the *escrow problem*. Absolute trust is placed in the third party, who could decrypt any message or sign on behalf of any entity. Partial solutions have been proposed to the escrow problem, particularly by distributing the power of the third party over several entities. The problem is present in a particularly acute way in Ding and Tsudik's identity-based mediated cryptosystem; compromise of the SEM gives away all messages ever encrypted for every party.

Recently there have been schemes proposed to overcome the escrow problem in a more complete way. Certificateless cryptography proposed by Al-Riyami and Paterson [2] is a hybrid between identity-based schemes and traditional schemes using public key certificates. Entities have public keys but they do not have certificates. Instead the identity string is used to ensure that only the correct entity can be in possession of the private key corresponding to the public key. The scheme is attractive, but does not address how to provide instant revocation when desired. This is the problem that we solve in this paper.

CONTRIBUTIONS. We introduce the notion of *Security-Mediated Certificateless (SMC) cryptography*. The major properties that the proposed notion achieve are:

- no certificates are used (in contrast with PKI-based schemes).
- user private keys are not escrowed (in contrast with identity-based schemes).
- instant revocation is provided (in contrast with certificateless schemes).

No previously proposed cryptosystem can provide all these properties together. We first provide a generic construction for security-mediated certificateless encryption. Then we provide a concrete scheme for security-mediated certificateless encryption with better efficiency based on pairings. Security can be proven in the random oracle model is given. Our concrete scheme has the following properties:

- it is secure in a powerful security model against a fully adaptive rogue key generation centre, or any coalition of fully adaptive rogue users, which can replace the public key of any user and ask for decryption oracle queries even when the public key is replaced.
- it is more efficient[1] than the known identity-based mediated scheme in a similar security model.
- it can be extended to support distributed SEMs, essential for availability.

PAPER STRUCTURE. In the following section we compare related proposals' properties with our proposal. Section 3 discusses the building blocks used by our proposals. The security model for our proposed notion of security-mediated certificateless encryption is discussed in Section 4. Section 5 details our generic construction. In Section 6 a concrete scheme from pairings achieving a higher efficiency than the generic construction is proposed. Finally we conclude our work and discuss some future work of SMC cryptography.

2   Related Work

Our new cryptographic model has strong similarities to a number of previous proposals. It is important to understand our contribution in the context of this previous work. Before discussing each of these in turn we consider a number of prominent features which can be used to differentiate the various models.

---

[1] Our concrete scheme is *not* a trivial extension from existing identity-based mediated scheme and existing certificateless public key encryption scheme.

SEM free. We use this term to indicate that a scheme does *not* use a security mediator. Generally we may regard this feature as an advantage.

Predefined keys. In traditional public key systems, public and private keys generally need to be generated together. An attractive feature of identity-based and related schemes is that encryption can be done before the corresponding private key has been generated. As discussed in [2], this allows "cryptographic work-flow", such that one must satisfy some condition in order to perform a certain cryptographic function (e.g. encryption). We say a system has predefined keys if part of the key can be predefined, which is sufficient for the interesting applications based on control of work-flow.

Instant revoke. As already discussed, in some applications it is important to have the feature to instantly revoke public keys.

Escrow free. Escrow freeness means the user's secret is not (completely) computable by a certain party other than the user. As discussed previously, identity-based cryptography and some related schemes do not achieve this property since they require some (possibly distributed) third party to compute all entities' secrets. The scheme in [7] is also not escrow free since the private key is not generated by the user (a single party generates the RSA modulus for all users).

Implicit certificates. Explicit certificates are required for conventional public key systems. We say that a scheme has *implicit certificates* if there is no need for users of public keys (e.g. the sender of the message being encrypted) to use an explicit certified string. An implication is that there is no need for on-line verification of certificates. Another advantage of implicit certificates is a saving in storage and bandwidth.

We will consider the relevant previous work next in the context of these important features. Table 1 summarises which schemes provide which features. Notice that no scheme can satisfy all features at once, and therefore our security-mediated certificateless cryptography can be considered as a new compromise between the various desirable features.

Table 1. Properties of related paradigms

	SEM Free	Predefined Keys	Instant Revoke	Escrow Free	Implicit Certificates
Identity-based (ID-based) [8]	✓	✓	✗	✗	✓
Certificateless [2]	✓	✓	✗	✓	✓
Certificate-based [12]	✓	✓	✗	✓	✓
Security-mediated [7]	✗	✗	✓	✗	✗
ID-based security-mediated [10, 16]	✗	✓	✓	✗	✓
Security-mediated Certificateless	✗	✓	✓	✓	✓

CERTIFICATELESS CRYPTOGRAPHY. Al-Riyami and Paterson [2] proved that their encryption scheme provides a strong form of chosen ciphertext security. They also provide a key agreement protocol, and a hierarchical encryption scheme in the same model, although none of these extras comes with a formal security analysis. The signature scheme they proposed is later found to be insecure by [14]. More efficient constructions of certificateless public key encryption were proposed subsequently [1,3,9,18]. The improved encryption scheme by Al-Riyami and Paterson [3] is broken and fixed by Zhang and Feng [21].

It is possible to extend certificateless public key encryption (CL-PKE) to a security-mediated one which entails keeping the public key constant while requiring the encryption algorithm to append a changing information such as the current time period to the identifier of the recipient. The corresponding partial private key can then be issued to SEMs for the partial decryption in our scheme. This has similar interaction to our scheme. However, an important limitation of this solution is that the key generation centre needs to remain virtually permanently on-line. The point is that the master secret is needed for the creation of a huge number of partial private keys associated with the fine-grained time intervals. Moreover, this requires every sender to know what "changing information" should be used for each recipient every time, which is not a trivial assumption. In contrast, the mediators in our scheme do not use the master secret and so compromise of one mediator does not affect other mediators or the master secret. Besides, the identifier in our scheme remains unchanged.

The PhD thesis of Al-Riyami [1, Section 4.6.1] suggested a way to provide revocation in certificateless cryptography which entails changing the private key (and hence the public key) of the system at regular time intervals. The encryption algorithm must then retrieve the latest system parameters. Again, an important limitation of this solution is that the key generation centre needs to go on-line at the start of each time period. We also remark that Al-Riyami provides no formal model or proof for such a scenario.

DISTRIBUTED SEM. In any security-mediated schemes, every decryption must involve the help of an on-line SEM, distributing SEM-key across multiple SEMs is essential to ensure availability. Distributing duplicated copies of SEM-key may not be desirable since it introduces more sites for attacker to compromise. One of the standard solutions is to apply threshold cryptography to distribute the SEM-key. In [20], apart from assigning one of the SEMs to hold the original SEM-key, the SEM-key is replicated in the form of a number of shares across multiple SEMs. However, their solution have not considered obtaining partial token from the SEMs holding a share of the SEM-key. Instead, once the initial SEM (holding the original SEM-key) is temporary unavailable, SEM-key migration occurs. The SEM-key is reconstructed from the shares, resulting in an extra copy of a SEM-key. We will show how distributing of SEM-keys is possible for all our proposal.

3   Preliminaries

We review some general notions about public key encryption, one-time signature and identity-based encryption, which will be used in our generic construction. The cryptographic primitive used by our concrete scheme will also be discussed.

3.1 Public Key Encryption

Let $\mathcal{PKE}$ = (PKE.Gen, PKE.Enc, PKE.Dec) be a (standard) public key encryption scheme consists of the key generation algorithm PKE.Gen, the encryption algorithm PKE.Enc and the decryption algorithm PKE.Dec. PKE.Gen takes as an input security parameter 1^k and outputs an encryption/decryption key pair (EK, DK). PKE.Enc is a randomized algorithm taking EK, a label ℓ and a message m as input, outputs a ciphertext C. PKE.Dec is a deterministic algorithm taking DK, a ciphertext C and a label ℓ, outputs a message m or $\perp$ if C is invalid. We require $\mathcal{E}$ to be correct, i.e. $\text{PKE.Dec}_{DK}^{\ell}(\text{PKE.Enc}_{EK}^{\ell}(m)) = m$ for all message m and for all (EK, DK) generated by PKE.Gen. We also require $\mathcal{PKE}$ to be secure against adaptive chosen ciphertext attack, adapted to deal with labels [19].

3.2 One-Time Signature

Let $\mathcal{S}$ = (SGen, Sig, Vfy) be a public key signature scheme consists of the key generation algorithm SGen, the signing algorithm Sig and the verification algorithm Vfy. SGen takes as an input security parameter 1^k and outputs a signing/verification key pair (SK, VK). Sig takes SK and a message m as input, outputs a signature σ. Vfy is a deterministic algorithm taking VK, a message m and a signature σ, outputs $\top$ or $\perp$ depending whether the signature is valid. $\mathcal{S}$ should be correct such that $\text{Vfy}_{VK}(\text{Sig}_{SK}(m)) = \top$ for all message m and for all (SK, VK) generated by SGen. For security, we assume $\mathcal{S}$ is strongly unforgeable (cannot create a new valid signature even for previously-signed messages) under adaptive chosen-message attacks. We refer *one-time signature schemes* as a class of signature schemes with a slightly modified security model that an adversary can only request a signature on a single message.

3.3 Identity-Based Encryption

In 1984, Shamir [17] introduced the idea of identity-based cryptosystem. An identity-based encryption $\mathcal{IBE}$ consists of four algorithms: IBE.Set, IBE.Gen, IBE.Enc and IBE.Dec. In essence, IBE.Set takes as an input security parameter 1^k, outputs common public parameters params and master secret master-key. For simplicity we omit the inclusion of params in the description of the remaining algorithm. IBE.Gen takes user's identity ID, and master-key as input and generates the private key D_{ID} for each user; IBE.Enc produces the ciphertext C by taking the recipient's identity ID, and the message m as input. Finally, IBE.Dec recovers the original message by taking the recipient's private key D_{ID}, and the ciphertext C as input. We require the scheme to be correct, i.e. $\text{IBE.Dec}_{D_{ID}}(\text{IBE.Enc}_{ID}(m)) = m$ for all messages m and all ID such that $D_{ID} = \text{IBE.Gen}_{master-key}(ID)$. We assume $\mathcal{IBE}$ is secure against chosen-ciphertext-and-identity attack. By chosen-identity attack we mean the adversary can ask for the private key of any chosen identities except the one in the challenge.

3.4   Bilinear Pairings and Related Problems

We provide a brief overview of the main definitions and notation for bilinear maps based on elliptic curve pairings. More details and implementation options can be found in many recent papers [6, 8]. We also provide definitions for the BDH problem used by Al-Riyami and Paterson [2]. Using the notation of Boneh and Franklin [8], we let $\mathbb{G}_1$ be an additive group of prime order q and $\mathbb{G}_2$ be a multiplicative group also of order q. We assume the existence of an efficiently computable bilinear map $e : \mathbb{G}_1 \times \mathbb{G}_1 \to \mathbb{G}_2$. Typically, $\mathbb{G}_1$ will be a subgroup of the group of points on an elliptic curve over a finite field, $\mathbb{G}_2$ will be a subgroup of the multiplicative group of a related finite field, and $\hat{e}$ will be derived from the Weil or Tate pairing on the elliptic curve. We assume that an element $P \in \mathbb{G}_1$ satisfying $\hat{e}(P, P) \neq 1_{\mathbb{G}_2}$ is known. By $\hat{e}$ being bilinear, we mean that for $Q, W, Z \in \mathbb{G}_1$, both $\hat{e}(Q, W+Z) = \hat{e}(Q, W) \cdot \hat{e}(Q, Z)$ and $\hat{e}(Q+W, Z) = \hat{e}(Q, Z) \cdot \hat{e}(W, Z)$. When $a \in \mathbb{Z}_q$ and $Q \in \mathbb{G}_1$, we write aQ for Q added to itself $a - 1$ times, also called scalar multiplication of Q by a. As a consequence of bilinearity, for any $Q, W \in \mathbb{G}_1$ and $a, b \in \mathbb{Z}_q$: $\hat{e}(aQ, bW) = \hat{e}(Q, W)^{ab} = \hat{e}(abQ, W)$.

Throughout this paper we assume that suitable groups $\mathbb{G}_1$ and $\mathbb{G}_2$, a map $\hat{e}$ and an element $P \in \mathbb{G}_1$ have been chosen, and that elements of $\mathbb{G}_1$ and $\mathbb{G}_2$ can be represented by bit strings of the appropriate lengths.

Bilinear Diffie-Hellman(BDH) Problem: Let $\mathbb{G}_1$, $\mathbb{G}_2$, P and $\hat{e}$ be as above. The BDH problem in $\langle \mathbb{G}_1, \mathbb{G}_2, e \rangle$ is as follows: Given $\langle P, aP, bP, cP \rangle$ with $a, b, c \in \mathbb{Z}_q^*$, compute $\hat{e}(P, P)^{abc} \in \mathbb{G}_2$. An algorithm $\mathcal{A}$ has advantage ϵ in solving the BDH problem if $\Pr\left[\mathcal{A}(\langle P, aP, bP, cP \rangle) = \hat{e}(P, P)^{abc} \right] = \epsilon$. Here the probability is measured over random choices of a, b, c in $\mathbb{Z}_q^*$ and the random bits of $\mathcal{A}$.

4   Security-Mediated Certificateless Cryptography

Security-mediated certificateless encryption is a seven-tuple (Setup, Set-Private-Key, Set-Public-Key, Register-Public-Key, Encrypt, SEM-Decrypt, User-Decrypt). The players are the key generation centre (KGC), security mediators (SEMs) and a set of users. The KGC runs the setup phase. It takes a security parameter k as input and generates system parameters (we omit the inclusion of system parameters as the input of the rest of the algorithms). A master-key s that is used to generate a SEM-key is randomly selected.

Following this users can generate their private and public key pairs, using Set-Private-Key and Set-Public-Key. Users need to register their identities and the public keys with the KGC by Register-Public-Key, which is a protocol initiated by the user. This requires the KGC to identify the user and receive an authentic version of the public key. At the same time the user must prove knowledge of the private key corresponding to its public key, although the value of the private key remains secret to the user. The KGC then uses the master secret s to generate the SEM-key required during decryption time by the SEM. This key needs to be authentically and confidentially transferred to the SEM. It is quite possible for one user to register different public keys (or even the same one) with multiple SEMs. Notice that SEMs are not given access to the master secret s at any time.

Encrypt takes a message, an identity and a registered public key to produce the corresponding ciphertext. SEM-Decrypt is executed by the SEM using the SEM-key to do the partial decryption for the user. Finally User-Decrypt takes the partial decryption results and the user's private key to get back the message.

4.1   Security Model

Existing security-mediated schemes are of different security levels. The identity-based scheme of Ding and Tsudik [10] uses a common RSA modulus for all users, and hence a collusion between a user and the SEM would result in a total break of the scheme. So the security of the scheme requires a strong assumption that the SEM is totally trusted or remains secure throughout the life of the system.

The security model used by Libert and Quisquater [16] has the restriction that the adversary cannot ask for the private key (i.e. the adversary can still ask for the SEM-key) of the target user in the challenge phase of the game. Although their scheme do not have the drawback of Ding and Tsudik's [10], trust is moved to the user as the scheme is insecure against chosen-ciphertext attack by the attacker who possesses the user part of the private key. Since it is assumed that the adversary do not equipped with the user part of the private key, the notion is termed as *weak semantic security against insider attacks*. Generally speaking, it is easier for an attacker to compromise the key for users' side than the SEM's one. The assumption is still a strong one.

We use a similar security model to that used by the identity-based scheme of Baek and Zheng [5], which is secure against chosen-ciphertext attack by insiders. However, a more powerful adversary should be considered in our scenario. The differences are firstly that we allow the adversary access to the master secret s, and secondly that we provide extra queries which allow the adversary to extract and replace public keys. No such queries are relevant to schemes in [5, 16] since identities are used in place of public keys.

The security model also reflects the similarity with Al-Riyami and Paterson's certificateless encryption [2]. An adversary against our scheme should be allowed to make a number of queries. Some of these are the same as those used in the CL-PKE model but we also need to allow queries for partial and complete decryption. The following are the queries available to the adversary. There are some restrictions on when these can be used which will be detailed below.

1. **Extract SEM-key:** On input an identity ID_A the adversary is returned with D_A, which is the key held by SEM for doing the partial decryption on behalf of the user A.
2. **Request public key:** On input an identity ID_A the adversary obtains user A's public key P_A
3. **Replace public key:** On input an identity ID_A and a valid public key P_A, the public key of A is replaced by this new one (and the SEM-key is also updated if the system bundles the public key with the identifier for SEM-key

creation). The replaced version will be used in the rest of the game (unless replaced again), e.g. the **User decrypt** query to be described below.

4. **Extract private key:** On input an identity ID_A, the adversary gets user A's private key x_A. This query is reasonably disallowed if the public key of A has already been replaced by the adversary.

5. **SEM decrypt:** On input a ciphertext C and identity ID_A, the adversary is returned with the partial decryption result C' by using the SEM-key D_A.

6. **User decrypt:** On input a ciphertext C' and an identity ID_A, the adversary is returned with the decryption of C' (which could, of course, be simply $\perp$). Similar to the proof of security for CL-PKE in [2], we have the luxury of allowing this query even in the case that the public key of A has been replaced by the adversary.

7. **Complete decrypt:** It can be done by executing the above two queries in sequence, subject to the restriction (if any) imposed to either one of them.

As in the CL-PKE model, the adversary is forbidden from both making an **Extract SEM-key** query and making a **Replace public key** query for the same identity. We consider two types of adversary, modelling a rogue key generation centre or any coalition of rogue users.

Type-I adversaries do not have access to the master secret s, but are allowed to choose any public key to be used for the challenge ciphertext.

Type-II adversaries have access to the master secret s, but only a registered public key can be used for the challenge ciphertext. (We do not consider a rogue SEM explicitly since it is weaker than the Type-II adversary.)

4.2 Definition of Security

The definition of security follows a well-known pattern in which the adversary plays a game in two phases against a challenger. In each phase the adversary is allowed to make queries to the challenger subject to any restrictions. At the end of the first stage the adversary outputs a pair of plaintexts and an Identifier, and the challenger returns the encryption of one of these. At the end of the second phase the adversary has to output a bit predicting which plaintext was chosen. It wins the game if it gets the bit correctly. The scheme is secure if no efficient adversary exists which can win the game with probability significantly bigger than $1/2$. More formally the game proceeds as follows.

Setup: System parameters are generated according to the setup procedure of the cryptosystem. The parameters are given to $\mathcal{A}$.

Phase 1: The adversary $\mathcal{A}$ is allowed to make any of the queries detailed above. These queries may be made adaptively.

Challenge phase: The adversary outputs an identity ID_{ch} and a pair of plaintexts m_0, m_1. If $\mathcal{A}$ is a Type-I adversary, it also chooses a public key P_{ch} (by the last **Replace public key** query); otherwise, the public key of identity ID_{ch} cannot be replaced. Important restrictions on key extractions include disallowing **Extract private key** query for ID_{ch} if $\mathcal{A}$ is a Type-II adversary, and disallowing making both of the **Extract SEM-key** query and **Extract private key** query (which is assumed to be issued implicitly if $\mathcal{A}$ has issued a **Replace public key** query) for ID_{ch} if $\mathcal{A}$ is a Type-I adversary. A ciphertext C_{ch}, which is the encryption of m_b (where b is a random bit) under the public key P_{ch} for ID_{ch}, is generated and passed to $\mathcal{A}$.

Phase 2: $\mathcal{A}$ can continue to make queries but cannot make both **Extract SEM-key** query and **Extract private key** query for ID_{ch}. If $\mathcal{A}$ has requested the private key corresponding to the public key P_{ch}, which is registered as the public key of ID_{ch} at the challenge phase, then **SEM decrypt** of the challenge ciphertext by the SEM-key corresponding to ID_{ch} is not allowed. On the other hand, $\mathcal{A}$ cannot ask a **User decrypt** query for C'_{ch} where C'_{ch} is the result of **SEM decrypt** of C_{ch}, if $\mathcal{A}$ has requested the SEM-key corresponding to ID_{ch} (which is assumed to be requested implicitly if $\mathcal{A}$ is a Type-II adversary).

Guess: When it has finished with Phase 2, $\mathcal{A}$ must output a guess bit b'. $\mathcal{A}$ wins the game if $b' = b$ and $\mathcal{A}$'s advantage is defined as $2 \times |Pr[b' = b] - 1/2|$.

Definition 1. *A security-mediated certificateless encryption scheme is IND-CCA secure if there is no efficient adversary in the above game with non-negligible advantage in the security parameter k.*

5   Generic Construction from Multiple Encryption

Multiple encryption refers to the encryption of the same piece of data using multiple and independent encryption schemes. Dodis and Katz [11] proposed a strong chosen-ciphertext secure multiple encryption (refer to [11] for the security definition). We follow their construction and explain our generic security-mediated certificateless encryption scheme. In essence, the multiple encryption includes one instance of identity-based encryption (for SEM side) and one instance of public key encryption (for user side). We illustrate our construction by a bitwise-OR operator instead of the (t, n) threshold secret sharing[2] in their settings. Here the (t, n) notation means at least $t + 1$ decryption keys out of the set of n decryptions keys can recover the ciphertext from the n-times-encryption. In the rest of the paper, we will abuse this notation to refer to a similar meaning that t is the confidentiality threshold of different threshold schemes.

5.1   Encryption Algorithm

Setup:

1. On input a security parameter k, execute IBE.Set to generate system parameters **params** and the **master-key**.
2. Sample H from a family of collision-resistant hash functions.

---

[2] Dodis and Katz's scheme actually offers four parameters: (t_p, t_f, t_r, t_f), referring to the threshold for privacy (confidentiality), fault-tolerance, robustness and soundness.

Set-Private-Key and Set-Public-Key: In this generic construction, this two algorithm may be necessary to combined into one if we treat PKE.Gen as a black-box.
On input a security parameter k, execute PKE.Gen to generate the user's pub-
lic/private key pair (EK, DK).

Register-Public-Key: Inputs are the public key EK and an identity ID_A and the
master secret master-key. The SEM $-$ key for A is set as $D_A = $ IBE.Gen$_{params}$
(ID_A). As part of the registration process we assume that A proves the knowledge
of the private key DK corresponding to the registered public key EK.

Encrypt: Inputs are a message $M \in \{0,1\}^n$, an identity ID_A and public key EK.

1. Generate one-time signature keys (SK, VK) using SGen.
2. Choose a random label ℓ.
3. Choose random $s_1 \in \{0,1\}^n$ and set $s_2 = M \oplus s_1$.
4. Compute $C_1 = $ IBE.Enc$_{params}(ID_A, s_1)$.
5. Compute $C_2 = $ PKE.Enc$_{EK}^{\ell}(s_2)$.
6. Compute $\alpha = H(C_1, C_2, \ell)$.
7. Compute the one-time signature $\sigma = $ Sig$_{SK}(\alpha)$.
8. Output the ciphertext $C = \langle C_1, C_2, VK, \sigma, \ell \rangle$.

SEM-Decrypt: Inputs are a ciphertext $\langle C_1, C_2, VK, \sigma, \ell \rangle$, an identity ID_A, a public
key DK and SEM-key D_A.

1. Check that ID_A is a legitimate user whose key is not revoked.
2. Compute $\alpha = H(C_1, C_2, \ell)$.
3. Check that σ is a valid one-time signature on α by Vfy$_{VK}(\alpha, \sigma)$.
4. Output $\perp$ if verification fails.
5. Otherwise, compute $V_1' = $ IBE.Dec$_{D_A}(C_1)$ and output V_1'.

User-Decrypt: Inputs are a ciphertext $\langle C_1, C_2, VK, \sigma, \ell \rangle$, the token V_1' from the
SEM, and a secret DK.

1. Compute α and check σ similar to SEM-Decrypt.
2. Output $\perp$ if verification fails.
3. Otherwise, compute $V_2' = $ PKE.Dec$_{DK}^{\ell}(C_2)$
4. Output $M' = V_1' \oplus V_2'$.

5.2   Efficiency and Security Analysis

Encryption takes the time for an invocation of identity-based encryption and a
public key encryption, together with one signature generation. Decryption by
SEM and the user, apart from signature verification, takes one identity-based
decryption and one public key decryption respectively. The resulting ciphertext's length is the total length of the ciphertext produced by identity-based
encryption and public key encryption, together with the verification key of the

signature algorithm, a hash value and a label employed by the public key encryption. Note that the use of one-time signature offers fast signature generation/verification.

Due to the page limit we only outline how simulations in the security proof can be done. From the strong-multiple chosen-ciphertext (SM-CCA) security of the multiple-encryption scheme [11], it is easy to see that partial decryption by the SEM and the complete decryption can be supported in the simulation by querying the decryption oracle of $\mathcal{IBE}$ and $\mathcal{PKE}$ respectively. Type-I adversary's **Extract SEM-key** and **Extract private key** queries can be simulated by the corresponding corruption oracle of $\mathcal{IBE}$ and $\mathcal{PKE}$. The success of a Type-I adversary means breaking the security of either $\mathcal{IBE}$ or $\mathcal{PKE}$. For Type-II adversary, the simulator is only given with $\mathcal{PKE}$ and executes IBE.Set itself instead of relying on any $\mathcal{IBE}$'s oracles. Simulating in this way makes it possible to answer the queries revealing the master-key. Since our generic construction is a $(1, 2)$ instantiation of Dodis and Katz's scheme, winning the game in the security proof means the adversary made a successful $\mathcal{IBE}$ decryption and a successful $\mathcal{PKE}$ decryption, implying the security of the underlying $\mathcal{PKE}$ is broken.

5.3   Distributing the SEMs

Our proposed generic construction can be extended to support distributed SEMs in two ways. Suppose t out of n shares of SEM-key is needed for a successful SEM decryption for a particular user. Instead of the above $(1, 2)$ instantiation, the first method is to instantiate $(t, n + 1)$ Dodis-Katz multiple encryption, which includes n instances of IBE and one instance of PKE, i.e. the ciphertext contains n ciphertext from IBE and one ciphertext from PKE. Let $\{\mathsf{ID}_A\}$ be $\{(\mathsf{ID}_A||i), i \in \{0 \cdots 0, 0 \cdots 1, 0 \cdots 10, \cdots, 1 \cdots 1\}\}$, i.e. the identity string ID_A concatenated by the binary representations of the integers $\{1, n\}$. For the n instances of IBE, we encrypt n shares produced by a $(t, n + 1)$ secret sharing[3], (instead of a $(1, 2)$ secret-sharing used above) of the message m by the n identities $\{\mathsf{ID}_A\}$ and the remaining share by EK. There are n SEM-keys corresponding to each user, generated by the KGC according to the identity set $\{\mathsf{ID}_A\}$. Each of n SEMs holds one of them. For SEM decryption, t SEMs perform decryption of the corresponding part of the ciphertext, without interacting with other SEMs. After obtaining these partial decryption results, the user executes PKE.Dec and gets the final message by the recover algorithm of the $(t, n + 1)$ secret sharing.

However, this method inherits the linear ciphertext size and the linear number of encryption from Dodis-Katz's construction. Hereafter we describe our second extension to avoid these linear dependencies. Instead of using n identity-based encryption, we employ a (t, n) identity-based threshold decryption [5], so essentially we are using something similar to the $(1, 2)$ instantiation of the above generic method again. Notice that the threshold decryption scheme employed

---

[3] Again, four threshold parameters instead of one can be set in the original construction [11], we only include the confidentiality threshold for the sake of brevity.

should spilt the *user*'s key instead of *KGC*'s key, in order to support different threshold settings for different users.

By this approach, we achieve a constant size ciphertext, but the efficiency of the resulting scheme is still linearly with (and hence highly dependent on) the decryption efficiency of the underlying identity-based threshold decryption. This shortcoming motivates our concrete construction in the next section.

6   Our Concrete Scheme from Bilinear Pairings

This section explains our concrete security-mediated certificateless encryption scheme, followed by discussion on its efficiency and threshold extension.

6.1   Encryption Algorithm

Setup:

1. On input a security parameter k, generate system parameters $(\mathbb{G}_1, \mathbb{G}_2, \hat{e})$ where $\mathbb{G}_1$ and $\mathbb{G}_2$ are groups of prime order q and $\hat{e} : \mathbb{G}_1 \times \mathbb{G}_1 \to \mathbb{G}_2$ is a pairing. Also choose five hash functions $H_1 : \{0,1\}^* \to \mathbb{G}_1$, $H_2 : \{0,1\}^n \to \mathbb{Z}_q^*$, $H_3 : \mathbb{G}_1 \to \{0,1\}^n$, $H_4 : \mathbb{G}_2 \to \{0,1\}^n$, and $H_5 : \mathbb{G}_1 \times \mathbb{G}_1 \times \{0,1\}^n \to \mathbb{G}_1$, where n is the length of plaintexts. These hash functions will be modelled as random oracles in order to provide the security proof.
2. Choose an arbitrary generator $P \in \mathbb{G}_1$.
3. Select a **master-key** s uniformly at random from $\mathbb{Z}_q^*$ and set $P_{pub} = sP$.
4. Return the **master-key** and the public system parameters given by

$$\text{params} = \langle \mathbb{G}_1, \mathbb{G}_2, \hat{e}, n, P, P_{pub}, H_1, H_2, H_3, H_4, H_5 \rangle.$$

Set-Private-Key: Choose a secret value $x_A \in_R \mathbb{Z}_q^*$ as the private key of entity A.

Set-Public-Key: Given the private key x_A of entity A, set the public key of A to $P_A = x_A P$.

Register-Public-Key: Inputs are the public key P_A and an identity ID_A and the master secret s. The SEM-key for A is set as $D_A = s \cdot H_1(\text{ID}_A)$. As part of the registration process we assume that A proves the knowledge of the value x_A such that $P_A = x_A P$.

Encrypt: Inputs are a message $M \in \{0,1\}^{n-k_0}$, an identity ID_A and public key P_A.

1. Compute $Q_A = H_1(\text{ID}_A)$.
2. Choose random $\sigma \in \{0,1\}^{k_0}$ and set $r = H_2(M \parallel \sigma)$.
3. Compute $k = \hat{e}(Q_A, P_{pub})^r$, $U = rP$ and $U' = rP_A$.
4. Compute $V = (M \parallel \sigma) \oplus H_3(U') \oplus H_4(k)$ [4].
5. Compute $S = rH_5(P_A, U, V)$.
6. Compute the ciphertext $C = \langle S, U, V \rangle \in \mathbb{G}_1 \times \mathbb{G}_1 \times \{0,1\}^n$.

---

[4] CL-PKE in [3] employs a similar "exclusive-or structure" in the ciphertext, which is exploited by the attack in [21]. However, the non-malleability provided by the S component protects our scheme from their attack.

SEM-Decrypt: Inputs are a ciphertext $\langle S, U, V \rangle$, an identity ID_A, a public key P_A and SEM-key D_A.

1. Check that ID_A is a legitimate user whose key is not revoked.
2. Check that $\hat{e}(P, S) = \hat{e}(U, H_5(P_A, U, V))$.
3. Compute $V' = V \oplus H_4(\hat{e}(D_A, U))$ and output V'.

User-Decrypt: Inputs are a partial ciphertext U, the token V' from the SEM, and a secret x_A.

1. Parse M' and σ' from $M' \parallel \sigma' = H_3(x_A U) \oplus V'$.
2. Verify whether $H_2(M' \parallel \sigma') \cdot P = U$.
3. If the verification succeeds then output M'. Else output $\perp$.

It is easy to see that the proposed scheme is correct. Consider a valid ciphertext produced by our scheme; from the bilinearity of pairings, the checking done in SEM-Decrypt must pass. Consider the decryption step in SEM-Decrypt, we have $\hat{e}(D_A, U)) = \hat{e}(sQ_A, rP) = \hat{e}(Q_A, sP)^r = \hat{e}(Q_A, P_{pub})^r$. For the decryption step in User-Decrypt, $x_A U = x_A rP = rP_A$. Again, the checking in User-Decrypt must pass for a valid ciphertext since $U = rP$. The correctness thus follows.

6.2 Efficiency and Security Analysis

We make the focus of our comparison on the efficiency of identity-based threshold decryption by Baek and Zheng [5] for the following reasons. First, the second threshold extension of the generic scheme described in previous section requires the use of identity-based threshold decryption. To the best of authors' knowledge, Baek and Zheng [5]'s scheme is the only scheme that separating the private key of each user into shares instead of the private key of the KGC. Second, a $(1, 2)$ threshold decryption can be used as an identity-based mediated encryption (IDME) by delegating one share to the SEM and another to the user. Since their threshold decryption scheme is chosen-ciphertext secure, the resulting IDME offering a similar level of security as ours, in the sense that partial SEM decryption queries are allowed.

From the Table 2, we can see that our scheme offers a more efficient solution. In IDME, the checking on the SEM's decryption is not included as part of the protocol. As a consequence, the user will not notice if there is something wrong in the SEM's decryption. Yet, a zero knowledge proof for the equality of two discrete logarithms based on bilinear pairings [5, 16] can be used to ensure the consistency of SEM's decryption result. The notation $(+y)$ in Table 2 represents the number of additional operations required if such a proof is employed. In our proposed scheme, such a zero knowledge proof is not necessary since a mechanism of consistency checking is already incorporated.

The following theorem summarises the security of our proposed scheme. The proof can be found in the full version of this paper.

Theorem 1. *Our proposed scheme is IND-CCA secure against Type I and Type II adversary in the random oracle model, under the assumption that the BDH problem is intractable.*

Table 2. Efficiency Analysis of Security-Mediated Encryption Schemes

	Encryption			Decryption (SEM)			Decryption (User)		
	$\hat{e}(\cdot,\cdot)$	Exp	Hash	$\hat{e}(\cdot,\cdot)$	Exp	Hash	$\hat{e}(\cdot,\cdot)$	Exp	Hash
IDME	1	3	1	3 (+2)	0 (+1)	1	3 (+2)	0 (+2)	1
Proposed Scheme	1	3	1	3	0	1	0	2	0

6.3 Distributing SEMs

Since our proposed scheme is built on top of a variant of the identity-based threshold decryption scheme which is proven to be IND-CCA secure, the extension of our scheme to support distributed SEMs can be proven to be IND-CCA secure too. The idea of the extension is as follows. Instead of delegating a single SEM-key, the SEMs got a (t, n) share $D_A^{(i)}$ of the SEM-key D_A (by employing the sharing a point on $\mathbb{G}$ sub-routine in [5], which is a simple twist of the Shamir's polynomial secret sharing). The partial decryption result to be returned by the SEMs is no longer the hash value $H_4(\hat{e}(D_A^{(i)}, U))$ but $\hat{e}(D_A^{(i)}, U)$.[5] And the user reconstructs all these partial decryption results and performs the final decryption. As a result, the extended scheme offers higher availability without explicit replication of SEM-key. Indeed, the major portion of the pairing operations in our proposed scheme comes from the checking of the validity of ciphertext before SEM decryption, which is an essential step for the chosen-ciphertext security of distributed SEMs. Similar to our second extension of our generic construction, constant size ciphertext is achieved. Moreover, our concrete scheme has a higher efficiency as shown in Table 2.

7 Conclusion and Future Work

We introduce the notion of security-mediated certificateless (SMC) cryptography, which has instantiated one more of the set of compromises within the various desirable properties for solving the certification problem in public key cryptography. We have provided a generic construction and also a concrete encryption scheme. An attractive feature of our proposal is that it can use the same parameters used for most other identity-based and share the same key generation centre (KGC). Our scheme also supports distributed security mediators (SEMs).

A limitation of certificateless encryption (both ours and the original) is that in its basic form it fails to reach Girault's level 3 [13]. This means that although there is less trust placed in the authority than for identity-based schemes (users do not reveal their private keys to the KGC), there is more trust placed in the KGC than in traditional public key schemes. This is because if a malicious KGC distributes a bogus public key for a user, the KGC can obtain secrets intended for that user even though there is no evidence that can be used to prove that

---

[5] Note that there is no special handling for the simulation of H_4 in the security proof.

the KGC misbehaved. There are ways to achieve level 3 as discussed by Al-Riyami [1]. One way is to provide a proof of possession of the private key, which in turn provides the evidence of malicious behaviour if more than one is found. This can be achieved by providing a signature using the same key.

We discuss some of our future work in SMC cryptography. Naturally it would be nice to provide a complementary signature scheme with similar properties. We have a set of candidate signature schemes, including a variant of blind signature scheme that SEM can blindly issue a partial signature to users. Another challenge is to design a scheme with all the properties of ours but can achieve the level 3 of trust refined by Al-Riyami [1]. His work [1] also refined the CBE model [12], and generic construction of CBE in this new model from CL-PKE is proposed [1, 3]. However, their security evidence is questioned recently [15]. It is interesting to identify the relation between SMC encryption and CBE. Another related problem is to design SMC encryption without pairing [4].

Acknowledgement

This paper is an outgrowth of a short-term research project sponsored by Endeavour Australia Cheung Kong Award 2005. Sherman Chow would like to thank Australian Government Department of Education, Science and Training for the assistantship. He is grateful to his coauthors for offering this on-going project, and anonymous reviewers for helpful comments and the suggestion about generic construction in particular. He is also indebted to all the staff and students of ISI, QUT for their continuing support and kind hospitality during his visit there.

References

1. Sattam S. Al-Riyami. *Cryptographic Schemes Based on Elliptic Curve Pairings.* PhD thesis, Royal Holloway, University of London, 2004.
2. Sattam S. Al-Riyami and Kenneth G. Paterson. Certificateless Public Key Cryptography. In *Advances in Cryptology - ASIACRYPT 2003, 9th International Conference on the Theory and Application of Cryptology and Information Security, Taipei, Taiwan, November 30 - December 4, 2003*, volume 2894 of *LNCS*, pages 452–473. Springer, 2003. Full version at http://eprint.iacr.org/2003/126.
3. Sattam S. Al-Riyami and Kenneth G. Paterson. CBE from CL-PKE: A Generic Construction and Efficient Schemes. In *Public Key Cryptography - PKC 2005, 8th International Workshop on Theory and Practice in Public Key Cryptography, Les Diablerets, Switzerland, January 23-26, 2005*, volume 3386 of *LNCS*, pages 398–415. Springer, 2005.
4. Joonsang Baek, Reihaneh Safavi-Naini, and Willy Susilo. Certificateless Public Key Encryption Without Pairing. In *Information Security, 8th International Conference, ISC 2005, Singapore, September 20-23, 2005*, volume 3650 of *LNCS*, pages 134–148. Springer, 2005.
5. Joonsang Baek and Yuliang Zheng. Identity-based Threshold Decryption. In *Public Key Cryptography - PKC 2004, 7th International Workshop on Theory and Practice in Public Key Cryptography, Singapore, March 1-4, 2004*, volume 2947 of *LNCS*, pages 262–276. Springer, 2004.

6. Paulo S. L. M. Barreto, Hae Yong Kim, Ben Lynn, and Michael Scott. Efficient Algorithms for Pairing-based Cryptosystems. In *Advances in Cryptology - CRYPTO 2002, 22nd Annual International Cryptology Conference, Santa Barbara, California, USA, August 18-22, 2002*, volume 2442 of *LNCS*, pages 354–368. Springer.
7. Dan Boneh, Xuhua Ding, and Gene Tsudik. Fine-grained control of security capabilities. *ACM Transactions on Internet Technology*, 4(1):60–82, February 2004.
8. Dan Boneh and Matt Franklin. Identity-Based Encryption from the Weil Pairing. *SIAM Journal on Computing*, 32(3):586–615, 2003.
9. Zhaohui Cheng and Richard Comley. Efficient Certificateless Public Key Encryption. Cryptology ePrint Archive, Report 2005/012, 2005.
10. Xuhua Ding and Gene Tsudik. Simple Identity-Based Cryptography with Mediated RSA. In *Topics in Cryptology - CT-RSA 2003, The Cryptographers' Track at the RSA Conference 2003, San Francisco, CA, USA, April 13-17, 2003*, volume 2612 of *LNCS*, pages 193–210. Springer, 2003.
11. Yevgeniy Dodis and Jonathan Katz. Chosen-Ciphertext Security of Multiple Encryption. In *Theory of Cryptography, Second Theory of Cryptography Conference, TCC 2005, Cambridge, MA, USA, February 10-12, 2005, Proceedings*, volume 3378 of *LNCS*, pages 188–209. Springer, 2005.
12. Craig Gentry. Certificate-Based Encryption and the Certificate Revocation Problem. In *Advances in Cryptology - EUROCRYPT 2003, International Conference on the Theory and Applications of Cryptographic Techniques, Warsaw, Poland, May 4-8, 2003*, volume 2656 of *LNCS*, pages 272–293. Springer, 2003.
13. Marc Girault. Self-certified Public Keys. In *Advances in Cryptology - EUROCRYPT '91, Workshop on the Theory and Application of Cryptographic Techniques, Brighton, UK, April 8-11, 1991*, volume 547 of *LNCS*, pages 490–497.
14. Xinyi Huang, Willy Susilo, Yi Mu, and Futai Zhang. On the Security of Certificateless Signature Schemes from Asiacrypt 2003. In *Cryptology and Network Security, 4th International Conference, CANS 2005, Fujian, China, December 14-16, 2005*, volume 3810 of *LNCS*, pages 13-25. Springer, 2005.
15. Bo Gyeong Kang and Je Hong Park. Is it possible to have CBE from CL-PKE?. Cryptology ePrint Archive, Report 2005/431, 2005.
16. Benoît Libert and Jean-Jacques Quisquater. Efficient Revocation and Threshold Pairing based Cryptosystems. In *PODC 2003 of the Twenty-Second ACM Symposium on Principles of Distributed Computing (PODC 2003), July 13-16, 2003, Boston, Massachusetts, USA. ACM*, pages 163–171. ACM Press, 2003.
17. Adi Shamir. Identity-Based Cryptosystems and Signature Schemes. In *Advances in Cryptology of CRYPTO 1984, Santa Barbara, California, USA, August 19-22, 1984*, volume 196 of *LNCS*, pages 47–53. Springer-Verlag, 1985.
18. Yijuan Shi and Jianhua Li. Provable Efficient Certificateless Public Key Encryption. Cryptology ePrint Archive, Report 2005/287, 2005.
19. Victor Shoup. A Proposal for an ISO Standard for Public Key Encryption (Version 2.1). Cryptology ePrint Archive, Report 2001/112, 2001.
20. Gabriel Vanrenen and Sean Smith. Distributing Security-Mediated PKI. In *Public Key Infrastructure, First European PKI Workshop: Research and Applications, EuroPKI 2004, Samos Island, Greece, June 25-26, 2004, Proceedings*, volume 3093 of *LNCS*, pages 218–231. Springer, 2004.
21. Zhenfeng Zhang and Dengguo Feng. On the Security of a Certificateless Public-Key Encryption. Cryptology ePrint Archive, Report 2005/426, 2005.

k-Times Anonymous Authentication with a Constant Proving Cost

Isamu Teranishi and Kazue Sako

NEC Corporation

Abstract. A k-Times Anonymous Authentication (k-TAA) scheme allows users to be authenticated anonymously so long as the number of times that they are authenticated is within an allowable number. Some promising applications are e-voting, e-cash, e-coupons, and trial browsing of contents. However, the previous schemes are not efficient in the case where the allowable number k is large, since they require both users and verifiers to compute $O(k)$ exponentiation in each authentication. We propose a k-TAA scheme where the numbers of exponentiations required for the entities in an authentication are independent of k. Moreover, we propose a notion of public detectability in a k-TAA scheme and present an efficient publicly verifiable k-TAA scheme, where the number of modular exponentiations required for the entities is $O(\log(k))$.

Keywords: k-times anonymous authentication, efficiency, public verifiability.

1 Introduction

1.1 Background

A k-Times Anonymous Authentication (k-TAA) scheme [TFS04, NN05] allows users to be authenticated anonymously so long as the number of times that they are authenticated is within an allowable number. The scheme not only offers a time restriction mechanism to well-known group signature schemes [CH91, ACJT00, BBS04, BSZ05, CG04, KY05], but provides stronger properties of anonymity and traceability. Regarding anonymity, users who are authenticated within the allowable number times can enjoy anonymity even from an authority, whereas in a group signature scheme users are always identifiable by the authority. Regarding traceability, any verifier can trace a malicious "over-time" user (that is, a user who exceeds the time restriction) from an authentication log in a k-TAA scheme, whereas in a group signature scheme it is only the authority who has this capability. There are many applications of the k-TAA scheme, such as e-voting [SK94,OMAFO99,DJ01,FS01, Neff01], e-cash [CP92, B93, AF96, CFT98, PBF99], e-coupon [OO98, NHS99], and trial browsing of contents [TFS04]. Moreover, these various application services can be offered based on a single secret key issued to users at the joining phase. For example, a user who paid an annual membership fee can download up to 1000 titles of

M. Yung et al. (Eds.): PKC 2006, LNCS 3958, pp. 525–542, 2006.

digital music and 100 movie titles anonymously every year and can participate in anonymous questionnaires held every month.

We use the term "application providers" (APs) to refer to verifiers who wish to authenticate members and who want to restrict the number of times the members can use their service anonymously. In the previous example, the music downloading site is set to 1000, and the movie downloading site is set to 100, and monthly questionnaires site is set to 1.

A problem with the previous k-TAA schemes [TFS04, NN05] is that they require large computation when the number k becomes large, since $O(k)$ exponentiation is necessary for both users and AP.

1.2   Our Contributions

We propose, for the first time, a k-TAA scheme where the number of exponentiations required for users and AP for authentication is independent of k. The proposed scheme is constructed using a bilinear pairing [MSK02, BB04], and is secure under the SDH assumption [BB04], the DDHI assumption [BB04], and the random oracle assumption.

Moreover, we propose and formalize a stronger variant of the detectability requirement [TFS04] called the *public detectability*. It requires that anyone can verify that the AP indeed provided a fair limit to all users regarding the number of accesses to their service. For most applications such as e-coupon schemes and trial browsing, it is the APs that wish to restrict the number of times they offer service to a user, or else they will be paying for over-time users. So the property of the public detectability may not be necessary. However, in applications such as e-voting, one may want to publicly verify that the verifier has not accepted votes from the same user for more than a given number.

We also present an efficient and public detectable k-TAA scheme, where the number of exponentiations required for the user and verifier is $O(\log k)$. The scheme is secure under the same assumptions as those of the constant-cost scheme.

1.3   Key Ideas

We present here the ideas of the proposed schemes. First, we present the previous mechanism of detecting over-timed users [TFS04] at the cost of $O(k)$ exponentiations. We then show how this could be decreased to $O(\log k)$ and to $O(1)$. If an AP wishes to restrict the access time to be k, he publishes k public information items, namely, $r_1, \ldots, r_k$. In the authentication, a user picks one of the AP information items, say r_w, and sends a *tag* data $r_w{}^x$ using his secret key x. If a malicious user tries to be authenticated more than k times, the same tag $r_{w'}{}^x$ should appear in the authentication log and thus such a user will be detected. This is the mechanism to detect over-time users.

In the course of authentication a user needs to prove in zero knowledge that the tag is well-formed, that is, it is one of the public information items provided to his secret key. In the schemes of [TFS04, NN05], a user prove this using the 'OR proof', that is, a user proves that one of $\tau = r_1{}^x$, $\tau = r_2{}^x$, $\ldots$, or $\tau = r_k{}^x$ is satisfied. This resulted in the cost of $O(k)$ exponentiation.

In order to avoid the 'OR proof', we employ a deterministic function f_x to construct our tag. In the authentication, the user computes $\tau = f_x(ID_{AP}||k, w)$ using his secret key x, sends it to the verifier and proves the inequality $1 \leq w \leq k$. The user can prove the inequality more efficiently by committing each bit of w. This is our first scheme with the public detectability property at the cost of only $O(\log k)$ exponentiation.

In our second scheme, the AP publishes signatures $\mathsf{Sig}(1)$, ..., $\mathsf{Sig}(k)$ in advance. In the authentication, the user computes $\tau = f_x(ID_{AP}||k, w)$ but proves the knowledge of a signature $\mathsf{Sig}(w)$, instead of proving the inequality regarding w. Since only k signatures $\mathsf{Sig}(1)$, ..., $\mathsf{Sig}(k)$ are published, it indirectly ensures that $1 \leq w \leq k$. This resulted in the cost of only $O(1)$ exponentiation. However, this is not publicly detectable since a malicious AP may secretly reveal $\mathsf{Sig}(w)$ for $w > k$.

Based on the ideas above, we sought the best choice for the function f. We observed that a weakened pseudorandom function f is sufficient for our purpose and were able to choose efficiently computable f.

1.4 Related Works

E-cash schemes are similar to k-TAA schemes in the sense that they issue e-coins, or identification tokens, that can be used k times. A major difference between e-cash schemes and k-TAA schemes lies in the meaning of k, and who determines it.

In an e-cash scheme, the number k refers to the upper bound of the number of times the token issued by the Bank can be used. The Bank specifies k at the withdrawal phase, and the token can be spent in any shops. In contrast, in k-TAA schemes, Group Manager issues identification token at joining phase, but the use of this token is not limited. Instead, in k-TAA schemes, we want to limit the number of times this token is used in each shop, or in our term, each Application Provider. So it will be each AP that determines the number k, which is the upper bound of the number of times a user can use the token to received services from AP. There can be multiple APs and each of them can determine the upper bound independently. So a same token can be used at most say 100 times to Provider-1, 20 times to Provider-2 , and maybe once to Provider-3.

Having said the difference in the model, the techniques used in e-cash schemes and in our schemes is very similar. Independent to our work, Camenisch et. al. presented an e-cash scheme [CHL05] using similar ideas in our first scheme. The difference is in techniques in showing the inequality of $1 \leq w \leq k$. Although the smart use of Boudot scheme [B00] makes their scheme more efficient than our first scheme, it still requires number of exponentiations to be dependent of k, namely $O(\log k)$.

2 Definition of k-TAA Scheme

2.1 Modified Points

Our definition is based on that of Teranishi et.al. [TFS04] with generalizations of allowing an AP to publish its own public information besides its ID and its allowable number k.

The generalization requires us to modify the previous definition in two other points, which are concerned with the "public tracing" algorithm. This is an algorithm which enables anyone to identify a user authenticated more times than the allowable number. In the case where the identification of the user fails, it also enables anyone to know why it does so.

We next describe our modifications. Since we allow an AP to publish its public information, we add a new type of output "AP", which means "the identification fails since the AP publishes a maliciously generated public information items (or behaves maliciously in an authentication)", to a public tracing procedure. We also add new security requirements, called the exculpability for APs. This requires that the public tracing algorithm outputs AP only if the AP is dishonest.

We note that Nguyen and Naini [NN05] also adopt the definition which allows an AP to publish its own public information, but they do not adopt the other two modifications.

2.2   Model

Three types of entities take part in the model, namely, the *group manager* (*GM*), *users*, and *APs*. The k-TAA scheme comprises the three algorithms *GM setup* (GM-Setup), *AP setup* (AP-Setup), and *public tracing* (trace) and two pairs of interactive protocols *joining* (Join = (Join-U, Join-GM)), and *authentication* (Auth = (Proof, Verify)). In the definitions below, κ is a security parameter.

GM-Setup : The GM executes GM-Setup on inputting 1^κ and obtains a *GM public key*/*GM secret key* pair (gpk, gsk). Then it publishes gpk.

AP-Setup : Each AP v determines the *allowable number* $k = k_v$, which indicates how many times the AP v allows each user to access. The AP v executes the AP-Setup on inputting its ID v and k, and obtains an *AP public information* api.

Join = (Join-U, Join-GM) : A user who wants to be a *group member* executes a Join protocol with the GM. The user and the GM execute Join-U and Join-GM respectively. The user's ID and gpk are input to both the Join-U and Join-GM, and gsk is input only to the Join-GM. The aims of the protocol are to add new members to the group and to generate new *member public key*/*secret key pair* (mpk, msk). If the Join protocol is successful, the user obtains both mpk and msk, and the GM obtains only mpk.

The member public key mpk comprises two parts. One part mck is called the *member certificate key* and the other part mik is called the *member identification key*. The key mck is a certificate which proves that the user is a member of the group. The key mik is added to the public list List along with the user's ID and will be used in order to identify the user.

Auth = (Proof, Verify) : An AP executes an Auth protocol with a user who wants to access the AP. The user and the AP execute Proof and Verify respectively. The public information (gpk, v, k, api) are input to both Proof and Verify, and msk is input only to Proof. If the protocol is successful, the AP records the data sent by the user in its *authentication log* Log, and outputs accept or reject. Here accept means that "the user is a group member and has not accessed the AP more times than the allowable number k".

trace : Anyone can execute trace algorithm using only public information (gpk, List, v, k, api) and the authentication log Log of an AP. The output of trace algorithm is either some user's ID u, "GM", "AP", or "NoOne". These four types of output respectively mean "the algorithm finds a malicious user u who is authenticated by the AP more times than the allowable number", "the algorithm finds that the GM published maliciously generated public information (gpk, List)", "the algorithm finds that the AP published maliciously generated (api, k, Log) or behaves maliciously in an authentication", and "the algorithm could not find any malicious entity".

We note that an AP can always mask a malicious user and generate Log, such that trace algorithm with input Log outputs "NoOne". That is, the AP can delete entries of the over times users.

2.3   Informal Definition of Requirements

A *secure* k-TAA scheme has to satisfy the following requirements:

Correctness: An honest group member is always accepted in an authentication by an honest AP.
Total Anonymity: No one is able to identify any authenticated member, or decide whether two accepted authentication protocols are performed by the same group member or not, if the authenticated user(s) has followed the authentication protocol within the allowed number of times per AP. These are satisfied even if all other users, the GM, and all APs collude with one another.
Exculpability for Users: trace algorithm does not output the ID of an honest user who is authenticated within the allowed number of times. This is satisfied even if all other users, the GM, and all APs collude with one another.
Exculpability for the GM: trace algorithm does not output "GM" if the GM is honest. This is satisfied even if all users and all APs collude with one another.
Exculpability for APs: trace algorithm using an honest AP's authentication log does not output "AP". This is satisfied even if the GM, all users and all other APs collude with one another.
Detectability: trace algorithm using an honest AP's authentication log does not output "NoOne", if a colluding subset of group members has been authenticated more than kn times. Here k is the allowable number set by the AP and n is the number of colluders.

We stress that the detectability property is satisfied only if the AP is honest. For most applications such as e-coupon schemes and trial browsing, the AP does not have to be honest, since it is the AP itself who wishes to limit the number of times to serve a user. However in applications such as e-voting, one wants to publicly verify that the AP has not accepted votes from the same user for more than a given number. In order to meet such applications, we newly introduce the stronger detectability notion, *public detectability*:

Public Detectability: trace algorithm using an honest or dishonest AP's authentication log does not output NoOne, if the log contains more than kn malicious entries. Here k is the allowable number set by the AP and n is the number of the group members. This is satisfied even if every user and every AP collude with one another.

2.4   Formal Definition of Requirements

We modify the experiments for defining the requirements of the previous paper [TFS04] in order to suit the modification described in 2.1, but our experiments are essentially the same as those of [TFS04]. The major modification is that we introduce the oracles $\mathcal{O}_{\text{AP-Setup}}$ and $\mathcal{O}_{\text{VList}}$. Here the former is the oracle which executes AP-Setup honestly, and latter is the oracle which manages the public list VList of a pair of AP's IDs v, the allowable number k set by the AP, and its public information api. We will describe the details of $\mathcal{O}_{\text{VList}}$ later.

The experiments of our version of the total anonymity and the exculpability for users and for the GM are the same as those of [TFS04], except that an adversary is allowed to access the oracle $\mathcal{O}_{\text{VList}}$. Moreover, the definition of the experiment for defining the detectability is also the same as that of [TFS04], except an adversary is allowed to access oracle $\mathcal{O}_{\text{VList}}$ and the oracle $\mathcal{O}_{\text{AP-Setup}}$.

Before we describe the experiments, we first describe what $\mathcal{A}$ can do when it colludes with GM, users, and AP respectively.

- If $\mathcal{A}$ colludes with the GM, it can maliciously execute GM-Setup and Join-GM.
- If $\mathcal{A}$ colludes with a user, it can execute Join-U and Proof maliciously on behalf of the user.
- If $\mathcal{A}$ colludes with an AP, it can execute AP-Setup and Verify maliciously on behalf of the AP.

We next describe the oracles. Let $\mathcal{O}_{\text{Join-GM}}$ be the oracle which executes Join-GM procedures honestly. Let $\mathcal{O}_{\text{Join-U}}$ and $\mathcal{O}_{\text{Proof}}$ be oracles which execute Join-U and Proof procedures on behalf of honest users. Similarly, let $\mathcal{O}_{\text{AP-Setup}}$ and $\mathcal{O}_{\text{Verify}}$ be the oracles which execute AP-Setup and Verify on behalf of honest verifiers.

We also introduce the *list oracle* $\mathcal{O}_{\text{List}}(X, \cdot)$ [TFS04], which manages the public list List of a pair of user's IDs and his member identification key mik, and allows $\mathcal{A}$ to read List. Moreover, the oracle also manages the set X of IDs of entities who collude with an adversary $\mathcal{A}$, and it allows $\mathcal{A}$ to write an (honestly or dishonestly generated) pair (u, mik) if $\mathcal{A}$ colluded with the user u. The list oracle also allows $\mathcal{A}$ to delete entries of List if it colludes with the GM.

We also introduce the new list oracle $\mathcal{O}_{\text{List}}$, which manages the public list VList of pairs of AP's IDs and their public information. The definition of $\mathcal{O}_{\text{VList}}$ is quite similar to that of the original $\mathcal{O}_{\text{List}}$. However, $\mathcal{O}_{\text{VList}}$ does not allow the GM to delete the data of List. This is because, even in the actual scenario, VList is managed not by the GM, but by some trusted party (such as a Certified Authority of a PKI). Therefore the GM cannot delete entries of VList. See the full paper for the formal definition of $\mathcal{O}_{\text{List}}$ and $\mathcal{O}_{\text{VList}}$.

—**Exp**$_{\mathcal{A}}^{\text{anon-}(u_1,u_2,\beta)}(\kappa)$—
$(\text{gpk}, v, k, \text{api}, \text{St}) \leftarrow \mathcal{A}(1^\kappa)$
$\beta' \leftarrow \mathcal{A}^{\mathcal{O}_{\text{anon}}(\cdot)}(\text{St})$
If $(N_1, N_2 \leq k$ and $\beta = \beta')$ Return Win.
Return Lose.

—**Exp**$_{\mathcal{A}}^{\text{excul-}u_1}(\kappa)$—
$(\text{gpk}, \text{St}) \leftarrow \mathcal{A}(1^\kappa)$.
$(v, k, \text{api}, \text{Log}) \leftarrow \mathcal{A}^{\mathcal{O}_{\text{excul-}u_1}(\cdot)}(\text{St})$.
Return trace$^{\mathcal{O}_{\text{List}}(\emptyset,\cdot)}(\text{gpk}, v, k, \text{api}, \text{Log})$.

—**Exp**$_{\mathcal{A}}^{\text{detect}}(\kappa)$—
$(\text{gpk}, \text{gsk}) \leftarrow \text{GM-Setup}(1^\kappa)$
$\mathcal{A}^{\mathcal{O}_{\text{detect}}(\cdot)}(1^\kappa, \text{gpk})$.
If $(\exists (v, k) \in \text{VList}$ s.t. $\#\text{Log}_{v,k} > k \cdot \#\text{List})$
    Return trace$^{\mathcal{O}_{\text{List}}(\emptyset,\cdot)}(1^\kappa, \text{gpk}, v, k, \text{api}, \text{Log}_{v,k})$.
Return $\perp$.

—**Exp**$_{\mathcal{A}}^{\text{excul-GM}}(\kappa)$—
$(\text{gpk}, \text{gsk}) \leftarrow \text{GM-Setup}(1^\kappa)$
$(v, k, \text{api}, \text{Log}) \leftarrow \mathcal{A}^{\mathcal{O}_{\text{excul-GM}}(\cdot)}(\kappa)$.
Return trace$^{\mathcal{O}_{\text{List}}(\emptyset,\cdot)}(\text{gpk}, v, k, \text{api}, \text{Log})$.

—**Exp**$_{\mathcal{A}}^{\text{excul-AP-}(v,k)}(\kappa)$—
api $\leftarrow$ AP-Setup$^{\mathcal{O}_{\text{VList}}(\{v\},\cdot)}(1^\kappa, v, k)$.
$(\text{gpk}, \text{St}) \leftarrow \mathcal{A}^{\mathcal{O}_{\text{VList}}(\{v\}^c,\cdot)}(1^\kappa, v, k)$.
$\mathcal{A}^{\mathcal{O}_{\text{excul-AP-}(v,k)}(\cdot)}(\text{St})$.
Return trace$^{\mathcal{O}_{\text{List}}(\emptyset,\cdot)}(\text{gpk}, v, k, \text{api}, \text{Log})$.

—**Exp**$_{\mathcal{A}}^{\text{pub-detect}}(\kappa)$—
$(\text{gpk}, \text{gsk}) \leftarrow \text{GM-Setup}(1^\kappa)$
$(v, k, \text{api}, \text{Log}) \leftarrow \mathcal{A}^{\mathcal{O}_{\text{pub-detect}}(\cdot)}(1^\kappa, \text{gpk})$.
If $(\#\text{Log} > k \cdot \#\text{List})$
    Return trace$^{\mathcal{O}_{\text{List}}(\emptyset,\cdot)}(1^\kappa, \text{gpk}, v, k, \text{api}, \text{Log})$.
Return $\perp$.

Oracles:

$\mathcal{O}_{\text{anon}}(\cdot) = (\mathcal{O}_{\text{List}}(\{u_1, u_2\}^c, \cdot), \mathcal{O}_{\text{VList}}(\emptyset^c, \cdot), \mathcal{O}_{\text{JOIN-U}}(\text{gpk} \cdot), \mathcal{O}_{\text{Proof}}(\text{gpk}, \cdot),$
$\qquad\qquad \mathcal{O}_{\text{Query}}(\beta, \text{gpk}, (u_1, u_2), (v, k, \text{api}), (\cdot, \cdot)))$

$\mathcal{O}_{\text{excul-}u_1}(\cdot) = (\mathcal{O}_{\text{List}}(\{u_1\}^c, \cdot), \mathcal{O}_{\text{VList}}(\emptyset^c, \cdot) \mathcal{O}_{\text{JOIN-U}}(\text{gpk}, \cdot), \mathcal{O}_{\text{Proof}}(\text{gpk}, \cdot))$

$\mathcal{O}_{\text{excul-GM}}(\cdot) = (\mathcal{O}_{\text{List}}(\{\text{GM}\}^c, \cdot), \mathcal{O}_{\text{VList}}(\emptyset^c, \cdot), \mathcal{O}_{\text{JOIN-GM}}(\text{gpk}, \text{gsk}, \cdot))$

$\mathcal{O}_{\text{excul-AP-}(v,k)}(\cdot) = (\mathcal{O}_{\text{List}}(\emptyset^c, \cdot), \mathcal{O}_{\text{VList}}(\{v\}^c, \cdot), \mathcal{O}_{\text{Verify}}(\text{gpk}, (v, k, \text{api}), \cdot))$

$\mathcal{O}_{\text{detect}}(\cdot) = (\mathcal{O}_{\text{List}}(\{\text{GM}\}^c, \cdot), \mathcal{O}_{\text{VList}}(\emptyset^c, \cdot), \mathcal{O}_{\text{Join-GM}}(\text{gpk}, \text{gsk}, \cdot), \mathcal{O}_{\text{AP-Setup}}(1^\kappa, \cdot, \cdot), \mathcal{O}_{\text{Verify}}(\text{gpk}, \cdot, \cdot)$

$\mathcal{O}_{\text{pub-detect}}(\cdot) = (\mathcal{O}_{\text{List}}(\{\text{GM}\}^c, \cdot), \mathcal{O}_{\text{VList}}(\emptyset^c, \cdot), \mathcal{O}_{\text{Join-GM}}(\text{gpk}, \text{gsk}, \cdot))$

Comments:

1. To simplify, we abbreviate the hash oracle $\mathcal{O}_{\text{Hash}}$.
2. In the experiment **Exp**$_{\mathcal{A}}^{\text{anon-}(u_1,u_2,\beta)}(\kappa)$, N_i is the total number of times $\mathcal{O}_{\text{JOIN-U}}$ and $\mathcal{O}_{\text{Query}}$ executes Proof using using a public key/secret key pair of user $u_{\beta \oplus d + 1}$ and an APs public information (v, k, api).
3. In the definition of **Exp**$_{\mathcal{A}}^{\text{detect}}(\kappa)$, $\text{Log}_{v,k}$ is the log of $\mathcal{O}_{\text{Verify}}$ on the behalf of the AP v with the allowable number k.
4. In the definition of **Exp**$^{\text{excul-AP-}(v,k)}$, Log is the log of $\mathcal{O}_{\text{Verify}}$.

Fig. 1. The experiments

$\mathcal{A}$ is allowed to access oracles only sequentially. We describe when $\mathcal{A}$ is allowed to access the oracles.

- $\mathcal{A}$ is allowed to access the list oracles $\mathcal{O}_{\text{List}}$ and $\mathcal{O}_{\text{VList}}$.
- If $\mathcal{A}$ does not collude with the GM, it is allowed to access $\mathcal{O}_{\text{Join-GM}}$.
- If $\mathcal{A}$ does not collude with a user u, it is allowed to access $\mathcal{O}_{\text{Join-U}}$ and $\mathcal{O}_{\text{Proof}}$. Here these oracles take roles of the user u.
- If $\mathcal{A}$ does not collude with an AP v, it is allowed to access $\mathcal{O}_{\text{AP-Setup}}$ and $\mathcal{O}_{\text{Verify}}$. Here these oracles take roles of the AP v.

We now describe the experiments for defining the requirements. Figure 1 describes the security experiments formally. Here κ is a security parameter, (gpk, gsk) is a GM public key/secret key pair, mik is a member identification key, and api is AP public information.

Total Anonymity: In advance, two target users u_1 and u_2 are determined, and a secret number $\beta \in \{0, 1\}$ is selected randomly. An adversary $\mathcal{A}$ is allowed to collude with the GM, all APs, and all users except target users u_1 and u_2. First, $\mathcal{A}$ determines and publishes the group public key gpk, an AP's ID v, the allowable number k of the AP, and the AP's public information api. Next, $\mathcal{A}$ maliciously executes the Join and Auth protocols with $\mathcal{O}_{\text{Join-U}}$ and $\mathcal{O}_{\text{Proof}}$. These oracles execute protocols on the behalf of the target users.

Moreover, $\mathcal{A}$ is allowed to access the *query oracle* $\mathcal{O}_{\text{Query}}(\beta, \text{gpk}, (u_1, u_2), (v, k, \text{api}), (\cdot, \cdot))$. We give the definition of the query oracle. The oracle executes Proof algorithm on the behalf of a target user, but does not disclose which target user the oracle takes the role of. More precisely, if $\mathcal{A}$ sends (d, M) to oracle $\mathcal{O}_{\text{Query}}(\beta, \text{gpk}, (u_1, u_2), (v, k, \text{api}), (\cdot, \cdot))$, the oracle regards M as data sent by a user and executes Proof using a public key/secret key pair of user $u_{\beta \oplus d + 1}$ and an APs public information (v, k, api). $\mathcal{A}$ is allowed to execute the Auth protocol with the query oracle once only for each $d \in \{0, 1\}$. If $\mathcal{A}$ requires for the oracle to execute the Auth protocol for the same d twice, $\mathcal{O}_{\text{Query}}$ returns $\perp$.

In the experiment, $\mathcal{A}$ is not allowed to authenticate the target user u_i more than k times. This is because a k-TAA scheme provides anonymity to users only if a user has been authenticated less than the allowed number of times. More precisely, let N_i be the total number of times $\mathcal{O}_{\text{Join-U}}$ and $\mathcal{O}_{\text{Query}}$ execute Proof using a public key/secret key pair of user u_i. Then $\mathcal{A}$ must preserve $N_1, N_2 \leq k$.

The aim of $\mathcal{A}$ is to determine whether $\beta = 1$ or not. $\mathcal{A}$ wins if $N_1, N_2 \leq k$ is satisfied and $\mathcal{A}$ succeeds in outputting β.

Exculpability for Users: In the experiment for defining the exculpability for users, a target user u is fixed in advance. $\mathcal{A}$ is allowed to collude with all entities except the target user u. If $\mathcal{A}$ succeeds in computing the log with which the public tracing procedure outputs the ID u of the target user, it wins.

Exculpability for GM: $\mathcal{A}$ is allowed to collude with all entities except the GM. If $\mathcal{A}$ succeeds in computing the log with which the public tracing procedure outputs "GM", it wins.

Exculpability for APs: A target AP v is fixed in advance. $\mathcal{A}$ is allowed to collude with all entities except the target AP v. Let Log be the authentication log of $\mathcal{O}_{\text{Verify}}$. If a public tracing procedure using Log outputs "AP", $\mathcal{A}$ win. We stress that not $\mathcal{A}$ but $\mathcal{O}_{\text{Verify}}$ outputs Log in this experiment, although adversaries of the other two exculpability properties are allowed to output Log themselves.

Detectability: $\mathcal{A}$ is allowed to collude with all users. If $\mathcal{A}$ succeeds in being accepted by some AP in more than kn authentications, $\mathcal{A}$ wins. Here, k is the number of times the AP allows access for each user, and n is the number of users who collude with $\mathcal{A}$.

Public Detectability: $\mathcal{A}$ is allowed to collude with all users and all APs. $\mathcal{A}$ wins if $\mathcal{A}$ succeeds in outputting a tuple $(v, k, \text{api}, \text{Log})$ satisfying both of the following conditions: (1) the authentication Log contains more than $k \cdot \#\text{List}$ elements and (2) a public tracing procedure using $(v, k, \text{api}, \text{Log})$ outputs NoOne.

Definition 1. We say a k-TAA scheme satisfies the *total anonymity, exculpability for users, exculpability for GM, exculpability for APs, detectability* and *public detectability* properties if no adversary can win with a non negligible advantage

in the experiments for defining these requirements. More precisely, we say a
k-TAA scheme satisfies these requirements if $|\Pr(\mathbf{Exp}_{\mathcal{A}}^{\text{anon-}(u_1,u_2,0)}(\kappa) = \mathsf{Win})$
$- \Pr(\mathbf{Exp}_{\mathcal{A}}^{\text{anon-}(u_1,u_2,1)}(\kappa) = \mathsf{Win})|$, $\Pr(\mathbf{Exp}_{\mathcal{A}}^{\text{excul-}u_1}(\kappa) = u_1)$, $\Pr(\mathbf{Exp}^{\text{excul-GM}}$
$_{\mathcal{A}}(\kappa) = \mathsf{GM})$, $\Pr(\mathbf{Exp}_{\mathcal{A}}^{\text{excul-AP-}(v,k)}(\kappa) = \mathsf{AP})$, $\Pr(\mathbf{Exp}_{\mathcal{A}}^{\text{detect}}(\kappa) = \mathsf{NoOne})$
and $\Pr(\mathbf{Exp}_{\mathcal{A}}^{\text{pub-detect}}(\kappa) = \mathsf{NoOne})$ are negligible for security parameter κ, for
all $(\mathcal{A}, u_1, u_2)$, $(\mathcal{A}, u_1)$, $\mathcal{A}$, $(v, k, \mathcal{A})$, $\mathcal{A}$ and $\mathcal{A}$ respectively.

We say a k-TAA scheme is *secure* if it satisfies the first five requirements.

3   Proposed Schemes

We propose two schemes. Authentications of the first and the second schemes
require computing $O(\log k)$ or $O(1)$ exponentiations respectively. Although the
first scheme is less efficient than the second scheme, only the first scheme satisfies
the public detectability property. As in the previous schemes [TFS04, NN05],
our proposed schemes are based on a group signature scheme. We adopt the
Furukawa-Imai scheme [FI05], since it is one of the most efficient group signature
schemes. The GM setup and the joining procedures of our two schemes are similar
to those of [FI05].

3.1   Notations

Let κ be a security parameter. Let $(\mathcal{G}, \mathcal{H}, \mathcal{T}, q, \langle \cdot, \cdot \rangle, \phi)$ be a bilinear pairing tuple,
that is, a tuple satisfying the following properties: (1) q is a prime number whose
bit length is κ, (2) $\mathcal{G}, \mathcal{H}$, and $\mathcal{T}$ are cyclic groups of order q, (3) ϕ is a polynomial
time computable homomorphism from $\mathcal{H}$ to $\mathcal{G}$, (ϕ is called *distorsion map*), (4)
$\langle \cdot, \cdot \rangle$ is a polynomial time computable mapping from $\mathcal{G} \times \mathcal{H}$ to $\mathcal{T}$, (5) for all
$(a, b) \in \mathcal{G} \times \mathcal{H}$, if $\langle a, b \rangle = 1$ is satisfied, then $a = b = 1$ is satisfied, and (6) for all
$a \in \mathcal{G}$, $b \in \mathcal{H}$, and $x, y \in \mathbb{Z}_q$, $\langle a^x, b^y \rangle = \langle a, b \rangle^{xy}$ is satisfied.

Let $\mathcal{U}$ be a group on which the DDH problem is hard and whose order is the
same as that of $\mathcal{T}$. Although we can set $\mathcal{U}$ to $\mathcal{T}$ itself, the Furukawa-Imai scheme
and our schemes become more efficient if we set $\mathcal{U}$ to an elliptic curve on which
a pairing is not defined.

3.2   First Scheme

Let Hash denote a full domain hash function onto set $\mathcal{U}^2$. For a bit string X, let
(g_X, h_X) denote $\mathsf{Hash}(X)$. For $x \in \mathbb{Z}_q$, we set $f_x^\kappa : \{0, 1\}^* \times \mathbb{Z}_q \to \mathcal{U}$ to

$$f_x^\kappa : (X, w) \mapsto g_X{}^w h_X{}^{1/(x+w)}.$$

GM-Setup: The GM-Setup generates and outputs a GM public key $\mathsf{gpk} = (a_0, a_1,$
$a_2, b, b')$ and a GM secret key $\mathsf{gsk} = y$ following [FI05]. That is, the algorithm
selects $a_0, a_1, a_2 \in \mathcal{G}$, $b \in \mathcal{H}$, and $y \in \mathbb{Z}_q$ randomly, and computes $b' = b^y$.

Join: The Join protocol generates a member certificate key $\mathsf{mck} = (A, e)$, a member identification key $\mathsf{mik} = f_x^\kappa(0, 0)$, and the member secret key $\mathsf{msk} = (x, r)$,

534   I. Teranishi and K. Sako

following [FI05]. These keys satisfy the equation $\langle a_0 a_1{}^x a_2{}^r, b \rangle = \langle A, b^e b' \rangle$. The algorithm outputs (mck, mik, msk) for users and outputs only mck for the GM.

More precisely, the GM and a user perform as described in Figure 2, where u is the ID of the user, mik is the member identification key of the user, and List is the list of the user's ID and his member identification key. Then the user checks that $\langle a_0 a_1{}^x a_2{}^r, b \rangle = \langle A, b^e b' \rangle$ is satisfied.

User	GM
$x, r' \leftarrow \mathbb{Z}_q, A' \leftarrow a_1{}^x a_2{}^{r'}$	
mik $\leftarrow h \leftarrow f_x^\kappa(0,0)$	
Add (u, mik) to List. $\xrightarrow{\quad A', \text{mik} \quad}$	Check that (u, mik) is in List.
Proof the validity of $(A', \text{mik})) \longleftrightarrow$	Verify the proof.
	$r'', e \leftarrow \mathbb{Z}_q$
$r \leftarrow r' + r'' \bmod q \xleftarrow{\quad ((A,e),r'') \quad}$	$A \leftarrow (a_0{}^{1/(y+e)} A' a_2{}^{r''/(y+e)})$

Fig. 2. Joining of the First Scheme

Auth: In w-th authentication, a user and an AP first perform as in Figure 3. Here pf is a proof of knowledge of $((A^*, e^*), (x^*, r^*), w^*)$ satisfying the following conditions: (T1): $\langle a_0 a_1{}^{x^*} a_2{}^{r^*}, b \rangle = \langle A, b^{e^*} b' \rangle$, (T2): $(\tau, \hat{\tau}) = (f_{x^*}^\kappa(v||k, w^*), f_{x^*}^\kappa(0,0)^\ell f_{x^*}^\kappa(v||k, -w^*))$, and (T3): $1 \leq w^* \leq k$.

User	AP
	$\xleftarrow{\quad \ell \quad} \ell \leftarrow \mathbb{Z}_q$
$(\tau, \hat{\tau}) \leftarrow (f_x^\kappa(v||k, w), \text{mik}^\ell \cdot f_x^\kappa(v||k, -w))$	
pf $\leftarrow$ (Validity proof of $(\tau, \hat{\tau})$) $\xrightarrow{\quad ((\tau,\hat{\tau}),\text{pf}) \quad}$	Verify pf.

Fig. 3. Authentication

The AP next executes the following procedures. Let Log be the AP's authentication log. If $\text{Ver}(\text{pf}) = \text{accept}$ and $\tau \notin \text{Log}$ are satisfied, add $(\tau, \hat{\tau}, \ell, \text{pf})$ to Log and output accept. If $\text{Ver}(\text{pf}) = \text{accept}$ but $\tau \in \text{Log}$ are satisfied, add $(\tau, \hat{\tau}, \ell, \text{pf})$ to Log but output reject. Otherwise, add no data to Log and output reject.

trace: From Log, the trace algorithm searches entries $(\tau, \hat{\tau}, \ell, \text{pf})$ and $(\tau', \hat{\tau}', \ell', \text{pf}')$ satisfying $\tau = \tau'$. We first consider the case where such entries exist. Then the algorithm verifies pf and pf'. If $\ell = \ell'$ is satisfied, output AP and stop. Otherwise, the algorithm computes $\text{mik} = (\hat{\tau}/\hat{\tau}')^{1/(\ell-\ell')}$ and searches the ID corresponding with mik from List. If there is such an ID, the algorithm outputs the ID and stop, otherwise outputs GM and stops.

We next consider the case where there exists no pair of entries $(\tau, \hat{\tau}, \ell, \text{pf})$ and $(\tau', \hat{\tau}', \ell', \text{pf}')$ satisfying $\tau = \tau'$ in Log. Then in order to check that the AP added invalid entries to the Log, the algorithm verifies all proofs in Log. If some proof is invalid, output AP and stops. If all proofs in Log are valid, the algorithm outputs NoOne and stops.

We note that one must verify all proofs in trace in order to ensure the public detectability. One is not required to verify this if only normal detectability is required.

3.3   Second Scheme

By modifying the first scheme, we construct the second k-TAA scheme such that the numbers of exponentiations in an authentication is $O(1)$. In order to reduce the computational cost of an authentication, we use a signature scheme. In our second scheme, AP publishes signatures $\mathsf{Sig}(1)$, ..., $\mathsf{Sig}(k)$ in its setup. In the authentication, the user computes $(\tau, \hat{\tau})$ as in the first scheme, but proves the knowledge of a signature $\mathsf{Sig}(w)$, instead of proving the inequality $1 \leq w \leq k$. Since only k signatures $\mathsf{Sig}(1)$, ..., $\mathsf{Sig}(k)$ are published, it indirectly ensures that $1 \leq w \leq k$. This resulted in the cost of only $O(1)$ exponentiation. However, this is not publicly detectable since a malicious AP may secretly reveal $\mathsf{Sig}(w)$ for $w > k$.

We use the following Boneh-Boyen signature scheme (SGen, Sig, SVer) [BB04] in order to construct our second scheme. Here SGen, Sig, and SVer are respectively the key generation, the signing, and the verification algorithms:

SGen: The algorithm selects $s \in \mathcal{G}$, $t \in \mathcal{H}$ and $z \in \mathbb{Z}_q$ randomly and computes $t' = t^z$. Then it outputs the public key (s, t, t') and the corresponding secret key z.
Sig: If a message $w \in \mathbb{Z}_q$ is input, the algorithm output a signature $S = s^{1/(z+w)}$ on w.
SVer: The algorithm accepts (w, S) if and only if $\langle S, t^w t' \rangle = \langle s, t \rangle$ is satisfied.

We now describe our second scheme. Let f_x^κ be the deterministic function described in 3.2.

$\mathsf{GM\text{-}Setup}$ and Join : These are the same as those of the first scheme.

$\mathsf{AP\text{-}Setup}$: Let v be an AP's ID. The AP v determines the allowable number k. Generate a public key/private key pair $(\mathsf{spk}, \mathsf{ssk}) = \mathsf{SGen}(1^\kappa)$ of the signature scheme [BB04]. Then compute signatures $S_w = \mathsf{Sig}_{\mathsf{spk},\mathsf{ssk}}(w)$ on w for all $w = 1, \ldots, k$. The AP public information is $\mathsf{api} = (\mathsf{spk}, \{S_w\})$. Add (v, k, api) to the AP public information list VList.

Auth: The only difference from the first scheme is what the user proves. In the second scheme, pf is the proof of knowledge of $(\mathsf{mck}^*, (x^*, r^*), w^*, S^*)$ which satisfies (T1) and (T2) of 3.2 and (T3'): $\mathsf{SVer}_{\mathsf{spk}}(w^*, S^*) = \mathsf{accept}$.

trace: Search $(\tau, \hat{\tau}, \ell, \mathsf{pf})$ and $(\tau', \hat{\tau}', \ell', \mathsf{pf}')$, satisfying $\tau = \tau'$ from Log. If there exist such entries, subsequent procedures are the same as those of the first scheme. If there exist no such entries, output NoOne and stop.

We next show that the second scheme does not satisfy the public detectability property. Indeed, an AP is able to generate any number of signatures, and therefore a colluding subset of the AP and a user is able to generate any number of entries of the AP's authentication log.

However, if we allow APs to access the GM (or some third party) in their setup, we can improve the second scheme so that it satisfies the public detectability property. In an AP's setup of the improved scheme, not each AP but the GM (or the third party) generates the signatures $\{S_w\}$. Then no colluding subset of an AP and a user is able to execute the above attack, and therefore the improved scheme satisfies the public detectability property.

3.4 Selection of f_x^κ

The deterministic function f_x^κ plays central role in our protocol, and the choice of this functions influence the efficiency of our protocol. In this subsection, we discuss why we chose it to be $f_x^\kappa(X, w) = g_X{}^w h_X{}^{1/(x+w)}$, where g_X and h_X are deterministically computed from the value $\mathsf{Hash}(X)$.

The function takes two inputs, which is the identifier of AP, X, and the value w specifying that this is w-th authentication for the user. We represent the family of the set of the two inputs as $\{\mathcal{X}_\kappa\}$ and $\{\mathcal{Y}_\kappa\}$.

If we chose f_x^κ to be pseudorandom, namely its output is indistinguishable from random function then it would be sufficient to make our scheme secure. However, in our protocol we further need to prove knowledge of input to some output of function f_x^κ. We could not build an efficient proof if we choose f_x^κ to be one of the pseudorandom functions that we know of [BCK03, DN02, GGM86, NR97].

Instead, we introduce a non-pseudorandom function but one which we can construct an efficient proof, and one which we can prove the scheme to be secure. This property of this function can be generalized as to be called *partial* pseudorandom function family. That is, the function may not be pseudorandom, but if we restrict the domain of one of the input to be polynomial in regard to security parameter κ, the resulting function is pseudorandom. Since we only consider polynomial adversary, we can show that considering partial psuedorandom function is sufficient for the security of the schehe. The details of the proof is provided in the full paper.

Definition 2. Let $\{\mathcal{X}_\kappa\}$, $\{\mathcal{Y}_\kappa\}$, and $\{\mathcal{Z}_\kappa\}$ be families of sets, and $\{f_x^\kappa\}_\kappa$ be a function family of $f_x^\kappa : \mathcal{X}_\kappa \times \mathcal{Y}_\kappa \to \mathcal{Z}_\kappa$. We call the function family $\{f_x^\kappa\}_\kappa$ a *(secure) partial pseudorandom function family* if the following property is satisfied: for any polynomial $p(\kappa)$, and for any family $\{\mathcal{C}_\kappa\}$ of sets satisfying $\mathcal{C}_\kappa \subset \mathcal{Y}_\kappa$ and $\#\mathcal{C}_\kappa \leq p(\kappa)$, the family of restricted mappings $\{f_x^\kappa|_{\mathcal{X}_\kappa \times \mathcal{C}_\kappa}\}_\kappa$ is a secure pseudorandom function family.

The property of partial pseudorandomness is helpful in proving the property of the total anonymity. That is, if f_x^κ satisfies the partial pseudorandomness, the tag $(\tau, \hat\tau) = (f_x^\kappa(X, w), \mathsf{mik}^\ell f_x^\kappa(X, -w))$ is equivalent to some random pair. This means that $(\tau, \hat\tau)$ do not reveal who is authenticated.

We next discuss why we set (g_X, h_X) to a hash value of some data in our construction. If we arbitrary chose g_X and h_X, an adversary $\mathcal{A}$ can choose $((g_X, h_X), (g_{X'}, h_{X'}))$ satisfying some polynomial time checkable relation, such as $(g_X, h_X) = (g_{X'}{}^2, h_{X'}{}^2)$. Then the polynomial time checkable relation, such as $f_x^\kappa(X, w) = f_x^\kappa(X', w')^2$, is maintained. This means that f_x^κ does not satisfy the partial pseudorandomness. Restricting (g_X, h_X) to be generated from hash function prevents this kind of attack. Proofs regarding that the proposed function satisfies partial pseudorandomness is provided in the full paper.

We note another important property of the function is collision resistance, which is defined below.

Definition 3. We say that $\{f_x^\kappa(X, w)\}_\kappa$ satisfies *collision resistance*, if it satisfies the following: for all X, a mapping $(x, w) \mapsto f_x^\kappa(X, w)$ is collision resistant.

The collision resistant property is helpful to prove the exculpability for users or the GM. If we use not f_x^κ but another function F_x^κ which does not satisfy the collision resistant property, then an adversary $\mathcal{A}$ can find two pairs (x_1, w_1) and (x_2, w_2) satisfying $F_{x_1}(X, w_1) = F_{x_2}(X, w_2)$. Let mik_i be the member identification key corresponding to x_i, and $(\tau_i, \hat{\tau}_i)$ be a tag $(f_{x_i}^\kappa(X, w_i), \mathsf{mik}_i^{\ell_i} f_{x_i}^\kappa(X, -w_i))$. Then two tags $(\tau_1, \hat{\tau}_1)$ and $(\tau_2, \hat{\tau}_2)$ satisfy $\tau_1 = F_{x_1}(X, w_1) = F_{x_2}(X, w_2) = \tau_2$. However, $(\tau_1/\tau_2)^{1/(\ell_1 - \ell_2)}$ corresponds to neither mik_1 nor mik_2. Therefore, the tracing algorithm using (τ_1, τ_1') and (τ_2, τ_2') outputs some other user's ID or GM. This means that the k-TAA scheme does not satisfy exculpability for users or the GM.

We provide in the full paper that with this choice of the function the proposed scheme is secure.

3.5   Computational Costs of an Authentication

We show that the computational cost of an authentication of the first and the second schemes are $O(\log k)$ and $O(1)$ respectively. All we must show are that the condition (T1), (T2), and (T3') can be proved only with $O(1)$ exponentiations and that (T3) can be proved only with $O(\log k)$ exponentiations. See the full paper for the details of the validity proof.

The condition (T1) and (T3') can be proved only with $O(1)$ exponentiations, since this condition does not contain k. The condition (T2) is equal to the condition $(\tau, \hat{\tau}) = (g_{v||k}{}^w h_{v||k}{}^{1/(x+w)}, g_{v||k}{}^w h_{v||k}{}^{1/(x-w)})$. Since $(g_{v||k}, h_{v||k}) = \mathsf{Hash}(v||k)$ is public information, one can prove the condition (T2) with $O(1)$ exponentiations too.

The condition (T3) is able to be proved using commitments $K(w)$, $\{K(w_i)\}$, and $K(u_i)$. Here $K(w)$, $K(w_i)$, and $K(u_i)$ are Pedersen commitments [P91] of w, i-th bit w_i of w, and i-th bit u_i of $k - w$. More precisely, one can prove the condition (T3) by proving the knowledge of $(\{w_i\}, \{u_i\})$ satisfying the following conditions: $K(w) = \Pi_j K(w_j)^{2^j}$, $K(w)\Pi_j K(u_i)^{2^j} = K(k)$, $w_i, u_i \in \{0, 1\}$ for $i = 0, \ldots, \log_2 k$. Here $K(k)$ is a commitment of k. From the above discussion, (T3) can be proved only with $O(\log k)$ exponentiations.

4 Security

We can show that our schemes are secure based on the following assumptions:

Definition 4. *(Strong Diffie-Hellman (SDH) assumption [BB04] on $(\mathcal{G}, \mathcal{H}, \mathcal{T})$)*
Let ϕ be the distorsion map from $\mathcal{H}$ to $\mathcal{G}$. Let $n = n(\kappa)$ be a polynomial and
$\mathcal{A}$ be an adversary. Then $\mathsf{Prob}_{\mathcal{A}}(\kappa, n(\kappa)) = \Pr(v \leftarrow_R \mathcal{H}, u \leftarrow \phi(v), x \leftarrow_R$
$\mathbb{Z}_q, \mathcal{A}(u, v, v^x \ldots, v^{x^n}) = (u^{1/(x+\beta)}, \beta))$ is negligible for all $n(\kappa)$ and $\mathcal{A}$.

Definition 5. *(Decision Diffie-Hellman Inversion (DDHI) assumption [BB04]*
on $\mathcal{U}$) Let $n = n(\kappa)$ be a polynomial and $\mathcal{A}$ be an adversary. For $b = 0, 1$, we set
$\mathsf{Prob}_{\mathcal{A}}^b(\kappa, n(\kappa)) = \Pr(g \leftarrow_R \mathcal{U}, x \leftarrow_R \mathbb{Z}_q, \mathcal{A}(h_b, g, g^{x^1}, \ldots, g^{x^n}) = 1)$. Here h_0 is
a randomly selected element of $\mathcal{U}$ and h_1 is the element $g^{1/x}$. Then for all $n(\kappa)$
and $\mathcal{A}$, $\mathsf{Adv}_{\mathcal{A}}(\kappa, n(\kappa)) = |\mathsf{Prob}_{\mathcal{A}}^1(\kappa, n(\kappa)) - \mathsf{Prob}_{\mathcal{A}}^0(\kappa, n(\kappa))|$ is negligible for κ.

Our scheme satisfies the following:

Theorem 6. *Suppose that $\{f_x^\kappa(X, w)\}_\kappa$ is a secure collision resistant partial*
pseudorandom function family. Suppose also the SDH assumption [BB04] on
$(\mathcal{G}, \mathcal{H}, \mathcal{T})$ and the random oracle assumption. Then the first scheme is secure and
satisfies the public detectability. Suppose also that a signature scheme (SGen, Sig,
SVer) is existentially unforgeable even if an adversary knows signatures $S_1, \ldots,$
$S_{k(\kappa)}$ on known messages $1, \ldots, k(\kappa)$ for all polynomial $k(\kappa)$. Then the second
scheme is secure.

From [BB04], the signature scheme (SGen, Sig, SVer) satisfies the above condition
under the SDH assumption. We next consider the security of $\{f_x^\kappa(X, w)\}_\kappa$.

Proposition 7. *Under the random oracle assumption and the DDHI assump-*
tion [BB04] on $\mathcal{U}$, the function family $\{f_x^\kappa(X, w)\}_\kappa$ is a secure collision resistant
partial pseudorandom function family.

From the above discussion, we can conclude the following theorem:

Theorem 8. *Under the SDH assumption on $(\mathcal{G}, \mathcal{H}, \mathcal{T})$ and the DDHI assump-*
tions on $\mathcal{U}$, our two proposed schemes are secure in the random oracle. Moreover,
under the same assumptions and in the same model, the first scheme satisfies
the public detectability property.

4.1 Sketch of the Security Proof

We sketch the proof of Theorem 6. See the full paper for the detailed proof. We
first examine the security of the first scheme.

Total Anonymity: Let (x_u, r_u) be the member secret key of the target user
u. Subinformation about x_u which an adversary can obtain are the following:
(1) $A_u' = a_1^{x_u} a_2^{r_u'}$ and $\mathsf{mik}_u = f_{x_u}^\kappa(0, 0)$, generated in the user u's joining
protocol, and (2) $(\tau, \hat{\tau}) = (f_{x_u}^\kappa(v||k, w), \mathsf{mik}_u^\ell \cdot f_{x_u}^\kappa(v||k, -w))$ generated in each
authentication. Since r_u' is randomly selected, A_u' gives no information about x_u.

From Proposition 7, $f_{x_u}^{\kappa}$ satisfies the partial pseudorandomness. Since the adversary is polynomial time algorithm, the oracles computes $f_{x_u}^{\kappa}$ only a polynomial number of times. Therefore, $\mathcal{A}$ cannot distinguish mik_u and $(\tau, \hat{\tau})$ from random elements. Hence $\mathcal{A}$ cannot distinguish which user is authenticated.

Exculpability for Users: In order to be authenticated on the behalf of the target user, $\mathcal{A}$ has to obtain the target user's secret key x_u. Subinformation about x_u which an adversary can obtain is the (1) and (2) described in the security discussion of the total anonymity. As in the case of the total anonymity, no adversary is able to obtain the target user's secret key x_u. Therefore, no adversary is able to be authenticated on the behalf of the target user.

Exculpability for the GM: This followed from the *coalition resistance* property [ACJT00, NN04] of the Furukawa-Imai scheme. Here the coalition resistance is the following property: an adversary, not colluding with the GM, cannot obtain a member public key/private key pair not generated in the joining protocols with the GM. It is well known that a secure group signature scheme satisfies the coalition resistance property [BMW03, BSZ05]. Hence, the Furukawa-Imai scheme (and therefore our first scheme) satisfies this property.

Suppose that an adversary of the exculpability property for the GM wins. In other words, suppose that there exist $(\tau, \hat{\tau}, \ell, \mathsf{pf})$ and $(\tau', \hat{\tau}', \ell', \mathsf{pf}')$ in the authentication log of an AP such that $\tau = \tau'$ is satisfied and $(\hat{\tau}/\hat{\tau}')^{1/(\ell - \ell')}$ is not in the List. Since $\tau = \tau'$ is satisfied, and since f^{κ} is collision resistance, member public key/private key pairs used to compute τ and τ' are the same. Let $((\mathsf{mck}, \mathsf{mik}), \mathsf{msk})$ be this key pair. From the definition of $\hat{\tau}$ and $\hat{\tau}'$, $\mathsf{mik} = (\hat{\tau}/\hat{\tau}')^{1/(\ell - \ell')}$ is satisfied. From the coalition resistance property, this key was generated in a joining protocol with the GM. Therefore, mik is in List. It contradicts to the fact that $\mathsf{mik} = (\hat{\tau}/\hat{\tau}')^{1/(\ell - \ell')}$ is not in the List.

Exculpability for APs: This is clearly satisfied.

Public Detectability: Let N be the number of times an adversary $\mathcal{A}$ executes the joining with the GM. From the definition of the joining protocol of our first scheme, N is not more than the number of elements of List. Let k be the allowable number of an AP v colluding with $\mathcal{A}$. Suppose that $\mathcal{A}$ succeeds to output Log which contains more than kN elements. In each entry $(\tau, \hat{\tau}, \ell, \mathsf{pf})$ of Log, $(\tau, \hat{\tau}) = (f_x^{\kappa}(v||k, w), \mathsf{mik}^{\ell} \cdot f_x^{\kappa}(v||k, -w))$ has to be satisfied for some x and w, since $\mathcal{A}$ has generated the validity proof pf of $(\tau, \hat{\tau})$.

Since the coalition resistance property is satisfied, x is a part of a secret key generated in a joining with the GM. Hence, there are only N choices of x. Since $\mathcal{A}$ has proved the condition (T3) of 3.2, $1 \leq w \leq k$ is satisfied. Hence, there are only k choices of w. (We note that $1 \leq w \leq k$ has to be clearly satisfied even if $\mathcal{A}$ colludes with the AP). Therefore, the number of choices of x and w are respectively less than N and k. Therefore, an adversary generates at most kN elements $(\tau, \hat{\tau})$. This means that Log cannot have more than kN elements.

We now intuitively show the security of the second scheme. We only show that our second scheme satisfies the detectability property, since the proofs of the other requirements are similar to those of the first scheme.

Detectability: Let N be the number of times an adversary $\mathcal{A}$ executes the joining with the GM. In each authentication, $\mathcal{A}$ computes $(\tau, \hat{\tau}) = (f_x^\kappa(v\|k, w), \mathsf{mik}^\ell \cdot f_x^\kappa(v\|k, -w))$. Since $\mathcal{A}$ proves the condition (T3') of 3.3, $\mathcal{A}$ knows a signature S on w by the AP. Since the AP has published the signatures only on $1, \ldots, k$, and since $\mathcal{A}$ is not allowed to collude with the AP, $1 \leq w \leq k$ has to be satisfied. Hence, there are only k choices of w. Moreover, as in the case of the security discussion of the public detectability property of the first scheme, there are only N choices of x. Therefore, an adversary generates at most kN elements $(\tau, \hat{\tau})$. It means that Log cannot have more than kN elements.

5   Conclusion

We proposed two k-TAA schemes, one where the numbers of exponentiations in an authentication are $O(\log k)$ and the other $O(1)$. The proposed schemes are secure under the SDH assumption [BB04], the DDHI assumption [BB04], and the random oracle assumption.

We also proposed and formalized the *public detectability* requirement, and showed that the first scheme satisfies this requirement. The public detectability requires that anyone can verify that the AP indeed provided a fair limit to all users regarding the number of accesses to their service.

Acknowledgement

The authors would like to thank anonymous referees for their valuable comments and their help in improving the presentation of our paper.

References

[ACJT00]   Ateniese, Camenisch, Joye, Tsudik. A Practical and Provably Secure Coalition-Resistant Group Signature Scheme. CRYPTO 2000, pp. 255-270.

[AF96]   Abe, Fujisaki, How to Date Blind Signatures, In ASIACRYPT'96, pp. 244-251.

[AM03]   Ateniese Medeiros. Efficient Group Signatures without Trapdoors. ASIACRYPT'03, pp. 246-268.

[BCK03]   Bellare, Canetti, Krawczyk. Pseudorandom functions revisited: The cascade construction and its concrete security. FOCS'96, 514-523.

[BMW03]   Bellare, Micciancio, Warinschi. Foundations of Group Signatures: Formal Definitions, Simplified Requirements, and a Construction Based on General Assumptions In EUROCRYPT'03, pp. 614-629.

[BSZ05]   Bellare, Shi Zhang. Foundations of Group Signatures: The Case of Dynamic Groups. CT-RSA'05, pp. 136-153.

[BB04]   Boneh, Boyen. Short Signatures Without Random Oracles. EUROCRYPT'04, pp. 56-73.

[BBS04]   Boneh, Boyen, Shacham. Short Group Signatures. CRYPTO'04, pp. 41-55.

[B00]   Boudot. Efficient Proofs that a Committed Number Lies in an Interval. EUROCRYPT'00, pp 431-444.

[B93]   Brands. An Efficient Off-line Electronic Cash System Based On The Representation Problem. TR. CS-R9323, Centrum voor Wiskunde en Informatica.

[BCC04]   Brickell, Camenisch, Chen. Direct Anonymous Attestation. ACM-CCS'04, pp. 132-145.

[CDS94]   Cramer, Damgård, Schoenmakers. Proofs of partial knowledge and simplified design of witness hiding protocols. CRYPTO'94, pp. 174-187.

[CFT98]   Chan, Frankel, Tsiounis. Easy Come - Easy Go Divisible Cash. EUROCRYPT '98, pp. 614-629.

[CG04]   Camenisch, Groth. Group Signatures: Better Efficiency and New Theoretical Aspects. SCN'04, pp. 120-133.

[CHL05]   J. Camenisch, S. Hohenberger and A. Lysyanskaya. Compact E-Cash. EUROCRYPT'05, pp. 302-321.

[CL02]   Camenisch, Lysyanskaya. A Signature Scheme with Efficient Protocols. SCN'02, pp. 268-289.

[CL04]   Camenisch, Lysyanskaya. Signature Schemes and Anonymous Credentials from Bilinear Maps. CRYPTO'04, pp. 56-72.

[CH91]   D. Chaum, E. van Heijst. Group signatures. EUROCRYPT'91, pp. 257-265.

[CP92]   Chaum,Pedersen.Transferred Cash Grows in Size, EUROCRYPT'92, pp.390-407

[CT03]   Canard, Traoré. List Signature Schemes and Application to Electronic Voting. International Workshop on Coding and Cryptography 2003, pp.24-28.

[CT04]   Canard, Schoenmakers, Stam, Traoré. List Signature Schemes. Special Issue of the Journal Discrete Applied mathematics, 2005.

[DJ01]   Damgård Jurik. A Generalization, a Simplification and Some Applications of Paillier's Probabilistic Public-key system. PKC'01. pp. 119-136.

[DN02]   Damgård, Nielsen. Expanding Pseudorandom Functions; or: From Known-Plaintext Security to Chosen-Plaintext Security. CRYPTO'02, pp.449-464.

[DY05]   Dodis, Yampolskiy. A Verifiable Random Function with Short Proofs and Keys. PKC'05, pp.416-431

[FI05]   Furukawa, Imai. An Efficient Group Signature Scheme from Bilinear Maps. ACISP'05, pp.455-467.

[FS01]   Furukawa, Sako. An Efficient Scheme for Proving a Shuffle. CRYPTO'01,pp. 368-387.

[GGM86]   Goldreich, Goldwasser, Micali. How to construct random function. J.ACM. 33(4): pp.797-807, 1986.

[KY04]   Kiayias, Yung. Group Signatures: Provable Secure, Efficient Constructions and Anonymity from Trapdoor Holders. http://eprint.iacr.org/2004/076.ps

[KY05]   A. Kiayias, M. Yung. Group Signatures with Efficient Concurrent Join. EUROCRYPT'05 pp. 198-214. Full version: http://eprint.iacr.org/2005/345.

[MSK02]   Mitsunari, Sakai, Kasahara. A new traitor tracing. IEICE Trans. Vol. E85-A, No.2, pp.481-484, 2002.

[NHS99]   Nakanishi, Haruna, Sugiyama. Unlinkable Electronic Coupon Protocol with Anonymity Control, ISW'99, pp. 37-46.

[NR97]   Naor Reingold. Number-Theoretic Constructions of Efficient Pseudo-Random Functions. FOCS'97. pp.458-467.

[NN04]   Nguyen, Safavi-Naini. Efficient and Provably Secure Trapdoor-free Group Signature Schemes from Bilinear Pairings. ASIACRYPT'04, pp. 316-337.

[NN05]   Nguyen, Safavi-Naini. Dynamic k-Times Anonymous Authentication. ACNS'05, pp. 318-333.

[Neff01]   Neff. A Verifiable Secret Shuffle and its Application to E-Voting, ACM-CCS'01 pp. 116-125.

[OO98]   Okamoto, Ohta. One-Time Zero-Knowledge Authentications and Their Applications to Untraceable Electronic Cash. IEICE Trans. on Fundamentals of Electronics, Communications and Computer Sciences, vol E81-A, No. 1, pp. 2-10, 1998.

[OMAFO99]   Ookubo, Miura, Abe, Fujioka, Okamoto. An improvement of a practical secret voting scheme. ISW'99, pp. 37-46.

[PBF99]   Pavlovski, Boyd, Foo. Detachable Electronic Coins. ICICS'99, pp. 54-70.

[P91]   Torben P. Pedersen. A Threshold Cryptosystem without a Trusted Party. EUROCRYPT'91, pp.522-526.

[S00]   Sako. Restricted Anonymous Participation. SCIS'00, B12. (Japanese).

[SK94]   Sako, Kilian. Secure Voting using Partially Compatible Homomorphisms. CRYPTO '94, pp. 411–424.

[TF03]   Teranishi, Furukawa. Tag Signature. SCIS'03, 6C-2. (Japanese. Preliminary version of [TFS04]).

[TFS04]   Teranishi, Furukawa, Sako. k-Times Anonymous Authentication. ASIACRYPT'04, pp. 308-322.

Author Index

Lecture Notes in Computer Science

For information about Vols. 1–3851

please contact your bookseller or Springer